# HTML 4

*Rick Darnell, et al.*

sams
net

201 West 103rd Street
Indianapolis, IN 46290

UNLEASHED

# Copyright © 1997 by Sams.net Publishing

FIRST EDITION

International Standard Book Number: 1-57521-299-4

Library of Congress Catalog Card Number: 97-65136

2000   99   98   97            4   3   2

Interpretation of the printing code: the rightmost double-digit number is the year of the book's printing; the rightmost single-digit, the number of the book's printing. For example, a printing code of 96-1 shows that the first printing of the book occurred in 1996.

*Composed in AGaramond and MCPdigital by Macmillan Computer Publishing*

*Printed in the United States of America*

| | |
|---|---|
| **President, Sams Publishing** | *Richard K. Swadley* |
| **Publishing Manager** | *Mark Taber* |
| **Acquisitions Manager** | *Beverly M. Eppink* |
| **Director of Editorial Services** | *Cindy Morrow* |
| **Managing Editor** | *Brice Gosnell* |
| **Director of Marketing** | *Kelli Spencer* |
| **Product Marketing Manager** | *Wendy Gilbride* |
| **Assistant Marketing Managers** | *Jen Pock* |
| | *Rachel Wolfe* |

**Acquisitions Editor**
*David B. Mayhew*

**Development Editor**
*Bob Correll*

**Software Development Specialist**
*Bob Correll*

**Production Editor**
*Ryan Rader*

**Copy Editors**
*Kristen Ivanetich*
*Carolyn Linn*

**Indexers**
*Christine Nelsen*
*Erika Millen*
*Bruce Clingaman*

**Technical Reviewers**
*Karen Clere*
*Blake Hall*

**Editorial Coordinators**
*Mandi Rowell*
*Katie Wise*

**Technical Edit Coordinator**
*Lorraine Schaffer*

**Resource Coordinator**
*Deborah Frisby*

**Editorial Assistants**
*Carol Ackerman*
*Andi Richter*
*Rhonda Tinch-Mize*

**Cover Designer**
*Jason Grisham*

**Cover Production**
*Aren Howell*

**Book Designer**
*Gary Adair*

**Copy Writer**
*David Reichwein*

**Production Team Supervisor**
*Brad Chinn*

**Production**
*Mona Brown*
*Jennifer Dierdorff*
*Shawn Ring*
*Janet Seib*

# Overview

# Contents

## Part III  Extending HTML 3.2

# Dedication

*To Jane, Margaret, and Elizabeth. —Rick Darnell*

*To my brother, Steve; his wife, JoAnn; and their two daughters, Stephanie and Carrie, for consistently helping me keep two feet anchored to this planet. —Michael Larson*

*To my wife, Alina, and daughter, Sonya. —Dmitry Kirsanov*

# Acknowledgments

It's a Saturday night and I'm listening to the News from Lake Wobegon piped through a sound card on my computer. It seems somewhat ironic that I'm listening to stories about vegetable gardens from the "little town that time forgot and can't improve" while I'm finishing a book about the latest in technology standards from the Information Age. Yet, here it is. Words on paper about an electronic medium.

It's a contradiction reminding us that, although the Internet is an amazing set of technologies that enables us to communicate faster than ever before, there's still a real world outside of the wires. Cables can't pull weeds out of the garden, shovel snow from the driveway, or put a daughter to bed. The Internet is only technology. Life is what happens on the outside of the computer, not inside it.

For the last several years, while I've lived my life, I've also had this thing I call a career in writing. There are two really neat aspects about writing. The first is seeing your name in print. It's probably vain and self-serving, but I get great satisfaction from seeing my name attached to a tome such as this.

Second is the people you meet along the way, who make the whole process possible and enjoyable. Writers are pretty pointless without editors, and vice versa. It's one of those dichotomies that results in a certain tension, but also holds incredible satisfaction when both sides reach the end of the process and another book is born.

On this project, David Mayhew was the guiding hand that assembled the components, hired the writers, and made sure we delivered the goods. From what I can see, an Acquisitions Editor has a thankless job and doesn't get nearly the glory we writers do, but David certainly puts in every bit as much work. I'm not really sure why he does it, but he doesn't mind laughing and will even tolerate mindless tangents when we should be talking business.

Although not directly related to this project, Her Majesty Beverly Eppink also deserves a great deal of gratitude. She was generous and supportive as an Acquisitions Editor, and she appears to have retained those qualities during her recent promotion to Acquisitions Manager. She's certainly encouraged my development with editors at Sams.net and is responsible for a great deal of my success.

Many other people on the payroll at Macmillan make these projects happen, from the Publisher and lawyers, to technical and copy editors, production editors, designers, lawyers, secretaries, custodians, and many others. Although I don't know everyone's name, everyone makes a contribution to the finished product. Many thanks to you all.

Then, there are the other authors who participated in this project. I got to be lead author this time, but it wouldn't have been a book without the contributions of the others. It's good to be in the company of this many people working toward the same goal, even though we're in different states and on different continents.

I also extend thanks to Capt. Jess Mickelson of the Missoula (Montana) Rural Fire District, the head of our regional hazardous materials team. He's certainly been supportive and understanding when I've had to miss training for deadlines, and he's been quick to offer opportunities to gain additional experience through conferences and other assignments so that I can maintain my status as a HazMat Technician.

And then there are the many people who have fostered me along the way, giving me the needed guidance so that I could learn how to put the right words in the right order. This list includes Bonnie Montgall, David MacFarland, John Braden, and influences such as Edward Abbey, Kenneth Grahame, and A.A. Milne.

Last in this list of acknowledgments, but certainly not least, is you, the reader. Your investment in this book just made my bank account a few cents bigger. (Royalties aren't all they're cracked up to be.) I hope you find the book useful and worth the money you shelled out for it. If it makes your job easier or gives you new ideas for communicating with your fellow humans, then we've done our jobs on this end. Thank you.

—*Rick Darnell*

I would like to thank everyone who appreciates the massive potential for enrichment represented by the WWW and who will settle for nothing less than the most up-to-date HTML reference.

I also want to thank the many folks on the Sams.net editorial and publication staff for their direction, comments, dedication, and support. I especially want to acknowledge the primary editors for this compendium, Dave Mayhew and Bob Correll, for their tenacity in continually focusing the content of this book to optimize its usefulness and ensure that we are as far out on the cutting-edge of these topics as possible. Great job, guys.

—*Michael Larson*

I am thankful to Andrey A. Chernov (`ache@nagual.pp.ru`) for useful comments on the text of Chapter 39, "Internationalizing the HTML Character Set and Language Tags."

—*Dmitry Kirsanov*

# About the Authors

## Lead Author

**Rick Darnell** (darnell@montana.com) is a flatlander by nature, currently living with his wife and two daughters in the middle of a bunch of mountains in Montana. He began his print career at a small weekly newspaper after graduating from Kansas State University with a degree in broadcasting. While spending time as a freelance journalist and writer, Rick has seen the full gamut of personal computers since starting out with a Radio Shack Model I in the late 1970s. When not in front of his computer, he serves as a volunteer firefighter and member of a regional hazardous materials response team. Rick has authored several books for Sams.net Publishing and for Que. For this book, he wrote Part II, "Basic HTML," as well as Chapters 28, 29, 34, and 36.

## Contributing Authors

**Dennis Báthory-Kitsz** is a composer, performance artist, author, technologist, and teacher. His early writing about computers promoted open architectures and experimentation, and today he concentrates on uses of technology in business and performing arts. His music has been performed in North America and Europe, and he co-hosts the new-music radio show "Kalvos & Damian's New Music Bazaar," which is heard in New England and on the Internet. Malted/Media (http://www.maltedmedia.com/) is his home page. Dennis compiled the glossary of this book.

**J. Gregory Bryan** has worked for the past 16 years as a consulting scientist, manager, and technical writer in the energy exploration, environmental, and manufacturing industries. Throughout his background of business and technical experience, Gregory has also remained active in the digital processing, analysis, and interpretation of diverse integrated data. Fascinated by finding new methods of effective communication, Gregory currently works as a technical writer and consultant in South Carolina, where he is honing a new set of skills relating to digital video production and the Internet. He can be contacted by e-mail at GBRYAN1207@aol.com. Gregory wrote Chapter 37 of this book.

**Bruce Campbell** (bdc@hitl.washington.edu) lives in Seattle, WA and works with technologies related to 3D collaboration, such as VRML (Virtual Reality Modeling Language). He has contributed to three books for Sams.net Publishing: *Teach Yourself VRML 2.0 in 21 Days*, *Maximum Java 1.1*, and *Java 1.1 Unleashed, 3rd Edition*. When he is not writing, he is either teaching for Catapult training centers, performing VR-related research at the Human Interface Technology Laboratory at the University of Washington, or running around somewhere in North America. He can be found on the Web at http://www.hitl.washington.edu/people/bdc. Bruce wrote Chapters 22 and 31.

**Bob Correll** (bcorrell@sams.mcp.com) graduated from the Air Force Academy with a B.S. in History and served as an Intelligence Officer for more than seven years. After leaving the military, he delivered pizzas and helped in a warehouse for a short time before signing on with Sams.net Publishing as a Software Specialist. Now serving as a Development Editor, Bob discovered the joys and frustrations of HTML with the help of Laura Lemay's first two books, ironically enough, published by the same team within Sams.net of which he is now a part. Bob enjoys using both sides of his brain (in theory, at least) and also expresses his creativity by making bowls, vases, and yo-yos by wood turning. Bob wrote Chapter 17 of this book.

**Eric Herrmann** is the principal of Practical Internet, an Austin-based consultancy that develops Web sites and provides software support for businesses and other Web page developers. He has been a programmer in the defense industry for 10 years, specializing in TCP/IP and asynchronous parallel processing. Eric wrote Chapter 27.

**Molly E. Holzschlag**—author of *Laura Lemay's Web Workshop: Designing with Stylesheets, Tables, and Frames* and *Laura Lemay's Guide to Sizzling Web Site Design*—is a writer, instructor, and Web designer. Her Web design books and columns look at Web design holistically, examining the technical, artistic, commercial, and personal issues involved in this emerging field. She holds an M.A. in Media Studies from the New School for Social Research. She teaches Web design to content providers on the Microsoft Network, and she holds seminars and classes on a regular basis. For more information, visit Molly at http://www.molly.com/. Molly wrote chapters 19 and 20 of this book.

**John Jung** provides technical support for a wide variety of operating systems at his day job. He enjoys reading books, playing video games, and watching TV. In his spare time, he goofs off and write books. He's worked on almost a dozen books in various different capacities. John wrote Chapters 18 and 40.

**Will Kelly** (willk@tiac.net) is a freelance technical writer and consultant in the Washington, DC area, specializing in the Internet, networking, and emerging technologies. He has written technical documentation and courseware in support of projects for major government agencies and Fortune 1000 corporations. He has a B.S. in English from Frostburg State University. Will steps away from his normal role as technical editor for some Sams.net books to contribute Chapter 21 to this book.

**Dmitry Kirsanov** graduated in 1996 from St. Petersburg (Russia) University, Faculty of Languages. He worked first as a translator, then pursued the career of freelance writer, and published two books and numerous magazine articles on the Internet and the Web, all in Russian. Recently, he started to write for the Web in English by opening the *Design Lab* monthly column at http://www.webreference.com/dlab/. Dmitry wrote Chapters 3, 38, and 39.

**Michael Larson** has authored one previous book (*Teach Yourself Web Publishing with Office 97 in a Week*), several technical publications, and numerous technical reports for many audience types.

He has two technical degrees—a Bachelor's degree from Rocky Mountain College in Billings, Montana and a Master's degree from Montana State University in Bozeman, Montana. He can be reached by e-mail at `larsonm@ix.netcom.com`. His home page is at `http://www.webcom.com/larsonm/`. Michael's interests are reading, graphics (he is a certified Photoshop addict), Web page building, and hiking. He is currently enjoying a sunshine-filled life in Utah. For this book, Michael authored Part IV, "Effective Web Page Design Using HTML," and Chapters 33 and 35.

**Paul Lomax** is the technical director of Mentor Web (`http://www.mentorweb.net/`), a leading Web design and hosting company. He has been a programmer for more than 12 years and has been a dedicated fan of Visual Basic since version 1. Paul is the author of *Laura Lemay's Web Workshop: ActiveX and VBScript*, and he wrote Chapter 30 of this book.

**Dick Oliver** (`dicko@netletter.com` and `http://netletter.com`) is the author and co-author of numerous books on computer graphics and the Internet, including *Teach Yourself HTML in 24 Hours, Creating Your Own Web Graphics, Web Page Wizardry, Netscape Unleashed,* and *Web Publishing Unleashed.* He is also the president of Cedar Software and the publisher of a paper and online newsletter called *The Nonlinear Nonsense Netletter.* Dick lives in Elmore, Vermont, and commutes to work all over the world via the Internet. He wrote Chapter 41 and Appendix A of this book.

**Michael Sessums** (`msessums@fastlane.net`) is a Web site developer and publications editor for Lockheed Martin Tactical Aircraft Systems, and he is a charter member of the Lockheed Martin Web Authors Guild. Michael designs logos and Web sites for small businesses. He also conducts Internet training and maintains a community service site called "Dart's Pet Rescue and Adoption Page" (`www.startext.net/homes/petpage`). His wife, Brenda, keeps him happy with the latest free software upgrades and an endless supply of cats. Michael wrote Chapters 6 and 32.

**Phil Stripling** (`philip@cieux.com`) is a lawyer who lives and practices in the San Francisco Bay Area, near the intersection of Law and Internet. With an undergraduate degree in speech/drama, he is living proof that you don't need a degree in computer science to write HTML and that the originators of the World Wide Web got it right. Phil authored Chapters 1, 2, 4, and 5.

# Tell Us What You Think!

As a reader, you are the most important critic and commentator of our books. We value your opinion and want to know what we're doing right, what we could do better, what areas you'd like to see us publish in, and any other words of wisdom you're willing to pass our way. You can help us make strong books that meet your needs and give you the computer guidance you require.

Do you have access to CompuServe or the World Wide Web? Then check out our CompuServe forum by typing **GO SAMS** at any prompt. If you prefer the World Wide Web, check out our site at http://www.mcp.com.

> **NOTE**
>
> If you have a technical question about this book, call the technical support line at 317-581-4669.

As the team leader of the group that created this book, I welcome your comments. You can fax, e-mail, or write me directly to let me know what you did or didn't like about this book—as well as what we can do to make our books stronger. Here's the information:

FAX:     317-581-4669

E-mail:  newtech_mgr@sams.mcp.com

Mail:    Mark Taber
         Sams Publishing
         201 W. 103rd Street
         Indianapolis, IN  46290

# Introduction

The Internet has progressed at an amazing pace in recent months and years. Once the realm of academics and defense agencies, the Internet is rapidly becoming a mainstream media conduit for communication between individuals, companies, and global dwellers.

As part of the Internet, the World Wide Web is now the predominant force in growth. Its language is simple, its interface is attractive and friendly, and it is adaptable to a wide variety of uses.

There are now Web sites for selling products, selling ideas, maintaining appearances, informing publics, continuing education and knowledge, and just plain wasting time. And, in a growing trend, the Internet concept is being adapted to internal communications by establishing intranets inside companies.

HTML (Hypertext Markup Language) is the language that puts the face on the Web. It consists of a variety of elements called *tags*, which are used for everything from defining type styles and headings to inserting specialized content such as images, sounds, virtual reality worlds, and Java applets.

HTML is intimidating for many people simply because it includes language in its definition and because it has to do with the Internet. This doesn't need to be the case. HTML is relatively simple to learn, much like the old markup codes for WordPerfect and other word processors prior to WYSIWIG (What-you-see-is-what-you-get) editing.

This leads to the other drawback to working with HTML. Most editors don't display a Web page the way it will appear on a browser. Instead, HTML authors and designers must contend with the content of their page intermixed with the tags that control how the content appears to the user. The good news is that this situation is changing rapidly, with the advent of new WYSIWYG editors, which display a page using the standard accepted by most browsers.

So why learn HTML? There are several reasons. First, it only *looks* complicated. When you start working your way through the tags and using the various elements to build Web pages, you'll discover that HTML is as much an organizational tool as a design tool. The tags give structure and purpose to each part of the page and explain how it relates to the rest of the page.

Second, even some of the best WYSIWYG editors don't support all of the various tags that are a part of HTML at any given time. Sometimes, it's necessary to directly modify the source of the page to add or change tags and attributes. To do this, you need to know how the tags relate to each other.

The final reason for learning HTML is simply for the fun of it. You gain a certain satisfaction from building a Web page from the ground up. You'll know about every brick and board that went into it, and you'll have the know-how to tweak each one so that the result is just what you wanted. On the other side of that is the fun of seeing other Web pages and knowing how the page author and designer worked to develop the intended effect.

---

**HTML AS GENERAL CONVERSATION**

The World Wide Web is becoming more and more common as a topic of conversation at the dinner table, at cocktail parties and banquets, in car pools, and around the water cooler at work. After reading this book, we're sure you'll discover HTML is one of the most fascinating things on the planet and will want to discuss the nuances of each tag with those around you.

Don't do it. It's more than enough in general company to know what *HTML* means. If you try to discuss HTML in any detail, you'll only receive blank stares and suddenly find yourself standing in a corner by yourself holding a small plate of vegetables and runny ranch dressing with the host's dog hanging on your every word.

---

# How This Book Is Organized

This book is divided into seven different sections, plus five appendixes and a glossary. The book begins with basic concepts and foundations of HTML and then delves into the details of standard tags and their attributes, advanced features, and extensions. After the details of the language are covered, additional related topics are covered, including design, supporting technologies, tools, and a crystal ball (in Part VII, "The Future of HTML") for taking a look at what the future holds for new incarnations.

Here's a section-by-section look at what's in store in each Part of the book:

I. **Understanding HTML:** The chapters in this section cover the foundation and history of HTML, beginning with the concept of hypertext and extending into document types, document structure, and how different browsers and platforms fit into the Web picture.

II. **Basic HTML:** This section covers the standard tags supported by the latest HTML 3.2 specification and a peek into upcoming standards, including widely supported features such as text alignment and formatting, images, and anchors. It also shows how HTML supports advanced content such as virtual reality and sound, and how to build forms.

III. **Extending HTML 3.2:** The latest version of HTML includes advanced features that extend the power an author or designer can use to build a page. Frames and layers, style sheets, and dynamic HTML are all explained in these chapters, which give you a handle on some of the newest technology available for Web pages.

IV. **Effective Web Page Design Using HTML:** With the tools and bricks in place from sections II and III, you have the requisite technical knowledge to build Web pages with HTML 3.2. However, a technically correct page is not necessarily a user-friendly page. This section shows you how to build pages that are attractive and usable by including concepts and examples for designing user interfaces and navigation tools.

V. **Associated Technologies and Programming Languages:** HTML's capabilities are extended a great deal through the support of technologies that add interactive features to otherwise lifeless pages. This includes Common Gateway Interface (CGI) scripts for data transfer, Java and JavaScript, ActiveX, and Visual Basic Script. Other extensions to HTML are also included, such as the Virtual Reality Modeling Language (VRML) and browser plug-ins.

VI. **Development and Site Tools:** In the "old days" of the Web, building HTML pages typically involved typing the content and tags into a text editor. It worked, but it wasn't terribly easy to revise or troubleshoot for problems. This situation has changed dramatically with the introduction of a wide variety of programs to create, change, and validate Web pages. This section includes an overview of the best and brightest tools, including HTML editors and Web management tools, site management utilities, Web servers, and graphics programs.

VII. **The Future of HTML:** This section is where we dust off the crystal ball to see what lies in store for HTML in the future. The chapters in this section discuss new languages to augment or replace HTML, along with the evolution of standards for character sets and page representation in an international arena. Issues of standardization among browsers and platforms, and HTML's use in non-Web environments are also covered.

The appendixes in the back of the book include more reference information to help you with your day-to-day work using HTML 3.2. In addition to a quick reference of HTML tags, the appendixes also include the complete HTML 3.2 language and extensions specification, lists of color and character values, and online resources for more information.

We hope the combination of information in the chapters and references in the appendixes makes *HTML Unleashed* the most complete reference you have in your collection.

# How to Use This Book

Whether you're an old hand or a newbie, Chapters 1 through 6 are a good introduction and explanation of why HTML looks and acts the way it does, and how it works within the framework of the Internet and intranets.

Chapters 7 through 16 are the meat and potatoes of HTML 3.2. Every tag in the HTML 3.2 specification is covered in this area, along with their various attributes and behaviors. If you're a beginner, working through this section will give you a solid foundation for working with HTML.

Chapters 7, 11, and 12 will quickly get you up to speed in building Web pages with examples of good page structure and the two most-used and most-useful tags you'll see on any Web page. If you've already worked with the language, you should review this area to see what's new and how HTML elements are supposed to behave, including new attributes for text alignment and lists.

For advanced users, Chapters 17 through 22 show how to extend HTML beyond the elements illustrated in the previous chapters. Advanced concepts, including frames, layers, and style sheets are explained and illustrated here.

Web page design is useful for anyone who might need to build a page or entire Web site. Chapters 23 through 26 provide good information about designing pages to work with users, rather than pages that frustrate users. It's good reading for anyone, no matter how you use HTML.

An introduction to other technologies utilized within HTML is covered in Chapters 27 through 33. These chapters aren't meant to be a comprehensive reference or tutorial on working with the various languages, such as CGI, Java, or VBScript. But they do provide a good overview of each technology or language, where it's used, and how it fits within HTML.

If you don't already have a favorite program for working with Web pages, check out Chapters 34 through 37. These chapters include overviews of HTML editors such as HotDog, Hot Metal, and HomeSite, along with complete suites such as FrontPage and Backstage. You'll also find information on utilities to validate HTML pages and hyperlinks, along with Web servers and programs for creating Web graphics.

The last section is another good place to go regardless of your experience with HTML. It's where we take a step into the future to see where this language is going and consider some of the issues that it faces in order to grow. All predictions are presented with a special guarantee: If any turn out to be false, we won't say, "Told you so."

# Conventions Used in This Book

Sams.net has spent many years developing and publishing computer books designed for ease of use and containing the most up-to-date information available. With that experience, we've learned what features help you the most. Look for these features throughout the book to help enhance your learning experience and get the most out of HTML.

- Screen messages, code listings, and command samples appear in `monospace type`.
- Uniform Resource Locators (URLs) used to identify pages on the Web and values for HTML attributes appear in `monospace type`.

> **TIP**
>
> Tips present short advice on quick or overlooked procedures. This also includes shortcuts.

**NOTE**

Notes present useful or interesting information that isn't necessarily essential to the current discussion but might help you understand with background information or advice that relates to the topic.

**CAUTION**

Cautions warn you about potential problems that a procedure may cause, unexpected results, or mistakes that may prove costly.

# Who Should Read This Book?

This book has been planned and designed to fill a wide variety of needs, depending on your level of experience and knowledge with HTML.

For beginners, we offer an introduction into the basics of HTML, including basic page structure and all of the tags needed to build the page. Each HTML element is presented with its corresponding attributes, along with its default behavior and the minimum information it needs to function.

Casual and accomplished users will probably find it easier to jump around to the specific topics they need, such as tables, frames, or design. Remember that this book is a comprehensive resource for HTML 3.2, so you'll still want to glance at the other chapters to see what else you might be missing.

For experts, this book serves as an excellent reference to answer specific questions. The syntax, attribute listings, and examples provide plenty of opportunity to see variations on HTML implementation. The references at the back of the book put the technical information you require within easy reach.

We've worked hard to put together the most comprehensive HTML book available, and we hope you'll agree that it's not only an important addition to your collection, but also a valuable tool you'll use every day.

From all of the authors, thank you for choosing *HTML Unleashed.*

—*Rick Darnell*
(darnell@montana.com)

## IN THIS PART

# PART

# I

# Understanding HTML

# Hypertext Markup in Theory and Practice

*by Philip Stripling*

**CHAPTER 1**

## IN THIS CHAPTER

Although many of us think of Hypertext Markup Language as the tags that are put into a document to enable the document to be displayed on the World Wide Web, the concepts behind HTML have a long history. This chapter presents a look at some of the people and ideas that led to our present world of animation, sounds, and applets, considering why other attempts at nonlinear information systems might have failed while the World Wide Web has succeeded beyond its original purpose. I explore briefly the concept of a nonlinear information system—which is the basis of HTML and, perhaps, the key reason for its success.

Webmasters and authors who keep the theories of nonlinear information systems in mind can develop a plan that allows for uniform development of the site and of each page within it. An understanding of the theories of nonlinear information will provide a basis for preparing a Web site that is functional and fully accessible to a worldwide audience.

# The Theory of Nonlinear Information

Human beings have always used linear information to communicate and think. Linear information systems have led the world to its present condition; whether that is reason for change or celebration is left for the reader to decide. Because we use, and have always used, linear information in our daily lives, what would we gain by having a nonlinear information system?

Although unrecognized, nonlinear information has always been with us as well, and it often works better than linear information. We have attempted to create nonlinear systems within our linear worlds by using the materials at hand; for example, books and magazines have tables of contents so that we are not required to start at page 1 and read consecutive pages until we get to what we're interested in. (Did you start with page 1 of this book?) Books have indices so that we can find related topics quickly, regardless of their location in the book. Editors often suggest the use of sidebars, margin notes, and tables to present different sets of ideas simultaneously, allowing readers to compare and contrast information quickly. Computers once used magnetic tape to store information, and it was necessary to spin through an entire tape if the desired data was at the end. Computer users quickly saw the need for quicker access, and the disk drive was born, allowing access to any data directly rather than having to step through every sector on the disk to get to the data.

The problem is that although linear information systems worked very well for much of our history, there are some areas today where linear information systems break down, overwhelmed by linear information itself. Imagine a world where all data is stored on spools of microfilm. To obtain information, you must determine which spool contains the desired data, locate and retrieve the spool, and run through the frames until you find the information you seek. It may well be that the index to the spools and the spools themselves are not in your building, so in addition to the time spent looking for the data, you must also spend time and energy getting to the data because, in the world of paper, it does not come to you. This is not an imaginary world, by the way. Title companies use contractors to search recorded deeds, mortgages, and easements before issuing title policies. Not only must the searchers locate the microfiche, but they also must travel to different locations, often in different towns, for a full title search—the local courthouse, the county clerk's office, and the secretary of state. A visit to the office of the recorder of deeds will show you a nearly Dickensian world of people poring over huge index books filled in by hand, prowling through stacks of books and file cabinets, and sitting before hooded microfiche machines, notepads in hand.

Nonlinear information systems address many of the problems of information flow. They provide an exponential gain over linear systems used in research. In a typical law firm in 1985, a large room was devoted to the law library. Walls of volumes contained reported cases, statutes, regulations, and ordinances. Several companies provided loose-leaf binders with commentary on specialized areas of the laws, with daily, weekly, and monthly updates keeping the librarian always behind in posting the changes. Law clerks sat at carrels with stacks of books, taking notes and making photocopies for lawyers to use in preparing briefs and memoranda. Again, the researcher went to the resource and transcribed the information. A secretary would have used a computer to type and print the manuscript, but no other person would have been able to use a computer for research or for maintenance of the materials in the library.

### NOTE

Our lawyer in this example is limited in her resources to the material provided by her firm on its server. For the purposes of the lawyer and her firm, this is not likely a limitation. For others, however, this limitation could be as inhibiting as having to rely on paper-based information systems.

Today it is likely that the library is on CD-ROMs on a server in a closet. The lawyer has a computer on her desk, connected to the server. Research is accomplished by keyword searches. When using information in a nonlinear information system, researchers can request access to certain information and have that information located, retrieved, and displayed directly, without having to wade through information that, in our earlier world, would have "come first." In our nonlinear world, there is no "first," "next," or "previous" in context. Instead of looking up a case and reading through it for the relevant citation, the lawyer requests the display of all instances of the relevant keywords. Instead of manually transcribing or photocopying the material, the lawyer can use the computer to copy and paste the selection directly into her brief. The use of such a nonlinear information system means that much less time is used in getting to the information, locating the particular material required, and retrieving and placing that material in the final product.

Consider an institution where people conduct extremely expensive and time-consuming experiments. The people involved live and work in different countries, so getting together for research and meetings is difficult. The people want to have certain work done, but it might duplicate work done at a similar institution in another country; no information on whether that work has been done exists at the institution. A researcher is tasked to determine whether certain work was done and, if so, to obtain the raw data and parameters. She logs onto her computer and links to several search engines on the World Wide Web. After she keys in a search string, the search engine presents a list of links to pages containing that string. Now, instead of using a database query, the researcher chooses hyperlinks to other nodes, retrieving further information. This activity becomes the query mechanism; by choosing links, the researcher refines the query until she links to the node with the information sought or until the full answer has been obtained from access to several nodes. (This all sounds much more professional than the usual term—*browsing*.)

The links are to Web pages located in other countries, on other continents. There is no need to go to the data. The data available to the researcher is not limited to that provided to the researcher by the institution. And search engines with *robots* scan the Web looking for additional information, indexing it for the researcher. No one at the institution is required to maintain a library or card catalog of material.

Using nonlinear information, researchers can follow leads that persons creating tables of contents and indices would never imagine as connections. Authors can link by analogy and simple association, leaving a clear path of their thoughts that some may choose to follow and others may choose to ignore. Nonlinear information systems allow us to work as we think. Nonlinear text can provide choices for consumers to follow links to specific information made available by a business about its products. For the casual browser, nonlinear text can provide a truer representation of actual experience. Whether for work or leisure, links can take the reader to ever more specific data, making the world the repository of a database virtually sitting within the reader's monitor.

As the following history points out, key elements were always missing from proposed nonlinear information systems, keeping them from being successful. For some proposals, the hardware was impractical; for some, the software required was proprietary; for others, the available information was limited. The world has been waiting for a system of nonlinear information that is literally boundless, with no limits to the available data, no limits to connectivity, and no requirements of prescribed hardware, software, or data.

# The Evolution of Nonlinear Information Systems

Nonlinear information systems have been considered ever since humankind has had the leisure for tinkering. Many of the proposals were high-tech at the time, but fatal limitations that were insurmountable existed until very recently.

## Ancient Reading Machines

Most people now associate nonlinear information systems with the World Wide Web, but the concept is much older. In 1588, a book published in Paris called *Le diverse et artificiose machine del Capitano Agostino Ramelli* (*The Various and Artful Machines of Captain Agostino Ramelli*) presents the concept of "the reading wheel." An engraving shows a man sitting in his study before a wheel that resembles a waterwheel. Instead of paddles over which water would flow, the wheel is made up of lecterns with open books on them. The man could rotate the wheel up or down and have one of several books before him for reading. The books were affixed to the lecterns so that they not only remained on the lectern as the wheel rotated, but stayed open to the appropriate page. Ramelli apparently suggested the reading wheel both for scholars who had much reading and for those with gout who had trouble walking to their shelves for more reading material.

Ramelli seems to have grasped that nonlinear information systems would presume that the reader would not read from beginning to end. In fact, it has been suggested that a hypermedia document should not be read, but explored. In contrast, books and magazines are the archetypal linear information systems, with their numbered, sequential pages. In a magazine, if an article is continued on a later page, that fact is noted in the article, and most readers will turn immediately to the page to finish the article. And although it would be possible to read the pages of a novel in random order until they have all been read, it is unlikely that the reader would remember and understand the development of the plot or any of the characters because the author has presumed sequential reading and created a linear information flow.

Conversely, in a nonlinear information system, there would be no predefined order, and it would be presumed that the reader could mark passages for later study, add notes, and have a history of items read for later return, perhaps to follow other links. The World Wide Web is such a nonlinear information system, and the thread of its development can be followed from more recent times than Captain Ramelli's.

If we imagine our old world of linear information (beginning with such memorized heroic epics as *The Iliad*, and on to illuminated parchment scrolls, and ultimately to printed books) as the unspooling of the thread of the continuous context in which we live, hypertext becomes the web of, not discontinuity, but nonlinear context, in which we aren't required to read or view data in sequence. In life we make our own order out of our experience. With nonlinear text we have that choice as well.

## A Modern Attempt at a Nonlinear Information System

Entire philosophies and concepts of nonlinear information systems have been put to paper. But paper was the rub, the shortcoming of all the suggested systems. The requirement that nonlinear information systems be affixed to paper doomed them all to failure.

Some time ago, people kept track of research notes on index cards. One company made index cards with holes around the edges, allowing users to cut notches in the cards. The holes were numbered, so that researchers could assign certain topics to certain numbers. A person could put a knitting needle through a deck of the cards at the appropriate hole and shake the deck, and cards notched at that number would fall out. Voilà! All the research on that topic was in a pile on the desktop next to the typewriter. Those cards had to be subsorted by a second round of notching or by hand to bring them into usable order for drafting the paper.

This kind of nonlinear information system limited researchers in several ways. For one thing, the information did not come to the researcher; it had to be gathered, usually from a library. Thus, a researcher had to locate and travel to a library containing appropriate information for the topic at hand, consult the card catalogue, retrieve books and periodicals from the stacks, and read the appropriate pages. Only that data physically present with the researcher could be consulted and transcribed to the note cards. Each card had to be either written or typed with the notes from the readings. Then an index card had to be prepared, with topics set forth and numbered, and the note cards notched at the appropriate number on the edge. Only those cards physically present with the researcher could be consulted and transcribed to the type-written final draft. Any errors or missing information required another trip to the library. Paper-based nonlinear information systems posed problems.

With the advent of computers, imaginations were fired anew, but the early thinkers were brought up short by the hardware. Few people had access to mainframes, and mainframes had too little memory and were too slow and too limited in output (either on paper or on CRTs that were monochrome and displayed only text). But as Moore's Law came into play, computers shrank to the desktop, power increased exponentially, prices fell, and monitors glowed in color and showed more than ASCII text.

And, as often happens, the original, creative thinkers were left behind.

## Vannevar Bush, the Progenitor of Modern Nonlinear Information Systems

Vannevar Bush is often referred to as the modern progenitor of hypertext. Born in 1890, he taught at Tufts College and at MIT, where he was later appointed dean. He worked on optical devices and on machines for rapid selection of specified spools of microfilm. During World War II, he was appointed by Franklin Roosevelt as the Director of the Office of Scientific Research and Development.

In the 1930s, Vannevar Bush proposed a differential analyzer that he called a *memex*. This machine could store vast amounts of data, and Bush considered various means of providing links so that the information would be accessible to the user. Bush used such terms as *trails* and *footprints* to suggest where one could go and where one had been. While serving as science advisor to President Roosevelt, Bush had the opportunity to refine his thoughts on associative information, and in July of 1945 *The Atlantic Monthly* published the seminal work on nonlinear information, "As We May Think." Given the length of the article's gestation from Bush's conception of the differential analyzer in the 1930s, the maturity of thought expressed in the article should not be a surprise. It was recognized by the editors of the magazine as a call for a new relationship between humankind and knowledge.

As World War II ended, Bush realized that the tremendous advances in knowledge had not only left the individual behind, but were on the threshold of overwhelming the individual, who would retreat to ever-narrower specialties, leaving a chasm between disciplines that no one person could bridge. Bush viewed the loss of interdisciplinary knowledge and communication as no less than catastrophic.

Bush describes the "hardware" of the memex in the archaic terms one would expect of a writer living in 1945. It consists of a desk with translucent projection screens embedded in the top, a keyboard, and buttons and levers. Content is purchased on microfilm, ready for insertion and projection, but provisions are made on the desk for original work to be photographically reduced to microfilm for later display. Books are projected onto the screens, with a lever to control the speed of changing pages, much like microfilm projectors used today. Books and other materials are called up for display by typing in a code. When new material is created, it is assigned a code, and this code is stored in an index. There are several screens, so several items can be viewed at once. The reader is somehow given the ability to make annotations and marginal notes, as one would if holding a book. Bush envisioned miniature cameras the size of walnuts that scientists could wear on their foreheads to photograph the important things that they saw.

Although the descriptions of the desk, its mechanics, and the accessories are decidedly of their time, Bush transcends the 1940s with his next section: associative indexing. Any item at any time can be caused to select another immediately. Bush goes astray by trying to be specific in how links are to be established (dots on microfilm recognizable by a photocell); nevertheless, his concept is electrifying. The user can build a trail; items are forever joined and immediately recallable merely by tapping a button. Original material can be added to existing works. When many items have been thus joined to form a trail, that trail can be followed by the user at will. Trails can be connected, so that readers can branch off into interesting side excursions. Trails can be copied and transferred to acquaintances, who can incorporate them into their own trails, add original materials, and copy and transfer the expanded trails to others for further aggregation. Trails can be handed down to new generations, giving new users access to the knowledge and experience of those who have gone before. It was this concept and the promise of emerging technologies that kept the flame of nonlinear information systems burning in the minds of thinkers for the next 20 years.

Curiously, however, Bush seems to have neglected a key element of his great idea: the method of making the trail available to others. The memex user in Bush's article sits at the desk alone. Microfilm is purchased with material already recorded. Notes and memoranda can be added, but there is no clear idea as to how the trail would be handed on to others. Bush mentions earlier in the article that microfilm can be mailed; we are left to guess that the memex user would make microfilm copies and have them delivered to people. Ultimately, Bush leaves unresolved the problem of access to the nonlinear data. The memex is a one-person nonlinear system with no inherent means of transferring data to and from the desk. It is the user's responsibility to obtain new data (perhaps by mail, perhaps in stores), create trails, and find a method to transfer and share the data with others.

## Doug Engelbart, Developer of User Interfaces

Doug Engelbart read "As We May Think" while stationed in the Philippines after World War II. The ideas propounded by Bush remained with him, but it was not until the 1960s that the means of implementing a memex became possible. Working with William K. English and John F. Rulifson, Engelbart created the oN-Line System (called, of course, NLS), a system of collaboration for teams of workers located in different places. As part of NLS, the team created the concepts of using outline editors for developing ideas, what was later to be called hypertext linking, word processing, windowing, online help facilities, and consistency in the user interface; the hardware required and invented included the mouse as a pointing device for selecting areas on a CRT.

It is important to remember that in 1968 computers were mainframes and programming was generally done by punch cards or paper tape. Output was often printed on a teletype. Engelbart and his team saw that this was not an ideal environment for the enhancement of human thought. But they also had the means, for the first time, to create a new environment for the users of computers. As computing power increased, the ease of use increased as well. Engelbart's work was influential in research then being done at Xerox's Palo Alto Research Center—and on Ted Nelson's thinking.

In April of 1997, at the age of 72, Engelbart was awarded the Lemelson-MIT prize in recognition of his invention of the computer mouse and dozens of other devices and ideas that make the user interface easy and convenient. The award was established in 1994 by Jerome H. and Dorothy Lemelson to recognize U.S. inventors and scientific innovators; it is administered by the Massachusetts Institute of Technology. Engelbart now heads the Bootstrap Institute, a nonprofit, tax-exempt organization with offices provided at no charge by Logitech International, a mouse manufacturer.

# The Origins of Hypertext Markup

With the advent of computers, the limitations faced by inventors in mechanical times were no longer insurmountable. New obstacles remained to be overcome, however, including overcoming the concept of computers as number crunchers, developing friendly user interfaces, and bringing the nonlinear information system itself to a level where there were few barriers to its use.

## Ted Nelson and Xanadu

Ted Nelson is credited with coining the word *hypertext*. Nelson was born in 1934 and received his undergraduate degree in philosophy at Swarthmore College. Returning to college in 1960 for a masters in sociology, Nelson enrolled in a computer science course designed for humanities students. He realized the potential of computers in the areas of thought and writing—areas not often connected with computers at that time. Mainframe computers were not conducive to that use, but he continued to develop his ideas. In 1965, he presented a paper at a conference of the Association of Computing Machinery. Nelson had made the first use ever of the word *hypertext*.

Nelson has written frequently about his vision of hypertext, which he has called Xanadu. His book *Dream Machines* was published in 1974, and the book *Literary Machines* was published in 1988. He has written many articles as well. His conceptions include linked images, branching to other images, hypermaps with layers of detail, and linked moving video. Nelson has shown a remarkable prescience in his view of the world of hypertext.

Nelson's article "A New Home for the Mind" appeared in the March 1982 issue of *DATAMATION* magazine, its 25th anniversary issue. In this article, Nelson proposed nonsequential writing, saying that writing had always been sequential because pages had been sequential, and there was no alternative. (Whether sequential pages were the cause or the effect of sequential writing is left to the reader to ponder.) Nelson proposed using the computer to vault our minds into the hyperspace of thought. He called this new realm of immediately available texts and graphics the *hyperworld* and the storage system a *hyperfile*. (*Hyperbole* was not mentioned in the article.)

Unfortunately, he has failed to bring Xanadu from the hyperspace of thought into this world. He announced its release due in 1976, 1988, 1991, and 1995. Sadly, in juxtaposition to the article in the 25th anniversary issue of *DATAMATION*, *Byte* magazine, in its September 1995 20th anniversary issue, heralded Xanadu as its first example of vaporware.

Nelson named his system after ideas in Samuel Taylor Coleridge's "Kubla Khan":

> *In Xanadu did Kubla Khan*
> *A stately pleasure-dome decree:*
> *Where Alph, the sacred river, ran*
> *Through caverns measureless to man*
> *Down to a sunless sea.*

Legend has it that the poet wrote the poem under the influence of a drug, that he was interrupted before finishing the work, and that he was never able to regain his prior state of inspiration and finish it. Although Nelson intended to provide a system where literary memory never flagged, his choice of Xanadu as a name has come back to haunt him as surely as Xanadu haunted Coleridge, who was unable to regain the magic realm and finish the work.

Among the problems delaying Xanadu are the coinages of terms and the changes in terminology. Nelson proposes *xanalogics*, *humbers*, *docuverses*, and *tumbler arithmetic*. Understanding what Nelson means and keeping up with his new names for his concepts make public acceptance of Xanadu a daunting task. Although the overarching concepts of Xanadu remain alive in today's World Wide Web, Xanadu itself seems to have disappeared into *caverns measureless to man, down to a sunless sea.*

## Bill Atkinson and HyperCard

The following HyperCard script from John McDaid, "Uncle Buddy's Phantom Funhouse," published by Eastgate Systems, Inc., shows the ability of a skilled author to create a working script that also stands alone as a poem. (This code is copyright 1992 by John McDaid and used with permission.)

```
on mouseUp
Global thermoNuclearWar
put the script of me into tightOrbit
put tightOrbit into eventHorizon
put empty into first line of eventHorizon
put empty into last line of eventHorizon
put eventHorizon after line thermoNuclearWar of tightOrbit
set the script of me to tightOrbit
put thermoNuclearWar + 10 into thermoNuclearWar
click at the clickLoc
end mouseUp
```

Bill Atkinson created much wonderful software for Apple's Macintosh computer, including MacPaint and MultiFinder. In 1987, Apple Computer introduced Atkinson's HyperCard to the world. HyperCard uses the graphics capabilities of the Macintosh computer to show on its screen a virtual deck of cards; cards can contain text, sound, video, or pictures, along with buttons and other navigation aids for the user to go from one card to another.

HyperCards are created in an interpreted language called HyperTalk. As shown in the working script at the beginning of this section, HyperTalk is similar to English and can be read and understood without a great deal of study. Using HyperTalk, script authors can create cards, accept input from the user from the keyboard or mouse, act on that input, and display the results. People have scripted complex programs and games using HyperTalk, although it is an interpreted language and, thus, sometimes relatively slow.

HyperCard suffers from several limitations. It has search and history functions built into it, but not links. Worse, the author cannot build links into the text of a card; the author must provide clickable buttons, which must be placed so that they do not obscure the text. Addition of text to a card might require the author to rewrite the location of any navigation buttons. Originally, HyperCard supported only one size of card, only black and white, and only one visible card at a time. The cards could not contain scrolling windows. But HyperCard met an untapped need and became quite popular in spite of its limitations.

Competitors quickly appeared and addressed some of the shortcomings. Apple handed HyperCard off to Claris International, Inc., a subsidiary servicing Apple's software, and Claris has updated and extended HyperCard to include scrolling, variable card sizes, debugging tools, and better printing. However, the program is proprietary, and potential users of stacks must have acquired the program; data stored in stacks is not available to other programs that cannot interpret HyperTalk. Although HyperTalk allows calls to AppleScript, no easy method native to HyperTalk allows connection to other computers for locating and retrieving data. The HyperCard user is, essentially, at the same point as the memex user in 1945. Users can obtain and add to stacks or create their own, but they remain bound by the content physically present on the computer. The program has no inherent method of transferring data to and from the desktop.

HyperCard is now sold as a separate product, but its limitations will restrict its use as a nonlinear information system. It has served well, however, and it has shown the power of the modern computer—coupled with a consistent graphical user interface—to free the user from the linear demands of paper and of the early computers, where steps were relentlessly sequential. With HyperCard, authors could publish text, pictures, and even animation, with different paths for readers to follow. With some knowledge of scripting, readers could add text to the cards, create new cards, and add links to and from existing cards obtained from others. Bush's memex was, at last, in its infancy, built directly upon the work of Engelbart and NLS.

The foundations of hypertext were laid. It remained only to tie in the reality of the computer and software with the vision of Xanadu.

# The World Wide Web Becomes the First Practical Nonlinear Information System

With many of the ideas, hardware, and software in place for the first time, nonlinear information systems became workable. The last steps required seeing the pieces as part of a whole, putting them into place, and inventing the mortar to hold them all together to form the foundation for true and unbounded nonlinear use, unconstrained by platform or software.

## Tim Berners-Lee and the World Wide Web

Tim Berners-Lee was born in England and graduated from Oxford University with a bachelor of science degree in physics. After working at a few jobs involving text processing and communications, he landed at the European Particle Physics Laboratory at CERN. As Bush foresaw, scientists working for CERN in different countries were having trouble communicating with each other. Although Berners-Lee had been hired to work at one of the high-energy particle accelerators, he became involved in the effort to facilitate communication between the scientists at CERN.

Earlier, he had written a program called Enquire that allowed him to keep track of his personal notes and to create associations between related notes in an effort to make notetaking and notekeeping work more closely to the way we think. That idea carried over into his new concept for using computers to enable users to look at a database of ideas with hypertext as the query mechanism. In Berners-Lee's model, this "meta" database is made up of as many databases as necessary on as many computers as necessary, with no single person in charge of the data or the database. Everyone at CERN could keep his or her data current and make the results available by computer. Everyone would have access to all the data and could build relationships by linking and bookmarking links. There would be no chasm between disciplines; interdisciplinary knowledge would be readily available, searchable, and viewable; and the building of bridges from discipline to discipline would be as easy as making a link. All users at CERN could record everything they saw and did, and everyone else could see the data and make use of it in their own fields. (As a historical note, scientists at CERN are *not* walking around with walnut-sized cameras on their foreheads photographing things of interest to them. However, students at some universities *are* wearing video cams throughout their day, broadcasting the view live to the World Wide Web.)

Finally, the memex became reality.

It took a while longer and much more work, of course. Berners-Lee proposed the World Wide Web to CERN in 1989 and began work in earnest in 1990. The fear at CERN was one of the problems posited by Bush: the loss of information. The work at CERN is incredibly expensive and time-consuming. People were hired and began work with little introduction to the current state of research, and the average length of stay was two years. Technical details of work were often lost and were difficult and time-consuming to reconstruct. Duplication of effort was rampant.

In a stroke of brilliance, Berners-Lee transcended the problem at hand. He understood several problems that had to be overcome, and he went far beyond the immediate need of CERN with his solution. He saw that a hierarchical system of information would collapse under its own weight, if not in a year or two, then in 10 years; that the information in the system would not be limited to text; and that indexing would limit access to information and hide it from those who needed data from a different perspective. His answer to these problems was distributed hypertext, where people kept their data on their computer, but the computers were linked on a network with the data publicly available on the network. With the network grown to include the Internet, the information available on this system may have no bounds.

> **NOTE**
>
> Although many of us are familiar with URL, a Uniform (or Universal) Resource Locator, the more general term, URI (Uniform Resource Identifier), incorporated not only URLs but also Uniform Resource Names and Uniform Resource Citations. URNs and URCs will have wider use in later versions of HyperText Transfer Protocol. See Chapter 5, "Behind the Scenes: HTTP and URIs."

Given approval, Berners-Lee wrote the server and the client software on his NeXT computer. The software was made available at CERN, then to the world through the `alt.hypertext` newsgroup. His colleagues and he then grappled with the protocols, inventing URIs, HTTP, and HTML along the way. As discussed in later chapters, not all the difficulties have been (or ever will be) ironed out, but with the addition of a graphical user interface, the World Wide Web has exploded across the face of the planet, enabling everyone to become publishers and granting with a vengeance Bush's wish for people to be able to sit at a desk, record their thoughts and observations, and make that record available to following generations. We who now live among the mess ponder whether all those thoughts and observations are worthy of being in the record.

# A Theory of Practical Hypertext Markup

The author of the nonlinear information system must furnish a method of linking related ideas and a search mechanism for specific queries that may not have immediately obvious answers. Ultimately, the nonlinear information system can have no bounds. With a uniform linking mechanism, the reader is not restricted to an author's work but can follow links to source documents anywhere in the world. These benefits are also drawbacks if they are poorly implemented. Maintaining context in a hypertext world is difficult but necessary.

## Divide the Content into Manageable Nodes

As discussed in further detail in Part IV, "Effective Web Page Design Using HTML," effectively designing documents presenting nonlinear information is considerably more difficult than writing for narrative text. Theorists of hypertext have several constructs that are useful in designing Web sites. The first is the division of the text into *chunks* that deal with one theme, topic, or idea. After the material is chunked, it must be written so that it can be read as a standalone node by a reader who may have come to that node from any of several links provided by the author or from a search engine. The author cannot assume the reader has information from "earlier" passages, as is the case with narrative text writing. Poorly chunked nodes can result in a procession of sound bites with no context and little content or in a node that is an unreadable cacophony of links shouting for attention and overwhelming content.

## Provide Context for Your Reader in Each Node

Linear text is self-contextual. I can refer later in this paragraph to *chunking* and assume you are familiar with that term from a previous paragraph. In nonlinear information systems such as the Web, formerly simple words such as "later" or "previous" become context traps for the author. While we can mention here what we discuss later, in a hypertext situation such a discussion may never come before a reader who does not follow a particular set of links. (Indeed, a reader might follow a link prior to even finishing reading a node and never return. "Later" never comes.) Each node must, therefore, not only be correctly chunked, but it must also be written so as to provide a set of context clues that a reader with no prior link to that node can use to become oriented to the information being presented.

With the heavy use of search engines, the Web site author can no longer assume that the reader can use the "back" facility of the browser to return to a "previous" page. The reader might have come to a page from out of nowhere (from the author's point of view). It is imperative, therefore, that the page contains links to a hierarchy within the Web site where readers can orient themselves and go on to other relevant nodes. In addition, the links within the document must have a purpose that is obvious to persons coming into the node from another Web site. Each link should have a clear statement of its function in the context of the document and without further explanatory material.

Readers should be aware that they are within a set of nodes as they follow the trail established by the author. By providing a similar look to all the nodes on a Web site, an author can create a visual context with which the readers will grow comfortable—and they will be more likely to notice if they follow a link to another site with a different appearance. Navigation aids within the site should be consistent in all the pages; readers should not be burdened with having to remember how they got to a page, where to go to get back, or how to determine where next to visit. Having to remember the meaning of icons from one page to another, for example, could be distracting to a reader intent on gleaning information from the author's text. It is aggravating and confusing to find that different icons mean the same thing on different pages or that the same icon means different things.

## Provide a Context for the Author and Webmaster

As the author creates documents, the author must retain a clear understanding of the structure of the site. Naming the documents can be a great aid to both the author and the reader. Links to documents with names that indicate the purpose of the Web page are helpful in keeping track of the structure of the site and the location of both the reader and author in the great scheme of things. The site author might find it helpful to keep an outline of the structure, with links and document names handy, ensuring correct citation and the absence of links or documents without corresponding documents or links.

When a hobbyist is creating a site for pleasure, the author may well be able to create and publish the entire site while retaining the overall concepts and presentation in mind. Business sites, on the other hand, often have several persons authoring content and another person creating the Web site, its navigation aids, and overall interface. The group must have a person who can review (or have reviewed by appropriate persons) each document for technical accuracy, legal issues, management purposes, and consistent style in all documents. Such reviews are crucial for professional Web site authors. Additionally, someone must keep track of the Web site as a whole. Web sites have a tendency to grow, making changes more difficult (where are all references to Part Number 234-4433?) and navigation more complex (users might give up when they have to pursue an item that is buried under several layers of pages, each taking time to download). The Web site author planning a site must keep in mind the importance of designing for future maintenance of the site and of each document.

# Summary

The World Wide Web works as a nonlinear information system. The ideas and software and hardware that preceded it all lacked one or more crucial facets that are present in the Web. Some of them required proprietary software and ran on only one operating system. Some provided no inherent method of communicating ideas. The World Wide Web has proved successful because it is not proprietary and requires no particular hardware or software. It has inherent in its concept the free exchange of ideas, the capability to provide links to information that may be located anywhere in the world. "Content" becomes available to a reader without the requirement that it be stored in the reader's computer. Nonlinearity without boundaries has finally been achieved.

# The History of HTML

*by Philip Stripling*

## IN THIS CHAPTER

CHAPTER 2

When Tim Berners-Lee was faced with the many options available to implement his concepts, he chose Standard Generalized Markup Language (SGML), setting the stage not only for total independence from platform operating systems and languages, but also for often rancorous debate on the issue of just what HTML is supposed to be for.

On the surface, SGML is the ideal choice for the purposes envisioned by Berners-Lee. SGML is an internationally recognized standard for text information processing, providing distribution, search, and retrieval of electronically stored text. Documents marked up in SGML fashion have two elements:

- The content, which is the information to be conveyed.
- Information about the content, identifying the basic structure of the document (headings, paragraphs, lists). The format of the document is not, and cannot be, specified in SGML markup.

This was ideal for Berners-Lee's purposes. A scientist at CERN could create content, SGML markup could be added later, and the resulting document could be made available by network to all persons with network access. Because SGML is platform independent, anyone with a computer and appropriate software (this combination is sometimes called a *client*) that could parse SGML documents could then read the data. The software used to parse and present data marked up in SGML was personalized by the user, taking into account the hardware in use. A person using a dumb terminal had to have a way on that terminal to distinguish text that was marked as Header 1 from Header 2 and Header 3, and also to distinguish lists from paragraphs. Different fonts, different font sizes, colors, italics, and similar conventions now taken for granted were not available to all clients. Thus, users were expected to set their software to meet their needs and available equipment, which quite likely varied from lab to lab. Because SGML markup identified only the nature of the contents, it was the reader's responsibility to determine how to display the different levels of meaning. As a result of the limitations of some displays, the convention arose for client software to ignore markup it could not interpret, displaying the content without the benefit of that particular tag.

Before HTML, the author of a document was never concerned with how the document would appear on someone's monitor. It was accepted that appearance was the province of the user. Unlike authors using `trof`, for example, HTML authors could not specify font names, font sizes, margins, or white space between elements. Users set those specifications to their own satisfaction, allowing for monitor size and available fonts.

# The Development of Hypertext Markup Language

One of the requirements of creating a usable nonlinear information system is to make the system easy for non-experts to understand and use. Unlike AppleScript, HyperTalk, and WinHelp files, marking up text for presentation on the Web uses a limited set of tags that are simple and easy to understand. This seeming simplicity, however, was difficult to obtain and is proving difficult to maintain.

**2**

## A WORLD WIDE WEB TIME LINE

**1989**

*March*

Tim Berners-Lee circulates "Information Management: A Proposal" at CERN.

**1990**

*October*

Proposal redrafted; World Wide Web named.

*November*

Berners-Lee creates a WWW browser on his NeXT computer.

**1991**

*February*

Project presented to CERN.

*March*

www, a line mode browser, is written.

*May*

Stanford Linear Accelerator Laboratory sets up first U.S. server; general release of www over CERN network.

*August*

Information is posted to several newsgroups providing information on the World Wide Web, including a draft for HTML 1.0.

**1992**

*January*

www available generally by ftp.

*April*

Erwise, a Finnish graphical client for X, is released.

*May*

Viola graphical browser is released by Pei Wei at Berkeley.

**1993**

*January*

Other browsers are available; a few dozen Web servers are online.

*February*

NCSA Mosaic for X is released.

*continues*

*continued*

*September*

NCSA releases early versions of Mosaic for common operating systems.

*October*

Web servers are now estimated at 200.

*November*

HTML+ is made available for informal discussion.

**1994**

*January*

General releases of commercial software to allow home users to connect to the World Wide Web over Internet connections.

*March*

Andreessen, et al., leave NCSA for Palo Alto, California and Netscape.

*April*

Initial draft of HTML 2.0 released to the public.

*July*

CERN and MIT announce an agreement to form the W3C.

*October*

Netscape 1.0 beta released.

*December*

First meeting of the W3C held at MIT; Netscape 1.0 finalized.

**1995**

*February*

HTML 2.0 released as an RFC.

*March*

HTML 3.0 released as an RFC.

*April*

Netscape 1.1 released.

*May*

W3C announces selection of Cascading Style Sheets to provide visual effects and provides initial information on HTML 3.0.

*July*

Netscape 1.2 released.

*August*

Internet Explorer 1.0 finalized.

*September*

RFC for HTML 2.0 approved.

*October*

NCSA Mosaic 2.0 final beta released; Netscape 2.0b1 released.

*November*

W3C workshop on style sheets; Internet Explorer 2.0 finalized.

**1996**

*January*

NCSA Mosaic 2.1 released.

*March*

W3C announces that the "market leaders" will work with the W3C to establish interoperability standards; Netscape 2.0 finalized; Internet Explorer 3.0a1 released.

*April*

NCSA Mosaic 3.0 beta released; Netscape 3.0b1 released.

*May*

HTML 3.2 released as an RFC.

*July*

Cougar released to the public.

*August*

Netscape 3.0 finalized; Internet Explorer 3.0 finalized.

*October*

Internet Explorer 3.01 released.

*December*

W3C recommends Cascading Style Sheets, level 1; Netscape 4.0b1 released.

**1997**

*January*

W3C recommends HTML 3.2; NCSA ends development with Mosaic 3.0.

*February*

Netscape 4.0b2 released.

*May*

Internet Explorer 4.0 Developer Release announced.

# Level 0 of HTML

In using SGML to describe how to format content, Berners-Lee employed another aspect of SGML: It is a language used to define other languages. Berners-Lee and his colleagues used SGML to describe the rules for Hypertext Markup Language in a document type definition (DTD), the basis for the structure of documents on the World Wide Web. (DTDs are discussed in detail in Chapter 3, "SGML and the HTML DTD.") Under Berners-Lee, HTML followed the SGML rules of platform-independent content markup with no provisions for representation of the document in HTML itself. Users were to provide formatting through their clients—and the client would never be known at the time of document creation and markup.

In its first implementation in 1990, HTML was at level 0. At that time, the means of communication over the Internet included e-mail, ftp, and Telnet, using the TCP/IP protocol. Gopher was becoming a popular means of indexing information, and Gopher servers were being introduced to the Internet, along with Archie, Veronica, and Jughead. WAIS was also being introduced as a means of providing access, especially to students on college campuses. To allow worldwide access to HTML documents, Berners-Lee and his associates introduced the ideas of the Hypertext Transfer Protocol (HTTP) and URIs to provide addresses and a means for locating the data. (See Chapter 4, "The Structure of an HTML Document," for more information.)

At level 0, HTML provided a platform-independent means of marking data for interchange. The concept was that servers would store and provide data and that clients would retrieve and display them. The servers would send the data via HTTP, but other existing protocols were available; thus, HTML nodes could provide access not only to other HTML nodes but also to Gopher space, ftp, Network News, and so on.

HTML 0.0 was very close to SGML. Oddly, the only required element was the TITLE element, and many older pages still remain that start with a title, and then go straight into the text—no <HTML>, no <BODY>, and no </BODY></HTML>. These older documents often use <P> at the end of each paragraph; the closing paragraph tag was not required, and the paragraph element was viewed simply as a device to *separate* paragraphs rather than as a *container* of paragraphs. Level 0 provided six levels of header, but expected that each level would be used only once and that the levels would be used sequentially. Thus, <H1> would be first, and then, if necessary, <H2>, <H3>, <H4>, and so on. This requirement was imposed by SGML parsers of the day that used certain conventions to read and render the structure indicated by the markup. More than one header of the same magnitude or headers out of sequence could confuse the parsers and cause problems with the display.

> **NOTE**
>
> Although I have referred to "tags" in this chapter and in Chapter 1, "Hypertext Markup in Theory and Practice," it is time to become more formal in describing the parts of SGML and

HTML. Based on RFC 1866, an *element* is a component of hierarchical structure defined by a DTD. *Markup* is the syntactically delimited characters added to the data of a document to represent its structure. There are four different kinds of markup: descriptive markup (tags), references, markup declarations, and processing instructions. A *tag* is defined as markup that delimits an element, including a name that refers to an element declaration in the DTD, and may include attributes. *Attributes* are values within tags that allow for further refinement of the markup expressed by the tag. (See Chapter 3 for examples and further explanations.)

Level 0 allowed a `<BODY>` tag (even though it was not often used), and authors could have the following elements contained within the body element: address, anchor, blockquote, break, headings, horizontal rule, image, list (definition, directory, menu, ordered, unordered), paragraph, and preformatted text. Provisions were made for the inclusion of special characters through the use of escapes.

## TYPICAL SOURCE MARKUP IN 1992

A typical page of those days would look something like this in its source markup:

```
<title>New Page in a New World</title>
This is a new page in the new world of the Web. In this new world
we do not think of the &lt;p&gt; or paragraph tag as a container,
but as a means of introducing a gap in the flow of text.<p>

As a result, it was usually placed at the end of a paragraph,
telling the reader of the source mark up that the paragraph had
ended rather than that a new one was to begin.<p>

Since only the title element was required, pages were often
remarkably simple when viewed in the source mark up, and were
mainly narrative text explaining things just as in a book. Many
pages had no links, and the authors expected readers to be
approaching the page from another node and returning via the
"back" facility of the browser.
```

# Level 1 of HTML

The discussions of HTML 0 brought to light several shortcomings, and in 1992 Dan Connolly began development of HTML 1.0, which was released on the Internet that year. After months of discussions, Berners-Lee wrote an Internet draft Request for Comments (RFC), which was released in mid-1993. The idea of an HTML container was added, with a HEAD element separate from the BODY element. Opening and closing tags were required for some elements. Along with TITLE, the HEAD element could contain the attributes of ISINDEX, LINK, and BASE, giving the document a context within a larger universe. Along with the anchor element, the image element allows (at first) GIF files to be displayed within the text. The horizontal rule was also introduced, beginning the slide down the slippery slope of attempting to define the display.

Level 1 also introduced one of the most useful elements, FORM. Forms enabled authors to have input fields on their nodes, allowing feedback from users, opening the door to considerable interaction via Common Gateway Interface (CGI) scripting. The potential of forms and CGI is still being explored, with HTML 4.0 including additional functions.

Level 1 also added the elements CITE and CODE; certain style elements having nothing to do with marking structure such as emphasis, keyboard, sample, strong, and variable, and the character formatting elements for bold, italic, and teletype (to force a monospaced font where available). While Level 1 was being discussed in the newsgroups and on the e-mail list, additional elements and extensions to HTML were being proposed, and HTML+ was in the wings.

## HTML+ and the Introduction of Graphics

Dave Raggett proposed HTML+, incorporating graphical and display elements into HTML, taking fuller advantage of the capabilities of Mosaic and other graphics-based browsers then becoming available. HTML+ offered the means for linking to and accessing PostScript documents, JPEGs, MPEGs, and sounds as well as GIFs. MIME was used to allow the extension of HTML file types; the data available over the World Wide Web was not circumscribed by the 7-bit ASCII conventions of the Internet. Now, not only are there no limits to the number of computers and users and no limits to the amount of data, but there are no limits to the types of data available.

HTML+ was an important conceptual step forward for HTML. Raggett included elements and attributes for superscripting and subscripting, footnotes, margins, inserted and deleted text (for change logs of documents being drafted by different persons at different locations), alignment of content, tabs (with alignment), tables, mathematical formulae, an extended set of character entities (including fractions, and inverted exclamation and question marks), and figures.

Raggett grasped and understood the concept behind the World Wide Web. With HTML+, he sought to extend HTML beyond the pedestrian concept of an article placed on a computer with hyperlinks. He understood the use of the Web not only as a means to accomplish Bush's goal of bridging the knowledge chasm, but also as a distinct medium with uses even Nelson had not dreamed of. Raggett introduced in HTML+ the means to link not only to other text, but to sound files, moving image files, PostScript, and any format later introduced by the use of MIME extensions to describe the new file type.

But he remained true to the SGML background of HTML in this proposed implementation. HTML+ would not deal with instructions on appearance, but would leave those details to the specifications of the user to the client. Elements, attributes, and values remained case insensitive, in accordance with SGML rules. HTML+ parsers ignored tags they did not recognize, allowing authors and users to avail themselves of other SGML markup in HTML documents for indexing and other processing outside of HTML. To ensure that browsers would detect this new level of HTML and render the document correctly, it was suggested that a document identifier be used and that it precede all other information in the document, including the <HTML> tag.

With HTML+, Hypertext Markup Language took a giant step toward resolving the disparate demands of content-based markup with the newly born demands of authors for control over the layout of a page of text and graphics elements. Unfortunately, the step was too large. The proposed elements and attributes were difficult to implement; considerable effort would have been required to resolve the various issues, including representation of mathematical formulae on dumb terminals. There was disagreement within the developers' community on the need for tables, forms, math, and even inline images. Furthermore, as browser implementation expanded outside the close circle of HTML development, reasonable people disagreed on what interpretations should be given to the HTML DTD, and different browsers displayed the same markup differently.

## HTML 2

In response to demands for a standard for HTML, the development group, under the leadership of Dan Connolly, proposed HTML 2. The World Wide Web Consortium (W3C) was established to handle implementation of HTML standards, and a Request for Comments was drafted and published, setting the stage for formal acceptance of HTML 2.0 as a recognized standard for Web publishing.

Level 2 implemented the FORM element with INPUT, SELECT, OPTION, and TEXTAREA. It also added BR, for line breaks, and the META element, which allows for the description of the document and provides for indexing and cataloging of the contents. HTML 2.0 changed the descriptions of anchor, base, body, lists, head, image, link, and title.

> **NOTE**
>
> One of the benefits of the World Wide Web is the accessibility of the data. I had intended to mention where in the world Berners-Lee, Raggett, Connolly, and Muldrow were during these times to show how little physical contact there was among the team members. But they kept moving! And through the newsgroups and listserv, contributions were made by people in California, Massachusetts, Australia and—well, you get the picture. The very accessibility of information via the Internet and the Web made keeping track of people's locations impossible.

Working with Berners-Lee, Dan Connolly and Karen Muldrow crafted a workable draft that maintained backwards compatibility with existing proposals for HTML and included forms. The DTD provided for start tags only in some instances, required end tags in others, and made end tags optional in others. Thus, <P> became an optional container, with the end tag </P> available but inferred from context if omitted.

HTML 2 broke no new ground, essentially implementing the status quo. It was, however, immediately workable for all user agents, it followed the rules established by SGML, and it required no long debate on whether the proposed elements were necessary or workable. Furthermore, it allowed the W3C to make a structured response to Netscape Corporation's ceaseless promulgation of additions to HTML, a profligacy driving many developers of HTML and HTML documents crazy. HTML 2.0 became the benchmark against which browsers and markup were measured.

## HTML 3

HTML 3.0 was proposed as an attempt to address the competing demands for a markup language that operated across all platforms and for a page description language that was acceptable to software companies in addition to Netscape. The theory was that HTML 3.0 would be fully SGML-compliant, while allowing "hints" to browsers on how to display certain text. HTML 3.0 was developed under the stewardship of David Raggett, the author of HTML+. Among the elements proposed in 3.0 was the FIG element, with text flow supported around figures. Raggett proposed support for mathematical equations, a very useful feature for a system intended to support cross-discipline scientific research. HTML 3.0 also included the TABLE element, an alternative to the PRE element for formatting tabular data.

The ALIGN attribute was added to several elements, including IMG, P, and HR, allowing authors to provide for left, right, or center justification. On the character level, HTML 3.0 proposed a number of new logical elements, including tags for definitions, quotations, language, inserted text, and deleted text. Some of the proposed physical tags were underlined text, bigger text, smaller text, and subscript and superscript. HTML 3.0 also included attributes for a background image, tabs, footnotes, and banners (a section of the HTML document that would not scroll, but remain at the top of the window).

Furthermore, HTML 3.0 was designed to work with style sheets. By removing the display control elements from HTML and using them in style sheets, several agendas were served. Those who viewed HTML as an SGML language would not have to deal with efforts to control the appearance of a node. Those who wanted to do graphics design on the Web would have a better mechanism for rendering attractive Web pages with graphics, text, animation, sound, and so on, and some control over placement of images and the flow of text. And those without clients capable of displaying graphics elements would have properly marked up HTML for their clients to parse, with control over display safely in the hands of the user. Two methods of incorporating style sheets were considered: providing a link to a separate style sheet, or providing a STYLE element with internal style hints in the HTML document. To alert browsers to the differences between HTML 3.0 and its predecessors, it was proposed that a new extension be used, perhaps .ht3 or .html3.

Several books were written discussing the migration from Level 2.0 to Level 3.0 and the dangers of using markup not yet in an approved standard. The HTML 2.0 draft was formally approved, but the approval date for HTML 3.0 came and went. The draft expired. By this time, Microsoft had its Internet Explorer in the marketplace as a free download at the Microsoft Web site. Netscape's Navigator was nominally for sale at $49, but it was also available for download at the Netscape Web site, with payment on the honor system. Not only Webmasters, but authors of books were having fits keeping track of the varying standards of HTML. There was a great deal of confusion and aggravation in the marketplace.

# HTML 3.2

In the end, HTML 3.0 was too ambitious. HTML 3.2 was drafted in acknowledgment of reality, incorporating many of the tags already in heavy use on Web pages around the world. It added the tags <SCRIPT> and <STYLE> to pave the way for client-side scripts such as JavaScript and VBScript and for style sheets. HTML 3.2 formalized such practices as colors for backgrounds, text, and links, and width, height, alignment, and spacing for images.

HTML 3.2 became the standard, replacing HTML 2.0. HTML 3.2 provided many new elements and attributes that enlivened Web pages with animation, colors, and sound. It became possible to have attractive, dynamic pages that were compliant with an established standard. There was some disagreement on just who was setting the standards, but at least formally recognized DTDs existed for HTML.

# HTML 4.0

With HTML 4.0, the W3C has begun again to attempt to set standards that will divide the markup of content from the appearance of a Web page. As discussed more fully in Part III, "Extending HTML 3.2," HTML 4.0 separates physical styles from content markup by more reliance on style sheets. With both Microsoft and Netscape in on the discussions, we can hope that browsers will finally implement style sheets. Many see that as the best way to suggest appearance while still allowing full use of HTML as an SGML-compliant method of bridging the chasm between mind and knowledge as the level of data increases.

HTML 4.0, being written by David Raggett and Arnaud Le Hors, again recognizes widely used tags such as <FRAMES> and incorporates them into the standard. But Level 4 represents a change in the concept of HTML. Its elements and attributes are heavily skewed toward the use of style sheets, and they provide more diversity in languages and in meeting special needs. In addition, with HTML 4.0, the W3C introduces OBJECT, which is a new element taking the place of IMG, and also makes additional use of LINK, adds functions to forms, and incorporates frames. These new elements and attributes are covered in detail in Part II, "Basic HTML."

# Other Proposals

In addition to the new concepts introduced in HTML 4.0, style sheets using CSS1 will be more widely supported in this new version of HTML, and Netscape and Microsoft are proposing incompatible methods of bringing Web page construction and rendering to the client, called Dynamic HTML. Dynamic HTML should reduce the times now required to download graphic elements many authors use in an attempt to control layout. With Dynamic HTML, an author can use a combination of embedded objects and scripting to exert some influence over the contents and layout of a Web page. Contemplated uses of Dynamic HTML include determination of browser window size with the construction of layout to match and dynamic transfer of content depending on user requests with the construction of a table of contents to match the data.

The use of cascading style sheets should also lessen server loads. Some authors are using transparent GIF images to simulate indentation of paragraphs, as well as using other image devices to influence the layout of their pages. Aside from not working well on all brands of browsers, downloading the artwork takes up as much as half the total time spent transferring data. (The savings in arguments posted to the Usenet newsgroups on indenting paragraphs alone makes the use of style sheets to indent paragraphs worth hundreds of thousands of megabytes of postings.)

# Graphical Browsers

Access to the World Wide Web was on text-based browsers. The pages themselves were almost entirely text. There was no method of displaying images quickly and as part of the Web page with www or Lynx. With little but text available, the Web was not much better than the Internet and had nothing to recommend using it instead of Gopher, another text-based method of organizing information on the Internet. The advent of graphical browsers set off the explosion of the World Wide Web.

## The Early Browsers

In 1991, Pei Wei had written a program called Viola. It was a HyperText system somewhat like HyperCard and ran under UNIX for X11 workstations. In early 1992, Pei reworked Viola to be a graphical browser for HTML. Viola allowed the user to have more than one font, links were boxed and needed a click of the mouse button for actuation, there was a "history" for ready access to pages already visited, and Viola had the capability to bookmark pages and to display the source markup for the page being viewed. In addition to Viola, there were www, Erwise, and a CERN browser for the Macintosh. In January of 1992, an estimated 50 Web servers were in existence.

In the United States, the National Center for Supercomputing Applications (NCSA) had been given as one of its missions the creation of freely available software to aid the scientific research community. The NCSA at Urbana-Champaign, Illinois, began a project to create a graphical interface to the World Wide Web. In February of 1992, NCSA's Software Design Group (with Marc Andreessen) released an alpha version of Mosaic for the X Window System (Mosaic for X). By September, NCSA had released versions of Mosaic for X, Microsoft Windows, and Macintosh computers. In January of 1993, O'Reilly & Associates and Spry (licensee of the commercial version of NCSA Mosaic) released software aimed at providing all the software necessary for the home computer user to connect to the Internet and the World Wide Web. In February 1993, Andreessen and some of his colleagues left NCSA and formed Mosaic Communications Corp. (After a brief discussion with NCSA, the company was renamed Netscape.) By October, the Second International WWW Conference had to turn away hundreds of would-be attendees due to lack of room.

In three years, the World Wide Web had become reality—truly worldwide.

The free availability of Mosaic coupled with the capability to transmit graphics for (more or less) immediate display laid the groundwork for the explosion of the World Wide Web. At the time, browsers were freely available for downloading over the Web or by ftp through the good graces of programmers attuned to the convention of providing free software on the Internet or through companies that wished to provide data over the Web and that realized their potential customers needed software clients.

Web browsers were small in both hard disk and RAM requirements. Text and GIF images were generally displayed by the browser, but other data types required "helper applications," as the concept was to keep the browser agile and fast. Virtual Reality Modeling Language (VRML) had been proposed by this time, and JPEG images were often used instead of GIFs because of the larger color palettes and smaller image sizes (in some circumstances). Cottage industries sprang up writing free or shareware helper applications or converting text-based programs to run under graphical interfaces as helper apps.

## Mozilla Roars to Life

When Andreessen and his colleagues founded the predecessor to Netscape, they referred to their prototype browser as Mozilla and used a green dragon as their icon. The programmers frequented newsgroups, and their SIG files often used "It's spelled Netscape, but it's pronounced Mozilla." The rumor was that "Mozilla" meant "Mosaic killer." Mosaic at that time had the lion's share of the browser market, but the Netscape team was determined to build a better browser, hoping the world would beat a path to its doorstep. By introducing extensions to HTML that were specific to the Netscape browser, Netscape the company hoped to sell server software that could make full use of those extensions. `<BLINK>` was born.

### A NOTE ON NETSCAPE'S NAME

Netscape's name can become a point of confusion, so here is a little history to make it clear. When the company was formed as Mosaic Communications, the *browser* was called Netscape. When the company changed its name to Netscape, the browser was called Netscape for a while; in fact, one of the most stable releases was Netscape 1.1N. Some of you might remember the "breathing N" logo in the upper-right corner of the browser window. With the release of version 2, the browser was called Navigator and had a ship's wheel as its logo. With the program called Navigator, I can stop trying to distinguish between Netscape the browser and Netscape the company.

Netscape began its practice of releasing beta software to the public over the Internet and using early adopters to help in the beta testing. Netscape went through several iterations of its browser (by then called Navigator) in versions numbered less than 1. The new browser introduced, in addition to the BLINK element, attributes to the horizontal rule element, allowing the specification of its height and of its width in pixels or as a percentage of window width. Netscape aggravated many SGML users by providing proprietary attributes for presentation control over lists and line breaks and by providing for the REFRESH attribute, which automatically transferred the user to a specified link. Netscape also introduced CENTER, ALIGN, VSPACE and HSPACE, HEIGHT and WIDTH, SIZE, and TYPE (for bulleted lists), among other "unauthorized" extensions. Netscape further angered the World Wide Web community by failing to publish its DTDs for these tags, making it impossible to determine how the extensions should be treated by other browsers.

Netscape unilaterally implemented the following proprietary attributes, which are not included in the official RFC for HTML 2.0:

- <ISINDEX>: An attribute for a prompt that the author wished to have a user see.

- <HR>: The attribute SIZE=*n*, where *n* is an integer from 1 to 5, suggesting additional thickness to the rule. The attribute WIDTH=*n*¦%, where *n* is an integer giving a length in pixels or % is an integer giving the length as a percentage of the window's width. The attribute ALIGN=*left*¦*right*¦*center*, where a horizontal rule less than the entire window width can be aligned with the left or right margin or centered in the window. And finally, NO SHADE, where the rule is a solid color rather than giving the illusion of depth with shading.

- <UL>: The attribute TYPE, allowing the author to suggest a *disk*, *circle*, or *square* as the bullet.

- <OL>: The attribute TYPE, allowing the author to suggest numbering by lowercase or capital roman numerals or letters (in addition to the standard numbers). The attribute START, allowing the author to suggest beginning the sequence with other than *1*, *i*, or *a*.

- <IMG>: This element received the most attention, being given the attribute ALIGN with the following possibilities:

  `left¦right¦top¦texttop¦middle¦absmiddle¦baseline¦bottom¦absbottom`

  The attributes of WIDTH and HEIGHT actually provided a helpful addition to HTML by allowing the browser to download text and format the text around the space an image would occupy without having to wait for the actual image to finish downloading. Netscape also added the attributes of BORDER, VSPACE, and HSPACE to provide some relief around the image instead of having it in contact with surrounding text.

- <BR>: Netscape added the attribute CLEAR, suggesting that a line break would continue down past an image to the left margin of the window.

- `<NOBR>`: Strings of characters between the opening and closing tags would not be wrapped by the browser.

- `<FONT SIZE=n>`: *n* could be an integer from 1 to 7, either positive or negative; 3 was considered the default, allowing text sizes to be larger or smaller than the default. Another element, `BASEFONT`, was introduced to set the base font size in the document as something other than the default.

Among the problems created by these additions were the lack of default values specified for many of the elements, such as `HR`—what was the default size, and what amount of increase in size did each increase in value suggest? Attribute values in SGML are not case sensitive, yet Netscape proposed having ordered lists be lettered, and it distinguished between the values `TYPE=A` and `TYPE=a`. `IMG` has no default alignment in HTML, and Netscape did not specify one as appropriate behavior when no attribute was given. Netscape also provided for characters in the attribute values that SGML required to be quoted, for example, +, -, and %. Netscape, however, ignored this requirement. Case sensitivity and violation of the SGML TOKEN rules meant that Netscape's additions could not be validated under SGML rules. Worse for people trying to make a living in the new World Wide Web, the onslaught of new additions meant that customers demanding the latest and trendiest features could never be satisfied. For those Webmasters attempting to maintain some compatibility with non-Netscape browsers, the Netscape additions often resulted in displays that were unreadable in Mosaic or Lynx.

With Version 2 of the Navigator, Netscape added the capability to run Java applets and a scripting language named JavaScript, along with several HTML 3.0 tags. The final release of Version 2 was followed the next month by the first release of Version 3.0b1, which added plug-ins and support for color backgrounds in tables. Other beta versions followed, incorporating the `FACE` attribute for `FONT`, and support for columns and spacing. The final release of 3.0 was in August 1996; version 4.0 saw its initial release in December of that year. Version 4.0b1 introduced the `LAYER` tag, which is an attempt to control the layout of elements of a Web page. Version 4.0b2 added support for cascading style sheets and Netscape's proprietary JavaScript style sheets. `LAYER` has been proposed to the W3C for acceptance as a standard for layout control.

**NOTE**

Debates raged in the newly formed newsgroup `comp.infosystems.www.authoring.html`. It was often stated that attempts to control appearance of a page using HTML were "doomed to failure." In the early 11th century, Canute was king of England, Norway, and Denmark. People began to say that King Canute was divine, which was a heresy. To prove his subjects wrong, Canute had his throne taken to a beach at low tide and placed near the water. He commanded the tide to remain at ebb. As the incoming tide reached him sitting in his throne, he made a kingly retreat to his castle, having no need to prove further his lack of divinity. Although people looked to the foundation of the World Wide Web Consortium (W3C) to bring commercial proprietariness to a halt, the commercial tide continued, and it was the W3C that retreated to the castle.

## The Sleeping Giant Is Awakened: Microsoft

Microsoft's Bill Gates had been saying that the Internet had insufficient bandwidth to become viable as a consumer marketplace. When he changed his mind, Microsoft turned on the proverbial dime and within a month made the Internet an extension of the Windows desktop. Microsoft started MSN, an online content provider with Internet access, provoking complaints to the United States Justice Department by competitors because Windows 95 loaded with an icon for MSN on the desktop for users to link to automatically.

Microsoft licensed Mosaic from Spyglass, rewrote some of the appearance features, and released it as the Internet Explorer. Microsoft quickly refined its version of Mosaic, making it more Microsoft and introducing the Microsoft way of doing things, such as using tags proprietary to the Internet Explorer. As time passed, more and more proprietary features were added, without the blessing of the W3C. Microsoft introduced its answer to BLINK, the relentlessly scrolling MARQUEE, background sounds that played over the computer, new controls for IMG, new attributes for background images, new coloring schemes for tables, ActiveX controls, and on and on.

Version 1 of the Internet Explorer was followed in only a few months by Version 2, which added support for tables and additional HTML 3.2 tags. In another few months, Internet Explorer 3.0 alpha and beta versions were released, adding proprietary tags for table specifications, frames, support for scripting (JScript, a Netscape JavaScript-compatible language, and VBScript, based on Microsoft's own Visual Basic), and limited support for style sheets. Version 4 was announced in May of 1997 and provides support for proprietary dynamic HTML, which Microsoft has implemented and proposed to the W3C as a standard.

Both Microsoft and Netscape joined the W3C, and their competition entered a new arena. They each proposed competing additions to HTML, but implemented them unilaterally without approval. Each pledged to support all approved standards. The W3C was overwhelmed.

# The World Wide Web Consortium

During a workshop in July of 1993, Berners-Lee proposed founding a consortium to handle the problems inherent in establishing the standards for HTML and HTTP. Berners-Lee and CERN were not the proper entities for this development. It was suggested that the consortium establish a reference model for the standards, test proposals to determine compliance, and provide a stamp of approval.

## Charter of the W3C

In 1994, the W3C was formed to attempt to bring some much needed order to the world of HTML. Founded as an industry consortium, W3C has as its goal developing common standards for the evolution of the World Wide Web. Members of the consortium may propose standards for adoption; once adopted, those standards are to be implemented by members in their software, whether server or client. The W3C is attempting also to promulgate protocols that are faster and more efficient in the use of the Web for images, sounds, and video.

## The Work of the W3C

With both Netscape and Microsoft on the W3C, that body became the battleground for the hearts and minds of the World Wide Web. The charter of the consortium to bring order to the growth of HTML and HTTP protocols took a backseat to the commercial interests of some of the consortium's members. Although many had predicted that bringing Netscape into the fold would force it to give up its renegade ways, the tide of commerce inexorably flowed into the conference room, lapping at the feet of the conferees. A retreat to the castle was crafted: HTML 3.2 was proposed in lieu of 3.0. Level 3.2, being a compromise, pleased no one, but it bowed to reality and incorporated formerly proprietary Microsoft and Netscape tags. That round of the debate of HTML for appearance or content was given to appearance.

With HTML 4.0, known informally as Cougar, the W3C has begun again to attempt to set standards that will divide the markup of content from the appearance of a Web page. As discussed more fully in Part III, "Extending HTML 3.2," Cougar proposes the separation of physical styles from content markup by more reliance on style sheets. With both Microsoft and Netscape involved in the discussions, we can hope that browsers will finally implement style sheets. Many see that as the best way to suggest appearance while still allowing full use of HTML as an SGML-compliant method of bridging the chasm between mind and knowledge as the level of data increases.

# Summary

A combination of three factors made Berners-Lee the creator of the Web. First, he worked during a time when computers were powerful enough, small enough, and cheap enough to be used as the infrastructure of the World Wide Web. That was chance. The second factor was the ability to see beyond a particular need and a particular solution to that need; to see instead the realization of a great theme reaching down through time to the right moment with the right tools; to see instead an overarching answer to a question that was unasked at the time, but which had been asked and unanswered for generations. By chance, Berners-Lee was at the right place and time to have the tools lacking to Vannevar Bush. Berners-Lee had Bush's insight, but Berners-Lee also had the means. The third factor, however, is what distinguishes Berners-Lee from many great thinkers and idealists: Berners-Lee saw the answer and put it into effect. Instead of talking and writing about his concept, Berners-Lee went about the daily grind of using what existed, inventing what did not, writing software, drafting proposals, and coordinating the efforts of a team to put his idea into working order and to get it used. We must not neglect the team that worked with him. I have mentioned Dan Connolly, Karen Muldrow, and David Raggett, but there were many others who made major contributions of time, thought, and effort.

I cannot overstate the importance of the theories that preceded Berners-Lee, especially those of Bush and Nelson. It is not incorrect to say that this is another case of vision increased by standing on the shoulders of giants. But Berners-Lee then got down off their shoulders, dug the foundation, laid the footings, and began bricking in the walls of his vision. As a result of this founding work, the World Wide Web spans the seas, linking not countries, but people who are now empowered for the first time in history with the ability to publish work with a worldwide audience without having to own the printing presses and the means of distribution.

# CHAPTER 3

# SGML and the HTML DTD

*by Dmitry Kirsanov*

## IN THIS CHAPTER

SGML is the substratum on which HTML was conceived and, therefore, is responsible for many of HTML's strengths and weaknesses. SGML stands for Standard Generalized Markup Language; this is a formal system designed for building text markup languages. It is not a markup system by itself, however; think of it as a programming language to build working programs (HTML being one of them) rather than a program by itself.

In this chapter, you'll learn the foundations of SGML to see how (and why) HTML was built on top of it. It's very instructive and engaging to trace the roots of the language and explore the conceptions of its creators. In fact, you can't say you know HTML unless you're at least sketchily acquainted with its SGML heritage.

We'll analyze the definition of HTML in terms of SGML, consisting of SGML Declaration and document type definition, both for HTML Version 4.0. You'll see what valuable information can be elicited from these formal constructs and how they can be used for authoritative reference on HTML topics. You'll also learn why an HTML document should conform to a DTD and how to ensure this using a validation service.

Knowledge of basic SGML concepts and syntax will provide you with a solid foundation for mastering HTML and will help you understand some of the peculiarities of the language. The goal of this chapter, however, is not to teach you SGML or how to write SGML applications, but to show you how understanding SGML may aid in learning and applying HTML.

# Procedural and Descriptive Markup

Any document can be thought of as consisting of *content* and *markup*. The content is relatively straightforward; it bands together all the characters of text, images, and the rest of the meat that delivers the message of your document. However, if you just add together all this stuff you won't get a readable document. You need to mark it up—that is, to introduce some new information into it that couldn't be automatically deduced from the content.

In fact, even a plain ASCII text, often cited as an example of pure text without any formatting, contains a fair amount of markup. For instance, it is markup that allows you to determine what the width of text column in a plain text file is, or where the boundaries between paragraphs lie. Of course, the inventory of markup instructions (called *tags*) that you can apply is determined by the format of your document and the tools you use to work with it.

So what is the purpose of markup? In other words, what information can, and should, be conveyed by a document beyond its content? This extra information can be divided into two groups: *structure* and *formatting*. Structure tells us how the document logically breaks down into parts (paragraphs, sections, chapters) and how these parts are hierarchically organized, from the document itself at the very top to the atoms of content at the very bottom. Formatting (in a broad sense) governs presentation of the document: which fonts to use to display it, in what tone of voice to read it aloud, how to break it into pages for printing, and so on.

Here enters the Great Markup Controversy that was one of the main driving forces behind the creation of SGML and whose backwashes are still disturbing the HTML community. Its essence, without the fear of oversimplification, can be reduced to the question of which of the two markup types is more important and should be given priority.

Obviously, many contemporary text processing systems are heavily biased toward marking up formatting aspects of a document in the first place (this sort of markup is often called *procedural* or *presentational*). The reason is obvious: What an average user needs most often is a formatted document, not a structural diagram of its parts.

However, the bitter truth is that procedural markup may actually impede using and reusing the document if not accompanied, and even preceded, by proper structural (often called *descriptive* or *generic*) markup. For instance, if a document file contains instructions to set a line of text in Times Roman, size 12 pt, and left-aligned, but never hints that this line is a heading or a figure caption, then this markup is very restrictive.

You won't be able to change formatting of all headings in a document at once. You'll have difficulty exporting the document into another format or another medium (such as a voice synthesis system), which may be using different means of formatting headings. You cannot even automatically generate a table of contents. To put it simply, unless you know what this part of text is supposed to *be*, information on how to *render* it is of very limited value.

On the other hand, after you have added information about the logical role of every element in the text, the natural next step is to attach the presentational markup to these logical tags rather than actual parts of the text. Now you don't have to specify font size for a heading in your text anymore; it is enough to mark it up as a heading, and the rest is taken care of automatically (provided that someone has associated certain formatting parameters with the structural heading tag).

This concept, called "separation of presentation from content," is the major advantage of all systems that put descriptive markup first. When separated, both content and formatting can be developed by different people and modified much more easily. Thus, one of the roles of descriptive markup is to serve as an intermediate layer separating content and formatting of a document.

It should be admitted that text processing systems that are in common use now (such as office word processors) do not completely ignore the benefits of descriptive markup. The named styles that you apply to paragraphs in, say, Microsoft Word, represent some sort of descriptive markup units with certain formatting tags associated with each of them. Moreover, users can create new styles as needed for their documents. This provides for a certain level of separation of presentation from content.

However, such a solution is only partial because style tags do not impose any restrictions on the structure of your document. For example, it's no problem to assign a heading style to a paragraph inside a figure caption or a footnote—which is pretty much senseless. Also, you are in no way discouraged from making direct changes to text attributes, such as font face or size, thereby overriding their values in a style. Styles in word processors are mere containers for presentation attributes and not a means to impose some prescribed structure on a document being created or processed.

You might wonder, do we really need to impose any structure on the document contents? Yes, and here's why: You can't predict what uses will be made of your document tomorrow or in a year, what formats it'll need to be converted to, or what media it'll be put onto. By using a strictly defined set of hierarchical descriptive tags, you ensure that the text can be processed automatically without any need to manually disambiguate cases such as a heading inside a footnote. I could say that descriptive markup reveals the immaterial soul of a document so that any program or person can then conveniently incarnate it into a body of choice.

The provision for automatic processing is the advantage that outshines all others. It is difficult to imagine how many resources humankind spends annually on preparation, processing, and interchange of documents. Office computing and desktop publishing software made this work easier, but, in many cases, proprietary and presentation-oriented tools put more handicaps than benefits in the flow of documentation. An open and extensible system of descriptive markup would thus be invaluable in many situations.

To summarize, what we need is a markup system focusing on structure of a document rather than its formatting. It should allow us to build a hierarchy of descriptive tags so that they could serve not only to separate and describe different parts of a document but also to formally prescribe its structure.

An equally important requirement is that the system should provide for easy extension and modification. Ideally, a user should be able to define a completely new set of tags if such a need arises. Finally, this system should not be proprietary; it is important that anyone be free to create and use markup tools based on this system and to produce software implementing these tools.

SGML is the system designed to satisfy all of these requirements, as well as many others. SGML is strictly descriptive and contains no means to mark up presentational aspects of documents. However, SGML can be easily interfaced to external procedural markup systems and style sheets.

It is the customizability area where SGML reveals its real power. In fact, SGML is not a markup system by itself; it is, rather, a *metasystem* enabling users to create such systems for particular types of documents. Its flexible syntax makes it possible to build markup languages (HTML being one of the examples) to match any imaginable demand. Moreover, any single SGML document can be provided with its own "local" markup definitions fine-tuned for the particular purpose.

Just like HTML, SGML is a computer language rather than a data format. This means that you can create SGML files manually in a text editor, although there exist software tools that facilitate the task. A piece of software that reads and analyzes an SGML document (for example, for transformation or validation) is called an SGML parser. A parser by itself, however, is not very useful because of the purely descriptive nature of SGML, so most often a parser is a part of a bigger document processing or browsing application.

# A Brief History of SGML

The roots of SGML go back to the late 1960s when the concept of descriptive markup saw the light for the first time. After companies started using computers for document processing, it soon became obvious that a storage format should contain not only formatting codes interpreted by the computer itself, but also descriptive human-legible information about the nature and role of every element in a document.

The first working system that used these concepts was the Generalized Markup Language (GML) developed by Charles Goldfarb, Edward Mosher, and Raymond Lorie at IBM. This system was the direct predecessor of SGML and contained prototypes for many of its major features, such as hierarchical document structure and document type definition. IBM adopted GML and built mainframe-based publishing systems on it that were widely used to produce technical documentation in the corporation.

In 1978, American National Standards Institute (ANSI) started research in the field of generic document markup pursuing the goal of establishing a nationwide standard for information interchange. Later, Dr. Goldfarb joined the ANSI working group, and in 1980 the first draft was published. It was finalized in 1983 as an industry standard named GCA 101-1983.

In 1984, the International Standards Organization (ISO) joined the activity and started preparation of an international version of the standard. The first draft of the ISO standard was published in 1985 and the final version appeared a year later. The standard bears the full name "ISO 8879:1986 Information processing—Text and office systems—Standard Generalized Markup Language (SGML)." The full text of the specification is available from ISO for a fee. (See `http://www.iso.ch/cate/d16387.html`.)

The best use of SGML is generally made in big corporations and agencies that produce a lot of documents and can afford to introduce a single standard format for internal use. Besides IBM, early applications of the new technology include the projects developed by Association of American Publishers (AAP) and the U.S. Department of Defense. Finally, in 1991, researchers at the European Laboratory for Particle Physics (CERN) chose to build a hypertext markup language that they called HTML as an SGML application. But that's another story…

# How to Define an SGML Application

From SGML's point of view, a document is a hierarchical structure of nested *elements* (chapters, sections, paragraphs, and so on). SGML has no means—and was not intended to have—for specifying any presentational aspects of these elements. However, strictly speaking, SGML cannot tell you about the meaning or role of any element, either. This information is implied by the creator of an SGML application and is usually provided in comments or in the documentation accompanying the formal specification.

SGML realizes the maxim of Wittgenstein, who said, "The meaning of a word is its use." In SGML, the only information that can be formally communicated about an element is in what contexts and levels of document hierarchy it can or must occur. This means that you cannot build an interpreter that could apply a meaningful formatting to a document based only on its SGML markup. However, the purely formal dissection that SGML performs on a document is still surprisingly useful in many situations.

All documents that can be marked up with the same hierarchy of elements are said to belong to a certain *document type.* Rather than describe a set of tools to mark up documents, SGML defines the structure of a particular type of documents via what is called document type definition (DTD). A part of this chapter (see the section called "Document Type Definition for HTML 4.0") is devoted to analyzing the DTD for one particular SGML application, HTML 4.0 (code-named Cougar). Besides (and before) the DTD, some general features of an SGML application are specified in another formal construct called the SGML declaration, which is detailed in the next section, "SGML Declaration for HTML 4.0."

As for SGML syntax, suffice it to say beforehand that it is pretty close to the syntax of HTML. You will see that SGML statements, like HTML tags, are enclosed in angle brackets (<>) and contain a keyword or name followed by one or more parameters separated by spaces. The only consistent difference is that SGML statements commonly have the ! character inserted between the open delimiter < and the statement keyword, for example:

```
<!ELEMENT IMG - O EMPTY -- Embedded image -->
```

You must already be familiar with one type of statement that uses the <! syntax, namely comments in HTML documents that are enclosed in <!-- and -->. That's because the comment syntax of HTML is directly borrowed from SGML, where everything within a <! statement enclosed in double hyphens (--) is ignored by the SGML parser. For example, the words Embedded image in the preceding code line are intended as a comment for human readers only.

One more <!-type declaration that needs to appear in HTML files is DOCTYPE, discussed briefly later in this chapter in the "Public Identifiers" section.

# SGML Declaration for HTML 4.0

SGML declaration is a formal construct used to specify some general information about an SGML application and its associated document type. The following sections list and analyze the SGML declaration for HTML 4.0 provided by W3C. (It can be found at http://www.w3.org/TR/WD-html40/.

The SGML declaration is contained in the SGML statement, which has the following syntax:

```
<!SGML  "ISO 8879:1986" ...  >
```

The ellipsis here represents the body of SGML declaration, and the string ISO 8879:1986 is meant to denote the *level* of SGML standard that this declaration conforms to. In our case, this is the original ISO specification published in 1986.

In the body of the declaration, first comes the comment part:

```
--
    SGML Declaration for HyperText Markup Language version 4.0

    With support for Unicode UCS-2 and increased limits
    for tag and literal lengths etc.
--
```

The rest of the declaration body is divided into sections that are described next.

## CHARSET Section

The CHARSET section of SGML declaration is used to specify the *character set* to be used by the documents conforming to this document type. So what is a character set?

You probably know that the characters that appear on your display are coded inside the computer by some bit combinations, usually *bytes* consisting of eight bits. Unfortunately, different computers and operating systems sometimes use the same bytes to represent different characters on the screen. The most frequent reason for this is that localized versions of programs and operating systems need to represent non-Latin characters of a particular language's alphabet (such as Cyrillic alphabet for Russian).

Thus, to make the SGML document as unambiguous as possible, SGML declaration defines exactly what *character set* it uses, that is, what bit combinations (or *codes*) are allowed within a conforming document and what characters they are intended to mean. To define a character set, you need to specify three things: first, the set of codes used; second, the set of characters represented; and third, the mapping between these two sets.

The set of codes is easy to specify by simply listing these codes in decimal or hexadecimal form. The set of characters, or *character repertoire*, is more tricky. You cannot simply "draw" a character in the specification because the SGML declaration itself is represented by a plain-text file where every character is coded by a bit combination not guaranteed to mean the same on all systems. One possible way to overcome this difficulty is to give a textual description for every character in the repertoire (for example, "CYRILLIC CAPITAL LETTER A").

However, SGML creators have chosen a less complicated way of dealing with the problem. SGML declaration makes use of other character set standards that already have been adopted by standard-setting bodies (mostly ISO) and that can provide us with a full specification of nearly any character in the world. Having made a reference to such a standard, you can then use character numbers in that standard to clearly identify what character you need for your document's character set. Here's how this is done.

First comes the CHARSET keyword that marks the beginning of the corresponding section. It is followed by the BASESET keyword that contains the name of the character set standard referred to thereupon:

```
CHARSET
       BASESET   "ISO 646:1983//CHARSET
                 International Reference Version
                 (IRV)//ESC 2/5 4/0"
```

The standard specified here, commonly referred to as "ISO 646," is practically indistinguishable from what is called "7-bit ASCII." Its 128 characters cover all Latin alphabet characters, digits, punctuation, and some special characters. It is the greatest common subset for nearly all character sets in use now, and you're unlikely to find a computer or a program (even a localized version) that uses something other than ISO 646 for its first 128 byte codes.

However, SGML declaration for HTML 4.0 does not use all this character set, but only a certain part of it. The selection is done using the DESCSET keyword:

```
DESCSET
       0    9    UNUSED
       9    2    9
       11   2    UNUSED
       13   1    13
       14   18   UNUSED
       32   95   32
       127  1    UNUSED
```

Here, the target HTML character set that we need to define is divided into subranges, with a clear identification of where characters in each subrange come from. The first number in each line specifies the starting code of the subrange; the second, its length; and the third position is occupied either by a number that identifies the code to start copying characters from the reference standard, or the UNUSED keyword, which means that the characters in this subrange are not allowed.

Thus, the first line in the preceding code means that the codes in the range 0–8 inclusive (decimal) cannot be used within documents conforming to the HTML 4.0 specification. The second line says that, starting from code 9 onward, we borrow 2 characters that are coded 9 and 10 in the ISO 646 standard (in other words, within this two-character range our character set is identical to ISO 646). The next two characters are again unused, and then we take one character with code 13, skip 18 more characters, and so on.

So, we have defined the first 128 characters of the HTML 4.0 character set. However, to specify the remainder of the code table, we have to refer to another standard. The syntax of the CHARSET section allows the specification of as many external standards as needed and the borrowing of characters from each of them (that is, to have as many BASESET/DESCSET pairs as necessary).

```
BASESET   "ISO Registration Number 176//CHARSET
           ISO/IEC 10646-1:1993 UCS-2 with
           implementation level 3//ESC 2/5 2/15 4/5"
DESCSET   128 32     UNUSED
          160 65375 160
```

The previous version of HTML, 3.2, referred to the standard named "ISO 8859-1" or "ISO Latin-1" to define the characters beyond 7-bit ASCII. ISO Latin-1 uses 8-bit codes and, therefore, accommodates the total of 256 characters (coded 0–255 inclusive), with the range 128–255 containing letters with diacritical marks used in different European languages as well as some special symbols (trademark, copyright, fractions, and so on). The first 128 characters of Latin-1 are identical to those of 7-bit ASCII.

However, the need for better support of languages other than English and Western European languages led to the development of a set of provisions commonly referred to as *HTML Internationalization*, initially described in RFC 2070 (which can be found at http://ds.internic.net/ rfc/rfc2070.txt) and then incorporated into HTML 4.0. One of the key features of the internationalized HTML is the extended character set that makes use of the Unicode coding standard. Unicode uses 16-bit (two bytes) codes and, therefore, covers as many as 65,536 characters, including nearly all national alphabets of the world and hordes of special symbols.

More precisely, HTML 4.0 refers to the ISO standard named "ISO/IEC 10646-1:1993" or simply "ISO 10646," which is a superset of Unicode and generally uses four-byte codes. However, the UCS-2 in the preceding BASESET statement identifies a special mode of ISO 10646, which uses two-byte codes and is in effect indistinguishable from Unicode. All these coding standards and related issues are covered in much more detail in Chapter 39, "Internationalizing the HTML Character Set and Language Tags."

One question that you might have by now, however, needs to be answered immediately. Does the SGML declaration imply that with HTML 4.0, you have to use Unicode for your documents? No, because the *document character set* we're defining is different from the *external character encoding* that the document is in when created, stored, and served over the network. For the external character encoding, you can use any character set standard that is best suited for the document's content. In practice, the only area affected by the document character set as per SGML declaration is numerical character references such as   that must, in HTML 4.0, point to Unicode code positions. Again, for more details on these issues, refer to Chapter 39.

Unicode itself is a superset of Latin-1, because the first 256 characters of Unicode are identical to those of Latin-1. Also, the latter is likely to remain for a long time the most popular choice for the external character encoding of HTML documents. Table 3.1 lists the first 256 characters of the HTML document character set specified by SGML declaration for HTML 4.0.

**Table 3.1. The first 256 characters of the HTML document character set as specified by SGML declaration for HTML 4.0.**

| Character (or its name for nonprinting characters) | Code (in the form of character reference) | Mnemonic Entity (if any) |
|---|---|---|
| UNUSED | &#0;–&#8; | |
| [tabulation] | &#9; | |
| [line feed] | &#10; | |
| UNUSED | &#11;–&#12; | |
| [carriage return] | &#13; | |
| UNUSED | &#14;–&#31; | |
| [space] | &#32; | |
| ! | &#33; | |
| " | &#34; | &quot; |
| # | &#35; | |
| $ | &#36; | |
| % | &#37; | |
| & | &#38; | &amp; |
| ' | &#39; | |
| ( | &#40; | |
| ) | &#41; | |
| * | &#42; | |
| + | &#43; | |
| , | &#44; | |
| - | &#45; | |
| . | &#46; | |
| / | &#47; | |
| 0 | &#48; | |
| 1 | &#49; | |
| 2 | &#50; | |
| 3 | &#51; | |
| 4 | &#52; | |
| 5 | &#53; | |
| 6 | &#54; | |

| Character (or its name for nonprinting characters) | Code (in the form of character reference) | Mnemonic Entity (if any) |
|---|---|---|
| 7 | &#55; | |
| 8 | &#56; | |
| 9 | &#57; | |
| : | &#58; | |
| ; | &#59; | |
| < | &#60; | &lt; |
| = | &#61; | |
| > | &#62; | &gt; |
| ? | &#63; | |
| @ | &#64; | |
| A | &#65; | |
| B | &#66; | |
| C | &#67; | |
| D | &#68; | |
| E | &#69; | |
| F | &#70; | |
| G | &#71; | |
| H | &#72; | |
| I | &#73; | |
| J | &#74; | |
| K | &#75; | |
| L | &#76; | |
| M | &#77; | |
| N | &#78; | |
| O | &#79; | |
| P | &#80; | |
| Q | &#81; | |
| R | &#82; | |
| S | &#83; | |
| T | &#84; | |

3

**SGML AND THE HTML DTD**

*continues*

**Table 3.1. continued**

| Character (or its name for nonprinting characters) | Code (in the form of character reference) | Mnemonic Entity (if any) |
|---|---|---|
| U | &#85; | |
| V | &#86; | |
| W | &#87; | |
| X | &#88; | |
| Y | &#89; | |
| Z | &#90; | |
| [ | &#91; | |
| \ | &#92; | |
| ] | &#93; | |
| ^ | &#94; | |
| _ | &#95; | |
| ` | &#96; | |
| a | &#97; | |
| b | &#98; | |
| c | &#99; | |
| d | &#100; | |
| e | &#101; | |
| f | &#102; | |
| g | &#103; | |
| h | &#104; | |
| i | &#105; | |
| j | &#106; | |
| k | &#107; | |
| l | &#108; | |
| m | &#109; | |
| n | &#110; | |
| o | &#111; | |
| p | &#112; | |
| q | &#113; | |
| r | &#114; | |

| Character (or its name for nonprinting characters) | Code (in the form of character reference) | Mnemonic Entity (if any) |
| --- | --- | --- |
| s | &#115; | |
| t | &#116; | |
| u | &#117; | |
| v | &#118; | |
| w | &#119; | |
| x | &#120; | |
| y | &#121; | |
| z | &#122; | |
| { | &#123; | |
| \| | &#124; | |
| } | &#125; | |
| ~ | &#126; | |
| UNUSED | &#127;–&#159 | |
| [nonbreaking space] |   |   |
| ¡ | &#161; | &iexcl; |
| ¢ | &#162; | &cent; |
| £ | &#163; | &pound; |
| ¤ | &#164; | &curren; |
| ¥ | &#165; | &yen; |
| ¦ | &#166; | &brvbar; |
| » | &#167; | &sect; |
| ¨ | &#168; | &uml; |
| © | &#169; | &copy; |
| ª | &#170; | &ordf; |
| « | &#171; | &laquo; |
| ¬ | &#172; | &not; |
| - | &#173; | &shy; |
| ® | &#174; | &reg; |
| ¯ | &#175; | &macr; |
| ° | &#176; | &deg; |

*continues*

**3**

**SGML AND THE HTML DTD**

**Table 3.1. continued**

| Character (or its name for nonprinting characters) | Code (in the form of character reference) | Mnemonic Entity (if any) |
| --- | --- | --- |
| ± | &#177; | &plusmn; |
| ² | &#178; | &sup2; |
| ³ | &#179; | &sup3; |
| ´ | &#180; | &acute; |
| µ | &#181; | &micro; |
| ¶ | &#182; | &para; |
| · | &#183; | &middot; |
| ¸ | &#184; | &cedil; |
| ¹ | &#185; | &sup1; |
| º | &#186; | &ordm; |
| » | &#187; | &raquo; |
| ¼ | &#188; | &frac14; |
| ½ | &#189; | &frac12; |
| ¾ | &#190; | &frac34; |
| ¿ | &#191; | &iquest; |
| À | &#192; | &Agrave; |
| Á | &#193; | &Aacute; |
| Â | &#194; | &Acirc; |
| Ã | &#195; | &Atilde; |
| Ä | &#196; | &Auml; |
| Å | &#197; | &Aring; |
| Æ | &#198; | &AElig; |
| Ç | &#199; | &Ccedil; |
| È | &#200; | &Egrave; |
| É | &#201; | &Eacute; |
| Ê | &#202; | &Ecirc; |
| Ë | &#203; | &Euml; |
| Ì | &#204; | &Igrave; |
| Í | &#205; | &Iacute; |
| Î | &#206; | &Icirc; |

| Character (or its name for nonprinting characters) | Code (in the form of character reference) | Mnemonic Entity (if any) |
|---|---|---|
| Ï | &#207; | &Iuml; |
| Ð | &#208; | &ETH; |
| Ñ | &#209; | &Ntilde; |
| Ò | &#210; | &Ograve; |
| Ó | &#211; | &Oacute; |
| Ô | &#212; | &Ocirc; |
| Õ | &#213; | &Otilde; |
| Ö | &#214; | &Ouml; |
| × | &#215; | &times; |
| Ø | &#216; | &Oslash; |
| Ù | &#217; | &Ugrave; |
| Ú | &#218; | &Uacute; |
| Û | &#219; | &Ucirc; |
| Ü | &#220; | &Uuml; |
| Ý | &#221; | &Yacute; |
| Þ | &#222; | &THORN; |
| ß | &#223; | &szlig; |
| à | &#224; | &agrave; |
| á | &#225; | &aacute; |
| â | &#226; | &acirc; |
| ã | &#227; | &atilde; |
| ä | &#228; | &auml; |
| å | &#229; | &aring; |
| æ | &#230; | &aelig; |
| ç | &#231; | &ccedil; |
| è | &#232; | &egrave; |
| é | &#233; | &eacute; |
| ê | &#234; | &ecirc; |

*continues*

**Table 3.1. continued**

| Character (or its name for nonprinting characters) | Code (in the form of character reference) | Mnemonic Entity (if any) |
| --- | --- | --- |
| ë | &#235; | &euml; |
| ì | &#236; | &igrave; |
| í | &#237; | &iacute; |
| î | &#238; | &icirc; |
| ï | &#239; | &iuml; |
| ð | &#240; | &eth; |
| ñ | &#241; | &ntilde; |
| ò | &#242; | &ograve; |
| ó | &#243; | &oacute; |
| ô | &#244; | &ocirc; |
| õ | &#245; | &otilde; |
| ö | &#246; | &ouml; |
| ÷ | &#247; | &divide; |
| ø | &#248; | &oslash; |
| ù | &#249; | &ugrave; |
| ú | &#250; | &uacute; |
| û | &#251; | &ucirc; |
| ü | &#252; | &uuml; |
| ý | &#253; | &yacute; |
| þ | &#254; | &thorn; |
| ÿ | &#255; | &yuml; |

**NOTE**

Note that the commonly deployed symbols of trademark (™), en dash (–), and em dash (—) do not belong to the Latin-1 range and therefore are not included in the table. To access these symbols, you must use their Unicode codes, which yield &#8482;, &#8211;, and &#8212; correspondingly or their mnemonic entities &trade;, &ndash;, and &mdash;.

## CAPACITY Section

This section is meant to provide a rough estimate of the system resources (more specifically, different types of memory) that an SGML parser will need to allocate in order to process the DTD. This is not very reliable information, however, because the memory usage is largely dependent on the internal architecture of the parsing application. Most SGML parsers do not take these values into account, and HTML creators simply assigned big enough numbers to these parameters to ensure that processing the DTD won't be aborted because of exceeding one of the CAPACITY values. The CAPACITY parameters are not discussed individually here; you can refer to the SGML specification for details.

```
CAPACITY    SGMLREF
            TOTALCAP        150000
            GRPCAP          150000
            ENTCAP          150000
```

The SGMLREF keyword means that all CAPACITY types that are not indicated here should take their default values from the SGML reference concrete syntax. (See the next section for more on this.)

## SYNTAX Section

The next major section of SGML declaration is introduced by the SYNTAX keyword. It is provided to define various syntax features of the SGML application, such as naming rules, delimiter and control characters, reserved names and limits used by the DTD and conforming SGML documents. This syntax is called "application concrete syntax" as opposed to "reference concrete syntax" of SGML itself, which is used in the SGML declaration (but not the DTD, as specified by the SCOPE parameter). As you'll see shortly, in the case of HTML, the differences between these syntaxes are minimal.

## SCOPE Declaration

Immediately before the SYNTAX section comes the SCOPE DOCUMENT declaration:

```
SCOPE       DOCUMENT
```

Its sole purpose is to specify that the application concrete syntax to be declared will be used not only by the conforming SGML documents but also by the DTD of this SGML application.

## Shunned Characters Declaration

The SYNTAX section starts with the list of shunned characters' codes preceded by the SHUNCHAR keyword:

```
SHUNCHAR CONTROLS 0 1 2 3 4 5 6 7 8 9 10 11 12 13 14 15 16
         17 18 19 20 21 22 23 24 25 26 27 28 29 30 31 127
```

"Shunned" doesn't mean "prohibited," and the list of shunned character codes doesn't fully coincide with the UNUSED codes in the character set declaration. In fact, some of the shunned characters (for example, the carriage return and line feed characters) are outright necessary in any text file, SGML document being no exception.

However, these characters should be used with care as their meaning and usage may depend on the computer environment in which the text is processed (for example, although a text line in MS-DOS and Windows is terminated by a pair of carriage return and line feed characters, UNIX systems use single carriage return). The keyword CONTROLS means that if a particular computer system uses some other characters as control codes (and not displayable characters), these should be added to the SHUNCHAR list.

## Syntax Character Set Declaration

Next comes what may be considered a duplicate of the CHARSET section—a BASESET/DESCSET pair defining a character set (see "CHARSET Section," earlier in this chapter):

```
BASESET   "ISO 646:1983//CHARSET
           International Reference Version
           (IRV)//ESC 2/5 4/0"
DESCSET   0 128 0
```

What is the purpose of this additional definition?

The character set defined in the SYNTAX section is used only within that section and nowhere else. This reminds us once again of the fact that any text document, SGML declaration included, is actually nothing but a sequence of codes, and to get to the meaning we need to know which character corresponds to each code. Having provided a separate character set declaration within the SYNTAX section, we can ensure that the syntax definition is completely independent of the document character set (defined in the CHARSET section). In other words, we won't have to rewrite the SYNTAX section when the content of CHARSET section is changed.

## Function Characters Declaration

The FUNCTION keyword is used to identify the character codes for so-called *function characters*:

```
FUNCTION
          RE           13
          RS           10
          SPACE        32
          TAB SEPCHAR   9
```

Function characters are special characters that can affect on syntax. All function characters defined here are *separators* whose role is identical to that of a white space. The RE and RS identifiers denote simply carriage return and line feed characters; they are short for Record End and Record Start, respectively. (In SGML, a line in a text file is sometimes termed a *record*, similar in a way to a database record.) TAB (tabulation character) is not recognized as a separator by SGML standard, that is why it is accompanied by the additional classifier SEPCHAR.

## Naming Rules Declaration

Next comes the NAMING declaration, which regulates usage of characters in element and entity names and as names' start characters:

```
NAMING   LCNMSTRT  ""
         UCNMSTRT  ""
         LCNMCHAR  ".-"      -- ?include "~/_" for URLs? --
         UCNMCHAR  ".-"
```

To facilitate recognition of a name by the parser, the repertoire of characters allowed in the first position of a name is limited as compared to the rest of the name. SGML standard itself allows Latin letters only as name start characters and Latin letters plus digits as ordinary name characters, so here we only need to specify additions to these sets. The characters are specified by using strings in quotes (called *literals*), and separate parameters are provided for indicating uppercase and lowercase character versions in each class.

Thus, the preceding lines tell us that in HTML, only Latin letters are allowed as name first characters (the corresponding parameter strings are empty) while the repertoire of ordinary name characters is extended by the period and the hyphen. These characters are caseless and thus are shown the same in both LCNMCHAR (LowerCase NaMe CHARacters) and UCNMCHAR (UpperCase NaMe CHARacters) parameters.

```
NAMECASE GENERAL YES
         ENTITY  NO
```

The NAMECASE declaration governs case sensitivity of the SGML application concrete syntax. It is further subdivided into ENTITY, which applies to entity names only (for more on entities, see the "Entities" section later in this chapter), and GENERAL, which covers all the rest, including element names. Here's the answer to the question of why <img> and <IMG> are treated the same in HTML while &eacute and &Eacute; aren't.

## Delimiters Declaration

The DELIM declaration allows you to change the character sequences used as tag delimiters in the SGML application.

```
DELIM    GENERAL  SGMLREF
         SHORTREF SGMLREF
```

The values SGMLREF indicate that in this respect HTML syntax is no different from SGML syntax; you use < as start delimiter of an opening tag, </ as start delimiter of a closing tag, > as end tag delimiter, and so on. This part of SGML declaration adds very little information on HTML syntax, so it need not be discussed in detail.

## Reserved Names Declaration

The NAMES keyword can be used to change some of the reserved SGML names that will be used in DTD declarations.

```
NAMES    SGMLREF
```

Again, the SGMLREF value indicates that the list of these reserved names is exactly that provided by SGML specification. Many of these reserved names are discussed later in the section on DTD.

## Quantity Limits Declaration

The last declaration in the SYNTAX section is the QUANTITY declaration:

```
QUANTITY SGMLREF
        ATTSPLEN 65536    -- Implementors are recommended --
        LITLEN   65536    -- to avoid fixed limits but --
        NAMELEN  65536    -- this is the best we can say here --
        PILEN    65536
        TAGLVL   100
        TAGLEN   65536
        ATTCNT   100
        GRPGTCNT 150
        GRPCNT   64
```

This declaration sets limits for some lengths and counters used by the parser in processing the DTD and conforming documents. Just like in the CAPACITY section, many of these parameters are assigned arbitrary big values that effectively mean "no limit at all;" it is difficult to imagine that one might need, for example, an element name (governed by the NAMELEN parameter) that is 65,536 characters long. Most HTML browsers disregard these limitations (or have their own instead), so the different QUANTITY parameters aren't discussed here.

## FEATURES Section

The section of SGML declaration introduced by the FEATURES keyword contains parameters that turn on or off some of the features of SGML syntax; that is, they allow or disallow using these features in the SGML application being defined. These features are divided into three classes: MINIMIZE, LINK, and OTHER. Following the HTML-oriented approach used throughout the chapter, only those features that are turned on in the SGML declaration for HTML 4.0 are considered here.

## MINIMIZE Class

The MINIMIZE class contains the markup minimization features that are intended to facilitate using SGML markup and to make it more readable for humans. Minimization features allow you to omit tags and other markup instructions in certain situations where context is sufficient to resolve the resulting ambiguity.

- The OMITTAG YES feature allows the DTD to specify that for certain elements, start and end tags can be omitted. Such an element will be opened or closed based on matching the context against the corresponding content model. (See the upcoming "Elements" section.) The most common example in HTML is the <P> tag, whose closing tag </P> can always be safely omitted.

- The SHORTTAG YES feature is very interesting. In fact, it contains a whole bunch of different features that could save a lot of typing when marking up a document. With

SHORTTAG YES, you can use empty open tag <>, empty closing tag </>, type pairs of tags in the form <TAGNAME/.../, omit attribute names, and so on, with all missing information implied by the parser through simple and effective rules. Unfortunately, common browsers do not support these features, so they are mostly of theoretical interest for HTML users.

## LINK Class

The LINK class contains features that affect processing attributes of elements. None of these is allowed in HTML.

## OTHER Class

The OTHER class contains miscellaneous features that didn't fit into MINIMIZE or LINK classes:

■ The FORMAL    YES feature indicates that the PUBLIC entity declarations (covered in the "Public Identifiers" section later in this chapter) should use formal syntax of public identifiers to enable automatic substitution of external sources by the parser.

# Document Type Definition for HTML 4.0

Now that we've examined the SGML declaration and found answers to a number of general questions about HTML formation, it's time to get to the details of its tags, entities, and the related document structure. All of this is defined in document type definition (DTD) for HTML 4.0. (See http://www.w3.org/pub/WWW/MarkUp/Cougar/Cougar.dtd and Appendix B in this book.)

The HTML DTD analyzed in this chapter is too long to be listed in its entirety. Instead of going through the DTD from top to bottom, I discuss the major concepts and syntax features of an SGML DTD in their logical order exemplifying them by excerpts from the HTML 4.0 DTD. This approach will enable you to understand any given part of the DTD without the chapter being too encumbered.

## Entities

Before we start investigating elements that form an HTML document and the tags that delimit these elements, let's discuss another SGML concept named *entities*. If tags can be likened to named styles in word processors, then entities are a direct analog of *macros* that may expand to text strings or markup instructions.

In HTML documents, entities are used to invoke characters that either are absent on a computer keyboard (such as &eacute;) or have special meaning and thus cannot be typed directly (such as &lt;). In the DTD itself, as you'll see later, entities play a more important role helping to make all sorts of declarations more concise and readable. The entities used in DTD are called *parameter entities*, as opposed to *general entities* intended for use in HTML documents and not in DTD. These two types of entities are declared in a slightly different manner, as shown in the next three sections.

3

SGML AND THE
HTML DTD

## Parameter Entities

The very first declaration in the HTML 4.0 DTD is an entity that expands into a formal reference (in this case, a URL) of the DTD:

```
<!ENTITY % HTML.Version
 "http://www.w3.org/pub/WWW/MarkUp/Cougar/Cougar.dtd"
   -- Typical usage:

     <!DOCTYPE HTML SYSTEM "http://www.w3.org/pub/WWW/MarkUp/Cougar/Cougar.dtd">
     <html>
     ...
     </html>
   --
 >
```

Let's consider, in this example, the syntax of an entity declaration. It uses the ENTITY statement that, like all other SGML statements, requires a ! after the start delimiter <. After the ENTITY keyword comes the % character indicating that the entity in question is a parameter entity rather than a general entity.

Separated from % by one or more spaces is the entity name that is later used to invoke the entity. Note that the name contains a period, thus making use of the NAMING section settings in the SGML declaration. (See "Naming Rules Declaration," earlier in this chapter.) Also recollect that entity names are different from element names in that they are case sensitive.

The last obligatory component of an entity declaration is the string enclosed in quotation marks (*data string*) that shows what this entity stands for and what it will expand to when invoked. Here's how the entity we have defined can be used later in the DTD:

```
%HTML.Version;
```

Note that this time, there is no space between the % and the entity name. The trailing semicolon may be omitted in certain contexts.

Unfortunately, this part of SGML syntax clashes with one of the Netscape HTML extensions, namely using the % character for specifying sizes of images and other elements as percentages of window dimensions. This is why HTML validators that check an HTML document against a DTD sometimes have trouble with this feature. (For more information, see http:// www.webtechs.com/html/mozilla.html#percent.)

## Public Identifiers

The last part of the %HTML.Version; entity declaration is the comment that reminds us about the necessity (unambiguously stated in HTML specification) to start any HTML document that is intended to be a valid SGML document with a DOCTYPE declaration. This allows an SGML parser to know at once that the structure and tags of the document it's about to process are described in the DTD identified by the string "http://www.w3.org/pub/WWW/MarkUp/Cougar/ Cougar.dtd". Of course, HTML (not SGML) browsers could also make use of this information to select the level of HTML support needed for the document (although only a few of them really do).

The use of a URL as a DTD identifier is rather unusual. (It is probably explained by the fact that, at the time of this writing, HTML 4.0 DTD was still evolving.) More often, to refer to external information sources, SGML documents use *public identifiers* of a special form. For example, in HTML 3.2 DTD the `%HTML.Version;` entity expands into the string `-//W3C//DTD HTML 3.2 Final//EN`, which is the public identifier of this version's DTD. Another example is the identifier string of a character set standard used for the `BASESET` parameter in SGML declaration. (See "CHARSET Section," earlier in this chapter.) Any DTD or related standard has a unique public identifier assigned in order to allow referring to this standard from other SGML documents. Such references are usually made via parameter entities.

If the data string in an entity declaration is preceded by the additional keyword `PUBLIC`, this means that the string is not the entity value but a public identifier pointing to an external information source. For example, the HTML 4.0 DTD is accompanied by a set of general entities for accessing characters of ISO Latin-1 (as discussed under "CHARSET Section," earlier in this chapter) isolated in a separate document (detailed at the address `http://www.w3.org/pub/WWW/MarkUp/Cougar/ISOlat1.ent`) with its unique public identifier. Here's how this document is incorporated into HTML DTD:

```
<!ENTITY % HTMLlat1 PUBLIC
    "-//W3C//ENTITIES Latin1//EN//HTML">
```

Here, the string in quotes contains the public identifier of the external resource whose contents will be substituted for each occurrence of the entity `%HTMLlat1;`. To make the mentioned document part of the DTD, it is now enough to invoke the defined entity (actually, this is done right after its declaration):

```
%HTMLlat1;
```

Formal rules for constructing public identifiers need not be detailed here. A fairly complete catalog of public identifiers can be found at `http://www.webtechs.com/html-tk/src/lib/catalog`.

## General Entities

General entities are declared in the DTD similarly to parameter entities, but they have a number of differences:

- A general entity cannot be used in the DTD but only in the documents conforming to this document type (in our case, the HTML documents).

- A general entity does not have the `%` character in its declaration.

- A general entity is invoked using the `&` character rather than the `%` character used for parameter entities—for instance,

  ```
  &lt;
  ```

  As with general entities, the trailing semicolon sometimes may be omitted (although I wouldn't recommend doing this).

- A general entity usually contains the `CDATA` keyword, inserted in its declaration before the data string. This keyword indicates that the string should not be interpreted as

SGML data; that is, any markup instructions it might contain should be ignored and treated as ordinary text characters.

For an example, consider the entity declarations provided in the DTD for accessing four special characters:

```
<!ENTITY amp    CDATA "&#38;"   -- ampersand       -->
<!ENTITY gt     CDATA "&#62;"   -- greater than     -->
<!ENTITY lt     CDATA "&#60;"   -- less than        -->
<!ENTITY quot   CDATA "&#34;"   -- double quote      -->
```

This example also shows us one special kind of entity called *character reference* that does not require any declaration. If the entity opening delimiter & is immediately followed by the # character and a number, this number is interpreted as character code (from the document character set as defined in the SGML declaration, see "CHARSET Section") and the whole entity is replaced by the character having this code. This is one of the two methods to access characters that are beyond the reach of a computer keyboard; the other method uses the *mnemonic* character entities defined in the DTD, such as &amp; or &eacute;.

You might wonder how the entities in the preceding example could expand to special characters if the CDATA keyword prohibits any SGML instructions, character references included, from having effect in the data string. The answer is that this string is in fact read twice: the first time when the entity declaration is interpreted, and the second time when the entity is used in the document and its data string is substituted. The CDATA keyword affects only the first reading. As a result, the DTD is protected from the special characters, while in the document the references are expanded to the characters intended.

## Elements

As I've already mentioned in the "How to Define an SGML Application" section earlier in this chapter, a document marked up with an SGML application is thought of as consisting of a hierarchy of nested elements. A marked up element is usually enclosed in a pair of start and end tags. The ELEMENT statement in SGML defines both start and end tags (but not their attributes) and prescribes what may be the content of this element by defining its content model.

Here's an example of element declaration:

```
<!ELEMENT P - O (%text)*>
```

Here, P is the element name (short for Paragraph). The two characters following the element name are *minimization indicators* specifying whether it is possible to omit start or end tags for this element. The first indicator refers to the start tag, and the second, to the end tag.

In place of a minimization indicator, you can put either a hyphen (-), meaning that the tag is obligatory, or the letter O, meaning that the tag is omissible. Thus, the preceding statement declares that a P element (a paragraph) must be preceded by the <P> start tag, but the </P> end tag can be omitted.

It is possible to have both start and end tags omissible. For example, the declaration

```
<!ELEMENT HTML O O (%html.content)>
```

indicates that both `<HTML>` and `</HTML>` tags around the content of an HTML document can be dropped.

## Content Model Keywords

The last component in the previous section's element declarations is the *content model* specification. (Here, it is done via parameter entities, and to see what they expand to we should find the corresponding `ENTITY` statements in the DTD.) Content model declares what can, what must, and what must not go inside the element.

The simplest type of content model is specified by a single keyword from the following list:

CDATA
: Stands for Character DATA. This keyword means that the SGML parser suspends its processing for the content of the element. Whatever other tags or entities are contained in the element, they won't have any effect and will be treated as ordinary data characters. The only tag that SGML parser reacts to when skipping over CDATA content is the end tag of the element that switched to CDATA mode.

    HTML DTD uses CDATA content model for the obsolete elements XMP, LISTING, and PLAINTEXT that were intended for inserting preformatted text into HTML document without the need to escape any special characters. Also, the CDATA mode is used for STYLE and SCRIPT elements whose content is to be processed by external programs rather than SGML parser.

RCDATA
: Stands for Replaceable Character DATA. This keyword introduces content model that is only different from CDATA in that it expands all general entities and character references, but ignores markup statements. RCDATA is not used in HTML DTD.

EMPTY
: Means that the content of the element is empty. Naturally, this is always accompanied by the permission to omit the end tag. Here is an example:

    ```
    <!ELEMENT IMG - O EMPTY -- Embedded image -->
    ```

ANY
: Allows any markup and data characters within the element. ANY is not used in HTML DTD.

## Content Model Groups

Sometimes, however, it is necessary to be more specific in defining content model of an element. This is done via *content model groups* whose syntax deserves a more thorough examination.

The simplest model group is one element name enclosed in parentheses, which means that the element being defined must contain one occurrence of the element specified in content model and nothing else. This is a rather artificial situation, as more often a model group contains two or more element names—for example,

```
<!ELEMENT HTML O O  (HEAD, BODY)>
```

Here, the comma between HEAD and BODY is a *connector* used to indicate the relations between the elements listed. Possible connectors include the following:

- A comma (,) indicates that the elements listed in the content model should both be present within the element exactly in the order specified.

- A vertical bar (¦) is the "exclusive or" connector. It indicates that one and only one of the elements can occur. However, it is often more practical to use the "simple or" relation allowing any one, or both, or even none of the elements to be present. This is why ¦ is often combined with the occurrence indicator *, for example:

```
<!ELEMENT APPLET - -  (PARAM ¦ %text)*>
```

Here the content model specification says that within the APPLET element, any number of PARAM elements mixed with any number of text fragments (this is what the %text; entity effectively expands to) may occur.

- An ampersand (&) is the "and" connector. It indicates that all the elements listed must occur, but in any order. It is often combined with the ? occurrence indicator. Here's how the DTD defines the %head.content; parameter entity that is later used in content model specification for the HEAD element:

```
<!ENTITY % head.content "TITLE & ISINDEX? & BASE?">
```

Here's the list of occurrence indicators used to show how many times the elements can occur in a content model:

- A question mark (?) means that the element may occur either once or not at all.

- A plus sign (+) means that the element may occur one or more times. Here is an example:

```
<!ELEMENT OL - -  (LI)+>
```

This means that an OL element may consist of an arbitrary number of LI elements, but at least one must be present in any case.

- An asterisk (*) means that the element may occur any number of times or not at all.

Model groups can be nested, and the occurrence indicators may apply to an entire group rather than a single element:

```
<!ELEMENT DL - -  (DT¦DD)+>
```

This means that within a DL (Definition List) element, at least one (but possibly more) DT or DD elements must be present.

Besides element names, you can use the #PCDATA (Parsed Character DATA) keyword in model groups. It refers to "usual" characters of the document without any markup tags and can be used to explicitly allow or disallow plain text within an element.

It is different, however, from the CDATA keyword discussed earlier. First, #PCDATA can be used only within a model group and not on its own as CDATA (that is, #PCDATA should be enclosed in parentheses even when it stands alone). And second, #PCDATA does not imply ignoring markup; if a tag is encountered in the context where only #PCDATA is allowed, a compliant SGML parser should fix an error rather than ignore this tag.

Together with the connectors and occurrence indicators listed, #PCDATA can limit the set of elements allowed inside another element without prohibiting plain text from appearing there. For example, here's how the %text; entity is defined via a number of subordinate classifying entities:

```
<!ENTITY % font "TT ¦ I ¦ B ¦ U ¦ S ¦ BIG ¦ SMALL ¦ SUB ¦ SUP">
<!ENTITY % phrase "EM ¦ STRONG ¦ DFN ¦ CODE ¦ SAMP ¦ KBD ¦ VAR ¦ CITE">
<!ENTITY % special
    "A ¦ IMG ¦ APPLET ¦ OBJECT ¦ FONT ¦ BASEFONT ¦ BR ¦ SCRIPT ¦
    MAP ¦ Q ¦ SPAN ¦ INS ¦ DEL ¦ BDO ¦ IFRAME">
<!ENTITY % formctrl "INPUT ¦ SELECT ¦ TEXTAREA ¦ LABEL ¦ BUTTON">
<!ENTITY % text "#PCDATA ¦ %font ¦ %phrase ¦ %special ¦ %formctrl">
```

Thus the %text; entity stands for, in plain English, "either a chunk of text or one of all these listed elements." Obviously, it'll most often be used with the * occurrence indicator. For an example, see how the preceding declarations are used once more to define quite a number of elements in one snap:

```
<!ELEMENT (%font¦%phrase) - - (%text)*>
```

As you see here, both parameter entities and groups can be used for specifying element names in declarations, not only in their content models.

SGML syntax also allows notation of the addition or subtraction of model groups, which is very convenient if these groups are specified via entity references. For instance, the FORM element is allowed to contain anything that can occur within a block-level element (that is, an element that starts a new paragraph) except for the FORM element itself (which means that FORMs cannot be nested). Rather than define the new content group from scratch, we can make use of the already defined %block.content; entity by subtracting the single FORM element from it:

```
<!ELEMENT FORM - - %block.content -(FORM)>
```

Analogously, we can sum up two model groups:

```
<!ELEMENT HEAD O O  (%head.content) +(%head.misc)>
```

## Attributes

An element is not fully described by its name and content model. Many elements have associated *attributes* that serve to provide additional information for rendering the element. Attributes for each element should be declared in the DTD via ATTLIST statements.

Here's a typical attribute declaration for an element:

```
<!ATTLIST AREA
    shape       %SHAPE      rect       -- controls interpretation of coords --
    coords      %COORDS     #IMPLIED   -- comma separated list of values --
    href        %URL        #IMPLIED   -- this region acts as hypertext link --
    target      CDATA       #IMPLIED   -- where to render linked resource --
    nohref      (nohref)    #IMPLIED   -- this region has no action --
    alt         CDATA       #REQUIRED  -- description for text only browsers --
    tabindex    NUMBER      #IMPLIED   -- position in tabbing order --
    onClick     %script     #IMPLIED   -- intrinsic event --
    onMouseOver %script     #IMPLIED   -- intrinsic event --
    onMouseOut  %script     #IMPLIED   -- intrinsic event --
    >
```

Right after the ATTLIST keyword, the name of the element for which we're defining attributes is specified. Next comes several three-component groups, each defining one attribute. The first identifier in each group is the attribute name. The other two specify the type of value for the attribute and its default value, as detailed in the next sections.

## Type of Attribute Value

After the name of each attribute in the ATTLIST declaration comes a keyword describing its type. This keyword is usually taken from the following list:

CDATA
: Here again, CDATA means that the value of this attribute may be any string of characters (as well as an empty string) and should be ignored by the parser. CDATA is used in situations where it is impossible to force more strict limitations on the attribute value with one of the following keywords.

NAME
: This keyword indicates that the value of the attribute is a name conforming to SGML naming rules as defined by the SGML declaration. (See the "Naming Rules Declaration" section, earlier in this chapter.) The following fragment of an ATTLIST declaration is an example:

```
<!ATTLIST META
...
    http-equiv  NAME        #IMPLIED   -- HTTP response header name --
    name        NAME        #IMPLIED   -- metainformation name --
...
    >
```

NMTOKEN
: This keyword is similar to NAME with the exception that there's no requirement to start the name with the name start character. (See "Naming Rules Declaration," earlier in this chapter.) This keyword is not used in HTML 4.0 DTD.

NUMBER    This keyword allows the parameter to take numeric values. The following
ATTLIST fragment is an example:

```
<!ATTLIST OL -- ordered lists --
...
   compact    (compact)  #IMPLIED  -- reduced interitem spacing --
   start      NUMBER     #IMPLIED  -- starting sequence number --
...
     >
```

ID    This keyword indicates that the attribute value is an *identifier* satisfying
two requirements: First, it is a valid SGML name (as in the case of NAME),
and second, it is unique across the document (that is, it cannot be assigned
to any other attribute within the same document). This value type is
specified for the ID attribute of the style sheets mechanism applicable to
the majority of HTML elements.

Besides these keywords, you can specify the list of possible values directly using the group notation that you've already seen applied for model groups in this chapter. Thus, in the preceding ATTLIST declaration for the OL element, the COMPACT attribute may only take as value the
character string "compact" or have no value at all, as in the example

```
<OL START=1 COMPACT>
```

which is equivalent to

```
<OL START=1 COMPACT=COMPACT>
```

Here's an example from the DTD with an attribute taking one of three possible values:

```
<!ATTLIST table
...
     align        (left¦center¦right)    #IMPLIED
...
>
```

## Default Value Specification

Finally, for each attribute in an ATTLIST declaration, either a default value is provided or a keyword is specified indicating whether this attribute is changeable and whether it is required. In
this position, character strings need not be enclosed in parentheses (although they should be
put in quotes if they contain spaces or delimiters), but the keywords require using a # escape
character as in the #PCDATA keyword mentioned earlier.

Here's a part of ATTLIST for TH and TD elements showing default values for ROWSPAN and COLSPAN
attributes:

```
<!ATTLIST (th¦td)                 -- header or data cell --
    ...
     rowspan NUMBER    1          -- number of rows spanned by cell --
     colspan NUMBER    1          -- number of cols spanned by cell --
    ...
>
```

More often, however, you'll see in place of the default value a keyword from the following list:

#FIXED    This keyword must precede the actual default value and is used to specify that the value cannot be changed by the user. It is used by the DTD only once, in the declaration for VERSION attribute of the HTML element:

```
<!ATTLIST HTML
        VERSION CDATA #FIXED "%HTML.Version;"
    ...
>
```

This means that the only possible value of the VERSION attribute is the string substituted for the %HTML.Version; parameter entity. (See "Parameter Entities," earlier in this chapter).

#IMPLIED    This keyword indicates that the attribute is optional.

#REQUIRED    This keyword indicates that the attribute is obligatory. For example:

```
<!ATTLIST PARAM
        name    CDATA   #REQUIRED  -- property name --
        value   CDATA   #IMPLIED   -- property value --
    ...
>
```

## Deprecated Features

Sometimes, a part of the DTD must be processed in a way different from the rest of it. For this, SGML offers the generic mechanism of *marked sections* that make it possible to isolate any markup statements and declarations in order to control their processing. HTML DTD uses this mechanism to mark its *deprecated features* that should be avoided in documents but are kept in the DTD for backwards compatibility. Here's what a marked section looks like:

```
<![ %HTML.Deprecated [
    <!ENTITY % preformatted "PRE ¦ XMP ¦ LISTING">
]]>
```

The %HTML.Deprecated; entity expands into the special keyword that tells the parser what to do with the contents of the section. The two keywords used in various HTML DTDs are IGNORE and INCLUDE. The IGNORE keyword allows you to ignore the marked section completely, and the INCLUDE keyword prescribes its contents should be processed on equal terms with the rest of DTD. So, to get a "strict" version of a DTD, all you need to do is to change the declaration

```
<!ENTITY % HTML.Deprecated "INCLUDE">
```

to

```
<!ENTITY % HTML.Deprecated "IGNORE">
```

# Other DTDs and Related Resources

You are probably aware that, besides consecutive HTML versions (the latest being 4.0), there exists a number of HTML "flavors" deviating from the standard in the scope of supported features. The most notorious of these flavors is "Netscape HTML", a vague term used to circumscribe the suite of HTML extensions ("netscapisms") introduced by different versions of Netscape Navigator browser and now making their way to other browsers and HTML flavors.

Unfortunately, Netscape HTML extensions aren't officially documented in the form of a DTD. Other companies, as a rule, are more reliable in this respect; for example, the DTD for the version of HTML supported by Microsoft Internet Explorer can be found at `http://www.microsoft.com/workshop/author/ref/ie3dtd.htm`.

There were also independent attempts to provide DTDs for various HTML flavors, including Netscape extensions; one of the best collections can be found at `http://www.webtechs.com/html`. The HTML Pro project at `http://www.arbornet.org/~silmaril/dtds/html/htmlpro.html` attempts to combine in one gigantic DTD all HTML variants and extensions proposed by standard-setting organizations and browser manufacturers.

Certainly, the whole wizardry of DTD syntax would be pointless if there were no programs to automatically parse the DTD declarations. The most sensible purpose of such parsing (as well as of formally defined syntax in general) is to check HTML documents against the DTD to ensure they are valid SGML documents using only declared elements and attributes.

The confusion of HTML flavors notwithstanding, it is always a good idea to make sure that your document is formally correct from the viewpoint of at least one of the DTDs out there, preferably the DTD of the current official HTML version adopted by a standard-setting body. (To watch for latest developments in this area, visit the W3C page at `http://www.w3.org/pub/WWW/MarkUp/` or the home page of IETF at `ftp://www.ics.uci.edu/pub/ietf/html/index.html`.)

Such a validation also can be helpful by ensuring that the document contains no syntax errors such as unclosed tags or delimiters. Validation packages are sometimes combined with functions to check for broken links, estimate download time, examine images, check spelling, and so on.

Some of these validators are accessible over the Internet. The WebTechs validation service at `http://www.webtechs.com/html-val-svc/` is a pure SGML validator without any extras, but it offers a big collection of DTDs to choose from and can check not only HTTP-accessible documents but also HTML fragments entered interactively. The site also offers a handy hypertext version for each of the DTDs it uses. (See, for example, `http://www.webtechs.com/sgml/Wilbur/DTD-HOME.html`.)

# Should HTML Continue Developing as an SGML Application?

It is true that one can create an HTML browser without it being an SGML parser (or even its proper subset). Equally true is that the overwhelming majority of HTML users are quite comfortable without the least notion of DTD intricacies. As you've seen in this chapter, a DTD is not very helpful in respect to the meaningful aspects of HTML, being limited to its formal syntax only. So what is the value that SGML adds to HTML development? Is it perhaps time to leave the SGML heritage behind?

Quite a lot can be said to advocate SGML importance. To begin with, SGML is an authoritative international standard that makes an SGML-supported argument especially strong in the modern world torn apart by browser wars and incompatible HTML extensions. After all, SGML has been proving its usefulness during more than a decade while HTML is much younger and, alas, significantly less stable.

SGML has a great potential outside of the HTML arena. Many important SGML applications have been and are being created for various documentation projects around the world. The SGML users community is strong and influential. HTML development can profit only by drawing from the mainstream of SGML philosophy and practice. Examples of promising SGML-inspired developments that may someday change the HTML world include Document Style Semantics and Specification Language (DSSSL), a versatile style language for use with SGML, and Extensible Markup Language (XML), a subset of SGML designed for use over the Internet. (See Chapter 21, "JavaScript Style Sheets and Other Alternatives to CSS," and Chapter 38, "The Emergence of Extensible Markup Language.")

The importance of a clear and unambiguous syntax specification should not be undervalued, either. Not only does a DTD, if present for a specific HTML flavor, give ultimate answers to many syntax-related questions, it also enables automatic checking of HTML documents in a robust and reliable way. I'd say that an HTML version without a DTD is like a language without a dictionary: Not everyone speaking the language needs to consult the dictionary, but those who really influence its advancement will hardly do without a good reference book.

The final, and probably the most important, argument is that it's SGML, not HTML, that was designed to ensure document portability and easy transformability. One of the main SGML missions is to guarantee that the content we create is accessible to everyone in spite of incompatible proprietary technologies. From this viewpoint, the HTML of nowadays with its flavors and browser feuds can hardly be named a deserved heir. However, by sticking to the SGML roots of the language, we can still considerably facilitate automatic handling of HTML files and using them in a diversity of environments, with the final effect of improving longevity of our information.

# Summary

In this chapter, you've learned the foundations of SGML, a metalanguage of logical markup, and you've analyzed the HTML DTD, the definition of HTML syntax in terms of SGML. In particular, the following questions were answered:

■ What is the difference between presentational and generic markup, and what is the importance of the latter?

■ What was the purpose of creating SGML and how did the history of its development progress?

■ What information on the properties of HTML can be elicited from the SGML declaration for HTML?

■ How does HTML DTD define entities, elements, and elements' attributes, and how do you parse the content model specification for an element?

■ Where on the Internet can you find additional information and DTD-related resources?

■ What are the benefits of maintaining HTML as an SGML application?

# The Structure of an HTML Document

*by Philip Stripling*

## IN THIS CHAPTER

CHAPTER 4

In order to be displayed on the World Wide Web, files must be saved in text format, and they must contain the tags to inform browsers how to render the page on a reader's computer monitor. The insertion of those tags is called *marking up* the document, a carryover from the days of typesetting. When marking up a document, the author must consider the needs of the reader, just as did the typesetter of old, working with molten lead to form each letter of a printed document.

Unlike typesetters printing on paper, however, new authors never know for certain how their Web pages will appear. By using Hypertext Markup Language (HTML), which is platform independent, an author can ensure that the Web page will be rendered in a readable fashion, with no loss of content. In this chapter, I discuss the benefits of platform independence and how to put together a Web page that will be rendered correctly by any brand of browser running on any computer.

The discussion of markup elements, tags, and attributes goes into some detail, especially on those attributes that cause problems for many authors. Although the use of proprietary markup is discouraged, the information is available for you to make your own choice based on your needs. You are encouraged to know the rules of appropriate, platform-independent HTML and to use them to design simple, elegant, readable Web pages.

# HTML Documents Are Platform Independent

Hypertext Markup Language is a data format that enables the exchange of information via the World Wide Web. To achieve this, the format must be recognized on all available computing platforms using available software. With platform independence, persons in different locations can exchange information, collaborate on authoring articles, publish data, and carry on a robust discourse without regard to time and space, and without having to pay for specific hardware and software with proprietary schemes.

With nonlinear information systems, it is important to provide users with a consistent view of the incredibly diverse data and data types available through the World Wide Web. Authors creating Web sites must satisfy the needs of users to have reliable, understandable access not only to the nodes of information, but also to the different protocols and applications that may be necessary to provide the data to the user. Authors who mark up text in a manner that limits usable access to their data may unwittingly exclude some persons from beneficial and useful information. In some circumstances, proprietary markup or design for specific window sizes may be perfectly acceptable—on a LAN or WAN where hardware and software are prescribed and set up for all users, for example, or where the purpose of the Web site is to present information to (or obtain information from) self-selecting patrons who will be using certain proprietary hardware or software and who are the target of the site. Authors who wish a wider market, however, should very carefully consider the use of proprietary extensions of HTML that will not degrade gracefully on other hardware or software than the proprietor's and the use of designs that presuppose the existence of a particular size of window for display.

HTML markup is the most hotly debated topic in the conferences of the World Wide Web Consortium (W3C). Because HTML is simple enough for all persons to learn and write, and because browsers that interpret HTML are going to be similar, the makers of browsers have sought to differentiate their programs by creating extensions to HTML that only their programs can interpret and display. This marketing ploy has aggravated many people. HTML is a simple method of presenting data to the world, and it is remarkably easy to learn and remarkably rich in its powers of expression.

By providing markup on a Web site using proprietary extensions or by designing to certain display sizes and resolutions, authors cease to serve the needs of their users and begin to serve the marketing interests of a particular software or hardware company. Nonlinear information systems have been proposed for some time, and several systems were implemented on proprietary hardware or software. They did not succeed because they did not transcend the platform for which they were written. The utility of HTML and the Hypertext Transfer Protocol is that they offer distributed data, wherein anyone can store and publish data on whatever system is at hand. Everyone can safely assume that any other person with any other hardware and software combination can have access to and provide links to other data anywhere in the world using the standard system of markup and transfer protocol. It is this utility that brings the World Wide Web to life, a life which no one person, corporation, or nation can give or take away. It is this utility that prevents the World Wide Web from being defined, limited, and bent to the will of any person, corporation, or nation.

At the moment, the open standards allow anyone to go online, search the World Wide Web, and find all the information that is necessary to mark up a file and publish it as a Web page. Many of the tools for doing this are freely available on the Internet. The standards for markup are public and freely available as well. HTML tutorials and guides are available at Web sites all over the world and as FAQs that are available for downloading as text files via FTP. As a result, the barriers to entry to the World Wide Web are remarkably low. No one has to be a "certi-fied" professional to create a Web page and to make it available on the Web. All of us are free to write and publish Web sites on our own interests and make them available to others. The standards, the tools, and the lessons are free. We do not have to buy a particular brand of software to write the page, and we do not have to own a particular brand of hardware to see the page.

One problem of standards is that growth and evolution may be stunted even by the small bureaucracy of the W3C. Netscape and Microsoft, two companies offering Web browsers, have proposed, and in many cases unilaterally implemented, proprietary extensions to HTML that are useful, some say even necessary. Although not all agree with particular choices, examples of interesting and useful extensions might include color for backgrounds and text, width and height attributes for graphics, frames, and embedded sound files. By having commercial interests push for acceptance of otherwise proprietary extensions to HTML, the W3C may be pushed to consider more proposals and different issues than it otherwise would. On the whole, this tension between the W3C and its commercial members will work to the benefit of users of HTML, so long as the parties remain on roughly equal footing.

4

THE STRUCTURE OF
AN HTML
DOCUMENT

During the process of standardization, however, authors are torn between the *demands* of their customers for the latest and trendiest Web sites and the *needs* of their customers for reliable and valid HTML to preserve the value of the content. Prior to HTML 3.2, making Web sites conform to valid HTML was seen as condemning the site to staid, static pages that caused readers' eyes to glaze over, while using proprietary extensions allowed glitz, animation, and placement of text and images, drawing customers in droves. Although there may have been some truth to that, currently accepted HTML includes a great many ways of enhancing appearance and providing the glamour long relegated to the trendier sites that often sported a logo indicating that the site was best viewed with a particular brand of browser. Commercial software companies continue to push proprietary tags, however, and the temptation is for Web authors to comply with their customers' requests to keep up with the competitors using such extensions and, presumably, drawing more hits.

As a Web author, you should know which elements and attributes are "standard" HTML and which are proprietary. Furthermore, you should know the effect of using a proprietary tag and viewing the page with a browser that cannot interpret the tag. If information is lost or rendered in a manner that makes it unintelligible, you do your customer a disservice. If, for example, you use the BLINK element, you may be assured that those browsers that do not interpret that tag will ignore it, but that no information will be lost as a result. On the other hand, if you mark up a page using frames and do not use the NOFRAMES element, you may rest assured that those persons using browsers that do not implement frames will be presented with a blank page.

In addition to being aware of the results of using nonstandard markup, you should be aware that not only do different browsers render the same markup differently, but the same brand of browser on different computer operating systems will render the same markup differently. Thus, in addition to validating your work, you should view (or have your acquaintances view for you) your marked up pages on different platforms with different software. You will not be able to cover all the bases, but you should cover as many as possible, so that your customer is not faced with e-mails complaining that the pages are not readable on a certain computer with a certain browser.

# HTML Markup Elements and Tags

This section presents a close look at the elements that make up an HTML document. You will learn the definition of element, how to distinguish an element from its tags, and how to specify the attributes that may be available in certain elements to affect their rendering. Part II, "Basic HTML," provides further information on the use of the elements available.

## Elements

If you look at this book, you will find a title page, a table of contents, chapters, and an index; those are some of the elements of the book. With SGML, you define the presentation of those elements when they are rendered by the browser on a computer screen. In HTML, elements are delimited by the tags that are the symbols for beginning an element and for ending it. The elements of an HTML page are described as containers delimited by those tags. An element is not the tag to which we all refer. It is the device used to present the concepts that you want the document to communicate when someone downloads your Web page and views it.

HTML elements are identified in a start tag that gives the element name and any attributes. (Element and attribute names are not case sensitive.) Tags themselves are delimited by the < and > symbols, as in <HTML>. You use elements to cause the browser to render the concept of a heading, a paragraph, a link, or an image. Although it might be convenient to use the words *tag* and *element* interchangeably, it is important to know the difference.

Some elements, such as anchors, cannot contain other elements. Some elements have only a start tag—such as BR and its tag,<BR>—denoting a line break. Some elements have end tags that may be omitted—such as the paragraph and its tag, <P>. Chapter 3, "SGML and the HTML DTD," contains a full listing of the elements, and Chapter 7, "Structural Elements and Their Usage," contains a full explanation of structural elements and their use.

> **NOTE**
>
> The contents of an element are a string of characters and nested elements (where permitted). Keep in mind that the element is not the tag; it is the content.

I've classified elements into three groups for discussion: document type, comment, and structure. The elements for document type and comment are SGML statements and must begin with <! and end with >.

## The DOCTYPE Element

Current HTML requires a document type (DOCTYPE) declaration before the use of any tags. This declaration provides an alert that the document conforms to SGML and specifies the DTD governing the document (which must conform to the DTD stated). A sample DOCTYPE declaration for HTML 2.0 would be

```
<!DOCTYPE  HTML PUBLIC "-//IETF//DTD HTML 2.0//EN">
```

This declaration informs the browser that the document to follow is HTML; that the document type definition is public (and, presumably, widely available; private DTDs exist, but the declaration would either have to give the URL of the private DTD where the user agent could access it or enclose it with the HTML document for proper parsing by the user agent); that the public DTD is maintained by the Internet Engineering Task Force; that the DTD is for HTML 2.0; and that the DTD is written in English.

## The COMMENT Element

The COMMENT element is also a declaration, so it, too, is opened by <! and terminated by >. However, the COMMENT element itself begins with -- and includes all text up to and including the next --. This is confusing to many people, who have come to expect that a comment is opened by the symbols `<!--` and closed by `-->`. This belief is incorrect, and the incorrect use of dashes in comments may cause the comments to be displayed by browsers. The COMMENT element may be placed anywhere within the HTML element. Comments will not be displayed by the browser and, because nothing between (and including) two pairs of `--` will be displayed, authors may incorporate comments that are several lines in length.

### Structural Elements

The remaining elements are the heart of HTML. Used properly, the structural elements will create a page that is interesting, readable, and portable to all browsers, rendered with clarity, regardless of the software and hardware of the reader. *Success.* Used poorly, information meant to be hidden will be displayed, information meant to be seen will be hidden, and the page will be a jumbled mess with the rendering varying from browser to browser. *Disaster.*

I do not attempt to list and describe all the structural elements in this chapter; Part II goes into greater depth on the use of these elements. I do, however, mention briefly some of the elements that cause new authors problems and show how to put a Web page together while avoiding the traps new authors sometimes fall into.

# Attributes

Attributes are the parts of elements that provide for author-specified values. Under the DTD specified in the DOCTYPE declaration, some elements may have no attributes. In a properly drafted DTD, those elements that have or can have attributes will have a *default* attribute for those instances when the author makes no declaration. Under the rules of SGML, attributes that have not been declared in the DTD noted in the DOCTYPE declaration should be ignored.

---

**CAUTION**

Commercial browsers with proprietary extensions to markup fail to follow this rule as to their own markup. As a result, the author who uses attributes that are proprietary to one browser may have different results in the display of that same markup by other brands of browsers.

---

Attributes enable an author to suggest characteristics and properties of an element that can be different from other instances of that element. Where they are allowed, attributes must appear in the opening tag of an element. An attribute is generally specified by an attribute name, an equal sign (=), and a value. In some instances, only the name of the attribute is required. The SGML declaration limits the length of an attribute value to 1,024 characters (including spaces).

It is possible to place an image in the body of an HTML document, so let's look at a sample of the markup for that placement to explore the definition of attribute. I don't discuss the specific attributes for the IMG element using this example—just the mechanics of specifying an attribute and its value.

This code line includes the element IMG and three of the available attributes (SRC, ALT, and ALIGN):

```
<IMG SRC="alfa.gif" ALT="This is the &quot;7% cereal&quot; model" ALIGN="left">
```

Each attribute has values. An equal sign follows the name of each attribute (whitespace on either side of the equal sign is allowed). Following the equal sign is the value of the attribute.

The method of stating the value of an attribute is the cause of some confusion. Authors may use a string of characters as the value, but may not use a >, as it will terminate the tag. If the string of characters contains only letters, numerals, periods (ASCII decimal 46), or hyphens (ASCII decimal 45), the string need not be surrounded by quotation marks (single or double quotation marks may be used). It is never incorrect to use quotation marks, however, and it is suggested that they be used at all times to prevent their inadvertent omission in those cases when they are necessary. In our example, it is not necessary to quotation the values of SRC and ALIGN. However, the ALT value contains spaces and a percent sign and so must be quoted. Furthermore, two quotation marks are included in the value for ALT. To prevent premature termination of the value, I have used entity references for those quotes (but I could have used single quotation marks).

# Putting the Pieces Together

After this review of the elements, tags, and attributes, you may feel that you are writing in a restrictive environment and that much of your freedom of expression has been curtailed. In fact, the situation is the opposite. By giving yourself rules to follow, you are encouraged to be creative and thoughtful. You will be able to provide content and information to your audience, assured that it will reach the largest possible number of readers. By working within the rules, you will be encouraged to create a document that is not only easy to read, but easy to write and maintain. (If you have plans for permanence on the World Wide Web, maintenance will quickly become important.)

## The HEAD

Using HTML 4.0, the HEAD section of your HTML file can contain the following elements:

-  BASE
- FRAMESET
- ISINDEX
- META

- LINK
- SCRIPT
- STYLE
- TITLE

**CAUTION**

Although material within the HEAD section is not normally displayed, failing to enclose text within the elements allowed in the HEAD might confuse the browser; the presence of normal text not within tags or tags not allowed in the HEAD section might cause the browser to conclude that the HEAD has terminated and that the BODY has begun.

The HEAD element of an HTML file contains information about the file itself. The HEAD tags are optional and consist of opening and closing tags—<HEAD> and </HEAD>. The order of the elements contained in the HEAD is not prescribed, so they may be listed in the order the author finds useful. With the exception of TITLE, the elements of HEAD are optional. The information contained within the HEAD is used by browsers in various ways, and all the elements available for use in the HEAD element can cause problems, so they are discussed in some detail in the following sections.

## BASE

The BASE element has only the attribute HREF, and it is used to set the base URL of the document. Relative URLs used within the document are resolved using the URL given in BASE. A sample BASE is

```
<BASE HREF="http://www.foo.com/~bar/index.html">
```

The HREF attribute is required, it must contain a fully specified URL, and the URL given must be where the document is located. If BASE is not used, the browser will resolve relative URLs using the URL it used to locate the document. BASE is not required, and it may be annoying in mirror sites where relative URLs then require a browser to go off site to locate images or even to retrieve the page being viewed to move to a named anchor within the page. This is particularly aggravating when the "mirror site" is the author's fixed drive and the computer is not connected to the Internet at the time the browser starts looking for www.foo.com.

## FRAMESET

The FRAMESET element is used to divide the browser window into two or more document windows, which are then used to display different files or different parts of one file. These different windows are referred to as *frames*, and their size, shape, and relative locations are controlled by three elements: FRAMESET, FRAME, and NOFRAMES. Every page that uses frames must have a NOFRAMES element to provide content for browsers that do not support the FRAMESET tag. The use of frames is covered in detail in Chapter 18, "Creating Sophisticated Layouts with Frames and Layers."

## ISINDEX

ISINDEX was proposed in the very early stages of HTML. Its purpose was to make a document searchable. An author would use <ISINDEX>, causing the user to be presented with a default prompt. The user would then type keywords that would be sent to the server. The server would execute the search and send the results back to the user. If the server did not have a search engine that could execute the search, it failed. The default prompt varied depending on the browser, and the attribute PROMPT was added to allow the author to suggest what was to be entered in the field. Because ISINDEX required a separate search engine, it never caught on. It has been replaced by the use of forms and the Common Gateway Interface.

## LINK

The LINK element is a reference to a related document. It has four attributes, HREF, REL, REV, and TITLE. LINK has not been widely used, but with the advent of style sheets, it may prove more popular. Lynx and later versions of NCSA Mosaic used the attribute REV to allow users to send comments to the author of the file via e-mail using the following tag:

```
<LINK REV="made" HREF="mailto:foo@bar.com">
```

REL will likely have wider application in providing links to style sheets:

```
<LINK REL="stylesheet" HREF="style.css" TYPE="text/css">
```

This link refers to an external style sheet that may be used to suggest how the document should be displayed. For more information on style sheets, see Chapter 19, "Introducing Cascading Style Sheets," and Chapter 20, "Cascading Style Sheet Usage."

The attributes REL and REV are confusing. It was originally suggested that REL would be a reference to "forward" relationships and that REV would refer to "reverse" relationships. Suggested uses for REL were to indicate a page that had the relationship of "home," "toc" (table of contents), "index," or even "up." REV, on the other hand, was supposed to be the reverse relationship. For example, if home.html were a document containing

```
<LINK REL="toc" HREF="toc.html" TITLE="Table of Contents">
```

then toc.html could contain the following LINK:

```
<LINK REV="previous" HREF="home.html" TITLE="Home Page">
```

At the time LINK was proposed, the thinking was that browsers could build navigation bars with the information from several <LINK> tags in a document, with users able to select links to navigate a site. (Although in our example relative URLs are given as the values in the examples, the URLs could be absolute and refer to documents located on another computer.) Later versions of NCSA Mosaic provided for the creation of a separate, nonscrolling pane in its browser window where an e-mail icon is located; this pane is created when the page being viewed has a LINK with a mailto: address. Presumably, if development of Mosaic had not been discontinued, other navigation aids would have been available when appropriate <LINK> tags were used.

## META

A META tag is referred to in RFC 1866 as "an extensible container for use in identifying specialized document meta-information." What else needs to be said?

Well, perhaps this could be expanded a little. The problem is that META has no strictly defined use and no strictly defined method of being accessed. In fact, access to and use of META information is not required. The META element has no closing tag, and it contains a name/value pair. Among the attributes of the META tag are HTTP-EQUIV, NAME, CONTENT, and SCHEME. CONTENT gives the value of the name/value pair, and it is required when HTTP-EQUIV or NAME is used. HTTP-EQUIV is a problem. Its use is supposed to be directed at the HTTP server containing the page, as in this example:

```
<META HTTP-EQUIV="Expires" CONTENT="Fri, 31 December 1999 23:59:59 GMT">
```

When a page is requested by a browser, the HTTP server can send the contents of the <META> tags as part of the HTTP protocol headers. (See Chapter 5, "Behind the Scenes: HTTP and URIs.") In that event, one of the protocol headers sent for this example would be

```
Expires: Fri, 31 December 1999 23:59:59 GMT
```

The use to be made of this header information is undefined at this time. If a page with an expiration date is cached by a browser, and the page is requested after the date in the expiry, the browser *should* request the page again from its source rather than display the cached version. Generally, however, it is ignored by browsers, leading to some irritation from authors who want to "expire" their pages so that they are never cached.

Several search engines have published information stating that their indexing algorithm uses META information to locate Web pages relevant to queries of their database. By following the instructions given at the search engine Web site, authors can have some assurance that their pages will be returned to people doing searches. Because there is no limit to the number of META elements you can insert in your HEAD, you might do well to read the help pages of several search engines and draft separate META tags that conform to each engine's requirements.

In an effort to assist robots in the indexing of pages, HMTL 4.0 has added several attributes to the META tag. The LANG attribute has been added, both to aid indexers in determining the appropriate language to present the search results and to facilitate the application of pronunciation rules for speech synthesizers. A SCHEME attribute should be used to indicate a method of describing a value. For example, if a book is referenced in a META tag by using the International Serial Book Number, that scheme would be denoted as follows:

```
<META NAME=identifier SCHEME=ISBN CONTENT="0-8230-2355-9">
```

Some of the elements that are used, always with NAME/CONTENT pairs, are the following:

> `<META NAME="author" CONTENT="Your Name">` to give the author's name.
>
> `<META NAME="keywords" CONTENT="A list of keywords for the search engine">`, but be sure to read the help file for each search engine, as there are limits on number of words and on number of repetitions.

`<META NAME="`*`description`*`" CONTENT="`*`Describe your web page`*`">`, as some engines will use that description when your site is listed in response to a query.

Another problematic use of `HTTP-EQUIV` was promulgated by Netscape. This is the use of `"REFRESH"`, as shown in the following example:

`<META HTTP-EQUIV="REFRESH" CONTENT="5; URL=http://www.foo.com/">`

For those using the Netscape browser, this tag will cause Netscape to load the page from the URL listed in the value of `CONTENT` 5 seconds after some point in time. The "meta refresh" is often used when an author has moved to a new site. The old URL containing a page with a meta refresh tag directs the reader to the new location. A text explanation should be furnished and a link should be provided for those who do not use a browser that will interpret and execute a meta refresh. Others have used meta refresh for "slide shows." A series of pages are displayed on the user's browser with no action required by the user. The problem for authors is that they cannot finally fix the amount of time the transfer will require, and an incoming page called by the meta refresh may interrupt the download of each page in the series.

> **CAUTION**
>
> The point at which the new page begins to load is unknown because of variations in the speed of the server, the speed of transfers over the Internet, and the speed of the user's modem. Thus, meta refresh will begin counting, presumably when the header is received, but the rest of the page being transmitted for display may be delayed in reaching the browser. If the page contains an image that takes longer to load than the allotted time, the new page will arrive and begin loading prior to the browser having fully rendered the page containing the meta refresh.

Meta refresh should be used with restraint and with caution. In addition to the problem of full transfer of the pages containing the meta refresh, users may have trouble going back to the page. If that is the introductory page to a series, and the meta refresh is very short, your readers may not have time to bookmark it. Meta refresh should be used, if at all, only with some thought as to the benefit of refresh. If your page has moved, leaving the user with a meta refresh does not encourage bookmarking the new page and deleting the old one.

As an aid in indexing its pages, resulting in wider access, the W3C recommends specifying the language of the document and providing keywords and a description of the contents. If different versions of the document are available in different languages, they can be referenced using `LINK` with the `REL` attribute.

## SCRIPT

The `SCRIPT` element was incorporated into HTML to accommodate scripting languages promulgated by commercial browser developers. There must be an opening `<SCRIPT>` tag and a closing `</SCRIPT>` tag, with the script placed between them. (Scripting is discussed in Part V, "Associated Technologies and Programming Languages.")

Scripting allows for considerable interactive content in a Web page. An advantage of scripting over CGI is that the processing of the script is done on the user's computer, not on the computer serving the page. In addition to conserving server processing, it enables persons to have dynamic pages posted to servers that do not allow Common Gateway Interface activities on the server.

With this power comes problems. Scripting languages are not universally understood. Some browsers do not recognize *any* scripts and will not execute them. The SCRIPT element is to ensure that *current* browsers hide the contents between the tags. Older browsers will display the contents if the script is not also enclosed in a comment. Yet another problem arises, however, if the script contains > or --. Some browsers interpret these characters as the end of the comment, resulting in the display of the parts of the script that follow.

The attributes of SCRIPT are as follows: TYPE (giving the media type specifying the scripting language: TYPE="text/tcl"), LANGUAGE (giving the scripting language; TYPE is preferred), and SRC (giving the URL for an external script; when SRC is used, the contents of the SCRIPT element should be ignored).

Web pages can contain more than one SCRIPT element, and they can be located in the BODY as well as in the HEAD. Scripts can be written to modify the document as it is being parsed—generating a table of contents, for example. Such scripts are, in effect, CGI scripts without server processing. Great care in crafting such scripts will be required, as will careful testing.

The use of the SCRIPT element might require the NOSCRIPT element in certain cases. NOSCRIPT has opening and closing tags, and its content will be rendered by browsers that do not support scripting or the language used by the SCRIPT element. Authors should never use the SCRIPT element as the sole element of a page without also using NOSCRIPT to provide content to users of browsers that do not support scripts or that have script support turned off for security reasons.

## CAUTION

Browsers that do not recognize the SCRIPT element will ignore the tag. The result is that the scripts placed between the tags will be displayed as plain text in those browsers, and the script will not be executed. Remember also that upon finding plain text within a header, some browsers assume that the HEAD element has been terminated. Avoid unexpected results by placing scripts within a comment to prevent older browsers from displaying them.

## STYLE

The STYLE element is another method of using a style sheet in an HTML document. STYLE has opening and closing tags, and it has the attribute TYPE. The LINK element discussed earlier will import style information from a separate style sheet, while the STYLE element allows the author to suggest presentation within the document itself. This has the advantage of requiring the download of only one document, and it has the further advantage of working when the server on which the page resides has not yet been configured to recognize the style sheet MIME type and cannot properly transfer an external style sheet. The syntax for a document-level style sheet is the same as for external style sheets, and the language used must be given in the TYPE attribute. (See Chapters 19 and 20.)

> ### CAUTION
>
> Browsers that do not recognize the STYLE element will ignore the tag. The result is that the style information entered between the tags will be displayed as plain text in those browsers, and the styles suggested will not be implemented. Remember also that upon finding plain text within a header, some browsers will assume that the HEAD element has been terminated. Avoid unexpected results by placing the style information within a comment to prevent older browsers from displaying them.

## TITLE

Although the <HEAD> tags are optional, current standards of HTML require a TITLE for your file. Although the contents of the HEAD section are not to be displayed, the TITLE element is often picked up by browsers and displayed in the title bar of the window. Some browsers use the TITLE for their list of bookmarks, and search engines often display the TITLE in their results, making a useful and informative title helpful for your readership. The TITLE element may contain text and escaped entities, but not markup. The <TITLE> tag requires a closing tag; it has no attributes, and it is to be used only once in the HEAD of the document.

## The BODY

The BODY element contains the text and other information that (it is hoped) will be displayed to the reader. BODY has opening and closing tags, but they may be omitted. If you have used the HEAD element and closed it properly, browsers should assume that termination of the HEAD element implies the opening of the BODY element. Do not rely on this assumption, however, as not all browsers properly follow the DTD.

The structure and appearance of the text within BODY are suggested by the elements that may be nested within the BODY element. The elements that may be contained within the BODY can be divided into block formatting elements and character formatting elements.

## Block-Level Formatting Elements

The block-level formatting elements include the following:

| Element | Function |
|---|---|
| ADDRESS | An address for further information. |
| BLOCKQUOTE | A quotation of several lines from another source. |
| CENTER | A centered division. |
| DIV | A logical division that can be rendered in a certain manner. |
| FORM | An area providing for interaction with the user. |
| H*n* | Headings, where *n* is an integer from 1 through 6. Headings are supposed to be used to indicate comparative importance of information through a hierarchy of prominence in the display of the heading, with H1 being the most prominent and H6 the least. |
| HR | A horizontal rule; that is, a line across the width of the page. (There are some attributes available to suggest different sizes and alignments of the line.) |
| P | A paragraph container. |
| PRE | For the display of text in a given format. |
| SPAN | For the application of a certain style to text that has no structural role or established rendering. For example, assigning <BIG> and <I> to the first three words of each paragraph could be done by defining such a style and then wrapping the words within <SPAN> and </SPAN>. |
| TABLE | For the display of text in a grid pattern. |
| Lists | For the display of items in lists, there is DIR, DL, MENU, OL, and UL; some of the list elements can contain subelements for list items (LI), definition terms (DT), and definitions (DD). |

These elements imply the closing of the preceding paragraph, although DIV does not imply the whitespace usually associated with paragraph breaks. With the exception of HR, block-level elements should be considered containers, requiring opening and closing tags. The proposed use of the horizontal rule is to indicate a change in topic. With the exception again of HR, block-level elements can contain character formatting elements.

## Character Formatting Elements

These elements are used to mark up text and should be contained within block formatting elements. Character formatting elements may be subdivided into logical markup, physical markup, and other markup, a category to pick up the remaining text-level elements.

The next sections distinguish between logical markup and physical markup, a distinction that may be dismissed superficially as mere semantics. The use of logical elements where possible, however, has advantages for authors wishing to assure hardware and software independence, and it allows the readers to define the method of display so that it is suitable for their needs.

### Logical Markup

Logical markup is the preferred method of defining the characteristics of text where possible. Logical markup elements include

- CITE to indicate a citation
- CODE to render computer language source code
- DFN to define a term
- EM to emphasize text
- KBD to mark text that the user is to enter on a keyboard
- Q to indicate inline quotes
- SAMP to indicate a sequence of literal characters
- STRONG to indicate strong emphasis
- VAR to indicate a variable used in computer code

The advantage of logical markup is that it can be used to define the meaning of the marked text. By defining certain characters as CODE, KBD, or VAR, you can give a reader information about the content of the text. Readers can configure their browsers to display those semantic elements so that they are in a particular font or a particular color and quickly scan the text to locate items of particular interest or to know which elements may be ignored. A similar situation often arises when authors use a program to write HTML and that program displays the elements in a different color and font style from the text portions of the document. Such devices are very helpful in separating markup from explanatory text, giving a quicker understanding of the meaning of the text and a quicker way to locate and resolve problems. Using logical markup enables your readers to have your text rendered with the same helpful clarity.

### Physical Markup

Writers and publishers in the print world have long used italics and bold to make text stand out. The appearance of such text can add meaning within the context of the document. Using markup that renders text in italics, for example, is not a contradiction of the SGML theory of marking for structure and content when that tag is used to indicate foreign words or magazine titles. The use of such physical markup to add emphasis, however, is discouraged.

The following elements are used for physical markup:

- B to display text as bold
- BIG to display text in a larger size than the default
- I to display text in italics
- SMALL to display text in a smaller size than the default
- STRIKE to display text with a horizontal line through the characters
- SUB to display text as a subscript
- SUP to display text as a superscript
- TT to display text in a monospaced font
- U to display text as underlined

Remember that readers may be using equipment that is incapable of rendering physical markup; the monitor might not be capable of showing superscripts and subscripts or different font sizes, for example. Because markup that cannot be rendered will be ignored, physical markup should be used only where its absence will not change the meaning of the text.

## Other Formatting Elements

Although this section is labeled "Other Formatting Elements," some may consider the following as the most interesting and useful elements. Here are the "other" elements:

- A is the anchor for links.
- APPLET is the container for Java applets.
- BASEFONT is the tag to set default font sizes.
- BR indicates line break.
- FONT is the tag to modify font display.
- FORM is the tag to allow user input for a variety of purposes.
- IMG is the element to display images and animation.
- MAP is the element to display client-side image maps.
- OBJECT is the new, more powerful element to display images, animation, and applets.

Several of these elements cause problems for beginning authors.

### BASEFONT

This tag is used to suggest a default font size. Its only attribute is SIZE, where the value must be an Integer from 1 through 7; the default size is 3. Beginners often use BASEFONT to set a larger-than-usual size, assuming that the large text will seem more important or exciting.

BASEFONT has only its opening tag, and there is no closing tag. BASEFONT affects normal and preformatted text. BASEFONT cannot be closed; therefore, it then affects all subsequent normal and preformatted text. Different browsers interpret what is "normal text" differently, however, and authors may find that the tag is ignored in certain nested elements that vary from browser to browser. Proprietary attributes other than SIZE are rendered by some browsers, but not others. Because of the differences in the treatment of the element and its attribute, its use is not recommended. To have text rendered in different sizes, the elements BIG and SMALL are recommended. To cause text to be emphasized, consider EM and STRONG instead. The heading level elements of H*n* should be considered where appropriate to indicate comparative importance of information. Remember also that some search engines index Web pages according to the six heading elements. BASEFONT is ignored in determining the index of your document.

## BR

Under normal circumstances, the user's browser will wrap text to fit within the user's window. On some occasions, an author may wish to have text forced into shorter lines than the window, but without the extra space between lines usually created by the paragraph element. A common example is an address:

> Joan Smith
> 123 Boulevard
> Orleans

The BR element has been described as the specification of a line break between words. Text with a BR inserted should end at the <BR> and continue at the beginning of the next line, with no whitespace between the two lines. Under that description, more than one <BR> in a series is undefined, as the succeeding line breaks would not be "between words." Undefined tags are to be ignored, so only the first <BR> should be given effect, and some browsers render it so. Because the use of multiple <BR> tags will not create whitespace for all browsers, BR's use for that effect should be discouraged. The BR element has no closing tag.

## FONT

The FONT element is a container requiring opening and closing tags. The attributes are SIZE and COLOR. SIZE sets the font's size for the text delimited by the tags. SIZE can be set to absolute sizes using the integers from 1 through 7, or it can be set to relative sizes with signed integer values from –7 through –1 and from +1 through +7; signed integer values must be quoted. FONT will override BASEFONT settings if the absolute size has been set with FONT, or FONT will use the BASEFONT SIZE value to determine the relative size if a signed integer has been used.

COLOR will set the color of the text. Colors may be set in RGB hexadecimal notation (#RRGGBB) or as a color name, using one of the 16 named values available. The named value is not as widely supported as RGB notation, and neither is broadly supported at this time. In addition, text may be inadvertently set to the color of the user's background, causing the text to disappear.

It is possible for users to override the background color set by an author, but not the FONT color; even though you have set the background, you cannot depend on the text color being readable. FONT size cannot be overridden, and the size you have chosen may be unreadable to the user for

4

THE STRUCTURE OF
AN HTML
DOCUMENT

a number of reasons—it did not scale well in the user's font, it is too small, it is too large and causes wrapping problems. The use of FONT is discouraged for the same reasons as the use of BASEFONT.

# Summary

If you are creating a page for your personal pleasure, go wild. Make the background a pattern, make the text the same shade as the background, use huge animation files that take forever to download, and make it all <BLINK>. You have wonderful choices to make, and you should try them all. This book explains how to create Web pages using the incredibly powerful tools not only of HTML, but style sheets, CGI, JavaScript, Java, ActiveX, and VBScript. You will learn how to create forms, do tables, and incorporate images, video clips, animation, and sound. You will be able to create background images, background sounds, and colored text of different fonts and sizes. Go for it.

However, if you are creating a page or Web site for a customer or for more serious purposes, and you want to incorporate all the trendy alternatives available on the World Wide Web, I have two words for you: Please don't.

When you are creating a page for the world to see and read, know the rules of standard HTML. Follow them to allow full accessibility to your page and the information it contains. Know the rules of standard HTML, but break them when you know what you are doing and what the results are likely to be. Let your failure to follow the standards be purposeful, not ignorant.

Create a page and a Web site with the simple elegance enforced by rules. You have been given a standard with many elements, and you may create a Web page in which the elements are unified and interrelated within the page and within a larger Web site. You may use the elements to create a page that is logically organized and logically displayed by readers who may come to your page from anywhere in the world and who may see your page as written in a foreign language. Use HTML to make your page easy to read.

As you read this book and apply its lessons, be constantly aware that your work will be published on the World Wide Web. It will be read by people who will not have particular hardware and software available to them. Your work may have valuable or entertaining information, and you should not restrict the access to your work. The World Wide Web rests on the notion that data should be freely available to all, regardless of platform. If you want to use proprietary markup, you are free to do so, but you should be aware of the consequences.

# Behind the Scenes: HTTP and URIs

*by Philip Stripling*

CHAPTER 5

## IN THIS CHAPTER

The World Wide Web is a nonlinear information system providing users with the facilities to search for and retrieve information sources anywhere in the world. With a uniform naming scheme for locating resources, recognized protocols for retrieving them, and a markup language supporting links within the documents, users have access not only to text-based documents, but also to still images, moving images, PostScript files, sound files, and more data formats than those that currently exist. The World Wide Web has no bounds; it has grown far beyond being the answer to the problem at CERN that it was intended to address.

By implementing the World Wide Web over the Internet as a public standard, Tim Berners-Lee provided for minimization of user effort through the use of URIs, embedded links, and consistent naming conventions. Both HTTP and URIs provided for platform independence to a remarkable degree, in part through the use of TCP/IP and in part through the use of hexadecimal encoding so that URIs can pass through all operating systems and still be read by the client and the server.

*Uniform* (sometimes called *universal*) *resource identifier* (URI) is the term used generically to identify *uniform resource locators* (URLs), *uniform resource names* (URNs) and *uniform resource characteristics* or *citations* (URCs). URIs are used to name, find, and retrieve information across the far reaches of the World Wide Web. A URL is just an extended filename; it tells your Web browser not only the name of the file you want to view, but also where it is and how to get it. For example, the URL for a hypertext file on another computer could be specified as

```
http://www.foo.com/~bar/file.html
```

The URI can specify any recognized protocol.

This chapter closely examines HTTP and URIs, and it shows how the two work together to enable cross-platform multimedia information exchange. You also learn about some of the problems in the implementation of HTTP and about proposals for the next generation.

# Hypertext Transfer Protocol

HTTP is not just for the transfer of hypertext documents. It is a protocol for the transfer of data formats between the server and the client (usually a browser). The data formats include plain text, hypertext, images, sound, and any other data formats that have been specified as MIME types, including proprietary formats such as Adobe Acrobat files. In addition to the data itself, HTTP transfers *meta-information* about the data.

HTTP operates over the Internet, where communication occurs between computers via TCP/IP. *TCP/IP* stands for *Transfer Control Protocol/Internet Protocol.* Understanding HTTP requires some understanding of how TCP/IP works, so this section covers how transfers take place over the Internet.

# In the Beginning...

Legend has it that the origins of the Internet lie in the need of the United States Department of Defense for a command-and-control system capable of surviving global thermonuclear war. This need was difficult to satisfy because different branches of the DOD had different computer systems and different network protocols, and no way existed to communicate between the networks. TCP/IP was introduced to allow a network of the networks with full communication between the nets, and with no set path in the event that global thermonuclear war destroyed parts of the network.

> **NOTE**
>
> Some people might not remember the debates on whether the United States could win a nuclear war, whether it could survive a nuclear war, and whether it was moral to think about winning or surviving a nuclear war. I recommend the novels *Dr. Strangelove, or How I Learned to Stop Worrying and Love the Bomb* (by Peter Bryan George), and *Fail-safe* (by Eugene Burdick and Harvey Wheeler). If you don't want to read about that time, you could rent the videos of the movies made of these two novels. (Interested persons might also want to research the suit and countersuit filed by each party alleging plagiarism—but that is another story. The time of the birth of the Internet was an interesting time in which to live.)

In those olden days, computers were mainframes, and they were always turned on and always on the Net (unless, of course, they crashed or were down for maintenance). The protocols developed for communication presumed the presence of many large computers that were completely self-sufficient. Among the early services run in the family of TCP/IP protocols were *ftp*, *rlogin*, and *mail*. With ftp, a user at a terminal to a mainframe started the program called `ftp` and used it to log on to a distant computer. The ftp session maintained its connection while the user transferred files to (using `put`) or from (using `get`) the distant computer. ftp required logging on with a known username and password, and the protocol handled any problems arising from the receiving computer having character sets and line endings different from the sending computer. The ftp session was terminated by logging off (the preferred method) or by inactivity for a certain period of time.

rlogin, now usually known as *telnet*, allows a person at one computer to log on to a distant computer and have the same access that would be allowed to a person logged in to a terminal directly connected to the distant computer. A username and password are generally required, and termination occurs by the same two methods used for ftp.

Computer mail allows a user to send a message to another computer for storage in a second person's mail file. Logging on is not required, and the second person need not be logged on to have the message received and stored.

The Internet now has personal computers, workstations, minicomputers, and dial-up Internet service providers (ISPs) connected. Not all the devices are turned on and functioning at all times, and in the case of ISPs, a user might not even be connected to the ISP when e-mail is received, for example. In these cases, the user calls on another computer for the provision of services in a client/server model of operation. The server provides Internet services for the computers that have access to the server. The client/server model still relies on the protocols of TCP/IP for the transfer of data across the network of networks with all the different operating systems that might be attached at any given point.

# TCP/IP

> **NOTE**
>
> Under the Internet Protocol, all computers with full-time access to the Internet are assigned a four-digit number. This IP number is 4 bytes, but, by convention, each byte is translated into a number between 0 and 255, and the bytes are separated by periods. The IP number is also referred to as a *dotted quad*.

The Internet is made up of hundreds of thousands of computers connected to networks, which in turn are connected to each other. The computers and connecting cables are the hardware, and the Internet Protocol is the method by which communications over the hardware are effected. It is the Internet Protocol that gives us dotted quad addresses: `123.456.789.123`. The domain name service provides a translation service so that we have to remember only `www.foo.com` instead of the four sets of digits with dots between them. Under the Internet Protocol, the route of delivery of data is not predetermined. Assume that a person at the Stanford Linear Accelerator starts her Web browser and connects to the Web page at CERN. When data is transferred from CERN in Switzerland to the Stanford Linear Accelerator in California, the packets of data do not travel in a straight connection, nor do all the packets travel along the same path. There are many networks, switches, and routers along the way, and any of these could be fully occupied or inoperative. IP ensures, however, that the packets will find alternative paths to the final destination. IP is called a *connectionless protocol* because it does not require a straight connection between sender and receiver; indeed, IP presumes that no particular path will exist during the transfer and that the data will pass through a dozen different networks on its way to the destination. (Remember that this process is the result of the Cold War and U.S. fears of a Soviet preemptive nuclear strike.)

Note that the user in Stanford does not log on to the computer at CERN. Her browser sends out a request for the page over the Internet, and the request is answered by the CERN computer sending the file back to her computer in packets. Each packet sent by CERN is addressed to her computer, but because the network does not know of the connection between any two packets, the order in which they arrive will be random, and they must be reassembled in order. This is handled by TCP.

Transport Control Protocol is the means by which a connection is established between the client and the server. When the server is ready to send data to the client, TCP breaks the file up into packets, each with an address and a number to allow reassembly in the correct order. TCP hands the packets to IP, which sends them out. The recipient uses TCP to reassemble the packets in order and to request retransmission of any missing packets.

TCP at the receiving end keeps track of packets by *demultiplexing* each packet. The information TCP needs in order to do this is contained in headers sent along with each packet and put there by the sending computer's version of TCP. Each computer maintains a conversation during the transfer, acknowledging receipt of packets, requesting retransfers of packets not received after a certain lapse of time, and maintaining flow. The combination of TCP/IP ensures, for the most part, that packets can be routed around congested nodes and that lost packets can be retransmitted; data loss is remarkably small.

As with HTML and HTTP, the TCP/IP is *open*. They are public standards supported by the Internet Engineering Task Force; the standards are published and freely available online. No commercial vendor owns the standards, and no payment or other fee is exacted for their use.

## HTTP—A Brief Overview

HTTP uses TCP/IP to transfer files over the Internet. One of the results of the use of TCP/IP is that HTTP is *stateless*. When a user requests a file by, for example, selecting a link, HTTP sets up a connection between the requesting computer and the sending computer via TCP/IP, it requests the file, the sending computer sends it, and the connection is then dropped. This has the advantage of not tying up Internet resources and the sending computer while the user reads a lengthy file and admires the tasteful rendering of the Web page. There is no "memory" of the transaction for either computer; if the user requests the page again (and it has not been cached), the sender will send it again, along with all its contents.

The basic transactions supported by HTTP are the connection, the request, the response, and the termination of the connection. The connection is the establishment of the TCP/IP connection over the Internet. This is a client/server mode; in some instances, such as a POST (which is covered in the "POST" section of this chapter), the roles of client and server might switch. HTTP specifically allows and provides for both sides of the connection to assume whichever role is necessary during a connection. Assuming that a person at Stanford has started her browser and selected her bookmark for a Web page at CERN, the browser will cause TCP/IP to establish a connection with the computer at CERN. In this example, the computer at Stanford is the client, and the computer at CERN is the server. It does not matter what brand of computer or what operating system is in use under the protocols of TCP/IP and HTTP. When it is notified that the connection has been established, the client (browser) sends a request to the server. This request includes certain information; the minimum request identifies the HTTP version as HTTP/0.9 and requests the contents of the Web page as text/html. The section "The Request" covers the additional information that can be included in a request. The response from the server will consist of the file requested if the request was a minimum request, or it will consist of a status line, header, and the response data if the request was under HTTP/1.0. When the response has been sent and acknowledged, the connection is terminated, generally by the server.

When our user at Stanford finishes rendering the Web page, she can then follow links on the page, and this entire set of transactions is repeated. If the followed link is on another computer, the transaction is initiated with this other computer as the server. The differences between HTTP/0.9 and HTTP/1.0 are outlined in more detail later, but I should mention here that under HTTP/0.9, no information is required to be transferred other than the request (which contains GET and the URL) and the response (which contains the Web page). The client transfers no information about itself to the server, and the server retains no trace of the transaction. This stateless protocol is in accordance with TCP/IP and was an intentional design of the drafters of HTTP. It has, however, led to some dissatisfaction among users, browser makers, and the Internet Engineering Task Force. You'll learn about the reasons for this dissatisfaction and proposed solutions in the section "HTTP/1.1 and HTTP-NG," later in this chapter.

# HTTP—A Detailed Examination

For those who want to use the Common Gateway Interface or scripting languages to extend HTML and provide interactivity on their Web pages, a more detailed knowledge of the rhythm of connect, request, respond, and terminate will be helpful. This section examines what goes on in this rhythm of HTTP in greater detail than the hobbyist requires, but it will be valuable for those of you who want to generate pages on the fly. As I discuss the details of the protocol, bear in mind that the identity of the client and the identity of the server may vary at any time. When I use the word *client*, I mean the application that establishes the connection and sends the request. When I use the word *server*, I mean the application that accepts the connection in order to respond to the request. Many applications are capable of playing both roles, but this discussion is limited to the particular example and takes no account of an application's other capabilities.

## The Connection

Let's assume that the HTTP communication is initiated by a Web browser and is a request for the service of a certain file on a server. The request might travel directly between the programs or, more likely, travel over several networks, through routers, switches, nodes, and gateways. Generally, the connection will be made through TCP/IP connections on the Internet. Currently, the protocol requires that the connection be established by the client before sending the request and that the connection be terminated by the server after sending the response. In the real world, the connection can be closed by either party due to failures of either program, user action, or automatic timing out of the connection due to inactivity. CGI interactions should take into account the possibility of premature termination.

If our person at Stanford has a connection to the Internet and has selected a bookmark in her browser with the URL `http://www.cern.org/pub/highenergy.html`, a connection is made via TCP/IP to the computer known as `www.cern.org`; when that connection is established, her application will send a request.

# The Request

The nature of the request depends on the version of HTTP in use. The version must be stated in the request as `HTTP/1.0` or `HTTP/0.9`. If no version is stated, version 0.9 is assumed. If you are writing a CGI program that expects to send a Full-Request or to receive a Full-Response, `HTTP/1.0` must be included or received in the request.

## HTTP/0.9

HTTP/0.9 understands only a Simple-Request, which is

```
GET [Request-URI] CRLF
```

where `Request-URI` is the relative path to the entity requested and `CRLF` is a carriage return/line feed, which is the HTTP end-of-line marker. There must be a space between `GET` and the `Request-URI`. In our example, the request will be

```
GET /pub/highenergy.html
```

with the CRLF not shown but present. Note that `GET` is issued to the path relative to the computer to which the connection has been made.

If an HTTP/1.0 server receives a Simple-Request, it *must* respond with a Simple-Response (which is described later in this chapter, in the section called "The Response").

## HTTP/1.0

An HTTP/1.0 application must generate a Full-Request; an HTTP/1.0 server receiving a Full-Request will then generate a Full-Response. Instead of a `GET`, the HTTP/1.0 Full-Request begins with a Request-Line such as this:

```
Method [Request-URI] HTTP/1.0 CRLF
```

Following the Request-Line are the request header fields. Those fields are `Authorization`, `From`, `If-Modified-Since`, `Referer`, and `User-Agent`. The following sections cover these in greater detail.

### The Request-Line

HTTP/1.0 offers a great deal more flexibility than HTTP/0.9, and one of the reasons is the availability of methods other than `GET`. The method specified can be `GET`, `HEAD`, `POST`, or an extension. Note that HTTP/1.0 must be specified in the Request-Line. There must be spaces between the method, the Request-URI, and the specification of the HTTP version. The Request-Line must end with a carriage return/line feed.

Allowable methods are established by the target resource. The client should be notified in the response if the method is not allowed or not recognized.

## GET

The GET method retrieves the data identified in the Request-URI. If the data is a Web page, the file constituting the page will be returned to the client, generally as text/html. If the GET points to a script or other process (rather than data), the result of the process will be returned. CGI programmers must be sure to include the necessary headers as part of the response.

If the request includes an If-Modified-Since header, GET requests that the file be transferred only if the date given in the If-Modified-Since field is earlier than the modified date of the file. This is called a *conditional* GET.

## HEAD

The HEAD method requests that the server should respond only with the information contained in the HTTP headers, generated by the META elements that may be contained in the file. The server is not to transfer any data contained in the BODY element of the file. This method is suggested for obtaining the meta-information from the file for use by search engines for indexing purposes and for use in testing links.

## POST

The POST method requests that the server accept data enclosed in the request as new data to be included in the file identified in the Request-URI. POST was designed to allow for adding data to existing resources; posting messages to newsgroups, mailing lists, or other similar groups; and transferring a block of data as the result of submitting a form to a script or other data process.

POST does not require that a file be created on the server. It often is merely the transfer of data from a form and can result in the search for and display of existing data. The response to such a POST should be either 200 (OK) or 204 (No Content), depending on whether the response will include any resulting data. If POST creates a file on the server, the response should be 201 (Created) and contain an HTML file noting the successful creation of the file and containing a link.

The data to be transferred in the POST is considered an Entity-Body. Therefore, POST requests must contain a valid Content-Length header; if the server cannot determine the length of the request, it should generate a 400 (Bad Request) error message. The Entity-Body is covered in the section "The Entity," later in this chapter.

# Request-URI

The Request-URI is a uniform resource identifier that identifies the file or data to which the request refers. An absolute URI is required when the request passes through a proxy. In all other cases, the URI must give the path to the URI relative to the server. The path of the URI cannot be empty. If the bookmark of our Stanford user were to `http://www.cern.org`, the path is the server root, denoted as / in UNIX parlance but *not* required for the HTTP protocol. (See the section "The File Path" for more information on the slash.)

CGI programmers should keep in mind that the Request-URI is transmitted as an encoded string, and arrange for the encoding or decoding of the URL as appropriate. See Chapter 27, "CGI Programming."

## The Request Header Fields

The client can include information in its request in addition to the method.

### Authorization

Occasionally, you might receive an error code `401` (Unauthorized) response when you try to access a Web page. The `Authorization` field is the companion to that response. A browser might authenticate itself by including the `Authorization` request header field with its request. The authorization process is determined by the server, and failure to provide the appropriate credentials in the `Authorization` field of the request will result in another `401` response. The authentication method is determined by the users. Note also that this is an instance where the roles of client and server are temporarily reversed.

The authentication scheme must be arranged before it is used. A server that receives a request for a file that has been identified as protected must send back a response with a WWW-Authenticate header (which is a challenge). This header must contain certain information in an arranged format. When the user agent receives the response with this header, it must generate a new request with an Authentication header containing the agreed upon response to the challenge issued by the server (the credentials). If the credentials are not within the defined protection scheme, the server must issue a `403` (Forbidden). The means for implementing authorization are not specified in the protocol. If you are interested, read RFC 1945, section 11, for additional information.

> **NOTE**
>
> `Authorization` is not secure and should not be relied on to prevent access to any information that should be kept private.

### From

The `From` request-header field contains the Internet e-mail address of the person running the user agent. This information can be given by a person when setting up an Internet browser, along with other information requested by the software to establish the preferences of the person using the program. I use the term *user agent* at the beginning of this paragraph because software other than browsers roams the Internet. Robot agents should include this field so that problems can be reported to the person responsible for the robot's actions.

### If-Modified-Since

I have already mentioned the use for this field—the conditional GET. If the file being requested has not been modified since the time specified in this field, a cached copy of the file might be used, and the file itself will not be transferred to the client. The proper response in that event is 304 (Not Modified). The field should be constructed as follows:

```
If-Modified-Since: Mon, 31 Dec 1999 23:59:59 GMT
```

When constructing a response to the conditional GET, the CGI programmer should bear in mind that a date later than the current time according to the server is invalid, and the If-Modified-Since field will be ignored. If the requested file has been modified since the If-Modified-Since date, the response is as if the request were a normal GET. If the resource has not been modified since the If-Modified-Since date, the response should be 304 (Not Modified).

Determining the date of modification is sometimes a problem. On some servers, it might be the file system last-modified time. If the file contains dynamically included parts, as is likely with CGI scripting, the date of modification might be the most recent of the last-modified times for the included parts. The format required for the date is discussed in the "Date" section, later in this chapter.

### Referer

The Referer is the URI from which the Request-URI was obtained; that is, if our person at Stanford clicked on the link to CERN while viewing a page located at http://www.leland.stanford.edu/slac/lowenergy.html, the Referer field will contain that URI. This field was intended to allow for optimized caching and tracing of mistyped or invalid links, but its use has raised concerns about revealing private information about personal interests.

If the Referer is on the same client as the Request-URI, a relative URI should be given; if the Referer is from another IP address, the absolute URI should be given. The field is not sent if the Request-URI was obtained from a source not having its own URI, such as keyboard input or bookmark.

### User-Agent

The User-Agent field usually contains the brand of the browser. This field is useful for determining protocol violations, but it is usually used to determine the popularity of particular brands of browsers. The User-Agent field can also be used to tailor a dynamic response to particular browsers, such as presenting text pages to Lynx users and animated graphics and scripts to Netscape and Internet Explorer browsers.

## The Response

Now that you have learned about the request side of the rhythm of HTTP, let's look at the partner's response to the request. After receiving the request message, the server must determine the version of HTTP being used by the client. If it is HTTP/0.9, the only response allowed is the Simple-Response. The client sends the BODY element of the page. The Simple-Response is terminated by the closing of the connection by the server. If the client has sent an

HTTP/1.0 request, but receives the BODY and not the Status Line, the client should presume the response to be a Simple-Response and treat the contents as an Entity-Body.

# Full-Response

A Full-Response begins with a status line and one or more of the following: General-Header, Response-Header, and Entity-Header. The headers will be followed by an empty carriage return/line feed and then the BODY of the page.

## Status-Line

The Status-Line of a Full-Response will contain the protocol version, a numeric status code, and a textual phrase associated with the status code. Each element of the Status-Line must be separated by a space; no carriage return or line feed is allowed until the end of the sequence:

```
HTTP/1.0 200 OK
```

The carriage return/line feed is present but not shown. This line alerts the browser that the response is a Full-Response, not a Simple-Response.

## Status Codes and Reason Phrases

The Status-Code element is a three-digit number sent in response to the request, alerting the browser to the success or failure of the request. The Reason-Phrase is a simple text explanation, which can provide some information for a person trying to make sense of what went wrong.

The 100 series of numbers is not used. The remaining series are as follows:

| Status Code | Reason Phrase |
| --- | --- |
| 200 | OK |
| 201 | Created |
| 202 | Accepted |
| 204 | No Content |
| 301 | Moved Permanently |
| 302 | Moved Temporarily |
| 304 | Not Modified |
| 400 | Bad Request |
| 401 | Unauthorized |
| 403 | Forbidden |
| 404 | Not Found |
| 500 | Internal Server Error |
| 501 | Not Implemented |
| 502 | Bad Gateway |
| 503 | Service Unavailable |

## General Header Fields

These headers are not restricted to either a request or a response, and they can be generated by the client, the server, or both, depending on circumstances at the time of the connection.

### Date

Date is a general header field, and its contents should give the date and time of the origination of the message. The date format for HTTP is specific; if the format is incorrectly stated, the Expires field should be considered to have passed its date and time of expiry. The allowable date formats are as follows:

> Sat, 01 Jan 1999 00:01:01 GMT
>
> Saturday, 01-Jan-99 00:01:01 GMT
>
> Sat Jan 1 00:01:01 1999

The first format is preferred. All HTTP/1.0 date and time indicators used within the protocol stream must be in Universal Time, formerly known as Greenwich Mean Time.

It is recommended that servers always send a Date header for use by the client in evaluating expiries of cached material. It is suggested that clients not include a Date header unless the message includes an Entity-Body (as in the case of a POST request). Messages without a Date header should be assigned one by the receiving application if the message will be stored in a cache or sent through a gateway using a protocol requiring a Date header.

### Pragma

Pragma is a general header field, and its contents should give directions for optional behavior within the protocol. The instructions in the Pragma header are implementation specific, and they can apply to any recipient within the request-response flow of traffic. The format for a Pragma header is

```
Pragma: [One or more pragma-directives] CRLF
```

A pragma-directive can be no-cache and can also include other extensions that are specific to a protocol. If the no-cache directive is used, the receiving application should send the request to the server even if the receiving application has a cached copy of the file containing the pragma-directive.

Because pragma-directives can apply to any or all recipients in the flow of traffic between the client and server, they should be passed through proxies and gateway applications. It is not possible to address a pragma-directive to a specific recipient, and it should be ignored by a recipient if the directive is not relevant to that recipient.

## Response Header Fields

The response header fields provide additional information about the response. The fields include Location, Server, and WWW-Authenticate. The WWW-Authenticate field was discussed earlier in this chapter in the section "Authorization."

### Location

The Location field specifies the exact location of the file identified in the Request-URI. For response codes in the 300 series, the location must give the URL for automatic redirection; only one absolute URL can be specified. Here is an example:

```
Location: http://www.foo.com/~bar/here.html
```

### Server

The Server field provides information about the software used by the server to handle the request. Here is an example:

```
Server: CERN/3.0 libwww/2.17
```

# The Entity

The file being transferred in response to the request is referred to as the Entity. It comprises Entity-Header fields and an Entity-Body.

## The Entity-Header Fields

The Entity-Header fields contain optional information about the Entity-Body or other resource identified in the request. The Entity-Header fields are Allow, Content-Encoding, Content-Length, Content-Type, Expires, and Last-Modified.

### Allow

The Allow field lists the methods supported by the resource identified by the Request-URI. If the request generating the response uses the POST method, the Allow header is not allowed; it should be ignored. Thus, the methods allowed by Allow are GET and HEAD. The client can attempt other methods, but a properly crafted program will follow the suggestion made by Allow.

### Content-Encoding

The Content-Encoding field indicates whether additional encoding (other than media-type encoding) has been applied to the file. Content-Encoding, for example, alerts the browser to the fact that a document has been compressed; the browser might then be able to handle the decompression itself or call upon a helper application to extract the file, rather than merely saving the contents to the would-be reader's disk.

### Content-Length

The Content-Length field indicates the size of the Entity-Body in a decimal number of octets. Here is an example:

```
Content-Length: 1066
```

> **NOTE**
>
> *Octet* is a byte made up of 8 bits. Using *byte* was considered, but some operating systems define bytes as being composed of other than 8 bits.

## Content-Type

The Content-Type field indicates the media type of the Entity-Body. Media types are open: There is no set number, limit, or definition of media types; there is only a method of describing them. This allows you to include media types as they are conceived; the number is boundless.

Media types are described as *type/subtype* (with no spaces allowed) and can have parameters. An example is text/html. Type, subtype, and parameter names are not case sensitive; however, the values of parameters can be. Media types are registered with the Internet Assigned Number Authority, and the use of nonregistered media types is discouraged.

## Expires

The Expires field indicates the date and time after which the file should be invalid. It is suggested that such files should not be cached; if a cached file is found in response to a request after the date in the Expires field, a fresh copy should be requested. Many Web authors know, however, that this field is frequently ignored by caching applications. See the "Date" section, earlier in this chapter, for formatting requirements.

## Last-Modified

The Last-Modified field indicates the date and time when the file appears to have been last modified. The problems with determining when a file was last modified, especially if parts of the entity have been created dynamically, have already been discussed.

# The Entity-Body

The Entity-Body is the file that is being requested. It is referred to as the Entity-Body because it can be a text file, a video clip, a PostScript file, an archive of compressed files, or an executable program; its exact format is unknown at the time the request is made. The Entity-Header fields give the format in the response. An Entity-Body is sent with the request message only if the request method requires it, and a Content-Length header field must be included in the request headers.

An Entity-Body must not be returned if the response is 204 (No Content) and 304 (Not Modified). Responses to the HEAD method must not include an Entity-Body. All other responses must include either the Entity-Body or a Content-Length header field of zero.

## Content-Type

The Entity-Body must carry with it a Content-Type field, which identifies the media type of the body. Designation of media type has been discussed in the section "The Entity Header Fields."

> **NOTE**
>
> If the media type is not given, the receiving program should examine the contents of the file and any name extension in an attempt to determine the media type. If the media type cannot be determined, the receiving application should treat the Entity-Body as "application/octet-stream." The person using a browser should have the program configured either to alert the user of that media type and ask for further instruction or to deal with that media type in a specified manner.

### Content-Encoding

If the Entity-Body has been encoded, the `Content-Encoding` field should be used to indicate the type of additional encoding applied. Examples of additional encoding include compression of a file and translation of an 8-bit binary file to 7 bits for transfer over the Internet.

### Content-Length

The length of the Entity-Body must be included in the `Content-Length` header field. If this field is not sent through error or because of a Simple-Request, the receiving application will determine body length as the total received at the time of termination of the connection by the server.

If an Entity-Body is included in a request message, the message *must* contain a `Content-Length` header field; brute force determination of body length by termination of the connection is not possible with a request, because the server would not be able to respond. If a request is sent with an Entity-Body and no (or an invalid) `Content-Length` header, the response should be `400` (Bad Request).

# HTTP/1.1 and HTTP-NG

To address some of the issues raised by statelessness, the World Wide Web Consortium (W3C) and others have been looking at the Hypertext Transfer Protocol and its weaknesses. HTTP opens only one connection per request and returns only one resource per request. Typically, a link is selected on a Web browser, the connection is established, and the server sends the Web page selected; the page, however, is likely to have a few icons, an image, an animation, a sound file, and so forth. The browser requests each object in turn, with a single connection, a single request, a single response, and termination. Although more than one request can be made at a time, a new connection must be established for each request, and the rhythm of request, response, and termination begins.

## HTTP/1.1

HTTP/1.1 proposes a persistent connection, where the client and server maintain their connection until all objects have been transferred. It is estimated that half the packet traffic under HTTP/1.0 is opening and closing connections. HTTP/1.1 also introduces pipelining, where the requests are issued in batches rather than serially (and waiting for the response/termination cycle). With multiple requests being sent in the same TCP packet, the number of packets sent is significantly reduced. Pipelining is the major factor in increasing the efficiency of HTTP/1.1 over HTTP/1.0.

## HTTP-Next Generation

The authors of HTTP-Next Generation (HTTP-NG) have the opinion that the constraints of HTTP and MIME are too great to be repaired. They propose to replace HTTP with a new generation of Web transport. HTTP-NG allows for multiple requests to be sent over a single connection, without the requirement of waiting for a response before sending a new request. As is the way on the Internet, the server need not respond to requests in the order in which they are received, and the responses can be interleaved.

HTTP-NG divides the connection into channels and sends control messages over a control channel and each object over its own object channel. This allows mixing protocols, by the way. After a connection is established, objects can be transferred over the connection in a channel using a protocol specifically suited to the transfer of that object. A test implementation has been set up, and early reports are that HTTP 1.0 used only a tenth of the bandwidth available for the test, but that HTTP-NG used the entire path bandwidth using multiple requests over one connection. Multiple requests over individual connections using HTTP 1.0 congested the available bandwidth and performance was degraded badly.

HTTP-NG is not compatible with HTTP/1.*x*. Its proponents are confident, however, that it can be implemented without loss of access to data residing on servers still operating under HTTP/1.*x* and without cutting those servers out of the part of the Web using the new generation of the protocol.

## MUX

There is also an experimental protocol for multiplexing transport over the Web (although it is generic and not restricted to the Web in any of its workings). MUX proposes to allow multiple protocols to be multiplexed over the same connection. This allows the server to send text, video, sound, and other files during the same connection, using the protocol best suited for each object. MUX also allows for files to be sent compressed, with an alert to the client of the method of compression. Because MUX works under HTTP, it does not obsolete current standards.

# Uniform Resource Identifiers—An Overview

Uniform (or sometimes *universal*) resource identifiers are strings of characters that identify the precise location of a resource available on the World Wide Web. URIs encompass not only the familiar uniform resource locators (URLs), but also uniform resource names (URNs) and uniform resource citations (URCs). URNs and URCs are discussed further in the "A Few Problems with URLs, and Some Proposals" section of this chapter. The syntax of a URI must not only encompass the currently available protocols for accessing data on the Internet (ftp, http, and gopher, for example), but it should also be capable of being extended to recognize new protocols as they come into general use.

The most common use of a uniform resource identifier these days is to locate a Web page using a URL. URLs are commonly thought of as pointers to a filename in a directory on a Web server. Most people think URLs look like this:

```
http://www.foo.com/~bar/file.html
```

To a large extent that is correct; however, URLs can also point to ftp sites, gopher space, newsgroups, and other resources using protocols other than HTTP. The preceding representation of a URL is called an absolute URL because it specifies the protocol to be used to make the connection, it states that the request for the resource complies with the Internet Protocol, and it states the path to be followed to locate and retrieve the resource. However, URLs can be *relative*, as shown in this example:

```
file2.html
```

In this case, the browser will look for `file2.html` in the same directory as the resource located at `~bar/file.html`.

The preceding section covers HTTP, but URIs can access files using other protocols as well. Generically, a URI consists of four parts: the protocol, the Internet node, the file path, and optional arguments. A URL looks something like the following:

```
[protocol]://[internet node]:[port][/file path/file path]?[optional arguments]
```

# Protocols

The protocol is the mechanism by which access to the Internet node is obtained. More than a dozen protocols are available, and a more detailed examination of a few of the more common ones can be found later in this chapter, in the section "The Syntax of Schemes."

# The Internet Node

The Internet node given for the connection is the fully qualified domain name (or IP number) of a computer with a permanent connection to the Internet.

# The File Path

The file path is optional. According to RFC 1738, the authority on the subject, if the file path is omitted, the slash is optional. Therefore, if you want to obtain a file from `www.foo.com`, the full Request-URI is blank. You would direct your browser to the following URI:

```
http://www.foo.com
```

**TIP**

Much discussion is waged on certain Usenet newsgroups concerning the need for a "trailing slash." The world of the World Wide Web exists mainly on the UNIX operating system. In UNIX, the slash has two functions. In one function, it acts as a separator between directories and files. The top directory, which contains all other directories, is called the *root directory*, or just *root*. The second function of the slash is to represent the *root directory*. The path to a file in a subdirectory could be represented as `/root/foo/bar/ralph.txt`. This is an *absolute pathname*, providing a complete and unambiguous name for the file `ralph.txt`. The first slash refers to root, and all the other slashes separate the names of directories, except for the last slash, which separates the filename from its directory.

Although URIs follow the UNIX convention of using a slash as a separator, a URI is not a UNIX filename. Using a slash as a URI separator works on all operating systems, even DOS and Macintosh. The slash in a URI is considered a separator of components of a hierarchical name known as the *url-path*. The slash preceding the url-path is not a part of the url-path. It is the indicator of the termination of the `<host>:<port>` part of the `<scheme-specific-part>`, and indicates the beginning of the url-path. The use of slashes in the url-path does not mean that the URI is a UNIX filename.

## Optional Arguments

The optional arguments must be preceded by a question mark. The optional arguments are often passed to a CGI script and contain, for example, an encoded string for which the CGI script will search.

# Uniform Resource Locators—A Detailed Examination

For most hobbyists, this brief overview will be more than sufficient. However, CGI programmers and others need to resolve a number of issues in order to create Web pages on the fly, create searchable databases, or receive and return information from forms on a Web page.

## The Parts of a URL

A generic URL can be represented as `<scheme>:<scheme-specific-part>`. The URL must contain the name of the scheme being used (which is what I called a *protocol* earlier in this section). The name of the scheme must consist of lowercase letters, numerals, the plus sign, the period, or the hyphen. Programs that receive scheme names in uppercase letters should treat them as lowercase.

## Character Encoding

Characters other than those listed in the preceding paragraph must be encoded. As I mentioned earlier, an octet is an 8-bit byte; the characters in a URL represent the octets used in Internet protocols. The US-ASCII coded character set defines the relationship between characters and octets representing those characters. Each octet can be encoded in hexadecimal using the percent sign and two hexadecimal digits. (The hexadecimal digits are 0123456789ABCDEF; lower-case letters are recognized.)

It is required that octets be encoded if they have no displayable character in the US-ASCII coded character set or if the character represented by the octet is "unsafe" or "reserved."

Characters that cannot be displayed range from hexadecimal 00 through 1F, 7F, and 80 through FF. Characters that are unsafe are those that have different uses in different situations. These characters include the space, <, >, the quotation mark, #, %, {, }, ¦, \, ^, ~, [, ], and '. All unsafe characters must be encoded within a URL by representing them as two hexadecimal characters preceded by the percent sign. Characters are reserved when their characters have specified meanings. If the character is reserved in a scheme, its octet must be encoded. Reserved characters are ;, /, ?, :, @, =, and &.

## The Syntax of Scheme-Specific Parts

Although the scheme comes first, it is inextricably bound to the *scheme-specific part*, which I will cover first. The scheme-specific part is presumed to use the Internet Protocol to access a specified host on the Internet to locate and retrieve specific data. The scheme-specific part must follow this syntax:

`//<user>:<password>@<host>:<port>/<url-path>`

The scheme-specific part must begin with a double slash, which indicates that it complies with the Internet scheme syntax. The following parts are optional and can be omitted: `<user>:<password>@`, `:<password>@`, `:<port>`, and `<url-path>`. The scheme-specific part must end with a carriage return/line feed not shown here.

The `<host>` portion must be a fully qualified domain name or its IP address (a dotted quad, which is four decimal digit groups separated by periods). `<port>` is the software port number to connect to. Most schemes have a default port specified; if no port number is given, the default is used. Omit the colon if omitting the port number. `<url-path>` is the location of the specified file to be retrieved.

**CAUTION**

The slash following the `<host>:<port>` is not part of `<url-path>`. See the discussion in the section "The File Path," earlier in this chapter. If only `<host>` or `<host>:<port>` is used, the slash can be omitted.

*url-path* is dependent on the scheme and is discussed with each scheme section.

# The Syntax of Schemes

Schemes (or protocols) are registered with the Internet Assigned Numbers Authority. A new scheme can be submitted for registry with a definition of the algorithm for accessing a resource and the syntax for representing the scheme. Rather than provide a full description of all the schemes, I've limited the discussion to the most common schemes.

## file

`file` is the method used to designate a file available on a local fixed disk; it cannot be used to identify a file accessible over the Internet. A typical `file` request looks like the following:

```
file://<hostname>/<path>
```

In this request, *<hostname>* is the fully qualified domain name of the system, and *<path>* is the hierarchical directory path residing on the host. *<hostname>* can be omitted, in which case *<path>* is resolved relative to the computer from which the URL is being resolved. `file` is unique in that it specifies neither an Internet protocol (such as `http`) nor an access method (such as `news`) for a resource.

## File Transfer Protocol

The `ftp` scheme is used to retrieve files from ftp servers. A username and password can be supplied to be passed to the server after the connection is made. If they are not supplied and one is requested, the username anonymous should be sent in response to the server's request for USER, and the Internet e-mail address should be sent in response to the server's request for PASS. A typical request for anonymous ftp would look like this:

```
ftp://ftp.foo.com/bar/MyPrize.gzip
```

The *url-path* for ftp is `<cwd1>/<cwd2>/<name>;type=<typecode>`. *<cwdN>* represents the directories to be entered as arguments to the change working directory command. *<name>* is the file to be retrieved, and *<typecode>* is one of a, i, or d, representing the type of transfer (ASCII, binary, or list). If a slash must be used in a *<cwd>* or *<name>* component, it must be encoded. For example, if the path sought is /pub/myfile.text, located on the server known as ftp.foo.com, the properly encoded URL is

```
ftp://myname:mypword@ftp.foo.com/%2Fpub/myfile.txt;type=a
```

This URL establishes a connection with the server, transmits the name myname and the password mypword in response to the requests, changes the directory to /pub, and retrieves myfile.txt in ASCII mode. If a username is supplied without a password, the user agent should prompt the user for a password. Unlike a true ftp connection, the connection will be terminated following the file transfer.

## Gopher

Gopher is a protocol that is used to provide indexing of information on the Internet, and it is text based. A gopher URL looks like this:

```
gopher://<host>:<port>/<gopher-path>
```

The default port is 70. *<gopher-path>* is one of the following:

```
<gophertype><selector>
<gophertype><selector>%09<search>
<gophertype><selector>%09<search>%09<gopher+_string>
```

The entire *<gopher-path>* may be empty; in that event, the slash is optional, and *<gophertype>* defaults to 1. *<selector>* is the gopher selector string. For specific details on gopher types and selector strings, see RFC 1436.

## Hypertext Transfer Protocol

HTTP is discussed in the first part of this chapter. The syntax of an HTTP URL is

```
http://<host>:<port>/<path>?<searchpart>
```

The default port is 80. No username or password is allowed. *<path>* and *?<searchpart>* are optional; if they are omitted, the slash can also be omitted. (See the discussion in the section, "The File Path," earlier in this chapter.) Within *<path>* and *<searchpart>*, the slash, semicolon, and question mark are reserved. The slash can be used to act as a separator in a hierarchical structure.

## `mailto`

The `mailto` scheme is used to designate an Internet e-mail address. The form is

```
mailto:<rfc822-address-specification>
```

There are no reserved characters, but RFC 822 addresses often contain a percent sign that must be encoded. Notice that the URL does not contain the double slash indicating compliance with the Internet Protocol. The `mailto` scheme does not request the retrieval of a file. The URL cannot contain any information other than an Internet e-mail address.

## news

The news scheme is used to access either a newsgroup or an article of news in Usenet form. The URL form required depends on whether a newsgroup or an article is to be accessed:

```
news:<newsgroup-name>
news:<message-id>
```

*<newsgroup-name>* is a period-delimited name such as *comp.infosystems.www.authoring.html*. *<message-id>* refers to the Message-ID header of a posted article without the enclosing angle brackets, along with the fully specified domain name. Notice that the URL does not contain the double slash indicating compliance with the Internet Protocol. The URL will refer to the newsgroup on the host of the user.

## telnet

The `telnet` scheme is used to institute a `telnet` session through the browser. The URL is

`telnet://<user>:<password>@<host>:<port>/`

The default port is 23. The `<user>:<password>`, `:<password>`, and slash portions are optional. The `telnet` scheme does not specify a path to a file. Remote logins vary in implementation and allowed activity.

# A Few Problems with URLs, and Some Proposals

Web browsers encounter problems with URLs. They reach dead links and have transfer times that stretch into infinity on overseas links and overloaded sites. Let's consider a frequent situation: A person has moved from one Internet service provider to a new one, and the original account has been terminated. The resource that person maintained on the first ISP has been moved, but there is no method of determining the new location until search engines have been updated. (This is sometimes referred to as a "lack of persistence." The URL can disappear without a trace just because it was relocated.) Uniform resource names have been proposed to solve this common problem. URNs would be permanently affixed to an object and resolved to the URL wherever the resource may happen to be. URNs can also be used to locate a copy of the resource nearest the requesting user agent, in the event of multiple copies. The goal is to provide persistence, cutting down on wasted requests for resources that have been relocated.

Another proposal is the uniform resource characteristic (or citation), where a resource would not only be described, but would also provide the author, title, and additional locations if available. A URC can also indicate data type, which is helpful in determining how to download a resource and how to handle it after it is obtained; or it can indicate copyright status, which is helpful in alerting users that the resource is not to be shared promiscuously (or alerting users that it can be so shared). A URC, when implemented, is likely to be a series of `<fields>=<values>` similar to the META element in HTML.

# Knowledge Representation

People with Web browsers can obtain information from databases located anywhere in the world. Overnight couriers have placed their status reports online, where anyone with the appropriate transit number of an overnight shipment can access the couriers' databases and determine the status of the delivery. Online services allow the order of automobiles without having to drive to a dealership. Bookstores are online. Large corporations represented by several law firms in different parts of the world now require the firms to make contract language, research, and legal memoranda available for other lawyers, reducing duplicate effort and duplicate billing on as many issues as possible. The amount and timeliness of business information available on the World Wide Web boggles the imagination, and much of the information is provided at no charge in the hopes that the user will buy other more timely or more proprietary information.

The use of HTTP and URIs on the World Wide Web enables an unbounded nonlinear information system. The protocols used by URIs provide us with access to resources that might be located anywhere in the world. By using standardized syntax in accordance with the registry maintained by the IANA, URIs are infinitely extensible. As new resources are invented, the method of locating and retrieving them can be specified and registered for worldwide use by all. By using the public protocols of TCP/IP and publishing the protocols of HTTP and URI, the W3C has attempted to ensure that the Web will remain accessible to all with no requirements of proprietary hardware or software.

In 1945, Vannevar Bush, President Roosevelt's Director of the Office of Scientific Research and Development, wrote an article in *The Atlantic Monthly* entitled "As We May Think." He proposed a mechanical contraption built into a desk, with information stored on microfilm and several projectors and screens available in the desk for viewing more than one resource at a time in a random fashion. He called this contraption a *memex*, which was short for *memory expander*. As Vannevar Bush imagined in 1945, we can access information on the Web in a random fashion, without having to wade through a serial retrieval process. We can add to the data by publishing our own Web pages, and have our information become a part of the rhythm of the Web. Unlike Bush's *memex*, however, our nonlinear information system is not limited in its resources to the material on our desktop.

As Ted Nelson foretold, we have available to us *hyperspace*. With links not only to text but to images, maps, sound, and whatever else can be imagined and implemented, our resources have become unbounded. Unlike early attempts at nonlinear information systems, with the World Wide Web we are not required to buy specific hardware or software for access to this new world of data, and we are not limited to resources that must be purchased and reside within our computers.

The steps leading to our present riches were certainly not inexorable. Vannevar Bush recognized that the explosion of new knowledge resulting from World War II would be impossible to keep track of. Bush's article suggesting a solution inspired Doug Engelbart, who happened to see the magazine half a world away in the Philippines and remember it until the 1960s. Engelbart's work on the mouse and collaborative authoring made it possible even to consider a computer as a support tool for just one person, something unheard of in the days of mainframes. Engelbart was awarded the Lemelson-MIT prize in 1997 in recognition of the advances based on his fundamental concepts. Ted Nelson and his Xanadu became a rich source of inspiration for supporters of nonlinear information, but it took the United States Department of Defense and its determination to survive—if not win—global thermonuclear war and all the destruction wrought by atoms to create a survivable network of networks on which such a system could run. And finally, it took high employee turnover at CERN to bring us to the beginning chapter of the World Wide Web: In the face of high employee turnover, how could CERN preserve the knowledge wrung at great cost from the destruction of atoms?

Today, we move information in myriad ways over the Internet and the World Wide Web. Our access is independent of any platform or software requirements, thanks to the public standards implemented by Tim Berners-Lee. We download text, images, video and sound clips, and executable programs that will run on any computer. None of this was possible with proprietary programs or proprietary hardware, and it is unlikely it would be possible today had the standards for doing so been proprietary. As you work through the chapters of this book, learning to create pages with HTML, to create scripts and programs for interactive pages, and to suggest design and layout, remember that accessibility for all users is fundamental to the existence of the Internet and is the foundation on which the World Wide Web is built.

# Summary

Hypertext Transfer Protocol and uniform resource identifiers work hand in hand to enable the transfer of data over the Internet through the World Wide Web. HTTP interfaces with TCP/IP to establish connections between computers and send packets of data back and forth, bringing us text, animated images, sound, and programs that run on virtual machines in our computers' memory. Uniform resource identifiers enable our computers to locate these resources for retrieval. Because these standards are publicly available, there are no restrictions on who can use them, and there are no restrictions on their use. Indeed, it is expected that they will be extended and improved as new ideas for data formats evolve.

Beginners in any subject always ask questions that begin with *how*. After they have learned how, they ask the interesting questions that begin with *why*. In this chapter, you have learned how HTTP and URIs work. As you read through the remaining chapters of this book and learn how to write CGI programs and style sheets, for example, you will already have the background to understand why CGI scripts must be structured to return certain information in response to a query, and why style sheets include a TYPE declaration. By having some of the why questions already answered, it will be easier to apply the lessons in learning how.

# Web Browsers and Platforms

*by Mike Sessums*

**CHAPTER 6**

## IN THIS CHAPTER

The user's platform and browser can affect how your page is viewed. It also determines what can be accessed on your Web site.

This chapter introduces you to HTML standards and browser extensions. It also helps you become familiar with the various platforms and browsers people are using to access the Web. Armed with this information, Web site developers can better plan their sites.

# Extensions Versus HTML Standards

Some people believe that it is all Microsoft's idea, but the W3 Consortium (W3C) sets the HTML standards for the World Wide Web (W3). Any browser that wants to survive must conform to the standards set by the W3C, not the other way around.

The W3C (www.w3.org) is composed of members from universities and leading-edge technology corporations around the world. Even with Microsoft and Netscape as members, the W3C tries to stay platform- and browser-neutral. This helps avoid a conflict of interest.

The consortium was created in 1994 in conjunction with CERN, the European Laboratory for Particle Physics in Switzerland. CERN (www.cern.ch) was the group that gave birth to the Web in 1989. Some of the W3C's goals include helping others realize the Web's potential by developing new standards, and making software to test those standards publicly available. (See Chapter 2, "The History of HTML," for more information on the roles that the W3C, Microsoft, and Netscape play in HTML development.)

Extensions are very hard to differentiate from standards. An example of an HTML standard is <HR>, meaning horizontal rule. A Netscape extension to this standard is SIZE=*n*. The latter allows you to specify how thick you want to make the horizontal rule.

Take a look at Listing 6.1 to see how these two tags are used.

**Listing 6.1. Horizontal rules: extensions vs. standards.**

```
<HTML>
<BODY bgcolor="ffffff">
<BR>
<HR>
<BR>
<HR SIZE=8>
</BODY>
</HTML>
```

The fourth line in Listing 6.1 shows the HTML standard, and the sixth line shows the Netscape extension. The <BR> gives your sample extra padding by using line breaks. The bgcolor="ffffff" attribute sets the background color to white, so that you can see the shaded horizontal rules better.

Figure 6.1 shows the difference that the extension makes when viewed with Netscape Navigator 4.0.

**FIGURE 6.1.**

*The results of HTML standard code for horizontal rule (top line) compared to the Netscape* size *extension to that code (bottom line).*

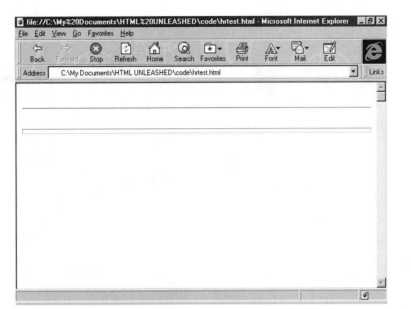

As you can see, browser extensions are coding additions that the browser manufacturers would like to see added to the current HTML standards. That is why some former browser extensions are now part of the HTML standards. Extensions are also a good way for one browser to try to outshine the others. This can be a real boon for Web site developers.

# HTML and Platform Idiosyncrasies

Not all platforms and their software support the latest HTML standards and browser extensions. Some plug-ins are available only on certain platforms.

The major platforms are either Windows-, Mac-, or UNIX-based machines. However, many other players are involved in the hardware and browser war, and with each come their own bonuses and drawbacks for Web site development.

Pixel size is a very confusing measurement when compared to physical display size, and it can be very deceptive. A 640×480 image fills the screen when display devices of different physical sizes are set to 640×480 pixel resolution. As an example of this, you could view the same page on a 14-inch monitor and a 20-inch monitor set at 640×480 pixels. They both fill the screen, but one physically displays six inches larger than the other (as shown in Figure 6.2).

A platform pixel comparison chart is located in Table 6.1.

**FIGURE 6.2.**

*Comparison of physical size to pixel size.*

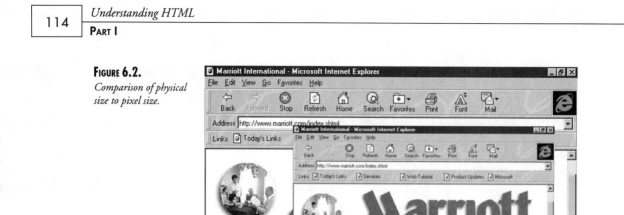

**Table 6.1. Platform and display size comparison in pixels.**

| Platform | Display |
|----------|---------|
| PC | 640×480/1024×768 |
| NC | 1280×1024 |
| Notebook | 640×480 |
| WebTV | 560×420 |
| Palmtop | 480×240 |

One thing to note on this chart is that even though the WebTV has a 560×420 display, the actual Web page design/display area is 544×378 with no horizontal scrolling.

Something else to consider when designing your site is what type of connection your target audience is using. If it is a T1 line typical of a corporate environment, you might be able to easily add plenty of graphics, background music, and VRML environments without worrying about load time. A link to a 10MB video is not a major problem and will probably load in just a couple of minutes.

However, if your target audience is accessing your site over a telephone line, you should think twice about overloading that site with frills. Even with a high-speed modem, a Web surfer will probably move on to another site long before your page gets a chance to load.

> **TIP**
>
> Although 300 dpi or higher resolution images might look great on paper, most computers can display only 90 dpi or less. Images much larger than this on your Web page are simply a waste of bandwidth. Saving your images at 90 dpi or 100 dpi will decrease load time and still deliver a quality image to your user's screen.

Now, let's take a closer look at the platforms people are using to access the Web, including personal computers (PCs), network computers (NCs), notebooks, laptops, Personal Digital Assistants (PDAs), and handheld PCs (HPCs). Each of these has its own operating system (OS), display, connection, and other features that can make Web site planning a challenge.

# Personal Computers

The biggest user base for most Web developers can be found in the *personal computer* (*PC*), which is popular in both corporate and home markets. The PC market is dominated by IBM clones and followed by PowerMacs, and some of the most innovative developments in Web software and support can be found here.

PCs in the U.S. have sported a variety of operating systems, including DOS, Windows, and OS/2 for the IBM and clones, and various System X incarnations for the Apple. In Japan, there were at least seven popular PCs and operating systems at last count.

Other PCs such as Atari, Amiga, and Commodore 64 and 128 are also being used to access the Internet, but in considerably fewer instances. Although their user base is not as large as the PC user base, computers such as the Commodores are still quite popular in several countries, mostly because of their price.

Luckily for Web developers, Microsoft has been able to use its Windows environment (in a variety of flavors, including 3.1, 95, and NT) to narrow the OS choices on IBM PCs and clones for a large portion of the world. Intense marketing by Microsoft and the waning popularity of the Apple PCs have also given Microsoft a strong hold on the PC market. Of course, this makes Web site planning and development easier, because it moves everyone closer to a standard.

However, Apple might not be down for the count just yet. Apple's Quicktime and QuicktimeVR formats have left their mark on many Web sites. The company's plans to team BeOS with its PowerMacs is one strategy it is using to get established in the consumer PC market again.

PC monitors are typically in the 14- to 20-inch range at 640×480 to 1024×768 pixels. The normal color range can be from 256 to 16 million colors. However, you might want to stay away from a 16-million color splash image because of the image file's considerable size.

PC users in the private sector usually connect to the Internet over residential phone lines. A much smaller number of users have high-speed ISDN connections. Corporate PC users, on the other hand, are usually connected to an intranet, just like their network computer cousins.

# Network Computers

Besides the PC, Web developers in a university or corporate engineering environment may also be catering to network computer (NC) users. The NCs can't match the popularity of the PCs for the general public. One reason is price, and the other is the use of a different marketing strategy than the PCs.

UNIX is the biggest OS player in this field, with Sun and Silicon Graphics leading the pack. Hewlett-Packard also produces UNIX workstations, but it has moved more toward the network PC in its partnership with Microsoft and Windows NT.

At one time, Digital's VAX VMS was the king of the NCs, but Web software development is almost nonexistent now. Many VAX users are still strapped with an archaic version of the Mosaic browser that doesn't support tables, forms, frames, Java, ActiveX, or the new HTML 3.2 standards. Web developers will find their options very limited when working with this target group.

NC monitors are typically in the 17- to 20-inch range at 1280×1024 pixels in both color and grayscale.

Most NC users are permanently connected to their school's or company's network (hence the name) or intranet.

# Laptops and Notebooks

Some of the new laptop and notebook computers sport awesome features that take full advantage of your Web site. Their performance typically rivals that of Pentium-based desktop computers.

One leading notebook is a true multimedia computer with a 12-inch SVGA screen, 16-bit sound system (with bass and treble controls), full-screen MPEG capability, and 128-bit graphics.

Color text and graphics are great on some of the SVGA screens but are difficult to see or totally washed out on others. Animation and other moving objects on Web pages have a tendency to blur or leave ghost image trails, especially when light-colored objects are used. Another drawback is that many users with 16-bit sound have only the tiny built-in speaker, which could make your site's sounds come out rather tinny.

The most common OS you will find in the notebook computer market is Windows. Notebook users can use the same browser software, browser plug-ins, and Web applications used by their desk-bound counterparts.

Notebook users generally connect to the Web through cellular phone hookups or anywhere they can find a place to "jack in."

# Micro Minis (Palmtops and PDAs)

Many of the Palmtops and PDAs (Personal Digital Assistants) that have cropped up over the years have been nothing more than glorified (and expensive) address books. However, newer models that have hit the shelves have been tagged with the acronym *HPC* (Handheld Personal Computer).

Although these little computers can't compare with the power of the standard desktop PC, their portability and compatibility with their bigger brothers make them an alternative to the notebook computer.

When PDA users were surveyed, one of the top items on almost everyone's wish list was a Web browser. Several of the PDAs do support some form of access to the Internet, thanks to pre-packaged, third-party, and home-grown software. Some of the manufacturers even include a programming language so that users can create their own software.

Currently, each HPC has its own proprietary operating system, but Microsoft might bring everyone back to standardization again. Based on a Windows 95 look and feel, Windows CE offers "pocket" versions of popular software such as Word, Excel, and Internet Explorer with Windows 95 file-sharing compatibility. A new version of Windows CE reportedly will support Java and DVD (Digital Video Disk). Many hardware and software developers have already jumped on the Windows CE bandwagon and pledged their support. Casio, alone, plans to ship 500,000 of its Windows CE–based Cassiopeias to consumers by next year.

These palmtop marvels sport only 2MB or 4MB of RAM and 4MB or 8MB of ROM ("the virtual hard drive"), making most graphic-laden Web sites a real burden, if not a downright impossibility to view. Rectangular 480×240 pixel backlit grayscale displays are typical of the HPCs.

Palmtop users make their connection to the Internet in a variety of ways, due to the portability of these little workhorses. They can be connected using cellular phones, wireless modems, and standard telephone lines. One company even offers a Windows CE-to-NT network connection. But here's the rub: Modems available for some of these units run as slow as 2400 baud, which makes text browsing the only option. Luckily, many users have access to 19.2Kbps or faster modems.

# Browser Heritage

Before the graphical environment of the Web came along, users happily surfed through text on the Internet with computers that emulated standard terminals such as the VT100.

This greatly limited the information that could be put on the Net. Content developers were restricted to a simple hyperlinked format for their documents and information. There were no sounds, animations, or virtual environments.

With CERN's development of the World Wide Web, all of that began to change. The new graphic environment allowed images to be added to information.

Lynx brought a little more style to text browsing, allowing users to access hypertext documents and the new formatting. Graphic browsers such as W3C's Arena, Cello, and the groundbreaking

Mosaic from NCSA really opened up a world of possibilities for a new breed of Net content authors.

Mosaic became the most popular Web browser, due to its free distribution, support, and availability on a wide variety of platforms. The Netscape Navigator grew out of this heritage and became the king of browsers.

The Netscape Navigator grew in circulation and support, bringing new innovations for how Web content could be shared. Microsoft had underestimated the importance and scope of the improvements in Web development and usage, so Netscape was able to get a firm hold on the market before Microsoft realized what had happened.

Finally realizing the enormity of its error, Microsoft had to make a mad dash to get a foothold in this rapidly growing market. Thus began the "browser wars."

Many graphic browsers are in circulation today, but none appear to be a serious challenge to either the Netscape Navigator or the Microsoft Internet Explorer.

# Two Top Contenders: Netscape Navigator and Microsoft Internet Explorer

Netscape and Microsoft are in a real power struggle to win the Web browser market. The good thing about their browser wars is that developers have seen some great innovations and advances in Web browsers and plug-ins as each company tries to outdo the other. To the victor belongs the Web.

Of course, there is a down side, too. Do you design your page to satisfy the Netscape Navigator users, or do you set your style around the Microsoft Internet Explorer? It is almost impossible to take full advantage of both on the same Web site, although some people try.

You can optimize your page using Netscape Navigator extensions, or you can make it "best viewed on Internet Explorer." Microsoft even offers special incentive programs to designers who put its Internet Explorer logo on their Web sites.

Even when a browser conforms to the W3C HTML standards, it might view the same page differently.

Figure 6.3 shows how Netscape Navigator 4.0 views a page that has a creative use of frames. The page looks nice, clean, and crisp. This really has all the makings of a perfect Web site.

Look at the same page with the Microsoft Internet Explorer (as shown in Figure 6.4), and you can see a world of difference.

**FIGURE 6.3.**

*The Netscape Navigator shows a clean page with no horizontal scrolling necessary.*

**FIGURE 6.4.**

*The same page shown in Figure 6.3 as viewed with the Microsoft Internet Explorer 3.02.*

The obvious difference in how the Internet Explorer 3.02 displays the page is the need for horizontal scrolling to see the whole picture in the frame on the right. Notice also how each frame element is clearly defined by hard lines that were not visible in the Navigator rendition of the page. Figure 6.3 looks like a professional publication, whereas Figure 6.4 looks like someone's TV dinner tray.

So why does the output from the same page differ so much? The answers can be found in how the browsers interpret the following code:

```
<frameset border=0 rows=90,*>
<frame src="lmclogo.html" scrolling="no" noresize>
<frameset border=0 cols=170,*>
<frame src="mainmenu.html" scrolling="no" noresize>
<frame src="composite.html" name="main" noresize>
```

The first and third lines of this excerpt of HTML code turn the border off with border=0. This works just fine in Navigator (as you saw in Figure 6.3), but it is ignored in Internet Explorer 3.02, where it shows up as a visible border (as you saw in Figure 6.4).

Lines two, four, and five are where scrolling is turned off with scrolling="no" and frame resizing is turned off using noresize. These last two bits of code are recognized by both browsers.

One negative thing you should notice about both pages in Figures 6.3 and 6.4 is that the information in the left frame spills off the screen. This is normal for images larger than the computer's display size. However, what makes it a bad design element is that the designer neglected to provide a scrollbar to let users with lower display settings access all the information he worked so hard to create. Figure 6.5 demonstrates how useful the scrollbar is in accessing important information in the frame on the right.

**FIGURE 6.5.**

*Using the scrollbar reveals navigation buttons and other links.*

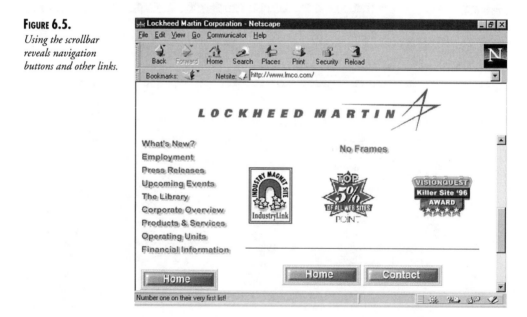

The addition of a scrollbar for the left frame may have been avoided for the sake of graphic design, but at the cost of functionality. If the user was able to change his display settings to at least 800×600, he could see the hidden Contact button on the fixed left frame (shown in Figure 6.6).

**FIGURE 6.6.**

*A Contact button appears when viewed at a higher resolution.*

A good solution to this problem would have been to make the elements in the left frame a bit tighter. Of course, the majority of users at Lockheed Martin, who have a mixture of PCs and NCs, are probably not viewing these sites at 640×480. However, the target audience for this Extranet page probably includes the general public and potential customers.

**TIP**

Be sure all of your page elements—especially those used for navigation—can be viewed on a screen set at 640×480. Add a scrollbar if needed, or make your page tight enough that viewers can see all of the elements without scrolling.

Scrollbars automatically appear on most browsers when the data or image areas are larger than the browser's viewing window. However, scrollbars can be turned off in the code as you have already seen.

Now look at that site with Microsoft Internet Explorer 4.0 (shown in Figure 6.7).

In Figure 6.7, you can see that Microsoft has cleaned up its act by recognizing the `border=0` tag. Also, notice that you can see the Contact button in the left frame without resetting the display to 800×600. Hey, this browser now has potential!

**FIGURE 6.7.**

*Look Ma, no frames! Internet Explorer 4.0 fixes some of the problems found in Internet Explorer 3.02.*

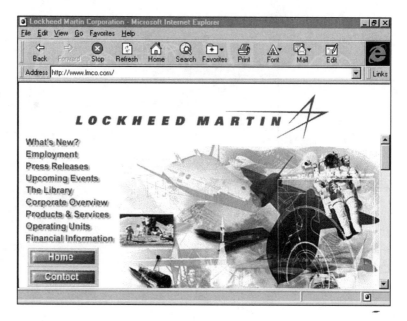

## Netscape Navigator

The Netscape Navigator was the first graphic browser to really take the Web by storm. Netscape Navigator 4.0 carries on the tradition as part of an integrated Web communications suite called Communicator 4.0.

Besides Navigator 4.0, this suite consists of Messenger, Collabra, Conference, and Composer. Messenger is the mail client, and Collabra Message Center is an integrated newsgroup reader and e-mail package.

Conference allows users to engage in voice chat and video teleconferencing. An interactive white board allows users to exchange ideas. Users can even exchange files easily while keyboard or voice chatting. One of the most exciting features of Conference is *collaborative browsing*. This feature allows one user to take others with whom he is chatting for a surf to his favorite sites on the Web.

Web sites could use some of these features to provide live, interactive customer feedback and technical support. Suppose that a user came to your site to locate a video driver for a card he just purchased from your site. He's totally lost, but a navigation button takes him to Netscape Conference and he's hooked up with technical support. While support and the customer are talking, support could engage collaborative browsing and take him directly to the right download page.

Netscape Composer is a full-featured WYSIWYG development tool with a toolbar that is typical of Web editing packages. (See Figure 6.8.)

**FIGURE 6.8.**
*Netscape Composer has
an easy-to-use, intuitive
interface.*

Well-defined buttons on the toolbar provide easy access to elements such as links, targets, images, horizontal rules, tables, and lists.

Of course, just about every plug-in imaginable is supported here, as are the W3C's Cascading Style Sheets (CSS).

Netscape Navigator has some of the most popular extensions to the HTML standards. These extensions give you ways to liven up unordered lists with various bullet shapes, have more control over image maps, and create special animations through a technique called *server push*. Of course, this only touches on a few of the capabilities that are possible. (See Table 6.2 for more Netscape Navigator extensions.)

**Table 6.2. Netscape Navigator extensions.**

| Extension | Description |
|---|---|
| `<area coords >` | Area coordinates for image map |
| `<area nohref>` | Defined area has no action |
| `<area shape>` | Area shape (such as circle) |
| `<basefont size>` | Specifies base font size |
| `<big>` | One size larger than base font |
| `<blink>` | Blinking text |
| `<body alink >` | Activated link color |

*continues*

**Table 6.2. continued**

| Extension | Description |
| --- | --- |
| `<body bgcolor >` | Background color |
| `<body link>` | Hypertext link color |
| `<body text>` | Normal text color |
| `<body vlink>` | Visited link color |
| `<caption align>` | Aligns table or figure caption |
| `<center>` | Center |
| `<div>` | Divisions |
| `<embed>` | Embed content |
| `<font size=value>` | Font size |
| `<hr align>` | Horizontal rule alignment |
| `<hr noshade>` | Horizontal rule shading off |
| `<hr size>` | Horizontal rule thickness |
| `<hr width>` | Horizontal rule width |
| `<img border>` | Image border size |
| `<img hspace>` | Image horizontal spacing |
| `<img usemap>` | Image map |
| `<img vspace>` | Image vertical spacing |
| `<isindex prompt>` | Text of new prompt to use |
| `<li type>` | Type of bullets to be used |
| `<map name>` | Image map name |
| `<nobr>` | No break |
| `<ol start>` | Starting ordered list number |
| `<ol type>` | Type of bullets for ordered list |
| `<server push>` | Animation by *pushing* data to browser |
| `<small>` | One size smaller than current font |
| `<sub>` | Subscript |
| `<sup>` | Superscript |
| `<ul type>` | Type of bullets for unordered list |
| `<wbr>` | Word break |

# Microsoft Internet Explorer

The word *free* is one of the big reasons that the Microsoft Internet Explorer has gained popularity so quickly. After all, that's how Netscape started out. Now that Netscape is charging for Navigator, and Microsoft has a feature-packed browser, more and more people are turning toward the Internet Explorer.

Internet Explorer CD-ROMs are getting almost as much circulation as AOL disks. Many CD-ROM magazines are including a gratis copy of Internet Explorer along with their other software on disk. Other computer magazines are getting into the act by providing browser CD-ROMs from Microsoft.

Let's face it. For most of the general public, it is hard to compete with free. That's why Netscape has found it impossible to dismiss the Internet Explorer. Of course, Microsoft has used this free browser to test some features and plug-ins (which Microsoft calls add-ons and ActiveX controls) that have made Netscape work even harder to keep its market share. According to industry leaders at a recent Web authoring convention, Netscape has fallen to about 60 percent over the past year, leaving Internet Explorer with a well-earned 30 percent. A scattering of other browsers make up the rest.

Microsoft's Internet Explorer 4.0 comes as part of an integrated communications package, much like in Netscape's Communicator 4.0. This new package contains e-mail, broadcasting, and a system shell that tries to fully integrate the Web with the user's desktop. This is very much in keeping with Microsoft Office 97 in making the Internet a seamless extension of Windows. In this new scheme of things, the Internet is accessible through hypertext links in applications such as Word, Excel, and PowerPoint. The Internet Explorer shell even adds the Internet as a "drive" that you can access through the Windows Explorer file manager (as shown in Figure 6.9).

The Microsoft Internet Explorer makes expanded use of Microsoft ActiveX, Active Video, Visual Basic, and Java support for added flexibility. It also can use many of the Netscape plug-ins and has plenty of its own add-ons, as well. These features make Internet Explorer 4.0 a Web designer's paradise.

All of these features and the desktop interface will definitely make the Microsoft Internet Explorer 4.0 tough competition to beat. After all, if you already have an integrated Web browser, why would you want to buy another one?

FrontPad, the Web authoring tool that comes with Explorer 4.0, is greatly underpowered compared to the many WYSIWYG authoring packages currently on the market. But, if they made it too powerful, no one would go out to buy Microsoft FrontPage or Publisher, would they?

Developers who have used Microsoft's Internet Assistants will find themselves on familiar ground. The current page being browsed comes up in FrontPad when the Edit button on the Explorer 4.0 toolbar is pressed. This gives you a semi-WYSIWYG environment that shows unknown HTML and other code as tags rather than integrating them seamlessly into the document while in edit mode. (See Figure 6.10.)

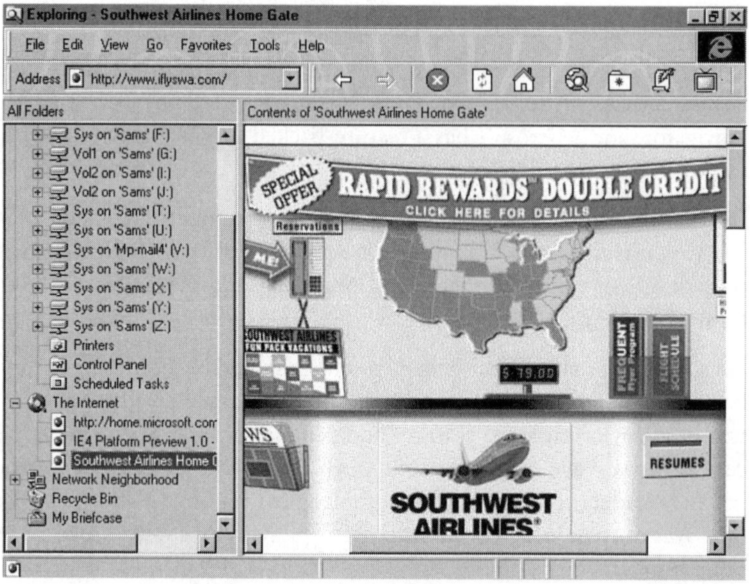

**FIGURE 6.9.**

*Connecting to the Net through the Windows Explorer file manager. This is just one of the slick features of Internet Explorer 4.0 shell.*

**FIGURE 6.10.**

*Microsoft Internet Explorer 4.0's FrontPage editor. Well, it's almost WYSIWYG.*

However, valid tags work just fine when you switch to browse mode (as shown in Figure 6.11).

**FIGURE 6.11.**

*Everything is sorted out
when the code shown in
Figure 6.10 is viewed
with Microsoft Internet
Explorer.*

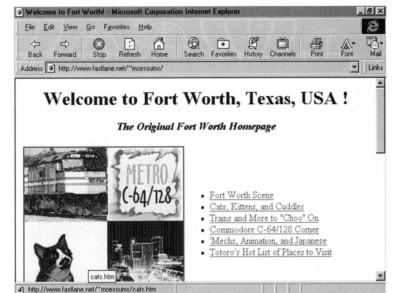

**TIP**

FrontPad is included in only the *enhanced* or *full* installation of Internet Explorer 4.0. If
you've chosen one of these installations and FrontPad isn't configured as your editor, you
can easily set it up yourself. Follow these steps from within Microsoft Internet Explorer:

1. Select the View pull-down menu.
2. Select Options from the list.
3. Choose the Programs tab.
4. Click the File Types button.
5. Choose Microsoft HTML Document 4.0 from the list.
6. Click the Edit button.
7. Choose edit from the list.
8. Enter the path of the FrontPad editor in the space labeled *Application used to perform
   action.*

One of the best things about the FrontPad editing interface is that you can directly publish
your Internet site without saving it to your local disk. Be aware, though, that if you make a
mistake in your edits, the mistake is already visible for the world to see when you save it. Be
sure to always test your updated pages before releasing them onto the Web.

Microsoft Internet Explorer has only a handful of extensions compared to Netscape Navigator. Marquees (those irritating little scrolling messages) and background sounds that sometimes seem to go on forever are just a couple of the extensions you'll find here. (See Table 6.3 for a look at some of the Internet Explorer's HTML extensions.)

**Table 6.3. Microsoft Internet Explorer extensions.**

| Extension | Description |
| --- | --- |
| `<bgsound loop>` | Background sound loop |
| `<bgsound src>` | Background sound URL |
| `<comment>` | Hidden text for comments |
| `<font color>` | Font color |
| `<font face>` | Font type face |
| `<img dynsrc>` | Inline video |
| `<img loop>` | Loop animated image |
| `<marquee align>` | Marquee alignment |
| `<marquee behavior>` | Marquee scrolling behavior |
| `<marquee bgcolor>` | Marquee background color |
| `<marquee direction>` | Direction of marquee movement |
| `<marquee height>` | Marquee area height |
| `<marquee hspace>` | Marquee horizontal spacing |
| `<marquee loop>` | Repeat marquee text message |
| `<marquee scrollamount>` | Marquee scroll speed |
| `<marquee scrolldelay>` | Marquee text blink |
| `<marquee vspace>` | Marquee vertical spacing |
| `<marquee width>` | Marquee area width |
| `<plaintext>` | Plain text |
| `<s>` | Strikethrough text |
| `<strike>` | Strikethrough text |
| `<table background>` | Table background |
| `<td background>` | Table data background |

Various versions of Internet Explorer are available for Windows (3.1, 95, NT), Mac, and UNIX.

# Other Browsers

You would think that, with the popularity of Netscape Navigator and Microsoft Internet Explorer, nobody would use anything else. However, a few other free and shareware browsers deserve to be mentioned. Of course, this is not a definitive list of browsers, but it covers some of the more popular ones.

## Amaya

This browser is the W3C's test bed for the HTML 3.2 standards and features. It replaces Arena, which is now being developed by a separate group. These users will probably not be the greatest target audience for your Web pages, because Amaya is available only on the UNIX-based platforms and doesn't have the support found in other browsers.

## AOL for Windows 3.0

There are more than 8 million potential users for your Web page at AOL. At one time, the AOL browser was pretty bad compared to more popular browsers such as Microsoft Internet Explorer and Netscape Navigator. However, AOL has teamed up with Microsoft to provide the AOL for Windows 3.0 browser. Compare the AOL browser in Figure 6.12 to the Microsoft Internet Explorer 3.02 in Figure 6.4.

**FIGURE 6.12.**
*AOL's browser looks suspiciously like Internet Explorer with a few extra buttons.*

AOL has also opened up its membership to people who already have Internet access. This allows them to use the browser of their choice, rather than AOL's proprietary browser.

> **NOTE**
>
> On some of the commercial services such as AOL and CompuServe, users sometimes connect at 2400 baud, so images can take a painfully long time to load.
>
> Offer a low-bandwidth alternative to your site, such as text-only or lower-resolution graphics pages.

No special Web site development should be necessary for this browser.

# Lynx

Here is another good reason to provide a text-only alternative to your site. Some people have only text-based access to the Web using text browsers such as Lynx. Although Lynx doesn't display graphics, it does recognize many of the HTML standard conventions. Other users may be connecting through a shell account with their terminals set to VT100 emulation. Web developers need to provide either text-only or text-alternate sites to support Lynx users.

Lynx is freely available for a variety of platforms including Amiga (Alynx), Atari, DOS (DosLynx), OS/2, PowerPC (Lynx), UNIX, Windows (Lynx 2.5), and VMS.

# Mosaic

The final version of Mosaic has been released, and there is no longer any official technical support from the NCSA Software Development Group.

Mosaic 3.0 is packed with features. It has support for animated GIFs, tables, frames, and client-side image maps—almost everything that Web developers and browser users demand. What you won't find is support for HTML standards higher than HTML 3.2, because no further versions have been planned past Mosaic 3.0, which was completed in late 1996.

This freeware is available for Windows, Macintosh, and UNIX. Some earlier versions are also available for the VAX VMS platform, but it is extremely crippled by today's browser standards.

Amosaic, a popular browser for the Amiga platform and based on NCSA's Mosaic, continues to receive support and development. This shareware package can be found at any Aminet site on the Internet.

# Microsoft Pocket Internet Explorer

Microsoft developed the Pocket Internet Explorer so that Windows CE-based palmtop users could surf the Web. (See Figure 6.13.)

The Pocket Internet Explorer does not support ActiveX, Java, JavaScript, plug-ins, VBScript, frames, or colored table cells.

**FIGURE 6.13.**
*Microsoft Pocket
Internet Explorer
developer's site.*

What is supported? Animated GIFs, background images, and the HTML tags that were supported by the full-size Internet Explorer 1.5. Microsoft does have plans for Windows CE to handle Java, so that could be a possibility in the future.

The Pocket Internet Explorer automatically resizes graphics to fit its 430-pixel display. Any text wider than this automatically wraps. However, Web designers can help speed up site access time by providing an alternate page in either text-only or reduced graphics. The Pocket Internet Explorer supports only 2-bit grayscale graphics. Microsoft has special charts and downloadable custom palettes to help site developers get the optimum results. If you don't want to go through that much trouble, don't worry. The Pocket Internet Explorer converts color graphics to the required 2-bit grayscale.

More information on developing sites for the Pocket Internet Explorer can be found at this address:

```
http://www.microsoft.com/windowsce/developer/data/designer/default.htm
```

## The Wave

Even little 8-bit machines will get into the act with the new Wave graphical Web browser for the Commodore 128D. Those equipped with GEOS, the new Super CPU, and a RamLink can have up to 32MB of RAM running at 20MHz. On the downside, there is no support for plug-ins or programming standards higher than HTML 1.5.

# WebTV

This is one of the first "Internet boxes" that is aimed at making the Net accessible to everyone. The WebTV Internet terminal is manufactured by Sony (www.sony.com) and Philips/Magnavox (www.philips.com). The WebTV has a browser-like interface and conforms to most HTML 3.2 standards. (See Figure 6.14.)

**FIGURE 6.14.**

*Net appliances such as WebTV give the masses access to your Web site. Here is an actual WebTV browser screen within a Netscape Window.*

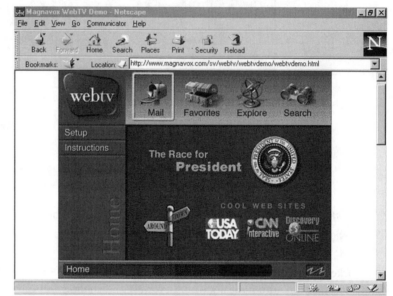

The WebTV Network (www.webtv.net) acts as the Internet service provider, and the Web terminal connects between the phone line and the TV. Microsoft has acquired the WebTV Network, so you can probably expect some interesting developments in the future.

The WebTV browser gives Web designers the best of both worlds, and then some. It conforms to most Microsoft Internet Explorer and Netscape Navigator extensions. And, as if that weren't enough, there are even WebTV extensions to offer greater flexibility for your site.

Remember that designing pages for a TV audience is a bit different from designing for a regular computer audience. Most don't have storage space for downloading files, so sites aimed solely at downloads will probably be passed over. However, if you have a product to sell, some of these devices have credit card slots for quick transactions.

The WebTV software automatically resizes your existing Web pages to fit the meager 544×378 pixel display. Vertical scrolling is allowed, but the width is fixed at 544 pixels. The idea is to keep the Net experience similar to regular TV programming. After all, when was the last time you had to scroll around while watching *Baywatch*?

Your pages should be as friendly as regular TV programming, because that is just what they have become. Design your WebTV pages as if you are making a TV commercial or series. Try to keep the load times short because the TV generation is not used to waiting for its entertainment. Keep the screen simple and uncluttered. Besides the faster load times, be sure to make your pages active and interesting.

Although the original version of WebTV didn't support much Web technology other than JPEG and GIF, the newer software reportedly will. Features such as MIDI, MPEG, WAV, AIFF, and Shockwave audio are tagged for support.

Don't use red or white backgrounds because they can cause distortions and audio noise on some equipment. If you must use these colors for background, choose a variation other than the full value of white or red. Charcoal makes an excellent background color and can be created by using `<body bgcolor=#191919>`. Choose light-colored text on dark backgrounds. However, be aware that full white text can bleed over into the background on some equipment.

Avoid large images and images that are very busy or complicated with too much data. These images can be too hard to see on a TV set. Text that is smaller than the base font of your site also can be too difficult to read. Text on image buttons can be a legibility nightmare.

More information on WebTV extensions, style guides, and system requirements can be found at this address:

`http://webtv.net/primetime/`

Cable and telephone companies have big plans to jump into the Web appliance market, so Web developers can look forward to an ever increasing audience for their sites.

# Summary

Great Web design starts by planning and knowing the capabilities of your target audience. The end user's level of expertise, connection speed, platform, and browser are just a few of the factors to consider during site development. Not only do you have to reach your audience, but your data also has to be accessible to them.

Remember that providing a text alternative to your home page will give more users access to your site. You can also offer "no frames" and low-resolution alternatives. Saving graphics at 640×480, 100 dpi, and 256 colors or less helps reduce load time. And load time is really the name of the game here. In this day of instant gratification, you will lose your audience quickly if your page doesn't get moving within just a few seconds. End users shouldn't have time to read a novel while they wait for your page to load. HTML standards set by the W3C and their Web-centric members such as Sun, Microsoft, and Netscape will help determine how your pages will look—now and in the future.

# IN THIS PART

# II
## PART

# Basic HTML

# Structural Elements and Their Usage

*by Rick Darnell*

CHAPTER 7

As explained in Part I of this book, "Understanding HTML," HTML documents are created by combining special markup codes called *tags*. Tags define the structure of the document and provide the framework for holding the actual content, which can be text, images, or other special content.

The elements covered in this chapter are called *structural* elements, because their primary purpose is to implement the form of the document. These include the document itself, the head and body sections, page titles, and other basic document identifiers.

> **NOTE**
>
> Actually, all HTML tags are structural in their purpose of defining the relations of elements to each other within the document. The reason this particular set is referred to as structural is because they really have no formatting purpose for what appears on the screen. All other tags control the appearance of the page in one form or another.

The easiest way to illustrate the purpose and form of structural tags is to begin with a page with no structure. (See Listing 7.1.)

**Listing 7.1. This HTML document lacks any HTML structural form.**

```
Missoula Rural Fire District Home Page
Welcome to the MRFD Home Page
Thank you for visiting our home page. From here, you can
link to several destinations, including fire safety
information, district budget, minutes from board meetings
and upcoming training.
```

If the code in Listing 7.1 were displayed on a browser, it would look something like the page in Figure 7.1. Note the complete lack of organization. In addition, it could also generate an error in a nonstandard Web browser because the type of content is not identified.

**FIGURE 7.1.**
*Without some basic structural elements in place, this Web page is formless and pointless.*

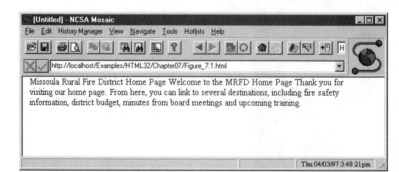

Good page design begins with good organization, and that's what the structural tags enable.

# The <!DOCTYPE> Declaration

Theoretically, the <!DOCTYPE> tag should be the first tag in your HTML document. This tag tells the Web server what it's dealing with when it delivers the document; in turn, the server informs the browser what kind of tags it can expect inside.

The usage is

```
<!DOCTYPE HTML idString>
```

where *idString* is a specification for the version of HTML in use within the document. For example, the following code identifies a document built according to the standards laid out for HTML 3.2:

```
<!DOCTYPE HTML PUBLIC "-//IETF//DTD HTML 3.2//EN">
```

> **TIP**
>
> A reasonably complete list of DOCTYPE declarations is found at the following address:
>
> `http://ugweb.cs.alberta.ca/~gerald/validate/lib/catalog`

In reality, use of <!DOCTYPE> is difficult. Many variations of HTML are in use, the standards are continuously evolving, and browser implementations continue to change the rules by which we play. The mix of extensions in a document can include tags from HTML 2.0 and 3.2 along with customized extensions from both Netscape and Microsoft. This is where the realm of universal standards and the rules of the marketplace meet head-to-head. As a practical matter, many browsers ignore <!DOCTYPE>, or just ignore the tags they don't understand, regardless of whether or not they're part of the standard expressed for the document.

> **NOTE**
>
> This tag is also used in customized forms by applications that need to identify product-specific content, such as Microsoft FrontPage.

With this bit of preamble out of the way, it's time to move on to the document itself.

# Setting the Boundaries with <HTML>

The first tag to be concerned with is <HTML>, which is the next line in a document after <!DOCTYPE>. It is paired with </HTML> to encase all other tags in an HTML page, and as such, the two mark the absolute beginning and end of the file.

The usage is

```
<HTML>
...document and tags...
</HTML>
```

where *document and tags* are the rest of your HTML document. Using these tags with the first example in this chapter results in the code shown in Listing 7.2.

**Listing 7.2. The first step in providing a structure for an HTML document is marking its beginning and end.**

```
<!DOCTYPE HTML PUBLIC "-//IETF//DTD HTML 3.2//EN">
<HTML>
Missoula Rural Fire District Home Page
Welcome to the MRFD Home Page
Thank you for visiting our home page. From here, you
can link to several destinations, including fire safety
information, district budget, minutes from board meetings
and upcoming training.
</HTML>
```

It is possible to create an HTML document without the <HTML> tags, and most browsers will know what to do with the document after it's loaded. However, there are a couple of good reasons to use them. First, HTML isn't the only markup language on the Web. Cousins of HTML, such as Extensible Markup Language (XML), are interpreted in slightly different ways. In the absence of this tag, most browsers default to HTML. Those that don't become confused when handed a document without any clear indication of type, resulting in a page that is displayed in an unpredictable manner, or one that refuses to load at all.

Second, using the <HTML> tag is good style and shows that whomever built the document had some idea what to do. And if you're taking the time to read this book, you know what to do.

The appearance of Listing 7.2 won't change on the browser with the addition of the opening and closing <HTML> tags, but at least now its boundaries are delineated and the browser knows what to do with the file after it's loaded.

Now that the document's type and boundaries are marked and identified, it's time to divide the HTML page into two operational parts—the header and the body. The tags and their compatriots, which govern these two major sections, are explained next.

# The HEAD Element

Theoretically, every document has a header and a body. The header of the document is where global settings are defined; it is contained within the <HEAD> and </HEAD> tags.

The usage is

```
<HEAD>
header content
</HEAD>
```

where *header content* includes one or more items from the six tags used exclusively within the header portion of an HTML document. It is also a favorite place to include scripting language function definitions.

The addition of these tags to our ongoing example results in the code shown in Listing 7.3.

**Listing 7.3. The HTML document has received an extra boost of structure with the <HEAD> tag.**

```
<!DOCTYPE HTML PUBLIC "-//IETF//DTD HTML 3.2//EN">
<HTML>
<HEAD>
Missoula Rural Fire District Home Page
</HEAD>
Welcome to the MRFD Home Page
Thank you for visiting our home page. From here, you
can link to several destinations, including fire safety
information, district budget, minutes from board meetings
and upcoming training.
</HTML>
```

Displayed on a browser, the results are made slightly clearer by the elimination of the first line, which has disappeared completely. It is destined for use within the next header tag.

Headers also serve another important function. Using the HTTP protocol, it's possible to download the header information only. The vast majority of users aren't aware of this capability and probably don't care. It is used primarily by search engines and automated robots, which can download a header and get some basic information about the page—title, file format, last-modified date, keywords— without spending the extra time to load or look at the rest of the document.

## Giving Your Page a <TITLE>

Probably the most commonly used HEAD feature in HTML is the <TITLE> tag.

Its syntax is

```
<TITLE>text</TITLE>
```

where *text* is a short, one-line name for the document that is displayed in the browser's title bar. Without a title, most browsers default to the HTML filename. Because filenames are not always terribly descriptive and often long and clunky, it's a good practice to provide a title for all HTML documents.

The addition of the <TITLE> tag to your HTML document results in the code shown in Listing 7.4 and the page shown in Figure 7.2.

**Listing 7.4. Adding a title to the HTML document reinforces the structure.**

```
<!DOCTYPE HTML PUBLIC "-//IETF//DTD HTML 3.2//EN">
<HTML>
<HEAD>
<TITLE>Missoula Rural Fire District Home Page</TITLE>
</HEAD>
Welcome to the MRFD Home Page
Thank you for visiting our home page. From here, you can
link to several destinations, including fire safety
information, district budget, minutes from board meetings
and upcoming training.
</HTML>
```

**FIGURE 7.2.**

*With the addition of some structural elements and a title (see the top bar of the browser), this Web page is beginning to take a recognizable shape.*

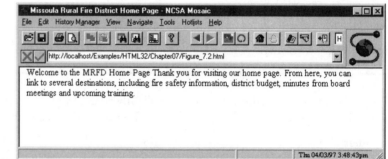

Only one title is allowed per document (as covered in the following Tip box), and its size is limited by the size of the user's browser window. You can include a title that is as long as you want, but it is truncated in the browser's title bar if it stretches beyond the limits.

---

**TIP**

To make your titles easier for the user, make sure they are short and to the point, but not so short as to be vague. For example, "MRFD" is not a good title. What does MRFD mean? Where are we? What are we doing here? On the other hand, "Missoula Rural Fire District Home Page" is a good title. You've identified the page and its purpose, which is what the user needs to know.

---

Keep in mind that many browsers keep their name in the title bar along with your title, leaving less space for the title of your page. Keep the title long enough to be useful but short enough to fit.

**ONE TITLE ONLY, PLEASE**

Once upon a browser, when Netscape 1.0 was the biggest show in town, there was a slight glitch with the `<TITLE>` tag. You could stack up a series of tags like this:

```
<TITLE>M</TITLE>
<TITLE>MR</TITLE>
<TITLE>MRF</TITLE>
<TITLE>MRFD</TITLE>
<TITLE>MRFD H</TITLE>
<TITLE>MRFD Ho</TITLE>
<TITLE>MRFD Hom</TITLE>
<TITLE>MRFD Home</TITLE>
<TITLE>MRFD Home </TITLE>
<TITLE>MRFD Home P</TITLE>
<TITLE>MRFD Home Pa</TITLE>
<TITLE>MRFD Home Pag</TITLE>
<TITLE>MRFD Home Page</TITLE>
```

The result would be a title that gradually built up across the title bar. This aberrant behavior was fixed in the next version, and the result was pages with some strange behavior. Different browsers interpret multiple titles in different ways. For example, Netscape 4.0 picks the first title from the list, and Internet Explorer 3.01 uses the last tag. For the preceding example, your document would appear to have a title of "M" or "MRFD Home Page," depending on which browser the user preferred.

The moral of this little story? Use one title in your document so that the browser won't have to guess, and your users won't have to wonder what's going on.

# A `<BASE>` for Hyperlinks

This tag controls the actions of relative hyperlinks in the body of the document. Relative links within a document by default refer to the same server where the page is located. However, with the `<BASE>` tag, you can define that the relative links are resolved relative to a different location, whether it's another directory on the host or a completely different server. (For more information on hyperlinks and anchors, see Chapter 11, "Linking Documents and Images.")

The `<BASE>` tag takes a single attribute, HREF, with the following syntax:

```
<BASE HREF="protocol://servername/path/">
```

In the preceding line, *protocol* is a valid Internet communication standard, such as HTTP; *servername* is a server name or address such as www.wossamotta.edu or 89.123.32.21; and *path* is any additional mapping on the server. The path is an optional value to the URL. If the path is included by itself, it refers to the host server.

For example, a page for an educational institution is located on the server at www.frostbitefalls.org. The page is copied straight off the university's server at www.wossamotta.edu and placed in the new location. Any relative links will no longer work because they're referring to locations at the home location.

If the user clicks on a link to look at the football schedule, the browser takes the content of the link, `/football/schedule.html`, and combines it with the host, `www.frostbitefalls.org`, to create `http://www.frostbitefalls.org/football/schedule.html`. But, alas, Frostbite Falls doesn't have this directory, and the user receives the dreaded `404 Not Found` error.

The `<BASE>` tag circumvents this problem, like so:

`<BASE HREF="http://www.wossamotta.edu/">`

Now, when a user clicks on a link for the football page, the base information is substituted for the host information, which results in `http://www.wossamotta.edu/football/schedule.html`—and now the information on the match-up versus Tick Tock Tech is easily accessed.

## `<ISINDEX>` for Searching with CGI

The `<ISINDEX>` tag is used during interactive searches of a Web page. Generally, it is placed in a document built by a special CGI script. It generates a prompt for the user to enter a search string. (See Figure 7.3.)

**FIGURE 7.3.**

*The `<ISINDEX>` tag results in a slightly different display, depending on the browser. In Mosaic, an additional bar is added to the bottom of the browser with a "Search Index" prompt.*

Any text provided by the user is appended to the document's URL and passed back to the CGI script for processing in the form *URL?search1+search2+...+searchN*. This is the standard syntax for return values to CGI scripts, with the question mark indicating the beginning of the string, and each plus sign marking a space.

The `<ISINDEX>` tag is typically inserted and handled exclusively by the CGI script. Customizing the search interface is accomplished by providing scripts with customized forms. (For more information on building forms, see Chapter 15, "Building and Using HTML Forms.")

This tag has one attribute, `prompt`, which changes the default message for the text field. The syntax is

`<ISINDEX prompt="string">`

where *string* is the new message. The length of the `prompt` string varies with individual browsers. For example, Navigator uses an HTML form to gather the index information, and Mosaic uses a custom browser element at the bottom of the screen. For this reason, try to keep the message as short as possible (about 35 characters) to retain compatibility with as many browsers as possible.

## Showing Relationships with `<LINK>`

The `<LINK>` tag has been around since the early days of HTML, although it has yet to earn acceptance or implementation from many browsers. In its current definition, `<LINK>` provides a media- and platform-independent method for defining relationships between the current HTML page and other documents and resources. All popular browsers, with the exception of Mosaic 3.0, still ignore the tag.

In theory, `<LINK>` is used to create document-specific toolbars or menus, to control how collections of HTML files are connected when printed, and to link associated resources such as style sheets and scripts. Five attributes are used with `LINK`:

| Attribute | Description |
| --- | --- |
| href | The URL of the linked document. This is provided in standard URL format, but it is typically a relative URL. |
| rel | This attribute and its value indicate the relationship of the current document to the document referenced in href. The values that are used include Precede, Annotation, Present, History, and Made. For example, the following line indicates that annotations (margin notes, footnotes, and so on) for the current document are located in a file called annotations.html:<br><br>`<LINK rel=Annotation href="annotations.html">` |
| rev | This attribute is similar to rel, except it indicates a reverse relationship between the document and the URL. For example, the following line indicates that the current document has annotations for the document specified in the URL:<br><br>`<LINK rev=Annotation href="chapter1.html">`<br><br>It accepts the same values as rel. |
| title | This attribute, related to href, is the name of the document referenced in href, and it must match the value contained in the `<TITLE>` tags in order to be valid. |
| name | Assigning a meaningful name to the link allows for easier reference elsewhere in the document. |

Currently, the only supported use for `<LINK>` is to specify style sheets as external to the document.

For more information on using <LINK> with cascading style sheets, see Chapter 19, "Introducing Cascading Style Sheets."

# Using <META> to Give More Information

Web servers send their own header with HTML documents to help clients interpret the document. This header is separate and different from the header you've been working on in this section.

Like the <!DOCTYPE> tag, the <META> tag is used to pass additional information about how the document should be handled, and it is often used with add-on content provided by applications such as Microsoft FrontPage and Macromedia Backstage. In addition, it is used to provide extra information about the document that can be used by search engines to classify and identify the document without downloading the entire document.

Three attributes accompany this tag:

- HTTP-EQUIV
- NAME
- CONTENT

## Sending Information: HTTP-EQUIV and NAME

The first two—HTTP-EQUIV and NAME —serve the same basic purpose, with one important difference. Any <META> tag using HTTP-EQUIV is added to the response header supplied to the browser. If the tag uses the NAME attribute, the information is available for reference in the document header but not included in the server-generated response header.

Keep in mind one important consideration when using the HTTP-EQUIV attribute. It should never override a standard header value such as last-modified or contenttype. This could result in a conflict with the server that prevents delivery of the document by the server or interpretation by the browser. Here are some examples of HTTP-EQUIV:

```
<META HTTP-EQUIV=refresh CONTENT=60>
<META HTTP-EQUIV=keywords CONTENT="fire department public safety">
<META HTTP-EQUIV=reply-to CONTENT="mrfd@montana.com">
```

The following list shows three of the most used variables for HTTP-EQUIV:

- Refresh implements a process called *client-pull*, which directs the browser to reload the document after the number of seconds specified in content. It is used in situations when the document is updated on a periodic basis. Content can also take the form $N$; URL=$url$, where $N$ is the number of seconds to wait, and $url$ is the new URL to load.
- Keywords specifies a list of words separated by spaces, which are used by some search engines to classify the document for quicker retrieval. Many search engines load only the head and not the body, so it's important to include the keywords in the <META> tag so that the engine knows what is found in your document.

■ `Reply-to` provides an e-mail address at which users can respond to the author or party responsible for the page. Its display is typically triggered by the server, which adds it as a server-side include. This attribute is not commonly used.

---

## WHAT IS CLIENT-PULL?

Client-pull provides a mechanism for pages to automatically reload after a certain amount of time has passed, or for a series of pages to automatically load themselves with a pause between them. If you want the browser to reload the current page in four seconds, you add this tag to your HTML page:

```
<META HTTP-EQUIV="Refresh" CONTENT=4>
```

If the value of CONTENT is 0, the page is refreshed as fast as the browser can retrieve it, which could be rather slow if the user has a slow or poor-quality connection. It's definitely not fast enough for any sort of quality animation.

After the REFRESH attribute is added to a page, the browser reloads it *ad infinitum*. To stop the process, you need to provide a hyperlink to another page without a client-pull tag.

Continuously loading the same page is useful for pages that are updated constantly—such as documents containing stock quotes or sports scores. However, you can also use client-pull to load a different page. Continuing the process of loading a new page allows you to automatically lead a user through a series of slides or instructions. The CONTENT attribute is modified to provide this capability:

```
<META HTTP-EQUIV="Refresh"
CONTENT="8;URL=http://www.mrfd.com/safety/tip2.html">
```

The URL must be a full URL. Relative URLs consisting of only pathnames are not allowed. Inside the target page, you can include a pointer to the next page, and so on. This technique allows you to load any number of pages in a sequence. However, it's still a good idea to provide a link to move out of the automatic process so that your readers aren't forced to sit through the entire show.

---

The NAME attribute is used to provide other information about the document that might be useful to someone looking at the document but not critical to deliver in the header. Here are some examples:

```
<META NAME=author CONTENT="Dave Herzberg">
<META NAME=description CONTENT="Home page for MRFD">
<META NAME=copyright CONTENT="Copyright 1997, Missoula Rural Fire Dist.">
```

The attributes in the following list are used more often by HTML editors:

■ `Author` identifies the person who created the page and sometimes includes the name of the HTML editor.

■ `Description` provides a one-line explanation of the page or its use. It is sometimes used by search engines to provide a summary of the page when it displays search results to a user.

■ `Copyright` is the official copyright notice for your page. Anything you create is subject to protection by copyright law, regardless of whether it has this statement. However, including this statement prevents the excuse of ignorance ("I didn't know") from would-be plagiarizers.

As seen in the preceding examples, `CONTENT` is the actual value that is contained in the tag. Although most browsers and servers don't require quotation marks around the value, it's a good practice to use them. This removes ambiguity and opportunity for misinterpretation, especially for values requiring more than one word.

## Defining a <STYLE> For the Page

The `<STYLE>` tag was included without a recommended implementation by the World Wide Web Consortium. It was intended to be a placeholder for introducing style sheets and client-side scripts in future versions of HTML. True to the form of the Web, the future is here, pushed along by Netscape and Microsoft.

You can find more about style sheets and using the `<STYLE>` tag in Chapters 20 through 22, which cover cascading style sheets (CSS) and their usage, JavaScript-based style sheets, and other alternatives to CSS.

# The BODY Element

Like the `<HEAD>` tag, the `<BODY>` tag's primary purpose is to delineate the main portion of the document—the part that is seen by the user. Its usage is

```
<BODY attributes>
...document contents...
</BODY>
```

where `attributes` includes any, all, or none of the six attributes controlling basic document display attributes, and the `document contents` is any valid HTML content, including text, forms, graphics, special content, and so on.

> **TIP**
>
> If omitted, the `<BODY>` tag is assumed by the browser after the `<HEAD>` tag. If the `<HEAD>` tag is also absent, the `<BODY>` tag is assumed immediately after the opening `<HTML>` tag.

In addition to marking the body of the text, the `<BODY>` tag is also used to set various display attributes for the document, including background colors and images, and the color of various types of text. These attributes are discussed in the following sections.

## Background Wallpaper Images: BACKGROUND

The first attribute to mention is BACKGROUND, which is used to identify a graphics image to tile behind the document (as shown in Figure 7.4), much like wallpaper forms a background for the crayon scribbles of a small child.

**FIGURE 7.4.**

*Use the BACKGROUND attribute to specify a graphics image for tiling in the background of the document.*

The syntax is

```
<BODY BACKGROUND="[url][path][filename]">
```

The first two values, *url* and *path*, are optional and default to the server and directory that contain the HTML document if omitted. The *filename* should be a GIF or JPEG image to ensure compatibility with all browsers. PCX and BMP are not universally accepted standards on the Web.

> **TIP**
>
> For best results, pick an image rendered in light, muted colors. Light grays tend to work best, although readable pages have also been produced with light blues and yellows. Backgrounds done in bright colors or designs are very distracting for readers and typically annoy them into not spending much time looking at what you produced.

## Background Colors: BGCOLOR

The next attribute sets the background color of the entire document, much like the BACKGROUND attribute sets the wallpaper. Its usage is

```
<BODY BGCOLOR="colorValue">
```

where *colorValue* is a recognized color literal such as black or aliceblue, or a hexadecimal triplet representing the red, green, and blue mix for the color. A pound sign (#) must precede the value if a hexadecimal number is used.

## WORKING WITH COLOR DEFINITIONS

The list of color literals is fairly extensive and should be more than adequate for most pages. Those who want precise control over colors can use the hexadecimal triplet definition.

A hexadecimal triplet is a set of three double-digit hexadecimal numbers. The first number corresponds to red, the next to green, and the last to blue. Each number ranges in value from 00 to FF, representing decimal 0 to 255. For example, 00FF00 is green, and FFFFFF is white. The total absence of color is 000000, or black.

In the ongoing battle between page authors and Web users, a custom color is not always accepted on browsers. Both Internet Explorer (2.0 and later) and Navigator (2.0 and later) include options to override a background color attribute on the page with the user's preferences set in the browser. If it's absolutely imperative that you have a specific color as the background, you need to use the BACKGROUND attribute with an image consisting solely of the desired color block.

In the same vein, inherent limitations are also set by the user's equipment. If old VGA monitors or black-and-white laptops are still in use, your color probably won't translate well. To be safe, let the user's machine set the background.

## TIP

If the image set with BACKGROUND is a transparent GIF file, any color set with BACKGROUND will show through it.

## Document Text Color: TEXT

The TEXT attribute sets the default color of any nonhyperlink text in the document. The default value is black. The usage is

```
<BODY TEXT="colorValue">
```

where *colorValue* is a recognized color literal such as black or aliceblue, or a hexadecimal triplet representing the red, green, and blue mix for the color. A pound sign (#) must precede the value if a hexadecimal number is used.

Take care when setting the default text color to make sure it doesn't conflict with the colors in the background. For example, red text on a green background might seem like a good idea at Christmas time. In reality, it's never a good idea. Viewing the results is like rubbing your eyes with a belt sander. On the other hand, proven combinations such as yellow on dark blue fare very well and can actually brighten a page beyond the typical default of black on medium gray.

> **TIP**
>
> Like the BGCOLOR attribute, any of the color attributes to the <BODY> tag can be overridden by any browser, such as recent versions of Internet Explorer, Navigator, and the various versions of Mosaic. The fact that you've picked a specific color scheme doesn't guarantee that the user will see it.

The TEXT color does not take priority over other formatting settings. Settings contained within the <FONT> tag override the values set in text attributes, including TEXT, LINK, ALINK, or VLINK.

## Hyperlink Color: LINK

In most browsers, the default value for hyperlinks not yet visited is dark blue. You can change this by using the LINK attribute. Its usage is

```
<BODY LINK="#0000FF">
```

where *colorValue* is a recognized color literal such as black or aliceblue, or a hexadecimal triplet representing the red, green, and blue mix for the color. A pound sign (#) must precede the value if a hexadecimal number is used.

Most browsers also specify an underline attribute for hyperlinks, but as yet that setting cannot be changed from within the HTML <BODY> tag. Underlining for a hyperlink is accessible from a style sheet, which is discussed in Chapter 19.

## Active Hyperlink Color: ALINK

Anyone who has used a browser for any length of time notices a color change when clicking on a text-based hyperlink. When the mouse button is depressed, the text color changes. The color varies from computer to computer and browser to browser, but the change is there—something different from both the link color and the visited link color. The ALINK (for *Active Link*) attribute is used to change this value from its default, which is usually red. The usage of this attribute is

```
<BODY ALINK="#FF00FF">
```

where *colorValue* is a recognized color literal such as black or aliceblue, or a hexadecimal triplet representing the red, green, and blue mix for the color. A pound sign (#) must precede the value if a hexadecimal number is used.

> **TIP**
>
> You can have a little fun with different settings for this attribute, but avoid setting a color equal to the background color. Having the link disappear for a moment is disconcerting to many users and makes them wonder about your intentions. After all, what are you trying to hide?

### Visited Hyperlink Color: VLINK

The last attribute of the `<BODY>` tag sets the color of hyperlink text after the hyperlink has been visited. This helps users differentiate between where they've been and where they haven't been. Its usage is

```
<BODY VLINK="#FF0000">
```

where `colorValue` is a recognized color literal such as `black` or `aliceblue`, or a hexadecimal triplet representing the red, green, and blue mix for the color. A pound sign (#) must precede the value if a hexadecimal number is used.

This color should be a contrasting color to the unvisited link color (`LINK`); otherwise, it's very hard for users to tell where they've been. Unless there is an overwhelming reason, don't set `VLINK` and `LINK` to the same value.

---

**TIP**

Keep in mind the differences in quality that Web users' displays are likely to have—everything from Super VGA to old EGA and CGA monitors. On lower-resolution monitors, the range of colors is much more limited. So, even though you've defined a light blue for `VLINK` and dark blue for `LINK`, the limitations of a graphics display could force both to a basic blue with no difference.

---

**WHEN DOES THE COLOR CHANGE BACK?**

Each browser handles this differently. Most browsers allow the user to set expiration dates on visited links, after which time they revert back to the original color. As a very general rule, this period is from two weeks to 30 days after the link is clicked, and it can be reset by the user to as little as a day.

---

# The SCRIPT Element

This particular element is a bit of a free spirit, and it is used in two ways. In either application, it indicates a specific scripting language that is being used in the document. At present, two scripting languages are in widespread use on the World Wide Web: JavaScript and Visual Basic Script (VBScript). This element's syntax is

```
<SCRIPT LANGUAGE="language">
```

where `language` is VBScript or JavaScript. If used without a closing tag, it indicates the scripting language used for any scripts throughout the entire document. More information on specifying and creating scripts is provided in Chapter 28, "Integrating JavaScript and HTML," and Chapter 30, "Integrating ActiveX and VBScript."

In its typical usage, <SCRIPT> is used in combination with a closing tag, </SCRIPT>, to contain a section of programming code. If this code is placed in the header, it's interpreted before the rest of the document is loaded. This is a common practice for segments of code that serve as functions, where it's imperative to have the function loaded and available before anything in the document has a chance to invoke it.

Code that is designed to execute when the document is loaded or to accept interaction from the user is placed in the appropriate part of the document, such as forms and hyperlinks.

Browsers that don't support scripting languages probably won't recognize the <SCRIPT> tag. If this happens, the contents of the tag are displayed as regular text, which results in a lot of strange reading for the user. To avert this problem, use this simple workaround:

```
<SCRIPT>
<!--
script stuff
-->
</SCRIPT>
```

When you encase the script in HTML comment tags within the <SCRIPT> tags, an incompatible browser will ignore the script contents. The script will ignore the comment tags and process normally.

# Summary

Structure tags set the stage for the rest of your HTML and provide its basic framework. They mark the beginning and end of the file, header, and body sections. Additional tags and attributes within the header set basic behaviors, define a title, and pass information to the browser. By using the <BODY> tag, you can also set background images and colors, and set default colors for various text items on the page.

Although these tags serve an important purpose in your HTML document, they're not the fun stuff. The meat and potatoes are next.

# Text Alignment and Formatting

*by Rick Darnell*

## IN THIS CHAPTER

CHAPTER

8

In Chapter 7, "Structural Elements and Their Usage," you saw how to build a frame for an HTML document. As you learned, the basic structure includes the boundaries of the HTML page, a header and a footer, and a handful of other items to provide a framework for the page content. With that little bit of HTML, you have more than enough to build a Web page.

There's a small problem, however. You could put all of your text between the two body tags, and the user could read it. But it would be a tedious task. Web browsers don't look at text the way a person does. When the browser sees the end of a line in your document, it adds a space and keeps right on going. The result is one long string of words on the page that is neither attractive nor friendly to use.

The HTML elements presented in this chapter are designed to do everything for your page. There are tags for headings, addresses, and quotations. There are tags to make the text bold, italic, and green. There are tags to begin new paragraphs, start new lines, and add horizontal lines to help divide the page.

This chapter presents the workhorses for organizing and formatting your document, and you'll find that virtually every page on the Web uses at least one or two of these tags, and many make liberal use of more than that. Read on to find out how to use HTML text formatting elements to give visual and logical structure to your pages.

# Headings <H1> through <H6>

You don't begin a newspaper story with the lead paragraph, you begin it with a headline. And that's where this chapter begins with the text formatting tags. The six HTML heading styles are a way of showing the level of importance among different parts of your page, much like this book uses different levels of headings to visually organize the information.

The syntax is

```
<Hn [align=left¦center¦right]>Heading Text</Hn>
```

where *n* is an integer from 1 to 6 indicating the level of heading used, with 1 being the most important and 6 being the least. The optional `align` attribute controls the horizontal alignment of the heading. If omitted, it defaults to left alignment.

Although browsers vary in the size and typestyle given to the six heading levels, every browser follows the basic rule of giving the biggest and boldest style to `<H1>`, and the smallest and most insignificant style to `<H6>`. (See Figure 8.1.)

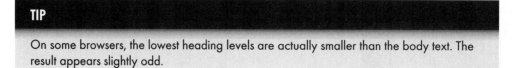

**TIP**

On some browsers, the lowest heading levels are actually smaller than the body text. The result appears slightly odd.

**FIGURE 8.1.**
*HTML heading styles show a descending level of emphasis and importance for the text they precede.*

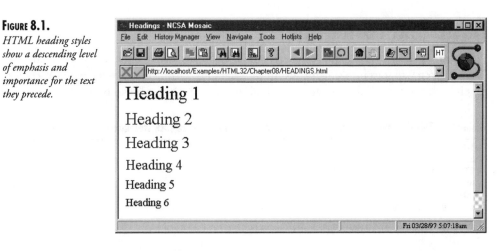

Headings allow for physical formatting within the container tags. You can set the style (bold, italic, or underlined) and typeface and size within a heading to give it additional emphasis.

```
Next on our site is <H1>Reflections on <I>The Devils
of Loudun</I></H1> followed by pictures of my cat.
```

Changing the style is possible within any of the heading styles, regardless of their level (as shown in Figure 8.2).

**FIGURE 8.2.**
*To further control the appearance of a heading, you can use physical formatting to control all or part of the text within.*

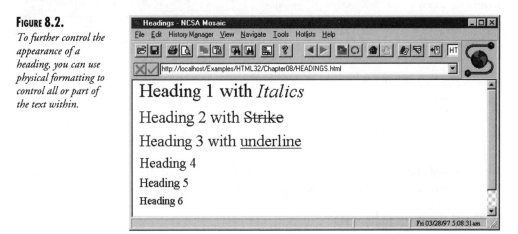

In Figure 8.2, note how the browser handles the text before and after the heading tags. A heading is always placed on its own line, even if it's placed inline with other material. A new paragraph is started for the heading, and any material following it is placed on the next new line.

# Basic Text Formatting

Now that the headings are in place, it's time to turn your attention to the rest of the document. The next step is to start breaking the text into paragraphs. Listing 8.1 appears to be a Web page that is broken into logical paragraphs, but look at Figure 8.3 to see how a browser interprets it.

**Listing 8.1. This document attempts to use extra hard returns to force each statement to its own line.**

```
<HTML>
<HEAD>
<TITLE>Hot Water Safety</TITLE>
</HEAD>
<BODY>
Hot water is dangerous.

Turn down the hot water heater thermostat.

Always supervise children in the bathtub.

Don't encourage children to play around the tub.
</BODY>
</HTML>
```

**FIGURE 8.3.**

*The code in Listing 8.1 creates a page that is formatted differently in the browser than it appears in the listing. The browser has ignored the extra line breaks and ran the lines together into one long paragraph.*

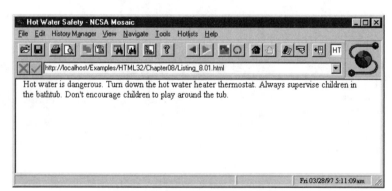

This obviously isn't what the designer had in mind, so check out the next three elements for methods to make the page conform to the way it should appear.

## A New Paragraph: <P>

The first way to break text into paragraphs is to use the paragraph tag—<P>. The syntax is

```
<P [align=left¦center¦right>...Text...</P>
```

where *Text* is a line or paragraph text, which should begin on a new line and remain together, and align sets whether the *Text* is aligned to the left (default), center, or right of the browser window. The closing tag is optional and can be omitted.

Using this tag on the preceding listing results in the code shown in Listing 8.2 and the page shown in Figure 8.4.

**Listing 8.2. This page is now divided into separate lines by defining each line as its own paragraph.**

```
<HTML>
<HEAD>
<TITLE>Hot Water Safety</TITLE>
</HEAD>
<BODY>
<P>Hot water is dangerous.</P>

<P align=right>Turn down the hot water heater thermostat.</P>

<P>Always supervise children in the bathtub.</P>

<P align=right>Don't encourage children to play around the tub.</P>
</BODY>
</HTML>
```

Notice the behavior of the alignment. A new paragraph supersedes any alignment settings in the previous paragraph. And, if an alignment is not specifically set, it defaults back to the left.

**FIGURE 8.4.**

*The code in Listing 8.2 is now interpreted the way you want it to be by using the <P> tag to mark each sentence as its own paragraph. Note that the extra return between lines is still ignored.*

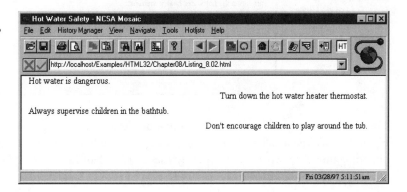

## A New Line: <BR>

A line break tag, <BR>, is similar to a paragraph tag, but it behaves slightly differently. It starts a new line within the current paragraph, but it doesn't start a new paragraph. The syntax is

```
<BR [clear=left|right|all]>...Text...
```

where *Text* is the material that should appear on the next line and the optional clear attribute defines how the following material should flow around floating images. An ending tag is not used.

Used with the preceding example, this tag creates the same basic effect as using a paragraph tag. (See Listing 8.3 and Figure 8.5.)

**Listing 8.3. Instead of new paragraphs, each line is started with a line break tag. This provides the same basic effect while keeping all of the text within the same paragraph.**

```
<HTML>
<HEAD>
<TITLE>Hot Water Safety</TITLE>
</HEAD>
<BODY>
<P>Hot water is dangerous.

<BR>Turn down the hot water heater thermostat.

<BR>Always supervise children in the bathtub.

<BR>Don't encourage children to play around the tub.</P>
</BODY>
</HTML>
```

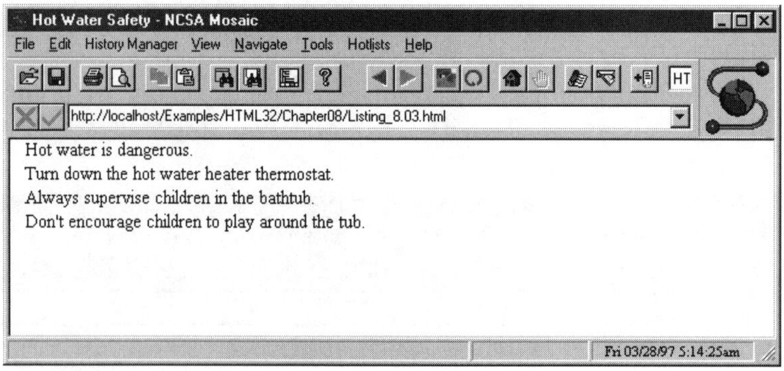

**FIGURE 8.5.**

*The code in Listing 8.3 creates a page with each sentence on its own line, although now the lines are slightly closer together because they're still within the same paragraph.*

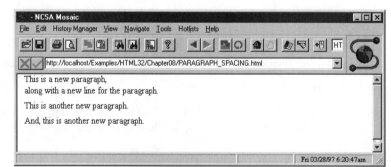

The big difference you'll notice between line breaks and new paragraphs is line spacing. (See Figure 8.6.) A line break uses the same spacing as if the line had just scrolled down from the preceding line. A new paragraph typically uses an extra half-line of space because the first line of a paragraph is not indented.

**FIGURE 8.6.**

*The primary difference between a line break and a new paragraph is how much space is left between the lines.*

Any alignment or other text formatting set previous to the line break within the same paragraph is carried to the new line.

The clear attribute is used to move past floating images on either margin. A value of left moves the text after the line break past any floating images on the left margin (as shown in Figure 8.7), while a value of right performs the same function for floating images on the right. As you might expect, all does the same for floating images on either margin. Other options for causing text to flow around an image are covered in Chapter 12, "Adding Images to Your Web Page."

**Figure 8.7.**

*Using the clear attribute allows text to move past a floating image.*

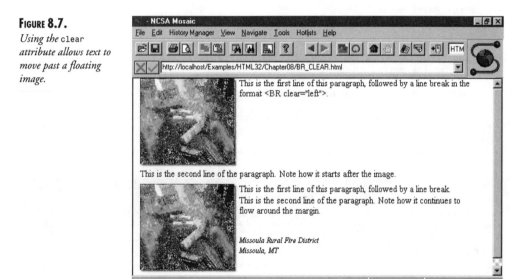

Standard inline images don't "float," so they're not affected by the clear attribute. An inline image, by definition, appears only on the line where it was inserted.

## Preformatted Text, Spaces and All: <PRE>

The last method for making your four lines of text appear the way you want is to mark the whole section as preformatted text. The syntax is

```
<PRE [width=characters]>...Text...</PRE>
```

where *Text* is any text, including returns, spaces, and other hard formatting. The width attribute tells the browser how wide of a space, in *characters*, to leave for the text.

The width attribute allows the browser to choose an appropriately sized font or indent as necessary so that the text is properly displayed. It is not supported by many browsers.

There are several key differences between this method and the two preceding tags. Look at Listing 8.4 and Figure 8.8. All of the text is contained by the <PRE> tags, which causes the browser to display everything in between *exactly as it finds it*. It also uses a monospaced font for display, which facilitates formatting of the text into rows and columns for data presentation.

**Listing 8.4. Instead of new paragraphs, each line is started with a line break tag. This provides the same basic effect while keeping all of the text within the same paragraph.**

```
<HTML>
<HEAD>
<TITLE>Hot Water Safety</TITLE>
</HEAD>
<BODY>
<PRE>Hot water is dangerous.

   Turn down the hot water heater thermostat.

      Always supervise children in the bathtub.

         Don't encourage children to play around the tub.</PRE>
</BODY>
</HTML>
```

**FIGURE 8.8.**

*The code in Listing 8.4 uses preformatting to display the lines exactly as they were typed in the file. The monospace font preserves character spacing for accurate display of indents and other formatting.*

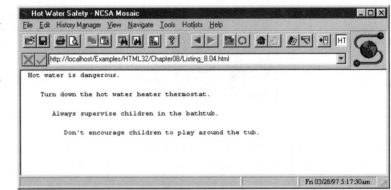

**TIP**

For browsers that aren't compatible with tables, preformatted text is an effective way to display a table made out of textual elements representing the border lines.

The monospaced font helps when preserving the line breaks and spaces inserted by the user. If you start a new line, insert five spaces and then start typing; that's exactly how your text appears using the <PRE> tag. Browsers disable automatic word wrap to further ensure that your text is displayed exactly as you typed it.

## Obtaining Preformatting the Old-Fashioned Way: <XMP>, <LISTING>, and <PLAINTEXT>

An old-fashioned way of doing something on a Web page usually means one thing: The old way is obsolete, and its tags are just kept around to be compatible with as many pages as possible. This is the category to which <XMP>, <LISTING>, and <PLAINTEXT> belong.

They work the same as <PRE>, requiring an opening and closing tag. However, according to the HTML 3.2 specification, browsers can support these for backward compatibility. To be safe, avoid usage of these items.

## Breaking a Document into Divisions: <DIV>

The <DIV> element is used to structure an HTML document into a series of divisions. Its syntax is

```
<DIV [align=left¦right¦center>...Text...</DIV>
```

where *Text* is one or more lines of text that comprise the division. The align attribute is optional; it sets the horizontal alignment for text within the block and behaves the same as the attribute used in the <P> tag.

The <DIV> tag is a block element that acts very similarly to a <P> tag. If a <P> tag doesn't have a closing </P>, <DIV> effectively closes it and starts a new paragraph. Other than this behavior, <DIV> doesn't generate paragraph breaks before or after its placement.

---

### USING <CENTER> INSTEAD OF <DIV align=center>

The <CENTER> tag is identical to <DIV align=center>. This duplication occurred because the <CENTER> tag was introduced by Netscape at about the same time the <DIV> element was added to the HTML 3.0 specification.

Both tags are included in the HTML 3.2 specification, although using the align attribute of <P> or <DIV> is the preferred way to center text. The <CENTER> tag was placed in the specification due to its widespread implementation.

---

# Formatting Text by Its Usage

One of the ways HTML defines the appearance of text is by its use within the document. This is a little difficult to understand for people just getting started with putting together pages.

In the traditional world of word processing and publishing, people tend to think in physical styles—font, size, bold, italic, and so on. But remember that HTML is a way of defining structure as much as appearance. HTML is a simple markup language used to create hypertext documents that are portable from one platform to another. Within this limitation, each browser is given a lot of latitude in how it interprets tags. The HTML 3.2 specification includes recommendations on preferred appearances, which browsers deviate from based on the needs and limitations of their respective platforms.

With that preamble out of the way, it's time to introduce the logical tags. These are the tags that describe the usage for a piece of text, rather than the physical attributes it should have. It's much the same as defining a style on your word processor for addresses. Every time you have an address, you apply the "address" style. You cease to think about the text in physical formatting by substituting the new style.

The big difference between your word processor and the browser is that the browser decides how it's going to display the address style, not you.

---

**TIP**

For each of the following styles, the preferred browser interpretation is listed even though this may vary across applications and platforms.

---

## Basic and Strong Emphasis: <EM> and <STRONG>

There are times when you need to make sure that the reader doesn't miss the point of your message. And in order to do that, you need to emphasize a word or more in a sentence. HTML provides the emphasis tag to fill this need. The syntax is

`<EM>...Text...</EM>`

where *Text* is the word or words to emphasize. Italics are the recommended rendering of emphasized text.

Related to the emphasis tag is the strong emphasis tag (<STRONG>), which should relate a higher level of importance to the reader. The syntax is

`<STRONG>...Text...</STRONG>`

where *Text* is the word or words needing extra emphasis. Boldface type is the preferred rendering of strong text. The difference between these two tags is illustrated in Figure 8.9.

---

**OTHER OPTIONS FOR EMPHASIZING**

Later in this chapter, you'll also see how the italic (<I>) and bold (<B>) tags are used to generate the same effects as emphasis and strong emphasis. So, why should anyone use the logical styles? They're longer and aren't as clear about their final appearance.

---

Remember that part of the purpose of HTML is to show structure and meaning within a document. This is the role the two emphasis tags play. Using the physical bold or italics tag would achieve the same visual effect, but using the logical tags also shows the intention and is stable across all platforms—not just the ones that support a variety of typestyles.

**FIGURE 8.9.**

*Emphasized text is usually displayed with italics to make it stand out from surrounding text, and strong text uses a bold presentation.*

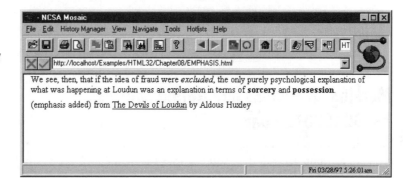

# Address Information: <ADDRESS>

The <ADDRESS> tag is used to mark contact information for the current document, whether it's an e-mail address or complete mailing address and phone number. It behaves much like the paragraph tag, forcing the text within its confines to be separated from surrounding material by additional line spacing. The syntax is

```
<ADDRESS>...ContactInformation...</ADDRESS>
```

where *ContactInformation* is the address information, along with any paragraph-level formatting such as line breaks. It is typically displayed as italic body text.

You can nest other items within the address tag, including hyperlink information. For example, one option for displaying e-mail contact information is

```
<ADDRESS><A href="mailto:sam@fairdeals.com">Sam Beauregard</A><BR>
Fair Deal Sam's Used Cars<BR>
"With Sam B., it's a guarantee"<BR>
Great Falls, MT
</ADDRESS>
```

This would create a hyperlink to connect to the user's e-mail software while maintaining the formatting for address information. (See Figure 8.10.) For more ideas on working with hyperlinks and mail-to destinations, see Chapter 11, "Linking Documents and Images."

8

TEXT ALIGNMENT AND FORMATTING

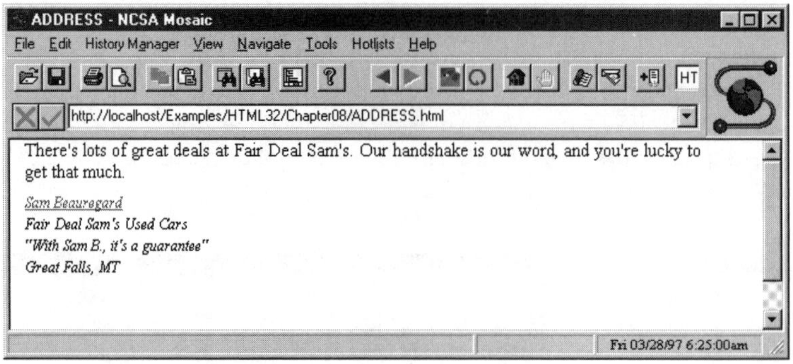

**FIGURE 8.10.**
*This text is formatted with the* <ADDRESS> *tag, and it also includes a nested tag for defining a hyperlink.*

## Marking Quotations and Noting Sources: <BLOCKQUOTE> and <CITE>

Sometimes when you are composing pages, you'll want to insert a quotation out of another work, or attribute facts to their sources. (See Figure 8.11.) Once again, HTML provides tags that identify how the text is being used, and leaves the details of its physical appearance to the browser.

For shorter quotations, it's certainly fine to use quotation marks and leave the text inline with the rest of the content. However, if the amount of text to quote exceeds more than a couple of sentences, it is easier for the reader to take note of the quote if it is separated from the rest of the text. This is when the <BLOCKQUOTE> element is used. The syntax is

```
<BLOCKQUOTE>...Text...</BLOCKQUOTE>
```

where *Text* is the quotation that should be separated from the rest of the surrounding material. This creates a separate paragraph for the text and, in most browsers, indents the entire paragraph from the left. (See Figure 8.11.) Some browsers also include a slight indent from the right, or set the text in italics.

The block quotation allows other formatting within its borders, including paragraphs, line breaks, and headings. Individual browsers vary in their handling of special formatting. Most will indent special formatting such as headings along with the rest of the block quotation.

Keep in mind that not all browsers handle the block quotation the same way, especially in regards to the type style (regular or italics). If you include formatting such as italics within a block quote, and the browser normally displays block quote in italics, then your added emphasis is lost to the reader. In some cases, the browser might change the typestyle of the rest of the block quotation.

**TIP**

For safety and consistency, try to avoid the use of other formatting within a block quotation.

**FIGURE 8.11.**

*A block quotation is separated from surrounding text by creating a new paragraph and indenting it from the left. The citation to the source of the quote is marked in italics.*

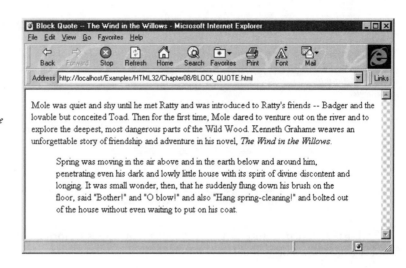

The citation tag, `<CITE>`, is used to identify sources of information outside the current document. It's used most often in research and professional papers, although you might find use in other areas such as book reviews and Frequently Asked Questions. The syntax is

`<CITE>Source</CITE>`

where `Source` is the name of the citation. The usual rendering for `<CITE>` is italics.

## Defining a Term: <DFN>

When you think about terms and definitions, a dictionary or glossary is the image that usually comes to mind. HTML offers one way of presenting this type of information through different types of lists, which are covered in Chapter 9, "Using Lists to Organize Information." Although HTML lists are the usual method used for presenting terms and definitions, there is also another alternative.

The other option for showing a definition term is using the `<DFN>` tag. Its syntax is

`<DFN>Term</DFN>`

where `Term` is the word that is defined. It's used to identify words within a body of text that are defined in the same sentence. (See Figure 8.12.) The typical rendering for a definition term is italics.

## Indicating Program Code: <CODE>

You've seen examples of syntax and usage of HTML code throughout this chapter, and you will continue to see it throughout the rest of the book. Sams.net uses a special monospaced typestyle to show these examples so that they stand out from the rest of the text.

8

**TEXT ALIGNMENT AND FORMATTING**

FIGURE 8.12.
*The italicized words
"Entry Team" are the
definition term, which
is defined within the
same sentence.*

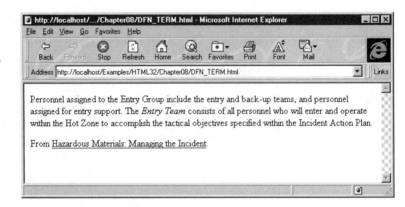

HTML has a similar feature in the <CODE> tag that it uses to format programming or other similar code lines. The syntax is

```
<CODE>...CodeLine...</CODE>
```

where *CodeLine* is the line or lines of code samples. If multiple lines of code are included, the line-break tag <BR> is also needed.

It's important to note that although the typical display of this element uses monospace text similar to the PRE element, <CODE> still requires the <BR> or <P> tags to force new lines. Except for the appearance of the text, anything within the <CODE> container behaves the same as other HTML text.

The <VAR> tag is often used in conjunction with the <CODE> tag to help explain the code. Its syntax is

```
<VAR>Variable</VAR>
```

where *Variable* is the name of a variable being described, much like <DFN> works for definition terms. The typical representation is italics, which is also the same as <DFN>.

<VAR> is similar to <DFN> in use; it explains a variable or argument of a piece of code within the context of a normal sentence or paragraph.

Figure 8.13 includes an example of using <CODE> and <VAR> together. After the code listing, there is a brief explanation of two of the variables.

Two more companions to the code elements are used in similar situations: <SAMP> and <KBD>.

**FIGURE 8.13.**

*The lines of Java code listed in this display are treated with a monospaced format to separate them from the explanatory text.*

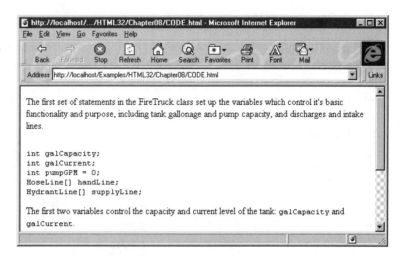

**Sample Output and User Typing: <SAMP> and <KBD>**

These two tags identify things the computer would say to the user and examples of what the user should say to the computer. Like <CODE> and <VAR>, they are hangers-on from the old days of the Internet, when just about everyone worked from a text-based UNIX system. The syntax is

<SAMP>*SampleOutput*</SAMP>

where *SampleOutput* is an example of a message the user might receive from the computer, and

<KBD>*KeyboardInput*</KBD>

where *KeyboardInput* is an example of something the user might type on the keyboard. The typical representation of sample output is monospaced text, while keyboard input is usually displayed with bold monospaced text. (See Figure 8.14.)

**FIGURE 8.14.**

*The simulated output from a computer is presented in monospaced type on a line by itself. The response requested from the user is presented in the text as monospaced bold type.*

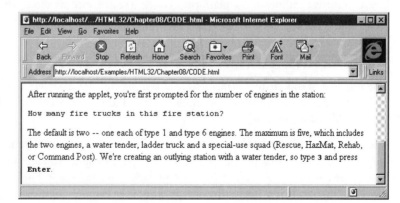

8

TEXT ALIGNMENT
AND FORMATTING

## A Quick Review of Logical Styles

You might have noticed that there is a lot of overlap in the way different HTML logical elements are represented within a browser. Although there is no set standard for these items, there are some commonly accepted conventions. Table 8.1 lists the logical styles and their typical rendering.

**Table 8.1. Logical element styles.**

| Element | Style |
|---------|-------|
| <ADDRESS> | *Italics* |
| <BLOCKQUOTE> | Normal with indent |
| <CITE> | *Italics* |
| <CODE> | Monospace |
| <DFN> | *Italics* |
| <EM> | *Italics* |
| <KBD> | **Bold Monospace** |
| <SAMP> | Monospace |
| <STRONG> | **Bold** |
| <VAR> | *Italics* |

The various browsers may interpret these items in a variety of ways, but remember that this is okay. Part of the purpose of HTML is to make documents that are platform independent. The end user really shouldn't care which style is used for which item, as long as it's consistent.

When you use the logical styles, the browser can decide how to display a certain type of text based on the capabilities of the platform, reducing your concerns about where your document can be viewed.

# Formatting Text with Physical Styles

The first half of this chapter is devoted to exploring the logical styles; now it's time to look at how to force text into a certain appearance. After all the reasons given for using logical styles, why would anyone do this?

Quite simply, the logical styles don't cover all the possibilities that designers and page authors seem to thrive on. Using physical styles allows a page designer to take control over many details of the page's appearance, including type style, size, and color. For users with compatible browsers, the result is a finely tuned page whose appearance begins to approach the quality found on the pages of many popular magazines.

## Basic Text Formatting Styles: `<I>`, `<B>`, `<U>`

The first three elements are standards in virtually all text-processing environments. They set the basic appearance of the text (as shown in Figure 8.15), and they are the basis for many of the logical styles.

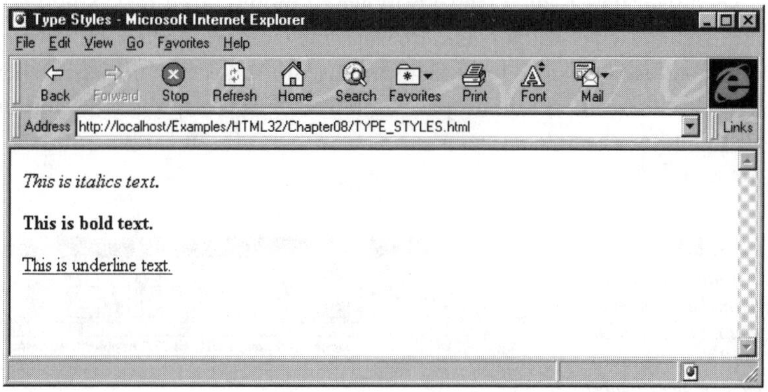

**FIGURE 8.15.**

*The three basic physical styles are italics, bold, and underline.*

The syntax for each of the elements is

```
<I>...Text...</I>
<B>...Text...</B>
<U>...Text...</U>
```

where `<I>` stands for italics, `<B>` stands for bold, and `<U>` stands for underline. In addition to using the tags individually, you can also nest them for a combined effect, like this:

```
This is <B>bold text with <I>bold and italics text</I></B>.
```

Use of the underline tag can confuse users because it is also used to mark hyperlinks to other documents. Use it sparingly, and try to limit its use to documents that don't also contain text hyperlinks.

---

### TIP

From the days of typesetting and proofreader marks, underlined text was used to indicate items that should be set in italics. This includes book and magazine titles.

---

## Strike-Through Text: `<STRIKE>`

Strike-through text is used more often in traditional word processing than in HTML pages. It indicates text that has been deleted but is still left on the page for review. This way other readers can review the changes and know how the revision of the document has progressed. The syntax is

```
<STRIKE>...Text...</STRIKE>
```

The HTML committee of the World Wide Web Consortium is considering replacing `<STRIKE>` with the shorter version `<S>`. This is only an idea; you can expect `<STRIKE>` to remain valid for at least another year or two.

## Teletype or Monospaced Text: `<TT>`

Several logical text styles take advantage of monospaced text. Simply stated, monospace text means that each character takes up the same width on the screen. Normally, graphical browsers use adjustable-width fonts. This means an *m* takes up more space than an *i*, which takes up less space than a *j*. In a monospace font, all three take up the same amount of space along with all the other characters, including spaces, periods, and other punctuation marks. (See Figure 8.16.)

**FIGURE 8.16.**

*The difference between normal and monospace font isn't very evident until they are viewed adjacent to each other.*

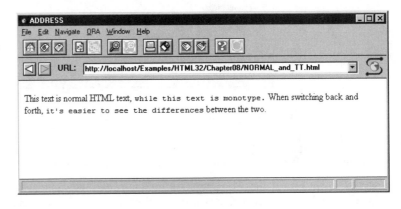

The syntax is

```
<TT>...Text...<TT>
```

where *Text* is the font to display in monospace font. The `<TT>` designation in the tag hearkens back to the days of teletype machines. Essentially, these were typewriters hooked up to networks that delivered news and bulletins. As was standard for typewriters at the time, they used a monospace type style.

## Superscripts and Subscripts: `<SUP>` and `<SUB>`

Next in the list of physical styles are the two tags for creating superscripts and subscripts. A superscript is text set slightly higher than the base text, and a subscript is set slightly lower. Both typically use a smaller typeface. The syntax for both is

```
<SUP>Text</SUP>
<SUB>Text</SUB>
```

In normal usage, a superscript or subscript is used for only a character or two. The following snippet uses this feature to indicate an endnote source (superscript) and notation for a chemical formula (subscript). (See Figure 8.17.)

```
The chemical formula<SUP>1</SUP> for Glacial Acetic acid
is C<SUB>2</SUB>H<SUB>4</SUB>O<SUB>2</SUB>.
<BR><SUP>1</SUP>Chemical Hazards Response Information System.
```

**FIGURE 8.17.**

*Superscripts and subscripts are typically used for small pieces of text, such as marking endnotes and other special notation.*

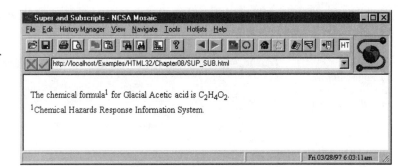

Like the other elements, you can nest these tags for additional usefulness. For example, you can make a reference to an endnote superscript also serve as a link to the actual endnote, like this:

```
The chemical formula<A HREF="#1"><SUP>1</SUP></A> for Glacial Acetic acid
is C<SUB>2</SUB>H<SUB>4</SUB>O<SUB>2</SUB>.
<BR><A NAME="1"><SUP>1</SUP></A>Chemical Hazards Response Information System.
```

Clicking on the superscript for the endnote moves the user to that location in the document. For more information on working with anchors and hyperlinks, see Chapter 11.

# Working with the Letters: <FONT>

With HTML 3.2, it's now possible to override the default size and color of text selections on a page. This is accomplished using the FONT element and its two attributes—size and color.

Some browsers also support a face attribute, which is used to specify one or more typefaces to use for the selection. It is not part of the HTML 3.2 specification, although it is currently supported by the two leading browsers. To specify the Garamond typeface as the first choice and Arial as the second, the tag would look like this:

```
<FONT face="Garamond,Arial">...text...</FONT>
```

If neither typeface is found on the user's browser, the default typeface for that particular application is used. If you choose to use the attribute, be sure that your page also displays correctly if the user's browser doesn't support it.

## Setting the Size: size and <BASEFONT>

The first attribute of <FONT> is size. This sets the size of the contents of the tag to a specific or relative size. The syntax is

```
<FONT size=number>...Text...</FONT>
```

where *number* is the desired size expressed as an integer from 1 to 7, or as a relative value from –6 to +6. If a relative value is used, it is added to the current setting for <BASEFONT>. (This is covered further later in this section.) Unlike the headings, where <H1> represents the largest heading and <H6> is the smallest, the size attribute uses 1 for the smallest type size and 7 for the largest. (See Figure 8.18.)

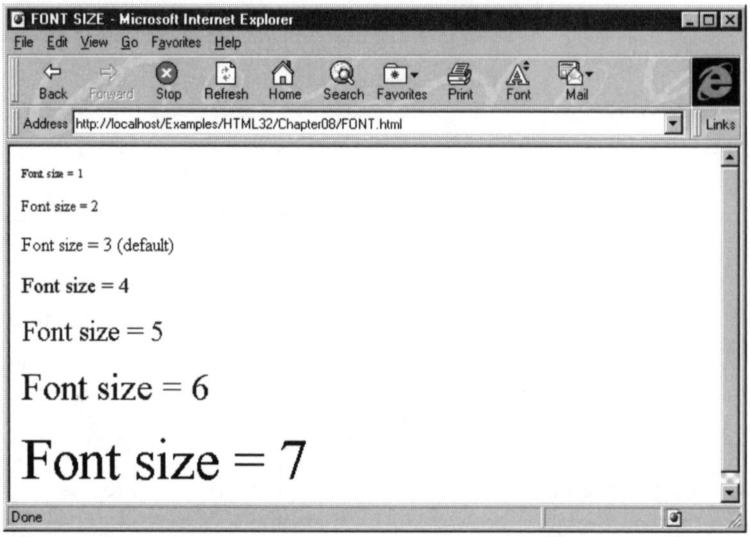

**FIGURE 8.18.**

*This is how different text sizes are represented using the FONT element.*

UNDERSTANDING HTML TYPE SIZES

For people used to dealing with type sizes represented in points, the range of sizes for HTML text doesn't appear practical. After all, a line of 1-point type creates fine print not even a lawyer could understand.

HTML type sizes do correspond to physical sizes, but the actual physical size varies between browsers and platforms. So, don't try to think of size 1 being equal to 6-point text. Instead, just think of size 1 as "really small," size 7 as "really big," and 2 through 6 as a range of "fairly small" to "fairly big."

As a companion to the size attribute of <FONT>, the BASEFONT element provides a way to set the base size of the body text. Its syntax is

```
<BASEFONT [size=number]>
```

where *number* is the size of the base font, expressed as an integer from 1 to 7. If omitted, it defaults to 3. It sets the base for all text following it and does not have a closing tag.

In addition to specifying an absolute text size, you also can use a relative number for <BASEFONT>. The syntax is the same, but a plus or minus sign is placed in front of the number. This method uses the default base size (3) and adds the value of the size attribute. (See Figure 8.19.)

**FIGURE 8.19.**
*No matter what the size of the previous font is, a relative value for the base font size is always added to the default size.*

Using relative sizes, the range of values for the base size attribute is –2 to +4. For both <BASEFONT> and <FONT>, relative values that result in a size less than 1 or more than 7 default to the minimum and maximum values for physical sizes.

## A Different Shade of Text: color

You can control the color of a block of text using the color attribute. The syntax is

```
<FONT color=name¦RGBValue>...Text...</FONT>
```

where the value of color is a *name* of one of the 16 standard colors, or an RGB hexadecimal triplet that specifies the mix of colors to use. Remember that default text colors for the entire document are set with attributes of the <BODY> tag, which was covered in the previous chapter.

> **NOTE**
>
> You can define a color in two ways. The first is the RGB hexadecimal triplet, which is very specific but not very friendly.
>
> Or, you can use the name of the color. It's much more friendly, but you can't use just any name. Personally, I really liked the color of my friend John's car. It was taupe. Unfortunately, I can't type <FONT color="taupe"> and expect the browser to understand.
>
> If you want to use color names, you'll need to stick to one of the 16 standard values—black, green, silver, lime, gray, olive, white, yellow, maroon, navy, red, blue, purple, teal, fuchsia, and aqua. Some browsers use other names. To be safe, use one of these names, or get out the old scientific calculator and start figuring 32 percent blue as a hexadecimal number.

Be careful when changing text colors, especially when using a non-default background such as an image or other color. Some colors don't work well together, such as green text on red, or red text on purple. The resulting effect will do more to drive your readers away than to illustrate your point.

# Other Special Text Formatting

In the world of HTML text formatting, some tags don't fit well into either logical or physical text styles. These include the tags for relative size changes and horizontal rules.

## All Text Great and Little: <BIG> and <SMALL>

An additional two tags in HTML control size. They are a hybrid between the logical styles and physical styles; they don't specify a size, but they don't indicate usage either. The syntax is

```
<BIG>...Text...</BIG>
<SMALL>...Text...</SMALL>
```

where the text is set to a smaller or larger size than currently set by the base font. Typical rendering is one size larger or smaller than the base font. (See Figure 8.20.)

**FIGURE 8.20.**

*Using <BIG> or <SMALL> results in the enclosed text being set one size larger or smaller than the base font, respectively.*

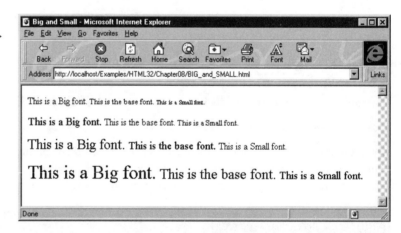

If the base font is set to the smallest size (1), <SMALL> defaults to a size of 3. The same occurs when the base is set to the largest size (7), when <BIG> also defaults to 3.

## Drawing a Line on the Page: <HR>

Horizontal lines are an easy-to-use element for dividing a page into logical sections. They signal the reader to be alert for a change in subject or style, or they can separate figures and captions from body text. Depending on your design needs, <HR> also includes several attributes to fine-tune its appearance. The syntax is

```
<HR attributes>
```

where *attributes* is one or more of four controls controlling height, width, alignment, and shading.

The first two attributes—height and width—set the basic size of the line. (See Figure 8.21.) The height of a horizontal rule is set in pixels, such as height=8. The width is set either in pixels or as a percentage of the browser window width. If you're using the percentage value, include a percentage sign (%) after the value. The typical defaults for height and width are 3 pixels high and 100 percent of page width.

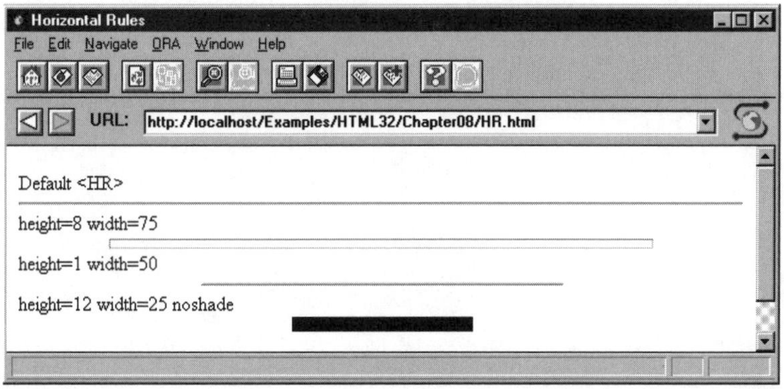

**FIGURE 8.21.**
*The first line on this page uses the browser size defaults. The subsequent lines adjust the* height *and* width *values for varying effects.*

The next attribute is align, which controls horizontal placement. The values for align are left, right, or center. Omitting this attribute usually results in left alignment of the line.

The last attribute is noshade. Normally, a browser displays a horizontal rule in some form of three-dimensional shading. This varies from browser to browser; some show it as depressed, some raised, some as an outline. Using noshade forces the horizontal rule to appear as a bold line. Again, this may vary among browsers. Some use black for the rule, and others use shades of gray.

# Summary

This chapter is designed to give you a head start in formatting text on your Web pages so that you can give your message the maximum impact. With the exception of a couple of tags for hyperlinks and images, this includes all of the most-used tags in HTML.

First and foremost are the tags to break the text into paragraphs and lines. Without them, every HTML document would just be one long, hard-to-read document. They give the basic structure to the page for the reader.

After breaking the document into paragraphs, HTML 3.2 offers two basic sets of choices to organize and format the text on your Web pages. First, you can use the logical styles. These format the text based on its purpose and usage, such as citations and addresses. They are typically supported across platforms and browsers, although the actual rendering might be atypical.

8

TEXT ALIGNMENT
AND FORMATTING

The physical styles don't necessarily give clues to the use or purpose of the text, but they do allow closer control over text appearance. You can define font size and color, along with using monospaced fonts and applying bold, italics, and underline styles.

A multitude of other HTML tags also control text appearance and formatting, but they are unique enough to deserve treatment by themselves. These include the list tags (Chapter 9, "Using Lists to Organize Information"), hyperlinks and anchors (Chapter 10, "Creating Tables for Data and Page Layout"), and forms (Chapter 15, "Building and Using HTML Forms").

# Using Lists to Organize Information

*by Rick Darnell*

**CHAPTER 9**

## IN THIS CHAPTER

Lists are everywhere. On the refrigerator for groceries, on a scratch pad for to-do lists, in the front of books as a table of contents, in lists of directions for accomplishing tasks. Lists are one of the most natural ways we organize our information.

HTML has a special set of tags just for the purpose of displaying lists, and HTML 3.2 has added additional attributes to some of these tags to give you greater control over their appearance.

At the most basic level, lists are divided into two categories:

- **Ordered Lists**. These lists are typically used to indicate a sequence of events or priorities. They're also used to specifically identify sections and relationships when creating outlines.
- **Unordered Lists**. An unordered list is typically used to display a group of items that are somehow related, but necessarily in a hierarchical fashion. Three special HTML subsets of unordered lists are illustrated later in this chapter—definitions, directories, and menus.

The next sections look at each type of list and the ways to customize them to your own specific circumstance.

# Ordered (or Numbered) Lists: <OL>

A list is defined by its opening and closing tags. For ordered lists, they are <OL> and </OL>. However, two tags do not a list make. If you're going to have a list, you'll need something to put in it. Look at Listing 9.1, which is a list encased with the ordered list tags.

**Listing 9.1. A simple ordered list enclosed with <OL> tags.**

```
<!DOCTYPE HTML PUBLIC "-//IETF//DTD HTML 3.2//EN">
<HTML>
<HEAD>
<TITLE>Basic CPR</TITLE>
</HEAD>
<BODY>
Basic CPR
<OL>
Use Body Substance Isolation Precautions
Determine Unresponsiveness
Open Airway
Look, Listen and Feel for Breathing
Ventilate Twice
Check for Pulse
If No Pulse, Begin Compressions
</OR>
</BODY>
</HTML>
```

> **NOTE**
>
> To save a little ink, examples and listings in this chapter won't explicitly include the basic structural codes (<HTML>, <HEAD>, and <BODY>). They're still assumed to be in place, and should be included if you enter the examples by hand.

Viewed on a browser, you can see where the text was indented in preparation for a list, but no actual numbering took place. (See Figure 9.1.)

**FIGURE 9.1.**

*A list of information enclosed with list tags doesn't result in an HTML list. Additional tags are needed to complete the formatting.*

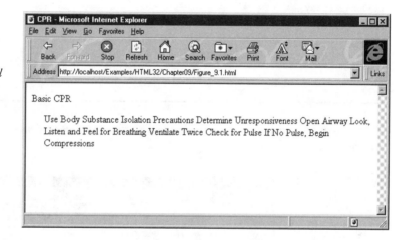

Why did this happen? Remember that HTML doesn't recognize line breaks unless it's told explicitly where they occur with the <P> or <BR> tags. The same principle applies to lists, although a different tag is used to tell the browser where each specific item begins. This is accomplished with the list item tag—<LI>.

With the <OL> and <LI> tags in hand, the basic syntax for an ordered list is as follows:

```
<OL>
<LI>ListItem1
<LI>ListItem2
...
<LI>ListItemN
</OL>
```

*ListItem* is each separate item in the list. See Listing 9.2 for an example of the usage of these tags.

9

USING LISTS TO
ORGANIZE
INFORMATION

**Listing 9.2. The same list shown in Listing 9.1, but now it has the beginning of each separate item marked with a list item tag.**

```
<!DOCTYPE HTML PUBLIC "-//IETF//DTD HTML 3.2//EN">
<HTML>
<HEAD>
<TITLE>Basic CPR</TITLE>
</HEAD>
<BODY>
Basic CPR
<OL>
<LI>Use Body Substance Isolation Precautions
<LI>Determine Unresponsiveness
<LI>Open Airway
<LI>Look, Listen and Feel for Breathing
<LI>Ventilate Twice
<LI>Check for Pulse
<LI>If No Pulse, Begin Compressions
</OR>
</BODY>
</HTML>
```

For each item identified with <LI>, the browser starts a new line, indents, and adds a number. (See Figure 9.2.)

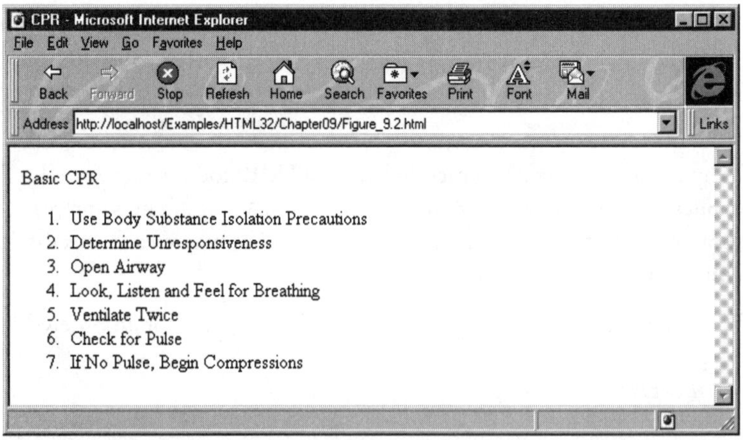

**FIGURE 9.2.**

*After each item is marked at the beginning with a list item tag, the browser completes the formatting with indenting and automatic numbering.*

**TIP**

Although some HTML editors include it, a closing </LI> tag is not required for each list item. However, you can include it if you want without adverse effect.

The line break tags—<P> and <BR>—are also allowed within the body of a list to further control its appearance and formatting (as shown in Listing 9.3).

**Listing 9.3. You can organize your list into headings and subtext using the <BR> and <P> tags.**

```
<!DOCTYPE HTML PUBLIC "-//IETF//DTD HTML 3.2//EN">
<HTML>
<HEAD>
<TITLE>Basic CPR</TITLE>
</HEAD>
<BODY>
Basic CPR
<OL>
<LI>Use Body Substance Isolation Precautions<BR>
If available, be sure to use latex or vinyl gloves,
goggles and a barrier device with one-way valve.<P>
<LI>Determine Unresponsiveness
<LI>Open Airway
<LI>Look, Listen and Feel for Breathing
<LI>Ventilate Twice
<LI>Check for Pulse
<LI>If No Pulse, Begin Compressions
</OR>
</BODY>
</HTML>
```

When viewed on a browser (as shown in Figure 9.3), the tags affecting line breaks don't affect the line numbering. When the list begins with the <OL> tag, only an <LI> tag will cause the browser to start a new line with the next number. You can force other lines to begin with the line break tags, but because it doesn't begin a new list item, the browser treats it like a continuation of the current item and doesn't add a number for the next item in the sequence.

**FIGURE 9.3.**

*Additional text formatting and page breaks are allowed within a list without affecting the basic list numbering or style.*

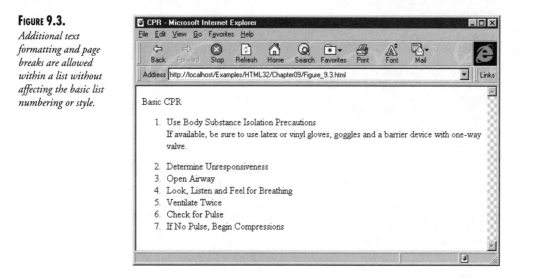

In addition to the formatting you can apply to individual list items, there are two other ways to customize an ordered list. This includes choosing a new beginning for list numbering (start) and the numbering characters used (type). These two attributes are covered in the following sections.

## Where to start a List

Sometimes it's necessary to interrupt a list for some explanatory text or other material where indenting isn't needed. Look at Listing 9.4 and its corresponding Figure 9.4.

**Listing 9.4. The second ordered list is a continuation of the first. It's interrupted by some explanatory text that you did not want indented.**

```
<!DOCTYPE HTML PUBLIC "-//IETF//DTD HTML 3.2//EN">
<HTML>
<HEAD>
<TITLE>Basic CPR</TITLE>
</HEAD>
<BODY>
<H2>Basic CPR</H2>
<H3>Airway and Breathing</H3>
<OL>
<LI>Use Body Substance Isolation Precautions<BR>
If available, be sure to use latex or vinyl gloves,
goggles and a barrier device with one-way valve.<P>
<LI>Determine Unresponsiveness
<LI>Open Airway
<LI>Look, Listen and Feel for Breathing
<LI>Ventilate Twice
</OL>
Look for chest rise and listen for exhalation while ventilating.
If no air enters, reposition the airway and try again. If the
airway is blocked, attempt to clear it using appropriate airway
obstruction maneuvers. If you can't get air into the patient,
circulation won't help. If the airway won't clear, you'll remain
in steps 3 through 5 until you can successfully ventilate the
patient, or they are transported to a hospital.
<H3>Circulation</H3>
<OL>
<LI>Check for Pulse
<LI>If No Pulse, Begin Compressions
</OR>
</BODY>
</HTML>
```

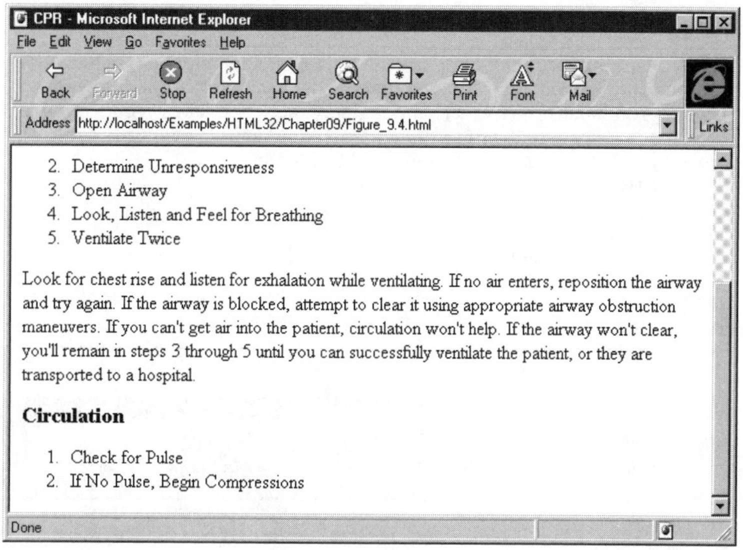

**FIGURE 9.4.**

*List numbering is not consecutive between individual lists. A new list starts the numbering process over from the beginning.*

Two sets of <OL> tags are used—one for the first half of CPR (airway and breathing), and another for the second half (circulation). Because each portion of the list is contained within its own pair of ordered list tags, the browser treats each as a separate list and begins numbering from 1 for the second list. The browser doesn't know it's really a continuation of the first list.

To work around this problem, use the start attribute for the <OL> tag to start numbering anywhere you want. (See Listing 9.5 and Figure 9.5.)

**Listing 9.5. The start attribute can be used to override default list numbering when a list is broken into multiple parts.**

```
<!DOCTYPE HTML PUBLIC "-//IETF//DTD HTML 3.2//EN">
<HTML>
<HEAD>
<TITLE>Basic CPR</TITLE>
</HEAD>
<BODY>
<H2>Basic CPR</H2>
<H3>Airway and Breathing</H3>
<OL>
<LI>Use Body Substance Isolation Precautions<BR>
If available, be sure to use latex or vinyl gloves,
goggles and a barrier device with one-way valve.<P>
<LI>Determine Unresponsiveness
<LI>Open Airway
<LI>Look, Listen and Feel for Breathing
<LI>Ventilate Twice
</OL>
Look for chest rise and listen for exhalation while ventilating.
If no air enters, reposition the airway and try again. If the
```

*continues*

### Listing 9.5. continued

```
airway is blocked, attempt to clear it using appropriate airway
obstruction maneuvers. If you can't get air into the patient,
circulation won't help. If the airway won't clear, you'll remain
in steps 3 through 5 until you can successfully ventilate the
patient, or they are transported to a hospital.
<H3>Circulation</H3>
<OL start=6>
<LI>Check for Pulse
<LI>If No Pulse, Begin Compressions
</OR>
</BODY>
</HTML>
```

**FIGURE 9.5.**

*Using the* start *attribute with the* <OL> *tag makes it possible to create lists that are interrupted by blocks of text or other material and then resumed with appropriate numbering.*

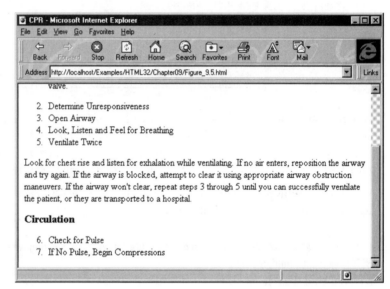

The syntax for start is

`<OL start=number>`

where *number* is any integer from 2147483647 to –2147483648. Be sure not to use commas in your numbers, because commas cause the numbers to be misinterpreted by the browser.

> **TIP**
>
> If numbers outside this range are used, the numbers "roll over" to the beginning. For example, if a list begins with 2147483647, the next number displayed in line is –2147483648. If your lists are hampered by a number system that extends to only approximately two billion, you probably have way too much time on your hands.

# What type of List Is Needed

In the early days of HTML, there was only one type of ordered list—with numbers beginning at 1 and ending wherever the list stopped. Then, as people began stretching its uses into things such as online books, the desire arose to use something other than numbers. The type attribute was developed in response.

The syntax of type is

```
<OL type=numberingSystem>
```

where *numberingSystem* is one of five characters—*1, A, a, I,* or *i.* Examples of the five numbering units are shown in Table 9.1.

**Table 9.1. Values and styles for the type attribute.**

| Value | Style | Example |
|-------|-------|---------|
| 1 | Arabic | 1,2,3,… |
| A | Uppercase alpha | A,B,C,… |
| a | Lowercase alpha | a,b,c,… |
| I | Uppercase Roman | I,II,III,… |
| i | Lowercase Roman | i,ii,iii,… |

The ability to use something other than numbers leads to a useful feature of ordered lists: nested lists. This is a list within a list, and can extend several levels. To create a nested list, include a new set of ordered list tags within the current list tags (as shown in Listing 9.6). The browser begins a new list for the new tags, while remembering where the parent list left off after the nested list ends. (See Figure 9.6.)

**Listing 9.6. A nested list is created by adding a new set of ordered list tags within existing list tags.**

```
<!DOCTYPE HTML PUBLIC "-//IETF//DTD HTML 3.2//EN">
<HTML>
<HEAD>
<TITLE>Patient Assessment</TITLE>
</HEAD>
<BODY>
<!--BEGIN MAIN LIST-->
<OL type=A>

<LI>Safety Considerations
<OL type=1>
  <LI>Body substance isolation
```

*continues*

9

**Listing 9.6. continued**

```
  <LI>Scene safety
  <LI>Initial size-up
</OL>

<LI>Initial Patient Assessment
<OL type=1>
  <LI>General Impression
  <LI>Unresponsiveness
  <OL type=i>
    <LI>Alert to person, place and time
    <LI>Verbal response to audible stimuli
    <LI>Pain evokes verbal or physical response
    <LI>Unresponsive to all stimuli
  </OL>
</OL>

<LI>Patient Critical Needs
<OL type=1>
  <LI>Airway
  <LI>Breathing
  <OL type=i>
    <LI>Use oxygen if indicated
    <LI>Consider use of assisting with bag valve mask
  </OL>
  <LI>Circulation
  <LI>Bleeding
</OL>

<!--END MAIN LIST-->
</OL>
</BODY>
</HTML>
```

**FIGURE 9.6.**

*Using the type attribute in conjunction with nested lists results in text formatted into outline form.*

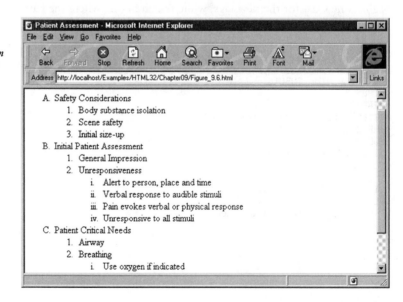

One of the main problems with nesting lists is the confusion they can generate. It's easy to lose track of which list is which and what's subordinate to what after the second or third embedded set of items. Remember that extra leading and trailing spaces are stripped from HTML along with extra carriage returns. Feel free to use extra returns and indenting in conjunction with comment tags to make your page's source code easier to read and edit.

---

**TIP**

If you use type in conjunction with start, be sure to use an integer with start regardless of the type specified.

For example, if you're including an ordered list that uses capital letters and begins at the letter *D*, the opening tag should be <OL type=A start=4>. The browser will translate the starting position into the appropriate letter.

---

Now that you've worked through the various types and variations of an ordered list, it's time to take a look at its half-sister—the unordered list.

# Unordered Lists: <UL>

Unordered lists are typically used to represent a set of items that are somehow related to one another, but don't necessarily need to follow a specific order. The syntax is similar to that of the ordered list:

```
<UL>
<LI>ListItem1
<LI>ListItem2
...
<LI>ListItemN
</UL>
```

*ListItem* is each separate item in the list. See Listing 9.7 for an example.

**Listing 9.7. Use of the unordered list is the same as the ordered list, with the substitution of <UL> for <OL>.**

```
<!DOCTYPE HTML PUBLIC "-//IETF//DTD HTML 3.2//EN">
<HTML>
<HEAD>
<TITLE>Jump Kit Inventory</TITLE>
</HEAD>
<BODY>
EMS Jump Kit Contents
<UL>
<LI>Rescue Scissors and Penlight
<LI>Stethascope and Sphygmanometer
<LI>Oxygen Bottle
<LI>Non-Rebreather Mask and Nasal Cannula
```

*continues*

**Listing 9.7. continued**

```
<LI>Oral and Nasal Airways
<LI>Gauze and Trauma Dressings
<LI>Sterile Saline and Water
<LI>Oral Glucose and Activated Charcoal
</UL>
</BODY>
</HTML>
```

As you can see in Figure 9.7, the unordered list is typically represented the same as an ordered list, except bullets are used instead of numbers.

**FIGURE 9.7.**

*An unordered list is displayed much like an ordered list, but it includes bullets in place of numbers.*

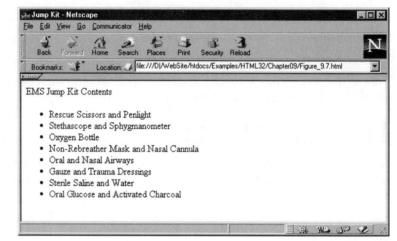

The actual appearance of the bullet varies from browser to browser. Internet Explorer uses small text bullets, and NCSA Mosaic uses a graphical bullet.

Numbering is obviously not an issue for an unordered list. However, HTML 3.2 offers some additional choices for the default bullet appearance with the type attribute.

## What type of Bullet Do You Want?

Three basic types of bullets are supported by HTML 3.2, although not all browsers support all three. If a browser doesn't recognize the attribute, the default bullet representation is used. The syntax for type is

```
<UL type=bulletType>
```

where *bulletType* is one of three values—circle, square, or disc. Their representations are displayed in Figure 9.8.

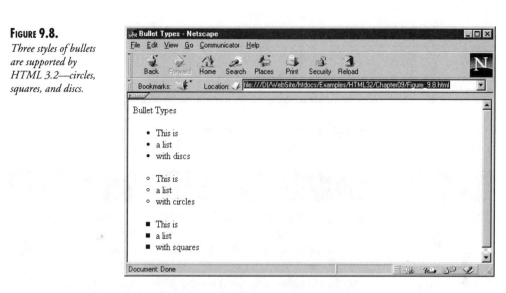

Also like the ordered list, an unordered list can contain other lists within a list. This helps to show relation among items, even though there isn't an underlying hierarchy. It is implemented in the same manner, with another set of list tags replacing a list item. (See Listing 9.8.) The type attribute helps to graphically differentiate the relationships.

**Listing 9.8. Using different types of bullets helps to graphically separate sublists.**

```
<!DOCTYPE HTML PUBLIC "-//IETF//DTD HTML 3.2//EN">
<HTML>
<HEAD>
<TITLE>Jump Kit Inventory</TITLE>
</HEAD>
<BODY>
EMS Jump Kit Contents
<UL>
<LI>Rescue Scissors and Penlight
<LI>Stethoscope and Sphygmanometer

<LI>Airway and Breathing Support
<UL type=square>
<LI>Oxygen Bottle
<LI>Non-Rebreather Mask and Nasal Cannula
<LI>Oral and Nasal Airways
</UL>

<LI>Gauze and Trauma Dressings
<LI>Sterile Saline and Water

<LI>Medications
<UL type=square>
<LI>Oral Glucose
<LI>Activated Charcoal
```

9

USING LISTS TO
ORGANIZE
INFORMATION

*continues*

**Listing 9.8. continued**

```
</UL>
</UL>
</BODY>
</HTML>
```

Notice that the list item preceding the embedded list also serves as a heading for the list. This is an aid to the reader because it identifies how the sublist relates to the main list.

---

**A LITTLE MORE ABOUT LISTS AND ATTRIBUTES**

One additional attribute is allowed for both types of lists, although its implementation in browsers is sparse at best. This is `compact`, which signals the client to try to display the list in the most space-efficient manner possible. Given the other possible variables within a list, most browsers ignore this attribute.

List items are also available for modification beyond their containing list tag. For ordered lists, the optional attributes for `<LI>` are `type` and `value`. The possible values are the same as the corresponding attributes in the `<OL>` tag, with `value` working the same as `start`.

For unordered lists, the lone optional attribute is `type`, with the possible values matching its `<UL>` counterpart.

The actual implementation of `<LI>` attributes varies from browser to browser, so be aware of differences. In Netscape Navigator, for example, setting an `<LI>` attribute in the middle of a list also affects the following list items.

---

# A Definition or Glossary List: <DL>

The last specialty list tag is `<DL>`, which stands for definition list. This tag is used to create a glossary-style listing, which is handy for items such as dictionary listings and Frequently Asked Questions pages.

It is used similarly to the unordered list tag, except that it doesn't use the `<LI>` tag to mark its various entries. This is because a definition list requires two items for every entry—a term and its definition. This is accomplished with the corresponding `<DT>` and `<DD>` tags. The syntax is

```
<DL>
<DT>Term1<DD>Definition1
<DT>Term2<DD>Definition2
...
<DT>TermN<DD>DefinitionN
</DL>
```

where *Term* is the word requiring a definition, and *Definition* is the block of text that serves the purpose. An alternate form of including the tags on the page places each `<DT>` and `<DD>` tag on separate lines, although the first method is a bit clearer in purpose. The browser presents the content in the same fashion, regardless of which way you choose.

Its implementation can vary a bit from browser to browser, but a common implementation is displayed in Figure 9.9.

**FIGURE 9.9.**

*A definition list is formatted slightly differently from other lists, with a series of hanging indents to separate terms from definitions.*

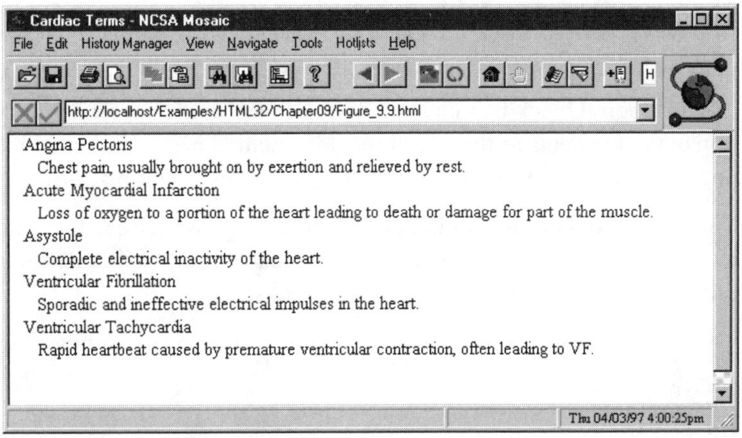

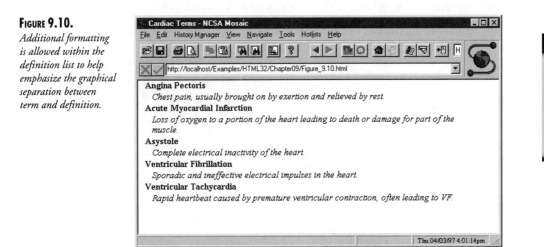

Like the other list tags and styles, it's also possible to include additional physical formatting tags within the terms or definitions.

```
<DT><B>Term</B>
<DD><I>Definition</I>
```

A popular method of implementing the definition list is to provide a bold style to the term, and regular or italics for the definition (as shown in Figure 9.10).

**FIGURE 9.10.**

*Additional formatting is allowed within the definition list to help emphasize the graphical separation between term and definition.*

Neither the `<DT>` nor the `<DD>` tag includes any attributes. Any additional formatting is handled through other tags, such as `<B>` (bold) or `<I>` (italic).

Now that you've seen the major styles for creating and displaying lists, it's time to take a look at the last two styles.

# Using Logical List Styles

HTML offers an additional set of list tags that don't dictate a corresponding physical style. Like the logical block tags illustrated in the preceding chapter, these tags help show the relation of the list items to the rest of the document. Their actual implementation and display is not strictly defined and varies with different browsers and platforms.

The logical list styles are not in as widespread usage as <OL> or <UL>, but you can still use them to make your HTML source code more readable. Each style uses the same <LI> tag to mark each separate item, except for the definition list.

The first two tags are <MENU> and <DIR>, and their syntax is the same as an unordered list.

```
<MENU> <!-- or DIR -->
<LI>ListItem1
<LI>ListItem2
<LI>ListItemN
</MENU> <!-- or /DIR -->
```

Neither item has any attributes, other than the often ignored compact. The first tag, <MENU>, represents a list of choices, such as those used with submitting a form or selecting a response to a question. It is typically rendered the same as an unordered list.

HTML standards from the World Wide Web Consortium recommend a multicolumn directory list rendering for the <DIR> tag. None of the graphics-based browsers follow this advice, and instead use the standard <UL> implementation.

The representation of both items, compared to an unordered list, is shown in Figure 9.11.

**FIGURE 9.11.**

*Although slightly different typefaces are used in Mosaic, the basic representation of a menu and directory list is still an unordered list.*

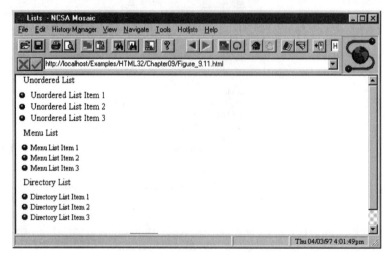

# Summary

Two main categories of lists are used with HTML. First is an ordered list, which can be used with its attributes to create a variety of formats for your information. Second is the unordered list, with its options for displaying unprioritized information.

Also in this grab bag of display items are the definitions. These are unique in that they don't require a list item tag, but rather use a pair of tags to delineate the term from the definition.

Two additional tags, now virtually obsolete but still part of the standard, are for menus and directory listings. Their preferred implementation is ignored by the vast majority of browsers, which tend to represent the two as simple unordered lists.

The next chapter, "Creating Tables for Data and Page Layout," adds another option for displaying text. Together with the text formatting tags in the preceding chapter and the various types of lists in this chapter, you're developing quite an arsenal to get your point across with HTML 3.2.

# Creating Tables for Data and Page Layout

*by Rick Darnell*

## IN THIS CHAPTER

CHAPTER 10

Tables are kind of like lists. We're introduced to them at an early age through the mirth of games such as tic-tac-toe and checkers. Later in life, someone forces us to use a spreadsheet, and suddenly tables are not so fun anymore—unless you're one of those folks who also enjoys things like actuarial tables relating sedentary lifestyles to colon polyps.

HTML tables have established themselves as one of the most used and powerful tools in formatting Web pages. Tables were originally introduced to facilitate formatting of tabular data, such as spreadsheet and database information.

Using a little creative thought, Web designers have implemented table tags and their various attributes to allow a variety of uses not directly supported by HTML, including formatting text into multiple columns and hanging indents. As you begin to explore the nuances of the various table tags and their attributes, you'll probably begin to see additional applications.

On the downside, table tags are also some of the most complicated to understand and use. In the linear space of a page of HTML coding, you must define a two-dimensional form. It's hard to keep track of which row belongs to which information, and how a particular cell will look in its final form. A table-enabled browser is crucial if you're not using a visual HTML editor.

With that preamble and warning out of the way, it's time to get out the angle iron, nuts, and bolts to build the basic frame for your new vehicle.

# Setting the Basic Constraints with <TABLE>

Like other block elements illustrated in earlier chapters, a table is marked at its beginning and end. The <TABLE> tag is used to fit this basic purpose. The syntax is as follows:

```
<TABLE attributes>
<CAPTION align=top¦bottom>captionText</CAPTION>
<TR attributes>
<TH>TableHeading</TH>
<TD>Cell1</TD>
<TD>Cell2</TD>
...
<TD>CellN</TD>
</TR>
...additional rows as needed...
</TABLE>
```

Each of the tags within the table is explained in this chapter, but here's a quick look at how each one relates to the whole:

- <TABLE> marks the beginning and end of a single table.
- <CAPTION> is an optional tag providing an attached caption for the table on the top or bottom.
- <TR> marks the beginning of a new row in the table.
- <TH> formats text as a heading in the affected row.
- <TD> defines the contents of a single cell within the table.

Following the sequence of tags, you can see that a table is constructed the same way a brick wall is made. Each row begins with a layer of cement (<TR>) and then adding bricks (<TD>) until the row is completed. Then, a new course is added until the wall is finished and capped (</TABLE>).

Now that the basic structure of a table has been explained, the next section looks at the basic attributes of <TABLE> for setting its overall appearance, both within the table itself and in relation to the browser window.

## The Table in the Browser: `align` and `width`

The first two attributes for <TABLE>—align and width—control how the table relates to surrounding text and other elements when displayed on the browser.

The syntax is

```
<TABLE align=left¦center¦right width=pixels¦percent%>
```

where align is the table's horizontal alignment on the page and width is the width of the table expressed in pixels or as a percentage of the browser window.

Let's take a look at align first. When this attribute is not included, the table defaults to the whims of the browser. Typically, this is flush with the left border, and surrounding text is interrupted by its presence. (See Figure 10.1.)

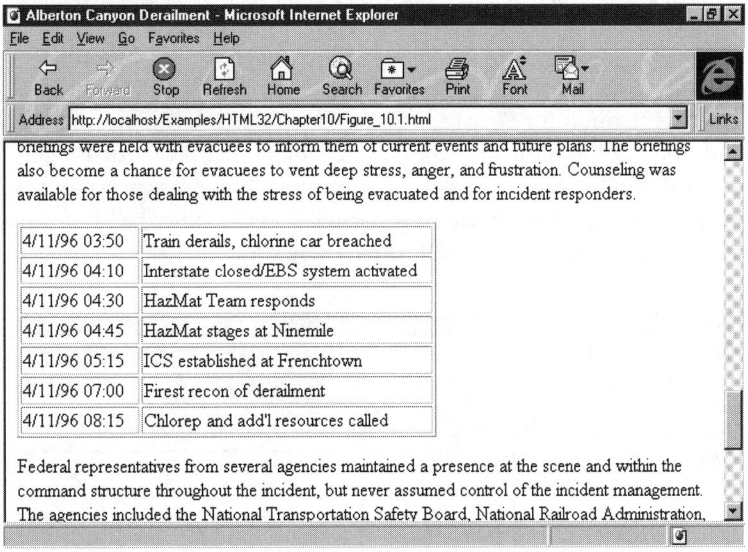

**FIGURE 10.1.**

*The default alignment for a table breaks text before the table and continues it afterward, keeping the table flush against the left margin.*

Using the values for the align attribute forces the table to one side of the browser window or the other, and the text now wraps around the outside border. (See Figure 10.2.)

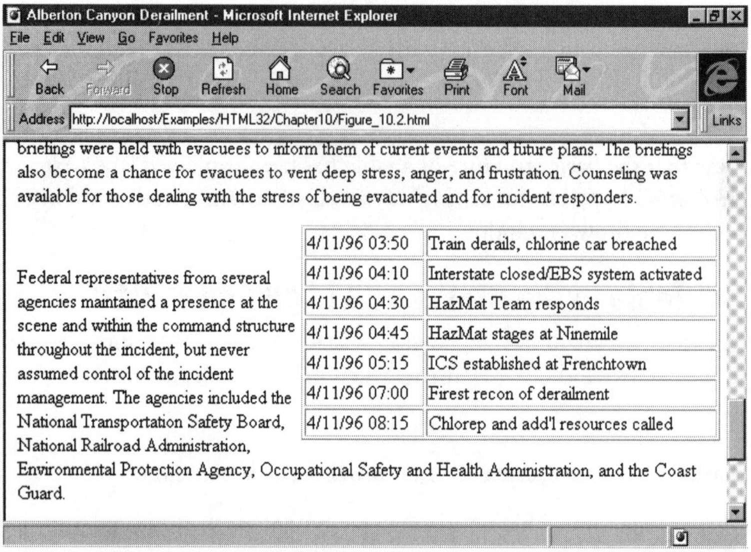
Alberton Canyon Derailment - Microsoft Internet Explorer
File Edit View Go Favorites Help
Back Forward Stop Refresh Home Search Favorites Print Font Mail
Address http://localhost/Examples/HTML32/Chapter10/Figure_10.2.html
Links
briefings were held with evacuees to inform them of current events and future plans. The briefings also become a chance for evacuees to vent deep stress, anger, and frustration. Counseling was available for those dealing with the stress of being evacuated and for incident responders.
Federal representatives from several agencies maintained a presence at the scene and within the command structure throughout the incident, but never assumed control of the incident management. The agencies included the National Transportation Safety Board, National Railroad Administration, Environmental Protection Agency, Occupational Safety and Health Administration, and the Coast Guard.
4/11/96 03:50 Train derails, chlorine car breached
4/11/96 04:10 Interstate closed/EBS system activated
4/11/96 04:30 HazMat Team responds
4/11/96 04:45 HazMat stages at Ninemile
4/11/96 05:15 ICS established at Frenchtown
4/11/96 07:00 Firest recon of derailment
4/11/96 08:15 Chlorep and add'l resources called

**FIGURE 10.2.**
*Adding* `align=right` *to the* `<TABLE>` *tag results in the table being forced flush right with the text flowing around the outside border.*

**TIP**

Although `center` is included as an option for the `align` attribute, it is not currently supported by any of the popular browsers. Using `align=center` results in a table that receives the browser's default treatment.

The next attribute for `<TABLE>` is `width`, which controls how much horizontal space is occupied in the browser window. By default, just enough space is allotted to display the widest value in each column. (See Figure 10.3.) For example, if the largest value in each column is a small integer, the table will be relatively narrow. On the other hand, if several columns have large obfuscated words, the table will be relatively wide.

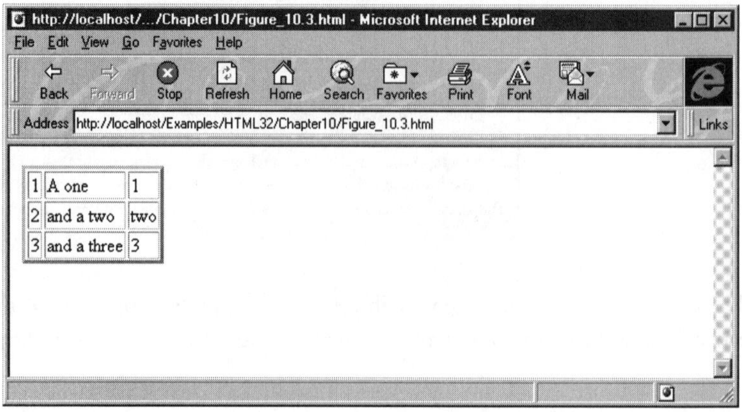
http://localhost/.../Chapter10/Figure_10.3.html - Microsoft Internet Explorer
File Edit View Go Favorites Help
Back Forward Stop Refresh Home Search Favorites Print Font Mail
Address http://localhost/Examples/HTML32/Chapter10/Figure_10.3.html
Links
1 A one 1
2 and a two two
3 and a three 3

**FIGURE 10.3.**
*The default width for a table is just enough space to display its contents. Each column is sized to accommodate the widest element in the column.*

The width attribute helps to remove some of the guesswork about just how wide a table should be. It can accept values in two measurements—pixels or a percentage of window space. To specify pixels, use a single integer. To indicate a percentage of the browser window, use a single integer followed by a percentage sign.

> ### TIP
>
> If the table contains graphics, go with pixels. This forces the table to be wide enough to contain your images. Otherwise, select the percentage value for compatibility with a wide range of user displays.

The main difference between the two forms of measurement is how they're treated when the browser window is resized. If a table is set to 400 pixels wide, it remains 400 pixels wide, whether the browser is full-screen or occupies only a narrow strip on the left side. (See Figure 10.4.)

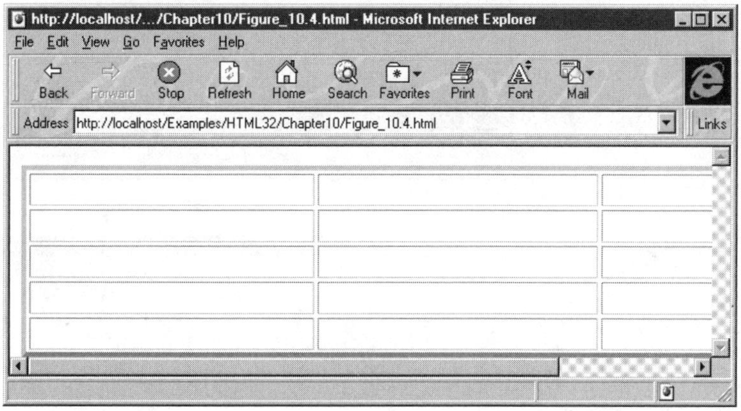

**FIGURE 10.4.**

*Setting a physical width in pixels results in a constant table width, regardless of browser window size.*

On the other hand, if a table is set to 100 percent of the browser window, its physical width will vary depending on the size of the browser window. (See Figures 10.5 and 10.6.) This ensures compatibility across different screens (VGA or SVGA) and browsers.

> ### NOTE
>
> Which measuring system should you use with your table? That's a hard call to make for Web authors because they have no control over the user's viewing environment, such as monitor resolution, color compatibility, browser window size, or whether the browser can handle tables at all. Make the best guess you can about the capabilities of your users, and

*continues*

10

CREATING TABLES
FOR DATA AND
PAGE LAYOUT

*continued*

tailor your system to fit those folks. You might also need to find a way to present the information in a nontabular format for those with less-endowed browsers.

The bottom line in all of this is one simple fact: Someone will be left out, and there's nothing you can do about it. So be as accommodating as you can, and don't lose too much sleep over those who can't see what you've done.

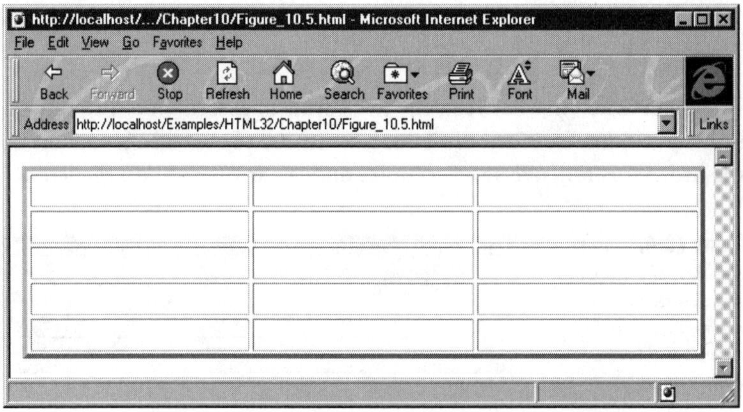

**FIGURE 10.5.**

*This table is set to 100 percent of the width of the browser window. See what happens when the window is resized in Figure 10.6.*

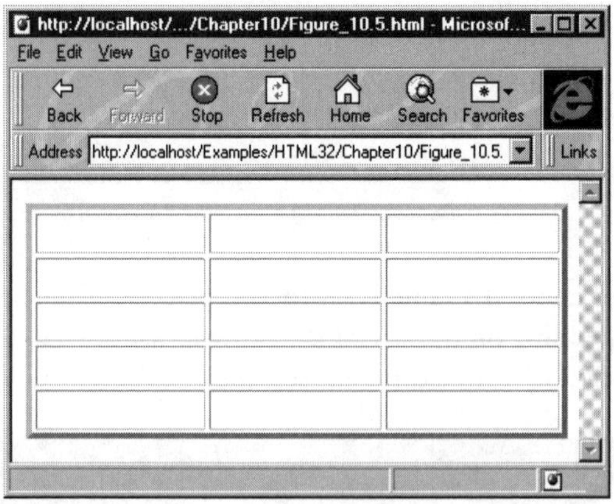

**FIGURE 10.6.**

*The table still fills the browser window, without spilling over. It is automatically resized to fit 100 percent of the new window's size.*

# General Table Appearances: border, cellspacing, cellpadding

The next set of attributes control how the table itself looks by setting the width of the outside border (border), the width of the border between cells (cellspacing), and the space between cell contents and corresponding borders (cellpadding) The syntax is

```
<TABLE border=size cellspacing=size cellpadding=size>
```

where size is a value in pixels. If an attribute is omitted, the typical defaults are no border, two pixels for cell spacing, and one for cell padding. This may vary slightly, depending on the browser.

> **NOTE**
>
> The user has a say in the matter, too.
>
> Many browsers have additional settings through preference dialogs that allow users to control the appearance of tables. Usually, this is limited to whether a table is displayed using one-dimensional lines or with the appearance of beveling and shading.
>
> Keep in mind that your tightly formatted table might not appear exactly as you expect, depending on the software preferred by the end user.

Many people confuse the purposes of the cellspacing and cellpadding attributes. If it helps to relieve the confusion, think about creating more space between inmates in padded cells, or some other equally innocuous illustration that makes it easier to imagine the spaces associated with each cell. For the purposes of illustration, I've included some examples in Figure 10.7.

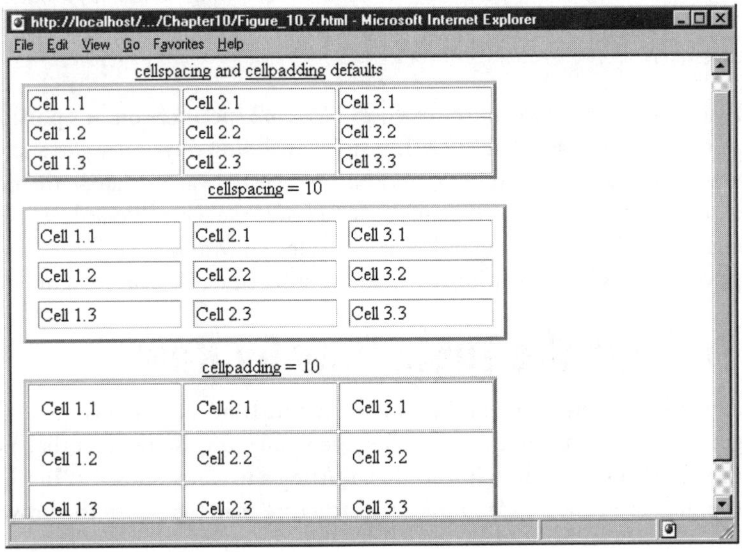

**FIGURE 10.7.**

*Three variations for a table include a version with default values, one with increased cell spacing, and another with increased cell padding.*

**NOTE**

Although not included in the HTML 3.2 specification, some browsers also support a bordercolor attribute to the <Table> tag. It takes a value of a recognized color literal (white, black, blue, and so on) or a hexadecimal color triplet preceded by #.

It's just one more control to further fine-tune the appearance of your Web pages and their contents, because the software manufacturers care so much about you.

## <CAPTION>

You can add a brief description for your table by adding a <CAPTION> tag immediately following the opening <TABLE> tag.

The <CAPTION> tag is to the table what the <TITLE> tag is to the <HEAD> of the document, except you can specify whether the caption appears on the top or bottom of the table. The syntax is

```
<TABLE>
<CAPTION align=top¦bottom>CaptionText</CAPTION>
...table elements...
</TABLE>
```

where *CaptionText* is the description for the text, and the align attribute indicates whether the caption is attached to the top or bottom of the table. The default placement for a caption if the align attribute is not used is at the top.

**TIP**

The three tables in Figure 10.7 all used a top caption to identify what each one was showing.

Although not recommended by the HTML 3.2 specification, it's possible to format a caption in the same way as other HTML text by including physical styles such as bold and italic, or using the <FONT> tag and its attributes. There is no way to change the horizontal alignment of a caption; the text always remains centered over the table. Block-level tags, such as the heading tags and logical formatting styles, are not allowed within a caption. More information on using physical styles for formatting text is found in Chapter 8, "Text Alignment and Formatting."

# Building the Table Row by Row

After the basic attributes of the table are defined and a caption is added (if desired), it's time to get down to the nitty-gritty of adding each table row. Remember that a table is built by marking a row, adding cells to it, and then starting a new row under it. In this way, the structure of the table in HTML code mimics the structure as it appears in the browser window.

# Where the Row Starts: <TR>

The beginning of a row is marked using the <TR> tag with this syntax:

```
<TABLE>
<TR align=left¦center¦right valign=top¦middle¦bottom>
<TD>Cell1.1<TD>Cell2.1<TD>Cell3.1

<TR align=left¦center¦right valign=top¦middle¦bottom>
<TD>Cell1.2<TD>Cell2.2<TD>Cell3.2

...Additional rows and cells...

<TR align=left¦center¦right valign=top¦middle¦bottom>
<TD>Cell1.N<TD>Cell2.N<TD>Cell3.N
</TABLE>
```

In this syntax, <TR> is the beginning of a row of cell definitions. The <TR> tag doesn't require a closing tag, although you can use one to help make the boundaries of each row easier to identify.

There are two attributes for <TR> that set the default behavior for all cells in that row. Individual cells can override the values of <TR>.

The first attribute is align. This is similar to the align in the <TABLE> tag, but it is limited to controlling the horizontal alignment of the material in cells. The available values are left (default), right, or center. Figure 10.8 shows a table with these three options.

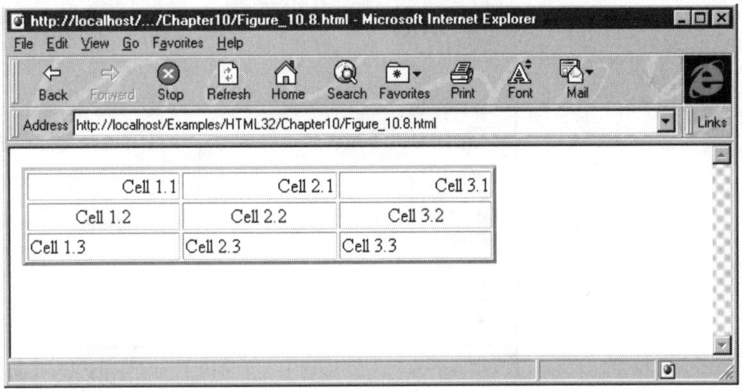

**FIGURE 10.8.**

*This table has three rows, with each one set to a different horizontal alignment with the* <TR align> *attribute.*

The next attribute, valign, controls the vertical placement of content in the cells. The default for most browsers is middle. As with most defaults, this isn't always the most aesthetically pleasing. (See Figure 10.9.)

As a general rule, rows should be set to valign=top. This is the way most people expect their tables to look. (See Figure 10.10.)

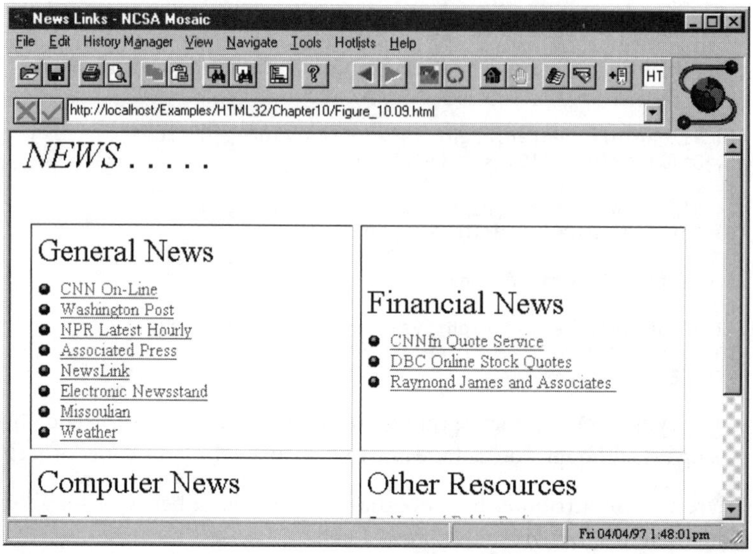

FIGURE 10.9.

*The default vertical alignment for a table places content in the middle of the cell. With differing content length in adjoining cells, the visual result isn't always appealing.*

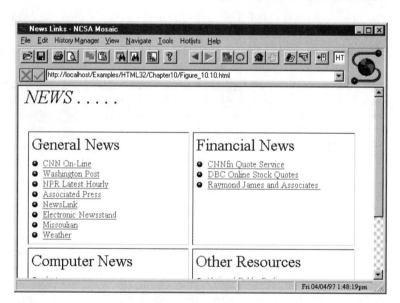

FIGURE 10.10.

*This is the same table displayed in the preceding figure with the* valign *attribute set to* top *in the* <TR> *tag.*

# Defining Table Cells

With the beginning of the row marked with <TR>, it's time to finally get down to the work of filling each cell. Two types of cell tags are used in a table. The first, <TH>, marks a header cell, which is similar to a heading tag on a Web page. The other is a data cell tag, <TD>, used for the body of the table.

## Header Cells: <TH>

A table header cell is much like any other table cell. Most browsers include a different font style for header cells to help reinforce their purpose to the user. (See Figure 10.11.)

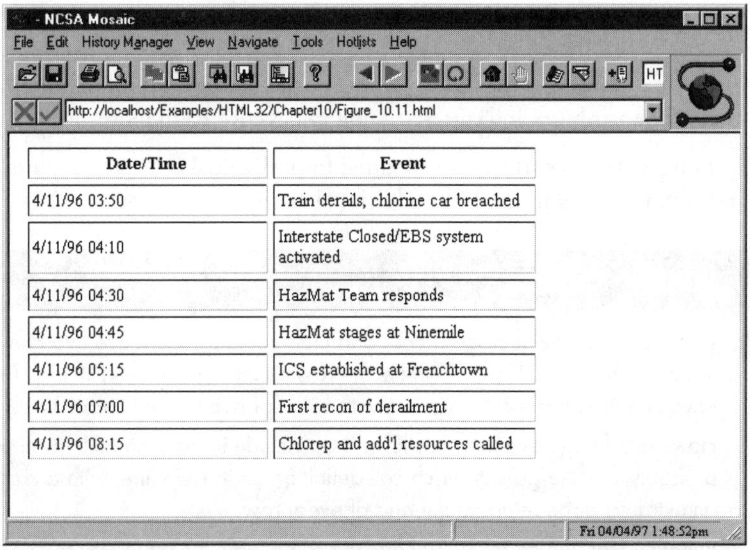

**FIGURE 10.11.**

*The first row in this table is defined using the <TH> tag, and the second uses the <TD> tag. The browser emphasizes the first row to show its status as a header.*

---

### TIP

Header cells are a logical definition, not a physical one. Interpretation of the <TH> tag is left up to the browser, and it varies across platforms and applications.

---

The syntax for <TH> is

```
<TABLE>
<TR><TH attributes>Cell Header
</TABLE>
```

where *Cell Header* is the header content of the cell, and *attributes* is blank or includes one or more of the attributes and its corresponding value. The various attributes are covered in detail in the next section.

Each header cell needs an opening tag, although a closing tag is not required. The cell can be placed at any point in the table, including mixed in on the same row with <TD> tags. A header cell has the same attributes as a content cell; content cells are covered in the following section on the table data tag.

## Table Data Cells: <TD>

It's taken a little time to get here, but after the table framework is in place, you can begin adding each brick of content. The syntax for <TD> is

```
<TABLE>
<TR><TD attributes>Cell Content
</TABLE>
```

where `Cell Content` is the actual content of the cell, and `attributes` is blank or includes one or more of the attributes and corresponding values covered in more detail in the following sections.

A closing </TD> or </TH> is not required for individual cells, although many HTML designers and editing programs use it for additional clarity.

> **NOTE**
>
> Depending on the number of cells and their contents, there are two conventions for <TD> tag placement. The first is on the same row as the container <TR> tag. This means you'll have one line of HTML beginning with <TR> for every row in your document.
>
> However, if you have many cells, or they include items such as hyperlinks or images, you'll probably want to go with each cell definition on its own line, with a closing </TR> tag and an extra carriage return at the end of every row.
>
> In both cases, the code will behave the same way. It's up to you to choose a format that helps to clarify the code for future editing and revision.

When considering formatting options for each cell, think of the <TD> and <TH> tags as <BODY> tags. Any tag valid for the body of an HTML document is valid within a cell. This means you can embed text, graphics, forms, plug-ins and objects, applets, and even other tables. This feature is what gives tables their power when used to format a page.

The attributes for table cells are divided into two broad categories—those that affect the cell's size, and those that affect the cell's contents.

## Cell Size Attributes: width, height, rowspan, and colspan

The first set of attributes set the size of a cell, including its capability to merge with an adjacent cell.

The syntax for the first two attributes is

```
<TD width=pixels¦percentage height=pixels>
```

where width is an integer representing a physical distance in pixels, or a portion of the overall table width followed by a percentage sign (%). The height of a cell is defined in pixels.

The default value for width is just wide enough to accommodate the cell's contents or the widest corresponding cell in the same position in another row.

The height attribute sets the height of a cell in pixels. The default value is just tall enough to contain the longest content in the current row. For example, if the row included a cell with one sentence and another cell with several paragraphs, both cells would be tall enough to accommodate the paragraphs. This of course leaves a great deal of white space in the cell with the single sentence.

The next two attributes—rowspan and colspan—are used to combine adjacent cells into larger cells. It's important to note that when you are using these attributes, the adjacent cells aren't eliminated; they're just "hidden" while the acquiring cell uses their space. The syntax is

```
<TD rowspan=numRows colspan=numCols >
```

where *numRows* is the number of rows, including the current cell, joined together. Likewise, *numCols* is the number of columns joined together. The default for both values is 1.

Spanning is a little tricky to plan and implement. For example, start with a 3×3 table. This requires three rows with three cells each. (See Listing 10.1.)

**Listing 10.1. Basic HTML for displaying a 3×3 table.**

```
<HTML>
<HEAD>
 <META HTTP-EQUIV="Content-Type" CONTENT="text/html">
</HEAD>
<BODY>
<TABLE border=3 width=75%>
 <TR> <TD>Cell 1.1   <TD>Cell 1.2   <TD>Cell 1.3
 <TR> <TD>Cell 2.1   <TD>Cell 2.2   <TD>Cell 2.3
 <TR> <TD>Cell 3.1   <TD>Cell 3.2   <TD>Cell 3.3
</TABLE>
</BODY>
</HTML>
```

Now you can begin merging cells by combining Cells 1.1 and 1.2. Because this reaches across columns, it's a column span. (See Listing 10.2 and Figure 10.12.) To do this, colspan=2 is added as an attribute to the table data tag for Cell 1.1.

**Listing 10.2. A column span across Cells 1.1 and 1.2 results in the addition of the colspan attribute.**

```
<HTML>
<HEAD>
 <META HTTP-EQUIV="Content-Type" CONTENT="text/html">
</HEAD>
<BODY>
<TABLE border=3 width=75%>
 <TR> <TD colspan=2>Cell 1.1   <TD>Cell 1.2   <TD>Cell 1.3
 <TR> <TD>Cell 2.1            <TD>Cell 2.2   <TD>Cell 2.3
 <TR> <TD>Cell 3.1            <TD>Cell 3.2   <TD>Cell 3.3
</TABLE>
</BODY>
</HTML>
```

**FIGURE 10.12.**

*The revised table with a column span. Notice what's happened with the bottom two rows of cells.*

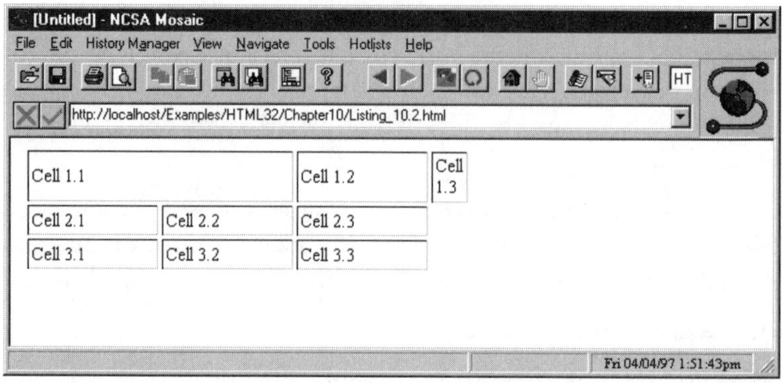

As you see in Figure 10.12, spanning cells isn't quite as simple as just adding the span attributes. Here's what happened. When the browser encountered `colspan=2`, it knew Cell 1.1 needed to take up the space of two cells, and it provided the space accordingly. Then, it continued across the row and finished adding the next two cells. The result was space for a total of four cells (two joined and two individuals).

At the next row tag, the browser started a new row by adding three cells. The browser didn't encounter a fourth `<TD>` tag, even though there was room in the table for one. Instead of adding a cell that the user didn't specify, it simply filled in with blank space. The final appearance was a 3×4 table with the bottom two rows only partially defined.

This feature of cell spanning is the cause for a great many headaches when you are working with tables. For each cell you span, you need to remove the corresponding cell definition. (See Listing 10.3 and Figure 10.13.)

**Listing 10.3. A column span across Cells 1.1 and 1.2 requires the addition of the `colspan` attribute and removal of the adjoining tag.**

```
<HTML>
<HEAD>
 <META HTTP-EQUIV="Content-Type" CONTENT="text/html">
</HEAD>
<BODY>
<TABLE border=3 width=75%>
 <TR> <TD colspan=2>Cell 1.1          <TD>Cell 1.3
 <TR> <TD>Cell 2.1        <TD>Cell 2.2  <TD>Cell 2.3
 <TR> <TD>Cell 3.1        <TD>Cell 3.2  <TD>Cell 3.3
</TABLE>
</BODY>
</HTML>
```

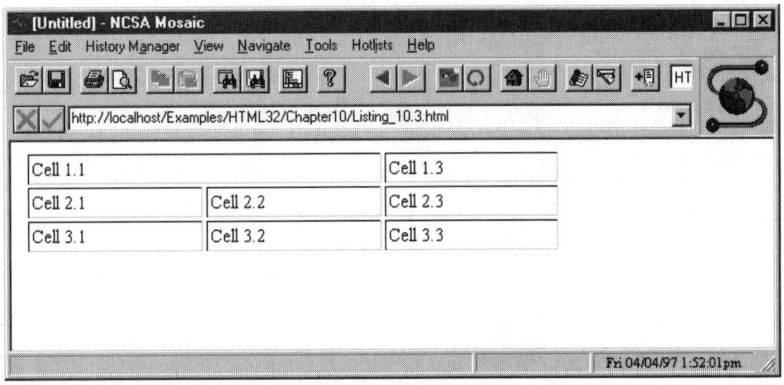

**FIGURE 10.13.**
*With the adjoining
data cell removed, the
table retains its original
3×3 appearance.*

---

**TIP**

It might be a bit awkward to edit tables in the graphical manner displayed in Listings 10.2 and 10.3, but it's very useful for determining which cells should be removed for spanning.

---

The same rules also apply for the rowspan attribute, except cells below the originating tag should be removed. It's also possible to combine the two attributes for other effects. (See Listing 10.4 and Figure 10.14.)

**Listing 10.4. Using the same basic table, the first cell is combined with the next row and next column. The result requires removing three adjoining cell tags.**

```
<HTML>
<HEAD>
 <META HTTP-EQUIV="Content-Type" CONTENT="text/html">
</HEAD>
<BODY>
<TABLE border=3 width=75%>
 <TR> <TD colspan=2 rowspan=2>Cell 1.1              <TD>Cell 1.3
 <TR>                                                <TD>Cell 2.3
 <TR> <TD>Cell 3.1                   <TD>Cell 3.2  <TD>Cell 3.3
</TABLE>
</BODY>
</HTML>
```

When spanning in two directions at once, you need to delete all the data cells in the path of the merge. This means removing cells from the right, left, and diagonal directions.

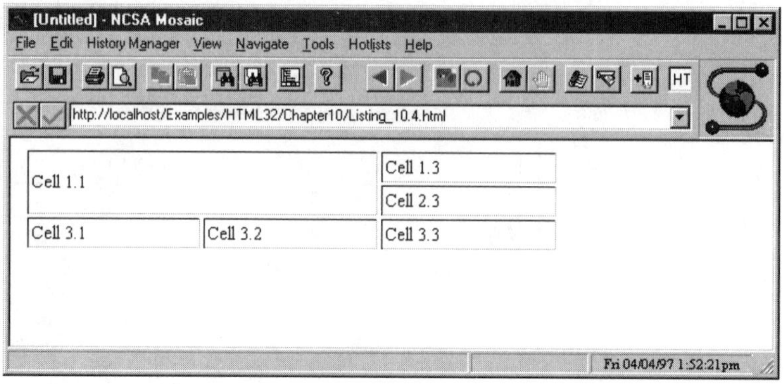

**FIGURE 10.14.**

*There are now four adjoining data cells, which have been combined into one large cell. Still, the table retains its original 3×3 appearance.*

## Cell Content Attributes: `align`, `valign`, and `nowrap`

The next group of attributes control how text and other content is placed within the cell. The syntax for these attributes is

```
<TD align=left¦center¦right valign=top¦middle¦bottom nowrap>
```

where `align` controls horizontal justification, `valign` controls the vertical justification, and `nowrap` forces text content within the cell to remain on one line.

The values and behavior for `align` and `valign` are the same as the `<TR>` tag, and they override its values for the current cell only.

The presence of the last attribute, `nowrap`, disables automatic word wrap within the cell's borders depending on other table settings, such as fixed or proportional width of a cell or the entire table. This is equivalent to using the ` ` character entity for inserting nonbreaking spaces within the content of the cell.

If the table doesn't have a specified width, the affected cell expands horizontally to accommodate the text. The same is true if the table width is specified as a percentage of the browser window, and the table's width will expand to accommodate the larger cell.

If the table `width` is set in pixels, the cell will expand to the pixel width, leaving the absolute minimum space necessary for other columns that don't have a `width` setting in pixels. If that's not enough space, the browser starts to insert line breaks as needed.

In short, if the `nowrap` attribute is used in conjunction with any `width` settings specified in pixels, the `width` settings have priority, and line wrapping is reinstated.

> **TIP**
>
> A similar effect is accomplished by omitting nowrap and using nonbreaking spaces ( ) between words that should remain together on the same line. This enables you to keep certain words together and allow the others to flow to a new line as needed.

## Whose Default Overrides Whose?

As you've seen in the tags leading to the actual cell data tag, there have been several opportunities to influence the width of a cell. So whose attribute takes precedence?

As a general rule, the last attribute encountered sets the standard for the rest of the table, although this is not always the case. Consider the following table definition:

```
<TABLE width=400>
<CAPTION>Table width=400, Cell width=500</CAPTION>
<TR><TD width=200>200 pixel-wide cell <TD width=300>300 pixel-wide cell
</TABLE>
```

In its definition, the table is set to 400 pixels wide. However, in the first two data cell definitions, the width is forced to 500 pixels. What happens? The `<TABLE>` tag takes control in this situation, with an interesting result. (See Figure 10.15.)

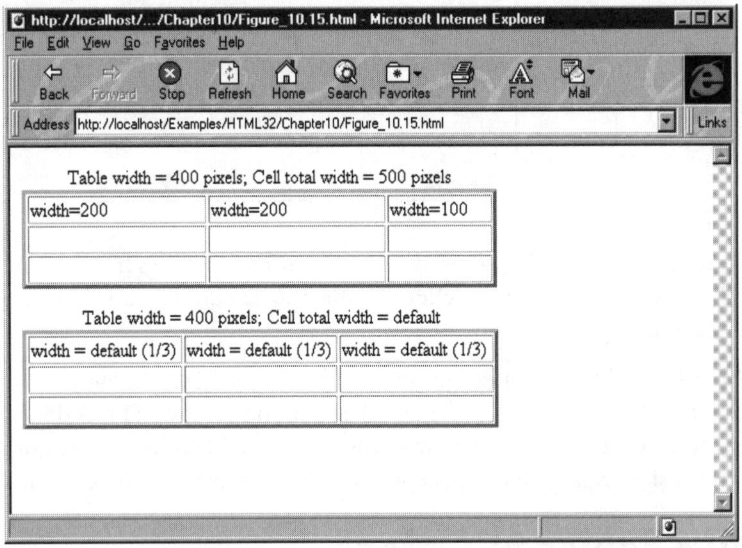

**FIGURE 10.15.**

*Compare these two tables. The first one is set to 400 pixels wide, although the data cells have width settings that add up to 500 pixels. The second table is the same as the first, without width settings for the data cells.*

Here's what happens. The width setting in the `<Table>` tag sets its physical width, which is cast in stone. When the browser encounters the data cells with their width attributes, it looks at the total pixels requested for the row. Because the value is greater than allowed, the browser does a little math and divides space between the two cells in the same proportion as their width attributes.

Now, look at another example, this time involving text alignment:

```
<TABLE>
<CAPTION>Align=right Valign=bottom</CAPTION>
<TR align=right valign=bottom>
  <TD height=50>Cell 1 (TR default)
  <TD align=left>Cell 2 (align=left)
  <TD valign=top>Cell 3 (valign=top)
</TABLE>
```

The height attribute is used to exaggerate the cell size for a better view of vertical alignment. The first cell in the table accepts the defaults from the <TR> tag. Cell 2 overrides the horizontal alignment and forces the text to the left, while Cell 3 overrides the vertical alignment and forces the text to the top. (See Figure 10.16.)

**FIGURE 10.16.**

*Although cell alignment is set to the bottom right, the next two cells each override one of the defaults.*

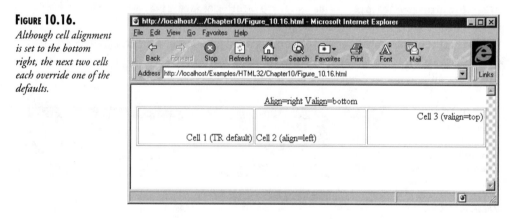

Note that the next cell in a row does not inherit any settings from the preceding cell. Each data cell starts with the defaults defined in the <TR> tag until an attribute is specifically overridden in the <TD> tag.

Alas, the world is full of exceptions to rules. In this case, the height attribute used in the first data cell also sets the height for all other cells in that row. This is done to ensure the integrity of the borders used to outline the cells. If each cell had its own height, the result would be a mishmash of zigzags and stairsteps as a line was drawn around each unique cell.

# Two Tables in Action

Now that you've been through the syntax for tables, it's time to take a look at some practical examples of how tables are used on the World Wide Web.

The exhibit begins with a basic table for displaying tabular data. (See Figure 10.17.) In this case, it's a list of events for a single user generated from a database with a CGI script. Although this wasn't a human-generated page, the table formatting follows the HTML standard. (See Listing 10.5.)

**FIGURE 10.17.**
*This page demonstrates one of the more traditional uses of a table—the display of raw data in table form.*

**Listing 10.5. This HTML page was generated by a CGI script and includes a table for displaying tabular information.**

```
<HTML>
<HEAD>
<!-- This page was generated by Macromedia's Backstage Object Server. -->
<META HTTP-EQUIV="Content-Type" CONTENT="text/html">
<TITLE></TITLE>
<BASE HREF="http://localhost/IncidentLog/">
</HEAD>
<BODY>
<H1><FONT FACE="Garamond" COLOR="Red">Volunteer Time Record</FONT></H1>
<TABLE BORDER="0" WIDTH="75%" CELLSPACING="0" CELLPADDING="0">
<CAPTION ALIGN="TOP"><B><I>Prepared for the
  month of February 1997</I></B></CAPTION>
<TR ALIGN="CENTER" VALIGN="CENTER">
  <TD WIDTH="50%" NOWRAP="NOWRAP"><B>Firefighter ID: 294</B></TD>
  <TD WIDTH="50%" NOWRAP="NOWRAP"><B>Report Date: 11-Mar-97</B></TD>
</TR>
</TABLE>
<B>F</B>=<I>Fire</I>  
<B>E</B>=<I>Emergency Medical</I>  
<B>H</B>=<I>HazMat</I>  
<B>T</B>=<I>Training</I>
<HR>
<TABLE BORDER>
```

10

CREATING TABLES
FOR DATA AND
PAGE LAYOUT

*continues*

**Listing 10.5. continued**

```
<TR>
  <TH>Incident Date
  <TH>Incident Time
  <TH>Incident Type
<TR>
  <TD ALIGN=LEFT>Feb 01, 1997
  <TD ALIGN=LEFT>09:00
  <TD ALIGN=LEFT>T
<TR>
  <TD ALIGN=LEFT>Feb 01, 1997
  <TD ALIGN=LEFT>22:00
  <TD ALIGN=LEFT>E
<TR>
  <TD ALIGN=LEFT>Feb 03, 1997
  <TD ALIGN=LEFT>19:00
  <TD ALIGN=LEFT>T
<TR>
  <TD ALIGN=LEFT>Feb 05, 1997
  <TD ALIGN=LEFT>19:00
  <TD ALIGN=LEFT>T
<TR>
  <TD ALIGN=LEFT>Feb 06, 1997
  <TD ALIGN=LEFT>15:10
  <TD ALIGN=LEFT>F
<TR>
  <TD ALIGN=LEFT>Feb 10, 1997
  <TD ALIGN=LEFT>19:00
  <TD ALIGN=LEFT>T
<TR>
  <TD ALIGN=LEFT>Feb 12, 1997
  <TD ALIGN=LEFT>19:00
  <TD ALIGN=LEFT>T
<TR>
  <TD ALIGN=LEFT>Feb 14, 1997
  <TD ALIGN=LEFT>18:00
  <TD ALIGN=LEFT>T
<TR>
  <TD ALIGN=LEFT>Feb 15, 1997
  <TD ALIGN=LEFT>09:00
  <TD ALIGN=LEFT>T
<TR>
  <TD ALIGN=LEFT>Feb 17, 1997
  <TD ALIGN=LEFT>12:30
  <TD ALIGN=LEFT>E
</TABLE>
<HR>
<P> </P><P> </P>
</BODY>
</HTML>
```

In addition to displaying the date, notice the use of the table header tag, <TH>, in the first row to identify the contents of each column. Other than alignment, no other text formatting is used in any of the cells; the difference between the <TH> and <TD> cells comes entirely from the browser's interpretation of each.

The next example is one developed to display information in a slightly different column format. It consists of a simple 2×2 table that includes a hanging headline in the left column and the corresponding story in the right column. (See Figure 10.18 and Listing 10.6.) The headlines are set with `valign` to the top of the cell so that they always appear at the beginning of the story, regardless of story length. The length of the text in the adjoining cell becomes irrelevant because it automatically grows to whatever is required.

No border is displayed, making the table's role in the formatting invisible to the user.

**FIGURE 10.18.**

*Although HTML doesn't directly support columns, the use of tables enables an author to create a page with vertical columns and hanging headlines.*

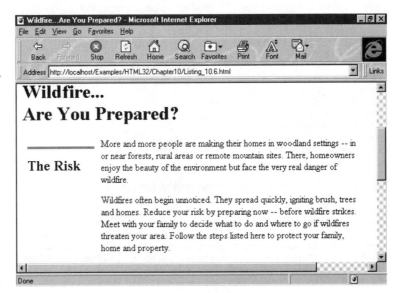

**Listing 10.6. This page uses a table to format two short articles with headlines that "hang" on the left side of the story.**

```
<HTML>
<HEAD>
<META HTTP-EQUIV="Content-Type" CONTENT="text/html; charset=iso-8859-1">
<TITLE>Wildfire...Are You Prepared?</TITLE>
</HEAD>
<BODY>
<IMG SRC="/ClipArt/Graphics/bar2.gif" WIDTH="720" HEIGHT="14">
<H1>
<IMG SRC="/ClipArt/Misc/Fire/fire1.jpg"
  WIDTH="214" HEIGHT="148" ALIGN="ABSMIDDLE" HSPACE="8">
  Wildfire...Are You Prepared?</H1>

<TABLE WIDTH=100% CELLSPACING=4" CELLPADDING=4>

<TR> <!--Begin Row 1-->
<TD VALIGN=TOP WIDTH=20%> <!--Headline 1-->
<HR NOSHADE SIZE=4 ALIGN=LEFT>
```

*continues*

**Listing 10.6. continued**

```
<H2>The Risk</H2>
<TD> <!--Content 1-->
<P>More and more people are making their homes in
woodland settings -- in or near forests, rural
areas or remote mountain sites.  There, homeowners
enjoy the beauty of the environment but face the
very real danger of wildfire.</P>
<P>Wildfires often begin unnoticed.  They spread
quickly, igniting brush, trees and homes.  Reduce
your risk by preparing now -- before wildfire strikes.
Meet with your family to decide what to do and
where to go if wildfires threaten your area. Follow
the steps listed here to protect your family, home
and property.</P>

<TR> <!--Begin Row 2-->
<TD VALIGN="TOP"> <!--Headline 2-->
<HR NOSHADE SIZE="4" ALIGN="LEFT">
<H2>Practice Wildfire Safety</H2>
<TD> <!--Content 2-->
<P>People start most wildfires...find out how you
can promote and practice wildfire safety around
your home and property.</P>
<UL>
<LI>Contact your local fire department, health
department or forestry office for information
on fire laws.
<LI>Make sure that fire vehicles can get to your home.
<LI>Clearly mark all driveway entrances and display your name and address.
<LI>Report hazardous conditions that could cause a wildfire.
<LI>Teach children about fire safety. Keep matches out of reach.
<LI>Post fire emergency telephone numbers.
<LI>Plan several escape routes away from your home -- by car and by foot.
</UL>
<P>Talk to your neighbors about wildfire safety.
Plan how the neighborhood could work together after
a wildfire.  Make a list of your neighbors' skills
such as medical or technical.  Consider how you
could help neighbors who have special needs such as
elderly or disabled persons.  Make plans to take
care of children who may be on their own if parents
can't get home.</P>

</TABLE>
</BODY>
</HTML>
```

# Summary

Tables are a series of nested tags, beginning with the initial <TABLE> tag, descending to the first <TR> tag, and culminating with a series of <TD> tags. Building a table requires the use of a fistful of tags and their associated attributes, but keeping the basic order in mind makes the process easier.

Tables are one of the container classes in HTML that have the most associated tags and attributes, which also makes tables one of the hardest HTML elements to master. However, if you take the time to build up your tables row by row and cell by cell with a clear mind toward your goal, you'll find them to be one of the most powerful and useful tags in the HTML arsenal.

## Summary

# Linking Documents and Images

*by Rick Darnell*

**CHAPTER 11**

What made the World Wide Web such a popular place? Was it the easy-to-remember URLs for finding resources? Was it the site dedicated to the Homemakers for Psychokinesis Society? Was it a million-and-one personal home pages that begin with, "Here are some pictures of my cat?" To be sure, those parts certainly had an effect. But probably the biggest draw to the Web was (and continues to be) the ability to wander around and encounter new things that look interesting.

From a page on astrophysics, it's possible to jump to a page about the moon, and from there to a page on Neil Armstrong, then on to information about Congress, and finally to a company that sells paper shredders. All of this is possible via hypertext—interconnected pages of information embedded with bits of highlighted text called *hyperlinks* to click for navigation. For users, the best thing about hyperlinks is that users don't have to know about how to construct a URL. They simply begin with a home page, a search engine, or a list of bookmarks, and start clicking.

I think it's safe to say at this point that anchors are probably the most important tags on the World Wide Web, and they are in large part the reason for the Web's overwhelming success and the acceptance of hypertext as a way to navigate documents.

## WHAT EXACTLY IS HYPERTEXT?

*Hypertext* refers to a way of preparing and publishing documents that enables readers to follow their own paths through the information. The traditional path through a published document is sequential—beginning at page 1 and continuing through to the end. Hypertext allows the reader to jump around within the document and, often, to completely different documents. This method of working through material is well suited to an electronic format.

There are two basic components to hypertext: nodes and hyperlinks. A *node* is a unit of information, such as a Web page. It is small enough to manage and stand on its own. A *hyperlink* is a navigation tool that enables the reader to jump to a new document; typically, it is embedded in the text. A collection of nodes connected by hyperlinks is known as a *web*. Is this all starting to sound familiar? Moving between nodes on a web is called *browsing*.

For example, suppose you were looking at a page (node) about John Wesley that was talking about his influences and place within the Anglican church. The word "Anglican" could be a path (hyperlink) to another document that specifically talks about the Anglicans and their structure and role in 17th century England.

Hypertext lends itself very well to a variety of applications, including large amounts of information (encyclopedias, dictionaries, and other reference books) and multivolume series (magazines, newsletters, and digests).

Each hyperlink is put in place with a special tag, called an *anchor*. Depending on its attributes, an anchor has two functions. First, as explained, it's a path to another document, part of a document, image, sound, or any other file. Second, an anchor marks a destination in a document that is accessible by using the hyperlink version of the tag elsewhere.

# The Anchor Tag: <A>

An anchor is a special text element that requires an opening and closing tag. If it is used as a hyperlink, there should be something in between, such as text or an image. When used to mark a destination, an anchor can be included with nothing in between. (For more information on using anchors to mark destinations, see "Creating Anchors to Locations Within Documents," later in this chapter.)

The syntax is

```
<A attributes>[HTMLcontent]</A>
```

where `attributes` are one of five choices (`name`, `href`, `rel`, `rev`, or `title`) and `HTMLcontent` is an optional value, which can include text, graphics, or other valid Web page content.

These tags cannot be nested within each other. Other text formatting tags are allowed within anchors, and anchors are allowed within other HTML elements such as tables and headings.

## Picking a Destination with `href`

The first and most often used attribute is `href`, used to create a hyperlink to another document. The syntax is

```
<A href="URL">HTMLcontent</A>
```

where `URL` is an absolute or relative URL to another document or anchor tag within a document, and `HTMLcontent` is the material that appears on the user's browser to click.

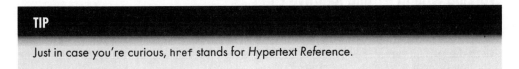

**TIP**

Just in case you're curious, `href` stands for *Hypertext Reference*.

The URL can take several forms, depending on the desired destination. For a location outside the realm of the host server, use a complete URL such as

```
http://www.wossamotta.edu/frostbitefalls/flash.html
```

> **TIP**
>
> Other Internet protocol designations are allowed within `href`, including FTP, Gopher, and Usenet. How these others are handled depends solely on the capability of the user's browser.
>
> As a general rule, most browsers support a wide variety of the most common protocols. All the same, it's a good idea to let users know your intentions before leading them outside the Web into other realms of the Internet.

The appearance of the text between an opening and closing anchor tag with the `href` attribute depends on the link's status, and it varies across browsers and platforms. A general standard has evolved of underlined blue text for unvisited links, although this is not a hard and fast rule. Most browsers allow users to change this setting, and additional attributes of the `<BODY>` tag also permit changing the hyperlink's appearance.

A general color standard for active hyperlinks (the mouse button is clicked on the link, but not yet released) and visited hyperlinks has not been established. For more information on changing the appearance of hyperlink text, see Chapter 7, "Structural Elements and Their Usage," or Chapter 19, "Introducing Cascading Style Sheets."

Nontextual content contained by anchor tags is handled in a slightly different manner. The browser often puts a border around the content with the link color corresponding to the current status. Like other browser features, this feature can be modified within the browser settings or by HTML attributes for the tags that inserted the content.

You can also use the `href` attribute to create hyperlinks to non-HTML content, such as electronic documents and virtual reality pages. For more information on creating these links, see Chapter 13, "Integrating Multimedia and Other File Types."

## Working with `href` and Relative Links

A complete URL is not needed for the `href` attribute to identify a Web page. If the Internet protocol and server address are omitted from the URL, the `href` value is treated as a value relative to the current server. For example, the host server www.wonka.chocolate.com has a home page with the following lines of HTML:

```
<A href="/newproducts/everlasting.gobstopper.html">Perfect Candy</A>
for children with very little pocket money.
```

When clicked by the user, the URL loaded by the browser is

```
www.wonka.chocolate.com/newproducts/everlasting.gobstopper.html
```

The leading slash (`/`) in the `href` value tells the browser to go to the root directory of the current server and build a path to the file from there.

*Linking Documents and Images*

**CHAPTER 11**

225

**11**

LINKING
DOCUMENTS
AND IMAGES

The value of the base URL changes after connecting to the Everlasting Gobstopper page. Suppose that an anchor tag is on the Gobstopper page that looks like this:

```
<A href="fizzy.lifter.drink.html">It's a gas!</A> Look for the newest Wonka soda.
```

Without any other URL information—no server address or path information—the relative link assumes the path from the current page, leading the browser to load the following address:

```
www.wonka.chocolate.com/newproducts/fizzy.lifter.drink.html
```

For a final wrinkle in this whole relative URL business, assume that a new path called /comingsoon/ is created for the Fizzy Lifter Drink under New Products. The anchor tag for the Fizzy Lifter page from the Gobstopper page now looks like this:

```
<A href="newproducts/fizzy.lifter.drink.html">It's a gas!</A>
Look for the newest Wonka soda.
```

What does the browser do with this? The same thing it did when the filename stood on its own: It adds all the current path information from the current document to the front, and uses the result to retrieve the target document. The value of the complete URL is now

```
http://www.wonka.chocolate.com/newproducts/comingsoon/fizzy.lifter.drink.html
```

## The <BASE> Tag Revisited

Back in Chapter 7, you learned a little about the <BASE> tag. This tag is part of the HTML document's head when a new starting point for the relative tag is needed. The syntax is

```
<BASE HREF="protocol://servername/path/">
```

where *protocol* is an Internet communication standard such as HTTP, *servername* is a server name or address such as www.wossamotta.edu or 89.123.32.21, and *path* is any additional mapping on the server. The path is an optional value to the URL. If the path is included by itself, it refers to the host server.

Its use follows the same principles illustrated in the preceding section for relative links. For example, all of the hyperlinks on the Wonka Chocolate Factory home page are relative links. If the Wonka Chocolate Factory received space on the Loompa Land server (www.oompaloompa.lo) to place a copy of the Wonka home page, all the original hyperlinks on the mirrored home page would need to be rewritten because the rest of the site remains at Wonka's server. As it stands, without the <BASE> tag and the page in its new location, the hyperlink

```
<A href="/favorites/wonkabar.html>Our bestselling candy</A>
```

would be interpreted by a browser as http://www.oompaloompa.lo/favorites/wonkabar.html and generate a 404 Not Found error for the user.

To avoid the hassle of rewriting the links, Wonka adds a new line to the <HEAD> of the document, which is placed on the Loompa Land server:

```
<BASE href="http://www.wonka.chocolate.com">
```

Now, all relative links on that page are accessed using Wonka's location instead of Loompa Land. Essentially, by adding one line to the remote Wonka home page, an entire site was mirrored on another server with just one file. Using the preceding example, the link is now interpreted correctly by the browser as

```
http://www.wonka.chocolate.com/favorites/wonkabar.html
```

> **TIP**
>
> The value of <BASE> is ignored by anchor tags when the anchor's href attribute includes a full URL. Remember that a relative link is used only when a server name or path is not used.

## Picking a target Frame

HTML 3.2 brings with it the formal advancement of frames, following the lead of frame implementation in popular browsers such as Netscape Navigator and Microsoft Internet Explorer. Frames allow subdividing of the browser window into separate sections. Each section can load and display a different document independent of the other frames on the page. Its primary use in HTML has been for placing information required for a range of pages, such as a table of contents or advertising. For more information about working with frames, see Chapter 18, "Creating Sophisticated Layouts with Frames and Layers."

As a companion to the frame implementation, the target attribute was added to the anchor tag. This enables you to specify a place other than the current window to load a URL. The syntax is

```
<A href="URL" target="frameName">AnchorText</A>
```

where *URL* is the location of the destination document and *frameName* is the name of the frame that will load the destination document. When the user clicks *AnchorText*, the current frame is unaffected while the destination document is loaded in the target.

This assumes that the target frame has been named as part of the <FRAME> tag. Without using a scripting language, it's impossible to identify individual frames without a unique name.

## Sending E-mail with an Anchor Tag

As you've probably seen on some HTML pages, it's possible to include a hyperlink whose destination is an e-mail address. This is accomplished with a special protocol—mailto:.

The e-mail protocol is used slightly differently than other protocols. Its syntax with an anchor tag is

```
<A href="mailto:name@domain">AnchorText</A>
```

where `name@domain` is an e-mail address such as `charlie@chocolate.factory.com`, and `AnchorText` is a line of text or image that the user clicks to activate the link.

On e-mail–enabled browsers, such as NCSA Mosaic, Netscape Navigator, or Microsoft Internet Explorer, the integrated mail program is started. In any case, the e-mail address is automatically loaded into the "send to" field. NCSA Mosaic and Netscape both support an additional feature to place a default subject line in the message.

Mosaic makes use of the `title` attribute for e-mail; it's the only browser that does so. The syntax is

```
<A href="mailto:emailAddress" title="SubjectLineText">AnchorText</A>
```

where `emailAddress` and `AnchorText` are the same as the standard syntax for `mailto:`, and `SubjectLineText` is what will appear in the subject line of the message, such as "About the Wonka Bar page."

For Netscape, the syntax is slightly different. The subject line is appended to the e-mail address and the `title` attribute is not used. The syntax is

```
<A href="mailto:emailAddress?SubjectLineText">AnchorText</A>
```

For future compatibility, it's a good idea to stick with the `title` attribute and forgo the Netscape method. Using the e-mail extension is not guaranteed unless you can guarantee that all of your users are using Netscape. With other browsers, the entire e-mail address and extension is placed in the "send to" field, which could cause problems with mail servers.

The `title` attribute for the anchor tag is a recognized part of the HTML standard and stands a better chance of eventual integration in the majority of browsers. Plus, if a browser doesn't support it, no problems are created for the user in the address field.

## Defining Relationships with `rel` and `rev`

These two tags are used to define the type of hyperlink specified with the `href` attribute. As such, `rel` and `rev` are used only in conjunction with `href`. The syntax is

```
<A href="URL" rel=type rev=type>AnchorText</A>
```

where `type` defines the relation of the current document to the link specified in `href`. The first, `rel`, indicates a forward relationship; its counterpart, `rev`, shows a reverse relationship.

The attributes can be used alone or together. Like their counterparts in the `<LINK>` tag, `rel` and `rev` are not supported by the vast majority of browsers, including the most popular offerings. More information about using the `<LINK>` tag is found in Chapter 7.

## Identifying an Anchor by Its name

This attribute is most commonly used by anchors marking a hyperlink destination within a document, although it can also be used to name href hyperlinks. Its syntax is

```
<A name="AnchorName">[HTMLcontent]</A>
```

where *AnchorName* is a string unique to the current document and *HTMLcontent* is optional material associated with it that is viewed by the user.

When used in conjunction with the href tag, the name attribute creates a dual-purpose anchor. The anchor is both a destination and a hyperlink, such as the following:

```
What's new on the <A href="www.wossomatta.edu" name="wossomatta">
Wossomatta Virtual Campus</A>
```

For more information on linking to specific points within a document, see "Creating Anchors to Locations Within Documents," later in this chapter.

Unique naming is important for anchors. Having the same name for a variety of anchors leads to unpredictable results, depending on the browser. Some browsers pick the first anchor that matches, others pick the last, and still others won't pick anything at all.

Although they are permitted by many browsers, avoid using spaces and slashes in the anchor name. This can create confusion and errors when users attempt to type the name directly or create a bookmark to the location. As a form of generally accepted syntax, use an underscore character (_) instead of a space in anchor names.

## Preview a Hyperlink with Its `title`

The title attribute is used only in conjunction with the href to provide information about the link. When used, it should provide the same name that is contained in the <TITLE> tag of the document specified with href. The syntax is

```
<A href="URL" title="documentTitle">
```

where *URL* is the document's address and *documentTitle* is its formal title specified in the HTML head.

On some browsers, including the title in the hyperlink enables the document title's display in the browser title bar as the Web server starts to deliver the document. However, not all document types support titles. For example, Gopher and FTP directory listings don't provide titles as part of their information.

NCSA Mosaic supports the title attribute to specify an e-mail message subject when used with mailto references. For more information about this usage, see "Sending E-mail with an Anchor Tag," earlier in this chapter.

*Linking Documents and Images*

CHAPTER 11

229

11

LINKING
DOCUMENTS
AND IMAGES

# Creating Anchors for Locations Within Documents

Some documents are well-served by having internal bookmarks to facilitate navigation within the document itself. This includes FAQs (Frequently Asked Questions), glossaries and definition lists, and long documents covering several topics or subtopics.

The syntax for creating a destination anchor is

```
<A name="UniqueName">[AnchorText]</A>
```

where *UniqueName* is a name for the anchor that is unique to the document and *AnchorText* is optional text displayed on the screen. Duplicate names can cause unpredictable behavior or errors.

There are two generally accepted methods for marking anchors within a document. The first is to place the anchor tag immediately before the content you're marking, without enclosing it. This means the closing tag, </A>, is placed immediately following the <A> tag. (See Listing 11.1.)

**Listing 11.1. The first method for marking an anchor is to place the tags immediately before the heading of the destination, but not enclosing it.**

```
<HTML>
<HEAD>
<TITLE>Anchors</TITLE>
</HEAD>
<BODY>
<A name="Topic_1"></A><H2>Topic 1</H2>
Topic 1 stuff.
<A name="Topic_2"></A><H2>Topic 2</H2>
Topic 2 stuff.
<A name="Topic_3"></A><H2>Topic 3</H2>
Topic 3 stuff.
</BODY>
</HTML>
```

This is an effective way to mark anchors within a document, but it does have a drawback. Because the anchor tags don't contain anything, they are sometimes inadvertently separated from the places they're supposed to mark.

The other method is similar to marking text for a hyperlink. (See Listing 11.2.)

**Listing 11.2. Another method for marking an anchor is to enclose the heading of the destination.**

```
<HTML>
<HEAD>
<TITLE>Anchors</TITLE>
</HEAD>
<BODY>
<A name="Topic_1"><H2>Topic 1</H2></A>
Topic 1 stuff.
```

*continues*

**Listing 11.2. continued**

```
<A name="Topic_2"><H2>Topic 2</H2></A>
Topic 2 stuff.
<A name="Topic_3"><H2>Topic 3</H2></A>
Topic 3 stuff.
</BODY>
</HTML>
```

This method works well with sections that have their own headings, such as the document in Listing 11.2, or within blocks such as definition lists. Unlike using tags for hyperlinks, creating a destination anchor does not change the appearance of any enclosed text.

Marking anchors this way is recommended only if you're enclosing short pieces of text. Blocking entire pages is not desirable, especially because it's easy to lose track of the closing </A> tag.

# Linking to Anchors Within a Document

The tags for linking to an anchor within an HTML document are identical to the tags for creating a hyperlink to an external document, with an additional piece of address information. The syntax for the hyperlink to a new location is

```
<A href=[URL]#anchorName>AnchorText</A>
```

where *URL* is an optional value indicating an external document followed immediately by a pound sign (#), called a hash, and the name of the anchor within the document. *AnchorText* is the text or other content that the user clicks to activate the hyperlink.

The first and most common method of connecting to an internal anchor is by using the hash and the anchor name without a URL. (See Listing 11.3.) This jumps to the desired location without reloading the document.

**Listing 11.3. The three hyperlinks at the beginning of this document link to the three anchors within the document by referencing only the anchor names.**

```
<HTML>
<HEAD>
<TITLE>Anchors</TITLE>
</HEAD>
<BODY>
Read about <A href="#Topic_1">Topic 1</A>.
Read about <A href="#Topic_2">Topic 2</A>.
Read about <A href="#Topic_3">Topic 3</A>.
<HR>
<A name="Topic_1"><H2>Topic 1</H2></A>
Topic 1 stuff.
<A name="Topic_2"><H2>Topic 2</H2></A>
Topic 2 stuff.
<A name="Topic_3"><H2>Topic 3</H2></A>
Topic 3 stuff.
</BODY>
</HTML>
```

This is a simple solution for linking to internal anchors. On pages that are developed with a CGI script, this solution doesn't always work. In that case, it becomes necessary to add the filename to the URL. (See Listing 11.4.)

**Listing 11.4. The three hyperlinks at the beginning still link to the three anchors within the document, but now the entire page is reloaded at the same time.**

```html
<HTML>
<HEAD>
<TITLE>Anchors</TITLE>
</HEAD>
<BODY>
Read about <A href="Anchors.html#Topic_1">Topic 1</A>.
Read about <A href="Anchors.html#Topic_2">Topic 2</A>.
Read about <A href="Anchors.html#Topic_3">Topic 3</A>.
<HR>
<A name="Topic_1"><H2>Topic 1</H2></A>
Topic 1 stuff.
<A name="Topic_2"><H2>Topic 2</H2></A>
Topic 2 stuff.
<A name="Topic_3"><H2>Topic 3</H2></A>
Topic 3 stuff.
</BODY>
</HTML>
```

This method also has a drawback. Every time the user clicks one of the links, the browser reloads the page before moving to the desired anchor. For large pages, or pages with lots of graphics, this means a much slower response time. However, you can use this behavior to your advantage by linking to a specific location in an external document. (See Listings 11.5 and 11.6.)

**Listing 11.5. This page includes a paragraph with a hyperlink to a definition term in a separate document.**

```html
<HTML>
<HEAD>
<TITLE>Fire Behavior</TITLE>
</HEAD>
<BODY>
One of the most dramatic and publicized fire behaviors is
<A href="glossary.html#backdraft">backdraft</A>. Backdraft is
 extremely rare, and many firefighters will never have
the opportunity to witness its effects firsthand.
</BODY>
</HTML>
```

**Listing 11.6. This is the glossary page referred to in the preceding listing. Note the anchors defined for each definition term.**

```html
<HTML>
<HEAD>
<TITLE>Fire Glossary</TITLE>
```

*continues*

**Listing 11.6. continued**

```
</HEAD>
<BODY>
<DL>
<DT><A name="fire_triangle">Fire Triangle</A><DD>The minimum requirements of
combustion and the basis for all extinguishment techniques. Its sides
represent fuel, heat and oxygen.
<DT><A name="fire_tetrahedron">Fire Tetrahedron</A><DD>A four-sided figure
representing the three elements of the <A href="fire_triangle">Fire Triangle</A>
plus an extra element for the chemical process causing flames.
<DT><A name="backdraft">Backdraft</A><DD>An explosive condition created when
oxygenated air is suddenly introduced to a superheated flammable atmosphere
with deficient oxygen for combustion.
<DT><A name="incipient">Incipient</A><DD>The initial stage of a fire, when
its size is still relatively small and temperatures are low. A fire is most
easily extinguished at this phase.
<DT><A name="flashover">Flashover<DD>The point at which all the combustible
material in a room reaches its ignition temperature and ignites simultaneously.
</DL>
</BODY>
</HTML>
```

When the user clicks the term Backdraft in Listing 11.5, the browser loads the glossary document and navigates to the anchor named after the hash in the hyperlink URL.

# Summary

Hypertext is the key to the World Wide Web's success. The use of hyperlinks to other documents turns the typical dead-end page of information into a major crossroads, with a multitude of destinations from one leaping-off point.

Anchor tags are the key to how the Web implements hypertext. As their primary usage, anchors mark hypertext links that connect with other Web nodes and resources. In its typical form, the anchor tag encases a small snippet of text and includes a single attribute, href, which identifies the destination.

In its other form, the anchor tag also marks a destination within a document. This is accomplished by using the name attribute without href. The result is a location that is accessed using a hyperlink anchor tag.

With these two basic capabilities, the anchor tag is the backbone of World Wide Web navigation, making jumps between pages, Web sites, and continents as easy as clicking a mouse.

# Adding Images to Your Web Page

*by Rick Darnell*

## IN THIS CHAPTER

**CHAPTER 12**

Once upon a time, before the World Wide Web got its name, there was a network that looked and acted like the Web, but it wasn't available to everyone. It was pretty limited in scope and appearance and was used by a bunch of guys with funny hats and whose hobbies included missile button design. These folks didn't care much for aesthetics and entertainment, so their Web didn't support images. Besides, they were still working in the days of yore when computer screens were green. Their browsers only displayed text, and there was no need or demand for presenting graphics across the network connection.

Some of the people with access to the early incarnations of the Web were at universities and other institutions of higher learning. As more and more people came into contact with the Web, it became more popular and more ideas surfaced about other uses and how it could look much nicer than it looked.

But all of the browsers in those early days were text-based. As the desire to share ideas grew, someone came up with the bright idea of including images as part of a Web page.

> **TIP**
>
> One of the most popular choices at the time was Lynx. It's still around today and in wide use among people who use nongraphics-based computer systems, and those who just prefer not to bother with all of the Web adornments such as images, applets, virtual reality, and so on.

Enter the National Center for Supercomputing Applications at the University of Illinois (NCSA). They put together a little program called Mosaic that supported the display of images right on the page with the rest of the text. Thus, the graphical browser was born, and this first work became the basis for virtually every other browser created since, including Netscape Navigator and Microsoft Internet Explorer.

NCSA added an additional tag called <IMG> to the fledgling HTML, which enabled early authors to insert a picture inline with the rest of the text. That tag is still around, and it has some brand new tricks, which I show you in this chapter. This chapter also includes some friends and relations of the tag that also relate to images. This feature has come a long way since its first inception, and you'll learn a multitude of ways to manipulate appearance and placement.

# The Basic <IMG>

The <IMG> tag is an empty element used to insert inline images. This includes items such as small icons and graphics, in addition to large image maps that occupy most of the browser window. Because the tag is a single resource element (one tag for one image), an ending tag is not supported.

In addition to identifying which image to use, the tag also has various attributes for defining its position relative to the surrounding text and Web content. This includes floating the image in the left or right margin, or placing it on top of, below, or centered on the textline it appears on.

The syntax for an image tag is

```
<IMG src="[URL]filename" [alt="textDescription">
```

where the `src` attribute identifies the image *filename* through a physical or relative URL and filename. The `alt` attribute is used to define a brief text description of the image or its use for browsers that don't load the image.

> **TIP**
>
> Browsers don't load images for a variety of reasons. First, the browser could be a nongraphical browser such as Lynx. Second, the user might have image autoloading turned off to speed up download time. Providing a value for `alt` ensures that the user has some idea of what's supposed to be going on with that big blank space.
>
> The attribute is vital for interoperability with speech-based and text-only user agents. For disabled persons, the `alt` value can provide a brief description of what the image is. For text-only browsers, it's the only indication that the user is missing any content.

The `src` attribute is required for every image. It identifies the specific image to use and its type. The two most popular image file types are GIF (Graphics Interchange Format) and JPEG (Joint Photographic Experts Group, also used as JPG), although PNG (Portable Network Graphic) images are starting to gain acceptance and wider usage.

The second attribute in the syntax definition, `alt`, is optional but recommended. It provides a textual description of the image and is the only portion of the tag used by browsers that don't support inline images.

## Where to align the Image

The `align` attribute controls how the image is positioned in relation to the line of text in which it occurs. Unlike other alignment attributes for items such as tables, `align` controls both the horizontal and vertical placement. Its syntax is

```
<IMG src="URL" align="position">
```

where *URL* includes the name of the file, and *position* is one of five values: `top`, `middle`, `bottom`, `left`, or `right`. The specific action of each value is as follows:

■ `top` positions the top of the graphic with the top of the current line. (See Figure 12.1.) If the text line is formatted with a tag such as `<H1>`, the image will appear to occupy more space within the line itself than if it occurs within a line of standard body text.

**FIGURE 12.1.**

*Top alignment causes the top of the image to line up with the top of the current line. Note the position of the top border of the image in relation to the letters next to it.*

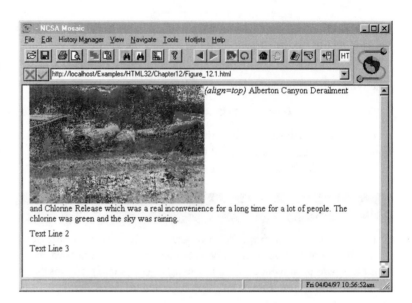

Browsers differ concerning whether the line immediately preceding or following is used to determine alignment.

■ `middle` is similar to `top`, but the vertical midline of the image is aligned with the baseline of the current line. (See Figure 12.2.) Its interpretation is consistent across browsers.

**FIGURE 12.2.**

*Middle alignment matches the vertical halfway point of the image to the baseline of the current line of text.*

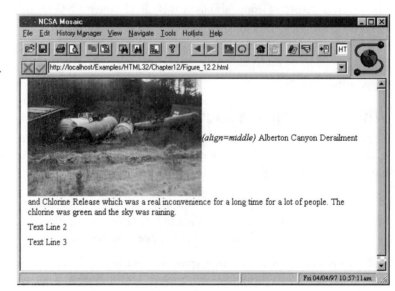

■ bottom is the default value if align is omitted from the <IMG> tag. (See Figure 12.3.) In this case, the bottom of the image rests on the baseline for the current line.

12

ADDING IMAGES
TO YOUR WEB
PAGE

**FIGURE 12.3.**

*Bottom alignment is the default placement for images. The bottom of the image rests on the baseline for the current line of text.*

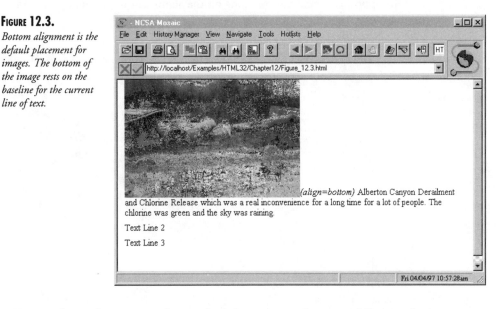

■ left forces the image to the current left margin, and any text following the image flows around the right margin of the image. (See Figure 12.4.) Its interpretation depends on whether any images or other material with left alignment appear earlier. Preceding text generally forces the image to wrap to a new line, with the subsequent text continuing on the line preceding the image.

**FIGURE 12.4.**

*Left alignment results in the text following the <IMG> tag flowing around the right side of the image.*

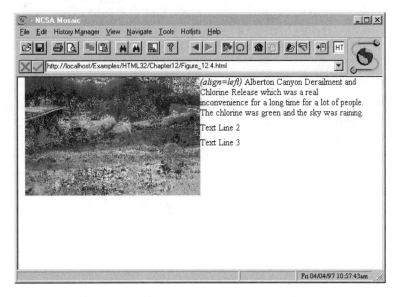

■    `right` is similar to `left`, but the image is forced to the right margin. (See Figure 12.5.) Any following text is wrapped along the image's left side. It exhibits the same behavior as `left` in the opposite direction, depending on the alignment of preceding text and other material.

**FIGURE 12.5.**

*Right alignment is the same as left, only the subsequent text flows around the left side of the image.*

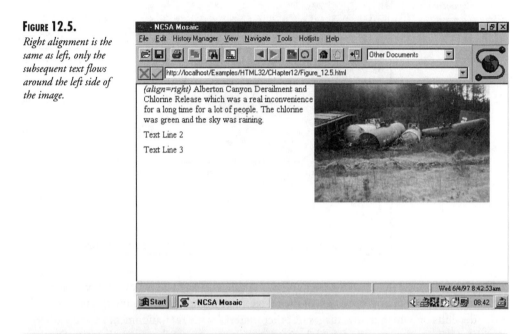

> **TIP**
>
> Some browsers introduce extra line spacing with multiple images using `left` or `right` alignment. Don't depend on the spacing to be uniform across all browsers and all platforms. For more information on controlling text flow, see Chapter 8, "Text Alignment and Formatting."

When placing an image on a page, remember that it is an inline feature that is displayed right along with any text on the same line. If it's not separated from surrounding material with a line break or paragraph, the image is placed on the same line as the current line of text according to the `align` attribute. This can lead to some rather undesirable appearances for images.

# Making Space with `width` and `height`

The two size attributes set the desired horizontal and vertical space for the image in pixels. They are typically used as a pair to reserve space in the browser window before the image is loaded. The syntax is

```
<UMG src="URL" width=pixels height=pixels>
```

where *URL* is the name and *pixels* is the amount of space reserved for the image.

There are a couple of reasons why you'll want to specify a size for your image. The first, already mentioned, is that it can speed display time for the rest of the page. When size information is omitted, some browsers set aside a minimal amount of space and then begin downloading the first bit of the image, which includes its size information. While the browser is working on that, it doesn't work on downloading any more of the body of the page.

Depending on the browser, the rest of the page might not display until it knows how much space each image needs. Or, the display might update and reload as each piece of information is acquired. Using the `width` and `height` attributes removes the guesswork for the browser.

The two attributes also preserve page formatting. If your page's overall appearance is dependent on the size and relation of the images to the text (like a newspaper or magazine), specifying the image size ensures that the proper amount of space is blocked. Although the image still won't appear, the right amount of space is held open to ensure the desired effect.

## Would You Care for a border with That Image?

When an image appears as part of a hypertext link, the browser usually responds by drawing a colored border (usually blue) around the image. The width of this border is set using the border attribute. The syntax is

```
<IMG src="URL" border=pixels>
```

where URL is the path and name of the image file, and *pixels* is the width of the border in pixels. Use a value of 0 to hide the border. The color of the border is controlled by the link color attributes in the <BODY> tag. For more information, see Chapter 7, "Structural Elements and Their Usage."

> **TIP**
>
> Most browsers also indicate a hyperlink image by changing the mouse pointer when it passes over the graphic, so that the user doesn't have to guess whether the borderless image is a hyperlink.

## Give the Image a Little hspace and vspace

The space attributes set up a *buffer zone* around the perimeter of the image. This is very useful when white space is needed immediately adjacent to the image. The hspace and vspace attributes set the width of this white space in pixels. The syntax is

```
<IMG src="URL" hspace=pixels vspace=pixels>
```

where URL is the image file and *pixels* is the number of pixels added to the appropriate side. By default, both are small nonzero numbers. This provides just enough white space to keep the image from touching adjacent text.

> **NOTE**
>
> White space is a design term meaning "space without anything in it." The space doesn't necessarily have to be white. Depending on the background color of the page, it could also be green, blue, pink, or any other color.

The space is added to both sides of the attribute. Therefore, if you include a value of 40 for hspace, 40 pixels of space will be added to the right and left sides of the image. This will make the image appear not in alignment with the other margins on the page.

# `ismap` for Server-Side Maps

The `ismap` attribute identifies the image as an image map. Image maps enable you to associate specific areas of an image with hyperlinks to other documents.

In order to have validity, an `<IMG>` element with `ismap` is encased with a hypertext anchor tag. When the user clicks the image, the `ismap` attribute passes the x and y location of the click to the server. The syntax is

```
<a href="URL/file.map"><img src="imageURL" ismap></a>
```

where `URL/file.map` is the name of the MAP file with the coordinate information and `imageURL` is the name of the actual image. This is called a *server-side* image map because all of the hyperlink information is processed by the Web server.

> **TIP**
>
> The `ismap` attribute is used only with server-side image maps. In order to function, the server must have the appropriate CGI software to process the image map information and the file that defines each of the hot spots.

The location on the image where the user clicks is passed to the server by creating a new URL from the URL specified in the anchor tag. A question mark is added to the end, followed by the value of the x and y coordinates separated by a comma. The link is then followed using the new URL. For example, if the user clicks the location x=10 and y=27, the URL sent to the server is `/cgibin/navbar.map?10,27`.

> **TIP**
>
> It is a good idea to use `border=0` with the image and use graphical clues to let the user know that the image is a clickable map. Otherwise, it's easy to confuse an image map with a one-shot hyperlinked image. Graphical clues include techniques such as bold shapes with descriptive text, or a long horizontal shape in the traditional navigation bar layout.

A recent feature added to browsers is the capability to interpret an image map without any help from the server. These are called client-side image maps, and they include all the necessary information to process their hyperlinks without further communication from the server. This type of image map is covered with the next attribute—usemap. More information on image maps is provided in Chapter 14, "Creating Image Maps."

## usemap for Client-Side Image Maps

The usemap attribute is used to mark an image as a client-side image map that is used with a <MAP> element. In most cases, a client-side map is preferable to a server-side map because it requires no communication across network lines and no additional support from the server to operate. The syntax is

```
<IMG src="URL" usemap="[mapURL.html]#mapName">
```

where *URL* is the image file and *[mapURL.html]#mapName* is an incomplete URL specifying the location of the <MAP> element that has the coordinate and hyperlink information, and is identified similar to a target anchor. If the filename is omitted, the <MAP> element is assumed to be in the current HTML file.

### A MAP FOR A FILE

Note the difference between the extension of the file specified for the hyperlink anchor on ismap and the source of the coordinates for usemap. The former requires a MAP file, which consists of a collection of coordinates and hyperlinks. The latter is a block of HTML tags within an HTML file. The file can contain other content, or it can exist solely for containing the map information.

The various active regions of the image map are described for the browser using <MAP> and <AREA> tags. This information is usually placed inside the HTML file with the <IMG> tag that requires it, although it can be placed in a separate file if the same map is used on several pages.

To ensure compatibility across browsers and platforms, ismap and usemap can be used on the same image. This allows the browser to choose which way it wants to interpret the image map, giving the document the maximum chance for compatibility.

# Background Images

Although they are not directly related to the <IMG> tag, this seems like a good place to mention the use of background images for Web pages. These images are placed on a page through an attribute of the <BODY> tag. The syntax is

```
<BODY background="[URL]filename">
```

where *URL* is the location of the image specified with a complete URL including server name and path or a relative URL with or without a path, and *filename* is the name of the image to use. For more information on relative pathnames, see Chapter 11, "Linking Documents and Images."

> **TIP**
>
> For compatibility, limit the file type to GIF or JPEG. Image files in these formats are supported by virtually every graphical browser in use.

The image is placed in the background of the Web page, similar to hanging wallpaper in a bedroom. If the image is smaller than the space occupied by the browser window, it's tiled to fill the entire background. Use care to ensure that the image isn't so bold or distracting as to make the rest of the page unreadable. For more information on using background and other color attributes of <BODY>, see Chapter 7.

# Using Images as Substitute Content

With the wide variety of browsers and capabilities on the Web, it's increasingly hard to make one page work for everyone. This is especially true when including content such as Java applets, ActiveX controls, and Netscape plug-ins. If a browser doesn't recognize your special content, it ignores it and either leaves a big hole or a blank space in your layout.

You can use browser tag incompatibility to your advantage by placing an image tag just before the closing tag of the specialized content. The format is

```
<APPLET attributes height=contentHeight width=contentWidth>
<PARAM attributes>
…other applet-specific lines…
<IMG src="URL" height=imageHeight width=imageWidth>
</APPLET>
```

where the applet tag is any of the specialized content container tags and the parameter tags are any of the tags subordinate to the container. As a matter of style and convention, the <IMG> tag is placed immediately preceding the closing container tag, and the content and image size attributes have the same value.

When this set of tags is encountered by a browser that doesn't support applets, the following is what happens:

- The opening container tag is not understood, so the browser ignores it and does nothing.
- Likewise, the subsequent tags that support the container tag are ignored. So far, the browser has done nothing but throw away the material that it doesn't understand.
- When the <IMG> tag is encountered, the browser suddenly has something it can work with. It interprets this tag and loads the image into the document in the space that was originally designed for the specialized content.
- The closing container tag is reached. Because it closes something the browser never understood, it is ignored, too.

This technique ensures that everyone who views your page has something to see, even if it's a large graphic that says, "You need a Java-compatible browser for this page." Another common usage is to use a screen capture from a video or VRML for the image. Even though the image is static, the user still gets a taste of what was intended.

# Summary

Use of inline images in Web pages is part of what made the World Wide Web such a popular place to spend time. Use of the image tag depends on only one attribute, src, to identify the graphics file. Although plug-ins and different browsers support a wide variety of image formats, GIF and JPEG are the most popular and are supported in virtually every setting.

With the advent of HTML 3.2, additional capabilities within the <IMG> tag are officially extended to make it easier to control the appearance and behavior of graphics on the Web page. Using alignment and spacing attributes enables you to left- or right-justify an image while causing the surrounding text to wrap around the margins.

Mapping attributes set the graphics as an image map. Graphical image maps are one of the more popular uses for graphics files, including menu bars and full-screen images for site navigation.

Additional attributes of the <IMG> tag are covered in the next chapter, including those used to insert virtual reality worlds and aviation clips. Read on for more information on making your graphical Web page really graphical.

# Integrating Multimedia and Other File Types

*by Rick Darnell*

**CHAPTER 13**

What is multimedia? The technical definition, for people who wear pocket protectors, goes something like this: A computer-based method of presenting information by using more than one medium of communication, such as text or graphics and sound, and emphasizing interactivity.

That's a mouthful, but what does it all mean? It's the difference between looking up Zanzibar in your 1973 edition of the World Book Encyclopedia and dropping a CD-ROM in your computer and watching a clip of Zanzibar farmers harvest and package cloves for export. If you want to see what cloves are for, you'd need to pick up volume 3 of the encyclopedia or click a hyperlink on the computer to see and hear another clip of Julia Child talking about the wonders of cloves for desserts and pork.

Multimedia reaches its fullest potential when it's implemented in a standalone form—all of the graphics, sound, and video are contained on a CD-ROM that is connected directly to the computer. Web-based multimedia tends to pale in comparison, due to the inherent limitations of network connections and modem speeds. Many developers are working hard to bring Web-based multimedia up to the same level as a CD-ROM, however.

At the time when HTML 3.2 was released, multimedia was just beginning to get a serious hold on the World Wide Web. Standards are still not entirely in place to support this specialized content across all browsers and platforms, but as usual, browser vendors are working hard to make sure you have access to the latest and greatest in multimedia and interactive content.

Initially, Web multimedia was limited to simple animations and links to sound files. Recent advances have expanded this to full-motion video and sound, virtual reality, and interactive games. This chapter takes a look at some of the ways this content is implemented through HTML.

# External and Internal Content

Multimedia on the Web is divided into two basic categories—things that can be displayed in-line or as an integrated part of the browser (internal), or content that is handled outside the browser (external).

Implementing both plug-in content and external applications requires the user to have the necessary software already installed on his or her system. This can lead to some problems, because not all content is available for all platforms and browsers. Using specialty items such as multimedia means that you have to leave behind some people who won't have the chance to appreciate all of your site's features.

## Implementing Internal Content

With the advancement of browsers and supporting applications, the list of internal content is growing week by week. This content includes items directly supported by a browser, such as animated GIFs, Java applets, and virtual reality. It also includes items supported through helper applications and plug-ins, which are special applications that the browser allows to run in the browser window. Both Netscape plug-ins and Microsoft ActiveX components are examples of this kind of content. Sometimes, internal content consumes the entire browser, such as display for an Adobe Acrobat document. Other times, it only takes up as much space as an icon, such as for specialized video.

With HTML 3.2, two primary tags are used for both items. First is the `<APPLET>` tag for Java applets. The other is `<IMG>` for inserting graphic images. A couple of other tags are used by other browsers, including `<EMBED>` for Netscape plug-ins and `<OBJECT>` for ActiveX controls.

Depending on the browser's capabilities, each of these items may in turn be handled internally by the browser, or a helper application may be invoked. In both cases, the content remains as part of the rest of the Web page.

### HOW DOES A BROWSER KNOW WHAT TO DO?

When your browser loads any particular file—whether it is an HTML file, image, or multimedia—how does it know what to do with it? The browser's reaction is determined by two things: the filename extension and the file's content type.

You'll see a lot of file extensions tossed around in examples throughout this book, including HTML (Web pages), GIF (images), DCR (Shockwave), and WRL (virtual reality). The browser uses the file extension to determine what to do when it retrieves a file from your local disk.

The content type is used when the browser receives a file from a Web server, because the Web server doesn't always send a filename. In some cases, the server sends only data with no file information. Instead of a filename and extension, it sends a special code called the content type, which identifies the information it's sending. Content types include `text/html`, `image/gif`, `application/mpe`, `application/msword`, and so on.

Both the browser and server contain lists of file extensions and content types. The server uses the list to determine which content type to send with a given file. The browser's list includes an additional entry for helper applications that corresponds to content types.

One of the proposals for HTML 4.0 is an expansion of the `<OBJECT>` tag to encompass all internal content. The new version of `<OBJECT>` could apply to applets, plug-ins, ActiveX, images, and any future type of embedded content.

The basic proposed syntax is

```
<OBJECT data=filename type=MIMEtype height=pixels width=pixels>
<PARAMETER name=paramName value=paramValue>
</OBJECT>
```

where `data` is the name of the file, such as `image.gif`, and `type` is the Internet content type, such as `image/gif`, followed by the height and width of the object's area in pixels. This is followed by any number of `<PARAMETER>` tags, for additional control of the content, and a closing

</OBJECT>. You can insert alternate content for incompatible browsers immediately before the closing object tag.

How does <OBJECT> work with applets, plug-ins, and ActiveX controls? Let's take a look, beginning with a Java applet. Syntax using the <OBJECT> tag is slightly different from the <APPLET> tag, shown here side by side:

```
<APPLET CLASS="driverOperator.class" CODEBASE="http://host/somepath/"
        HEIGHT=100 WIDTH=100>
   <PARAM NAME="start" VALUE="1">
   This browser doesn't drink Java.
</APPLET>

<OBJECT CLASSID="java:driverOperator.init" CODETYPE="application/java-vm"
        CODEBASE="http://host/somepath/" HEIGHT=100 WIDTH=100>
   <PARAM NAME="start" VALUE="1">
   This browser doesn't drink Java.
</OBJECT>
```

Here's what is happening attribute by attribute. The first attribute is the CLASSID. This identifies the program type (java), followed by the applet name (driverOperator) and the first method to execute (init). Note that it doesn't name the .CLASS file explicitly, as the <APPLET> tag does.

Next comes the CODETYPE. This is similar to the TYPE attribute for other Internet content, but it applies only to files containing code that must be interpreted on the client's computer. The CODEBASE is the URL where the class file is located. The last information is the height and width of the applet on the page.

After the opening <OBJECT>, you see any parameters in the same basic format as all HTML parameters and then any text content to use if any of the other tags are not recognized by the browser. This ensures compatible content for everyone, regardless of their browser or platform choice. Last is a closing </OBJECT>.

For another example, let's look at a multimedia plug-in for a Shockwave file:

```
<EMBED src="bounce_logo.dcr" alt="Hockey Pucks" width=400 height=150>
   <img src=shocknew.gif alt="Best viewed with Shockwave">
</EMBED>

<OBJECT data=bounce_logo.dcr type="application/director"
        standby="Hockey Pucks" width=400 height=150>
   <img src=shocknew.gif alt="Best viewed with Shockwave">
</OBJECT>
```

This is similar to the applet, with a couple of notable exceptions. The first exception is the data tag, which identifies the plug-in content file. It uses the type to tell the browser which helper application needs to be run. The <EMBED> tag uses alt to display a message while the content is loading, whereas <OBJECT> uses standby, although alt should still be included for nongraphic browsers.

The <EMBED> tag is followed by the old <IMG> tag, which provides alternate content for browsers that don't support objects or Shockwave. You see that even the image tag includes alternate content for˜nongraphical browsers. This set of tags provides content that degrades in a predictable manner, depending on the capabilities of the user's browser.

Finally, the following example shows how <OBJECT> works with an ActiveX control:

```
<OBJECT id="oompa_1" classid="clsid:663C8FEF-1EF9-11CF-A3DB-080036F12502"
   DATA="http://www.loompa.com/ole/oompa.stm">
</OBJECT>

<OBJECT id="oompa_1" classid="clsid:663C8FEF-1EF9-11CF-A3DB-080036F12502"
   data="http://www.loompa.com/ole/oompa.stm">
</OBJECT>
```

As you can see, ActiveX is the only content that isn't affected by the change to the new tag.

Now that you understand the internal content, let's move outside of the browser's sandbox.

## Implementing External Multimedia Content

The browser starts external applications (also known as *helper applications* or *helper apps*), but the browser doesn't give the applications space within the browser window to do their stuff. The applications start a separate program that then loads and displays the content for the user. One popular application that fits this category is RealAudio. RealAudio is a way to deliver streaming audio (prerecorded or live) to the user across the Internet. When a user clicks a RealAudio link, the RealAudio Player launches and takes over receiving and playing the audio stream (as shown in Figure 13.1).

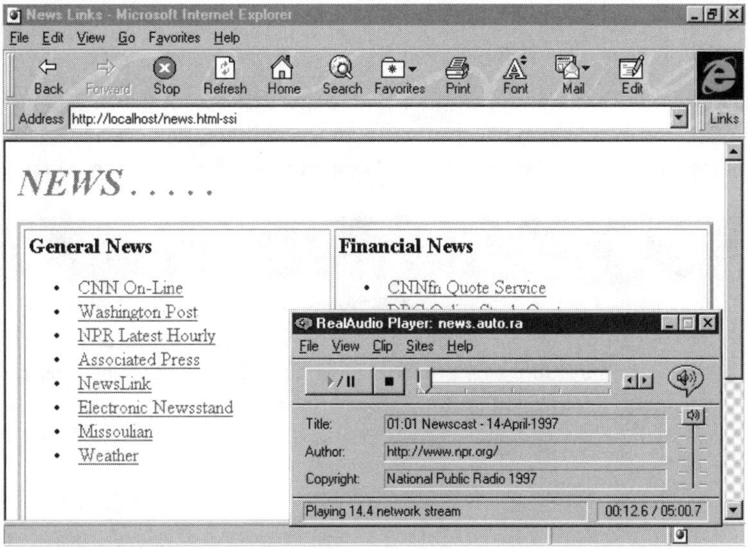

**13**

INTEGRATING
MULTIMEDIA AND
OTHER FILE TYPES

**FIGURE 13.1.**

*RealAudio is an example of multimedia content that is accessed via a link on a Web page but delivered outside the browser via a separate application.*

To connect to external media from a Web page, use the `<A REF="`*URL*`">` tag. The path to the external file is a URL similar to an HTML page, except you're pointing to something that doesn't end in HTML. Here is an example:

```
<A HREF="volcano.mpeg">Mount St. Helens (3.6 MB)</A>
```

When the user clicks the preceding link to a video file, one of two things happens. If the content is something the browser can understand, such as some types of images or text files, the browser loads the file into its current window. If the browser can't handle it directly, it downloads the file and passes it off to the application on the user's system that is designed to read and handle that file.

A convention is used in the hyperlink, especially for large multimedia files—a notation of the file size. For users still relying on slower modem connections, this notation is a polite way of letting them know they'll be sitting and waiting a while for the content to load.

# HTML 3.2 Options for Multimedia

HTML standards directly support only two technologies that are capable of delivering some form of multimedia content. The first is Java. Java is a programming language that provides methods for integrating graphics and sound into synchronized displays, complete with the capability for user interaction.

## Including Animation and Sound with the Java Animator

As part of its release for Java, Sun included a variety of applets to demonstrate Java's capability. Some of these applets are strictly demonstrations that really don't serve any useful purpose. Then there's the Animator applet, which anyone can use to add animation and sound to his or her Web page. (See Figure 13.2.)

To use the Animator applet on a Web page, make a copy of it and all its support files to the same directory as your Web page or in a subdirectory such as `/Animator`. The files include `Animator.class`, `ParseException.class`, and `DescriptionFrame.class`.

---

**TIP**

The location of the Animator applet depends on your system and where the Java Development Kit (JDK) files are located. Look for a `/samples/Animator` path on your computer or search for the actual `Animator.class` file. If you don't have the most recent JDK, you can download it for free from `www.javasoft.com`.

---

**FIGURE 13.2.**

*The Animator applet enables page developers to assemble images and sound into a synchronized animation sequence for their Web pages.*

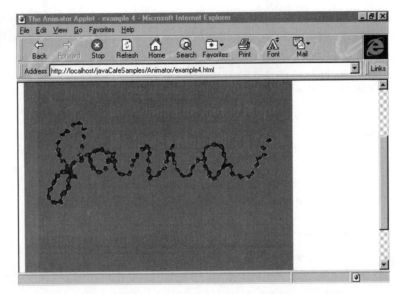

For the easiest operation, just copy the CLASS files to the same directory as your Web page, and then create two subdirectories: /images, to hold the animation graphic files, and /audio, to hold any sound files. When you're finished, the directory structure should look something like this:

```
/MyWebPages
    MyAppletPage.html
    Animator.class
    DescriptionFrame.class
    ParseException.class
/MyWebPages/images
/MyWebPages/audio
```

Next, copy the graphic files to the /images directory. Animator supports both GIF and JPEG file formats. The names of the files don't matter, but a couple of conventions are built into Animator to make your life easier.

The default name that the applet looks for is T#.gif, in which # is a series of numbers beginning with 1 for the first image and continuing in order to the last image. I'll use this default for the examples.

You can also use your own name with the same naming convention, such as dance0.gif, dance1.gif, and so on. The last option is to give each animation a unique name, such as first.gif, second.gif, and so on, although I don't recommend this because it requires a lot more typing for a couple of the parameters.

Repeat the process for any sound files. The naming conventions for images don't apply to sound files.

> **TIP**
>
> Currently, Java supports only one sound format: 8-bit, 8,000 Hz, one-channel, AU files. You can create these on a Sun workstation using the AudioTool application or convert files from other formats using an audio format conversion utility.

With all of your files in the proper place, it's time to get to work building the HTML code to implement the animation. Using the information from the example so far, you can build the tags to implement the Animator. This example assumes eight images with eight sound files that correspond to each image. The line numbers are not part of the HTML; I added them to help in the subsequent explanation.

```
1: <applet code="Animator.class" width=460 height=160>
2:    <param name=imagesource value="images">
3:    <param name=endimage value=8>
4:    <param name=soundsource value="audio">
5:    <param name=sounds value="1.au¦2.au¦3.au¦4.au¦5.au¦6.au¦7.au¦8.au">
6:    <param name=pause value=200>
7:    <param name=repeat value="true">
8: </applet>
```

Here's what this section of HTML does, line by line:

1. The applet filename (`Animator.class`) is identified and the size is defined. Note that the other two CLASS files are not listed. They are referenced directly by Animator and don't need their own `<APPLET>` tag.

2. The directory of the images is specified with the `imagesource` parameter.

3. The last file is identified by its number, `10`. Because you're using the default naming convention, Animator will load 10 files beginning with `T1.gif` and ending with `T10.gif`.

4. The directory for the audio files is specified with the `soundsource` parameter.

5. Each of the audio files is matched with an image in the animation using the `sounds` attribute. The files are matched in order and separated with a vertical bar. If you didn't desire a sound for one of the images, you would leave its spot blank, such as `1.au¦¦3.au`. Because the sounds must be listed by filename, it's a good idea to keep the names as short as possible.

6. The `pause` parameter indicates how long, in milliseconds, the applet should wait before displaying the next image. This example uses a delay of 200 milliseconds (0.2 seconds).

7. The last parameter is `repeat`, which tells the applet whether this is a continuous loop animation or a one-time shot. Most Web animations are loops, so the default is `true`. However, I encourage you to use this parameter to avoid ambiguity when reviewing the code later.

8. As the last step, the <APPLET> tag is closed. If you wanted to include any alternate content, you would place it immediately before the closing tag.

## HTML APPLET SYNTAX

The World Wide Web Consortium now officially supports Java with their HTML 3.2 standard, which includes the specifications for including Java applets using the <APPLET> tag. A complete overview of this tag is provided in Chapter 29, "Integrating Java Applets and HTML," but I've provided a quick overview here to help you understand what's happening with the Animator applet.

The basic syntax for a Java applet is

```
<APPLET code="appletName.CLASS" width="wPixels" height="hPixels">
</APPLET>
```

in which code is the name of the Java CLASS file and width and height specify the space in pixels that the applet should occupy on the Web page. The applet file must be of the type CLASS or it will not work.

The browser makes an important assumption when you use this simple version of the <APPLET> tag: The Java CLASS file *must* be located in the same directory as the Web page. If it is located somewhere else, such as in a special directory on the server that is dedicated to holding Java applets, you'll need to use the codebase attribute.

The codebase attribute identifies the path to the CLASS files. It is added to the <APPLET> tag as a relative path (/java_applets/class_files/) or a complete URL (http://www.grace.net/java/class/animator/). It's important to note that codebase is used only to specify a path to the applet; it doesn't identify the applet file. The CLASS file must still be identified using the code attribute.

The <APPLET> tag also includes several other attributes that are identical to their counterparts in the <IMG> tag: alt, align, hspace, and vspace. For anchor or script references, you can also specify a name.

To pass parameters to the applet, use the <PARAM> tag. The syntax is

```
<PARAM name="paramName" value="paramValue">
```

in which the name is one of the applet's parameters and value is what is being submitted. If the applet does not recognize the parameter name, the tag is ignored. Remember that each applet is a little application unto itself and can have as many parameters as it needs or have none at all.

After any <PARAM> tags, you can also include alternate text or images to display. Any valid HTML text formatting is allowed, including block quotes, images, and hyperlinks.

Anything other than the <PARAM> tags within the <APPLET> tags is ignored by a Java-compatible browser. Because an incompatible browser ignores the <APPLET> and <PARAM>

*continues*

*continued*

tags, you can use this feature to display other HTML content in lieu of the applet. This is a good place to provide a snapshot of what the applet looks like (with <IMG>), admonishing the user to get a Java-compatible browser (with HTML text such as <BLOCKQUOTE> or hyperlinks to a source for a Java browser [with <A href>]).

Although the basic syntax serves most purposes, Animator includes a host of parameters to fine-tune its operation. These parameters are listed in Table 13.1, along with the parameters used in our basic example.

**Table 13.1. Java Animator parameters and their use.**

| Parameter | Value |
| --- | --- |
| imagesource | Directory that contains the animation frames. |
| namepattern | Template for creating names of image files to load, in the form *prefix%N.suffix*, in which *%N* is the number of the file. |
| startup | URL of the image to display at load time. |
| background | Background image for frames. |
| backgroundcolor | Background color for frames. |
| startimage | Number of the starting frame. |
| endimage | Number of the ending frame. |
| images | Explicit order for animation frames by their number, such as 1¦2¦3¦2¦1. |
| positions | The x and y positions for each frame in the form *x1@y1¦x2@y2¦xN@yN*. A blank value uses the previous value. |
| pause | Number of milliseconds to pause between all images, unless otherwise specified by pauses. |
| pauses | Number of milliseconds to pause between frames in the form *pause1¦pause2¦pauseN*. Omitting a value defaults to the pause value. |
| soundsource | Directory containing audio files. |
| sounds | List of audio files to synchronize to individual frames in the form *sound1.au¦sound2.au¦soundN.au*. |
| soundtrack | Audio file to play in a continuous loop throughout the animation. |

| Parameter | Value |
|-----------|-------|
| `repeat` | Query whether to repeat the animation sequence answered with `true` or `false`. |
| `href` | URL of a page to visit when the user clicks the animation. If not set, a click toggles pausing of the animation. |

If you use the default naming convention, `endimage` is the only attribute that Animator requires.

---

**TIP**

To view the Java Animator on your browser, you'll need a recent version of Netscape Navigator (2.0 or later) or Microsoft Internet Explorer (3.0 or later). Or, you could use Sun HotJava, the first browser to support Java, which also happens to be written in Java.

Microsoft Internet Explorer is available through www.microsoft.com/. Netscape Navigator is located at home.netscape.com/. Sun HotJava is located at the JavaSoft site at www.javasoft.com/.

---

For the work involved, Animator is really a simple way to offer multimedia content to your Java-enabled users. It especially becomes handy when you throw the synchronized sound component into the bag. It might not be the equivalent of CNN film footage, but it's an ideal tool to put together an animation to make a point or illustrate a process, or even animate a hyperlink button.

## Including Animated GIF Files

The other technology HTML indirectly supports through its `<IMG>` tag is animated GIF files. An animated GIF file contains several images combined into one package that are then displayed in turn to create a simple animation.

There are some good and bad points to this technology. The good news is that it is even simpler to implement than the Java Animator, although you lose the sound component. The bad news is that it creates very large GIF files, which can take a long time to download. In a GIF animation, all of the images it includes are saved within the same file, along with the instructions about how many times to display it.

By displaying only the first image in the file, an animated GIF will also work with browsers that don't support the animation portion. Of course, the user still must wait for the other images that are included in the animation package.

To create an animated GIF, you need the set of image files and a utility to assemble them together. You have the following options, depending on your platform:

- Windows: The most popular tool is Alchemy Mindworks GIF Construction Set, which also supports creating transparent and interlaced images. It's available from `www.mindworkshop.com/alchemy/`.

- Macintosh: GIFBuilder is a freeware utility with which you can assemble a set of GIF, PICT, or TIFF files into an animated GIF file. It's available from `www.mid.net/ INFO-MAC/`.

- UNIX: With a command-line utility called whirlGIF, you can assemble a set of GIF files into an animated GIF. It includes a variety of options for the animation, which are explained at `www.msg.net/utility/whirlgif/`.

At this point, you might be wondering why you can't just use your old reliable image editor. Animation has been a capability of GIF files for quite a while, but it hasn't been supported in very many places. Its newfound popularity on the Web has caught graphics programs unprepared.

After you assemble the animation, attempt to load it with your browser. If nothing happens, you need to make sure you're using the latest version of Navigator, Internet Explorer, or Mosaic.

# Non-HTML 3.2 Options for Multimedia

Other multimedia options are also covered in this chapter, including RealAudio, QuickTime movies, and virtual reality, although they are not currently part of the HTML 3.2 specification. I'll also spend a little time with browser-specific attributes to existing HTML tags.

## Adding Video with `dynsrc`: Internet Explorer

Although Internet Explorer is not widely supported by other browsers, Microsoft has equipped it to handle its native AVI video files. Microsoft accomplished this by adding the `dynsrc` attribute to the `<IMG>` tag. The syntax for an image then becomes

```
<IMG src="imageURL" dynsrc="video.avi">
```

If the browser doesn't support `dynsrc`, it ignores `dynsrc` and uses the image identified in `src`.

In addition, Microsoft added several other attributes to go along with `dynsrc` to help control its display, including the following:

- `controls`: This set of controls added to the bottom of the video frame direct fast-forward, rewind, stop, and play.

- ■ loop: This value determines how many times the video should replay. For example, a value of 3 causes the video to repeat three times and then stop. A value of -1 or INFINITE causes it to play in an endless loop.

- ■ start: The video can be started in two ways. The first is FILEOPEN, which causes the video to begin as soon as the entire HTML page and AVI file are loaded. The other option is MOUSEOVER, which prevents the video from starting until the user passes the mouse over the top of the frame.

## Adding Background Sounds: Internet Explorer

Another option Microsoft added for its browser is the capability to play a sound file as a soundtrack for a page. This is accomplished with the <BGSOUND> tag, which has the following syntax:

```
<BGSOUND src="soundURL" loop=##¦INFINITE>
```

In this syntax, the src is a WAV, MIDI, or AU sound file, and loop specifies how many times the sound should play. If loop is omitted, the default is one time. Otherwise, select -1 or INFI-NITE to play the sound in an endless loop.

## Scrolling Marquees: Internet Explorer

One other Microsoft innovation that has yet to catch on with other browsers is a tag to create a scrolling display. The basic syntax is

```
<MARQUEE>Text</MARQUEE>
```

Any text between the two tags appears on its own line, scrolling from right to left at a pace slow enough to read. When the message completely disappears on the left, it starts over from the right again, and so on, ad infinitum. Incompatible browsers simply show the text within the tags inline with surrounding text.

The formatting of the surrounding text determines the appearance of the marquee text. If the marquee happens to be in the middle of body text, it appears in the same size and face as the body text. If the marquee is enclosed in a heading element, it appears in the heading typeface.

A couple of restrictions are made on this formatting. You can't change the font color or make formatting changes within the marquee tag. All HTML tags within <MARQUEE> are ignored.

A Microsoft marquee includes the following optional attributes to fine-tune its behavior, depending on your intended effect:

- ■ behavior: This attribute determines how the message moves, either SCROLL, SLIDE, or ALTERNATE. The default is SCROLL. A SLIDE behavior is when the message comes in from the right and stops when the first letter touches the left margin. An ALTERNATE behavior is when the message comes in from the right, touches the left margin, and then moves back to the right margin. It then continues to bounce back and forth between the two margins.

- ◼ `direction`: This attribute, used only with `behavior=SCROLL`, determines the direction in which the marquee text moves. The default is `RIGHT`, which specifies text moving from the right side to the left. The other possible value is `LEFT`.

- ◼ `loop`: Like the attribute of the same name for AVI files and background sounds, this attribute determines how many times the marquee will scroll. The default is `INFINITE`, which also can be represented by `-1`. After a marquee stops, the message remains on the screen.

- ◼ `scrollamount`: This attribute determines the number of pixels by which to increment the text at each step in the scrolling process. Higher numbers mean faster scrolling, although it might not appear to move as smoothly.

- ◼ `scrolldelay`: This attribute determines the number of milliseconds to delay between each step in the scrolling animation. Larger numbers result in slower and less smooth scrolling.

- ◼ `bgcolor`: Normally, the marquee is transparent to the page behind it. The `bgcolor` attribute specifies a color for the space behind the marquee and is represented using a color name or an RGB hexadecimal number.

- ◼ `height`, `width`: These two attributes set the size occupied by the marquee. Either value can be set in pixels or as a percentage of the screen size. The default size is 100 percent of screen width and one text line of height.

- ◼ `hspace`, `vspace`: These attributes determine the amount of space (in pixels) between the edges of the marquee's space and other elements on the page. `hspace` stands for horizontal space (left and right), and `vspace` stands for vertical space (above and below).

- ◼ `align`: This attribute sets how text and other material adjacent to the marquee will align with the marquee's area. The values are `TOP`, `MIDDLE`, and `BOTTOM`. It does not affect text within the marquee, which is always aligned to the top of the available space.

**NOTE**

You also can include a marquee using one of the many Java applets designed for the purpose. The applet method guarantees compatibility with at least three browsers, while the `<MARQUEE>` tag limits your users to Internet Explorer.

It's unknown whether the `<MARQUEE>` tag will gain widespread acceptance. Sites that are designed specifically for Internet Explorer use `<MARQUEE>` widely, but outside of those situations, its use is rare.

## Plug-ins: Navigator and Internet Explorer

In the early days of Mosaic and other early Web browsers, for new additions to Web technology, you had to wait for a new version of the browser. If a new type of content was introduced, such as video or virtual reality, you had to wait until a new version of the browser that supported it was introduced.

Then, Netscape developed the plug-in concept with the 2.0 version of Navigator. Plug-ins add capability to a browser without changing the browser itself by directing the browser to use helper applications. This allows the browser to display a variety of content inline with other standard Web content. Plug-ins are available for displaying and editing spreadsheets, viewing any kind of graphics file imaginable, listening to sounds in varying formats, and displaying multimedia presentations.

---

### TIP

Netscape includes several of the more popular plug-ins, including plug-ins for virtual reality and Web chat, with its standard software release.

---

### NOTE

The HotJava browser is designed for Java developers and programmers for customization and expansion. By adding new classes to the base browser, developers can extend HotJava without completely rewriting the code.

This is similar to the plug-in concept, but it's actually the browser that is changing; the add-on becomes part of the browser rather than a helper application.

Sun doesn't expect HotJava to become a general-use browser like Navigator or Internet Explorer. Instead, it's hoping it will become the base for corporate intranet applications, because it is easily customizable to specific situations and circumstances.

---

One key problem with plug-ins is that they require your users to have a browser that supports plug-ins and have the proper plug-in installed. Many plug-ins are available for only one or two platforms, leaving another chunk of users out in the cold. And, you must coordinate with your system administrator to make sure the Web server knows how to deliver the goods.

If all of these items are in place, the user is set to receive the advanced content you want to deliver. One of the most popular multimedia plug-ins available is Shockwave from Macromedia, which enables page authors to display multimedia content developed using Shockwave Director. This content can take the form of animations, electronic books, games, or other items requiring synchronized sound and video with interactivity.

To place a plug-in on a page, use the `<EMBED>` tag. Three attributes are required, with the syntax

```
<EMBED src="URL" width=wPixels height=hPixels>
```

in which src is the location of the plug-in file and width and height define how much space the plug-in will occupy on the Web page. For plug-ins that require additional parameters, add additional attributes to the `<EMBED>` tag. Check the documentation for the specific plug-in you're using to see what it requires.

To support users who aren't using plug-in–capable browsers, use the `<NOEMBED>` tag immediately following the `<EMBED>` tag. This creates a place to provide a snapshot of the plug-in in action, alternate text, or a hyperlink to the application home page. The syntax is

```
<EMBED src="URL" width=wPixels height=hPixels>
<NOEMBED>
...substitute content...
</NOEMBED>
```

Plug-in–compatible browsers ignore everything between the `<NOEMBED>` tags. If a browser doesn't recognize the `<EMBED>` tag, it also won't recognize the `<NOEMBED>` tag or display anything within its borders.

## ActiveX Controls: Internet Explorer and Netscape

ActiveX is yet another option by which Web page designers can deliver specialized content to the user. This standard, developed by Microsoft, is a bit of a cross between Java and plug-ins. Like Java, it is loaded automatically when it encounters the browser. Like a plug-in, after it's loaded on the user's system, it stays there for the future and doesn't have to be reloaded.

**TIP**

Only Internet Explorer and Netscape Navigator support ActiveX. Other browsers might follow their lead, but there's no indication of that happening any time soon.

ActiveX controls also offer a variety of content options, including Shockwave, spreadsheets, and Windows-type controls. To include an ActiveX control, use the `<OBJECT>` tag with the syntax

```
<OBJECT classid="classID" data="contentFile" height="114" width="101">
</OBJECT>
```

in which `classid` is a 36-character string that identifies the control and `data` identifies the file that contains the content, such as a DCR file for a Shockwave Director movie. The `height` and `width` features set the space the object will occupy.

> **TIP**
>
> Class IDs are available from the software vendor who developed the ActiveX control.

> **NOTE**
>
> The World Wide Web Consortium is considering using the `<OBJECT>` tag for all specialized content, including Java applets, plug-ins, ActiveX controls, and other specialty items that have yet to be created. This would make life easier for page designers because several tags would be combined under one umbrella.

You also can use the following attributes with an ActiveX control:

- `codebase`: This attribute is the URL for the source of the control. Every Windows machine has a registry that includes virtually every bit of information about hardware and software for that particular machine. When a browser loads the class ID, it looks in the registry to see whether it's already loaded on the machine. If it is, it uses the local version. If it is not, the browser uses `codebase` to load it from the network.

  Because `codebases` can change with new versions of software, be sure to check with the software vendor to make sure you're using the right version.

- `codetype`: This attribute is an alternative method for the browser to determine whether it can handle the ActiveX object. The content type for ActiveX is `application/x-oleobject`.

- `align`: As with other content based on the `<IMG>` tag, you can use the `align` attribute to control the alignment of the ActiveX space in relation to surrounding text. The choices are `LEFT`, `RIGHT`, `TOP`, `MIDDLE`, and `BOTTOM` (default).

You should consider two final issues with ActiveX, the first of which is passing parameters to the control. To do this, use the <PARAM> tag between the <OBJECT> tags. The syntax is

```
<PARAM name="parameter" VALUE="content">
```

in which name is the parameter identifier and value is its setting. Parameter names and values will be unique for each control, so you need to consult any documentation for your specific circumstance.

Next is the issue of alternative content. As in a Java applet or Netscape plug-in, the <OBJECT> tag also supports content for incompatible browsers by inserting the appropriate HTML text, anchors, or image tags immediately before the closing </OBJECT>.

# Summary

In this chapter, you learned about several options for multimedia, including external and internal media, HTML-supported options, and browser-specific extensions.

Your Web browser cannot read external media files directly. Instead, your browser links to an external file to start up a helper application to view or play those files. The link is created using the existing hyperlink anchor tag—<A href="URL">.

Inline multimedia is directly supported by HTML 3.2 in only two ways. The first is through Java applets, which use the <APPLET> tag to insert small Java programs that provide a variety of capabilities. One example provided with the Java Development Kit is Animator, which is a utility to provide synchronized sound and animation on a Web page.

The other multimedia method that HTML 3.2 directly supports is GIF animation. Animated GIFs are created with a separate utility that packages several image files into one and that is then interpreted and played back by the browser.

In HTML 4.0, you can expect the <OBJECT> tag to replace all of the other current tags used to insert inline content, including images, sounds, Java applets, plug-ins, and ActiveX controls. The tag, as proposed by W3C, includes all of the attributes needed by all of these items so that you'll retain the same control over their appearance and behavior.

Netscape and Internet Explorer support a variety of new tags and capabilities of those browsers, including tags for scrolling marquees, inline video, ActiveX controls, and plug-ins.

# Creating Image Maps

*by Rick Darnell*

## IN THIS CHAPTER

Image maps are one of the most useful navigation tools developed in recent years. The first step toward this feature was simple. It was a row of separate images, each with its own hyperlink anchor. It looked something like this:

```
<A HREF="home.htm"><IMG SRC="home.gif"></A>
<A HREF="search.htm"><IMG SRC="search.gif"></A>
<A HREF="next.htm"><IMG SRC="next.gif"></A>
```

This worked well for navigation bars, but it still was a little unwieldy with the number of tags, and it slowed down the browser with three additional images to load. It also didn't allow images to be embedded inside each other.

Enter the image map concept. An image map is a graphics image (GIF, JPEG, or other) that is subdivided into regions called *hotspots*. Each of the hotspots corresponds to a different URL, enabling one graphics file to lead to many destinations. For example, you can use a geographic map of the Rocky Mountain region to create an image map that offers site-specific weather forecasts, allowing users to click on the area for the information they need. Or, you can create an image map from a picture of several people, so that a click on a person's image brings up information about that person.

Image maps are implemented in two ways. The first way is through a *server-side* map. While the image is loaded on the user's browser, the hotspot coordinates are located on the Web server. When the user clicks on an area, the coordinates are passed to the server, where they are interpreted and the corresponding URL is sent back to the URL. The browser then requests the document at the URL from the server.

The other method is through a *client-side* map. A client-side map has all of the hotspot information included as part of an HTML page. Usually, this is on the same page as the image, but it can reside elsewhere. When the user clicks on the image map, the browser does all the work to determine the URL, which is then passed to the server.

Client-side image maps are the preferred option because they are quicker and require less work from the server. Most browsers support client-side maps, although there are still many in use that support only server-side maps.

---

**TIP**

Whichever method of image mapping you use, it's a good practice to include text hyperlink versions of the links contained in the image map. If a browser doesn't support images or images are turned off, the browser still has access to the links.

---

# Server-Side Image Maps

As mentioned in the introduction, server-side image maps are the way that this technology was introduced to the Web. The user clicks on an image, and the x,y coordinates are sent to a special program on the server. Other than actually creating the image map information, it is a simple matter to include on the Web page. The syntax is

```
<A href="/scriptURL/imageMapURL">
<IMG src="imageSource" ismap></A>
```

where *scriptURL* is the path to the script that interprets image maps, and *imageMapURL* is the path to the MAP file containing the hotspot coordinates. The construction of the MAP file is covered in the next two sections under each server type.

The path to the script file varies depending on the type of Web server in use. On an NCSA server, the path is probably something similar to /cgi-bin/imagemap, while a CERN typically uses /htbin/htimage. In both cases, the script file is immediately followed by the path to the image map information.

### TIP

Your map file cannot reside in the top document directory of your server because there is no way to specify this directory in the concatenated format. The map coordinates *must* be in a subdirectory. Many authors include the MAP file in the same directory as the image for easy identification.

So far, the first three steps of creating a server-side image map have been covered in this chapter:

1. Select a graphics file to use for the image map. This can be any browser-compatible image file, but GIFs and JPEGs are the most common and widely supported.
2. Insert the image file using the HTML <IMG> tag with the ismap attribute. For more information on using this tag, see Chapter 12, "Adding Images to Your Web Page."
3. Enclose the image tag with a hyperlink anchor using the server image map script URL combined with the path to the image MAP file for the href attribute.

Now comes the last step—actually creating the MAP file. The method differs slightly depending on the type of server you're using. The two predominant options are CERN and NCSA.

### NOTE

CERN stands for *Conseil European pour la Recherche Nucleaire*, or in English, *European Laboratory for Particle Physics*. It is based in Geneva, Switzerland, and is the birthplace of the World Wide Web. Researchers at CERN developed the Web in 1989 as a collaborative network.

*continues*

**14**

CREATING IMAGE
MAPS

*continued*

NCSA stands for *National Center for Supercomputing Applications*. It is a research center affiliated with the University of Illinois at Urbana-Champaign and specializes in scientific visualization. NCSA labored in relative obscurity until it developed NCSA Mosaic, the first graphical browser for the Web.

Knowing what these two organizations are won't make you any richer, but it might win you a dozen donuts on a radio quiz show sometime.

Most servers in the United States use the NCSA HTTP standard, although CERN servers are still widespread. You'll need to check with your Internet service provider or system administrator to see which format you'll need to use.

Before you begin creating your image map, you'll need a copy of the image you're using and a way to identify pixel coordinates within it. Most popular graphics programs support this capability, including PaintShop Pro and xRes.

## Creating a MAP File for CERN

There are many utilities you can use to create a MAP file, and three are covered at the end of this chapter. For now, let's leave utilities behind and work with the MAP at its lowest level. If you're using a mapping utility, these details are typically handled by the program.

At its basic level, a MAP file is simply a text file with a list of shapes, coordinates, and URLs. Four keywords are used with a CERN MAP:

- ▪ `rectangle`: Indicates a rectangular area by defining two opposite corners (usually the left top and bottom right). It can be abbreviated as `rect`:

  ```
  rectangle (25,50) (35,70) http://www.wossomatta.edu/
  rect (25,50) (35,70) http://www.wossomatta.edu/
  ```

- ▪ `circle`: Indicates a circle by defining the center and a radius. This is for circles only; image maps don't support ovals. It can be abbreviated as `circ`.

  ```
  circle (25,50) 30 http://www.wossomatta.edu/
  circ (25,50) 30 http://www.wossomatta.edu/
  ```

- ▪ `polygon`: Defining a polygon is a lot like creating a dot-to-dot puzzle. It includes a list of coordinates that are connected in turn until the last. If the figure isn't closed by a set of coordinates identical to the first, the script automatically connects the first and last set of coordinates, as in this example:

  ```
  polygon (25,50) (35,60) (25,70) (15,60) http://www.wossomatta.edu/
  poly (25,50) (35,60) (25,70) (15,60) http://www.wossomatta.edu/
  ```

- ▪ `default`: This specifies a URL to use if a mouse click doesn't land within any of the other shapes. It is always a good idea to add this item, even if the URL just points back to the current page:

  ```
  default http://www.wossomatta.edu/
  def http://www.wossomatta.edu/
  ```

The shapes are checked individually in the order in which they appear in the MAP file. Searching stops at the first match, and the corresponding URL is returned to the browser. This process has an interesting effect when used to define overlapping areas. The following snippet defines two areas—a red circle and a blue rectangle covering the circle's lower-right quarter:

```
rect (94,95) (290,213) /blue_rect.html
circ (103,93) 77 /red_circ.html
```

The image is represented in Figure 14.1. When the mouse is clicked on the overlapping area, the mapping information is evaluated in the order in which it appears in the file. Because the rectangle is listed first, its URL is returned after the click, and the information for the circle is never reached.

**FIGURE 14.1.**

*Overlapping hotspots are handled by placing the topmost element in the MAP file first and following with each lower element.*

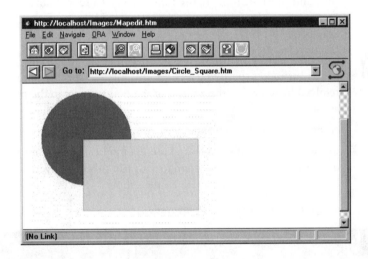

The last step is to locate the `imagemap.conf` system file on the Web server. This file includes entries for every image map located on the server. You'll need to add a line with the name and location of the MAP file. Using the preceding circle and rectangle example, the entry would look like this:

```
Circle_Square : /images/Circle_Square.MAP
```

The downside to all of this work is that it can be a problem getting access to the `imagemap.conf` file if your pages are on someone else's server. Chances are you won't have the rights to modify system files. And, if your pages move from a CERN server to an NCSA server, you'll need to change the syntax of your MAP file.

## Creating a MAP File for NCSA

The syntax for creating a MAP file for an NCSA server is similar to the syntax for a CERN server. However, a couple of key differences prevent a MAP file created for one type of server from working on the other.

14

CREATING IMAGE MAPS

The format of the file is the same—a text file with a list of shapes and coordinates. The following five types of values are allowed in the file:

- `rect`: Indicates a rectangular area by defining the top left and bottom right corners. Here is an example:

  ```
  rect http://www.wossomatta.edu/ 25,50 35,70
  ```

- `circle`: Indicates a circle by defining the center and an outside point on the circle. This is for circles only; image maps don't support ovals. Here is an example:

  ```
  circ http://www.wossomatta.edu/ 25,50 55,30
  ```

- `poly`: A polygon includes a list of up to 100 pairs of coordinates that are connected in turn until the last. If the figure isn't closed by a set of coordinates identical to the first, the script automatically connects the first and last set of coordinates. Here is an example:

  ```
  poly http://www.wossomatta.edu/ 25,50 35,60 25,70 15,60
  ```

- `point`: Instead of specifying an area, this method specifies one point. The URL is resolved by returning the address of the point closest to the mouse click. Here is an example:

  ```
  point http://www.wossomatta.edu/ 25,50
  ```

- `default`: This specifies a URL to use if a mouse click doesn't land within any of the other shapes. It is always a good idea to add this item, even if the URL just points back to the current page. Here is an example:

  ```
  default http://www.wossomatta.edu/
  ```

### TIP

It doesn't make a lot of sense to include only one point with a default line in an image map. Anywhere the user clicks will be closer to the point, and the default URL will never be returned.

Like the CERN MAP file, each set of coordinates is evaluated in the order in which it was placed in the file. This means that overlapping images also are handled in the same manner.

# Client-Side Image Maps

Most major browsers now support client-side image maps. This is a method by which the browser handles all the work of associating URLs with image hotspots. This is a preferable option because it doesn't place an extra load on the server and it is faster.

An additional benefit of client-side maps appears in the status bar of the user's browser. In a server-side map, the only URL that appears when the mouse is passed over the image is the path to the CGI script and MAP file. In a client-side implementation, the URL represented by the hotspot is displayed in the status bar.

> **TIP**
>
> Don't forget that the URLs in an image map can point to any Web resource, including sound files, video files, and FTP servers.

A client-side image map is enabled by adding the `usemap` attribute to the `<IMG>` tag. The syntax is

```
<IMG src="imageURL" usemap="mapName">
```

where *imageURL* is the location of the image file, and *mapName* is the URL of the mapping tags. As you'll see in the next section, every set of client-side mapping information is given a unique name. For the `<IMG>` tag, this name is referenced the same as an anchor. If the map information is located in the same file as the image tag, the format is `usemap="#mapName"`. If the information is located in a different file, the format is `usemap="URL#mapName"`.

With the `<IMG>` tag in place, it's time to actually assemble the shapes and coordinates that define the hotspots in the image.

## Defining a <MAP>

Creating a client-side image map requires a set of HTML tags that define the hotspots and their corresponding URLs. This utilizes the `<MAP>` and `<AREA>` tags. Their syntax is

```
<MAP name=mapName>
<AREA shape="rect¦circle¦poly" coords="pixelCoordinates" HREF="URL">
...
</MAP>
```

where *mapName* is a required attribute with a unique name for the map. This name must not conflict with other named elements on the page, such as anchors or applets; otherwise, unpredictable behavior could result.

The `<AREA>` tag requires three attributes. The `shape` attribute determines the basic shape of the hotspot and is one of four values: `rect`, `circle`, `poly`, or `default`. The `size` attribute also determines the formatting of *pixelCoordinates* in the `coords` attribute. The format for each of the values is slightly different, as you see in the following list:

- `rect`: A rectangular area defined by the area extending from the top left to the bottom right. Here is an example:

  ```
  <AREA shape="rect" coords="25,50 , 55,80" href="http://www.wossomatta.edu/">
  ```

- `circle`: A circle (no ovals) defined by the center of the circle and the radius in pixels. Here is an example:

  ```
  <AREA shape="circle" coords="25,50 , 30" href="http://www.wossomatta.edu/">
  ```

■  poly: An irregular shape defined by a series of coordinate pairs, resulting in a dot-to-dot area. The polygon is closed by connecting the last set of coordinates to the first. Here is an example:

```
<AREA shape="poly" coords="25,50 , 35,60 , 25,70 , 15,60"
      href="http://www.wossomatta.edu/">
```

■ default: The default URL for a click that doesn't land in any of the defined hotspots. An alternate attribute for href is nohref, which indicates that nothing should happen:

```
<AREA shape="default" href="http://www.wossomatta.edu/">
<AREA shape="default" nohref>
```

## A PROPOSED METHOD FOR IMAGE MAPS

One of the new tags under consideration for subsequent versions of HTML is the <FIG> element. It supports client-side image maps in a way that is slightly different from the <IMG> and <MAP> combination.

The basic format for inserting an image with <FIG> is

```
<FIG src="Image.gif" width=150 height=50>
</FIG>
```

Note the closing tag. This is where the functionality for image maps comes into play:

```
<FIG src="Image.gif" width=150 height=50>
<H3>Destinations</H3>
<UL>
<LI><A href="http://www.wossomatta.edu/football"
      shape="rect 25,50 , 55,80" >Football</A>
<LI><A href="http://www.wossomatta.edu/fight_song"
      shape="rect 55,50 , 85,80" >Fight Song</A>
<LI><A href="http://www.wossomatta.edu/coach_canute"
      shape="rect 85,50 , 115,80" >Our Leader</A>
</UL>
</FIG>
```

There are several things to pay attention to with the new proposal. First, you can embed any HTML within the <FIG> elements. If the browser doesn't support images, the text is displayed instead.

Second, an additional attribute is added to the anchor tag to convert it into an image map parameter. If the image is displayed, the information in the shape attribute is used to define the hotspots. If the text is used, the shape information is ignored, and the anchor is treated as any other hyperlink.

These two features of <FIG> are especially useful for speech-based browsers for the sight impaired and for people still using text-only browsers who would normally miss the links offered in the image.

After you assemble a client-side map, the next question is how do you know if the user's browser will know what to do with it? Basically, you don't. Too many browsers are surfing the Web to guarantee compatibility with a client-side solution. Therefore, to ensure that everyone can use your image map, use a client-side and server-side map.

This doesn't require two images for each one. You can combine all the tags and necessary attributes within one image:

```
<A href="/cgi-bin/images/Circle_Square.MAP">
<IMG src="/images/Circle_Square.gif" usemap="#Circle_Square" ismap>
</A>
```

When interpreted by a browser that doesn't support client-side maps, the usemap attribute is ignored and the server-side map is used.

Another option for supporting browsers that are incompatible with client-side maps is to provide a hyperlink to the choices that would have been available through the map. The preferred location for these choices is in the same file, although they could be in a separate file. Here is an example:

```
<A href="#imageMapText">
<IMG src="/images/Circle_Square.gif" usemap="#Circle_Square">
</A>
```

In this case, if the browser doesn't support usemap, clicking on the image will lead the user to the location with the choices.

# Image Map Editing Tools

Many applications are available for a multitude of platforms that make the process of generating image maps much easier than working with a text editor and an image editor to determine coordinates and syntax. The choices are by no means limited to the applications I've reviewed here, nor are these necessarily the best utilities. This should just give you an idea of what is available for use.

Two of the easier-to-use applications are discussed in the following sections. The last includes more advanced features but isn't as easy or intuitive to use.

## MapEdit

MapEdit is one of the more popular applications for making image maps. It provides a WYSIWYG (what you see is what you get) interface and comes in versions for both UNIX and Windows. (See Figure 14.2.)

**FIGURE 14.2.**

*MapEdit is a simple visual editor for creating image maps, but it is more than adequate for most users.*

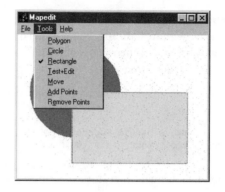

MapEdit loads the image into a scrollable and resizable window, where you can draw polygons, circles, and rectangles; a URL is specified for each. It also allows you to go back, delete each hotspot, and set a default URL for clicks outside of any of the hotspots.

You can also associate comments of arbitrary length with each object if you are creating an NCSA-format map. If you are creating a client-side image map, you can provide alternate text (using the alt attribute) to be shown to users of nongraphical browsers.

Although you can save any of your maps as client-side HTML files, MapEdit allows you to load only maps formatted for server-side mapping.

MapEdit is available on the Web at http://www.boutell.com/mapedit/.

## Map This!

Map This! is a complete mapping utility that supports all three map formats—CERN, NCSA, and client-side—in a graphics format. (See Figure 14.3.) After reading any of the three formats, Map This! can convert it to either of the remaining two.

**FIGURE 14.3.**

*Map This! is a freeware program that includes support for all three image map formats.*

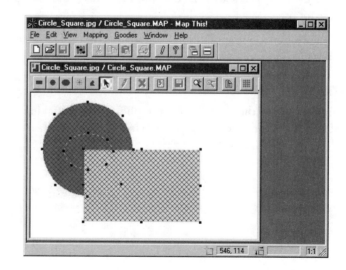

Like other image map programs, Map This! doesn't verify URLs. It is up to you to verify that you're providing valid values. Map This! also doesn't check values for your hotspots. Because of a glitch in its editing interface, it will allow you to identify hotspots in "offscreen" areas that will never be hit.

After the initial hotspots are defined, you can resize, reshape, move, or delete them. In addition to specifying the URL, Map This! also supports an additional line of explanation where you can enter a brief note. This additional information is embedded with special codes so that it won't interfere with the operation of your MAP file.

The program supports up to 1,024 areas per map. If you try to load more, it generates an error. This shouldn't be a limitation for the majority of these situations because most servers will choke before processing that many URLs.

Map This! is available on the Web at

```
http://galadriel.ecaetc.ohio-state.edu/tc/mt/
```

## Live Image

Live Image is a similar product to Map This!, except it's shareware instead of freeware and offers a few more features. (See Figure 14.4.) Live Image includes an Image Map wizard for easier creation of any type of image map. You can create your first image map in just a few minutes by answering a few questions. For general editing, Live Image also supports dragging and dropping of URL links from Netscape and Internet Explorer.

**FIGURE 14.4.**

*LiveImage includes all of the basic features of an image map editor, plus wizards to help with common tasks and easy creation of button bars.*

14

CREATING IMAGE MAPS

The program supports three file formats—GIF, JPEG, and PNG. Other file formats are available via application plug-ins. Images can also be converted between formats.

Another very useful feature is a wizard for creating button bars. LiveImage includes several predefined button images that can be put in a row, stacked, or placed in columns to create a custom button bar. The images are joined together, along with labels and links you provide, into one image file along with a companion map file. The map file can be in HTML, NCSA, or CERN format.

LiveImage is available on the Web at `http://www.mediatec.com/`.

# Summary

Image maps enable you to turn a GIF or JPEG into a clickable map by designating polygons, circles, and rectangles within the image and specifying a URL for each spot. The two different kinds are server-side and client-side. A server-side map requires a special script on the Web server to interpret the coordinates from the user's mouse click, and it is slower due to the extra time needed for client/server communication. Client-side maps do the same thing server-side maps do, without the help of a special program on the server.

If you're using a server-side map, you'll need to create a MAP file that contains all of the image coordinates and URLs. The syntax for relaying the shape, coordinate, and URL information varies depending on whether you're using a CERN or NCSA-based server.

A client-side image map includes all of the mapping information embedded in the <MAP> and <AREA> tags. This enables the browser to handle all of the processing for the user's clicks without extra communication with the server. To be safe, you can combine server-side and client-side mapping information for the same image. This ensures compatibility, no matter what browser is in use.

Image maps are a powerful feature provided by HTML for your graphics. They can turn your images into powerful navigation tools that users will appreciate.

# Building and Using HTML Forms

*by Rick Darnell*

**CHAPTER 15**

## IN THIS CHAPTER

So far, the HTML elements covered in this book have been static creatures. You put them on a page and the user can look at them, but not much else. That all changes in this chapter.

Forms are the most important interactive feature HTML has to offer. With a form, users can give feedback and comments, submit orders and queries, or provide registration information. In short, forms open a two-way dialog between you and your users. You ask the questions by designing a form, and the user answers by filling out the form.

HTML form elements were added with HTML 2.0. All the basic features were added that computer users are already familiar with, including lists, buttons, checkboxes, and text fields. The contents are sent to a CGI script for processing or e-mailed directly to one or more recipients.

Creating a form is a two-part process. First, there's the form itself, which is a set of tags and attributes contained within a pair of <FORM> elements. That part is covered in this chapter. The next step is putting together a CGI script on the server to handle the form's contents. More information about processing HTML forms with databases is covered in Chapter 27, "CGI Programming," and Chapter 33, "HTML and Databases."

# Beginning with Basics: <FORM>

All forms have one thing in common: They include an opening and closing <FORM> tag. What happens between the tags is as varied as any set of HTML. Any other text or form element is allowed within a form, including paragraphs, tables, images, and multimedia. The only thing that is *not* allowed is another form.

The usual syntax for the <FORM> tag is

```
<FORM method="get¦post" action="scriptURL">
```

where method determines how the information is sent to the script, and action sets the path to the CGI script that will process the contents. The URL can be a relative path for a script located on the same server as the form, or a complete URL including protocol and server name.

There are two choices for method—GET or POST. If the method is not specified, it defaults to GET. Data sent using the GET method is appended to the script URL. When it arrives at the server, it is separated and assigned to two variables—the script URL (SCRIPT_NAME) and the string of data (QUERY_STRING). It is limited by constraints on the length of the URL that can be handled by the server, which is usually 255 characters.

The other method, POST, is becoming the preferred method for sending information. The data is sent as a separate stream of information to the script. This enables the script to directly receive information without passing through a decoding process in the server, so the script can read an unlimited amount of information.

The script will dictate the method used, but here's a simple rule of thumb if you're offered a choice. Use GET only when the length of data input is small.

You can use the POST method to test your forms, depending on the type and brand of Web server you're using. Most NCSA-type servers include a script called post-query in their cgi-bin directory. WebSite has a program script called cgitest.exe or cgitest32.exe in the cgi-win directory, depending on the platform and version.

To use these testing scripts, make sure your opening form element looks similar to this:

```
<FORM method="POST" action="/cgi-bin/post-query">
```

The NCSA version is usually accessed by using /cgi-bin/post-query, while the WebSite version uses /cgi-win/cgitest32.exe/Form. Check your server documentation or ask your system administrator for the path and name of the script for your site.

When a generic test script is used, its output usually resembles what you see in Figure 15.1. It consists of a list of each of the form fields and the corresponding value that was sent with it.

**FIGURE 15.1.**

*A form-testing script on the WebSite server returns each of the form element names and values it received to make sure the form is working properly.*

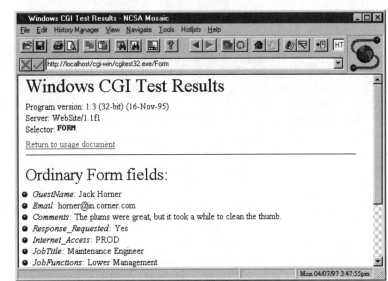

The last attribute to use with <FORM> is enctype. This attribute specifies the MIME content type for encoding the form's data. In short, it tells the browser how to format the information before passing it to the server. The default value is x-www-form-encoded. This is also referred to as URL encoding, and it is discussed in greater detail in Chapter 27.

Theoretically, you could use any valid MIME type, such as text/plain. However, most forms use the default encoding to avoid problems in manipulating data that is not encoded in some form. Form data is not encoded to keep it secret; it is encoded to ensure that input fields are easily matched to their values.

# Giving a Place to <INPUT> Content

The elements for use within a form are simple but include enough variety to fit most any situation that will arise during form design. The base tag for defining each element is the <INPUT> tag, which is used to add buttons, images, checkboxes, radio buttons, passwords and text fields. The base syntax is

```
<INPUT type="elementType" name="fieldName">
```

where `elementType` defines how the input field looks on the screen, and `fieldName` assigns a keyword to the field that is used to reference its value within the CGI script. The <INPUT> tag also can have other attributes, depending on the value of the type attribute. The type-specific attributes are covered for each item.

Although the appearance of each type of input item is different to the user, they are all submitted to the CGI script as pairs of names and values.

Two other types of form elements are not implemented through <INPUT>—text boxes and lists. These are covered in their own respective sections later in this chapter.

## FORM ETIQUETTE

You should follow a few simple rules with any form you put on your Web page. These aren't hard and fast rules; rather, they are just some suggestions to make your life easier—kind of like knowing which fork to use first at a fancy restaurant.

First, make the form as short and simple as possible. A form that stretches for more than a couple of pages or screens is awfully cumbersome and wears down users before they reach the end. The more questions you ask, the more users won't hang around to complete the form.

Second, plan, plan, plan. Know what information you want from the user and why you want it. If your reason for asking for a particular item, like age, is "just because," then it's probably a good idea not to ask.

Sketch your form on paper the way it should appear on the user's screen. There should be some kind of flow to the form. One element should lead to another, so that the user doesn't skip anything. If users have to guess where to go next, chances are higher that they won't get to the end of the form to press the Submit button.

It's always a good idea to tell the user why you're asking for the information. Is this to register software or to be on a mailing list? Is it to sign a guest book or provide an opinion? There are a lot of reasons for people not to trust what they see on their browser. Give them a reason to trust your request.

By the same token, don't lock them into submitting your form. Always give users a Reset button to clear the information and a link to more information about the form.

The eight values for type are covered in the following sections. Table 15.1 presents a rundown of each; Figure 15.2 shows their basic appearances.

**Table 15.1. The eight values for input type.**

| *Type* | *Description* |
|---|---|
| TEXT | One-line text field |
| PASSWORD | One-line text field where the input is masked with asterisks |
| HIDDEN | One-line text field that is not displayed but sent to the script |
| CHECKBOX | Yes/no or on/off choice |
| RADIO | One or more checkboxes grouped together |
| SUBMIT | Button to submit form contents |
| RESET | Button to clear the form contents to default values |
| IMAGE | Image to click instead of a Submit button |

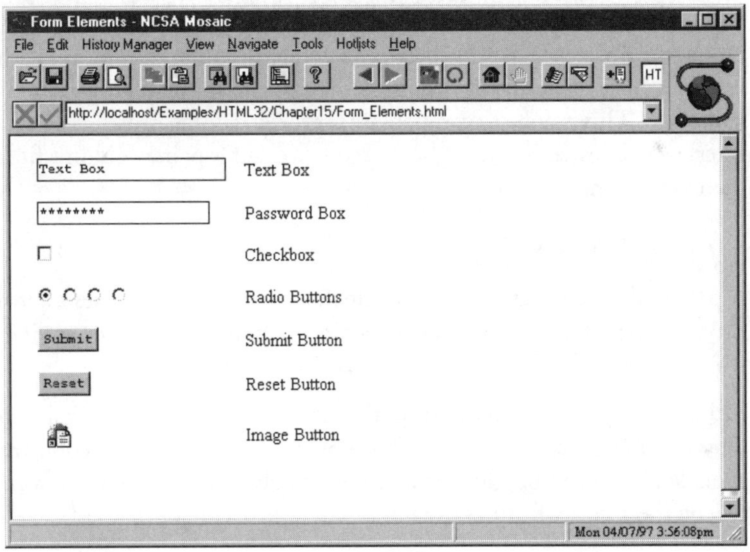

**FIGURE 15.2.**

*Seven of the eight input types are shown in this figure. Because it's not displayed by the browser,* HIDDEN *is not shown.*

## type="TEXT"

Text fields are used for any information that doesn't fit within the confines of the other types. This includes information such as names, addresses, job titles, telephone numbers, and so on. Because a text field accepts virtually any type of input, it is one of the most versatile elements.

Here are the three additional attributes that can be used with a text field:

| | |
|---|---|
| maxlength | This attribute sets the maximum allowable length of the field, specified in characters. If this value is not specified, there is no limit. |
| size | This controls how wide, in characters, the box appears on the Web page. How many characters are actually displayed at one time varies because many browsers use proportional instead of fixed-width typefaces. |
| value | This is used to initialize the fields with a default string of text. The user can add, change, or delete the information if needed. If a Reset button is used, the contents of value are reloaded back into the field. |

The following example shows a text field that allows 35 characters but displays only 20 at a time. It doesn't have a default value:

```
<INPUT type="TEXT" name="NameFirst" maxlength="35" size="20">
```

The next example is a text field that includes a default value for a state name:

```
<INPUT type="TEXT" name="State" maxlength="2" size="4" value="WY">
```

Notice the difference in value between maxlength and size. The size attribute is larger, allowing for a little more display room, although the input is still limited to two characters by maxlength. This is done to compensate for the way some browsers handle the text. If two characters were allowed for size also, certain two-letter pairs wouldn't fit in the box for display, such as "WY" and "MA".

## type="PASSWORD"

A password field is a special type of single-line text box that uses asterisks to mask the input. Anything typed in a password field is hidden from view to keep prying eyes away from passwords, account numbers, and other guarded information.

Although the display is masked on the screen, the actual transmission of password field contents is not encoded in any way. This provides security against people who look over the user's shoulder. It doesn't provide security for actually transmitting the information. You'll need to rely on the security features of your server to take care of that task.

In its other behavior, a password field includes the same attributes as a text field: maxlength, size, and value.

> **TIP**
>
> A default value for a password might seem a little strange, but it is actually pretty useful for things such as visitor passwords.

## type="HIDDEN"

This is another type of text field, but nothing is shown on the screen. It provides a way to send additional information to the CGI script that cannot be changed by the user. For example, to send the name of an HTML file, you could use a line such as

```
<INPUT type="HIDDEN" name="File" value="survey.html">
```

Some CGI programs use hidden fields to pass information from one page to another. If a user types a name or account number on one form, the CGI script processes it and includes it on a second follow-up form that retains the information in a hidden field. This makes it easier for the users because they don't have to supply the information again.

> **TIP**
>
> Even though the field is hidden from view on the browser, it can still be examined by the user through looking at the HTML source code. The hidden input field is not a good place to mumble nasty things under your breath.

## type="CHECKBOX"

Checkboxes are used to record yes/no or true/false information such as the following:

■ Do you want to receive more information about our products?

■ Are you age 18 or older?

■ Do you own a car?

The checkbox is typically represented as a small box that the user clicks to place or remove an *x* or checkmark. This type of input element returns a value to the CGI script only if it's selected. If the box isn't checked, no value is returned to the script.

There are two attributes to consider with a checkbox. The first is value. This is the value sent to the CGI script if the checkbox is selected. If omitted, the default value is "on".

The other attribute is checked. This controls the initial status of the checkbox. The following example is for a field that a user selects to be placed on a company mailing list. The element defaults to "yes":

```
<INPUT type="checkbox" NAME="send_mail" VALUE="yes" checked>
```

## type="RADIO"

Radio buttons are similar to checkboxes, but they present a range of choices. Only one radio button in a group is selected at a time. Selecting another button in the same group deselects the current choice.

The first attribute to use with radio buttons is name. This is used to identify each of the buttons in the group. One <INPUT> tag is required for each button, with each button having the same name. Then, each button is assigned a value to return if it is selected, as shown in the following:

```
Cash <INPUT type="radio" name="payment_type" value="Cash">
COD <INPUT type="radio" name="payment_type" value="COD">
Visa <INPUT type="radio" name="payment_type" value="Visa">
Mastercard <INPUT type="radio" name="payment_type" value="Mastercard">
American Express <INPUT type="radio" name="payment_type" value="Amex">
```

The preceding set of radio buttons presents a list of payment options. However, if the user doesn't select one of the payment types, nothing is returned to the CGI script. You can specify a default value by adding the checked attribute to one of the buttons.

Only one button in a group can be initially selected, although it's possible to include the checked attribute with more than one button. This situation is usually resolved by the browser by selecting the last button with checked. However, this is not consistent across all browsers and versions. Usually, the last item is marked for selection, but Netscape and Microsoft occasionally use the first, depending on the version. For consistent results, make sure only one button is marked as default.

## type="SUBMIT"

Although it is included with input types, the SUBMIT type results in a button that, when pressed, sends the contents of the form to the CGI script specified in the action attribute of the <FORM> tag.

**NOTE**

Scripting languages such as JavaScript and Visual Basic Script can add additional functionality to buttons and forms beyond just submitting the contents to a URL. You can calculate totals, load pages, create frames, and perform other activities besides the basic submit and reset functions.

See Chapter 28, "Integrating JavaScript and HTML," and Chapter 30, "Integrating ActiveX and VBScript," for more information.

The default label on a Submit button is Submit. You can use the `value` attribute with a Submit button to change the default to something else, as shown in the following

```
<INPUT type="submit" value="Place your order">
```

The button will grow in width to accommodate any text you add. If the available width is constrained by another element, such as a table, the button's height will also adjust until all text fits.

# type="RESET"

Clicking a Reset button restores any default values specified in individual form elements. If a default value is not defined, any content within the element is erased.

Like the Submit button, you can also change the name of the Reset button using the `value` attribute.

# type="IMAGE"

The image type is similar to the Submit button, but it uses a graphic instead of a button. One attribute is required and two attributes are optional. The base syntax for the image type is

```
<INPUT type="IMAGE" src="ImageURL">
```

where *ImageURL* is the location and name of the image file. In addition, you also can control the alignment of the image in relation to other items around it by using the `align` attribute. The legal values are TOP, MIDDLE, and BOTTOM, and they behave the same as the corresponding values for the <IMG> tag, described in Chapter 12, "Adding Images to Your Web Page."

One of the features of using an image is that the coordinates of the pointer's x and y position on the image are sent to the browser, allowing you to use it as an image map for different processing options depending on where the user clicked.

The last attribute is `name`. The name assigned to the image is also sent to the CGI script in the form

```
Name.x=xPosition
Name.y=yPosition
```

where *Name* is the name assigned to the image, and *xPosition* and *yPosition* are the x and y coordinates where the user clicked. This allows an additional degree of control over processing by providing the CGI script a way to differentiate between images and areas within the images.

# <TEXTAREA>

The <TEXTAREA> input type uses its own tag. It is related to <INPUT type="TEXT"> in that it receives free form text input. (See Figure 15.3.) However, a text area allows the user to enter larger amounts of information with multiple lines.

**FIGURE 15.3.**

*A text area form element allows an unlimited amount of input using multiple lines within a scrolling box.*

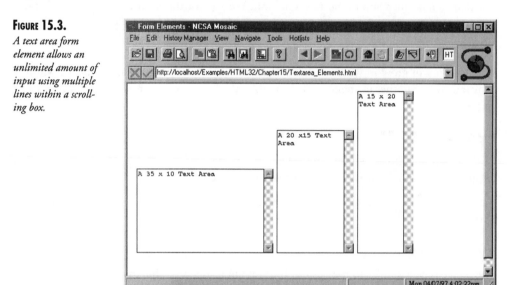

The first attribute of <TEXTAREA> is the same as other input types. This attribute is name, which assigns a keyword to the field that is used to reference its value within the CGI script.

The next two attributes set the visible size of the text area—rows and cols. As you can discern from the names, rows describes how high the area is in text lines, while cols sets the width of the area in characters. Because a user can enter text beyond the horizontal or vertical constraints of the box, the user's browser will provide scrollbars to assist in editing.

A text area form element requires an opening and closing tag. Between the opening and closing tags, you can provide a default set of text to use when the form is first displayed, which is also reinstated if the Reset button is pressed. If no default text is desired, the closing tag immediately follows the opening tag.

# <SELECT>

The last type of form element is a selection box. It can take the form of a drop-down list or a menu of items. (See Figure 15.4.) It is similar to the radio button input type, although it is easier to create and more flexible to use. The syntax for a selection box is

```
<SELECT name="selectionName" [size=visibleItems][multiple]>
<OPTION [selected]>Option1 Text
...Add'l options...
</SELECT>
```

where name is used the same as other form input items, size determines how many options are visible at one time, and multiple controls whether more than one item can be chosen at one time.

**FIGURE 15.4.**

*The selection box on the left includes the* multiple *attribute, and the one on the right does not.*

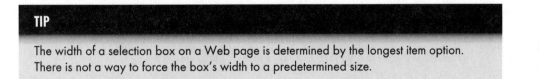

The default value for size depends on the browser and whether multiple is used. On any browser, if multiple is not used, the default size is one line. A button with an arrow on it is provided to display the rest of the list.

If multiple is used, on the other hand, the behavior depends on the browser. On some browsers, such as NCSA or Spyglass Mosaic, the default for size becomes the number of items on the list. On Internet Explorer, however, the default is four lines, with a scrollbar provided to access the rest. If you need a consistent appearance, use the size attribute.

> **TIP**
>
> The width of a selection box on a Web page is determined by the longest item option. There is not a way to force the box's width to a predetermined size.

Each item in the list is specified using an <OPTION> tag. The text to the right of the tag is treated the same as value is in other form items such as text boxes. Alternatively, you can use the value attribute with <OPTION> to specify the text to send to the CGI script, and then the text is treated like a label.

If the selected attribute is included, that item is chosen initially. More than one item can be marked with selected if the multiple attribute is also used in the <SELECT> tag.

# A Completed Form

Now that you've been through each of the form elements and their various and sundry attributes, it's time to take a step back and look at an entire form. This form is designed to connect with a CGI script that will post the contents to a guest book database.

The guest book includes requests for a wide variety of information, including the user's name and e-mail address, requests for a reply, comments, and some demographic information.

First, create the opening form tag. Because this form has the potential to return a lot of information, use the POST method. The name of the script is guest_register.pl, which is located in /cgi-bin:

```
<FORM method="POST" action="/cgi-bin/guest_register.pl">
```

With the container tags for the form in place, it's time to start adding individual elements. Three things are wanted the most from this form—the user's name, e-mail address, and comments. The first two items are handled with text fields. The name is limited to 50 characters, and the e-mail address should not be longer than 35 characters:

```
Your name: <INPUT type="TEXT" name="GuestName" maxlength="50">
Email address: <INPUT type="TEXT" name="Email" maxlength="35">
```

Note the text placed to the left of the input tags. These are labels to let the user know what is desired for each box. The next field to include is a text area for comments. This is placed on its own line:

```
<BR>Comments: <TEXTAREA name="Comments" rows=5 cols=60>(No comment.)</TEXTAREA>
```

Before you start adding elements to gather demographic information, make sure the important items are emphasized. First, a pair of Submit and Reset buttons have been included right after the text area, followed by a horizontal rule to separate the section from the one below it. Then, some text is added below the horizontal rule to tell the user that completing the demographic information is purely optional:

```
<P><INPUT type="SUBMIT"><INPUT type="RESET"></P>
<HR>
<P>In addition to your comments, we'd also like to ask you a few questions
about who you are and how you found us. If you don't want to complete
this information, use the Submit button above. Thank you.</P>
```

With the first three items in place, turn your attention to some demographic information that is wanted from the user. Because this form is only an example, the demographic information will include several types of form elements so that you can see how they would look in actual usage.

Start with a checkbox and a set of radio buttons:

```
Would you like for a response to your comments?
<INPUT type="CHECKBOX" name="Response_Requested" value="Yes">
 <TABLE WIDTH="30%">
  <CAPTION>Who do you use for Internet/ World Wide Web access?</CAPTION>
  <TR>
   <TD WIDTH="5%">
   <INPUT TYPE="radio" NAME="Internet_Access" VALUE="LISP" SELECTED="selected">
   <TD>Local ISP
  <TR>
   <TD><INPUT TYPE="radio" NAME="Internet_Access" VALUE="RISP">
   <TD>Regional ISP
  <TR>
   <TD><INPUT TYPE="radio" NAME="Internet_Access" VALUE="AOL">
   <TD>America Online
  <TR>
   <TD><INPUT TYPE="radio" NAME="Internet_Access" VALUE="CIS">
   <TD>Compuserve
  <TR>
   <TD><INPUT TYPE="radio" NAME="Internet_Access" VALUE="MSN">
   <TD>Microsoft Network
  <TR>
   <TD><INPUT TYPE="radio" NAME="Internet_Access" VALUE="PROD">
   <TD>Prodigy
 </TABLE>
```

The checked attribute is not part of the checkbox, so the default answer for requesting a reply is "no." A table is used to format the radio buttons so that they line up in a neat vertical column with their labels adjacent. Next on the agenda is a drop-down list for the user's job title and a menu list for their job functions. Another table is used to make sure these two items appear on the same horizontal line:

```
<TABLE width="100%">
<TR>
<TD>Your job title:<SELECT NAME="JobTitle">
  <OPTION VALUE="">Owner</OPTION>
  <OPTION VALUE="">President</OPTION>
  <OPTION VALUE="">CEO</OPTION>
  <OPTION VALUE="">Supervisor</OPTION>
  <OPTION VALUE="">Maintenance Engineer</OPTION>
  <OPTION VALUE="">Flight Attendant</OPTION>
  <OPTION VALUE="">Firefighter</OPTION>
  <OPTION VALUE="">Counterespionage Agent</OPTION>
</SELECT>
<TD>Your job duties (select all that apply):<BR>
<SELECT NAME="JobFunctions" MULTIPLE>
  <OPTION VALUE="">Upper Management</OPTION>
  <OPTION VALUE="">Middle Management</OPTION>
  <OPTION VALUE="">Lower Management</OPTION>
  <OPTION VALUE="">Receivables</OPTION>
  <OPTION VALUE="">Payables</OPTION>
  <OPTION VALUE="">Global Terrorism</OPTION>
</SELECT>
</TABLE>
```

With the addition of a little thank-you and a closing </FORM> tag, the form is completed. The entire finished document is shown in Listing 15.1 and Figure 15.5.

**Listing 15.1. An HTML document with a form to gather guest book information.**

```
<HTML>
<HEAD>
<TITLE>Guest Book</TITLE>
</HEAD>
<BODY>
<H1>Please sign our Guest Book...</H1>
<FORM method="POST" action="/cgi-bin/guest_register.pl">
Your name: <INPUT type="TEXT" name="GuestName" maxlength="50">
Email address: <INPUT type="TEXT" name="Email" maxlength="35">
<BR>Comments: <TEXTAREA name="Comments" rows=5 cols=60>(No comment.)</TEXTAREA>
<P><INPUT type="SUBMIT"><INPUT type="RESET"></P>
<HR>
<P>In addition to your comments, we'd also like to ask you a few
questions about who you are. If you don't want to complete
this information, use the Submit button above. Thank you.</P>
Would you like for a response to your comments?
<INPUT type="CHECKBOX" name="Response_Requested" value="Yes">
<BR>Who do you use for Internet/ World Wide Web access?
<TABLE WIDTH="100%">
<TR>
  <TD><INPUT TYPE="radio" NAME="Internet_Access"
             VALUE="LISP" SELECTED="selected">Local ISP
   <BR><INPUT TYPE="radio" NAME="Internet_Access" VALUE="RISP">Regional ISP
  <TD><INPUT TYPE="radio" NAME="Internet_Access" VALUE="AOL">America Online
   <BR><INPUT TYPE="radio" NAME="Internet_Access" VALUE="MSN">Microsoft Network
  <TD><INPUT TYPE="radio" NAME="Internet_Access" VALUE="CIS">Compuserve
   <BR><INPUT TYPE="radio" NAME="Internet_Access" VALUE="PROD">Prodigy
</TABLE>
<TABLE>
<TR valign="TOP">
<TD>Your job title:
<BR><SELECT NAME="JobTitle">
  <OPTION>Owner
  <OPTION>President
  <OPTION>CEO
  <OPTION>Supervisor
  <OPTION>Maintenance Engineer
  <OPTION>Flight Attendant
  <OPTION>Firefighter
  <OPTION>Counterespionage Agent
</SELECT>
<TD>
<TD>Your job duties (select all that apply):<BR>
<SELECT NAME="JobFunctions" MULTIPLE>
  <OPTION>Upper Management
  <OPTION>Middle Management
  <OPTION>Lower Management
  <OPTION>Receivables
  <OPTION>Payables
  <OPTION>Global Terrorism
</SELECT>
</TABLE>
<H3>Thank you for taking the time to answer these questions.
Your time and input is appreciated.</H3>
</FORM>
</BODY>
</HTML>
```

**FIGURE 15.5.**

*The finished guest book form as it appears on a user's browser.*

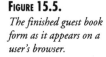

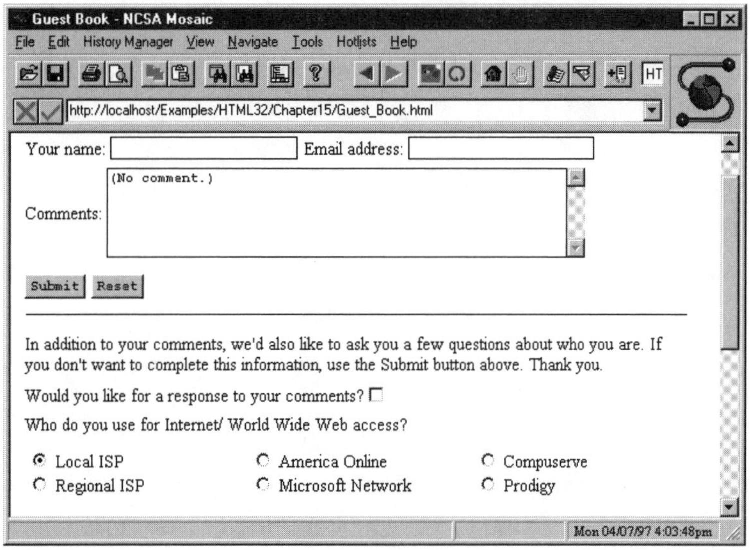

# Summary

Forms are a way of gathering information from the user that is processed through a CGI script. An HTML form consists of a pair of <FORM> tags that encase one or more elements, including text boxes, menus, checkboxes, and buttons. Other HTML elements can also be used to label and format the form items, such as text, images, horizontal rules, and tables.

Forms were implemented in HTML 2.0, and the tags for creating forms are widely supported in just about every available browser. There might still be a problem in some older browsers with compatibility with a couple of tags—primarily the checkbox and radio button.

In this chapter, you learned how to include each form element in a Web page, as well as how to construct the form itself so that when it's submitted it calls the right programs on the server to process the information.

# Putting It All Together: Basic HTML

*by Rick Darnell*

## IN THIS CHAPTER

**CHAPTER 16**

You've spent several chapters learning about the various elements of HTML—what each element does and how to make it work. You've learned about headers, footers, text alignment, lists, tables, links, images, multimedia, image maps, and forms.

Now it's time to put all these elements together to assemble Web pages that do something useful—deliver your message to the world. If you've never worked with HTML 3.2 or are just looking for a few new ideas, this chapter is for you.

This chapter focuses on building several HTML pages that incorporate most of the standard features of HTML 3.2, including home pages, directories, and news and information items. I'll introduce basic HTML design, a topic that is further addressed in Chapters 23 through 26, which cover effective Web page design in much more detail.

> **NOTE**
>
> All of the examples in this chapter are from a real Web site for the Missoula (Montana) Rural Fire District. You can view this site at www.montana.com/mrfd/.

# Basic Page Layout Issues

Before beginning to create your page, you must answer two important questions:

- What do you want to say?
- To whom do you want to say it?

Although these are two separate questions, they are hard to separate. What you want to say depends on to whom you want to say it. As you try to answer these questions, more questions arise. The following questions help focus your efforts even more:

- Are you targeting your pages to potential customers?
- Do you want to provide unique information on a special topic or issue?
- Is this a method of keeping employees and other company personnel informed of developments and news companywide?

If you don't have an audience or a message, there's a good chance you'll end up saying nothing to anyone. This is also related to the topics covered in Chapter 15, "Building and Using HTML Forms." Form follows function, and the lack of one shows up in the other.

After you know what your basic message is and how it should be organized for delivery to your audience, it's time to plug the individual parts of the message into the framework. If the Web site is the bell, the pages are the hammers that make the sound.

Before you start a new page, remember that the overall design and layout of your page is how your message is communicated to the user. Good design and layout is not an end in itself. Looking at many pages on the Web, you'll see the full gamut—from bland pages with no thought given to their appearance to pages whose only message is to show off how artistic a designer can be. As you start to play with the design, remember one cardinal rule of layout: Self-indulgence is a message-killer.

It's a good idea to flip through magazines, books, and brochures before you start. Web page design evolves from printed page design, and the printed page is a good place to start looking for ideas.

Although the number of formatting options and capabilities are growing for Web pages, they are still limited in comparison to their printed cousins. With a little creativity, however, it's possible to make your page stand out.

---

### A FEW WORDS ABOUT A LOT OF SPACE

Space is an important part of every page. It gives breathing room in the midst of a crowd of information. Effective use of space can help a page as much as ineffective use can hurt a page.

Having too much space causes the user to waste time with the scroll bars to get to the next piece of the page. Having too little space causes everything to run together like gumbo. An extra set of eyes can help judge the overall effect. Enlist the help of friends and coworkers to critique your work. It's some of the best advice you can get free of charge.

---

The following five layouts use the default font the browser provides and the same image and headline size. Even with this limitation, different uses of headline, text, images, and white space result in a very different look and feel for each. Depending on your use and placement of the four page elements, each layout can take on its own personality, which you can harness to help reinforce your message.

## A Conventional Page

The first style of page is one that is seen all too often on the Web. It is also the easiest to construct and doesn't really require any knowledge of design or HTML. It consists of a heading at the top, followed by the bulk of the text, and perhaps an image included at the end or somewhere else along the way. (See Listing 16.1 and Figure 16.1.)

**Listing 16.1. A conventional page doesn't take advantage of any of HTML's formatting capabilities. It is also the most compatible with all browsers and platforms.**

```
<!DOCTYPE HTML PUBLIC "-//IETF//DTD HTML 3.2//EN">
<HTML>
<HEAD>
 <TITLE>Conventional</TITLE>
</HEAD>
<BODY>
<H1>The Alberton Canyon Derailment</H1>
<P>In the early morning hours on Thursday, April 11, 1996, an east-bound
Montana Rail Link (MRL) train derailed in western Montana approximately
two miles west of Alberton,  and immediately adjacent to the Clarks Fork
River and I-90.  Eighteen cars derailed from the 71-car train, including six
cars carrying hazardous materials. Four contained chlorine; one contained
potassium cresylate; and the sixth contained sodium chlorate.</P>
<P><IMG SRC="/mrfd/Alberton/albert8.jpg" WIDTH="300" HEIGHT="197"></P>
<P>To compound the problem further, another MRL train derailed near Noxon,
Mont., spilling 1,000 gallons of diesel fuel and overturning another chlorine
car.  The additional confusion caused by the diversion and rerouting of
resources slowed the initial response of personnel and equipment.</P>
<P>One of the chlorine cars and the potassium cresylate car were breached,
resulting in the release of approximately 100,000 lbs. of deadly chlorine
gas. The cloud drifted over the highway and through the town of Alberton
forcing the evacuation of more than 1,000 people in a 100 square-mile area.
Half of these were kept out of their homes for 17 days.  An estimated 350
people were treated for health and respiratory problems in Missoula hospitals,
35 miles to the east. A lone fatality occurred when a transient riding in a
box car walked into the cloud after surviving the crash.</P>
</BODY>
</HTML>
```

**FIGURE 16.1.**

*A conventional page: thick with text, heading at the top, and picture at the bottom.*

Although you wouldn't want all of the pages in your site to look like this one, it is a quick and dirty way of putting a page together to disseminate information until you can put something else together. It is also a good alternative page to use if you're developing a mirror for older browsers that might not support HTML 3.2 advanced features.

## A Modern Layout

A modern layout is similar to the text-heavy conventional layout, but uses horizontal rules to mark the beginning and end of the page and images that extend into the text. (See Listing 16.2 and Figure 16.2.) A true modern layout would also include extra space between each of the text lines, but this is not yet possible with HTML 3.2.

**Listing 16.2. The main feature of a modern layout is the use of left- and right-alignment on images, allowing text to flow around the picture rather than stay inline.**

```
<!DOCTYPE HTML PUBLIC "-//IETF//DTD HTML 3.2//EN">
<HTML>
<HEAD>
 <TITLE>Modern</TITLE>
</HEAD>
<BODY>
<HR WIDTH="75%" NOSHADE SIZE="8" ALIGN="LEFT">
<H1>The Alberton Canyon Derailment</H1>
<P>In the early morning hours on Thursday, April 11, 1996, an east-bound
Montana Rail Link (MRL) train derailed in western Montana approximately
two miles west of Alberton,  and immediately adjacent to the Clarks Fork
River and I-90.  Eighteen cars derailed from the 71-car train, including six
cars carrying hazardous materials. Four contained chlorine; one contained
potassium cresylate; and the sixth contained sodium chlorate.
<IMG SRC="/mrfd/Alberton/albert8.jpg" ALIGN="RIGHT" WIDTH="300" HEIGHT="197"></P>
<P>To compound the problem further, another MRL train derailed near Noxon,
Mont., spilling 1,000 gallons of diesel fuel and overturning another chlorine
car.  The additional confusion caused by the diversion and rerouting of
resources slowed the initial response of personnel and equipment.</P>
<P>One of the chlorine cars and the potassium cresylate car were breached,
resulting in the release of approximately 100,000 lbs. of deadly chlorine gas.
The cloud drifted over the highway and through the town of Alberton forcing
the evacuation of more than 1,000 people in a 100 square-mile area. Half of
these were kept out of their homes for 17 days.  An estimated 350 people were
treated for health and respiratory problems in Missoula hospitals, 35 miles to
the east. A lone fatality occurred when a transient riding in a box car walked
into the cloud after surviving the crash.</P>
<HR WIDTH="75%" NOSHADE SIZE="8" ALIGN="RIGHT">
</BODY>
</HTML>
```

You can easily convert a conventional layout to a modern layout simply by adding LEFT or RIGHT to the image's align attribute. It significantly improves the appearance of the page with minimal effort.

# A Classic Layout

Adding columns to a page does two things. First, it shortens line length, making it easier for the user to read the text. This is especially important on a Web page, where most users are reading a screen, which causes greater eyestrain than looking at a page.

Second, columns conserve space in larger documents. Although it seems though it takes up more space, it actually reduces the total length of the document. This is part of the reason why newspapers use multiple columns.

A classic layout is one of the simplest implementations of columns in a Web page. (See Listing 16.3 and Figure 16.3.) Because HTML 3.2 doesn't directly support columns, however, tables fit the purpose quite nicely to achieve the same effect.

**Listing 16.3. This is the first layout that makes use of tables to create columns on a Web page. The headline is placed outside of the table and centered to give it prominence.**

```
<!DOCTYPE HTML PUBLIC "-//IETF//DTD HTML 3.2//EN">
<HTML>
<HEAD>
 <TITLE>Classic</TITLE>
</HEAD>
<BODY>
<H1 ALIGN="CENTER">The Alberton Canyon Derailment</H1>
<HR WIDTH="75%" SIZE="8" ALIGN="CENTER" NOSHADE>
<TABLE WIDTH="100%" BORDER="0" CELLSPACING="15">
 <TR VALIGN="TOP">
  <TD WIDTH="50%">
    <P>In the early morning hours on Thursday, April 11, 1996, an east-bound
    Montana Rail Link (MRL) train derailed in western Montana approximately
```

```
two miles west of Alberton,  and immediately adjacent to the Clarks Fork
River and I-90.  Eighteen cars derailed from the 71-car train, including six
cars carrying hazardous materials. Four contained chlorine; one contained
potassium cresylate; and the sixth contained sodium chlorate.
<P><IMG SRC="/mrfd/Alberton/albert8.jpg" WIDTH="300" HEIGHT="197"></P>
<TD WIDTH="50%">
<P>To compound the problem further, another MRL train derailed near Noxon,
Mont., spilling 1,000 gallons of diesel fuel and overturning another
chlorine car. The additional confusion caused by the diversion and rerouting
of resources slowed the initial response of personnel and equipment.</P>
<P>One of the chlorine cars and the potassium cresylate car were breached,
resulting in the release of approximately 100,000 lbs. of deadly chlorine
gas. The cloud drifted over the highway and through the town of Alberton
forcing the evacuation of more than 1,000 people in a 100 square-mile area.
Half of these were kept out of their homes for 17 days.  An estimated 350
people were treated for health and respiratory problems in Missoula
hospitals, 35 miles to the east. A lone fatality occurred when a transient
riding in a box car walked into the cloud after surviving the crash.</P>
</TABLE>
</BODY>
</HTML>
```

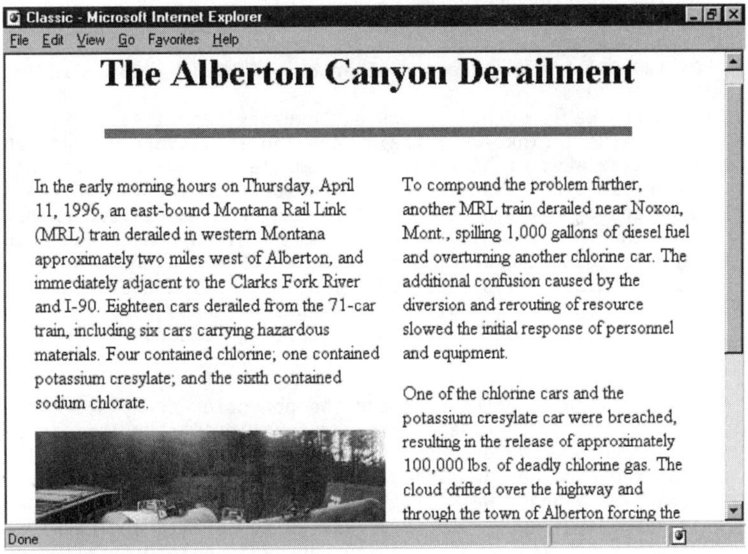

**FIGURE 16.3.**

*This classic layout is often used in varying forms. It is a simple, two-column format with a centered headline and image set into the text.*

The two columns should be of equal width, and only one requires the width attribute. However, both <TD> tags include the width specification, which helps you to avoid ambiguity during later review and revision.

## A Technical Information Page

The layout for technical documents evolved out of a need for practical features. Originally, many of these pages were closer in appearance to the conventional design. This meant a lack of space to make notes or comments about the contents, however. By shifting to a three-column format and leaving one of the outside columns open for diagrams and illustrations, additional white space was acquired.

The resulting design is very angular, and the ample white space results in a clean and strong appearance. (See Listing 16.4 and Figure 16.4.)

**Listing 16.4. The technical page design is similar to the two-column classic, except a third column is added to the table to hold images.**

```
<!DOCTYPE HTML PUBLIC "-//IETF//DTD HTML 3.2//EN">
<HTML>
<HEAD>
 <TITLE>Technical</TITLE>
</HEAD>
<BODY>
<TABLE BORDER="0" WIDTH="100%" CELLSPACING="15">
 <TR>
  <TD>
  <TD COLSPAN="2" WIDTH="33%">
   <H1>The Alberton Canyon Derailment</H1>
 <TR VALIGN="TOP">
  <TD VALIGN="MIDDLE">
   <P><IMG SRC="/mrfd/Alberton/albert8.jpg" WIDTH="225" HEIGHT="148"></P>
  <TD WIDTH="33%">
   <P>In the early morning hours on Thursday, April 11, 1996, an east-bound
    Montana Rail Link (MRL) train derailed in western Montana approximately
    two miles west of Alberton, and immediately adjacent to the Clarks Fork
    River and I-90. Eighteen cars derailed from the 71-car train, including
    six cars carrying hazardous materials. Four contained chlorine; one
    contained potassium cresylate; and the sixth contained sodium chlorate.</P>
   <P>To compound the problem further, another MRL train derailed near Noxon,
    Mont., spilling 1,000 gallons of diesel fuel and overturning another
    chlorine car.  The additional confusion caused by the diversion and
    rerouting of resource slowed the initial response of personnel and
    equipment.</P>
  <TD WIDTH="33%">
   <P>One of the chlorine cars and the potassium cresylate car were breached,
    resulting in the release of approximately 100,000 lbs. of deadly chlorine gas.
    The cloud drifted over the highway and through the town of
    Alberton forcing the evacuation of more than 1,000 people in a 100
    square-mile area. Half of these were kept out of their homes for 17 days.
    An estimated 350 people were treated for health and respiratory problems in
    Missoula hospitals, 35 miles to the east. A lone fatality occurred when a
    transient riding in a box car walked into the cloud after surviving the
    crash.</P>
   </TABLE>
</BODY>
</HTML>
```

FIGURE 16.4.

*This design is good for
technical information.
It combines some of the
features of the
conventional and
modern layouts, but
uses more white space.*

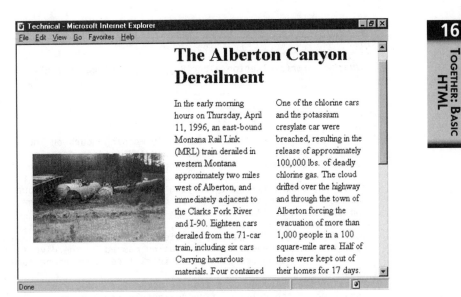

# A Formal Page

Formal pages aren't necessarily the most space-efficient designs in the world, but they do have a certain style that fits the bill for major announcements, such as the naming of a new chief or the receipt of a new fire truck.

The design is created using a table with three columns. The width of the outside two columns is 25 percent of the table width, leaving half of the table width for the center column and the text (as shown in Listing 16.5 and Figure 16.5). Then, each content element is placed in its own cell—first the headline, then the image, and finally the text.

**Listing 16.5. In a formal design, three columns create the space on the left and right of the text and control the headline and initial image space.**

```
<!DOCTYPE HTML PUBLIC "-//IETF//DTD HTML 3.2//EN">
<HTML>
<HEAD>
 <TITLE>Formal</TITLE>
</HEAD>
<BODY>
<TABLE BORDER="0" WIDTH="100%" CELLSPACING="3">
 <TR>
  <TD WIDTH="25%">
  <TD>
   <H1 ALIGN="CENTER">The Alberton <BR>
    Canyon Derailment</H1>
  <TD WIDTH="25%">
 <TR>
  <TD>
```

*continues*

**Listing 16.5. continued**

```
 <TD>
  <P ALIGN="CENTER">
   <IMG SRC="/mrfd/Alberton/albert8.jpg" WIDTH="300" HEIGHT="197" VSPACE="24">
  </P>
 <TD>
<TR>
 <TD WIDTH="25%">
 <TD>
  <P><FONT SIZE="+3">I</FONT>n the early morning hours on Thursday, April 11,
    1996, an east-bound Montana Rail Link (MRL) train derailed in western
    Montana approximately two miles west of Alberton, and immediately adjacent
    to the Clarks Fork River and I-90. Eighteen cars derailed from the 71-car
    train, including six cars carrying hazardous materials. Four contained
    chlorine; one contained potassium cresylate; and the sixth contained
    sodium chlorate.</P>
  <P>To compound the problem further, another MRL train derailed near Noxon,
    Mont.,spilling 1,000 gallons of diesel fuel and overturning another
    chlorine car.  Theadditional confusion caused by the diversion and
    rerouting of resources slowed the initial response of personnel and
    equipment.</P>
  <P>One of the chlorine cars and the potassium cresylatecar were breached,
    resulting in the release of approximately 100,000 lbs.
    of deadlychlorine gas. The cloud drifted over the highway and through the
    town of Alberton forcing the evacuation of more than 1,000  people in a 100
    square-mile area. Half of these were kept out of their homes for 17 days.
    An estimated 350 the east. A lone fatality occurred when a transient riding
    in a box car walked into the cloud after surviving the crash.</P>
  <TD WIDTH="25%">
</TABLE>
</BODY>
</HTML>
```

**FIGURE 16.5.**

*This formal design is for those moments in which dignity is everything. A large initial capital letter, central placement of text and image, and lots of space give this page its grace and simplicity.*

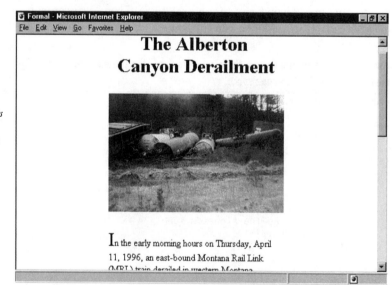

As an added touch, you can increase the size of the first letter in the text using the <FONT size> tag. If you require additional text formatting and fonts, you should create the text portion in a program designed for the job, such as Macromedia FreeHand, and export it to a GIF or JPEG file. However, doing so will adversely affect page download time.

# Page 1: A Template

With some of this basic layout information in hand, it's time to roll up your sleeves and get to work. Using the Missoula Rural Fire District site as an example, you'll begin with a template, which will become the basis for your other pages.

> **NOTE**
>
> An HTML template serves as a guide to other HTML pages, much like a pattern for sewing or tracing outlines. Templates are useful for maintaining the same design and image across multiple pages, without guesswork, by providing much of the underlying structure and formatting before you begin.

The Fire District uses its site to communicate a variety of information to the public, including safety tips and date-dependent news. The District also uses the site to develop general awareness about the District and its varying roles and responsibilities in the community. As such, the Web pages need to offer a professional attitude in a friendly matter.

For this purpose, we'll opt for a design that is a cross between the classic and technical layouts. It includes ample white space on the left side, interrupted only by hanging headlines and an appropriate image, combined with a bold banner across the top.

Construction of the page begins with the basics—a structure for the document (as shown in Listing 16.6).

**Listing 16.6. The beginning of the template for a set of Web pages.**

```
<!DOCTYPE HTML PUBLIC "-//IETF//DTD HTML 3.2//EN">
<HTML>
<HEAD>
<TITLE>MRFD - a title</TITLE>
</HEAD>
<BODY bgcolor="#FFFFFF">
</BODY>
</HTML>
```

Structure does not a page make, but even a castle needs a foundation before the flags fly from the towers. In short, every Web page should start at the beginning and work up from there. In addition to the structure, we'll specify a default background color in the <BODY> tag using the RGB hexadecimal triplet for white. The placeholder <TITLE>, which contains the format for the Web page titles, is also added so we don't forget to add a title for other pages later.

> **TIP**
>
> It's a good idea to begin a page title with a common identifier for your site. This makes it easier for the user to identify it if he or she includes a bookmark for a page on his or her home browser.

Now that the first bit of detail is completed, it's time to move to formatting for the top of the document. For consistency, we'll give every page the same banner across the top using a simple table with text and an image, as described in Chapter 10, "Creating Tables for Data and Page Layout." (See Listing 16.7 and Figure 16.6.)

**Listing 16.7. The first part of the page includes a two-column table with one row.**

```
<!DOCTYPE HTML PUBLIC "-//IETF//DTD HTML 3.2//EN">
<HTML>
<HEAD>
<TITLE>MRFD - a title</TITLE>
</HEAD>
<BODY bgcolor="#FFFFFF">
<TABLE border="0" cellspacing="15" width="100%" bgcolor="#000000">
 <TR>
  <TD align="RIGHT" valign="BOTTOM" width="75%">
   <H1><FONT color="White">...Subject Title...</FONT></H1>
  <TD align="LEFT" valign="BOTTOM">
   <IMG src="/mrfd/images/fire2.jpg" HEIGHT="158" WIDTH="149">
</TABLE>
</BODY>
</HTML>
```

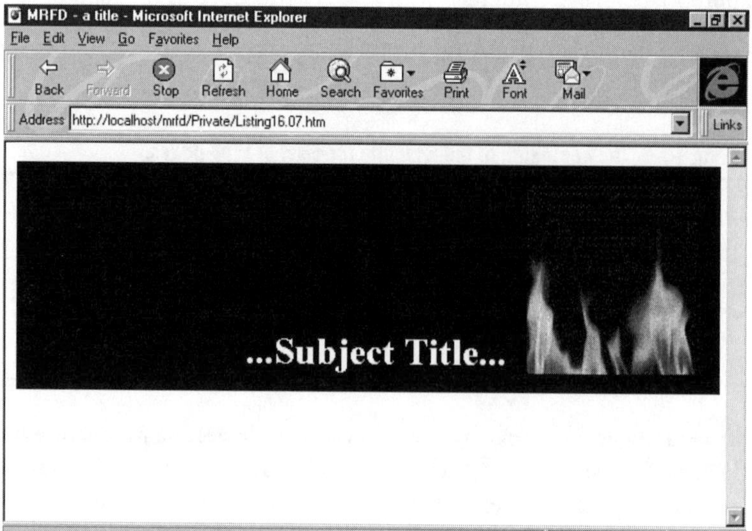

**FIGURE 16.6.**

*The template as it appears so far, with a document title and heading for the top of the document.*

You should note several things concerning the opening table tag. First, the borders are invisible (`border="0"`), which ensures that only the formatting is apparent to the user. The method of the formatting remains hidden. Next, the `cellspacing` attribute uses a larger-than-normal figure to help pad the contents of the two data cells. The table will always occupy 100 percent of the available window width with a black background (`bgcolor=#000000`).

The first cell has contents that are forced to the bottom and right margins and that occupy 75 percent of the available table width. Then, the page title is added in white to contrast against the black background. Because it's the main title, you use the `<H1>` tag.

The second cell's contents are aligned to the bottom and left margins. The `width` attribute is not used, because the browser will automatically assign it the remaining 25 percent of the table. Its content is a JPEG image with a specified height and width, as discussed in Chapter 12, "Adding Images to Your Web Page."

Because there's no way of telling where a document based on the template could appear, it uses an `src` URL, which is relative to the document root of the Web.

> **TIP**
>
> The height and width for the image are the same as its actual dimensions. These attributes help speed the page display time by alerting the browser to how much space is needed before the image begins to download.

> **TIP**
>
> The image of the flame could just as easily be an animated GIF or a Shockwave animation, as described in Chapter 13, "Integrating Multimedia and Other File Types." Place the special content in a common directory so the browser cache can recognize the file, no matter what page it appears on. This will dramatically speed download time for subsequent pages.

After the banner for the page is completed, insert the area where the content will appear. To do this, use another table with opposite column width settings to add interest and balance to the layout (as shown in Listing 16.8 and Figure 16.7).

**Listing 16.8. Add the area for content using another table, with 25 percent of the width allowed for a headline and the balance for body text.**

```
<!DOCTYPE HTML PUBLIC "-//IETF//DTD HTML 3.2//EN">
<HTML>
<HEAD>
```

*continues*

**Listing 16.8. continued**

```
<TITLE>MRFD - a title</TITLE>
</HEAD>
<BODY bgcolor="#FFFFFF">
<TABLE border="0" cellspacing="15" width="100%" bgcolor="#000000">
 <TR>
  <TD align="RIGHT" valign="BOTTOM" width="75%">
   <H1><FONT color="White">...Subject Title...</FONT></H1>
  <TD align="LEFT" valign="BOTTOM">
   <IMG src="/mrfd/images/fire2.jpg" HEIGHT="158" WIDTH="149">
</TABLE>
<TABLE BORDER="0" CELLSPACING="15" WIDTH="100%">
 <TR>
  <TD WIDTH="25%" VALIGN="TOP">
   <H2>Topic Title
    <IMG SRC="/ClipArt/Earth/Landscp/Wildrnss.jpg" WIDTH="162" HEIGHT="122">
   </H2>
  <TD VALIGN="TOP">
   <P>Body text...</P>
</TABLE>
</BODY>
</HTML>
```

**FIGURE 16.7.**

*With the two main elements in place, the Web page template begins to take shape. Notice the placeholder text, which will be replaced for each Web page as it is developed from the template.*

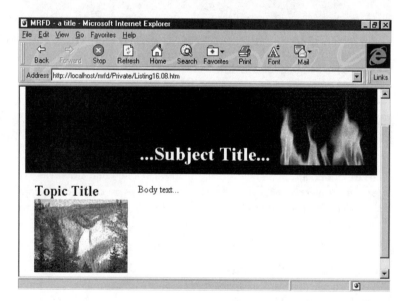

Now, the structure tags are in place, the page has a banner heading, and the table is formatted to receive content. The last step is to add a few details to finish the job, including a horizontal rule at the bottom of the page and a link back to the home page. With all of these pieces in place, the completed template file appears in Listing 16.9 and Figure 16.8.

**Listing 16.9. The `template.htm` file includes all of the components for the other Fire District Web pages.**

```html
<!DOCTYPE HTML PUBLIC "-//IETF//DTD HTML 3.2//EN">
<HTML>
<HEAD>
 <TITLE>MRFD - a title</TITLE>
</HEAD>
<BODY BGCOLOR="#FFFFFF">
<TABLE BORDER="0" CELLSPACING="15" WIDTH="100%" BGCOLOR="#000000">
 <TR>
  <TD ALIGN="RIGHT" VALIGN="BOTTOM" WIDTH="75%">
   <H1><FONT COLOR="White">...Subject Title...</FONT></H1>
  <TD ALIGN="LEFT" VALIGN="BOTTOM">
   <H1><IMG SRC="/mrfd/images/fire2.jpg" HEIGHT="158" WIDTH="149"></H1>
</TABLE>
<TABLE BORDER="0" CELLSPACING="15" WIDTH="100%">
 <TR>
  <TD WIDTH="25%" VALIGN="TOP">
   <H2>Topic Title
     <IMG SRC="/ClipArt/Earth/Landscp/Wildrnss.jpg" WIDTH="162" HEIGHT="122">
   </H2>
  <TD VALIGN="TOP">
   <P>Body text...</P>
</TABLE>
<HR>
<P ALIGN="RIGHT">
<A HREF="/mrfd/index.htm"><STRONG>MRFD Home</STRONG>
 <IMG SRC="/mrfd/Images/cross.gif" WIDTH="113" HEIGHT="97" ALIGN="MIDDLE">
</A></P>
</BODY>
</HTML>
```

**FIGURE 16.8.**

*The completed file,* template.htm, *illustrates the basic appearance of any Web page created for the Fire District. Through the use of invisible borders for the table, advanced formatting techniques are implemented without distracting the user.*

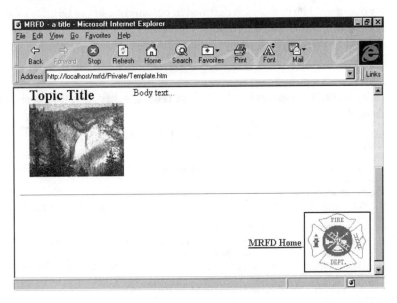

> **NOTE**
>
> If a picture is worth a thousand words, it can seem to take at least a thousand minutes to load. For that reason, most of the pages within the Fire District site include only three relatively small images—one in the banner, one under the document title, and one for the link to the home page.
>
> Because the banner image and home page image are the same on virtually every page, the user's browser should maintain its respective files in a cache that will further speed download time. The only new file the browser needs to download for each page is the one under the document title.
>
> Why all this emphasis on limiting images? Because a lot of ISDN and 28.8Kbps modems are on the market, as are a lot of 14.4Kbps and 9600 modems. This limit is an attempt to be sensitive to the download time for all users while still including enough images to make the pages interesting.

Save the template as `template.htm`. Every time a new page is needed, you can place a copy of `template.htm` in the appropriate directory and rename it. Then, you can open it for editing and replace the placeholder contents with the real thing. Because it's a utility file not meant for display to users, it is kept on the local drive and not on the Web site.

## Creating a Real Page from the Template

After the template is created, we'll make copies that are then modified to create the real pages for our users. The first copy is destined to become one of the District's safety pages. First, we'll rename it, and then add the content. Other than changing the title and adding the appropriate content in the body, no other modifications to the page are needed. (See Listing 16.10 and Figure 16.9.)

**Listing 16.10. This page was based entirely on `template.htm`. Only the title and body content was changed.**

```
<!DOCTYPE HTML PUBLIC "-//IETF//DTD HTML 3.2//EN">
<HTML>
<HEAD>
 <TITLE>MRFD - Living in the Wildland/Urban Interface</TITLE>
</HEAD>
<BODY BGCOLOR="#FFFFFF">
<TABLE BORDER="0" CELLSPACING="15" WIDTH="100%" BGCOLOR="#000000">
 <TR>
  <TD ALIGN="RIGHT" VALIGN="BOTTOM" WIDTH="75%">
   <H1><FONT COLOR="White">...Summer Fire Safety...</FONT></H1>
  <TD ALIGN="LEFT" VALIGN="BOTTOM">
   <IMG SRC="/mrfd/images/fire2.jpg" HEIGHT="158" WIDTH="149">
</TABLE>
<TABLE BORDER="0" CELLSPACING="15" WIDTH="100%">
 <TR>
  <TD WIDTH="25%" VALIGN="TOP">
```

*Putting It All Together: Basic HTML*
CHAPTER 16

307

16

PUTTING IT ALL
TOGETHER: BASIC
HTML

```
 <H2>Living in the wildland/urban interface
 <IMG SRC="/mrfd/images/Wildrnss.jpg" WIDTH="162" HEIGHT="122"></H2>
<TD VALIGN="TOP">
 <P>Wildfire is a natural element in all ecosystems and environments, and
 Montana is no different. Our climate conditions lead to flammable ground
 cover such as grass, brush and trees. Everyone who has lived in Missoula
 County for any length of time can attest to smoky summer days, or may even
 have seen some of the larger wildfires visible from the valley. Fire is
 a part of our history and a naturally occuring element where we live.</P>
 <P>A new dimension is added to wildfires by the presence of homes. Wildfire
 quickly threatens homes and homeowners, and create a new set of issues for
 firefighters.</P>
 <P><FONT COLOR="Maroon">Missoula Rural Fire District</FONT> has firefighters
 trained for containing fires in the wildland/urban interface. But compared
 to a wildfire, they are very limited in manpower and equipment, and in the
 distances and terrain they protect. The first homes to burn in the recent
 Pattee Canyon fire were lost while firefighters were still en route to the
 scene.</P>
 <P>If you're in an area that has a potential for wildfire, you can call
 for a representative from <FONT COLOR="Maroon">Missoula Rural Fire
 District</FONT> to come to your home and make
 <A HREF="/mrfd/Seasonal/Summer/Wildfire_Tips.htm">suggestions for creating
 defensible space</A> around your structures. <CITE>Defensible space</CITE>
 is an <DFN>area of reduced fuel</DFN> which gives your home greater odds
 of surviving a fire. This is a service provided free of charge to district
 homeowners. For more information, call 549-6172 or
 <A HREF="mailto:mrfd@montana.com">send us a note</A>.</P>

</TABLE>
<HR>
<P ALIGN="RIGHT">
<A HREF="/mrfd/index.htm"><STRONG>MRFD Home</STRONG>
 <IMG SRC="/mrfd/Images/cross.gif" WIDTH="113" HEIGHT="97" ALIGN="MIDDLE">
 </A></P>
</BODY>
</HTML>
```

Several features were included within the content. First, any mention of Missoula Rural Fire District was highlighted in maroon to emphasize who was providing the information without being intrusive. A color such as red or pink would stand out more, but would also interfere with the user trying to read. This use of the <FONT> tag is covered in Chapter 8, "Text Alignment and Formatting."

Next, two hyperlinks were added within the text, following the syntax discussed in Chapter 11, "Linking Documents and Images." The first was a link to a related page, /mrfd/Seasonal/ Summer/Wildfire_Tips.htm. If the user wanted more information on this topic, he or she could click the hyperlink. The second was a link to send e-mail, mailto:mrfd@montana.com. If a user wanted to provide feedback, he or she had the option of doing so immediately rather than looking for a feedback page elsewhere on the site.

**FIGURE 16.9.**

*The finished product, which was created using the template as its starting point, took only a few minutes to create.*

Another feature used the logical tags for citations and definitions. The <CITE> tag was used to highlight the term *defensible space,* and the <DFN> tag was used to mark the definition within the same sentence. In most browsers, this would probably appear the same (italics). The logical tags indicate usage if the page is edited or changed at a later time.

This is a simple page, but it represents most of the content on this site. The total time used to create it—including copying and renaming the template, typing the text, and finding an appropriate image to use under the document title—was 10 minutes.

# A Home Page from the Template

Creating a home page from the template is similar to creating the standard page. Some hyperlinks within the document are added, plus a graphic image for a bullet. The hyperlink at the end of the template is replaced with author and copyright information.

The District home page (shown in Listing 16.11 and Figure 16.10) is basically the same as any other page but with a few additional features. First is an unordered list that uses graphical bullets instead of the <UL> tag. This is the only additional graphic used on this page beyond the three called for in the template. It's a small image that you can download quickly and that doesn't seriously interfere with download time.

**Listing 16.11. The home page is also created from the template with some additional minor style changes.**

```
<!DOCTYPE HTML PUBLIC "-//IETF//DTD HTML 3.2//EN">
<HTML>
<HEAD>
 <TITLE>Missoula Rural Fire District — Home Page</TITLE>
```

```
</HEAD>
<BODY BGCOLOR="#FFFFFF">
<TABLE BORDER="0" CELLSPACING="15" CELLPADDING="1"
➥WIDTH="100%" BGCOLOR="#000000">
 <TR>
  <TD ALIGN="RIGHT" VALIGN="BOTTOM" WIDTH="75%">
   <H1><FONT COLOR="White">...Missoula Rural Fire District<BR>
    ...<A HREF="#NAME">Point of Origin</A></FONT></H1>
  <TD ALIGN="LEFT" VALIGN="BOTTOM">
   <IMG SRC="/mrfd/images/fire2.jpg" HEIGHT="158" WIDTH="149">
</TABLE>
<TABLE BORDER="0" CELLSPACING="10" CELLPADDING="5" WIDTH="100%">
 <TR>
  <TD WIDTH="25%" VALIGN="TOP" ALIGN="CENTER">
   <H2 ALIGN="CENTER"><A NAME="TOP"></A>Missoula Rural
    <IMG SRC="Images/MRFD-BADGE.JPG" ALIGN="MIDDLE" WIDTH="127" HEIGHT="149">
    Fire District</H2>
   <P> </P>
   <P ALIGN="LEFT"><B> <I>Point of origin</I></B><BR>
        <I>Where a fire begins</I></P>
  <TD WIDTH="75%" VALIGN="TOP">
   <H3>
    <IMG SRC="Images/BL-HELMT.gif" WIDTH="61" HEIGHT="59" ALIGN="MIDDLE">
    <A HREF="#SPARKS">What's New</A></H3>
   <UL>
    <LI>
     <P><A HREF="#SPARKS1"><STRONG>Burning season open</STRONG></A></P>
    <LI>
     <P><A HREF="#SPARKS2"><STRONG>Flood plain information</STRONG></A></P>
   </UL>
   <H3><IMG SRC="Images/BL-HELMT.gif" WIDTH="61" HEIGHT="59" ALIGN="MIDDLE">
    <A HREF="/mrfd/Seasonal/Summer/index.htm">Summer safety</A></H3>
   <BLOCKQUOTE>It may not feel like it yet, but the summer season is almost upon
    us. Here are some things to  keep in mind to keep you safe.</BLOCKQUOTE>
   <H3><IMG SRC="Images/BL-HELMT.gif" WIDTH="61" HEIGHT="59" ALIGN="MIDDLE">
    <A HREF="General_Information/Property_Taxes.htm">How
    we spend the taxes you pay</A></H3>
   <BLOCKQUOTE>Every year, a part of your property taxes goes towards
    fire protection in the Missoula Rural Fire District. Here's how that
    amount is determined.</BLOCKQUOTE>
   <H3><IMG SRC="Images/BL-HELMT.gif" WIDTH="61" HEIGHT="59" ALIGN="MIDDLE">
    <A HREF="Alberton/">The Alberton Canyon Derailment</A></H3>
   <BLOCKQUOTE><FONT COLOR="Maroon">Missoula Rural Fire District
    </FONT>was a key player in this incident. The Regional Hazardous
    Materials Response Team was involved during the entire incident. MRFD
    also supplied the Operations Chief, Public Information Officer, a Liaison
    Officer and many other positions during this incident.</BLOCKQUOTE>

   <H3><IMG SRC="Images/BL-HELMT.gif" WIDTH="61" HEIGHT="59" ALIGN="MIDDLE">
    <A HREF="General_Information/Staff_Directory.htm">Who</A> and
    <A HREF="General_Information/Station_Directory:htm">where</A> we are</H3>
   <BLOCKQUOTE>MRFD covers a lot of ground, so we've provided a
    <A HREF="General_Information/Station_Directory.htm">station</A>
    and <A HREF="General_Information/Staff_Directory.htm">staff</A>
    directory to help figure out who's who and what's what.
    </BLOCKQUOTE>
   <HR>
 <TR>
```

*continues*

**Listing 16.11. continued**

```
<TD>
<TD>
  <H3><IMG SRC="Images/BL-HELMT.gif" WIDTH="61" HEIGHT="59" ALIGN="MIDDLE">
    <A NAME="SPARKS"></A>Sparks</H3>
  <H4><A NAME="SPARKS1"></A>Burning permits available</H4>
  <BLOCKQUOTE>The Spring burning season is now open. Stop by any
   <A HREF="General_Information/Station_Directory.htm">fire
   station</A> between 8 a.m. and 5 p.m. to pick up a burning permit
   and a copy of the rules to keep your flames legal. The permit and
   advice are free of charge.</BLOCKQUOTE>
  <H4><A NAME="SPARKS2"></A>Flood plain maps posted</H4>
  <BLOCKQUOTE>Each <A HREF="General_Information/Station_Directory.htm">fire
   station</A> in the District now has a copy of the Missoula County flood
   plain maps posted for public review. If you want to know  where you'll be
   standing when the water comes, come by and take a look.</BLOCKQUOTE>
   </TABLE>
<HR SIZE="4" noshade>
<P><CITE><IMG SRC="Images/cross.gif" WIDTH="113" HEIGHT="97" ALIGN="LEFT">
 &copy;1996, 1997 Missoula Rural Fire District, Missoula, Montana.</CITE>
 <BR><CITE>Page layout and construction by Rick Darnell and Dave Herzberg.
    </CITE></P>
<ADDRESS>Send comments to <A HREF="mailto:mrfd@montana.com">MRFD</A>.</ADDRESS>
<HR>
<P ALIGN="CENTER"><EM>For more information about the fire service and
 other departments<BR> around the country, be sure to stop by</EM><BR>
  <A HREF="http://www.firelink.com/">
   <IMG SRC="Images/SMALLFIRELINK.GIF" WIDTH="140" HEIGHT="43">
  </A></P>
</BODY>
</HTML>
```

**FIGURE 16.10.**

*The Fire District home page also uses the template as its base. To increase its color, it includes graphical bullets for each of the list items.*

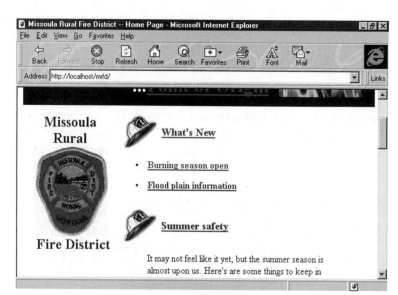

*Putting It All Together: Basic HTML*

CHAPTER 16

311

16

PUTTING IT ALL
TOGETHER: BASIC
HTML

Each list item is a link to another page on the site and is followed by a brief summary paragraph marked with <BLOCKQUOTE>. This indents the text and gives further emphasis to the bullet and link.

The home page also includes a news briefs section, a quick summary of items of interest that is individually hyperlinked using anchor tags (<A *name*>) as the destination. Because this is separate from the main section of the home page, an additional row is added to contain the briefs.

The last item added to the page is copyright and author information. This is added in lieu of the hyperlink to the home page and provides the legal information that most documents should include.

# A Page with a List

The next page created using `template.htm` is a directory of the fire stations that are a part of the District. After copying the template, the banner headline and page title are both changed and the lists are added for the body text, which is illustrated in Chapter 9, "Using Lists to Organize Information." (See Listing 16.12 and Figure 16.11.) A set of nested lists is also added.

**Listing 16.12. The outer list in this set is a definition list that includes an ordered list as a part of each definition (<DD>).**

```
<!DOCTYPE HTML PUBLIC "-//IETF//DTD HTML 3.2//EN">
<HTML>
<HEAD>
 <TITLE>MRFD — Station Directory</TITLE>
</HEAD>
<BODY BGCOLOR="#FFFFFF">
<TABLE BORDER="0" CELLSPACING="15" CELLPADDING="1"
➥WIDTH="100%" BGCOLOR="#000000">
 <TR>
  <TD ALIGN="RIGHT" VALIGN="BOTTOM" WIDTH="75%">
   <H1><FONT COLOR="White">...Directory...</FONT></H1>
  <TD ALIGN="LEFT" VALIGN="BOTTOM">
   <IMG SRC="/mrfd/images/fire2.jpg" HEIGHT="158" WIDTH="149">
</TABLE>
<TABLE BORDER="0" CELLSPACING="10" CELLPADDING="5" WIDTH="100%">
 <TR>
  <TD WIDTH="25%" VALIGN="TOP">
   <H2>Missoula Rural Fire District Station Directory</H2>
  <TD WIDTH="75%" VALIGN="TOP">
   <DL>
    <DT><STRONG>Station 1</STRONG> (Administration and Maintenance)
    <DD><EM>2521 South Ave. West, Missoula<BR>
     (406) 549-6174</EM>
    <OL>
     <LI>Engines 311, 312, 316
     <LI>Water Tender 317
     <LI>Staff vehicles 301, 302, 303, 305
    </OL>
```

*continues*

**Listing 16.12. continued**

```
    <DT><STRONG>Station 2</STRONG>
    <DD><EM>6550 Highway 10 West, Missoula<BR>
     (406) 549-3601</EM>
     <OL>
      <LI>Engines 321, 326
      <LI>HazMat Response 328
      <LI>Staff vehicle 304
     </OL>
    </DD>

    <DT><STRONG>Station 3</STRONG>
    <DD><P><EM>Closed June 1995</EM></P>

    <DT><STRONG>Station 4</STRONG>
    <DD><EM>9480 Highway 10 East, Bonner<BR>
     (406) 258-6061</EM>
     <OL>
      <LI>Engines 341, 346
      <LI>Water Tender 347
      <LI>Truck 348
     </OL>

    <DT><STRONG>Station 5</STRONG>
    <DD><EM>12221 Highway 93 South, Lolo<BR>
     (406) 273-2551</EM>
     <OL>
      <LI>Engines 351, 356
      <LI>Water Tender 357
     </OL>
    </DD>

    <DT><STRONG>Station 6</STRONG>
    <DD><EM>8455 Mullan Road, Missoula<BR>
     (406) 542-0366</EM>
     <OL>
      <LI>Engines 361, 366
     </OL>
    </DD>
   </DL>
</TABLE>
<P ALIGN="RIGHT"><A HREF="/mrfd/index.htm">
<STRONG>MRFD Home</STRONG>
<IMG SRC="/mrfd/Images/cross.gif" WIDTH="113" HEIGHT="97" ALIGN="MIDDLE">
</A></P>
</BODY>
</HTML>
```

Each list entry consists of two parts—the name of the station and its address and assigned apparatus. The only list available in HTML that serves a term-definition relationship is the definition list. The list of apparatus is created using a numbered list within the definition.

**Figure 16.11.**

*Several directory pages are similar to this one. Where additional information is needed for each list entry, the definition list tags are used.*

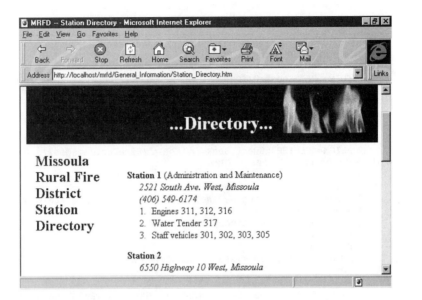

# A Feedback Form

Last on our list of projects for the MRFD site is a guest book. We're not looking for anyone's life story with this feature—just a few basic demographic bits of information. If more information is needed, we can always add more fields, as demonstrated in Chapter 15, "Building and Using HTML Forms."

This page continues to use tables to control its formatting, including a table within a table. This occurs in the main body of the document, where the form contains a table to control the formatting of its elements. (See Listing 16.13.)

**Listing 16.13. The guest book form page gathers basic information from the user and retains formatting using tables.**

```
<!DOCTYPE HTML PUBLIC "-//IETF//DTD HTML 3.2//EN">
<HTML>
<HEAD>
 <TITLE>MRFD - Guest Book</TITLE>
</HEAD>
<BODY BGCOLOR="#FFFFFF">
<TABLE BORDER="0" CELLSPACING="0" WIDTH="100%"
➥BGCOLOR="#000000" CELLPADDING="10">
 <TR>
  <TD ALIGN="RIGHT" VALIGN="BOTTOM">
   <H1><FONT COLOR="White">...Thanks for visiting...</FONT></H1>
  </TD>
  <TD ALIGN="LEFT" VALIGN="BOTTOM" WIDTH="110">
   <P><BR>
```

*continues*

**Listing 16.13. continued**

```
    <IMG SRC="/mrfd/Images/pointsource-posterized_92x139.jpg"
➡HEIGHT="139" WIDTH="92"></P>
  </TD>
  <TD WIDTH="25"> </TD>
 </TR>
</TABLE>
<TABLE BORDER="0" CELLSPACING="15" WIDTH="100%">
 <TR>
  <TD WIDTH="25%" VALIGN="TOP">
   <H2 ALIGN="CENTER">Guest Book<IMG SRC="/FireDept/Images/fd-foot.jpg"
➡WIDTH="128" HEIGHT="205"></H2>
  </TD>
  <TD VALIGN="TOP">
   <H3>Thanks for visiting our Web site. Please take  a few minutes to tell
   us about yourself.</H3>
   <FORM ACTION="/cgi/guestbook.exe">
    <TABLE BORDER="0" CELLSPACING="2" CELLPADDING="1">
     <TR>
      <TD>Do you live in Missoula County?</TD>
      <TD>
       <P ALIGN="LEFT">
        <INPUT TYPE="checkbox" NAME="CheckBox" VALUE="CheckBox">
        Yes</P>
      </TD>
     </TR>
     <TR>
      <TD>Are you a member of any fire service agency?</TD>
      <TD>
       <P ALIGN="LEFT">
        <INPUT TYPE="checkbox" NAME="CheckBox" VALUE="CheckBox">
        Yes</P>
      </TD>
     </TR>
     <TR>
      <TD>If so, paid or volunteer?</TD>
      <TD>
       <P ALIGN="LEFT">
        <INPUT TYPE="radio" NAME="PaidVolunteer" VALUE="Paid">
        Paid  <BR>
        <INPUT TYPE="radio" NAME="PaidVolunteer" VALUE="Volunteer">
        Volunteer</P>
      </TD>
     </TR>
     <TR>
      <TD>How did you find us?</TD>
      <TD>
       <SELECT NAME="Where">
        <OPTION VALUE="FL">FireLink</OPTION>
        <OPTION VALUE="MC">Missoula County</OPTION>
        <OPTION VALUE="MT">Montana Territories</OPTION>
        <OPTION VALUE="YL">Yahoo/Lycos/Etc.</OPTION>
        <OPTION VALUE="OT">Other</OPTION>
       </SELECT>
      </TD>
     </TR>
     <TR>
```

```
      <TD VALIGN="TOP">Anything you'd like to tell us? (What you'd like
       to see<BR>on the site, what you thought of our pages, etc.)
      </TD>
      <TD>
       <TEXTAREA COLS="20" NAME="comments" ROWS="10"></TEXTAREA></TD>
     </TR>
    </TABLE>
    <P ALIGN="CENTER">
     <INPUT TYPE="SUBMIT" NAME="Submit" VALUE="Sign the Book">
     <INPUT TYPE="RESET" NAME="Reset" VALUE="Never mind...">
    </P>
   </FORM>
  </TD>
 </TR>
</TABLE>
<HR SIZE="8" NOSHADE>
<P ALIGN="RIGHT">
 <A HREF="/mrfd/index.htm"><STRONG>MRFD Home</STRONG>
 <IMG SRC="/mrfd/Images/cross.gif" WIDTH="113" HEIGHT="97" ALIGN="MIDDLE">
 </A></P>
</BODY>
</HTML>
```

Like the parent table, the form's table has the borders suppressed so only the formatting is seen, not the mechanism for creating it. Also, note the use of alternative labels for the submit and reset buttons. Although *Submit* and *Reset* are fine and acceptable names, sometimes it's nicer to include something a little more personal. However, the buttons still work the same.

# Summary

This chapter has given you a look into the way one organization uses HTML 3.2 to build its Web pages. The process began with experimenting with the four basic design elements—headlines, text, images, and space. These elements led to a simple design that fit the needs of the Fire District and became the basis of a Web page template.

From there, various HTML 3.2 elements were added to the pages, including hyperlinks, font sizes and colors, lists, and inline images. The result is a uniform image for the Web site that requires little time to implement. This feature is especially useful because this site is maintained by people with other demands on their time.

It is possible to use combinations of graphics, tables, and frames to build more elaborate and fancy page designs, but you should get a feel from these examples for what is possible by remaining within the constraints of the standard HTML elements. Chapter 18, "Creating Sophisticated Layouts with Frames and Layers," covers extended HTML features beyond what I've discussed in this section. Chapter 19, "Introducing Cascading Style Sheets," focuses on design, showing you how to further use HTML's capabilities to deliver your message to an eager audience.

III

PART

# Extending HTML 3.2

# Introducing HTML 4.0

*by Bob Correll*

## IN THIS CHAPTER

**CHAPTER 17**

To say that HTML is evolving is undeniably true. We've had about a year to enjoy the new capabilities HTML 3.2 gave us as Web developers and gnash our teeth at what it couldn't do. Netscape and Microsoft each upped the ante with their third generation of Web browsers in the summer of 1996, seeking to implement what was then the draft version of HTML 3.2. It wasn't until January 1997 that the specification for HTML 3.2 was approved by the World Wide Web Consortium (W3C), and true to the fast pace of free-market competition, the fourth generation of browsers and the next HTML specification is here.

The fact that Netscape and Microsoft are battling for control of the browser market has tremendous influence over the shape of HTML and the rapidity of change in the specification, a standard that has been trailing the browsers in the race to the market. Get used to it if you haven't already. Without browsers, we would have no use for HTML, and despite the feeling that sometimes the cart is preceding the horse, I would argue that this external contest is, on the whole, beneficial.

Enter HTML 4.0. This chapter is an overview of the latest developments in the HTML specification from the W3C and an entry point to the other chapters that cover these items in more depth. Some of the items I introduce will undoubtedly be familiar to you, and perhaps you are already using some of them. In these areas, the W3C is catching up with HTML elements already in widespread use and making the *de facto* standard official. Other areas, such as the Object Model, are more forward-looking and lay the groundwork for the future of HTML. A full understanding of these areas is critical for you to get the most out of HTML as you develop your Web pages and sites.

# What Is HTML 4.0?

HTML 4.0 is the code name for a collection of material under review by the World Wide Web Consortium HTML Working Group for potential incorporation into the next version of HTML, most likely version 4.0. This material has been released to the public, and much discussion will precede the eventual acceptance or rejection of each proposal (or part thereof).

> **NOTE**
>
> This chapter relies heavily on the draft HTML 4.0 material from the W3C, and therefore some of the information is subject to change. You should regularly visit the W3C site at
>
> `http://www.w3.org/TR/WD-html40/cover.html`
>
> This site, shown in Figure 17.1, keeps you abreast of developments and modifications.

**FIGURE 17.1.**
*You should become familiar with the Cougar page at the World Wide Web Consortium.*

The 10 documents, each with a different focus, that were under consideration by the W3C as Cougar are summarized here:

- Creating "index-friendly" Web pages
- Fully extending HTML support for style sheets
- Fully extending HTML support to client-side scripting lanuages
- Standardizing frame usage
- Enhancing forms
- Inserting objects into HTML
- Enlarging supported character sets
- Allowing file uploads
- Enhancing tables
- Internationalization

As was the case with HTML 3.2, several months may go by before the process of reviewing and debating the different proposals culminates in an official W3C Recommendation. As this discussion progresses, versions 4 of Microsoft Internet Explorer and Netscape Navigator (in the form of Netscape Communicator) will be released—before the standard has been set! This will result in a period of time when neither major browser meets the precise requirements of HTML 4.0 but implements only select portions, some of which probably will not be included in the final HTML standard.

# Linking and Indexing Mechanisms

The first draft under consideration, Hypertext Links in HTML, describes the current use of hypertext links and resource descriptions used in HTML 4.0. It offers several techniques for Web developers that will help indexing engines better catalog your site. I won't go into the descriptive aspects here because these are fully covered in Chapter 11, "Linking Documents and Images," and Chapter 7, "Structural Elements and Their Usage."

The first two recommended methods for making your site friendlier to indexing engines involve language. Given the internationalization of the Web, it is becoming more important that you know in which language a page was originally written. Therefore, you should define the language in the document HEAD, or as required in the BODY element if you depart from your default language, as shown in this snippet of code:

```
<HEAD>
<META HTTP-EQUIV=Content-Language CONTENT=en>
</HEAD>
<BODY LANG=en>
[content of Body is English]
<SPAN LANG=fr>
[content to be displayed in French]
</SPAN>
[body language reverts back to English]
</BODY>
```

You should also specify any language variants of the document using the LINK element to refer to your different translations. This allows search engines to offer the results in the preferred language of the user if a translation exists.

---

**NOTE**

Internationalization is a major theme of HTML 4.0. More than ever before, the fact that it is a *World Wide* Web is being recognized, and HTML 4.0 has language-identifying attributes sprinkled throughout.

---

The remaining recommendations suggest methods to construct your Web page in a way that improves indexing by search engines. As you might know, searching the Web can be a daunting task, and many vendors are expending tremendous amounts of energy attempting to catalog and index the vast number of Web pages currently online. You can help ensure that your site stands a chance of being properly indexed by using the META element with descriptive keywords, providing a logical content description, and specifying which areas of your site can be indexed.

# Support for Style Sheets

Style sheets represent a major advancement in the ability of HTML authors to control the appearance and layout of their work. This change has been driven in part by the increasing importance of the Web to business and entertainment, whose content developers were not satisfied with the standard heading tags and rudimentary layout possibilities that HTML offered. With style sheets, you can specify different font faces, sizes, and colors; control your margins; insert padding; and much more. Some of these effects are shown in Figure 17.2, the W3C informational Web page on style.

**FIGURE 17.2.**

*You can create appealing visual effects using style sheets. This Web page is from the W3C.*

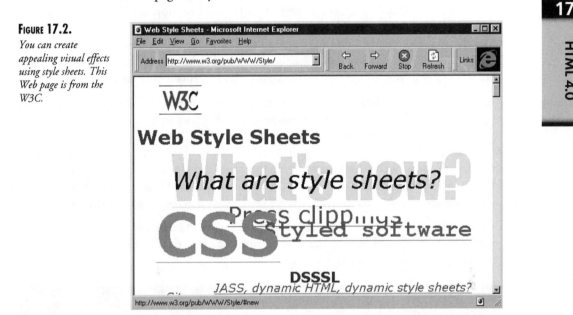

On December 17, 1996, the W3C officially released its recommendation on style sheets, entitled "Cascading Style Sheets, level 1." HTML 3.2 made provisions for the introduction of style sheets with the STYLE tag but did not flesh out the necessary HTML to completely integrate them into the standard. HTML 4.0 addresses this fact and more fully describes how to incorporate style sheets into your HTML documents.

Style sheets are more fully covered in Chapter 19, "Introducing Cascading Style Sheets," Chapter 20, "Cascading Style Sheet Usage," and Chapter 21, "JavaScript Style Sheets and Other Alternatives to CSS."

# Conceptual Framework for Style Sheets

Several rules of thumb drive the implementation of style sheets in HTML. The first is a commitment to support the flexible placement of style information. Instead of being forced to define a style in a single manner and in one designated location, you have the freedom to choose from several methods depending on the circumstances and your inclinations. You might want to include style information in a variety of places, either external to the HTML document or within it. The freedom to refer to an external style sheet, include style information in the HEAD element of a document, or place it inline ensures that you can find a method to suit your needs.

Second, HTML 4.0 does not specify a single style language to support. You can use cascading style sheets, level 1 (which has the recommendation of the W3C and is supported by both major browsers) or any alternative. This has opened the door to JavaScript-based style sheets as well as a few others. However, before you decide that "Joe's Friendly Style Sheets, level 42" are the ones you like best, you should ensure that your target audience's browser can interpret them.

Third, the concept of cascading style sheets (in general, as opposed to the specific Cascading Style Sheets, level 1 implementation) is supported. This allows style elements from a number of external sources to be included—thus, the term *cascading*. By using cascading style sheets of one form or another, you can put together multiple styles of your choosing, independent of the content of your Web page, and you can apply them depending upon design you are looking for. This permits you to reuse your styles with a minimum of fuss. You should refer to the documentation of your chosen style, because not all style languages support this usage.

Fourth, you can define a broad category of media (such as a PC monitor, WebTV, print-based browser, or speech-based browser) to which your style applies. This warns certain users that they are unable to support a particular style.

### NOTE

This is another major theme of HTML 4.0—improving support for nonvisual browsers or those with capabilities different from most standard PC monitors.

Finally, multiple styles can be supported to give users the flexibility of choosing one that suits their needs. This permits for the "graceful degradation" of your style depending on the limitations of a diverse audience. A person with limited vision might be able to choose an alternate style that you have provided with larger fonts to improved legibility.

Now that you've seen the conceptual framework, let's look briefly at a few of the proposed elements that make this possible.

## The LINK Element

Using the LINK element, you can refer to a style sheet that is external to the HTML document. You can reference multiple external style sheets if necessary (which is called cascading), with the last LINK taking precedence over those before it.

The syntax for using LINK is

```
<LINK attributes>
```

No closing tag is required. The LINK element supports the following six attributes:

- href provides the URL for the linked style sheet.
- title is used to group various LINK and STYLE elements together under a common name such as "Corporate Standard."
- rel stands for *relationship value* between the LINK element and the external style sheet and must be included for your external style to be recognized as a style sheet. The values are stylesheet and alternate stylesheet.
- rev defines the relationship opposite to REL, which would be from the style sheet to the LINK element. This is not necessary if you are linking to an external style.
- type specifies the Internet Media type, allowing users to disregard if they do not support your media type.
- media defines the medium to which your style sheet applies. The media attributes are print, screen, projection, braille, aural, and all. Multiple options are permissible when separated by commas.

Suppose that you have multiple styles you want to incorporate into your document. Using the LINK element to reference them would look like the following:

```
<LINK REL=stylesheet MEDIA=aural HREF="soundsgood.css">
<LINK REL=stylesheet MEDIA=braille HREF="feelsgood.css">
<LINK REL=stylesheet MEDIA=screen HREF="looksgood.css">
<LINK REL=stylesheet MEDIA=all HREF="allgood.css">
```

Depending on the media of the target browser, one or more of the style sheets would be applied.

## The STYLE Element

The STYLE element enables you to include your style in the actual HTML document. The element must be in the document HEAD, and multiple declarations are allowed. The syntax is

```
<STYLE attributes>
[style data]
</STYLE>
```

A closing tag is required. The STYLE element has only the following three attributes:

■ type is the Internet Media type, such as "text/css".

■ title is similar to the title attribute for the LINK element. This allows you to group your styles together under a common name.

■ media allows you to identify the media for which your style is designed. This attribute can take the same values that were used in the LINK element.

If you want to define a style to apply to your different headings, it would look like this:

```
<STYLE TYPE="text/css">
    H1 {color: red }
    H2 {color: blue}
    H3 {color: black}
</STYLE>
```

## Generic Attributes

In order to define a style across a document, a method for identifying each style-capable element must be created. This allows you to apply your style to a defined object in the page. The following generic attributes have been proposed for most elements in HTML:

■ id defines a unique identifier that applies to the entire document.

■ class allows you to define a class of elements that will be formatted as you define in your style declaration.

■ style provides rendering information that is specific to the element to which it is attributed.

### The SPAN and DIV Elements

What if you want to change the style of some text in the middle of a paragraph? The text is not a complete element and would not have a unique ID. Therefore, the SPAN element has been proposed to allow you to apply a style to text that is otherwise not an element. After defining the SPAN style in the STYLE element, you can use SPAN wherever you would use the <EM> tag.

The DIV element is proposed to handle situations when you have multiple elements to which you want to apply a style. It is used wherever the <P> tag is used, and it can be nested.

# Support for Scripting

Although you might have used JavaScript and VBScript for some time, you might be interested to know that the SCRIPT element in HTML 3.2 was simply a placeholder reserved for future use. Your ability to incorporate these technologies into your Web pages has been at the discretion of the large browser vendors—Netscape and Microsoft. This has caused considerable trouble in terms of standardization, as each company has attempted to evangelize its chosen language. You now have a more fully developed scripting interface into HTML in which you can insert client-side scripting.

This is certainly good news, but perhaps the real significance is the fact that scripting will be the glue that holds many of the proposed elements of HTML 4.0 together. For example, scripting will be able to manipulate style sheets, and a large part of what is called Dynamic HTML relies upon scripting to provide the dynamism.

Because HTML does not define a standard scripting language, implementation across browsers between the differing scripts might not be uniform, but it appears that JavaScript is currently the most widely supported script.

**NOTE**

The SCRIPT element illustrates another focus of HTML 4.0–building the framework for the inclusion of a language or object while remaining neutral to the implementation. This neutrality has its good and bad points. It allows you the flexibility to choose a language you desire, but it does not ensure that all browsers will support it.

Knowing how to use the SCRIPT tag and taking advantage of these events is dependent on your knowledge of a chosen scripting language. Therefore, I encourage you to read Chapter 28, "Integrating JavaScript and HTML," and Chapter 30, "Integrating ActiveX and VBScript," for further details.

## The SCRIPT Element

Multiple instances of the SCRIPT element can be located in both the document HEAD or BODY. The SCRIPT element has the following syntax:

```
<SCRIPT attributes>
[script and HTML content]
</SCRIPT>
```

Here are the available attributes:

- type is the MIME type that specifies the scripting language, such as "text/javascript" or "text/vbscript".
- language is the name of the scripting language, which is deprecated in favor of the type attribute.
- src allows you to give a URL for access to external script.

**NOTE**

Accessing external scripts requires you to set up a MIME attribute for the type of document that contains the script.

## Intrinsic Events

Intrinsic events are easy to define. A user has done something that you can track and have the Web page respond to through the appropriate script. Having the capability to track these events allows you to build dynamic Web pages. The current list includes the following events:

- onLoad occurs when the page has finished loading or all frames defined within a frameset have loaded. You can use this attribute only within the BODY or FRAMESET.

- onUnload occurs when a user exits the document. This attribute is available only within the BODY or FRAMESET elements.

- onClick occurs when the user clicks on an anchor or form field. The anchor refers to a hypertext link and the form field consists of buttons, checkboxes, radio buttons, reset buttons, and submit buttons.

- onMouseOver occurs when the mouse is moved over an anchor or TEXTAREA element.

- onMouseOut occurs, conversely, when the mouse has moved out of an anchor or TEXTAREA element.

- onFocus occurs when a form field is selected by tabbing or clicking with the mouse.

- onBlur happens when a form field loses its focus.

- onSubmit means, simply, that a user has submitted a form.

- onSelect, as opposed to onFocus, occurs when the text has been selected within a single or multiline field.

- onChange occurs when a form field has lost its focus and the data has been changed.

Intrinsic event handling and Dynamic HTML are covered in Chapter 22, "Dynamic HTML."

# Frame Implementation

Frames—devices used to divide a Web page into separate regions for navigation and layout purposes—were ushered in by the release of versions 3 of Netscape Navigator and Microsoft Internet Explorer during the summer of 1996. Figure 17.3, a Web page from Netscape's site, is an excellent example of using frames to divide a Web page into regions that each have a distinct navigational or layout purpose. Despite their widespread use, frames were not a part of the official HTML 3.2 specification, which followed six months later.

HTML 4.0 rectifies that fact by standardizing the use of frames and also introducing a new element called IFRAME, for *inline frame*. Users of Microsoft's Internet Explorer will undoubtedly recognize IFRAME as the floating frame introduced in version 3 (which is not supported by Netscape). Support for this might be short-lived, because the same document that proposes it also discusses an alternative, based on the OBJECT element, and never comes to a definitive conclusion.

**FIGURE 17.3.**
*The use of frames greatly enhances page layout possibilities.*

Frame syntax and usage is covered in Chapter 18, "Creating Sophisticated Layouts with Frames and Layers."

# The Inline Frame

The usage of IFRAME is similar to that of a normal frame but distinct in a few areas. With a normal frame, you replace the body tag with a frameset and then create frames within that structure. Inline frames are designed to actually reside inside the BODY element of a Web page, with text and other elements flowing around them accordingly. The syntax for IFRAME is

```
<IFRAME attributes>
    [HTML content]
</IFRAME>
```

Here are the available attributes:

- src is the address of a document to be displayed in an inline frame.
- name names the frame so that you can direct content into it.
- frameborder displays a border around the frame. Values are "1", which is the default and turns the border on, and "0", which turns the border off.
- marginwidth inserts the specified number of pixels between the frame border and content.
- marginheight inserts the specified number of pixels between the frame border and content.

- scrolling allows scrollbars to be displayed. Values are "auto" (default), "yes", and "no".
- width determines the frame width in pixels.
- height determines the frame height in pixels.
- align is an additional attribute that allows you to position the frame in relation to the line of text where it is located. Allowable values are left, middle, right, top, and bottom.

An example of usage might be to display another local Web page or link to an external Web site in order to create the effect of a picture within a picture, similar to what many televisions can do.

**Listing 17.1. The main page that calls the inline frame.**

```
<HTML>
<HEAD>
<TITLE>Inline Frame Test</TITLE>
</HEAD>
<BODY>
This is a test for the inline frame
<IFRAME src="iframe1.htm" name="iframe1" frameborder=1 scrolling=no
 width=100 height=50 align=middle></IFRAME>
Notice how it's aligned in the middle of the text and that text
automatically wraps around it.
<P><IFRAME src="http://www.samspublishing.com" name="iframe2"
frameborder=1 width=600 height=200 align=top></IFRAME>
<P>Here I've directed the Sams.net web site into the frame.
</BODY>
</HTML>
```

In Listing 17.1, I created two inline frames within the main.htm file. The first is a small frame that calls another HTML file and displays it within the inline frame. The second case links to the Sams.net Publishing Web site and displays it within a larger inline frame. The output of Listing 17.1 is shown in Figure 17.4.

**NOTE**

As of this writing, the inline frame feature works only with Microsoft Internet Explorer 3 and 4.

**FIGURE 17.4.**

*Two inline frames—
one containing another
HTML document and
the second linking to a
Web site.*

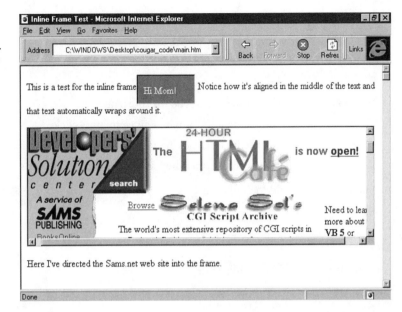

## Form Extensions

HTML forms have existed for some time now, and the current proposal seeks to improve interactivity by including intrinsic events and providing better support for speech-based browsers. Three new elements have been proposed, and this section briefly describes the attributes associated with each.

### The LABEL Element

The LABEL element provides speech-based browsers with the means to describe an element, and it incorporates intrinsic events to enhance interactivity. (See the "Support for Scripting" section earlier in this chapter.) Labels used to enclose a single form control are called *implicit* while those that are defined separately are called *explicit*.

The syntax is

```
<LABEL attributes>
[FORM Controls or field label text]
</LABEL>
```

Here are the available attributes:

- `for` is the ID of a form control.
- `id` is a document-wide identifier.
- `class` is a list of class names to be used in style sheets.
- `style` is element-specific style information.

- **title** provides additional information in relation to a particular element.
- **dir** specifies the directionality of the text.
- **lang** indicates the language used.
- **disabled** is used to disable form controls.
- **accesskey** is used to provide a keyboard shortcut.
- **onClick** is used to execute a script when an element is clicked.
- **onFocus** is used to execute a script when an element receives the focus.
- **onBlur** is used to execute a script when an element loses the focus.

An implicit label would look like this:

```
<LABEL>
    City
    <INPUT TYPE="TEXT" NAME="CITY>
</LABEL>
```

An explicit label would look like this:

```
<LABEL FOR="CITY">City</LABEL>
<INPUT TYPE=TEXT NAME=CITY ID=CITY>
```

Using an explicit label allows you to place the label and the associated input element in separate locations on the page, such as in different columns of a table.

## The BUTTON Element

The new BUTTON element enables you to create more than the two standard buttons available now: Submit and Reset.

Here are the BUTTON element attributes:

- **id** is a document-wide identifier.
- **class** is a list of class names to be used in style sheets.
- **style** is element-specific style information.
- **title** provides additional information in relation to a particular element.
- **dir** specifies the directionality of the text.
- **lang** indicates the language used.
- **disabled** is used to disable form controls.
- **tabindex** is an integer that sets the tab order.
- **onClick** is used to execute a script when an element is clicked.
- **onFocus** is used to execute a script when an element receives the focus.
- **onBlur** is used to execute a script when an element loses the focus.

## The FIELDSET Element

The FIELDSET element has been proposed in order to group related fields together to give speech-based browsers the capability to describe the different groups and let the user move from group to group.

Here are the attributes:

- ■ id is a document-wide identifier.
- ■ class is a list of class names to be used in style sheets.
- ■ style is element-specific style information.
- ■ title provides additional information in relation to a particular element.
- ■ dir specifies the directionality of the text.
- ■ lang indicates the language used.

HTML forms are more fully covered in Chapter 15, "Building and Using HTML Forms."

# Inserting Objects

The draft currently under consideration by the W3C discusses ways to insert additional types of content (such as Java Applets or ActiveX Controls) into HTML documents. What about the APPLET tag? It is still supported but obviously is specific to Java Applets; no other objects can use the APPLET tag to gain entry into a Web page. Instead of creating a new element for every object or plug-in that could conceivably be used in a Web page, the W3C has chosen to create a single OBJECT element that functionally replaces the IMG element for inserting media into an HTML document and can be extended if necessary.

## The OBJECT Element

The OBJECT element has the following syntax:

```
<OBJECT attributes>
    [Parameters]
    [alternate content for those without the capability to view your media-type]
</OBJECT>
```

Here are the available attributes:

- ■ id is a document-wide identification.
- ■ declare allows you to imply an object without actually creating or instantiating it until needed.
- ■ classid is a URL identifying the class identifier or implementation of an object.
- ■ codebase is a URL pointing to the location of the code.
- ■ data is another URL that points to any data an object might require.
- ■ type identifies the Internet Media type for the data as referenced in the DATA attribute.

- codetype identifies the Internet Media type of the code as referenced in the CLASSID attribute.
- standby allows the display of a short message to be shown while the object is being loaded.
- align specifies how to align the object relative to the current text line or aligned as a separate entity. Possible values are texttop, middle, textmiddle, baseline, textbottom, left, center, and right.
- width specifies the width allotted to the object within the browser window.
- height specifies the height allotted to the object within the browser window.
- border shows a border around the object when the value is "1", and it shows no border when set to "0".
- hspace is similar to what is used in an inline image. It allows you to insert extra space to "cushion" the object.
- vspace is similar to what is used in an inline image. It allows you to insert extra space to "cushion" the object.
- usemap attributes the object's URL if the object is a client-side image map.
- shapes is used in conjunction with objects that have anchors or links defined by shaped areas.
- name is used with HTML forms that might contain an object, in order to determine whether that object should send data to the server when the form is submitted.
- alt is alternate content to be displayed if the user can't or doesn't want to display the object.
- title is the title of the object to be displayed.

Here is an example of how to insert a QuickTime movie into a Web page:

```
<OBJECT data=Apollo13.mov
     type="video/quicktime"
     alt="Problem"
     title="Apollo 13">
  <img src=Bang.gif alt="Problem">
</OBJECT>
```

The image, bang.gif, is displayed if the user can't view the QuickTime movie.

## The PARAM Element

The PARAM element, which is a list of named parameters to be passed to initialize an object, is associated with the OBJECT element.

The syntax is

```
<PARAM attributes>
```

You should note that there is no closing tag.

Here are the attributes:

- name defines the property name.
- value is the data you will be passing to the object.
- valuetype defines the type of value to be passed. Allowable values are REF, which indicates a URL; OBJECT, which points to the URL of an OBJECT element in the document; and DATA, the default value, which is passed directly to the OBJECT as a string.

# Other Items Under Consideration

*WD-entities, Additional Named Entities for HTML* extends HTML support for all characters in ISO 8859-1, Adobe Symbol font characters representable by glyphs, characters required for internationalization, and characters that lie outside of ISO 8859-1 but are included in CP-1250.

*RFC 1867, Form-based File Upload in HTML* recommends two changes to HTML 3.2 and would add a new MIME media type in order to enable the user to submit a file for upload from an HTML form.

*RFC 1942, HTML Tables* was also used as the basis for and considered a superset of the HTML 3.2 Recommendation. Improvements to the HTML 4.0 specification are focused on supporting style sheets and improving accessibility issues. You can turn to Chapter 10, "Creating Tables for Data and Page Layout," for further information.

*RFC 2070, Internationalization of the Hypertext Markup Language* discusses the issue of internationalization of HTML and is more fully covered in Chapter 39, "Internationalizing the HTML Character Set and Language Tags."

# Dynamic HTML

Dynamic HTML is not mentioned by name in HTML 4.0, but the mechanisms have been put in place to change the way you create—and experience—Web pages. The combined effects of the proposed style sheet implementation, improvement of the HTML support for scripting languages, and the use of a wider variety of objects to be created within a Web page gives you the power to dynamically manipulate items in a Web page without accessing the server.

When you use style sheets and take advantage of the generic attributes that have been proposed, you are able to uniquely identify virtually everything in a Web page. Having done this, you can call on your favorite scripting language to change an element (such as a font face or the color of a heading) in response to a user action (such as onMouseOver, which is an intrinsic event).

However, HTML 4.0 is language-neutral. It creates a standard that specifies the interface between scripting/programming languages and HTML with complete neutrality and leaves implementation issues to be hammered out by other parties. Netscape and Microsoft might be able to claim compliance with the HTML 4.0 standard while still not supporting rival scripting languages or style sheet implementations.

# Summary

As you have seen, HTML 4.0 is an ambitious attempt to improve HTML support for a wide range of HTML elements and techniques, and this chapter has just touched the surface. Aside from "housekeeping" improvements, HTML 4.0 seems to have three main themes: accessibility, dynamism, and neutrality. Whether it takes the form of internationalizing HTML or providing means for nonvisual browsers (or those with differing capabilities) to meaningfully interpret a Web page, the push is on to be able to reach the largest audience possible. In addition, through the use of style sheets, scripting, and the Object Model, Dynamic HTML is made possible.

Most striking is the move to integrate a wide variety of media types, styles, and scripts—much of which is outside of HTML proper—with HTML without attempting to restrict which type the developer can use. This doesn't mean Netscape will ever buy into ActiveX or Microsoft will stop trying to market its programming and scripting technologies to developers, but HTML is steering a course between these two giants, hoping to preserve the openness of HTML.

# Creating Sophisticated Layouts with Frames and Layers

*by John Jung*

## IN THIS CHAPTER

There are times when using the basic HTML tags that you've learned simply isn't enough to get what you want. Sometimes you really want your Web page to stand out and truly be different. Many people turn to Java and JavaScript in such situations. Although those are generally adequate solutions, they aren't the only ones. A number of HTML extensions that are being proposed for the next update to HTML are available to you. Two such concepts and extensions are frames and layers.

# Frames

Frames are the implementation of a concept currently under discussion at the World Wide Web Consortium (W3C). With frames, you can separate Web pages into distinct sections. These sections can be any size within the browser window and, if allowed, can be resized. Also, the content in one frame can be independent of other frames if the Web author so desires. It's also possible to have the user's actions in one frame affect the content of other frames.

## What Are Frames Good For?

Because the contents in each frame are separate and distinctive of each other, you get better control over the information presented. For example, a commercial Web site could put the logos of its big advertisers in separate frames. Whatever the user does at such a site won't make the logos disappear. This way, you can provide free advertising to your big sponsors and not worry about someone missing it.

But frames give you far more functionality, rather than just control over what is presented. With the frames extension, you can change the content of other frames, which makes it possible for you to use frames as a navigation tool. You could display the main menu for your site in one frame and the contents in another. When the user makes a selection on the main menu, the contents frame will be updated. In fact, many such cool Web sites do precisely this (as shown in Figure 18.1).

## Considerations of Frame Use

Frames can be a useful tool, but you shouldn't just rush out and start using them. You need to take some considerations into account before using frames. First, frames are a relatively new idea. As a result, some older browsers don't even support frames. For example, Lynx, the text-only Web browser, provides limited support for frames. As a result, if you use frames, many Lynx users will have problems getting around your site. Additionally, moderately older browsers have a poor user interface for navigating through frames. Netscape Navigator 2.0 was the first Web browser to support frames. Everything was fine, unless you wanted to go back a frame configuration or two.

**FIGURE 18.1.**

*Frames provide an excellent way to navigate through your site.*

This is the logo for where you're at in the Netscape Web site.

This frame is your main navigation tool. Click a link and the other frames update.

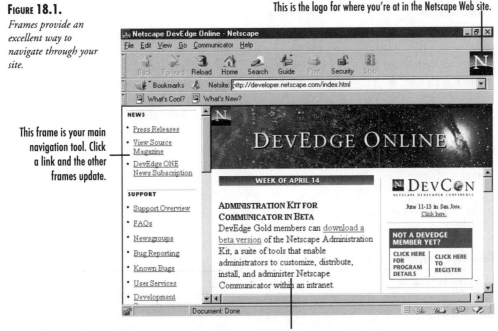

The actual contents of this Web page are displayed here.

Another consideration in using frames is whether they're really necessary. Although frames are a good tool, they aren't appropriate for all Web sites. If you're creating your own personal Web page, you can probably get away with using frames. After all, you want the Web page to impress only yourself and maybe your friends. You're not trying to ply any goods, so you're not really losing out on anything. If your company has a history of being a "hip" and "with-it" type of company, you could also use frames. If you're selling airplanes or power tools, however, you probably don't need them. So when should you use frames? Look at the following criteria. If you meet any of them, you should consider using frames:

- It's a personal Web page.
- Your company has a maverick/independent image.
- Your target audience will most likely be using the latest browser.

# Syntax of Frame Creation

Like working with most other building blocks of HTML, creating frames isn't terribly difficult. In fact, I found tables a bit harder to create than frames. The frame extension is made up of three new HTML tags and one new attribute. The easiest of the three tags to understand is the `<NOFRAMES></NOFRAMES>` container. Basically, only Web browsers that don't support frames will display whatever is between those tags. You can use these tags to tell users what browser you prefer them to use so that they can view your frames.

# <FRAMESET>...</FRAMESET>

The <FRAMESET>...</FRAMESET> container is the starting point for designing your frame lay-out. Use this container to specify the relative and absolute size of each frame. You can use only the <FRAME> tag and the <NOFRAMES> and <FRAMESET> containers within these tags. When creat-ing any Web page with frames, you must first define a top-level frameset. You can create this top-level frameset only if you use the <FRAMESET> container instead of the <BODY> container. Table 18.1 details the attributes for the <FRAMESET> tag. Generally, the syntax for the <FRAMESET></FRAMESET> group of tags is as follows:

```
<FRAMESET frame_configuration...>
<FRAME SRC=URL1...>
<FRAME SRC=URL2...>
...
<FRAME SRC=URLn...>
...Additional <FRAMESET></FRAMESET> tags as needed...
</FRAMESET>
```

**Table 18.1. Attributes for <FRAMESET>.**

| Attribute Name | Acceptable Values | Purpose |
| --- | --- | --- |
| BORDER | Any integer number | Indicates the border thickness for all child frames. |
| COLS | A number that may or may not have a percentage sign (%) or asterisk (*) | Defines the number and size of the columns you want to create. A number without a percentage sign indicates the size of the column in pixels. A number with a percentage sign indicates the width of the frame relative to the width of the browser. An asterisk indicates that the frame is sized proportionately to other frames. Specify multiple columns by quoting the size in a comma-separated list. |
| FRAMEBORDER | 1 or 0 | Specifies whether frames are displayed with a border. A value of 1 indicates the presence of a frame border and 0 disables the frame border. Individual frames can override this attribute. |

| Attribute Name | Acceptable Values | Purpose |
|---|---|---|
| ROWS | A number that may or may not have a percentage sign (%) or asterisk (*) | Defines the number and size of the rows you want to create. A number without a percentage sign indicates the size of the row in pixels. A number with a percentage sign indicates the height of the frame relative to the width of the browser. The asterisk indicates that the frame is sized proportionately to other frames. Specify multiple columns by quoting the size in a comma-separated list. |

18

CREATING LAYOUTS WITH FRAMES AND LAYERS

## The <FRAME> Tag

After you specify a frameset, you must define the content of those frames, which is where the <FRAME> tag comes in. The <FRAME> tag controls various attributes for a particular frame, such as the content, color, and border width. For every row or column you define in the frameset, you must have a corresponding <FRAME>. The first frame, specified by either COLS or ROWS, will use the first <FRAME> tag (as shown in Listing 18.1). You can create complicated frame layouts using the <FRAMESET> container tags instead of the <FRAME> tag. (See the section "Creating Fancy Frame Layouts," later in this chapter.) Table 18.2 completely lists all the attributes that the <FRAME> tag uses.

**Listing 18.1. Code to create a frame layout.**

```
<HTML>
<HEAD>
<TITLE>Sample Frameset</TITLE>
</HEAD>
<FRAMESET ROWS="50%,50%">
  <FRAME SRC="agenda.html">
  <FRAME SRC="minutes.html">
</FRAMESET>
</HTML>
```

**Table 18.2. Attributes for <FRAME>.**

| Attribute Name | Acceptable Values | Purpose |
| --- | --- | --- |
| FRAMEBORDER | 1 or 0 | Specifies whether frames are displayed with a border. A value of 1 indicates the presence of a frame border and 0 disables the frame border. Individual frames can override this attribute. |
| MARGINHEIGHT | Any integer number | Indicates the height of the top and bottom margins in pixels. |
| MARGINWIDTH | Any integer number | Indicates the height of the left and right margins in pixels. |
| NAME | Any string beginning with a letter | Identifies the name of the frame for reference. There are four reserved names: _blank, _parent, _self, and _top. The _blank name opens a new window with the specified URL. The _parent name opens the URL in the parent frame of the current frame. If you call a _self frame, the URL replaces the frame the link was originally in. The _top name displays the URL in the full window. |
| NORESIZE | None | Simply acts as a toggle switch. When present, it prevents the user from resizing the frame. |
| SCROLLING | Yes, No, or Auto | Specifies whether a scrollbar appears in the frame. When set to Auto, the browser determines whether a scrollbar should be created. Auto is the default behavior. |
| SRC | Any URL | Specifies the file to be displayed within the frame. If you do not specify a SRC attribute, the space where the frame would appear will be blank. |

## The New Attribute

The final addition to HTML that the frames extensions made was to add a new extension. That extension, TARGET, was added to the Anchor element. This attribute takes a single string that specifies the name of the frame to display the contents. The <FRAME> tag, using the NAME attribute, defines the name of the frame (as shown in Listing 18.2). This enables you to change the contents of a frame by using hypertext links. For example, Figure 18.2 shows a framed Web page and the names for each. If you click a link in the left frame, named left, the right frame, named right, is updated appropriately. The HTML source for the left frame is shown in Listing 18.1. Frequently using the TARGET attribute updates the frame. The TARGET attribute isn't part of the <FRAMESET> or <FRAME> tag definition. Rather, it's an attribute for the <A> tag, used for navigation purposes. The TARGET attribute is entirely optional, and not using it would make each frame update independently. The last link in the left frame of Figure 18.2 updates the contents of its own frame.

> **NOTE**
>
> To create a new window, specify an invalid frame name.

**FIGURE 18.2.**

*In this simple framed page, the contents on the right are updated by the links on the left.*

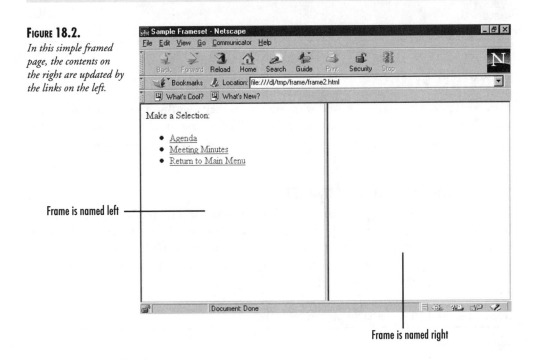

Frame is named left

Frame is named right

**Listing 18.2. The HTML source for the entire Web page shown in Figure 18.2.**

```
<HTML>
<HEAD>
<TITLE>Sample Frameset</TITLE>
</HEAD>
<FRAMESET COLS="50%,50%">
  <FRAME SRC="left.html">
  <FRAME SRC="right.html">
</FRAMESET>
</HTML>
```

**Listing 18.3. HTML source for the frame Left shown in Figure 18.2.**

```
<HTML>
<HEAD>
<TITLE>This title doesn't show up in the browser window</TITLE>
</HEAD>
<BODY BGCOLOR="#FFFFFF">
Make a Selection:
<UL>
<LI><A HREF="agenda.html" TARGET="right">Agenda</A></LI>
<LI><A HREF="minutes.html" TARGET="right">Meeting Minutes</A></LI>
<LI><A HREF="mainmenu.html" TARGET="_self">Return to Main Menu</A></LI>
</UL>
</BODY>
</HTML>
```

# Making Frames

Now you know what frames are and what arguments they use. But it takes a lot more than simply knowing the tags to be able to create frame layouts. You need to be able to put what you've just read about into practice. I'll give you some simple frame layouts and show you how they would look in a Web browser.

## Creating Simple Frame Layouts

Let's start out on applying your frame knowledge by creating a simple Web page. It should have two frames—one on top and one on the bottom. You won't care about the content in each frame because those are just regular Web pages. Also, you won't have any links that update each other; I already covered that. Figure 18.3 shows what your Web page should look like, and Listing 18.4 shows how it was done.

**Listing 18.4. The HTML source for the page shown in Figure 18.3.**

```
<HTML>
<HEAD>
<TITLE>Two Frame Web Page</TITLE>
</HEAD>
```

```
<FRAMESET ROWS="50%,50%">
  <FRAME SRC="top.html">
  <FRAME SRC="bottom.html">
</FRAMESET>
</HTML>
```

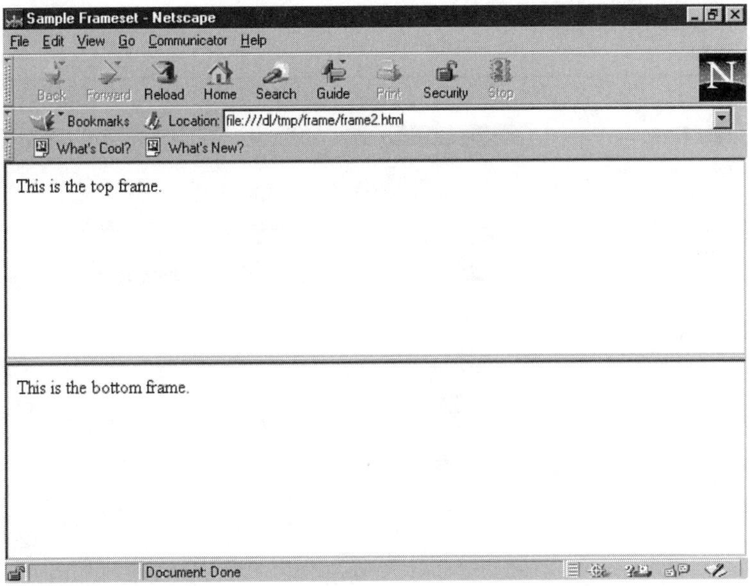

**FIGURE 18.3.**

*This simple frame layout has only two frames.*

Maybe that was a bit too easy. I think you could figure out the appropriate values to plug into the ROWS attribute. Also, with two frames, it's not hard to guess which Web page goes into which frame. Let's try something more difficult. Let's try three frames—two next to each other and the third under both of them. (See Figure 18.4.) Take a look at Listing 18.5 to see how it should be done. Basically, you first create a <FRAMESET> that encapsulates the general look of the Web page, such as splitting it horizontally in this case. Next, instead of using a <FRAME> to specify the Web page to be presented in the frame, you specify another <FRAMESET>. This nested <FRAMESET> further subdivides the region, allowing you to display even more Web pages. Because you are splitting the top frame region, the nested <FRAMESET> will be split vertically. This nested <FRAMESET> receives its contents from the two <FRAME> tags between the beginning and ending tags. Finally, to specify the Web page for the bottom frame, you simply use a regular <FRAME> tag.

**Listing 18.5. HTML source for the page shown in Figure 18.4.**

```
<HTML>
<HEAD>
<TITLE>Three Frame Web Page</TITLE>
</HEAD>
```

*continues*

**Listing 18.5. continued**

```
<FRAMESET ROWS="70%,30%">
  <FRAMESET COLS="70%,30%">
    <FRAME SRC="left.html">
    <FRAME SRC="right.html">
  </FRAMESET>
  <FRAME SRC="bottom.html">
</FRAMESET>
</HTML>
```

**FIGURE 18.4.**

*This frame layout, which can be a little tricky, uses three frames.*

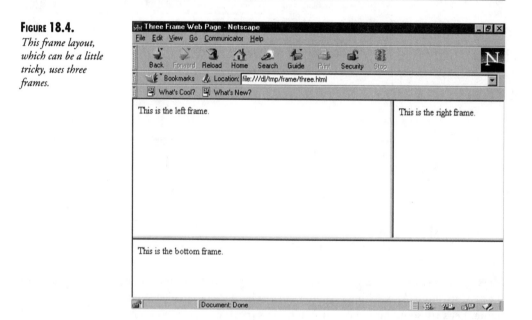

The important part to remember about this example is that you nested <FRAMESET> tags, which is how you were able to have the left and right frames. You now have the basics of creating nice, functional layouts. With these ideas, you can create truly advanced frame layouts if you think about how to lay out a page beforehand. The next section deals with creating sophisticated frame layouts.

## Creating Fancy Frame Layouts

It's quite possible, by using frames, to have really cool-looking frame layouts. Earlier, I briefly mentioned that you could nest <FRAMESET> tags. This procedure is the heart of making a truly spectacular Web page. Because <FRAMESET> uses the currently available window space, nesting enables you to further subdivide the window. For example, consider how Figure 18.5 was created. Or, you can cheat and look at Listing 18.6. Basically, you split the window into three horizontal frames, leaving the bottom frame alone. You subdivide the top frame into four nested frames, all of them next to each other. You then split the middle region into two nested frames, leaving the left frame region alone. Finally, you split the middle left frame region into four frames, one on top of each other.

**Listing 18.6. HTML source for the frame layout in Figure 18.5.**

```
<HTML>
<HEAD>
<TITLE>Advanced Frame Layout</TITLE>
</HEAD>
<FRAMESET ROWS="33%,33%,33%">
  <FRAMESET COLS="25%,25%,25%,25%">
    <FRAME SRC="blank1.html">
    <FRAME SRC="blank2.html">
    <FRAME SRC="blank3.html">
    <FRAME SRC="blank4.html">
  </FRAMESET>
  <FRAMESET COLS="80%,20%">
    <FRAME SRC="blank5.html">
    <FRAMESET ROWS="25%,25%,25%,25%">
      <FRAME SRC="blank6.html">
      <FRAME SRC="blank7.html">
      <FRAME SRC="blank8.html">
      <FRAME SRC="blank9.html">
    </FRAMESET>
  </FRAMESET>
  <FRAME SRC="blank10.html">
</FRAMESET>
</HTML>
```

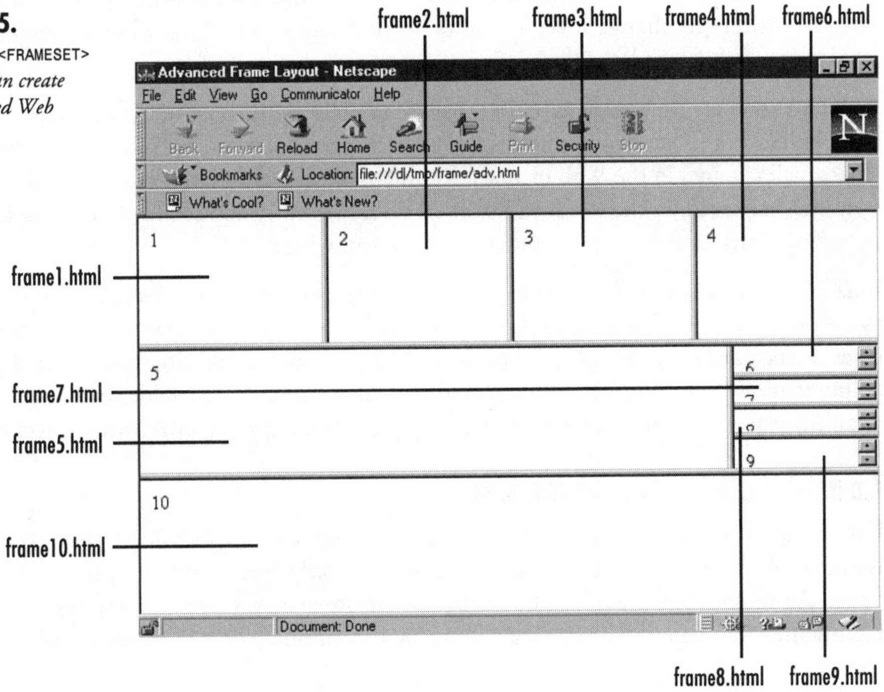

**FIGURE 18.5.**
*By nesting <FRAMESET> tags, you can create sophisticated Web pages.*

# Layers

Layers are a very new set of tools that help make neat-looking Web pages. Layers, created by Netscape, enable Web authors to define any number of *sub-Web pages*—pages whose content is independent of each other and the main Web page. They can show any URL, just like a Web page, or a frame, but also have much flexibility. Frames can be positioned, sized, and moved around with various JavaScript code. Further, you can put layers on top of each other, and have only certain ones showing their content. Hence, they're called "layers." When you use layers correctly, you can create some outstanding Web pages. Currently, only Netscape Navigator 4.0 will support the layers, although Internet Explorer 4.0 will probably do so as well.

## Differences Between Frames and Layers

"Layers sound a lot like frames," I hear you saying. Not at all. Layers and frames are different in numerous respects. First, you can't simply have one frame; you must have at least two. That means that the frame layout takes up the entire Web browser window. Layers, on the other hand, are separate entities that take up only a certain amount of space. If the Web author desires, he or she can use a layer that takes up the entire Web browser window space. But perhaps more importantly, layers have two functions that frames simply lack.

First, you can control the visibility of a layer. In other words, you can show or hide any and all layers. This is quite different from frames, which simply must take up the entire Web browser window space. You cannot create a frame that takes up only a certain portion of the browser window. Furthermore, you can use JavaScript (as discussed in the section "Layers and JavaScript" in this chapter) to change layer visibility so that—depending on what a user does with JavaScript—a different layer shows.

A second and very important function that frames lack is the precise layout control that you have with layers. That is, with frames, as with all other HTML tags, the browser determines where each tag goes in the Web browser. With layers, you can specify exactly where you want a layer to be placed on the window. You don't have to worry about a layer showing up in different locations on different computers. *You* control where it goes.

Finally, with layers, you also have the built-in ability to change their positions. So, if you were to use JavaScript, you could control not only which layers are seen but where they appear. This gives you unparalleled control over how your Web page looks. Additionally, you could use this ability to move layers to create neat animations. For example, you could create a set of images of an airplane, put each on a separate layer, and use JavaScript to control which layer is visible.

## Considerations for Layer Use

For all the neat functionality of layers, there are some reasons you don't want to use them immediately. The primary reason is that, currently, only Netscape Communicator supports layers. Although there are a lot of Netscape Navigator users, there aren't necessarily a lot of Communicator owners. The fact that Netscape Communicator is released doesn't mean that all Navigator users will rush out and use it. As a result, by using layers, you could be aiming for a rather small market. Almost all corporate sites should avoid layers until other browsers start to support them. You can probably get away with using layers in personal Web pages, but don't be surprised if you get some complaints. The primary reasons you would want to use layers are the same as those for wanting to use frames. If you meet any of the following criteria, you should probably use layers:

- You are creating a personal Web page.
- Your company has a maverick or independent image.
- Your target audience will most likely be using the latest browser.

Another consideration in using layers is that JavaScript handles most of its functionality. That means that along with further alienating some users, you should watch the content. It's too easy for developers to overload their JavaScript Web pages with graphics and sound. Layers makes it all the more tempting to put up really cool Web pages and not consider the user. Far too many Web pages today, without layers, have large Java applets and large images. It can take a considerable amount of time, even with intranet-level connections, to retrieve some of these pages. This situation can only get worse if people don't think about the consequences of using layers.

An additional consideration for the usage of layers is that the W3C hasn't agreed on its specifications. Although this isn't surprising for cutting-edge HTML code, the standards committee has also shelved discussion on layers, so it's possible that the W3C has completely lost interest in the idea of layers. Therefore, it's possible that the W3C will simply drop the proposed layer tags entirely. You have no guarantee that layers *will* be dropped, but you also have no guarantee that they won't.

Yet another consideration in using layers is how much work you want for yourself. If you intend to use layers extensively, you must remember that it will create a bit of work. Because layers can be anywhere on the screen, they are out-flow layers, which means that any HTML code after a layer will appear exactly where it would go if the layer tags weren't used. For example, suppose you give a title to a Web page, define a layer, and then add a bulleted list of items. The bulleted list of items would come immediately below the title of the Web page, not after the layer. You might want to use an in-flow layer for such a purpose.

## What Are In-Flow and Out-Flow Layers?

In this section, I talk about how to create layers. The new layer specifications allow for two different types of layers: out-flow and in-flow layers. An out-flow layer—probably what you, like most people, will use—is positioned exactly where the Web author wants it to be. To create an out-flow layer, use the `<LAYER>...</LAYER>` container tags. An in-flow layer is offset from the last HTML tag or text. To create in-flow layers, use the `<ILAYER>...</ILAYER>` container tags. The `<ILAYER>` tag has exactly the same argument as the `<LAYER>` tag. Because the syntax for using both are the same, for simplicity's sake I'll talk about only out-flow layers.

# Attributes and Methods of Layers

Layers are of a similar nature to frames in that they divide the Web browser window into distinct objects. You can't change frames dynamically. Therefore, when a user selects a particular link, you should have a frame change its size. Layers are simply the next progression from frames, allowing you to modify their attributes based on user events. In creating layers, you can set a number of possible attributes. In addition, each layer you create has a number of predefined methods associated with it. *Methods* is just another name for *functions* or *subroutines*, if you prefer. Neither layer attributes nor methods were created for frames.

## Layer Attributes

You can set a certain number of attributes for each layer you create. These attributes are just like regular HTML tag attributes, with one big difference: For almost every attribute available, a corresponding layer property is available. I'll talk more about layer properties in the next section, "Layer Properties and Methods." Table 18.3 lists all the attributes for the `<LAYER>`... `</LAYER>` container tags. The general `<LAYER>` tag can be broken down as follows:

```
<LAYER layer_attributes>
...HTML code or plain text...
</LAYER>
```

**Table 18.3. Attributes for `<LAYER>` and `<ILAYER>` container tags.**

| Attribute Name | Acceptable Values | Purpose |
| --- | --- | --- |
| ABOVE | Any layer name | Indicates that the current layer is above the specified layer name. |
| BACKGROUND | Any URL | Specifies the background image to be displayed in the layer. |
| BELOW | Any layer name | Indicates that the current layer is below the specified layer name. |
| BGCOLOR | #RRGGBB | Identifies the background color for the layer. RR, GG, and BB are hexadecimal numbers that give the intensity of the red, green, and blue values of a color. You can specify only two digits for the hexadecimal numbers. |
| CLIP | Integer,Integer, Integer,Integer | Specifies the left, top, right, and bottom coordinates by four-integer numbers for the layer in pixels. Whatever is in the layer contained in the CLIP rectangle is displayed. |

| Attribute Name | Acceptable Values | Purpose |
|---|---|---|
| LEFT | Any integer value | Specifies the left edge of the layer in pixels from the left side of the browser window. For <ILAYER>, this attribute specifies the offset from the previous HTML tag or text. |
| NAME | Any string beginning with a letter | Identifies the layer for Java or JavaScript referential use. |
| TOP | Any integer value | Specifies the top edge of the layer in pixels from the top of the browser window. For <ILAYER>, this attribute specifies the offset from the previous HTML tag or text. |
| VISIBILITY | SHOW, HIDE, or INHERIT | Determines whether the layer is visible. The INHERIT value causes the layer to take the visibility attribute of its parent. |
| WIDTH | Any integer value | Indicates the width of the layer in pixels. |
| ZINDEX | Any integer value | Indicates the index value for the layer for stacking and displaying. |

## Layer Properties and Methods

Because Netscape intended layers to enable you to create dynamic Web pages, layers have a few extra features. All of these features provide hooks for scripting languages into accessing aspects of the layer. The script can change values of some properties or call some layer methods. Table 18.4 shows all the properties for all layers. Table 18.5 gives you a list of methods available to all layers.

**Table 18.4. The <LAYER> tag properties.**

| Attribute Name | Can Be Changed? | Acceptable Values | Description |
|---|---|---|---|
| above | No | Any layer name | Specifies the parent layer of the current layer for nested layers. |
| background | Yes | Any URL | Specifies the background image to be displayed in the layer. |

*continues*

**Table 18.4. continued**

| Attribute Name | Can Be Changed? | Acceptable Values | Description |
|---|---|---|---|
| below | No | Any layer name | Specifies the child layer of the current layer for nested layers. |
| clip.top, clip.left, clip.right, clip.bottom, clip.width, clip.height | Yes | All properties accept any integer value | Control the various aspects of the clipping rectangle. |
| bgColor | Yes | #RRGGBB | Identifies the background color for the layer. RR, GG, and BB are hexadecimal numbers that give the intensity of the red, green, and blue values of a color. You can specify only two digits for the hexadecimal numbers. |
| height | No | Any integer value | Indicates the height of the layer in pixels. |
| layers | No | An array | Stores the index and name for each defined layer. |
| left | Yes | Any integer value | Specifies the number of pixels, from the left edge of the browser window, where the layer should start. |
| name | No | Any string beginning with a letter | Identifies the layer for Java or JavaScript referential use. |
| sibling.Above | No | Any layer name | Indicates that the current layer is above the specified layer name. A null value indicates the top-level layer. |

| Attribute Name | Can Be Changed? | Acceptable Values | Description |
|---|---|---|---|
| sibling.Below | No | Any layer name | Indicates that the current layer is below the specified layer name. A null value indicates the bottom-most layer. |
| top | Yes | Any integer value | Specifies the number of pixels from the top of the browser window, where the layer starts. |
| visibility | Yes | show, hide, or inherit | Determines whether the layer is visible. The INHERIT value causes the layer to take the visibility attribute of its parent. |
| width | No | Any integer value | Indicates the width of the layer in pixels. |
| zINDEX | Yes | Any integer value | Indicates the index value for the layer for stacking and displaying. Layers with a higher zINDEX value will be stacked above lower zINDEX numbered layers. |

**18**

CREATING LAYOUTS
WITH FRAMES AND
LAYERS

**Table 18.5. The <LAYER> tag methods.**

| Method Name | Parameters | Parameter Data Type | Description |
|---|---|---|---|
| offset | (x,y) | integer, integer | Causes the layer to be offset on the left by the specified x value. The top is similarly offset by the specified y value. |
| moveAbove | (layer_name) | string | Adjusts the stacking array to place the current layer above the specified layer. Both layers will have the same parent. |

*continues*

**Table 18.5. continued**

| Method Name | Parameters | Parameter Data Type | Description |
|---|---|---|---|
| moveBelow | (layer_name) | string | Adjusts the stacking array to place the current layer below the specified layer. |
| moveTo | (x,y) | integer, integer | Places a layer at a precise screen location. You specify the exact position at which you want the upper-left corner of the layer to be placed. |
| resize | (width, height) | integer, integer | Resizes the current layer. The first value is the desired width of the layer and the second is the desired height. |

## Layers and Languages

One nicer aspect of layers is that it has built-in support for languages. You can use just about any scripting language, such as JavaScript, to expand the capabilities of layers. You can dynamically turn layers on or off when the user moves his or her mouse. You can exploit the features of both the language and layers. The first part in accessing the features of layers is to be able to look at and change its properties. You can do this by using the following syntax:

```
document.layername.property
```

Here, document is the required string, but layername and property are variables. The layername represents the name that you've given to the layer, and property is the property of the layer that you want to access. (See Table 18.4.) Similarly, you can access the methods of a particular layer with the following syntax:

```
document.layername.method(params)
```

Once again, document is a required string, and layername is the name of the layer. This time, method is the name of the method you want to access, and params are the parameters you're passing. Table 18.5 completely lists all the methods and their parameters built into all layers. I'll talk more about using properties and methods later in this chapter.

# Creating Layers

So now that you know the technical syntax of creating layers, it should be a snap to create them, right? Well, not always. Sometimes, it helps to try out what you know before you put it into your Web page. As a result, I'll go through a couple of examples of using layers. I'll show you a Web page with some layers and then show you how it was done.

## Basic Layer Use

In some ways, creating layers is much easier than creating frames. With layers, you can specify the exact size and position you want the layer to be. Also, all HTML code between the <LAYER>...</LAYER> container is processed as usual. So, let's start by trying to create three layers, each next to each other. Figure 18.6 shows you the look to strive for, and it was created with the code in Listing 18.7. In this example, you use three out-flow layers and simply specify their background color. Out-flow layers are used because they give you very precise control over where the layers are placed. In this example, the layers are simply positioned next to each other, so that it is easier to see all of them.

**Listing 18.7. HTML source for the page shown in Figure 18.6.**

```
<HTML>
<HEAD><TITLE>Sample of Three Layers</TITLE></HEAD>
<BODY BGCOLOR="#FFFFFF">
<H1><CENTER>Three Layers Next to Each Other</CENTER></H1>
<LAYER NAME="red" LEFT=50 TOP=50 WIDTH=50 HEIGHT=50 VISIBILITY=SHOW
  BGCOLOR="#FF0000">
</LAYER>
<LAYER NAME="green" LEFT=100 TOP=50 WIDTH=50 HEIGHT=50 VISIBILITY=SHOW
  BGCOLOR="#00FF00">
</LAYER>
<LAYER NAME="blue" LEFT=150 TOP=50 WIDTH=50 HEIGHT=50 VISIBILITY=SHOW
  BGCOLOR="#0000FF">
</LAYER>
</BODY>
</HTML>
```

**18**

CREATING LAYOUTS
WITH FRAMES AND
LAYERS

**FIGURE 18.6.**

*Although they look like blocks, they're three separate layers.*

Layer with a red background

Layer with a green background

Layer with a blue background

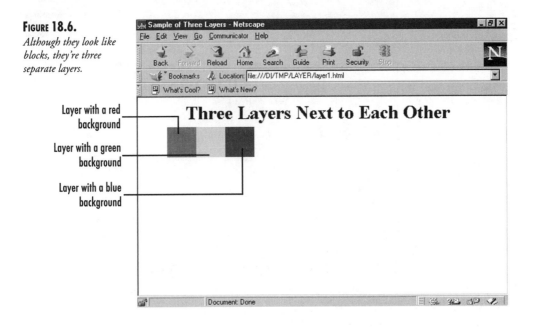

That wasn't terribly hard, was it? Let's go on to something a little bit trickier—stacking the order of the layers. This is an important exercise to understand because you can use it to script. You could easily have multiple layers on top of each other and simply choose which one you want on top. Figure 18.7 shows two layers, one slightly offset from the other, which create a drop-shadow effect. Listing 18.8 shows you how it was done. In this example, you first create a layer that will act as the shadow of the second layer. Because it's a shadow, use a gray color as the background, although black would work as well. Next, create an out-flow layer for the layer that's getting the shadow, and position it up and to the left from its shadow. This makes only a small part of the shadow layer appear from underneath the green layer.

**Listing 18.8. HTML source for the page shown in Figure 18.7.**

```
<HTML>
<HEAD><TITLE>Sample of Two Layers</TITLE></HEAD>
<BODY BGCOLOR="#FFFFFF">
<H1><CENTER>Two Layers</CENTER></H1>
<LAYER NAME="grey" LEFT=60 TOP=60 WIDTH=400 HEIGHT=100 VISIBILITY=SHOW
  BGCOLOR="#888888" zINDEX=3>
</LAYER>
<LAYER NAME="green" LEFT=50 TOP=50 WIDTH=400 HEIGHT=100 VISIBILITY=SHOW
  BGCOLOR="#00FF00" zINDEX=1>
  <CENTER>This is the green layer</CENTER>
</LAYER>
</BODY>
</HTML>
```

**FIGURE 18.7.**

*By controlling the stacking order of the layers, you can create nice special effects.*

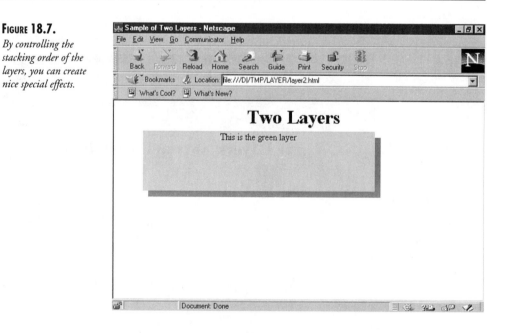

This might seem rather simple and straightforward—because it is. Layers aren't that hard to understand or to use. Their syntax is similar in nature to that of frames. As a result, if you know how to manage frames well, you should be able to manage layers pretty well, too.

## Layers and Clipping Rectangles

Another useful aspect of layers is the ability to define clipping rectangles. A clipping rectangle is a specified region in which only contents in that region are displayed. You could have a layer with lots of HTML tags but only display part of it. When the user makes a particular selection, you could simply move the clipping rectangle. Take a look at Figure 18.8 and notice that some of the text is cut off. That's the clipping rectangle in action, even though you don't see a border around it. You can see how I created that figure by looking at Listing 18.9.

**Listing 18.9. HTML source for the page shown in Figure 18.8.**

```
<HTML>
<HEAD><TITLE>Sample of Clipping</TITLE></HEAD>
<BODY BGCOLOR="#FFFFFF">
<H1><CENTER>Using the Clipping Rectangle</CENTER></H1>
<LAYER NAME="green" LEFT=50 TOP=50 WIDTH=200 HEIGHT=200 VISIBILITY=SHOW
  CLIP="0,0,150,50" BGCOLOR="#00FF00">
This is a long line of text that <B>will</B> get cut off somewhere along the
 way.
</LAYER>
</BODY>
</HTML>
```

**FIGURE 18.8.**

*The clipping rectangle cuts off some of the text.*

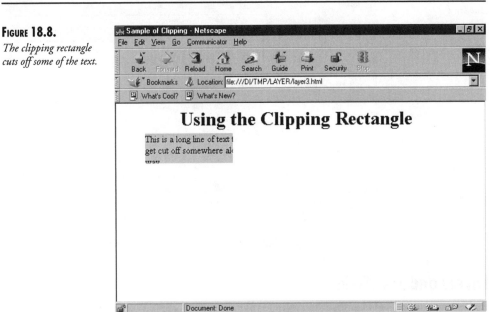

## In-Flow Layers

So far, I've shown you how to use only out-flow layers. What about the layers that simply start off where the last bit of HTML code ends? These in-flow layers are equally easy to manage and create. Look at Figure 18.9 and you'll notice that some of the text appears to be on a colored block. That green block is actually an in-flow layer. Notice that the text before and after the layer continues as usual, with no break-up. Listing 18.10 shows you how the in-flow layer was created.

**Listing 18.10. HTML source for the page shown in Figure 18.9.**

```
<HTML>
<HEAD><TITLE>Sample of In-Flow Layers</TITLE></HEAD>
<BODY BGCOLOR="#FFFFFF">
<H1><CENTER>In-Flow Layers</CENTER></H1>
This is a line of text that will be followed by
<ILAYER VISIBILITY=SHOW WIDTH=50 HEIGHT=50 BGCOLOR="#00FF00">
<B><U>a layer</U></B>
</ILAYER>
, and then some more text.
</BODY>
</HTML>
```

**FIGURE 18.9.**

*Some of this text is actually part of an in-flow layer.*

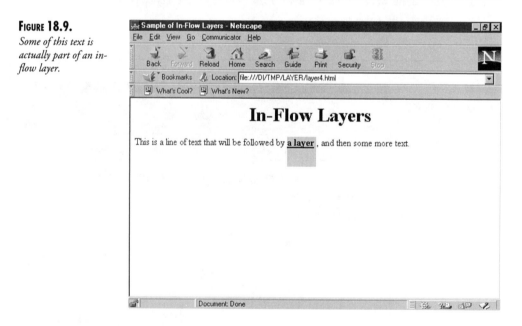

## Layers and JavaScript

As I've mentioned, you can use a scripting language with layers. With this combination, you can create an extremely impressive looking Web page. It makes it possible to have floating help that describes what each link does. Also, you can provide a great deal more interaction with the user than regular HTML allows.

Figure 18.10 gives an example of a Web page with links on the left side. When the user moves his or her mouse over each link, the help layer on the right changes. The right layer gives specific information for the purpose of the link on the left. Listing 18.11 shows you the entire Web page that I used to accomplish this feat. This trick is accomplished by using a separate layer for each link. When the cursor is over a particular link, all layers are hidden except for the appropriate one. Also, when the mouse is moved off the link, the generic description layer is displayed.

### Listing 18.11. HTML source for the page shown in Figure 18.10.

```
<HTML>
<HEAD><TITLE>Layers and JavaScript</TITLE></HEAD>
<BODY BGCOLOR="#FFFFFF">
<LAYER name="helplayer0" LEFT=300 TOP=50 WIDTH=200 VISIBILITY=SHOW
  BGCOLOR="#00FF00">
This layer gives you a description of where the link you're over, will take
  you.
</LAYER>
<LAYER name="helplayer1" LEFT=300 TOP=50 WIDTH=200 VISIBILITY=HIDE
  BGCOLOR="#FFFF00">
The agenda from the last meeting are available.
</LAYER>
<LAYER name="helplayer2" LEFT=300 TOP=50 WIDTH=200 VISIBILITY=HIDE
You can read the last meeting minutes.
</LAYER>
<LAYER name="helplayer3" LEFT=300 TOP=50 WIDTH=200 VISIBILITY=HIDE
  BGCOLOR="#00FFFF">
  BGCOLOR="#FF00FF">
Take a look at enclosure #1 from the last meeting.
</LAYER>
<LAYER name="helplayer4" LEFT=300 TOP=50 WIDTH=200 VISIBILITY=HIDE
  BGCOLOR="#F0F0F0">
Take a look at enclosure #2 from the last meeting.
</LAYER>
<LAYER NAME="linklayer" LEFT=50 TOP=50 WIDTH=200 VISIBILITY=SHOW
  BGCOLOR="#00FF00">
  <A HREF="agenda.html" onMouseOver="changeLayer(1)"
  onMouseOut="changeLayer(0)">Agenda</A><BR>
  <A HREF="minutes.html" onMouseOver="changeLayer(2)"
  onMouseOut="changeLayer(0)">Meeting Minutes</A><BR>
  <A HREF="encl01.html" onMouseOver="changeLayer(3)"
  onMouseOut="changeLayer(0)">Enclosure #1</A><BR>
  <A HREF="encl02.html" onMouseOver="changeLayer(4)"
  onMouseOut="changeLayer(0)">Enclosure #2</A><BR>
</LAYER>
<SCRIPT>
function hideLayers ()
{
```

*continues*

**Listing 18.11. continued**

```
    document.layers["helplayer0"].visibility = "hide";
    document.layers["helplayer1"].visibility = "hide";
    document.layers["helplayer2"].visibility = "hide";
    document.layers["helplayer3"].visibility = "hide";
    document.layers["helplayer4"].visibility = "hide";
}
function changeLayer (n)
{
    hideLayers();
    document.layers["helplayer" + n].visibility = "inherit";
}
</SCRIPT>
</BODY>
</HTML>
```

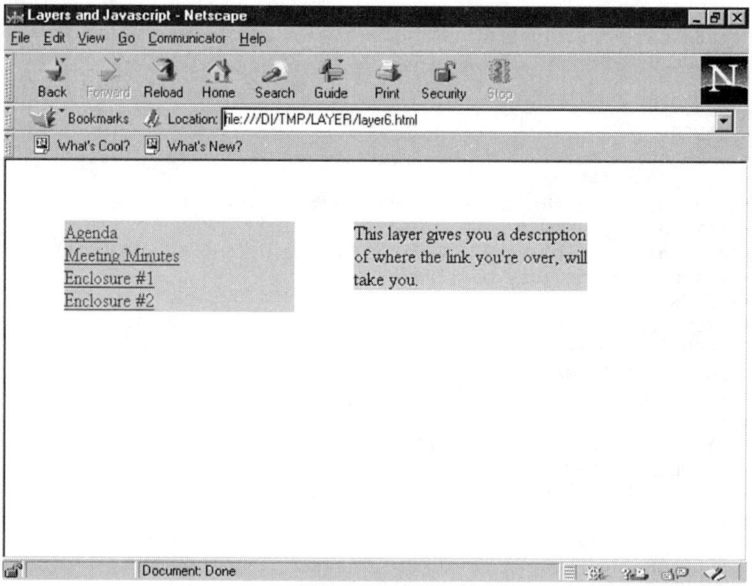

**FIGURE 18.10.**

*The text on the left is contained within its own layer.*

The key parts of this listing are the onMouseOver and onMouseOut attributes in the anchor elements. Netscape proposed these extensions to provide a better mechanism for event handling. You'll also notice that all I'm really doing is hiding all the layers and then revealing the correct layer. Therefore, when the user positions the mouse over a particular link in the left layer, the corresponding right layer is exposed. Furthermore, a "default" generic layer explains how to get more help on each link. So, whenever the user moves off of any link in the left layer, the generic layer is displayed. With this approach, you don't need to keep track of which layer is currently visible.

Obviously, this is just the tip of the iceberg for the functionality of layers and JavaScript. You really modified only one attribute—the `visibility` attribute—and used JavaScript code to modify the values. It's possible to expand this Web page to do much more. You could simulate nested menus with floating help simply by adding the `moveTo()` or `offset()` methods. Or, you could have a layer on the screen and, depending on the user input, resize it to show more information. You could even create a simple game just by messing around with layers, their visibility, and their positions.

## Summary

In this chapter, I covered some of the cooler HTML extensions that Netscape proposed. I talked about frames and layers and the pluses and minuses of each. Also, I gave you a comprehensive list of the attributes and syntax for creating such elements. I provided you with some examples on how to create sample Web pages with these elements. You can take these examples and expand on them, based on what you learned here.

## What's Next?

The next chapter focuses on a new development created for HTML: cascading style sheets. Style sheets are a way of providing a uniform look and feel to all your Web pages. For corporate Web sites, this takes a lot of the work needed to make a site look consistent. But cascading style sheets also give you some extra functionality that you might not have thought about.

# Introducing Cascading Style Sheets

*by Molly E. Holzschlag*

## IN THIS CHAPTER

CHAPTER 19

Style sheets have been available for several years, but only recently has their power been recognized with a new eagerness to push the design of Web pages to new limits. Style sheets were at first overlooked in lieu of proprietary extensions offered by Netscape, because Netscape's solutions were available to more people for viewing and style sheets weren't. With style sheets, Web designers are gaining the ability to control how both text and design elements are laid out on pages through HTML, with a level of sophistication beginning to approach many word processors.

Style sheets are a means of controlling the way HTML tags are formatted. Because many Web designers have come from a graphic design or desktop publishing background, style control is part of the natural approach to design. But style tools were unsupported by browsers for HTML. Even before the invention of style sheets, HTML specifically avoided advanced style options, offering instead only very standard or rudimentary means of creating style elements such as color, headers, and margins. Special effects such as text shadowing required graphic images, which in turn slowed down pages with extra data passed from server to client.

*Cascading* refers to the fact that not only can multiple styles be used in an individual HTML page, but the browser will follow an order (a cascade) to interpret the information. This means that, out of the three types of currently available style sheets, a designer can choose to use all three simultaneously. The browser then looks for information in an orderly and predetermined fashion, delivering the pervading style sheet.

# Style Sheets and Style Control

Before style sheets, style control with HTML was clumsy at best, and nonexistent at worst. Style sheets give a Web designer better ways of working with critical issues such as fonts, and the designer also has a means to control other traditional graphic design issues such as typeface, style and size, font weight, and leading (pronounced "ledding").

Internet Explorer set the pace by introducing style sheets in the Internet Explorer 3.0 release, and now Netscape has incorporated style sheets into its Communicator 4.0 release.

**TIP**

Ironically, when a page using style sheets without other HTML formatting is viewed by Netscape 3.0 or below or Internet Explorer 2.0 or below, the page reverts to the old reliable, and nasty gray background with demoted fonts and other styles. (See Figures 19.1 and 19.2.)

**FIGURE 19.1.**

*A page using cascading style sheets, as it appears in Internet Explorer 3.0.*

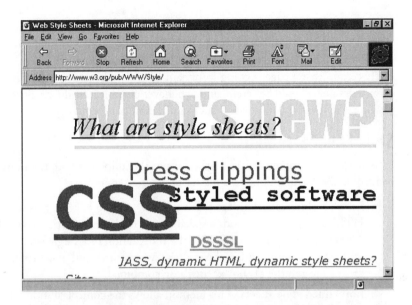

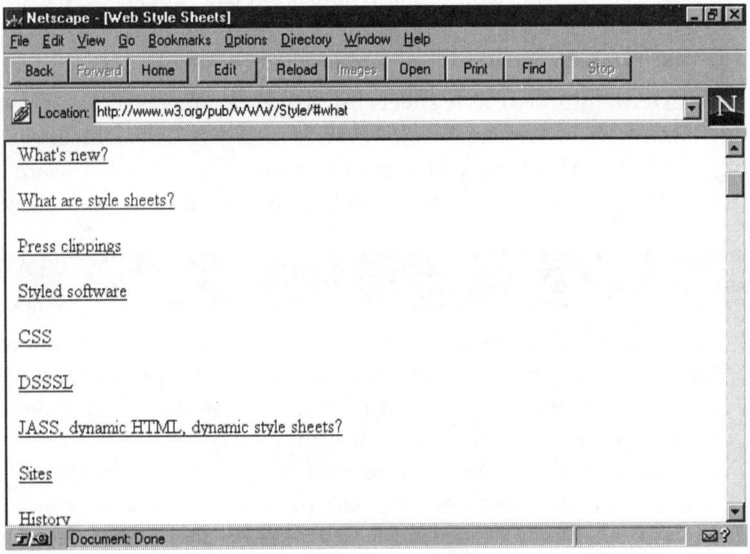

**FIGURE 19.2.**

*The same page reverts to bare-bones defaults in any Netscape browser below version 4.0.*

This doesn't mean that certain challenges aren't inherent in cascading style sheets. These challenges include issues such as the difference between various fonts loaded on different machines. Font style, including face and weight, can be called by a style sheet, but if the font and font weight isn't on the visitor's machine, the browser cannot interpret the style you've set up.

Conveniently, there are workarounds for this type of problem. Wise designers stack information into the style argument strings, and the browser will seek out the information it can interpret. This is good, but some control is lost as a result because the designer can never be absolutely certain that a page is going to remain consistent regardless of where it's viewed. As always, a designer should be careful and, whenever possible, test the results of his or her work by viewing it in a variety of browsers and on different platforms.

## Style Sheet Essentials

Style sheets can be used in three primary ways: the inline method, the individual page or embedded method, and linking to a master or external style sheet.

- **Inline style sheets.** This approach exploits existing HTML tags within a standard HTML document and adds a specific style to the information controlled by that tag. An example would be controlling the indentation of a single paragraph using the `style="x"` attribute within the `<p>` tag. Another method of achieving this is with the `<span>` tag and the `style="x"` attribute combined.

- **Embedded style sheets.** This method allows the control of individual pages. It uses the `<style>` tag, along with its companion tag, `</style>`. This information is placed between the `<html>` tag and the `<body>` tag, with the style attributes inserted within the full `<style>` container.

- **External (linked) style sheets.** All that is required is to create a style sheet file with the master styles you want to express—using the same syntax you would with embedded style. This file uses the `.css` extension. Then, simply be sure that all of the HTML documents that require those controls are linked to the style sheet.

### NOTE

With embedded and linked style sheets, the attribute syntax is somewhat different from standard HTML syntax. Attributes are placed within curly brackets; where HTML uses an equals sign (=), a colon (:) is used instead; and individual, stacked arguments are separated by a semicolon rather than a comma. Also, several attributes are hyphenated, such as `font-style` or `margin-left`. A style sheet string would then look like this: `{font-style: arial, helvetica; margin-left}`. Still, as with HTML, style sheet syntax is very structured. As you work with the examples in this chapter, you should become quite comfortable with the way style sheets work.

The following examples introduce you to the basics of each type. Although you'll be using some style sheet syntax to create the examples, detailed syntax will be covered later in the chapter.

## Using Inline Style

Creating inline style sheets is a simple matter of adding a style attribute to individual tags within the document.

Look at the following lines of HTML, paying attention to how the style attribute and the <span> tags are used:

```
<p style="font: 18pt garamond">
This paragraph was created using inline cascading style sheets
with the style attribute used within the paragraph tag.
</p>

<span style="font: 32pt arial">
This section's style was created with the span tag and the style
attribute combined.
</span>
```

When viewed on a browser that supports cascading style sheets, the lines appear as those in Figure 19.3.

**FIGURE 19.3.**

*The results of inline style sheet commands.*

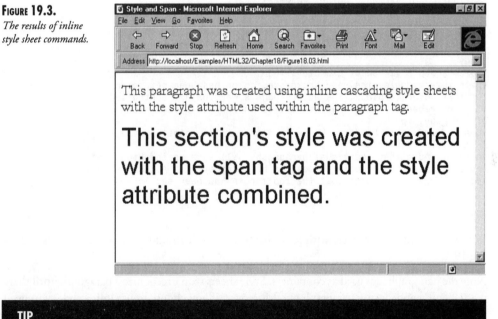

**TIP**

The <div> (division) tag can be used like the <span> tag for inline control. The <div> tag is especially helpful for longer blocks of text, whereas <span> is most effective for adding style to smaller stretches of information, such as sentences, several words, or even individual letters within a word.

In a sense, the inline method of style sheet control defeats the ultimate purpose of cascading style sheets. The main point of the technology is to seek style control of entire pages or even entire sets of pages. The inline method treats the capabilities more like a <FONT> tag, and should be used only where touches of style are required.

## Using the Individual Page Style

This section focuses on what is known as *embedding* a style sheet. Embedding sets the standards for an entire page. Look at the following basic document with embedded style, noting the addition of the <style> tags between the </head> and <body>.

```
<html>

<head>
<title>Embedded Style Sheet Example I </title>
</head>

<style>
BODY {background: #FFFFFF; color: #000000;
margin-top:.25in; margin-left:.75in; margin-right:.75in}
H3 {font: 14pt verdana; color: #0000FF}
P {font: 12pt times; text-indent: 0.5in}
A {color: #FF0000}
</style>

<body>
<h3>Embedded Style Sheet Example I</h3>
<p>In this example, the body background color has been set to white,
the text color to black. The entire page's margins are controlled
with the embedded style sheet to 3/4 of an inch on either side
of the page.</p>
<p>All third-level headers (H3) will appear in 14 point Verdana,
in the color blue.</p>
<p>You'll note that individual paragraphs will each be indented _ of an inch,
and will appear in 12 point Times. <a href="other.htm">A link</a> will
appear in red. Also note that the top margin has been set to 1/4 of an inch.</p>
</body>

</html>
```

When displayed on a browser with style sheets, the result should look like the results in Figure 19.4.

Note the paragraph tags used as containers. Style sheets won't recognize a paragraph until there is an opening and closing paragraph tag. Moreover, if you choose to use inline style, you need to use the container code for paragraphs as well.

Embedded style sheets will probably be the type of style sheet you find yourself using most often. Because of their page-by-page control, embedded style sheets enable a designer to modify the look and feel of pages within a site. However, if strong uniformity is required, linking to a master style sheet is in order.

**FIGURE 19.4.**

*The results of individual, or embedded, style sheet commands.*

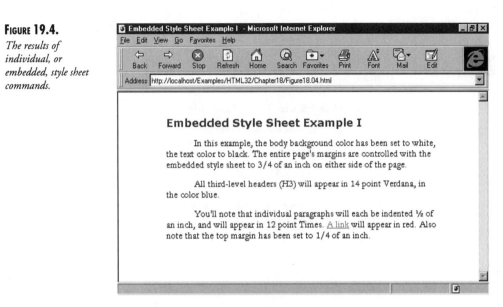

## Creating the Cascading Style Sheet Master File

Creating linked style sheets is the focus of this section. This type of style sheet is a master document, controlling all documents that are linked to it. First, create a file that contains a set of `<style>` tags as well as any other style sheet definition:

```
<style>

BODY {background: #FFFFFF; color: #000000; margin-top:.25in;
margin-left:.75in; margin-right:.75in}
H3 {font: 14pt verdana; color: #0000FF}
P {font: 12pt times; text-indent: 0.5in}
A {color: #FF0000}

</style>
```

This file is saved with a .css extension. For this example, we'll call it `style.css`. This file can now be used to control the style attributes it defines, in as many individual HTML pages as you want to link to it.

After you've created the master file, you need to add a line to the document it affects so the styles can be used when the page is loaded. After you've opened the HTML file, place the following line somewhere between the `<head>` tags:

```
<link rel=stylesheet href="style.css" type="text/css">
```

All of the data within the actual `html` file will now interpret the styles you've set forth in the .css file. An example of an HTML page using externally linked style sheet controls is shown in Figure 19.5.

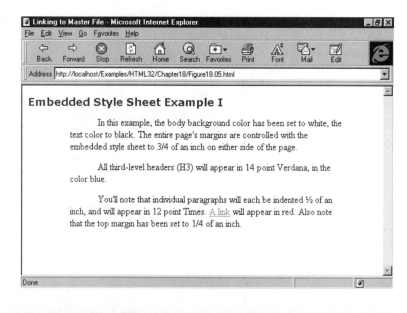

> **Embedded Style Sheet Example I**
>
> In this example, the body background color has been set to white, the text color to black. The entire page's margins are controlled with the embedded style sheet to 3/4 of an inch on either side of the page.
>
> All third-level headers (H3) will appear in 14 point Verdana, in the color blue.
>
> You'll note that individual paragraphs will each be indented ½ of an inch, and will appear in 12 point Times. A link will appear in red. Also note that the top margin has been set to 1/4 of an inch.

---

**TIP**

If your server requires you to register the MIME (Internet Media) type for style sheets, note that the suffix is .css, the MIME type is text/css, and it is considered an 8-bit (ASCII) file type.

---

## Combining Style Sheet Techniques

Designers who have complex requirements will benefit from mixing style sheet techniques. Mixing takes full advantage of the cascade element of style sheets. When multiple techniques are combined, the browser looks for the information in the following cascading order:

- Linked style sheets will be employed globally.
- If an embedded style sheet exists on a page with a linked style sheet, the embedded style sheet will override a linked style sheet.
- Inline styles will override the preceding two points.

This way, you can set a single style sheet for an entire site, change a few pages here and there for individual style with embedded style, and use inline style to override both.

With so many sites, it's difficult to keep up with which style overrides which, and it can become confusing! Designers and developers using style sheets recommend that you select a favorite technique and stick with it; apply other style sheet techniques only if they are required for distinct assignments.

# Text-Specific Style Attributes

Some graphic designers dedicate entire careers to the study of typography. It is undeniably an art, comprised of being familiar with countless font faces and related attributes such as weight, size variations, styles, families, and how to artistically use all of these aspects in attractive combinations.

The face of the Web can't change for the better if designers don't understand some text-based fundamentals before putting style sheets to use. The remainder of this chapter concentrates on the text and other formatting attributes that are available for use in all methods of style sheets. We'll begin by working with fonts:

- `font-family`. This attribute controls the face of the font by arguing for these items:

  - The name of the typeface you want to use. Here is a sample-style specification for Times:

    `{font-family: Times}`

  - The addition of a series of alternative fonts in those cases mentioned early in the chapter. Because an individual computer might not have the installed font of your preference, you might want to add a similar alternative:

    `{font-family: times, garamond}`

  - The name of a typeface family name:

    `{font-family: serif}`

The following typefaces, or type *families*, can be called for with style sheets:

- Serif. Serif fonts are a good choice for long sections of text. Popular serifs include Times New Roman and Garamond. Serifs are actually the little accents at the ends of the lines, which make up the letterform, such as the little horizontal line at the top and bottom of an uppercase *I*.

- Sans Serif. This font family includes popular choices such as Arial, Helvetica, and Avante Garde. *Sans* means *without*, so sans serif faces don't have the little adornments.

- Cursive. These are script fonts—fonts that appear as though they have been hand-written.

- Fantasy. Fantasy fonts are decorative in nature and very useful for stylish headings and titles. They are typically not practical for body text.

- Monospace. You're most likely to be familiar with monospace fonts from the days of the typewriter. Monospace means that every letter takes an equal amount of space. An *a* takes as much space as an *m*. Most fonts are proportional; each letter takes up a space that is proportional to the individual letter's size and style, rather than forcing it to fit in an exact amount of space.

**NOTE**

The standard design guideline for selecting serif versus sans serif fonts is to use serifs for body text, and use sans serifs for headers or small blocks of text.

However, although studies suggest that serif fonts are easier to read, sans serif fonts are becoming increasingly popular as common text fonts within Web browsers. It's an interesting phenomenon, but no one quite understands why it's occurring! Designers have to use good judgment, basing the use of serif or sans serif fonts on whether the pages are easy to read as well as attractive.

**TIP**

Using a typeface family as a default is an excellent idea, because it covers the designer's font choices as completely as possible. Even if a specific font face is unavailable on a given computer, it's likely that a similar one in that font's family is available. A savvy designer will place his or her first choice first, second choice second, and so forth, with the family name at the end. If I'm arguing for two serif fonts, my final string would be {font-family: times, garamond, serif}.

- `font size`. Sizing in style sheets gives the designer the choice to size his or her fonts using five size options:
  - Points. To set a font in point size, use the abbreviation `pt` immediately next to the numeric size:

    `{font-size: 12pt}.`
  - Inches. If you'd rather set your fonts in inches, simply place `in` and the numeral size, in inches, of the font size you require:

    `{font-size: 1in}.`
  - Centimeters. Some designers might prefer centimeters, represented by `cm` and used in the same fashion as points and inches:

    `{font-size: 5cm}.`
  - Pixels. Pixels are argued with the `px` abbreviation:

    `{font-size: 24px}.`
  - Percentage. You might want to set a percentage of the default point size:

    `{font-size: 50%}`

Designers will most likely find themselves more comfortable with the point values for setting font sizes. However, if you prefer another method, that's fine. If you choose a method, stick to it. Consistency is a smart approach to the creation of your own individual design and coding style.

■ `font-style`. This attribute typically dictates the style of text, such as placing it in italics. The appropriate syntax is as follows:

`{font-style: italic}`

Another font style is bold, but, interestingly, no current style sheet attribute can achieve this. The only other legal attribute for style is `normal`, which simply places the typeface in normal default status. It's unclear when support for more font styles will become available, although it seems only natural that they will at some point be added to the specifications.

■ `font-weight`. The thickness of a typeface is referred to as its *weight.* As with font faces, font weights rely on the existence of the corresponding font and weight on an individual's machine. A range of attributes is available in style sheets, including the following:

    `extra-light`

    `demi-light`

    `light`

    `medium`

    `extra-bold`

    `demi-bold`

    `bold`

Before assigning font weights, make sure that the font face to which you are applying the weight has that weight available. Always check your work on a variety of platforms and machines to see whether you can achieve strong design despite the fact that some machines might not support the font or the font weight in question.

■ `text-decoration`. This attribute decorates text with options such as the following:

    `none`

    `underline`

    `italic`

    `line-through`

**19**

---

**NOTE**

With cascading style sheets, designers can use the `{text-decoration: none}` attribute and argument to globally shut off underlined links. In embedded and linked style sheet formats, the syntax would follow the A value: A `{text-decoration: none}`. For inline style, simply place the value within the link you want to control: `<a style="text-decoration: none" href="my.html">this link has no underline</a>`.

■ line-height. To set the leading of a paragraph, use the line-height attribute in points, inches, centimeters, pixels, or percentages in the same fashion you would when describing font-size attributes:

```
P {line-height: 14pt}
```

This attribute is the same as *leading*, which refers to the amount of line spacing between lines of text. This space should be consistent, or the result is uneven, unattractive spacing. The line-height attribute allows designers to set the distance between the baseline, or bottom, of a line of text.

After learning some of the basics, it's time to see how style sheets are actually used.

## Using Text Attributes in Embedded Style Sheets

Now you can employ attributes discussed in the previous section in an embedded style sheet. Begin with a fresh page in your HTML editor, and a set of basic structure tags with <style> tags.

```
<html>

<head>
<title>Text Style Example: Embedded Style Sheets</title>
</head>

<style>
</style>

<body bgcolor="#ff9933">
</body>

</html>
```

Then, add the style syntax between the <style> tags. You'll see the font family, size, weight, and style specified for headers; family, size, and style in paragraphs; and underlining removed from links with the text-decoration attribute. Note the stacking of font faces and families to ensure as close a match as possible to the intended style:

```
H1 {font-family: lucida handwriting, arial, helvetica, cursive, san-serif ;
➥font-size: 16pt; font-style: normal}
H2 {font-family: lucida handwriting, arial, helvetica, cursive, san-serif;
➥font-size: 14pt; font-style: normal}
P {font-family: garamond; font-size: 12pt; font-style: normal;
➥line-height: 11pt}
A {text-decoration: none; font-weight: bold}
```

With the style in place, you can add the body of the document. I've included some dummy content just for illustration purposes.

```
<h1>Duis Autem Vel</h1>

<p>
Duis autem vel eum iriure dolor in hendrerit in vulputate velit esse molestie
consequat, vel illum dolore eu feugiat nulla facilisis at vero eros et accumsan
et iusto odio dignissim qui blandit praesent luptatum zzril delenit augue duis
```

```
dolore te feugait nulla facilisi. <a href="other.htm"> Nam liber </a> tempor
cum soluta nobis eleifend option congue nihil imperdiet doming id quod mazim.
</p>

<h2>Vendrerit In Vulputate</h2>

<p>
Eros Et Accumsan dignissim qui blandit praesent luptatum zzril delenit augue
duis dolore te feugait nulla facilisi. Nam liber tempor cum soluta nobis
eleifend option congue nihil imperdiet doming id quod mazim placerat
<a href="other1.htm"> facer possim assum. </a>  Iusto odio dignissim qui blandit
praesent luptatum zzril delenit augue duis dolore te feugait nulla facilisi.
</p>
```

When the file is viewed on a browser, you can see how the headers, paragraphs, and links have obeyed the style sheet's commands, as demonstrated in Figure 19.6.

**FIGURE 19.6.**

*This is an example of using an embedded style sheet. A variety of text controls are applied to the text on this page.*

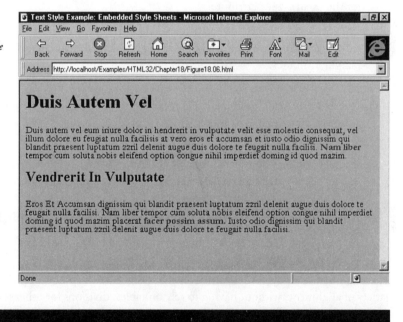

**NOTE**

The gibberish used in place of text is referred to as *greeking*. It's not really Greek, but a latinesque style of word placement designers use when creating mock-ups and dummy text.

Remember that a linked style sheet is simply the information in an embedded style sheet placed in its own file and given the extension `.css`. Then, all pages that you want to draw from the information in that file are simply linked to that file.

Now you have a page that has successfully employed simple embedded style sheets. The next section covers margin, indent, and text-alignment attributes to help add texture and white space to the page.

## Margins, Indents, and Text-Alignment Attributes

All critical elements of controlling page layout, margins, indents, and text alignment can help bring a sophisticated look to your pages. Here are some examples:

- `margin-left`. To set a left margin, use a distance in points, inches, centimeters, or pixels. The following sets a left margin to ¾ of an inch:

  `{margin-left: .75in}`

- `margin-right`. For a right margin, select from the same measurement options provided for the `margin-left` attribute:

  `{margin-right: 50px}`

- `margin-top`. Top margins can be set using the same measurement values used for other margin attributes:

  `{margin-top: 20pt)`

- `text-indent`. Again, points, inches, centimeters, or pixel values can be assigned to this attribute, which serves to indent any type of text:

  `{text-indent: 0.5in)`

  Internet Explorer allows for negative margin and text indent values. This exciting feature enables the designer to create interesting and unusual effects, including overlapping text for contemporary, stylish design.

- `text-align`. This feature allows for justification of text. Values include left, center, and right:

  `{text-align: right}`

Text alignment is a powerful layout tool, and designers will enjoy being able to place text in a variety of alignments without having to rely on tables, divisions, or other less graceful HTML workarounds (they still exist). Designers should remember that justification of text requires a fine eye. Left justification is the only reasonable choice for long selections of text, because it is much more readable. Right justification comes in handy for short bursts of text, such as pull-quotes. Centered text should be used sparingly. Even though it seems natural to want to center text, it is actually more difficult to read.

To add margin control to the previous example, add the following line to the beginning of the style section:

`BODY {margin-left: 0.75in; margin-right: 0.75in; margin-top: 0.10in}`

The new file should match what you see in Figure 19.7.

**FIGURE 19.7.**

*Margins create attractive white space.*

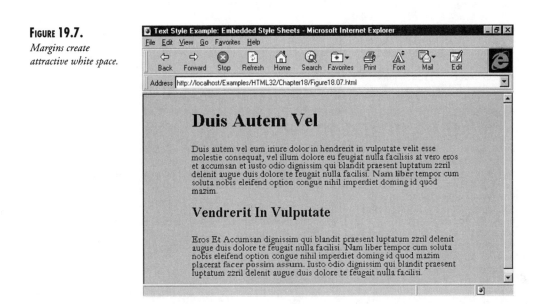

Although margin values are added to the entire page with the BODY attribute, you can add margins to any HTML tag you choose. For example, if you want to control the headers with different margins, place the margin values in the string next to the header of your choice. Similarly, you can adjust margins on individual paragraphs by adding the margin values you seek to the paragraph string.

For a practical example, replace the style definitions in the previous example with the following attributes, which include margin and justification syntax for the borders of the page:

```
BODY {margin-left: 0.75in; margin-right: 0.75in; margin-top: 0.10in}
H1 {font-family: lucida handwriting, arial, helvetica ; font-size: 16pt;
➡font-style: normal; text-align: left}
H2 {font-family: lucida handwriting, arial, helvetica; font-size: 14pt;
➡font-style: normal; text-align: right}
P {font-family: garamond; font-size: 12pt; font-style: normal;
➡line-height: 11pt}
A {text-decoration: none; font-weight: bold}
```

Because individual paragraphs should be justified in this example, that information is placed inline, and the browser will know what to do. The full HTML code looks like this:

```
<html>

<head>
<title>Text Style Example: Embedded Style Sheets</title>
</head>

<style>
BODY {margin-left: 0.75in; margin-right: 0.75in; margin-top: 0.10in}
H1 {font-family: lucida handwriting, arial, helvetica ; font-size: 16pt;
➡font-style: normal; text-align: left}
```

```
H2 {font-family: lucida handwriting, arial, helvetica; font-size: 14pt;
➡font-style: normal; text-align: right}
P {font-family: garamond; font-size: 12pt; font-style: normal;
➡line-height: 11pt}
A {text-decoration: none; font-weight: bold}
</style>

<body bgcolor="#ff9933" link="FF0033">
<h1>Duis Autem Vel</h1>
<p style="text-align: right">
Duis autem vel eum iriure dolor in hendrerit in vulputate <a href="other.htm">
velit esse molestie </a>consequat, vel illum dolore eu feugiat nulla facilisis
at vero eros et accumsan et iusto odio dignissim qui blandit praesent luptatum
 zzril delenit augue duis dolore te feugait nulla facilisi.</p>
<h2>Vendrerit In Vulputate</h2>
<p style="text-align: left">
Eros Et Accumsan dignissim qui blandit praesent luptatum zzril delenit augue
duis dolore te feugait nulla facilisi. Nam liber tempor cum
<a href="other1.htm">soluta nobis eleifend </a> option congue nihil imperdiet
doming id quod mazim placerat facer possim assum.</p>
</body>

</html>
```

The look and feel of this page is becoming much more interesting, as shown in Figure 19.8.

**FIGURE 19.8.**

*Visual texture makes a Web page more interesting, even without graphics.*

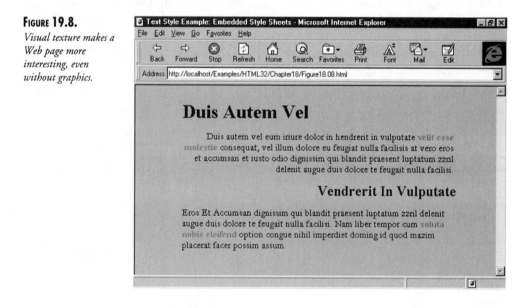

Another method to justify individual paragraphs is by defining classes. I'll introduce style sheet class variations toward the end of this chapter.

# Color and Background

 If you've checked these pages with the examples on the CD-ROM, or noticed the <body> tag syntax, you have noticed the background color defined within traditional HTML rather than in the BODY attribute available to style sheets. Internet Explorer 3.0+ has a bug in the software that results in the browser ignoring this basically legal attribute, and the bug appears to also exist in Netscape's 4.0 pre-release. As a workaround, I define a background color for the body in a traditional fashion.

All bugs and browser headaches aside, background color can be added to actual attributes including other HTML tags used in style sheet formats. For example, you can have a paragraph or a header splashed with color by simply placing the appropriate syntax in that area.

Furthermore, you can change the text color in any field you specify. This is particularly satisfying for Web designers who are constantly seeking to employ browser-based color to enliven pages rather than relying on time-consuming graphics.

The syntax required to create background color—again, with the one exception that Internet Explorer versions below 4.0 ignore the attribute if placed in the BODY string—is the style sheet background: convention and a hexadecimal triplet color argument:

```
{background: #FFFFFF}
```

Similarly, background graphics can be called upon using this attribute. Merely replace the hex argument with a URL:

```
{background: http://myserver.com/cool.gif}
```

For text color, simply use the color attribute and a hex argument:

```
{color: #FF6633}
```

Internet Explorer allows the use of color names in the case of color and background arguments. Such color names include black, silver, gray, white, maroon, red, purple, fuchsia, green, lime, olive, yellow, navy, blue, teal, and aqua. My advice is to stick to hexadecimal values. Not only do you have a better selection, it also helps keeps your coding consistent and professional-looking.

To add splashes of background color to fields in the file you've created, use the following style syntax in our ongoing sample file. The result is shown in Figure 19.9:

```
BODY {margin-left: 0.75in; margin-right: 0.75in; margin-top: 0.10in}
H1 {font-family: lucida handwriting, arial, helvetica; font-size: 16pt;
font-style: normal; text-align: left}
H2 {font-family: lucida handwriting, arial, helvetica; font-size: 14pt;
font-style: normal; text-align: right; background: #99CCCC}
P {font-family: garamond; font-size: 12pt; font-style: normal;
line-height: 11pt}
A {text-decoration: none; font-weight: bold}
```

FIGURE 19.9.

*Notice the splash behind the text. Is it distracting or enhancing? Designers must choose background splashes carefully.*

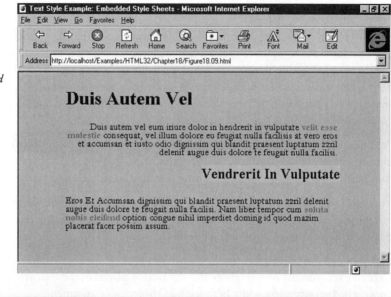

**TIP**

You'll need to view these examples on a computer with a color monitor to see the full color effect.

Contrast gained by using background splashes can be very effective, but designers can quickly get in trouble by overusing them. Be careful and consistent with your color palettes, and select splashes that provide visual accents rather than detract the eye from what is important. You'll note that I selected the header to highlight; in another case, maybe only a line or phrase of text would be important.

To liven up sections of text, follow the same style guidelines to set for background color, but use the color: attribute:

```
H2 {font-family: lucida handwriting, arial, helvetica; font-size: 14pt;
➡font-style: normal; text-align: right;
background: #99CCCC; color: #FF0033}
```

View it in your browser. You now have an interesting, textured page completely designed with style sheets!

# Additional Functionality

Two additional techniques can assist you in making style sheets more functional. The first is *grouping*, which allows for the reduction of attributes and arguments by creating logical groups. Another way to expand function is through the use of *classes*. This technique allows you to assign variations to individual HTML tags, giving you tremendous flexibility in terms of creating variations within page attributes.

## Grouping Style Sheets

To group style sheets, you can follow these guidelines:

- Group multiple tags together. If you want to assign the same attributes to all header styles, you can group them together. Here's an example without grouping:

```
H1 {font-family: arial; font-size 14pt; color: #000000}
H2 {font-family: arial; font-size 14pt; color: #000000}
H3 {font-family: arial; font-size 14pt; color: #000000}
```

Here's the same example grouped:

```
H1, H2, H3 {font-family: arial; font-size 14pt; color: #000000}
```

- Group attributes by dropping them into specific families of information. Without grouping, an example of font attributes and arguments would look like this:

```
BODY {font-family: arial, san-serif; font-size: 12pt;
➥line-height: 14pt; font-weight: bold; font-style: normal}
```

With grouping, I can simply name the attribute font: and then stack the arguments like this:

```
BODY {font: bold normal 12pt/14pt arial, san-serif}
```

When grouping attributes, be sure to remember that attribute order is significant. Font weight and style must come before other font attributes; the size of the font will come before the leading, and then you can add additional information to the string. Note that there are no commas between the attributes, except in the case of font families.

Grouping attributes can be done with margins, using the margin: argument followed by the top, right, and left margin values in that order. Be sure to specify all three values, unless you want the same value applied to all three:

```
BODY {margin: .10in .75in .75in}
```

Note again that there are no commas between the attributes.

## Assigning Classes

To get the most variation in style, assign classes to individual HTML tags. This is done very simply by adding a named extension to any HTML tag. If you have two headers and two paragraph styles that you want to attribute, you can name each one and assign style to the individual paragraphs. You then call on the name within the specific HTML tag in the body of the document:

```
H1.left {font: arial 14pt; color: #FF0033; text-align: left}
H2.right {font: arial 12pt; color: #FF6633; text-align: right}
```

In the HTML, you would place the class name:

```
<h1 class=left>This is my Left Heading</h2>
```

All of the H1 headers you name class=left will have the H1.left class attributes. Similarly, the H2.right headers named class=right will have the attributes defined for that class.

Grouping and class allow for very flexible use of style sheets. Begin with the following style definition in the sample file:

```
BODY {margin: 0.10in 0.50in 0.50in}
H1.left {font: 16pt lucida handwriting; text-align: left}
H2.right {font: 14pt lucida handwriting; text-align: right; color: #FF0033}
P.left {font: 12pt/11pt garamond; text-align: left}
P.right {font: 12pt arial; text-align: right; margin: 0in .75in .50in}
A {text-decoration: none; font-weight: bold}
```

Then, within each of the appropriate tags, add the class names to complete the process:

```
<H1 class=left>Duis Autem Vel</h1>

<p class=right>
Duis autem vel eum iriure dolor in hendrerit in vulputate <a href="other.htm">
velit esse molestie </a>consequat, vel illum dolore eu feugiat nulla
facilisis at vero eros et accumsan et iusto odio dignissim qui blandit
praesent luptatum zzril delenit augue duis dolore te feugait nulla facilisi.
</p>

<h2 class=right>Vendrerit In Vulputate</h2>

<p class="left">
Eros Et Accumsan dignissim qui blandit praesent luptatum zzril delenit augue
duis dolore te feugait nulla facilisi. Nam liber tempor cum
<a href="other1.htm">soluta nobis eleifend</a> option congue nihil imperdiet
doming id quod mazim placerat facer possim assum.
</p>
```

An incompatible browser will ignore the attributes it doesn't recognize, while a browser such as Internet Explorer 4 will display the file shown in Figure 19.10.

If you're placing margins in the BODY attribute as well as in the P attribute, be sure your paragraph margins are larger than those you've selected for the entire body of text. Otherwise, the point is moot! The browser will ignore the lesser margins and use the greatest available value.

**FIGURE 19.10.**

*The resulting page is a collection of style that defies the standard HTML.*

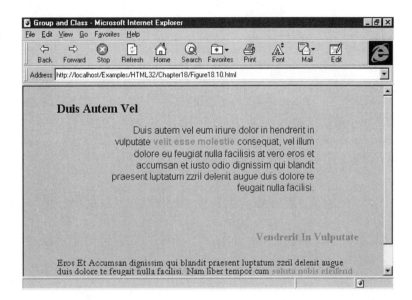

# Summary

Style sheets are both sophisticated and infantile in their behavior. The concept is extremely advanced, allowing designers to do things never dreamed possible in the young history of HTML. However, the actual application is in its infancy. As with many layout options available to designers, this is more the fault of browser technology than the reality of the tool.

If you begin to use style sheets to work with your design, you are certain to be challenged by the limitations of browsers. That problem will last for some time, but invariably in your favor is the fact that you started learning and using the technology early, giving you an edge. I encourage you to think about the power of the system rather than the limitations, because those limitations will gradually subside. Your skills can only improve with time and practice.

Moreover, there's the thrill of being able to actually design without ever opening up a graphics program. Color, font, text control—they're all yours now to use and enjoy. The next chapter gives a few more examples and moves into page design with style sheets for you to examine and work from. This includes mastering text-heavy documents with style sheet control.

**19**

INTRODUCING
CASCADING STYLE
SHEETS

# Cascading Style Sheet Usage

*by Molly Holzschlag*

**CHAPTER 20**

Because style sheets are so flexible, this chapter of the book is included so that you can spend a little time designing a variety of templates for a hands-on feel. More importantly, these designs are applicable to a range of common Web design jobs. By changing some of the style attributes, such as fonts, colors, alignment, headers, or paragraph styles, you can stock up on a very diverse collection of style sheet–based offerings.

All of these examples use embedded style sheets. In some cases, the style is extrapolated so that you can see how to make a linked style sheet to control numerous pages with the same style elements. There's a lot of variation within the style sheets themselves. Sometimes tables are used to lay out a page, and other times the page is a straightforward HTML document. This chapter also includes demonstrations on the use of grouping and class, as well as examples of how to override style sheet calls by reverting to traditional HTML tags.

> **TIP**
>
> It cannot be said enough: Know your audience. This will help determine how much you can realistically employ style sheets.

This chapter should serve not only as a practical taste of what style sheets can do, but also as inspiration to spend time on your own using style sheets in creative design applications. You will see how to use classes to create an untold variety of styles within the same page.

# Business Page

The first template is a business page. This can be used for commercial business purposes or for an intranet application. The design consists of a splash of color on the left margin that contains a summary or subtitle, with the headline and text on the right. The headline color matches the background color on the left to add an extra sense of consistency to the page.

The style container to create this page looks like this:

```
<style>
BODY {background: #CCCCCC; color: #000000; margin-top:0.00in;
➥margin-left: 0.20in; margin-right:0.20in}
H1 {font: 24pt Garamond; color: #669966; text-align: right}
P {font: 12pt Verdana; color: #FFFFFF; text-align: right;
➥text-indent: 0.5in}
P.1 {font: 11pt verdana; color: #000000; text-align: right;
➥text-indent: 0.5in}
</style>
```

> **CAUTION**
>
> A bug in both Internet Explorer 3.0 and Navigator 4.0 causes the browser to ignore body colors in the style sheet. To be safe, you must put the color in the <body> tag. It's a good idea to put the color attributes in the style sheet as well, because the problem is in fact a bug and not a style sheet idiosyncrasy. It's always a good idea to do both anyway. Many people don't upgrade browsers in a timely fashion, and reasonable backwards compatibility is always a good idea.

With the style in place, you can turn your attention to the table, table cells, and content. Place all three within the <BODY> container tags. Pay careful attention to the use of table cell color definitions, which override the style background just as if this were a standard HTML page.

```
<table border=0 width=575 cellpadding=10 cellspacing=0>
  <tr>
    <td valign=top width=150 bgcolor="#99CC99">
      <p style="line-height: 0.5in">Duis autem in hendrerit in vulputate
      molestie consequat vel feugiat nulla facilisis
    </td>
    <td valign=middle width=425>
      <h1>The Multi Group</h1>
      <p>s e n s e . a n d . s e n s i t i v i t y<br>
      <i>in</i> the market place</p>
      <p class=1>
      Eros Et Accumsan <b>dignissim qui</b> blandit praesent
      luptatum zzril delenit augue duis dolore te feugait
      nulla facilisi. Nam liber tempor cum soluta nobis
      eleifend option congue nihil imperdiet<b> doming id
      quod mazim</b> placerat facer possim assum. Iusto odio
      dignissim qui blandit praesent luptatum zzril delenit
      augue duis dolore te feugait nulla facilisi. Nam
      <i>liber tempor </i>cum soluta nobis eleifend option
      congue nihil imperdiet doming id quod mazim placerat
      facer possim assum. Accumsan et iusto odio dignissim
      qui blandit. Eros Et Accumsan dignissim qui blandit
      praesent luptatum zzril delenit augue duis dolore
      <b>te feugait nulla</b> facilisi. Nam <i>liber
      tempor</i> cum soluta nobis.</p>
    </td>
  </tr>
</table>
```

View the assembled product in a style sheet–compliant browser. Figure 20.1 shows the results.

The Multi Group example is very consistent with a splash or front page. Suppose you are designing different levels of a company's Web site. You can use this style at each level, embedding the same style in those specific pages, or linking those pages to a master style sheet.

FIGURE 20.1.

*A business-oriented
splash page.*

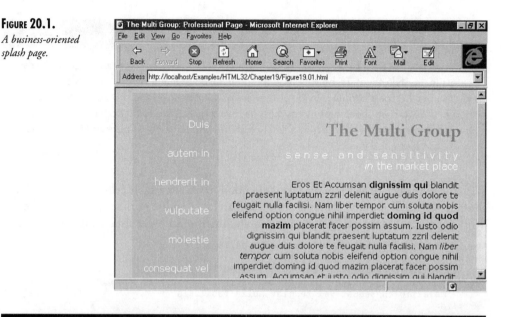

Don't forget the limitation of font styles. Not all users will have the same fonts on their computers that you have on yours. These examples are based on using fonts in one machine—mine. You'll need to look at the fonts on your system for compatibilities that will complement the style.

# Employee Newsletter

The following steps help you to implement a simple HTML newsletter layout, which relies on justification to create an interesting and dynamic look. Each story is separated by a horizontal rule, and the headings alternate between the left and right margins.

The embedded style sheet focuses on color and alignment implemented through classes:

```
<style>

BODY: {color: #000000; margin-left: 0.75in; margin-right: 0.75in;
➥margin-top: 0.00in}
H1.right {font: 18pt "lucida handwriting"; color: #999966;
➥text-align: right}
H1.left {font: 18pt "lucida handwriting"; color: #999966;
➥text-align: left}
P {font: 12pt "arial narrow"; color: #CCCC99; margin-indent: 0.5in}
P.1 {font: 11pt/11pt "arial narrow"; color: #FFFFFF}
HR {color: #CCCC99}

</style>
```

The styles are implemented in the body without the use of tables or other tricks to force the formatting.

```
<h1 class=right>P.J. Dailey News . . .</h1>
<p>Eros Et Accumsan <b>dignissim qui</b> blandit praesent
luptatum zzril delenit augue duis dolore te feugait
nulla facilisi. Nam liber tempor cum soluta nobis
eleifend option congue nihil imperdiet<b> doming id
quod mazim</b> placerat facer possim assum.</p>
<hr>
<h1 class=left>te feugait</h1>
<p class=1>Eros Et Accumsan <b>dignissim qui</b> blandit
Praesent luptatum zzril delenit augue duis dolore te feugait
nulla facilisi. Nam liber tempor cum soluta nobis
eleifend option congue nihil imperdiet?</p>
<hr>
<h1 class=right>liber tempor</h1>
<p>Eros Et Accumsan <b>dignissim qui</b> blandit praesent
luptatum zzril delenit augue duis dolore te feugait
nulla facilisi. Nam liber tempor cum soluta nobis
eleifend option congue nihil imperdiet<b> doming id
quod mazim</b> placerat facer possim assum.</p>
```

View the assembled results in your browser, which should match the example in Figure 20.2.

**FIGURE 20.2.**
*An interoffice
newsletter example.*

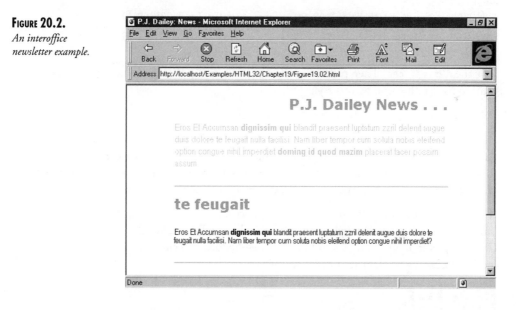

The P.J. Dailey page provides a great example of how to combine headers and body text. With very few exceptions, you don't want to separate a header from the related text with a horizontal rule. This is a mistake that many people make. Furthermore, this example shows how horizontal rules can successfully be used without appearing cliché.

The addition of style breaks the typical, and ugly, use of horizontal rules on the Web. When you define color and have plenty of white space, the problems seen with most rules disappear. At all costs, avoid using horizontal rules that stretch from margin to margin. Also, the use of headers and text together creates a rationale for not using the rules at all. If a paragraph break is what you're after, use extra spacing between the paragraph and the next line of text—whether a header or another paragraph.

## Creating a Linked Style Sheet

Because the P.J. Dailey example could be applied to many pages, I'll show you how to create a linked page. All you need to do then is link the individual pages to this page, and all pages will pick up the styles defined within the sheet.

Begin by taking the embedded style out of the originating page, and place it into a file by itself:

```
<style>
BODY: {color: #000000; margin-left: 0.75in; margin-right: 0.75in;
➥margin-top: 0.00in}
H1.right {font: 18pt "lucida handwriting"; color: #999966;
➥text-align: right}
H1.left {font: 18pt "lucida handwriting"; color: #999966;
➥text-align: left}
P {font: 12pt "arial narrow"; color: #CCCC99; margin-indent: 0.5in}
P.1 {font: 11pt/11pt "arial narrow"; color: #FFFFFF}
HR {color: #CCCC99}
</style>
```

Save the file as pj.css. Then place the following link within the <HEAD> tag on every page you want to have influenced by this style:

```
<link rel=stylesheet href="pj.css" type="text/css">
```

Because you're linking styles, it's not necessary to embed this information in any of the individual pages that will be influenced by the link. However, if you want to alter individual pages that will take on most of the attributes of the linked style sheet yet contain a few individual changes, you can embed a style sheet into that page with the minor changes.

If you want to alter only one or two smaller sections in a handful of pages, drawing from the linked page and embedded style, you can use inline style to cover that smaller section. The CSS-compliant browser will read inline before embedded and embedded before linked, resulting in a cascading implementation of your style.

# Price List

The following example uses a bordered table within the page as a grid. Pay specific attention to the classes defined for the table cells. This further demonstrates the power and flexibility of style sheets and their ability to influence any of the HTML tags. Here's the style definition:

```
<style>
BODY {background: #CCCC99; color: #000000; margin-left: 0.5in;
```

```
➥margin-right: 0.5in}
H1 {font: 20pt "book antiqua"; color: #666633; text-align: left}
H2 {font: 18pt "book antiqua"; color: #666633; text-align: left}
P {font: 12pt arial; color: #000000}
B {font: 12pt "book antiqua"; color: #666633; font-weight: bold}
HR {color: #CC9999}
TD {font: 11pt "book antiqua"}
TD.grey {background: #999999; font: 11pt arial}
TD.mauve {background: #CC9999; font: 11pt arial}
A {text-decoration: none; color: #CC9999; font-weight: bold}
</style>
```

To implement the style within the document, use the tags and classes in the following manner:

```
<h1>Beautiful Dreamer Music</h1>
<p>Eros Et Accumsan dignissim qui blandit praesent luptatum
zzril delenit augue duis dolore te feugait nulla facilisi.
Nam liber tempor cum soluta nobis eleifend option congue
nihil imperdiet doming id quod <a href="nil.htm">mazim
placerat facer</a> possim assum.</p>
<hr width=45%>
<h2>Prices:</h2>
<table border=1 width=500 cellpadding=10 cellspacing=0>
  <tr>
    <td class=mauve width=50><b>Eros</b></td>
    <td class=grey width=50><b>Qui </b></td>
    <td class=mauve width=50><b>Zzril </b></td>
  </tr>
  <tr>
    <td class=mauve width=50>
      Eros<br>
      dignissim <br>
      blandit <br>
      luptatum
    </td>
    <td class=grey width=50>
      Eros<br>
      qui <br>
      blandit <br>
      luptatum
    </td>
    <td class=mauve width=50>
      Accumsan<br>
      dignissim <br>
      praesent <br>
      zzril
    </td>
  </tr>
  <tr>
    <td colspan=3 align=right>
      <i>eros et accumsan dignissim, st.</i>    Total: $18,000.00
    </td>
  </tr>
</table>
</div>
```

Save the completed file and compare it with the example in Figure 20.3.

FIGURE 20.3.

*Price sheet page,*
*version 1.*

## Price List in a Reverse Style

Now let's have some fun by reversing the headers and body text of this example. The following steps show how dramatic variation can be achieved quite simply with the same style sheet with the following changes to the style:

```
<style>
BODY {background: #CCCC99; color: #000000; margin-left: 0.5in;
➥margin-right: 0.5in}
H1 {font: 20pt "arial"; color: #666633; text-align: left}
H2 {font: 18pt "arial"; color: #666633; text-align: left}
P {font: 12pt "book antiqua"; color: #000000}
B {font: 12pt "arial"; color: #666633; font-weight: bold}
HR {color: #CC9999}
TD {font: 11pt "arial"}
TD.grey {background: #999999; font: 11pt "book antiqua"}
TD.mauve {background: #CC9999; font: 11pt "book antiqua"}
A {text-decoration: none; color: #CC9999; font-weight: bold}
</style>
```

Next, apply the style to the body of the document:

```
<body bgcolor="#CCCC99">
<h1>Beautiful Dreamer Music</h1>
<p>Eros Et Accumsan dignissim qui blandit praesent luptatum zzril delenit augue
duis dolore te feugait nulla facilisi. Nam liber tempor cum soluta nobis
```

```
eleifend option congue nihil imperdiet doming id quod <a href="nil.htm">mazim
placerat facer</a> possim assum.</p>
<hr width=45%>
<h2>Prices:</h2>
<table border=1 width=500 cellpadding=10 cellspacing=0>
  <tr>
    <td class=mauve width=50>
      <b>Eros</b>
    </td>
    <td class=grey width=50>
      <b>Qui </b>
    </td>
    <td class=mauve width=50>
      <b>Zzril </b>
    </td>
  </tr>
  <tr>
    <td class=mauve width=50>
      Eros<br>
      dignissim <br>
      blandit <br>
      luptatum
    </td>
    <td class=grey width=50>
      Eros<br>
      qui <br>
      blandit <br>
      luptatum
    </td>
    <td class=mauve width=50>
      Accumsan<br>
      dignissim <br>
      praesent <br>
      zzril
    </td>
  </tr>
  <tr>
    <td colspan=3 align=right>
      <i>eros et accumsan dignissim, st.</i>    Total: $18,000.00
    </td>
  </tr>
</table>
</div>
```

Save the file and view it in your browser. It should appear similar to the example in Figure 20.4.

Some people use comment tags around their style sheet calls. This hides the style sheets from non-style sheet browsers. You can then design the page to be viewable in a non-compliant browser, but still allow for readability and some semblance of style.

**FIGURE 20.4.**
*Price sheet page,
version II.*

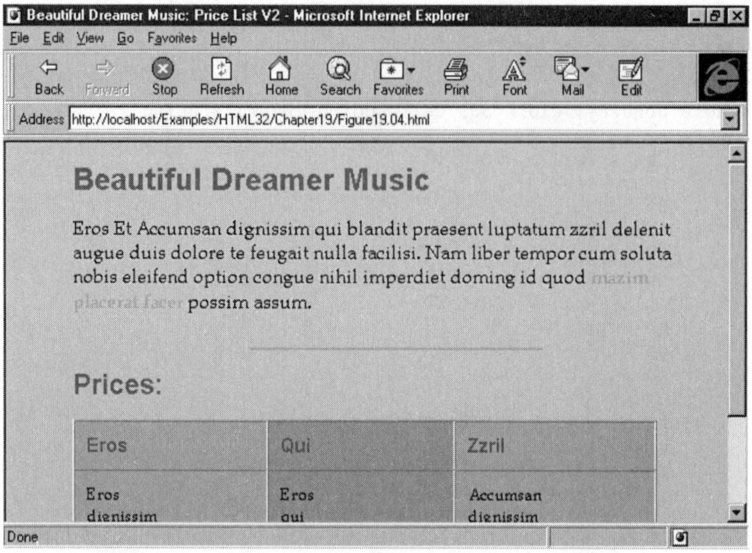

# Creating a Party Invitation Using Style Sheets

Want to get colorful? The following tags use style sheets to achieve a fun and colorful design without the use of any graphics:

```
<style>
BODY {color: #FFFFFF; margin: 0.0 0.05 0.05}
H1 {font: 25pt "LasVegasD"; color: #FF3333; text-align: right}
H2 {font: 20pt "LasVegasD"; color: #FF3333; text-align: left}
P {font: 13pt "verdana"; color: #333399}
HR {color: #FF3333}
A {color: #FFCC33; text-decoration: none}
</style>
```

The page is formatted with a table in addition to the application of styles:

```
<table border=0 width=580 cellpadding=10 cellspacing=0>
  <tr>
    <td width=400 bgcolor="#FFFF00">
      <h1>Viva Las Vegas Party!!!</h1>
      <p><b>Las Vegas-style</b> party for all employees of AJbest Books. Eros
      Et Accumsan dignissim qui blandit praesent luptatum zzril delenit augue
      Duis dolore te feugait nulla facilisi.</p>
      <p><b>Nam: </b>liber tempor cum soluta nobis</p>
      <p><b>Nam: </b>liber tempor cum soluta nobis</p>
      <p><b>Nam: </b>liber tempor cum soluta nobis</p>
    </td>
    <td width=170>
      <h2>win big . . .</h2>
      <p align=right>Eros Et Accumsan dignissim qui
```

```
            <a href="http://win.htm/">blandit praesent</a> luptatum zzril
            delenit augue duis dolore te feugait nulla facilisi. Nam liber
            tempor!</p>
            <hr>
            <p align=right><i>email: <a href="mailto:helene@ajbooks.biz">
            helene@ajbooks.biz</a></i>
        </td>
    </tr>
</table>
```

Save the file and view it in your browser. Figure 20.5 shows the layout of this bright, online invitation.

**Figure 20.5.**

*A business party invitation.*

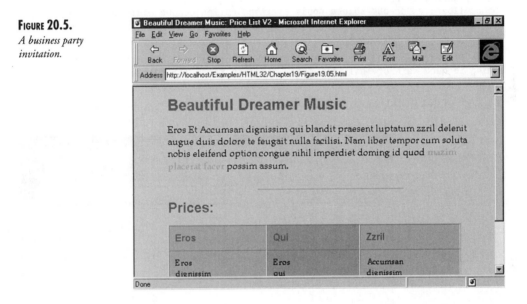

If you're beginning to be intrigued by the possibilities, you might want to check out some additional references and examples. For an official view, look at what the World Wide Web Consortium has to say at `www.w3.org/ub/WWW/Style/`, which includes a large list of links to other sites. Another good resource is located at `www.htmlhelp.com/reference/css/references.html`.

# Kid's News

Here is another example of a standard HTML design using rules that creates an attractive, vivacious, and very fun page through the use of a few basic styles:

```
<style>
BODY {color: #FFFFFF; margin: 0.05in 0.75in}
H1 {font: 20pt "Kids"; color: #663366; text-align: right}
H2 {font: 18pt "Kids"; color: #663366; text-align: left}
```

```
P {font: 13pt "arial narrow"; color: #009933}
HR {color: #FF9900}
A {color: #FF9900; text-decoration: none}
</style>
```

Next, create the layout and content with HTML in the body:

```
<h1>KidTIME!</h1>
<blockquote>
<p><b>Hey Kids!</b> Nam liber tempor cum soluta nobis eleifend option congue
nihil imperdiet doming id quod <a href="nil.htm">mazim placerat facer</a>
possim assum.</p>
<hr>
<h2>You Know It!</h2>
<p>Nam liber tempor cum soluta nobis eleifend option congue nihil imperdiet
doming id quod <a href="nil.htm">mazim placerat facer</a> possim assum.</p>
<hr>
<h2>Cool KATsss</h2>
<p>Nam liber tempor cum soluta nobis eleifend option congue nihil imperdiet
doming id quod <a href="nil.htm">mazim placerat facer</a> possim assum.</p>
</blockquote>
```

View the completed file in your browser, and compare it to the example in Figure 20.6.

**FIGURE 20.6.**

*Light and bright kid's page.*

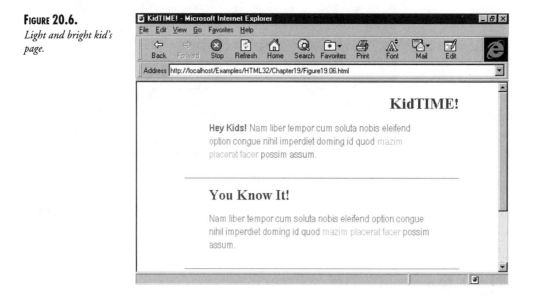

With the completed style sheet in hand, it's time to create the preceding fun kid's magazine in the linked style.

Take the embedded style out of the originating page, and place it into a clean file:

```
<style>
BODY {color: #FFFFFF; margin: 0.05in 0.75in}
H1 {font: 20pt "Kids"; color: #663366; text-align: right}
H2 {font: 18pt "Kids"; color: #663366; text-align: left}
```

```
P {font: 13pt "arial narrow"; color: #009933}
HR {color: #FF9900}
A {color: #FF9900; text-decoration: none}
</style>
```

Name this file `kids.css`. Place the following link in the `<HEAD>` of every page you want to have influenced by this style:

```
<link rel=stylesheet href="pj.css" type="text/css">
```

Then, save and test your files to be sure you've typed everything correctly.

# Online Book Cover

This task shows you a very sophisticated look and feel gained through style. Pay special attention to another way of using class. In this case, I've defined attributes, not tags, and given them a name in the `.namegoeshere` style. This allows me to call that class within any HTML section I choose; therefore, the style that string contains will be used. Also note the use of graphics. Even with three graphics on the page, the total HTML and graphic combination results in only 11KB.

Begin with the style, paying attention to the defined classes `.HEAD` and `.SUB`:

```
<style>
BODY {font: 16pt "garamond"; font-style: "italic";color: #66CCCC;
➥ text-align: center; background: #000000}
.HEAD {font: 15pt "arial narrow"; font-weight: bold; text-align: center;
➥ font-style: none}
.SUB  {line-height: 20pt}
</style>
```

Next, add the table and contents, noting the use of class each step of the way:

```
<table border=0 width=500 cellpadding=5 cellspacing=0>
  <tr>
    <td width=200 class=head>
      d a r e   t o   d r e a m
    </td>
    <td width=200>
      <img src="images/wow1.gif" width=100 height=147>
    </td>
  </tr>
  <tr>
    <td width=200>
      <img src="images/wow2.gif" width=75 height=116>
    </td>
    <td class=sub width=200>
      . . . a journey into<br> lives <br> and lifetimes
    </td>
  </tr>
  <tr>
    <td width=200>
      a series of poems<br>
      ~ by ~ <br>
```

```
      women of war
    </td>
    <td width=200>
      <img src="images/wow3.gif" width=175 height=110>
    </td>
  </tr>
</table>
```

Save the file and view it in your browser. Compare the results with the example in Figure 20.7.

**FIGURE 20.7.**

*An elegant, artistic book cover.*

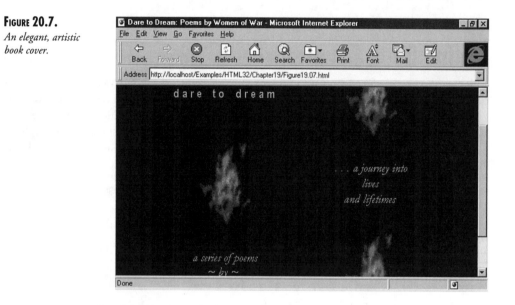

## Summary

By now, you should have a taste of what style sheets can do, how they work, and the many flexible ways of using them.

As always, you have to determine how to apply style sheets in your own work. For the purposes of this chapter and the previous chapter, you should have enough information and examples to get you started. Remember that although style sheets are gaining support, usage, and popularity, they still aren't predominant enough for you to depend on them exclusively. Either design the page so that it looks good regardless of the browser, or provide a mirror set of pages in non-style sheet versions.

If you are definitely considering working with style sheets more regularly, you should visit the World Wide Web Consortium at `www.w3.org` for very explicit discussions regarding style sheet development, implementation into browsers, and use in design.

# JavaScript Style Sheets and Other Alternatives to CSS

*by Will Kelly*

## IN THIS CHAPTER

CHAPTER 21

JavaScript style sheets are another option to control formatting in a Web document. Style sheets are a real boon to Web publishing because they offer more control over formatting than just HTML. JavaScript style sheets utilize JavaScript to specify element styles in an HTML document.

---

**NOTE**

Chapter 19, "Introducing Cascading Style Sheets," provides a strong introduction to the basics of style sheets. JavaScript style sheets are introduced here.

---

JavaScript style sheets are still coming into use on the Web. More sites are due to spring up as Netscape Communicator becomes more stable and becomes a shipping product. In the past, the release of a Netscape Navigator browser was accompanied by brand new Netscape Extensions to HTML. The release of Netscape Communicator also brought with it JavaScript style sheets.

When the Web took off as a communications medium, one of the biggest complaints from communicators was the lack of formatting options available in Hypertext Markup Language. HTML, though a powerful tool for multiplatform content, has never been known to be designer friendly. This is changing for the better, just like everything else on the Web.

Netscape Communications Corporation was the first commercial company to seize upon the lack of creative options in HTML with the introduction of its proprietary HTML extensions, called Netscape Extensions. These extensions gained popularity with designers who wanted more control over formatting HTML documents. Netscape continued to push the envelope for designers with new extensions with each release of Netscape Navigator. Though Netscape releases new HTML extensions with each release of its browser, it is also the brains behind JavaScript style sheets.

With the release of Netscape Communicator, Netscape debuted JavaScript style sheets, the next era in formatting control for HTML documents.

This chapter provides an introduction to JavaScript style sheets and their major elements.

# What Are JavaScript Style Sheets?

JavaScript style sheets are style sheets that use JavaScript to set style properties. They aren't the same as cascading style sheets (CSS), though they serve the same role as CSS. You need to know JavaScript to use JavaScript style sheets to format your documents; you manipulate the style sheets through the JavaScript language. The JavaScript style sheet syntax offers control over the specific style for a particular HTML element. For example, suppose you are developing a corporate home page and want to format the page with the company's colors, which are dark blue, white, and black. You can set individual styles to cover the corporate colors. You can specify headings to display in blue. You could specify paragraph text to display in black.

You might already have been introduced to style sheets through word processing and desktop publishing. This crossover in publishing technology is understandable considering the migration of designers and other publications professionals to the Web. As a technical writer, I spent my fair share of time producing manuals with word processing style sheets. The power of style sheets offered the ability to combine multiple formatting elements in one style. I could create styles that could cover the font, font size, margins, and any other formatting element I needed to set. When JavaScript style sheets became a reality, I was ecstatic to learn that the power of style sheets was introduced to Web design and publishing.

> **NOTE**
>
> JavaScript style sheets are a particular application of JavaScript. If you need to learn more about JavaScript, refer to Chapter 28, "Integrating JavaScript and HTML."

JavaScript style sheets enable you to set classes that can cover multiple formatting requirements. The simple example I just mentioned talked only about colors, but you can carry the styles further. For the paragraph text, you can set a class for the headings that could cover the font, bolding, and centering of the headings. This class, which you could name something like CORPHD, can help you maintain a consistent organizational identity between online and print publications. It is also a labor-saver because it sets all the styles at once, rather than having to set each style individually. The CORPHD class takes care of the work of three tags:

- ■ The <FONT> tag to set the font of the heading
- ■ The <B> tag to set the heading as bold
- ■ The <CENTER> tag to specify the centering of the heading

You implement JavaScript style sheets via in-line style sheets to control the format of existing HTML tags present in your Web project.

Netscape Communicator supports both JavaScript and cascading style sheets. Microsoft Internet Explorer 3.0 and 4.0 support cascading style sheets.

Older browsers like NCSA Mosaic and Cello don't support style sheets. Then what happens when a user running an older browser hits my site, which is equipped with JavaScript style sheets? The browser will be able to interpret only the HTML code present in the Web page.

# New HTML Tags for Style Sheets

JavaScript style sheets don't replace HTML. They format HTML. But just as you need an HTML tag to support any element on a Web page, HTML tags support JavaScript style sheets. These tags enable the browser to interpret the style sheet and thus the document formatting. Three new HTML tags were introduced to support JavaScript style sheets: the <STYLE> tag, which indicates a document is formatted with a style sheet; the <LINK> tag, which specifies a link to an external style sheet in a document; and the <SPAN> tag, which specifies the beginning and end of a styled piece of text.

# The <STYLE> Element

The opening and closing <STYLE> tags indicate that a style sheet is being used to format the HTML document. Between the <STYLE> and </STYLE> tags, you can establish styles for use in an HTML document, including styles for elements, classes, IDs, and general styles.

The <STYLE> tag is just not particular to JavaScript style sheets; it is also used for cascading style sheets. When you use the <STYLE> tag to support a JavaScript style sheet, you need to specify the TYPE attribute as "text/javascript".

> **NOTE**
>
> The <STYLE> tag is always implemented within the HEAD element.

Listing 21.1 shows an example of how to implement the <STYLE> tag in an HTML document.

**Listing 21.1. The <STYLE> tag in action.**

```
<HTML>
<HEAD>
<STYLE TYPE= "text/javascript">
tags.BODY.marginRight=10
tags.BODY.marginLeft=10
CorpHD.align="center"
CorpBD.align="left"
</STYLE>
</HEAD>
```

# The <LINK> Element

The <LINK> element links to an external style sheet to format the HTML document. Listing 21.2 shows an example of how to implement the <LINK> element.

**Listing 21.2. The <LINK> tag in action.**

```
<HTML>
<HEAD>
<TITLE>The <LINK> Tag in Action</TITLE>
<LINK REL=STYLESHEET TYPE= "text/JavaScript"
HREF= "http://samplesite.com/exstyles" TITLE= "example"
</HEAD>
```

> **NOTE**
>
> The <LINK> tag is always implemented within the HEAD element.

## The <SPAN> Element

The <SPAN> element indicates the beginning and end of styled text. Text within the <SPAN> and </SPAN> tags is the text to which the style is applied. Listing 21.3 shows an example of what the <SPAN> tags can do in an HTML document.

**Listing 21.3. The <SPAN> tag in action.**

```
<P><SPAN style=color= 'red' fontWeight= 'bold' fontStyle= 'italic'>
Blivits Communication </SPAN>is a full service technical and Web
communications firm composed of communicators drawn from business and government.
We do documentation, Websites, and most any communications piece</P>
```

# Style Sheets and Existing HTML Tags

The introduction of the JavaScript style sheet as a formatting tool, besides using newer HTML tags, has also introduced new attributes for existing HTML tags. These new attributes primarily focus on style issues. The new attributes follow:

- ■ STYLE: The STYLE attribute is an important new attribute because it enables you to specify the style for a specific element.
- ■ CLASS: The CLASS attribute enables you to define classes for styles.
- ■ IDS: The IDS attribute enables you to specify exceptions to styles. Stylistic exceptions come into play when you want to designate a slight change to the default style for a class. An example would be italicizing a particular word or words when the rest of the text is just in a normal typeface.

> **NOTE**
>
> The IDS attribute is not the same as the IDS JavaScript object. The IDS HTML attribute specifies a unique style for the HTML element, whereas the IDS JavaScript object enables you to create a unique style identification.

# JavaScript Style Sheet Properties and Values

This section gets into the nitty-gritty of JavaScript style sheets. You format via properties that actually specify the format. For instance, the font properties govern the formatting of fonts in a Web document, including font type, size, and appearance.

We've already introduced you to some of the basics behind style sheets in Chapter 19. Many of those same rules apply here, except that JavaScript is the programming language controlling the formatting.

## Font Properties

One chief formatting complaint in days of yore, when you could only produce Times New Roman as a body font for HTML documents, was the lack of choice in font styles. This has improved with advancements in HTML and proprietary HTML extensions. Style sheets such as JavaScript style sheets also contribute to the improvements in font formatting. In fact, one of the most common applications of style sheets is formatting fonts.

### The `fontSize` Property

The `fontSize` property controls the setting of font size and related characteristics. Four possible values apply to all elements:

- `absolute-size`: The `absolute-size` value contains the index to a table of font sizes computed by the rendering program for the style sheet. It includes the following possible values: `xx-small`, `x-small`, `small`, `medium`, `large`, `x-large`, and `xx-large`.

- `relative-size`: The `relative-size` value is designated in reference to the table of font sizes and the parent element's font size. The relative-size value has the value of either `smaller` or `larger`.

- `length`: The `length` value is the absolute value of the line height.

- `percentage`: The `percentage` value is the percentage of the line height of the parent element.

### The `fontFamily` Property

The `fontFamily` property designates the font family that is used for the style, such as Courier or Arial. The `fontFamily` value is the only possible value for the property. The property can apply to all elements.

Sometimes a font is not available to a user. Configuration management is impossible in a world-wide enterprise environment such as the World Wide Web. You need to be aware of five generic font families, including serif, sans-serif, cursive, monospace, and fantasy. I am not going to start a lesson on typography; I'll keep it simple. The five generic family names are guaranteed to indicate a font on every system. This guarantee is platform-independent, so it covers Windows, Macintosh, Unix, OS/2, and the other client operating systems that are plugged into the Internet.

## The `fontStyle` Property

The `fontStyle` property controls the style of fonts in the HTML document. This property has five possible values: `normal`, `italic`, `italic small-caps`, `oblique`, `oblique small-caps`, and `small-caps`. The `small-caps` value can also encompass the `italic` and `oblique` values. On some systems, capital letters of a smaller font size will not be rendered correctly if you do not correctly set the resolution for the output medium.

# Text, Classes, and ID Properties

JavaScript style sheets also enable you to set text properties, such as text decoration and line height.

## The `lineHeight` Property

The `lineHeight` property sets the distance between the baselines of two adjacent lines. This property applies only to block-level elements. The `lineHeight` property has three possible values:

- `number`: The `number` value specifies the line height as computed by the font size of the current element multiplied by the numerical value. The numerical value is not the same as the percentage value because of how it inherits. Inheritance takes place when the numerical value is specified; then child elements will inherit the factor and not the resultant value.

- `length`: The `length` value is the line height's absolute value.

- `percentage`: The `percentage` value is the percentage of the parent element's line height.

## The `textDecoration` Property

The `textDecoration` property describes the decorative elements applied to an element's text. This property has five possible values: `none`, `underline`, `overline`, `line-through`, and the ever-fabulous `blink`. If the element has no text, the `textDecoration` property has no effect, which would happen with elements such as IMG and Bold.

## The `verticalAlign` Property

The `verticalAlign` property designates the vertical positioning of text. This property has nine possible values:

- `baseline`: The `baseline` value aligns the element's baseline with the parent element's baseline.

- `sub`: The `sub` value displays the element in subscript style.

- `super`: The `super` value displays the element in superscript style.

- `top`: The `top` value aligns the top of the element with the tallest element present on the line.

- `text-top`: The `text-top` value aligns the top of the element with the parent element's font top.

- `middle`: The `middle` value aligns the element's vertical mid-point with the baseline plus half the parent's x-height. The x-height is defined as the height of the character x.

- `bottom`: The `bottom` value aligns the element's bottom with the line's lowest element.

- `text-bottom`: The `text-bottom` value aligns the element's bottom with the bottom of the parent element's font.

- `percentage`: The `percentage` value refers to the element's line height.

## The `textTransform` Property

The `textTransform` property indicates the text case of a font. The property has four possible values and applies to all elements:

- `capitalize`: The `capitalize` value displays the first character of each word in uppercase.

- `uppercase`: The `uppercase` value displays all letters of the element in uppercase type.

- `lowercase`: The `lowercase` value displays all the element's letters in lowercase.

- `none`: The `none` value neutralizes any and all inherited values.

## The `textAlign` Property

The `textAlign` property specifies how text is aligned within the element. This property has four possible values: `left`, `right`, `center`, and `justify`.

The alignments that the values represent are relative to the width of the element. If the client system does not support the `justify` element, it will supply a replacement. In the case of the western languages that dominate so much of the World Wide Web, the substitution will be the `left` value.

## The `textIndent` Property

The `textIndent` property designates the indent that appears before the first formatted line of text. This property has two possible values:

- `length`: The `length` value defines the length of the indent as a unit-based numerical value.

- `percentage`: The `percentage` value defines the length of the indent as a percentage of the width of the parent element.

> **NOTE**
>
> An indent is never inserted in the middle of an HTML element that is broken by another element, such as the `<br>` tag.

# Block-Level Element Format Properties

The block-level elements, as defined by JavaScript style sheets, govern such elements as headings and paragraphs as boxes that can include borders, paddings, and margins.

## The Margin Properties

The margin properties encompass the following:

- `marginLeft`
- `marginRight`
- `marginTop`
- `marginBottom`
- `margins()`

These properties specify the margin of an element. The margin is specified via individual values. The `margins()` value sets the margins for all four sides at once. These margins designate the minimal distance between adjoining element borders.

## The Padding Element Properties

The padding element properties encompass the following:

- `paddingTop`
- `paddingRight`
- `paddingBottom`
- `paddingLeft`
- `paddings()`

The padding element properties specify how much space to insert between the border and the content of the document. You can set the values for padding by specifying values.

## The Border Element Properties

The border element properties encompass the following:

- `borderTopWidth`
- `borderRightWidth`
- `borderBottomWidth`
- `borderLeftWidth`
- `borderWidths()`

The border properties specify the border width around an object in pixels, em units, or points. By specifying values for the elements, you can set the border width.

### The borderStyle Property

The borderStyle property specifies the style of a border around a block-level element. This property has three possible values: none, solid, and 3D.

### The borderColor Property

The borderColor property specifies the color of the element's border. You can specify the color to be a named color or a six-digit hexadecimal color value.

### The width Property

The width property designates the width of an element. This property is typically applied to text elements, but it is best used when applied to in-line images and other media insertions. The width property has three possible values: length, percentage, and auto.

### The height Property

The height property specifies the height of the element. This property works best when you apply it to in-line graphic images and similar media insertions. You can also apply this property to textual elements, however. The height property has only two values: length and auto.

### The align Property

The align property specifies the element's alignment. This element can include text or an in-line image. The align property has three possible values: left, right, and none.

> **NOTE**
>
> The align property is somewhat related to cascading style sheets: it corresponds to the CSS float property. The term float is a reserved term in JavaScript and can't be used for a property name.

The align property is most often implemented with in-line images and can make an element float to either the right or left. It also controls how other content wraps around the property.

### The clear Property

The clear property specifies whether an element allows floating elements on all of its sides. It has four possible values: none, left, right, and both.

# Color and Background Properties

You can set color and background properties for block-level elements just as you can set them for an entire HTML document.

## The color Property

The color property specifies the element's text color. The color specified is the foreground color, rather than the background color. Text is always at the foreground of a document. This property's only possible value is the color value.

## The backgroundImage Property

The backgroundImage property specifies the background image of an element. The url value is its only possible value.

# Classification Properties

The classification properties classify properties into appropriate categories and don't set element appearance.

## The display Property

The display property specifies whether an element is one of the following possible values:

- in-line element is like the <B> HTML tag.
- block-level is like the <P> HTML tag.
- block-level list item is like the <LI> HTML tag.

The initial value for the property is drawn from the HTML specification. If the none value is implemented for this property, the display of the element is turned off.

## The listStyleType Property

The listStyleType property specifies the formatting of list items in HTML documents. List items would be classed as items with a display value of list-item. This property has nine possible values: disc, circle, square, decimal, lower-roman, upper-roman, lower-alpha, upper-alpha, and none.

You can specify this property on any element. It will inherit down the tree normally.

### NOTE

The list is displayed only on elements with list-item as its display value.

## The whiteSpace Property

The whiteSpace property specifies how white space inside the element should be handled. This property has two possible values: normal and pre. The normal value specifies that white space is collapsed. The pre value works the same way as the <PRE> HTML tag.

# Precedence Order

The precedence order is determined for tags, classes, and IDs via an algorithm. The algorithm works as follows:

- It finds all declarations applying to the specific element/property.
- It sorts all declarations by their explicit weight.
- It sorts by the origin. Via this sorting, the style sheets developed by the given Web site's author override the reader's style sheet. This override works as a default.
- It sorts by the selector's specificity, with more specific selectors overriding the general selectors.

# Other Alternatives to CSS

JavaScript style sheets aren't the only game in town as far as alternatives to cascading style sheets. The World Wide Web Consortium (http://www.w3.org) is currently developing the next version of Hypertext Markup Language with input from the online community. The new version includes a specification for styles. Netscape Communicator introduced Dynamic Fonts with Preview Release 3. This powerful feature, though not a style sheet per se, enables developers to have more control over the fonts in their HTML documents than has ever been offered before.

## Cougar

The new version of HyperText Markup Language, code named *Cougar*, introduces many new features to HTML including its own version of styles and style sheets. The standards are all in the draft stage. With this style specification, you no longer have to extend HTML code when you need new presentation styles to get the job done. Now, you can include style rules as a group in the document header, as part of individual HTML elements in the document, or as part of associated style sheets.

This new style sheet draft has influenced both CSS and JavaScript style sheets by providing the specs for the <LINK>, <STYLE>, and <SPAN> elements. The basic concepts of style sheets as set out by Cougar are as follows:

- Style information placement: One of the charms of style sheets is the developer's ability to reuse them. Style sheets are placed in separate files and are not embedded into an HTML document like traditional Web formatting.
- Style sheet language independence: The Cougar specification for style sheets doesn't tie HTML into a particular style sheet language. Remember, JavaScript style sheets use the JavaScript language to control formatting. With this specification, you have more options to use other languages to specify formatting.
- Cascading style sheets: This feature of the specification enables you to use style information from multiple sources to format an HTML document.

■ Media dependencies: This feature enables you to define styles for media types in an HTML document.

■ Alternative styles: The Cougar style specification provides readers with alternative styles for viewing style sheet–formatted Web content.

Point your browser to `http://www.w3.org/pub/WWW/TR/WD-style` to learn more about this emerging standard.

## Dynamic Fonts

I have the tendency to be a font monger. Not that I use them all the time, but there is a certain sense of security that they are available and at my beck and call. When I was poring over the specs for Netscape Communicator (`http://home.netscape.com/inf/comprod/products/communicator/index.html`), I was happy to learn about Communicator's support of Dynamic fonts. Dynamic fonts enable you to include fonts dynamically in your HTML documents. This dynamic link is accomplished via an author-defined link to a URL containing the font files.

To learn more about Dynamic fonts, and what they have to offer the Web developer, consult the following address:

`http://developer.netscape.com/library/documentation/communicator/jsss/index.htm`

# Future of JavaScript Style Sheets

JavaScript style sheets are closely tied to Netscape Communicator and other Netscape Web publishing technologies. Netscape will drive JavaScript style sheet development to compete against Microsoft's support of cascading style sheets. Marketing is certainly driving the technology, but it is also good to know that Netscape Communicator supports CSS, making Netscape prepared to support either way.

# Summary

This chapter covered the basics of JavaScript style sheets and offered an introduction to some of the other options to cascading style sheets that are becoming available for Web development.

JavaScript style sheets offer Web developers control over formatting Web pages that they could never have had with plain HTML. The introduction of JavaScript style sheets will also help the Web mature even more as a communications and creative medium because more options are now available to the artists and Web developers developing content for the Web.

# Dynamic HTML

*by Bruce Campbell*

## IN THIS CHAPTER

CHAPTER 22

# Introduction to Dynamic HTML

HTML, as defined in the 3.2 specification, standardizes the creation process of static documents that are accessed from the Web and consumed by a Web audience. Scripting languages, programming languages, user controls, and plug-in applications are incorporated into Web pages by Web page designers to add animation, database access, sound, video, and interactive applications. Dynamic HTML is an enhancement to HTML that provides a group of technologies designed to create and display more interactive Web pages within the .htm or .html file itself, avoiding the complexity of requiring additional plug-in applications, add-on controls, and multiple Web server requests. Microsoft is leading the way in providing Dynamic HTML enhancements by including the Dynamic HTML technologies in the Internet Explorer 4.0 Web browser. Microsoft continues to work closely with the World Wide Web Consortium, or W3C (http://www.w3.org/pub/WWW/), the governing body of the HTML standard, to provide an open standard that other Web browser developers can incorporate into their applications. Netscape (http://www.netscape.com) is incorporating many features of Dynamic HTML into its upcoming Communicator product. In fact, Netscape has drafted additional functionality for Dynamic HTML that shows innovative and useful characteristics. As the W3C incorporates the innovations from Microsoft and Netscape, other groups and individuals are sure to further refine Dynamic HTML as well.

Included in Dynamic HTML is a new object model designed to make HTML objects more accessible to scripting functions that take advantage of the existing HTML <SCRIPT></SCRIPT> tag pair. Using the new object model to create Web pages and a new Web browser to surf Dynamic HTML-based Web content, developers can get a head start on learning the promises Dynamic HTML holds for the Web.

## Benefits of the New Object Model

The new object model provides the following benefits examined in detail in the four HTML examples provided in this chapter:

- Access to all page elements for dynamically changing page appearance
- Instant client page update without additional server services
- An exciting event model tracking mouse usage and page state
- HTML text ranges that can be changed on the fly to dramatically change content

Any Web page element can be identified as an object using HTML's ID attribute. For example, a paragraph of text can be instantiated through the ID attribute of the following HTML line:

```
<P ID=ParagraphX STYLE="font=weight: normal">
```

Using the ID attribute value, a function within a <SCRIPT></SCRIPT> tag pair can then instantly change the page as a result of an event, such as the following:

```
ParagraphX.style.fontstyle = "Italic"
```

Any ID attribute value can be instantiated to receive messages from other script-based functions on the HTML Web page.

## Available Events in Dynamic HTML

Client-based interactive Web pages are made possible by the events incorporated into Dynamic HTML. Table 22.1 presents the available events provided by the Internet Explorer 4.0 implementation at press time. Follow the Reference link on Microsoft's Dynamic HTML Web page for new developments.

> **NOTE**
>
> At press time, the URL for Dynamic HTML information at Microsoft was http://www.microsoft.com/workshop/prog/ie4. Any changes to the Dynamic HTML specification since this chapter was written should be documented at Microsoft's Web site.

**Table 22.1. Dynamic HTML events.**

| | | |
|---|---|---|
| onabort | onfocus | onmouseup |
| onafterupdate | onhelp | onreadystatechange |
| onbeforeupdate | onkeydown | onreset |
| onblur | onkeypress | onrowenter |
| onbounce | onkeyup | onrowexit |
| onchange | onload | onscroll |
| onclick | onmousedown | onselect |
| ondblclick | onmousemove | onstart |
| onerror | onmouseout | onsubmit |
| onfinish | onmouseover | onunload |

The user's mouse and keyboard actions, as well as the current state of the active Web page, generate events. You can embed event handling directly into an HTML tag, as in the following code:

```
<P ID=ParagraphX STYLE="font=weight: normal"
onmouseover="Italicize();"
onmouseout="Normalize();"
>
```

Passing the mouse over and off the paragraph text that follows this `<P>` tag in an HTML Web page invokes the `Italicize()` and `Normalize()` functions. Both functions are written in the same .htm file as the `<P>` tag using a scripting language within the `<SCRIPT></SCRIPT>` tag pair.

With the new object and event model in hand, developers can provide the following features in a single HTML Web page:

- Dynamically changing styles
- Dynamically changing content
- Dynamic positioning of graphics
- Dynamic data-awareness

I will review each feature in this chapter by way of an example created for the Internet Explorer 4.0 pre-release version provided by Microsoft for download through its Web site. I have coordinated the examples to reflect four pages of the same Web site.

## DYNAMIC HTML: MICROSOFT, NETSCAPE, AND THE W3C

To be honest, I am using Microsoft's IE4 for this chapter's examples because it appears to be a bit more mature than Netscape's implementation at the time of this book's publication. The examples definitely give you a flavor for the kind of things that will be available from Dynamic HTML even if the name is changed to reflect HTML 4 or some other buzzword.

Both Netscape and Microsoft are admitting allegiance to the W3C as the final arbiter of any official specifications that come out as a result of these Dynamic HTML features. I definitely suggest that you check out Netscape's implementation if you really like authoring for the Navigator browser—especially if you are already using the LiveConnect API architecture. You should check out Microsoft's implementation if you really like authoring for Internet Explorer and you've invested substantial time in learning ActiveX and Visual Basic. But regardless of your situation, you should always read the technical papers at the W3C Web site because they define the reasons behind the decisions to make changes for the mutual progression of the Web. Check out the current Cougar project for some very important papers on HTML's development. For now, if your Web site exists for general consumption, be sure to test your Dynamic HTML files with both browsers.

Because the examples from this chapter lean so heavily toward Microsoft's vision of Dynamic HTML, I include the following list so that you can ponder Netscape's vision. Within Netscape's implementation are the following sample features:

- Netscape defines a <LAYER> tag that you can use to set up independent regions of a Web page and position them independently.
- Netscape defines a standard, vectored font specification that can be downloaded with a page to create a font that is not resident on the reader's machine.
- Netscape defines another scripting language, called JavaScript, that can be used to handle dynamic events.
- Netscape is considering changes to its plug-in architecture to take advantage of new Dynamic HTML features.

Both Microsoft and Netscape are committed to developing Dynamic HTML features that behave well in older browsers that can't use all of the Dynamic HTML functionality. Significant work must be done in order to keep that promise, but I suspect features that work in one browser should not detrimentally affect the other. If they do, the public at large should give that browser developer a hard time.

The examples are interactive Web pages designed using Dynamic HTML for the fictitious Web Baseball League (WBL), which consists of eight baseball teams playing a 112-game season of virtual baseball over the Web. The site has been designed for fans of the league to keep abreast of league standings and interact with the pages from their computers.

The following list summarizes the features of the sample WBL pages by each listing number that you can reference in this chapter:

- Point and click team names to see expanding and collapsing current information sections on each team. (See Listing 22.1.)
- Drag and drop team logos into an interactive form to participate in a contest of predicting future team standings. (See Listing 22.2.)
- Click buttons to enter each team's electronic locker room with data-awareness enabled for local data manipulation. (See Listing 22.3.)
- Use dynamic table interaction to sort current league standings by team name, wins, losses, batting averages, and earned run averages. (See Listing 22.4.)

Now let's investigate the code behind the examples. Consider that all code is integrated with HTML tags in a single .htm file. No additional plug-ins, helper applications, or virtual machines are necessary to create the dynamic effects of each page. The Web server is contacted only once to present the information to the Web browser client. With Dynamic HTML, Internet packet traffic is reduced significantly and a considerable burden is taken off the Web server.

# Creating Dynamic Text

Dynamic HTML sets up event handling in the Web page itself. You can handle events that dynamically change the text on the Web page as the user moves, clicks, or double-clicks the mouse, or presses a key on the keyboard. The effect can be dramatic because you can change the HTML tags that format a paragraph as well as the text itself on the fly.

The example in Listing 22.1 builds a Web page that league fans can visit daily to get up-to-date information on each team. Perhaps you could have similar pages for injury reports, upcoming weekly schedules, or insider's gossip.

The page is set up to track the user's mouse clicks. As the user clicks a team name, the team name expands to present detailed information for that team. The user can click again to collapse the detail. Such page behavior presents an uncluttered Web page, avoids unwanted detail, and reduces the need to scroll to find information at the site. Dynamic text is a powerful feature in combating information overload for the casual Web surfer, but also can be used to anticipate the needs of the audience. Figure 22.1 shows the team page before a user has clicked a team. Figure 22.2 shows the page after a user has clicked the Spiders team name. The page returns to appear as in Figure 22.1 when the user clicks anywhere on the Spiders detail text.

**Listing 22.1. Example of dynamic text.**

```html
<HTML>
<BODY TOPMARGIN=0 LEFTMARGIN=40 BGCOLOR= "#FFFFFF" LINK= "#000066"
 VLINK= "#666666" TEXT= "#000000">
<HEAD>
<FONT FACE="verdana,arial,helvetica" SIZE=3>
<TITLE>The WBL Daily Update</TITLE>
</HEAD>
<BODY>
<STYLE>
.redText {color:Red}
.blueText {color:Blue}
</STYLE>
<H3>The Web Baseball League Daily</H3>
<IMG SRC="Bears.jpg" ALIGN=LEFT HEIGHT=32><P CLASS="blueText">
 Bears
<IMG SRC="Tigers.jpg" ALIGN=LEFT HEIGHT=32><P CLASS="blueText">
Tigers
<IMG SRC="Robins.jpg" ALIGN=LEFT HEIGHT=32><P CLASS="blueText">
Robins
<IMG SRC="Lions.jpg" ALIGN=LEFT HEIGHT=32><P CLASS="blueText">
Lions
<IMG SRC="Rhinos.jpg" ALIGN=LEFT HEIGHT=32><P CLASS="blueText">
Rhinos
<IMG SRC="Frogs.jpg" ALIGN=LEFT HEIGHT=32><P CLASS="blueText">
Frogs
<IMG SRC="Sharks.jpg" ALIGN=LEFT HEIGHT=32><P CLASS="blueText">
Sharks
<IMG SRC="Spiders.jpg" ALIGN=LEFT HEIGHT=32>
<P id=spider CLASS="blueText" onclick="expandP();">
Spiders</P>

<SCRIPT LANGUAGE=VBScript>
function expandP()
   dim r
   set r = document.rangeFromElement(spider)
   if (spider.className="blueText") then
      r.pasteHTML("<B><I>Spiders</I></B><BR>Wins: 4<BR>Losses: 14<BR>
        ➥Batting Average: .212<BR>Earned Run Average: 3.86<BR>")
      spider.className="redText"
   else
      r.pasteHTML("Spiders")
      spider.className="blueText"
   end if
end function
</SCRIPT>
</FONT>
</BODY>
</HTML>
```

**FIGURE 22.1.**
*Before clicking* Spiders.

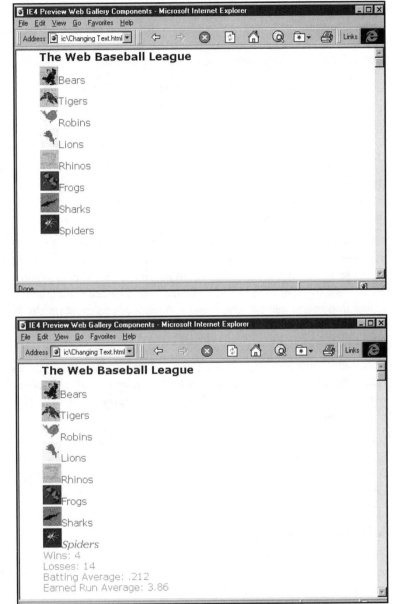

**FIGURE 22.2.**
*After clicking* Spiders.

The <STYLE></STYLE> tag pair defines two styles to be used in the page according to the specification for cascading style sheets presented in Chapter 19, "Introducing Cascading Style Sheets." The style redText colors text red. The style blueText colors text blue.

A paragraph is created for each team, including a thumbnail of the team logo and the team name. The blueText style is applied to each paragraph using the CLASS attribute of the <P> tag. In this example, the dynamic text feature is enabled for the Spiders team paragraph only. To enable dynamic text, the following steps are executed:

1. The ID=spider attribute of the <P> tag instantiates the paragraph as a dynamic object.
2. The onclick="expandP();" attribute of the <P> tag establishes the click event.
3. The expandP() function is created and inserted in a <SCRIPT></SCRIPT> pair tag using an appropriate scripting language such as JavaScript or, in this case, VBScript.

The expandP() function obtains a handle to a range of HTML text in the Web page by calling the rangeFromElement() method of the document and passing it an object that specifies a range in the Web page. In this case, the spider object defines a paragraph of text. Every Web page is instantiated as a document object upon loading in the Web browser.

The expandP() function interrogates the CLASS attribute value of the spider paragraph. If the bluetext style is active for the spider paragraph, the function calls the pasteHTML() method of the range handle it obtained and stored in variable r. The singular argument of the pasteHTML() method is a string of valid HTML tags and text. The detailed HTML tags and text string are pasted into the spider paragraph and dynamically presented on the Web page by the Web browser. The HTML syntax replaces the HTML tags and text that had been initially loaded by the browser following the spider <P> tag.

In contrast, if the redtext style is active for the spider paragraph, the pasteHTML() method is called with the original HTML tags and text to reset the spider paragraph back to its original contents. As the HTML contents change for the spider paragraph, the style toggles between red and blue.

Inherent in this example are two features of Dynamic HTML that you can use independently. First, you can change styles dynamically. Second, you can change the HTML tags and text contents for a text range (such as a paragraph or heading) on the fly, based on the available Dynamic HTML Web page events presented in Table 22.1.

# Creating Dynamic Graphics

The cascading style sheet model introduced in Chapter 19, includes details for defining a ZINDEX value for a Web page graphic. Z-indexing enables a Web author to identify which graphic should appear in front of another if they share the same (x,y) coordinates. The object with a lower ZINDEX value is presented in front of objects with higher ones. This example builds on other dynamic graphic placement features added by Dynamic HTML.

The HTML Web page detailed in Listing 22.2 contains eight .jpg graphic files—one for each team logo in the Web Baseball League. The logos are presented on the page shown in Figure 22.3 with the expectation that a user will drag and drop the logos on the page to place them in the order he believes the teams will finish after the upcoming season. Perhaps the contest could be held weekly or monthly instead.

**Listing 22.2. Example of drag-and-drop graphics.**

```
<HTML>
<HEAD><TITLE>WBL Standings Contest</TITLE></HEAD>
<BODY BGCOLOR="#FFFFFF">
<H2>Predict The Web Baseball League Standings</H2>
<FONT FACE="Verdana, Arial, Helvetica" SIZE="4">
<B>Use the mouse to position the team logos
 in order of finish</B><BR><BR></FONT>
Then predict the number of wins and losses for the 112 game schedule<BR>
Click OK to submit your selections<BR>

<SCRIPT LANGUAGE="VBScript">
function document_onmousemove(button, shift, x,y)
dim newleft, newtop, srcElement
  if (button = 1) then
    set srcElement = window.event.srcElement
    ' if mouse is dragging and IMG, move it.
    if srcElement.tagname="IMG" then
        ' move team logo
        newleft=x-document.all.OuterDiv.docLeft-(srcElement.docWidth/2)
        if newleft<0 then newleft=0
        srcElement.style.pixelLeft= newleft
        newtop=y-document.all.OuterDiv.docTop-(srcElement.docHeight/2)
        if newtop<0 then newtop=0
        srcElement.style.pixelTop= newtop
        window.event.returnValue = false
        window.event.cancelBubble = true
    end if
  end if
end function
</SCRIPT>

<DIV ID=OuterDiv style="position:relative;width:100%;height:600px">
    <IMG ID="bear" STYLE="container:positioned;position:absolute;TOP:58pt;
      LEFT:0px;WIDTH:64px;HEIGHT:64px;ZINDEX:-1;" SRC="Bears.jpg">
    <IMG ID="frog" STYLE="container:positioned;position:absolute;TOP:58pt;
      LEFT:66px;WIDTH:64px;HEIGHT:64px;ZINDEX:-2;" SRC="Frogs.jpg">
    <IMG ID="lion" STYLE="container:positioned;position:absolute;TOP:58pt;
      LEFT:134px;WIDTH:64px;HEIGHT:64px;ZINDEX:-3;" SRC="Lions.jpg">
    <IMG ID="robin" STYLE="container:positioned;position:absolute;TOP:58pt;
      LEFT:202px;WIDTH:64px;HEIGHT:64px;ZINDEX:-4;" SRC="Robins.jpg">
    <IMG ID="rhino" STYLE="container:positioned;position:absolute;TOP:58pt;
      LEFT:270px;WIDTH:64px;HEIGHT:64px;ZINDEX:-5;" SRC="Rhinos.jpg">
    <IMG ID="shark" STYLE="container:positioned;position:absolute;TOP:58pt;
      LEFT:338px;WIDTH:64px;HEIGHT:64px;ZINDEX:-6;" SRC="Sharks.jpg">
    <IMG ID="spider" STYLE="container:positioned;position:absolute;TOP:58pt;
      LEFT:406px;WIDTH:64px;HEIGHT:64px;ZINDEX:-7;" SRC="Spiders.jpg">
    <IMG ID="tiger" STYLE="container:positioned;position:absolute;TOP:58pt;
      LEFT:474px;WIDTH:64px;HEIGHT:64px;ZINDEX:-8;" SRC="Tigers.jpg">

  <H1> --1-- --2-- --3-- --4-- --5-- --6-- --7-- --8--</H1>
  <PRE>
```

22

DYNAMIC HTML

*continues*

**Listing 22.2. continued**

```
</PRE>
<TABLE>
<TR>
<TD WIDTH=64><INPUT TYPE=text NAME="wins1" SIZE=5 VALUE="" MAXLENGTH=3></TD>
<TD WIDTH=64><INPUT TYPE=text NAME="wins2" SIZE=5 VALUE="" MAXLENGTH=3></TD>
<TD WIDTH=64><INPUT TYPE=text NAME="wins3" SIZE=5 VALUE="" MAXLENGTH=3></TD>
<TD WIDTH=64><INPUT TYPE=text NAME="wins4" SIZE=5 VALUE="" MAXLENGTH=3></TD>
<TD WIDTH=64><INPUT TYPE=text NAME="wins5" SIZE=5 VALUE="" MAXLENGTH=3></TD>
<TD WIDTH=64><INPUT TYPE=text NAME="wins6" SIZE=5 VALUE="" MAXLENGTH=3></TD>
<TD WIDTH=64><INPUT TYPE=text NAME="wins7" SIZE=5 VALUE="" MAXLENGTH=3></TD>
<TD WIDTH=64><INPUT TYPE=text NAME="wins8" SIZE=5 VALUE="" MAXLENGTH=3></TD>
<TD WIDTH=64><< Wins</TD>
</TR>
<TR>
<TD WIDTH=64><INPUT TYPE=text NAME="loss1" SIZE=5 VALUE="" MAXLENGTH=3></TD>
<TD WIDTH=64><INPUT TYPE=text NAME="loss2" SIZE=5 VALUE="" MAXLENGTH=3></TD>
<TD WIDTH=64><INPUT TYPE=text NAME="loss3" SIZE=5 VALUE="" MAXLENGTH=3></TD>
<TD WIDTH=64><INPUT TYPE=text NAME="loss4" SIZE=5 VALUE="" MAXLENGTH=3></TD>
<TD WIDTH=64><INPUT TYPE=text NAME="loss5" SIZE=5 VALUE="" MAXLENGTH=3></TD>
<TD WIDTH=64><INPUT TYPE=text NAME="loss6" SIZE=5 VALUE="" MAXLENGTH=3></TD>
<TD WIDTH=64><INPUT TYPE=text NAME="loss7" SIZE=5 VALUE="" MAXLENGTH=3></TD>
<TD WIDTH=64><INPUT TYPE=text NAME="loss8" SIZE=5 VALUE="" MAXLENGTH=3></TD>
<TD WIDTH=64><< Losses</TD>
</TR>
</TABLE>
<INPUT TYPE=submit VALUE="OK">
</FONT>
</BODY>
</HTML>
```

**FIGURE 22.3.**
*WBL standings.*

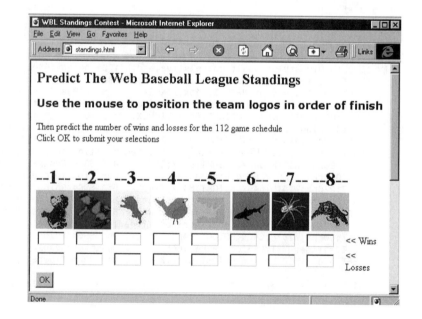

The HTML Web page in Listing 22.2 includes a script function that sets up an onmousemove event for the whole page. The Web page is instantiated as a document object when the Web browser loads the page. The document_onmousemove() function contains four arguments: the mouse button the user is currently holding down, the state of the Shift key on the keyboard, the x location of the mouse pointer, and the y location of the mouse pointer. This function is available for any Web page taking advantage of Dynamic HTML.

If the user is dragging an object by the left mouse button (button 1), the function associates that object with an srcElement variable declared in the function body. Next, the srcElement is interrogated to determine whether the object being dragged was created as the result of an <IMG> tag. If so, it is a graphical object and the script continues. If not, the function exits without interest in the mouse movement.

If the function determines that the user is dragging a bitmap with the left mouse button, the bitmap location is changed dynamically on the screen to reflect the current x and y values of the mouse pointer.

I have declared two variables in the function body—newleft and newtop—that I use to determine where the bitmap should be placed. The movement of the bitmaps is constrained by a region created by the Web author in an OuterDiv object identified with the ID=OutDiv attribute. The region is the full width of the Web page wide (100%) and is 600 pixels (px) high at the relative point in the page where it is encountered when parsing the .htm file.

The line window.event.cancelBubble = true tells the browser window to refrain from bubbling up the event in the case that the document cannot handle the event. The concept of bubbling has to do with the automatic passing of events up to a parent class of an object when an object is not equipped to handle that event. Bubbling helps reduce the amount of function writing that is necessary in cases where some objects on a page can handle an event by themselves. Objects that can't handle the event can use the same function and the event is automatically passed up the class hierarchy until it can be handled.

The rest of the HTML Web page after the </SCRIPT> tag is standard cascading style sheet and HTML syntax. I create and position the team logo bitmaps initially using the STYLE attribute of the <IMG> tags, I create a heading to mark the positions of the bitmaps from first to eighth, and I add a table of input text areas to accept the guesses of the user. The user submits his or her choices by clicking the OK button.

Substantial interactivity is added to Web pages by allowing for the dragging and dropping of component objects. Such interactivity is critical if the Web is to be able to compete with successful CD-ROM titles.

# Creating Dynamic Data-Aware Pages

Data-awareness is a powerful enhancement that Dynamic HTML provides. With Dynamic HTML, you can access a data source anywhere on the Web with a Web browser, deliver it locally to the requesting client, and then interactively present it to an audience without any additional network traffic.

To make a data-aware Web page, use the data source control specified within the `<OBJECT>` `</OBJECT>` tag pair. The Web browser can provide the data source control as a browser class or user control. Dynamic HTML coordinates the binding of the HTML page elements to the data source. Typical data sources that Dynamic HTML handles include comma-delimited files, SQL query dynasets, and other open database connectivity sources.

Data-aware Web pages using Dynamic HTML have the following features:

- Automatically generating table rows from data records
- Dynamically expanding tables
- Interactively filtering and sorting table contents
- Binding HTML elements to a specific record
- Data-binding form fields

The example in Listing 22.3 covers binding of HTML elements to a specific record and the example in Listing 22.4 reviews automatic generation of table rows and interactive sorting.

## Binding HTML Elements to a Specific Data Source Record

Dynamic HTML provides a method of downloading a substantial data source from the Web, maintaining the data in computer memory, and presenting the data in smaller, comprehensible pieces. Such a feature has two main benefits: one-time Web server access and manageability to avoid user information overload. Traditionally, users have accessed multiple pages from a Web site to fulfill their information consumption needs. Web authors have provided these smaller pages to keep the presentation clean and to limit the need for scrolling the text (as well as to present well on WebTV). With Dynamic HTML, the author can still present the information in smaller chunks, but the Web server can deliver it all at once to avoid multiple request servicing.

As an example, Listing 22.3 creates a Web page that enables a new visitor to the Web Baseball League Web site to learn about the teams in the league one team at a time. Instead of requesting eight different pages from the Web server over time, the user is provided buttons to access the rows of a data source one row at a time. The whole data source is delivered to the user as a result of the client making a single server request. Figure 22.4 shows the Web page for the Frogs team row of the data source, which, in this case, is a simple comma-delimited text file named `wblteam.txt`. The `wblteam.txt` file is provided in Listing 22.5 later in this chapter.

**Listing 22.3. An example of dynamic record presentation.**

```
<HTML>
<HEAD>
<BODY TOPMARGIN=0 LEFTMARGIN=40 BGCOLOR="#FFFFFF" LINK="#000066"
VLINK="#666666" TEXT="#000000">
```

```
<FONT FACE="verdana,arial,helvetica" SIZE=2>
<TITLE>WBL Team Records</TITLE>
</HEAD>
<H2>Web Baseball League Teams</H2>
<BODY BGCOLOR="#FFFFFF">
<HR>
<P>Click the buttons below to investigate the teams of the Web Baseball League.
<P>
<OBJECT ID="teamlist"
        CLASSID="clsid:333C7BC4-460F-11D0-BC04-0080C7055A83"
        BORDER="0" WIDTH="0" HEIGHT="0">
  <PARAM NAME="DataURL" VALUE="wblteam.txt">
  <PARAM NAME="UseHeader" VALUE="True">
</OBJECT>

<TABLE>
  <TR>
    <TD ALIGN=RIGHT><INPUT TYPE=BUTTON ID=backward VALUE="   <   "></TD>
    <TD ALIGN=LEFT><INPUT TYPE=BUTTON ID=forward VALUE="   >   "></TD>
  </TR>
</TABLE>
<P>
<IMG ID=Picture SRC="Tigers.jpg" BORDER=4 HEIGHT=128 WIDTH=128 ALIGN=LEFT>

<SCRIPT LANGUAGE=VBScript>
function document_onclick()
    Picture.src = team.value + ".jpg"
end function
</SCRIPT>

<TABLE ALIGN=CENTER CELLSPACING=0 CELLPADDING=0>
<TR>
<TD ALIGN=RIGHT VALIGN=TOP><LABEL FOR=team>Team Name: </LABEL></TD>
<TD ALIGN=LEFT VALIGN=TOP WIDTH="10"></TD>
<TD ALIGN=LEFT VALIGN=TOP>
<INPUT ID=team TYPE=text DATASRC=#teamlist DATAFLD="Team"></TD>
</TR>
<TR>
<TD ALIGN=RIGHT VALIGN=TOP><LABEL FOR=wins>Current Number of Wins: </LABEL></TD>
<TD ALIGN=LEFT VALIGN=TOP WIDTH="10"></TD>
<TD ALIGN=LEFT VALIGN=TOP>
<INPUT ID=wins TYPE=text DATASRC=#teamlist DATAFLD="Wins"></TD>
</TR>

<TR>
<TD ALIGN=RIGHT VALIGN=TOP>
<LABEL FOR=losses>Current Number of Losses: </LABEL></TD>
<TD ALIGN=LEFT VALIGN=TOP WIDTH="10"></TD>
<TD ALIGN=LEFT VALIGN=TOP>
<INPUT ID=losses TYPE=text DATASRC=#teamlist DATAFLD="Losses"></TD>
</TR>

<TR>
<TD ALIGN=RIGHT VALIGN=TOP>
<LABEL FOR=BA>Current Team Batting Average: </LABEL></TD>
<TD ALIGN=LEFT VALIGN=TOP WIDTH="10"></TD>
```

*continues*

**Listing 22.3. continued**

```
<TD ALIGN=LEFT VALIGN=TOP>
<INPUT ID=BA TYPE=text DATASRC=#teamlist DATAFLD="BA"></TD>
</TR>

<TR>
<TD ALIGN=RIGHT VALIGN=TOP>
<LABEL FOR=ERA>Current Team Earned Run Average: </LABEL></TD>
<TD ALIGN=LEFT VALIGN=TOP WIDTH="10"></TD>
<TD ALIGN=LEFT VALIGN=TOP>
<INPUT ID=ERA TYPE=text DATASRC=#teamlist DATAFLD="ERA"></TD>
</TR>
</TABLE>

<SCRIPT LANGUAGE=VBSCRIPT>
function backward_onclick()
  if teamlist.recordset.AbsolutePosition > 1 then
    teamlist.recordset.MovePrevious
  else
    msgbox "At First Team"
  end if
end function

function forward_onclick()
  if teamlist.recordset.AbsolutePosition <> teamlist.recordset.RecordCount then
    teamlist.recordset.MoveNext
  else
    msgbox "At Last Team"
  end if
end function
</SCRIPT>
</FONT>
</BODY>
</HTML>
```

The data control object in this example is an ActiveX control that a user can download once from the Internet to extend the capabilities of his or her Web browser. I use the same control in Listing 22.4. The <OBJECT></OBJECT> tag pair includes the data control object in the HTML page. The <OBJECT></OBJECT> pair is the HTML specification's attempt to standardize a tag that encompasses browser-specific tags of the past, such as the <EMBED></EMBED> tag pair that Netscape uses to enable the plug-in architecture in HTML Web pages. Here are the ActiveX control identification lines from Listing 22.3:

```
<OBJECT ID="teamlist"
        CLASSID="clsid:333C7BC4-460F-11D0-BC04-0080C7055A83"
        BORDER="0" WIDTH="0" HEIGHT="0">
  <PARAM NAME="DataURL" VALUE="wblteam.txt">
  <PARAM NAME="UseHeader" VALUE="True">
</OBJECT>
```

**FIGURE 22.4.**
*Dynamic record presentation.*

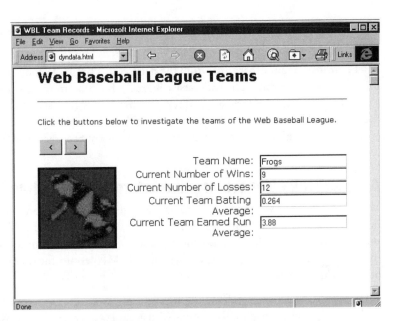

The ID attribute value instantiates teamlist as the data source object. The CLASS_ID attribute value of the <OBJECT> tag is a sophisticated code with embedded security used to select the appropriate ActiveX control for data set management. The control requires two parameters identified in <PARAM> tags with NAME and VALUE attributes. The DataURL parameter supplies to the Web browser the URL of the data source. The UseHeader parameter identifies whether or not to use the header row of the data set as useful information.

The Web page includes a table with two buttons to provide the user with controls to move from team to team. I instantiate both buttons as objects with the ID attribute. I instantiate one button as backward and the other as forward.

I place the bitmap image for the Tigers team logo on the page in an <IMG> tag as an object that the ID=Picture attribute instantiates. The Tigers team information is the first row of the data set wblteam.txt. The document_onclick() function is available to any Web page loaded in a Web browser supporting Dynamic HTML. In this case, I create it to keep the team logo being displayed in agreement with the current data row shown on the Web page. The single line Picture.src = team.value + ".jpg" handles every mouse click on the page for every team. It changes the SRC attribute for the Picture object based on the team field of the current data row. The team field is instantiated with the ID=team attribute of its <INPUT> tag.

The tags for each data set field are similar. For the team field, the connection with the data source is made in the <INPUT ID=team TYPE=text DATASRC=#teamlist DATAFLD="Team"> tag. The TYPE attribute identifies the presentation type for the field. The DATASRC attribute

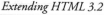
identifies the source of the data. The DATAFLD attribute identifies the field in the data source from which the input box expects to get data.

After I create the four other fields from the data set in a similar fashion, I create two functions for the two user buttons. The backward_onclick() function moves the user back up the data set to the first row. The forward_onclick function moves the user down the data set rows to the last row. The fact that the functions start with the same string as existing instantiated objects is critical. Unless you use exactly the same strings of backward and forward, the function would not be valid.

# Automatically Generating and Interactively Sorting Table Rows

With Dynamic HTML, you can automatically generate tables from data sets. As Dynamic HTML creates and places the table on the Web page, the rest of the Web page continues to present its content. Table generation does not stop a user from continuing to read further down the page. After the table is generated, Dynamic HTML permits the user to sort the table based on any field in the table.

The example in Listing 22.4 dynamically produces a table on a Web page based on the current standing data source that a URL on the Web accesses. Users can access Web Baseball League standings on a daily basis in this manner and can sort the standings based on team name, wins, losses, batting averages, and earned run averages (ERA). In the future, the WBL intends to develop the page further to present individual player statistics and daily box scores. Figure 22.5 shows the Web page after table generation.

**Listing 22.4. An example of dynamic sorting.**

```
<HTML>
<BODY TOPMARGIN=0 LEFTMARGIN=40 BGCOLOR= "#FFFFFF" LINK= "#000066"
VLINK= "#666666" TEXT= "#000000">
<FONT FACE="verdana,arial,helvetica" SIZE=2>
<HEAD><TITLE>WBL Current Standings</TITLE></HEAD>
<H2>WBL Current Standings</H2>
<HR>
<P>
<OBJECT ID="teamlist"
       CLASSID="clsid:333C7BC4-460F-11D0-BC04-0080C7055A83"
        ALIGN="baseline" BORDER="0" WIDTH="0" HEIGHT="0">
    <PARAM NAME="DataURL" VALUE="wblteam.txt">
    <PARAM NAME="UseHeader" VALUE="True">
</OBJECT>

This Table is Sortable By Clicking on the Column Header<P>
<TABLE BORDER="1" ID="elemtbl" DATASRC="#teamlist">
<THEAD>
<TR>
<TD><FONT COLOR="#0000FF"><B><U><DIV ID=team>Team</DIV></U></B></FONT></TD>
<TD><FONT COLOR="#0000FF"><B><U><DIV ID=wins>Wins</DIV></U></B></FONT></TD>
```

```
<TD><FONT COLOR="#0000FF"><B><U><DIV ID=losses>Losses</DIV></U></B></FONT></TD>
<TD><FONT COLOR="#0000FF"><B><U><DIV ID=BA>Batting Avg</DIV></U></B></FONT></TD>
<TD><FONT COLOR="#0000FF"><B><U><DIV ID=ERA>ERA</DIV></U></B></FONT></TD>
</TR>
</THEAD>
<TBODY>
<TR>
<TD><SPAN DATAFLD="Team"></SPAN></TD>
<TD><DIV DATAFLD="Wins"></DIV></TD>
<TD><SPAN DATAFLD="Losses"></SPAN></TD>
<TD><DIV DATAFLD="BA"></DIV></TD>
<TD><DIV DATAFLD="ERA"></DIV></TD>
</TR>
</TBODY></TABLE>

<SCRIPT LANGUAGE="VBSCRIPT">
function team_onclick()
  teamlist.SortColumn = "Team"
  teamlist.Reset()
end function

function wins_onclick()
  teamlist.SortColumn = "Wins"
  teamlist.Reset()
end function

function losses_onclick()
  teamlist.SortColumn = "Losses"
  teamlist.Reset()
end function

function ba_onclick()
  teamlist.SortColumn = "BA"
  teamlist.Reset()
end function

function era_onclick()
  teamlist.SortColumn = "ERA"
  teamlist.Reset()
end function
</SCRIPT>
<HR>
</FONT>
</BODY>
</HTML>
```

Again, an <OBJECT></OBJECT> tag pair identifies the data control as it was previously reviewed in Listing 22.3. The table is set up to autogenerate through the DATASRC="#teamlist" attribute of the <TABLE> tag and the use of the DATAFLD attribute for each <DIV> or <SPAN> tag in the second row of the table definition. Through the DATAFLD attribute, each cell in the second row of the table identifies its respective data set field.

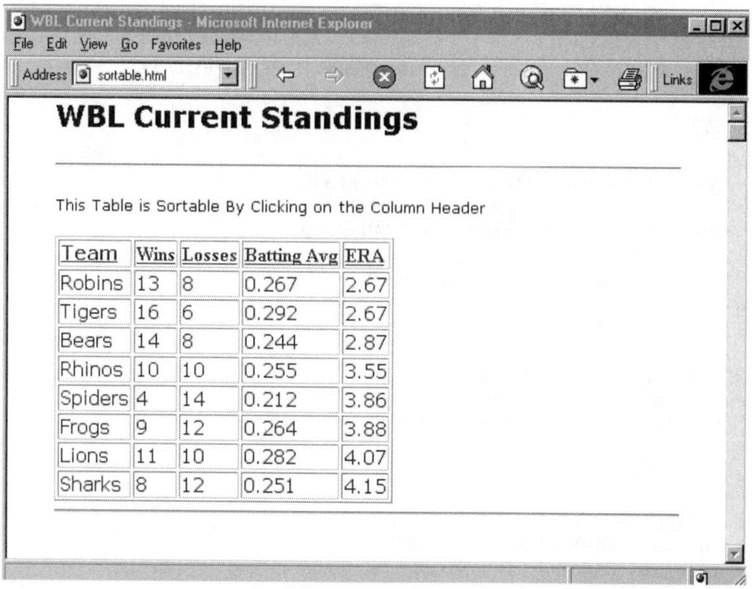

**FIGURE 22.5.**

*Dynamic standings sorting.*

When specifying the first row of the table, the ID attribute of the <DIV> tag instantiates each cell as an object. The value for each ID attribute is used as the value of the SortColumn attribute of the teamlist data source object for its respective function. Within each onclick function, the Reset() method is called for the teamlist object, which performs the sort based on its current SortColumn attribute value.

Sorting simple league standings is a straightforward use of the technology. The four examples presented in Listings 22.1, 22.2, 22.3, and 22.4 present features that you can mix and match on the same Web page to produce some elaborate, yet manageable, results. Listing 22.5 presents the simple text file used as the data set source of Listings 22.3 and 22.4.

**Listing 22.5. The contents of wblteam.txt.**

```
Team,Wins:INT,Losses:INT,BA:FLOAT,ERA:FLOAT
Tigers,16,6,.292,2.67
Bears,14,8,.244,2.87
Robins,13,8,.267,2.67
Lions,11,10,.282,4.07
Rhinos,10,10,.255,3.55
Frogs,9,12,.264,3.88
Sharks,8,12,.251,4.15
Spiders,4,14,.212,3.86
```

# The Future of Dynamic HTML

Dynamic HTML intends for the features provided in this chapter to simplify compound Web-based document composition into a single file format. By providing a reasonable object model and common event handling in the Web page itself, HTML can stand on its own to deliver powerful information content.

The presentation in Chapter 31, "VRML Primer," reflects a phenomenon in which other technologies have been developed for integration with VRML to add functionality not covered by the standard. VRML supporters continue to present enhancements to incorporate the best inventions into the standard itself. Now, with Dynamic HTML, the HTML standard might be following a similar course. The functionality of plug-in applications has added tremendous value to the presentation of Web-accessed information in a Web browser. HTML supporters should continue to find ways to integrate those ideas into the HTML standard itself. Because things move so rapidly on the Web, it makes sense that both HTML and VRML should vigorously continue to entertain new enhancements. Dynamic HTML is a big step forward in providing a vision for HTML-based interactivity, just as the VRML 2 standard is a big step forward in providing a vision for VRML-based interactivity. By the time bandwidth is no longer an issue, the standards should be there to support the development of technologies imagined by optimistic visionaries.

# Summary

Dynamic HTML is an enhancement to HTML that adds interactivity and dynamic changes to the Web page. Using the Dynamic HTML syntax, Web authors can compete with CD-ROM titles and traditional business applications to provide value on the Web that the home and office markets demand. Dynamic HTML instantiates Web page components through the ID attribute, which is used with many HTML tags. After a component is instantiated, user events can trigger changes to the component such as font, style sheet, size, and (x,y,z) location changes.

Dynamic HTML manages data awareness that enables Web pages to filter and sort a data set accessed over the Web. This chapter showed two powerful examples of data awareness in Listings 22.4 and 22.5.

Finally, Dynamic HTML allows for wholesale addition and deletion of HTML tags and text through a document object that is always instantiated for the active Web page. With a substantial number of events from which to choose and the power to swap tags in and out, it might take a while until the best uses of Dynamic HTML emerge. Perhaps this is just the start of a new growth for HTML syntax. An interested reader can keep up to date by finding helpful references on Web sites at Microsoft (`http://www.microsoft.com`), the World Wide Web Consortium (`http://www.w3.org`), and Netscape (`www.netscape.com`).

**22**

**DYNAMIC HTML**

# IV
## PART

# Effective Web Page Design Using HTML

# CHAPTER 23

# Interface Design

*by Michael A. Larson*

## IN THIS CHAPTER

Knowing the HTML tags and their attributes fills only part of the toolbox that you need to build Web pages. Your next step will be to learn how to utilize HTML and related tools to build usable, good-looking, and fast-loading Web pages that effectively fulfill the purpose of your Web site. In many ways, designing Web pages is akin to home construction. To build a house you would use many similar tools and materials: wood, concrete, sheet rock, nails, paint, and so on. Yet there is an almost infinite variety in floor plans and architecture.

In the four chapters of Part IV, "Effective Web Page Design Using HTML," you will learn the techniques for producing clear, informative, easy-to-navigate, and entertaining Web pages.

This chapter deals with the interface of your Web page, so let's assume that someone has decided to visit your Web site. This person might be coming in through the front door—that is, your home page (`index.html`, `default.htm`, `welcome.html`, and so on)—or she might be coming in through a side door, probably from one of the Internet search engines such as Alta Vista, Lycos, or HotBot. It's likely this person also has a mission in mind—to find information or be entertained—or she could simply be curious.

No matter how people get to your Web site or why they come, they must immediately understand what they are looking at when your page loads, or even during the process of loading. They have to know where they are, what that means in relation to their mission, and where they need to go if they can't accomplish their mission on this first page. If you have a good interface design, your visitors will immediately find their information or know where to get it in as few steps as possible. If your visitors can't understand what to do next to accomplish what they came for, they might leave your site frustrated or disappointed—and you have failed in your mission as a Web site designer, whether that is selling a product or distributing important information. Success on a Web site means getting people to visit, making their visit productive, and having them return. To accomplish this, you must pay close attention to a critical factor: interface design.

In this chapter, you will see what elements you need to think about as you brainstorm your Web site theme. You'll also learn about some of the major components of interface design, including controls, color, and style. By combining all these elements, you will be able to build an attractive, utilitarian, and consistent interface into your Web site that will never leave your visitors feeling confused or lost.

# What Is Interface Design?

Interfaces are everywhere, incorporated into items you use every day. The dashboard, pedals, gear shift, and steering wheel on your car comprise the interface between you and the essential mechanisms in your vehicle that must work together to get you places every day. The remote control is the interface between you and your evening of entertainment at home after work. Books have an interface (words, ink, and paper) for optimal communication of written material. Even your washer and dryer have an interface. Many of the items you use every day have interfaces. If you think about it, you don't even notice many of these interfaces, because they are so simple and intuitive to use—like a light switch. When you design an interface for your Web site, you want it to be intuitive and natural. A good interface is

- Easy to use. A visitor can tell at a glance the function of each section of a Web page and intuitively know what to do next.
- Always available without being intrusive. Important items are placed within easy reach.
- Immediately understandable. Everything is logically arranged and well organized in relation to the purpose of your site.

A well-designed interface also can be

- Entertaining or interesting. For instance, having an unusual image in the middle of a business site can coax visitors to see parts of your company that they normally would pass up.
- Colorful or beautiful and nonirritating. Images enhance text and vice versa. Animated GIFs can be irritating to many people trying to read text on a page.

An example of an attractive and useful interface is found on the Microsoft SiteBuilder site (`http://www.microsoft.com/sitebuilder`) as shown in Figure 23.1.

**FIGURE 23.1.**

*The Microsoft SiteBuilder home page. When the mouse passes over a menu option, the color of the menu text changes.*

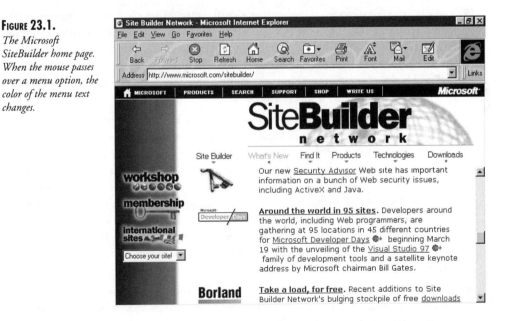

Underneath the SiteBuilder logo at the top of the page is a series of six text choices with small arrows beneath them. When the mouse passes over one of the words, the text color changes from black to light blue, indicating that the choice is available for selection if the mouse is clicked.

This is an excellent example of a successful interface. Visitors have nothing new to learn and the interface is always there—at least as long as you stay in the SiteBuilder section of the Microsoft site. The text defining each choice is clear; there are no cryptic icons to decipher. The color change is also attractive and provides some minor entertainment. This enhanced functionality is added with Visual Basic Scripting. Similar functionality (that uses completely different technology) can also be added with Macromedia Flash or Director Shockwave plug-ins.

The first thing you have to keep in mind when designing your interface is the medium of your method: Your Web site will be read off a screen, most likely a PC monitor, although it could be anything from a television screen to a simple PDA (personal digital assistant) LCD (liquid crystal display) screen. You might also want to keep in mind that the contents of any given Web page may also be printed, but this should be of secondary concern in most cases. Here are some characteristics of screen technology that you need to keep in mind:

- Most monitors and TV screens have color capabilities, but to varying degrees. Many PC systems are limited to 256 colors, whereas TV signals are 24-bit or true color (I'll talk more about color models later). Many PCs are also capable of 24-bit color display, but you don't know what a visitor to your site may be using. If you think some of your visitors will come in through the PDA avenue, consider how your site will look on a PDA.

- The sharpness of different screens varies significantly. Most PC monitors have a much higher resolution than TV, but TV gains a higher level of apparent resolution from its fast frame rate. The graphic you just designed may look great on the high-resolution, small-dot-pitch monitor you are using in True color mode, but how much information will be lost from your graphic for people using poorer-quality monitors or TVs, or fewer than 16 million colors (24-bit color)?

- Screen sizes and resolutions also vary significantly. TV screens come in sizes from 2-inch portable LCD displays to 56-inch or greater monster rear-projection units. PC monitors and graphics cards also have a wide range of resolutions. The baseline resolution for many systems is 640×480 pixels, but higher resolutions are also common, including 800×600, 1024×768, and upward. Monitor sizes also vary from 14 inches for PCs and 12 inches for the Macintosh, through 21 inches. (Larger monitors are also in use, but they are much less common due to their expense.) Additionally, you have to think about laptop screens. Some are strictly grayscale (or only black-and-white) LCD screens, some have color, some are dual-scan, and some have the brighter active-matrix screens.

- Most monitors and TVs have brightness, contrast, and color controls that may or may not be properly adjusted. Will all elements of your Web pages still be visible and usable under less-than-ideal conditions?

As a Web designer, you have to write to a medium that you cannot completely control or define. People creating print documents have exquisite control over their paper and ink, so they can control every part of their information. TV producers also program to the constant standard of color TV resolution (with a nice decay to the black-and-white standard) and have a high level of control over what their content will look like. The WWW presents a unique challenge for the Web designer: access from multiple devices with different characteristics. What this means is that your Web page interface has to be readable/understandable under a variety of conditions. You must have a rugged, simple design in order to reach the widest possible audience.

So with your medium in mind, how do you design an effective interface? First of all, don't reinvent the wheel. Much interface design research and development has already been done by software manufacturers, and you have seen their results in Windows, Macintosh, OS/2, and UNIX X-Windows. They use a variety of interface controls to allow the user to interact with software and hardware on the computer. Some useful lessons can be learned from these common operating systems.

# Brainstorming Your Site Theme

The most important component of designing your interface controls is laying a solid foundation for your Web site. This involves setting a Web site theme. A theme is a combination of colors, imagery, and styles that sets the tone of your Web site. A theme is often noticed on both a conscious and subconscious level. Setting a Web theme is a multistep process:

1. Set the goals of your Web site.
2. Define the audience you want to address with the content of your site.
3. Outline the content you want to place on your Web site.
4. Define the look and feel of your Web site.

## Setting Your Site Goals

Your site goals can have goals as simple as "I want to tell the world about me" or as complex as "I want a commercial site for selling products, distributing a wide variety of company information, interacting with customers and suppliers, and incorporating support for multiple databases." The key is to clearly define your goals. Get as much input from as many people as possible at this stage. The clearer your goals, the easier it will be to build your Web site.

Here are some questions that you might want to ask to determine your goals:

- Why am I creating this Web site?
- Do I want to concentrate on a single goal or multiple goals? Why? If I decide on multiple goals, what are they, and how can I make them distinct from one another?
- Will these goals always be the same, or will they change over time? How will this influence the Web site, its initial design, and its future maintenance?

You might want to write down as many ideas as possible and then rewrite them clearly and concisely, discarding and narrowing choices as you go along. You will also want to do your first reality check: Are adequate resources available to accomplish the goals set forth? Obviously, you will need to balance your goals with your resources. It is also a good idea at this point to set up a tentative time frame for getting everything done, and see how that reflects on the original set of goals. You might want to design a complex, multitiered site but start out by erecting only a simple site and building on it over time.

An excellent example of using a site to meet multiple goals at a corporation is the Novartis site, which can be found at `http://www.novartis.com`. Their corporate goals are listed on the page entitled Who We Are (at `http://www.novartis.com/weare/index.html`).

If you go back to the company's graphical home page (at `http://www.novartis.com/index2.cgi?4`), you will notice that all its corporate goals have their own link. The company's corporate identity is accurately reflected by its Web site.

## Defining Your Audience

After defining the "why" of your Web site, you need to decide which audience to build it for. Your goals will make this step fairly easy. If you're setting up a commercial site for selling products, you should design your site to appeal to the profile of your typical customers. If you are putting up a home page, you might want to decide on a more broad cross-section of the Internet audience. Here are some audience characteristics to keep in mind:

- **Age.** Do you want to appeal to a narrow age group (children, teenagers, the elderly, and so on) with your Web site content or have an "ageless" format that appeals to everyone?

- **Language.** Do you need a multilingual site—with an English version and a Japanese version, for instance—or will one language reach most of your desired audience?

- **Culture or subculture.** People from different cultures will see things differently from how you see them as the Web page author. (This is especially true of icons.) One way to address the widest audience is to avoid slang.

- **Affluence.** If your business is going after sales to a particular income group via the Web, your Web page designs should be crafted to appeal only to this group.

- **Educational sophistication.** If your Web site is scientific or technical in nature, you might want to make sure textual content is very high and graphical content is low to emphasize your theme.

- **Estimated attention span.** For a broad audience, this could be just about anything, and the best thing you can do is to make sure your Web pages load fast. For a narrower audience, try to design your pages to fit what you think the audience's average attention span might be.

Any or all of these audience characteristics may be relevant. Knowing your audience will help you as you write your content, build your interface controls, and design the look and feel of your site. Keeping a particular person in mind when you are actually building site components will help you build a consistent site. (How would so-and-so see this? Would so-and-so understand this? Is this clear enough for so-and-so?) Getting feedback from people who fit your audience type at this stage in the process can be invaluable for deciding on content, writing style, and appealing imagery, and it can have a significant bearing on the ultimate success of your site.

For instance, the Novartis site is primarily aimed at a broad audience of adults around the world. It is geared to be informational, rather than entertaining, in nature. The interface (found at `http://www.novartis.com/agri/index.html`) reflects this in terms of the simple graphics chosen and the wording of the text.

Also note that Novartis attempts to appeal to the widest browser-type audience by allowing the user to choose a text-only or graphical version of the Web site from its home page (at `http://www.novartis.com`).

## Outlining Your Content

Now that you know the purpose of your site and your audience, you need to organize and define the content of your site. It is very tempting to dive right in and start experimenting with graphics and styles and fonts after you've gone through the first two planning steps. Try to hold off for just a bit longer and write the outline for your content.

Write down each major topic and subtopic. Decide whether you want to make each major topic a separate Web page (which is recommended) and how many subtopics deserve their own page. You might want to start diagramming your entire Web site as a way to organize your thoughts. This gives you some idea of how much effort will be needed to flesh out the content of the site. Start considering whether some content can best be addressed by hyperlinking to another site, and also what level of detail you want for the content of each section.

## Designing the Look and Feel of Your Web Site

This is the stage at which you pour your own personality or your company image into the Web site. If someone visits your Web site and then visits your company in the real world, he or she should immediately feel familiar with the surroundings. You want to communicate not only the hard-wired side of your company or self (logo, product, name, store locations, and so on), but also the qualities that make you unique, and any qualities or accomplishments of which you are particularly proud. Your Web site is the place to strut your stuff. Let the whole world know you are proud of your unique identity by using it to influence the look and feel of your Web site.

You can use all the tools that HTML has available to project your image onto a Web site. This means selecting appropriate fonts, colors, and graphics. For a company, these might revolve around existing objects that already are used in print or other media. For an individual, it might be your favorite colors or the colors of something that means a lot to you, such as your favorite football team or flower. Also, when you think about color, don't forget black and white. You can create some very dramatic and compelling content with these colors.

Now that you have outlined your site, its content, and its image, you can design your interface controls as the finishing pieces. Decide whether you will be using photos, illustration, text, or some combination of these. If you make extensive use of hyperlinked images or image maps in your interface, decide whether you also want to include complementary text hyperlinks. Because text hyperlinks load so much more quickly than images, these are prized by Web surfers who know exactly where they want to go. Also note that up to 30 percent of people surf the Web with graphics turned off in their browsers, and graphically challenged browsers are still used. Again, know your audience.

If you are using a template file to prepare all your Web pages, you need to prepare your interface graphics or hyperlinked text interface and place them on the template properly before preparing the remaining graphics on the site. You can do this before or after you have fleshed out the text content of the site. I don't recommend preparing the remainder of the graphics for your site until all or most of the text content has been written and finalized. This will save you from having to redo any graphics if a new and compelling idea is suggested by the text.

Consider the Novartis site again. What look and feel do you think Novartis is using for its site and why? In my opinion (because I haven't talked with the Novartis Webmaster), the site uses a paper-brochure paradigm. White space is heavily used, and the pages are very simple and uncluttered. The idea, I think, is to emphasize a small amount of important information rather than overwhelm the reader with too many facts and figures.

# Interface Controls

Interface controls have two elements: hardware elements and software elements (menus, buttons, dialog boxes, and so on).

For hardware elements, most people will be interacting with the controls in any given Web site interface via the keyboard and some type of pointing device, usually a mouse. The mouse is greatly favored by both Web surfers and Web designers as the primary means of interaction on a Web site. As a Web designer, however, you should also make any controls on a page accessible via the keyboard, if possible, for those few users who don't have a pointing device or for those who might have difficulty using one. Usually the Tab key, Spacebar, and arrow keys step a user through a set of controls or menus. Keep in mind that Java applets or other specialty programs (such as the Visual Basic scripting program mentioned earlier) may only be interactive via the mouse.

The software elements that make up interface controls are by far the most important part of interface design. Most operating systems today are based on a GUI (Graphical User Interface) design that contains the following common elements:

- ■ Menus, usually drop-down
- ■ Toolbars
- ■ Standard dialog boxes for messages
- ■ Controls in dialog boxes for data entry or choice selection
- ■ Onscreen buttons that perform one or more actions
- ■ Icons to represent programs or processes
- ■ Resizable, named windows, usually one window per process or program, usually with scrollbars
- ■ Sound or animations associated with system events
- ■ Fonts for displaying text
- ■ Some way to assign colors, fonts, or styles to various GUI elements

These elements have been around for more than a decade in most major computer operating systems. The other predominant interface, the command-line text interface, is still used in operating systems but is of lesser importance to the Web designer because most Web site access these days is through GUI-based browsers sporting the preceding list of controls.

Unfortunately, there is no way to universally implement many of the interface controls found in GUI operating systems from a Web site. Menus, dialog boxes, associating sounds or animations with events, and other common GUI elements can be added to a Web site via Java, JavaScript, or ActiveX. Not all browsers, however, support part or all of these elements (Internet Explorer comes closest at the present time), so you end up having to build two sites: one that supports the GUI controls, and a second that uses standard HTML elements.

Toolbars and icons can be difficult to implement on a Web site because of a lack of context. Many toolbars are icons only, and without some previous experience, a visitor could be unsure of their meaning. If you're sure that the icons will be understood, you can use image maps to duplicate the toolbar function.

Dialog boxes with data entry fields can be duplicated, without the free-floating characteristic, with HTML forms. This is also true of radio buttons, check boxes, and drop-down list boxes.

For other GUI elements, to some degree, you can duplicate multiple open windows of various sizes by spawning multiple copies of a browser or by using frames. To get around the problem of whether a particular font is present on a user's machine, you can use graphical text, although this quickly becomes bandwidth intensive if overused. As cascading style sheets become more common (and if a Web fonting standard is ever established), this problem will disappear.

For instance, Figure 23.2 shows the use of the GUI menu paradigm on the main page of the Fractal Design Corporation Web site (at `http://www.fractal.com`).

FIGURE 23.2.

*The main menu on the Fractal Design Corporation home page.*

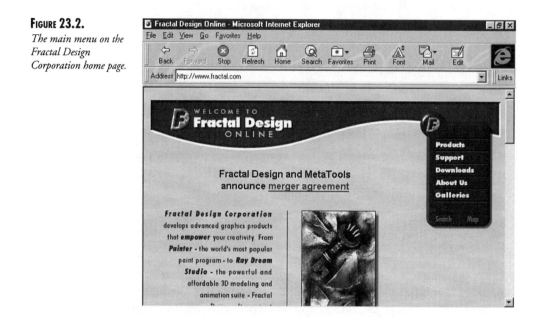

If you elect to go to the Products page, the menu changes; the color of the text, Products, changes from white to yellow, which appears as a different shade of gray in Figure 23.3.

FIGURE 23.3.

*The Fractal Design Corporation Products page menu.*

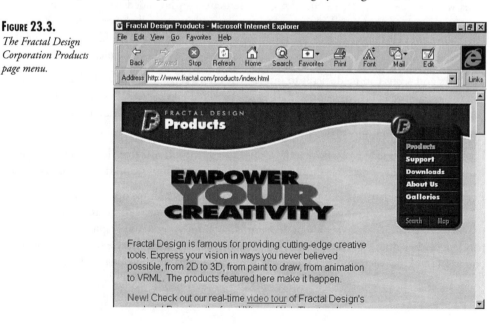

Using standard HTML, Fractal Design has made a GUI-style menu and has been able to demonstrate a menu selection by changing the color of the graphical text. Using common GUI paradigms means that the visitor does not have to spend time figuring out controls and can pay more attention to your content.

Note that the Fractal Design Corporation menu also displays several other characteristics of a good interface control: First, the menu selections are clearly labeled; there is no ambiguity about where you will go when you choose a selection. The menu itself is easy to find in the upper-right corner of the page. The menu design also fits the look and feel of the rest of the page. Also note that the menu has enough contrast to be easily identified against the rest of the page. This is especially essential for laptops, PDAs, or other computers with limited colors or resolution.

> **NOTE**
>
> If you want GUI controls that can't be crafted in HTML, you can build or obtain custom-built controls using Java Applets or ActiveX controls and get the exact control you want with much greater functionality. The disadvantage to this approach is that Java is not supported by many older browsers and ActiveX is currently supported only by Microsoft browsers. Using either can also lead to much larger Web page sizes, slowing page loading time for your visitors. Some security and certification issues are also left to be ironed out for ActiveX controls. As faster access to the Internet becomes available and fixes are made for security problems, using Java and ActiveX to customize your site will become a much more attractive option.

Keep the following concepts in mind when you are thinking about which interface control elements to place on your Web site:

- Unlike an operating system GUI, most of the action on a Web site involves moving the surfer from Web page to Web page or from one part of a page to another. Most controls in your Web site interface will be heavily navigational. Most of the controls in an operating system GUI revolve around modifying some element or initiating some action within an open program, rather than taking a user from program to program.

- Make your controls' functions obvious. Although icon-style graphics on buttons may look attractive, icons can have vastly different meanings to different people. (Remember, the Internet is a global, cross-cultural phenomenon.) Thus, your controls' functions will be clearer if you use text alone or text plus an image to label them.

- You can place your controls just about anywhere on a page. Your choice of location depends on how available you want your controls to be and how the location fits in with the rest of the page. Many people place their prime controls at the top of the page, as you've seen in earlier figures from the Microsoft SiteBuilder site and the Fractal Design Corporation site. It is also common to place a master menu on the left side, both with and without frames.

- The size of your controls in relation to the rest of your page can also vary greatly. If you make your controls too large, they might overshadow other important content on your page. Making them too small means that they might be difficult to find or read. Size your controls for clarity and usefulness.

- Your decision on whether to have multiple sets of controls or menus on the same page depends on the complexity of your site and the number of interactive elements in it. For instance, a very large site, such as the Microsoft home page, shown in Figure 23.4, has a consistent set of controls across the top of every page, each pointing to a different, major function (such as searching) or section. The pages within a section are further indexed by a menu off to the left. No matter what system of controls you decide on, keep them consistent throughout your Web site for optimal clarity.

**FIGURE 23.4.**

*The Microsoft home page demonstrating the placement and use of multiple menu systems necessary for a large, complex site.*

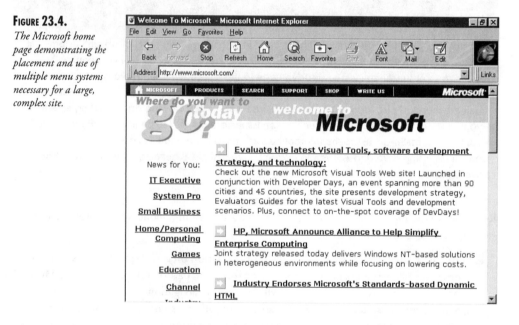

The controls you use on your site should probably take up only a small part of any given Web page and should complement the colors and the style or mood of your Web site.

# Using Color in Your Interface

Color is both the complement and the contrast you need for your interface controls. Effective use of color will give people the visual cues they need to quickly be aware of your interface controls, as well as blend them attractively with the rest of your Web site. Although having good instincts about color is helpful, you should also know how color is defined and used on the WWW.

The first thing you have to learn about is color models. There are two major models—one for the print world, CMYK (cyan-magenta-yellow-black), and one for displays, RGB (red-green-blue). There are also several other important models, but for the purposes of designing Web pages, the RGB model is the one that merits examination. In the RGB model, each color is expressed as a combination of red, green, and blue in either decimal or hexadecimal notation. Whenever color is used in an HTML page, such as designating the color of the font, it is in hexadecimal. For instance, pure red is `FF0000`; each pair of digits represents the red, green, and blue components of each color, respectively. White is `FFFFFF`, and black is `000000` (the absence of any color). Some paint and graphics programs designate each RGB component using decimal notation, so you will need a conversion calculator if you want to apply a particular color from an image to a font or to the HTML page background. You can find online hex-to-decimal (and vice versa) conversions at `http://sicg.calstate.edu/htmlcase/`. You can also find a nice table listing all 216 colors of the Web palette and their hex and decimal equivalents at `http://babeard.simplenet.com/decimal.htm`.

When you are working with a video card displaying 24-bit color, all RGB combinations are available for use. In the Web world, however, many browsers use a 216-color palette called the "Web" or "Netscape" palette. Whenever possible, you should limit your GIF images to these 216 colors (you cannot change the palette in JPG files; they are 24-bit color by definition) for optimal display. Pixels present in an image that are not one of the 216 colors in the palette are dithered. You want optimal control over the appearance of your image rather than depending on a dithering algorithm, so stick with the 216-color palette. Most paint or graphics programs have the Netscape palette built into them.

You can do an entire study on how colors influence people's perception of an image. For instance, red and orange are warm colors that immediately draw people's attention. Blues are cooler, more distant colors. Colors also have a cultural element. In the United States, for instance, brown is associated with soil, nature, and wholesome goodness. Mostly, however, you will want to use color to enhance the appearance of your Web site. As with menu elements, be consistent with the use of color throughout your site. If you choose to use colored text, make sure it contrasts well with its background for easy readability.

Now that you know what colors you have available, how do you choose which colors to apply to your interface controls? Because the interface controls are closely tied to the overall style of your site, you usually let your site style be your guide. You want your interface controls to be recognizable as controls and yet not detract from the layout or appearance of your site by being too utilitarian. For instance, if your site has a desert theme, you could have an image map control that imitates a red rock canyon color to stay within the same theme and provide contrast. You want enough contrast to your controls that people know what they are, but you don't want them to be "other-worldly"—that is, outside of your site's theme. Also, be consistent with the color themes you choose for your controls throughout the site. If you want to tell people what page they are on by "graying out" or changing the color of the menu choice, make sure the color is different enough that it stands out from the remainder of the menu choices. Try not to use subtle shades in this situation; they might be missed by visitors who have poorer resolution displays or fewer colors.

# Incorporating an Image Style

Another part of your interface is the selection of an image style. An image style is merely a definition of how you want to use images to enhance the overall theme or content of your site. If you have a site about astronomy, your images will probably be of various heavenly bodies and spacecraft. The style of the images that you use for controls can vary greatly, depending on your site's tone and intended audience. You can use illustrations of heavenly bodies for the controls, even though much of the content of your site will be actual photos of space phenomena.

How you choose the style of the images and text you use for your controls depends on the content of your site and how you want to communicate that content. Consider these questions:

- Do you want to be formal or informal, even playful, in your approach? If you are being more formal, as in the Novartis site discussed earlier in this chapter, you should choose images with the same tone. On the other hand, if you are authoring an e-zine (electronic magazine) for teenagers, you can use much more outrageous material.

- What audience are you aiming for? Everyone? A particular age group? Use images attractive to your intended audiences.

- Do you want to use photographic images or clip art? Which is more readily available and easier for you to use? Which works better with your site theme? If you're putting together a site about mountain climbing, having a picture gallery of the highest mountains in the world makes more sense than using clip art. If you are putting up an instructional Web page, you might be able to spice it up with some clip art to add variety, especially if your topic is a bit dry. Remember to respect the copyrights on any images you use on your Web site.

- How does the placement of your interface controls on the page influence whether you can use text only, images, or both? Usually placing your controls won't interfere with the rest of your Web page content. The main consideration is that you don't want your controls to be hard to find because of too much clutter on the page.

After you've decided on an image style, you will usually find it easier to settle on a particular file format for generating your interface controls. If you will be using fewer colors, such as illustrations, the GIF format will give you the smallest image size with the highest quality. This is especially helpful if you will be using graphical text (text that is built in a graphics program and exported as a bitmap graphic), because this will give you crisper text. Using JPG files in this situation will blur your text. On the other hand, if you will be using photographs or photo-realistic images, you will usually get smaller file sizes with JPG compression and the blurring effect of this file format will not be as apparent.

A new file format, PNG (Portable Network Graphics), has been approved for use on the WWW, and support for it should start with version 4 of both the Netscape and Microsoft browsers. This file format will address many of the shortcomings found in the GIF format. JPG will still probably be the format of choice for photographs. PNG will support up to 48-bit color (GIF supports only 8-bit); a good, lossless compression algorithm; an alpha channel (for transparency and other effects); and a gamma correction feature to compensate for gamma differences between platforms for improved image appearance. PNG can also be used freely without a license, unlike the GIF format that is now owned by Unisys. The use of PNG probably will not become widespread on the WWW until more of the older browsers go out of circulation. This format will probably eventually supplant the GIF format on the WWW with its superior features and free licensing. You can obtain more information on PNG at `http://www.w3.org/Graphics/PNG/Overview.html`.

---

**TIP**

If you currently use a graphics editor that supports PNG (such as Adobe Photoshop) to edit or produce the graphics for your Web site, you can get ahead of the game by saving a copy of your graphics files as PNG before you reduce colors for GIF conversion or increase compression for JPGs. Then when PNG becomes more common, you need to just upload the PNG files, change the file extensions in your HTML files, and you're immediately up to date.

---

**23**

**INTERFACE DESIGN**

# Summary

Defining your site's interface involves deciding what controls you need and how best to make them easily understood and readily available to all visitors to your Web site. The design of your interface controls should be tightly integrated with the style of your site. Because the majority of interface controls on a Web site are navigational, make sure it is clear where they lead. Make sure your interface is both consistent and attractive, even if you just use hyperlinked text interface controls. Spend as much time as possible thinking about control placement and how the controls relate to the content of your site. Build your interface controls based on the GUI paradigm for maximum familiarity. A lost or confused surfer is not a happy surfer, no matter how beautiful your controls are.

# CHAPTER 24

# Layout Design

*by Michael A. Larson*

## IN THIS CHAPTER

In the print and desktop publishing world, page layout is an art form. You can literally craft documents with sub-millimeter precision to obtain that perfect integration of text and graphics. You have access to myriad fonts and tools for touching them up, or even creating new ones. Control over text is unparalleled. You can control the placement of each letter, the distance between each letter (kerning) and line (leading), and easily add drop-caps and callouts. Then there's the color and picture elements. You can control colors almost exactly (with the help of a good print shop) and nudge and size graphics to place them precisely on the page for maximum impact. On top of all of this, you have exact control over the type of ink and paper. A wide array of tools is available to perform these many tasks, all with many powerful and time-saving features.

Layout for Web pages is, unfortunately, not in such an advanced state of development as printed page layout. Mainly, this is because of the nature of the medium of Web pages (computer screens rather than paper) and the current status of HTML. Also, many users have only 256 colors available on their monitor. Additionally, most monitors are not color calibrated against a color standard. A Web designer simply cannot expect to achieve an exact and reproducible effect on everyone's monitor. HTML was also never designed to be a precise page layout language, but it is certainly evolving in that direction. As such, it is necessary to use several clever workarounds to achieve maximum page layout control. If you're used to exacting page layout control, you will need to lower your expectations a bit or wait until enough browsers support cascading style sheets (CSS) on the WWW. (See Chapter 19, "Introducing Cascading Style Sheets," or Chapter 20, "Cascading Style Sheet Usage.")

You need to remember three things when laying out pages in HTML:

- HTML is relatively new and continually developing. Paper has been around since the Egyptians laid papyrus reeds next to each other for scrolls. HTML has been around for less than 10 years.

- HTML is universal. The language was designed for the lowest common denominator (see next point) so that it could be used by the greatest number of people. Although this is great for communication (and actually fueled the Internet explosion), it is bad news for the sophisticated desktop publisher or artist.

- Computers are not universal. The world is in a sad state of affairs. We have mainframes, minicomputers, UNIX workstations, Macintoshes, PCs (DOS and Windows), and many assorted "miscellaneous" computers of all kinds of different flavors, ages, and capabilities. Some still use monochromatic monitors, and some still don't even have hard drives or wheeze along on a 20MB monster. But they all share one commonality: the capability to run a browser.

This is the "paper" you will be printing to. It is inconsistent and is ever-changing. Screen sizes, screen resolutions, and color support can vary dramatically—and that is just for the one company's computers. The art of page layout in HTML is trying to take some of the design principles from the print world and use them to maximize communication in this chaotic situation.

This chapter reviews the typical elements that you will lay out on an HTML page, including text, fonts, graphics, and other multimedia. You'll see what you can do with HTML page structure without using tables, and then you'll see why tables are a godsend for page layout and how to maximize their use, including nested tables. You'll also look at crafting all of the content on an HTML page as an image in a separate paint or illustration program, and then piecing it together using HTML tables. The chapter ends with a discussion of the way CSS will make many of these page-layout workarounds unnecessary as it ushers in a new age of Web page design.

# Layout Elements

Just as in the print world, you are usually faced with a blank page when you open your favorite HTML editor. You need to fill this page with some or all of the elements available to an HTML author. Here's a list of many of the elements that are available for building a Web page:

- Text
- Fonts
- Style sheets
- Static graphics
- Animated or moving images
- Page background
- Tables
- Sound
- Programming and form elements
- Hyperlinks
- Page dimensions
- Specialty elements available only via a browser plug-in

Most of the preceding elements are covered in depth in other chapters in this book, so in this chapter, I simply review how each element influences page layout and some of the things you need to keep in mind as you're laying out a coherent and attractive Web page.

## Text Elements

The core of most HTML pages is the textual content. Most people will probably be visiting your Web site because they want to read what you or your company has to say about certain items of interest to them. This is not a book on writing copy, so I can't help you write text. I assume you already know how to write concise copy, it will be provided to you by someone else, or you will obtain it from other documents. In any case, you need to decide how much text to place on a page, how the text relates to the graphical elements, and how you want the text to look. You have some basic control over the appearance of your text, such as a few sizes, bolding, italicizing, and color. Use typical writing rules to decide which control element to use where. You will not have precise control over kerning or leading. You cannot use textual drop caps or small caps, although you can use graphical representations. In many respects, you have to go back to a typewriter model of producing text for an HTML page. You have a few different heads for your typewriter, and you can change the color of your ribbon.

## Fonts in Your Page Layout

Fortunately, starting with version 3 of Navigator and Internet Explorer, you could start to specify font faces by name. If a font is specified in the HTML code and the machine with the browser doesn't have that font, the text will "decay" back to the default fonts specified on that machine. You will not lose information, but the appearance of your page may suffer dramatically, depending on what those default fonts are. The up side of this scenario is that if your target machine does have the fonts installed, they will be used to display the HTML page. Because the vast majority of users will be accessing your Web page from a GUI operating system (OS) with a certain number of basic fonts installed, you can specify several different OS-specific font names each time you use fonts, and the chances of one of them being present is very good. Later browser versions will even let you make fonts available to browsers that don't have them. Be aware that font names aren't standardized. A typical sans serif font might be called Helvetica, MS Sans Serif, Swiss, or Arial depending on the platform. Unless you're targeting a specific type of OS with your Web or intranet site, specifying text fonts is risky.

## Cascading Style Sheets

The next page layout element, cascading style sheets, finally gives you the page-layout tool you need to precisely control margins and text elements. At this time, unfortunately, most browsers (Internet Explorer 3 being the main exception) have no support for style sheets. New versions of Internet Explorer and Netscape Communicator (both version 4) will both have built-in support for CSS. Until these and later browsers that support CSS become more widespread, using style sheets exclusively won't be a practical alternative for designing Web sites. If you are working with a narrower audience, such as in an intranet, however, you can start using style sheets right away.

If you have a choice between using style sheets or using many of the page-layout techniques described later in this chapter, you will usually find style sheets to be the better alternative. One significant advantage of style sheets is that the same style sheet can be referenced by multiple HTML pages. This makes it easy to specify the look and feel for an entire Web site from a single style sheet, saving countless hours of work on the page layout side.

While you are waiting for browsers that support CSS to become widely used, an interim solution might be to combine style sheets with your existing Web page layouts or to run two separate Web sites—one with style sheets and one without (similar to running a frames version and a no-frames version of the same site). Using style sheets is a win-win situation for both Web authors and Web surfers: Authors have more tools for design, and surfers see a considerable improvement in Web-page appearance. The sooner Web designers start using CSS, the more quickly surfers will see the benefits and start discarding older browsers in favor of ones that support CSS.

The new HTML 4.0 specification for style sheets adds even more page control for fonts and page display. You can allow the viewer to switch between small or larger fonts depending on the resolution of their current monitors. You can also use style sheets to define which medium is covered by them and have a different style sheet for Web TV, for low-resolution or mono-chrome monitors, for PDAs or laptops, and so on. With these capabilities, you can finally optimize your site for viewing from most common devices hooked to the WWW. Instead of rewriting many HTML pages—one set for each medium—you need just one set of style sheets to cover them all.

## Static Graphics

Static graphics can include images that convey content, ornamental pictures (buttons, bars, and so on), images that can be tiled for the page background, and image maps. The only current standard is two bitmap formats, GIF and JPG. Generally, you will want to keep your image file sizes as small as possible and use images sparingly to improve page load time. When you've decided which graphics to use for a particular page, how large you want them to be, and how many to use, your next question will be where to place them in relation to the text or to other graphics. You will usually employ the same principles for placing graphics as you do text: Keep it in context, make sure it has a use, and make sure it enhances and fits into the current page. Remember, you cannot let text overwrite graphics (except in the case of the page background image), nor can you have text follow a complex path determined by a graphical element (fitting text to paths). You also cannot overlap images (again, except for placing a graphic over the background image), unless you are designing pages that use JavaScript layers and your audience has browsers that support this feature.

## Animated or Moving Images

The most common moving pictures used in Web pages are animated GIFs. Moving video, such as AVI or QuickTime movies, are usually not directly incorporated into Web pages because of their huge file sizes. Streaming video technology combined with push technology means that you may eventually be able to incorporate a news feed from CNN into your Web page. For now, animated GIFs can add some action to your Web page. Most animated GIFs need to be quite small in image size because the presence of multiple frames in the file quickly swells the file size. Remember to use animation to emphasize a point or attract attention. There is a fine line between emphasizing something and distracting the user from the remainder of your page. Many people are very irritated by movement on a page. Try looping your animation so that it plays only a certain number or times, or build in a long cycle time between loops. Use the same logic for placing an animated GIF on your page that you use with any other graphic. It also operates under the same restraints.

# Page Background

A page background color or image is probably the single easiest-to-implement element of your Web page that can have maximum impact for setting the mood or style of your page. You can use a small graphic to add paperlike textures and colors, add an interesting border to the left side of the screen, or add a simple repeating logo. Any GIF (except an animated one) or JPG can be used. Here are two rules to keep in mind:

- Keep your background image or color in line with the theme for your site.
- Make sure that the text color or font face you are using is easily read against the background.

It's very tempting to use the coolest textures for page backgrounds, but think about whether you want to be remembered as the Web designer who gave someone a headache or eye strain. There are enough problems in everyone's lives without adding one more. Also, some browsers do not support background images. For these browsers, also set a background color that is similar to the color in your image so that visitors will be able to read your text.

# Tables

Tables are great for displaying rows and columns of data, textual or graphical. When you're adding a table of data to your Web page, your primary layout concern is whether you want your table to have a relative width (the cells will change size depending on the width of the browser) or an absolute width in pixels, in which case your visitors will need to use the horizontal scrollbar to view all of the table contents if their browser window is narrower than the width of the table. This decision depends on how critical the layout of the table is to the readability of your data, and how much using a relative table will distort other elements on your page if your visitor has a fairly narrow window. Tables are also used as a complete HTML page layout tool; I'll discuss this later in the section "Page Layout with Tables."

Again, the new HTML 4.0 specification adds more features to tables, including the following:

- You now can align columns of data on a decimal point, a colon, or any specified character. This will be useful for people who deal with financial or technical data in HTML tables.
- More options will also be available for defining table rules, which are the horizontal and vertical lines surrounding the cells.
- You won't have to wait for a large table to be completely downloaded into your browser before seeing the data. The data will be displayed as it is received by the browser.
- You can have a fixed header row and scroll the table data below it. No more jumping back and forth to the header row to see the column title. This is a terrific feature for large tables of data.

■ You can specify default alignments for entire columns in your table, rather than having to do it on a row-by-row basis. This is a much more logical and useful way to build a table.

## Sound

Because sound does not effect any of the display elements on your page, the only layout-related question to ask is when you want the sound to load in relation to the other page elements. If you place the tag earlier in the page, it will play while the rest of the page loads; if you place it later, it will load after other elements. The choice depends on how important the sound is to your Web page.

## Programming and HTML Form Elements

Programming script is usually placed into the HTML code before any of the controls it is attached to so that it can be properly initialized before a visitor has a chance to interact with the controls. Tables provide a convenient means of organizing and aligning HTML form controls and their text descriptions. Wherever you decide to place programmed controls or HTML forms, make sure any associated descriptive text will always stick with the control or that the purpose of the control is obvious.

## Hyperlinks

You will almost certainly be using text hyperlinks, so you need to decide how you want them to look and how this will influence your page layout. Do you want to stay with the default blue underlined text or use another color? I prefer red underlined text, because it stands out more and encourages clicking. Make sure your choice of hyperlink color is easily visible against your background color or image. Your visited hyperlink color can tend to blend into your background (you probably don't want to make it invisible by blending it in completely) for a grayed-out effect.

## Page Dimensions

Unlike the world of paper, where human handling limitations and product use determine the page size, HTML pages have no defined page size and can scroll on indefinitely (you've probably seen some of these mega-pages). Because most people have grown up under the paper book/page paradigm, you will probably want to limit the length of your screen to no more than three to five page-down commands. It is also a good idea to design your page width to not exceed 550 to 600 pixels, because this allows the many people using 640×480 resolution monitors to view your entire page without horizontal scrolling. Another practical limit on page size is to limit the sum of the file sizes on a page to 50KB or less. In other words, add the size of the HTML file with the text elements to the file size (not pixel size) of all the graphics on a given page and any other elements (such as sound files), and that total should not exceed 50KB. This will ensure a snappy response for all the pages on your Web site for the surfer attached to a modem. It takes a lot of planning and strict graphics guidelines to meet this requirement, but that's part of being an effective page designer.

## Specialty Elements Only Available Via a Plug-in

Plug-ins can add some very interesting content and pizzazz to a Web page. If viewing a Web page requires a plug-in, make sure you have a download link to wherever the plug-in is located. ActiveX controls will automatically download and install (with user permission, of course) into browsers that support this standard. Be sure to follow the manufacturer's instructions closely for placing the appropriate code or tags needed to support a plug-in into your HTML file. Otherwise, it is just another page element (albeit one that might help separate your site from the rest of the pack).

Now that you know how each of the elements discussed in the preceding sections might influence your page design or layout, you're ready for a look at what tools are available for page layout without resorting to tables as a layout tool.

# Page Layout Without Tables

Prior to the introduction of tables, content developers relied on other means to control alignment and spacing. It's still a good technique to use if your page content is predominantly text or if you don't want to spend a lot of time tweaking page structure. You can still obtain some very acceptable and readable designs using these techniques.

First, here is a brief list of the page organization elements you have access to with this technique:

- Indents
- Lists (ordered and unordered)
- Paragraph breaks
- Line breaks
- Sentence justifications
- Horizontal rules
- Some control of text wrapping around graphics
- Tables used for data elements
- Some special layout control with a single-pixel transparent GIF, a spacer image

Most of these elements have been described in other chapters in this book (except the spacer image), so in this chapter I'll only review what each of these elements does with text and/or graphics in HTML pages. Then I'll show you how to use the spacer images for improved appearance.

Figure 24.1 shows some basic uses of indents, lists, paragraph breaks, and justifications.

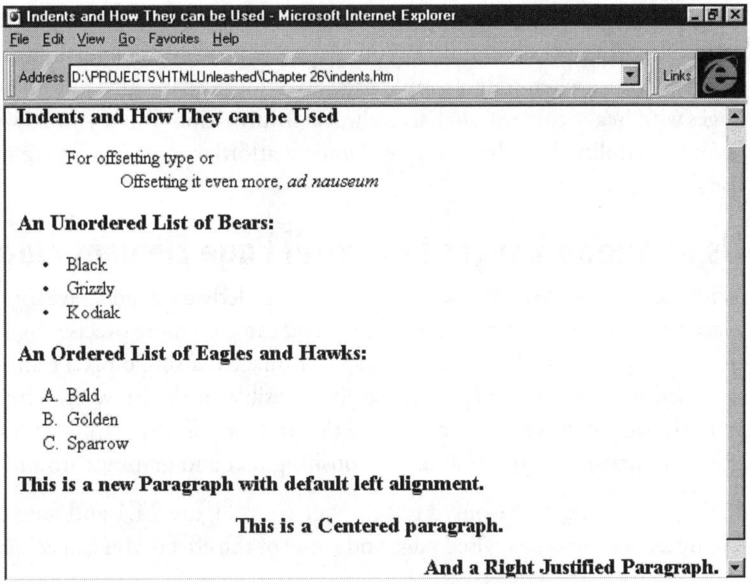

**FIGURE 24.1.**
*Some simple text ordering techniques using HTML.*

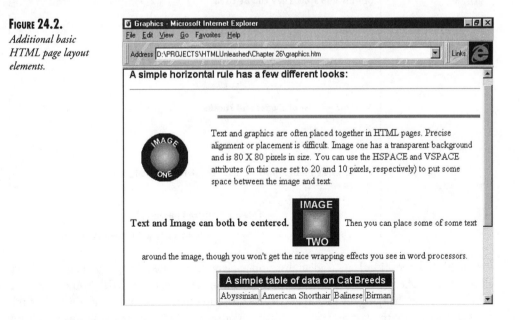

Figure 24.2 shows some of the possible uses of horizontal rules, images and their alignment, text wrapping around images, and a simple table of data.

**FIGURE 24.2.**
*Additional basic HTML page layout elements.*

For the greatest speed in getting information up on your Web site, these simpler page organization elements will often suffice. Your page will probably not win any design awards, but there are many times when only a simple page layout is needed, such as for late-breaking news or on pages with heavy content, such as technical information. But if you do want or need more page layout capability than these simple elements afford, spacer images are the next easiest item to use for page layout.

## Using Spacer Images to Control Page Element Placement

With standard HTML techniques, you can get orderly pages and have some control over graphics placement and text/graphics interaction. You can gain more precise alignment and control over placement by using spacer images. A spacer image is a single-pixel transparent GIF image that is loaded just like any image but that isn't visible in the browser. The other elements in the HTML page, however, will respond to the presence of this graphic and shift accordingly. This gives you many "invisible hands" for pushing text and graphics around the page.

Let's go back to the text-only HTML page from Figure 24.1 and redo it using spacer images. Figure 24.3 shows the revised page and some of the effects you can achieve with spacer images.

**FIGURE 24.3.**

*Using spacer images for aligning text and other special effects.*

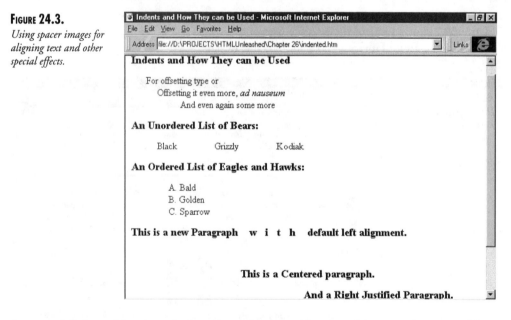

I removed all the positional tags (indent, list, and paragraph) and used the spacer image to achieve all the effects. The spacer image is a one-pixel-by-one-pixel transparent GIF. You can achieve different sizes by changing the HEIGHT and WIDTH attributes in the <IMG SRC> tag. To achieve the stepladder effect for the first three sentences about offsetting, I placed the spacer image in front of each sentence using standard image-insertion techniques, and then edited the WIDTH to 20,

**40**, and **80** pixels, respectively, for each of the three sentences. This pushed each sentence out by that predetermined distance. This level of control isn't possible using the HTML indent. I used a <BR> after each sentence to keep the text close together. I changed the list of bears from a vertical list to a horizontal one by using a 40-pixel WIDTH spacer image before the first word and a 60-pixel WIDTH spacer image between each of the bear species. This type of horizontal listing can also be done using a table with BORDER=0, although sometimes it's easier to use the spacer image. I used the spacer image to offset the list of eagles. I had to type in the list letters (A, B, C) because the spacer image will offset the list letter from the list item rather than offsetting them both from the left margin. The sentence about left alignment shows the use of the spacer for changing the space between letters for the word *with*. I used a spacer image with a WIDTH of five pixels before and after each letter. You can also use the spacer image for vertical space control, as you can see from the next sentence. This "centered paragraph" was vertically offset from the paragraph above it by changing the HEIGHT in the spacer image to 50 pixels. The last right-justified paragraph has a spacer image with a WIDTH of 50 pixels after the period to shift the paragraph away from the right margin by that amount.

As you can see, the spacer image is a handy way to push text around. But how about other elements? First of all, spacer images will not work in concert with horizontal rules for horizontal offset, although you can use them to control vertical offset. You can also use a spacer image to add both horizontal and vertical offset between two images; this works much as the spacing you saw between the bear species text.

One major use of spacer images might be to add custom spacing between text sections on an HTML page. For instance, if you have a heading, some text, and then another heading, rather than adding two paragraph tags between the last of the text and the second heading, you could add one paragraph tag and a spacer image with a HEIGHT of your choosing for finer control over the spacing between your sections. This will improve the overall attractiveness of your page. The spacer image is also a very useful and powerful tool when used in concert with a page layout table.

# Page Layout with Tables

A very powerful tool that should occupy a place of importance in the toolbox of all HTML authors is using the HTML table for page layout. This tool will eventually be replaced by style sheets, but for now it represents the easiest and most flexible manner for placing and aligning all the elements on a Web page. This is made even easier by the fact that almost every HTML editor in the marketplace has easy-to-use features for building and modifying tables. With little more than a click or two, you can merge cells, delete cells, add or subtract entire columns or rows, change element alignment (both vertical and horizontal) within a cell, change background colors in groups of cells, and even create new tables within existing tables (that is, nested tables). By using tables, you will finally feel like you have some serious control over the appearance of an HTML page.

I assume that you know basic HTML table structure and use. If you are unfamiliar with tables, read Chapter 10, "Creating Tables for Data and Page Layout," before proceeding.

## General Page Layout with HTML Tables

So what is page layout with HTML tables? It involves placing some portion of a Web page or the entire Web page completely inside one or more tables. The tables will have their borders set to zero, so they are invisible when the page is loaded into a browser. Figure 24.4 shows an example of using a table for page layout inside FrontPage 97 so that you can see the individual cells.

**FIGURE 24.4.**

*Using a table for basic page layout in FrontPage 97.*

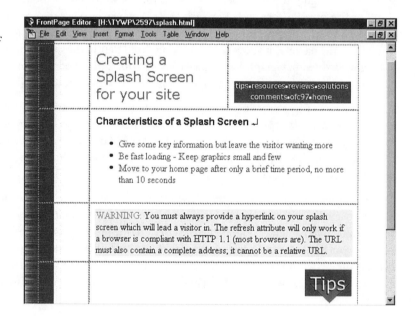

Here are some general guidelines for using page layout tables effectively:

- Use one image per table cell. You can then optimally align the image in the cell, both vertically or horizontally, without influencing any other elements.

- Do not mix text and images in the same cell. Cells should contain an image only or text only. It's easy to create extra cells. Again, this gives you maximum flexibility in aligning elements.

- Use cells for white space. Use a spacer image inside a cell to exactly control the height and/or width of the cell. Leave entire rows or columns empty to separate key sections.

- Fix the width of your layout table to an absolute pixel value; don't set it at 100 percent relative. When you use a fixed width, the structure of your table will not distort if your page is being viewed through a narrow browser window. Your table width should not exceed 600 pixels (I use 550 pixels to be safe). This width is based on the fact that many people still have their screen resolutions set at 640×480 pixels. One note: If personal digital assistants (PDAs) become commonly used to surf the Web, what will the newest lowest common denominator in screen width become—200 pixels?

■ Use the cell background color to emphasize text or to add a simple colored division line between sections on your page. This is an easy way to add inverse text for emphasis or interest without having to create a separate image in a bitmap editing program.

Building on the white-space idea, play your table structure off of your page background image for added impact, as shown in Figure 24.4. You will see this idea all over the WWW. By using a background image that tiles to create an interesting element to the left of the page, you can overlay this with a table. By placing a spacer image that is slightly wider than the left element created by your page background image in the far-left cells of the table, and fixing the width of your table with an absolute width rather than a relative width, you can guarantee that any text or elements on your page won't run over your left element. Or, better yet, instead of placing a spacer image in the far-left cells of your table, you can include some image elements in those cells. This will give you access to some interesting blending or offsetting features, sort of a primitive layers capability.

## Adding Newspaper-Style Columns for Text Using Tables

Another capability that tables can add to a Web page is the capability to give you pseudo-newspaper columns. This is shown in Figure 24.5.

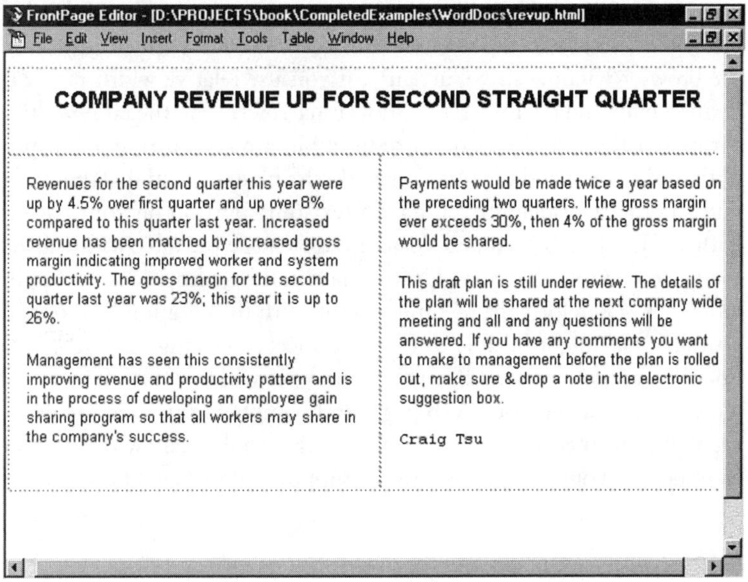

**FIGURE 24.5.**

*Adding newspaper-style columns with tables in FrontPage 97.*

**COMPANY REVENUE UP FOR SECOND STRAIGHT QUARTER**

Revenues for the second quarter this year were up by 4.5% over first quarter and up over 8% compared to this quarter last year. Increased revenue has been matched by increased gross margin indicating improved worker and system productivity. The gross margin for the second quarter last year was 23%; this year it is up to 26%.

Management has seen this consistently improving revenue and productivity pattern and is in the process of developing an employee gain sharing program so that all workers may share in the company's success.

Payments would be made twice a year based on the preceding two quarters. If the gross margin ever exceeds 30%, then 4% of the gross margin would be shared.

This draft plan is still under review. The details of the plan will be shared at the next company wide meeting and all and any questions will be answered. If you have any comments you want to make to management before the plan is rolled out, make sure & drop a note in the electronic suggestion box.

Craig Tsu

**24**

LAYOUT DESIGN

Of course, text will not flow from cell to cell as you edit it. You will need to do everything manually. After you have completely written and edited your text, you will need to do a word count, place the first half of the words in the left column, and place the last half in the right column (or some variation thereof if you use more than two columns).

## Nested Tables

Even finer page layout control can be gained through nested tables. Nested tables are created by placing an entirely new table within the confines of a single cell in an existing HTML table. Nested tables are useful for special layouts in the following situations:

- Subsectioning portions of a Web page already laid out with a table. If you want to lay out the sections of a Web page by topic, for instance, you could control the layout of each subsection with a separate nested table.

- Adding tables of data (with or without borders) in a Web page already laid out with a table. This would be a convenient way to associate an athlete's statistics with a picture of the athlete.

Don't forget that the background color of the cell into which you place a nested table becomes the default background color for the nested table. Also remember that some older browsers (now fairly rare) do not support nested tables and that any information in a nested table will not be seen by that browser.

A new capability of tables in the HTML 4.0 specification will be useful in page layout—the use of the relative width characteristics to specify the relative width of both the columns and the font sizes so that the data and table columns will both cleanly scale up or down to match the browser window size. Currently, if you use relative width rather than absolute width to define a table and the browser window is narrower than the table width, the table columns will shrink but the text won't, often resulting in a messy, unaligned display. Under HTML 4.0, both the columns and the text size would shrink or expand together to fill the screen and maintain an orderly display. If you have a text-only portion on your page that you are laying out with an HTML table, you no longer need to make the table width absolute, which could force many viewers to scroll more. Unfortunately, this scaling does not apply to images placed into table cells. Therefore, the text might scale with the columns, but the graphics will not. Theoretically, you might be able to use style sheets to change the WIDTH and HEIGHT attributes of images to accommodate differences in browser window sizes. If you used the new relative table width for laying out your Web pages and combined this with the new HTML 4.0 style sheet capability, in theory, your entire Web page would scale with every browser window size—assuming, of course, that the browser supports these new HTML 4.0 features.

After you've decided on a page layout using tables, it's very easy to set up a template and fill in the cells with content. Tables give you good alignment and placement control for all of the elements in a Web page. But for even more control, you need to be more of an artist than an HTML author.

# Page Layout Using Graphics Only

If you must use an uncommon font to achieve a specific effect, or you have a variety of graphics that must be aligned down to the last pixel, you may be a candidate for graphics-only page layout. What this means is that you create your Web page in another program using all the layout tools therein and then export your completed page, text and graphics, as a single graphic or several graphics. These are then assembled into an HTML shell page (which may or may not use tables for layout). The browser will display the graphic as it would any other graphical element, but this graphic will contain most of the richness of the page you created in your original graphic editing program.

This approach has several advantages:

■ You can leverage all of your skills with desktop publishing programs into the world of Web publishing.

■ You have as much control as your creation program, such as Quark XPress, gives you. You are not bound by the limitations of the HTML language.

There are two major disadvantages: You still have only 216 colors to work with, and you will have file size limitations. Because you most likely will be mixing text and images on your page, the final image should be in GIF format, because JPG will blur your text if you use any compression at all. Making a full-page graphic can lead to huge file sizes very quickly, especially if you want to stay under 50KB for your total HTML page size. These two disadvantages mean that some of the richness of your page will be lost, but you will gain access to more layout tools. You have to balance which is most important to you.

## Programs Needed for Building Graphics-Only Web Pages

If you are going to try to build a Web page using graphics only, you must have, at a minimum, the following:

■ A program that is capable of exporting an entire page in a bitmap format.

■ A paint or utility program for reducing the colors in your graphic to the 216-color Netscape palette and for translating files to GIF, if necessary.

■ An HTML editor that easily creates image maps. This will be the means for adding hyperlinks to your pages.

Making Web pages from desktop publishing programs is not just a matter of exporting pages to a bitmap format. Don't forget the following:

- The text in your exported file must be viewable under several different screen resolutions; there is no way for browsers to zoom in on text that is too small. With this in mind, you will probably want to use a larger font size than you would for print media and place less text information on a page. You will probably have to experiment to find your optimal font size.

- You want to export your page at the size, in pixels, that you will be using on your Web page. You want to do minimal resizing of the final graphic to maintain maximum readability of your text. Your desktop publishing program must give you this control during the exporting step.

- The background color of the HTML page that you place your graphic into should be the same as the graphic's background color. Some browsers offset their pages differently than others. Keeping the HTML page background color and the graphic background color the same will minimize any artifacts (lines, border effects, and so on).

- Make sure the type of image map you select will work on your Web server. Most browsers support client-side image maps that do not require any interaction with the Web server to read the coordinates of the hotspots. If you want or need to use a server-side image map, make sure your HTML editor or image-map-making program supports that coordinate system.

By using the graphics-only approach with care, you can build your entire Web site this way. You may also want to build a text-only version for text-only browsers or for people who surf with graphics turned off. An alternative might be to add text hyperlinks to your pages that reproduce any image map hyperlinks.

Be on the lookout for programs that can significantly simplify the process of creating graphics-only Web pages. For instance, in CorelDRAW! 7 and Corel PhotoPaint, you can assign URLs to any object. If you then publish that image to the Web, any objects with URLs become hotspots on an image map. These programs do all the coordinate drawing and also save an HTML file with the map coordinates in addition to the graphic as a GIF image.

# Summary

As you can see, page layout under HTML can be approached from several different directions. It can be as simple as adding some text and graphics and using some basic justifications, paragraphs, and horizontal rules. Or it can be as complex as doing all your page design in a desktop publishing or drawing program and exporting it to a Web-compatible bitmap format as a large image map. Tables are a good in-between choice, because they have excellent alignment and organization capabilities and are easy to use. Tables also give you access to some special effects, such as crude layering with patterns in the page background image. The spacer image is also a useful tool for moving text around a page or for filling in a table cell to prevent it from moving. Cascading style sheets provide the most control and the cleanest appearance with the least effort and will probably become the predominant means of page layout in the very near future.

Try to keep page layout in perspective with your needs. If it is critical to get information out to an audience quickly, you may want to use simpler page layout techniques and forget using tables or CSS. If a more complex layout is critical to communicating the information on your Web page, pull out your whole arsenal of tools. Good use of page layout tools and design is essential if you want eye-catching pages that will attract more users and keep them on your site. A well-organized page also makes it easier for your users to find the information they want. Remember: Page layout should add to the enjoyment of your Web pages and complement your content.

# User Navigation

*by Michael A. Larson*

## IN THIS CHAPTER

**CHAPTER 25**

No matter how beautiful your graphics, how powerful your prose, or how cool your Web site, if visitors can't find their way around or to an important part of your site, all your efforts have been for naught. If you have a large Web site and someone has followed one train of thought through your site and then needs to get to an entirely different part of your site but can't see an easy way to get there, again you have failed in the navigation design of your Web site. Most visitors do not want to play Dungeons and Dragons through your Web site (unless you are sponsoring a treasure hunt or other game), finding information by solving the maze that is your navigation interface design. Visitors who become frustrated because they can't get around easily can negate all of the time, effort, and expense that you put into crafting your site.

Each Web site is like a little town. Towns have many obvious and intuitive similarities. They all have streets, houses, businesses, and vehicles. Most people can figure out the basics of how to get around a new town because they know the common elements of all towns. But people might have trouble finding the details, because on the Web each "town" or Web site can have a very different purpose.

As the Chamber of Commerce for your town, you must make sure to give your visitors an understandable and quick (with as few clicks as possible) means of navigating through your particular street layout, pointing out attractions as well as preventing your visitors from ending up in dead-end alleys. Most visitors will know the basics of Web site navigation, hyperlinks, buttons, and image maps, just as they know the basics of getting around a town using street signs, roadmaps, billboards, and phone books. Do not assume that your visitor understands your town as well as you do. Be courteous, and think about the best way to guide your visitors.

This chapter explains the underlying principles of optimal site navigation design. You will look at ways to incorporate navigation systems into your Web site, including using text hyperlink menus, groups of images and/or graphical text with hyperlinks, image maps, or some combination of these items. You'll also see examples of these systems and how they can be applied to an entire site, whether you're building a small Web site or a megalith. Finally, you'll see how having your own search engine can enhance the ease of navigation at your site with a minimum of HTML programming.

# Fundamentals of Navigation Design

A Web site navigation system consists simply of a set of hyperlinks that enables a visitor to view and select all the different content sections of a Web site. The design of the navigation system varies with every Web site. The process of building Web site navigation systems involves both laying the roadway and clearly marking it. The navigation system must also be integrated with the other components of your site. Site navigation should be a clearly visible, integral part of your Web town. Don't forget that your Web site navigation system can be both attractive and useful; you do not have to sacrifice beauty for utility.

The first step in designing a navigation system is to create an outline for your Web site. The content and design of your Web site will often suggest the best means to navigate it.

During the process of outlining your site, write down the structure and relationships between parts of your site. You can do this with words, symbols, or a combination of words and symbols. (Flowchart programs are very helpful here.) I find it easiest to approach outlining by topic. I usually list all of the major topics, and then place the subtopics under the major topics. After that, I prioritize the topics by how interesting I think they will be to my visitors and how important each topic is to me. You might also end up with more branches under your subtopics. The number of branches often suggests whether you can get by with a simple navigation system or whether you need multiple navigation systems to help visitors get around your site.

After you have your site outlined, consider the following questions to define your navigational needs:

- Do you see your Web site structure (not content) changing with time? That is, do you see yourself erecting whole new sections and tearing down others, or will you mostly just be changing or updating the content of existing sections?

- How will most users travel around your site? Can you see any obvious traffic patterns? Do you have a major theme that will attract the majority of users?

Answers to these questions will help you determine what navigation system (or systems) to build. For instance, if you have just a few sections, one navigation menu will easily lead the user around your site. If you have a larger site with more sections and subsections, you may need two separate navigation systems—one for major topics, and one for subtopics. If your site structure is fairly fluid, you will want to use a navigation system that is easy to change. If you want to direct visitors to an important feature of your site, you may want to emphasize it in your navigation menu by using a brighter color or bolder text.

**TIP**

For a small Web site with just a few topics, you might need only a simple set of text hyperlinks or a small image map (or both) placed across the top or bottom (or both) of each page. When your needs grow past one menu, you need to think more about placement, how to relate your navigation menus to each other, and what visual cues to give your readers as to their location at any given time. For instance, you could build a primary navigation menu composed of text and icons. Then for each page under this main topic, you could place the icon on the same place on every page. This icon could then be hyperlinked back to the beginning page for this section, no matter how deep your visitor goes. This uses the visual cue idea, and it provides a convenient navigation means for your visitors. Whatever system you finally choose, remember to keep your navigation system as simple and easy to use as possible.

Two other items will influence your choice of navigation systems: placement and clarity.

How and where you place your navigation system will very much depend on your content. For instance, if you have a mostly textual or a linear site (the content of one page leads to the next and so on to the last page of the site), placing the navigation system at the bottom of each page may be the easiest for your user. If you have major sections and/or subsections, placing the navigation system to the side (usually the left) or across the top of a page may work better. For a complex site, you may need to have multiple points on the page (top, side, and bottom) available for navigation selection, as well as a page dedicated to mapping your site or searching it using keywords. Your choice of navigation systems will be suggested by traffic patterns, your content, and how complex or large your Web site is.

Another key element in choosing your navigation system design is to define the level of clarity and understanding you want from your navigation system. By clarity, I mean, "How easy is it for anyone to understand your navigation system?" You need to balance clarity with the design or theme of your Web site. Remember, the WWW is global in nature, and many of the visual shapes and colors common in your culture will not mean anything (or worse, will mean something very different) to visitors from other countries. If you have a site that depends heavily on graphics, using a graphical-style navigation system will enhance your site's appearance, but you may sacrifice some clarity. You can usually obtain the best clarity with text hyperlinks. If your text is well written, most people will immediately understand where a hyperlink leads within the context of your site. Images are not usually as obvious as text to a visitor, although they maximize the design and beauty of your site.

A good compromise is often a combination—an image with text incorporated into the graphic. The images can then be color-keyed or be simple shapes that represent each area of your Web site as an additional visual hint. You can see an example of this in Figure 25.1. Say you own an automobile painting business, and you want people to be able to request quotes from a page on your Web site. Which of the three navigational choices shown in Figure 25.1 best conveys the content of this quotes page to the visitor?

**NOTE**

Don't forget that navigation applies to moving through a single page as well as between Web pages. If your content requires you to build long pages with multiple sections, use the HTML bookmark to build a navigation menu of the sections at the top of the page. Some people also place a "Back to Top" hyperlink after each section and at the bottom of the page.

You've seen some of the factors influencing the placement and clarity of your navigation system. The next step is to look at some of the navigation systems commonly used on a Web site.

**FIGURE 25.1.**
*Three ways to steer a visitor to the "Request for a Quote" page.*

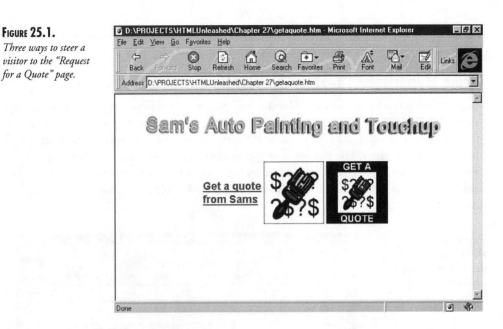

# Navigation Systems

Navigation systems must fulfill a variety of demanding roles. First-time visitors to your site must be able to easily find everything. Repeat visitors should have an easy route to get to their favorite part of the site without going through 20 hyperlinks to get there. The navigation system should be easy to use and complete, but shouldn't contain too many selections. Putting together an effective navigation system is one of the many balancing acts that a Web author has to go through. There are four universal systems that you can mix and match for a navigation system:

- Text hyperlinks, separate or grouped together
- Hyperlinked, individual images
- Image maps
- The Submit button on an HTML form

The Submit button is usually not thought of as a navigation aid, although after clicking the Submit button as part of the transaction with the Web server, you are usually served a new HTML page; that is, you have essentially navigated somewhere. HTML forms can be used for restricting access to some parts of your site. (Registration may be required, for instance.) Don't forget to include these restricted routes when you're mapping out the navigation for your site.

There are also two, nonuniversal, special containers for navigation systems to consider:

- Frames
- Specialty programs such as Java, JavaScript, ActiveX controls, or other specialty programs supported by a plug-in

Some combination of these six items will likely comprise your navigation system. Let's look at the strengths and weaknesses of each in detail.

## Using Hyperlinked Text for Navigation

Hyperlinked text is by far the easiest kind of navigation system to put together. You just type some descriptive text and add the hyperlink. The default style of the hyperlink (usually a blue, underlined font) is automatically applied to the text. You're done. It's easy to go back and tweak the text for more clarity. You can sprinkle hyperlinked text throughout your Web pages. For a more formal menu appearance, you can combine a set of common destinations in a list, in a table, or in a nested table. Figure 25.2 shows a navigation table of text hyperlinks at the bottom of a Web page.

**FIGURE 25.2.**

*Hyperlinked text selections grouped in a table create a basic navigation system.*

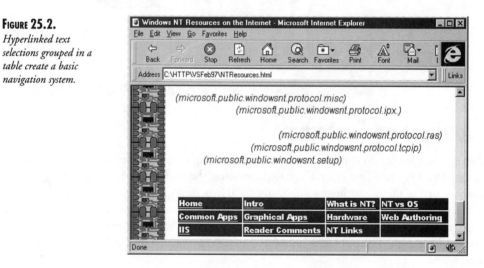

Text also loads very quickly, leaving you more room to use graphics for other things on your Web page. Text hyperlinks, of course, can be viewed and used by every browser on the market. The only disadvantage of hyperlinked text is that you have limited control over its appearance under HTML.

### NOTE

When you have more than about 10 text hyperlinks in your navigation menu, you need to start thinking about breaking up the menu by topic. This will speed users to their destination on your site. If your text hyperlink list becomes too long, you might tire your visitors by making them read every item.

## Using Hyperlinked Images for Navigation

The next most commonly used navigation elements are hyperlinked images. These act in much the same way as icons do: Clicking on them produces one action. You can sprinkle these throughout your pages or put a hyperlinked image in the same place on every page to point, for example, to the site home page. You can string these together in a table to perform a function similar to that of an image map. Images can be graphical text (text saved as a bitmap image from a graphics editing program), an elaborate, irregularly shaped image, or some combination of the two. The main advantage of hyperlinked images is their excellent combination of design and usefulness. Their main disadvantages are that they take up more bandwidth than text, it is very difficult to make an icon (without text) that everyone understands, and you need a bitmap editing program if you ever need to tweak them. Don't forget to use the ALT= attribute in the <IMG SRC> tag for adding descriptive text so that browsers that don't support graphics or have graphics turned off know where the hyperlink leads.

## Using Image Maps for Navigation

Image maps are arguably a Web designer's most useful and beautiful navigation aids. (See Chapter 14, "Creating Image Maps," if you need more information about image maps.) When visitors see an image with many easily identifiable parts, they know immediately that this is probably a navigation menu. There is also no restriction on the shape of the hot zone you can map out for each part of the image, so you have complete freedom in designing the image. An image map is fairly easy to build using any modern HTML editor. Some paint programs let you associate layers or image objects with URLs and create the image map code for you. Often, the primary disadvantage of an image map is its file size. Because there are usually multiple and differing parts to the image map, it is difficult to reduce it in size or color and maintain enough detail to make it usable. It takes careful planning to avoid this pitfall.

**TIP**

Don't forget to start using cascading style sheets to supplement your navigation menus as soon as enough browsers support them. With CSS, you can layer text over your images. This means you no longer have to decide whether to use GIFs for optimal text clarity or JPEGs for optimal photographic quality in your image maps. Now you can have both. The use of PNGs will also eliminate the need to choose between GIFs and JPEGs for image maps.

One disadvantage to using image maps is that you can use only one ALT= attribute in the <IMG SRC> tag for the entire image. People surfing with graphics turned off won't be able to use an image map to navigate, because they won't be able to see the image sections or hot spots based on the ALT= attribute. You need to have backup text hyperlinks or a separate text-only version of your Web site.

## Using Frames for Navigation

Hyperlinked text and images or image maps can all be used in concert with frames (see Chapter 18, "Creating Sophisticated Layouts with Frames and Layers," for more information) to build a complete navigation system. Frames are a natural for this. You can place menus across the top, across one or both sides, and/or across the bottom of the frameset page. These menus remain static while the results of any menu selection can be displayed in a central window. Figure 25.3 shows one way to use frames to display navigation menus and content in one browser window.

**FIGURE 25.3.**

*Using frames to display both the navigation menu and the contents of any selection.*

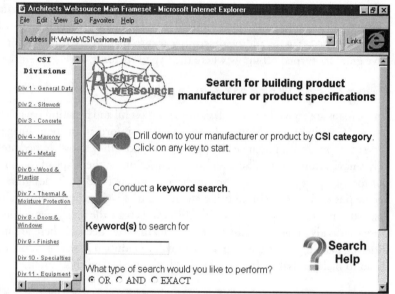

With frames, you don't need to include a copy of your navigation menu(s) on every page of your Web site. Also, changing or expanding your navigation menu(s) involves changing only one page and one set of hyperlinks. This helps reduce the onerous task of Web site maintenance.

Although frames are very useful from the Web designer's perspective, they meet with mixed results in reality. You have to be careful in programming the target frame for each of your hyperlinks, or you can end up loading multiple copies of the frameset page and get the dreaded "hall of mirrors" effect. Also, a fair number of browsers don't support frames, which means that you need to produce both a frames version and a no-frames version of your Web site. Frames also seem to be a sore point with some users; the number of user complaints about this feature in newsgroups is exceeded only by complaints about animated GIFs. Given these drawbacks, many Web authors have removed frames from their pages, returning to the use of nested tables or Java applets to achieve similar effects. However, many sites still successfully use frames.

In the HTML 4.0 specification, a new element called `iframe` is added to frames. An `iframe` is an independent HTML document window that appears within the body of another HTML document rather than as part of a frameset. Using an `iframe` brings up interesting navigation possibilities. You could have a small `iframe` in every Web page, which could contain navigation menus. This `iframe` could contain a main navigation menu in the `iframe` and have secondary navigation menus in the HTML page containing the `iframe`. Or the navigation menu in the `iframe` could be different for every page on your Web site, which means that you could essentially have a rolling, customized navigation menu for every page on your site if you choose. An `iframe` would also make an excellent container for specialty navigation systems built using Java, JavaScript, or ActiveX controls.

## Using Java, JavaScript, and ActiveX Controls for User Navigation

The last type of navigation systems container uses Java programs, JavaScript, CGI scripts, ActiveX controls, or plug-ins. Some extremely useful and unique effects can be achieved using these controls. There are ActiveX controls that act like Windows Explorer: When you click on the top menu choice, a sublist appears, allowing you to place and organize many choices into a relatively small area on your page. Macromedia Director and Flash, via their Shockwave technology, enable you to design multimedia components that respond with a color change or movement when you pass the mouse cursor over them.

All these components allow a greater degree of interaction and entertainment than is possible with text hyperlinks, image hyperlinks, or image maps. Unfortunately, they are not universally supported. Java probably comes the closest to being universal, but you must be a trained programmer or be able to purchase the program to get that interactivity. ActiveX is currently only supported by Microsoft browsers. Plug-ins are not something that you can expect your visitors to have available with their browsers. In addition, many plug-ins may not be supported across every platform. If you choose to use any of these options on your site, make sure that you make available alternative pages that don't contain these options, or warn your visitors that they need a special component to view the page. It is also often possible to detect browser types (and to a lesser degree, plug-ins) using JavaScript or VBScript and send the browsers to the appropriate page.

Although it is extra work to support all of these specialty programs, the effects are often unmatched. Using these components is one way to build a site that stands out.

## Adding Visual Cues to Your Navigation Menus

The means by which you show visitors which page or section of the Web site they are currently on is another important factor. With a text-based hyperlink system, you can remove the hyperlink from the text selection for the page you are on. For instance, in Figure 25.2, the visitor knows that he is on the page with NT Links because it is the only selection without a hyperlink and it is also a different color.

Instead of removing the hyperlink, you could change the color of the text to a color more closely approximating the background color, giving it a grayed-out effect.

This system can be applied to hyperlinked images. If your images are colored, you might have a grayscale version indicating the current page. Or if the image has text in it, you might want to blur it. Another option would be to apply another color. Whatever indicator system you use, make sure it is the same for all pages in your site.

Image maps are the easiest to modify in this manner, although it is usually not practical to change the image. To indicate which page or section is being viewed, all you have to do is remove the hotspot coordinates for that section from your image map. I don't recommend changing the image used for the image map unless you have a very small graphic. If you do have a small image file size, it certainly gives your visitors more information if you can change the color or style of the image map to represent the section they are currently in.

# Navigating Through an Entire Web Site

This section discusses tools that help users get around a huge Web site. You can use standard navigation menus for small or medium-sized sites. It is also often possible to make all of the Web site pages or sections available from one or two menus. But when your site swells to several hundred pages or more, trying to include links to all sections becomes cumbersome; you need to offer other options for getting around your site. The two commonly used options are

- A site map
- Your own search engine

## Using and Building Site Maps

A site map consists of one or more pages whose primary function is to give a user a quick, at-a-glance view of your site. The site map, also called a *site atlas*, is usually based on some type of hierarchical structure. It can be an image map, a strictly text-based outline of your site, or both. The idea is to let users see your entire site outline and be able to go directly to the areas that interest them most.

If you decide on a text-only site map, you can build it with a variety of techniques. You can use the listing capabilities in HTML coupled with indenting (<BLOCKQUOTE>) and font sizes to quickly build a useful site map, as demonstrated in Figure 25.4.

You can also use tables to organize your text-based site maps and add some small images to generate interest or draw attention to the major section headers, as shown in Figure 25.5.

**FIGURE 25.4.**

*A text-based site map using lists, indents, and font sizes for organization.*

**FIGURE 25.5.**

*Using a table to organize a combination of text and small graphics for your site map.*

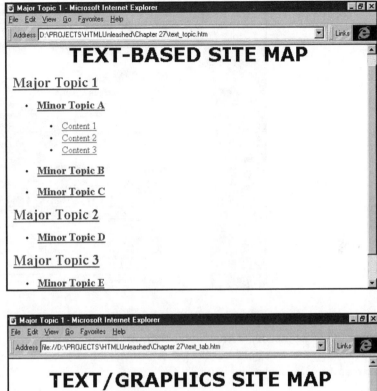

The more commonly implemented site maps are image maps with hot spots leading to the various sections of the site. Your image map can mimic a text-based hierarchy by using a flow-chart metaphor. This is illustrated by the Lycos (http://www.lycos.com) search engine's site map, shown in Figure 25.6.

25

USER
NAVIGATION

FIGURE 25.6.

*Lycos uses a flow-chart metaphor for its site map.*

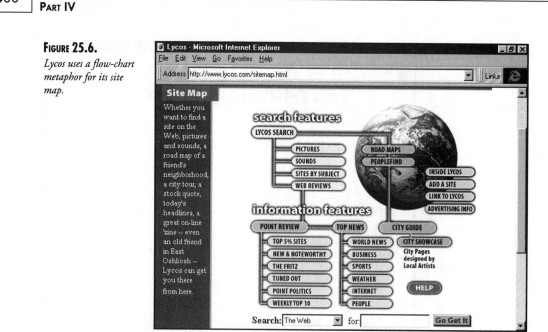

Just because site maps that use image maps need to be clear doesn't mean that they can't be interesting. The Indian government used one of the country's national treasures as the background for a site map that leads the visitor through a budget report (`http://www.m-web.com/sitemap.html`), as shown in Figure 25.7.

FIGURE 25.7.

*The Taj Mahal acts as a backdrop for a site map.*

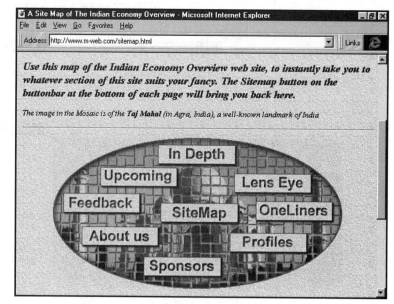

A good site map should have the following characteristics:

■ It should be easy to follow.

■ It should have enough detail to be informative without being either too verbose or too succinct.

■ It should have a help page available, if necessary.

■ If the site map is multipage, the navigation system to move around the index should be distinct from the index itself or from any other navigation menus you use on your site.

Color-coding the graphics or text for each section of your site map will make it easier to follow. Also, decide whether you want to arrange your site map content alphabetically or topically. Typically, a topical arrangement will work better for a Web site. Your help page should include an overview of how your content is arranged and why it is arranged that way, as well as any hints for moving through it.

> **CAUTION**
>
> One fact to keep in mind as you decide whether to have a site map is that a site map will increase your Web site maintenance requirements. Every time you add or delete a page, you will have to update the site map. For a site with rapidly changing content, this may prove more burdensome than any convenience or usefulness the site map offers visitors. This factor should also influence how you design your site map. You may want to separate the site map hyperlinks leading to rapidly changing parts of your Web site from the more static portions of your site map. There is no requirement that all of your site map has to be on one page.

## Adding a Search Engine to Aid Navigation

When your Web site becomes too large or too active to adequately describe with a site map, you might consider using a search engine. The same technology used by Alta Vista (`http://www.altavista.digital.com`), Lycos, Excite (`http://www.excite.com`), or any of the other major Internet search engines can be used to index all of the text content on your Web site. This index would then be searchable by anyone on your site from an HTML form using keywords. A list of "hits" from your site is returned by your local search engine. The hits are active hyperlinks to other pages on your site. Using a search engine has several advantages:

■ Visitors can use their own words for searching.

■ You probably won't need a hierarchical site map.

■ Search engines are usually faster to use than site maps.

■ Search engines require little maintenance or attention.

■ Search engines automatically update themselves.

Almost all Web servers support at least one search engine. If your Web site is hosted by an ISP, the ISP will usually have a search engine that you can use with instructions on how to add it to a Web page. It takes only a few lines of HTML code to add a search box to your HTML page. For instance, Microsoft uses Index Server as the search engine in support of their Internet Information Server (IIS) Web server. To add a keyword search box to an HTML page, you need only the following few lines of code:

```
<FORM ACTION="/scripts/samples/search/query.idq" METHOD="GET">
    Enter your query below:
    <TABLE>
        <TR>
            <TD><INPUT TYPE="TEXT" NAME="CiRestriction" SIZE="60"
            ➥ MAXLENGTH="100" VALUE=""></TD>
            <TD><INPUT TYPE="SUBMIT" VALUE="Execute Query"></TD>
            <TD><INPUT TYPE="RESET" VALUE="Clear"></TD>
        </TR>
        <TR>
            <TD ALIGN=right><A HREF="/samples/search/tipshelp.htm">
            ➥ Tips for searching</A></TD>
        </TR>
        <INPUT TYPE="HIDDEN" NAME="CiMaxRecordsPerPage" VALUE="10">
        <INPUT TYPE="HIDDEN" NAME="CiScope" VALUE="/">
        <INPUT TYPE="HIDDEN" NAME="TemplateName" VALUE="query">
        <INPUT TYPE="HIDDEN" NAME="CiSort" VALUE="rank[d]">
        <INPUT TYPE="HIDDEN" NAME="HTMLQueryForm"
        ➥ VALUE="/samples/search/query.htm">
    </TABLE>
</FORM>
```

A table is used to organize the elements in the preceding HTML form. The form from this code as it looks from a browser is shown in Figure 25.8.

**FIGURE 25.8.**

*Adding a keyword search text box to an HTML form.*

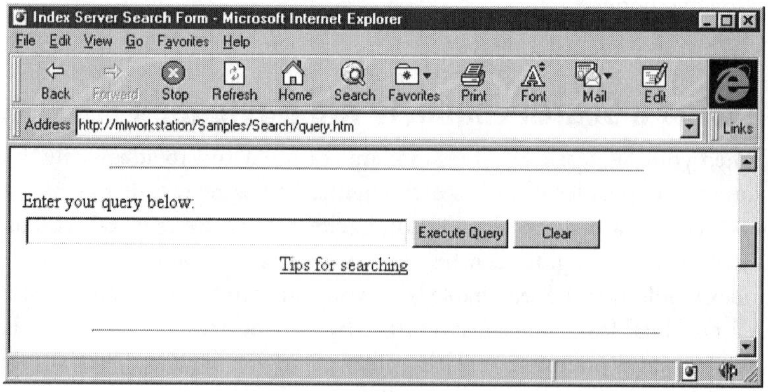

Notice from the HTML code that you can customize a number of options for the output of the form, including the following:

■ `CiRestriction` enables you to exclude certain parts of your Web site from being searched or to exclude certain users from searching.

- ◼ `CiMaxRecordsPerPage` controls how many hits per page are displayed. The default is 10.
- ◼ `CiScope` defines the starting point for the search, typically the root of your Web site.
- ◼ `CiSort` indicates how to sort the returned information, by rank or filename.
- ◼ `HTMLQueryForm` is the path to the template.

You can allow a visitor to specify some of these parameters by adding other controls to your HTML search form.

Most of the other search engines have similar parameters, such as the following:

- ◼ Whether to search by a single word, several words, or a phrase
- ◼ Options to match your search keywords along a scale from exactly to very loosely
- ◼ Whether to return hits with brief or verbose descriptions
- ◼ The capability to search the entire Web site, parts of it, or specific elements of it, such as images
- ◼ The capability to filter pages by date
- ◼ The capability to have the results displayed in a new browser window

Be sure to include a link to a help page for tips on using your search engine.

Most indexes automatically update themselves and do not add much to your site-maintenance duties. As such, they are often much easier to use on a Web site than a complete site map. I have seen numerous Web sites that provide both search capability and a site map. This gives visitors the greatest flexibility and the most options in finding something on a site. Within reason, you cannot have too many navigational aids.

# Summary

Thinking about navigation systems is not very exciting, but your Web site will quickly become useless without one. Currently there is no single standard for designing and building a navigation system; Web authors must devise their own. There are, however, some essential guidelines to follow. If you incorporate good design techniques with the utilitarianism of the navigation system, the navigation system becomes unobtrusive, yet easy to find and use. Remember that a navigation system should never lose any of its clarity or ease of use during the creation process.

Though graphics or graphical text give you the most attractive navigation systems, don't forget to use text in your basic navigation systems or site maps. Many Web surfers know exactly where they want to go and don't want to wait for graphics. Text hyperlinks speed these users to the key information, and they will (hopefully) remember your site because of it. Have you ever visited a site where you just didn't have time for some large image map to download, so you went to the next site instead? Your navigation system should never be a reason from someone to leave your site. Give people the text navigation choices, at least until more people have faster connections to the WWW.

# Putting It All Together: HTML Design

*by Michael A. Larson*

## IN THIS CHAPTER

CHAPTER

26

Knowing about design theory, page layout techniques, color models, and Web site navigation systems is all fine and good. Effectively applying these principles, however, is where the tread meets the road. If you know how to combine these principles with your site content, you will be building an excellent Web site in no time.

So, what makes one Web site excellent and another not so excellent? Discerning this takes a practiced eye, and the best way for you to practice is to dive into a couple of well-designed Web sites and take them apart to see what makes them tick. I have found two superb Web sites just waiting for your review: Travelution (`http://www.rosenbluth.com/`) and CyberMad (`http://www.CyberMad.com`). Travelution is a one-stop shop on the Internet, providing extensive travel tips, package tours, and reservations under one roof. This large, fairly complex business site put together by a third-party Web development company for Rosenbluth, International and currently under the care of webmaster Kate Urzillo is representative of a well-done corporate site. CyberMad is an award-winning electronic magazine (e-zine) by Christopher Parr. This Web site is moderately large and extremely diverse in its content and presentation styles; it is more representative of the entertainment genre on the WWW. The entire contents of both Web sites are on the CD-ROM accompanying this book. They are completely browsable from the CD-ROM (using Netscape or Internet Explorer, both Version 3.0 or later, is strongly recommended) with hotlinks to their current versions on the WWW.

In this chapter, you play the role of a Web site reviewer. Using the principles from the earlier three chapters as guidelines, I take you through some of the pages from each Web site, examining many aspects of both of these sites to see how true they are to the guidelines. The main lesson for you to learn here is how to determine why these are excellent Web sites. After you can recognize what goes into a successful Web site, you can build your own top-notch site.

I strongly encourage you to browse the Web sites on the CD-ROM. The grayscale screenshots in this chapter do not do justice to the Web author's skill in using color within each page to communicate or entertain. Before you get to the CD-ROM Web sites, you will run across an introductory page. This page contains hyperlinks to the Web pages I used for each of the screenshots in this chapter. You might want to view the actual Web pages before you read this chapter or read this chapter with your computer nearby. As you browse the sites on the CD-ROM, any time something catches your eye, make sure to view the HTML source. In fact, if you want to forget about reading the rest of this chapter, and just dive into the CD-ROM sites, I won't be offended. Both sites are so interesting, you might need to view them twice, once to read the content and a second time to review the design. If, at the end of your tour, you know what makes each site superb, you've learned all I've wanted to show you. If you'd rather undertake a more structured review of each site, then just read on.

# Examining a Corporate Internet Site

The Internet was once the domain of universities, government, and the military, but it is now the next market in the business world and businesses are flocking to it in unprecedented numbers. Some businesses are on the WWW because it's cool. Some see it as another means of advertising, like TV or radio. Some see it as a library, a place to deposit information about themselves that anyone can read. Some businesses have more vision and see it as a unique means of tying together themselves, their vendors, and their clients for improved competitiveness and service. And, of course, for many, their business is the Internet.

For all of the tens or even hundreds of thousands of businesses on the Internet, I had a very difficult time finding business-oriented Web sites that made good use of all of the design principles presented in the last three chapters—namely, an attractive and useful interface, good use of page layout, and easy to use navigation systems. I am very puzzled by this because most businesses are very savvy about their other media advertising. They will spend top dollar on materials and talent to put out ads, brochures, posters, and billboards displaying their products or services. Yet when these same companies enter the Internet world, the company logo, a picture of the company president, and a few pages of text are somehow supposed to be enough. Obviously, many businesses have not yet adapted to this medium.

I did finally find a company that understood the Internet audience, how to use Web technology, and how to adapt its business to it. This company, Rosenbluth International, built the Travelution Web site, `http://www.rosenbluth.com`. Travelution is basically your very own online travel agent. All of the resources and information that you need to plan a personal or business trip, whether domestic or international, are available from this site. And, the company used a variety of approaches to optimize this information for use over the Internet and add some services unique to the Internet. Rather than just trying to reproduce its paper, radio, or TV ads, the company has used the design principles discussed in the earlier chapters to good effect.

Before I discuss how these principles were used, I'll first give you some background from Susan Steinbrink, director of Consumer and Strategic Marketing at Rosenbluth International, on the factors that influenced the building of Travelution:

> Rosenbluth was a pioneer in the travel industry as it specifically relates to electronic commerce. In 1988, Rosenbluth Vacations established its presence on Prodigy. In May, 1995, Rosenbluth's site was launched on the Internet. This past November, the site was enhanced by Rosenbluth International. The core competency behind the site was twofold—increase brand awareness and seek a new audience (from corporate travel to the general traveling consumer). Through the Internet, we hope for Rosenbluth International to become the trusted advocate of travel information for Internet users, as we have for millions of corporate travelers worldwide. Rosenbluth International's Web site offers the general traveling consumer a fresh alternative to value-added travel data and services, including the ability to book air, car, hotel, cruise, and tour reservations, and browse specific destination information.

Building Travelution was a team effort that included not only the Web site builders, but also many key personnel at Rosenbluth International:

> Our Web site was developed by a third party Web development company who worked closely with our IS and marketing group to ensure that the design met our expectations. Even Hal Rosenbluth, the president and CEO of our company, was involved in how the site looked. He had final approval on all design aspects prior to the launch.

Even though Rosenbluth was an early pioneer in electronic business, the company still took seriously the updating of its Internet site:

> We spent a good deal of time ensuring that we had a good handle on exactly what we wanted to end up with. In order to accomplish this, we developed detailed Web site specifications and detailed flowcharts, offering up every page that we wanted to create. Then, the work began.

Even though Internet technology is constantly changing, the team kept things in perspective:

> Our goals for our Web site are constantly being refined. We, of course, took into consideration new technologies, versions of browsers, and the like. It was important for us to be cognizant of the lowest common denominator with all of our decisions.

> When designing our site, great measures were taken to create a Web site that would not be voluminous, but rather informative and fun. Easy navigation was a priority during the design, as well as the moderate use of graphics to ensure speed. The text on the site is light, as well, to insure that the information is not overwhelming to visitors. We know that travel is stressful enough; we wanted our Web site to help travelers "de-stress" their trip by providing only the information that would be the most useful and easy to use.

According to Steinbrink, here are some of the future directions Travelution will be exploring:

> Recently, we integrated Rosenbluth International's patented E-Res Electronic Reserva-tion System, which allows Rosenbluth International corporate clients the opportunity to utilize the Internet as a means to book their travel plans online by incorporating negotiated fares and travel policy. Currently, there is a fear in the business travel industry of travelers booking online, if they use a system that does not incorporate travel policy.

> We will also explore push marketing through the Web site in the future. For example, if a traveler is in the cruise and tour section and requests specific information about a supplier, we will be able to push information to them via the telephone lines.

## Interface Design at Travelution

Before proceeding, note that it is best to view Travelution with Netscape Navigator, version 3 or better. Although the site displays quite nicely in Internet Explorer, some special effects added using JavaScript will not work with IE, version 3 or earlier.

*Putting It All Together: HTML Design*

CHAPTER 26

489

26

PUTTING IT ALL
TOGETHER:
HTML DESIGN

A good interface

- Is consistent
- Is easy to use
- Is colorful or beautiful and nonirritating
- Can be seen on a variety of monitors with different resolutions and color depths
- Has well placed and appropriately sized controls

Travelution receives an A+ for consistency. Its home page, shown in Figure 26.1, is a good example of the consistency used through the whole site.

**FIGURE 26.1.**

*The Travelution home page.*

A background image is used to set the color tone throughout the majority of the site. The left portion of the page is a textured blue; the larger, central portion is white; and the right side is a neutral yellow. Both the blue and yellow portions make good use of shadows to add some attractive and simple 3D effects. The colors visually organize the information for you. The right side is for placement of the main navigation menu. The middle contains the bulk of the information you will read or respond to. The left side is for secondary navigation menus or miscellaneous information. This design is used on almost every page of the site, even forms.

Most readers will understand this simple and easy-to-use interface completely after traveling through only two or three screens. The strength of this design is in its simplicity and good use of color. Notice how any elements placed over any of the three color regions have good contrast with that region, which means good visibility with a variety of monitor settings and color depths. As if this layout isn't enough, further graphical hints as to your location are given throughout the site. For instance, if you click on Escapes from the home page, you will see the main screen for the Escapes section as shown in Figure 26.2.

FIGURE 26.2.

*The main page for the Escapes section of Travelution.*

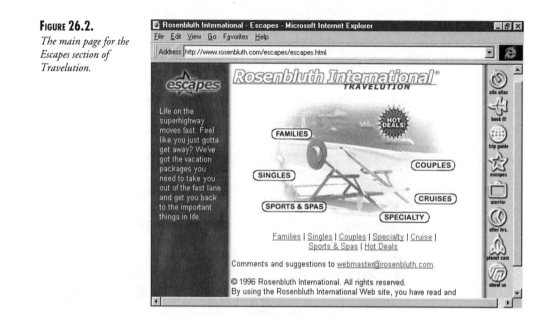

An attractive graphic, using the word "escapes," is placed in the upper-left blue portion of every page in this section. The star graphic that represents the Escapes menu item in the main navigation menu to the right is included in the graphic as an additional visual cue. Additionally, if you explore the Escapes section further, the Escapes graphic becomes a hyperlink back to the main Escapes page. More location hints are also incorporated into the company logo. You can see how this is effectively used by going back to the home page, clicking Book It, and traveling to the Flights screen shown in Figure 26.3.

Note the word "Flights" has now been added to the company logo at the top of the page. This has the added advantage of keeping the user's visual attention on your company logo. Because the logo is present on every page, it might tend to fade out of the visual attention of most visitors after awhile. Because it's an active part of the site with these location hints, however, visitors will automatically check the company logo on every page. This is an excellent use of advertising technique in the Internet medium.

As an aside, also notice how the page layout shown in Figure 26.3 no longer has the blue-white-yellow background pattern nor the navigation menus seen on the rest of the site. This is another visual cue to visitors that they are about to leave the site and enter the reservation computers.

**FIGURE 26.3.**
*Adding site location hints to the company logo.*

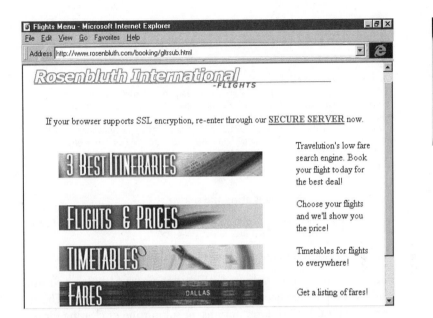

One interesting use of the browser interface is spawning off a new browser window (via JavaScript) and resizing it to display additional navigational information not directly available from the page. For instance, from the Travelution home page, if you click Site Highlights, a new browser window is opened and filled with an HTML page as shown in Figure 26.4.

**FIGURE 26.4.**
*Spawning a new, customized browser window.*

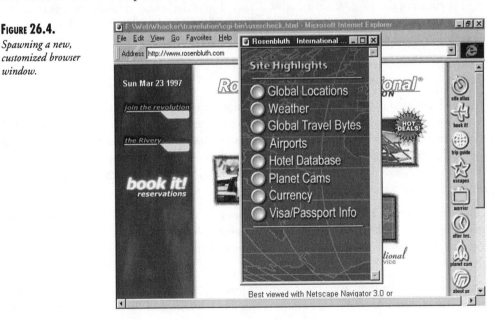

Notice how the new browser window has no controls or address bar and has a specific window size. As taken from the Travelution home page, the JavaScript code for spawning the new window is

```
function WinOpen() {
 /* Turn status, toolbar, directories, etc. off by replacing
     yes with no. Modify the HEIGHT and WIDTH calls to suit
➥your needs for this window. */
  var msg = window.open("../global.html","DisplayWindow","HEIGHT=360,WIDTH=230,
➥status=no,toolbar=no,scrollbars=yes,directories=no,menubar=no,location=no");
  if (navigator.appName == "Netscape" )     {
  msg.creator = self;
  }
```

The hyperlink code for initiating the spawn is

```
<A HREF="usercheck.html" onClick="WinOpen();"><IMG SRC="../images/main_03b.gif"
➥WIDTH="250" HEIGHT="96" BORDER="0"></A>
```

This new window disappears after a hyperlink within it is selected.

The vast majority of controls used at Travelution are related to navigation and are discussed in a later section of this chapter, "User Navigation at Travelution." The only other interface controls are typical HTML form buttons for submitting or clearing forms.

## Page Layout Techniques Used at Travelution

As you might have guessed by now, tables are used at Travelution for most page layout. The home page uses a container table three columns wide to lay out the contents of the left and right portions of the page. A nested table is placed into the center column and contains the content shown in the white section of the page. This nested table effect is shown on the Travelution home page in more detail in Figure 26.5.

In this figure, I changed the table border width for the container table to two and for the nested table to five for display purposes.

This same layout is used throughout much of the site, making maintenance and changes quite easy. Most changes will be made to the content of the nested table. Any content can be added to the nested table without disturbing the layout or appearance of the content of the left and right columns in the container table. Many times the content of the central column does not need the additional organization of a nested table, and the content of the central column is simply placed into the container table.

Only one simple font face, Arial, is used throughout the site to improve page appearance. This gracefully decays to default fonts if the user does not have Arial on his or her machine, ensuring that no information will be lost to any user and that the basic flow of text will not be affected.

Graphics are for the most part small and fast-loading, leading to a quick response for most pages. The largest (file size) image on the whole site is 59KB, and that is a weather map over which Travelution has no control. The Web site builders followed the general rule of thumb of keeping most pages under 50KB in size. Graphics are used well to inform or entice the visitor. The enticement part is especially important for a travel-oriented site. It is much easier to fantasize about running down a white sand beach if you can see a picture of it. In fact, it would be quite easy to try to overload Travelution with too many images or images that are too large. The builders struck a good compromise between the need to display pictures of travel locations and the limited Internet bandwidth available to many visitors.

**FIGURE 26.5.**

*Using nested tables to lay out Travelution.*

Interestingly, only one animated GIF and no video is used on the entire site. The animated GIF is the centerpiece of the opening page; it does not compete with any text. Again, in a business situation, having a potential customer leave the site because he or she is irritated by animated GIFs is unacceptable. In my opinion, Travelution does not suffer any ill effects in appearance or usefulness by not having more animated GIFs or video. There is one short audio clip with a warm welcome from the Rosenbluth CEO. You can find this on the About Rosenbluth part of the site.

Neither style sheets nor frames are used at Travelution. This ensures compatibility with the maximum number of browser types. This compatibility is essential for a business site because any browser not served means potential lost business and revenue. Travelution also does not use spacer images for pushing text or graphics around a page. This keeps page building simple, and means more time can be spent placing content onto the site.

There is only one small layout flaw at Travelution, and I only point it out because it can become a major problem in certain situations. You will need to view the file `tip_int.html` in the tips folder on your screen to actually find this flaw; it will not show up in a screenshot. If you look on the left blue side, below the navigation text, you will see a text hyperlink about a Big

Mac. The problem here is that the blue hyperlink color blends in with the blue page background color. On many monitors, you might not even notice this hyperlink. In this case the hyperlink is more entertainment-oriented and does not detract from the information on Travelution, so little is lost. But what if the hyperlink were more important? Whenever you think about the colors to use for hyperlinks or text, think about what might happen if your text shifts around in a browser. Will that text or hyperlinked text end up over a background element that will camouflage it? If you think your text or hyperlinked text will end up camouflaged, you might consider replacing them with graphics (for Travelution, a piece of hamburger clip art and some graphical text would do nicely) or changing the default text or hyperlink colors. Another possibility is using nested tables to ensure that a particular background color is always associated with certain text or text hyperlinks.

## User Navigation at Travelution

I don't know any other way to say it except that the navigation system at Travelution is simply one of the best I've seen on the WWW. Every single navigation system you read about in Chapter 25, "User Navigation," is attractively represented, consistent, and well placed on most of the pages of the Travelution site.

Take another look at the main navigation menu that travels down the yellow, right side of most Travelution pages. (Refer back to Figure 26.1.) First, all choices on this menu fit comfortably in a 640×480 screen. Next, the navigational choices are represented by both text and interesting icons. The ALT field in <IMG SRC> is also filled in appropriately in case a surfer has images turned off or is using a text-based browser. The menu choices are arranged in a descending order, from most likely to be used to least likely. As if that isn't enough for a navigation menu, a special effect using JavaScript is built in for users of Netscape 3 or later. On the mouseover() event, the button appears to shrink as if it has been pushed. This improves the interactivity of this menu while providing some simple entertainment.

Can't find what you want from the main navigation menu? Go straight to the first choice in the navigation menu, the site atlas, which is shown in Figure 26.6.

This site map makes excellent use of graphics and text to outline the site. A user is able to take everything in quickly and clearly and click to a destination in short order. The icons and most of the main headers match those found in the main navigation menu along the left side. Other nice touches include a "You are here" note and inclusion of important non-Travelution sites, including After Hours and the Currency converter under Trip Guide.

Clicking on one of the major sections, in this instance Escapes, takes you to the Escapes opening page, shown earlier in Figure 26.2.

Here, an attractive image map is backed up by text hyperlinks that will take you to any of the listed escapes. The Escapes graphic is in the upper left as a further indicator of your location, as noted earlier. The main navigation menu is always to your right if you change your mind. Clicking on one of the Escapes, such as Cruises, takes you to the main menu for cruises shown in Figure 26.7.

*Putting It All Together: HTML Design*

CHAPTER 26

495

26

PUTTING IT ALL
TOGETHER:
HTML DESIGN

**FIGURE 26.6.**

*The site atlas at
Travelution.*

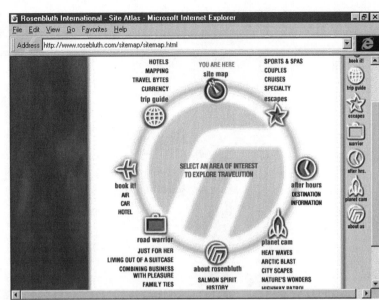

**FIGURE 26.7.**

*Choosing a cruise in
the Escapes menu at
Travelution.*

Notice how the navigation menu to the left has changed. Now you have graphical text, with the text highlighted (in this case, yellow) for the Escapes subsection you are in. Each of the choices on the left represents one part of the image map from the Escapes page. This is included below the Escapes graphic as further emphasis that you are in a subsection of the Escapes section of Travelution. In the middle of the page you can choose from any of the four cruise packages. If you click on the Glacier Bay cruise, you will see the screen shown in Figure 26.8.

**FIGURE 26.8.**

*One of the cruises offered at Travelution.*

Notice here that none of the navigation menus changed even though you've gone another level deeper into the site. Of course, the question is, where would you put another navigation menu, or is it even appropriate here? Do you now change the left side navigation menu to reflect the four cruises, or leave it as is to provide a means of visiting other Escapes? Because there are no more levels to drill down through (an HTML form to request more price information is the next and last level from this page), an additional menu is optional here. There is no right answer here in my opinion. This is a judgment call and should be based on how you think most users will want to navigate through this section (feedback or user testing would provide invaluable information here).

This style of navigation is used through most of Travelution and makes it almost impossible for even the most novice surfer to become lost. The vast amount of travel information on Travelution is well organized using these many navigation menus, emphasizing the point that your next trip to Glacier Bay will be as well planned and organized by Rosenbluth International as your trip around the Travelution Web site has been.

## Other Notable Design Highlights at Travelution

In addition to good page layout, navigation, and interface design, I was drawn to Travelution because the designers sprinkled it all with a bit of well-placed fun. If you go to the Road Warrior section, for example, you will see a picture of a cow with the phrase underneath "Feeling stressed?" (See Figure 26.9.)

**FIGURE 26.9.**
*A cow on a travel site?*

You don't really expect to see a cow on a travel site, so it is immediately eye catching. Clicking on the cow brings up a list (again, using the spawned browser window technique mentioned earlier) of 10 reasons to visit a resort ranch. Any road warrior will empathize with at least one of the reasons and be encouraged to investigate this particular travel package by clicking a button at the bottom of the list. Although this is simply good advertising technique, it is executed well within a Web site and adds to the enjoyment of Travelution.

Another excellent blending of Web technology with the travel theme of Travelution is an entire section called Planetcam. Here you can find lists of hyperlinks to various Webcams around the Internet that are pointing at items of interest to the traveler. One of these lists, Heat Waves, is shown in Figure 26.10.

These hyperlinks will load the latest picture for wherever the Web camera is pointed to give you immediate feedback on what's happening. Going to Maui tomorrow? Don't rely solely on a weather map or atlas. See for yourself by checking out the Maui Web cameras. Where else can you get this type of immediate feedback, day or night, from the comfort of your computer chair? Travelution did not skimp on its selection of locations to choose from, either, with a total of 60 cameras from around the world. This is an excellent example of putting the unique features of the Internet (Web cams everywhere) to work for your business. It also shows the Internet savvy at Rosenbluth International.

Rosenbluth International has effectively demonstrated that a Web site can be attractive, well designed, and even a little fun without sacrificing any business usefulness. Building a site like this takes a commitment in time and resources, but if a business is serious about its presence on the WWW, why should it settle for a mediocre site? A quality business should have a quality Web site. You can build an effective business presence on the Web using mostly HTML and some sound design principles, as you've seen well demonstrated at the Travelution site.

**FIGURE 26.10.**

*Web camera sites of interest to travelers.*

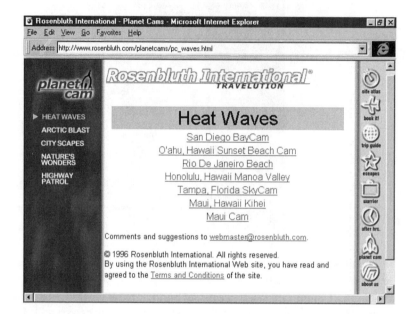

# Examining an E-zine

Before I review the CyberMad Web site, you need to remember that this is an entertainment-oriented Web site. Although content clarity and ease of navigation are still important, there is much more room for a broader interpretation of the guidelines. On a business site, a word that is not understood or a user who becomes lost can cost the business many dollars—and that is completely unacceptable for a business site. For an e-zine, missing a word or sacrificing some clarity for art might actually contribute to the entertainment value of a particular page. Remember, your design guidelines must be tightly integrated with the flow of your Web site content. Design techniques used on a corporate site can devalue the content (that is, lead to terminal boredom) on an entertainment site, and entertainment techniques can lead to misunderstandings on a business site (that is, lost dollars and upset clients). A particular approach to designing any Web site is successful because the content and the design work together in synergy. Either one alone is insufficient to achieve greatness for a Web site.

Because Web site design and content are so tightly interwoven, in order to effectively study CyberMad, we first need to hear from Christopher Parr, Creator and Executive Producer, as to why he created the site:

CyberMad evolved due to the lack of quality sites. Either they had no content or the graphics were pulled straight out of the clip art books. Being a writer with experience in theater and TV, I constructed the CyberMad project as a similar medium—kind of like "Saturday Night Live" meets *Alice in Wonderland* online. Since then, the style and influence has been repeated in what has been dubbed as an *e-zine.* I never once considered it as your standard static Web site. CyberMad morphed into a dynamically changing and inviting presence, showcasing something unique and strange without a corporate presence.

The majority of CyberMad was written solely by Christopher Parr with some CGI scripts from a UNIX guru, and later, inclusion of the works of various artists. Parr says that after he had decided on his goals, his Web site started this way:

> CyberMad is a constantly evolving presence. At the beginning, the project was fairly thin, but after a few weeks of conceptualization, I constructed a solid skeleton— designed for growth and expansion. Currently, the site consists of many layers— getting deeper and deeper every month.

Concerning the problem of designing Web pages in relation to constantly changing Web technology, Parr says this:

> It is difficult to tolerate old browsers, but you need to think of the audience. If one person with Netscape 1.0 is turned away, that's one person who will never experience your presence. Web technology grows too fast and doesn't coexist with the reality that most people are still connected with 14.4 modems.

As your Web site evolves, Christopher Parr recommends, "Watch the trends, but don't always follow everyone's advice. Stay true to your identity and get online."

## Interface Design at CyberMad

With these site goals in mind, let's look at how some of the interface controls at CyberMad are designed and placed to meet these goals. The interface controls that are primarily navigational in flavor are discussed later in this chapter. Our first stop is the Hollywood Geek Machine, the first screen of which is shown in Figure 26.11.

As you can see, there are only two obvious controls, Push and Exit, both part of a generic machine image. Because most people come here out of curiosity, the Push button is the most obvious next choice. When Push is clicked, a page with a JavaScript random number generator is loaded and a random "geek" image is displayed, as shown in Figure 26.12.

In this second screen, the leftmost button now reads Again rather than Push. Clicking on Again takes you back to the first screen and you can loop through these two screens until you've seen all the geeks. Then you can exit back to the Culture Department page.

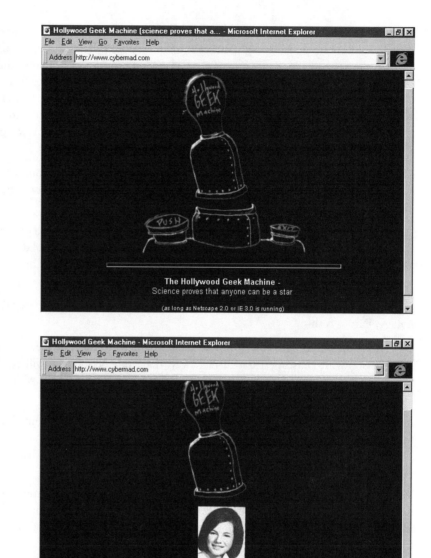

From an interface design perspective, this is perfectly done. The controls are obvious, relatively easy to read (acceptable for an entertainment site), cleverly incorporated into a machine-style image (maintaining the machine context of this area of the site), and consistent in style and color with the rest of the page. There is no clutter on this page to distract you from the machine, so it will clearly be the focus of attention. The color scheme is simple (red, black, and

*Putting It All Together: HTML Design*

CHAPTER **26**

501

26

PUTTING IT ALL
TOGETHER:
HTML DESIGN

white), so it should be readable on almost any monitor at any resolution. The entertainment value of this section is enhanced by the excellent use of these controls, making the experience of the Hollywood Geek Machine that much more enjoyable.

Our next stop as we examine interface design at CyberMad is the Hype Monster, screen one of which is shown in Figure 26.13.

**FIGURE 26.13.**

*Screen one of The Hype Monster.*

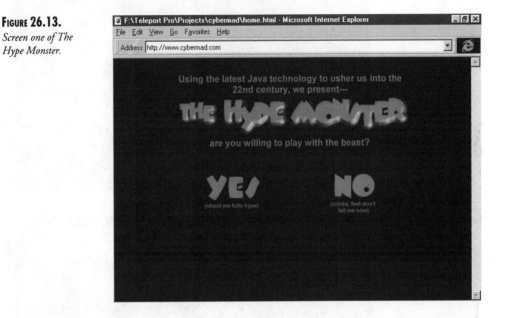

Again, this mostly black and red interface has only two obvious choices, Yes and No responses to the single question posed on the page. Again, the controls are easy to find, entertaining in themselves, and well integrated with the page theme and style. The small point text under the responses might be a bit hard for some readers to see, but it is not essential to operating the controls. True to form, clicking on the Yes response brings up the next page, shown in Figure 26.14, which contains a Java applet scrolling through a number of hype phrases.

The single interface control on this page is a skillful combination of a color reversed image and some text. Again, even though this control is not quite the same style as the Yes and No responses on screen one (the font used in the text is the same) of The Hype Monster, it is immediately apparent that it is a control because little else is on this page. The control is again well integrated with and adds beauty to the page. When you've seen most of the hypes, you assume you can return by clicking this control. Surprise! This control takes you down another path and you come to the screen shown in Figure 26.15.

**FIGURE 26.14.**
*Screen two of The Hype Monster.*

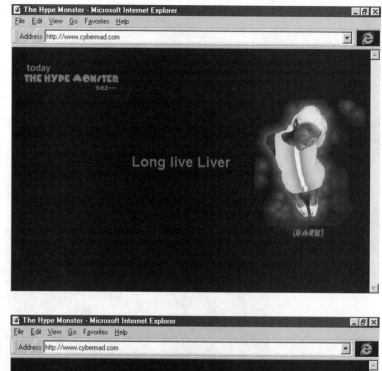

**FIGURE 26.14.**
*Screen two of The Hype Monster.*

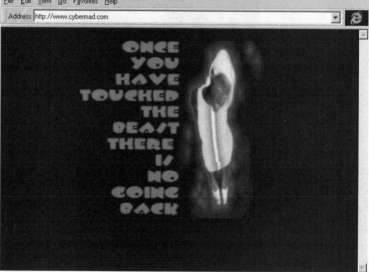

**FIGURE 26.15.**
*The Hype Monster won't let go.*

Where are you now? Obviously, you can use your browser Back button to back out of all of this, but this is one instance where the mystery of The Hype Monster is enhanced by offering no alternative controls or navigation. This heightens your curiosity because you thought you had seen all The Hype Monster had to offer when you were watching the hype phrases go by in the last screen. This is an excellent example of taking an interface no-no, offering only one poorly marked path, and making it work for you. You have little choice but to click the image and continue forward even though you don't know where you are or where you're going. The final satire for this piece of CyberMad becomes evident from the last screen of The Hype Monster, shown in Figure 26.16.

**FIGURE 26.16.**

*The final message of The Hype Monster.*

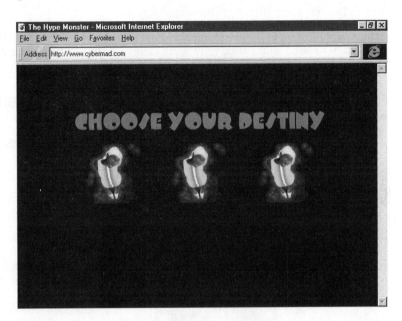

If your browser is set to display the URL in the status bar, you will notice that you can go to Microsoft, Netscape, or back to the CyberMad Culture page. Again, the interface is consistent with that found in the rest of The Hype Monster. It is interesting to note that on this page, the same image is used to represent all three destinations with no text explanation. Yet the rest of the controls in The Hype Monster were very clearly marked. Why do you think Christopher Parr left the text out? In my opinion, he is again using mystery to emphasize the lessons The Hype Monster has just taught you. Sometimes as much of a message is communicated by the lack of clear interface controls as is communicated using clearly marked controls.

There are many other excellent examples of well-integrated, beautiful, and yet very useful interface controls throughout the CyberMad site. I recommend visiting and examining Movie Central and Insult-a-rama for further examples in the excellent use of interface controls and design. As you surf through the site, notice how each section has its own unique flavor and how the interface is crafted as an integral part of the flavor for that section.

## Page Layout Techniques Used at CyberMad

Page layout techniques vary tremendously at CyberMad, as you might expect given the wide range of topics. In this review of layout techniques, I provide the HTML filename under discussion so that you can examine the HTML source on the CD-ROM for more detail on how a particular page was built.

The first screen of the Hollywood Geek Machine (geek.html), which you saw in Figure 26.11, simply centers a series of images and builds the machine without having to resort to a table for layout. The second screen (geeks.html) continues with this simple layout scheme even with a JavaScript routine inserting an image.

Simplicity within a table rules in the Reviews section (reviews.html) of Movie Central. Figure 26.17 shows a fixed width table (300 pixels) with a white cell background centered against a black page background (the left and bottom menus on the page are navigation menus in frames).

**FIGURE 26.17.**

reviews.html *uses a single cell table for page layout.*

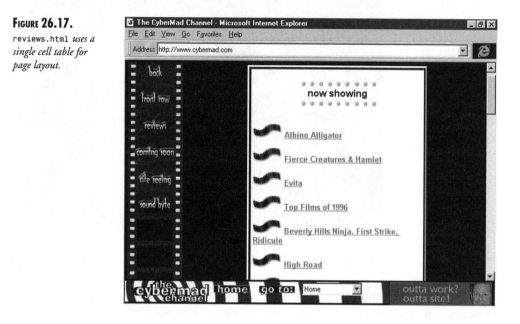

This table is unique in that it is composed of only a single cell and all of the text and graphics are included in this single cell. Here is the HTML code for much of the table:

```
<CENTER><TABLE CELLPADDING=3 CELLSPACING=3 BORDER=3 WIDTH=300>
<TR><TD COLSPAN=2 ROWSPAN=2 ALIGN=left VALIGN=MIDDLE BGCOLOR=#FFFFFF>
➥<font face=arial size=3>
<CENTER><br><img border=0  src="flick.gif"  width=150 height=13><br><b>
➥now showing</B><br><img border=0  src="flick.gif"   width=150
➥height=13></CENTER></FONT><P>
<BR><b>
<font size=2 face=arial><b>
<a href="gator.html"><img src="film-1.gif" border=0>Albino Alligator</a><P>
<a href="fierce.html"><img src="film-1.gif" border=0>Fierce Creatures
➥& Hamlet</a><P>
 ---- SNIP ----    THE REMAINING REVIEWS    ---- SNIP ----
</TD></TR>
</TABLE>
```

Notice how the film strip image opposite each review is inserted in the hyperlink anchor with the text, allowing one anchor set to work for both the text and the graphic. This saves a lot of

coding time. Even though it is common practice to include graphics in their own table cell, there are instances, such as this, when good organization can be achieved without the hassle of working with many table cells.

CyberMad also makes good use of nested tables for page layout in The Culture Dept. (`culture.html`). First, the page background (`backcine.gif`) is a simple black and white (4 pixels high by 640 pixels wide) line. The width of the black (182 pixels) and white (458 pixels) sections acts as a simple grid for placing the graphics and text elements. The container table, within which two nested tables are placed, is set at 600 pixels wide to constrain the page size for easy viewing by people at 640×480 monitor resolution. The container table is again composed of a single cell. The first nested table is composed of four cells and contains the back button and the graphic at the top of the page. (See Figure 26.18.)

**FIGURE 26.18.**

*The first nested table in* `culture.html`.

Again I turned on the table borders for improved viewing. The table cell widths and cell justifications are used together to determine whether an element is placed against the black portion or white portion of the page background image.

Below the first nested table, a graphic (`culture.gif`) is simply placed into the container table. If you load this image into a bitmap editor that displays transparency, you will notice that Christopher Parr leaves transparent the portion of the image that crosses the black/white boundary of the page background image. (See Figure 26.19.)

This is a simple way to allow for slightly different browser offsets without worrying about whether the image will stay aligned against the page background.

**FIGURE 26.19.**

*Leaving a transparent hole in* culture.gif.

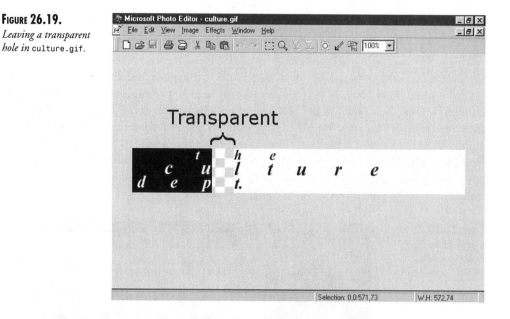

The second nested table contains the bulk of the elements seen on The Culture Dept. page. This table is four columns wide but again contains only a single row, as shown in Figure 26.20.

**FIGURE 26.20.**

*Using nested tables in the Culture Dept. at CyberMad.*

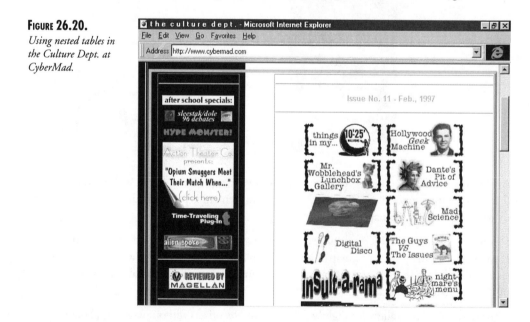

The first column is used to add an offset (seven pixels) to the left of the table. The second column (width=128) contains all of the text and graphics that display against the black portion of

*Putting It All Together: HTML Design*
CHAPTER **26**
507

**26**
PUTTING IT ALL
TOGETHER:
HTML DESIGN

the page background. The third column (width=70) spans the black/white transition of the page background. The final column (width=398) contains all of the elements that display against the white portion of the background. Again, even though each text and graphics element in culture.html is not placed into its own table cell, the page is still well organized.

As Christopher Parr has demonstrated here, you should use the simplest page layout design possible. This will save you time and give you an attractive page. You've also seen how the page layout is tightly integrated with the content of the page and how it can enhance the content. Also notice that no long, run-on pages are found on CyberMad. Even at lower monitor resolutions, you seldom have to page down more than three times to read an entire page. This keeps the reader constantly interacting with the material, which is a primary goal for an entertainment site.

## User Navigation of CyberMad

CyberMad uses a drop-down list box in a frame at the bottom of the browser window to make all of the major CyberMad site sections available to visitors at all times. The Table of Contents page, including the bottom frame, for CyberMad is shown in Figure 26.21.

**FIGURE 26.21.**

*The two main navigation menus at CyberMad.*

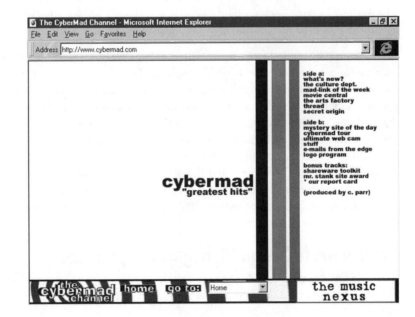

Christopher Parr used JavaScript to build the drop-down list box navigation menu in the bottom frame. This makes the control available to the vast majority of browsers. This also makes excellent use of the GUI paradigm, building on most people's familiarity with a windowing environment. The JavaScript code can be seen in nav.html. Note that the original JavaScript included the complete URL for the page to be accessed. I had to change this to include only the filename so that the site could be placed on the CD-ROM. A new page is loaded simply by selecting an item from the drop-down list. Also notice the "Home" graphic that returns the user to the Table of Contents page (shown in Figure 26.21).

The Table of Contents page emphasizes the navigation menu in the upper frame through good use of white space and the unique placement of the vertical stripes down the page. Anyone using any monitor resolution or color depth will be able to read and find this menu. The menu itself is an image map, and a page layout table is used to align the image map against the background stripes.

Notice how there are no backup text hyperlinks for either menu. Although an informational or business-oriented Web site would have back up text hyperlinks to ensure navigability by all browsers (especially when each browser is a potential client), on an entertainment site, they are again optional. Because so much of the CyberMad content is based on graphics (think back on how the Hollywood Geek Machine would look without graphics), there is no need to design for browsers that can't handle graphics. Even though Christopher earlier stated his commitment to maximizing browser compatibility, the entertainment goals of CyberMad simply cannot be met using text. For instance, the Culture page shown in Figure 26.20 is almost completely dependent on graphics for navigation.

The site author does, however, make good use of the ALT attribute for labeling images. Again, let your site content dictate your selection of navigation tools.

Throughout the remainder of the site, Christopher Parr uses a wide variety of text and graphical hyperlinks to keep the user from getting lost. He adds another frame to Movie Central. He uses a slide show paradigm (Back and Next buttons) in many parts of the CyberMad Tour. As you browse the site, also notice how Christopher Parr uses the hyperlinked word "Back" rather than "Home" as his primary means of returning to an index page. This builds on the browser paradigm for navigation because everyone knows where the Back key is on a browser within five minutes of learning how to use a browser for the first time. This makes navigating CyberMad even more intuitive. The hyperlinked "Back" graphic is also not placed in the same location on every page, nor does it look the same. This shows good integration of navigation with the design of each individual page or section. Very few pages in this entire site required the use of the browser's Back button to leave.

## Other Notable Design Highlights at CyberMad

CyberMad makes good use of an entrance or cover page to introduce you to the site. This page, shown in Figure 26.22, immediately sets the irreverent tone for the site and invites further exploration.

Animation and video are sparsely but effectively used throughout the site. The Culture Page has a scrolling marquee of the e-zine volume and date for browsers that can view it. Some of the animated GIFs include Mr. Wobblehead (how could you not animate this?), several other unintrusive animations on the Culture Page, and a marquee of lights on many pages in Movie Central. My favorite animation was the rotating nut used as the "o" on the Arts Factory page.

*Putting It All Together: HTML Design*

CHAPTER **26**

509

26

PUTTING IT ALL
TOGETHER:
HTML DESIGN

FIGURE **26.22.**

*The entrance to CyberMad.*

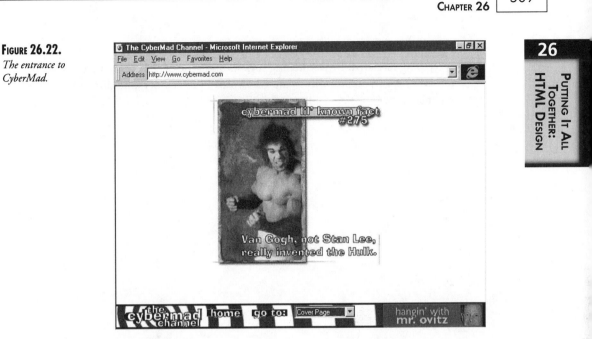

Parr also uses Java applets for The Hype Monster and in `guyindex.html`. There are also a number of sounds (as WAV files) sprinkled through the site. The only video is a very short AVI file connected via the `DYNSRC` attribute in the `<IMG SRC>` tag to a hyperlinked "Back" graphic on many pages. The only overly annoying movement I found on the whole site was the ubiquitous ads in the lower navigation frame.

Even with some of the pages shouting with oversaturated colors, CyberMad is still one of the best examples I have seen of the use of standard HTML to match content with Web page design. The many different page designs and techniques throughout the site were always matched to their content, enhancing the entertainment experience at CyberMad and, ultimately, making a unique contribution to the new media that is the WWW. The medium, of the WWW is not paper, it is not TV or the movies, and it is not radio. The WWW is a unique medium, and Christopher Parr has shown us one way to master it.

# Summary

The lessons in this chapter are best summarized by a few more words of wisdom from Christopher Parr:

> Reaction was initially positive, with the site being selected for the standard recognition with "Cool Site of the Day" and "USA's Hot Site." Then, for about five months, nothing happened. Visitors were still coming, but it seemed as if there was no buzz about the site in the press. I actually considered canceling the site. Then, all of a sudden, CyberMad won the 1996 NetBest Award (`http://www.ypn.com/netbest`) and

I was in Boston being introduced by author Douglas Coupland. After that point, everything escalated. I was catching reviews and articles about the site everywhere I turned. *Tenacity* and *dedication* are two words to remember, and don't expect overnight success.

# V
## PART

# Associated Technologies and Programming Languages

# CGI Programming

*by Eric Herrmann*

## IN THIS CHAPTER

**CHAPTER 27**

*HTML Unleashed* has everything you need to know about HTML—so what does CGI have to do with HTML? Not only will you learn what CGI has to do with HTML in this chapter, you will also learn how to use CGI to create interactive Web pages and get the detail you need for later reference. In the next few pages you will learn enough to build your own interactive Web pages, and gain an understanding of why CGI is extremely important to anyone building HTML Web pages. It's important, that is, if you want your Web page to sell products, interact with your Web page visitor, or provide any type of dynamic Web experience on your Web site. Finally, this chapter provides the details of CGI protocols of the CGI environment. If your only resource for CGI programming is *HTML Unleashed*, you will be able to refer to this chapter again and again to get the details about HTTP headers, environment variables, and decoding data from the all the interactive forms on your Web site.

# What CGI Programs Do on Your Web Site

CGI programs act as a special interface between your Web page and your Web server. CGI stands for Common Gateway Interface, and the name describes exactly what CGI programs are doing on your Web site. A CGI program receives the data from your Web page. Usually, a Web page uses an HTML <FORM> tag to initiate the CGI program. The HTML <FORM> tag has become the method of choice for sending data across the Net because of the ease of setting up a user interface using the HTML <FORM> and <INPUT> tags. Your CGI program interprets the data passed to it. It can then manipulate that data and return another Web page, or it can pass that data to another program, acting as an interface between the Web and other programming environments.

Putting databases, catalogs, and company information on the Web has become big business for lots of Web designers in the 1990s. The database and other programs don't typically interact directly with the Web; they use a CGI program to read the incoming data and another CGI program to return the data in HTML format. The terms *gateway* and *interface* come from this common use of CGI programs. The programs act as a gateway by reading incoming data from your HTML pages, and again as a gateway when they send new HTML pages back to your Web client. They also act as an interface when they send incoming data or receive outgoing data from other more complex programs, such as database servers.

# HTML and CGI

HTML, the language that gathers the data for CGI programs, is primarily designed for formatting text. So, how does it get involved with your CGI program? The primary method is through the HTML <FORM> tags. However, it's not required that your CGI program be called through an HTML <FORM> tag; your CGI program can be invoked through a simple hypertext link using the anchor tag, perhaps like so:

```
<a href="A CGI program"> Some text </a>
```

The CGI program in this hypertext reference or link would be called, or activated, in a manner similar to being called from an HTML <FORM> tag.

You can even use a link to pass extra data to your CGI program. All you have to do is add more information after the CGI program name. This information is usually referred to as extra path information, but it can be any type of data that might help identify to your CGI program what it needs to do.

The extra path information is provided to your CGI program in a variable called PATH_INFO. PATH_INFO is any data after the CGI program name and before the first question mark (?) in the href string. If you include a question mark after the CGI program name and then include more data after the question mark, the data would go in an environment variable called the QUERY_STRING. The environment variables available to your CGI program are covered later in this chapter. So to put this all into an example, if you created a link to your CGI program that looked like

```
<a href=www.practical-inet.com/cgibook/chap1/program.cgi/
extra-path-info?test=test-number-1> A CGI Program </a>
```

then when you selected the link A CGI Program, the CGI program named program.cgi would be activated, the environment variable PATH_INFO would be set to extra-path-info, and the QUERY_STRING environment variable would be set to Test=Test-number-1.

Normally, this is not considered a very good way to send data to your CGI program. For the programmer, it's harder to modify data hardcoded into an HTML file because it can't be easily done on the fly, and it's easier to modify for the Web page visitor who is a hacker. Your Web page visitors can download the Web page onto their own computers, modify the data your program is expecting, then use the modified file to call your CGI program. Neither of these scenarios seems very pleasant. And lots of other people felt so also, so this is where the HTML <FORM> tag steps in.

The HTML <FORM> tag is responsible for sending dynamic data to your CGI program. The basics just outlined are still the same. Data gets passed to the server for use by your CGI program, but the way you build your HTML <FORM> tag defines how that data will be sent. And your browser does most of the data formatting for you.

However, the most important feature of the HTML <FORM> tag is that the data can change based on user input. This is what makes the HTML <FORM> tag so powerful. Your Web page client can send you letters, fill out registration forms, use clickable buttons and pull-down menus to select merchandise, or fill out a survey.

To sum up, HTML, and in particular the HTML <FORM> tag, is responsible for gathering data and sending it to your CGI program. HTTP headers are covered in more detail later in this chapter.

The next section explains how the data collected by your browser is formatted and sent to the Web server. After you know how the data collected by your Web page is formatted, you can use a CGI program to decode the data when it gets to the server.

# What Happens to the Data Entered on Your Web Page

The GET method is the default method for sending data gathered by the <FORM> tag to the server. The URL-encoded string passed to your server is limited by the input buffer size of your server, which can be as small as 256 bytes. This means that the URL-encoded string can get too big and lose data. That's bad.

The data entered on your form is URL-encoded into name/value pairs and appended after any path information to the end of the URL identified in the ACTION field of your opening <FORM> tag.

Name/value pairs are the basis for sending the data entered on your Web page form to your CGI program on the server. These pairs are covered next in detail. The browser takes the following steps to get your data ready for sending to the server:

1. The browser takes the data from each of the TEXT entry fields and separates them into name/value pairs.

2. The browser encodes your data. URL encoding is covered last in this section.

3. After the data is URL encoded, the data is appended to the end of the URL identified in the ACTION field of your FORM statement. A question mark is used to separate the URL and its path information.

The data after the question mark is referred to as the query string.

Whether you use the GET method or not, the URL encoding of the query string is consistent for all data passed across the Internet. QUERY_STRING, by the way, is one of the environment variables that is discussed later in this chapter.

The HTML used to create the form is shown in Listing 27.1, and the form itself is shown in Figure 27.1. Listing 27.2 contains the data from a registration form. You can see the name/value pairs separated by the ampersand (&) and identified as pairs with the equal sign (=).

**Listing 27.1. The HTML for a registration form.**

```
01: <html>
02: <head><title> HTML FORM using Text Entry</title></head>
03: <body>
04: <h1> A FORM using the Get method for text entry </h1>
05:
06: <hr noshade>
07: <center>
09 : <FORM Method=GET Action="/cgi-bin/nph-get_method.cgi">
10: <table border = 0 width=60%>
11: <caption align = top> <H3>Registration Form </H3></caption>
12: <th ALIGN=LEFT> First Name
13: <th ALIGN=LEFT colspan=2 > Last Name <tr>
14:
```

```
15: <td>
16: <input type=text size=10 maxlength=20 name="first" >
17: <td colspan=2>
18: <input type=text size=32 maxlength=40 name="last" > <tr>
19: <th ALIGN=LEFT colspan=3>
20: Street Address <td> <td> <tr>
21:
22: <td colspan=3>
23: <input type=text size=61 maxlength=61 name="street"> <tr>
24: <th ALIGN=LEFT > City
25: <th ALIGN=LEFT > State
26: <th ALIGN=LEFT > Zip <tr>
27: <td> <input type=text size=20 maxlength=30 name="city">
28: <td> <input type=text size=20 maxlength=20 name="state">
29: <td> <input type=text size=5 maxlength=10 name="zip"> <tr>
30:
31: <th ALIGN=LEFT  colspan=3> Phone Number <tr>
32: <td colspan=3> <input type=text size=15 maxlength=15
➥name="phone" value="(999) 999-9999"> <tr>
33: <td width=50%> <input type="submit" name="simple"
➥value=" Submit Registration " >
34: <td width=50%> <input type=reset> <tr>
35: </table>
36: </FORM>
37: </center>
38: <hr noshade>
39: </body>
40: </html>
```

**FIGURE 27.1.**
*The registration form.*

**Listing 27.2. Registration form data encoded for the server.**

```
QUERY_STRING  first=Eric&last=Herrmann&street=255+S.+Canyonwood+Dr.&city=
Dripping+Springs&state=Texas&zip=78620&phone=%28512%29+894-0704&simple=
+Submit+Registration+
```

# Name/Value Pairs

All of the data input from a form is sent to the server or your CGI program as name/value pairs. The preceding registration example used only TEXT input, but even the Submit button is sent as a name/value pair. You can see this at the end of the line of Listing 27.2. The Submit button name is simple and the value is Submit Registration. Notice that case is maintained in the value fields.

Name/value pairs are always passed to the server as *name=value* and each new pair is separated by an ampersand (&) like so: *name1=value1&name2=value2*. This arrangement allows you to perform some simple data decoding and have a *variable = value* already built for your Bourne or C-shell script to use. Using Perl, you can filter out name/value pairs with just a little bit of effort.

Notice on line 16, <input type=text size=10 maxlength=20 name="first" >, that the name attribute is added to the input type of text. In programming, the name is the formal parameter declaration, and the value, whether given by default or by entering data into the entry field, is the actual parameter definition.

Put in another way, the name is your program's way of always referring to the incoming data. The name field never changes. The data associated with the name field is in the value portion of the name/value pair. The value field changes with every new submittal. In the sample name/value pair first=Eric, the name is first, and the value is Eric.

Just remember that whether you use text entry, radio buttons, checkboxes, or pull-down menus, everything you enter on your Web page form will be sent as name/value pairs.

# Path Information

Path information can be added to the action string identifying your CGI program. You can use path information to give variable information to your CGI program. Let's assume you have several forms that call the same CGI program. The CGI program could access several different databases, depending on which form was submitted.

One way to tell your CGI program which database to access is by including the path to the correct database in the form submittal.

You add path information in the ACTION field of the opening HTML <FORM> tag.

First, as usual, you identify your CGI program by putting into the ACTION field the path to your CGI program and then the program name itself. For example:

```
<FORM METHOD=GET ACTION="/cgi-bin/database.cgi/">
```

Next, you add any additional path information you want to give your CGI program. If you wanted to add path information to one of three databases in the preceding URL, it would look like this:

```
<FORM METHOD=GET ACTION="/cgi-bin/database.cgi/database2/">
```

The path information in this example is `database2/`.

When the Submit button (in line 33 of Listing 27.1) is clicked, the browser appends a question mark (?) to the ACTION URL; the name/value pairs are appended after the question mark.

# URL Encoding

By now you have figured out that in order to send your data from the browser to the server, some type of data encoding must have occurred. This is called URL encoding.

The convention of URL encoding Internet data was started to handle sending URLs by electronic mail. Part of the encoding sequence is for special characters like tabs, spaces, and periods. E-mail tools have problems with these and other special characters in the ASCII character set. The URL gets really confused if you used the reserved HTML characters within a URL. So if the URL you're referencing includes restricted characters like spaces, they must be encoded into the hex equivalent.

URL encoding is important to your CGI program for the following two reasons:

- Several reserved characters must be URL encoded if you include them in the URL string in the ACTION field. Spaces, the percent sign (%), and the question mark (?) are examples of special characters. (More about these characters in the next section.)
- All data is URL encoded, and if you want to be able to decode it when it gets to your CGI program, you need to understand it.

## Reserved Characters

So what is this set of characters that can't be included in your URL? One of the simple ones is the space character. If you own a Macintosh computer, you know that spaces in filenames are a common and convenient feature of the Apple operating system. However, when shipped on the Internet, they confuse things. So if you had a file called `Race Cars`, you would need to encode that into `Race%20Cars`.

The percent sign (%) tells the decoding routine that encoding has begun, and the next two characters are hex numbers that correspond to the ASCII equivalent value of a space.

If you were trying to send HTML tags as part of your data transfer, the < and > symbols would need to be encoded. They encode as `%3C` for <, and `%3E` for >.

Hex is simply a numbering system with values ranging from 0 to 15, where the numbers 10–15 are encoded as the letters A–F. So the hex range is 0–F. A code is always made up of a percent sign followed by two hex values. You don't really need to understand hex values any better than that—just read the numbers from the table and encode them as needed.

Table 27.1 lists the ASCII characters that must be encoded in your URL. It lists both the decimal and hex values. The decimal values are only included for your information; you must use the hex values.

**Table 27.1. URL characters that must encoded.**

| Character | Decimal | Hex |
|-----------|---------|-----|
| tab       | 09      | 09  |
| space     | 16      | 20  |
| "         | 18      | 22  |
| (         | 40      | 28  |
| )         | 41      | 29  |
| ,         | 44      | 2C  |
| .         | 46      | 2E  |
| ;         | 59      | 3B  |
| :         | 58      | 3A  |
| <         | 60      | 3C  |
| >         | 62      | 3E  |
| @         | 64      | 40  |
| [         | 101     | 5B  |
| \         | 102     | 5C  |
| ]         | 103     | 5D  |
| ^         | 104     | 5E  |
| `         | 106     | 60  |
| {         | 113     | 7B  |
| ¦         | 114     | 7C  |
| }         | 115     | 7D  |
| ñ         | 116     | 7E  |

In addition to the reserved characters listed in Table 27.1, there are several other characters that should be encoded if you don't want them to be interpreted by your server or client for their special meaning.

- Encode the question mark (?) as %3F; otherwise, you will begin a query string too early.
- Encode the ampersand (&) as %26; otherwise, you start the separation of a name/value pair when you don't want to.
- Encode the backslash (/) as %2F; otherwise, you will start a new directory path.
- Encode the equal sign (=) as %3D; otherwise, you may bind a name/value pair when you don't want to.

- Encode the number sign (#) as %23. This is used to reference another location in the same document.
- Encode the percent sign (%) as %25; otherwise, you will really confuse everyone. Decoding will start at your unencoded %.

If you want to look at the gory details of MIME/URL encoding, you can get RFC 1552, the MIME message header extensions document, off the Net. It has the encoding format in section three and is available with the other Internet RFC documents at http://ds.internic.net/ds/dspg1intdoc.html.

## The Encoding Steps

So now you know the basis for encoding all the data. Remember that all data sent on the Internet is URL-encoded. The steps used for getting your data encoded follow. These steps work for both the POST and the GET methods.

1. Data is transferred as name/value pairs.
2. Name/value pairs are separated from other name/value pairs by the ampersand.
3. Name/value pairs are identified with each other by the equal sign. If no data is entered and a default value is defined, the value will be the default value. If no default value is defined, the value will be empty but a name/value pair will be sent.
4. Spaces in value data are a special case. They are converted to the plus sign (+).
5. Reserved characters cannot be used in the URL; they must be encoded.
6. Characters that have special meaning must be encoded before being sent to the browser.
7. Characters are encoded by being converted to their hex values.
8. Encoded characters are identified with a percent sign and two hex digits (%*NN*).

# Decode FORM Data

Now that you know the steps for encoding the data that's sent from the browser to your server, the decoding is easy. This section presents the basic steps of decoding the data sent from your HTML form to the Web server. This is where you put your new knowledge of CGI programming and its environment to work.

Your CGI program will be activated based on the ACTION field in the HTML <FORM> tag on your Web page. The data from your form will be available either in the environment variable QUERY_STRING or at STDIN. Thus, step one of decoding the incoming URL-encoded FORM data is figuring out how the form sent your data. To do this, you read the environment variable REQUEST_METHOD. Your CGI programs rely on the environment variable for a lot of information; the environment variables available to your programs are covered in the last sections of this chapter. The REQUEST_METHOD environment variable should equal GET or POST, the two methods for sending data from an HTML form. If the REQUEST_METHOD isn't set, the default method for sending data from your HTML form is the GET method.

Step two in decoding the incoming form data is to read the data into a common variable your code can process. If the data was sent using the GET method, your program needs to copy the environment variable QUERY_STRING into your decoding variable. If the data was sent using the POST method, the data is available at STDIN. The environment variable CONTENT_LENGTH contains the amount of data your program needs to read from STDIN. Your CGI program could be written in Perl 5, C/C++, Java, TCL, Visual Basic, or some other language of your choice. You might use a loop, a simple read, or some other function to move the data from STDIN into your decoding variable. Just remember that the amount of data you need to move from STDIN is available in the CONTENT_LENGTH environment variable.

 Now that you have the data from your form, step three starts the actual decoding process. Remember that the first step of sending URL-encoded data was placing the data into name/value pairs and that name/value pairs are separated by an ampersand. If your CGI program is written in Perl 5, use the split function to separate name/value pairs based on the ampersand. Save the split data into an array for further decoding. If you're using Java, the stringTokenizer function performs a similar function, separating the data into tokens based on the ampersand. C has a similar tokenizing function called stoken for tokenizing strings. At the end of this section is part of a program written by Steven E. Brenner, cgi-lib.pl. This program is included on the CD-ROM (and can be found online at www.bio.coma.ac.uk/cgi-lib) and illustrates the steps you're learning about here. I've included this program because it is well commented, so even if you're unfamiliar with Perl, you should be able to understand the program.

The fourth step in decoding the data is converting the plus signs back into spaces. Use a straightforward substitution function for this action. In Perl you could use tr or s. In C you might just search for the plus sign and replace it with a space. Regardless of the method, the plus sign is replaced with a space character, as it was before it was URL encoded.

Step five separates the name/value pair based on the equal sign. In Perl and Java, you can again use the split or stringTokenizer functions, respectively, to separate the data.

Step six involves converting all those hex-encoded special characters shown in Table 27.1 back into their normal state. Remember that all the hex-encoded characters begin with a percent sign. Your code should look for that first percent sign, and you know the next two characters will be hex values. Convert these hex values back to their ASCII equivalent, and your data is now URL decoded.

In Perl and Java, a convenient storage place for name/value pairs is in an associative array. Save the URL-decoded name/value pairs and begin the decoding steps on the next set of URL encoded name/value pairs. When your code has processed all the name/value pairs, you can take the data and do as you please with it.

As promised, part of Steven E. Brenner's code for reading and decoding form data is shown in Listing 27.3.

**Listing 27.3. Reading and decoding form data in Perl 5.**

```perl
sub ReadParse {
  local (*in) = shift if @_;    # CGI input
  local (*incfn,                # Client's filename (may not be provided)
     *inct,                     # Client's content-type (may not be provided)
     *insfn) = @_;              # Server's filename (for spooled files)
  local ($len, $type, $meth, $errflag, $cmdflag, $perlwarn, $got);

  # Disable warnings as this code deliberately uses local and environment
  # variables which are preset to undef (i.e., not explicitly initialized)
  $perlwarn = $^W;
  $^W = 0;

  binmode(STDIN);    # we need these for DOS-based systems
  binmode(STDOUT);   # and they shouldn't hurt anything else
  binmode(STDERR);

  # Get several useful env variables
  $type = $ENV{'CONTENT_TYPE'};
  $len  = $ENV{'CONTENT_LENGTH'};
  $meth = $ENV{'REQUEST_METHOD'};

  if ($len > $cgi_lib'maxdata) { #'
      &CgiDie("cgi-lib.pl: Request to receive too much data: $len bytes\n");
  }

  if (!defined $meth || $meth eq '' || $meth eq 'GET' ||
      $type eq 'application/x-www-form-urlencoded') {
    local ($key, $val, $i);

    # Read in text
    if (!defined $meth || $meth eq '') {
      $in = $ENV{'QUERY_STRING'};
      $cmdflag = 1;  # also use command-line options
    } elsif($meth eq 'GET' || $meth eq 'HEAD') {
      $in = $ENV{'QUERY_STRING'};
    } elsif ($meth eq 'POST') {
        if (($got = read(STDIN, $in, $len) != $len))
      {$errflag="Short Read: wanted $len, got $got\n";};
    } else {
      &CgiDie("cgi-lib.pl: Unknown request method: $meth\n");
    }

    @in = split(/[&;]/,$in);
    push(@in, @ARGV) if $cmdflag; # add command-line parameters

    foreach $i (0 .. $#in) {
      # Convert plus to space
      $in[$i] =~ s/\+/ /g;

      # Split into key and value.
      ($key, $val) = split(/=/,$in[$i],2); # splits on the first =.

      # Convert %XX from hex numbers to alphanumeric
      $key =~ s/%([A-Fa-f0-9]{2})/pack("c",hex($1))/ge;
      $val =~ s/%([A-Fa-f0-9]{2})/pack("c",hex($1))/ge;
```

*continues*

**Listing 27.3. continued**

```
    # Associate key and value
    $in{$key} .= "\0" if (defined($in{$key})); # \0 is the multiple separator
    $in{$key} .= $val;
}
```

# The HTTP Headers

If HTML is responsible for gathering data to send to your CGI program, how does it get there? The data gathered by the browser gets to your CGI program through the magic of the Hypertext Transport Protocol request headers, or HTTP headers for short. The HTML tags tell the browser what type of HTTP header to use to talk to the server, your CGI program. The basic HTTP headers for beginning communication with your CGI program are GET and POST.

If the HTML tag calling your program is a hypertext link, such as <a href=www.domain.com/ progam.cgi>, call a CGI program </a>, then the default HTTP request METHOD GET will be used to communicate with your CGI program. If instead of using a hypertext link to your program, you use the HTML <FORM> tag, then the METHOD attribute of the <FORM> tag defines what type of HTTP request header will be used to communicate with your CGI program. If the METHOD field is missing or set to GET, the HTTP METHOD request header type is GET. If the METHOD attribute is set to POST, then a POST METHOD request header will be used to communicate with your CGI program.

After the method of sending the data is determined, the data is formatted and sent using one of two means. If the GET METHOD is used, the data is sent via the URL field. If the POST METHOD is used, the data is sent as a separate message, after all the other HTTP request headers have been sent.

After the browser has determined how it is going to send the data, it creates an HTTP request header identifying where on the server your CGI program is located. The browser sends this HTTP request header to the server. The server receives the HTTP request header and calls your CGI program. Several other request headers can go along with the main request header, providing to the server and your CGI program useful information about the browser and this connection.

Your CGI program performs some useful function, and then it tells the server what type of response it wants to send back to the server.

So where are we so far? The data has been gathered by the browser using the format defined by the HTML tags. The data/URL request has been sent to the server using HTTP request headers. The server used the HTTP request headers to find your CGI program and call it. Now your CGI program has done its thing and is ready to respond to the browser. What happens next? The server and your CGI program collaborate to send HTTP response headers back to the browser.

What about the data, the Web page, your CGI program generated? Well, that is what the HTTP response headers are for. The HTTP response headers describe to the browser what type of data is being returned to the browser.

Your CGI program can generate all of the HTTP response headers required for sending data back to the client/browser by calling itself a nonparsed-header CGI (nph-cgi) program. If your CGI program is an nph-cgi program, then the server will not parse or look at the HTTP response headers generated by your CGI program. The HTTP request headers will be sent directly to the requesting browser, along with data/HTML generated by your CGI program.

However, the more common form of returning HTTP response headers is for your CGI program to generate the minimum required HTTP request headers; usually just a `Content-Type:` HTTP response header is required. The server then parses or looks for the response header your CGI program generated and determines what additional HTTP response headers should be returned to the browser.

The `Content-Type:` HTTP response header identifies to the browser the type of data that will be returned to the browser. The browser uses the `Content-Type:` response header to determine the types of viewers to activate so the client can view things like inline images, movies, and HTML text.

The server adds the additional HTTP response headers it knows are required and then bundles the set of the headers and data up in a nice TCP/IP package and sends it to the browser. The browser receives the HTTP response headers and displays the returned data as described by the HTTP response headers to your customer.

# The HTTP Headers

HTTP headers are the language your browser and client use to talk to each other. Think of each of the HTTP headers as a single message. In the client and server sense, first there are a bunch of questions, which are the request headers, and then there are the answers to those questions, the response headers.

## Status Codes in Response Headers

Status codes in the response header tell the client how well your request for a URL went. There are five basic types of HTTP status codes. A status code is always included in the HTTP response headers returned from the HTTP request headers. The status codes are shown in Tables 27.2 and 27.3.

The following information is a subset of an Internet draft known as Hypertext Transfer Protocol, and is available at

`http://www.ics.uci.edu/pub/ietf/http/draft-ietf-http-v10-spec-01.html`

The status code element is a three-digit integer result code of the attempt to understand and satisfy an HTTP request header. The reason phrase is intended to give a short textual description of the status code.

The first digit of the status code defines the class of response. The last two digits do not have any categorization role. There are five values for the first digit, as listed in Table 27.2.

**Table 27.2. Status codes and their meanings.**

| Numeric | English | Meaning |
|---|---|---|
| 1xx | Informational | Not used, but reserved for future use. |
| 2xx | Success | The action was successfully received, understood, and accepted. |
| 3xx | Redirection | Further action must be taken in order to complete the request. |
| 4xx | Client error | The request contains bad syntax or cannot be fulfilled. |
| 5xx | Server error | The server failed to fulfill an apparently valid request. |

The individual values of the numeric status codes defined for HTTP/1.0 are presented in Table 27.3.

**Table 27.3. The status codes and the reason field and its meaning.**

| Code | Reason field | Meaning |
|---|---|---|
| 201 | Created | The request has been fulfilled and resulted in a new resource being created. The newly created resource can be referenced by the URL(s) returned in the URL header field of the response, with the most specific URL for the resource given by a Location header field. |
| 202 | Accepted | The request has been accepted for processing, but the processing has not been completed. |

| CODE | Reason field | Meaning |
|------|-------------|---------|
| 203 | Non-authoritative information | The returned meta-information in the entity header is not the definitive set as available from the origin server, but is gathered from a local or a third-party copy. |
| 204 | No content | The server has fulfilled the request, but there is no new information to send back. |
| 300 | Multiple choices | The requested resource is available at one or more locations and a preferred location could not be determined via content negotiation. |
| 301 | Moved permanently | The requested resource has been assigned a new permanent URL and any future references to this resource should be done using one of the returned URLs. |
| 302 | Moved temporarily | The requested resource resides temporarily under a different URL. |
| 303 | See other | The requested resource resides under a different URL and should be accessed using a GET method on that resource. |
| 304 | Not modified | If the client has performed a conditional GET request and access is allowed, but the document has not been modified since the date and time specified in the If modified since field, the server shall respond with this status code and not send an entity body to the client. |
| 400 | Bad request | The request could not be understood by the server because of a malformed syntax. |

27

CGI
PROGRAMMING

*continues*

**Table 27.3. continued**

| CODE | Reason field | Meaning |
|------|--------------|---------|
| 401 | Unauthorized | The request requires user authentication. The response must include a WWW authenticate header field containing a challenge applicable to the requested resource. |
| 402 | Payment required | This code is not currently supported, but is reserved for future use. |
| 403 | Forbidden | The server understood the request but is refusing to perform the request because of an unspecified reason. |
| 404 | Not found | The server has not found anything matching the request URL. |
| 405 | Method not allowed | The method specified in the request line is not allowed for the resource identified by the request URL. |
| 406 | None acceptable | The server has found a resource matching the request URL, but not one that satisfies the conditions identified by the accept and accept encoding request headers. |
| 407 | Proxy authentication required | This code is reserved for future use. It is similar to 401 (Unauthorized), but indicates that the client must first authenticate itself with the proxy. HTTP/1.0 does not provide a means for proxy authentication. |
| 408 | Request timeout | The client did not produce a request within the time that the server was prepared to wait. |
| 409 | Conflict | The request could not be completed because of a conflict with the current state of the resource. |

| CODE | Reason field | Meaning |
|------|-------------|---------|
| 410 | Gone | The requested resource is no longer available at the server and no forwarding address is known. |
| 411 | Authorization refused | The request credentials provided by the client were rejected by the server or insufficient to grant authorization to access the resource. |
| 500 | Internal server error | The server encountered an unexpected condition that prevented it from fulfilling the request. |
| 501 | Not implemented | The server does not support the functionality required to fulfill the request. |
| 502 | Bad gateway | The server received an invalid response from the gateway or upstream server it accessed in attempting to fulfill the request. |
| 503 | Service unavailable | The server is currently unable to handle the request due to a temporary overloading or maintenance of the server. |
| 504 | Gateway timeout | The server did not receive a timely response from the gateway or upstream server it accessed in attempting to complete the request. |

# The Method Request Header

Status codes are part of the server's response to an HTTP request header. The client makes the request of the server, and the server builds the response headers. The most common request header is the GET method request header.

The client sends to the server several request headers defining to the server what the client wants, how the client can accept data, how to handle the incoming request, and any data that needs to be sent with the request.

The first request header for every client/server communication is the Method request header. This request header tells the server what other types of request headers to expect and how the server is expected to respond.

The most common request methods are GET, POST, and HEAD. The HTTP specification also allows for the PUT, DELETE, LINK, and UNLINK methods, along with an undefined extension method. You will be dealing primarily with the GET and POST methods, so this chapter focuses on them.

Each of the request headers identifies a URL to the server. The difference between GET and POST is the effect on how data is transferred. The HEAD request method affects how the requested URL is returned to the client.

The next section discusses the FULL request method line. This is the request header that includes the type of access (GET, POST, HEAD, and so on) that the client is requesting. Of all the request headers, this is the one that really makes things work. This is the request header that tells the server which Web page you want returned to the browser. Without this header, no data will be transferred to the calling client.

## The Full Method Request Header

The FULL Method request header is the first request header sent with any client request. The FULL request method line is made up of three parts separated by spaces: the method type, the URL requested, and the HTTP version number.

The syntax of the FULL Method request header is as follows:

```
Request_Method URL HTTP_Protocol_Version \n (newline)
```

For example:

```
GET http://www.practical-inet.com/index.html HTTP/1.0
```

The Request_Method can be any of the following method types: GET, POST, HEAD, PUT, DELETE, LINK, and UNLINK.

The URL is the address of the file, program, or directory you are trying to access.

The HTTP_Protocol_Version is the version number of the HTTP protocol that the client/browser can handle.

## The GET HTTP Header

The GET method is the default method for following links and passing data on the Internet. When you click on a link, your browser is sending a GET method request header. When you click the Submit button on a form, if the method is undefined in the ACTION field of the <FORM>, the GET method request header is used to call the CGI program that handles the <FORM> data.

When you click on a URL, it usually is of the form `http://www.somewhere.com/filename.html`. A `GET` method request header is generated along with any other request header the browser might want to send. The URL is located and returned by the browser, unless an If-Modified-Since request header was sent along with the other request headers.

When the If-Modified-Since header is included in the request headers, the browser will check the modification date of the requested URL and only return a new copy if it has been modified after the date specified.

When you click on a URL and that URL is a request for another Web page, you have sent a `GET` method request header and lots of other headers to your server.

## The Requested URL

The second field in the first line of the `FULL` method request header is the Requested URL field. The URL tells the server what file or service is requested.

Normally, the `FULL` Method request header is for a file on the server. When this is the case, the absolute path of the file/URL is included in the Method request header. An example of a `GET` Method request header is `GET / HTTP/1.0`

The format of the requested URL is the absolute pathname of the document root. Consider this sample `GET` method request header:

```
/~yawp/test/env.html/
```

The following bullets refer to the preceding example to explain what the document root pathname means:

- The absolute pathname is the directory and filename of the URL, beginning at the `/` directory. For this example, I show the absolute pathname to my personal directory `~yawp` with a subdirectory of `test`, and a filename of `env.html`.

- This `/` directory is defined by your server administrator as the starting location for all Web pages or URLs on the server. This is also called the document root.

- On my server, the server administrator has defined a public Web directory within every user's home directory, so the actual path to the `env.html` file is `yawp/public-web/ -test/env.html`. On my commercial server, the document root looks like `www-practical- inet.com`, but the real path is `/usr/local/business/http/practical-inet/.2`.

## The Proxy GET Method Request Header

If the target of the URL is a proxy server, it should send an absolute URL. An absolute URL includes the domain name and the full pathname to the requested URL. The domain name in the following example is `www.w3.org`:

```
GET http://www.w3.org/hypertext/WWW/TheProject.html HTTP/1.0
```

## The HTTP Version

The last field in the FULL Method request header is HTTP version. The only valid values at this moment are HTTP/1.0 followed by a CRLF.

Table 27.4 summarizes the request/response headers used by the server and client to communicate with each other. They are defined completely in the HTTP specification. This chapter covers several of the more common headers. Several of the headers, such as the Method header are covered in detail in the following sections. A summary of those headers is included in Table 27.4.

The most important thing to remember is that the request/response headers are the means your client and browser use tell each other what is needed and what is available.

**Table 27.4. A summary of the HTTP request/response headers.**

| Request/response header | Meaning |
| --- | --- |
| Accept | This header tells the server what type of data the browser can accept. Examples are text, audio, images. |
| Accept-Charset | This header tell the server what character sets the browser prefers. The default is US-ASCII. |
| Accept-Encoding | This header tells the server what type of data encoding the browser can accept. Examples are compress and gzip. |
| Accept-Language | This header tells the server what natural language to the browser prefers. The default is English. |
| Allow | This header tells the browser what request methods are allowed by the server. Examples are GET, HEAD, POST. |
| Authorization | This header is used by the browser to authenticate itself with the server. It is usually sent in response to a 401 or 411 code. |
| Content-Encoding | This header is used to identify the type of encoding used on the data transfer. An example is compressed. |
| Content-Language | This header identifies the natural language of the data transferred. |
| Content-Length | This header identifies the size of the data transfer in decimal bytes. |
| Content-Transfer-Encoding | This header identifies the encoding of the message for Internet transfer. The default is binary. |
| Content-Type | This header identifies the type of data being transferred. An example is text/html. |

| Request/response header | Meaning |
|---|---|
| Date | This header identifies the GMT date/time the data transfer was initiated. |
| Expires | This header identifies the date/time the data should be considered stale. This header is often used by caching clients. |
| Forwarded | This header is used by proxy servers to indicate the intermediate steps between the browser and server. |
| From | This header should contain the Internet e-mail address of the client. This header is no longer in common use. |
| If-Modified-Since | This header makes the request method a conditional request. A copy of the requested URL is only returned if it was modified after the time specified. |
| Last-Modified | This header identifies the date/time when the URL was last modified. |
| Link | This header is used for describing a relationship between two URLs. |
| Location | This header is used to define the location of a URL. Typically this header is used to redirect the client to a new URL. |
| MIME-Version | This header is used to indicate what version of the MIME protocol was used to construct the transferred message. |
| Orig-URL | This request header is used by the client to specify to the server the original URL of the requested URL. |
| Pragma | This header is used to specify special directives that should be applied to all intermediaries along the request/response chain. This header is usually used to provide directives to proxy servers or caching clients. |
| Public | This header is used to list the set of nonstandard methods supported by the server. |
| Referer | This request header identifies to the server the address (URL) of the link that was used to send the method request header to the server. |
| Retry-After | This response header is used to identify to the client a length of time to wait before trying the requested URL again. |

*continues*

**Table 27.4. continued**

| Request/response header | Meaning |
| --- | --- |
| Server | This response header identifies the server software used by the server. |
| Title | This header identifies the title of the URL. |
| URL-Header | Uniform resource identifier. |
| User-Agent | This request header identifies the type of browser making the request. |
| WWW-Authenticate | This response header is required when status response headers of Unauthorized (401) or Authorization Refused (411) occur. This header is used to begin a challenge/response sequence with the client. |

# The HTTP Response Header

After the server receives the request headers, it begins to generate the correct response. The server starts by looking up the URL in the GET Method, and then generates the response headers. The GET Method request header tells the server what URL is desired; the other request headers tell the server how to send the data back to the client.

After the server gets a request in, it must choose a valid response. It starts with a response status line, which gives the protocol version followed by a status code. The format of a response status line is as follows:

```
PROTOCOL/Version_Number Status_Code Status_Description
```

The only valid protocol right now is HTTP, and version 1.0 is the standard at the moment.

Figure 27.2 shows the response headers generated when the server receives a GET Method request header.

The following sections briefly discuss these response headers. These are the basic ones that will be returned from almost any request header.

## Status Response Line

The Status response line is

```
HTTP/1.0 200 OK
```

Nothing to write home about in this response header. Simple and straightforward. The HTTP version number is 1.0. The status is 200. The status description is OK. So this means our server found our requested URL and is going to return it to the browser.

**FIGURE 27.2.**

*The server response
headers to a* GET
*Method request header.*

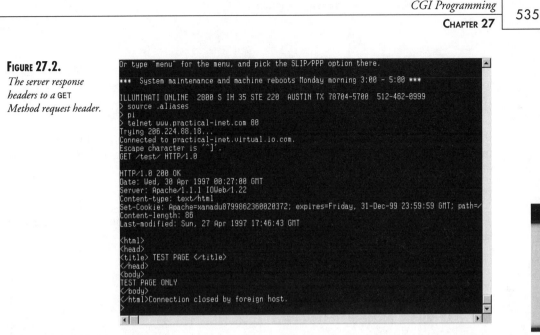

```
Or type "menu" for the menu, and pick the SLIP/PPP option there.

*** System maintenance and machine reboots Monday morning 3:00 - 5:00 ***

ILLUMINATI ONLINE  2800 S IH 35 STE 220  AUSTIN TX 78704-5700  512-462-0999
> source .aliases
> pi
> telnet www.practical-inet.com 80
Trying 206.224.88.18...
Connected to practical-inet.virtual.io.com.
Escape character is '^]'.
GET /test/ HTTP/1.0

HTTP/1.0 200 OK
Date: Wed, 30 Apr 1997 00:27:00 GMT
Server: Apache/1.1.1 IOWeb/1.22
Content-type: text/html
Set-Cookie: Apache=xanadu87998623600020372; expires=Friday, 31-Dec-99 23:59:59 GMT; path=/
Content-length: 86
Last-modified: Sun, 27 Apr 1997 17:46:43 GMT

<html>
<head>
<title> TEST PAGE </title>
</head>
<body>
TEST PAGE ONLY
</body>
</html>Connection closed by foreign host.
>
```

## The Date Response Header

This is the Date response header:

```
Date: Wed, 09 Apr 1997 22:41:26 GMT
```

This is the time that the server generated the response to the request header. The date must be
in Greenwich Mean Time (GMT). The date can be in one of three formats, as described in
Table 27.5.

**Table 27.5. Greenwich Mean Time (GMT) format.**

| Format example | Format description |
| --- | --- |
| Sun, 13 Apr 1997 06:15:10 GMT | Originally defined by RFC 822 and updated by RFC 1123, this is the preferred format. |
| Sunday, 17-Apr-97 06:15:10 GMT | Defined by RFC 850 and made obsolete by RFC 1036, this format is in common use; it's based on an obsolete format and lacks a four-digit year. |
| Sun Apr 17 06:15:10 1994 | This is the ANSI standard date format represented in C's asctime() function. |

Only one Date response header is allowed per message. Because it is important for evaluating
cached responses, the server should always include a Date response header. Cached responses
are beyond the scope of this book but, in short, can be part of a request/response chain, used to
speed up URL transfers.

## The Server Response Header

This is the Server response header field:

```
Server: Apache/1.1 IOWeb/1.22
```

It contains information about the server software used to create the response. If you are having problems with your CGI working with a particular site, this header field can identify the type of server software your CGI is failing with.

## The Content-Type Response Header

The Content-Type header field tells your browser what type of media is appended after the last response header:

```
Content-type: text/html
```

Media types are defined in an appendix at the end of the book.

## The Set-Cookie Response Header

The Set-Cookie header is used as a state maintaining header. It is critical to Shopping Cart and other Electronic Commerce CGI applications. The Set-Cookie header is always set by your ISP. You can add Set-Cookie headers just like other HTTP headers. This is the Set-Cookie response header:

```
Set-Cookie: Apache=pentagon21775860625686440;
expires=Friday, 31-Dec-99 23:59:59 GMT; path=/
```

## The Content-Length Response Header

The Content-Length header field indicates the size of the appended media in decimal numbers, in 8-bit byte format, referred to in the HTTP specification as OCTETS:

```
Content-length: 1529
```

This header is often used by the server to determine the amount of data sent by the client, when posting <FORM> data.

## The Last Modified Response Header

In this example we are passing a file, URL, that is of type text/html, so the Last Modified field is the time the file was last modified:

```
Last-Modified: Wed, 09 Apr 1997 22:37:43 GMT
```

This field is used for caching information. When an If-Modified-Since request header is sent, this field is used in determining whether the data should be transferred at all.

## The Enclosed URL

The last line of the response headers is blank; after that, the requested URL is shipped to the client. This is the blank line just before the opening <HTML> tag in Figure 27.2.

All of your HTTP response and request header chains must end with a blank line.

The last `print` statement of an HTTP header program you write should print a blank line:

```
print "Last-modified: $last_modified_variable\n\n";
```

Notice in the preceding example that two new lines (\n) are printed. One is always required for every HTTP header, but the second new line indicates to the server or client the end of any incoming or outgoing HTTP headers. Everything after that first blank line is supposed to be in the format defined by the Content-Type header.

# Environment Variables

Not all environment variables are created equal. The environment variable is the server's way of communicating with your CGI program, and each communication is unique.

The uniqueness of each communication with your CGI program is based on the request headers that are sent by the Web page client when it calls your CGI program. If your Web page client is responding to an Authorization response header from the server, then it will send Authorization request headers. Because the request headers define a number of your environment variables, you can never be sure which environment variables are available.

## Environment Variables Based on the Server

However, some of the environment variables are always set for you and are not dependent on the CGI request. These environment variables typically define the server on which your CGI program runs. The following environment variables are based on your server type and should always be available to your CGI program.

### GATEWAY_INTERFACE

The environment variable GATEWAY_INTERFACE is the version of the CGI specification that your server is using. The CGI specification is defined at `http://hoohoo.ncsa.uiuc.edu/cgi/`. This is an excellent site for further information about CGI. At this time, CGI is at revision 1.1.

### SERVER_ADMIN

The environment variable SERVER_ADMIN should be the e-mail address of the Web guru on your server. When you can't figure out the answer yourself, this is the person to e-mail. Be careful, though. These people are usually very busy. You want to establish a good relationship early, so he or she will respond to your requests later. Make sure you have tried all of the simple things, everything you know first, before you ask this person questions. This is definitely an area where "crying wolf" can have a negative affect on your ability to get your CGI programs working. When you have a really tough problem that no one seems able to figure out, you want your server administrator to respond to your questions.

## SERVER_NAME

The environment variable SERVER_NAME contains the domain name of your server. If a domain name is not available, it will be the IP number of your server. This should be in the same URL format as your CGI program was called.

## SERVER_SOFTWARE

The environment variable SERVER_SOFTWARE contains the type of server your CGI program is running under. You can use this variable to figure out what type of security methods are available to you—whether server-side includes are even possible, for example. This way you don't have to ask your Webmaster these simple questions.

# Environment Variables Based on the Request Headers

This next set of environment variables give your CGI program information about what is happening during this call to your program. These environment variables are defined when the server receives the request headers from a Web page.

## SERVER_PROTOCOL

The SERVER_PROTOCOL environment variable defines the protocol and version number being used by this server. For the time being, this should be HTTP/1.0. The HTTP protocol is the only server protocol used for the WWW at the moment. But like most good designs, this environment variable is designed to allow CGI programs to operate on servers that support other communication protocols.

## SERVER_PORT

The SERVER_PORT environment variable defines the TCP port that the request headers were sent to. The port is like the telephone number that is used to call the server. The default port for server communication is 80. When you see a number appended after the domain name server, this is the port number that the request was sent to, for example, www.io.com:80. Because the default port is 80, it is not generally necessary to include the port number when making URL links.

## HTTP REQUEST_METHOD

The HTTP REQUEST_METHOD environment variable is the HTTP Method request header converted to an environment variable. As explained earlier in this chapter, the following request methods are possible: GET, POST, HEAD, PUT, DELETE, LINK, and UNLINK. GET and POST are certainly the most common for your CGI program and define where incoming data is available to your CGI program. If the method is GET, the data is available at QUERY_STRING. If it is POST, the data is available at STDIN and the length of the data is defined by the environment variable CONTENT_LENGTH. The HEAD request method is normally used by bots searching the Web for page links. The other methods are not quite as common and tell the server to modify a URL/file on the server.

# PATH_INFO

The PATH_INFO environment variable is only set when there is data after the CGI program (URL) and before the beginning of the QUERY_STRING. Remember, the QUERY_STRING begins after the question mark (?) on the link URL or ACTION field URL. PATH_INFO can be used to pass any type of data to your CGI program, but it is usually used to send information about finding files or programs on the server. The server strips everything after it finds the target CGI program (URL) and before it finds the first question mark (?). This information is URL decoded and then placed in the PATH_INFO variable.

# PATH_TRANSLATED

The PATH_TRANSLATED environment variable is a combination of the PATH_INFO variable and the DOCUMENT_ROOT variable. It is an absolute path from the root directory of the server to the directory defined by the extra path information added from PATH_INFO. This is called an *absolute* path. This type of path is often used when your CGI program moves in and out of different directories or different shell environments. As long as your server doesn't change, you can use the absolute path regardless of where you put or move your CGI program. Sometimes absolute paths are considered bad because you cannot move your CGI program to another server. You have to decide which is more likely:

1. Your CGI program will change directories.
2. You will change servers.
3. The absolute path will change on your existing server. This can happen when your server adds or removes disks.

# PATH

The PATH environment variable is not strictly considered a CGI environment variable. This is because it actually includes information about your UNIX system path.

# SCRIPT_NAME

The SCRIPT_NAME environment variable gives you the path and name of the CGI program that was called. The path is a relative path, which starts at the document root path. You can use this to build self-referencing URLs. Suppose you want to return a Web page and you want to generate HTML that includes a link to the called CGI program. The print string would look like this:

```
print "<a href=http://$SERVER_NAME$SCRIPT_NAME>
This is a link to the CGI program you just called </a>";
```

# SCRIPT_FILENAME

The SCRIPT_FILENAME environment variable gives the full path to the CGI program. You do not want to use this when building a self-referencing URL. Remember, the server is making some assumptions about how you will access your CGI program. The full pathname would be appended onto the server's full pathname and totally confuse your poor server. The server starts with the SERVER_NAME; from there it determines the document root, and then it adds on the path to your CGI program.

## QUERY_STRING

The QUERY_STRING environment variable contains everything included on the URL after the question mark. The setup for a QUERY_STRING is normally performed by your browser when it builds the request headers. However, you can create the data for your own QUERY_STRING if you want to by including a question mark in your hypertext reference and then URL encoding any data that is included after the question mark. This is just one more way to send data to your program. Two big drawbacks to using the QUERY_STRING are the YUK! factor and the size of the input buffer. The YUK! factor means your data will be displayed back to your client in the Location field. The size problem means you have a limitation on how much data you can send to your program using this method. The amount of data you can send without exceeding the input buffer is server specific, so I can't give you any hard rules. But you should try to limit all data you send using this method to under 1024 bytes.

## REMOTE_HOST

The REMOTE_HOST environment variable contains the domain name of the client accessing your CGI program. You can use this information to help figure out how your script was called. If the domain name is unavailable to your server, then this field will be left empty. However, if this field is empty, the REMOTE_ADDR environment variable will be filled in. Your program can read this environment variable from right to left. There can be more that one subhierarchy after the first period (.), so be sure to write your code to deal with more than one level of domain hierarchy to the left of the period.

## REMOTE_ADDR

The REMOTE_ADDR environment variable has the numeric Internet Protocol (IP) address of the browser or remote computer calling your CGI program. Read the REMOTE_ADDR from right to left. The right-most number defines today's connection to the remote server. Or at least, this will be the case when your Web browser client connects from a modem to a commercial server.

## AUTH_TYPE

The AUTH_TYPE environment variable defines the authentication method used to access your CGI program. The AUTH_TYPE will usually be basic, because this is the primary method for authentication of the Net right now. The AUTH_TYPE defines the protocol-specific authentication method used to validate the user.

## REMOTE_USER

The REMOTE_USER environment variable identifies the caller of your CGI program. This value is only available if server authentication is turned on. This is the username authenticated by the USERNAME/PASSWORD response to a response status of Unauthorized Access (401) or Authorization Refused (411).

## REMOTE_IDENT

The REMOTE_IDENT environment variable is only set if the remote username is retrieved from the server using the identd. This only occurs if your Web server is running the identd identification daemon, a protocol that identifies the user connecting to your CGI program. However, just having your system running identd is not sufficient; the remote server making the HTTP request must also be running identd.

## CONTENT-TYPE

The CONTENT-TYPE environment variable defines the type of data attached with the request method. If no data is sent, then this field is left blank. The content type will be application/x-www-form-urlencoded when posting data from a form.

## CONTENT-LENGTH

The CONTENT-LENGTH environment variable specifies the amount of data attached after the end of the request headers. This data is available at STDIN and is identified with the POST or PUT method.

# Summary

The fundamental building blocks for CGI programming are outlined in this chapter. The client, your Web browser, sends HTTP request headers to your Web server. The Web server calls your CGI program. Your CGI program uses environment variables to interpret the request from the Web browser and then processes the data (making a sale), collects data from a database, puts an item in a shopping cart, or answers a question from a customer—the possibilities are endless. After the request is processed, your CGI program returns HTTP response headers and HTML to the Web browser.

An entire book could be devoted to the topic of CGI programming, and many books have been written just about CGI—in fact, I wrote one myself, *Teach Yourself CGI Programming with Perl 5 in a Week.* In the 500 pages of this tutorial-style book, you can learn the details of CGI programming and work through lots of CGI programming examples, including mail tools, image mapping, shopping carts, and much more.

# Integrating JavaScript and HTML

*by Rick Darnell*

## IN THIS CHAPTER

CHAPTER

28

JavaScript is a scripting extension to HTML that extends your ability to respond to user events without the need for client/server communication or CGI scripting.

Before scripting languages, material such as HTML forms was typically submitted to the server for all processing, whether it meant checking a ZIP code or putting information in a database. The process bogged down each time information was passed back and forth between client and server due to inherently slow communication lines. JavaScript eliminates much of the client/server communication by shifting responses to user events to the client side. Because network transmission is not required, the process goes much faster.

# Getting to Know JavaScript

JavaScript is more closely related to a programming language than to HTML tags. However, JavaScript cannot exist outside of HTML. To function, it must be included as part of a page.

## What Is JavaScript?

JavaScript was developed by Netscape in conjunction with Sun's Java. You may also know it as LiveScript—the first name it had before the collaboration with Sun.

### JAVASCRIPT ISN'T JAVA

Java is an object-oriented programming language used to create standalone applications and applets, special mini-applications for Web pages. Java is compiled into machine-independent byte codes, which are in turn interpreted by the Java virtual machine on the host computer. Writing Java programs is easiest when you have some background in programming languages, such as C or C++.

JavaScript shares some of the same syntax and structure as Java, but provides a much smaller and simpler language for people with HTML or CGI experience. It is interpreted along with the rest of the page at load time. JavaScript only resides within an HTML document and provides for greater levels of interactivity than basic HTML commands.

For example, JavaScript enables the HTML author to respond to user-initiated events, such as mouse clicks and form activity, without the need for client/server interaction. The result provides quicker operation for the end user, and less load on the server.

Although similarities exist between Java and JavaScript, the languages are different and are intended for different uses. A simple form-handling routine that would require a significant amount of coding in Java represents a basic task for JavaScript, but creating a browser such as HotJava in JavaScript is impossible.

Java applets occupy a defined space on the screen, much as an image or other embedded item. Though a Java applet can communicate with another applet on the same page, communication with a page's HTML elements requires a substantial amount of code. For more information about Java, see the next chapter, "Integrating Java Applets and HTML."

JavaScript does not represent a watered-down version of Java for programming beginners. Although related to Java, it provides a solution for client-side scripting in an era when users with high-powered machines get bogged down by client/server communication.

Although many ways exist to control the browser from within a Java applet, simple tasks such as computing a form or controlling frame content can become complicated affairs. JavaScript bridges the gap by enabling HTML authors to implement basic HTML functionality and interactivity without hours and hours of writing code.

A narrower focus and application for JavaScript means there is a much smaller set of objects, methods, and properties to work with, and they are all focused towards dealing with HTML content. For example, JavaScript does not have the capability to control network connections or download files.

## Why Should I Learn JavaScript?

Although based on programming, JavaScript is simple enough to be within easy reach of anyone who feels comfortable with HTML coding. It greatly expands the capabilities of typical HTML pages, without a great deal of hassle.

Take the following example:

```
<SCRIPT LANGUAGE="javascript">
document.writeln("This page last changed on "+document.lastModified());
</SCRIPT>
```

When the page loads, some basic information about itself is also included, such as the time and date the page was saved. Without any further communication with the server, JavaScript accesses the date and displays it for the user. You don't need to remember to update a line of HTML or include a link to a CGI script—the process is automated with the JavaScript line.

With JavaScript, you can also effectively manage multiple frames. You can control the content in other frames by loading them with new URLs or managing form input. For more information on creating and working with HTML frames, see Chapter 18, "Creating Sophisticated Layouts with Frames and Layers."

One major power of JavaScript is revealed in its capability to handle forms and their elements. Using JavaScript, it's possible to validate and check information on a form before it is sent to the server, saving valuable network bandwidth and processing time on the server. Client-side form processing also localizes validation of potentially destructive content, making it much harder for end users to send incompatible data that could cause damage to the server.

Additional characteristics represent form elements in the shape of events and event handlers. For INPUT TYPE= tags such as BUTTON and TEXT, the page author can check for mouse clicks, changed text, focus, and even change the content of form elements. Submission of forms and other information is also controlled by substituting custom actions for the standard submit button formats.

## How to Use JavaScript Now

Most HTML editors that handle nonstandard HTML tags will allow creation and editing of JavaScript sections to your pages. Several resources available for learning the syntax and idiosyncrasies of JavaScript appear at the end of this chapter.

### TIP

One of the most useful sites is the JavaScript online documentation at `http://home.netscape.com/eng/mozilla/Gold/handbook/javascript/index.html`, which is also available as a downloadable file.

For users to take advantage of your JavaScript-empowered pages, they need to use a compatible browser. Currently, the list is limited to the two most popular selections—Netscape Navigator (Version 2.0 and later) and Microsoft Internet Explorer (Version 3.01 and later). Other lesser-used choices, such as NCSA Mosaic and Sun HotJava, can also be expected to follow suit, although no timetable is available for JavaScript implementation.

### WARNING

The JavaScript API is not entirely stabilized yet. As Netscape continues its own development and collaboration with Sun and Microsoft, the implementation and workability of some features may change. You should always try your script on more than one browser and platform combination to ensure that your solutions function as planned.

### NOTE

JavaScript is JavaScript, whether it appears on Internet Explorer or Navigator, right? Wrong. JavaScript is essentially Netscape's invention, and they call the shots on its evolution. That would leave Microsoft stuck in an eternal game of catch-up, except that Microsoft developed its own version of JavaScript called JScript.

The two implementations are very close—both include objects such as *window* and *document*, both support user events, and their basic syntax is the same. However, Netscape supports several objects not included by Microsoft, and Microsoft includes an expanded set of user events not supported by Netscape.

One of the most significant differences is in case-sensitivity. Microsoft is much more forgiving in its use of capital letters for objects and methods. Therefore, if you write a script that should work for both Microsoft and Netscape, it may crash on Netscape because of the difference in capitalization.

> If you're developing for both browsers, start by testing your work on Netscape. When it's stable, move it to the Microsoft platform and check it there. Netscape is driving the train, so you'll want to stay current with their work, and then make sure it's compatible with other implementations.

As do many sites that provide a host of compatibilities, some of which are mutually exclusive, it shows good manners to offer your page in a generic version if crucial content is not usable with a non-JavaScript browser. You can also offer a link to sites where a compatible browser is available for downloading.

# Creating Scripts

Creating scripts is really quite simple, although you must use proper syntax to ensure success. Although a knowledge of object-oriented programming is useful to anyone creating functions with JavaScript, it is not a necessity.

## New Language, New Terminology

Objects, methods, properties, classes—an object-oriented world has taken off, and a whole new batch of terminology has cropped up to go with it. This section provides a quick primer on the basic terms that are used in conjunction with an object-oriented language such as JavaScript.

> **TIP**
>
> JavaScript is case-sensitive. For example, if your variable is called Skunk, you can also have SKUNK, skunk, and skunK, and each one will have its own unique smell.

## Object

Objects are at the heart of any object-oriented programming language, and JavaScript is no different. An *object* is a software model, typically used to represent a real-world object along with a set of behaviors or circumstances. In JavaScript, built-in objects can also represent the structure, action, and state of an HTML page.

In object-oriented terminology, the actions are called *methods* and the states are called *properties*. Both of these terms are covered later in this section.

To build an object, you need to know something about it. Consider a squirrel as an example. A squirrel has several physical properties, including sex, age, size, color. It also has properties relating to its activity, such as running, jumping, eating peanuts, or tormenting dogs. Its methods relate to changes in behavior or state, such as run away, stop and look, or twitch tail and chatter.

This example may seem all well and good, but how do you represent this idea as an object in JavaScript? The basic object creation is a two-step process, beginning with a defining function that outlines the object, followed by creating an instance of the object. Using some of the properties listed in the preceding example, you make a JavaScript squirrel. (See Listing 28.1.)

**Listing 28.1. A JavaScript object definition for a squirrel.**

```
function squirrel(color) {
    this.color = color;
    this.running = false;
    this.tormentingDog = false;
}

var groundSquirrel = new squirrel("brown")
```

The first part of the script with the `function` tag outlines the initial state for any given squirrel. It accepts one parameter, called `color`, which becomes a property, and adds two more properties called `running` and `tormentingDog`, both set to false by default. If you don't understand all the syntax and notation, don't worry. We'll get into those details just a little bit later in this chapter.

By itself, the function does nothing—it has to be invoked and assigned to a variable. This is what happens in the next step, where a variable called `groundSquirrel` is created and given the color brown. The following code shows how the object and its properties are represented:

```
groundSquirrel.color // "brown"
groundSquirrel.running // false
groundSquirrel.tormentingDog // false
```

Now, to implement the object as part of an HTML page (as shown in Figure 28.1), include the object definition between the `<HEAD>` tags. (See Listing 28.2.)

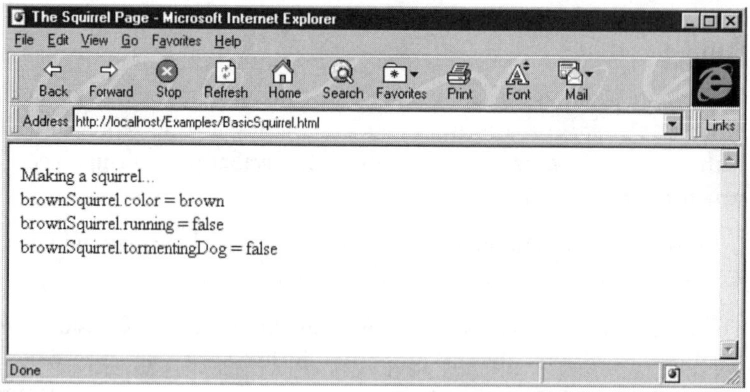

**FIGURE 28.1.**

*The squirrel page creates a simple object and displays its properties.*

```
Making a squirrel...
brownSquirrel.color = brown
brownSquirrel.running = false
brownSquirrel.tormentingDog = false
```

The two slashes (//) are used to include comments in your JavaScript code. Anything after them is ignored by the interpreter.

**Listing 28.2. Use the JavaScript definition of a squirrel in an HTML document similar to this one.**

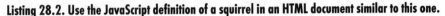

```
<HTML>
<HEAD>
<TITLE>The Squirrel Page</TITLE>
<SCRIPT language="javascript">
<!--
function squirrel(color) {
    this.color = color;
    this.running = false;
    this.tormentingDog = false;
}

// -->
</SCRIPT>
</HEAD>
<BODY>
Making a squirrel...
<BR>
<SCRIPT LANGUAGE="javascript">
var brownSquirrel = new squirrel("brown");
document.writeln("brownSquirrel.color = "+brownSquirrel.color);
document.writeln("<BR>brownSquirrel.running = "+brownSquirrel.running);
document.writeln("<BR>brownSquirrel.tormentingDog = "
                 +brownSquirrel.tormentingDog);
</SCRIPT>
</BODY>
</HTML>
```

## Class

A *class* represents the definition for a type of object. Although classes are in Java and not in JavaScript, it is helpful to understand classes because many discussions about either language may refer to them.

Simply stated, a class relates to an object as a pattern for a stuffed squirrel relates to the actual toy. The pattern contains all the information about the stuffed squirrel, but you can't play with it. To play with the stuffed squirrel, you need to create an instance of it. In object-oriented terminology, this process is called *instantiation*.

Classes can also have inheritance, which means they take on the behavior of other classes. A gray squirrel and a red squirrel both have basic squirrel characteristics, but different specific traits and behaviors. They are considered subclasses of the squirrel class.

Although a JavaScript function has a definition similar to a class, it can operate without instantiation.

28

INTEGRATING
JAVASCRIPT AND
HTML

## Property

*Properties* are the individual states of an object, typically represented as variables. In the squirrel example, `color`, `running`, and `tormentingDog` all represent properties of squirrel. An object's properties can include any of the valid JavaScript variable types.

### WHICH TYPE IS WHICH?

A variable's type is the kind of value it holds. Several basic variable types are offered by JavaScript, including string, Boolean, integer, and floating-point decimal.

JavaScript utilizes loose casting, which means a variable can assume different types at will, as in the following example:

```
squirrel.color = "pink"
...statements...
squirrel.color = 30
```

Both color values are valid. In Java, this would cause an error because it incorporates tight casting. After a variable is assigned a type in Java, it can't be changed.

Loose casting can make life easier when working with JavaScript. When building strings, for example, you can add a string to an integer, and the result will be a string:

```
value = 3;
theResult = value + "is the number." //Results in "3 is the number."
```

The downside is that sometimes you can easily forget what a variable thinks it is. It's a good idea to try to keep variables to their original type unless absolutely necessary.

Object properties are accessed using the object's name, followed by a period and the name of the property:

```
squirrel.color
```

Assigning a new value to the property will change it:

```
squirrel.color = "pink"
```

## Function

A JavaScript *function* is a collection of statements that are invoked by using the name of the function and a list of arguments, if used. As a general rule, if you use a set of statements more than once as part of a page, it will probably be easier to include them as a function. Also, any activity used as part of an event handler should be defined as a function for ease of use.

Functions normally appear in the HEAD portion of the HTML document to ensure that they are loaded and interpreted before the user has a chance to interact with them.

The syntax to define a function is

```
function functionName ([arg1] [,arg2] [,...]) {
...statements...
}
```

An example of a function that automatically generates a link to an anchor called top at the top of the current page could look like this:

```
function makeTopLink (topLinkText) {
    var topURL = "#top";
    document.writeln(topLinkText.link(topURL));
}
```

This function accepts a text string as its one argument and generates a hypertext link, similar to using the HTML <A HREF> tags.

```
makeTopLink("Return to the top.");
makeTopLink("top");
```

## Method

If properties represent the current conditions of the object, methods serve as the knobs and levers that make it perform. Consider the squirrel example again. Defining a squirrel seemed easy enough, but what about making it do something? First, the methods need to be defined as JavaScript functions.

The first method for the squirrel makes him run and quit tormenting the dog:

```
function runAway() {
    this.running = true;
    this.tormentingDog = false;
    document.writeln("The squirrel is running away.");
}
```

The second method makes the squirrel stop moving and tease the dog:

```
function twitchTailChatter () {
    this.tormentingDog = true;
    this.running = false;
    document.writeln("The squirrel is being annoying.");
}
```

One more method would help you see what happens to the squirrel as his state changes:

```
function showState() {
    document.writeln("<HR><BR>The state of the squirrel is:<UL>")
    document.writeln("<LI>Color: "+this.color+"</LI>");
    document.writeln("<LI>Running: "+this.running+"</LI>");
    document.writeln("<LI>Tormenting dog: "+this.tormentingDog+"</LI>");
    document.writeln("</UL><HR>");
}
```

> **TIP**
>
> You can include HTML tags in text written to the browser screen using JavaScript's write and writeln methods. These methods are interpreted like any other HTML text, so formatting can occur for generated content.

Now that you have three methods defined, you need to make them a part of the object. This step amounts to including the method names as part of the object definition:

```
function squirrel(color) {
    this.color = color;
    this.running = false;
    this.tormentingDog = false;
    this.runAway = runAway;
    this.twitchTailChatter = twitchTailChatter;
    this.showState = showState;
}
```

Finally, the last step is to include the whole package as part of an HTML document, such as Listing 28.3, and see whether it works. (See Figure 28.2.)

**Listing 28.3. Using the JavaScript definition of a squirrel and its behavior requires an HTML document similar to this one.**

```
<HTML>
<HEAD>
<TITLE>The Squirrel Page</TITLE>
<SCRIPT language="javascript">
<!--
function runAway() {
    this.running = true;
    this.tormentingDog = false;
    document.writeln("The squirrel is running away.");
}

function twitchTailChatter () {
    this.tormentingDog = true;
    this.running = false;
    document.writeln("The squirrel is being annoying.");
}

function showState() {
    document.writeln("The state of "+this.name+" is:<UL>")
    document.writeln("<LI>"+this.name+".color: "+this.color+"</LI>");
    document.writeln("<LI>"+this.name+".running: "+this.running+"</LI>");
    document.writeln("<LI>"+this.name+".tormenting dog: "+
                    this.tormentingDog+"</LI>");
    document.writeln("</UL><HR>");
}

function squirrel(color,squirrelName) {
    this.name = squirrelName;
    this.color = color;
    this.running = false;
    this.tormentingDog = false;
    this.runAway = runAway;
    this.twitchTailChatter = twitchTailChatter;
    this.showState = showState;
    document.writeln("A squirrel is born...");
}
```

```
// -->
</SCRIPT>
</HEAD>
<BODY>
<SCRIPT LANGUAGE="javascript">
var brownSquirrel = new squirrel("brown","brownSquirrel");
brownSquirrel.showState();
brownSquirrel.twitchTailChatter();
brownSquirrel.showState();
brownSquirrel.runAway();
brownSquirrel.showState();
</SCRIPT>
</BODY>
</HTML>
```

**FIGURE 28.2.**

*The browser screen displays the activity of the JavaScript object as each method is executed.*

The Squirrel Page - Microsoft Internet Explorer

File Edit View Go Favorites Help

Back Forward Stop Refresh Home Search Favorites Print Font Mail

Address http://localhost/Examples/IntermediateSquirrel.html

A squirrel is born... The state of brownSquirrel is:

- brownSquirrel.color: brown
- brownSquirrel.running: false
- brownSquirrel.tormenting dog: false

The squirrel is being annoying. The state of brownSquirrel is:

- brownSquirrel.color: brown
- brownSquirrel.running: false
- brownSquirrel.tormenting dog: true

The squirrel is running away. The state of brownSquirrel is:

Done

**28**

INTEGRATING
JAVASCRIPT AND
HTML

# The <SCRIPT> Tag

As seen in the earlier examples in this chapter, JavaScript requires its own special tag to mark its beginning and end. The basic form of the tag appears in the following code:

```
<SCRIPT [LANGUAGE="JavaScript"]>
...statments...
</SCRIPT>
```

A problem can develop when users view a page embedded with JavaScript statements with a noncompatible browser.

Note that Figures 28.3 and 28.4 both use the same HTML document (shown in Listing 28.4), which includes JavaScript statements; however, Figure 28.3 is viewed with Internet Explorer 3.0 and Figure 28.4 is viewed with NCSA Mosaic.

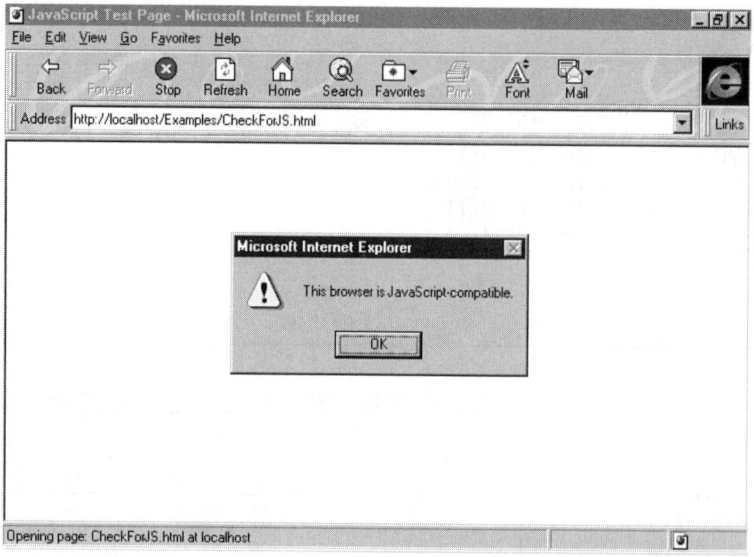

**FIGURE 28.3.**

*JavaScript-compatible Internet Explorer 3.0 displays this HTML document and processes the JavaScript commands contained in it.*

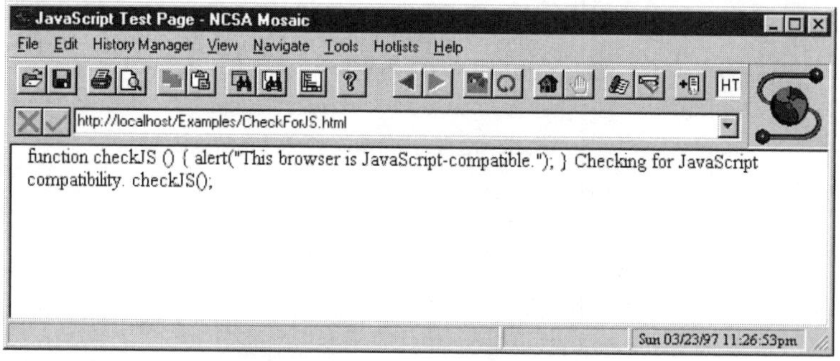

**FIGURE 28.4.**

*The NCSA Mosaic browser is not yet JavaScript compatible. The SCRIPT tags are ignored and the commands are processed as any other text.*

## Listing 28.4. The contents of the HTML document used in Figures 28.3 and 28.4.

```
<HTML>
<HEAD>
<TITLE>JavaScript Test Page</TITLE>
<SCRIPT>
function checkJS () {
    alert("This browser is JavaScript-compatible.");
}
</SCRIPT>
</HEAD>
<BODY>
Checking for JavaScript compatibility.
<SCRIPT>
checkJS();
</SCRIPT>
</BODY>
</HTML>
```

A noncompatible browser ignores the `<SCRIPT>` tags and displays the JavaScript commands as any other text. For a document including any length of JavaScript, the result produces a screen full of commands and characters otherwise unintelligible to the user.

## Hiding Scripts from Incompatible Browsers

To prevent an older or noncompatible browser from incorrectly processing your JavaScript code, you must use HTML comment tags correctly.

To hide your JavaScript, you must nest a set of HTML comment tags inside the `<SCRIPT>` tags. A JavaScript comment tag (two forward slashes) must appear just before the closing comment tag to prevent it from being processed as another line of JavaScript and causing a syntax error. (See Figure 28.5.)

```
<SCRIPT LANGUAGE="JavaScript">
<!-- Note: An opening HTML comment tag.
...statements...
// Note: A JavaScript comment tag (two forward-slashes),
// followed by a closing HTML comment tag.
// -->
</SCRIPT>
```

**FIGURE 28.5.**

*NCSA Mosaic with the additional HTML comment tags displays the non-JavaScript content and passes over the part it can't interpret.*

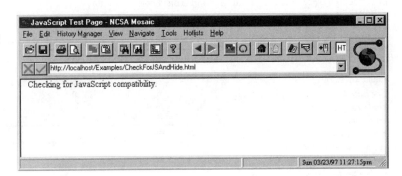

With proper placement and usage, JavaScript can add vital functionality to your HTML pages without interfering with the capability of noncompatible browsers to interpret the document. Remember, however, that if your page depends on JavaScript for including crucial information or operability, it shows common courtesy to warn users and, if possible, supply a generic version of the document.

## Placing Scripts on the Page

The `<SCRIPT>` tag can appear in either the HEAD or BODY section, although its placement will determine when and how the script is used.

If placed in the HEAD portion of the document, the script is interpreted before the page is completely downloaded. (See Listing 28.5 and Figure 28.6). This order works especially well for documents that depend on functions. The script is loaded and ready before the user has a chance to interact with any event that actually invokes the function. (See Figure 28.7.)

**Listing 28.5. Placing functions in the HEAD portion of the document ensures that they are interpreted and ready for use before the rest of the document can access them.**

```
<HTML>
<HEAD>
<SCRIPT LANGUAGE="javascript">
function printMessage(msgStr) {
    document.writeln("<HR>");
    document.writeln(msgStr);
    document.writeln("<HR>");
}
alert("The function is loaded.")
</SCRIPT>
</HEAD>
<BODY>
Welcome to the body of an HTML page.
<SCRIPT LANGUAGE="javascript">
printMessage("I just called a function from the body.")
</SCRIPT>
</BODY>
</HTML>
```

**FIGURE 28.6.**

*The initial screen displayed by Listing 28.5. Note that the alert box with our message has appeared, but the text contained in the* BODY *portion of the document has not.*

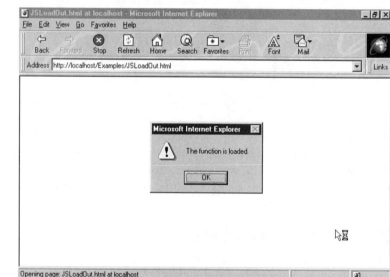

**FIGURE 28.7.**

*The rest of the display generated by Listing 28.5 shows the HTML text in the body of the page and executes the function that was defined in the head.*

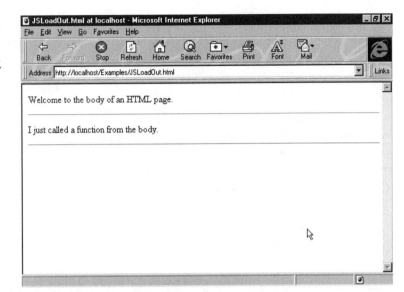

# Using JavaScript in Your Web Page

Many uses exist for JavaScript, and more continue to appear all the time as developers experiment with the possibilities opened with interactive HTML.

This section presents a few uses and examples to get you started.

## SCROLLING TICKER DISPLAYS

A JavaScript ticker, which scrolls a message across the status bar, is absent from this list of applications. With Internet Explorer's <MARQUEE> tag and the availability of multifeatured Java ticker applets, the JavaScript ticker no longer provides an efficient use of browser capability.

## Validating Forms

Using CGI scripts to validate forms wastes precious user time and server time to conduct a process that is now easier and faster on the client's computer. The time required for client/server communication is reduced, along with the lengthy development necessary for CGI scripts.

With its capability to interact with form elements, JavaScript seems ideally suited to validate information directly on the HTML page. This setup localizes the process and takes advantage of the under-utilized client machine. Checking information on the client side also makes it much harder for users to send incompatible or damaging data to the server.

Several methods exist to implement form validation, and most include adding a JavaScript function as the action of a Submit button. The HTML definition of the Submit button could look like this:

```
<INPUT TYPE="BUTTON" NAME="SUBMIT" VALUE="SUBMIT"
    onClick="checkInformation(this.form)">
```

checkInformation is a function that provides verification for the form to ensure that the information meets CGI script expectations. If not, it should return to the document without submitting the form contents to the server. It can also return focus to the offending items. If everything passes inspection, the function can also use the submit method.

```
function checkInformation(thisForm) {
    ...validation statements ...;
    if (validationPassed) {
        thisForm.submit(); }
    return;
}
```

Each form element becomes part of a form object with JavaScript. By using the name of the form as the name of the object, you can access each of the elements. If a name is not used, you can also use the forms array. The first form on the page is forms[0], the next is forms[1], and so on.

For an example, look at the following form definition:

```
<FORM NAME="validation">Enter your user name and identification in the boxes.<BR>
Your name: <INPUT TYPE="text" NAME="userName" VALUE=""><BR>
User ID: <INPUT TYPE="text" NAME="userID" WIDTH="9" VALUE=""><BR>
<INPUT TYPE="button" NAME="button" VALUE="Submit" onClick="checkID(this.form)">
</FORM>
```

Each element in this form is represented in JavaScript, as follows:

```
document.validation.userName
document.validation.userID
document.validation.button
```

The last element, a button, includes an event handler that calls the function checkID with the current form as the argument. Note that you don't need the name of the form in the call because the contents are passed as an argument in this.form. In the function shown in Listing 28.6, the form is referred to as the name of the argument, formID.

**Listing 28.6. A function that checks to make sure the length of two form elements are correct before submitting the form.**

```
function checkID(formID) {
    val validUser = true;
    val validID = true;
    if (formID.userName.length != 10) {
        validUser = false;
        formID.userName.value = "Invalid Entry"; }
```

```
        if (formID.userID.length != 9) {
            validID = false;
            formID.userName.value = "Error"; }
        if (validUser && validID) {
            formID.submit(); }
        else {
            alert("Please try again."); }
}
```

To understand the function, you work through it section by section. First, two Boolean variables are initialized. These flags indicate whether or not the validation has been passed when it comes time to check at the end of the function.

Next, the length of a form element named userName is checked. If the value doesn't equal (represented in JavaScript by !=) 10, the valid flag is set to false, and the form element receives a new value, which is reflected immediately on the page.

The same process is repeated for the next form element, userID. At the end, if both flags are true (logical and is represented by &&), the form is submitted using the submit method. If either or both of the flags are false, an alert screen appears.

## Random Numbers

JavaScript includes a method of the Math object that generates random numbers, but in its current form, it only works on UNIX machines. Another way of generating somewhat-random numbers exists using a user-defined function instead of the built-in method. It is referred to as a calculated random number, and can reveal its biases and true nonrandom nature if used repeatedly over a short period of time.

To ensure compatibility for a script across platforms, any script depending on random numbers shouldn't depend exclusively on the random method, and, instead, should rely on a generated number created by a function similar to the following random number function:

```
function UnixMachine() {
    if (navigator.appVersion.lastIndexOf('Unix') != -1)
        return true
    else
        return false
}

function randomNumber() {
    if UnixMachine()
        num = Math.random()
    else
        num = Math.abs(Math.sin(Date.getTime()));
    return num;
}
```

If the client machine has a UNIX base, randomNumber will use the built-in function. Otherwise, it generates a number between 0 and 1 by generating a sine based on the time value.

28

INTEGRATING
JAVASCRIPT AND
HTML

**JAVASCRIPT TIME**

Time in JavaScript is measured as the number of milliseconds elapsed since midnight on January 1, 1970, and is accessed by using the Date object or an instance of it. The Date object is dynamic, ever changing with the time. An instance of the object returns a static value, depending on the current value of Date or the date parameter passed to it.

The time is based on the client machine, not the server. One idiosyncrasy occurs in JavaScript's representation of time elements. The getMonth and setMonth methods both return a value from 0 (January) to 11 (December). When using these two methods, make sure to convert to the 1-12 system the rest of the world recognizes, as in the following example:

```
var birthday1 = new Date(96,1,11);
document.writeln(birthday1.getMonth()); //Returns a 1 (February)
var birthday2 = new Date("January 11, 1996 06:00:00");
document.writeln(birthday2.getMonth()); //Returns a 0 (January)
```

If you need a constant stream of random numbers, a sine wave pattern will become evident. In this case, it becomes necessary to show some variation in the process by adding more variation into the calculation. You can do this by substituting a different computation (cos, log) at various intervals of time.

## Status Bar Messages

With event handlers and the window.status property, JavaScript enables your browser to display custom messages in the status bar that respond to user actions. One of the most popular implementations is a descriptive line for hyperlinks:

```
More information is available from
<A HREF="http://www.microsoft.com"
onMouseOver="window.status='The Microsoft Home Page';return true">
Microsoft Internet Explorer</A>.
```

One problem with the status property is that it becomes the default message until a browser-generated message overrides it, or status is set to a different value. In the preceding example, The Microsoft Home Page remains in the status bar until another message preempts it.

Working around this problem requires the use of a timer. After the mouse is passed over the hyperlink, the message displays, but only for a short time, after which the status bar is reset to a blank display. This setup requires two functions—one to write the message and set the timer, and one to erase the message.

```
timerLength = 1.5;
function writeStatus(str) {
    timeoutVal = timerLength * 1000;
    setTimeout("clearStatus()",timeoutVal);
    window.status = str;

}
function clearStatus() {
    window.status = "";
}
```

This method of generating status bar messages requires more lines of code, but results in a cleaner operation for custom hyperlink messages. The message appears for the number of seconds assigned to `timerLength`, after which the `clearStatus` function is called to write a null string to the display. To invoke the new method, use the following example:

```
<a href="http://www.microsoft.com/"
onMouseOver="writeStatus('Microsoft Home Page'); return true;">
Microsoft</A>
```

Another possibility for this method of generating status bar displays includes making a copy of the old value of `window.status` and restoring it when the timer expires.

# Controlling Browser Behavior

One of the important and powerful capabilities of JavaScript is controlling various aspects of browser behavior and appearance. This feature comes in handy for implementing demonstrations and tours by adding the capability to spawn new browser windows with controllable levels of functionality.

The command syntax to create a new browser window is

```
windowVar = window.open("URL", "windowName" [, "windowFeatures"])
```

`windowVar` represents the name of a variable that holds the information about the new window.

`URL` refers to an address for the contents of the new window, and can be blank.

`windowName` represents how the window will be referred to in frame and window references.

`windowFeatures` provides a list of the individual features of the browser that should be included or excluded. If blank, all features are enabled. If only some features appear, any unmentioned features are disabled.

To include a feature, use the syntax `windowFeature=yes` or `windowFeature=1`. Conversely, to disable a feature, use `windowFeature=no` or `windowFeature=0`.

The features include `toolbar` for the row of buttons at the top of the screen, `status` for the status bar at the bottom, `scrollbars` for the buttons and slides to control the part of the document viewed, `resizable` for user control over the size of the browser, and `width` and `height` in pixels for the initial size.

To open a plain window with hotlink-only navigation, use this code:

```
//Note: Setting one feature automatically sets all non-mentioned features to false.
window.open("URL", "windowName", "toolbar=no")
```

# JavaScript Resources on the Internet

JavaScript is used and talked about on the Internet frequently, making the Internet one of the first stops for information. You can find up-to-the-minute information on current implementations, bugs, workarounds, and new and creative uses.

## Netscape

One of the first stops you make should be the home of the people who developed and implemented JavaScript. The Netscape site provides a place to look for new developments and documentation about JavaScript features.

The complete JavaScript online documentation (shown in Figure 28.8) also appears here. The online manual is also available in a ZIP file that you can download.

You can access Netscape at `http://home.netscape.com/`.

The manual is located at `http://home.netscape.com/eng/mozilla/3.0/handbook/javascript/index.html`.

**FIGURE 28.8.**

*The Netscape site has an online manual on JavaScript, including objects, methods, and event handlers. It is also available for download.*

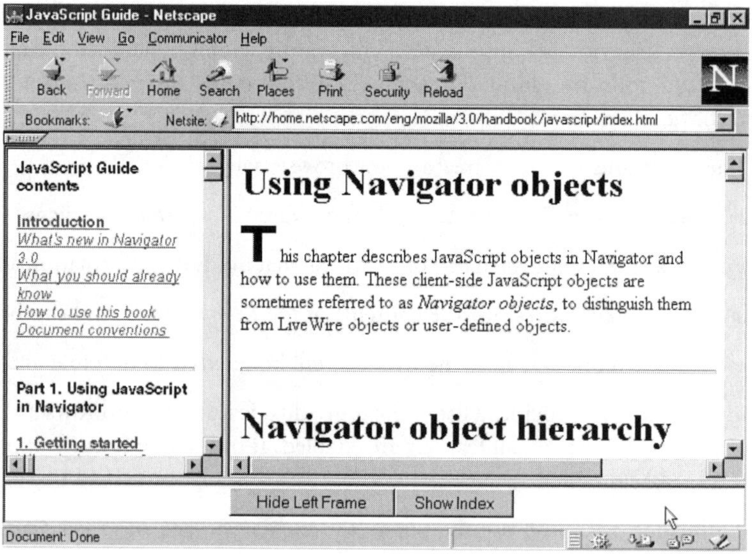

## Gamelan

This site provides one of the best places for examples of what other people are doing with JavaScript on the Web. Though Gamelan is more geared towards Java, it also includes one of the largest listings of JavaScript sites found anywhere on the Web. By perusing the examples here (as shown in Figure 28.9), you can gain insight from others who have gone before you.

You can access Gamelan at `http://www.gamelan.com/`.

## A Beginner's Guide to JavaScript

The JavaScript Index (shown in Figure 28.10) has a collection of real-life JavaScript examples and experiments, including a list of Web pages that illustrate some of JavaScript's features and capabilities. It includes tips and code snippets that are available for use by the author in other Web pages.

**FIGURE 28.9.**

*The Gamelan site offers one of the premier sites for JavaScript resources on the World Wide Web.*

You can access the Beginner's Guide at `http://www.geocities.com/SiliconValley/Park/2554/`.

**FIGURE 28.10.**

*The JavaScript Index has a solid source of examples and successful experiments from developers who are making JavaScript one of the fastest growing languages on the Internet.*

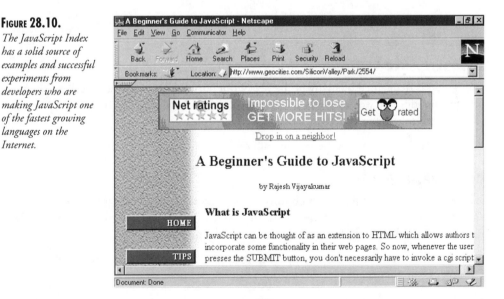

# Voodoo JavaScript Tutorial

The Voodoo JavaScript Tutorial (shown in Figure 28.11) contains a set of lessons covering the various aspects of including JavaScript on your Web pages. This project continues to evolve with new lessons added periodically, so you may want to check back periodically to see what's new.

You won't find much in the way of advanced material here, but what you find gives you more than enough to get beyond the beginner level.

You can access the site at `http://rummelplatz.uni-mannheim.de/~skoch/js/index.htm`.

FIGURE 28.11.

*The Voodoo JavaScript tutorial provides a good place to pick up the basics of working with JavaScript, in addition to other HTML features such as frames.*

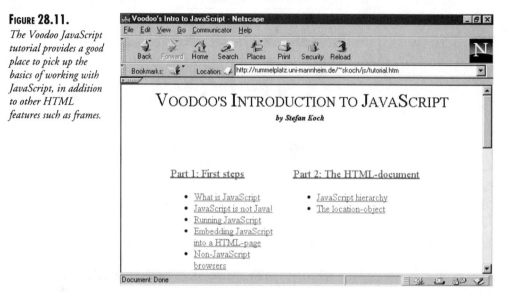

## JavaScript Newsgroup

This group is frequented by many of the JavaScript gurus and provides an excellent source of information, tips, and workarounds. A high level of activity occurs and the threads move quickly, so make sure to check every day, if possible.

You can reach the JavaScript Newsgroup at `news://comp.lang.javascript`.

## netscape.navigator

It never hurts to have a direct line monitored by the folks who developed JavaScript at Netscape, and netscape.navigator remains the closest thing to that line. JavaScript topics are definitely in the minority in this group, but you can find them if you look.

Note the different news server. The title implies it's secure, but it seems to be readily available for browsing and posting.

It's address is `news://secnews.netscape.com`.

# Summary

JavaScript adds new functionality and interactivity to HTML pages that in the past you could only attain through learning CGI scripting languages such as Perl. By switching the bulk of interactive behavior to the client side, it has also improved the perceived speed of World Wide Web sites as seen by the user.

Although it does have its nuances and idiosyncrasies, taking the time to learn JavaScript will pay off in supporting Web pages with dramatically improved features and functions that users will want to revisit again and again.

# Integrating Java Applets and HTML

*by Rick Darnell*

## IN THIS CHAPTER

**CHAPTER 29**

Java is one of the hottest topics on the World Wide Web, and for good reason. It offers expanded portability for Web content, including sound and animation, without the use of plug-ins or other helper applications, and independent of host hardware. In this sense, Java has helped promote a change in the way page developers think about content on the World Wide Web, similar to the way the World Wide Web changed the way people think about the Internet.

Java holds a great deal of promise for the World Wide Web, and computers in general, because it provides a solution to the problem of incompatible platforms. Internets and intranets are no longer expected to include similar or directly compatible machines (all UNIX, all Macintosh, or all PC). Because it has a neutral architecture, the same application written in Java can be used by anyone on the network, without concern for what kind of machine the developer used.

This is the same as HTML—a Web page will work on a PC just as well as UNIX. But, Java is a programming language capable of much more than a Web page. Although it's virtually impossible to build a spreadsheet program with HTML, it's very possible with Java.

For standalone applications, Java's object-oriented structure provides an easy method to upgrade. The class for the upgrade or extension of the application is downloaded into the appropriate class library; then you can run the updated features.

With its modeling capabilities, Java represents a good choice for implementing advanced Web capabilities and content, such as virtual reality sites or Web crawlers powered by intelligent agents.

# Getting to Know Java

Java is an object-oriented programming language developed by Sun Microsystems, Inc. Although not initially conceived as a way to expand the interactivity and capability of Web pages, it didn't take long for people to see how the platform-independent nature of Java was an ideal fit with the nature of the Internet.

In the past, when an author developed a page with special content beyond the constraints of HTML, an important decision had to be made—either use helper applications or shift the necessary processing to the server. The first solution meant that some content would be inaccessible to some users if they didn't have the helper application or if a helper was unavailable for their system. The second solution meant excluding some content because inherently slow modem lines made animation and sounds unworkable over normal network connections.

Enter Java from Sun. By utilizing a key feature of Java—platform independence—Java applets can implement sound, animation, and other user interactivity, regardless of platform. You still have to have a compatible browser for your machine, however. Java is currently supported by at least three browsers—HotJava from Sun (which is written in Java, also), Netscape Navigator 2.0 or later, and Microsoft Internet Explorer 3.0 or later.

# What Is Java?

According to Sun Microsystems, "Java is a simple, robust, secure, object-oriented, platform-independent, dynamic programming environment."

At first, all of this Java talk can sound like a lot of voodoo. After you strip away the hype, however, it's easy to see how Java works effectively for implementing simple solutions to potentially complicated challenges in a distributed environment.

Platform independence is probably one of Java's most important features. One compiled piece of Java code can run on any platform with a Java compiler. Currently, the list of platforms includes Windows 95, Solaris, and Macintosh, but that list should grow significantly in the near future. By its very nature, Java does not contain any "implementation-specific" syntax. This format means a byte is an 8-bit integer and a float is a 32-bit IEEE 754 floating-point number, no matter where the applet runs.

Java was designed with C and C++ programmers in mind. C and C++, however, had many hard-to-understand, rarely used features that Java developers felt caused more pain than benefit. Important functions that come standard to every program, such as memory allocation and pointer arithmetic, are automatically handled by objects in the Java system without needing any acknowledgment from the programmer.

## WHAT DOES *Object-Oriented* MEAN?

*Object-oriented*, probably one of the most overused and confusing terms in computer lingo, really has a simple and easy-to-understand meaning. It facilitates creating clean and portable code by breaking software down into coherent units.

In other words, object-oriented programming focuses on the ways of interacting with data, rather than the programming language. For example, if you're going to mow the lawn, are you going to be concerned about starting the lawnmower or about the type of socket used to install the spark plug? In object-oriented programming, the focus is on the lawnmower.

Objects become the basic building blocks of the application. Because of their modularity, an object can change without requiring major revision of the other program elements.

One benefit of the object-oriented code is the dynamic nature of the resulting programs. A programmer can use inherited interfaces—a set of methods without instance variables or implementation—to update a class library and not worry about affecting the capability of the rest of the program to interact with it.

In addition, Java is relatively small. Because of the need to run on a wide variety of platforms, Java applications tend to be smaller than the multimegabyte applications that predominate the marketplace. The overhead to run a Java program includes 40KB for the basic interpreter and classes, plus an additional 175KB for the standard libraries and threading.

Java programs must be inherently reliable because any piece of Java byte must be capable of running on any platform. For this reason, a great deal of emphasis is placed on checking for bugs and problems early in the development process, beginning with basic language implementation.

The Java compiler checks for a wide variety of errors beyond basic syntax, including type casting and method invocations. If you make a mistake or mistype, chances are good that your mistake will be flagged by the compiler, which is a far better place than by the interpreter at runtime.

## Java and Security

Running in a distributed environment, such as an intranet or the World Wide Web, requires safeguards for client computers; a potentially hostile piece of code can do a great deal of damage by erasing files, formatting disks, and creating other types of damage. Given the way applets are implemented—automatic load and run—you need to ensure the integrity of any piece of code distributed to a broad and uncontrolled audience. Java uses three security procedures to make the end user safe from malicious attacks:

- Byte code verification
- Memory layout control
- File access restrictions

### Byte Code Verification

After a piece of Java code is loaded into memory, it enters the interpreter, where it is checked for language compliance before the first statement is executed. This process ensures against corruption or changes to the compiled code between compile time and runtime.

### Memory Layout

Next, the memory layout is determined for each of the classes, preventing would-be hackers from forging access by deducing anything about the structure of a class or the machine it's running on. Memory allocation is different for each class, depending on its structure and the host machine.

### File Access Restrictions

After that, the interpreter security continues to monitor the activity of the applet to make sure it doesn't access the host file system, except as specifically allowed by the client or user. You can extend some implementations of this specific feature to include no file access.

Although no system can guarantee 100 percent security, Java goes a long way to ensure the protection of client systems from its applets.

## How to Use Java Now

The simplest way to implement Java with your HTML Web pages is through embedding applets. A wide variety of applets are already available for inclusion, including the animation applet included with the Java Development Kit, and a plethora of "ticker" display applets.

### WATCH WHICH BROWSER

Although spreading quickly, Java applets do not come with all browsers. Netscape Navigator, Microsoft Internet Explorer, and Sun HotJava support Java applets. NCSA Mosaic added Java compatibility to its wish list for future upgrades to its product, but no word has been given on when that might happen.

If your browser is not Java-compatible, the applet section of the HTML page is ignored.

# How Applets and Applications Are Different

Java applications work similarly to standalone programs, such as your browser or word processor. They don't require a third-party intermediary, such as HotJava or the applet viewer. Applets require a Java-compatible browser or the applet viewer for viewing. They operate similarly to other objects imbedded in HTML documents, such as Shockwave or RealAudio files, which require assistance to run.

### NOTE

The HotJava browser developed by Sun is a Java application that was written and implemented entirely in the Java language.

Applets run on a host system; this fact makes them especially suspect and leads to several key security restrictions. Applets have limited capability to interact with the host platform. An applet cannot write files or send files to a printer on the local system. In addition, it cannot read local files or run local applications. Although no system is 100 percent secure, Java goes to great lengths to ensure the integrity of applets generated under its banner.

Java is not bulletproof, however. As quick as it was proclaimed "secure," a dedicated group of programmers went to work to find security holes. And they found them. Through cooperative efforts between Sun, Netscape, Microsoft, and others, these are being corrected, but it's still a dangerous world. There are reports of "black Java" applets that are hostile enough to format system drives and pass secure information across the Internet.

As discussed in the introduction, the compiled byte code is checked extensively for illegal operations and is verified again on the host system before the applet is run. Although these security features limit the scope and capabilities of an applet, they also help ensure against "Trojan horse" viruses and other shenanigans by less-than-scrupulous programmers.

With all of the security features built in, you don't want to implement word processors, spreadsheets, or other interactive applications in Java applets. If you require these programs, consider building a full Java application, which does not contain the security restrictions of an applet.

## JAVA APPLETS AND JAVASCRIPT

It has been said a million times, but if you have just started using Java, it bears repeating. Java isn't JavaScript. JavaScript isn't Java.

Java, in applet or application form, is a compiled language with classes and inheritance. HTML pages can include a reference to Java applets, which are then downloaded and run when a compatible browser finds the tag.

JavaScript is an object-based, client-side scripting language developed by Netscape, but it does not include classes or inheritance. JavaScript exists on the HTML page and is interpreted by a compatible browser along with the rest of the page.

Although they share some common syntax and terminology, the two work differently and have different uses. Confusing Java and JavaScript only leads to a steeper learning curve.

# Java Applet Viewer

During applet development and testing, sometimes it's easier to bypass the unnecessary overhead of a browser. If your browser doesn't support applets, you still need a way to view the applets. At this point, the Java Applet Viewer (shown in Figure 29.1) comes in handy.

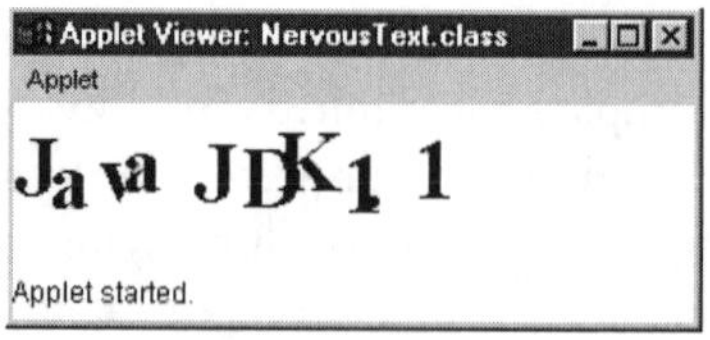

**FIGURE 29.1.**

*The Java Applet Viewer enables the programmer to view embedded Java applets, such as NervousText, without using a browser. Only the embedded applet is displayed; the rest of the HTML around the applet is not even acknowledged.*

## Using the Applet Viewer

The Applet Viewer searches the HTML document for the <APPLET> tag. Listing 29.1 is an example of an HTML document that contains an <APPLET> tag.

For more information on the <APPLET> tag, see the "Using an Applet on a Web Page" section, later in this chapter.

**Listing 29.1. A simple HTML document containing an <APPLET> tag.**

```
<HTML>
<HEAD>
<TITLE>The animation applet</TITLE>
</HEAD>
<BODY>
<APPLET CODE="Animator.class" WIDTH=460 HEIGHT=160>
<PARAM NAME=imagesource VALUE="images/beans">
<PARAM NAME=endimage VALUE=10>
<PARAM NAME=pause VALUE=200>
</APPLET>
</BODY>
</HTML>
```

Using the information contained within the tag, the Applet Viewer opens a window on the user's system, and then runs the applet. Other HTML information on the page is ignored; only the applets appear.

The Java Applet Viewer is distributed with the Java Development Kit and is found in the same directory as the Java compiler and interpreter. To run the Applet Viewer, use the following steps:

1. Create a document that references your applet with the appropriate tags and parameters. (See Listing 29.1 for an example.)

2. From a command line prompt, type appletviewer *[path/]filename*.html.

   If the Applet Viewer launches from the same directory as the HTML document, you don't need the pathname. Otherwise, the path is relative to your current location in the directory structure. The extension .htm is also valid for the viewer.

3. Any applets found in the HTML document are loaded and run, with each applet in its own instance of the Applet Viewer.

4. Although you cannot change the initial parameters contained within the HTML page from the Applet Viewer, you can start the applet from the beginning by choosing Applet¦Restart from the menu. To load it again from memory, select Applet¦Reload.

5. Leave the applet by choosing Applet¦Quit.

> **TIP**
>
> The Applet Viewer Reload function will not work if the application was launched from the same directory as the HTML document and classes. For applets, create a subdirectory from your class directory called HTML and place all of your classes and HTML files in it. Call the Applet Viewer from the parent directory by using `appletviewer html\`*`filename`*`.html`. This way, you can make changes to the applet, compile it, and use the Reload function to see your changes.

# Creating Java Applets

Creating Java applets is easier if you already have a background in programming. With Java's tight structure, the basic format of an applet is fairly straightforward. You walk through an example here.

> **TIP**
>
> You can access online tutorials and documentation for Java and object-oriented programming from the Sun site, `http://java.sun.com/`.

## Applet ABCs

At its simplest, an applet consists of two parts—the class declaration and a paint method. The following snippet contains a breakdown of the common elements for any applet:

```
Import java.applet.Applet;
import java.awt.Graphics;

public class MyApplet extends Applet {
    public void paint (Graphics g) {
        your statements here;
    }
}
```

The first line includes a copy of the `Graphics` class from Java's Abstract Windowing Toolkit (AWT), which contains the methods needed for putting graphics, including text, lines, and dots, on the browser screen. This line may also be represented as `import java.awt.Graphics` if more than the `Graphics` class will be used.

Second, the actual applet is declared. It is `public`, meaning it is available to any other class, and it is a subclass of Java's Applet class, which provides the behavior necessary for interaction with the host browser.

The third section defines a method called `paint`, which the Java interpreter looks for to put the information on the screen. It is public to the class, and `void` indicates it does not return a value when it is completed. Its one parameter is an instance of the `Graphics` class imported on the first line of the program, which is referred to as `g`. This reference could just as easily be called `bob` or `hammer`, but `g` is the commonly used convention.

# Displaying with `paint`

Now that the applet is defined, you need to make it do something. For the `paint` method, include the following line:

```
g.drawString("Hava a nice day.",50,25);
```

After compiling the code and inserting it into an HTML document (as shown in the "Using an Applet on a Web Page" section, later in this chapter), you get something that looks like the message shown in Figure 29.2.

**COMPILING AN APPLET**

To convert your source code into a usable class, type `javac MyApplet.java` at the command prompt. If any errors are reported, check your spelling and syntax and try again.

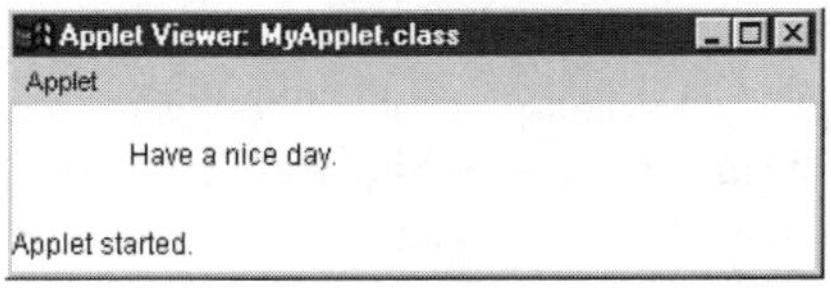

**FIGURE 29.2.**

*MyApplet displays a simple message on the screen.*

Of course, applets can do much more. The text can look better if some other AWT classes are included. First, you need the classes that control the font and display color:

```
import java.awt.Font;
import java.awt.Color;
```

After the class declaration, create a variable to hold a new setting for the text:

```
Font f = new Font("TimesRoman",Font.ITALIC,24);
```

After the `paint` method declaration, use the `Graphics.set` methods to set the display before writing to the screen:

```
g.setFont(f);
g.setColor(Color.red);
```

With this extra bit of effort, the applet looks like the one in Figure 29.3.

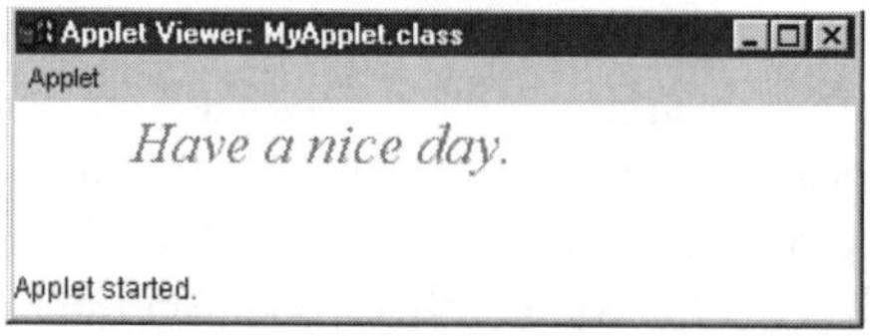

**FIGURE 29.3.**

*MyApplet displays in a larger font in red after some minor revisions to the code.*

Again, this example is limited. The addition of a parameter to control the string would make it more useful to the HTML author. After the class declaration, declare the message as a variable:

```
String message;
```

A new method is also required to initialize the value of `message`.

## APPLET ACTIVITIES

In addition to `paint`, four major activities exist in the life of an applet. If any are omitted, default versions are provided in the `Applet` class. This setup is called *inheritance*. Providing new methods in the applet is called *overriding*.

The first activity is *initialization*, accomplished with the `init` method: `public void init() {...}`. This activity occurs once, immediately after the applet is loaded. Initialization includes creating objects, setting graphics, or defining parameters. It can only happen once in the applet's life.

The second activity is *starting*, accomplished with the `start` method: `public void start() {...}`. After initialization, activity begins. This activity can also happen if a user activity stopped the applet. Starting can happen many times in the life of an applet. The `paint` method is invoked somewhere in this method.

The next activity is *stopping*, accomplished with the `stop` method: `public void stop() {...}`. This activity can be an important method to include because, by default, the applet continues running and using system resources, even after the user has left the page with the applet. Like `start`, stopping can occur many times in the course of execution.

The last activity is *destroying*, accomplished with the `destroy` method: `public void destroy() {...}`. Destroying occurs when an applet throws out its own garbage after completing execution—when the applet is no longer needed or the user exits the browser. Java provides adequate coverage in this department, so you don't need to override this method unless you want to return specific resources to the system.

To initialize the message parameter, the `init` method for the applet must be overridden:

```
public void init() {
    this.message = getParameter("message");
    if (this.message == null) {
```

```
        this.message = "Your message here."; }
    this.message = "A note from Java: " + this.message;
}
```

This method retrieves the value of the parameter in the HTML document. If a parameter named message is not found, the value is null and message is set to the default string.

---

**TIP**

Java is case sensitive for all of its variables, even when passed back and forth as parameters. Remember, a Rose by another name is not a rose.

---

Next you need to update the paint method so that it uses the string defined in init rather than the literal string in the drawString method:

```
g.drawString(this.message);
```

Using the Applet Viewer again generates the results in Figure 29.4.

To place your own message in the applet, add a <PARAM> tag to the HTML source containing the applet. For more information, see "Passing Parameters to Applets," later in this chapter. The complete listing for MyApplet appears in Listing 29.2.

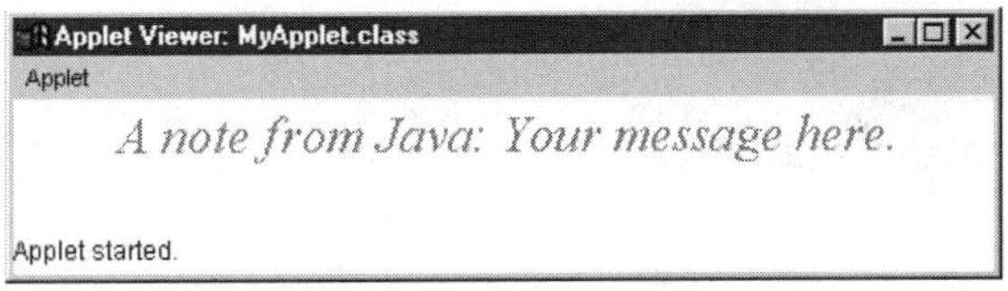

**FIGURE 29.4.**

*The default message generated by MyApplet, after checking for a message parameter and finding none.*

**Listing 29.2. A simple applet for displaying text onscreen. Note the use of the parameter in the init method.**

```
import java.awt.Graphics;
import java.awt.Font;
import java.awt.Color;

public class MyApplet extends java.applet.Applet {
    Font f = new Font("TimesRoman",Font.ITALIC,24);
    String message;

    public void init() {
        this.message = getParameter("message");
        if (this.message == null) {
```

*continues*

**Listing 29.2. continued**

```
            this.message = "Your message here."; }
        this.message = "A note from Java: " + this.message;
    }

    public void paint(Graphics g) {
        g.setFont(f);
        g.setColor(Color.red);
        g.drawString(this.message,50,25);
    }
}
```

> **TIP**
>
> Listing 29.3 is a sample HTML file that can be used as the basis for inserting or testing applets. Saved in a generic form, it is a very reusable piece of code.

**Listing 29.3. A sample of an HTML document that can display MyApplet.**

```
<HTML>
<HEAD>
<TITLE>The MyApplet</TITLE>
</HEAD>
<BODY>
<HR>
<APPLET CODE="MyApplet.class" WIDTH=400 HEIGHT=50>
<PARAM NAME=message VALUE="Here I am.">
</APPLET>
<HR>
</BODY>
</HTML>
```

# Using an Applet on a Web Page

Using applets on a Web page involves a two-part process. First, you must make sure your classes and related files, such as images and audio clips, appear in a directory accessible to the HTML page. One common location is in a `classes` subdirectory of the HTML documents.

Second, the <APPLET> tag that refers to the class must be inserted in the Web page, along with any parameters the applet needs to function.

## All About the <APPLET> Tag

The <APPLET> tag is used to insert the applet on a page, and it takes the following syntax:

```
<APPLET CODE="appletName.class" [CODEBASE="pathToClass"]
WIDTH=xxx HEIGHT=xxx [ALIGN= ]>
```

```
[<PARAMETER name=parameterName value=parameterValue>]
</APPLET>
```

The required line of code identifies the name of the applet, CODE, and the size it will appear on the page.

The optional parameter CODEBASE indicates a relative path to the class if it is not stored in the same directory as the HTML file. ALIGN works much like the parameter in the <IMG SRC> tag by controlling the positioning of HTML text adjacent to the applet's space.

## Passing Parameters to Applets

Parameters are used to pass information to an applet about its environment and how it should behave in the current HTML document. Some applets have one method of running and don't accept any parameters. Most, however, contain some user-definable parameters that can be changed.

The <PARAM> tag enables you to pass information to the applet. The syntax is this:

```
<PARAM NAME=paramName VALUE=paramValue>
```

The parameter of the name is case sensitive and must exactly match the parameter name in the applet. The value of a parameter is a different matter. All parameters passed from an HTML page to an applet are passed as strings, no matter what it is or how it's formatted on the page. Any conversion to other types (integer, Boolean, date) must happen within the applet itself.

For example, `<PARAM NAME="speed" value=100>` and `<PARAM NAME="speed" value="100">` both pass the string `"100"` to the applet. This cuts a lot of guesswork between the browser and the applet because neither one has to guess what kind of value is being sent. Everything is converted to a string, and the programmer can take care of casting the value to a new type after it enters the applet.

## Controlling Applets with Scripts

Controlling a Java applet with a scripting language such as JavaScript is a fairly easy matter, but it does require some knowledge of the applet you're working with. You have to know which methods, properties, and variables in the applet are public. Only the public items in an applet are accessible to JavaScript.

**29**

INTEGRATING
JAVA APPLETS
AND HTML

---

**TIP**

Two public methods are common to all applets and you can always use them—start() and stop(). These methods provide a handy way to control an applet when it is active and running.

With this information in hand, start with the `<APPLET>` tag. It helps to give a name to your applet to make script references to the applet easier to read. The following snippet of code shows the basic constructor for an HTML applet tag that sets the stage for JavaScript control of a Java applet. The tag is identical to the tags you used in previous chapters to add applets, except that a new attribute is included for a name:

```
<APPLET CODE="UnderConstruction.class" NAME="AppletConstruction"
WIDTH=60 HEIGHT=60>
</APPLET>
```

Assigning a name to your applet isn't absolutely necessary because JavaScript creates an array of applets when the page is loaded. However, doing so makes for a much more readable page.

To use a method of the applet from JavaScript, use the following syntax:

```
document.appletName.methodOrProperty
```

---

**TIP**

Beginning with version 3.0, Netscape Navigator uses an `applets` array to reference all the applets on a page. The `applets` array is used according to the following syntax:

```
document.applets[index].methodOrProperty
document.applets[appletName].methodOrProperty
```

These two methods also identify the applet you want to control, but the method using the applet's name without the `applets` array is the easiest to read and requires the least amount of typing.

Like other arrays, one of the properties of `applets` is `length`, which returns how many applets are in the document.

The JavaScript `applets` array is currently available only in Netscape Navigator 3.0 or later, and not Microsoft Internet Explorer. This doesn't leave Internet Explorer completely out in the cold–JavaScript can still reference an applet in Explorer using the applet's name.

---

One of the easy methods of controlling applet behavior is starting and stopping its execution. You start and stop an applet using the `start()` and `stop()` methods that are common to every applet. Use a form and two buttons to add the functions to your Web page. (See Figure 29.5.) The following code snippet is a basic example of the HTML code needed to add the buttons, with the name of the applet substituted for *appletName*:

```
<FORM>
<INPUT TYPE="button" VALUE="Start" onClick="document.appletName.start()">
<INPUT TYPE="button" VALUE="Stop" onClick="document.appletName.stop()">
</FORM>
```

**Figure 29.5.**

*One of the simplest methods of controlling an applet is to use buttons that start and stop it.*

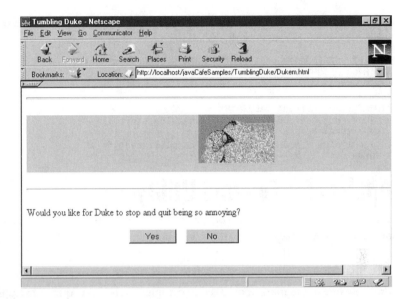

You can also call other methods, depending on their visibility to the world outside the applet. JavaScript can call any Java method or variable by using a public declaration.

> **TIP**
>
> Any variable or method within the applet that doesn't include a specific declaration of scope is protected by default. If you don't see the public declaration, it's not.

The syntax to call applet methods from JavaScript is simple and can be integrated with browser events, such as the button code snippet just shown. The basic syntax for calling an applet method from Java is

```
document.appletName.methodName(arg1,...,argx)
```

To call the stop() method from the underConstructionApplet applet within an HTML page, the syntax is as follows (assuming that the applet is the first one listed on the page):

```
document.underConstructionApplet.stop();
```

Here's how you do it with Navigator (again, assuming that the applet is the first one listed on the page):

```
document.applets[0].stop();
```

Integrating the start() and stop() methods for this applet with the applet tag and button code snippet used earlier results in the following code:

```
<APPLET CODE="UnderConstruction" NAME="underConstructionApplet"
WIDTH=60 HEIGHT=60>
</APPLET>
<FORM>
<INPUT TYPE="button" VALUE="Start"
onClick="document.underConstructionApplet.start()">
<INPUT TYPE="button" VALUE="Stop"
onClick="document.underConstructionApplet.stop()">
</FORM>
```

# Applets for Fun and Utility

This section provides a selection of applets available on this book's CD-ROM that you can use on your own Web pages.

## Animator

Probably one of the most frequently used applets is the Java Animator Applet (shown in Figure 29.6), which comes with the Java Development Kit and provides a quick-and-easy way to add animation to your Java-powered page. You can find it at http://localhost/javaCafeSamples/Animator/example1.html.

**FIGURE 29.6.**

*The Animator Applet is used to display a series of images with an option for frame-specific sounds and soundtracks.*

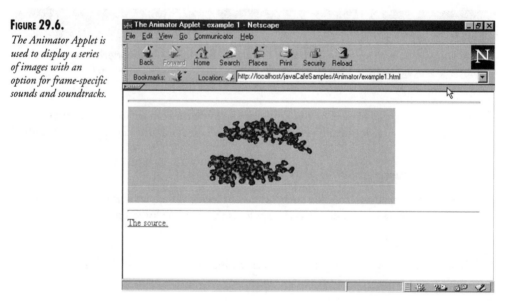

Animator also supports synchronized sound with the animation, but the sound must use the Sun.AU format. No other sound formats are supported yet.

Implementing the applet requires a set of GIF or JPG files containing the images that form the animation.

---

**TIP**

Try to keep the size of the images as small as possible. Each image has to be down-loaded to the client machine, adding significantly to the time required for the applet to load and run.

---

A wide variety of parameters exist that control the operation of Animator. Here's the break-down and syntax (with the explanation following each line of code):

```
<APPLET CODE="Animator.class" WIDTH=number HEIGHT=number>
```

Width should be at least the width in pixels of the widest frame, whereas height should reflect the size of the tallest frame. Smaller values will result in the image being clipped.

```
<PARAM NAME=IMAGESOURCE VALUE="pathInfo">
```

Points to the directory that contains the animation frames. The default directory is the same as the HTML document. By default, the files are named T1.gif, T2.gif, and so on.

```
<PARAM NAME=STARTUP VALUE="filename">
```

An image that is displayed while the applet loads and prepares to run.

```
<PARAM NAME=BACKGROUND VALUE="filename">
```

An image file for use as a background for the animation.

```
<PARAM NAME=BACKGROUNDCOLOR VALUE="color,color,color">
```

The color for the animation background, represented as an RGB value with a number from 0 to 255 for each of the settings.

```
<PARAM NAME=STARTIMAGE VALUE=number>
```

The first frame in the animation, by default 1.

```
<PARAM NAME=ENDIMAGE VALUE=number>
```

The last frame in the animation.

```
<PARAM NAME="NAMEPATTERN" VALUE="dir/prefix%N.suffix">
```

A pattern to use for generating names based on STARTIMAGE, ENDIMAGE, or IMAGES.

```
<PARAM NAME="PAUSE" VALUE=number>
```

Number of milliseconds to pause between images default—can be overridden by PAUSES.

```
<PARAM NAME="PAUSES" VALUE="number¦number¦...">
```

Millisecond delay per frame, with each value separated by a vertical bar. Blank uses a default PAUSE value.

```
<PARAM NAME="REPEAT" VALUE=true>
```

If true, the animation will continue as a loop.

```
<PARAM NAME="POSITIONS" VALUE="x@y¦x@y...">
```

Screen positions (X@Y) for each frame, represented in pixels and separated by vertical bars. A blank value will use the preceding frame's position.

```
<PARAM NAME="IMAGES" VALUE="number¦number¦...">
```

Used to define an explicit order for frames, which becomes useful if your frames are out of order or if you want to reverse the sequence (such as "1¦2¦3¦2¦1").

```
<PARAM NAME="SOUNDSOURCE" VALUE="aDirectory">
```

Indicates the directory with the audio files. The default is the same directory as the class.

```
<PARAM NAME="SOUNDTRACK" VALUE="aFile">
```

An audio file to play throughout the animation as background music.

```
<PARAM NAME="SOUNDS" VALUE="aFile.au¦¦¦¦¦bFile.au">
```

Plays audio files keyed to individual frames.

```
<PARAM NAME="HREF" VALUE="aURL">
```

The URL of the page to visit when user clicks the animation (if not set, a mouse click pauses/resumes the animation).

## Calendar Applet

The Calendar Applet (`http://localhost/javaCafeSamples/Calendar/Calendar.html`) displays a calendar for the current month with a button for each day and a scrolling message across the top. The month is changed via a pair of buttons at the bottom of the applet. (See Figure 29.7.) As a button for a specific day is pushed, the applet displays any events on that day.

```
<APPLET CODE=Calendar.class WIDTH=300 HEIGHT=275>
</APPLET>
```

The events are set using HTML parameters.

```
<param name=EVENTnum value="mm/dd/yy:Message">
```

First is the parameter name. Each EVENT is numbered sequentially, so the first is EVENT1, the second is EVENT2, and so on. The value of the parameter is in two parts, separated by a colon. The first part identifies the date value for the button in MM/DD/YY format. This is followed by a colon and the text of any string you want to display:

```
<param name=EVENT1 value="02/14/97:February 14, 1997 - Happy Valentine's Day">
```

In this example, EVENT1 corresponds to 2/14/97. Clicking the button for that day results in "February 14, 1997—Happy Valentine's Day" scrolling across the top of the calendar.

FIGURE 29.7.

*The Calendar Applet.*

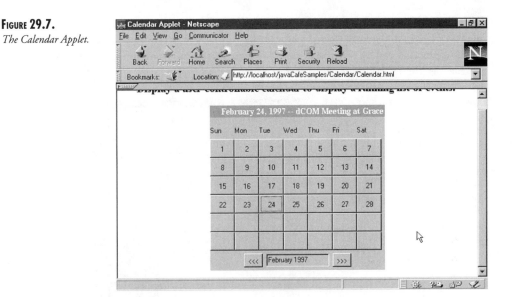

## Macromedia ImageMap PowerApplet

The Macromedia ImageMap PowerApplet (http://www.macromedia.com) is an example of some of the creative things you can do with Java for client-side image maps. The applet enables you to define hot areas in a GIF image that act as hyperlinks to other Web pages. In addition to the basic hyperlink activity, it can also provide simple animation by replacing portions of the original image with another image, display pop-up text, and produce other effects. (See Figure 29.8.)

FIGURE 29.8.

*The ImageMap applet is using the splash screen from AppletAce. Placing the mouse over the Ace's eyes makes them "pop out," instead of their normal appearance.*

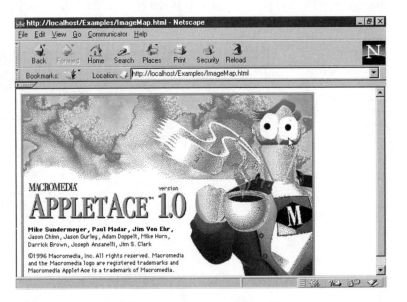

29

INTEGRATING
JAVA APPLETS
AND HTML

To make working with ImageMap easier, Macromedia has also developed a handy utility (written in Java) called AppletAce. (See Figure 29.9.) AppletAce is configured to each of the four PowerApplets offered by Macromedia and makes the process of defining hot areas and actions much easier than working directly with parameter tags.

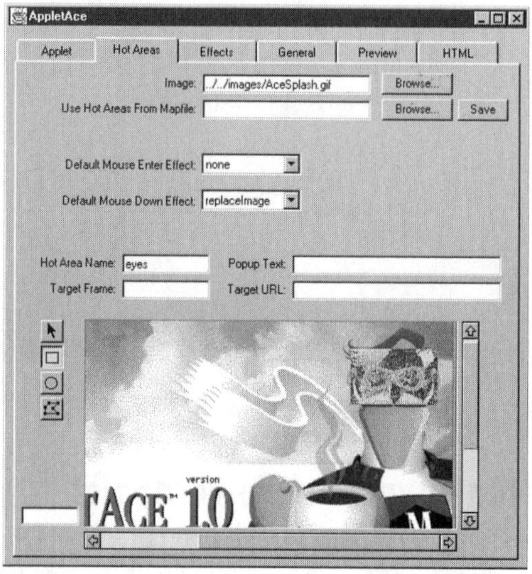

FIGURE 29.9.

*AppletAce provides an easy-to-use interface for generating the HTML* <APPLET> *and* <PARAM> *tags needed for customizing Macromedia's ImageMap and other PowerApplets.*

## Ticker

The Ticker applet (http://www.sbk-ks.de/~twe/e/ticker.html) provides one example of the many "ticker tape" applets available. It is one of the improved versions, which has made the extra effort to reduce flicker and provide additional control over the text. (See Figure 29.10.)

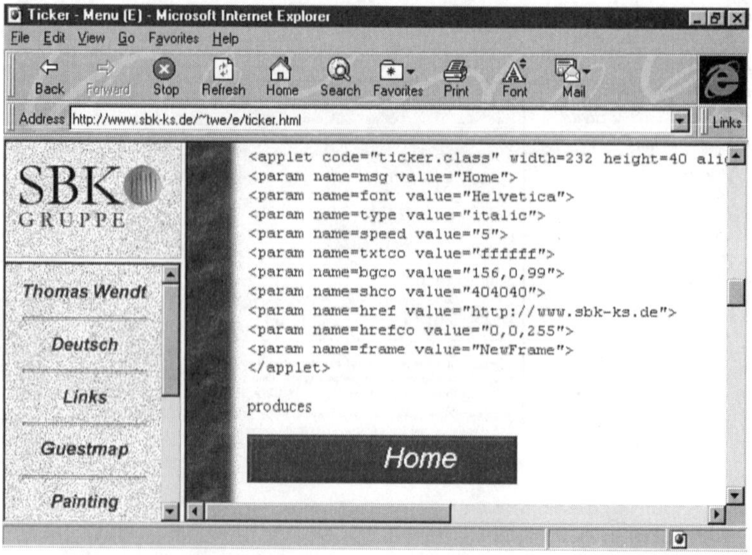

FIGURE 29.10.

*The Ticker applet provides a flexible way to display scrolling messages on the browser screen.*

```
<applet code="ticker.class" width=232 height=40 ali
<param name=msg value="Home">
<param name=font value="Helvetica">
<param name=type value="italic">
<param name=speed value="5">
<param name=txtco value="ffffff">
<param name=bgco value="156,0,99">
<param name=shco value="404040">
<param name=href value="http://www.sbk-ks.de">
<param name=hrefco value="0,0,255">
<param name=frame value="NewFrame">
</applet>
```

produces

Home

The Ticker applet takes a variety of parameters, listed here with an explanation of each following the parameters:

```
<PARAM NAME=msg VALUE="string">
```

The message to display.

```
<PARAM NAME=speed VALUE=number>
```

The animation speed, expressed as the number of pixels per 100 milliseconds. The default is 10.

```
<PARAM NAME=txtco VALUE="r,g,b">
```

The color of the message, expressed as an RGB value with numbers from 0 to 255. If omitted, the default is black.

```
<PARAM NAME=bgco VALUE="r,g,b">
```

The color of the background. If omitted, the default appears as light gray.

```
<PARAM NAME=shco VALUE="r,g,b">
```

The color of the message shadow. If omitted, no shadow appears.

```
<PARAM NAME=href VALUE="URL">
```

The ticker can also serve as a hyperlink if the user clicks the ticker. A relative or complete URL is legal.

```
<PARAM NAME=hrefco VALUE="r,g,b">
```

The color of the URL frame. If omitted, the default is blue.

```
<PARAM NAME=start VALUE="yy, mm, dd">
<PARAM NAME=exp VALUE="yy, mm, dd">
```

Dates to start and stop displaying the applet. If the page is viewed outside of these dates, as determined by the host machine, the ticker will not display its message. It will still occupy space on the screen, however. You can use either date parameter by itself.

```
<PARAM NAME=exfill VALUE="r,g,b">
```

If the local date falls outside of the start and stop parameters, the box becomes filled with this color.

## J-Track

J-Track (`http://liftoff.msfc.nasa.gov/home/mission/jtrack/welcome.html`) is an interesting little piece of work that tracks several prominent satellites and the space shuttle when in flight. (See Figure 29.11.) After the applet is loaded and initialized, it displays the position and path of each satellite. The tracking information is updated in real-time, so if you just sit and watch, you can see the position of each target change. When the space shuttle is orbiting the earth doing repairs on the Hubbel telescope or docking with the space shuttle, you can track the progress from your desktop and be the first one on your block to know when to look out your window and wave.

# Applet Sources on the Web

Many sources exist on the Web for applets that you can use. Make sure to check the licensing on the applet. Just because an applet appears on a page doesn't mean you can freely use it.

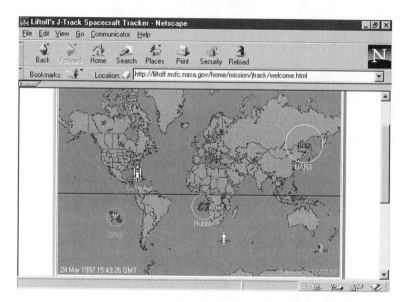

## JavaSoft

JavaSoft, a subsidiary of Sun Microsystems, handles the Java products. Go to its Web site (`http://java.sun.com/`) first when looking for information, documentation, updates, downloads, and other feedback.

Originally part of the Sun Web site, JavaSoft received its own space to handle the dramatic increase in attention Java has received since its release.

## The Java Applet Rating Service (JARS) World

JARS (`http://www.jars.com/`) is an independent organization devoted to promoting excellence in Java applet programming. Developers submit their work to the folks at JARS, who evaluate the applet, give it a rating, and then post the results on their site along with links to the developer's home page and applet example.

The number of applets rated through JARS has continued to grow, so it's a good place to look for some of the best in applet programming.

## Gamelan

The Gamelan site (`http://www.gamelan.com/`) shows you what the rest of the world is doing with Java. Links appear here to some of the best applets to date for the viewing, and you can download some for use on your pages. It also includes a page devoted to JavaScript for links devoted to pages utilizing Java's cousin.

Some of the innovative productions found here include animators, tickers, network utilities, and a "Learn to Dance" applet.

## alt.lang.java

Although not technically a source for applets, the `alt.lang.java` newsgroup provides a great source of information about Java and its uses. Following the threads can also lead to Java applets and applications, where you can learn from people already making the most of this new language.

# Summary

With Java, you can embed customized applications within your Web page that expand the capabilities of HTML beyond its traditional static nature. Applets are available for enabling on-line shopping, database searching, player-to-player gaming over the Internet, and gathering guestbook information (without using CGI scripts).

Anything you do with a traditional application—word processing, spreadsheets, database access, and so on—you can do with Java. And with Java, you approach a write-once, run-anywhere capability. You don't have to provide a separate applet for Macintosh machines, another for PCs, and a third for UNIX. One applet will fit all three.

Java was, in its early days, primarily used for animations, tickers, and other multimedia-type content. Although these take advantage of some of Java's capabilities, you should also consider using Java for database applications, such as user registration and guestbook applications, on-line shopping, and computer-to-computer communication over network lines.

Java has been embraced by the major developers of hardware, including Intel, IBM, and Macintosh, and additional support from software developers, including Microsoft, Netscape, Sun, Macromedia, and Symantec. You can expect Java's use to continue spreading as more and more hardware and software manufacturers pledge support to the language and concepts. Even if you never have the chance to delve deeply into the intricacies of building an applet or application from scratch, an understanding of the basics will help you take full advantage of Java's powerful capabilities.

# Integrating ActiveX and VBScript

*by Paul Lomax*

## IN THIS CHAPTER

CHAPTER

30

In this chapter, you learn about the importance of the latest Microsoft ActiveX and VBScript technologies and how you can use them to create stunning Web applications. You learn how to add VBScript to your Web pages to interface and manipulate HTML intrinsic controls, ActiveX controls, and even the browser itself. You learn how to incorporate ActiveX controls and HTML layout controls to give your Web page the look and feel of a Windows application.

# The Importance of ActiveX and VBScript

When Microsoft discovered the Internet in late 1996, the world was to change forever. Too dramatic? Maybe, but at least the world of computing, which is not known for staying put in one place for more than a few seconds, was about to undergo a revolution. Still too dramatic? Not really. This revolution was to be more a renaissance than an advent.

The renaissance is really in the form of centralized processing power. Over the past few years, corporations have been busy upgrading the specification of client machines, decentralizing processing, placing more and more work on the workstation, taking the load from the server and distributing it throughout the organization. However, the upsurge in the popularity of the intranet—with good reason—is, in part, from putting that processing back onto the server through the use of small, self-contained, componentized applications that run on the server, querying databases, and passing no more than a text-based HTML page to the client. But, of course, this is only part of the picture. If this were taken to its logical conclusion, we'd end up with Network Computer and Super Server, which as we all know is not what Bill Gates is aiming for.

So what exactly is Microsoft doing to computing?

Over several frantic months, Microsoft engineers adapted and modified their tried and tested technologies and added Internet capabilities to virtually anything that moved. In fact, more than adding Internet capability, the previous situation of a Web-enabled desktop application is actually reversed; it's now more common to ask whether a product can run as a standalone on the desktop as well as on the Web. (I exaggerate a little, but you get the point.) This change has been brought about by the progressive development of a technology that is now called *ActiveX*.

ActiveX is a way of distributing processing power once again. In fact, such is the flexibility of the technology that the decision about where a control (or script, for that matter) should execute is where it should be—in the hands of the developer. The developer decides—sometimes from experience, sometimes from trial and error—where the application should run. So what does this mean for the Web and, in particular, Web page design?

# A New Era for Web Pages

Windows applications have for several years taken advantage of component object model (COM) objects, which are reusable software building blocks that are glued together by developers using languages such as Visual Basic to create complete applications.

COM has recently been given a facelift. Distributed COM (DCOM) enables developers to create an application, some part of which can be on a completely different machine. An extension of this idea is ActiveX. So rather than being a brand new untried technology, ActiveX is the logical progression of the very thing that Windows itself is based upon.

From an HTML developer's point of view, the best thing about ActiveX is that it can be glued into an HTML Web page.

ActiveX controls come in all shapes and sizes; at first glance, some might not even appear to be ActiveX controls at all. Consider, for example, the Forms2 controls that Microsoft includes with the full install of Microsoft Internet Explorer (MSIE). The text box, combo box, list box, and so on are all ActiveX controls. Then there are the third-party controls, everything from database controls to Scratch 'n' Sniff controls. (Okay, so I made that one up.) There are also ActiveX data controls to make the retrieval and display of data from the server that much easier, and ActiveX controls that operate on the server itself, even to the point of controlling the Web server.

Many ActiveX controls are self-contained, but the vast majority require some user interaction; they need some input to process and then output. This interaction is made possible by the glue that goes between the user interface (the browser) and the control. The glue that holds the HTML page and ActiveX control together is VBScript. Although it is a fully functional language in its own right and can be used to write all sorts of applications, its most popular use at the moment is to control the ActiveX controls.

# Using VBScript with HTML Documents

When you add VBScript to your Web page, you create an interactive application. Like all programs, VBScript is used to provide an automated solution to a problem. For example, your problem might be figuring out how to communicate with the user quickly and without sending data back and forth between the server and the browser. The solution to this problem could be to write a script that displays a customized message box in response to a particular event, like this:

```
<SCRIPT LANGUAGE="vbscript">
    Sub cmdButton1_OnClick
        Alert "Thank you for clicking this button"
    End Sub
</SCRIPT>
```

Now let's look at the elements you use to create interactive scripted HTML documents.

## The <SCRIPT> Tag

New for scripting is the <SCRIPT> tag, which does use a closing tag, </SCRIPT>.

The <SCRIPT> tag has one main element, LANGUAGE=. The current values for this are JavaScript, VBScript, or VBS. In Microsoft Internet Explorer Version 3.*x* and later, the default scripting language is JScript; if you don't use the LANGUAGE= element, your script will be compiled as

JavaScript; and if you've written in VBScript, all you get for your troubles is an error. To compile as VBScript, therefore, you must start your script with this line:

```
<SCRIPT LANGUAGE="vbscript">
```

> **TIP**
>
> Remember that, as with all HTML elements, the <SCRIPT> tag and the script it contains are not case sensitive; vbscript is the same as VBScript and vBscRiPt.

The <SCRIPT> tag tells script-enabled browsers to get ready to compile a script from the code that follows, but what if the browser (Netscape Navigator, for example) doesn't understand VBScript? Because you've used the LANGUAGE= element, the complete script block is ignored.

But what about browsers that aren't script-enabled at all? Well-behaved browsers will ignore the <SCRIPT> tag, but they won't ignore the script it contains and will treat the script like text and show it on the page. It's prudent, therefore, to always enclose your scripts within HTML comment markers, like this:

```
<SCRIPT LANGUAGE="vbscript">
    <!--
        your script goes here
    -->
</SCRIPT>
```

The comment markers are ignored by the scripting engine, so don't worry about your script being overlooked. This way, your Web page won't look like hieroglyphics to someone with an older browser.

You can have as many <SCRIPT> tags within one HTML page as you like, or need, or you can consolidate all your subroutines and functions for the page into one script tag block. Furthermore, it doesn't matter where on the page you place your script block, in the <HEAD> or <BODY>; wherever it is, it will be compiled.

So, you've got your script block, but when is your script going to execute? That depends on what you want the script to do. Here are the three options:

- A script that automatically executes as the page is downloading into the browser
- A script that executes as the result of an action taken by the user
- A script that executes because it has been called by another script

Allowing your script to run automatically as the page is loading into the browser entails a degree of risk, if only because you have lost control over its execution. However, sometimes you need to have a freely running script, such as when you need to print some variable text into the HTML page at a particular place.

> **CAUTION**
>
> Always ensure that scripts that will run as the page is downloading do not reference controls that have not yet been downloaded. In other words, a script that references a control must be placed after the control's definition on the page unless the script is held within an event handler or a subroutine.

To create a script that executes automatically, use the <SCRIPT> tag without any event handler or subroutine definition, like this:

```
<SCRIPT LANGUAGE="vbscript">
  <!--
    Document.Write "<CENTER><H3>Hey this is Cool!<H3></CENTER>"
  -->
</SCRIPT>
```

What's an event handler? An event is something that the user causes to happen or that a change in a control generates. A click on a button is an event; typing text into a text box is an event; the page downloading into the browser is an event. The code you write that executes in response to an event is called an *event handler.*

Unfortunately (or fortunately), you can't create your own events; you have to use the events available for the particular control or object. Here's how you define an event handler for an HTML button's Click event:

```
<SCRIPT LANGUAGE="vbscript">
  <!--
    Sub myButton_OnClick
        Alert "Hello World"
    End Sub
  -->
</SCRIPT>
```

myButton is the name of the control. (See the next section, "The <INPUT> Tag," for more information about how to name controls.) _OnClick is the event name. Note that the event handler is finished with the End Sub statement.

The final way to add scripting is by writing a subroutine, of which there are two types. A subroutine is a standalone piece of code that is called by some other code within your script. There are two types of subroutines: the function, which returns a value to the calling code; and the sub, which, when it's finished, simply hands back execution to the calling code without passing back a value. Here's how you define both:

```
<SCRIPT LANGUAGE="vbscript">
  <!--

    Sub myButton_OnClick
        Call mySubRoutine()
    End Sub
```

```
Sub mySubRoutine()
    Alert timesTwo(4)
End Sub

Function timesTwo(someValue)
    timesTwo = someValue * 2
End Function
-->
</SCRIPT>
```

In the preceding code snippet, you can see all three types of scripted routines in action. First, the OnClick event handler for the button called myButton calls the sub mySubRoutine, which passes the value 4 to the timesTwo function. The timesTwo function multiplies the incoming value (whatever it is) by two and returns the result. In this case, the result is shown in an alert box, which you'll learn more about later in this chapter.

As you've seen, apart from writing scripts that execute on download to the browser, it is most likely that a script will at least start executing as the result of some user action—an event. The next section offers a look at the easiest way to create a dynamic, interactive, scripted user interface using normal HTML form elements.

## The <INPUT> Tag

The <INPUT> tag will be familiar to anyone who has authored an HTML form. It defines the user interface items that you place within the form, such as the text box or option button.

A list of HTML form controls known as *elements objects* or *intrinsic controls* can be found later in the chapter in the section called "Referencing the Elements Objects."

VBScript can be used to interface with these HTML controls, just as easily as it can with ActiveX controls. In fact, you can gain a large advantage simply by adding scripting to your current HTML forms.

To attach script to an HTML form control, you simply need to give the control a name using the NAME= element of the <INPUT> tag. Be careful, however, to give your controls different names because the scripting engine must have a unique name to reference a control.

There are two methods of attaching a script to an HTML control. The first, and the easiest to read and maintain, is to create an event handler within a <SCRIPT> block. Listing 30.1 shows how to place the contents of one text box into another text box at the click of a button.

**Listing 30.1. A simple script attached to the click event of a button.**

```
<HTML>
 <HEAD>
  <SCRIPT LANGUAGE="vbscript">
  <!--
   Sub cmdButton1_OnClick
       frmForm1.txtText2.Value = frmForm1.txtText1.Value
```

```
        Alert "Hello World"
        Status "VBScript in Action"
    End Sub
  -->
  </SCRIPT>
 </HEAD>
 <BODY BGCOLOR="white">
  <CENTER>
   <FORM NAME="frmForm1">
    <INPUT TYPE="text" NAME="txtText1">
    <INPUT TYPE="text" NAME="txtText2">
    <INPUT TYPE="button" NAME="cmdButton1">
   </FORM>
  </CENTER>
</HTML>
```

When the user clicks the cmdButton1 button (which, by the way, is not the usual Submit that you're probably used to using on an HTML form), the cmdButton1_onClick event is fired. In the simple script attached to this event, the Value property of the text box txtText1 is assigned to the Value property of text box txtText2, thus displaying the contents of txtText1 in txtText2. Just for good measure, the message Hello World then pops up on the screen in a small alert box, and the message "VBScript in Action" is displayed in the status bar along the bottom of the browser.

The other method of attaching code to a control's event is somewhat trickier to write, read, and maintain. Basically, you write the complete event handler within the control's HTML definition. Listing 30.2 is the same example as the one used in Listing 30.1, except the event handler is written inline.

**Listing 30.2. A script written inline with the control's definition.**

```
<HTML>
<HEAD>
</HEAD>
<BODY BGCOLOR="white">
<CENTER>
    <FORM NAME="frmForm1">
        <INPUT TYPE=text NAME="txtText1">
        <INPUT TYPE=text NAME="txtText2">
        <INPUT LANGUAGE="VBScript" TYPE=button ONCLICK="frmForm1.txtText2.value
➥=frmForm1.txtText1.value
Alert &quot;Hello World&quot;
 Status &quot;VBScript in Action&quot;"
        NAME="cmdButton1">
    </FORM>
</CENTER>
</HTML>
</BODY>
```

As you can see, the cmdButton1's HTML <INPUT> definition is now creaking under the weight of compact, yet illegible coding. The LANGUAGE= tag is there, as is the ONCLICK event, only this time as an ONCLICK="". The complete event handler must be written within quotation marks, which means that any quotation marks used within the event handler must be implicit; in other words, you have to use the &quot; HTML code.

More than one inline event handler can be placed in a control's HTML definition to handle different events.

Later in the chapter, you'll see the ActiveX Control Pad in use. This tool enables you to add ActiveX controls to an HTML document with ease and to attach scripts to the control's events. You can also use the ActiveX control pad's Script Wizard to add scripts to HTML form controls, and by default it will generate the inline type of event handler seen in Listing 30.2.

# Using VBScript with the HTML Object Model

VBScript is an event-driven language. Unlike scripts that run automatically as the page is downloading into the browser, VBScript programs are launched by an event—for example, when a user clicks a button or changes the value of a text box. Which events you can use to start a script executing depends on which events have been built into the objects that make up the environment in which you are working—in this case, the browser.

> **NOTE**
>
> Until Netscape launches a browser that supports both ActiveX and Active scripting (VBScript and JScript), when I mention the browser for VBScript, I mean Microsoft Internet Explorer 3.x (MSIE).

It follows, therefore, that to use VBScript successfully, you must understand the objects that make up the browser—the HTML object model.

A browser application that supports Active scripting must adhere to the HTML object model specification, a standard that allows for the consistent operation of client-side scripting languages such as VBScript.

The HTML object model defines several main objects and the properties, events, and methods associated with those objects. Because these objects expose their properties, events, and methods via a programmable interface, it is possible for scripting languages such as VBScript to interact with the object model by reading and setting an object's properties, responding to an object's events, and calling an object's methods.

The HTML object model is arranged in a hierarchy of objects, with the main browser window at the top and the form elements (such as text boxes) at the bottom. When you reference an HTML object in your script, you must follow the hierarchy; otherwise, you will generate an error.

**TIP**

The most common error that comes up when you are trying to reference an HTML object's property or event is `Property or Method Not Supported by this Object`. This means that you haven't followed the logical path of the hierarchy and thus have called a property or method that is not recognized by the stated object. You will usually find the solution by starting at the top of the hierarchy and working your way down toward the object you're trying to reference. You will come across an object that either doesn't appear in your reference or isn't being referenced properly.

## The Object Hierarchy

To create a reference in your script to a particular HTML object, you must build the reference from the top of the hierarchy downward, using dot notation to separate the objects. Here is a list of the objects:

| Object | Description |
| --- | --- |
| Window | The `Window` object is at the top of the tree in the object hierarchy; all other objects are child objects of the `Window` object. In most instances you don't have to specifically use the `Window.` reference in your script because it is implicit in all HTML object script references. Another way to use the `Window` object in your script is through the `Top.` reference. |
| Frame | The `Frame` object is actually an array of `Frame` objects. One way to reference them is by their ordinal numbers in the window, in which case the first frame is referenced as `Frames(0)`, the second frame is referenced as `Frames(1)`, and so on. The other way to reference a `Frame` object is by its name, assuming that you have used the `Name=` parameter when defining the frame in your `Frameset` document. |
| Document | The `Document` is a child object of either a `Frame` or a `Window`. Each `Frame` or `Window` object can contain only one `Document` object. As you might have guessed, the `Document` object represents the actual HTML document itself. You can use the `Document.Write` method to create dynamic HTML pages writing text to the document as it downloads to the browser, even creating completely new HTML documents at the browser from VBScript. After the document has been downloaded into the browser and displayed to the user, its content is fixed. |

**30**

INTEGRATING
ACTIVEX AND
VBSCRIPT

**NOTE**

Forthcoming developments from Microsoft will allow you to change the HTML page using VBScript even after it has been downloaded into the browser, giving almost unlimited flexibility and dynamism to HTML.

Form
: Like the `Frame` object, the `Form` object is an array of `Form` objects. A `Form` object can be referenced by its ordinal number in the array, starting with 0 or by its name. You can use the `Form` object to programmatically set the `Method` and `Action` parameters of the form and to submit the form data to the server. If the form and script reside on the same HTML page, you can reference a `Form` object without using a `Window.Document.` prefix; however, if the script and form are on separate documents (for instance, in two separate frames), you must use `Document.` as a prefix to the form reference. See "Scripting with the HTML Object Model" and "Working with Frames," later in this chapter, for more information.

**NOTE**

For the sake of clarity and understanding of the HTML object model, the little-used `Location`, `Navigator`, and `History` objects have been left out of this discussion.

Element
: The `Element` object is an array of form elements that includes `Text`, `Hidden`, `Password`, `Radio`, `Checkbox`, `Button`, `Submit`, and `Reset`. There is also one other main form element, `Select`, which creates a drop-down or selectable list of options. Although this is not defined using the `<INPUT>` tag as the other HTML form controls are, for all intents and purposes, the `Select` control can be treated like all the other form controls. Again, `Element` objects can be referenced by their names or by their ordinal numbers in the `Elements` array. You must note, though, that all the elements in a single form are placed in the same array; therefore, if you want to reference them by number, you need to code some method of distinguishing which type of element you are currently referencing.

## Scripting with the HTML Object Model

To illustrate how you can use the HTML object model in your scripts, here are a few examples of each object. All the following examples assume that the object and the script are within the same window or frame; a separate section, "Working with Frames," has been devoted to the particularly tricky subject of creating scripts that have the object and the script located in different frames.

## Referencing the Window Object

To display a quick message box to the user, you can call the Window object's Alert method:

```
<SCRIPT LANGAUGE="vbscript">
   Sub cmdMyButton_OnClick
       Alert "You clicked me?"
   End Sub
</SCRIPT>
```

Note that the Window object is implicit and does not need to be referenced. This means that the code

```
Alert "You clicked me?"
```

is the same as

```
Window.Alert "You clicked me?"
```

## Referencing the Document Object

The most common use of the Document object is to create dynamic content via its Write method. To use this, simply add a script that will execute automatically on download within your HTML, and the resulting HTML text will appear in the completed document in the browser. Here's a quick example:

```
...
<BODY BGCOLOR="white">
<CENTER>
<H2>Welcome to my Dynamic Website</H2>
</CENTER>
<P>
Today is;
<SCRIPT LANGUAGE="vbscript">
    Document.Write WeekdayName(Now()) & "" & Now()
</SCRIPT>
<P>
...
```

Again, because the use of the Window object is implicit, you can simply start your reference to the Write method with the Document object.

## Referencing the Form Object

The Form object is a child of the Document object, and you should therefore reference the Document object prior to referencing the Form object. There are many occasions when you will need to reference the Form object, most of which involve reading the value of text boxes and other elements of a form. However, you can both read and set two properties of the Form object itself. The Action property is the URL of the server-side script or CGI program that will receive the form's data; the Method property determines whether the form data should be sent to the server in a GET or POST HTML transaction.

The following example shows how you can dynamically change the Action property of a form:

```
<SCRIPT LANGUAGE="vbscript">
Sub cmdSubmit_OnClick
    If x = True then
        Document.frmForm1.Action = "http://www.justanycom.com/anasp.asp"
    End If
End Sub
</SCRIPT>
...
<FORM NAME="frmForm1" METHOD="POST">
...
</FORM>
```

Now here's the same code, but this time the reference to the form uses its ordinal position rather than its name:

```
<SCRIPT LANGUAGE="vbscript">
Sub cmdSubmit_OnClick
    If x = True then
        Document.Forms(0).Action = "http://www.justanycom.com/anasp.asp"
    End If
End Sub
</SCRIPT>
...
<FORM METHOD="POST">
...
</FORM>
```

You can also use the Form object to programmatically submit the form data, perhaps based on the outcome of a data validation routine, as the following example shows:

```
<SCRIPT LANGUAGE="vbscript">
    Sub cmdSubmit_OnClick
        If isDataValid = True Then
            Document.frmForm1.Submit
        Else
            Alert "Data not submitted"
        End If
    End Sub

    Function isDataValid()
        If IsDate(Document.frmForm1.InvDate.Value) Then
            isDataValid = True
        Else
            Alert "Value must be a date"
            isDataValid = False
        End If
    End Function
</SCRIPT>
<FORM NAME="frmForm1" ACTION="http://www.www.net/www.asp" METHOD="POST">
  <INPUT TYPE="text" NAME="InvDate">
  <INPUT TYPE="button" NAME="cmdSubmit" VALUE="SUBMIT">
</FORM>
```

In the preceding example, an HTML button has been used rather than the normal HTML Submit. The code attached to the button's OnClick event calls a function, which checks that the data input in the InvDate text box is a valid date; if it is, the function returns True and the form data is submitted using the Form object's Submit method.

## Referencing the Elements Object

Elements objects are the intrinsic HTML controls that you place on an HTML form to solicit data from the user of the page. The object itself is an array and is a child of the Form object. Therefore, to reference an individual control, you use this syntax:

`Document.form.control`

With so many cool ActiveX form controls to choose from, you might wonder why you should even bother with HTML controls. There are a couple of good reasons. First, you might already have spent time developing your HTML forms, and you might want to leverage this investment by simply adding scripts to your existing forms. Second, not everyone will have loaded the full install of MSIE; those who didn't would not have the ActiveX Forms 2.0 controls, and therefore you would have to make them available for download from your Web site—which will take time and bandwidth. At least you can be sure that everyone can use intrinsic HTML controls. Here's a list of the intrinsic HTML controls (Elements controls). The following intrinsic HTML controls are all defined using the <INPUT> tag:

- Button: This Windows-style command button is similar to the popular Submit button. You can add scripts to the Button's Click event.
- Checkbox: Use this to allow the user to make selections when more than one item can be selected.
- Hidden: No control is displayed on the page. Use this to "hold" data to be submitted to the server within a form.
- Password: This is similar to the text control, except characters typed into the control appear as asterisks.
- Radio: This is an option button, which is used when only one of a range of choices is allowed.
- Reset: This clears all form controls.
- Submit: This button control has one purpose—to submit the form data to the server.
- Text: This is a good old-fashioned text box control for entering data. It's important to remember that all data passed from a textbox to a script is in the form of a string, even if the data is numeric.

The Select control, which creates a selectable list, is not defined with the <INPUT> tag, but it can be treated like the rest of the intrinsic controls when creating scripts.

Let's first look at an event that all the text-based HTML controls support: the OnChange event. It's fired when the user moves away from a control after changing its value from the last time the OnChange event was fired for the particular control. You can use this event to validate the data as the user is completing the form, like this:

```
<SCRIPT LANGUAGE="vbscript">
   Sub txtQuantity_OnChange
      If Not IsNumeric(Document.frmForm1.txtQuantity.Value) Then
         Alert "Quantity must be numeric"
      End If
   End Sub
</SCRIPT>
```

The preceding code also demonstrates how to read the value of a text-based control using its
`Value` property. You can also set the `Value` property, automatically filling in parts of a form:

```
<SCRIPT LANGUAGE="vbscript">
   Sub Window_OnLoad
      Document.frmForm1.txtTodaysDate.Value = Now()
   End Sub
</SCRIPT>
```

In the preceding example, the code executes after the page has completed downloading into
the browser by being attached to the `Window`'s `OnLoad` event. The code assigns the current date
and time to the text box's `Value` property using the VBScript `Now()` function.

---

## USING OBJECT VARIABLES

You might have noticed by now that when you reference individual controls on an HTML
form, the code line can become quite long and unwieldy; furthermore, every dot that
separates the individual objects in the hierarchy represents a function call deep inside the
scripting engine. This becomes even more of a problem when you start adding frames into
the equation. For example, this line of code references a value in a text box in the frame
adjacent to the one containing the script:

```
dateValue = Top.frRightFrame.Document.frmForm1.txtDateVal.Value
```

See what I mean? If you had to write similar code for many fields on a form, not only would
it take a lot of coding time and space, but it is also difficult to read. A solution is to use
object variables. An object variable is simply a pointer to a particular object that you can
use in place of the object. You create object variables using the VBScript SET command,
like this:

```
Dim myForm
Set myForm = Top.frRightFrame.Document.frmForm1
```

Now, every time you use the variable, it is the same as using the complete hierarchical path
to the object:

```
dateValue = myForm.txtDateVal.Value
```

---

# Working with Frames

HTML frames are a popular method of creating easy-to-use Web applications. They can also
be a boon for the script writer, enabling you to place all your scripts within one of the frame
documents. However, care must be taken when you reference HTML objects in other frames.

The key to referencing the controls in one frame from a script in another frame is to always remember to start your reference from the topmost object in the HTML object hierarchy and work your way down the hierarchy until you arrive at the particular control.

For example, if you have a FRAMESET document like

```
<FRAMESET COLS=50%,50%>
  <FRAME NAME="frLeftFrame" SRC="scripts.htm">
  <FRAME NAME="frRightFrame" SRC="adoc.htm">
</FRAMESET>
```

the document adoc.htm contains a form like this:

```
<FORM NAME="frmAnyForm" METHOD=POST ACTION="something.asp">
Quantity <INPUT TYPE="text" NAME="txtQuantity">
<BR>
EMail Address <INPUT TYPE="text" NAME="txtEMail">
</FORM>
```

For a script within the left frame (scripts.htm) to reference the controls on the frmAnyForm, you must begin your reference with the Window object, then reference the right-hand frame, followed by the Document, Form, and finally the control itself:

```
Window.frRightFrame.Document.frmAnyForm.txtQuantity.Value
```

Just as frames can be nested (a frameset within a frameset), so too can Frame objects. Suppose that you had a further frameset within the right frame—the two frames called frTopFrame and frBottomFrame. If the form resided in the bottom right frame, you would reference the control like this:

```
Window.frRightFrame.frBottomFrame.Document.frmAnyForm.txtQuantity.Value
```

A sound understanding of the HTML object model will enable you to update your HTML Web pages with Active scripting; you will be able to control the browser, the document, the forms, and the intrinsic controls. With very little effort, you'll be able to turn once flat, lifeless HTML pages into dynamic applications that take advantage of the speed that client-side scripting can bring. However, to really bring your pages up-to-date with the very latest Active content, you need to go one step further and add ActiveX controls.

# Adding ActiveX Controls to HTML Documents

The scripting techniques you've seen so far have revolved around the built-in functionality of the Web browser. To improve on this functionality, you must add new and exciting controls to your Web pages. Microsoft has leveraged years of development to bring you ActiveX controls that can add the sort of functionality normally associated only with a Windows desktop program.

# What Is an ActiveX Control?

An ActiveX control is a program, or an executable file that exposes certain methods, properties, and events through a programmable interface. ActiveX controls have been around for quite a while, but have only recently been referred to as ActiveX controls. They adhere to the component object model (COM) standard; this standard has been amended recently to allow slimmer controls to be created for ease of download across the Internet.

An ActiveX control is built in such a way that other programs that are also built to the COM interface standard can interface with it. In this way, VBScript can read and set its properties, handle its events, and call its methods.

Here are some of the many different types of ActiveX controls:

- User-interface controls are the text boxes and other forms controls and buttons that you probably are used to using in Windows desktop applications. Other user-interface controls include menu bars, image controls, and hotspot controls.

- Server-side components are ActiveX controls that have no graphical user interface (GUI). These controls are called into action by a server-side script to perform a particular function (such as interfacing a database). They execute and return a result to the calling script. These components used to be known as remote automation servers or OLE servers.

- Client-side components are a special type of controls that, like the server-side components, have no visible interface for the user; they are simply add-on programs that you as a script writer can use to enhance the range of functionality in your script. An example of this type of ActiveX control is the Timer, which fires an event at specified periods.

It's impossible to know how many ActiveX controls are available from third-party software vendors, but it runs into many thousands, and more are coming to market every day. It is also possible for you to create your own controls using the Control Creation Edition (CCE) of Visual Basic 5.

# Built-In ActiveX Controls

The full install of MSIE installs a range of commonly used ActiveX forms controls. The built-in ActiveX controls include these:

- The *checkbox* control allows the user to select a number of options.

- The *combobox* is a basically a single control, which is a combination of a text box and a drop-down list.

- The *commandbutton*—just click it!

- The *hotspot* control enables you to create programmable graphical areas.

- The *image* control lets you create a graphical area on the HTML page that is much more flexible than the HTML <IMG> tag.

■ The *label* control is a text area that cannot be amended by the user; it is entirely under the programmer's control.

■ The *listbox* control presents a list of values.

■ The *optionbutton* control enables the user to select one of a number of options.

■ Both vertical and horizontal *scrollbars* are available from a single control.

■ The *spinbutton* control is used to increment and decrement a specific user-definable value.

■ The *tabstrip* control enables you to include the now familiar notebook metaphor in a Web page.

■ The *textbox* control is the ubiquitous data entry element.

■ The *toggle button* control is a dual on and off button that the user can click to switch on and click again to switch off.

## Third-Party ActiveX Controls

If you have a particular requirement that can't been fulfilled using the Forms 2.0 controls, you have to either create your own control using VB5 CCE or Visual C++, or look around the marketplace for an off-the-shelf solution. The best place to commence your search is the Microsoft ActiveX Gallery within the Microsoft Site Builder Network, from where you can download both fully functional and trial versions of some of the very best ActiveX controls.

## Using the ActiveX Control Pad

To include an ActiveX control on a Web page, you must refer to it using the control's unique 128-bit ID. I don't know about you, but I'm not too hot at remembering 128-bit IDs like 978C9E23-D4B0-11CE-BF2D-00AA003F40D0. Luckily, Microsoft's developers can't remember these IDs either, and they quickly realized that a tool was needed for us all to be able to add ActiveX controls to a Web page. Thus the ActiveX Control Pad, shown in Figure 30.1, was born.

The ActiveX Control Pad can be downloaded for free from Microsoft's Web site, and it is also included on the CD-ROM that accompanies this book.

As shown in Figure 30.1, an HTML template is opened automatically when you launch the program. You can close this if you wish and open your own HTML page using the File|Open command.

To illustrate how easily you can create dynamic Web pages using the ActiveX Control Pad, the following example takes you through adding a couple of ActiveX controls to a new HTML page, then shows you how to attach some VBScript using the Script Wizard that is part of the ActiveX Control Pad. You'll be creating a page that contains a Label control and a ComboBox control. The ComboBox will contain a list of font sizes from 8–24; when the user of the page makes a selection from the ComboBox, the font size of the label's caption changes to that selected by the user.

**FIGURE 30.1.**

*The ActiveX Control Pad.*

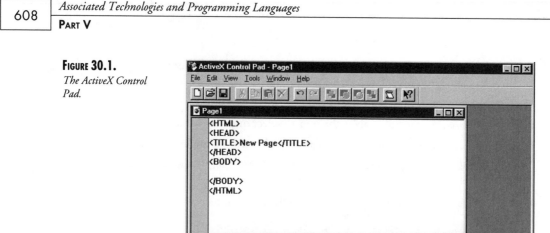

First, launch the ActiveX Control Pad. Before you start with any active content, you need to make these changes to the HTML template:

1. Change the title to something like "Test ActiveX Page."

2. Add a `BGCOLOR="white"` parameter to the `<BODY>` tag.

3. Add a `<CENTER>` tag under the `<BODY>` tag.

Now you're ready to start adding the ActiveX controls. The Label control is the first to be added, as follows:

1. Place your cursor under the `<CENTER>` tag.

2. Select Insert ActiveX Control from the Edit menu.

3. From the list of available controls, select the Microsoft Forms 2.0 Label and click OK.

A Design window and Properties window for this Label control will now be displayed. You can use the Design window to drag the size of the label and the Properties window to set the properties you need for this control.

## Setting a Control's Properties

Change these properties for this control:

1. `BackColor`: This is the background color of the label itself. Click on the property name; the property value will be repeated in a drop-down list at the top of the Properties window. To the right of the down arrow button is a button with three dots (an ellipsis) on it. Click this button to display the Color dialog. Select the White color block and click OK. Click the Apply button.

A special selection dialog is displayed whenever you click a button with an ellipsis.

2. `Caption`: This is the text that is displayed on the label. Select the `Caption` property, type the required caption, `"My Test ActiveX Control"`, in the property setting box at the top of the Property window, and click Apply.

3. `ForeColor`: This is the color of the caption on the label, and you set it just like you did `Backcolor`: Make it a shade of blue.

4. `Height`: This property determines how tall the label will be; set it to `100`.

5. `TextAlign`: You can choose to align the caption to the Left, Center, or Right of the label. For this example, set it to Center by selecting the `TextAlign` property, then selecting Center from the list of options.

6. `Width`: This property determines the how wide the label is; set it to `300` pixels.

Your label is now customized for this example. To add the code to the HTML page that will define this label, close the Label Design window by clicking the X button in the top right corner. The `<OBJECT>` tag and the required parameters are now generated automatically by the Control Pad and pasted into the page at the point where your cursor was placed. Your page should now resemble Figure 30.2.

**FIGURE 30.2.**

*The HTML definition for the ActiveX label.*

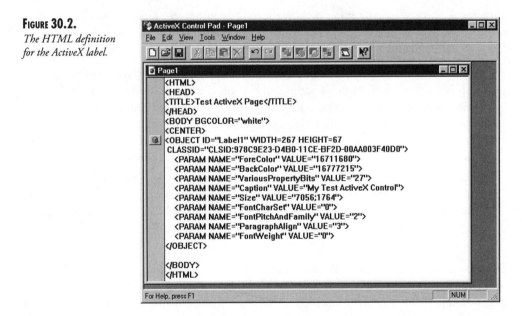

```
<HTML>
<HEAD>
<TITLE>Test ActiveX Page</TITLE>
</HEAD>
<BODY BGCOLOR="white">
<CENTER>
<OBJECT ID="Label1" WIDTH=267 HEIGHT=67
  CLASSID="CLSID:978C9E23-D4B0-11CE-BF2D-00AA003F40D0">
    <PARAM NAME="ForeColor" VALUE="16711680">
    <PARAM NAME="BackColor" VALUE="16777215">
    <PARAM NAME="VariousPropertyBits" VALUE="27">
    <PARAM NAME="Caption" VALUE="My Test ActiveX Control">
    <PARAM NAME="Size" VALUE="7056;1764">
    <PARAM NAME="FontCharSet" VALUE="0">
    <PARAM NAME="FontPitchAndFamily" VALUE="2">
    <PARAM NAME="ParagraphAlign" VALUE="3">
    <PARAM NAME="FontWeight" VALUE="0">
</OBJECT>

</BODY>
</HTML>
```

You now need to add your second control, the ComboBox control, by following these steps:

1. Place a `<P>` tag after the `</OBJECT>` tag to create a little room on the page between the controls. Now press the Enter key to move the cursor to the next line.

2. Select Insert ActiveX Control from the Edit menu.

**30**

**INTEGRATING ACTIVEX AND VBSCRIPT**

3. From the list of available controls, select Microsoft Forms 2.0 ComboBox and click OK.

4. A Design window and Properties window for this ComboBox are now shown. You don't need to change any of the properties for this control, so simply close the control design window to generate the HTML definition code for the ComboBox.

With the controls added, you now need to attach some scripting to the page and the ActiveX controls to achieve the desired results.

## Attaching Scripts to ActiveX Controls: The Script Wizard

The ActiveX Control Pad includes a Script Wizard that simplifies the writing of most scripts. However, you must bear in mind that because of the nature of wizards, not every possible scenario can be catered for, and sometimes you might need to manually attach code directly onto the HTML page. This is particularly true of scripts that you need to execute on download.

For this example you need to first populate the ComboBox with even values from 8 to 24. You need to add code to the ComboBox's Click event so that when the user selects a font size from the list with the mouse, the font size is translated to the Label control's caption.

Launch the Script Wizard by either clicking the toolbar button that looks like an ancient scroll or selecting Script Wizard from the Tools menu. You need to note a couple of things about the Script Wizards defaults:

- Ensure that the Script Wizard's default is VBScript. The Script Wizard has the capability to generate both VBScript and JScript. Change the default language by selecting Script... from the Options menu, which you access from the Tools menu; then select the desired default scripting language. Some very strange folk might choose to default their Script Wizard to JScript (though I can't think why!); however, because we're talking VBScript here, it might benefit you to default yours to VBScript.

- Second, when the Script Wizard launches, use the Code View option. The List View option is quite honestly less than useless. To see what I mean, after you've written the scripts shown in Listing 30.3, try to switch to List view and you'll be told that because a custom script has been written, the List view cannot work. But aren't all scripts custom?

Okay, back to the job in hand… You need the ComboBox to be populated only once. You can only reference the control after it has been created, which means that you have to wait for the page to complete downloading. The ideal event to use in this situation is the Window's OnLoad event. This is fired after the page has been displayed and the script has been parsed through the scripting engine. Follow these steps to add your code to the OnLoad event:

1. In the events pane of the Script Wizard, click the plus sign (+) to the left of the Window object. This displays the two Window object events, Onload and OnUnLoad.

2. Select the OnLoad event.

3. Type the following code in the code window:

```
Dim i
For i = 8 to 24 step 2
        ComboBox1.AddItem CStr(i)
Next
```

The first line of this code declares a local variable, i. The next line starts a loop that will execute eight times. 8 to 24 Step 2 specifies that on the first iteration, the counter i will have a value of 8, and it will increase by 2 on each subsequent iteration until it has a value of 24, after which time the loop will terminate. On each iteration, the counter i will be converted to a string value using the CStr() function, and then added to the ComboBox list with the AddItem method.

Your Script Wizard window should now resemble Figure 30.3.

**FIGURE 30.3.**

*The Window* OnLoad *event handler.*

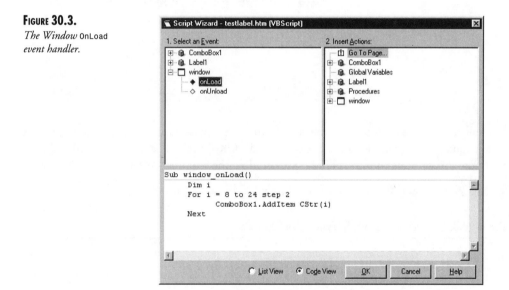

The next stage is to create an event handler for the ComboBox control's Click event.

1. In the events pane of the Script Wizard, click the plus sign to the left of the ComboBox1 object. This displays all the ComboBox events.

2. Select the Click event.

3. Type the following code in the code window:

```
Label1.Font.Size = CInt(ComboBox1.List(ComboBox1.ListIndex))
```

ComboBox1.ListIndex returns the index number of the item selected by the user. This is then used to return the text from the list that relates to this index. Because the value returned will be a string value and font sizes are numbers, you have to convert the value to an integer using the CInt function. This number is then assigned to the Size property of the label's Font object.

Your Script Wizard window should look like the one in Figure 30.4.

**FIGURE 30.4.**

*The ComboBox* Click *event handler.*

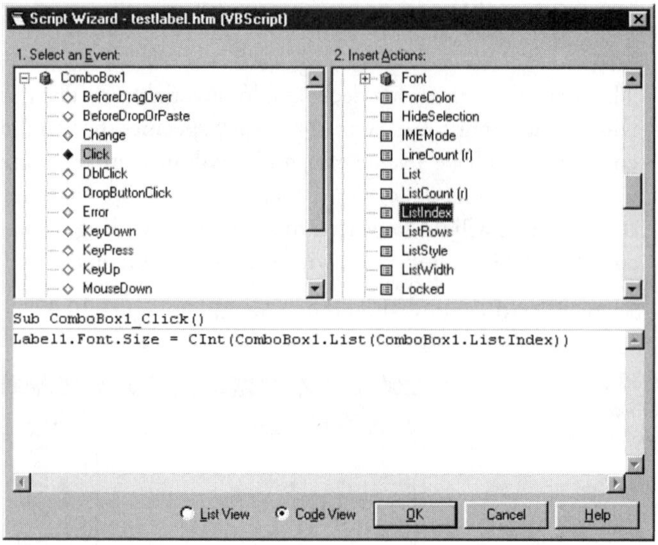

Now all you need to do is transfer the code from the Script Wizard to the HTML page. This is done quite easily by clicking the Script Wizard's OK button. The Script Wizard will then transpose the scripting into the HTML page, adding the required <SCRIPT> tags and so on.

Listing 30.3 contains the complete source code for this example.

**Listing 30.3. An example of using dynamic ActiveX controls.**

```
<HTML>
<HEAD>
    <SCRIPT LANGUAGE="VBScript">
<!--
Sub window_onLoad()
    Dim i
    For i = 8 to 24 step 2
        ComboBox1.AddItem CStr(i)
    Next
end sub
-->
    </SCRIPT>
<TITLE>Test ActiveX Page</TITLE>
</HEAD>
<BODY BGCOLOR="white">
<CENTER>
    <OBJECT ID="Label1" WIDTH=400 HEIGHT=60
 CLASSID="CLSID:978C9E23-D4B0-11CE-BF2D-00AA003F40D0">
    <PARAM NAME="ForeColor" VALUE="16711680">
    <PARAM NAME="BackColor" VALUE="16777215">
    <PARAM NAME="VariousPropertyBits" VALUE="27">
```

```
        <PARAM NAME="Caption" VALUE="My Test ActiveX Control">
        <PARAM NAME="Size" VALUE="10583;1588">
        <PARAM NAME="FontCharSet" VALUE="0">
        <PARAM NAME="FontPitchAndFamily" VALUE="2">
        <PARAM NAME="ParagraphAlign" VALUE="3">
        <PARAM NAME="FontWeight" VALUE="0">
</OBJECT>
<P>
  <OBJECT ID="ComboBox1" WIDTH=96 HEIGHT=24
    CLASSID="CLSID:8BD21D30-EC42-11CE-9E0D-00AA006002F3">
        <PARAM NAME="VariousPropertyBits" VALUE="746604571">
        <PARAM NAME="DisplayStyle" VALUE="3">
        <PARAM NAME="Size" VALUE="2540;635">
        <PARAM NAME="MatchEntry" VALUE="1">
        <PARAM NAME="ShowDropButtonWhen" VALUE="2">
        <PARAM NAME="FontCharSet" VALUE="0">
        <PARAM NAME="FontPitchAndFamily" VALUE="2">
        <PARAM NAME="FontWeight" VALUE="0">
  </OBJECT>

  <SCRIPT LANGUAGE="VBScript">
<!--
Sub ComboBox1_Click()
Label1.Font.Size = CInt(ComboBox1.List(ComboBox1.ListIndex))
end sub
-->
  </SCRIPT>
 </BODY>
</HTML>
```

All that needs to be done now is to save the file and run it through the browser—as long as the browser is MSIE. When you select a font size from the list, the label's caption immediately resizes itself to the new font. Figure 30.5 shows how the page should look in the browser.

**FIGURE 30.5.**

testlabel.htm.

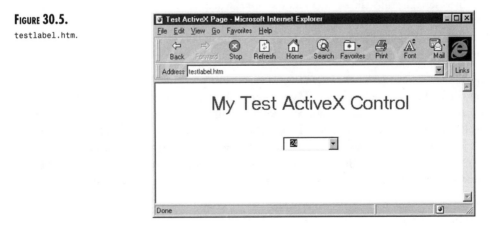

## Making Controls Available to Your Users

Although this is not relevant for the preceding example, there are many occasions when you will need to make a control you are using available to the users of your Web page.

Suppose, for example, you decided to use the new SuperWiz WebMenu control throughout your Web site, you design your pages using the control, and you try the pages on your local machine and are ecstatic with the results. You upload the Web pages to your server, ready to win award after award for the coolest Active Content Web site. There's just one slight problem: If your users don't have the SuperWiz WebMenu on their machines, too, all they will see is…nothing!

If you go back to the properties page for one of the controls you added in the example from the preceding sections (you can click the cube icon at the side of the Object definition to edit a control), you will see a property called CodeBase. This tells the client browser where it can find the control in question.

In fact, what actually happens is that the browser first checks in a cache directory where it keeps downloaded controls. If it finds the control locally, it ignores the CodeBase tag—unless there is a difference in the version information. CodeBase can be either a path relative to the HTML file or it can be an absolute path.

## ActiveX and Active Scripting Security Issues

Before moving on to look at a way you can create a true Windows type form in an HTML document, let's stop for a moment and consider some security aspects.

First, consider the case of all Active Scripting; I use the generic here because this material applies equally to VBScript and JScript. Client-side scripts are safe. They cannot operate outside of the browser. The only time a client-side script can access a hard drive is via the document's Cookie property, and even then it is the browser, not the script, that is accessing the hard drive. VBScript on the client side is prevented from creating any object that would allow it access to anything outside of the browser.

An ActiveX control, on the other hand, is an executable program; as such, it has the potential to contain malicious code. However, Microsoft has put in place the code signing system, which warns the user when an ActiveX control is being downloaded from a new source. If you aren't sure of the source of the control, you should take precautions. One problem for the developer of Active Content pages, though, is that some individuals and organizations have taken their Web security to such a point that they automatically refuse any ActiveX control. When designing Active Content pages, therefore, you should bear this in mind and provide an alternative.

# The Microsoft HTML Layout Control

Not very long ago, I was asked to put together a Web site for a company; they wanted the site to mimic one of their in-house Windows applications. The application's user interface was a complex affair, providing many various and dynamic options—that is, options that generated further options.

At the time all I had to work with was the good old HTML form controls, which where just not up to the job, at least not without many trips back and forth to the server in the course of completing just one set of data input. I can still remember wishing that I could replicate the functionality of a Windows application on a Web page.

Those wishes have now been answered by the HTML Layout control, an ActiveX control that you create yourself in less time than it takes to say "graphical user interface."

## What Is the HTML Layout Control?

The Layout control is a blank form. Sounds exciting, huh? Let me put it another way. It's like a blank canvas ready and waiting for you to express your innermost creativity in form and application design through the medium of the Web page. Okay, so it's a blank form.

The Layout control is a true Window. It accepts and sends Windows messages like the desktop Windows applications written in C++ or VB. It allows you, therefore, to create applications that look, feel, and actually are true Windows programs.

After you drag and drop the form and other controls you need onto the canvas of the Layout control, you can place the controls with pixel accuracy—something that is nearly impossible on a normal HTML document. You then add your VBScript code to the Layout control, save it as one single ALX file, and insert the ALX file into the HTML page just like any other ActiveX control.

## Designing Forms with the HTML Layout Control

To give you just a taste of what you can do with the HTML Layout control, the following example will take you through the process of designing a simple input form, adding some validation code, and then adding the Layout control to an HTML page.

To start with, you need to launch the HTML Layout control designer. Launch the ActiveX Control Pad, then select New HTML Layout from the File menu. The Layout Control designer, shown in Figure 30.6, is launched, containing a blank form ready for you to start work.

**FIGURE 30.6.**

*The HTML Layout Control designer.*

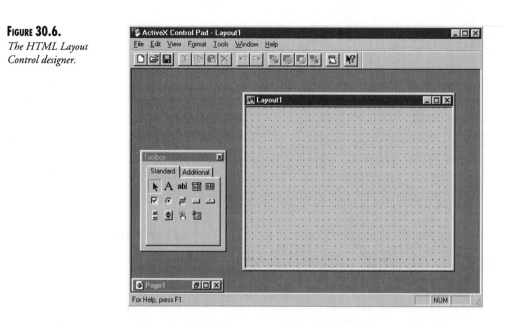

Adding controls to the Layout control is easy. Simply click on the control in the toolbox you wish to add, then click on the Layout background in roughly the area where you want the control, hold the mouse button down, and drag the control to the size you require. After a control has been placed on the Layout background, it can be resized and moved using the mouse. To add the controls for your sample application, follow these steps:

1. Select the TextBox control in the toolbox, click and hold the mouse button down on the Layout background, and drag the new text box into position. For this example, you're going to need two text boxes, one under the other, so add another text box under your first one.

2. Add two labels, one for each text box.

3. Add two list boxes; space them at the bottom of the form with a gap between.

4. Add three command buttons; place them between the two list boxes.

5. Add two additional command buttons at the bottom of the form.

6. Add two additional labels—one for each list box.

7. Save as `inputform.alx`. Your form should resemble Figure 30.7.

**FIGURE 30.7.**

inputform.alx.

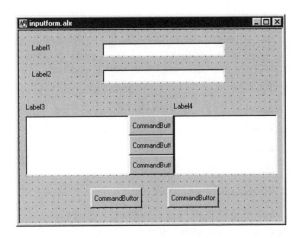

# Setting Properties of Controls in an HTML Layout

You now need to change certain properties of the controls you've just added. You need to change the caption properties of the labels and buttons to be somewhat more meaningful than simply the control's name. You can also change the color scheme to something more appealing than the standard gray and black. The HTML Layout control enables you to change the properties of several similar controls with one command, as you're about to see. Follow these steps:

1. Select all the labels and buttons by first selecting one label or button, then hold down the Ctrl key while you click on the other labels and command buttons. Notice that all the controls you've clicked on have sizing blocks on their edges, indicating they have been selected. While still holding the Ctrl key down, you can deselect a control by clicking it a second time. With all the labels and command buttons selected, right-click one of them and select Properties from the pop-up menu.

2. The properties shown in the Properties window are common to both the Label and TextBox controls. You can now change the Font property and have that change reflected in all the currently selected controls. Select Font from the properties list and click the ellipsis button to display the Font properties dialog. Change the font to 10 point, bold. Click OK and click Accept at the top of the Properties window.

3. You now need to set the captions for each of the labels and buttons. Start by selecting the top label (label1); right-click to display the properties window. Select the Caption property, change the caption to "Your Name". Click Accept to translate the property change to the control.

4. Similarly, change the caption properties of the other labels and controls as follows:

| Change This: | To This: |
|---|---|
| Control | Caption |
| Label2 | Your EMail |
| Label3 | Favorite Programs |
| Label4 | Your Choice |
| CommandButton1 | >> |
| CommandButton2 | << |
| CommandButton3 | All |
| CommandButton4 | Submit |
| CommandButton5 | Clear |

5. The final part of this beautification process is to change the color scheme. Select all the label controls, and change the BackColor property to White.

6. Right-click the layout background, select Properties, and change the BackColor property to White. Your form should now look like the one in Figure 30.8.

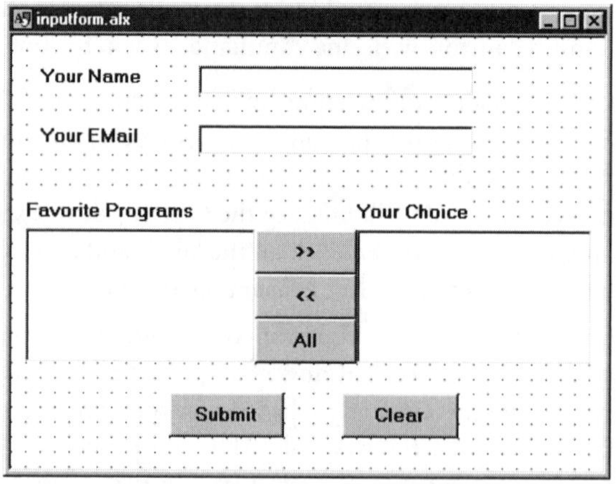

**FIGURE 30.8.**

*The completed user interface.*

## Attaching Scripts to the Layout Control

Of course, without some scripting behind the controls, there is very little that the form can do. This particular example is an input form in which users can enter their names and e-mail addresses, and select their favorites from a range of programs. You're going to make the following changes to bring the form life:

■ Populate the Favorite Programs list as the layout completes downloading into the browser.

■ Add the item selected by the user to the Your Choice list.

■ Add all Favorite Programs items to the Your Choice list.

■ Remove an item from the Your Choice list if necessary.

■ Validate the e-mail address.

■ Clear all controls.

All this functionality is going to be added to the form using the Script Wizard, so first, click the Scroll button on the toolbar to launch the Script Wizard. Follow these steps:

1. To code the populating of the Favorite Programs list, in the events pane, click the plus sign to the left of Layout1 and select the OnLoad event. Enter the following code in the script window:

```
Dim sPrograms
sPrograms = Array("Microsoft Visual Basic", "Borland Delphi", _
                "Pegasus Mail", "Internet Explorer", _
                "Netscape Navigator", "Visual Interdev")
ListBox1.List = sPrograms
```

This defines a variable that will hold the list in memory ready to assign to the list, and then the list of values is created using the Array() function. The List object is itself an array, so you can simply assign the array of values to the Listbox1.List.

2. Now for some very rudimentary data validation. Here you're going to check that the e-mail address entered contains an at symbol (@); this, of course, is the very minimum requirement for a valid e-mail address. Again in the events pane, click the plus sign to the left of the TextBox2, select its Exit event, and enter this code in the script window:

```
If InStr(TextBox2.Text, "@") = 0 Then
    Alert "This Email Address appears to be invalid"
End If
```

The preceding code uses the InStr() function, which returns the position of the specified character within a string, or returns 0 if it is not found.

3. After the user has chosen a particular item from the Favorite Programs list, he/she clicks the >> button to add the selected item to the Your Choice list. In the events pane, click the plus sign to the left of CommandButton1 and select its Click Event. Enter this code in the script window:

```
If ListBox1.ListIndex <> -1 Then
    For i = 0 To ListBox2.ListCount - 1
        If ListBox2.List(i) = ListBox1.List(ListBox1.ListIndex) Then
            Exit Sub
        End If
    Next
    ListBox2.AddItem ListBox1.List(ListBox1.ListIndex)
End If
```

The code should look like the code in the script window in Figure 30.9.

**30**

INTEGRATING
ACTIVEX AND
VBSCRIPT

**Figure 30.9.**

*The* CommandButton1
Click *event.*

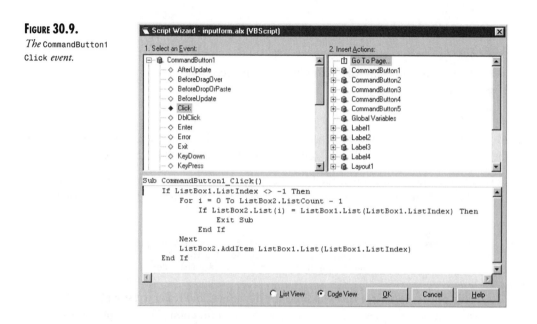

In this code, you are first checking that a selection has been made. If no selection has
been made by the user, the list box's ListIndex property will return −1. If this is the
case, your script need go no further. However, assuming that the user has selected an
item from the list, you must then check that the selection hasn't already been added to
ListBox2 by iterating through the items in the list. If a match is found, this item has
already been added and the Exit Sub terminates execution of the event handler. If the
selected item isn't found in ListBox2, you can safely add the item to the list.

4. You can add some extra speed functionality by allowing the user to double-click the
   Favorite Programs list to add an item to their choices list. Rather than rewriting the
   preceding code in the double-click event of the list box, you can simply call the
   button's Click event, which replicates the user clicking the button. To code this, click
   the plus sign to the left of the ListBox1 object in the events pane and select the
   DblClick event. Move to the actions pane and click the plus sign to the left of the
   Procedures item and double-click the CommandButton1_Click item. This will automatically place a line of code in the event handler:

```
call CommandButton1_Click()
```

Thus, whenever a user double-clicks an item on the list, it has exactly the same effect
as first selecting the item and then clicking the button.

5. You now need to give the user the ability to remove an item from the list of chosen
   programs. To do this, add the following code to the Click event of CommandButton2:

```
If ListBox2.ListIndex <> -1 Then
    ListBox2.removeItem ListBox2.ListIndex
End If
```

Again, you must first check that a selection has been made, then you can call the list box's `removeItem` method, passing it the index number of the item to be removed.

6. As with the favorites list, you can include a `DblClick` event for the choices list that will call the `CommandButton2 Click` event:

```
Sub ListBox2_DblClick(Cancel)
    call CommandButton2_Click()
end sub
```

7. To add all items from the favorites list to the choices list, you need to assign the `ListBox1.List` property to the `ListBox2.List` property; however, you should first clear out any items currently in `ListBox2`. Add the following code to `CommandButton3`'s `Click` event:

```
call ListBox2.Clear()
ListBox2.List = ListBox1.List
```

8. This example isn't actually going to do anything with the form data, so just add an alert box to the `Click` event of `CommandButton4`:

```
Alert "Submitting data"
```

9. The final code will reset all the controls by assigning zero length strings to the text boxes, clearing the Choices list box, setting the `ListIndex` of `ListBox1` to –1 (no items selected), and finally placing the cursor in `TextBox1` using the text box's `setFocus` method. So, you need to add the following code to the `Click` event of `CommandButton5`:

```
TextBox1.Text = ""
TextBox2.Text = ""
ListBox2.Clear
ListBox1.ListIndex = -1
TextBox1.SetFocus
```

When that's done, all that remains is to click the OK button on the Script Wizard to transpose all of the code you've entered into the ALX Layout control file. Save the Layout control, and you're now ready to add it to the HTML page. Before you do that, though, just make a few amendments to the standard HTML template provided in the Control Pad.

Give it a title of "Sample ALX Form," add a `BGColor ="white"` parameter to the `<BODY>` tag, then under the `<BODY>` tag add the following lines of HTML:

```
<CENTER>
<FONT FACE="arial">
<H2>Computer Users Survey</H2>
```

## Inserting the Layout Control into an HTML Page

Place the cursor on an empty line under the `<H2>` heading and select Insert HTML Layout from the Edit menu. This activates a File Open dialog, which should be defaulted to the current directory. Select the `inputform.alx` file and click OK. The ActiveX Control Pad will then insert the HTML code to define your Layout control, and your HTML page should now look like Figure 30.10.

**FIGURE 30.10.**

*The HTML object definition for the Layout control.*

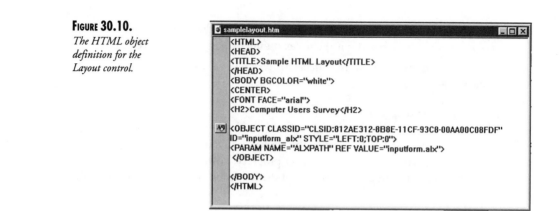

```
samplelayout.htm
<HTML>
<HEAD>
<TITLE>Sample HTML Layout</TITLE>
</HEAD>
<BODY BGCOLOR="white">
<CENTER>
<FONT FACE="arial">
<H2>Computer Users Survey</H2>

<OBJECT CLASSID="CLSID:812AE312-8B8E-11CF-93C8-00AA00C08FDF"
ID="inputform_alx" STYLE="LEFT:0;TOP:0">
<PARAM NAME="ALXPATH" REF VALUE="inputform.alx">
</OBJECT>

</BODY>
</HTML>
```

Save the HTML File as `samplelayout.htm`, and you're ready to run it though the browser. The complete listing for both the `inputform.alx` Layout control file and `samplelayout.htm` are shown in Listings 30.4 and 30.5, respectively. Figure 30.11 shows the Layout control within the HTML page running in the MSIE browser.

**FIGURE 30.11.**

samplelayout.htm *running in the browser.*

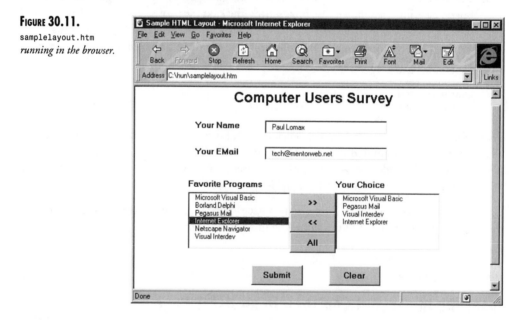

## Listing 30.4. inputform.alx.

```
<SCRIPT LANGUAGE="VBScript">
<!--
Sub Layout1_OnLoad()
  Dim sPrograms
  sPrograms = Array("Microsoft Visual Basic", "Borland Delphi", _
                "Pegasus Mail", "Internet Explorer", _
```

```
                              "Netscape Navigator", "Visual Interdev")
    ListBox1.List = sPrograms
end sub
-->
</SCRIPT>
<SCRIPT LANGUAGE="VBScript">
<!--
Sub TextBox2_Exit(Cancel)
    If InStr(TextBox2.Text, "@") = 0 Then
        Alert "This Email Address appears to be invalid"
    End If
end sub
-->
</SCRIPT>
<SCRIPT LANGUAGE="VBScript">
<!--
Sub CommandButton1_Click()
    If ListBox1.ListIndex <> -1 Then
        For i = 0 To ListBox2.ListCount - 1
            If ListBox2.List(i) = ListBox1.List(ListBox1.ListIndex) Then
                Exit Sub
            End If
        Next
        ListBox2.AddItem ListBox1.List(ListBox1.ListIndex)
    End If

end sub
-->
</SCRIPT>
<SCRIPT LANGUAGE="VBScript">
<!--
Sub ListBox1_DblClick(Cancel)
    call CommandButton1_Click()
end sub
-->
</SCRIPT>
<SCRIPT LANGUAGE="VBScript">
<!--
Sub CommandButton2_Click()
    If ListBox2.ListIndex <> -1 Then
        ListBox2.removeItem ListBox2.ListIndex
    End If
end sub
-->
</SCRIPT>
<SCRIPT LANGUAGE="VBScript">
<!--
Sub CommandButton3_Click()
      call ListBox2.Clear()
      ListBox2.List = ListBox1.List
end sub
-->
</SCRIPT>
<SCRIPT LANGUAGE="VBScript">
<!--
Sub ListBox2_DblClick(Cancel)
    call CommandButton2_Click()
```

**30**

INTEGRATING
ACTIVEX AND
VBSCRIPT

*continues*

**Listing 30.4. continued**

```
end sub
-->
</SCRIPT>
<SCRIPT LANGUAGE="VBScript">
<!--
Sub CommandButton4_Click()
    Alert "Submitting Data"
end sub
-->
</SCRIPT>
<SCRIPT LANGUAGE="VBScript">
<!--
Sub CommandButton5_Click()
    TextBox1.Text = ""
    TextBox2.Text = ""
    ListBox2.Clear
    ListBox1.ListIndex = -1
    TextBox1.SetFocus
end sub
-->
</SCRIPT>
<DIV BACKGROUND="#ffffff" ID="Layout1" STYLE="LAYOUT:FIXED;WIDTH:338pt;
HEIGHT:241pt;">
    <OBJECT ID="ListBox1"
      CLASSID="CLSID:8BD21D20-EC42-11CE-9E0D-00AA006002F3"
STYLE="TOP:107pt;LEFT:8pt;WIDTH:132pt;HEIGHT:74pt;TABINDEX:0;ZINDEX:0;">
        <PARAM NAME="ScrollBars" VALUE="3">
        <PARAM NAME="DisplayStyle" VALUE="2">
        <PARAM NAME="Size" VALUE="4657;2619">
        <PARAM NAME="MatchEntry" VALUE="0">
        <PARAM NAME="FontCharSet" VALUE="0">
        <PARAM NAME="FontPitchAndFamily" VALUE="2">
        <PARAM NAME="FontWeight" VALUE="0">
    </OBJECT>
    <OBJECT ID="ListBox2"
      CLASSID="CLSID:8BD21D20-EC42-11CE-9E0D-00AA006002F3"
STYLE="TOP:107pt;LEFT:198pt;WIDTH:134pt;HEIGHT:74pt;TABINDEX:1;ZINDEX:1;">
        <PARAM NAME="ScrollBars" VALUE="3">
        <PARAM NAME="DisplayStyle" VALUE="2">
        <PARAM NAME="Size" VALUE="4710;2619">
        <PARAM NAME="MatchEntry" VALUE="0">
        <PARAM NAME="FontCharSet" VALUE="0">
        <PARAM NAME="FontPitchAndFamily" VALUE="2">
        <PARAM NAME="FontWeight" VALUE="0">
    </OBJECT>
    <OBJECT ID="TextBox1"
      CLASSID="CLSID:8BD21D10-EC42-11CE-9E0D-00AA006002F3"
STYLE="TOP:17pt;LEFT:107pt;WIDTH:157pt;HEIGHT:17pt;TABINDEX:2;ZINDEX:2;">
        <PARAM NAME="VariousPropertyBits" VALUE="746604571">
        <PARAM NAME="Size" VALUE="5530;582">
        <PARAM NAME="FontCharSet" VALUE="0">
        <PARAM NAME="FontPitchAndFamily" VALUE="2">
        <PARAM NAME="FontWeight" VALUE="0">
    </OBJECT>
    <OBJECT ID="TextBox2"
      CLASSID="CLSID:8BD21D10-EC42-11CE-9E0D-00AA006002F3"
```

```
STYLE="TOP:50pt;LEFT:107pt;WIDTH:157pt;HEIGHT:17pt;TABINDEX:3;ZINDEX:3;">
        <PARAM NAME="VariousPropertyBits" VALUE="746604571">
        <PARAM NAME="Size" VALUE="5530;582">
        <PARAM NAME="FontCharSet" VALUE="0">
        <PARAM NAME="FontPitchAndFamily" VALUE="2">
        <PARAM NAME="FontWeight" VALUE="0">
    </OBJECT>
    <OBJECT ID="Label1"
     CLASSID="CLSID:978C9E23-D4B0-11CE-BF2D-00AA003F40D0" STYLE="TOP:17pt;
LEFT:17pt;WIDTH:66pt;HEIGHT:17pt;ZINDEX:4;">
        <PARAM NAME="BackColor" VALUE="16777215">
        <PARAM NAME="Caption" VALUE="Your Name">
        <PARAM NAME="Size" VALUE="2328;583">
        <PARAM NAME="FontEffects" VALUE="1073741825">
        <PARAM NAME="FontHeight" VALUE="200">
        <PARAM NAME="FontCharSet" VALUE="0">
        <PARAM NAME="FontPitchAndFamily" VALUE="2">
        <PARAM NAME="FontWeight" VALUE="700">
    </OBJECT>
    <OBJECT ID="Label2"
     CLASSID="CLSID:978C9E23-D4B0-11CE-BF2D-00AA003F40D0" STYLE="TOP:50pt;
LEFT:17pt;WIDTH:83pt;HEIGHT:17pt;ZINDEX:5;">
        <PARAM NAME="BackColor" VALUE="16777215">
        <PARAM NAME="Caption" VALUE="Your EMail">
        <PARAM NAME="Size" VALUE="2911;582">
        <PARAM NAME="FontEffects" VALUE="1073741825">
        <PARAM NAME="FontHeight" VALUE="200">
        <PARAM NAME="FontCharSet" VALUE="0">
        <PARAM NAME="FontPitchAndFamily" VALUE="2">
        <PARAM NAME="FontWeight" VALUE="700">
    </OBJECT>
    <OBJECT ID="CommandButton1"
     CLASSID="CLSID:D7053240-CE69-11CD-A777-00DD01143C57"
STYLE="TOP:107pt;LEFT:140pt;WIDTH:58pt;HEIGHT:25pt;TABINDEX:6;ZINDEX:6;">
        <PARAM NAME="Caption" VALUE="&gt;&gt;">
        <PARAM NAME="Size" VALUE="2037;873">
        <PARAM NAME="FontEffects" VALUE="1073741825">
        <PARAM NAME="FontHeight" VALUE="200">
        <PARAM NAME="FontCharSet" VALUE="0">
        <PARAM NAME="FontPitchAndFamily" VALUE="2">
        <PARAM NAME="ParagraphAlign" VALUE="3">
        <PARAM NAME="FontWeight" VALUE="700">
    </OBJECT>
    <OBJECT ID="CommandButton2"
     CLASSID="CLSID:D7053240-CE69-11CD-A777-00DD01143C57"
STYLE="TOP:132pt;LEFT:140pt;WIDTH:58pt;HEIGHT:25pt;TABINDEX:7;ZINDEX:7;">
        <PARAM NAME="Caption" VALUE="&lt;&lt;">
        <PARAM NAME="Size" VALUE="2037;873">
        <PARAM NAME="FontEffects" VALUE="1073741825">
        <PARAM NAME="FontHeight" VALUE="200">
        <PARAM NAME="FontCharSet" VALUE="0">
        <PARAM NAME="FontPitchAndFamily" VALUE="2">
        <PARAM NAME="ParagraphAlign" VALUE="3">
        <PARAM NAME="FontWeight" VALUE="700">
    </OBJECT>
    <OBJECT ID="CommandButton3"
     CLASSID="CLSID:D7053240-CE69-11CD-A777-00DD01143C57"
STYLE="TOP:157pt;LEFT:140pt;WIDTH:58pt;HEIGHT:25pt;TABINDEX:8;ZINDEX:8;">
```

*continues*

**Listing 30.4. continued**

```
            <PARAM NAME="Caption" VALUE="All">
            <PARAM NAME="Size" VALUE="2037;873">
            <PARAM NAME="FontEffects" VALUE="1073741825">
            <PARAM NAME="FontHeight" VALUE="200">
            <PARAM NAME="FontCharSet" VALUE="0">
            <PARAM NAME="FontPitchAndFamily" VALUE="2">
            <PARAM NAME="ParagraphAlign" VALUE="3">
            <PARAM NAME="FontWeight" VALUE="700">
        </OBJECT>
        <OBJECT ID="Label3"
         CLASSID="CLSID:978C9E23-D4B0-11CE-BF2D-00AA003F40D0" STYLE="TOP:91pt;
LEFT:8pt;WIDTH:116pt;HEIGHT:17pt;ZINDEX:9;">
            <PARAM NAME="BackColor" VALUE="16777215">
            <PARAM NAME="Caption" VALUE="Favorite Programs">
            <PARAM NAME="Size" VALUE="4075;583">
            <PARAM NAME="FontEffects" VALUE="1073741825">
            <PARAM NAME="FontHeight" VALUE="200">
            <PARAM NAME="FontCharSet" VALUE="0">
            <PARAM NAME="FontPitchAndFamily" VALUE="2">
            <PARAM NAME="FontWeight" VALUE="700">
        </OBJECT>
        <OBJECT ID="Label4"
         CLASSID="CLSID:978C9E23-D4B0-11CE-BF2D-00AA003F40D0" STYLE="TOP:91pt;
LEFT:198pt;WIDTH:66pt;HEIGHT:17pt;ZINDEX:10;">
            <PARAM NAME="BackColor" VALUE="16777215">
            <PARAM NAME="Caption" VALUE="Your Choice">
            <PARAM NAME="Size" VALUE="2328;583">
            <PARAM NAME="FontEffects" VALUE="1073741825">
            <PARAM NAME="FontHeight" VALUE="200">
            <PARAM NAME="FontCharSet" VALUE="0">
            <PARAM NAME="FontPitchAndFamily" VALUE="2">
            <PARAM NAME="FontWeight" VALUE="700">
        </OBJECT>
        <OBJECT ID="CommandButton4"
         CLASSID="CLSID:D7053240-CE69-11CD-A777-00DD01143C57"
STYLE="TOP:198pt;LEFT:91pt;WIDTH:66pt;HEIGHT:25pt;TABINDEX:11;ZINDEX:11;">
            <PARAM NAME="Caption" VALUE="Submit">
            <PARAM NAME="Size" VALUE="2329;873">
            <PARAM NAME="FontEffects" VALUE="1073741825">
            <PARAM NAME="FontHeight" VALUE="200">
            <PARAM NAME="FontCharSet" VALUE="0">
            <PARAM NAME="FontPitchAndFamily" VALUE="2">
            <PARAM NAME="ParagraphAlign" VALUE="3">
            <PARAM NAME="FontWeight" VALUE="700">
        </OBJECT>
        <OBJECT ID="CommandButton5"
         CLASSID="CLSID:D7053240-CE69-11CD-A777-00DD01143C57"
STYLE="TOP:198pt;LEFT:190pt;WIDTH:66pt;HEIGHT:25pt;TABINDEX:12;ZINDEX:12;">
            <PARAM NAME="Caption" VALUE="Clear">
            <PARAM NAME="Size" VALUE="2328;873">
            <PARAM NAME="FontEffects" VALUE="1073741825">
            <PARAM NAME="FontHeight" VALUE="200">
            <PARAM NAME="FontCharSet" VALUE="0">
            <PARAM NAME="FontPitchAndFamily" VALUE="2">
            <PARAM NAME="ParagraphAlign" VALUE="3">
            <PARAM NAME="FontWeight" VALUE="700">
        </OBJECT>
    </DIV>
```

**Listing 30.5. samplelayout.htm.**

```
<HTML>
<HEAD>
<TITLE>Sample HTML Layout</TITLE>
</HEAD>
<BODY BGCOLOR="white">
<CENTER>
<FONT FACE="arial">
<H2>Computer Users Survey</H2>

<OBJECT CLASSID="CLSID:812AE312-8B8E-11CF-93C8-00AA00C08FDF"
ID="inputform_alx" STYLE="LEFT:0;TOP:0">
<PARAM NAME="ALXPATH" REF VALUE="inputform.alx">
 </OBJECT>

</BODY>
</HTML>
```

# Summary

VBScript and ActiveX enable you to create state-of-the-art, dynamic, and interactive HTML pages and Web applications. Whether you're looking to create an outstandingly creative Web site or translate a current Windows application to the Web, Microsoft Active Content is the fastest and most highly developed path to take.

You can use VBScript to interface the browser, HTML Intrinsic form controls, and ActiveX controls. The VBScript language and syntax is straightforward and relatively easy to learn. VBScript also has the advantage of being a subset of Visual Basic; therefore, the millions of VB programmers in the world will be able to get up and running with VBScript in no time at all. Most of the VBScript language actually pre-dates Windows, giving you the benefit of many years of development behind the code you create.

ActiveX controls have been with us for much longer than most people realize. They are, in essence, the very building blocks of Windows itself. The available pool of ActiveX controls is immense, and tools such as the new VB5 CCE allow you to create your own ActiveX controls.

The possibilities of what you can achieve with VBScript and ActiveX are endless and are governed only by your own imagination. Enjoy!

# VRML Primer

*by Bruce Campbell*

## IN THIS CHAPTER

CHAPTER 31

If the success of a computer language is determined by the number of people using and writing about it, HTML is a very successful electronic information presentation language. Tens of millions of electronic files available on the World Wide Web are formatted following the rules and syntax of HTML outlined in this book. And, HTML is evolving as new developments such as cascading style sheets (see Chapter 19, "Introducing Cascading Style Sheets,") and Dynamic HTML (see Chapter 22, "Dynamic HTML") add new capabilities to the language. There is a second Web language, the Virtual Reality Modeling Language (VRML), which continues to be successful in adding a third dimension to information presentation on the Web. VRML files exist alone on the Web to provide navigable 3D scenes to a Web audience or, as focused on in this chapter, VRML files are embedded within HTML Web pages to present information based on the best of each language.

# Adding the Third Dimension

Depth is usually considered the third dimension. Depth is often ignored when designing computer applications because the computer screen is only two dimensional. The third dimension was ignored in the first cave paintings produced by human beings, probably because the flat cave walls had two dimensions, width and height. But as the study of art progressed, intricate theories of building three-dimensional images on two-dimensional canvases were developed, and depth was added to painted images. Today's Web pages are created using a language that handles two dimensions quite adequately for the information presentation techniques of today, but is the Web at the same point analogously as painting was in the days of the cave painter?

# What the Third Dimension Does for the Web

Web authors use HTML to provide tours of interesting places to visit. Universities put virtual tours of their campuses on their Web servers so surfers can point and click through digitally scanned photographs of key buildings and green spaces. NASA provides pictures of Mars, Jupiter, Saturn, and other heavenly bodies on its Web pages. City governments do the same to provide virtual tours of their cities. The technique is a successful one because so many Web navigators have used the same presentation formats in their own vacation scrapbooks and have learned to click like crazy when using the mice attached to their computers.

Yet, something is lost in the translation of three-dimensional places into sample photographs placed with text on a Web site. There is no sense of continuity of the pictures into a coherent whole. No easy way to put the whole place in the mind at once. The audience often imagines a place that is laid out quite differently in reality. Mars and Jupiter appear to be the same size and very close to each other when viewed as two successive pictures on a Web site. In fact, they are millions of miles apart and Jupiter is thousands of times larger than Mars.

Visualization is considered one of the most important aspects in the progression of science. Physics, chemistry, genetics, and astronomy all are explained in terms of mathematical concepts that are very difficult to understand. Without understanding the existing theories, scientists cannot support, improve upon, or debate against the current body of knowledge in their fields. Presenting scientific theories as three-dimensional, interactive models is often more useful for an audience's understanding than a series of pictures supported by text.

The Web is ripe for 3D content that the world can visit and navigate from within a Web browser. Although most people have traditionally learned through text, pictures, and movies and readily accept the same format for Web-based learning, learning through experiencing 3D models compliments other methods quite well. People experience 3D models in six directions: right, left, up, down, forward, and backward. Interacting with 3D models can be as simple as using the arrow keys on a standard 84- or 102-key keyboard and as complex as manipulating sophisticated onscreen controls with the mouse and keyboard.

Imagine two brain surgeons. One has learned to remove tumors dangerously close to the brain stem by studying a series of pictures provided in a medical textbook. The other has actually practiced performing the surgery on a virtual 3D model of a brain with a tumor placed in a very dangerous location. In an emergency, which brain surgeon would most people want if they were to be the doctor's first patient? No doubt about it, people understand the benefit of the third dimension in this case.

Imagine a virtual tour of a new ballpark for the favorite sports team of someone who has held season tickets for 10 seasons. One tour lets the fan click to see pictures of different parts of the stadium. The other lets the fan move around the ballpark to sit in any seat by moving up, down, forward, backward, right, and left within a 3D model. No doubt, most season ticket holders would prefer the second method of checking out the new park.

The third dimension helps the human mind organize information in a format it understands well on a daily basis: a model of the location of a work cubicle within a building, the look of a loved one from any angle. Humans are built to encounter new information in three dimensions and digest it directly in the mind. If only there were a way to use the Web to provide navigable 3D places in a Web browser. Then, for much subject matter, Web authors would have an option to let viewers choose the order in which they experience a new place on the Web, yet still have an organized visit.

# VRML Fits the Bill

The Virtual Reality Modeling Language is growing up on the Web as a common interest of people who understand the workings of HTML, support the World Wide Web, understand computers, computer networking and computer graphics, and want the Web to have a standard way to become a navigable place people can visit and do things in. Computers are evolving quickly and finally have the capability to perform desktop virtual reality (VR). Science fiction books such as *Neuromancer* by William Gibson and *Snow Crash* by Neal Stephenson provide the imaginative vision of what a 3D navigable Web could be. There is talk of a second Web continually navigable in three-dimensional space.

VRML has already been standardized twice. VRML 1 defined standard syntax for creating three-dimensional models that could be created by combining 3D models of objects from all over the Web. VRML 2, finalized in August 1996, redefines the syntax a bit and adds an event model to the objects in a VRML model. The event model was necessary because VRML enthusiasts were concerned that VRML 1 output was too stagnant and didn't provide enough interactivity to capture a person's attention. Yet, as creative artists and scientific visualization folks began to use the standard, some very impressive VRML 1 worlds were created and made available on the Web.

# How a Web Surfer Sees a VRML Model

VRML files are stored on and delivered from Web servers that need no additional software, just HTML Web servers. Yet, a Web surfer needs additional software to be able to view a VRML file from within a Web browser. The additional software is called a VRML *viewer* and works with both the Netscape Navigator and Microsoft Internet Explorer Web browsers as a *plug-in* application. (Plug-in applications are covered in detail in Chapter 32, "Plug-ins.") During installation of a VRML viewer, the installation routine communicates with the Web browser to set up a new x-world/x-vrml MIME type associated with `.wrl` and `.wrz` file extensions. The `.wrz` extension is an explicit extension for a VRML world file that has been compressed using a common compression algorithm called gzip. Yet today, even WRL files can be compressed and the VRML viewer recognizes that fact when it opens the file in a Web browser.

Figure 31.1 shows an example of an embedded VRML file in an HTML document. The VRML creates a billiard table as part of a billiard arcade. The VRML appears in a square area on the HTML page as defined with the following `<EMBED>` tag of the HTML Web page:

```
<embed src="pool.wrl" border=3 height="500" width="500" align="right">
```

Complete HTML examples follow later in the chapter.

In Figure 31.1, the Web surfer has previously downloaded the latest copy of the CosmoPlayer VRML 2 viewer from Silicon Graphics Inc.'s Web site using the URL `http://vrml.sgi.com/cosmoplayer`. During installation, CosmoPlayer registered itself to Netscape Navigator, the Web browser. Then, the user downloaded the VRML billiard table from another Web site. CosmoPlayer provides the onscreen controls that the user can manipulate with the mouse to move forward, backward, up, down, right, and left within the billiard arcade scene. In fact, the ball middle control allows the user to spin the world in order to quickly examine its geometry.

The Web is full of HTML pages that document the history of VRML and compare, contrast, and explain VRML viewers. The VRML page at the San Diego Supercomputer Center, called the VRML Repository, is often recommended as a starting place for first-time VRML investigators. The URL for the VRML Repository is `http://www.sdsc.edu/vrml`. Home pages for the most popular VRML 2 viewers also include independent VRML information as well as links to interesting 3D worlds. Silicon Graphic's VRML café at `http://sgi.vrml.com/cafe` is another VRML Web site that focuses on current events and white papers about the further development of VRML and related technologies.

**FIGURE 31.1.**
*A VRML file embedded in an HTML document.*

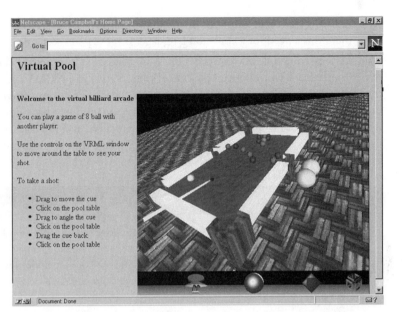

VRML 2 has become the most used Web language for presenting interactive 3D content to a Web visitor. It is capable of providing a virtual 3D worm for dissecting, a virtual new Tiger Stadium, a virtual coffee house, a virtual galaxy, and a virtual DNA double helix. VRML viewers let Web surfers interact with scenes like these in intuitive ways. Web authors can add text narrative on the same Web page using HTML with VRML embedded.

# The History of VRML and the VRML Community

The history of VRML is most interesting for the fact that much of the work in creating the standard was done on the Internet. Using electronic mail through a simple, yet heavily sub-scribed to, mailing list and a couple of usenets, anyone interested in helping guide the standard had an outlet for voicing an opinion and responding to others' opinions. The Internet proved a successful medium for getting the right minds together with the right critical thoughts. Pro-posals for the continual improvement of VRML were promoted by many different individuals and organizations, and the VRML community together discussed and voted on the best sug-gestions. The VRML Architecture Group (VAG) evolved as a group of individuals responsible for the recording of the standard and its promotion. Their Web site at `http://vag.vrml.org/` still maintains old documents that track the history of the VRML standard as well as the final VRML 2 specification. The history document is especially helpful if you are interested in the history of VRML. For example, the history link at the VAG Web site begins like this:

> In 1994, Tim Berners-Lee (the founder of HTML) invited Mark Pesce to present a paper at the First International Conference on the World Wide Web. Pesce and partner Tony Parisi had developed Labyrinth, a prototype three-dimensional interface

to the Web. His presentation sparked a consensus: the conference attendees agreed there was a need for a common language to specify 3D scene descriptions.

Many impressive people have helped VRML become what it is today; I consider them impressive because they have volunteered hours of time evangelizing VRML as an important tool in the road to human expression, creativity, learning, communication, networking, and socializing (as well as a tool for Earth conservation) while continuing to provide solid technical expertise. The center of the VRML universe is San Francisco, and the lead evangelist definitely is still Mark Pesce. Beyond that, referring to any specific names in a short history section would undoubtedly leave important people out.

---

**NOTE**

How can VRML help with Earth conservation? The idea is that VRML models of the Earth can be developed to track depletion of the rain forests over time, current pollution levels, current birth rates, and so on. In fact, in the future, with the appropriate sensors and modeling in place, all kinds of interesting scientific data could be accessible in real-time through a VRML model.

---

Geographical pockets of VRML interest are truly worldwide. Many of the members of the VRML community are compelling writers whose visionary papers have helped VRML gain acceptance and, perhaps more important, enthusiasm. There are many books on VRML 1 that still should be read for the vision they provide for VRML. Yet, to be technically astute with the current language, a VRML 2 book is a must.

The Java development team at Sun has recently (May 1997) introduced a 3D API as a specification for creating and manipulating 3D applications within the Java language itself. I talked with a representative from Sun, who assured me that the intent was not to compete with VRML 2. (SGI has supported Sun in developing the 3D API specification.) Still, a 3D interface from Sun is worth investigating. OpenGL is another 3D graphics API that has a lot of supporters. In fact, many graphics acceleration boards are created primarily to enhance the OpenGL 3D function calls.

The VRML standard has reached a plateau; any technology is finally considered big business. With the World Wide Web Consortium (W3C) as a template, the VRML Architecture Group is maturing to become the VRML Consortium with a more formally recognized governing body. The formal organization should prepare it for what no doubt is on the horizon: new features in the standard, venture capital to be directed, and ISO standard recognition. These days are an important time in VRML's development, and changes are in the works (which, by the way, is nothing new here).

The next section takes a look at what VRML 2 is today and how it can be mixed with HTML.

# VRML Scenes

Creative VRML-based Web content is stored as one or more WRL files. These files contain text following the UTF8 convention that HTML also subscribes to. UTF8 covers a larger character set than ASCII but is similar in purpose, with a more international focus. These WRL files are often called *worlds* by their creators because they focus on the virtual reality aspect of their design. Authors hope their audience feels so immersed in the content that they feel like they are in a different place—not sitting in front of a computer screen—and that their actions as they use the computer are an extension of their bodies. Immersion is a word used by virtual reality developers to describe the degree to which the computer's reality gains the attention of the user's senses. In immersive VR, immersion of sight and sound is aided by a head-mounted device (HMD) that becomes the user's sole field of vision and source of sound.

Web browsers are currently not run immersively by most people. Instead, VRML content is shown via desktop VR, and a user is more apt to think of the content as a model when compared to an immersively experienced world. Somewhere between the world and model descriptions of VRML content is the concept of a scene. In the long run, I suspect, the word *model* might become the accepted term as a descriptor of the output of a VRML file. However, I find that the word *world* is still the most commonly used term.

VRML scenes are created out of *nodes* the VRML-enabled viewer program parses and presents on the Web page. These nodes are put together to define hundreds of different possible features of a 3D scene. Each node has a list of *fields* that can be used to subdefine the properties of the node. The order in which the nodes and fields are listed is significant in many cases, and the aggregation of them all is called a *scene graph*. It is called a graph in the same vein as a mathematician refers to a graph: as a way to describe an organization of objects that possess certain characteristics. Understanding HTML is helpful in learning VRML. The syntax of the two languages has many similarities.

# Similarities Between VRML and HTML

Besides being created as text-based files following the same UTF8 standard, VRML and HTML syntax are similar in the following ways:

- VRML uses short text strings to identify the appearance or behavior of every node that makes up a VRML scene; similarly, HTML uses short text strings to declare tags that dictate the appearance of objects on a Web page. For example, VRML uses the word Sphere to tell the Web browser to draw a sphere as part of a VRML scene, and HTML uses the string BR to tell the Web browser to make a line break in written text.

- VRML nodes have a start and end point; HTML tags have pairs that dictate the start and end of a tag's influence. For example, the Transform node in VRML transforms only the objects inside of its braces, and the <B> tag in HTML boldfaces only the words between the <B> and </B>.

- VRML fields help subdefine the node; HTML attributes subdefine the tag. For example, the `transform`, `scale`, and `rotation` fields of a VRML `Transform` node dictate how the objects inside the node are presented in a way similar to how the `BGCOLOR`, `VLINK`, `LINK`, `TEXT`, and `BACKGROUND` attributes of a `<BODY>` HTML tag dictate how the body of an HTML page is presented.

- Both languages read their content sequentially from top down, left to right, and both languages ignore white space such as spaces, carriage returns, and line feeds beyond one white space character unless it is within quotes. Text placement is flexible so that the author can organize the text in any way deemed appropriate.

- Both languages lend themselves to editor applications that can be used to make the text creation process easier. HTML editors enable an author to use buttons and drop-down lists in conjunction with the mouse to create Web pages. VRML editors, often called modeling packages, enable an author to create 3D geometries and color or texture them using drag-and-drop techniques involving the mouse with buttons and drop-down lists. Both languages have many programmers working at making better tools for content creation, yet both allow an author to use a cheap, simple text editor to create the content. Cheap is important if everyone is to have access to authoring on the Web.

# Differences Between VRML and HTML

Although VRML and HTML coexist nicely on a Web server and the language mindset is similar, the two languages look dramatically different in syntax, and their domains overlap only slightly in places. VRML does have a `Text` node that places text in a VRML scene. VRML has an `Anchor` node used to provide hyperlinking from VRML scenes to other Web objects such as Web pages or other VRML scenes. But so many VRML nodes are foreign to an HTML expert. HTML is concerned with text, related text objects such as lists and tables, and 2D pictures called bitmaps. VRML, on the other hand, is concerned with representing a three-dimensional model, explicitly defining a z direction perpendicular to the plane of a traditional computer screen. VRML nodes, once learned, are natural and provide insight as to how the human mind organizes 3D information encountered in day-to-day living. Learning VRML makes one ponder human physiology and the human mind.

Visual objects in VRML scenes are made of shapes that are the combination of primitive geometries provided by the language or hand crafted by connecting points together counterclockwise in 3D space. Primitive geometry nodes include the `Box`, `Sphere`, `Cone`, `Cylinder`, and `ElevationGrid`. 3D space is defined along three axes—x (left to right), y (down to up), and z (back to front). Points in space defined as x,y,z coordinates are combined using the `IndexedFaceSet` node in order to create polygons that are combined to create solid objects. For example, the point (10,3,−4) refers to a point 10 units from the right of the origin, 3 units above the origin, and 4 units back from the origin.

Each visual object has an appearance that is defined by colors and textures. Textures are created the same way HTML graphics are created and a Web author can often take advantage of the same HTML background tiling technique in VRML to keep texture file sizes small. An author's VRML textures can also take advantage of the same transparency available to HTML graphics to overcome burdensome shape detail such as that required by a tree or mountain range.

VRML contains different lighting nodes to provide lighting effects, a Fog node to vary clarity of the scene, a Background node to simplify the creation of objects off in the distance, and sound nodes to incorporate sound into a scene and even associate the sound to a specific 3D location.

VRML Viewpoint nodes provide convenient camera coordinates and directions that can be used to move to significant locations within the VRML scene. The VRML viewer is always showing a viewpoint to the Web surfer, yet many of the intermediary viewpoints are reached dynamically by the user's actions. Viewpoint nodes are convenient bookmarks in the scene that can be accessed by a visitor who is unsure of where to go.

Many of the new nodes of VRML 2 track the user's viewpoint or user's actions through the mouse or other pointing device to allow a visitor to interact with other nodes. For example, a TouchSensor node can be associated with a doorbell object that, when clicked, opens up a door object. A PositionInterpolator node identifies how the door should open, and a Timer node keeps track of how long it should take to open. Separate nodes can set up a close event for the door. A SphereSensor node can set up an event based on the user's current location, triggering an event when the user moves within the hidden geometry of the SphereSensor located in 3D space.

Events associate VRML nodes with each other through a ROUTE statement. A ROUTE statement connects the nodes that can trigger events with nodes that control the timing of the event or the actual transformation of the objects involved in the event. Transformations available in VRML 2 include change of location (called translation in the VRML specification), change of scale, change of orientation, change of appearance, as well as lighting and camera transformations for any one or more objects associated within the same object group.

# An Overview of VRML Syntax

A working knowledge of VRML syntax can be quickly gained by learning the nodes that make up the language. There is no need to memorize all the details because there are many reference documents available on the Web, with http://vag.vrml.org/VRML2.0/FINAL being the most official. Instead, learning is best done by reading a good book and making small changes to example VRML scenes to see the effect of the changes. After a quick introduction to some key nodes, this section moves on to the VRML billiard table example so you can learn by focusing on the process.

> **NOTE**
>
> A book I co-authored with Chris Marrin, *Teach Yourself VRML 2 in 21 Days,* demonstrates each feature of VRML 2 that enables creative 3D Web page interactivity. Many book titles on VRML 1 and VRML 2 can be found at the VRML Repository Web site at the San Diego Supercomputer Center (http://www.sdsc.edu/vrml). The VRML Repository Web site is worth investigating for its wealth of information on VRML and its unbiased presentation style.

The key organizing nodes of the VRML 2 standard are the Transform, Inline, and Group nodes. These nodes are parent nodes to the other nodes that define a VRML scene. A Transform node associates one or many children nodes together so that they can be manipulated together as a single object when desired. A group node associates children as well, but without providing any manipulation at that level. An Inline node associates other nodes together and provides a URL to get those nodes from another file that is located on the Web; the Inline node is important for taking advantage of the unique features of the Web for sharing information and collaborating.

Initially, the children nodes of interest are the ones that add visual objects to the scene. In the case of the following billiard table example, each component of the table is added as a child object to the same Transform node. After the components are associated with each other in the same Transform, they can be manipulated as a group to change their location, size, or orientation uniformly for all components. For a simple billiard table, the visual objects include a slate surface, six bumper cushions, six pockets, and a table base, as well as 16 balls. To start slowly, the first code example, Listing 31.1, has only one pocket, one bumper, and a solitary cue ball. Figure 31.2 shows the partial billiard table.

**Listing 31.1. A primitive VRML billiard table.**

```
#VRML V2.0 utf8
DEF overview Viewpoint {
    position        200 250 500
    orientation     0 0 1 0
    fieldOfView  0.785398
    description     "OVERVIEW"
}
DEF Billiards_Table Transform {
    children [
        DEF Slate Transform {
            children [
                DEF TSB TouchSensor {}
                Shape {
                    appearance Appearance {
                        material Material {diffuseColor 0 .2 0 }
                        # texture ImageTexture {url "green1.gif" }
                    }
```

```
                    geometry Box {size 312 512 .05 }
                }
            ]
            translation 156 256 -12
        },
        Transform {
            children [
                DEF Bumper Shape {
                    appearance Appearance {
                        material Material {diffuseColor .8 .7 .7 }
                        # texture ImageTexture {url "pink1.gif" }
                    }
                    geometry Box {}
                }
            ]
            scale 125 15 15
            translation 154 -15 2
        },
        Transform {
            children [
                DEF Pocket Shape {
                    appearance Appearance {
                        material Material {diffuseColor .1 .1 .02 }
                        # texture ImageTexture { url "brown1.gif" }
                    }
                        geometry IndexedFaceSet {
                            coord Coordinate {
                                point [ 0 0 0, 30 0 0, 20 20 0,
                                        20 30 0, 30 40 0, 40 40 0,
                                        60 30 0, 60 60 0, 0 60 0,
                                        0 0 -80, 0 60 -80,
                                        60 60 -80, 60 0 -80 ]
                            }
                            coordIndex [ 0, 1, 2, 3, 4, 5, 6, 7, 8, -1,
                                         0, 8, 10, 9, -1, 9, 10, 8, 0, -1,
                                         7, 8, 10, 11, -1,
                                         11, 10, 8, 7, -1,
                                         11, 10, 9, 12, -1 ]
                        }
                }
            ]
            translation -30 480 20
        },
        DEF Ball Transform {
            children [
                DEF TSC TouchSensor {}
                Shape {
                    appearance Appearance {
                        material Material {diffuseColor 1 1 1 }
                    }
                    geometry Sphere {radius 10 }
                }
            ]
            translation 150 400 0
        },
    ]
} # end Billiards_Table
```

**FIGURE 31.2.**

*A partial billiard table
showing one pocket, one
bumper, and the cue
ball.*

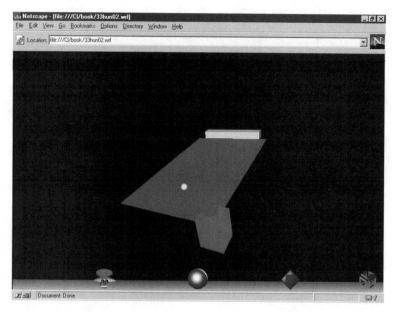

The first line in Listing 31.1 is called the header line. The header line identifies the version of the VRML standard to which the file format is complying. Its syntax is very specific, including the # character, which anywhere else in the file acts solely as a comment identifier. A comment is active until the next line feed is encountered. The second line starts the Transform node for the billiard table. The DEF keyword allows a node to be named and then reused according to name. Corresponding Transform nodes for the Slate, Bumper, Pocket, and Ball are also named using the DEF keyword.

> **NOTE**
>
> The DEF keyword acts like an object identifier in an object-oriented programming language. The node it defines becomes reusable in the rest of the VRML scene. As mentioned in the "The Future of VRML" section later in this chapter, other programming languages are being used to manipulate objects in a VRML scene. These languages interface with the VRML file through the nodes defined with DEF keywords.

Each visual object is a child Transform node of the Billiards_Table Transform node. Each visual object contains a Shape node as a child of the Transform node, as well as potential translation, scale, and rotation fields to be discussed after the Shape node discussion. Each Shape node has two fields: an appearance field that specifies the color or texture of the object and a geometry field that specifies the area of physical coordinates the object occupies in 3D space.

The appearance field expects an Appearance node to follow. Yet, this field-node relationship allows flexibility in the future of VRML development when other node types may be appropriate for the appearance field. The Appearance node contains a texture and/or material field that specifies the color and texture of the Shape node it is a part of. In Listing 31.1, the ImageTexture nodes are commented out, so only the effect of the Material node is seen in Figure 31.2. Textures use external bitmap files specified using their absolute or relative URLs. The bitmaps are wrapped around the geometry defined in the same Shape node. Still, the bitmaps can be the exact files used in the <IMG> tag of an HTML Web page. They are traditionally JPG and GIF files. The Material node defines a diffuseColor field that gives a Shape node its predominant color. Textures and materials are a significant part of the VRML specification; several additional fields and transformations are available to the Shape node.

> **NOTE**
>
> The hierarchical ordering of the nodes and fields presents the best opportunity for reuse because any node can be defined with a DEF keyword at any point in the hierarchy. In this case, the whole Billiards_Table can be reused to create multiple tables in the arcade, the Bumper can be reused to create six of them on a single table, or an Appearance node can be reused to create the same look to other visual objects. The hierarchy also works well inside the computer after the scene has been parsed and stored internally because it is designed to take advantage of a stack and its related algorithms.

The geometry field of the Shape node is different for each visual object on the billiard table. For the Slate Transform and Bumper Shape nodes, the geometry is defined as a Box node. The Slate box has dimensions of 312 units in the x direction, 512 units in the y direction, and .05 units in the z direction. For the Cue Transform node, geometry is defined as a Sphere node with a radius of 10 units.

> **NOTE**
>
> Using the primitive shapes of Box, Sphere, Cylinder, and Cone reduces the VRML file size, yet is very constricting to the exact shapes. These shapes contain many polygons, and polygon counts are a significant indicator of performance in the Web browser. So, they must be used with caution in a VRML scene.

The geometry field of the Pocket Shape node uses an IndexedFaceSet node to derive a very specific shape out of coordinates in 3D space. Each point is separated by a comma, and the points are connected using the list of indexes in the coordIndex field. Each component polygon of the shape is created by a list of point indexes that all end with a −1 and are connected counterclockwise. Five polygons create the corner pocket seen in Figure 31.2. Points are reused in different polygons to guarantee a solid seam around the object. The pocket is not completely closed off because the neighboring bumpers will make the pockets appear solid. The `IndexedFaceSet` node is at the heart of every unique VRML object shape encountered on the Web. It can be expanded to show incredible detail by connecting tens of thousands of points. Detail requires associated computer processing power that is not always available to each Web site visitor, but the VRML standard is poised for the future through the `IndexedFaceSet` node.

The `translation`, `scale`, and `rotation` fields are critical to the flexibility of the VRML scene. Any group of objects nested in the `children` field can be manipulated together using the other fields of the `Transform` node. The `translation` field defines the point in 3D space around which the objects are centered. The `scale` field defines the relative x, y, and z size of the objects as multipliers of their `Shape` nodes' defined `geometry` fields. The `rotation` field defines the orientation of the objects relative to their `Shape` nodes' defined `geometry` fields. These three fields become necessary when an object is reused in the VRML scene. They also allow for the manipulation of an object defined in an external file that is being added to the scene using the `Inline` node.

The other three corner pockets in the billiard table are similar to the first one defined in Listing 31.1. Instead of creating them from scratch, they are included as child `Transform` nodes of the `Billiards_Table` `Transform` node based on the original `Pocket` `Shape` node. For example, the opposite corner pocket looks like this:

```
Transform {
    children [
        USE Pocket
    ]
    rotation 0 0 1 3.14
    translation 340 30 20
},
```

Here, the `Pocket` shape is reused by referring to it with the `USE` keyword. The shape is placed in a `Transform` node in order to rotate the pocket 180 degrees and move it to its appropriate location relative to the `Slate` `Transform` node. The other five bumpers can be created like this:

```
Transform {
    children [
        USE Bumper
    ]
    scale 15 105 15
    translation 324 375 2
},
```

For the bumpers, the shape is reused by referring to the `Bumper` `Shape` node definition with the `USE` keyword. Each bumper is scaled from the default `Box` node size of 2 by 2 by 2 by using the `scale` field of the `Transform` node. In this example, the final dimensions will be 30 (2 times 15) by 210 (2 times 105) by 30 (2 times 15). The center location of this bumper will be 324 units to the right, 375 units above, and 2 units in front of the (0,0,0) origin.

Nodes reused by reference to a defined node must appear after the defined node in the text file, so the preceding two reuse examples would appear as child nodes of the `Billiards_Table Transform` node after the child `Transform` nodes containing the `DEF` keyword. Six other child nodes taking advantage of reuse would create the last two corner pockets and four bumpers seen in Figure 31.1. Fifteen additional billiard balls could be created as well as child `Transform` nodes of the `Billiards Table Transform` node. The side pockets could be created using a different `IndexedFaceSet` node. Figure 31.3 shows an improved VRML billiard table after taking advantage of VRML node reuse.

**FIGURE 31.3.**

*A VRML billiard table with object reuse.*

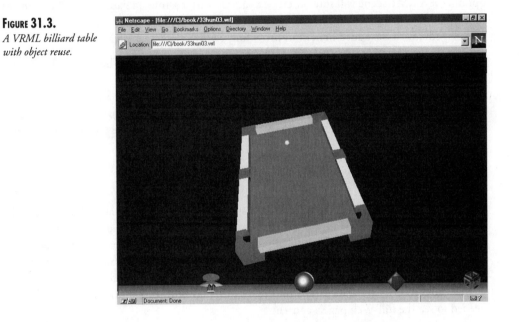

Two last points of interest are related to Listing 31.1: First, a `Viewpoint` node was added to explicitly start the VRML viewer camera at a specific location and orientation in the scene. Without it, different VRML viewers start at different viewpoints. Second, `TouchSensor` nodes were added as children to the `Slate` and `Ball Transform` nodes to set up an expectation for user interaction with the scene. `TouchSensor` nodes make the objects in which they are contained aware of the mouse pointer. VRML specifies events that can be triggered by passing the mouse over or clicking upon objects that contain the `TouchSensor` node.

The example in Listing 31.1 is typical of basic VRML syntax and functionality. VRML 2 has an impressive list of nodes and fields that could build this billiard table into an interesting billiard world to explore and interact with. The most likely would include adding lights and simple events. Although some of the vision for enhancing this VRML scene is discussed in the section "The Future of VRML," I encourage you to explore other books for explicit examples. The next section focuses on adding the VRML scene to an HTML Web page assuming the VRML file has been saved in a text editor with a `.wrl` extension.

# Adding VRML to a Web Page

VRML can be added to an HTML document using two distinct approaches. The first approach embeds a VRML scene within a rectangular area of the Web page as if it were a bitmap image. In a single Web page, multiple VRML scenes can be added this way. As a Web surfer scrolls a larger Web page, the VRML scene will scroll off the page just as a picture would. The alternative is to load the VRML scene in a separate frame, set up with a frame definition document as described in Chapter 18, "Creating Sophisticated Layouts with Frames and Layers." With this option, the VRML scene will stay onscreen as a Web surfer scrolls a related HTML document in a separate frame. Either approach can be used to set up the look and feel of an electronic encyclopedia with the added benefit of providing a fully interactive VRML scene.

Any method of adding a VRML scene to a Web page usually reduces the size of the VRML scene to appear less than full screen to the audience. VRML viewer plug-ins are programmed to scale the opening viewpoint relative to the available presentation size and resolution of the VRML scene; the smaller the area, the better the VRML scene will perform in responding to the user's manipulation of the scene. Reducing the size also reduces the visitor's sense of immersion.

# Embedding VRML in an HTML Page

Figure 31.1 presents a VRML billiard table that has been embedded in an HTML page. The HTML text could continue for many screens worth of information on the rules of play, details about interacting with the world, and even a physics lesson on the dynamics of billiard balls colliding in a constrained area. As the viewers wish to read more, they could scroll down below the VRML scene, read more information, and then scroll back up to continue playing with the scene. The scrollbars are added dynamically by the Web browser window whenever they are needed to see the full Web page's content.

The HTML syntax for the Web page presented in Figure 31.1 is provided in Listing 31.2. The HTML tags used for the text presentation are very common. The file pool.wrl is the VRML billiard arcade scene that is embedded into the Web page at the point it is encountered within the HTML file. The <EMBED> tag uses an SRC attribute that sets up the pool.wrl relative URL as the source of the contents of the area created with a HEIGHT attribute of 500 pixels high and a WIDTH attribute of 500 pixels wide. The VRML scene is aligned along the right of the Web browser window by way of the ALIGN attribute. A BORDER with thickness of 2 is set up around the VRML scene to keep it from running close to text on the rest of the page.

**Listing 31.2. The VRML billiard table embedded in an HTML page.**

```
<HTML>
<HEAD>
<TITLE>VRML Billiards</TITLE>
</HEAD>
<BODY>
```

```
<EMBED SRC="pool.wrl" HEIGHT="500" WIDTH="500" ALIGN="RIGHT"  BORDER=2 >
<P>
You can play a game of 8 ball with another player.
<P>
Use the controls on the VRML window to move around the table to see your shot.
<P>
To take a shot:
<UL>
<LI>Drag to move the cue
<LI>Click on the pool table
<LI>Drag to angle the cue
<LI>Click on the pool table
<LI>Drag the cue back
<LI>Click on the pool table
</UL>
</BODY>
</HTML>
```

Multiple VRML scenes could be added in this fashion by adding more <EMBED> tags, similar to adding multiple <IMG> tags to an HTML Web page.

# Adding a VRML Frame

To add a VRML scene as a separate frame, a frame definition document, as described in Chapter 18, is created to house the VRML scene. In Listing 31.3, three frames are created: A description frame named DESC shows narrative about the game of billiards, an index frame named INDEX provides a permanent list of different narrative documents available for reading from the DESC frame, and the VRML frame named VRML shows the VRML scene.

**Listing 31.3. The HTML frame definition document.**

```
<HTML>
<HEAD>
<TITLE>VRML Billiards</TITLE>
<FRAMESET ROWS="*,50">
<NOFRAMES>
</NOFRAMES>
<FRAMESET COLS="300,*">
<FRAME SRC="overview.htm" NAME="DESC">
<FRAME SRC="pool.wrl" NAME="VRML">
</FRAMESET>
<FRAME SRC="index.htm" NAME="INDEX">
</FRAMESET>
</HEAD>
</HTML>
```

The INDEX frame has a fixed height of only 50 pixels, which is sufficient to print a line of text. The DESC frame is 300 pixels wide and fills the rest of the browser window vertically based on the current window size. The VRML frame takes up the rest of the browser window, to the right of the DESC frame, dynamically obtaining whatever room is left over. The order of the DESC and VRML frame <FRAME> tags can be switched to move the VRML frame to the left of the DESC frame.

In that case, the VRML frame has a fixed width. Figure 31.4 shows the presentation of the billiard world in a frame definition document.

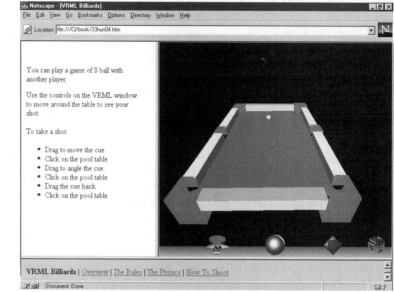

# Communications Between VRML and HTML

After a VRML scene has been added to a frame definition document, the scene can communicate with the other frames from within the VRML file itself. The Anchor node within the VRML specification is responsible for setting up hyperlinks in a VRML file. An Anchor node can be added as a child node to a VRML Transform node in the same manner the TouchSensor node is added to the Slate Transform node in Listing 31.1. A new HTML document containing information on the rules of pool could be opened in the DESC frame when a visitor clicks on the slate of the billiard table by replacing the TouchSensor node of the Slate Transform node in Listing 31.1 with the following Anchor node:

```
Anchor {
    url [ "http://www.officialpoolsite.com/rules.html" ]
    parameter ["target=DESC"]
}
```

In this case, the rules.html document opens in the DESC frame when the geometry of the Transform node is clicked on by a visitor.

Any HTML hyperlink set up using an <A></A> tag pair can refer to a WRL file in its SRC attribute. When the hyperlink is clicked, the VRML scene is loaded on top of the current Web browser window contents. This technique is used when a VRML scene is intended to be explored by itself without any accompanying HTML text. VRML scenes encountered on the

Web are usually presented in this manner because many Web surfers haven't yet set up a VRML viewer for use with integrated pages.

# The Future of VRML

VRML fills a current need on the Web to present three-dimensional content that can be explored by a Web audience following a walking or flying analogy. HTML has nothing currently in its specification that formats information along those lines. VRML-based content appears to rival CD-ROMs, video games, and interactive television in terms of the market it addresses. But, VRML is integrated with the Web, and Web delivery introduces network latencies not acceptable for many audiences that use CD-ROMs and video games or watch television.

In this regard, VRML seems to be an extension of HTML as an information delivery vehicle. HTML syntax is similar enough to VRML syntax to entertain the thought of merging the two. VRML could refer to HTML content as a special form of texturing scrollable information on simple rectangular polygons. Web browsers could be created to parse one file containing nodes of both HTML and VRML types. This would be worth doing if a significant proportion of the population were willing to immerse themselves on the Web by wearing a special head-mounted device. Yet, there is little talk of merging the two, nor are there any attempts at mass producing virtual reality HMDs.

Instead, the future of VRML seems to be progressing in two directions: increased interactivity and multiuser worlds.

## Increased Interactivity in VRML Scenes

As the example of creating a VRML billiard table shows, VRML files are very hierarchical, which allows for any node to be defined with the DEF keyword and be reused locally or across the Web. VRML viewer developers are rapidly improving external interfaces to their viewers that let a programmer access defined objects in the VRML file after the file has been loaded in the browser. The VRML community is pushing for standardization of a Java-based Application Programming Interface (API) that passes VRML nodes to Java classes as variables that can be manipulated from within a Java program. VRML 2 standardizes many simple object behaviors inside the VRML nodes and fields specification. VRMLscript adds even more capabilities. VRMLscript is a scripting language similar to JavaScript that is included in the WRL file through use of a Script node. It is different from JavaScript in that it is streamlined for VRML consideration only.

Because well-developed networking, scripting, and embedded physics classes already exist in Java, a Java API included in a VRML viewer lets these classes update VRML objects dynamically inside the Web browser. In the case of the billiard table example, the embedded physics classes can be associated with the billiard cue stick and the 16 balls to create a realistic VRML billiard game inside the VRML viewer. Although there are valid reasons to try instead to include these embedded physics within the WRL file itself, the standardization process takes some time while the Java solution is becoming more defined daily.

VRML is Web aware, so interactive VRML worlds could theoretically use information from all over the Net, including other VRML WRL files and databases accessed through Java database APIs. VRML worlds that change based on stock exchange, sports score, or planetary data are possible through a valid API.

Developing APIs include node methods such as `addChildren` and `removeChildren`, and browser methods such as `createVrmlFromString` and `createVrmlFromURL`, which allow new VRML objects to be added and deleted from the current scene on-the-fly based on other variables in the Java program.

Understanding the uniqueness of the Web provides an upper hand in creating new VRML scenes and Web pages that are interactive in ways that are different than today's popular CD-ROM, video game, and television show titles. So far, little has been done to create interactive pages that truly take advantage of the one-to-one connections of person to person, person to server, and server to server available on the Web. This is no surprise, given the history of other new technologies that struggled to define their uniqueness before capitalizing on it.

## Multiuser Worlds Using VRML

One unique facet of the Web is being recognized more often in magazine articles and technology reviews: The Web is a powerful facilitator of virtual communities. Chat rooms dedicated to specific purposes where repeat visitors get to know each other are just the start of the realm of virtual communities on the Web.

VRML scenes that are stored on a server, allow multiple people to enter them simultaneously, and then pass 3D locations of each participant to each connected VRML viewer are called multiuser worlds. In many of these multiuser worlds, the location in the scene of each user is represented by a 3D model of a token being, called an avatar. Avatars are represented by talking heads, monopoly tokens, fully fashion-designed humans, and anything the imagination can dream up. Some form of text or voice communication service is provided so that the visitor can chat with others from within the world.

The biggest criticism of 3D modeled virtual communities is that the third dimension adds little value and slows things down appreciably. Sometimes the third dimension is just too literal and leaves less to the imagination. People like to imagine. Perhaps the third dimension is dismissed because the worlds being created do not present a powerful three-dimensional backdrop such as those provided for scientific visualizations. Or, perhaps, because current mass-produced technology is limited to one small world at a time being active in computer memory, the ability to navigate a large, interesting landscape continuously in 3D is not perceived as important only because it cannot currently be done effectively. VRML presents an amazing range of possibilities that are only now being explored. As people continue to develop their VRML skills, the worlds will get better. Add better communications capabilities and integrate some powerful Java scripting, and the sky's the limit.

Enough is being done with artistic VRML worlds to suggest that visiting a Web space with another person will be an exciting adventure in the future if not today. As the right interactions are added to the worlds, multiuser worlds may become even more popular. To finish the billiard arcade example, add eight or more `Billiards_Table Transform` nodes to the VRML scene, with artistically textured walls and ceilings, embedded physics and rules on all the cue sticks and balls, and avatar services enabled to be able to watch and communicate with anyone in the scene to play a game of billiards. This is a powerful vision of a probable future of VRML, possible because the physics are handled locally on each browser and not dependent on short latency communications from the server.

# Summary

This chapter introduced a quick primer on VRML 2, the second specification of the Virtual Reality Modeling Language. VRML allows a Web author to exploit the third dimension in providing Web content that is experiential in a personal manner. VRML worlds are navigable by a user, becuase the user has control of her viewpoint and travels up, down, forward, back, right, and left to investigate the scene.

VRML skills are great to acquire as a complement to HTML skills. With both in hand, you can decide whether the third dimension will add or detract from your information presentation and create the best Web page for the occasion. If you already have extensive programming skills, VRML can be extended through scripting in Java to provide Web pages that appear more as applications than as static information presentations.

This chapter is by no means a complete reference of all the workings of VRML, but you have learned enough to get your feet wet. To learn more, open your favorite Web search engine and enter the keywords `VRML` or `Virtual Reality`. Plenty of new and interesting VRML sites are provided on the Web weekly.

# Plug-ins

*by Mike Sessums*

## IN THIS CHAPTER

**CHAPTER 32**

Browser plug-ins can increase your site's versatility and make it stand out from the rest. This chapter takes a look at the most popular plug-ins and some of those on the rise, as well as some of the tools you'll need to make them useful.

Third-party plug-in developers concentrate on the Microsoft Internet Explorer and Netscape Navigator, so I do the same.

Plug-ins are pretty amazing. They enable users to hear a new song at a Web music store before buying the CD. (See Figure 32.1.)

**FIGURE 32.1.**

*An audio control pops up to play a demo clip from a new music CD.*

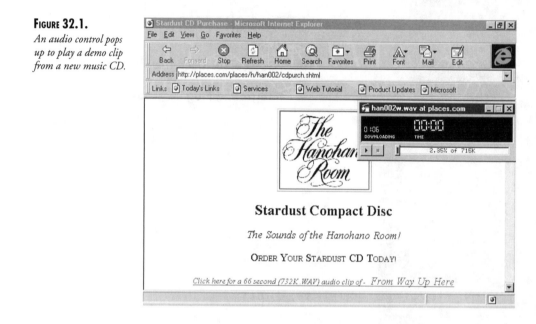

Plug-ins let potential students tour a college campus to check out the facilities without having to buy a plane ticket. (See Figure 32.2.) The possibilities are almost endless.

Plug-ins are also known as *add-ons* and *helper applications*. Many plug-ins are automatically installed, or plugged in, when Microsoft Internet Explorer or Netscape Navigator is set up. Others are available for plug-in at the Microsoft and Netscape browser Web sites, as well as some third-party sites.

There are around 90 plug-ins for Netscape Navigator, and the number is growing. Generally, plug-ins are made for one browser or the other, and are not interchangeable. However, Microsoft now boasts that you don't have to throw away those plug-ins just because you picked the "right" browser (meaning Internet Explorer). Through its ActiveX programming language, the Microsoft Internet Explorer will automatically check the user's hard drive for plug-ins installed on the Netscape Navigator as sites require it. (However, this feature doesn't always work.)

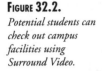

**FIGURE 32.2.**

*Potential students can check out campus facilities using Surround Video.*

Microsoft also says there are more than 1,000 ActiveX controls aimed at doing the same thing plug-ins do: delivering "active" content to the user. Movies and animations are examples of active content. An example of static content is standard HTML.

# Fads Versus Useful Tools

You might think it would be difficult to keep up with the latest plug-ins, but actually only a few are widely used. The most popular ones are covered in this chapter.

One way to find out whether a plug-in is genuinely useful or merely a fad is to check out what other sites are using. Of course, what constitutes a useful plug-in for one site might be totally inappropriate for another.

A good example of this is VRML. There is no doubt about it: VRML is cool. It's fun. On some sites, it is downright awesome. But here is the test: After playing around with a site's virtual world, what did you learn from it? I mean, what was it there for? Is it just to dazzle, or did it really serve a purpose?

Streaming video is another example. This one's not really so much a fad as it is technology that just isn't quite ready for prime time. The video quality is generally quite poor and choppy. If the technology catches up, streaming video will be the most ideal method for delivering large video content over the Web.

Live Web camera sites border on the fad category because many of them show the Web author's room or fish aquariums. (See Figure 32.3.) Oh, there's a lot of excitement there. Of course, many other people have discovered this technology's great potential.

FIGURE 32.3.

*A very clever use of the Web camera: Netscape's Fishcam.*

When you design your page, don't include the need for very many of the plug-ins that are out of the mainstream. Otherwise, your audience will have to download and install new plug-ins before they can take advantage of your Web site. An exception to this might be a very specialized audience, such as heart surgeons, who might require very specialized plug-ins that the public doesn't normally use.

# Integrating Plug-ins

Browser plug-ins enable the Web audience to experience the content on your Web pages. However, plug-ins are only part of the picture.

Before you can integrate these plug-ins on your home page, you will need to create the content or locate stock items to include on your pages. These could include video, audio, animation, external applications, multilingual support, or Net communications, to name a few.

## Video

Whether you want to use stock videos or digitize your own, there are several ways you can include video in your Web site. Video plug-ins (see Table 32.1) help make this possible.

**Table 32.1. Video plug-ins.**

| Plug-in | Platform | Company |
|---------|----------|---------|
| ActiveMovie | Windows 95, Windows NT | Microsoft (www.microsoft.com) |
| CineWeb | Windows 3.1, Window 95, Windows NT | Digigami (www.digigami.com) |
| ClearFusion | Windows 95 | Iterated Systems (www.iterated.com) |
| InterVU Player | Windows 95, Windows NT, Mac 68K, PowerMac | InterVU (www.intervu.net) |
| LiveVideo | Windows 3.1, Windows 95, Windows NT | Netscape (www.netscape.com) |
| Maczilla | Mac 68K, PowerMac | Knowledge Engineering (maczilla.com) |
| Moviestar | Mac 68K, PowerMac, Windows 3.1, Windows 95, Windows NT | Intelligence at Large (www.ialsoft.com) |
| Net Toob Stream | Windows 3.1, Window 95, Windows NT | Duplexx Software (www.duplexx.com) |
| Quicktime | Mac 68K, PowerMac, Windows 3.x, Windows 95, Windows NT | Apple (www.apple.com) |
| RealVideo | Windows 95, Windows NT, PowerMac, UNIX | Progressive Networks (www.real.com) |
| VDOLive | Windows 3.x, Windows 95, Windows NT | VDONET (www.vdonet.com) |
| ViewMovie | Mac 68K | Ivan Cavero Belaunde (www.well.com/~ivanski/ viewmovie/docs.html) |
| ViVoActive | Windows 3.x, Windows 95, Windows NT, PowerMac | Vivo Software (www.vivo.com) |
| Web Theater | Windows 95, Windows NT | Vxtreme (www.vxtreme.com) |

**32**

PLUG-INS

The video standards for the World Wide Web are Video for Windows (AVI) and Quicktime (QTW). MPEG video has also gained some popularity. However, you're more likely to see videos saved as or converted to animated GIFs because this type is seeing wider use on Web sites.

You can include video links in your Web pages, or you can choose some of the more exciting methods of streaming video and live Web cameras.

The simplest way to add video is to just provide a hypertext link to your video file, in this case, an AVI:

```
<A href="video/yfronts.avi">Mr. Humphries</A>
```

The user clicks the link, Mr. Humphries, and the file called `yfronts.avi` starts downloading from the video directory. An external player starts up outside of the browser.

Streaming Video is a video-on-demand concept that holds some great potential. No longer do users have to wait to view a video. Streaming video starts playing after only a short portion is downloaded. Data continues to download while the user experiences the video.

Corporations such as Sybase are using RealVideo to deliver messages from their CEOs. (See Figure 32.4.) Their employees also use the RealPlayer plug-in as a company training device.

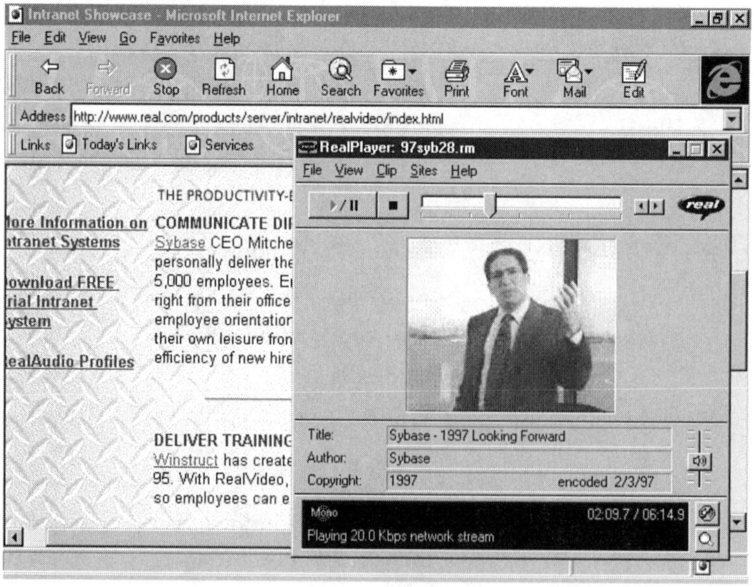

**FIGURE 32.4.**

*Sybase CEO, Mitchell Kertzman, uses RealVideo to deliver his 1997 outlook message to employees.*

The problem with plug-ins such as RealVideo is that the technology isn't quite there yet. Play-back speed is considerably less than 30fps (frames per second), the normal speed required to give the appearance of motion. Many of the RealVideos on the Web right now resemble low-quality slide shows when viewed over regular telephone lines. If there is a lot of motion or are a lot of screen transitions, the viewer almost needs Dramamine.

For about $1000, you can get Progressive Networks' EasyStart Server to run your own stream-ing video and audio solutions. A free alternative is pseudo-streaming over a standard HTTP Web server. No additional software or hardware is required for this method. However, Pro-gressive Networks calls it *pseudo-streaming* because, although you get streaming media, the quality is not optimized like it would be on one of their servers. That's a scary thought—especially when you view some of the bad video samples running from their servers. But the company insists that the pseudo-streaming should be good enough for personal Web sites running on a standard Web server.

If you go this last route, you will need to get your ISP system administrator to set up the RealVideo MIME types for the server. (You might also have him set up the RealAudio MIME types.)

After you have the server question solved, you're ready to add the streaming video to your home page. For this example, we'll link over to an existing RealVideo site by placing the anchor ref-erence on our home page:

```
<a href="http://ramhurl.real.com/cgi-bin/ramhurl.cgi?ram=comea.rm">Dr. Katz</a>
```

When selected, this link executes a CGI script on the `ramhurl.real.com` server. The actual stream-ing video link is located in a metafile called `comea.rm`, and the RealPlayer plug-in is launched when it encounters the `.rm` file extension.

The Dr. Katz video (see Figure 32.5) has good timing and pacing that makes good use of RealVideo's shortcomings. But then, a good comedian is an expert in the art of timing. This video and the Comedy Central site are worth checking out.

RealVideo has strong support from studios showing trailers of upcoming movies, TV networks trying to give an ailing sitcom new life, and recording artists looking to boost sales and air time. The RealVideo guide (shown in Figure 32.6) lists more than 60 sites that take advantage of the RealPlayer plug-in's video capabilities.

Web cameras, or Web cams for short, use a live Internet link to provide "as it happens" video for the Web voyeur. The problem is, there usually isn't much happening.

Visitors to the Netscape Fishcam spend most of their time waiting for the fish to cross in front of the camera. When one finally does, there is a sense of elation similar to the rare sighting of Bigfoot.

**FIGURE 32.5.**
*Comedy Central's Dr. Katz RealVideo cartoon.*

**FIGURE 32.6.**
*The RealVideo video guide to program listings.*

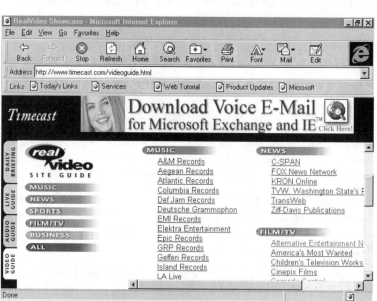

Many of the Web cameras are positioned on street corners, classrooms, and people's computer rooms. Some are used for scientific purposes in sort of a time-lapse photography method of observation.

One site that has an excellent use of the Web cam is the Interactive Model Railroad at the University of Ulm in Germany. (See Figure 32.7.)

**FIGURE 32.7.**

*A live Web camera lets armchair engineers operate model trains in Germany.*

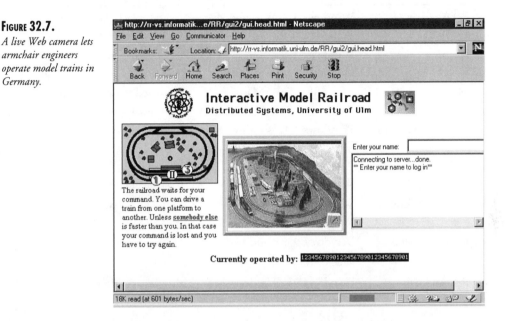

This great little site gives you a clickable map of stations so that you can tell the engineer to which station you want the train moved. You can also select which train you want moved. The video of the train layout refreshes every few seconds to show you the trains switching tracks and moving to the new destination station. Not even Gomez Addams could crash a train on this layout.

## Audio

Audio is being used in a variety of ways. There is background audio that plays a music track or sound when a page is loaded. There are live and prerecorded broadcasts of nightly news and events. Table 32.2 shows some of the audio plug-ins available.

**Table 32.2. Audio plug-ins.**

| Plug-in | Platform | Company |
| --- | --- | --- |
| Crescendo Plus | Windows 3.1, Windows 95 Windows NT, Mac 68K | Liveupdate (`www.liveupdate.com`) |
| Digital Sound & Music Interface | OS/2 | Julian Pierre (`www.polsci.wvu.edu/Madbrain/ npdsmi.html`) |

*continues*

**Table 32.2. continued**

| Plug-in | Platform | Company |
|---------|----------|---------|
| Echospeech | Windows 3.1, Window 95, Windows NT | Echo Speech (`www.echospeech.com`) |
| Koan | Windows 3.1, Windows 95, Windows NT | Sseyo (`www.sseyo.com`) |
| Maczilla | Mac 68K, PowerMac | Knowledge Engineering (`maczilla.com`) |
| Media Player | Windows 3.1, Windows 95, PowerMac, UNIX | Netscape (`www.netscape.com`) |
| MIDIPLUG | PowerMac, Windows 3.1, Windows 95 | Yamaha (`www.yamaha.co.jp/english`) |
| Net Toob Stream | Windows 3.1, Window 95, Windows NT | Duplexx Software (`www.duplexx.com`) |
| RapidTransit | Windows 95, Windows NT, Mac 68K | Fastman (`www.fastman.com`) |
| RealAudio | Windows 95, Windows NT, Mac 68K, PowerMac, UNIX, OS/2 | Progressive Networks (`www.real.com`) |
| WebTracks | Windows 3.1, Windows 95, Mac 68K | Wildcat Canyon Software (`www.wildcat.com`) |

If you have a sound card, you already have the ability to record your own music and sounds for inclusion in your Web pages. Many sound cards, such as the SoundBlaster AWE 32, come with recording studio software. There are also many royalty-free audio clips already available on CD-ROM or on the Net.

The simplest way to take advantage of audio plug-ins is to provide a hypertext link to your sound file, in this case, a wave file (.wav).

```
<A href="audio/dangle.wav">Mrs. Slocombe</A>
```

The user clicks on the link, Mrs. Slocombe, and the file called dangle.wav starts downloading from the audio directory. An external player will pop up outside of the browser. (Refer back to Figure 32.1.)

If you wanted the controls embedded within the browser window (see Figure 32.8), you can use the <EMBED> tag, as follows:

```
<EMBED SRC=" audio/dangle.wav" AUTOSTART=TRUE LOOP=FALSE WIDTH=145 HEIGHT=55>
</EMBED>
```

The EMBED SRC= tag works just like the IMAGE SRC= tag and tells the browser where to find or search for the file. It always works in pairs and ends with the </EMBED> tag. The AUTOSTART=TRUE attribute tells the browser to play the wave file when it loads the page. If you change the attribute to AUTOSTART=FALSE, the user has to click the Play button to hear the sound. The LOOP=FALSE attribute sets the sound file to play through only once. The WIDTH=145 and HEIGHT=55 attributes tell the browser what pixel size to make the audio player's control bar. You could also add alignment attributes such as ALIGN="CENTER".

**FIGURE 32.8.**

*This is how the Audio control appears when embedded within the Web page.*

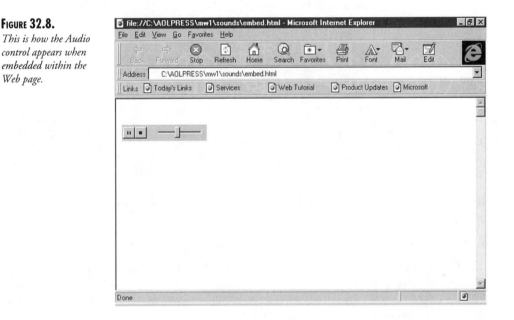

Background audio is also a relatively easy feature to integrate into your Web pages:

```
<bgsound src=totoro.wav loop=3>
```

This code calls out the background sound, totoro.wav, and plays it three times using the loop=3 attribute. Please note that <bgsound> only works with Microsoft Internet Explorer.

**TIP**

Keep background sound files small to reduce your page's load time.

Streaming audio like RealAudio works the same way as its partner, RealVideo. And just like RealVideo, RealAudio files can be played using the RealPlayer. (See Figure 32.9.)

32

PLUG-INS

**FIGURE 32.9.**

*Get the latest ABC Internet Hourly News at 15 minutes past the hour with streaming RealAudio.*

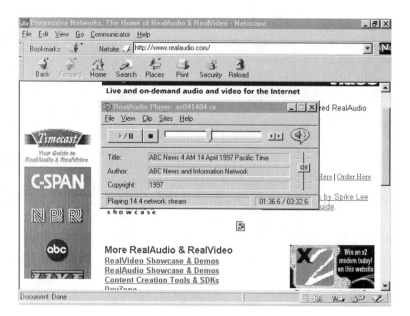

RealAudio files are as easy to include in your Web pages as RealVideo. For this example, we create a link to the ABC Internet News:

```
<a href="http://www.real.com/contentp/abc24/ramfiles/az041612.ram"></a>
```

The RealAudio Player plug-in is automatically started when files with the `.ram` extension are encountered. Actually, this link is to a text metafile that contains the hostname and path or location of the `.ra` (RealAudio) file. In the preceding example, the RealAudio metafile (RAM file) is called `az041612.ram`. This file would only contain a single line of text, such as

```
http://www.startext.net/rafiles/news.ra
```

In this example, the RealAudio file is called `news.ra` and is located in the `rafiles` subdirectory on the Startext ISP server.

Top radio and news networks have joined the RealAudio bandwagon. At the RealAudio home page (`www.realaudio.com`), you will find information heavyweights such as C-SPAN, NPR, and ABC. You can even download a trial version of Progressive Network's EasyStart Server and the free RealAudio Encoder from the RealAudio site.

The RealAudio Encoder enables you to create streaming audio easily. I took a 4MB stereo file and used the Encoder to compress that down to 100KB. Total conversion time was less than five minutes. Even though the encoder saved the audio file as mono, the RealPlayer did some channel magic that still made the sounds in the new file shift around just like they did in the larger original file.

After you create the RealAudio file, you can use HTTP pseudo-streaming to deliver your audio over standard Web servers. (See the earlier discussion in the "Video" section about pseudo-streaming RealVideo.)

The free RealAudio Encoder 3.0 is available for Windows 95, Windows NT, Macintosh PowerPC, Linux, FreeBSD and various UNIX platforms.

# Animation

People traditionally think of Mickey Mouse and Disney when anyone mentions animation. However, Web animation is a huge melting pot of traditional animation, 3D, and multimedia experiences. Plug-ins like those listed in Table 32.3 give Web site developers flexibility as never before.

**Table 32.3. Animation, 3D, and multimedia plug-ins.**

| Plug-in | Platform | Company |
|---------|----------|---------|
| AnimaFlex | Windows 3.1, Windows 95, Windows NT, Mac 68K, PowerMac | RubberFlex Software (www.rubberflex.com) |
| Apple Electrifier | PowerMac | Lari Software (www.electrifier.com) |
| Bubbleviewer | Windows 3.1, Windows 95, Windows NT, PowerMac | Omniview (www.omniview.com) |
| Cosmo Player | Windows 95, Windows NT, UNIX | Silicon Graphics (www.sgi.com) |
| CyberAge Raider | Windows 95, Windows NT | CyberAge Communications (www.miint.net/cyberage) |
| CyberHub Client | Windows 95, Windows NT | Black Sun Interactive (www.blacksun.com) |
| DeepV | Windows 95 | Heads Off (www.headsoff.com) |
| Enliven Viewer | Windows 95, Windows NT | Narrative Communication (www.narrative.com) |
| Flying Carpet | Windows 95, Windows NT | Accelgraphics (www.accelgraphics.com) |
| HyperStudio | Windows 95, Mac 68K, PowerMac | Roger Wagner Publishing (www.hyperstudio.com) |
| IconAuthor | Windows 3.1, Windows 95 | Aimtech (www.aimtech.com) |

*continues*

32

PLUG-INS

**Table 32.3. continued**

| Plug-in | Platform | Company |
|---------|----------|---------|
| Jutvision | Windows 95, Windows NT | Visdyn Software Corp. (www.visdyn.com) |
| Live3D | Windows 3.1, Windows 95, PowerMac | Netscape (www.netscape.com) |
| mBED | Windows 95, Windows NT, Mac 68K, PowerMac | mBED (www.mbed.com) |
| Multimedia Home Space Viewer | Windows 3.1, Windows 95, Windows NT, Mac 68K, PowerMac | Paragraph International (www.paragraph.com) |
| Surround Video | Windows 95, Windows NT, PowerMac | Black Diamond (www.bdiamond.com) |
| NetMC | Windows 95, Windows NT | NEC Systems Laboratory (netmc.neclab.com) |
| OLiVR Viewer | Windows 95, Windows NT, PowerMac | OLiVR (www.olivr.com) |
| RealiView | Windows 95, Windows NT | Datapath Limited (www.realimation.com) |
| RealVR | Windows 95, Windows NT, PowerMac | RealSpace (www.rlspace.com) |
| Shockwave | Windows 3.1, Windows 95, Windows NT, Mac 68K | Macromedia (www.macromedia.com) |
| Shockwave Flash | Windows 3.1, Windows 95, Windows NT, Mac 68K, PowerMac | Macromedia (www.macromedia.com) |
| Sizzler | Windows 3.1, Windows 95, Windows NT, Mac 68K, PowerMac | Totally Hip Software (www.totallyhip.com) |
| SmoothMove | Windows 95, Windows NT | Infinite Pictures (www.smoothmove.com) |
| TopGun | Windows 95 | 7th Level (www.7thlevel.com) |
| Viscape | Windows 95, Windows NT | Superscape (www.superscape.com) |
| VR Scout | Windows 3.1, Windows 95, Windows NT | Chaco Communications (www.chaco.com) |

| Plug-in | Platform | Company |
|---------|----------|---------|
| Vrealm | Windows 95, Windows NT | Integrated Data Systems (`www.ids-net.com`) |
| Web-Active | Mac 68K, PowerMac | Plastic Thought (`www.3d-active.com`) |
| WebXpresso | Windows 95, Windows NT, UNIX | Dataviews (`www.dvcorp.com`) |
| Whurlplug | PowerMac | Apple (`www.apple.com`) |
| WIRL | Windows 95, Windows NT | VREAM (`www.vream.com`) |

Three of the most popular animation and interactive plug-ins are Shockwave, Surround Video, and WIRL.

## Shockwave

The Shockwave plug-in enables users to experience "shocked" pages. (See Figure 32.10.) Shocked sites can have interactive animation, audio, and multimedia. The newest version of the Shockwave plug-in also gives the Web site visitors all this in a streaming format. AOL, Pointcast, and Marimba's Castanet are just some of the more well-known sites that contain Shockwave content.

**FIGURE 32.10.**

*This shocked page lets kids play dress up with gapgirl.*

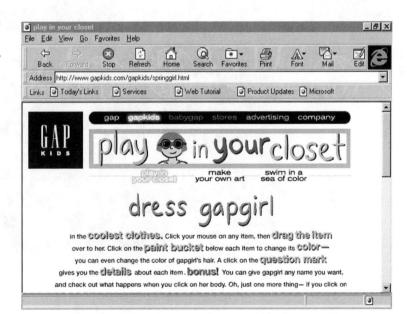

Director from Macromedia (www.macromedia.com) is one of the most popular methods for creating high-quality streaming interactive multimedia for games, interactive presentations, and CD-quality audio and movies for shocked Web pages.

One problem with Shockwave presentations on shocked pages is they usually take so long to load that you've lost your audience. Most people won't wait five minutes for a page to load, and I've found most pages with Shockwave movies take much longer than that. Shockwave has excellent potential, but it is best to keep the "shocking" simple and the files small.

## Surround Video

Surround Video is a rising star in the 3D video arena. So why isn't this plug-in listed in the video category? Well, Surround Video works more like a photo-realistic 3D world viewer or animation than a true video.

Black Diamond (www.bdiamond.com) has created the Surround Video SDK (software developers kit) that can create 360-degree interactive panoramic video from any film-based, digital, or 360-degree camera. Surround Video also supports Visual Basic and JavaScript for added flexibility. Many educational and commercial groups have already found an application for this new technology. At CarPoint, potential buyers can use the Surround Video plug-in to check out the luxurious interior and instrumentation of a BMW. (See Figure 32.11.)

**Figure 32.11.**

*An interactive Surround Video inside a BMW 5-Series at CarPoint.*

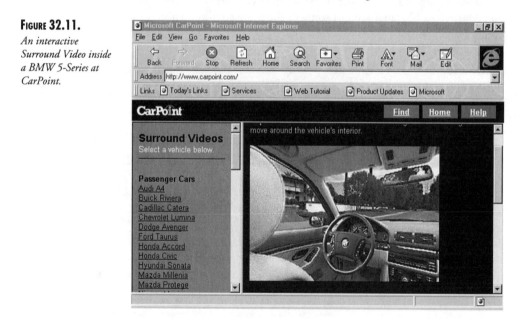

Surround Video loads quickly enough to get users into the driver's seat before they get a chance to surf on to the next site.

## WIRL

Plug-ins like VREAM's WIRL immerse users in VR (Virtual Reality) Worlds. An excellent Titanic site created by Macedon Mediature Inc. (`www.mediature.com/titanic/`) has several VRML images of the Titanic. (See Figure 32.12.)

**FIGURE 32.12.**

*VR plug-ins let users check out a virtual Titanic.*

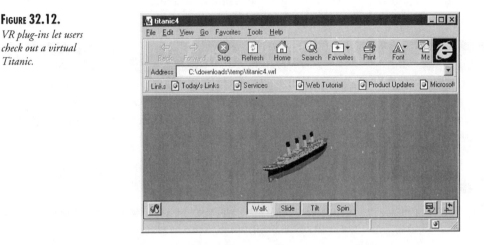

Getting VR worlds onto your home page is as easy creating a hypertext link:

```
<a href="vrworlds/titanic4.wrl">
```

The VRML plug-ins will launch a new browser frame or start up its own external viewer when it encounters the `titanic4.wrl` file. One of the most common file extensions for virtual worlds is `.wrl`.

## Cosmo Player

One of the most popular VRML world viewers is Cosmo Player from Silicon Graphics (SGI). SGI really put its graphics technology background to work in the Cosmo Player and 3D world authoring tools.

Many VR worlds are limited to a clunky environment with the occasional 2D photo and HTML site link. However, one slick feature of the Cosmo Player and the Cosmo VR creation tools is the capability to create worlds containing 3D spatialized audio. Video can also be embedded into these virtual worlds.

Unlike some VR viewers, the Cosmo Player's constant frame rates translate to smoother interaction with large VR worlds. A few other viewers appear to have problems even at the most simple object level. Count in Java support with the package, and you walk away with some awesome authoring possibilities.

## Animated GIFs

Some tools can convert AVIs to Animated GIFs, such as GifBuilder 0.4. This freeware package enables Macintosh users to create animated GIFs from a variety of input. It can import PICT, GIF, TIFF, or Photoshop images and convert Quicktime movies. Smartdubbing is another freeware Mac package for converting Quicktime movies to animated GIFs. GIF Construction Set is a great animated GIF authoring tool for Windows.

> **NOTE**
>
> Animated GIFs play back at a higher rate on the Microsoft Internet Explorer than on Netscape Navigator. Consider which browser you want your audience to use when creating animated GIFs. Also, be sure to include one of those "This site best viewed with..." statements so that the animation will play back as intended.

## External Applications

Still haven't found a plug-in to match up with what you need? Maybe you should roll your own. An easy way to do this is to use existing applications as plug-ins.

Almost any software application can be used as a plug-in for graphical browsers. Good examples are Microsoft Word and Microsoft PowerPoint files.

Say I have a family history database that was created in Family Tree Maker for Windows. I want to share this database with other users of the same software package. To do this, I would just copy the Sessums data file to my Web site and provide a link from my home page, such as this:

```
<a href="tree/sessums.ftw">Kader Sessums database for Family Tree Maker</a>
```

With the user's browser properly configured, Family Tree Maker for Windows is opened when the browser encounters a file with the `.ftw` extension.

Microsoft's Internet Explorer is more application savvy than Netscape Navigator. Most registered file types, such as `.doc` for Word or `.ppt` for PowerPoint, will make Internet Explorer 4.0 launch the appropriate application without asking the user any questions. Netscape Navigator, however, requires the user to configure these helper applications manually.

We can't leave a discussion on application plug-ins without looking at the most widely accepted one, Adobe's Acrobat Reader. Many documents are being converted to Adobe's Portable Document Format (PDF) for presentation and delivery on the Web. The point of PDF is to let documents keep the same look and feel as the original document. Images, layout, and fonts stay intact.

One easy way to get your documents into PDF is to save them as PostScript. You can then use a product such as Distiller to convert the PostScript files into PDF. These files are then viewed with the Acrobat Reader plug-in from Adobe (www.adobe.com).

To include an Acrobat file in your home page, simply make a link to your PDF document:

```
<a href="documents/nascar.pdf">Nascar Season Stats</a>
```

In this example, the nascar.pdf file would launch Acrobat Reader and open the file in my documents directory. My Web visitor could now view my Nascar Season Stats.

So what is the benefit of serving up your existing documents as PDF rather than in their native file format? The biggest advantage is universal acceptance.

Not every user will have the software package in which you created your file. Most will not run out and purchase the software just to view it. On the other hand, if your document were available in PDF, the user could view it with the free Acrobat Reader. The reader is available for Windows 3.1, Windows 95, Windows NT, OS/2, and various flavors of UNIX.

## Multilingual Support

Some sites need to publish their information in languages other than English. Companies looking toward world trade and individuals looking for rich Web content in their own language can all benefit from multilingual Web pages.

However, the special characters involved in some languages can present a real problem. Luckily, Microsoft Internet Explorer 4.0 and Netscape Navigator 4.0 include multilingual support, so a Japanese Web site looks like Japanese and not gibberish.

The Microsoft Internet Explorer 4.0 supports 98 language character sets from Afrikaans to Zulu. I never realized there were 19 varieties of Spanish! Compare this to Internet Explorer 3.0, which only supports five language character sets: Chinese (simplified and traditional), Japanese, Korean, and Pan European. Users also are required to install the separate Multilingual Support packs just like they would regular plug-ins for earlier versions of Netscape.

Netscape Navigator 4.0 supports only 10 language character sets. These include Western (Latin), Central European, Japanese, Chinese, Korean, Cyrillic, Greek, and Turkish. The editor on Netscape Navigator Gold even supports multibyte input for creating Japanese, Korean, and Chinese pages.

Figure 32.13 shows what happens when your browser doesn't support a Web site's character set.

Figure 32.14 shows what you will see when your browser is savvy enough to speak the language.

32

PLUG-INS

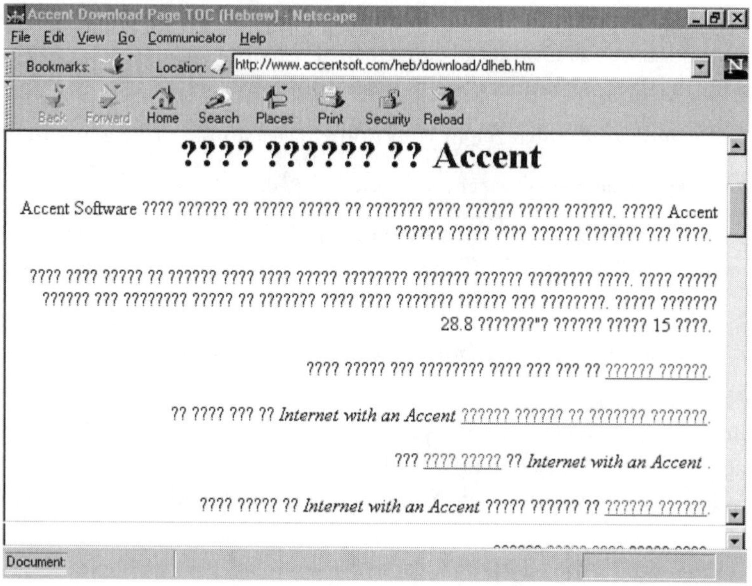

**FIGURE 32.13.**

*Netscape Navigator 4.0
doesn't support
Hebrew.*

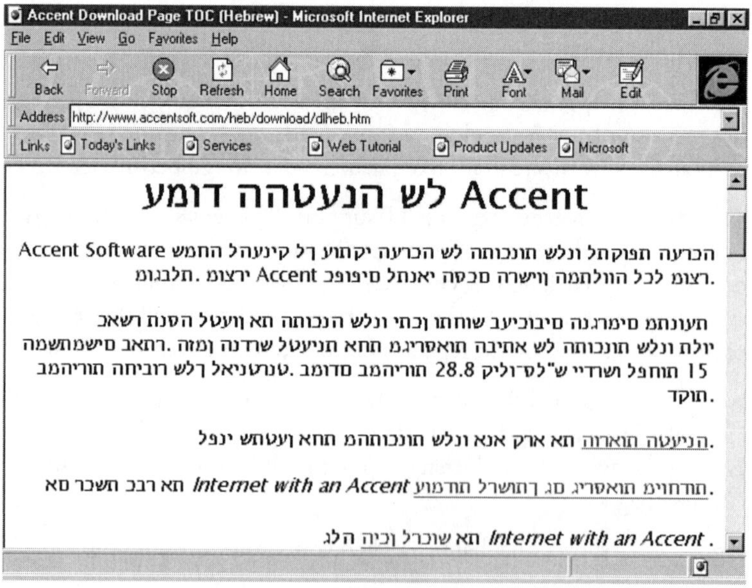

**FIGURE 32.14.**

*Internet Explorer 4.0 is
at home even with
Hebrew.*

A possible solution for the Netscape Navigator problem would be to seek out yet another plug-in by a third-party software group. Navigate with an Accent, available from Accent Software (www.accentsoft.com), extends Netscape Navigator's language savvy from 10 to 30. Quite a nice add-on for the world traveler. It even includes Hebrew.

Now that you've found the multilingual plug-ins, you need to create some content to take advantage of them. One Web authoring package that lets you do this is Internet With An Accent by Accent Software. Its Accent Global Author enables you to create Web pages in 30 different languages. Of course, you have to be able to write and understand those languages.

> **NOTE**
>
> Although Accent Global Author is designed to work under any language version of Windows 3.1 or Windows 95, it has only been tested under English and Hebrew versions of these operating systems. Web authors using other language versions might want to download the free demo from Accent Software before making a commitment.

Web authors might find translation software such as Power Translator 6.0 from Globalink very handy. This package handles translation of English, French, German, Italian, and Spanish at up to 20,000 words per hour. Thank goodness most Web sites aren't that wordy! Be aware, though, that translation software like this uses templates for translation and might not be 100 percent accurate. The only way to be sure is to be somewhat familiar with the language to which you are translating.

After you get your alternate page created, you'll want to create a link on at least your home or top-level page that enables users to quickly switch to the language of their preference. Accent Software uses national flags as clickable links to make language identification and navigation easy. (See Figure 32.15.)

**FIGURE 32.15.**

*Users click a flag to get a duplicate of this page in that country's native language.*

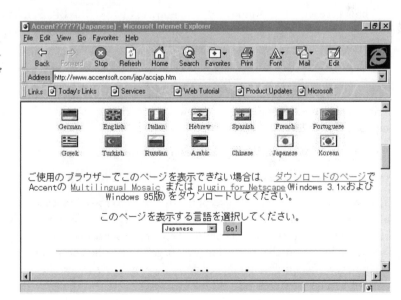

By providing a multilingual site, you will not only increase the audience for your message or product, you will gain appreciation from users whose primary language is not English.

## Net Communications and Power Meetings

A new level of technical support and site interaction has arrived, thanks to Net communication tools. Tables 32.4 and 32.5 show a few of the more popular communication plug-ins.

**Table 32.4. Video teleconferencing.**

| Plug-in | Platform | Company |
| --- | --- | --- |
| CU-SeeMe | Windows | Cornell University (`cu-seeme.cornell.edu`) |
| NetMeeting | Windows | Microsoft (`www.microsoft.com`) |
| VideoPhone | Mac, Windows | Connectix (`www.connectix.com`) |
| WebPhone | Windows, OS/2 | NetSpeak (`www.netspeak.com`) |

**Table 32.5. Net phones and text conferencing.**

| Plug-in | Platform | Company |
| --- | --- | --- |
| OnLive! Talker | Windows 95 | OnLive Technologies (`www.onlive.com`) |
| PhoneFree | Windows 95, Windows NT | Big Bits Software (`www.phonefree.com`) |
| PowWow | Windows, OS/2 | Tribal Voice (`www.tribal.com`) |

Tribal Voice, the developer of PowWow, uses its chat tool to offer interactive, live technical support. (See Figure 32.16.)

It is easy to add Web phone and chat capabilities to your own site with PowWow. Here's how:

```
<a href="powwow:msessums@fastlane.net">Call Me on PowWow!</a>
```

This works like any other link, except the user links to powwow:msessums@fastlane.net instead of the usual file location. This portion tells the PowWow plug-in to look up user msessums@fastlane.net on the PowWow server. If msessums@fastlane.net is logged on to the server, the PowWow client software will "page" him. When he answers the page, chatting can begin. If the target user is not logged on to the PowWow server, the user who clicked the chat link will receive a User is not online message.

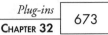

**FIGURE 32.16.**

*PowWow users can get Web phone (voice) support anywhere in the world.*

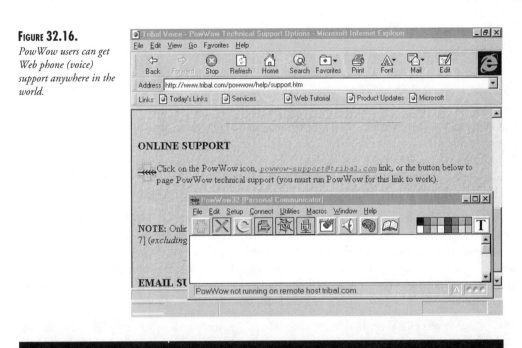

**32**

**PLUG-INS**

---

**TIP**

You might want to include a note that PowWow must be started before Netscape Navigator or Microsoft Internet Explorer for the chat link to work.

---

Network administrators who want to run a private PowWow server on their corporate intranet or from behind their firewall can use the PowWow User Location Server (PULS). This server, which runs on Windows NT networks, costs as much as the regular PowWow client software—it's free.

PowWow users on the public Internet don't see it, but when they start up a PowWow session they are connected to a public PowWow server. This server acts as a transparent-to-user locator service that registers a user's IP address in a look-up table each time the user logs on. A white pages listing at Tribal Voice lets users look up the last 100 users who started up (logged on to) PowWow. Users do one of the following: click the name of the party from the PowWow listing, click a PowWow link from a home page, or type an e-mail address.

---

**NOTE**

PULS is only required to run the PowWow client software on intranets. You don't need PULS to take advantage of PowWow's registration and lookup feature if you are running on a public network. For most Web developers, PowWow is the only software that is needed.

Conference, included in Netscape Communicator 4.0, lets you talk by either voice or keyboard. The problem with the keyboard chat is that you must press the Send button before the other party can see your text. PowWow, on the other hand, allows anyone to whom you are connected simultaneous viewing of any text you type. No Send button to press. Of course, this can be embarrassing if you're a bad typist!

Conference also allows file transfer between users, collaborative browsing, and a white board for sharing ideas (just like on PowWow). By the way, *collaborative browsing* is just a white collar term for group surfing. One person acts as sort of a tour guide and takes control of everyone else's browsers during the surfing session. They can still talk by voice or keyboard chat while they are surfing. The PowWow plug-in is great for this type of interaction, and they did it first.

Microsoft's NetMeeting features file transfer, white board, and keyboard chat, just like Tribal Voice PowWow and Netscape Conference. It also uses directory servers to keep track of users' addresses, similar to those of the PowWow server. But what really sets it apart from the other conference plug-in tools is that users can experience video teleconferencing, share Windows 95 applications, and do some collaborative work on shared files. These features alone make NetMeeting worth checking into, especially for business applications.

CU-SeeMe was one of the first video teleconferencing tools and is still very popular. Combine the freeware or shareware versions of this software with the Connectix QuickCam and video couldn't be easier.

Users can hold a conference with up to eight CU-SeeMe users at a time. The conference display is reminiscent of "Hollywood Squares," where the player boxes are stacked on top of each other.

CU-SeeMe uses reflector sites to connect users. They can also connect one on one if they know the other user's IP address.

Connectix also has its own conferencing software, VideoPhone 2.0. This tool has some basic features of NetMeeting (although Connectix had it first). Users have a shared white board and can use direct-dial connections.

Web browsers can be configured to automatically start Connectix VideoPhone or Connectix VideoPhone Viewer when they encounter files with the .cvp extension on a Web page.

## Other Plug-ins

Other plug-ins are available for various image types (see Table 32.6) and specialized business and professional applications. (See Table 32.7.) These tables in no way constitute a definitive list. Many more plug-ins exist and are being registered with Netscape and Microsoft all the time.

**Table 32.6. Image plug-ins.**

| *Plug-in* | *Platform* | *Company* |
|---|---|---|
| ABC QuickSilver | Windows 95, Windows NT | Micrografx (www.micrografx.com) |
| CMX Viewer (vector graphics viewer) | Windows 95, Windows NT | Corel (www.corel.com) |
| CPC View (TIFF, PBM, and CPC viewer) | Windows 95, Windows NT | Cartesian Products (www.cartesianinc.com) |
| CyberSleuth (displays image author and other data) | Mac 68K | Highwater FBI (www.highwaterfbi.com) |
| Dr. DWG Netview (AutoCAD image viewer) | Windows 3.1, Windows 95, Windows NT | Dr. DWG (www.cswl.com) |
| DWG/DXF (AutoCAD image viewer) | Windows 95, Windows NT | Softsource (www.softsource.com) |
| Fractal Viewer (true-color image viewer) | Windows 3.1, Windows 95, Windows NT, Mac 68K | Iterated Systems (www.iterated.com) |
| Imaging for Internet (FlashPix viewer) | Windows 95, Windows NT | Hewlett-Packard (www.hp.com) |
| InterCAP Inline (CGM viewer) | Windows 95, Windows NT | InterCAP Graphics Systems (www.intercap.com) |
| Lightning Strike (wavelet image codec) | Windows 3.1, Windows 95, Windows NT, Mac 68K, UNIX | Infinop (www.infinop.com) |
| LuRaWave (wavelet image viewer) | Windows 95, Windows NT, PowerMac | LuRaTech (www.luratech.de/ luratech_e.html) |
| MetaWeb CGM Viewer (CGM viewer) | Windows 3.1, Windows 95, Windows NT | Ematek/HSI (www.ematek.com) |

*continues*

**32**

PLUG-INS

**Table 32.6. continued**

| Plug-in | Platform | Company |
|---------|----------|---------|
| NetWriter Viewer (view NetWriter images) | Windows 3.1, Windows 95, Windows NT | Paragraph International (www.paragraph.com) |
| Pegasus (JPEG viewer) | Windows 3.1, Windows 95 | Pegasus Imaging (www.jpg.com) |
| PNG Live (PNG viewer) | Windows 95, Windows NT, PowerMac | Siegel & Gale (www.siegelgale.com) |
| SVF (CAD viewer) | Windows 95, Windows NT | SoftSource (www.softsource.com) |
| TruDef (views 12 graphics formats) | Windows 3.1, Windows 95, Windows NT | TruDef Technologies (www.trudef.com) |
| ViewDirector (TIFF viewer) | Windows 95, Windows NT | TMS Inc. (www.tmsinc.com) |
| Visual WebMap 2D (CAD, IGDS, DGN, and GIS map viewer) | Windows 3.1, Windows 95, Windows NT | Project Development (hem.passagen.se/project) |
| Watermark Webseries (TIFF viewer) | Windows 95, Windows NT | FileNet (www.filenet.com) |
| Wavelet Image Viewer (Wavelet viewer) | Windows 3.1, Windows 95, Windows NT, Mac 68K, PowerMac | Summus Ltd. (www.summus.com) |
| Whip! (AutoCAD viewer) | Windows 95, Windows NT | Autodesk (www.autodesk.com) |

**Table 32.7. Business and professional plug-ins.**

| Plug-in | Platform | Company |
|---------|----------|---------|
| AboutPeople (dynamic address book) | Windows 95, Mac 68K, PowerMac | Now Software (www.nowsoft.com) |
| AboutTime (dynamic calendar) | Windows 95, Mac 68K, PowerMac | Now Software (www.nowsoft.com) |
| Autodesk MapGuide (vector-based mapping solution) | Windows 3.1, Windows 95, Windows NT | Autodesk (www.autodesk.com) |

| *Plug-in* | *Platform* | *Company* |
|---|---|---|
| Carbon Copy/Net (remote Windows access) | Windows 3.1, Windows 95 | Microcom (www.microcom.com) |
| Chemscape Chime (views 2D/3D chemical structures) | Windows 3.1, Windows 95, Windows NT, Mac 68K, PowerMac | MDL Information Services (www.mdli.com) |
| Citrix Winframe Client (Windows apps interface) | Windows 3.1, Windows 95, Windows NT | Citrix (www.citrix.com) |
| Day-Timer Organizer (electronic organizer) | Windows 3.1, Windows 95 | Day-Timer Technologies (www.daytimer.com) |
| EarthTime (world time) | Windows 95, Windows NT | Starfish Software (www.starfishsoftware.com) |
| Envoy (document viewer) | Windows 3.1, Windows 95, Windows NT, Mac 68K, PowerMac | Tumbleweed Software (www.tumbleweed.com) |
| Intermind Communicator (electronic communications automation) | Windows 3.1, Windows 95, Windows NT | Intermind (www.intermind.com) |
| Netopia Virtual Office (collaborative Web office) | Windows 3.1, Windows 95, Windows NT | Farallon (www.farallon.com) |
| Nobelnet Opener (Web distribution for apps) | Windows 3.1, Windows 95 | Noblenet (www.noblenet.com) |
| PointCast Network (receives news and information) | Windows 3.1, Windows 95 | PointCast Inc. (www.pointcast.com) |
| Quick View Plus (manipulates more than 200 file formats) | Windows 3.1, Windows 95, Windows NT | Inso Corp. (www.inso.com) |
| ScriptActive (active scripting solution) | Windows 95, Windows NT | Ncompass (www.ncompasslabs.com) |
| Surfbot (auto Web site content retrieval) | Windows 95, Windows NT | Surflogic (www.surflogic.com) |

**32**

**PLUG-INS**

# Summary

You've seen that a multitude of plug-ins support just about every conceivable Web application. It's even possible to set up various programs as plug-ins if you still can't find the one you need.

Although it would be impossible to keep up with all the plug-ins and controls available, you've also seen that only a few have gained wide acceptance.

One thing to remember when developing your Web site is don't use a feature supported by plug-ins simply to use it. Plan out what you want to do on your Web site, and then check to see whether there are plug-ins and creation tools to make your plans a reality.

# HTML and Databases

*by Michael A. Larson*

**CHAPTER**

**33**

With the popularity of the Internet and the rise in use of intranets, many people, individually or in a variety of institutions, are trying to find the best means to take the massive amount of information they have in their databases and make it available to people via a browser. These people run into a problem because most databases, both large and small, were never designed to dish out HTML pages or work with a Web server. Fortunately, a wide range of solutions are available to meet the wide range of needs—from someone on a standalone computer converting database forms, reports, and queries to HTML all the way up to the enterprise level where information systems (IS) personnel have to port very complex, standalone mission-critical applications over to a Web server/browser environment.

HTML is, unfortunately, of little help to database engineers. The language was not designed with database integration in mind. The closest database functionality you can find in HTML proper is the table structure of rows (records) and columns (fields). Another structure, HTML forms, also mimics some of the capability of a database form but with far less functionality and flexibility, and often requiring a whole lot more non-HTML programming to perform simple database-like tasks such as entering the contents of an HTML form into a database. The only other benefits of HTML in relation to databases are that it is a simple set of tags and its file format is straight ASCII, which most databases can easily write to.

One means of communication between databases and HTML that is widely used today is the common gateway interface (CGI). Many lines of CGI script, however, are needed to link each field in an HTML form to a database. This requires a great deal of programming and any modifications can be very labor intensive. This particular problem might be one of the main reasons for the slow integration of databases onto Web sites by commercial and business enterprises.

So you end up with a gulf between databases (many originally engineered to be proprietary, closed systems) not designed to be used in the open environment of the Web and a Web language that was never designed to be used with databases. The means by which many vendors have chosen to fill this gulf is the subject of this chapter.

As I mentioned earlier, there is a broad gradient of problems and needs when an individual or an enterprise thinks about putting database information on a web. Some common problems discussed in this chapter include

- How to get information from established database forms, reports, or queries into the HTML format—at a minimum, into an HTML table and preferably into a customized, more attractive format, such as those typically generated with database report modules.

- How to dynamically query a database from a Web browser and return the results in real-time in a format the browser can read, which is usually HTML.

- How to port a proprietary, enterprise-wide database application into a Web environment.

- Figuring out how to use the Web as a cross-platform tool for tying together the hodgepodge of database systems and platforms typical of many enterprises today. In this case, the problem is actually turned to become the solution.

If you have done any database programming at all, you know that solutions to any of the preceding problems have to be accomplished with a high level of security and confidence that the information in any given database will not be compromised, corrupted, or accessed without permission. Internet proponents tout the need for the ultimate in data availability: Make all information available all of the time to everyone. Database engineers have a very different requirement, often imposed by the institution owning the database: Maintain the integrity of databases that may contain decades of valuable information, and make information available only to those who have the necessary clearance to view it. Bringing these two opposing approaches together in a harmonious solution is a significant challenge, requiring unique approaches and development tools.

I discuss these integration problems on a vendor-by-vendor basis. Each vendor has a solution that addresses all or part of the gradient of problems for getting database information onto a web. Most vendors not only offer a solution for their particular databases, but also one that is inclusive of a wide variety of other databases, database types, and platforms. I discuss the databases and solutions only as they relate to getting database information to HTML and to a lesser degree, to using Java applications to establish communication between the database and browser. Due to both the breadth and depth of currently available database applications and the relative newness of trying to get database information into HTML, I can only cover a few select databases and vendor solutions. My criteria for selecting which vendor solutions to review include the following:

- Market share. Databases that are used by the most people or businesses.
- Increasing market presence. Database solutions that appear to be gaining on the more popular systems.
- Unique technology or approach to tying databases and the Web together.

Be sure to do your own investigations if this is a critical component of your mission. This is by no means the final word. Databases and HTML are a moving target. HTML is also only one component of a web solution involving databases. The solution you choose should also incorporate any other individual or enterprise requirements of the database information.

# Lotus Approach 97

This database component to Lotus SmartSuite (`http://www2.lotus.com/approach.nsf`) has some basic and some very advanced HTML publishing capabilities. For the basic capability, this database represents the simplest solution: Any Approach form, report, table, or chart can be saved to HTML without requiring you to know HTML coding. This is called a static solution because it involves only the single step of translating database objects to HTML. The HTML output will usually be in a less elegant form than its equivalent database object because HTML has fewer formatting options and less flexibility than is built into most databases.

The advanced publishing capabilities in Approach are closely linked with Net.Data, a very powerful Internet tool associated with the IBM DB/2 database; Net.Data is discussed later in this chapter.

Approach also has a built-in Web site database where users can store their favorite URLs as hyperlinks and associate them with keywords of their choosing for easier searching.

# Microsoft Access

In its latest version, Access 97 (`http://www.microsoft.com/access/`) contains a variety of means for getting information from an Access database to a browser. Some solutions work closely with Microsoft's Internet Information Server (IIS), which is related to Peer Web Services on Windows NT Workstation and Personal Web Server under Windows 95, and some do not require a Web server to work.

Access uses two basic approaches to getting database information to Web users: static and dynamic. The *static approach* involves using the Save as HTML wizard from the menu in Access 97 to translate Access reports, queries, and forms to HTML tables. You can insert tables into HTML template files with the use of a special placeholder tag in the template file showing Access where the HTML table should be placed. With the addition of the new Hyperlink data type in Access 97, you can now store active hyperlinks in an Access database. These hyperlinks remain active in native Access objects such as forms and reports or when any Access objects containing them are translated to HTML via the wizard. Access 97 also enables you to import HTML tables or lists (even over the Internet) into existing Access tables, or you can create new tables. You can also link to HTML table data if you don't want to import the data into your database.

Microsoft has two technologies that work in conjunction with its Web server to provide a more dynamic and real-time interaction between a user with a browser and an Access database. The older of these two technologies is called IDC/HTX and the newer is ASP.

IDC is short for Internet database connector. HTX is merely an HTML file that has placeholders telling Access where to place the returned records. IDC/HTX works as a process involving many different parts. The IDC file is a plain-text file containing the data source and the SQL query. An IDC request is initiated from a browser via a request that looks like this:

```
http://MSWebservername/scripts/somefile.idc
```

The file causes a special library called `httpodbc.dll` to be loaded. This library loads the appropriate ODBC (open database connectivity) driver for the data source. The ODBC driver connects to the Access database, enabling the library to send the SQL query in the IDC file to the database. Access runs the query based on the content of the IDC file and sends the result back through the ODBC driver to the library. The library looks in the IDC file to determine which HTX file to use. The library adds the records at the placeholder locations in the HTX files and returns the now complete HTML file to the Web server. The server passes this file back to the browser that initiated the IDC request. This process is not limited to use with Access databases but can also be used with FoxPro, Oracle, and SQL Server databases. It even works with non-database sources such as Excel spreadsheets or delimited text files. As long as you have the proper ODBC driver, have the data source registered with the ODBC driver, and use the proper syntax in the IDC file, you can get data from the data source to a browser. The IDC also provides a means of passing a username and password to the database if this is required.

Microsoft recently put out a similar, but more powerful, technology called ASP (active server pages). ASP uses a process similar to the IDC/HTX process but utilizes only one plain-text file (.asp extension) for both the requesting file and the HTML template return file. In addition to having to deal with only one text file, you can also add programming logic to your requests using either Visual Basic Script or JavaScript. You can also create server-side objects or add ActiveX controls. This is a much more powerful and flexible system than IDC/HTX. Again, this approach relies on Microsoft Web servers and will not work with any other type of Web server at this time.

These two dynamic approaches enable the database designer to add hyperlinks to a Web page pointing toward fixed queries that will return the latest, most commonly requested reports. Or you can couple these technologies with HTML forms to enable a user to specify one or more parameters for the query and have a special report returned to them.

The Access Save as HTML wizard will generate IDC/HTX file pairs or ASP files from Access queries or forms. This wizard can also start the Publish to the Web wizard that will publish an entire set of HTML-translated objects to the Web server, as opposed to saving them locally and then uploading them to your Web site via FTP.

# Sybase

Sybase (http://www.sybase.com) uses a technology called NetImpact Dynamo (http://www.sybase.com/netimpact/internetapps.html) to Web-enable its own databases—Sybase Anywhere and Sybase SQL Server Professional—as well as many others. NetImpact Dynamo uses a dynamic approach for interacting with the database. SQL commands, scripts, and host-variable macros can be placed into any HTML file (called a template) for processing. NetImpact Dynamo also provides tools for HTML authoring, including wizards for producing templates, site management tools, and a Personal Web Server for offline use. The DynaScript language in NetImpact Dynamo is compatible with JavaScript and can be placed either in a module separate from the HTML page or in the HTML page.

When a browser requests an HTML file that is a template, the Web server passes the request to NetImpact Dynamo, which pulls the template from a template repository, processes any scripts or SQL commands via an ODBC source, and passes the results back to the Web server as an HTML page, which is then passed back to the browser.

NetImpact Dynamo supports multiple gateways including CGI, ISAPI (Internet Server Application Programming Interface), and NSAPI (Netscape Server Application Programming Interface) on Windows 95 or Windows NT platforms.

Sybase also has a similar technology for Sun Solaris, IRIX, HPUX, and Windows NT called web.sql. This program also works in a dynamic manner but does not require a gateway to the database; it is directly connected to the Web server and supports its own inline scripting for improved performance. The HTML files processed by web.sql can contain SQL queries and perl5 scripts. The web.sql engine uses the Sybase Open Client API, which allows connections to a wide variety of major databases. CGI and NSAPI are also supported.

# SQL Server

Microsoft's SQL Server (http://www.microsoft.com/sql/inetOverview.htm) dishes out its database information via SQL Web Assistant. The SQL Web Assistant takes a slightly different approach to publishing dynamic information. It uses a wizard-style interface to build and schedule a query. The data source can be selected from a table with a point and click interface, using an SQL statement, or from a stored procedure. The results of that query are then published on a schedule as frequently as needed or in response to data updates in the database. This means that you can publish your data very frequently—which is useful, for instance, in the case of stock quotes—or infrequently, maybe once a week as you might need in the case of summary financial reports. This approach works well for publishing large lists of information such as catalogs, price lists, or inventory.

SQL Server database information can also be placed into a Web environment using the same technology discussed earlier under Microsoft Access, namely using IDC/HTX or ASP dynamic queries in conjunction with ODBC and Microsoft Web servers. Note that the Web Assistant is more of a push model for distributing data, whereas IDC/HTX and ASP represent more of a pull model, providing multiple options for getting information from an SQL Server database into a form viewable by anyone with a browser.

# Oracle

Oracle's solution for getting database information into HTML centers around its Developer/ 2000 report writing module (http://www.oracle.com/support/products/dev2k/win/html/index.html). This product can be used with Oracle databases or as a standalone application compatible with many other database systems on many platforms, including all flavors of Windows, Macintosh, and UNIX/Motif, as well as the new networking computers (NCs), also known as thin clients. Developer/2000 performs two Web-related functions: generating HTML output for any report (PDF output is also available) and processing HTML forms.

HTML reports are generated by simply telling Developer/2000 to output to the HTML format. Any chart can also be output as a GIF for use on an HTML page. As in Microsoft Access, any layout object can have a URL associated with it. In addition to generating HTML reports, Oracle's newer WebServer Version 3.0 contains the Web Library. This library is a repository for all Web site objects (HTML, images, Java applets, and so on) that provides security, version-stamping, and other site or file management features.

An HTML form built by Developer/2000 contains an embedded Java applet (the Forms Client) that is downloaded to the browser when the HTML page with the form is called. The Web server then serves as an intermediary between the Forms Client and the Oracle Forms runtime engine (the Application server). In an intranet situation, the Application Server communicates with the database via a remote procedure call (RPC) and back directly with the Forms Client. In an Internet situation, communication between the Web server and the application server is via CGI or a cartridge mechanism if the Web server is an Oracle product. Both of these situations provide a convenient means of using a browser to trade information directly with an Oracle database. This model is an Internet extension to the idea of building and deploying customized database applications, usually on an enterprise-wide basis.

# IBM DB/2

Big Blue has updated and enhanced its DB/2 WWW Connection program and renamed it Net.Data (`http://www.software.ibm.com/data/net.data/`). Net.Data covers a wide range of functions, from creating dynamic Web pages via SQL to building enterprise-strength Web applications. Net.Data includes native support (read "faster performance") for DB2, Oracle, and Sybase as well as ODBC access to other data sources, including Lotus Notes, Microsoft databases, SQL Server, and Informix. Flat file data can also be accessed and updated. Net.Data supports APIs for IBM Internet Connection Web Servers (ICAPI), Netscape Servers (NSAPI), and Microsoft Internet Information Servers (ISAPI). Net.Data has several language environments from which to access DB2 databases—REXX, Perl, Java, or C++ applications—for maximum flexibility.

A key component to the cascade of events that Net.Data uses to obtain information from the database or applications is a Web macro. A Web macro is a combination of HTML, a macro language, and language environment-specific statements that can be from SQL, Perl, or REXX. An `.INI` file also is needed for details on your language environment, paths, and so on.

Several layers of security in Net.Data make it a very security-conscious environment for these types of database and browser interactions. Not only can you have authentication (username/password), but you can encrypt data with Secure Sockets Layer (SSL) or Secured HyperText Transfer Protocol (SHTTP). The system also works effectively behind a firewall.

Because you can call just about any application or library from within the Web macro as well as perform SQL queries, Net.Data is ideally suited for enterprise applications. It leverages your existing applications and databases, providing a straightforward means to make a wide variety of information available on the Internet or the company intranet. This package is well-suited for the professional programmer and might be daunting for the casual database user or programmer.

# Centura (formerly Gupta)

The Centura Web Developer (`http://www.centurasoft.com/products/development/web_developer/`) can be used to build applications that generate static HTML pages, dynamic HTML pages, or full-blown business enterprise applications, which is the main focus of the package. It can use ODBC interfaces or use NSAPI or ISAPI across many different database types.

The Web Developer system requires a Web server, an application server, and a data server. After a Web Developer application has been built, debugged, and compiled, it is placed on the application server. A URL request from a browser for the application passes to the Web server, which passes the request to the application server, and the application is started. The application server returns the "address" of the application process to the browser via the Web server, and any subsequent interaction occurs directly between the browser and the application process. When the process is completed, results are returned to the browser, or another process is started.

Web Developer supports multiple levels of security, including authentication, encryption, and firewalls. Again, this package is geared toward professional programmers who need to produce complete business solutions that might include a Web component.

For optimal security, Centura recommends replicating your databases to an SQLBase that lives on the Web server outside the firewall to make your database information available to Internet users and leave your primary databases untouched behind a firewall.

# Computer Associates International

CAI has two major solutions for deploying database information on a web: OpenIngres/Internet Commerce Enabled (ICE) (`http://www.cai.com/products/unicent/ice.htm`) and Jasmine (`http://www.cai.com/products/jasmine.htm.bkp`) databases. As with many other packages, solutions developed with these systems will work across databases in a variety of formats, both SQL and nonrelational databases, and across many platforms.

ICE supports both static and dynamic HTML report generation through its Report Writer. Dynamic reports utilize all of the conditional processing and multimedia available to its standard database reports. The output of existing Report Writer files can be wrapped in HTML with Report Writer.

ICE also provides an additional level of interactivity via Dynamic SQL that allows for the easy integration of commercial, online transactions or ordering systems into a Web site. ICE is closely tied with the Spyglass Web server or can use CGI on other Web servers to parse the HTML file or initiate the Report Writer for HTML output back to the browser.

CAI's second solution, Jasmine, specializes in handling multimedia content. The Jasmine Application Development Environment (JADE) will build rich multimedia applications that can be deployed on any web and viewed in a browser through the use of a plug-in. JADE is the database equivalent to Macromedia's Director, but it has more of a business and technical orientation. JavaScript or VBScript can be used to interact with the Jasmine application within a browser.

CAI's Unicenter (`http://www.cai.com/products/unicent/unicpd.htm`) enterprise-level management systems also have some powerhouse Web site management capabilities for those dealing with complex and fast-growing Web sites. With extensive monitoring, reporting, and administrative capabilities, you can watch all aspects of your web for problems. Event and security management tools enable you to define the severity of any problems, allowing you to apply the proper solution in the proper time frame. You can define all objects on a Web site as assets and control access to them by developers and reviewers, even on a scheduled basis. Other tools are available for performance and storage management. This represents the widest extension of database technology to cover all aspects of Web site development and maintenance.

# Informix

Informix (`http://www.informix.com`) has allied itself with Netscape to provide an Internet solution from an application perspective rather than as a means of generating HTML pages. The Informix database is the foundation of 20 out of the 21 business applications that compose Netscape's AppFoundry. These applications in turn are based on Netscape ONE technologies, providing nonplatform-specific business applications. AppFoundry also includes several powerful enterprise development tools—Borland's IntraBuilder and NetObjects Fusion, among others—for building entire Web sites, Internet or intranet, based on Netscape ONE.

The Informix OnLine Workgroup Server database is also ODBC-compliant and can be used as a data source for IDC/HTX or ASP queries for publishing dynamic content.

# Summary

As you've seen, a vast array of solutions are available for getting database information into HTML. Interestingly, most of the solutions are not locked into a single database on a single platform but usually cover a wide range of databases including relational, flat-file, and nonrelational types. This is probably indicative of the fact that any enterprise that has been integrating computers into its processes over the last 20 years or even longer has a menagerie of systems and databases and thus needs a wide-ranging solution if it wants to make much of its information available on the Internet.

Solutions start with the simple, static translation of database objects (forms, reports, tables, queries, and so on) to HTML pages with varying degrees of control over the output. In fact, the simplest HTML solution available for turning a database report into an HTML file is to use the `Print#` command found in most databases to hardcode the HTML tags into the report and output the report to disk. Of course, you have to learn HTML tags.

Dynamic solutions enable users to send variables to a database and receive information that they can read from a browser. This solution is the most powerful because the user can be on a completely different platform from the database and still have access to that information, which creates an instant cross-platform solution with minimal programming. Cross-platform solutions with tighter integration between the client browser and the database are possible by sending Java applets to the client machine. You can even use targeted database tools to manage an entire Web site.

With this range of solutions, any business, government agency, institution, or individual can make a database available on the Internet. Good security and flexibility is now built into many browser/database interactions, which means there is minimal threat to the integrity of the database being queried. Custom solutions using multiple programming languages can provide an even tighter link between the browser and the database for companies using the Internet as a wide-area network. There is no technological reason for not deploying a database on the World Wide Web. The simple HTML language and its associated browser has finally made universal database distribution and availability a reality after decades of struggle by monolithic companies with armies of programmers failed. Truly a David and Goliath epic.

# PART

# VI

# Development and Site Tools

# HTML Editors and Utilities

*by Rick Darnell*

There are two ways to create and check HTML. The first is to get your old reliable text editor, type in the tags and content, and then view the results on a browser. If you need to check it for compliance with one of the HTML standards, you get your source code in one hand and the standards in the other.

Although this method certainly works, it's kind of like digging a lateral field for your septic tank with a shovel. It gets the job done, but you expend a lot more time and energy than is really required.

Luckily, we live in a world filled with people who think there are easier ways to do everything. Some of these people have turned their energies to creating editors designed especially for producing HTML and engaging in related activities such as updating pages and verifying syntax.

This chapter covers a handful of those tools. It is by no means a comprehensive list, but it covers the major players and popular products available to Web developers. I've included a range of editors for a variety of platforms, plus a few utilities to help with some of your other tasks. In this and the following chapters, you will get a feel for the many options available to fill your HTML and Web publishing needs.

A wide range of tools is covered here, including the old reliable text-based editors and some of the newest offerings in the WYSIWYG (What You See Is What You Get) category. Web editors haven't really kept up with the pace of the World Wide Web up to this point. But, as you can see with recent offerings from Netscape and Adobe, that situation is quickly changing.

# HTML Editors

There are two basic kinds of editors—HTML source and WYSIWYG. HTML source editors are similar to customized text editors. These editors enable you to insert and edit various tags and content, but you're still working with a bunch of text and tags. You'll need some knowledge of HTML to work with a source editor. Even though many are well documented and provide intuitive support for many tags, a working knowledge of HTML will make the process much easier.

*WYSIWYG* is synonymous with graphical editors. When you add a horizontal rule, you see a horizontal rule on the page, not the <HR> tag. Knowledge of HTML is not as important with this kind of editor, although it never hurts. Depending on the sophistication of the editor, you may want to work directly with the source HTML code to tweak the page to correct idiosyncrasies, such as where tags are nested or to remove empty tags like <H1></H1>.

## PageMill

Long the sole domain of the Apple Macintosh, Adobe PageMill is now also available for Windows 95. It is one of the most popular HTML editing tools on the Macintosh platform and is now making a run at the PC market.

> **TIP**
>
> PageMill is available from Adobe Corporation at www.adobe.com.

Those who use the Macintosh version will recognize their old friend in its new environment. (See Figure 34.1.) The power and functionality are the same, with the addition of several new features. Creating a Web page is as easy as typing and watching the results take shape through the WYSIWYG option. You can switch with a single keystroke to a source-edit mode with color-coded HTML tags. PageMill also provides options for importing word-processing files from several different formats, including Microsoft Word and WordPerfect.

**FIGURE 34.1.**

*PageMill, the popular Web page editing software developed for the Macintosh, is now available for PC users.*

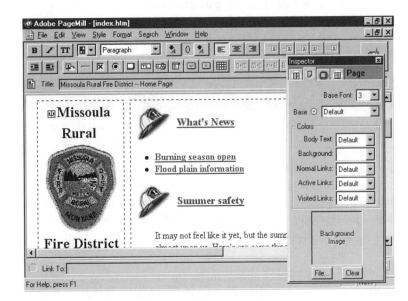

One distinctive editor option is the hidden HTML option, with which you can view items that are normally not displayed for the end user while you edit, such as comments, scripts, and anchors. As with many graphic HTML tools on the market, PageMill also supports the creation of image maps. You can add hyperlinks manually or by dragging them from a browser. Links are live within the editor, which means that you can check them while editing without switching to a browser.

Standard features include spell check, search and replace, and intuitive support for frames and tables. You can create frames and tables using a drag-and-drop interface for both content and specifications, and the results are immediately visible on your editing screen. PageMill also supports importing information from Excel files into HTML table format.

**34**

**HTML EDITORS AND UTILITIES**

Adobe's program has a few quirks. First, it implements HTML headings a bit oddly. Instead of using <H1> through <H6>, PageMill uses Smallest through Largest. Ironically, the world's leading font supplier didn't include support for the <FONT face> attributes.

# HomeSite

The story of HomeSite for Windows is one of those "only in America" stories about a guy and an idea. The guy was a cartoonist who was publishing his work on the World Wide Web but wasn't very happy with the tools he had to work with, beginning with a text editor and moving up to some of the more complex software suites. Nothing had the range of capabilities and features he was looking for, so he set out to create his own.

The result is an author's authoring program that is full featured, easy to use, and sells for a low shareware price. It is every bit the equal of other more sophisticated HTML source authoring tools, but costs much less. It is one of the grassroots favorites among Web authors and is commonly recommended in the HTML newsgroups.

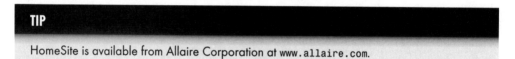

**TIP**

HomeSite is available from Allaire Corporation at www.allaire.com.

Its user interface provides easy access to virtually every HTML element. (See Figure 34.2.) The process is intuitive—place your cursor where tags should appear, and then click a button or select an item from a menu. HomeSite supports the most popular content items, including Java, Netscape plug-ins, and ActiveX, in addition to JavaScript tools for developing scripts. Dialog boxes are provided for most of the tags with extended options, such as <FONT> and <APPLET>.

HomeSite also provides extended support for HTML beyond 3.2, including access to browser-specific tags such as <BGSOUND> for Internet Explorer and <EMBED> for Navigator. In addition, it provides a complete set of additional tools, such as search and replace, spell check, color-coded tags, and document weight. It also includes link validation and frame wizards for quicker construction and maintenance of HTML pages.

**NOTE**

A document's *weight* is the amount of time it requires to download from server to browser. Checking a document's weight is a good rule of thumb to see whether your pages are too loaded with graphics and other special content.

Internet Explorer was apparently the browser of choice for HomeSite's developer because HomeSite defaults to Internet Explorer to view completed pages.

**FIGURE 34.2.**

*HomeSite is an authoring program created by a bona fide HTML author and is one of the grassroots favorites on the World Wide Web.*

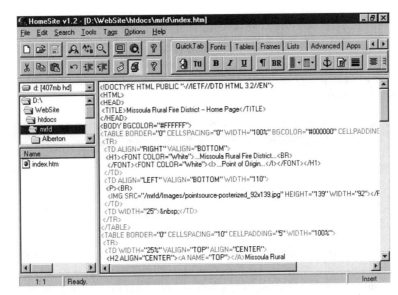

Some of HomeSite's drawbacks come in the site management area. It relies on FTP programs or Microsoft's Web Publishing wizard to move files from the local computer to the Web site. HTML validation is not supported, although you can still use third-party utilities such as HTML Validator.

## BBEdit

BBEdit is the premier text editor for Macintosh programmers and HTML authors. What BBEdit lacks in WYSIWYG (which is currently nonexistent in this product), it makes up for in sheer editing power. BBEdit is fully AppleScriptable, has the capability to find and replace text within many documents at once (which is handy if a link changes or a common element must be updated), and is fully compatible with the Internet Config application to allow simple and seamless integration with your favorite Internet tools including FTP and Web browsers.

A number of BBEdit extensions (most of which you can easily download from the Bare Bones Web site) integrate features found in most other text-based HTML editors. The current champion of the bunch is arguably Lindsay Davies' HTML Tools extensions. This set of extensions allows fast and easy HTML markup using a customizable floating palette and supports most of the HTML tags and attributes used today. These extensions also allow for the addition of user-customized tags with limited scripting. These particular extensions, however, are available and compatible only with the BBEdit Pro version.

As you might have guessed, BBEdit comes in two versions. BBEdit Lite is 100% free and is highly recommended for any Macintosh. BBEdit Pro is not free, but it adds a plethora of features and ships with some of the greatest HTML extensions available. More information, as well as BBEdit Lite and a selection of BBEdit extensions, can be found at http://www.barebones.com/.

# Netscape Navigator Gold

Netscape put together an interesting combination with its Gold version of Navigator, available for Windows, Macintosh, and a variety of UNIX platforms. Netscape combined one of the most popular browsers with an editor to provide integrated page creation and testing under one umbrella.

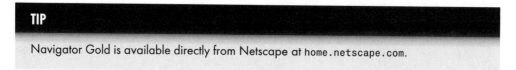

**TIP**

Navigator Gold is available directly from Netscape at home.netscape.com.

Navigator Gold includes support for many HTML 3.2 tags and is tightly integrated with Navigator to easily test and review the finished project.

Working with Navigator Gold is quite easy. It can work with any HTML page—as you surf the Web with the browser side of Navigator Gold, you can click the pencil icon on the toolbar to download the page and its graphics for modification. (See Figure 34.3.) As with any editor, you can also begin with a blank page or work from the various templates and wizards located on Netscape's Web site.

**FIGURE 34.3.**

*Navigator Gold is an enhanced version of the standard Netscape Navigator software. It is a quick and easy way to create Web pages but lacks support for advanced HTML, such as frames and forms.*

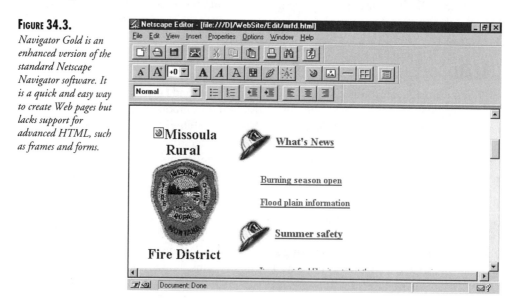

Netscape Gold includes support for editing HTML tables. The formatting commands are quite extensive and cover all of the current attributes HTML 3.2 supports. The WYSIWYG interface very accurately represents what will appear on the user's browser.

By entering a server name and password, Navigator Gold can also take care of the work of posting your pages to their ultimate destination. In addition to the actual HTML file, the editor also takes care of including all of the related accessories, such as image files.

The editor component of Gold seems to run a version behind the browser. Even though the browser includes support for frames, forms, or typefaces, the editor doesn't support any of these options. It does include an option to insert custom tags by hand, however.

The editor is also short in its list of amenities; it only includes spell check, image map creation, and drag-and-drop operation for items such as hypertext links.

## Netscape Composer

Netscape Composer, a part of the Netscape Communicator (4.0) release, is the newest HTML editing program. It is available for all major platforms, including Windows, Macintosh, and UNIX. Composer includes a simpler and more intuitive interface than the Netscape Gold editor, although it includes capabilities beyond its predecessor. Like its counterpart, Composer is geared toward creating individual pages and includes no support for any site management activities. It does provide remote publishing features through FTP and HTTP protocols.

> **TIP**
>
> Composer is available directly from Netscape at home.netscape.com.

Composer's editing screen is similar to the Navigator browser window, with additional toolbars for HTML features such as links, tables, and character and paragraph formatting. (See Figure 34.4.) Although Composer supports Java and JavaScript, it doesn't support frames or forms.

You don't need any knowledge of HTML to work with Composer's dialog boxes. For instance, when formatting a graphic, the user is presented with a set of thumbnail diagrams that illustrate how each option affects the relation of the image to the text. You use a similar method for illustrating the result of editing actions as when you work with tables and paragraphs.

Composer is a WYSIWYG editor. If you need to work directly on the HTML source code, use a menu option to start an external text editor. After completing any changes, Composer gives you the option of updating the view in the editing area.

Like its cousin, Navigator Gold, Composer offers tight integration with Netscape browsers, which enables authors to drag and drop links from remote pages directly into an HTML page in progress. You can also drag image files from the browser into the editor or send HTML documents as e-mail or newsgroup messages.

No templates or wizards are included with Composer to make creating Web pages easier, though a resource is located on Netscape's site to make this possible. To do so, download sample pages to edit. Your other option is to use a CGI-driven wizard on Netscape's site to create a page with the desired headlines, text, images, and bullets that you can then download to your computer to edit.

Without forms, frames, or site management capability, Composer is not effective for complex pages or for working with entire Web sites, but it is a good tool for quickly building and publishing basic HTML pages.

## HotDog

Once upon a time, HotDog was relegated to the world of "Oh, isn't that cute." It was a basic little HTML editor that depended more on an entertaining canine theme than on actual function and utility. But that's all changed. HotDog includes support for the full range of HTML content, including Java, plug-ins, and style sheets. It runs on Windows 95 and NT.

**TIP**

HotDog is available from Sausage Software at www.sausage.com.

One of HotDog's strongest features is its customizable interface. (See Figure 34.5.) You can add or remove virtually anything from its toolbar, which makes it especially useful for people with special needs or patterns to their HTML page construction.

**FIGURE 34.5.**

*HotDog, one of the many available shareware HTML editors, has grown into one of the strongest offerings among its compatriots.*

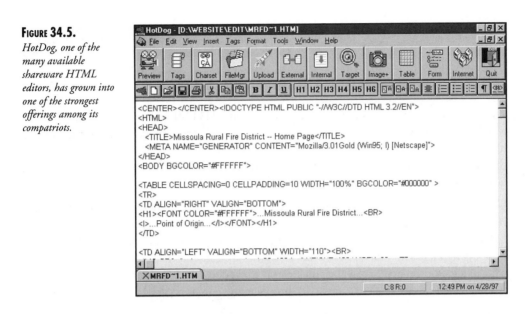

The standard edition links to a browser (usually Internet Explorer) to view what a page will look like when it is completed. The professional version includes Rover, a browser interface that behaves very similarly to Internet Explorer.

An important addition to HotDog's capabilities is its support for style sheets, with which you can implement font or page characteristics for an entire page without working through the entire document. There is also a Resource Manager that integrates all page components for link checking, file management, and graphics preview.

HotDog includes FTP capability to easily transfer files when you're finished editing. This capability also includes the ability to work on files from remote locations, spell check, HTML verification, page wizards, and table and frame tools.

# HTML Utilities

The following set of programs doesn't actually create original HTML pages. The utilities make it easier for you to manage your site and the pages within it. To that extent, you might find this selection of programs useful in your day-to-day HTML production.

## CSE 3310 HTML Validator

HTML Validator for Windows helps you check HTML documents for correct syntax according to HTML 3.2 and 2.0. Direct it to look at an HTML page, and it produces a list of messages based on what it finds, including whether it finds nothing wrong. It also supports Netscape and Microsoft extensions, current with each company's 3.0 release, plus tags for tables and frames. It includes an option to add your own tags and attributes, so you can update it to any HTML 4.0 features you want to use.

You cannot check your document for syntax in a standard HTML browser because the browser is only designed to view HTML documents. If syntax errors exist in a document, the browser usually only attempts to guess how the document should appear, which results in documents that display in a variety of ways, depending on the browser. If a document has enough errors, it might not display at all.

Some HTML editors currently include HTML validation, including FrontPage and Backstage. But many don't, including the editors I discussed earlier in this chapter. Before publishing HTML documents, especially those you create manually or with a dumb HTML editor (*dumb* meaning that it has no validation or other checking), you should check for syntax errors. That's where Validator comes into play, helping to ensure that documents are written in correct HTML syntax, which in turn enables a variety of browsers to view your pages.

Use the syntax error list that Validator generates to correct your document before publishing it. (See Figure 34.6.) The list is stored in a text file for printing and use, complete with validation process information and line-by-line document listings.

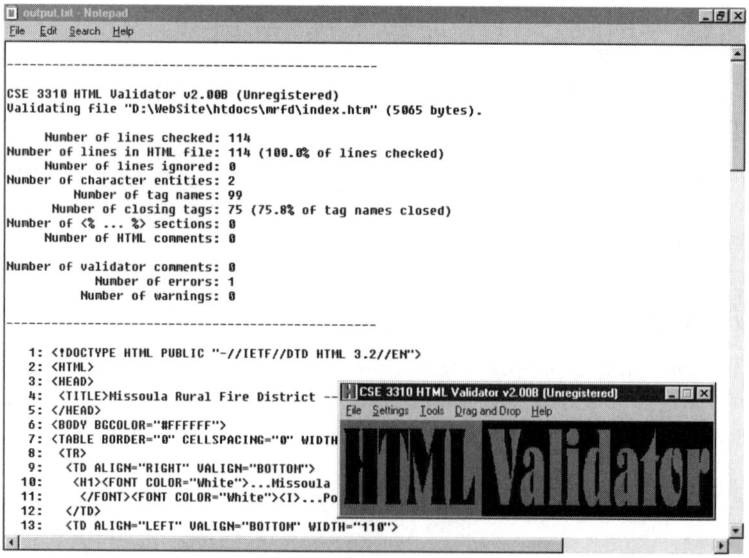

**FIGURE 34.6.**

*The result of validation is a text file that includes Web page statistics and a line-by-line listing with error messages.*

HTML Validator also includes tools that change HTML tags and attributes to uppercase or lowercase, convert different operating system text file formats to other text file formats, and enable you to use templates in your documents.

**TIP**

Using a validation program doesn't guarantee that a document will be perfect in its syntax. Although Validator finds the vast majority of errors, some will fall through the cracks, especially in HTML code, which is sloppy to begin with. Programs such as Validator will find most syntax errors, especially if you use it after each revision of a document.

Validator finds a majority of HTML syntax errors, including common mistakes such as missing double quotation marks and closing tags, mismatched < and > characters, and tags in incorrect locations. When it encounters an unknown attribute, Validator generates an error message or ignores what it can't understand, and gives the offending item the benefit of the doubt.

HTML 3.2 does not require <HEAD> and <BODY> tags, but Validator requires them for successful validation. This should not be a problem because using them benefits page structure and construction. You might need to close some tags for proper validation, such as table data (<TD>), even though it's not required as part of HTML 3.2. Including them will not adversely affect table display, though having to go back to insert them could be a major inconvenience.

**WHAT ABOUT THE NAME CSE 3310 HTML VALIDATOR?**

There are lots of strange names for computer software, including HotDog, Fusion, Packrat, xRes, and so on. For this application, CSE 3310 HTML Validator comes from the University of Texas at Arlington college course for which it was created—Computer Science Engineering 3310 (software engineering).

HTML Validator is shareware. After validating 150 HTML documents, it disables itself and requires that you pay a registration fee.

## InContext WebAnalyzer

InContext WebAnalyzer—which is available for Windows 3.1, 95, and NT—clearly identifies any broken links on your site so that you can resolve them and spare your users from the agony of Error 404: Not Found. Its straightforward operation results in more information about a Web site and its individual pages than you could ever use.

**TIP**

InContext WebAnalyzer is available for demonstration or purchase at www.incontext.com.

The bright side of gathering all of the information is that it doesn't take very long, depending on the speed of your modem and the load on the Web server. When WebAnalyzer is finished with its detective work, you have two graphical displays of the links and resources to which your site refers, plus a text listing of all the files. (See Figure 34.7.)

**FIGURE 34.7.**

*InContext WebAnalyzer's interface and functionality is similar to Microsoft FrontPage Explorer's, but InContext WebAnalyzer is quicker and offers more flexibility.*

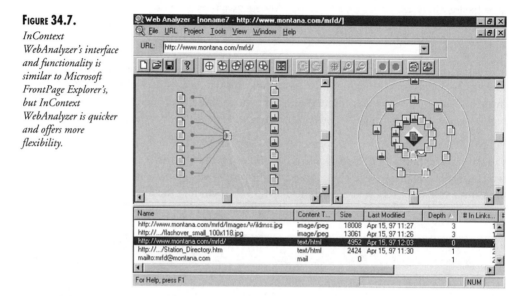

The great strength of WebAnalyzer's intuitive graphical display is not its only asset. The display is interactive. Clicking a node in the WaveFront or file list makes it the center of attention in the individual node view. A special icon represents each link and element external to the page, including hyperlinks, e-mail addresses, images, and other objects.

A text icon with a circle and slash represents unresolved or broken links. Place the pointer over any of the icons to show its URL so you know where to look for the problem. When you specify the problem area, you can launch an HTML editor of your choice to edit the offending link and correct the problem.

Using a browser you specify, WebAnalyzer also presents a comprehensive set of reports in HTML format. (See Figure 34.8.) These reports are a verbose presentation of the information from the graphical views. They include summary reports of indexes and sites plus page-by-page summaries of the links and resources used.

Setting options on WebAnalyzer is especially important. After you give a starting URL, the program begins to crawl outward, following each link and resource. It gradually mushrooms as each page goes in more and more directions. A realistic limit to this mushrooming is two to three levels out for Internet-based sites and four to five levels for intranets. Beyond these levels, too much information to be useful in resolving broken links is returned.

**FIGURE 34.8.**

*You can view all reports generated by WebAnalyzer through a standard browser. These reports include extended information about a page or site, including thumbnail images of graphic files.*

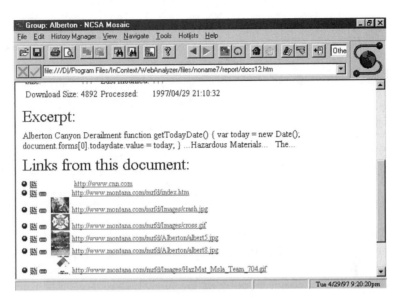

# Xpire Plus

Often, information on a Web page is only valid for a limited time. To help point out new material, many people place NEW! tags in front of hyperlinks. But as time goes by and the information isn't "new" anymore, you have to constantly search through all of your HTML files to look for outdated information. If you have several pages, this search can be very time-consuming, boring, and error-prone.

> **TIP**
>
> Find Xpire Plus on the World Wide Web at www.kagi.com/bungalow.

The Xpire Plus HTML utility, which runs only on Windows 95, assists in this facet of Web site maintenance by helping you keep pages up to date and preventing expired links. Instead of manually searching through each individual HTML file for outdated information, Xpire prompts you for a directory and then takes over checking its entire contents for old information. (See Figure 34.9.) The utility also supports the creation of sections that appear after a certain date.

To do this, encase the time-sensitive items with a pair of comment tags. For example, place `<!--XPIRE10/31/97 -->` at the beginning of a section that should end on Halloween and immediately follow it with `<!--ENDX-->`. You would handle sections that should appear on a certain date similarly, such as `<!--XON 10/31/97 _Today is Halloween_ XON-->`.

**34**

**HTML EDITORS AND UTILITIES**

FIGURE 34.9.

*Using Xpire with*
*specially coded HTML*
*pages can automate the*
*process of making sure*
*content appears and*
*disappears at its*
*appointed times. It also*
*removes NEW! flags*
*when the content is no*
*longer considered new.*

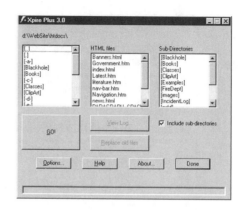

The last feature handles NEW! tags or icons. Xpire uses another comment tag, `<!--XNEW 10/28/97-->`, immediately before the program preferences, and operates it in conjunction with program preferences to remove each item after a predetermined time. You can set the number of days an item is considered new and how many lines to delete following the `<XNEW>` tag.

After you have marked the HTML documents, just run Xpire periodically to make sure each section is added or removed as necessary.

The downside to Xpire is that you have to get used to including the tags with your pages as you're editing them. If your HTML editor automatically generates comment tags, this might not be too big of a problem. Some editors, however, such as FrontPage Editor, include other information within the comment tag to help you with formatting while editing.

## Bandwidth Buster

Bandwidth Buster, available for Windows 3.1 and 95, modifies HTML files with tags and features to reduce the download time users need to view your pages. The whole concept is to take advantage of all the little quirks and browser features to optimize file size and efficiency as an HTML file is retrieved from the server.

### TIP

Bandwidth Buster is available for download from Sausage Software at www.sausage.com.

Bandwidth Buster uses several methods to trim your site and reduce your page's download and layout time. First, it can replace GIF images with compressed JPEG images using a compression ratio that you select. This occurs through a batch conversion process so you don't have to specify each file. It also adds HTML image size and alternate content tags to speed up your page on most browsers, and, optionally, it can create low-resolution copies of your images to insert as LOW SRC images in your HTML files. The LOW SRC images are very small and loaded first by the browser. After the browser retrieves all other content, it loads the full image.

Lastly, Bandwidth Buster can create a text-only alternative Web site. It removes all references to any images and saves all files with their directory structures to a separate location.

You can access all options from a simple interface. (See Figure 34.10.) After the conversion has taken place, Bandwidth Buster offers an additional feature to measure the download time of specific pages based on preset modem speeds.

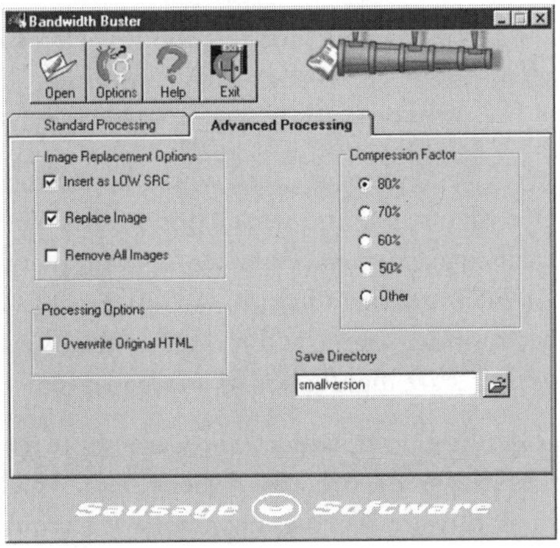

**FIGURE 34.10.**

*Bandwidth Buster, developed by Sausage Software (makers of HotDog), optimizes Web pages for download and display time on most browsers.*

Consistent with Sausage's usual style, several entertaining little animations and sound effects are tossed into the bundle for various activities. For example, the start-up flash screen includes a dog grabbing the "Internet cable," complete with the sound of electrical zapping. Though these features aren't entirely necessary, they use minimal system resources and are only slightly annoying in terms of time.

# Crunch!

Crunch! is a command-line utility that scans HTML files for unnecessary information. Because it's a command-line utility, you can get Crunch! for Windows 3.1, 95, NT, and even OS/2. If you use a Web authoring system such as Microsoft FrontPage or Netscape Gold or even if you write your own Web pages, you're likely to end up with files that contain many unnecessary characters and tags, such as comments.

> **TIP**
>
> Crunch! is available on the Web from Tennyson Maxwell at www.tenmax.com.

Crunch! strips these unnecessary characters and tags from your Web pages, reducing their size by up to 50 percent. It also helps you spot HTML coding errors. After crunching, links with missing quotation marks or incorrectly terminated HTML tags show up as errors when you view them with a browser or pass them through a validator.

After crunching, your HTML files are virtually unreadable, so you must back up your files if you plan to edit them later. The crunched format places all tags and content on one continuous line, making it virtually unreadable in source view, which the Crunch! developers tout as a great way to stop data pirates.

# Reading More About Your Choices

Several good sources of news and reviews about what's happening in the HTML editor market—along with other categories such as Web utilities, image editors, and related items—are available online.

The first source is *c\net* (www.cnet.com), which has established itself as a leading online information source for what's new and what's hot on the World Wide Web. You can hook up directly to their reviews page at www.cnet.com/Content/Reviews. Another source is the "Internet User" section of *PC Magazine Online* (www.pcmag.com/iu). It includes lists of new products, reviews, product roundups, and a "Product of the Week" feature. HTML editors and site management packages are highlighted at www.pcmag.com/iu/author/htmledit.

Other services offer links to download software, short reviews, and individual rating systems, including services such as Tucows (www.tucows.com), which serves as a collection point for a lot of Internet-related software. Tucows now works on a mirror system, in which other Web sites such as our beloved Sams.net (www.mcp.com/sams) copy its files and structure.

# Summary

HTML editors come in many different sizes and with many different strengths. Each is different in the way it supports creating and editing Web pages, beginning with basic appearance (HTML source or WYSIWYG), type and format of toolbars, and menu commands. The differences grow as extended features are added, such as publishing to remote sites or spell-check capability.

Which editor you choose depends on your needs and your HTML comfort level. If you're new to page editing, you'll probably want to start with a simpler editor, such as Netscape Gold, Composer, or HomeSite. More advanced users will look to options such as PageMill or HotDog. Whichever you choose, make sure the editor extends and simplifies your capability to create Web pages, and doesn't limit your options with a difficult interface or inadequate support for the tags you use.

After you create your pages and Web site, you'll want to look at some of the many utilities designed to keep them up to date and usable. From HTML validators to link checkers to page optimization, don't overlook some of the solutions to common problems. Many utilities are free or very inexpensive via shareware.

Like any good book about emerging technologies, this book will contain several outdated items by the time it hits the bookshelves and your hands. So, even though I've reviewed current software in this section, it's important that you keep in mind that new tools and new revisions of existing tools may have already appeared by the time the ink on this page dries.

For the latest and greatest news about capabilities and features, you need to head straight for the horse's mouth. Of course, even though this chapter supplies URLs so you can get in touch with the respective developers, remember that the developers will tell you that their software is the greatest thing since sliced bread. For that reason, it's good to get a second or third opinion.

# Graphics Programs

*by Michael A. Larson*

## IN THIS CHAPTER

**35**

**CHAPTER**

A large part of the appeal of HTML is its capability to place both text and images on the same page. Unless you are transcribing old political speeches to the WWW, eventually you will need to make or modify an image for use in your Web page. Images can add an extra point of interest, summarize a large amount of data, or emphasize some point in your text.

Using graphics does not necessarily mean you have to draw them yourself. Large collections of bars, buttons, and backgrounds are available on the WWW (as discussed in Appendix D, "HTML Resources") for noncommercial use or available for purchase. To a lesser degree you can find collections of images, clip art, and animated GIFs on the Internet that can also be freely used.

But you will almost certainly come to a moment when you need a particular graphic of a particular size, color, or certain "look," and it just isn't out there. If you have the budget, you can hire an artist or get the advertising department to create the graphic you need. A less expensive route might be to purchase an image from a stock photo catalog or buy a clip art collection. Or you might have the image already available, perhaps as a large scanned image. With the aid of the many graphics programs I discuss here, you might be able to draw it yourself, even if you are artistically challenged. Remember that even though these programs are good, you shouldn't expect the next Mona Lisa to flow from your fingertips.

No matter where your image comes from, chances are good it will not be in a form that is ready for use in your Web page. Placing a 10MB scanned image in your Web page will not improve the popularity of your Web site. Minimally, you will need to reduce the size of your image and probably put it into the correct file format. Moreover, you will probably need to put some creative touches on your image by cropping, rotating, changing colors, applying filters, combining it with other images, adjusting the palette or number of colors, adding shadows or transparency, and so on. You need to learn one or more graphics packages to accomplish all this.

The majority of graphics packages, both vector and bitmap, are available for the Windows and Macintosh platforms. There are far fewer native UNIX and OS/2 graphics packages. In this chapter, I review the more popular graphics programs available for all four common computing platforms, discussing their features, ease-of-use, strengths and weaknesses, and the unique capabilities that make a given package stand out from the crowd, especially as it relates to the needs of the Web author. Moving pictures can also be inserted into Web pages, so this chapter includes information about packages that you can use to make animated GIFs or to add streaming video to a page.

I don't discuss the following:

■ Fonts, except as they relate to 3D rendering.

■ High-end graphics packages such as Pixar or most multimedia authoring tools. Though these packages are extremely interesting and capable, using them for Web images is usually overkill. These packages may become more interesting to the Web author as their prices drop and the bandwidth problems on the Internet ease.

■ Making AVI or Quick Time movies. These require special hardware and the current bandwidth problems on the Internet generally make the use of these files in their native format undesirable.

# Choosing a Graphics Package

Graphics packages come in many different types on many different platforms. Choosing a package will depend on the following factors:

■ Your budget

■ The complexity and types of image modifications you want to perform

■ How much time you have to master the graphics packages

■ The capabilities of your hardware

Graphics packages covering a wide range of sophistication are available for all common computing platforms. Packages that used to be available on the Macintosh have been ported only to Windows and, in many instances, to UNIX. It is unlikely that you will need to purchase a special computer platform exclusively for graphics, although you may need to upgrade existing hardware on your HTML authoring machine.

If you intend to do extensive graphics work, two hardware items that you should give serious consideration to are your monitor and video card. Try not to work with any monitor smaller than 17 inches (diagonal) and get the highest vertical scan rate you can afford in order to reduce eye strain. Make sure that your video card has sufficient RAM to support 24-bit color at whatever screen resolution you generally work at. It is also handy to be able to change color depth and/or resolution on the fly (without rebooting your system) to check how your Web pages look under 256 colors at 640×480.

Graphics packages generally fall into one of two types: vector and bitmap.

## A Brief Overview of Vector and Bitmap Editors

*Vector* programs, often called *drawing* or *illustration* programs, use equations to define the placement of lines, colors, and objects. As such, their native file sizes are very compact and the images scale well; that is, there is no loss in real resolution (apparent resolution might suffer) no matter how large or small you make the image. Vector packages are commonly used by professional illustrators to create images from scratch. Many packages also come with extensive, ready-to-use clip art collections. CorelDraw and Adobe Illustrator are vector packages. From the perspective of putting graphics on a Web page, the strengths of vector programs include

■ Nondestructive image scaling

■ Fine control over shape

■ Many ready-made objects that can be easily disassembled, moved, and distorted

■ Responsiveness (except for very complex images or operations)

**35**

**GRAPHICS PROGRAMS**

■ Lower hardware requirements than bitmap editors

■ Ease of exporting the final image to a file format usable on a Web page

The major disadvantages are

■ Native vector file formats are not usable on the Web without browser plug-ins.

■ Many packages have a steep learning curve.

■ Colors might shift during export, requiring touch up in a bitmap editor.

Bitmap editors work with bitmap images, which also are called *raster* images. A bitmap is a pixel-by-pixel definition of a picture. The total number of pixels (image size) is fixed in any given file, as are the color and placement of each pixel in the image. Image size is dependent upon the number of colors and pixels, although some bitmap file formats use compression algorithms to reduce their size. Bitmap editors work by manipulating each pixel in an image. Adobe Photoshop and PaintShop Pro are bitmap editors. Paint programs, such as Fractal Painter, are also bitmap editors. Some of the strengths of bitmap programs are as follows:

■ You can work directly with GIF or JPEG images.

■ A wide variety of special effects is available, including drop shadows and transparent GIFs.

Some of the disadvantages of bitmap editors include the following:

■ They can be very CPU-, disk-, and RAM-intensive, requiring more hardware than vector packages.

■ Many packages have a steep learning curve.

■ Image information is lost due to pixel interpolation when an image is resized.

These package definitions, vector and bitmap, are not strict: You can import bitmaps into most vector packages and draw vector curves in some bitmap packages. There are also related types of graphics packages that have special capabilities such as ray-tracing, 3D rendering, or fractal generation programs. If you will be generating or manipulating large numbers of graphics for Web use, graphics utilities such as Debabelizer are also essential.

# Bitmap Packages

The vast majority of graphics on the WWW are in GIF or JPG bitmap formats, so bitmap packages are a Web author's first tools of choice. Bitmap packages generally fall into two categories: editing programs and paint programs. Editing programs, typified by Adobe Photoshop, have an extensive array of filters and functions available for modifying existing images. They have fewer tools for drawing or creating images. On the other hand, paint programs, such as Fractal Painter, have an extensive array of "media" (chalk, charcoal, multiple paintbrushes, pencils, papers, and so on) available for drawing, creating, or modifying images. Base your decision of whether to go with an editing or paint program on whether you will be spending more time editing existing images or creating new ones. You might even need both types in your graphics toolbox to give you the most options.

Most bitmap editors have many tools and capabilities in common, including these:

- Selection tools, including a marquee selection box, lasso, magic wand, and selection by color range.
- Basic drawing tools, including a pencil and paintbrush at a minimum.
- Filters, which can range from touch-up filters for sharpening or blurring an image through special effects such as creating drop shadows or applying light sources.
- Support for scanners.
- Support for common bitmap file formats and flavors including BMP, TIF, RLE, GIF, JPG, PCX, PCD, PSD, PNG, and TGA.
- The capability to open images from many different bitmap file formats and save them to many different bitmap formats.
- The capability to flip, mirror, and rotate (in degree increments) images.
- Cloning, which uses one part of an image as the "paint" for another part or another image.
- Retouching, which includes changing colors, color replacement, brightness, resizing, cropping, contrast, hue, or saturation among others.
- Masks for protecting one part of an image while another part is changed.

Many more packages out there are similar in functionality to the ones discussed in the following sections. It is simply not possible to be exhaustive on this topic. I chose the ones I did because of their popularity and features. Even if you find none of the packages featured here to be suitable for your uses, you will at least know what to look for in other bitmap editing or paint programs.

## Adobe Photoshop

The latest incarnation of Adobe Photoshop (`http://www.adobe.com/prodindex/photoshop/main.html`) for Macintosh and Windows (95 and NT) is Version 4.0. Photoshop is the most widely used bitmap editor among graphics professionals. Its popularity is due to its combination of incredible power and a well laid out, elegant interface. The program is also highly extensible with a wide array of filters and add-ons available. Adobe Photoshop comes on a CD-ROM with an excellent printed user guide and a second tutorial CD-ROM with beginning-to-advanced lessons.

In addition to the usual bitmap editing features already mentioned, Photoshop has

- Layers and ways to merge them or change transparency.
- Adjustment layers for adjusting color, hue, and so on without modifying the underlying image. Great for experimentation.

■ Automation. You can record a set of actions on one image and apply the actions to another group of images.

■ Grids for precisely placing and aligning the parts of your image.

■ A very intuitive and wide-ranging zooming tool.

■ The capability to save selections in the file for later recall.

■ A path drawing tool and the capability to export the path to Adobe Illustrator.

■ An easy way to create shadows for any text or object and make any color or the background transparent for a transparent GIF.

■ Gradient fills with more than two colors and the capability to adjust transparency anywhere along the gradient.

■ Thirteen categories of filters, each with multiple capabilities—for example, artistic filters (neon glow), rendering filters (lens flare), and texture creating filters (stained glass)—for a total of more than 90 filters.

More filters are available from a variety of vendors, including the famous Kai's Power Tools. Adobe defined the standard format for filter plug-ins; most plug-ins are written to this standard first and most other bitmap packages support this standard.

As you can see, Photoshop is feature-laden, and this is its greatest strength. This wide-ranging capability provides the ultimate in flexibility for artistic design. You can do almost anything with a bitmap under Photoshop.

This also leads to its two primary weaknesses:

1. It is a resource hog. It is not comfortable with less than 32MB of total RAM on any platform. And, of course, 24-bit color bitmap files can eat gigabyte hard drives for lunch. Photoshop needs a muscle car to run; otherwise, don't even try it. On the positive side, it can handle more than one CPU under Windows NT.

2. It has a significant learning curve. Not only will you need to learn what the features are and how to use them, but you must also learn when it is appropriate to use them and what the artistic effects of their use will be. This is a significant time commitment unless you are already a creative artist.

This program is not for the casual user. The time investment to learn and use it will only pay off if you spend a great deal of time creating or modifying images or need to have a large variety of modification options available for any given image. On the other hand, huge amounts of information are available about using Photoshop, including books, mailing lists, newsgroups, and many Web sites that are repositories of Photoshop tips and tricks. Here are some URLs on the Internet that are dedicated to Photoshop:

■ PC Resources for Photoshop specializes in filters and Photoshop plug-ins. It is found at http://www.netins.net/showcase/wolf359/adobepc.htm.

■ You can find the Ultimate Compendium of Photoshop Sites (yes, that is the name of the Web site) at http://www.sas.upenn.edu/~pitharat/photoshop/.

■ Stop by Andy's Photoshop tips at `http://www.andyart.com/photoshop/index.htm`.

■ My favorite Usenet newsgroup dedicated to Photoshop is `comp.graphics.apps.photoshop`.

■ A huge Photoshop site, Photoshop Paradise, is at `http://desktoppublishing.com/photoshop.html`.

■ If you want to join a Photoshop mailing list, go to `http://www.csua.berkeley.edu:8000/~kima/photoshop/`.

■ The definitive online reference guide to Photoshop, Web Reference, is at `http://www.duke.edu/~ac10/photoshop/index.html`.

Note that many of the Web sites in this list also contain extensive lists of Photoshop sites on the WWW. The preceding list is just a sampler to get you started.

The minimum system requirements for using Photoshop on a Macintosh are the 68030 processor or a Power Macintosh with 16MB of RAM available for Photoshop and System 7.1 or later. For Windows 95 or Windows NT, the minimum is a 486 processor (a Pentium or Pentium Pro is highly recommended) and 16MB RAM. For both platforms, increasing the RAM to a minimum of 32MB is recommended. If you can afford more RAM, get it.

## PaintShop Pro

This very affordable shareware package from JASC, Inc. (`http://www.jasc.com/psp.html`) has a wide following among casual-to-intermediate users and is quite popular with people doing typical Web graphics. This package combines ease of use with many of the sophisticated capabilities found in Photoshop. Version 4.12 also reads a wide variety of file formats, including several vector formats: CorelDraw (CDR and CMX), Micrographx Designer (DRW), AutoCAD (DXF), and WordPerfect Graphics (WPG). It also reads Photoshop (PSD) native files. You can easily convert batches of files between different graphics formats with this program. Some other features useful for Web authoring include

■ Screen capture capability, full screen or only a selected portion

■ Several different drawing media, including crayon and charcoal

■ Drop shadows and the capability to create transparent GIFs

■ A thumbnail image browser

■ Support for Photoshop filters

■ The easy creation of image masks

The main strengths of this program are that it is easy to use and learn without leaving out many important high-end features—and it is affordable to boot. Its main weakness is that is has fewer features than Photoshop, including far fewer default filters. Most sorely missed are layers and the step automation for applying the same modifications to a group of images.

The minimum system requirements for this Windows 95 or NT only (a Windows 3.1 version is also available) program again include a 486 with 8MB RAM, but I recommend a Pentium or better and 16MB RAM.

# Fractal Painter

If you like to draw, pen, doodle, sketch, do origami, woodcarve, make snow angels, or have any shred of artistic inclination, you are going to love this program. Fractal Painter (http://www.fractal.com), currently in Version 4.0 on both Macintosh and Windows platforms, has the widest array of drawing media available in a mainstream computer program. You have over 150 brushes available, and you can modify any one of them. There are six different pencils, chalk, watercolor, pens for calligraphy, felt pens, oil paint, cloners, and airbrushes. You can even paint with more than half a dozen liquids. To complement this, you have a wide array of surfaces to paint on, including many different types of papers, weaves, and colors. Some of Fractal Painter's features are

- Layers (called floaters) and masks.
- An image can become a painting element (random or ordered) with the Image Hose brush. Each image is a separate Nozzle.
- You can create image maps inside the program.
- Capability to read Photoshop 3 files, preserving the layers.
- Support for Photoshop filters.
- Support for collaborative painting, which means several artists can work on the same canvas at the same time.
- Many of the media features can be applied on a frame-by-frame basis to QuickTime or Video for Windows files.
- Capability to import and perform vector editing on files from CorelDraw, Adobe Illustrator, or Macromedia FreeHand.

This vector file import and vector editing is unique to Fractal Painter. Other bitmap editors can import vector files but convert them to a raster format.

Fractal Painter definitely shines as an artistic paint program while supporting most of the basic bitmap editing functions. Its support of multiple media (both paint and canvas types) is unparalleled. Anyone familiar with traditional painting or drawing techniques and tools will find this program very intuitive to use; others will find it moderately difficult to learn. If you prefer to draw more of the graphics for your Web pages, you need look no further. If you can master much of the media, you also will have many more options available for editing existing images than are provided by filters.

For the Macintosh, you'll need a 68030/40 processor or Power Macintosh with 8MB RAM for the application and System 7.0 or later. For Windows (3.1, 95, or NT), you'll need a 486 or Pentium with 8MB RAM (16MB recommended). A Math coprocessor (FPU) is required on both platforms to support some operations.

# General Image Manipulation Program (GIMP) for UNIX

If you're doing most of your HTML writing on a UNIX box and are tired of running to a Windows machine or a Mac to do your graphics, there is finally a good, general-purpose bitmap editor for you. This program currently exists as freeware (Version 0.54, soon to go commercial at Version 1.0, `http://www.xcf.berkeley.edu/~gimp/`) with compiled versions and source code available for Linux, Free BSD, HPUX, and Solaris.

This program makes good use of the unique and robust capabilities of the UNIX operating system. You can have multiple views of the same image on the screen at the same time and multiple undo levels, limited only by available RAM memory. It also supports most of the same, common capabilities as other bitmap editors, including masking and layers. Extensions have been written into the program so that custom plug-ins can be added. The freeware comes with 40 plug-ins. File support is available for GIF, JPEG, PNG, TIF, and XPM formats.

If you like to or have to work on a UNIX box, this program will be of great interest to you for getting your basic Web graphics work done. If your UNIX box is also your site's Web server, you are now in a one-stop shopping situation where you can write HTML and compose graphics on the same machine on which you're hosting your site.

GIMP requires support for shared memory from the operating system. It also requires X11 (R5 or R6) and Motif 1.2 or above.

# ColorWorks for OS/2

SPG (`http://www.spg-net.com/products.html`) has put together a powerful bitmap editor in ColorWorks, Version 2. Rather than defining a standard set of tools like most other editors, this program allows you to "paint" with any effect or combination of effects, essentially giving you a limitless toolbox. It is also possible to save these combinations as a Graphics State file. SPG provides a number of predefined files for immediate use. ColorWorks is also the only bitmap editor I've seen so far that truly supports multithreading; that is, you can initiate multiple editing effects and each will spin off on its own thread. You do not have to wait for one thread to finish before starting another. You can also manage your threads much as you would manage print jobs through a print spooler, deleting or pausing them at will. Because OS/2 supports multiple CPUs, the multiple threads from ColorWorks will efficiently use all of the CPU power you have available. ColorWorks also uses extensive memory-managing techniques to maximize the RAM you have and the program itself uses only 1MB of RAM.

ColorWorks supports masking and multiple undo, although it lacks the capability to handle multiple layers. This graphics package is a good selection for the Web author working under OS/2 and will allow you to meet most common graphics creation and editing needs. Any PC that will run OS/2 Version 2.1 or higher will run ColorWorks.

# Other Bitmap Editors

Several other bitmap editors are of note because they are written almost completely for Web use (Microsoft Image Composer, free at `http://www.microsoft.com/imagecomposer`) or because they are bundled with major vector graphics editors that are discussed next in this chapter. There are many more editing packages available, each with its own combination of features, price, and platform availability. Whichever bitmap editor you choose, make sure it is one you enjoy. The process of creating and editing graphics should give you a sense of accomplishment and not be an exercise in frustration from software that is ill-suited to your work style.

## Microsoft Image Composer

This rewrite of the Altamira Composer editing package by Microsoft for Windows 95 and NT specifically emphasizes the needs of the Web author. This package is bundled and integrated with Microsoft FrontPage 97 and Visual InterDev. With Image Composer, any image brought into the program is converted to a sprite (not to be confused with sprites used in game programming). A *sprite* makes use of the alpha channel to basically define an area of transparency around the main objects, allowing for nonrectangular images. For instance, a picture of a potted plant will have the shape of the pot and the leaves; the background is not a part of the sprite. This sprite or a group of sprites can then be used to create a composition that can be saved in the native MIC file format or as a transparent GIF for use on a Web page. A sprite is roughly equivalent to a layer.

Image Composer contains a number of built-in filters and supports Photoshop plug-ins, the use of masks, and the easy creation of drop shadows. You cannot build animated GIFs, although Microsoft gives away a free GIF animation builder at its Internet site that works closely with this program. Because you can move individual sprites or groups of sprites in Image Composer, you can easily save a series of frames that can then be built into a GIF animation. Again, hardware requirements are a bit steep, with 32MB RAM recommended and up to 300MB of disk space needed if you install all of the images that come with the program.

## Macromedia xRes

This very capable bitmap editor (`http://www.macromedia.com/software/xres/`) for Windows 95 or NT and the Macintosh can be purchased alone or as part of a bundle with Macromedia Director or Macromedia FreeHand. In many respects, this program is similar to PaintShop Pro, but it contains more high-end features such as layers and paths. Its tight integration with other Macromedia products makes it especially attractive for people working with Director or FreeHand on graphics for Shockwave-enhanced Web sites. In addition to support for Photoshop plug-ins, xRes has the special capability to interpret single-page PostScript files. As with Fractal Painter, you can create image maps directly in the program.

## Corel Photo-Paint

This bitmap editor (`http://www.corel.com/products/graphicsandpublishing/`) comes bundled with CorelDraw and is currently at Version 7 on Windows 95 and NT, at Version 6 on the Macintosh as a similar application (Artisan), and at Version 3.5 on UNIX (Xpaint and

Photo-Paint). Most of the following comments relate to the Windows Version 7. Corel Photo-Paint can also be purchased as a standalone product for the Windows platform.

Photo-Paint is a high-end bitmap editor supporting layers, masks, and grids for object placement. Photo-Paint gives you very fine control over transparency and has made adding drop shadows automatic. It supports the Adobe Photoshop plug-in standard and comes with a large number of built-in filters. It also includes an image painter similar to the Image Hose found in Fractal Painter. For Web images, it supports the Web color palette, image map creation, transparent and animated GIFs, and the newer Progressive JPEG image format. If you purchase the CorelDraw software bundle, you probably won't need to look at other bitmap editors. Hardware requirements are a bit steep, with 32MB RAM recommended for Windows and 20MB minimum for the Power Macintosh with System 7.5 or later.

# Vector Packages

Vector graphic files are not directly supported as image types under HTML 3.2. Presently, there is no Internet-native file format for vector images filling the same role as GIF or JPG files do for bitmap graphics. In many ways, vector graphics are ideal for Web use. Their file size is usually smaller than bitmap files, improving browser page load times, and they are infinitely scalable without resolution loss, which would banish the "jaggies" from Internet graphics forever. For the time being, however, if you create a graphic with a vector package, you will need to export the file to a raster format or use a file conversion utility to rasterize it to a GIF or JPG. Browser plug-ins are available that will allow viewing of a vector file from its native format within a browser, but for an Internet site, it can be a great inconvenience to require all visitors to have a particular plug-in. This can be accomplished, however, within the narrower confines of a company intranet. I fervently hope that a standard vector format is adopted in the near future for use in HTML pages.

Because the vast majority of graphics on the WWW currently are in a bitmap format, you might be wondering why you should even consider shelling out the money and time to learn a vector package. Vector packages give the Web author some unique advantages:

- Most clip art is in some kind of vector format, and many vector editors come with large libraries of clip art images.

- You can easily disassemble, modify, or combine clip art images or parts of images to get more unique images.

- It is very easy to create primitive shapes such as circles, squares, or polygons.

- You can resize vector files without resolution loss and export them as a bitmap image in the precise dimensions you need for your Web page. This avoids extensive resizing in a bitmap program, which can lead to a loss of detail and a nasty eruption of the "jaggies."

If these capabilities look appealing to you and you want to add them to your bag of tricks, please read on; otherwise, you might want to proceed to the next section on an essential graphics utility for the Web author.

**35**

GRAPHICS
PROGRAMS

As with bitmap packages, vector packages have many types of tools in common. Some of the common features that you should look for are

- A pencil or line drawing tool and extensive means to modify line thickness and color
- A shape drawing tool or group of tools
- A node editing tool to modify curves and lines
- Transformation tools, including those for rotation, mirroring, and flipping
- A zooming and magnification tool
- A text tool for adding and manipulating text
- The capability to fit text to shapes, objects, or paths
- The capability to trace or outline bitmap files to create a vector file
- The capability to fill images with color, gradients, textures, or bitmaps
- The capability to combine, group, and ungroup elements
- Page layout tools and grids for precise placement of elements
- The capability to export images at a user-specified size to a bitmap format
- Special effects, including fitting text to a curve, extruding, perspective, and defining clipping paths

You do not need to subdivide vector graphics programs into those with an editing or painting emphasis as you do bitmap programs. Vector programs use more of the drawing metaphor and have fewer of the painting capabilities seen in bitmap paint programs. This is starting to change, however, most notably with Fractal Expression (`http://www.fractal.com`), which allows many special painting capabilities (using oil, watercolor, chalk, and so on) to enter the vector world for the first time.

Again, I've chosen the vector packages discussed in the following sections based on their popularity and capabilities. All vector programs I've found run under Windows or on the Macintosh. There are UNIX versions for each of the two most popular vector programs, Adobe Illustrator and CorelDraw. I am not aware of any vector editors for use under OS/2.

# CorelDRAW!

CorelDRAW! (`http://www.corel.com/products/graphicsandpublishing/`) is a high-end vector program that comes in a bundle by the same name along with Photo-Paint, Dream 3D (a 3D rendering program based on Ray Dream Designer), and Presents (a multimedia presentation program). In addition to improved performance over earlier versions, Version 7 for the Windows platform contains several new features, including enhanced and flexible transparency controls and the capability to apply Photoshop plug-ins to imported bitmaps. There are also several new capabilities geared toward the Web graphics user. You can directly export a vector graphic as a transparent GIF or in Progressive JPEG. You can also export an entire page as HTML or to Barista, Corel's new Java-based format.

The bundle also includes 32,000 pieces of clip art or symbols, 1,000 photos, and 1,000 TrueType and Type 1 fonts. It also contains Corel Depth, which allows the quick and easy creation of 3D text, and Texture for creating an infinite number of natural textures. There is also a Script editor and a multimedia manager.

CorelDRAW! is a moderately difficult program to learn, but worthwhile when you consider the entire package and the unique Web capabilities not found in other vector packages.

Recommended system requirements include Windows 95 or NT on a Pentium with 32MB RAM. Version 6 requires a Power Macintosh, System 7.5 or later and a minimum of 20MB RAM. The UNIX Version 3.5 will run under HP UX 9.0 or greater, a DEC ALPHA OSF/1, Version 2 or higher, Sun Solaris 2.3 or higher, IBM AIX 3.2 (RS/6000) or greater, and IRIX 5 (SGI) or higher. The Macintosh and UNIX bundles differ in content from the Windows Version 7 bundle.

## Adobe Illustrator

As an Adobe application, Illustrator (http://www.adobe.com/prodindex/illustrator/main.html) started life on the Macintosh and now also runs under Windows. Currently, at Version 7 on both platforms, this program has a unique knife tool that can cut objects along a freeform path. You can mask objects with any shape and convert spreadsheet data to graphs. You can import bitmap images and apply any Photoshop plug-in filter effect to bitmaps imported into Illustrator. You can export images to GIF or transparent GIFs and read and edit PDF files.

The program is moderately difficult to learn. Features of interest to the Web author include

- The capability to assign a URL to an object and have the program create a link to an image map
- The built-in 216-color Web palette
- Export files to JPG or GIF89a
- Opens and exports to the PNG format

The recommended system for the Macintosh is a 68030 processor or better with 16MB of install RAM and 8MB of RAM available for the application or a Power Macintosh with 32MB of installed RAM. For Windows 95 or NT, the recommended system is a Pentium under Windows 95 with 32MB of RAM. The program will not run under Windows 3.1. For UNIX (Solaris 2.3 or 2.4), a Sun SPARCstation 2, IPX, or faster processor workstation with OpenWindows or Motif and 32MB of RAM is needed.

## Macromedia FreeHand

FreeHand 7 for Windows or Macintosh (http://www.macromedia.com/software/freehand/) can be purchased alone or as part of the FreeHand Graphics Studio that also includes xRes, Fontographer (for creating and modifying fonts), and Extreme 3D (for 3D rendering and animation). FreeHand graphics can be added to "shocked" Web pages, which incorporate

35

GRAPHICS PROGRAMS

Macromedia's Shockwave technology. Shockwave is a plug-in that maintains the vector nature of FreeHand files, allowing for image zooming on a Web page and for independent treatment (such as hyperlinks) of each object in the graphic.

FreeHand supports multiple levels of undo and has the unique capability to make styles that include both text and graphical style elements such as spacing and line specifications. These styles can then be applied to other objects or text. You can import bitmaps into FreeHand and apply Photoshop standard plug-in filters. You can do Search and Replace operations on graphics items. Scripting in Java or AppleScript is available. You can also save graphics as PDF files.

In addition to the applications mentioned, the FreeHand Graphics studio also contains 10,000 pieces of clip art, 500 fonts, many templates, stock photographs, and 3D models.

Recommended system requirements for Windows 95 or NT include 16MB of RAM; for the Macintosh, System 7 or higher and 6MB of application RAM are required.

## Other Vector Packages

The number of vector-style graphics programs not already mentioned is far smaller than the bitmap crowd. Some packages contain fewer features than those discussed, but they might be easier to learn. Corel Xara (`http://www.xara.com/corelxara/`) fits into this category. Other very high-end programs, such as CAD programs, have little day-to-day utility for most Web authors. No matter which program you choose, I do recommend that you obtain a vector-style graphics program to give yourself the most capability and flexibility in editing or creating graphics for your HTML pages.

# An Essential Graphics Utility for the Web Author: Debabelizer

Even if you have high-powered bitmap and vector editors, you still might not have all of the tools you need for preparing Web graphics. Most traditional editing programs concentrate on maximizing content and detail, both of which are usually essential for sharp-looking graphics. This, unfortunately, often leads to large file sizes. Most users on the WWW, however, will not tolerate slow downloads, no matter how good looking your graphics might be. Until this bandwidth problem goes away, you have to make graphics that are small and fast loading as well as attractive. You can reduce GIF or JPEG file size using one of three methods:

- Have fewer pixels; that is, make the image smaller.
- Reduce the number of colors.
- Use compression techniques.

This is all complicated by the fact that many browsers support only a 216-color palette (the "Netscape" or "Web" palette), which means that for optimal viewing on all browsers, all of the graphics that you use need to be mapped or dithered to this palette. The need to make some combination of these problems work together for all of the graphics you use on any particular Web site and still have your graphics look good has opened a niche market for programs that optimize graphics for use on the Internet. The first horse out of the gate, and, in this case, the best tool to get this done, is Debabelizer.

This product by Equilibrium (`http://www.equilibrium.com`) has long been the target of envy from Windows users because it initially was available only for the Macintosh. Now it is also available for Windows 95 and NT. Its capability to automate many of the image reduction steps saves you countless hours in adding graphics to your Web site and ensures that your graphics will be of the smallest possible size and have the same appearance across different browsers.

You can use the SuperPalette in Debabelizer to create an ideal palette for a group of images and map them all to it. An HTML parser will place all of the files from a Web page onto a list for SuperPalette creation. You can use scripts in Debabelizer to automate the performance of a series of effects to a group of images, such as changing file formats to transparent GIF or Progressive JPEG, reducing colors, palette mapping, and so on. The number of ways to change and customize palettes is unrivaled by any bitmap editor. The Windows version also provides a wizard to optimize graphics for Web use.

Debabelizer also has basic bitmap editing functions and supports the Photoshop plug-in standard. Other non-Web capabilities in the program include a host of capabilities for applying effects to video, including text overlay and blue screen removal.

Recommended system requirements for the Macintosh are at least 2.5MB of application memory and System 6.0.7 or higher. For Windows 95 or NT, a Pentium and 32MB RAM are recommended.

# Animation and Video Packages

Moving graphics on a Web page can be a major source of interest, perhaps drawing attention to an important item, or they can be irritating, even going so far as driving the user off your page. If used properly, moving images, whether they be graphics or video clips, can add considerable interest and content to a Web site. So you will need to know what tools to use to create or modify moving picture content for use on an HTML page.

Four primary types of moving picture technology are available for use in a Web page:

- Animated GIFs
- Standard video files, Video for Windows (AVI), or QuickTime movies (MOV)
- Plug-in support for proprietary animated graphics packages
- Streaming video

Each of these involves a trade-off in file size versus frame rate versus picture quality. Using AVI and MOV files in Web pages isn't discussed in detail here because relatively few users on the Internet have the bandwidth to view these in real-time at an acceptable frame rate. Most users have the ability to download and view these files, but their large file sizes for even short clips makes even this offline viewing inconvenient.

# GIF Animation

Animated GIFs are composed of multiple GIF frames in one file, as supported under the GIF89a file format. Because even a single GIF file can easily exceed 50KB, the size restraints on animated GIFs are fairly severe. Most animations are small, or only a small part of the image is animated. And the number of frames must be minimized to maintain a small file size. The process of making an animated GIF is very laborious. You must plan the animation (how many frames, what will move, how will it move, and so on), generate each frame in a bitmap editor or paint program, assemble the files in an animation construction program, and add the display time for each frame. This process is very similar to how cartoon animation was done several decades ago. If you want to try your hand at it, there are several packages available to choose from.

## GIF Construction Set

This shareware package from Alchemy Mindworks (`http://www.mindworkshop.com/alchemy/gifcon.html`) for Windows 95 or NT gives you complete control over all aspects of the animation. After you have created all of the frames for your animation as separate GIF images, you can open a new image in GIF Construction Set and begin inserting the frames one by one. GIF Construction Set has several palette options, including the capability to generate a global palette based on your first image and map the remaining images to that palette. A block metaphor is used to build the animated GIF. A header block is created in a new file and contains some basic file information, such as image size. A comments block can be added for notes (text will not display). Each frame image is an image block, and a control block is needed for each image to control the frame display time for that block. Plain text blocks enable you to add text that will display in the animated GIF, and a loop block will control how often the animation loops or plays. After you get the animation to run as you wish, GIF Construction Set will save the file in the 89a format so that it will run as an animation in a browser.

## GifBuilder

This freeware program for the Macintosh, authored by Yves Piquet (`http://iawww.epfl.ch/Staff/Yves.Piguet/clip2gif-home/GifBuilder.html`), makes it easy to create an animated GIF. After you have your frames, open GifBuilder and start dragging and dropping your files into it from their folder. You can change the order by dragging the filenames around if you need to. You can then use the Options menu to set the looping, palette, and interframe delay. You can select all of the files and set the same delay time or select individual files and set a separate time for each frame. You can also easily change the background of the animation to transparent. Save your file and you're finished.

# Microsoft GIF Animator

Microsoft offers a high-quality GIF animation program for free on its site at `http://www.microsoft.com/imagecomposer/gifanimator/gifanin.htm`. This program is designed to work optimally in tandem with Microsoft Image Composer, but it can easily be used as a standalone program.

The program is very easy to use. You can import any image that you can paste to the clipboard, import any GIFs, or drag and drop from Image Composer. You also can import the image palette or select a browser palette. You can resize your animations and select the number of times they will loop. You can select one color to be transparent. After you've added all of your frames, you can easily rearrange them by selecting a frame and clicking on an up or down arrow. Animated GIF building doesn't get much easier than this, and you can't beat the price.

## Other GIF Animation Programs

The preceding are just two programs of many available on the Internet. For UNIX, MultiGIF by Andy Wardley (`http://www.peritas.com/~abw/code/multigif.html`) works as a command-line utility to generate an animated GIF. Source code is also available. Consult Appendix D for more links to GIF animation builders.

## Macromedia Flash: Proprietary Animation on the Web

This recent addition to Macromedia's line (`http://www.macromedia.com/software/flash/`) came from the purchase of FutureSplash. It requires a browser plug-in (80KB to 150KB in size depending on platform) to work but produces such high-quality, low-bandwidth animations that it should be seriously considered by Web authors as an alternative to animated GIFs. A major advantage to this format is that it streams, giving the user some immediate visual feedback, and continues to play as it downloads. Creation of animations is also eased by use of *Motion Interpolation*. All you need to do is define the starting and ending points and rotation for the object and Flash generates the in-between files. No need to laboriously create each frame as with an animated GIF, so you can spend more time experimenting. You can also embed links in any portion of the animation.

Recommended system requirements for authoring on a PC are a 486 or faster and 16MB RAM; For the Macintosh, a 68040 processor or faster, System 7.5 or later, and 16MB of RAM are required.

## Macromedia Director: Proprietary Multimedia for the Web

This package (`http://www.macromedia.com/software/director/`) is a full-featured, multimedia authoring package for doing things such as producing CD-ROMs. This high-bandwidth technology is of interest to Web authors because of the availability of a Shockwave plug-in and Macromedia's Afterburner technology, which can compress a Director file to a size acceptable for Internet use. This gives you the option of putting more sophisticated media on your Web site. The program is based on a theater metaphor and allows you to combine a wide variety of media types—including audio, video, graphics (2D and 3D), text, and database objects—and script them with a built-in language, Lingo. Director is used by many Web sites to produce games and simulations. Because of its many features, the program will be moderate-to-difficult to learn.

System requirements for Windows 95 and NT are a 486 processor or better with 16MB RAM. For the Macintosh, a 68040 or faster, System 7.1 or higher, and 16MB RAM are required.

## Streaming Video

The high bandwidth requirements of playing standard video in real-time at an acceptable frame rate makes the process unavailable to most Internet users. New technologies that stream and compress video, however, now make it possible to use video in real-time broadcasts or to play video clips to users who only have modem connections to the Internet. Although the video quality, size, and frame rate are all only of medium quality in the best of situations, look for this important technology to improve with time. I have chosen VivoActive and RealVideo as examples of this genre of applications.

### VivoActive

VivoActive (http://www.vivo.com) is an example of *serverless video*, meaning that you don't need a special Web server to feed the video to the browser and RealVideo, which uses the server form of video streaming.

VivoActive from Vivo Software uses a program, VivoActive Producer, to transform AVI or QuickTime Movie video clips to a new format. Compression rates are quite impressive, with a 30MB AVI file reduced to less than 100KB by Producer. This compressed file is then read and streamed through the Vivo browser plug-in when a link is clicked or a page is loaded. If you have a modem connection to the Internet at less than 28.8kbps, you can expect significant delays during the playing of the Vivo clip. Video and audio quality are both acceptable. Unfortunately, at this time, players are available for only Windows and Macintosh platforms. A MIME entry is also needed in the Web server table. The authoring software, Producer, is available for Windows and Macintosh.

### RealVideo

RealVideo (http://www.realvideo.com) is a recent development from the folks at Progressive Networks who brought you RealAudio. This form of video requires a dedicated video server to stream the video in response to a browser request. Video is processed using a set of Encoder tools before being placed on the server. Many high-end, professional options are available for processing, including support for Adobe Premiere plug-ins and Terran Interactive's Movie Cleaner Pro, among others. Command-line batch processing is available for automation of the process. Efficient playback often requires using the UDP protocol rather than TCP, which may necessitate reconfiguring any firewalls. The player will not work if the user connection is substantially below 28.8kbps. Players are currently available only for Windows and Macintosh, but this is sure to change.

# Ray Tracing, 3D Rendering, and Fractals

At times you might not be able to get the effects you want with regular bitmap or vector graphics programs, especially when it comes to generating 3D images or fractals. Programs that render in 3D also enable sophisticated lighting and texturing support, which adds a very realistic touch to an image. Fractals can be used to generate textures, generate landscapes, or just to make that cool graphic you need to decorate a particularly blah part of your Web site.

# POV-Ray

POV-Ray (Persistence of Vision Ray-Tracer) is freeware (`http://www.povray.org/index.html`) and belongs to a group of programs called *ray tracers*. A ray tracer renders a scene by shooting rays into it. A scene is built from shapes, lights, a camera, textures, and other items. POV-Ray uses ASCII scripts to define each of these elements. The elements are then rendered into a very high quality and, often, attractive 3D image. You can generate many types of effects including fog, fire, and steam. Simple and advanced primitives are available, as are many predefined patterns and textures. Many example files are included with the program. It is not difficult to learn how to build the scripts using the tutorial. This program has proven addictive for many people, so handle with care.

POV-Ray runs on Macintosh, Windows, and UNIX boxes. For PCs, you need Windows 3.1 or later, a 386 or better CPU and 8MB RAM minimum. A DOS version is also available. For the Mac, you need a 68020 CPU (with or without FPU) or Power Mac, System 7 or better, and at least 8MB or RAM; for Linux, you need a minimum 386 with 4MB RAM. POV-Ray also is available for the Sun OS and the Commodore Amiga.

# Ray Dream Designer

Ray Dream Designer (`http://www.fractal.com/products/rds/index.html`) from Fractal Design Products (the same engine is also used in Corel Dream, part of the CorelDraw bundle) is a visual 3D modeling program. You use many of the same elements as POV-Ray such as lights, cameras, and textures (called shaders here). But you interact with the shapes and other elements on the screen in whatever level of detail you want, from a wire frame view to a mostly rendered view. You can grab the 3D object and rotate it, apply different textures, try different lights or camera angles, and so on. Then when you have it just the way you want it, you can render it into a final image. The package comes with several hundred premade models and two wizards: one for automatically creating indoor or outdoor scenes and another that will lead you step-by-step through building your model. If you purchase Ray Dream Designer as part of Ray Dream Studio, you can also animate almost all aspects of your 3D model and scene. Scenes from this program can be directly exported to VRML as well as GIF or JPG.

To run this program on the Macintosh, you need a 68040 processor or Power Mac (no FPU required), System 7.0 or higher, and a minimum of 12MB application RAM; for Windows 3.1, 95, or NT, you need a 486 or Pentium CPU with 16MB RAM for best performance.

# Fractint

Fractal images are the pictorial representation of fractal geometry or sets of mathematical points. These iterative formulas can generate very complex, abstract, and beautiful graphics. Using Fractint (DOS) or Winfract (both freeware from The Stone Soup Group), you don't have to worry about drawing anything; let the equations do it for you. By using different equations, changing parameters in the equation, or using different color maps, you can generate some striking images. You do not need to be a math wizard to do this. All of the equations and color maps are named. The images can then be saved as GIFs and used on your Web page. You can find the DOS or Windows version at many file archives on the Internet such as `http://filepile.com`.

Similar programs are available for UNIX. Xfractint (`http://spanky.triumf.ca/www/fractint/xfractint_port.html`) is an X-windows port of Fractint and Xmfract is a Motif, multiwindowed version. A Macintosh version is not available. Only basic system resources (no FPU required for most equations) are required on all platforms.

# Summary

The choices for graphics packages are many and varied. In this chapter, you've seen

- Bitmap editors and paint programs
- Vector-style graphics packages
- A key graphic utility, Debabelizer
- How to add moving pictures to a Web page with GIF animation or streaming video
- Some proprietary solutions for adding animated graphics or multimedia
- 3D rendering programs and fractals

If you work with a team and most of the drawing or graphics creation is done by a professional, you might need Debabelizer only for palette touch-up or image resizing. If you plan on creating more graphics yourself, choose the set of tools that will help you get your job finished the easiest and fastest. If you have no formal artistic training and find yourself doing a lot of graphics creation, I highly recommend learning more about color and design techniques either through further reading, hanging out with artistic types, visiting award-winning Web sites and examining their appeal, or taking courses at your local institution of higher learning. Unfortunately, many Web authors understand how to use many high-powered graphic packages to create very low-powered Web garbage graphics. Learning to create effective graphics is just as important as having the right tools. Give a hoot—don't pollute the Web.

# Advanced Web Authoring Tools

*by Rick Darnell*

In the previous chapters of this section, we've discussed various tools and utilities that help you manage your Web site and pages, including creating pages, creating images, checking links, and validating HTML.

Currently, three major Web authoring suites are available to developers on Windows and Macintosh platforms. The first is Microsoft FrontPage, which Vermeer Technologies originally developed and then Microsoft purchased. Microsoft has since integrated the package with its other software applications, including the popular Microsoft Office.

Another option is Macromedia Backstage. Backstage doesn't offer the additional feature of integration with other applications, but it is still a powerful set of programs in its own right. It includes an add-on server that supports the Web server in delivering dynamic content and supports HTML files located on the local machine and on remote Web servers.

The third Web development suite is NetObjects Fusion by NetObjects software. This package, like Microsoft FrontPage, is available for both Macintosh and Windows users. Furthermore, it's currently the only suite that provides for pixel-level precision of your Web page design.

> **NOTE**
>
> Both Web management programs I discuss in this chapter provide options for creating dynamic HTML pages. A traditional HTML page is a static creature. After it's created, it doesn't change, similar to a newspaper, in which the words don't change after they are set on the page in ink. You can go back to look at the words as many times as you want, but they'll still be the same pages in the same order.
>
> A dynamic HTML page can be different every time you see it, similar to the difference between the five and ten o'clock evening news on television. The format is the same, but many of the stories are changed or updated from the earlier broadcast.

# Microsoft FrontPage

FrontPage, an advanced Web management and authoring tool, features an integrated set of tools that are designed to help you in creating, implementing, and managing Web sites.

It includes multiple author and administrator capabilities, enabling system administrators to spread tasks across a larger group of people and still maintain a grasp on what needs to be done and what is complete.

FrontPage has two major components: FrontPage Editor, a WYSIWYG HTML editor that eliminates the need to remember the nuances of each markup tag, and FrontPage Explorer,

*Advanced Web Authoring Tools*

CHAPTER 36

731

36

ADVANCED
WEB AUTHORING
TOOLS

which provides a visual and intuitive interface that tracks links, pages, images, and other page components.

---

**NOTE**

How do you want to Explore today? With FrontPage, Microsoft now has three applications that go by the name *Explorer*: the file management utility packaged with Windows 95, Windows Explorer; the browser known as Internet Explorer; and, included with FrontPage, FrontPage Explorer. Any mention of Explorer in this chapter is a reference to FrontPage Explorer. I will refer to all other Explorers by their full name.

---

**TIP**

The three primary FrontPage components—Explorer, Editor, and To Do List—won't work without a connection to your Web site through a Web server. FrontPage provides the Personal Web Server for use on individual computers. For actual deployment and use, you'll want to use a more advanced server, such as Microsoft Internet Information Server or O'Reilly WebSite. For more information on the strengths and weaknesses of various servers, see Chapter 37, "Web Servers."

---

FrontPage also provides a set of Web robots, commonly referred to as Web bots, which are specialized CGI scripts that provide implementation for discussion groups, full-text Web searches, and form handling.

As with many Microsoft products, FrontPage makes extensive use of wizards to convert tasks into a series of questions and choices, such as creating Web sites and pages.

## FrontPage Explorer

The central component to the FrontPage suite is Explorer. Explorer provides a visual interface for administering your Web projects. Depending on your Web site's size and organization—whether it's an Internet site or an intranet implementation—Explorer provides an intuitive interface for creating, editing, and deleting pages and verifying hyperlinks. (See Figure 36.1.)

Explorer's initial view serves as a type of Web control panel. It shows your Web in Hyperlink View, which is divided into two parts. On the left side of the screen is an outline view that shows each page included as part of the site. Clicking a page in this view makes it the center of the link view on the right side of the screen.

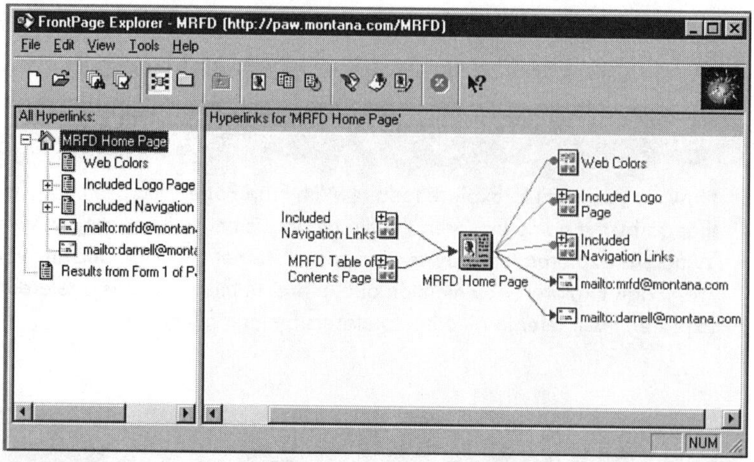

**Figure 36.1.**

*FrontPage Explorer serves as the front end to all other FrontPage applications in addition to providing a graphical view of your site's construction and links.*

**Figure 36.1.**

*FrontPage Explorer serves as the front end to all other FrontPage applications in addition to providing a graphical view of your site's construction and links.*

**NOTE**

Which web is which? FrontPage refers to each set of related directories and files as a web. So, if you've created an area on your company server for each of three departments using FrontPage, each area is its own web.

In essence, each of the FrontPage webs is a Web application—a group of HTML pages that serve a specific purpose, whether it is customer service, corporate presence, or hosting a discussion group.

The link views show a page and all links to and from it. All items to the left of the page are links from another source on the current web, and all items to the right are destinations from the current page. If a page has more links that are not displayed, it is marked with a plus sign (+).

You can also display the Web site as a series of directories by selecting the Folder View button. Initially, doing so only displayed other HTML pages and CGI scripts. You can also choose to display links to images, multiple links to the same page, and links to anchors within the current document.

You can add specialized items to any web. For example, if you're creating a department site on an intranet and need a discussion group, you would start the Discussion Web Wizard and select the checkbox for adding it to the current web. Any web can be moved to a server for publication on an intranet or Internet.

One of FrontPage's strongest features is its selection of wizards and predefined Web templates to quickly and easily build a Web-based application.

*Advanced Web Authoring Tools*

CHAPTER **36**

733

**36**

ADVANCED
WEB AUTHORING
TOOLS

## Explorer Templates

Templates are preconstructed webs with a predetermined set of pages already in place. FrontPage includes the following four templates that fit this description, plus an option to create a Web site completely devoid of any page:

- Normal Web: A web template that consists of a single page and a folder for images.

- Customer Support Web: This template is designed for Web sites that serve a high volume of technical support inquiries. This web helps to organize and improve Web-based customer service.

- Project Web: This template creates a web for a specific project, including lists of contributing members, status reports, schedules, discussions, and archives.

- Personal Web: This template is a starting point for creating a set of personal Web pages, including a home page. In effect, it's the same as the Normal Web.

FrontPage also includes an Empty Web, which sets up the necessary support directories for a FrontPage web but doesn't include any HTML pages.

## Explorer Wizards

Web Wizards are similar to templates, but instead of a one-size-fits-all approach, it generates a customized set of pages based on your response to a set of questions about your intent for the new web.

- Corporate Presence Wizard: This wizard generates a set of pages and directories to establish a basic Web presence for a company. You can also tailor it for individual departments on an intranet server. It provides templates for products, services, department information, mission statements, and personnel directories.

- Discussion Web Wizard: This wizard sets up a portion of your server for hosting a Usenet-type discussion group without installing a dedicated news server. It includes support for threads, tables of contents, text searching, and administration.

There's a third Web Wizard, the Import Web Wizard, although it is slightly different in purpose than the first two. The Import Web Wizard creates a place for a new FrontPage Web and then copies files from another directory on your system or from a remote server.

## FrontPage Security

When you use Explorer to manage a site, you must ensure that every web has at least one administrator who is identified with a name and password when the web is first created. The web administrator controls access by setting permissions for end users, authors, and other administrators, such as the following:

- End users: By default, a web is open to everyone. If it's necessary to control who has access to a web, administrators can identify individuals to be excluded or included for browsing. If a user attempts to browse a protected web, he or she is prompted for a username and password before he or she is granted any access.

■ Authors: Web authors can create, edit, or delete pages, but they cannot create, change, or remove webs. By virtue of this level, they're also included as end users.

■ Administrators: Administrators have permission to create and delete webs, pages, and authors, and to designate other administrators. (See Figure 36.2.) They also set which users have access to browse the finished product.

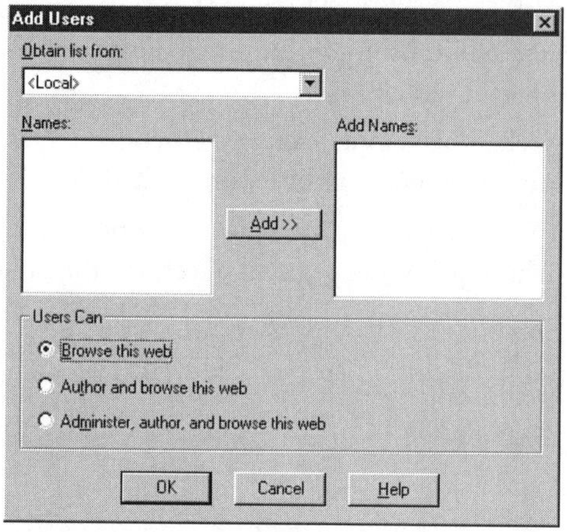

**FIGURE 36.2.**

*In the Add Users box, define which users have access to manage or browse the Web site.*

By default, security settings are inherited from the root web. All administrators, authors, and end users defined for the root web are valid for any other web created under the root web unless otherwise specified. A user's permission level is checked any time a web page is accessed for any reason.

In addition to screening name and password information, you can screen all permissions by entering a mask IP address. Using a series of numbers and wildcards, you can restrict access to specific computers or groups of computers on the network. Even if a perpetrator knows a name and password combination, he or she must still use the right computer to gain access.

## FrontPage Editor

FrontPage was one of the first HTML editors to offer a WYSIWYG interface for creating Web pages. It doesn't require that you have any knowledge of HTML, even to create complex pages that include forms and embedded objects such as ActiveX controls and Java applets.

To launch Editor from Explorer, click its icon from the toolbar or double-click a page icon. When it is opened, Editor manages virtually all page editing tasks from the toolbar, which includes buttons for text formatting, hyperlinks, tables, forms, Web bots, and embedded objects. (See Figure 36.3.) Access other page features, such as a page title, default text and link colors, and background color, from the Edit menu.

**FIGURE 36.3.**

*FrontPage Editor provides a graphical interface for creating Web pages with text, graphics, forms, tables, and other specialized content.*

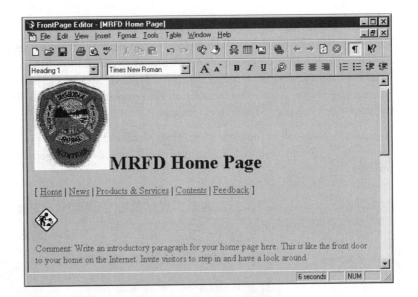

Working with Editor is much like working within a word processor. You can type, cut, and paste any text on the page. It also provides advanced formatting of the text, including changes in size, color, and typeface.

---

**TIP**

Even though FrontPage supports advanced text formatting features, the final results might not appear as you expect on all browsers. Be sure to test your pages on a variety of Web browsers to ensure consistency and compatibility.

---

One feature that makes Editor especially easy to use is drag-and-drop hyperlink creation. If you need to copy links from Explorer or other Web pages, click and hold the desired page or link and drag it to the appropriate location in the editing window.

Editor supports forms in two ways. First is the Form Page Wizard (described later in this chapter). Through a series of questions and checkboxes, the wizard asks which kind of information you need and assembles the elements into a finished HTML page. You can also create a form manually by inserting individual HTML form elements. After the first form element is inserted, it's surrounded by dotted lines to denote the boundaries of the form. Then, you can specify which CGI script will process the form's contents.

Like Explorer, one of Editor's strongest features is its use of templates and Wizards to speed the development of individual pages.

## Editor Templates

FrontPage Editor includes a set of templates that cover virtually any page publishing need. Its options include bibliography, employee directory, feedback form, frequently asked questions, glossary of terms, guest book, office directory, event registration, software data sheet, table of contents, and what's new. Also included in the template selection is a "Normal page," which includes only the basic HTML structure tags.

In other templates, all of the basic formatting, placeholder text, and graphics are in place. (See Figure 36.4.) All you have to do is substitute your content for the generic material that Editor provides.

**Figure 36.4.**

*FrontPage templates are ready-made Web pages, which make it faster to develop new pages.*

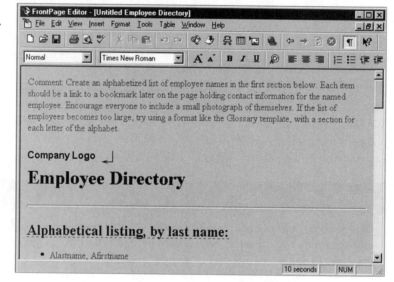

## Editor Wizards

Editor includes four wizards to walk you through creating pages that normally require extensive HTML coding or CGI scripting. The following are the four wizards:

■ Database Connector Wizard: Using an ODBC connection and a special template file created with Editor, a developer can create an Internet Database Connector (IDC) file. The IDC enables Structured Query Language (SQL) queries (including database additions and modifications) to any compliant database accessible from the Web server machine.

■ Form Page Wizard: Similar to the Home Page Wizard (discussed in the last bullet), this Wizard prompts you for the kind of information you want to collect from users. You can choose to submit the information to an e-mail address or CGI script or post it to a Web page for later viewing. The wizard completes the process by adding text and formatting the page, which results in an attractive, immediately usable form. (See Figure 36.5.)

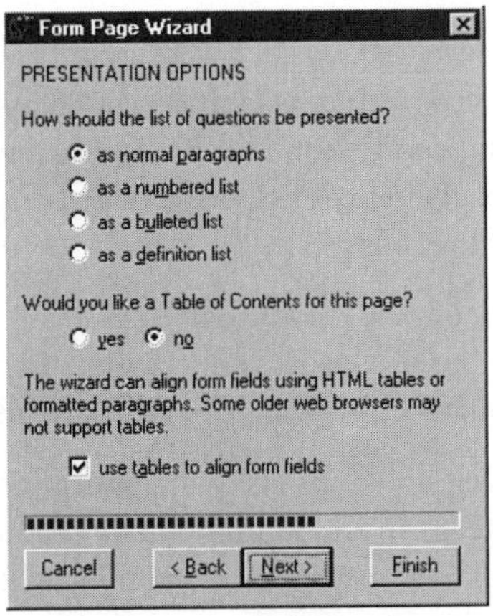

*Advanced Web Authoring Tools*

CHAPTER 36

737

36

ADVANCED
WEB AUTHORING
TOOLS

FIGURE 36.5.
*The Form Page Wizard is one example of a tool that builds a ready-to-use form based on your answers to a series of questions.*

Form Page Wizard

PRESENTATION OPTIONS

How should the list of questions be presented?

- as normal paragraphs
- as a numbered list
- as a bulleted list
- as a definition list

Would you like a Table of Contents for this page?

- yes  - no

The wizard can align form fields using HTML tables or formatted paragraphs. Some older web browsers may not support tables.

☑ use tables to align form fields

Cancel    < Back    Next >    Finish

■ Frames Wizard: Frames are becoming more accepted as a serious design tool for Web pages. The Frames Wizard visually defines how the frames should be placed within the browser window (as shown in Figure 36.6) and creates the HTML code to implement the result. Chapter 18, "Creating Sophisticated Layouts with Frames and Layers," provides more information about using frames.

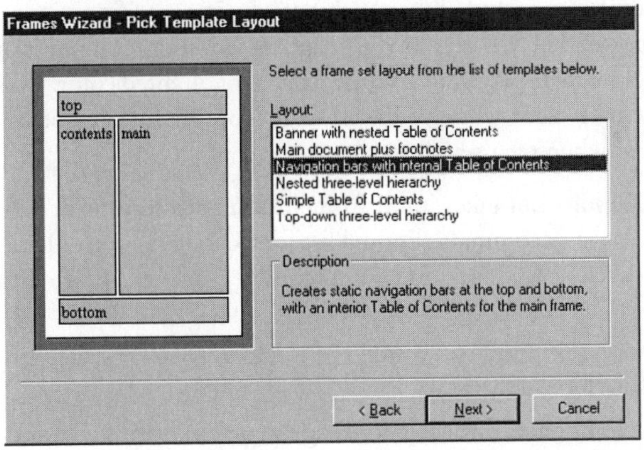

FIGURE 36.6.
*The Frames Wizard builds the HTML needed to present a series of frames to the user in one of several predetermined layouts.*

Frames Wizard - Pick Template Layout

Select a frame set layout from the list of templates below.

top
contents | main
bottom

Layout:
Banner with nested Table of Contents
Main document plus footnotes
Navigation bars with internal Table of Contents
Nested three-level hierarchy
Simple Table of Contents
Top-down three-level hierarchy

Description
Creates static navigation bars at the top and bottom, with an interior Table of Contents for the main frame.

< Back    Next >    Cancel

■ Personal Home Page Wizard: By asking a series of questions about you and your activities and interests, this Wizard constructs a one-page document that serves as your personal Web page. There are enough options that you can use this either for a strictly personal situation or as an online biography/resume for corporate and business situations.

# Web Bots

Web robots, also called Web bots, are objects that you insert on a page to include capabilities that would normally require extensive CGI programming. The list of capabilities includes inserting other Web pages, scheduled images and text, discussion groups, tables of contents, time stamps, and other functions.

You can implement some of these capabilities (time stamps, scheduled images, inserting other Web pages) by placing a Web bot directly on the page, but to implement others, you must integrate them through Web wizards and form handling (discussion groups, feedback forms).

After you insert a Web bot on a page, a dialog appears to collect the configuration information that the Web bot needs to function. For example, if you insert an Include Web bot, you're prompted for the URL of the page that will show when the page is displayed. (See Figure 36.7.)

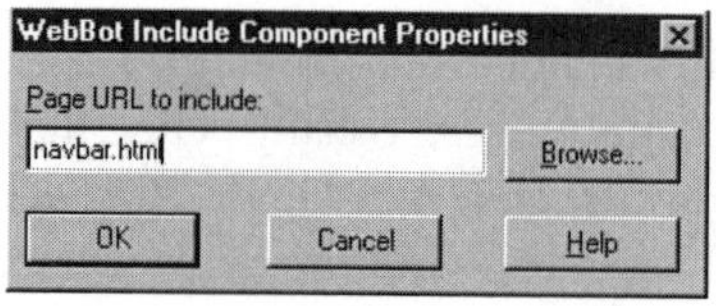

**FIGURE 36.7.**

*FrontPage uses Web bots to add functionality to Web pages, such as inserting another Web page at runtime.*

You would also include other Web bots during specific actions, such as adding comments or unsupported HTML tags to your page. By adding a comment to a Web page, you put a Web bot in place to display your comments in a highlighted color. This means that you can see what notes you've made while you're actually working on the document, even though they're not displayed when the user views the page.

A Save Results Bot takes input from a form and stores it in a location you define, such as an HTML page or comma-delimited list for a database to use. This makes it easy to collect information such as feedback and comments, registration information, and other end-user information.

# To Do List

The Explorer and Editor in FrontPage share an integrated To Do list to help with delegation and tracking of Web editing tasks. The list includes the task, who is supposed to do it, and the priority for completion. (See Figure 36.8.)

To more easily work directly from the list, you can highlight any linked job and click the Do Task button to launch Editor and load a copy of the page for editing. When the page is saved, you're prompted to remove the associated item from the To Do list.

You can extend the usefulness of the To Do list by using Editor to include comments to the affected Web page and to describe in greater detail what needs to be done or corrected on the page. The comments will only appear during editing, not when the page is displayed.

*Advanced Web Authoring Tools*

CHAPTER 36

739

36

ADVANCED
WEB AUTHORING
TOOLS

**FIGURE 36.8.**
*The To Do List provides a way of tracking assignments on your Web site.*

| Task | Assigned To | Priority | Linked To | Description |
|---|---|---|---|---|
| Replace Logo Image | RDarnell | High | Included Logo Page | replace the image on this page with |
| Customize Home Page | RDarnell | High | MRFD Home Page | replace generic text with something |
| Customize News Page | RDarnell | High | MRFD News Page | add your own public relations text |
| Customize Products Page | RDarnell | High | MRFD Products Page | create data sheets for your own proc |
| Customize Feedback Fo... | RDarnell | Medium | MRFD Feedback Page | adjust input areas in the form |
| Customize TOC Page | RDarnell | Medium | MRFD Table of Contents P... | describe sections in more detail |

FrontPage To Do List - MRFD

☐ Keep window open   ☐ Show history

Do Task | Details... | Complete... | Add... | Close | Help

# Bonus Pack Add-ons

In addition to the three core components of FrontPage, Microsoft also includes several additional programs and features with its product. These include a Web server specially designed for standalone or small group operation, a wizard for posting pages to your Internet Service Provider, and a new image utility. And, like every other Microsoft product available on the market, it includes a copy of the latest version of Internet Explorer.

## Personal Web Server

Many Web authors are learning the usefulness of having a Web server installed on their desktop computer to develop and test their pages. The Microsoft Personal Web Server, a 32-bit Web server, is a useful answer to this need.

You can also use the Personal Web Server to operate a small Web site for a workgroup or small peer-to-peer intranets. This 32-bit application runs on either Windows 95 or Windows NT and requires a minimum of 8MB RAM and 1MB of hard disk space. It requires more disk space to hold Web pages.

Although it doesn't include many of the advanced features of a full-fledged Web server, it is more than adequate for developing and testing Web pages and forms. It includes support for handling pages for the HyperText Transfer Protocol (HTTP) and for working with forms and data for the Common Gateway Interface (CGI).

The Personal Web Server does not support secure transaction options. Although its official limit is five users, two to three is a more realistic option, depending on the operating system and available resources.

You can automatically install the Personal Web Server through the FrontPage setup window or by downloading the software from Microsoft at www.microsoft.com/ie/iesk/pws.htm. You manage the Personal Web Server through the Windows Control Panel and a browser interface. (See Figure 36.9.) Use forms and hyperlinks to gather information and update the server configuration files.

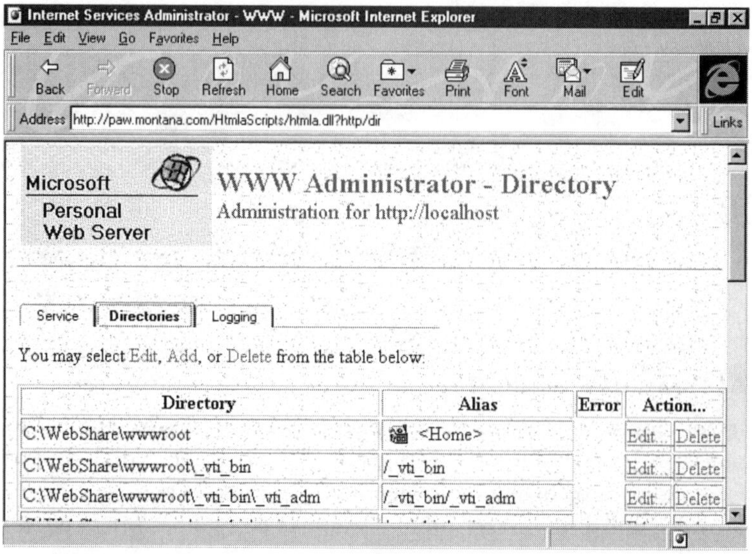

**Figure 36.9.**

*Instead of a standard dialog box, a series of forms manages the Personal Web Server through a browser interface.*

## Web Publishing Wizard

After your Web pages are ready for viewing by the rest of the browsing world, you'll need a way to transport them to your Internet service provider. Using an FTP program can be a clunky process, so Microsoft developed the Web Publishing Wizard. This handy little utility enables users to easily post Web pages to their ISP or intranet site. It supports a wide range of providers, including CompuServe, Sprynet, and America Online, in addition to compatibility with Apache Web server, Microsoft Internet Information Server, and Internet servers that conform to NCSA HTTPD. (See Figure 36.10.)

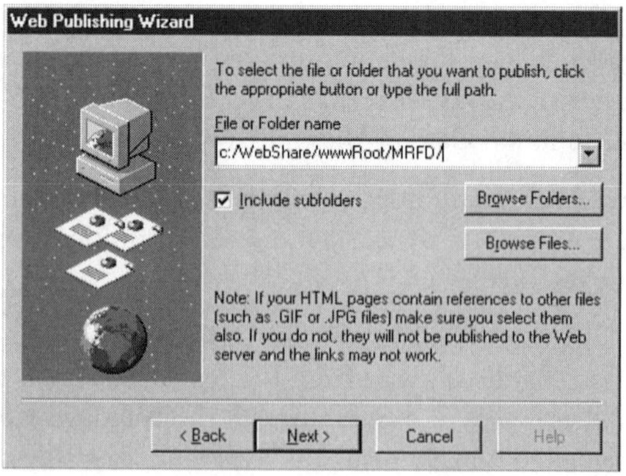

**Figure 36.10.**

*The Web Publishing Wizard simplifies the process of posting a set of files or directories to a remote Web site.*

The Web Publishing Wizard connects to the ISP, determines the protocol it needs to copy the files, and then uploads the files to the appropriate directory on the Web server. To further simplify the process, the Web Publishing Wizard uses the same connection information as your browser. If you can connect to your ISP to browse, you can connect to update your Web pages.

## Image Composer

With its new Image Composer software, Microsoft has moved past the Paint program it shipped as standard equipment with Windows. Where Paint is a multipurpose tool for print or screen, Image Composer is designed explicitly for screen images.

Like many other image editing utilities on the market, Image Composer treats bitmap images like objects, which makes editing and combining images for different effects easier. More than 600 images are included with the program, which you can layer or combine to create complex collages and effects that you can then use in your Web pages. In addition to the images, Image Composer also includes 500 graphic effects with which you can easily alter a picture's appearance to the desired effect. (See Figure 36.11.)

**FIGURE 36.11.**

*Microsoft Image Composer is a graphics tool designed specifically for creating on-screen images, including GIF animations.*

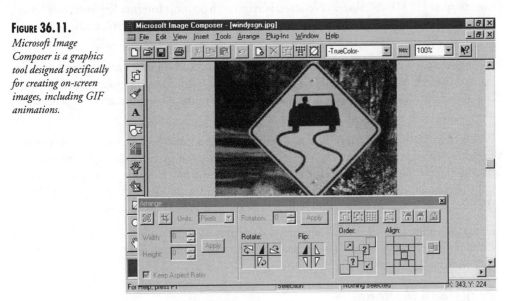

Although the available effects are on par with professional image programs such as Photoshop, they are easier to use thanks to a simplified pushbutton interface. This could lead to abuse and convoluted finished products if it is not used carefully.

# Macromedia Backstage

Macromedia Backstage is the latest entry into the growing field of Web site development applications. Backstage draws its name from its behind-the-scenes approach to implementing Web pages and features. Using Backstage to create Web pages on a local or remote server is only the beginning of its capabilities, although it is an important capability.

Perhaps Backstage's strongest feature is its full support for database connectivity through simple-to-use objects. This enables you to post user information directly to a database from a Web page and generate reports directly from the data into other Web pages, all without learning a CGI scripting language.

Backstage is designed for both first-time Web authors and experienced developers. You can complete a basic site including advanced features and make it available to the browsing public in hours, not days.

HTML files created with Backstage are compatible with any Web server and any browser that can interpret HTML 2.0, such as Netscape Navigator, Microsoft Internet Explorer, and NCSA Mosaic. Support is also included for some HTML 3.2 extensions, such as tables, advanced image handling, and logical formatting codes.

A complete set of Backstage objects supported through an add-on server offer insertion of specialized content on your pages, including hit counters and discussion groups. In addition, a "conditional include" object enables you to tailor individual pages on the fly, depending on who views them.

Packaged together as Backstage Desktop Studio and Enterprise Studio, the basic elements—Backstage Designer, Manager, Server, and objects—are the foundation applications of the Backstage line. To make the Web development process a one-stop-shopping process, Backstage also includes a Web-optimized version of Macromedia xRes, a full copy of O'Reilly WebSite Web server, PowerApplets, clip art library, and HTML templates.

Desktop Studio works with desktop-based databases, such as Access, FoxPro, dBASE, and Paradox. Enterprise Studio extends database connectivity to client-server databases such as Oracle, Sybase, and Informix.

## Backstage Manager

With Backstage Manager, you can administer your Web site and individual projects from a bird's eye view. You can create new content and edit existing files on local or remote Web sites.

Backstage Manager gives a structural view of your Web with each set of pages included in its own *project folder*. (See Figure 36.12.) This provides a central point for creating, editing, and managing your Web projects. As you use Backstage to navigate through different Web sites, local or remote, you can launch Designer to edit pages or other image, sound, and multimedia applications for other content items.

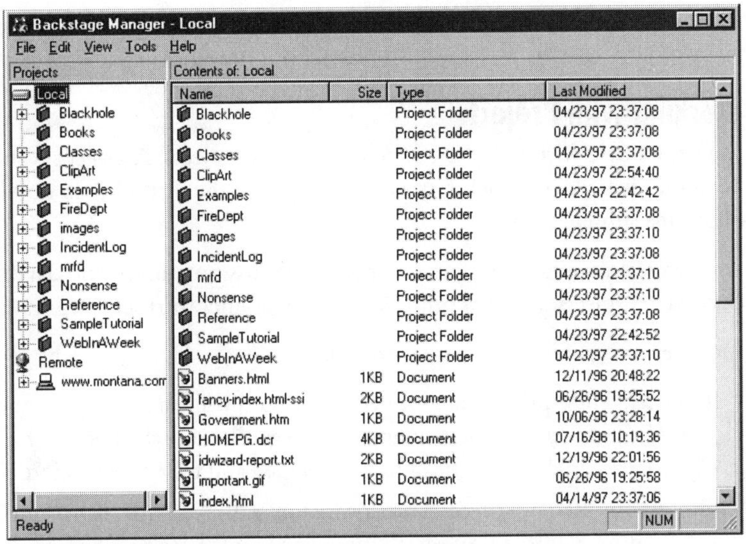

**FIGURE 36.12.**

*Backstage Manager is a project-level tool that manages a Web site and some of its more advanced features, such as discussion groups and user profiles.*

Most sites are administered through local access, but Manager can work with sites in remote locations through FTP server access. You can download an entire site for editing, disconnect from the server, and upload it later. Or, you can directly edit a page for spot changes.

One option for working with Manager for remote projects is to create all the files and structure you need on the local host. Then, copy the completed project to the remote site by dragging and dropping it onto the appropriate remote server icon. When you connect to the remote site, Manager will automatically upload the new files without working through a tedious FTP process.

Backstage divides each project into four elements:

■ Web pages: These pages are HTML files and the related content within in them, such as images, applets, and plug-ins.

■ Discussion groups: A Backstage discussion group, similar to a Usenet newsgroup, includes a series of messages about a particular topic. Unlike FrontPage's method of creating an HTML file for each posting, Backstage maintains the messages using a simple database and displays them using a small group of pages.

■ Database queries: Every project includes a set of queries used to access the databases that project needs. If more than one project needs a query, you must duplicate the query in each project that needs it.

■ User profiles: As with a Web server, you can include a list of users who have special privileges within a Backstage project. These users, whom you manage separately from the Web server, are unique to each project.

Using these four elements, each project becomes a web application that stands on its own for its own purpose, whether it is customer service, intranet departments, or a personal Web site.

## Working with Projects

Manager works with HTML and related files as projects. A project is the starting point of any Web site created with Backstage, which gives you the flexibility to develop unique sites or applications simultaneously.

Each project maintains its own set of users, discussion groups, and database access and queries. Backstage Objects, inserted on pages using Designer, further support each of these features.

Manager recognizes two types of projects:

- Local: These projects are located entirely on your machine. They stay on your computer, and you can access them at any time, regardless of whether you have access to the network. Web sites typically are developed and tested here before they are deployed.

- Remote: Remote projects are located on a Web server that is not a part of your local machine. Remote projects are organized by the server where they are deployed. To connect to the remote site, you need to have FTP server software installed on your local machine.

Clicking any of the project icons within a local or remote server shows an expanded view of the project's contents in the right pane of the Manager window.

The project directories further divide into public and private parts. When you install Backstage on your computer, it creates a `Private` subdirectory parallel to your document subdirectory (such as `html` or `htdocs`) within your Web site. The `Private` subdirectory contains information about discussion groups, queries, and users. For security, this information is kept in `Private`, which you can access through the Web and FTP server only by Backstage Manager and Server. Although you can browse these files directly using other software, editing them directly can compromise their integrity and prevent the project from working properly.

## Keeping Links Current

Part of the problem in maintaining a Web site is keeping the hyperlinks within the site valid and working. If you move or delete files or restructure project folders, hyperlinks within the site can suddenly point to pages that no longer exist. Maintaining these links is one of the most important aspects of site management; nothing says poor craftsmanship like lumpy duct tape and broken hyperlinks.

To help keep a handle on this problem, Manager has two built-in functions to track links and pages. The first is an automatic link update utility for files that are moved via the drag-and-drop feature.

*Advanced Web Authoring Tools*

CHAPTER 36

745

36

ADVANCED
WEB AUTHORING
TOOLS

**NOTE**

Dragging and dropping files from project to project and folder to folder within Backstage doesn't perform a traditional move. (The file is not cut from its old location and pasted in the new one.) Instead, it acts as a copy operation, leaving the file in the original location and adding a new copy of it to the destination.

Whenever you move a file with the drag-and-drop feature in Manager, a dialog box appears to update the hyperlinks for the file in its new location. This box looks at each relative link on the Web page that moved, ignoring links that consist of a complete URL, and updates the links to reflect the new path to their targets from the Web page's new location.

This feature is limited to one-way updating; it updates the links only within the page that moved. It does not change hyperlinks to that page from other pages because the original file is left in its original location. If you delete the original file, the links to it are no longer valid, which presents another problem: How do you find out which pages have hyperlinks affected by missing pages?

Manager includes a utility called the Link Wizard that looks at every hyperlink in the Web site to confirm its validity. You then have the opportunity to provide new address information for each hyperlink.

At your choosing, Backstage Manager can automatically fix broken links. The only way an automatic fix occurs is if it finds only one file on the Web site that matches the name of the missing link. The spelling is case-sensitive and must match exactly. The other option gives you the choice of specifying a new file for every broken link.

If you move a large number of files using a file manager or change your site in other substantive ways, the Link Wizard helps you keep a handle on maintaining the integrity of hyperlinks within your Web site. If you use the Link Wizard regularly, the result is a user-friendly site that doesn't leave people frustrated by the message `Error 404: File Not Found`.

## Backstage Designer

Backstage Designer, the HTML editor of the Backstage suite, provides a graphical interface so that you can see what your page will look like on the browser with a set of powerful tools with which to use HTML tags in the HTML 2.0 specification. (See Figure 36.13.) This spec includes images, links, tables, forms, and buttons, in addition to newer items from HTML 3.2 and custom extensions, such as Java, ActiveX, and Netscape Plug-ins.

**FIGURE 36.13.**

*Backstage Designer is an HTML editor that displays your pages as they're likely to appear on a browser, rather than as a list of tags and attributes.*

**NOTE**

Backstage does not yet support frame tags, one of the newer items on the list of HTML tags.

Some pages use tags in slightly different ways that Backstage does not entirely understand. For example, many editors don't close the new paragraph tag, `<P>`, with a closing tag, `</P>`. Backstage reports formatting errors on these pages and adds or removes tags as it sees necessary.

These inconsistencies between the way different editors format their pages are an inconvenience at times, but Backstage can still open the pages for editing.

The Backstage Designer toolbars and graphical editing area provide access to virtually every HTML feature available. You also have access at any time to the HTML source code for adding advanced items, such as JavaScript and browser-specific extensions.

## Designer's Text Capabilities

Not so long ago, your choice of text formatting was limited to whatever the browser used for its default. With the evolution of HTML, it is now possible to define a wide range of custom attributes using the `<FONT>` tag. This tag gives you a lot of flexibility in controlling exactly what font face you want to use, as well as its size. Unfortunately, learning all of the nuances for the tag's attributes can be a time-consuming process.

With Backstage Designer, it's all a matter of point and click. Highlight the text you want to change, click the palette button, and select a color from the list.

Other attributes are as simple to assign using point and click. You can access headings, fonts, font styles, justification, numbered lists, and unordered lists from the toolbars, in addition to special-use tags such as citation, definition, emphasis, and strikeout.

## Working with Images and Image Maps

Graphics are now an integral part of a Web page, whether they're simple bullets, company logos, navigation bars, or complex image maps.

Designer supports GIF and JPEG images in all of these roles through its point-and-click interface. Designer controls all the basic features of a graphic through a properties box. These features include image alignment, borders, horizontal and vertical spacing, and scaling.

Designer also provides an editing screen for creating an image map. An image map is a graphic with hyperlinks embedded in various areas. It offers a great opportunity for creativity and functionality when you can create multiple links within an image.

Images and image maps are covered in more detail in Chapter 12, "Adding Images to Your Web Page."

## Adding Specialized Content

One of the fastest growing areas of Web page development is specialized content, including real-time sound, animation, virtual reality, and other non-HTML items.

> **NOTE**
>
> For the latest on the W3C proposals and developments on working with objects embedded in HTML, check out the W3C Web site for ActiveX and Java at www.w3.org/pub/WWW/OOP/. For the latest on real-time audio and video content, see www.w3.org/pub/WWW/Consortium/Prospectus/RealTime.html.

Backstage Designer directly supports the inclusion of Java applets, ActiveX controls, and Netscape Plug-ins.

To include a Java applet, the class and related files, such as images and audio, should reside somewhere in the root web. After specifying the location of the class, add additional parameters through a tab in the dialog box. (See Figure 36.14.) At the time of this writing, Netscape Navigator 2.0 and later, Microsoft Internet Explorer 3.0, and Sun HotJava support Java applets. Java applet support is included on a "wish list" for NCSA Mosaic, but no timetable is available for when it might be implemented.

Microsoft developed ActiveX controls to provide advanced object linking and embedding control for content from other applications, such as Excel and Word. Like Java applets, the various aspects of ActiveX controls are controlled through a dialog box.

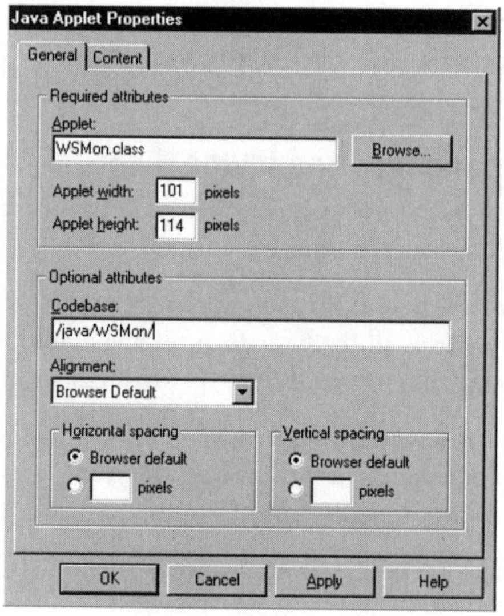

**FIGURE 36.14.**

*The Java Applet Properties dialog box provides an interface to control the attributes and parameters, including an image to display if the browser is not Java-compatible.*

In addition to support for embedding traditional applications such as word processing and spreadsheets, ActiveX controls are available for linking Netscape Navigator Plug-ins with Microsoft Internet Explorer. Functionally, ActiveX controls extend the capability of the browser the same way as a Netscape Plug-in, in addition to providing a way to include standard Windows interface items (buttons, window layouts, and menus) within the Web page. Controls are loaded into the browser automatically when needed and don't require a separate installation process.

Netscape Plug-ins provide inline support for third-party add-on content such as VRML, RealAudio, and animation. Without Netscape Plug-ins, to view content not directly supported by the browser, you must launch an external application. When you use a plug-in, the content is included inline with the rest of the document without the need for switching to an external application.

## Going Beyond HTML

For features that Backstage toolbars or menus don't support, such as frames, Backstage Designer includes an HTML source-edit mode (shown in Figure 36.15) to view or change the source code for the page. When you save the changes, the modifications are displayed in the editing window. If you put in HTML tags that Backstage doesn't recognize, the style does not appear, but the text still appears.

*Advanced Web Authoring Tools*

CHAPTER 36

749

36

ADVANCED
WEB AUTHORING
TOOLS

**FIGURE 36.15.**

*The HTML source edit window enables the page designer to view or change the base code, including adding unsupported items such as JavaScript or VBScript.*

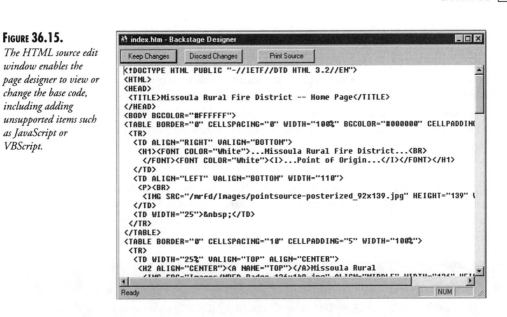

Designer also goes one step further to ensure correct HTML code by performing HTML validation. If it detects a formatting tag that was not closed or an incompatible nesting of tags, it corrects the errors and alerts you to the inconsistencies.

Because of its capability to edit the source code, Designer will support future extensions of the HTML specification without requiring an immediate upgrade to a new version of Designer, although these extensions won't display on the editing screen as they were intended to appear.

The script editor, related to the source-edit window, includes JavaScript and VBScript code for the page. This free-form text window encases its contents in <SCRIPT> tags on the page. Although scripts are invisible to the user, they appear within Designer as a small yellow icon. Double-clicking the icon enables you to edit the code.

> **TIP**
>
> Even though Designer directly supports editing scripts, you still need a compatible browser to test the script's operation. Designer doesn't include any provision for interpreting and executing content within <SCRIPT> tags.

## Backstage Server

If you want the full power of Backstage Objects, you'll need the Backstage Server to work in conjunction with your existing Web server. The Backstage Server is the key to providing dynamic Web pages and content, including database access and discussion groups.

It is also one of Backstage's most confusing features. It is *not* a Web server. It's an add-on that enables an existing Web server to provide the content that Backstage objects generate.

The Backstage Server does not replace an existing Web server; it only provides functionality for the Backstage objects and database features. The Backstage Server services the object library. Backstage objects are small applications that generate HTML content at runtime (another way of saying "dynamic page creation"). These objects include simple functions such as the current date and page hit counter, and advanced features such as posting information to a database or generating custom reports.

Backstage requires that you install 32-bit ODBC drivers for the databases you'll be using with your Backstage applications. Backstage is compatible through ODBC with database applications from Oracle, Microsoft, Sybase, Informix, CA-Ingres, and Borland. Most vendors' ODBC drivers require that you own a 32-bit version of their product before you install it.

> **NOTE**
>
> Microsoft developed Open Database Connectivity (ODBC) as a standard interface for databases. It uses Structured Query Language (SQL) for retrieving, updating, and posting data. Using ODBC, a single application such as Backstage can access a multitude of different databases using a single set of commands, enabling developers to build client/server applications without becoming tied to a specific database program.

You'll need to install and configure a separate Web server, such as those that Microsoft, Netscape, or O'Reilly WebSite, bundled with Studio, offer. Chapter 37 provides more information. Backstage Server works as a companion to the Web server to dynamically create pages at runtime.

## Server Administrator

As information about your Web server changes, you can change the Backstage server to match. To make sure Backstage knows how to work with your server, the Administrator provides a means to enter information about the server root directories, logging requirements, and CGI virtual path mapping.

The Administrator provides no direct control over the Web server; you must use the Web server's configuration programs to control it. You will find details on configuring the Backstage Server and a variety of Web servers in Chapter 12.

## Basic Requirements and Configuration Considerations

Backstage Server runs on Windows NT and Windows 95. Its memory requirements depend on which Windows system you use—24MB for NT or 16MB for Windows 95.

Designer and Manager also run on Windows 3.1. The minimum processor required is a 486 processor running at 33MHz. The memory requirements for these two programs are the same as for the Backstage Server. If you run Designer under Windows 3.1, you will need 8MB of RAM.

> **TIP**
>
> As with many applications, Backstage's performance will improve with additional memory. You can never have too much memory.

You must have an HTTP-compliant Web server on the same machine as Backstage Server. Several products are available, including offerings from Netscape, Microsoft, NCSA, and O'Reilly and Associates.

A Web browser is also good to have on hand. If you include Java applets on your pages, your options are limited to Netscape Navigator (2.0 or later), Microsoft Internet Explorer (3.0 or later), or Sun HotJava. ActiveX controls and Netscape Plug-ins will work with both Internet Explorer and Navigator. You'll need a special ActiveX control from Microsoft to include Netscape Plug-ins in Internet Explorer, however, and a special Netscape Plug-in to use ActiveX controls in Navigator. Nobody ever said the Web was always going to be a simple place.

To work with remote projects, you must have an FTP server on the machine with the Web server. Backstage Manager includes built-in FTP client software but not a server.

## Bonus Add-ons

Backstage also includes a couple of items to increase its value as a turnkey solution to creating a Web site. As I mentioned earlier, the Backstage Server is designed to support an existing Web server. If you don't already have a Web server installed, Backstage includes a full-featured version of O'Reilly WebSite.

To aid in creating Web pages, Backstage also includes a large set of clip art and templates to speed the design process.

# NetObjects Fusion

NetObjects Fusion, another tool in the growing field of integrated Web tools, features a site and HTML editor and graphics manager. It emphasizes site structure and style and offers tools with which you can control and implement sitewide elements such as page borders, styles, banners, navigation bars, and hyperlinks. Editing one of these site features automatically updates the entire site.

Fusion is a site-oriented tool that works with your Web pages as a whole, rather than as a collection of HTML pages that happen to link to each other. In the site context, Fusion generates a map of the entire site structure and allows global changes from a centralized location. This approach encourages top-down design and planning, which results in sites that are more intuitive and easier to browse.

NetObjects Fusion includes a graphical editor, database publishing, and asset management.

Although NetObjects Fusion is listed as a tool for users with a broad range of experience levels, it is primarily geared toward people with previous Web and graphic design experience. It requires Windows 95 or NT with at least 20MB of hard drive space and 16MB of RAM to run.

Rather than breaking down Fusion into a series of programs, I'll look at it in the variety of views it offers for your site and pages. Fusion offers five different views, each of which serves a different need.

## Site View

You use the Site view to create a hierarchical structure of Web pages or import an existing site (as shown in Figure 36.16). You can choose from one of Fusion's predefined formats or create your own.

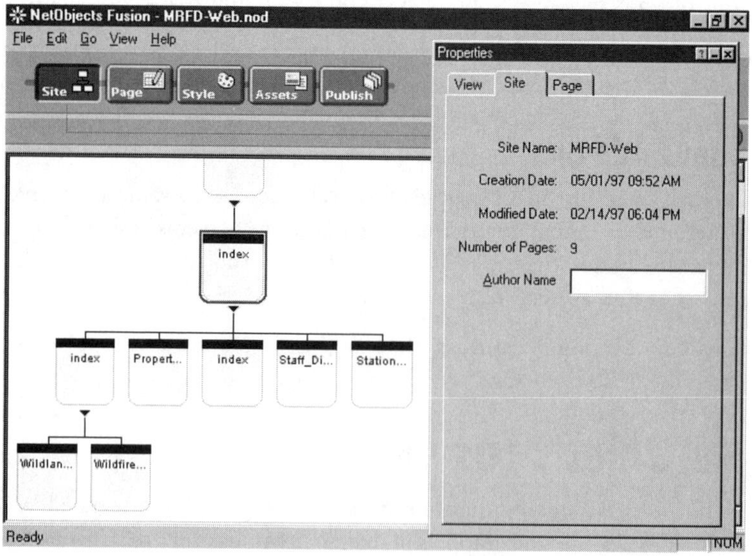

**FIGURE 36.16.**

*The Site view displays a hierarchy of your Web pages with parent, child, and sibling relationships that appropriately places links in each document.*

With the visual interface, you can change or revise the structure as needed to fit the needs of your site. If you're working from an existing site, NetObjects Fusion also includes an option to import the pages into its proprietary format. The conversion process has several holes but still enables you use Fusion's powerful site management features and layout tools.

# Page View

With the Page view, you can create layouts and add or edit content to Web pages. (See Figure 36.17.) One of the most intuitive editors on the market today, it gives the developer precise control over a page's appearance and maintains a graphical interface with drag-and-drop capability.

**FIGURE 36.17.**

*Fusion's use of HTML tables and other automatic formatting features precisely controls each page. A Properties palette controls the overall view of the page and its specific attributes.*

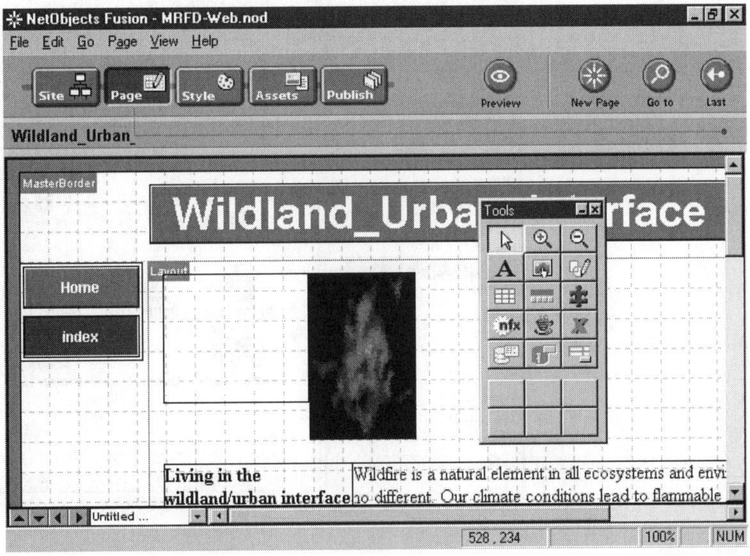

You perform most editing by dragging text, images, applets, or other content to the desired location on the page. Fusion automatically creates a section of HTML table code to ensure that the content appears correctly in a browser. Grids, guides, and snap-to features also aid in aligning different elements.

The drag-and-drop interface extends to interactive content. With Fusion, you can deposit Java applets, ActiveX controls, Netscape Plug-ins, and sound and video files. The program ships with six Java applets, called NetObjects Fusion Components, that fill needs such as tickers, site-mapping, and discussion groups.

NetObjects Fusion supports all basic HTML plus extended HTML and scripts for additional features. Its method for dealing with hyperlinks is both creative and practical. Smart Links defines hyperlinks by their relation to the destination. You can point links at a page's parent, child, or other relative, and Fusion will construct the appropriate link when the site is published. This enables you to rearrange files at will without worrying about redefining the links within it.

You gain database access through ODBC data-object controls, which fill in a table with information from a database table.

## Style View

The Style view is the access point for 50 prebuilt site styles that give a consistent look to your project's pages. (See Figure 36.18.) Style features that you can control from this view include color schemes and navigation icons.

**FIGURE 36.18.**

*With the Style view, you can define and edit the graphical standards that define your site.*

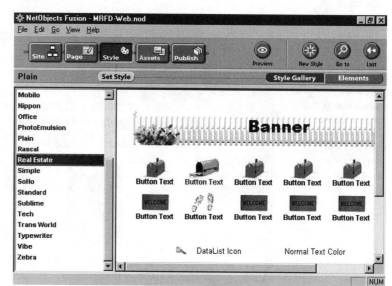

Several predefined site styles that you can override according to your own needs are included with Fusion. Each style is based according to a theme and provides a centralized method of managing and applying the overall graphical appearance of your site.

The predefined components available with each style from the Fusion Site Gallery include backgrounds, banners, primary and secondary navigation buttons, fonts, lines, icons, and text colors. You can also create new styles from scratch, if needed.

## Assets View

With the Assets View, you can track various files, links, and database information, including image files, applets, objects, and plug-ins. (See Figure 36.19.)

The best part about using the Assets view to change files is how it integrates with the rest of the program. For example, if you change the name of a GIF file, the Assets view also automatically changes any references to that file anywhere else in the site to the new value. It treats links to external resources in the same fashion and lists them with the rest of the other site assets.

The Assets view marks assets that are included as part of a site but not used within any pages, enabling you to easily identify these space-wasters and delete them, if appropriate. It also identifies broken links and missing files for appropriate action.

*Advanced Web Authoring Tools*

CHAPTER 36

755

36

ADVANCED
WEB AUTHORING
TOOLS

**FIGURE 36.19.**

*Whether it's a file, hyperlink, or database connection, the Asset view lists it for you to review or change.*

| Name | Link To | Type | Verify Status |
|------|---------|------|---------------|
| Home | index.html | Internal | |
| index | index2.htm | Internal | |
| index | index1.htm | Internal | |
| index | index.htm#SPARKS2 | Internal | |
| index | index.htm#SPARKS1 | Internal | |
| index | index.htm#SPARKS | Internal | |
| index | index.htm | Internal | |
| mailto:mrfd@montana.com | mailto:mrfd@montana.com | External | |
| NetObjects Home Page | http://www.netobjects.com | External | |
| Property_Taxes | property_taxes.htm | Internal | |
| Staff_Directory | staff_directory.htm#Board | Internal | |
| Staff_Directory | staff_directory.htm | Internal | |
| Staff_Directory | staff_directory.htm#Command | Internal | |
| Station_Directory | station_directory.htm | Internal | |
| Station_Directory | station_directory.htm#1 | Internal | |
| Wildfire Tips | wildfire_tips.htm | Internal | |

## Publish View

After all the work is completed on the site, use the Publish view to send the finished product to its final location. (See Figure 36.20.) You can publish a site in its original or text-only form. To decrease upload time, NetObjects Fusion gives you the choice of publishing the entire site or only the changes that have occurred since the last time the site was published.

**FIGURE 36.20.**

*The Publish view configures the final settings for the site and sends it to the server for publication and use.*

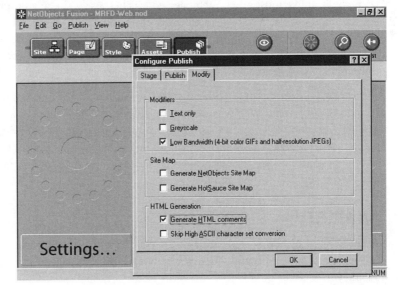

You have two options for configuring a site for publishing. First is a local staging server, with which you can test the site in the privacy of your home computer. The other is a remote Web server, with which the work is available for use by the rest of the world, your company, or whomever is the intended audience.

When you're ready to publish, click the Stage (local) or Publish (remote) buttons to compile the site and its elements into a set of HTML pages and associated files and send them to the server you designated. Other publishing options include text-only, grayscale, and low-bandwidth.

## Advanced Features

Functionally, Fusion gives you all the features you expect from a Web design suite. But it also has a number of advanced features, which aren't always inherently obvious to the casual user. Not all of these features are available in other Web development suites. Consequently, if you find some of these features particularly powerful, you might want to consider getting Fusion.

## O'Reilly WebSite

O'Reilly WebSite is a full-featured Web server that works hand-in-hand with the Backstage Server to provide the support that you need to run a basic Web site and the additional capacity and power to fully implement Backstage Server capabilities. It also includes several add-on applications to provide other services for your users, including the capability to index and search your entire Web site.

## PageDraw

PageDraw is unlike most other Web page editors because it doesn't simply provide access to tags. Rather, it treats a Web page as an entire entity, and you put HTML elements on it. This type of approach provides unprecedented pixel-level control over the display of a Web page. Rather than having to concern yourself with what the user's browser does, you can explicitly place an HTML element anywhere on the page.

All this control doesn't come without some sort of drawback, and the drawback of getting precision control over a Web page is that the HTML files tend to be much larger. This is because the fine level of control is accomplished by using a number of advanced HTML tricks. Furthermore, PageDraw also makes use of numerous transparent images to help it accomplish this type of control. Also, the Web pages created by PageDraw tend to be a bit more convoluted than if you do them by hand.

# Summary

Advanced Web authoring tools are an important item to consider when you're considering developing a Web site. Should you invest in one of these packages? That decision depends on you and your needs.

*Advanced Web Authoring Tools*

CHAPTER 36

757

36

ADVANCED
WEB AUTHORING
TOOLS

If you're just creating an occasional page or two for your department or company, a simple HTML editor will probably fit your needs. If you're responsible for managing the content of a folder or site, an application such as FrontPage, Backstage, or NetObjects Fusion will probably be a big help. If you're a webmaster, either for a department server on an intranet or for a Web server on the Internet, an integrated authoring tool will quickly become a necessity.

Remember that these applications don't do the management work for you. They provide a one-stop-shopping approach to the various tools that make establishing and maintaining a Web site an easier process.

FrontPage, Backstage, and NetObjects Fusion each have their strong points and weak points. FrontPage has a more intuitive interface for its management program (Explorer) and a more powerful editor than Backstage. Using wizards and templates to create Web sites is very helpful, especially when you're creating new Web sites from scratch. Database access requires much more knowledge of ODBC and SQL than the average user has. Its discussion group feature depends on HTML files, which can lead to problems if a message is deleted for inappropriate content.

Backstage excels in database access. It requires that you have only enough knowledge to set up an ODBC connection to a database (you can find directions in Windows help files) and a passing knowledge of SQL (provided in the manual). Designer then provides several ways to read and write information from databases as part of the HTML page. Backstage also has stronger user management features, including the capability to tailor a browsing session for each user. Manager and Designer are weaker tools in general than their counterparts in FrontPage and are not as intuitive to use. Designer also doesn't support frames.

Fusion takes the approach of creating integrated Web site management from that of the Web author. As a result, its features tend to focus more on the needs of the typical Web author. Web authors are concerned about the overall look and feel of their Web sites; for that, you have the SiteStyle Manager. Web authors are concerned about links breaking unexpectedly; for that, Fusion automatically updates all links. Some Web authors are interested in very precise placement of HTML elements; for that, PageDraw gives authors just that capability. The weaknesses of Fusion tend to lie in anything that isn't particularly important to the Web author. For example, few of the user and group security features that exist within FrontPage are included in Fusion. Also, Fusion does a lot of its automaintenance by keeping a private database of objects. If something happens to that database, you might lose a significant portion of your Web site.

Which application you choose depends on your specific needs. FrontPage is considerably less expensive than Backstage and is a good starting point for people just assuming Web management responsibilities. If your Web site requires any level of database interaction, such as online ordering, membership management, scheduling, or customer service, Backstage offers the best in features and ease of use.

# Web Servers

*by J. Gregory Bryan*

## IN THIS CHAPTER

Some things never change, which can be both a comfort and a curse when it comes to purchasing a new or improved computer system. In this chapter on Web servers, some of you may be comforted by the fact that in purchasing or upgrading a server system, you will be guided primarily by a solitary, yet very important question. It's one that should be comforting because you've heard it so many times before: *"What are you going to use it for?"*

Remember the first computer you ever bought? What did the salesperson ask you? *"What are you going to use it for?"* Right? How about the last equipment purchase you ran past your boss? Same thing? Even though it can be a little aggravating at times to have to explain the subtle complexities that led you to your triumphant conclusion that you must upgrade, it's still somewhat comforting to realize that—whether you're preparing to purchase a new Web server, a word processor, a microwave oven, or even a fancy fishing rod—you always have to ask yourself, *"What do I really need to get this job done?"*

It's especially true for something as complicated and potentially expensive as an in-house Web server system. And that brings us to why this question can also be a curse, or at least why it might make you curse before the decision-making process is over.

If you are already an experienced HTML programmer, a systems analyst, or some other type of Web developer or site administrator, you already know how fast the Internet industry is changing. Or should I have said *industries?* There are, and continue to be everyday, an increasing number of highly specialized hardware and software industries that are exploding into existence as the popularity of the Internet and the World Wide Web increases. At the very forefront of this tidal wave of technology is the humble Web server and everything associated with it.

In this chapter, I operate under two assumptions:

1. That you're already experienced enough with the Internet or intranets to know the value of broad scale, distributed computing
2. That your decision to purchase a new Web server or upgrade an existing one is for the general purpose of better exploiting the treasures of the Web

If you're nodding your head in the affirmative and thinking "yeah, that sounds about right," let me be the first to tell you—it's not going to be as simple as you think.

If, on the other hand, you already know how complex this decision can be, I'm sure you'll agree that there are several key factors on which you *must* be clear before making your decision. The first half of the chapter centers on these important considerations. Then, in the last half of the chapter, I show you the broad landscape of available options and focus on a variety of examples from several different product categories.

Okay. Let's get started.

Consider again the underlying question, *"What are you going to use this for?"* I must caution you not to answer too quickly. Obviously, if you've decided to set up a Web server, you have a primary interest in connecting to the Web. Maybe some of you have rented service at an Internet service provider (ISP) and have finally decided that to get the kind of hands-on control you need, you must have an in-house server. Some of you might have had an intranet in service for quite some time but now are ready to branch out onto the Internet for the very first time. In either case, I can virtually assure you that the things you want from your Web server today will not be the same things you'll be demanding from your server six months or a year from now.

Let's look at the big issues first and the factors that define them:

- Present purpose
- Future needs
- Cost

# Present Purpose

Your present purposes for upgrading or purchasing a new Web server are probably varied and readily justifiable. They might include any of the following:

- To connect the organization to the Web
- To take advantage of the content out on the World Wide Web
- To market and promote your own content
- To expand your marketing and customer service capabilities
- To compete more effectively

Now here are some questions you'll have to answer before you can do any of that:

- What kind of in-house system or facility do you currently have? Is it dedicated to one type of platform or many?
- How many different operating systems (OS) are currently in place?
- Does the organization have a preferred software standard (such as Microsoft, Lotus, Novell, and so on)?
- Will existing intranets, local or wide, be connected through the Web server?
- How many users will access the Internet internally? How many hits are expected from outside sources?
- What about security? Do you need a firewall? Multiple firewalls?
- Will you be engaging in any sort of electronic commerce over the Internet?
- Will you be transferring files, parts of databases, or applications through the server?

■ Are any of the transactions going to be of the "mission critical" type? How much fault tolerance can you afford?

■ How much storage space will you require? Do you need a sophisticated RAID (Redundant Array of Inexpensive Disks) system or would mirrored servers be more appropriate?

■ How are you going to communicate with the Internet—by modem, ISDN (integrated services digital network), T1s, T3s, frame relay?

■ How knowledgeable is your in-house staff in *all* aspects of network computing and telecommunications protocols?

■ Will you need a single-, double-, or triple-tiered system to adequately meet your needs?

■ What percentage of your IS budget is devoted to Internet-related activity? How many personnel will be assigned to manage the system full-time?

■ How well does your CEO really understand what you're trying to do?

Those are just a few questions to get you thinking. Chances are good that no matter what your level of sophistication is as a Web development professional, you never have had to deal with so many different issues surrounding one decision before. If you make your Web server decision in a responsible fashion, however, all these questions and more will come to bear on your selection.

You'll notice that I haven't spent any time at all talking about communication and transaction protocols (TCP/IP, CGI, FTP, HTTP, SMTP, NNTP, MOM, ORB, and so on). For one thing, the acronyms are piling up faster than anyone could hope to list them. Beside that, in spite of the plethora of protocols, a growing effort to standardize the most basic elements of internetwork communications has occurred in the last few years.

Practically every server you might possibly consider will accommodate an increasingly standardized set of communications protocols. There are a few remaining battles, to be sure, such as that being fought by the Object Request Brokers (ORBs) and the older but still entrenched Remote Procedure Calls made to the Message Oriented Middleware (MOM); but even the most aggressive and often prejudiced software designers are working hard to make sure these little skirmishes don't injure the would-be customer. Usually a variety of software patches are at hand for anyone who is inadvertently bruised in such conflicts.

Having said all that, however, it does behoove a Web server shopper to pay attention to the *kinds* of functions the various server applications can perform. An almost unimaginable variety of Web server vendors and Web server products is in the marketplace today. The prices vary from free to many thousands of dollars. Most of them do very similar things. None of them do everything.

Later on, I'll look at the features of some of the most popular Web servers. For now, let's think a little more about the questions at hand. Back in the early days of Web servers and the Internet (I'm talking less than a half decade ago), a would-be Web surfer had to have a different tool for every task. After the invention of the HyperText Markup Language, HTML, and the first GUI browser, MOSAIC, users quickly learned that by following the "Blue Text," they could go just about anywhere and find just about anything they wanted. Getting it, however, required very specialized tools and, frequently, completely different servers.

Here are just a few of the more common types of the original, independent servers:

- Gopher servers transport files of various types, which was fine as long as you had the proper application software to read them.
- File Transport Protocol (FTP) servers enable you to do basically the same thing as Gopher servers but with much greater flexibility.
- Network News Transport Protocol (NNTP) servers deliver Usenet or newsgroup messages and articles.
- Simple Mail Transport Protocol servers (SMTP) deliver electronic mail.
- Telnet servers are required to conduct remote operations on distant computer terminals.
- HTTP servers enable users to talk to one another.
- DNS servers keep the growing number of domain names organized.
- DBMS enables users to sample, calculate, or summarize from virtually any database located anywhere in the world.

I don't know how many different kinds of servers exist. I still remember when the newfangled print server was the greatest thing since sliced bread. The point here is that just couple of years ago, setting up a Web server that had even the slightest variety of functionality would have been beyond the means of most IS or DP departments, but that is not the case anymore. Most popular Web servers now feature a collection of the common server functions. Many even include sophisticated development tools, a variety of security options, and highly adaptable browsers. Again though, quite a lot of disparity still exists between the features of even the most popular Web server products. Even among those that offer exactly the same kinds of features, one can find significant differences in hardware requirements, maintenance requirements, ease of setup, administrative options, and scalability. It pays to be very clear about your present needs and the needs of the others who will ultimately visit your Web server.

Assuming that you wisely choose from your selection of desired server functions, you still must get a few other critical issues right. It goes well beyond the scope of this chapter to try to discuss them all. These are some of the more important factors to consider, however, regardless of your intended application:

- **Compatibility:** It will be particularly important for you to select a server that is compatible with your lead operating system (OS) or network operating system (NOS). Although you might at first intend for the Web server to run on a completely independent platform, that probably won't be the case for very long. You might need to interface with a mainframe to have access to existing files or databases. You might decide to connect the LANs in accounting, shipping, marketing, customer service, and credit to the Web server. If you plan to have a Web site with an artistic flare, you'll want to connect the people in the graphics department. They might have Macs and you might not.

It's clear to see that as the popularity and functionality of an in-house Web server grows, the compatibility issue will become more and more important. Equally to the point is the fact that by selecting compatible server software, you will avoid any unnecessary staffing or training problems. If you're in a house of many Windows, for example, you could be in trouble if you take a fancy to a UNIX-based Web server.

- **Platform requirements:** For many of the same reasons I previously stated, it is important that you select a Web server that will run either on an existing platform within your organization or at least on a platform that will be compatible and suitable for present and future needs. You must consider these questions: How many users are expected to transact with the server? Will it support a sufficient number of IP addresses? Will there be enough RAM? Can you add more? What sort of disk array is required for your purposes? How many CPUs will be required? Is that expandable? What about connectivity issues? Networking, telephony, and so on? The list goes on.

  Related and equally important to these questions is the question of fault tolerance. How well-integrated is your hardware and the required operating system? Is it extremely stable and capable of handling faults of all types without locking up or shutting down? If you have mission-critical or secure commerce requirements, will you need multiple backup systems to meet your Web server's needs?

- **Scalability:** The demands on your system will grow. It may be difficult to imagine in the beginning. And you might have other overarching considerations, such as a boss who is encouraging you to "just get the basics to get us started." In either case, however, you will be sorry if you don't select a server and platform combination that is at least 50 to 100 percent more capable than you initially require. Think about it. There's no room to elaborate here, but it's the same principle that was at work back when you thought it impossible to fill up that gigantic 20MB (!) hard drive. Enough said?

Of course, numerous other considerations are related to the hardware/software issue. I hope, though, that the notes and questions I gave you will stimulate sufficient discussion among the people in your organization so that you can avoid unnecessary pitfalls.

Speaking of discussions among people, it is likely that the move to an in-house Web server will require, at some point, a sales job on the executives who control the purse strings. It might have been a relatively easy sell, convincing the president of the company that you needed to put up a Web page when virtually all of his/her competition is represented on the World Wide Web. It will, no doubt, be a harder sell to get the *many* additional thousands required to build and properly maintain an in-house Web server.

In the recent article "Do Execs Get the Web?" in the November 1996 issue of *Internet World*, Joel Maloff touched on a number of very important topics concerning your impending sessions with upper management. His basic message is that, even today, most executives still don't "get the Web." As incredible as it may seem, most chief executives still think this Internet thing is some sort of fad that will soon go away. Those few who have seen the Web's potential, Maloff points out, are scared stiff. They don't understand it. They're afraid to get on it. They're afraid to stay off!

These are generalizations, of course. No doubt, a growing population of savvy executives out there have jumped on the wagon and are hanging on for dear life. The majority, though, must certainly fall into the categories described in Maloff's article. More than likely, your boss is in one of those categories as well.

Why have I chosen to dwell on this point? It's a topic you should be prepared to discuss before you endeavor to fling open your company's doors to the rest of the world.

"Flinging open the doors!" Indeed, that's the way most upper managers will see it. All the nightmares about computer hackers, industrial espionage, drug trafficking, child pornography, and whatever other unsavory evils one might imagine will be swirling through your boss's head as soon as you start talking about putting up an in-house Web server. Don't laugh! The boss has a good point and one to which you'd better be prepared to respond.

# Future Needs

You know there will be some future needs (and benefits), but have you written them down? Have you discussed the fact that company-wide e-mail will now be possible, whereas you might not have had it before? Does your customer service department really understand the fact that it will be able to double or triple the number of service inquiries to which it can now respond, and that with the use of autoresponders and FAQs, it can now provide 24-hour, worldwide service at virtually no extra cost? Does the marketing department appreciate the opportunity it will now have to study site usage reports and gain insight into prospective customers who think in ways never imagined before? Does the sales manager know she can now conduct interactive sales meetings worldwide or offer online tutorials while, at the same time, virtually eliminating the normal travel costs? Use your imagination.

To discuss the future needs and benefits issue, as well as the many other questions you will be asked to address, it makes sense to pre-plan your presentation and do so with the aid of professionals from other departments, such as Marketing, Customer Service, Shipping, and Accounting. Spend as much time as is required to educate these colleagues regarding the present and future benefits of the desired system. Spend a lot of time explaining security issues and the expected increases in teamwork and efficiency, especially when internal intranets will be connected with the Web server.

In other words, prepare a business plan surrounding your intended purchase. If you present a well-organized and professional plan that has the support of your company's key departments, you'll probably be surprised how agreeable upper management can be. Most executives have no trouble whatsoever investing in things that they feel will grow the business. *All* executives, on the other hand, will balk at spending a nickel on anything they don't understand or have doubts about. And speaking of spending, that brings us to the next topic: cost.

# Cost

Keep the following in mind. Regardless of whether you intend to use freeware on an existing platform or intend to string wire from here to Timbuktu and set up your own in-house ISP, you are going to spend some money. How much, of course, depends on the answer to that very first question I asked: *"What are you going to use it for?"*

It's only after answering this question as honestly as possible that you will be able to determine your costs. The dollars, from low-end to high-end, can easily range from $5,000 to $100,000. Those who intend to have a *big time* operation with multitiered systems, proxies, routers, high-end security, fully integrated enterprise, legacy, and commercial applications will spend hundreds of thousands. It all depends on your ultimate objective. If that objective is well-defined and understood, you can speak confidently about the numbers, knowing for certain well the benefits will greatly outweigh the costs.

Remember also that you must include the cost of personnel in your overall figures. One frequently made mistake is the assumption on the part of first-time site managers that they will be able to handle the whole operation by themselves, including site design, administration, maintenance and repairs, content preparation, content updates, programming, interdepartmental liaison duties, budgeting, purchasing, settling the inevitable squabbles and disputes, and so on.

Regardless of the kind of organization or type of operation that you intend to run, you will likely need the full-time assistance of several other people. Believe me, many more capable heroes have tried to go it alone. Interestingly, some of the best and most innovative developments in server technology have been made by super technicians who finally decided they needed to eat or go home and sleep! One person can't do it all. Don't sell your new Web server operation short by assuming that you can.

In your case, even if the boss is loathe to add additional staff, it's better to be honest about your staffing requirements rather than underestimate the venture and end up in abysmal failure. Besides, business executives hate being "nickeled and dimed" over things you should have warned them about in the first place. Don't get discouraged on this point. Being fiscally conservative is what good executives do best. That's their job and it's what they are expected to do. Do your job and prepare a good and thorough presentation. Speak in plain English. Address all the points. You'll get your new Web server—and maybe the Employee of the Year Award!

# Now, Let's Talk about Servers

As I prepared to write this chapter, purely by chance one of my colleagues was in the process of upgrading an important in-house server. In his case, it was a packing server that keeps track of all the orders being packed and shipped out of a busy warehouse. Although his particular server requirement was fairly limited in application but mission-critical in nature, I watched him go through a very similar process of defining his needs. The platform/server combination he chose was a highly compatible, fault-tolerant, and expandable system that will not only meet the present needs of the shipping department but will also provide the initial infrastructure for much more widespread server applications. The company, by the way, though large and very successful, has not yet reached the point of establishing an in-house Web server. It's still in the process of laying the appropriate groundwork.

It occurred to me while talking with my friend that probably many organizations are in a similar state of infrastructural development and that many such organizations might not even be as well versed in server technology as he is. These people (and perhaps readers of this book) might find themselves in the position of having to gather as much information as possible in a very short time to assist them with their Web server selection. In an industry that is changing as rapidly as this one is, you can never hope to know all there is to know. Using the Internet, however, the broad range of readily available magazines and newsletters, product brochures (which are just as easily acquired), and personal interviews with knowledgeable people—such as I have done to gather background information for this chapter—a person can educate himself very quickly.

## A NOTE TO FIRST-TIME WEB SITE DEVELOPERS

Although most of the information in this chapter has been slanted toward the experienced Web developer, many of the considerations required of people establishing in-house Web servers will also apply to the first-time developer. One additional consideration, however, is especially important for those who have never established or maintained a Web site.

First-timers should strongly consider the option of having their site hosted on a remote server operated and managed by a reputable Internet Service Provider (ISP) company. The main reasons for this suggestion are very important:

■ The cost of having a site hosted by an ISP is considerably less than building and maintaining an in-house system. Delaying those costs makes good sense for anyone who is still low on the learning curve. Additionally, the use of ISP servers at this stage of Web-presence gives the beginning Web developer an opportunity to test and compare different kinds of services and different kinds of server environments. This will be very useful information when the time comes to establish your own system.

*continues*

*continued*

■ The effective management and administration of a Web site requires knowledge and skills that cannot be gained without some experience. When your site is hosted by a professional service provider, you can begin developing your Web presence with the expert guidance from those who have performed the task many times before. A good ISP will make suggestions about site design and, perhaps even more importantly, will provide you with a wide range of administrative reports. Such reports might include the following:

- Usage statistics to show the number of hits your site experienced, the frequency of repeat visits, the amount of time spent on various pages, and the addresses of visitors
- Error logs
- Message logs, e-mail, and other items of use and interest

The study of administrative reports provided by the service provider yields valuable information regarding the function and effectiveness of your Web site.

In other words, learn all you can from the experience of others before you endeavor to set up your own internal Web server. Connecting your organization to the Internet is obviously an important venture. Mistakes avoided in the early development stage can save loads of aggravation and money down the road.

In the descriptions that follow, I will not attempt to cover all the possible platform/server combinations. That would be a multibook-scale project all its own. The information presented, however, is what I have gleaned from the variety of media sources I previously mentioned. These sources do an amazingly good job (collectively) of keeping abreast of new developments. For example, more than a hundred different magazines are devoted to computer technology and provide regular features on server- and Web-related technologies. Most of these magazines are staffed by good writers and editors who compete on a daily basis to bring you the most up-to-date information possible.

Likewise, many online magazines, user forums, and fact pages now tap into a broad range of Web-related topics in exceeding detail. Reading these materials is an educational experience for just about anyone. Another interesting outlet of information, also available across the Web, are those pages posted by site administrators and Webmasters, entitled "About this Server." You might be amazed by the variety of platform/server combinations that hundreds of other organizations just like yours have successfully deployed. Fire up your favorite search engine and have a look!

So, how many platform/server combinations are there? Probably nobody knows. There are some good, up-to-date sources, however, on the most popular combinations. I should note here that when "platform" is used, it really means the "platform environment"—the hardware and operating system combination on which the Web server will reside. Five minutes of research will reveal that hardware being used in server environments includes virtually every kind of machine still in use today—everything from DOS machines to Windows PCs, Macs, NT servers, Sun, Apollo and SGI workstations, IBM, VAX, DEC and HP minis and mainframes, as well as a hundred other types and brands not mentioned here. Basically any kind of computer with sufficient disk space, memory, and processing power can serve as a node on the Web. Your choice must obviously be based on your ultimate objectives for the Web server.

How about operating systems? Naturally, far fewer types of operating systems exist but, still, most of them are used. Using an often-cited survey from the WebCrawler, Steven J. Vaughan-Nichols, in his article entitled "At Your Service: The Right OS for Your Web Server" (*NetGuide*, 4/97), discusses the strengths and limitations of the most commonly preferred operating systems. Vaughan-Nichols' choice for high-end, high-volume sites is unequivocal: It's UNIX. For medium- to low-end sites, he prefers Windows NT. Looking at the WebCrawler survey, it appears that the rest of the world agrees with him.

Regenerated and generalized after the original data, the tally currently stands at

| | |
|---|---|
| UNIX: | 84% |
| Windows NT: | 7% |
| MacOS: | 5% |
| Windows 95, 3.1: | 2% |
| All others: | 2% |

The percentages shown here represent the distribution of the most commonly used operating system platforms for servers across the Web.

# UNIX

Most Internet aficionados probably could have made a good guess at the breakdown. UNIX far and away out-paces the rest of the pack for both historical and currently practical reasons. First of all, the Internet was born from UNIX-based parents, and for the first several years of its life, the only friends and family the youthful Internet knew were also of the UNIX persuasion. As years went by, the occasional odd operation system attempted to make its acquaintance, but even today, the vast majority of Internet-based activity takes place between UNIX machines.

UNIX (or UNIX derivatives) operate on a much wider variety of platforms than any other operating system. In fact, it is unlikely you could find a hardware platform in existence for which a UNIX-type OS hasn't been developed. Consequently, the greatest variety of Web server software has also been developed to run in the UNIX environment.

In addition to its sheer ubiquity, UNIX allows the greatest number of CPUs, the greatest number of IP addresses, and by far the most robust operating system, even in the *most* heavily trafficked networks. There is a downside, though.

The list of percentages shown in the previous section will probably begin to shift as "regular" people (non-computer types) become more and more attracted to the World Wide Web. The downside for UNIX is that in spite of its undisputed capabilities, it remains one of the *most* difficult operating systems to learn. You have to want to learn UNIX—really want to learn. With Windows or the MacOS, on the other hand, you hardly have to learn at all. You just sit down, point, click, and go to work. On top of this, UNIX-based Web servers traditionally have been difficult to install. Although this is changing, Windows-type servers, by comparison, almost install themselves.

# Windows

The strength of the Windows-based operating systems as Web server platforms lies in the sea of nontechnical users who are just now becoming acquainted with the Internet. If you are installing a Web server for a low- to medium-impact site and expect to interface with other people in your organization who normally use PCs for other types of applications, chances are good that a Microsoft operating system will be your best choice.

According to the Vaughn-Nichols article, though a surprising 19 Web servers have been developed for the Windows 95 system, most people who are experienced with Windows 95 in heavy-duty application software would agree that this popular operating system is probably not stable enough to support a good Web server site. Windows NT, however, has proven itself to be an extremely hardy contender and appears to be gaining in widespread popularity.

Windows NT not only enjoys a rapidly growing number of suitors in the server development community but far outstrips other OS types in its capability to run the most popular suites of business software. Also a powerhouse in the area of easy database management, NT's only apparent drawback is its scalability. No weakling in this area, it still falls short of the scalable capabilities of UNIX and IBM's OS/2. For sites expecting huge amounts of traffic, these others might be more appropriate.

> **NOTE**
>
> Here's an interesting note: The busiest site on the Web is `Microsoft.com`, which is powered by an NT-based server. Microsoft's database server, however, which is responsible for transferring millions of product-related requests per day, runs on a mainframe powered by a UNIX-based server.

# MacOS

The popularity of MacOS, not too far behind Windows with respect to UNIX, is a testament primarily to the number of Mac users who have discovered the Web. The MacOS has limited capability in heavy demand situations and is particularly clumsy in its interactions with dynamic sites. Of the 20 or so servers that have been developed for MacOS, only one (StarNine) seems to enjoy much enduring popularity. Mac owners are a loyal bunch, as everybody knows. MacOS may not be the absolute best choice for a Web server OS, but you can probably expect the number of Mac servers to remain pretty constant from one year to the next.

## OS/2

OS/2 is a great operating system for a Web server. It is robust, multithreaded, fast—all in all, a very stable platform. The only problem is that almost no one uses it anymore. Chalk another one up to IBM's marketing strategy. A half a dozen or so server packages have been designed for OS/2 systems. They work and will work for you if you already have an OS/2 shop. If you don't, you'll find many more software options and greater support with some other operating system.

> **NOTE**
>
> If you are planning to closely link your Web server to an internal intranet, you will want to read several good articles that have to do with the importance of picking the right NOS. OS/2 still makes a very strong showing in the intranet environment, a factor that might influence your Web server platform selection.

# Moving on to the Web Server Software

You can find one of the most informative surveys on the Web at http://www.netcraft.com/survey/. The Netcraft site maintains a hotlinked directory of Web server home sites, as well as up-to-date survey information about server and platform use across the Web.

The Netcraft, April, 1997, survey results shown in Tables 37.1 and 37.2 are based upon responses from 1,002,612 sites.

**Table 37.1. Top developers.**

| Developer | Mar-97 | % | Apr-97 | % |
|---|---|---|---|---|
| Apache | 356500 | 42.79 | 429049 | 42.79 |
| Microsoft | 97077 | 11.65 | 154653 | 15.43 |
| Netscape | 108933 | 13.07 | 121870 | 12.16 |
| NCSA | 74446 | 8.94 | 73881 | 7.37 |

**Table 37.2. Top servers.**

| Server | Mar-97 | % | Apr-97 | % |
|---|---|---|---|---|
| Apache | 356500 | 42.79 | 429049 | 42.79 |
| Microsoft-IIS | 78414 | 9.41 | 131718 | 13.14 |
| NCSA | 74446 | 8.94 | 73881 | 7.37 |
| Netscape-Communications | 37656 | 4.52 | 39572 | 3.95 |
| Netscape-Enterprise | 28418 | 3.41 | 37853 | 3.78 |
| Netscape-Commerce | 35041 | 4.21 | 35129 | 3.5 |

There are other excellent sources of current server use information as well. Many magazines devote a large effort to tracking server and other Internet-related topics on a monthly basis.

You can find one of the best running summaries at Meckermedia's iWORLD site (http://www.iworld.com), where you can find WebCompare, ServerWatch, and the Web Servers Feature Chart. In the following section, I'll highlight the main features of some of the most popular Web servers currently at the top of all the lists. These are not the only options but merely the tip of the iceberg, so to speak. Check out the previously mentioned sites, as well as the monthly Network Features sections in magazines such as *PC Magazine* for descriptions of other Web servers and server-related products.

# Features of Popular Web Servers

This section gives you an overview of the features of many Web servers that are currently in use.

## Apache

The most popular Web server worldwide is Apache. Lending to its unquestioned dominance is that it was developed for the most commonly used platform, UNIX, and that it is free. It's not your ordinary freeware, however; the organization that has developed and maintained this powerful package (located at www.apache.org) has produced a sophisticated, easy-to-use product that is packed full of features and is constantly being improved. The Apache Development Group is an international organization of seasoned volunteers who have developed this product for noncomercial distribution in the public domain. Formed under the auspices of Apache Digital Corporation of Durango, Colorado, The Apache http project depends on donations by members and users for its continued work.

The current version is a plug-in replacement for NCSA 1.3. It is highly configurable and offers DBM-based authentication databases and content negotiation. Apache efficiently uses system memory, and you can easily upgrade it by various, optional modules. It's fast, installs easily, and best of all, includes the source code.

The only real drawback is one that doesn't usually cause people much of a problem anyway. There is no *official* technical support service for this product. That doesn't mean, however, that you can't find good help and advice. You can find a list of known bugs at the Web site, and you can find third-party support services through the Apache mailing list at `comp.infosystems.www.servers.unix`, or by commercial parties such as UK Web Ltd. or Cygnus (`http://www.cygnus.com/product/idk/apache/`). *Apache Week*, a weekly digest for Apache developers, is another good source of support information. To subscribe to the mailing list, send a message to `majordomo@apache.org` with the words "subscribe apache-announce" in the body of the message.

## CERN httpd

The *CERN httpd*, also known as the *W3C httpd*, is an old standard for UNIX platforms that is in its final version with release of Version 3.0A. The W3C server is another of the well-known, public-domain programs that has been perfected by developers at MIT and CERN—the European Laboratory for Particle Physics near Geneva, Switzerland, which also happens to be the birthplace of the World Wide Web.

The CERN httpd is a full-featured, hypertext server that can serve equally well as a standalone HTTP server or as a proxy server within a firewall. A proxy server provides quicker document caching and sorting and can also provide access to the Internet from behind a firewall.

User guides, release notes, and installation and overview documents are all available from online sources (such as `www.w3c.org`), as are bug logs, utilities, and patches.

The main features of this server include the following:

- Functionality as a proxy server for HTTP, FTP, Gopher, WAIS, and news groups
- Server-side, executable scripting
- Established forms
- Clickable icon support
- A powerful index search interface
- Authorization checking and access protection
- Configurable file suffixes
- Capability of handling multiple file formats, encodings, and languages
- A number of highly flexible and configurable characteristics

## Microsoft Internet Information Server (IIS)

A relative newcomer in the market place is Microsoft's Internet Information Server (IIS), the commercial Web server integrated into NT Server 4.0. Though IIS's popularity accounts for only about 9.4 percent of the market (compared to Apache's 42 percent), the growing popularity of PC platforms and the growing number of PC users on the Internet seems to suggest that we'll be seeing more widespread use of this versatile Web server.

The IIS runs on the Windows 95 and NT platforms, although as I discussed earlier, NT provides much greater fault tolerance and overall stability. User feedback suggests that the overall performance of IIS is close to that of Apache in terms of reliability and overall satisfaction. For users already committed to the NT platform, the additional cost (free!) is just as compelling, because it comes bundled with the NT Server package.

Drawbacks include a lack of capability to support NFS drive security, given its dependence on Windows NT networking and security. Also, it is not easily customized for varied access by Web-specific users or groups.

Technical support is abundant, however, by way of a thorough Installation and Planning Guide, online tech support, and on-board utilities and help files.

## NCSA

The next most popular server, whose popularity rivals Microsoft's IIS (at 8.9 percent of the market), is an old standard—NCSA HTTPD. Like its closely related cousin, NCSA HTTPD is also free (for noncommercial use). To access a copy on the Internet, go to `http://hoohoo.ncsa.uiuc.edu/docs/setup/Download.html`.

NCSA is another UNIX-based server that is known to be highly functional, reliable, and easily supported, but, like Apache, no commercial support is available. You can readily address most support issues through online information including complete user documentation, installation guides, and tutorials, as well as an active user discussion forum. Reports of known bugs are tracked at `httpd@ncsa.uiucc.edu`. The particular advantage to NCSA seems to be its capability to handle complex user-authentication issues at very large sites, where weekly accesses may number into the millions.

## Netscape Servers

Netscape sells a wide range of server products, including Communications, Commerce, FastTrack, and Enterprise. The variety and versatility of these products helps account for the more than 12 percent of the market that Netscape has conquered.

Competing well with all the major servers, Netscape provides versions that run on Windows 95, NT, and UNIX systems. Free evaluation copies are available for trial use at Netscape's Web site, `www.netscape.com`, and licensed copies begin at $495.

Like the popular Netscape browser, the Netscape servers rank high in customer satisfaction, ease of use, and reliability. Their greatest achievement, however, may lie in their highly integrated design. Although it's sometimes hard to tell who's pushing who, the Netscape products exemplify the recent trend among server software developers to blend high-end user functionality into a single-user interface. Dovetailing Internet-related functions with normal operating system functions is another related characteristic. New and experienced users alike can enjoy such features as built-in search engines, remote editing capabilities, automatic cataloging, and built-in log analysis tools.

Netscape rounds out the program by offering a comprehensive support package that includes

- Ninety days of free support
- Incident-based support ($89 per incident, or three for $199)
- Annual support ($399 for 12 hours per 5 days, and $599 for 12 hours per 7 days)
- Online Help

## WebSite

O'Reilly and Associates offers WebSite, the commercial server for Windows 95/NT, which is another of the new breed of servers offering multiple, integrated functionality. Chief among this package's capabilities are

- The capability for remote administration
- CGI 1.3 and Visual Basic toolkit
- HotDog editor
- Integrated indexing and search tools

WebSite Pro adds

- Enhanced crytographic security
- WebSite API (with Microsoft ISAPI-ISA compatibility)
- ODBC/SQL database access using API-integrated Cold Fusion 1.5
- API-integrated Perl 5
- Server-side Java SDK
- One-button publishing with Navigator Gold

WebSite is truly one of the most versatile of the server products currently available. You can download evaluation copies at the company's Web site: www.ora.com. Licensed copies are available from the vendor at the competitive price of $249 ($495 for the Pro version).

WebSite is highly regarded for its ease of installation and use, reliability, and overall functionality. Most notable are the very well-written user's manuals that are part of the package.

O'Reilly's tech support is also known to be of high quality, which lends credence to the old saying that you get what you pay for. The first 90 days of telephone support are free, but the same service will cost you $450 per year thereafter. You can also access online support and discussion groups and the newsletter, WebSite-talk.

Archive is available at http://www.ora.com/archives/website-talk/. Registered product owners are automatically entered on the mailing list.

## WebSTAR

The leading Macintosh Web server is WebSTAR by StarNine. The product's easy installation, ease of use, and readily accessible (and eager to help) support team are among its greatest strengths. Other notable features include

- Enables scripting and recording with AppleScript
- Performs faster than MacHTTP 2.0
- Supports WebSTAR API
- Supports thousands of connections per hour
- Integrates with both Mac and SQL databases
- Enables remote administration from anywhere on the Internet
- Controls multiple servers from Mac

Fully licensed copies are available from Apple for $499, and 30-day trial copies are available at `keys@starnine.com`. A serial number is required to activate the software.

### Sun Netra j Servers

Brand new in the market, and fully described at `www.sun.com`, is the Sun Microsystems Netra j server. The Netra j, according to a recent Sun press release, is designed to dramatically reduce the total cost of owning an IT infrastructure. The package is meant to complement the "zero-administration" JavaStation network computer. The Netra j server line features fully integrated software for Java computing, easy-to-use browser-based administration and management tools, secure access to data on other computers, and outstanding price/performance. The Netra j server is designed for transaction and process-oriented business applications. Netra j server configurations are available to support from tens to thousands of networked computers.

Designed exclusively to run on the Sun Solaris platform, this package is extremely pricey in comparison to virtually all other server packages. Sold as integrated hardware/software packages, the Netra j servers start at $7,695 and quickly go up to $200,000 and more. For those users who require the ability to do Java computing without jeopardizing previous investments in legacy applications and infrastructure, Sun and the Netra j server may offer some truly unique solutions.

This is a powerhouse product for existing Sun shops but is well beyond the range of what will probably remain the greatest majority of Internet users for quite some time.

## Summary

In their role as the engines for the traffic on the Web, Web servers are becoming more and more sophisticated with each passing month. The brief review in the previous section illustrates the fact that the most popular servers, whether free or quite expensive, all now employ a wide array of utilities that are designed to more fully integrate with existing systems and provide a broader range of functionality.

The latest developments in server technology are becoming so tightly integrated with operating system and network operating system software packages that eventually they will become one and the same. All of this points to the fact that the role of the Web server has merged into mainstream computing. Yesterday's computer users discovered the Web and, for a brief time, explored it haphazardly with no guarantee of success. Tomorrow's computer users, however, will expect the Web to be paved and the onramps and offramps to be wide, clear, and abundant.

General advice for those considering a Web server purchase or upgrade:

> Spend adequate time defining your present and future needs. Discuss the costs, benefits, and challenges of setting up an in-house Web server with colleagues from other departments. Explore all possible applications for a married Internet/intranet system within your organization.

Specific advice for those considering a Web server purchase or upgrade:

> Spend a considerable amount of time perusing the bookstore shelves and the magazine racks and browsing the Web for information relating to your intended purchase. The options available to you are numerous. Be certain that you've nailed down your server requirements and then select the most compatible, stable, well-integrated, multifunctional, expandable, and affordable system you can find.

Finally, take an active role in educating others in the use of this marvelous tool. After all, putting the world within everyone's grasp has become the overarching purpose of the World Wide Web. As a Web development professional, you have a unique opportunity to help others glimpse what you've already seen.

# VII
## PART

# The Future of HTML

# The Emergence of Extensible Markup Language

*by Dmitry Kirsanov*

Everyone interested in the future of the Web must be curious—and pretty uncertain—about what may be the outcome of the HTML case. Browser wars and incompatible extensions tearing apart the language are not only bad by themselves, they're a sure sign that something's going wrong with HTML in the first place. It may sound like heresy that the tongue spoken by millions of Web pages is approaching the end of its useful life, but many serious observers cannot suppress exactly that feeling.

If we strip away for a moment the innumerable struts, crutches, and sophisticated gizmos that make the HTML golem walk and speak and look alive, what we'll see will be a pretty simple (not to say primitive) markup language designed for basic documents of a quite predictable structure. Just headers, paragraphs, block quotations, and the good old ADDRESS at the end. Does *this* sound like a model structure for the whole world of information out there?

Of course, now HTML has tables and fonts and so on. Indeed, visual HTML extensions (or inline images, as the last resort) enable you to emulate any document structure—that is, make the document *look* as if it is properly structured. But as a result, the internal structure of the text will inevitably become illogical, cumbersome, presentation-oriented (and with images, the text may cease to be text at all). This is very likely to prevent reusing the document in the future; it becomes difficult even to convert it into another visually oriented format, not to mention isolate its logical elements.

Fortunately, there's a new important language designed to address this issue. XML (eXtensible Markup Language) is a simple and compact subset of SGML designed specifically for use on the Internet in the way that HTML is currently used. This new project of W3C is gaining momentum at a surprising rate, and everybody seriously concerned with HTML may want to check it out. Maybe someday, you'll find yourself saying, "back in those days when everyone was using HTML…"

# The Premises of XML

As with every new and promising technology, it is probably more important to explain what it isn't rather than what it is. XML, just like SGML, is not a page layout or graphics language. By itself, XML provides even fewer presentation tools than you have with HTML. Strictly speaking, it's not even a markup language, but rather a system making it possible to build such languages to match any conceivable document type.

Chapter 3, "SGML and the HTML DTD," explains the HTML document type definition (DTD), the specification of HTML tags and document structure written in SGML. Similarly, with XML you can build a DTD that exactly matches the structure of your document and introduces a set of self-explanatory, logically organized tags and attributes fine-tuned for your markup needs.

By attaching the DTD with the document sent over the network, you can ensure that the XML software reading the document can parse it correctly and thereby guarantee its correct formatting, conversion, adding to a database, or whatever the receiver will choose to do with the document. In short, with XML you can create your own HTML, or XYZML, or Whatever-You-Like-ML! (It's no surprise such a language was called "extensible" in the first place.)

It is important to understand that XML isn't better than HTML because it makes it easier to change fonts or position images. In the visual presentation realm, XML is not better than HTML (and some might say it's worse because it lacks all those neat Netscape enhancements—unless you've defined them in your DTD). It was the intention of the creators of the language that the visual presentation of an XML document can be (optionally) specified by an attached style sheet, which is an *external* mechanism for XML just as it is for HTML.

XML's visualization power is thus completely determined by the style sheet language you use—for example, Cascading Style Sheets (CSS) or Document Style Semantics and Specification Language (DSSSL)—and if you don't care about logical markup you can achieve exactly the same *visible* results by using this chosen style sheet mechanism with HTML. (Remember that you can use the neutral SPAN tag in HTML to apply any attributes, style names included, to arbitrary fragments of text.) It is when the proper internal structure of your data really matters that XML easily outshines HTML.

XML specification (found at `http://www.textuality.com/sgml-erb/WD-xml-lang.html`) defines the language in the terms of behavior of a *parser*, which is a piece of software whose sole purpose is to understand the element structure of your document and break it down into nested elements in accordance with the DTD. Another program (termed simply "application" in the XML specification) is supposed to obtain the document thus dissected from the parser and process it further. Exactly what the application performs on the document is outside the scope of XML; for instance, it may be a browser that displays the document using an appropriate style sheet.

Because XML is a subset of SGML, an XML document is almost always a valid SGML document; small discrepancies between these two languages are likely to be eliminated soon with the acceptance of certain amendments to the SGML standard. The relation between XML and HTML is more complex. With the capability to define new tags, XML documents are not likely to count as valid HTML very often; on the other hand, an HTML file is relatively easy to make XML-conformant on one of the two levels of conformance (described later in this chapter), depending on whether or not you provide a DTD for your document.

I don't attempt a real tutorial of XML in this chapter for two reasons. First, one chapter's space is surely insufficient to cover even the basics of the language, and second, the language itself is so young and unstable that it is probably untimely to start teaching it in a serious fashion. (A quote from the language specification: "Please be advised that the draft you are now reading is unusually volatile.") Instead, this chapter presents a couple of small examples that will help you to quickly grasp the "look and feel" of the language.

In a sense, XML is positioned somewhere in between SGML and HTML, with the intent of its creators being to combine the best features of these two languages. However, XML is much closer to SGML than to HTML, and although knowledge of HTML will help you understand the most obvious XML features, an acquaintance with SGML syntax and ideology would be of much more help. So I recommend that you brush up what you remember from reading Chapter 3 before proceeding to subsequent sections of this chapter.

# Well-Formed XML Documents

If you're scared by the prospect of learning the art of writing document type definitions, there's good news for you: With XML, you can create a document even without DTD. If the lack of a DTD is the sole violation of XML requirements, such a document is called *well-formed,* as opposed to a *valid* document that has a DTD provided (or referred to). Thus, well-formedness is the lower of the two levels of XML conformance, but although it is inferior to validity, it is still very useful.

The permission to omit the DTD means, in essence, that you are free to use *any* tags that seem necessary for your document. You may just go wild and write in plain English what each part of your text is supposed to represent. For example, if you're a grammarian, you could try the following:

```
<SENTENCE>
  <SUBJECT TYPE="COMPLEX">
    <ARTICLE TYPE="INDEFINITE">A</ARTICLE>
    <ADJECTIVE>quick</ADJECTIVE>
    <ADJECTIVE>brown</ADJECTIVE>
    <NOUN>fox</NOUN>
  </SUBJECT>
  <VERB TYPE="INTRANSITIVE">jumps</VERB>
  <PREPOSITION>over</PREPOSITION>
  <ARTICLE TYPE="INDEFINITE">a</ARTICLE>
  <OBJECT>
    <ADJECTIVE>lazy</ADJECTIVE>
    <NOUN>dog</NOUN>
  </OBJECT>.
</SENTENCE>
```

Given this well-formed document, an XML parser will be able to break the text into the elements that you deemed essential in this case and pass each element to the application along with its name (derived from the tag name) and attribute information you provided. It is the application, not the XML parser, that must be programmed to perform some useful tasks with this structured information. Most often, you'll need to provide the application with a style sheet that associates certain formatting parameters with each element. (In our example, the style sheet might specify displaying different parts of speech in different colors.)

In fact, even "plain English" is not an obligatory requirement for your tags. Creators of XML intended that the language must be international from the very beginning. They painstakingly identified all Unicode characters that may be called "letters" in some sense or in some language and included these characters in the set of characters allowed in element and attribute names. This means that you can write your tags in Russian or Chinese instead of English.

There are, of course, numerous restrictions that are imposed even on well-formed documents. Some of these requirements are even stricter than those of HTML and thus deserve special attention:

- In XML, *every* start tag must have a corresponding end tag (unless it is an empty tag that takes special form, as described in the next item). Tags should be properly nested; that is, you can't have an open tag within the scope of some other tag and the corresponding end tag outside that scope.

- If a tag is empty by its nature (in other words, the corresponding element can never contain any text), it must have a forward slash (/) before the closing greater than symbol (>), as in the following example:

```
<IMG alt="XML logo" src="http://www.ucc.ie/xml/xml.gif"/>
```

  Such tags are the only tags that do not have corresponding end tags.

- All attribute values without exception must be enclosed in quotes—either single quotes (' ') or double quotes (" ").

In fact, the preceding requirements are the *only* ones that you must satisfy to make your HTML files well-formed XML. It doesn't matter which browser's HTML extensions you use or whether you "abuse" HTML tags or not. XML is a truly liberal language; it makes you a creator of your own universe whose rules you're unlikely to break simply because you established them.

Those familiar with the material in Chapter 3 may be wondering about another essential part of any SGML application—the SGML declaration that always accompanies a DTD. Because XML is pretty simple compared to SGML, its authors decided to omit this part of the language; XML parsers (or SGML software processing XML documents) should behave as if all XML documents were assigned the same generic SGML declaration that is listed in an appendix to the XML standard.

# XML DTDs and Valid XML Documents

Although in many cases well-formed XML documents are sufficient for practical purposes, designing a DTD for your document has a number of advantages:

- First and foremost, a DTD allows an XML parser to *validate* your document (which is why such documents are called valid). When validating, the parser checks for misspelled tags or attributes, for errors in types of attribute values and in elements' content models (covered in Chapter 3), and so on. For HTML, similar validation services exist that will check your file against one of the existing HTML DTDs.

- For a human reader, a DTD is a convenient way to quickly learn the structure of the particular type of documents. Compared to SGML, the simplified DTD syntax of XML is very straightforward and unambiguous.

- With DTD, you can define not only elements and their attributes, but also *entities*. (See "Entity Declarations," later in this chapter.) Similarly to macros in word processors or #define preprocessor instructions in C, entities can be used to abbreviate text strings and markup instructions in an obvious and easy-to-modify manner. Also, you can use *external entities* to refer to other XML documents, DTDs, or binary data located in separate files.

## Accessing the DTD

Let's examine an example of a valid XML document, namely a play by Shakespeare (*The Tempest*) marked up by Jon Bosak, one of the authors of XML. The package (http://sunsite.unc.edu/pub/sun-info/standards/dsssl/egs/21_shaks/) includes, besides the XML document and its DTD, a DSSSL style sheet that contains formatting instructions for each element and a Postscript output of a DSSSL processor that formatted the play. (See Chapter 21, "JavaScript Style Sheets and Other Alternatives to CSS.")

Here's the very beginning of the XML document play.xml:

```
<?XML version="1.0"?>
<!DOCTYPE play PUBLIC "-//Free Text Project//DTD Play//EN">
```

The first line here is an *XML declaration,* a special instruction that is XML-specific and would not be recognized by an SGML parser because of the <? delimiter (which is not used in SGML). Here, the XML declaration provides information about the version of XML standard that the document conforms to.

Next comes the DOCTYPE statement that, like its namesake in SGML, provides the DTD for the document to be parsed. In XML, a DTD may be in two parts: *internal* is contained in the document file itself, and *external* is referenced by its URL or *public identifier* (covered in Chapter 3), with the internal part taking precedence over the external one in a case of conflict.

In our example, only the external part of DTD is present, which is referred to by the public identifier preceded by the keyword PUBLIC. An XML parser is supposed to be able to retrieve the text of the DTD using its public identifier (that is, to translate the identifier into a URL or some other sort of physical address). If the DTD you're using is not assigned a well-known public identifier, you should provide a URL instead of it, with the SYSTEM keyword instead of PUBLIC. Here is an example:

```
<!DOCTYPE HTML SYSTEM "http://www.foo.com/myfiles/html3x.dtd">
```

Finally, to provide an internal part for a DTD, you must put it in brackets within the DOCTYPE declaration. Such a declaration may also contain a SYSTEM or PUBLIC external reference, as in the following example:

```
<!DOCTYPE HTML SYSTEM "http://www.foo.com/myfiles/html3x.dtd"
[
  <!-- your DTD goes here -->
]>
```

## Element Declarations

The name right after the DOCTYPE keyword in the preceding statements is the name of the *root element* of your document type, the top-level element that encloses all other elements. In HTML, this element is named HTML, and in our Shakespearean example it is named PLAY. Here's how the PLAY element is defined in `play.dtd`:

```
<!ELEMENT play (title, fm, personae, scndescr, playsubt, induct?,
                                    prologue?, act+, epilogue?)>
```

You can see that the *content model* (discussed in Chapter 3) for this element is quite simple and immediately translatable into human talk: "A PLAY is formed by its TITLE, followed by the front matter (FM), followed by the list of dramatis PERSONAE, and so on." The question mark indicates optional elements, and the plus sign indicates the elements that may occur once or more. Note that the XML spec prescribes to drop the SGML minimization parameters that are useless in XML, which doesn't permit tag omission anyway.

One more excerpt from `play.dtd` shows a hierarchical set of related tags to mark a personage's speech:

```
<!ELEMENT speech   (speaker+, (line | stagedir | subhead)+)>
<!ELEMENT speaker  (#PCDATA)>
<!ELEMENT line     (stagedir | #PCDATA)+>
<!ELEMENT stagedir (#PCDATA)>
<!ELEMENT subhead  (#PCDATA)>
```

Thus a SPEECH is constituted by one or more SPEAKER elements followed by at least one of the LINE, STAGEDIR (stage direction), or SUBHEAD elements, in no particular order. (The | sign means that any one of the connected particles may occur.) The #PCDATA keyword has the meaning of "any character data without tags"; thus, the SPEAKER, STAGEDIR, and SUBHEAD elements are allowed to contain only text characters, while a LINE may have STAGEDIRs intermingled with text.

Note that nothing in the definition of LINE (except the name) suggests that what the element contains is really a line of verse. It is just implied to be so by the person who did markup, and it may be formatted as a line if an appropriate style sheet is used. However, XML only serves as an intermediator between the author and the formatter, and it is not intended to describe the nature of data elements that are marked up with it.

**38**

THE EMERGENCE OF
EXTENSIBLE MARKUP
LANGUAGE

Here's a SPEECH element exemplifying these DTD provisions:

```
<SPEECH>
<SPEAKER>PROSPERO</SPEAKER>
<LINE><STAGEDIR>Aside</STAGEDIR> The Duke of Milan</LINE>
<LINE>And his more braver daughter could control thee,</LINE>
<LINE>If now 'twere fit to do't. At the first sight</LINE>
<LINE>They have changed eyes. Delicate Ariel,</LINE>
<LINE>I'll set thee free for this.</LINE>
<STAGEDIR>To FERDINAND</STAGEDIR>
<LINE>A word, good sir;</LINE>
<LINE>I fear you have done yourself some wrong: a word.</LINE>
</SPEECH>
```

## Entity Declarations

Entities can be declared in a DTD as follows:

```
<!ENTITY me "Dmitry Kirsanov, St.Petersburg, Russia">
```

In the document, such an entity can be used similarly to mnemonic character entities of HTML:

```
This document was created by &me; on April 21, 1997
```

Another syntax is used to define entities that refer to external files or documents, as in the following example:

```
<!ENTITY mypage SYSTEM "http://www.symbol.ru/dk/index.xml">
<!ENTITY xml-logo SYSTEM "http://www.ucc.ie/xml/xml.gif" NDATA gif>
```

In the second declaration, gif is the name of a *notation* (similar to a data type), which must be declared somewhere in the DTD along with information on where an XML processor can access a helper software capable of handling data in this notation.

Now, &mypage; and &xml-logo; entities can be used in documents using this DTD. However, XML specification does not prescribe the exact behavior of the XML application on encountering such an entity. For example, it might incorporate it into the text of the current document, or it might present it as a link that the user can activate.

# Linking Capabilities of XML

The first part of the XML specification referenced earlier in this chapter (http:// www.textuality.com/sgml-erb/WD-xml-lang.html) fully describes the syntax of the language. However, a second part of the specification at http://www.textuality.com/sgml-erb/WD-xml-link.html is concerned with *linking capabilities* of XML documents similar to the hypertext features of HTML.

In some sense, this is beyond the scope of an SGML-like language, because the *semantics* of elements (including their capability to link) should be left to creators of SGML or XML applications. On the other hand, links are difficult to implement using common style sheet languages and therefore need support from a deeper level. For this reason (as well as, apparently, to make XML a better competitor to HTML), authors of the language chose to make linking provisions a part of the main body of the XML standard.

The linking model of XML (which can be used with SGML as well) is much more versatile than that of HTML. It is largely based on the efforts of other SGML projects such as HyTime and Text Encoding Initiative (TEI). I don't describe the detailed syntax here, because it is likely to change in subsequent drafts of the specification. It is worth noting, however, that all linking constructs are implemented on the level of reserved attributes and their values, not elements. This means that you can easily turn any element into a link by expanding its list of attributes.

A simple link intended to connect the XML document you're reading to some other Internet resource may be assigned a number of parameters, including the following:

- Strings describing the *role* of the link in the document and its associated *label* (for example, this information may be displayed by the browser in its status line)
- A parameter defining whether the linked resource should, upon activating the link, replace the current document, be opened in a new context (for example, in a new window), or be embedded into the current document in place of the link
- A parameter indicating whether the user can activate the link or it is activated automatically when encountered by the processing application

Very important, although perfectly backwards-compatible, enhancements are proposed for the syntax of URLs that are used in XML to address resources. Using search parts (separated by ?) or fragment identifiers (separated by #) of special form, you can access any part of another XML document without the necessity of attaching a label to it beforehand (such as <A NAME="...">
in HTML).

The syntax of such *extended locators* in XML is capable of expressing formally such requests as "everything from the third paragraph of the first chapter to the end of the chapter" or "the whole section to which the last sidebar belongs." Of course "chapters" or "sidebars" are to be declared as corresponding elements in the DTD of the linked document.

Moreover, you may prescribe whether the necessary fragment is extracted right on the server where the linked document is stored (which may result in considerable bandwidth savings) or whether the server sends you the whole document and your application needs to winkle out the part you requested.

XML links can be not only inline but also *out-of-line,* which means that they do not need to reside in one of the documents connected by the link. Links can be grouped so that all the links in a group are activated at once. Finally, you can create collections of interlinked documents and inform the processing application about what other documents contain links to the current one.

# The Prospects of XML

XML is really a quite recent development. Its basic principles were all worked out in 1996, and the first draft of the specification was presented to the public at the SGML 96 conference in November. A revised draft (still not final specification) was released in March 1997. As of this writing, software created for parsing XML files is all experimental and can fit on one 3.5-inch disk.

Nevertheless, this new development is likely to seriously impact the Web industry in the near future, and in the more distant future, it could completely change the landscape we're accustomed to. Here are several points that were chosen as the most important goals by the designers of the language. These could become the key advantages in the competition of XML with other technologies:

- **XML shall be straightforwardly usable over the Internet.** Web servers in use today require minimal configuration changes to be able to serve XML documents. The standard way to link and bind together XML documents and DTDs is via URLs that are understood by the majority of Internet software.

- **It shall be easy to write programs that process XML documents.** The experimental XML software mentioned earlier is all written in Java, with some of the experimental XML parsers being contained in class files of a few kilobytes in size.

- **XML documents should be human-legible and reasonably clear.** With the users of XML being able to create their own tags and attributes with self-explanatory names, an XML file is likely to be nearly as readable as (and in some cases, even more readable than) plain text.

- **The XML standard should be prepared quickly.** It is not yet finalized, but the amount of work done in such a short term is impressive.

- **The design of XML shall be formal and concise.** Syntax descriptions in XML specification use a formal grammar that is concise, easy to understand, and easy to translate into programming code.

- **XML documents shall be easy to create.** As you've seen in this chapter, the concept of well-formedness enables you to quickly mark up any document or translate it from HTML to XML.

- **Terseness in XML markup is of minimal importance.** Clear and unambiguous syntax was always given preference over the possibility of saving a few keystrokes.

The XML technology is in an embryonic state, so any attempts to augur its future are almost sure to not come true. However, the growing interest in XML shown by many people concerned with Web development is a clear indication that the Web is eager to try out something more powerful and elegant than the HTML of today.

# Summary

In this chapter, you've become acquainted with an important new development, the extensible markup language, that, combined with a style sheet language, has a potential to eventually replace the heavily overused HTML of nowadays. Because it is a simplified subset of SGML, XML allows you to create customized markup tags and specify the corresponding document strucure for any type of documents you might need to store or disseminate. In particular, you learned about the following topics:

- What XML is and isn't, in what aspects it is better than HTML, and why it is important to mark up the logical structure of a document in the first place.
- What are well-formed XML documents, and how they can be easily created from HTML documents.
- What are the advantages of providing an XML document with a DTD, and how to refer to the DTD file from within an XML document.
- How elements and entities are declared in an XML DTD and then used in the documents.
- What linking capabilities are provided by the XML standard, and how they extend the HTML hypertext model.
- What were the main goals of the creators of XML, and in what ways its design principles help it compete with HTML and other technologies.

# CHAPTER 39

# Internationalizing the HTML Character Set and Language Tags

*by Dmitry Kirsanov*

## IN THIS CHAPTER

No book on HTML is complete without a section on the ways to overcome the pronounced Western bias in the language and to provide for its fruitful application in the worldwide multilingual environment. This chapter covers the main approaches to this problem, both those used by practicing webmasters all around the world and those suggested by standard-setting bodies.

The primary problem related to HTML internationalization (or *i18n*, as it is often abbreviated: *i* plus 18 in-between letters plus *n*) is the correct rendering of characters used by other languages. This is why I start by examining different standards of character encoding (character sets). These standards are classified by the length of bit combinations they use, from 7-bit ASCII to Unicode and ISO 10646.

Various HTML internationalization issues were first crystallized in the important document RFC 2070 (`http://ds.internic.net/rfc/rfc2070.txt`). Then, RFC 2070 provisions were incorporated in the DTD for HTML version 4.0. However, I discuss, for the most part, the material of RFC 2070 and pay special attention to the cases where it is not identical to the declarations of HTML 4.0 DTD.

In the field of HTML proper, this chapter starts by investigating the new document character set as defined in RFC 2070 and HTML 4.0. You will be introduced to the important distinction between the document character set and external character encoding. You'll learn about existing methods of specifying external character encoding, proposed additions to handle multilanguage form input, as well as a number of real-world problems related to the HTML character set.

Another big part of the HTML internationalization problem is language markup, that is, specifying the language of a piece of text in order to help user agent software to render it, observing the typography conventions of that language. Some language-specific aspects of text presentation are also addressed in RFC 2070, which introduces tools to control writing direction, cursive joining, rendering of quotation marks, text alignment, and hyphenation. As a conclusion, I cover briefly the font issues related to HTML internationalization.

# Character Encoding Standards

It so happened that the computer industry has been flourishing in the country whose language uses one of the most compact alphabets in the world. However, not long after the first computers had learned to spell English, a need arose to encode characters from other languages. In fact, even the minimum set of Latin letters and basic symbols has been for some time the subject of controversy between two competing standards, ASCII and (now almost extinct) EBCDIC; no wonder that for other languages' alphabets, a similar muddle has been around for much longer (in fact, it's still far from over).

As explained in Chapter 3, "SGML and the HTML DTD," a character encoding (often called *character set* or, more precisely, *coded character set*) is defined—first, by the numerical range of codes; second, by the repertoire of characters; and third, by a mapping between these two sets. You see that the term *character set* is a bit misleading because it actually implies *two* sets and a relation between them. Probably the most precise definition of a character encoding in mathematical terms is given by Dan Connolly in his paper "Character Set Considered Harmful" (`http://www.w3.org/pub/WWW/MarkUp/html-spec/charset-harmful.html`): "A function whose domain is a subset of integers, and whose range is a set of characters."

The range of codes is limited by the length of the sequence of bits (called *bit combination*) used to encode one character. For instance, a combination of 8 bits is sufficient to encode the total of 256 characters (although not all of these code positions may actually be used). The smaller the bit combination size, the more compact the encoding (that is, the less storage space is required for a piece of text), but at the same time, the fewer total characters you can encode.

It is quite logical to codify characters using bit combinations of the size most convenient for computers. Because modern computer architecture is based on bytes (also called *octets*) of 8 bits, all contemporary encoding standards use bit combinations of 8, 16, or 32 bits in length. The next sections survey the most important of these standards to see the roles they play in today's Internet.

# 7-Bit ASCII

The so-called 7-bit ASCII, or US ASCII, encoding is equivalent to the international standard named ISO 646 (`ftp://dkuug.dk/i18n/ISO_646`) established by the International Standards Organization (ISO). This encoding actually uses octets of 8 bits per character, but it leaves the first (the most significant) bit in each octet unused (it must be always zero). The 7 useful bits of ISO 646 are capable of encoding the total of 128 characters.

This is the most ubiquitous encoding standard used on the overwhelming majority of computers worldwide (either by itself or as a part of other encodings, as you'll see shortly). ISO 646 can be called international in the sense that there are precious few computers in the world that use other encodings for the same basic repertoire of characters. It is also used exclusively for keywords and syntax in all programming and markup languages (including SGML and HTML), as well as for all sorts of data that is human-editable but of essentially computer nature, such as configuration files or scripts.

However, with regard to the wealth of natural languages spoken around the world, ISO 646 is very restrictive. In fact, only English, Latin, and Swahili languages can use plain 7-bit ASCII with no additional characters. Most languages whose alphabets (also called *scripts* or *writing systems*) are based on the Latin alphabet use various accented letters and ligatures.

The first 32 codes of ISO 646 are reserved for *control characters,* which means that they invoke some functions or features in the device that reads the text rather than produce a visible shape (often called *glyph*) of a character for human readers. As a rule, character set standards are reluctant to exactly define the functions of control characters, as these functions may vary considerably depending on the nature of text processing software.

For example, of the 32 control characters of ISO 646, only a few (carriage return, line feed, tabulation) have more or less established meanings. For use in texts, most of these codes are just useless. The code space thus wasted in vain is a holdover from the old days, when these control characters used to play the role of today's document formats and communication protocols.

# 8-Bit Encodings

The first natural step to accommodate languages that are more letter-hungry than English is to make use of the 8th bit in every byte. This provides for additional 128 codes that are sufficient to encode an alphabet of several dozens letters (for example, Cyrillic or Greek) or a set of additional Latin letters with diacritical marks and ligatures used in many European languages (such as ç in French and ß in German).

Unfortunately, many more 8-bit encodings exist in the world than are really necessary. Nearly every computer platform or operating system making its way onto a national market without a strong computer industry of its own brought along a new encoding standard. For example, as many as three encodings for the Cyrillic alphabet are now widely used in Russia, one being left over from the days of MS-DOS, the second native to Microsoft Windows, and the third being popular in the UNIX community and on the Internet. A similar situation can be observed in many other national user communities.

ISO, being an authoritative international institution, has done its best to normalize the mess of 8-bit encodings. The ISO 8859 series of standards (which is available at `http://wwwbs.cs.tu-berlin.de/~czyborra/charsets/`) covers almost all extensions of the Latin alphabet as well as the Cyrillic (ISO 8859-5), Arabic (ISO 8859-6), Greek (ISO 8859-7), and Hebrew (ISO 8859-8) alphabets. All these encodings are backward compatible with ISO 646; that is, the first 128 characters in each ISO 8859 code table are identical to 7-bit ASCII, while the national characters are always located in the upper 128 code positions.

Again, the first 32 code positions (128 to 159 decimal, inclusive) of the upper half in ISO 8859 are reserved for control characters and should not be used in texts. This time, however, many software manufacturers chose to disregard the taboo; for example, the majority of True Type fonts for Windows conform to ISO 8859-1 in code positions from 160 upward, but use the range 128–159 for various additional characters (notably the em dash and the trademark sign). This leads to the endless confusion about whether one can access these 32 characters in HTML (the DTD, following ISO 8859, declares this character range unused). HTML internationalization extensions resolve this controversy by making it possible to address these characters via their Unicode codes.

The authority of ISO was not, however, sufficient to position all of the 8859 series as a strong alternative to the ad hoc national encodings supported by popular operating systems and platforms. For example, ISO 8859-5 is hardly ever used to encode Russian texts except on a small number of computers.

On the other hand, the first standard in the 8859 series, ISO 8859-1 (often called ISO Latin-1), which contains the most widespread Latin alphabet extensions serving many European languages, has been widely recognized as *the* 8-bit ASCII extension. Whenever a need arises for an 8-bit encoding standard that is as international as possible, you're likely to see ISO 8859-1 playing the role. For instance, ISO 8859-1 served as a basis for the document character set in HTML versions up to 3.2. (In 4.0, this role was taken over by Unicode, as discussed next.)

## 16-Bit Encodings

Not all languages in the world use small alphabets. Some writing systems (for example, Japanese and Chinese) use *ideographs*, or hieroglyphs, instead of letters, each corresponding not to a sound of speech but to an entire concept or word. As there are many more words and especially conceivable ideas than there are sounds in a language, such writing systems usually contain many thousands of ideographs. An encoding for such a system needs at least 16 bits (2 octets) per character, which allows you to accommodate the total of $2^{16} = 65536$ characters.

Ideally, such a 16-bit encoding should be backward compatible with the existing 8-bit (and especially 7-bit ASCII) encodings. This means that an ASCII-only device reading a stream of data in this encoding should be able to correctly interpret at least ASCII characters if they're present. This is implemented using *code switching*, or *escaping* techniques: Special sequences of control characters are used to switch back and forth between ASCII mode with the 1 octet per character and 2-octet modes (also called *code pages*). Encodings based on this principle are now widely used for Asian languages.

Code switching works all right, but one interesting problem is that the technique makes it ambiguous what to consider a coded representation of a character—is it just its 2-octet code or the code preceded by the switching sequence? It is obvious that the "extended" national symbols and ASCII characters are not treated equally in such systems, which may be practically justifiable but is likely to pose problems in the future.

In late 80s, the need for a truly international 16-bit coding standard became apparent. The Unicode Consortium (`http://www.unicode.org`), formed in 1991, undertook to create such a standard called Unicode. In Unicode, every character from the world's major writing systems is assigned a unique 2-octet code. According to the tradition, the first 128 codes of Unicode are identical to 7-bit ASCII, and the first 256 codes, to ISO 8859-1. However, strictly speaking, this standard is not backward compatible with 8-bit encodings; for instance, Unicode for the Latin letter *A* is 0041 (hex), while ASCII code for the same letter is simply 41.

The Unicode standard deserves a separate book to describe it fully (in fact, its official specification is available in book form from the Unicode Consortium). Its many blocks and zones cover all literal and syllabic alphabets that are now in use, alphabets of many dead languages, lots of special symbols, and combined characters (such as letters with all imaginable diacritical marks, circled digits, and so on).

**39**

**INTERNATIONALIZING HTML**

Also, Unicode provides space for more than 20 thousand unified ideographs used in Asian languages. Contrary to other alphabets, ideographic systems were treated on a language-independent basis. This means that an ideograph that has similar meanings and appearance across the Asian languages is represented by a single code despite the fact that it corresponds to quite different *words* in each of the languages and that most such ideographs have country-specific glyph variants.

The resulting ideographic system implemented in Unicode is often abbreviated CJK (Chinese, Japanese, Korean) after the names of the major languages covered by this system. CJK unification reduced the set of ideographs to be encoded to a manageable (and codable) number, but the undesirable side effect is that it is impossible to create a single Unicode font suitable for everyone; a Chinese text should be displayed using slightly different visual shapes of ideographs than a Japanese text even if they use the same Unicode-encoded ideographs.

The work on Unicode is far from complete, as about 34 percent of the total coding space remains unassigned. Workgroups in both the Unicode Consortium and ISO are working on selection and codification of the most deserving candidates to colonize Unicode's as-of-yet wastelands. A good sign is that the process of Unicode acceptance throughout the computer industry is taking off; for example, Unicode is used for internal character coding in Java programming language and for font layout in Windows 95 and Windows NT operating systems.

# ISO 10646

Although Unicode is still not widely used, in 1993 ISO published a new, 32-bit encoding standard named ISO/IEC 10646-1, or Universal Multiple-Octet Coded Character Set (abbreviated UCS and outlined at `http://www.dkuug.dk/JTC1/SC2/WG2/docs/standards`). Just as 7-bit ASCII does, though, this standard leaves the most significant bit in the most significant octet unused, which makes it essentially a 31-bit encoding.

Still, the code space of ISO 10646 spans the tremendous amount of $2^{31}$ = 2147483648 code positions, which is much more than could be used by all languages and writing systems that ever existed on Earth. What, then, is the rationale behind such a huge "Unicode of Unicodes?"

The main reason for developing a 4-octet encoding standard is that Unicode actually cannot accommodate all the characters for which it would be useful to provide encoding. Although a significant share of Unicode codes are still vacant, the proposals for new character and ideograph groups that are now under consideration require in total several times more code positions than are available in 16-bit Unicode.

Extending Unicode thus seems inevitable, and it makes little sense to extend it by 1 octet because computers will have trouble dealing with 3-octet (24-bit) sequences; 32-bit encoding, on the other hand, is particularly convenient for modern computers, most of which process information in 32-bit chunks.

Just as Unicode extends ISO 8859-1, the new ISO 10646 is a proper extension of Unicode. In terms of ISO 10646, a chunk of 256 sequential code positions is called a *row*, 256 rows constitute a *plane*, and 256 planes make up a *group*. The whole code space is thus divided into 128 groups. In such terms, Unicode is simply plane 00 of group 00, the special plane that in ISO 10646 standard is called the *Basic Multilingual Plane* (BMP). For example, the Latin letter A (Unicode 0041) is in ISO 10646 fully coded 00000041. As of now, ISO 10646 BMP is absolutely identical to Unicode, and it is unlikely that these two standards will ever diverge.

ISO 10646 specifies a number of intermediate formats that do not require using the codes in the *canonical form* of 4 octets per character. For example, the UCS-2 (Universal Character Set, 2-octet format) is indistinguishable from Unicode as it uses 16-bit codes from the BMP. The UTF-8 format (UCS Transformation Format, 8 bits) can be used to incorporate, with a sort of code switching technique, 32-bit codes into a stream consisting of mostly 7-bit ASCII codes. Finally, the UTF-16 method was developed to access more than a million 4-octet codes from within a Unicode/BMP 2-octet data stream without making it incompatible with current Unicode implementations.

Most probably, ISO 10646 will be rarely used in its canonical 4-octet form. For most texts and text-processing applications, wasting 32 bits per character is beyond the acceptable level of redundancy. However, ISO 10646 is an important standard in that it establishes a single authority on the vast lands lying beyond Unicode, thus preventing the problem of incompatible multioctet encodings even before this problem could possibly emerge.

# MIME

MIME stands for Multipurpose Internet Mail Extensions. It is a standard developed originally to extend the capabilities of electronic mail by allowing e-mail messages to include virtually any type of data, not only plain text. However, the mechanisms of MIME proved so useful and well designed that they are now used in many other fields, including HTML. The latest MIME specification can be found in RFCs 2045 through 2049. (See `http://ds.internic.net/rfc/rfc2045.txt`, `http://ds.internic.net/rfc/rfc2046.txt`, and so forth.)

The existing e-mail transport systems, such as Simple Mail Transfer Protocol (SMTP) and Post Office Protocol 3 (POP3), do not accept anything but plain text in the body of a message. This means that a message should contain only printable (noncontrol) characters of 7-bit ASCII and the lines should not exceed some reasonable length. To overcome this limitation, MIME introduces methods to convert binary data or texts in more-than-7-bit encodings into "mail safe" plain ASCII text.

Special MIME header fields are added to such messages to specify what conversion method was used (if any) and what was the original type of the data sent in the message. For text messages, along with other parameters, the character encoding (character set, or *charset*) of the message body is specified. This mechanism is important for us because it is used not only in e-mail messages but also in HTTP headers for HTML documents transferred over the network. The `charset` parameter is a part of the `Content-Type` header field and takes the following form:

```
Content-Type: text/html; charset=ISO-8859-1
```

39

INTERNATIONALIZING
HTML

Here, `text/html` is the standard identifier of the "HTML source" data type, and `ISO-8859-1` indicates the character encoding used by the text of the HTML document. Both these values are taken from the official registry of content data types, character sets, and other MIME-related classifiers maintained by IANA (Internet Assigned Numbers Authority).

It is this official registry that makes MIME so useful beyond the e-mail realm. For our purposes, it is especially important that MIME has developed a standard way of communicating the character encoding of a document. The list of registered MIME `charset` values can be obtained from `ftp://ftp.isi.edu/in-notes/iana/assignments/character-sets`.

# HTML Character Set

Now that you are acquainted with various character encoding standards and the MIME-supplied method to indicate the standard in use, it's time to get to HTML and see how it is tweaked in version 4.0 to handle multilanguage data.

## Document Character Set Versus External Character Encoding

First of all, an important distinction should be made. Chapter 3 examines SGML declaration for HTML and, in particular, its CHARSET section. This section defines the single *document character set* to be used by all conforming HTML documents.

On one hand, this makes the choice of the document character set fairly obvious: It should be itself international, which means Unicode or, better yet, ISO 10646. Here's how the SGML declaration for HTML 4.0 defines the document character set (see Chapter 3 for syntax explanations):

```
CHARSET
     BASESET  "ISO 646:1983//CHARSET
              International Reference Version
              (IRV)//ESC 2/5 4/0"
     DESCSET  0   9   UNUSED
              9   2   9
              11  2   UNUSED
              13  1   13
              14  18  UNUSED
              32  95  32
              127 1   UNUSED
     BASESET  "ISO Registration Number 176//CHARSET
                 ISO/IEC 10646-1:1993 UCS-2 with
                 implementation level 3//ESC 2/5 2/15 4/5"
     DESCSET  128 32    UNUSED
              160 65375 160
```

Here, ISO 10646 is employed in one of its transformation formats, namely the UCS-2, which is a 2-octet format identical to Unicode.

RFC 2070 takes a more thoroughgoing approach and bases the document character set on the canonical 4-octet form of ISO 10646 only, without a reference to ISO 646 (which is a subset of ISO 10646 anyway) and with the upper limit of the code space raised to as much as 2147483646.

On the other hand, however, it is unrealistic to expect and fairly unreasonable to require that all HTML authors and browser manufacturers switch to Unicode in the next couple months (or years, for that matter). So how can we get the benefits of Unicode without making everybody change over to it?

RFC 2070 explains that this quandary is resolved by differentiating the document character set from the *external character encoding* of the document. The external encoding is applied to the document when it's stored on a server and transferred through the network; this encoding can be arbitrary, provided that it is sufficient to encode the character repertoire of the document and that both server and user agent software are capable of handling it properly.

Upon receiving the document, the user agent software should convert it from external encoding to the document character set, so that further SGML processing and markup parsing is performed in this character set only. Before displaying the parsed document, the user agent can recode it once again, for example, to comply to the encoding supported by the operating system (in order to call its display services) or to match the encoding of fonts that will be used for output.

Converting the document from external encoding to the SGML-specified document character set is done for two obvious purposes. First, it is necessary to ensure that all characters that have special meaning in HTML, such as letters in element names and < and > characters, are correctly recognized (although it is unlikely, external encoding could remap some of these characters to other bit combinations).

And second, remember that users can invoke characters using character references (as discussed in Chapter 3), such as &169; for the copyright sign. For these references to be unambiguous and not require changes when the document is recoded from one character set to another, it is declared that these explicit references always refer to the document character set—that is, Unicode.

This means that, for example, to access the CYRILLIC CAPITAL LETTER EF via a character reference, you should use its Unicode code, which yields &#1060;, *regardless* of what character encoding you work in when creating your document. It doesn't matter whether you use KOI8-R 8-bit Cyrillic encoding in which this letter is coded 230 (decimal) or ISO 8859-1 that has no Cyrillic alphabet at all. A compliant HTML parser should always resolve character references in terms of the document character set (Unicode) simply because, at the time of HTML-specific processing, the document should be already converted into the document character set.

Here are some advantages of using Unicode as the document character set and separating it from external encoding of a document:

- This solution is backward compatible to the previous versions of HTML standard. Indeed, character references in, say, HTML 3.2 were supposed to refer to ISO 8859-1, which is a proper subset of Unicode. (Whether a code is 8 or 16 bits makes no difference in this case because character references use decimal values of codes where padding zeroes can be dropped.)

■ The solution is also fairly flexible. International HTML authors can continue using the character sets that are widely supported by software and that minimize overhead for their languages. At the same time, they acquire the capability to directly access the entire character space of Unicode via character references.

■ Finally, implementing the technique should not be too bothersome for browser manufacturers. The RFC 2070 standard does not even require user agents (browsers) to be able to display *any* Unicode character, but offers instead a number of workarounds for the cases when a browser cannot generate a glyph for a particular Unicode code (for example, displaying the hexadecimal code or some special icon in place of the character).

## Specifying External Character Encoding

For an HTML browser to correctly translate the received document from external encoding into the document character set, it must know the external encoding beforehand. As of now, MIME is the only standard mechanism capable of communicating such information. As described earlier in this chapter, the charset parameter is included in the Content-Type field that must be a part of any HTTP header, that is, must precede any document sent via HTTP protocol (See Chapter 5, "Behind the Scenes: HTTP and URIs.") This field should also be included in the header of an e-mail message containing an HTML document. Currently, there is no way to indicate character encoding for an HTML document retrieved via FTP or from a local or distributed file system.

Common browsers such as Netscape and Internet Explorer recognize the charset parameter and try to switch to the requested character set before displaying the document (in Netscape Communicator 4, for example, you can open the Options|Document Encoding submenu to see the list of supported character sets). If no charset parameter is specified, ISO 8859-1 is assumed, and if it's not what the author planned for the document, the user will have to guess which encoding to switch to manually in order to read the document. (It is not unreasonable to claim that the very possibility of manually switching character sets in common browsers is to blame for the abundance of Web servers that never care to declare the character encoding of the documents they deliver.)

However, there's something more to character set negotiation. HTTP protocol allows a client program to list a number of character encodings it can handle, in the order of preference, right in an HTTP request using the Accept-Charset field. This enables the server to select the appropriate version of the document among those available or translate it to a requested character set on-the-fly. The standard declares that if no Accept-Charset value is given in the request, the user agent thereby guarantees that it can handle *any* character set. Unfortunately, the only browser (at this time) that allows a user to specify the Accept-Charset value to be inserted in HTTP requests is Lynx (whose Web site is at http://lynx.browser.org).

One more method to indicate the external character encoding of a document is by emulating the Content-Type header field in a META element. For this, you should place the following tag within the HEAD block of your HTML document:

```
<META HTTP-EQUIV="Content-Type" CONTENT="text/html; charset=KOI8-R">
```

if you need to specify that your document is in KOI8-R Cyrillic encoding. This is a handy choice for those who are unable or unwilling to change setup of the server that the document is stored on, but it has an obvious down side: Such a document, if automatically converted from one encoding to another, requires manually changing the <META> tag attributes. The META encoding indication is supported by most browsers, but beware of a pitfall: Contrary to the standard stating that the charset value in the HTTP header, if present, should override its META emulation, some browsers give preference to the META-supplied value.

## Forms Internationalization

When browsing on the Web, you not only download textual information, but sometimes upload it as well using the forms mechanism of HTML. Naturally, this mechanism needs adjustments to allow character set negotiation of the data submitted from the user agent software to the server. This section covers the new features introduced to meet this requirement.

In HTML 4.0, the FORM tag is given an additional ACCEPT-CHARSET attribute that is similar to the Accept-Charset HTTP field mentioned in the preceding section. The main difference is that the ACCEPT-CHARSET attribute in HTML works the other way around, specifying what character encodings the server is able to *receive* from the user. The value of the ACCEPT-CHARSET attribute is a list of MIME identifiers for character encodings the server can handle, in order of preference; usually this list contains at least the external character encoding of the document itself.

A browser could make use of the value of the ACCEPT-CHARSET attribute in several ways:

- A browser must configure the text input areas so that the text being typed in would display using appropriate glyphs. This is a minimal level of support (it is implemented, for example, in Netscape Navigator 3.0, although this browser uses the main document encoding for this purpose instead of the ACCEPT-CHARSET attribute value), because it leaves the user with the main problem of how to input text properly. If the operating system does not support the encoding, it might be necessary to use a specialized keyboard driver or copy and paste previously converted text. In certain cases, an HTML author could provide a clue right in the document as to which encoding is accepted in a particular input field.

- Better yet, a browser must take into account the character encoding supported by the operating system and convert, if it is possible (that is, if the encoding supported by the system and the encoding accepted by the server have identical character repertoires) and necessary (that is, if these two encodings are not the same), the text typed in by the user before sending it out. This makes the preceding item unnecessary because the operating system itself takes care of the proper display of characters in text input areas, provided that they use the native encoding of the system. This level of support is implemented in Microsoft Internet Explorer 4.0 and Netscape Communicator 4.0 (but again, both of these browsers ignore the ACCEPT-CHARSET value and consider the form charset the same as the document charset).

■ RFC 2070 suggests that a browser may restrict the range of characters that can be input in the text area in accordance with the encoding specified. In my opinion, this is rather useless if not accompanied by one of the other two provisions.

The second part of the form internationalization problem is how to submit the form data along with the information about its encoding. For the first of the two submission methods, POST, MIME is helpful once again. It is possible to add the charset parameter to the "Content-Type: application/x-www-form-urlencoded" header field that precedes any data sent with the POST method.

However, RFC 2070 gives preference to another technique that uses the "multipart/form-data" content type that was proposed in RFC 1867 (which is outlined at http://ds.internic.net/ rfc/rfc1867.txt) for form-based file uploads. (RFC 1867 provisions are also incorporated into HTML 4.0.) With this method, form data is not encapsulated in the form of a URL, and each name/value pair may have its own charset parameter attached. Currently, this technique is not supported by common browsers.

With the other form submission method, GET, data is encapsulated right in the URL that the browser submits to the server. In principle, URLs can contain any bit combinations, provided that they are encoded using the %HH notation. (See Chapter 5.) However, quoting RFC 2070, "text submitted from a form is composed of characters, not octets," and there's no easy way to incorporate information about the encoding of text data into an URL (other than by providing an additional input field that the user will need to manually set, which is pretty awkward).

RFC 2070 suggests that even with the GET method, user agent software could send the data in the body of the HTTP request instead of the URL, although currently no applications support this technique. Another solution with URLs might be using one of the special formats of ISO 10646; in particular, the UTF-8 format (which is outlined at http://ds.internic.net/rfc/ rfc2044.txt) preserves all 7-bit ASCII characters as is and encodes any non-ASCII characters using only the octets with the most significant bit sets—for instance, those outside the ASCII range. This makes UTF-8 completely backward compatible with the URL syntax. Because ISO 10646 is a superset of all other character encodings, a string in such a format doesn't require any further charset specifications (provided, of course, that the server is aware of using UTF-8).

# Real-World Character Sets Problems

In fact, differentiating the document character set from external encoding is nothing really new in HTML. Any numerical character references in a document conforming to HTML 3.2 or an earlier version must refer to the characters from the Latin-1 (ISO 8859-1) set, regardless of the external character set of the document. Unfortunately, this convention is ignored by many contemporary browsers, which leads to undesirable (although, admittedly, not too serious in the case of HTML 3.2 without internationalization extensions) consequences.

For instance, the KOI8-R character encoding as defined in RFC 1489 (which is outlined at http://ds.internic.net/rfc/rfc1489.txt) specifies code 191 (decimal) for the COPYRIGHT SIGN character. In ISO 8859-1, the same symbol is coded 169. Ideally, when a mnemonic entity &copy; or character reference &169; (which is what &copy; expands to, as defined by HTML DTD) is used in a KOI8-R document, the browser must resolve it with regard to ISO 8859-1 character set and display the copyright sign (for example, by accessing code position 191 in a KOI8-R font).

However, as most browsers are incapable of remembering anything about the ISO 8859-1 character set after being switched to KOI8-R or whatever external encoding is used for a document, an HTML author cannot rely any more on the table of Latin-1 mnemonic character entities. These entities or numeric character references are guaranteed to work only if the document itself is created (and viewed) in ISO 8859-1.

As a sort of a workaround, creators of several KOI8-R Cyrillic fonts for use on the Web chose to move the copyright sign from the standard-prescribed code 191 to the Latin-1-inspired 169. As Alan Flavell of CERN has put it, "Breaking your font in order to help a broken browser is a bad idea." It is obvious that, with the internationalized HTML gaining wide recognition, the problem could become more severe, as Unicode character references in conforming documents are much more likely to go out of sync with the external character encoding of a document.

In fact, support for nonstandard document encodings in browsers such as Netscape Navigator 3.0 is reduced to the capability to switch display fonts, in response to either the charset parameter in HTTP header or the user's having selected a command—and little else. As a result, Netscape Navigator 3.0 cannot display Russian texts in KOI8-R without KOI8-R Cyrillic fonts installed, even if it's working under a Russian version of Windows that provides Cyrillic fonts in Windows encoding.

There are still more problems related to document character encoding that many common browsers are unable to cope with, and that HTML authors should therefore beware of:

- Even when the text of a document is correctly displayed, its title, if it contains encoding-specific characters, may appear broken in the window title bar (apparently because the font used in window title bars is determined by the operating system, which may be completely unaware of the encoding of the document).

- ALT texts in place of inline images, as well as button labels in forms, might not display correctly if they contain encoding-specific characters (again, the reason is that many browsers use a system-provided font for these purposes).

- Text-oriented Java applets in Java-enabled browsers may have problems with displaying text in a nonstandard encoding.

# Language Identification

Character set problems constitute only a part of the whole HTML internationalization issue. Almost equally important is the problem of *language identification* of a document. Lots of aspects of document presentation depend not only on the character set, but also on the language of the text.

For example, as I've mentioned before, the same ideographs are used in many Asian languages, so that in each language they are rendered by slightly different glyphs and quite different sounds of speech. Also, different languages using the same character set may differ greatly in respect to hyphenation, spacing, use of punctuation, and so on.

To this end, HTML 4.0 introduces the new LANG attribute, which can be used with most HTML elements to describe the language of the element contents. A "language" in this context is defined as "spoken (or written) by human beings for communication of information to other human beings; computer languages are explicitly excluded." Here is an example:

```
<P LANG="fr">Ce paragraphe est en Français</P>
```

The LANG attribute can take as a value a two-letter abbreviated *code* (or *tag*) of the language. A list of these codes is defined by ISO 639 standard (outlined at ftp://dkuug.dk/i18n/ISO_639); these codes should not be confused with country codes (for example, uk as a language code means Ukrainian, not United Kingdom).

Also, *extended identifiers* can be used to designate different dialects or writing systems of a language, identify the country in which it is used, and so forth. These extended identifiers are based on two-letter codes with the addition of *subtags* separated by a hyphen (-). Here are some examples:

- en-US: English language of the USA (two-letter subtags are always interpreted as country codes)

- no-nynorsk: Nynorsk variant of Norwegian

- az-cyrillic: Azerbaijani language written in Cyrillic script

A registry of such extended language identifiers is maintained by IANA (at the address ftp://ftp.isi.edu/in-notes/iana/assignments/languages/). All LANG values are case insensitive; their complete syntax is defined by RFC 1766 (found at http://ds.internic.net/rfc/rfc1766.txt). Another useful resource is the document at http://domen.uninett.no/~hta/ietf/lang-chars.txt, where most known languages are listed along with the character sets they use.

# Language-Specific Presentation Markup

In a multilanguage environment, a need may arise to specify in HTML some aspects of text presentation, such as the writing direction (left to right or right to left), punctuation peculiarities, and so on. These aspects usually can be derived from the language of the text (as mentioned in the preceding section), but sometimes one might need to specify this information without specifying the language or to override the language default values. Also, some presentation aspects (such as quotation marks) require additional markup even if a language is specified.

RFC 2070 introduces and HTML 4.0 adopts a whole bouquet of new HTML elements, attributes, and entities for this sort of presentation markup. These new features are summarized in the following sections.

## Writing Direction

While most Western languages are written from left to right, languages such as Arabic and Hebrew are written from right to left. In situations when such text is intermingled with the text of the opposite direction (resulting in a bidirectional, or *BIDI*, text), a special markup might be necessary to resolve ambiguity.

Unicode standard has a number of direction-related provisions. Each Unicode character is assigned the *bidirectional category* parameter that may take a number of different values, such as left-to-right, right-to-left, number separator, or neutral (for example, whitespace). Some characters (such as parentheses) are marked as *mirrored* depending on the text direction (in right-to-left text, an opening parenthesis should take the appearance of a closing one and vice versa).

To support this behavior, RFC 2070 introduces directional markup tools of three types. The first type consists of the left-to-right and right-to-left marks that behave exactly as zero-width spaces having corresponding direction properties. These marks are taken directly from Unicode inventory, so in HTML they are implemented as entities expanding into corresponding Unicode characters:

```
<!ENTITY lrm  CDATA "&#8206;" -- left-to-right mark -->
<!ENTITY rlm  CDATA "&#8207;" -- right-to-left mark -->
```

Direction marks can be used when, for example, a double quote (which doesn't have a direction of its own, but is not a mirrored character either) sits between a Latin and a Hebrew character; in this situation, the actual place of the quote depends on whether it is assumed to belong to the left-to-right or the right-to-left text stream. By placing an invisible direction mark (&lrm; or &rlm;) on one side of the quote, you can ensure that the quote is surrounded by characters of the same directionality, thereby resolving the ambiguity.

The second type of direction markup is represented by the new DIR attribute that, like LANG, can be used with nearly all HTML tags to indicate the writing direction of the text in the element's contents. Sometimes you might need to indicate the basic writing direction of a piece of text; also, explicit direction markup is critical when there are two or more levels of nested contra-directional text (for an example, refer to RFC 2070).

39

INTERNATIONALIZING HTML

The two possible values for the DIR attribute are strings rtl (right-to-left) and ltr (left-to-right). As is the case with CSS attributes, you can use the DIR attribute when no element is normally discriminated by using the SPAN element as a sort of a neutral container. If the DIR attribute is omitted, the element inherits the writing direction of its parent element. The entire HTML document's default direction is left to right.

For brevity, definitions of the DIR and LANG attributes are packed into one parameter entity in the HTML 4.0 DTD:

```
<!ENTITY % i18n
  "lang        NAME      #IMPLIED  -- RFC 1766 language value --
   dir         (ltr|rtl) #IMPLIED  -- default directionality --"
   >
```

Later, the %i18n; entity is added to the ATTLIST declarations for the majority of HTML elements.

Finally, the third type of direction markup is represented by the new phrase-level BDO element (BDO stands for bidirectional override). It is used when a mix of left-to-right and right-to-left characters should be displayed in a single direction, overriding the intrinsic directional properties of the characters. For the BDO element, DIR is the only obligatory attribute.

## Cursive Joining Behavior

In some writing systems (most notably Arabic), a letter's glyph may be different depending on the context—that is, on whether the letter is preceded or followed by some other letters. Arabic letters are modeled after handwritten cursive prototypes, so a letter in a middle of a word is drawn joined to its neighbors and therefore might look quite different than it does when it is isolated.

As a rule, software capable of displaying Arabic handles these differences automatically. But sometimes it's necessary to control the joining behavior, for example, to exemplify a standalone letter with cursive joiners. For this, Unicode provides two special characters, both being invisible and having zero width, the first to force joining of adjacent characters where normally no joining would occur, and the second to prevent joining that would normally take place. HTML 4.0 provides means to access these characters in HTML via the &zwj; and &zwnj; mnemonic character entities:

```
<!ENTITY zwnj CDATA "&#8204;" -- zero width non-joiner -->
<!ENTITY zwj  CDATA "&#8205;" -- zero width joiner     -->
```

## Quotation Marks

A number of different styles exist to render quotation marks around short, in-text quotations. Although the English language always uses quotes "like this," French has « comme ça », and German prefers „wie hier". Moreover, nested comments sometimes use different styles; for example, Russian tradition uses French quotes (without separating spaces) on the upper level and German quotes for quotations within quotations. Finally, it is desirable to be able to render the same text with "rich" quotes in a graphics environment but with plain double quotes of 7-bit ASCII in text-mode browsers.

To account for these differences, HTML 4.0 offers the new phrase-level Q element whose content is surrounded by a pair of quotation marks rendered in accordance with the language of the text, the level of nesting, and the display capabilities available. Here is an example:

```
<P LANG="en">The English language always uses quotes <Q>like this</Q>,
French has <Q LANG="fr">comme &ccedil;a</Q>,
and German prefers <Q LANG="de">wie hier</Q>.</P>
```

Unfortunately, this solution is not backward compatible; most existing software will just ignore Q tags without displaying even the plain ASCII quotes, which can often damage the meaning of the text. Thus, practical use of Q elements is not encouraged until the majority of user agent software provides support for the feature.

## Alignment and Hyphenation

Traditions of using text justification modes in other languages may be quite different from those of English. That is why RFC 2070 introduces the optional ALIGN attribute that can be used with most block-level elements (namely P, HR, H1 to H6, OL, UL, DIV, MENU, LI, BLOCKQUOTE, and ADDRESS) with the values of left, right, center, and justify. RFC 2070 suggests that the default ALIGN value for texts with left-to-right writing direction should be left, and for right-to-left texts, right.

This is a significant improvement over HTML 3.2, where the list of elements supporting this attribute is shorter (only DIV, H1 to H6, HR, TD, and P) and the value "justify" is not allowed. Judging from the DTD, HTML 4.0 takes a halfway approach: It adopts the justify option but leaves the list of elements accepting the ALIGN attribute the same as in HTML 3.2.

As for hyphenation, user agents are supposed to apply language-dependent rules to break words if this is necessary for proper display. In complex or critical cases, RFC 2070 suggests that HTML authors use the mnemonic entity &shy; that invokes the SOFT HYPHEN character present in Unicode as well as all of the ISO 8859 family and other character sets.

This invisible character marks the point where a word break can occur; if the word is indeed broken, the character is visualized as a usual hyphen (-) character. Unfortunately, common browsers do not implement this behavior; what's worse, both Netscape Navigator and Microsoft Internet Explorer *always* display a - in place of a soft hyphen, thus preventing you from using this character whatsoever.

For better hyphenation control, the new HYPH element was proposed that is capable of handling complex cases when breaking a word is accompanied by a change in its spelling (for example, the German word *backen* becomes *bak-ken* when hyphenated). However, the HYPH element was not included in either RFC 2070 or HTML 4.0.

# Font Issues

Fonts lie on the boundary between visual presentation aspects of HTML documents and the problems of HTML internationalization. It's of little use to have HTML supporting Unicode if you cannot display its character repertoire (or at least, the part of Unicode that your document makes use of).

Of course the majority of users interested in non-English Web content already have some fonts installed on their systems. Often these fonts are supplied with localized versions of operating systems or other software, and implement encodings that are popular for a particular language. Common browsers such as Netscape Navigator allow using such fonts for viewing Web pages.

However, what we need is a method to ensure proper display of multilanguage data on any given system. One solution might be creating and distributing a free (or inexpensive) multilanguage font pack or, alternatively, a single font with Unicode character layout. A free Unicode font named Cyberbit is available from Bitstream at `http://www.bitstream.com/cyberbit.htm`.

The big down side to the single font solution is that the file size of a typical Unicode font is several megabytes (even without ideographs area). Probably the most practical solution for the Web today is a *glyph server*, a proxy server that substitutes inline bitmaps for all non-ASCII characters on the page you're viewing. Intermediation of such a server is a quick way to read a foreign-language page without any font headaches. Glyph servers now available include `http://www.lfw.org/shodouka/` (Japanese only) and `http://baka.aubg.bg`.

Recently, Microsoft and Adobe announced a merger of their proprietary font formats, True Type and Type 1, to create a new format called OpenType (which you can learn about at `http://www.microsoft.com/truetype/fontpack/opentype.htm`). Besides improved typographic control, this new format will make fonts readily available for many platforms with much less software support than before.

For the subject of this chapter, it is particularly important that the two companies have submitted a proposal to W3C aiming at developing a scheme to include with the page sent over the Web all the fonts (in OpenType format) necessary to view it. Microsoft intends to implement a preliminary draft of this specification in one of the forthcoming versions of Internet Explorer.

This development is likely to have great impact on HTML internationalization. On the one hand, the possibility to ensure proper display of any characters in a document on any system capable of handling outline fonts is a big plus. On the other hand, however, there are a number of dangerous pitfalls along this path.

First, being able to rely on supplied fonts, some HTML authors (as well as browser manufacturers) might really go wild in the area of character sets support. In fact, a character encoding of a document needs only to comply to that of the accompanying font, which makes nearly all

HTML internationalization provisions described in this chapter redundant—and, as a result, puts them in danger of death of neglect without software support. Of course fonts for Web distribution can use Unicode, but there's no guarantee that this will always be the case.

Second, the HTML font support puts additional emphasis on the visual presentation of a document, which is the aspect being already overemphasized with the proprietary HTML extensions now widely used. There are many documents on the Web today that are created without any concern for portability or SGML compliance, and it is not very likely that font embedding in HTML documents will ever improve the situation.

The future of HTML internationalization is quite obscure now. The standards surveyed in the chapter have just been finalized, and their implementations in software (even experimental) are few. Also, the big software companies are particularly known for poor support of official standards and pursuing their own proprietary extensions instead.

However, most national webs are now growing at a much greater rate than the Web as a whole, so that Internet-related products without at least some international support are likely to become rare very soon. In view of this, the package of RFC 2070 and related standards has, in addition to its thoughtful design, the clear advantage of being open, independent, and stable.

# Summary

This chapter examines the HTML internationalization provisions introduced in RFC 2070 and then adopted in HTML 4.0. This part of the HTML standard allows you to create and serve Web content in any language and using any writing system, maximizing the chances of your audience getting your message and not a mess of indecipherable characters. In particular, you learned about the following topics:

- What a coded character set is, what character set standards exist, and how they are used
- What MIME is, and how it helps to communicate information about the character set of a document
- Why it is important to differentiate the HTML document character set and the external character encoding of an HTML document
- What pitfalls of common browsers you should beware of when working with international HTML documents
- What tools are available in HTML 4.0 to specify the language of any document fragment and its language-specific presentation parameters (writing direction, cursive joining, rendering of quotation marks, text alignment, hyphenation)
- How the font accessibility problem might affect the future of HTML internationalization

# Point/Counterpoint: Pure HTML

*by John Jung*

## IN THIS CHAPTER

With the rush of the Internet and the Web, everything seems to be operating at a faster pace. Now, people think that any program six months to a year old is considered obsolete. Nowhere is this attitude more prevalent than in the software industry. Internet-related companies, in particular, feel pressure to keep releasing newer products faster. Indicative of this situation is the rapid release of newer versions of Web browsers. With these new releases come more, and newer, HTML extensions. But what do all these extensions give us? Are they helping or hurting Web authors?

# Definition of Pure HTML and Extensions

With all these HTML tags floating around, how can anyone tell which ones are extensions? Truth be told, there's no easy way. It's almost impossible to keep track of which tag is an extension and which one isn't. From a purely technical perspective, the best approach to answer the question is to ask the World Wide Web Consortium (W3C). W3C's Web page (`http://www.w3.org/`) makes the official specifications for HTML available. The problem is that the information is often presented in a very dry manner.

Fortunately, most people don't create Web pages by hand anymore, and there's a much more convenient solution: HTML editors. These programs used to be simple text editors that gave immediate access to HTML tags. They've evolved to the point that they keep track of which tags are extensions, and which aren't. Some of the better ones will even tell you which attributes within a tag are extensions. The problem is, extensions are created at a much faster rate than the programs are released.

## Where Do Extensions Come From?

Who's making up all these extensions? Anyone can make up any HTML extension and call it his own. The problem isn't creating the extension, but getting Web browsers to support it. Most Web browsers simply ignore any tag they don't recognize. As a result, even if you were to create your own extension, you'd never be able to see it. Chances are, no one would ever be able to see it. So the real power of creating extensions rests with the companies that make Web browsers. Because they create the browsers, they can create any extension they want and provide immediate support for it.

## Why Are Extensions Made?

You might wonder why so many extensions are being made. There are, generally, two reasons why companies are creating so many extensions. One is because they find a definite lack within HTML before they create their extension. Typically, extensions created out of this motive have been largely accepted. Usually, these extensions have offered better management of the HTML body itself than what was available. Sometimes these extensions are based on proposed standards, and so eventually get support.

But probably the main reason software developers create so many extensions is to be different. With the fast software development pace, each new version of the browser has to offer a new feature of some sort. The quickest way to accomplish this is to create an extension. It gives the browser an immediate feature that others lack, and it's easy. What needs to be done gets worked out inside the company. Best of all, if the extension gets very wide support, the company is hailed as a pioneer.

## How Does a Tag Become Pure?

A pure HTML tag is one that has its behavior and syntax formally defined by the W3C. For a tag to become pure, its purpose and syntax must be proposed to the W3C. In turn, the W3C debates the merits of the proposed tag and determines whether the tag is viable. After the proposed tag has been scrutinized, the entire W3C decides whether it should become a standard tag.

# Pros and Cons of Pure HTML

As mentioned, a pure HTML tag is one that is officially sanctioned by the W3C. But does a tag having this official sanction really offer any benefits? If extensions generally offer more capabilities than pure HTML, why not use them all the time? Also, are there any negatives to using pure tags?

## Pros of Using Pure HTML

There are several reasons for using pure HTML tags in your Web page. Almost all of them benefit, in some way, by being part of a standard. Because they must go through a rigorous review, standard tags are generally slower to come by. This means that when the tag is finally released, you can be sure that it wasn't thrown in as just a gimmick. The tag didn't show up, just because a new release of the browser dictated its existence. Also, standard HTML tags tend to provide support for all systems and configurations. HTML was initially created to disseminate information, and as a result, tries to reach the widest audience.

### Immediate Wide Support

One of the biggest benefits to using pure HTML tags in your Web page is immediate wide support. There is currently no known major Web browser company that isn't committed to the HTML standard. As a result, the standard tags almost guarantee that everybody will be able to see them. Part of the reason browser companies can support standard tags so quickly is because they are reviewed by the W3C, and the major browser vendors are members of the W3C. As a result, they know which tags are coming along and which ones will likely pass. Further, they can pass along such information to their own companies so that when a tag does become a standard HTML tag, everybody will have support for it.

Extensions, on the other hand, usually are created by a single company, so nobody else knows about them. Other Web browser companies find out about the extension the same time everybody else does. As a result, the other Web browser companies either have to wait for others to create extensions and support them or risk releasing a product that won't support the extensions of a different company. Thus, the other Web browser company either appears to lack initiative or is alienating potential customers.

## Platform Independence

The W3C is an independent standards body; that is, no one person dictates how it should operate. This is another definite reason to use pure HTML, because such tags tend to be *platform independent*—you don't need to have one particular system, or environment, to use the tag. It might seem unlikely that a company would introduce a tag that it couldn't widely support. After all, wouldn't that company be shooting itself in the foot? Absolutely. The problem is that it has already happened.

The DYNSRC attribute is probably the best example of an extension that was entirely too platform dependent. This attribute, proposed by Microsoft, was to allow video playback using the <IMG> tag. Unfortunately, it would only support AVI files. Not surprisingly, AVI files are most often found on Windows-based operating systems. There were no provisions in the extension to support other multimedia file formats. As a result, few people used it, preferring, instead, to use the <EMBED> tag. Ironically, the <EMBED> tag was another extension—introduced by Netscape.

How many problems did this problem cause for Microsoft? It's hard to say, but they introduced the extension, so it was up to them to support it. Although they supported it fine on the Windows operating systems, that was the whole extent of it. Internet Explorer, the Microsoft browser, was very slow in migrating to other operating systems. Compare that with Netscape Navigator, which was, and still is, available on numerous platforms. Not only was the DYNSRC attribute a failure for Microsoft, it probably cost them some business. Because Microsoft's browser was only on one platform, it was not a solution for many large businesses. Netscape, however, rapidly became the de facto Web browser in many large companies.

Did one extension cause all these problems? Probably not, but it probably didn't help, either.

## Feedback

Another advantage of using pure HTML tags in Web pages is that HTML tags tend to be more fleshed out. When a single company releases an extension, it might not have heard differing, or even helpful, opinions. As a result, if a shortcoming or flaw exists, it'll only be found after the extension is released. At least with pure HTML tags, there's the advantage of having more people look at the idea, increasing the likelihood that problems will be identified before the tag is released.

## Cons of Using Pure HTML

Although pure HTML tags are widely supported, there are some drawbacks to using them exclusively. In particular, many of the standard HTML tags are, relatively speaking, quite tame. The primary purpose of pure HTML is to get the text out—to present the content—not necessarily how it looks. Extensions are designed to present information well. Recent developments from the W3C have helped in this regard, but it's still far behind extensions.

## Creativity

People who make fun of committees often say that they eliminate creativity. Although this isn't really true, standards committees certainly do stifle creativity a bit. The problem is that standards bodies, such as the W3C, face very few pressures, which means that they have little motivation to create new tags. Contrast that against the Web browser companies such as Microsoft and Netscape. They almost have to create new HTML tags just to be different. They need to carve out some sort of niche so that people will choose their browser over the competition's.

Consider some popular extensions that have provided creativity that HTML tags didn't. Extensions such as the SIZE attribute for the <HR> tag have given us the capability to control the length and thickness of the horizontal rule. Extensions such as the ALIGN attribute for the <IMG> tag have also provided far better control over how text flows in relation to images. Similarly, the ability to specify different font sizes, which the SIZE attribute for the <FONT> tag accomplishes, was also largely overlooked by the W3C, and extensions filled the gap. Although many of these extensions have since gone on to become standards, they certainly didn't start out that way. They started out as extensions created by Netscape.

## Availability

Another shortcoming to using only pure HTML is that it takes so long for pure tags to become available. Because pure HTML tags must go through a long evaluation process, it can take several months before a tag actually becomes standard. Extensions, on the other hand, can be released whenever a new Web browser is released. There's no need to wait for an approval process—the extension is created, and support can be instantaneous.

If we simply waited for the W3C to create new standards, many popular features wouldn't be supported. For example, nobody would be able to create any Web pages with frames until now, when the W3C made them officially available. All Java applets wouldn't have existed until about the beginning of 1997, when the <APPLET> and <PARAM> tags became standards. In short, Web pages in general would have a lot less spunk and appeal if everybody just used pure HTML.

# Pros and Cons of Extensions

Anybody can create an HTML extension, so there are a lot of nonstandard tags out there. Extensions are a double-edged sword. On the one hand, they generally offer more features than pure HTML tags. On the other hand, there's no way of guaranteeing extensions will be supported by others. These are just some of the points discussed in the following sections.

## Pros of Using Extensions

Because extensions can be created on-the-fly, they offer a number of advantages over pure HTML. Extensions can respond quickly to what people want, providing immediate access to cutting-edge technology. Although a standards committee is still debating the viability of the technology, extensions are using it. Furthermore, some browser companies release extensions based on upcoming standards. This makes it possible to remain somewhat ahead of the game while ensuring that others will soon catch up. Finally, extensions also have the capability to direct a debated standard in a certain direction. Although it might not become a true standard, it comes close enough for most people.

## Cutting-Edge Technology

One of the best aspects of using HTML extensions is that you can use them right away. There's no need to listen to people debating the merits of a tag, or the technology it's based on. Simply use the tag and forget about it. For example, two years ago, Java was an emerging technology with some promise. With its potential to liven up Web pages and the right marketing, it caught on quickly. This was helped along by Netscape's introduction of the <APPLET> extension, which enabled Web authors to link their Java applets with their Web pages.

However, while Netscape's extension was taking over, the W3C committee was largely quiet. Even during the HTML 3.0 DTD proposal, almost a year later, there was no mention of Java. That's because they were still taking a "wait and see" attitude with it. Although this is an understandable position to take, it certainly wasn't what Web authors were looking for. They wanted to spice up their Web pages immediately, and they wanted to use Java.

## Future Standards

Another advantage of extensions is that they can be precursors to standards. Some browser companies are part of the W3C, and they know, in advance, what tags are coming. They also know how much support or opposition those tags are facing. As a result, they can often reasonably predict which tags will become standards and which ones won't. They can use this knowledge if they're releasing a new browser before the standard has been finalized. This, in turn, gives Web authors the assurance that they will eventually get support. Meanwhile, they can impress others and get their point across more effectively. It's just not a standard yet.

## Directing a Standard

Using HTML extensions can influence pure HTML. Standards committees can argue all they want about what should be a standard. However, if an HTML extension is in tremendously wide use, there's little reason to oppose the extension. It's far better to make the extension a pure HTML tag than to have so many Web pages be nonstandard. There might be a desire to fix certain aspects of, or even enhance, the extension. However, popular extensions will probably become standards.

An example of an extension controlling where the standard goes is the <FRAME> tag. Frames were introduced years ago, with Netscape Navigator 2.0. Presently, with Netscape Communicator soon to be released, the W3C is still debating whether or not it should support frames, and if so, how best to implement them. Only now, after Netscape Communicator, has the W3C decided to make frames offical. The W3C frame syntax is nearly identical to Netscape's extensions, which have been around for so many years. The only major difference between the W3C frames and Netscape's is the addition of inline frames. That is, frames that are contained within the body of the Web page. Did the grassroots support for <FRAME> help it gain stature? Possibly, but such support certainly didn't hurt the tag.

# Cons of Using Extensions

Although HTML extensions can give you capabilities you've never had before, using them also has its share of pitfalls. Some problems are small, such as modified syntax. For example, an extension might have a proposed attribute that ultimately gets changed when the tag becomes a standard. Other problems are much more serious, such as not getting support anywhere else. Such is the case with poorly thought out ideas for HTML tags. Most of these problems deal with issues of support and maintenance of Web pages.

## Change of Syntax

One problem with using extensions, particularly those expected to become standards, is that their syntax could change. Although a browser company might expect that its proposal will become standard, there are never any guarantees. As a result, if you follow the company too closely, you may create nonstandard Web pages.

An example of such a situation involves the ALIGN attribute of the <IMG> tag. Netscape proposed numerous additional values for it, such as texttop and absmiddle, and encouraged people to use them. However, the extensions were never approved. The W3C rejected those values, saying that the current ones were sufficient. Although this probably won't break any Web pages entirely, it might cause some inconvenience.

## Lack of Support

Another problem facing people who use extensions is that some extensions never get supported. Typically, this happens when extensions are poorly thought out and created for the sake of being different. The history of HTML extensions is rife with examples of failed extensions. Interestingly, many of the failed extensions came from Microsoft. In an effort to be different from Netscape, Microsoft created numerous extensions for its Web browser. Almost all of them were rejected by the W3C.

Among the more prominent HTML extensions that Microsoft proposed is the <BGSOUND> tag. A sound file had to be specified, and when the page was accessed, the sound file would be played. There were numerous problems with this simplistic approach, not the least of which was that there was no guarantee that everybody could hear the sound. Further, there were few Web sites that even had a desire, let alone a need, to use such a tag. Additionally, Netscape's <EMBED> extension was already in wide use as a general-purpose method of including files. As a result, this tag, and the DYNSRC extension attribute for the <IMG> tag, both failed. There was no reason to use two separate tags when one was sufficient.

# Which One to Use?

So which should you use, pure HTML or extensions? On the one hand, with pure HTML, you're pretty sure that your message will get out. The problem is that it might not look as nice as someone else's Web page. On the other hand, extensions can help you create those better looking, more dynamic pages. But if the extensions never get wide support, your message will never get out. There really is no easy answer because there are compelling arguments for both sides.

So what's the best solution for you? I don't know. Because I don't know you, I don't have a good answer just for you. The answer for the best approach to solving the HTML versus extensions debate lies entirely with you. If you're working on a corporate Web page and it is distributing public memos, you probably don't need to use extensions. Or, if you're trying to get a message out to as many people as possible, standard HTML tags are probably the best approach. On the other hand, if you have a personal Web page or one that is appropriate for your corporate image, you should probably opt for extensions. Also, you must remember that because HTML is constantly evolving, the answer is really a moving target. If you used a tag or attribute that was an extension, it might suddenly become a standard before you know it. Therefore, you would actually be using standard HTML tags to get high-impact Web pages. A number of different approaches to designing Web pages will fit most needs. Which one you choose depends on which one you feel is appropriate for your need.

## Multiple Web Pages

One way to get around the problem is to have multiple Web pages. You can have a Web page full of extensions and all the cutting-edge features you want, but if you do, be sure to always have a similar page for those who might not have the latest browser. Some people don't have a thirst to always have the latest piece of software, and you have to accommodate them as much as possible. For them, you can create a Web page that uses few or no images, and uses nothing but pure HTML code. Just be sure to put a link to the generic Web page on your main Web page. It's best to put such a link either at the top or the bottom, of the page. You should also provide links to your more sophisticated Web page on the generic page. (See Figure 40.1.) This method makes it possible for all visitors to your site, regardless of what they're using, to enjoy it.

## Common Extensions

Another way to get around the problem is to use only common extensions. Some extensions are in incredibly wide use even though they aren't standard. You can probably use such tags without worrying about breaking too many browsers. What makes an extension a common extension? That's hard to say because the HTML specifications are always changing.

CHAPTER 40

**FIGURE 40.1.**

*MTV takes an interesting approach to distinguish between its various Web pages.*

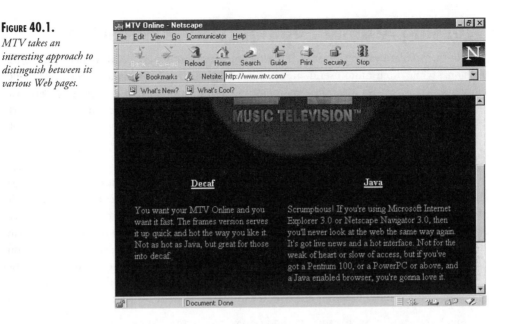

One way you can find common extensions is to create your Web page as normal and then, before you publish it, be sure to check how the page looks. Don't just use one browser, use two or three. Try to find a slightly older browser, or one that supports the most basic of features. Most browsers come with a free evaluation period, so you don't have to pay to try them out. Be sure that the information generally looks the same on all the browsers. Although the content might not appear the same, make sure that all the content is there for everybody to see.

## Try Using Pure HTML

A sure way of getting around the problem of using extensions is to use only pure HTML. If it sounds like I'm discouraging the use of extensions, that's because I am. Too often, when people aren't sure how to make a page look just right, they run straight for extensions. They immediately jump to JavaScript or Java applets and, consequently, alienate some users.

For various reasons, some people might not be able to access these extensions. For example, security warnings have been issued about possibly dangerous Java and JavaScript Web pages. You can be sure that some people have completely disabled Java and JavaScript on their modern browsers. And not everybody is using Netscape or Internet Explorer. There is still a handful of users with text-only browsers.

Therefore, I do recommend that you try to code your page in pure HTML. Although you might have to make a few compromises, such as not having a message scroll across the screen, it might not be so bad. You might actually be pleasantly surprised at what you can do simply by using tables and animated GIFs. They might not be as devastatingly impressive as extensions, but they can look pretty good just the same.

**40**

POINT/COUNTER-
POINT: PURE
HTML

# Working Around Popular HTML Extensions

Part of the problem with extensions is that people simply use them because they're there. Extensions, while often quite useful, aren't the only methods of solving a problem. There are numerous creative ways that you can accomplish a similar look using only pure HTML tags. This is worth the effort because if you can find the right combination that works, you can reach more people.

## Frames

Frames is one of the most widely used extensions around. People like to use them because they give strict control over the look of an entire window. You can have a menu on the left side of the window and a content window on the right. When the user clicks on an item in the left, the right frame automatically updates. It looks cool and makes it easy for people to navigate around. Best of all, frames can give an immediate look and feel to the site, such as using a frame for a navigation tool. Additionally, it's not that much work to provide support for frames. After the <FRAMESET> layout is complete, just make sure all the links point to the right TARGET. The problem is, many older browsers either don't support frames or support them poorly.

Although frames offer such a nice method of navigation, there are easier alternatives—not as snazzy looking as frames, but reasonable alternatives, nonetheless. One approach is to have a common page layout. This gives your site a common look and feel without frames. If you absolutely must have a common navigation tool, you can use tables. Have a row or column where the navigation buttons reside. (See Figure 40.2.) Although this requires you to duplicate some HTML code, it does make your site very accessible.

## Multimedia Files

I know what you're thinking, "Multimedia files aren't HTML tags!" You're right. Unfortunately, people use the <EMBED> extension to put a multimedia file on their sites. The file may be anything from a sound file that plays in the background to a full-fledged multimedia file. Although some file types need an extension to properly function, such as for Shockwave files, QuickTime movies, and other plug-ins, not all of them do. For what most people do with multimedia files, it's an unnecessary risk of possibly alienating users. There's also the problem that sufficiently large multimedia files could take a while to retrieve—so long that some people might give up on your site. In fact, some corporate sites that initially had multimedia files as part of their Web pages soon took them out. Chances are, people complained either because of inaccessibility or download time of the files.

FIGURE 40.2.

*CNET, a popular Web site, uses tables instead of frames for navigation.*

The best way to get around this problem is to simply not use multimedia files. I know you're going to complain, claiming that they're essential to your site. But are they really? Do you really need the music from Rocky playing when someone first accesses your site? Is it worth losing people who don't have sound capability or the latest browser? If you really need to have multimedia files in your Web page, there are two good alternatives for you.

One alternative is the multiple Web page solution mentioned earlier. You can have a list of available Web pages with duplicated contents. Furthermore, you can list the desired configuration for accessing each page. Users would simply click the one that best suits their conditions. Another alternative is to provide links to the multimedia files themselves. (See Figure 40.3.) Although your Web page won't look nearly as dynamic or exciting as it could, you will be reaching more people. With this solution anybody, with or without a recent browser, can experience your Web page. Additionally, with downloadable multimedia files, you also have another means of advertising. You might be able to put in a simple ad for your site or company at the beginning or end of a file.

**FIGURE 40.3.**

*Unlike some of its competitors, CBS lets you download its theme music.*

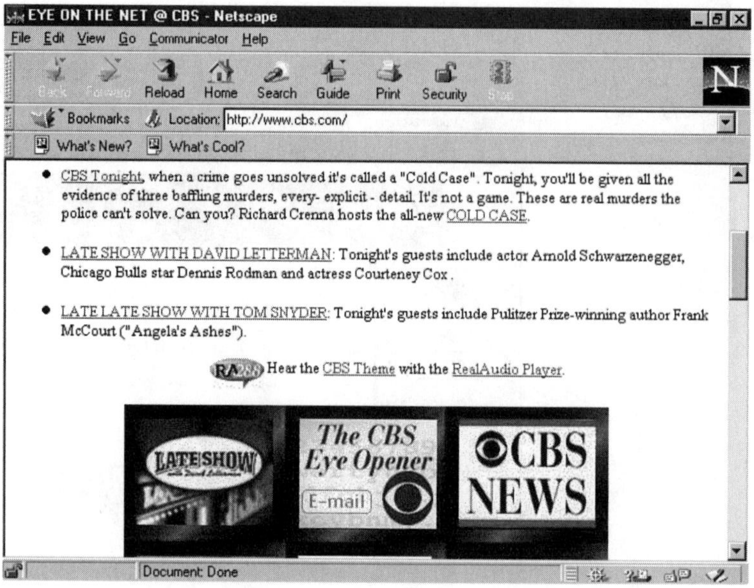

# Summary

This chapter explains what pure HTML and HTML extensions are and covers the benefits and drawbacks of using them. Ultimately, of course, the decision about which HTML tags to use is up to you. But perhaps the best piece of advice is to not work on the bleeding edge. HTML extensions can look really neat and give cool effects, but you won't be reaching the widest audience. Because not everyone will automatically upgrade to the latest version of a Web browser, you can't be sure how wide your audience will be. However, if you don't care about reaching everybody, then go nuts. Use all the extensions you want, and don't worry about anyone who complains about not being able to see your Web page.

# HTML Beyond the Web

*by Dick Oliver*

## IN THIS CHAPTER

CHAPTER **41**

If you've read even a few chapters from Parts III, IV, and V of this book, you have probably gotten the idea that HTML isn't just for Web pages any more. But you may not yet see how all these new extensions and technologies fit together into a cohesive future for HTML. This chapter steps back a bit and offers a big-picture view of where HTML is heading and the new role of HTML in today's high-tech world. You'll find out why most of the HTML pages you create in your lifetime will probably not be Web pages, and why the intimate familiarity with HTML you have gained from this book will be one of the most important (and profitable) skills that anyone can have in the next few years.

To pull that big picture together, first consider some of the pieces that you've seen in previous chapters:

- In Chapter 22, "Dynamic HTML," you learned that all future versions of the Microsoft Windows operating system will use HTML as a fundamental part of the user interface.

- In Chapter 17, "Introducing Cougar," and Chapter 38, "The Emergence of Extensible Markup Language," you discovered that HTML is being extended to give you precise control over the appearance and functionality of virtually any textual and graphical information.

- In Part V, "Associated Technologies and Programming Languages," you saw how all major programming languages, interactive media, and database formats can also be seamlessly integrated with HTML.

- And in Chapter 39, "Internationalizing the HTML Character Set and Language Tags," you found out that HTML can be used to communicate in the native script of any human language in the world.

New data security standards are also making it practical to carry out financial and other sensitive transactions with HTML, and the proposed Platform for Internet Content Selection (PICS) standard provides a highly flexible way for the content of any HTML page to be rated according to any criteria that a rating authority or individual user might select. Restricting access to adult-oriented or confidential information is one of many applications.

All this adds up to a very near future where HTML will without a doubt play a central role—it may even be accurate to say *the* central role—in the display and exchange of almost all information across all computers and computer networks on Earth. If this sounds important, well, it is. But this chapter makes a case that HTML will have an even more important role than that to play. To understand how that can be so, we need to take another step back to see an even bigger picture: the changing role of the computer itself in our society.

# From Calculators to Communicators

The computer was once considered a device for accounting and number crunching. Then it evolved into a device for "crunching" all types of information, from words and numbers to graphics and sounds. Today and tomorrow, the computer is above all a communications device; its primary use is the transmission of information between people.

Two major trends are dragging HTML out of its niche as a Web page language:

■ People from a wider variety of social, economic, and educational backgrounds are using information technology on a daily basis. Digital information is playing a greater role in all our lives.

■ Physical location is no longer the primary factor in the market that most businesses serve. To find customers and do business in a global marketplace, even the smallest companies need to be able to gather and distribute many different types of information.

These large social trends may not seem, at first glance, to have much to do with HTML, except that they cause people and businesses to access the Web more often. But they have directly led to two corresponding trends in technology:

■ Entry-level information technology is getting—and must continue to get—both easier to use and less expensive.

■ The distinctions between an individual computer, a local network, and the global Internet are blurring.

HTML is proving to be the dream technology that is enabling both of these trends to accelerate faster than anyone anticipated.

In many workplaces today, these two trends are already well established. You can use a computer to access business information every day without knowing much more than how to click links and scroll down through long pages. And you can do so without being at all sure which information is coming from your computer, which is coming from the server down the hall, and which is coming from other servers, perhaps thousands of miles away.

The direction that these trends are taking us is also already clear: Users who become used to seeing highly readable and attractive pages of information (such as Figure 41.1) on their computer screens will lose the tiny bit of tolerance they have left for cryptic icons, unadorned text messages, and idiosyncratic menu mazes. (See Figure 41.2.) They will soon expect their computer screens to *always* be as easy to read and interact with as the Web.

Those who make their millions supplying computer software are well aware of that expectation and are expending an unprecedented amount of research and development effort toward fulfilling it. Along the way, the central metaphor for interacting with computers has changed from the "window" of the 1980s "desktop" to the "page" of the 1990s "World Wide Web." It is in the process of changing even more radically, to a metaphor focused on direct communication instead of old-fashioned paper shuffling.

**FIGURE 41.1.**

*HTML's raison d'etre is to provide nicely formatted information that is easy to navigate.*

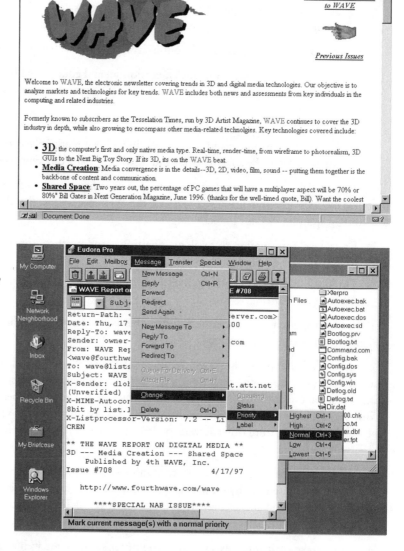

**FIGURE 41.2.**

*Today's computer interfaces are simply too confusing and hard to learn for many of tomorrow's applications. (Note that the actual information content shown here is the same newsletter as in Figure 41.1.)*

# From the Desktop to the Conference Table

When personal computers first started appearing on desks, people bought them to help with the kind of tasks that take place on a desktop: reading, writing, calculating, and shuffling pages of information around. This reflected the business model of the mid-20th century: Isolated workers and companies spent most of their time processing information in their own offices and a much smaller portion of their time directly communicating that information between individuals and companies.

As the century draws to a close, that business model is showing severe signs of strain. More and more time is spent in communication, and less and less in isolation. Workers who were trained in the older way of doing business complain that they now spend so much time attending meetings and conferences, or answering voice mail and e-mail, that no time is left to "get any work done." Those from the newer generation of employees and entrepreneurs, on the other hand, complain when coworkers or business associates create communication bottlenecks by being "out of touch" and "hard to reach."

The old desktop metaphor is increasingly useless for doing the most crucial tasks in a communications-oriented business world. As the personal computer becomes more of an interpersonal communicator, the interface must be more of a conference table than a desktop. Like a conference room, your computer is now primarily a place to exchange textual and graphical documents, audiovisual presentations, and verbal interaction. Unlike most conference rooms, your computer allows you to directly exchange information with hundreds of millions of people all over the world.

# HTML as the New User Interface

As the role of the computer evolves, HTML is becoming more and more central to nearly everything we do with computers. HTML is *the* global standard for connecting all types of information together in a predictable and presentable way.

HTML provides a painless and reliable way to combine and arrange text, graphics, sound, video, and interactive programs. And unlike older proprietary page layout standards, it was designed from the start for efficient communication between all kinds of computers worldwide. At this point, the likelihood of any other standard unseating it as king of the communications hill seems remote.

The prominence of HTML, however, does *not* mean that Web browsers will be a major category of software application in the coming years. In fact, the Web browser as a distinct program has already nearly disappeared. Microsoft Internet Explorer 4.0, for instance, does much more than retrieve pages from the World Wide Web. It lets you use HTML pages as the interface for organizing and navigating through the information on your own computer, including directory folders and the Windows desktop itself. In conjunction with HTML-enabled software such as Office 97, HTML becomes the common standard interface for word processing, spreadsheets and databases as well. The new Netscape Communicator 4.0 is also much more than a Web browser. It uses HTML to integrate all types of media into e-mail, discussion groups, schedule management, business documents, and collaborative project management. (See Figure 41.3.)

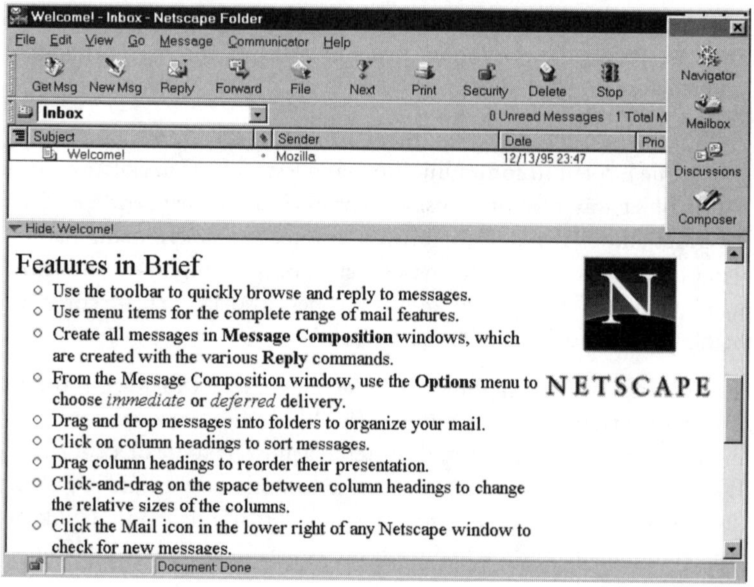

**FIGURE 41.3.**

*Netscape Communicator 4.0 offers a vision of the future by integrating HTML into e-mail, discussion groups, and other business communication.*

Meanwhile, HTML support is being included in every major software release so that every program on your computer will soon be able to import and export information in the form of HTML pages. In a nutshell, HTML is the glue that holds together all the diverse types of information on our computers and ensures that it can be presented in a standard way that will look the same to anyone in the world.

In a business world that now sees fast, effective communication as the most common and most important task of its workers, the information glue of HTML has the power to connect more than different types of media. It is the hidden adhesive that connects a business to its customers, and connects individual employees to form an efficient team. Knowing how to apply that glue—the skills you gained from this book—puts you in one of the most valuable roles in any modern organization.

# The Digital Media Revolution

The most important changes in the next few years may not be in HTML itself, but in the audience you can reach with your HTML pages. Many Web site developers hope that Internet-based content will have enough appeal to become the mass-market successor to television and radio. Less optimistic observers note that the global communications network has a long way to go before it can even deliver television-quality video to most users.

I won't pretend to have a magic mirror that lets me see how and when HTML becomes a mass-market phenomenon. But one thing is certain: All communication industries, from television to telephony, are moving rapidly toward exclusively digital technology. As they do so, the lines between communication networks are blurring. New Internet protocols promise to optimize multimedia transmissions at the same time that new protocols allow wireless "broadcasters" to support two-way interactive transmissions. The same small satellite dish can give you both Internet access and high-definition TV.

Add to this trend the fact that HTML is the only widely supported worldwide standard for combining text content with virtually any other form of digital media. Whatever surprising turns the future of digital communication takes, it's difficult to imagine that HTML won't be sitting in the driver's seat.

More than a million people can already access the Internet without a "real computer" through TV set-top boxes and from WebTV Inc., cable TV companies, and digital satellite services. These devices are only the first wave of much more ubiquitous appliances that provide HTML content to people who wouldn't otherwise use computers.

**NOTE**

The prospect of mass-market HTML access is obviously a great opportunity for HTML page authors. But it also presents a number of challenges when you are designing HTML pages because many people might see your pages on low-resolution TV screens or small hand-held devices. See the "What You Can Do Today to Be Ready for Tomorrow" section, later in this chapter, for some pointers on making sure your HTML pages can be enjoyed and understood by the widest possible audience.

# Unity in Diversity

So far in this chapter, I've noted how HTML is in the right place at the right time to enable several key changes in business and interpersonal communication. As the people and companies of the world becomes more interconnected and interdependent, HTML's capability to make all information technology easier to use and less constrained by geography seems almost magical.

Even more magically, HTML has enabled an explosion of new media formats and incompatible file types while at the same time providing the first truly universal format for exchanging all types of information.

But there is no secret mystical force behind this apparent paradox. The power of HTML comes from a very intentional (and seemingly mundane) aspect of its design. Quite simply, HTML standardizes the format of the most common types of information while freely allowing unlimited special cases for proprietary formats and new technology. This means that you can both ensure complete compatibility between the widest variety of software and easily develop unique information formats to meet your individual needs.

Early multimedia Web sites were perhaps the first examples of how to meet these two (apparently conflicting) goals simultaneously. Text and graphics were visible to all visitors (as shown in Figure 41.4), while Shockwave movies, Java applets, or other formats were used to provide additional audiovisual or interactive content for those who had the necessary plug-ins or helper applications (as shown in Figure 41.5). Though multimedia formats have come a long way toward standardization, you can still freely include proprietary file formats in ordinary HTML pages and use the helper app, Netscape plug-in, ActiveX object, or Java program of your choice to handle them.

**FIGURE 41.4.**

*This site uses HTML to present text and images that everyone can see.*

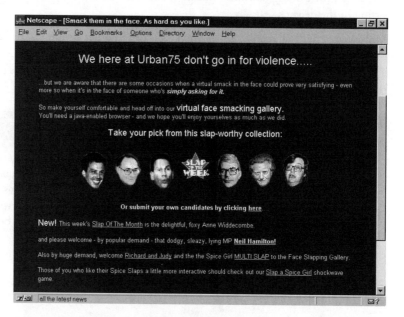

**FIGURE 41.5.**

*If you explore the site shown in Figure 41.4 further, you'll find multimedia elements that require custom applets and/or plug-ins.*

The ability to extend HTML pages with custom data types is far more than a way to embed a nifty movie or virtual reality scene into your Web page. To show how much more, the next two sections highlight some of the most exciting up-and-coming uses of HTML.

# HTML as a Programming Language

The near-universal compatibility of HTML provides a big incentive to format any important document as a Web page, even if you have no immediate plans for putting it on the World Wide Web. You can create a single page that can be printed on paper, sent as an e-mail message, displayed during a board meeting presentation, and posted for reference on the company intranet. Or, you can take the traditional route and format the page separately for each of these applications—and edit each file with a different software program when the information needs to be updated. Now that most business software supports the HTML standard, many organizations are trying to get employees to consistently use it for all important documents.

But the great migration to HTML goes beyond what you might have thought of as "documents" in the old days. Combined with Java, ActiveX and other new technologies, HTML is being used for creating full-blown software applications that would traditionally have been written in more unwieldy languages such as C++.

As one example, consider M. Casco Associates, a small technical software company based in rural Pennsylvania. For years, the company has developed and published a line of interactive science simulation software for the educational market using the C and C++ languages. Figure 41.6 shows the Windows version of one of their programs, called Order: A Closer Look at Chaos. (The program uses interactive simulations to teach the basics of chaos theory.)

Because they are a small company, Casco could not afford to develop for more than one operating system or computer type at a time, even though their potential market included DOS, Windows, Macintosh, and UNIX users. Creating an effective interface to combine the tutorial and interactive elements of their software was a significant part of the development effort.

Figure 41.7 shows the latest version of their software, which was rewritten as interactive Java applets embedded in an HTML tutorial and guide. Not only does this new version eliminate much of the interface programming, but it is also instantly compatible with any type of computer that can run a Java-enabled Web browser. As a bonus, M. Casco was able to put part of the program directly on the World Wide Web for potential customers to evaluate without rewriting a line of code. (See for yourself at `http://www.mcasco.com.`) The small Java modules and HTML tutorial are also considerably easier to debug and maintain than a large C++ program requiring a recompile every time a change is made.

Transferring traditional programs to HTML-based presentations usually involves a shift in how you think about the user's experience. Essentially, instead of an application with a hypertext help system, you have a hypertext help system with an application inside it. This gives new users an obvious and friendly way to get to know a program, and still allows the HTML to step out of the way whenever the Java applets or other interactive media should be the focus of the user's attention.

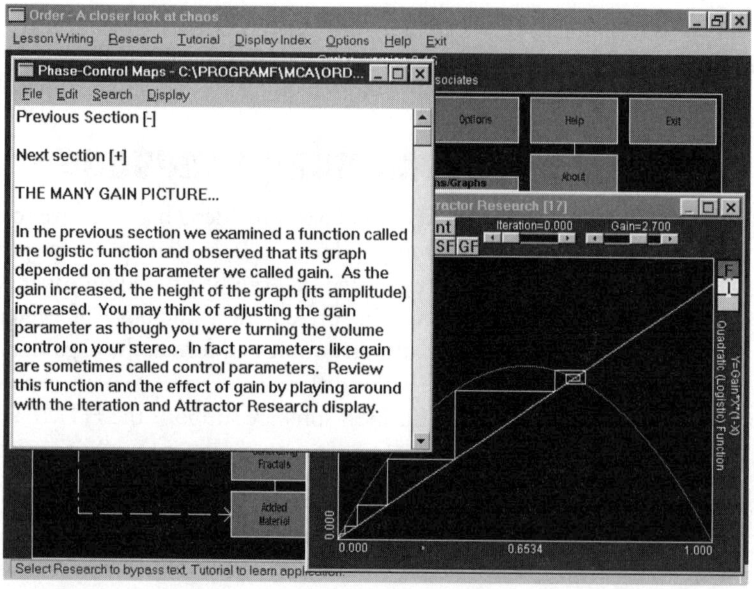

**FIGURE 41.6.**

*This fairly sophisticated Windows program includes both interactive scientific simulations and an extensive online help tutorial.*

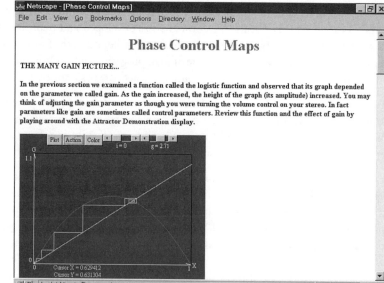

**FIGURE 41.7.**

*With HTML and Java, all the functionality of the large C++ program in Figure 41.6 can be implemented in simple, cross-platform compatible parts.*

# HTML Applications of the Future

You've seen that HTML-based presentations can in many cases replace what was once done with proprietary data formats, specialized software, or more traditional programming languages. Here are a few of the other areas where HTML is finding application beyond the Web:

■ Kiosks with HTML-based interactive content are popping up everywhere. They look like ATM machines on steroids, and they're helping sell records and theme park tickets, expand department store displays, and even automate the paying of parking tickets. The number of kiosks using intranet and/or HTML technology is projected to soar from under 90,000 today to more than 500,000 by the end of 1998.

■ Information-rich CD-ROM titles are migrating to HTML fast. Encyclopaedia Britannica is already entirely HTML based, which enables them to offer their content on CD-ROM, the Web, or a combination of both for maximum speed and up-to-the-minute currency. Because CD-ROM drives display multimedia so much faster than most Internet connections, dynamic HTML presentations become possible that just couldn't be done on today's World Wide Web. The new DVD-ROM drives will be even faster and will hold much more information, making them ideally suited to large multimedia "sites."

■ Corporate newsletters are now often created in HTML for the company intranet, and then printed on paper for delivery to employees or customers who wouldn't see them on the Web. The traditional difference between online and paper presentations was that graphics needed to be high-resolution black-and-white for printing and low-resolution color for computer screens. Today's inexpensive color printers, however, do a great job making low-res color images look great in an HTML-based newsletter.

■ Teachers are finding that tests and educational worksheets are easier to administer as HTML pages and can include many types of interactive content that wouldn't be possible on paper. Even for students who lack access to the Internet, simple HTML documents can be passed out on floppy disks.

■ Vertical market users often buy a computer specifically to run a certain custom-designed application or set of applications. The VARs and systems integrators that provide these systems are delivering machines configured to start up displaying HTML pages. This helps step users through the use of the machine, or replace old-fashioned "idiot menus" with a more attractive and sophisticated interface without sacrificing ease of use.

■ Even game developers are getting into the HTML act. While some programmers still contend that HTML-based content will never be the best solution for calculation-intensive applications, others have proceeded to produce Java and ActiveX modules that do high-speed 3D graphics rendering (which is arguably the most intensive application of all) quite nicely. These engines are being used for both Web-based *virtual reality* worlds and cutting-edge entertainment titles to be distributed on CD-ROM.

I could list many more creative and beneficial uses of HTML beyond run-of-the-mill Web pages, but the point should be clear: If you need to present any type of information, seriously consider HTML as an alternative to the software or programming tools that you would have used a couple years ago for the job.

# What You Can Do Today to Be Ready for Tomorrow

If you've made your way through most of the chapters of this book, you already have one of the most important ingredients for future success in the new digital world: a solid working knowledge of HTML.

Chances are that your primary reason for learning HTML at this time is to create some Web pages, but I hope this chapter has convinced you that you'll be using HTML for far more than that in the future. Here are some of the factors your should consider when planning and building your Web site today, so that it will also serve you well tomorrow:

- The multimedia and interactive portions of your site are likely to need more revisions to keep up with current technology than the text and graphics portions. When possible, keep the more cutting-edge parts of your site separate and take especially good care to document them well with the <COMMENT> tag.

- Though new technologies such as Java and Shockwave may be the wave of the future, avoid them today except when developing for disk-based media or a fast local intranet. Even when everyone is using the new 33Kbps and 56Kbps modems, many people still will move on to a different site before they'll wait for an applet or interactive movie to download, initialize, and start working.

- Because style sheets will soon give you complete control over the choice and measurements of type on your Web pages, it would be a good idea to study basic typography now if you aren't familiar with it. Understanding and working with things such as *leading, kerning, em spaces,* and *drop caps* have long been essential for producing truly professional quality paper pages. It will soon be essential for producing outstanding Web pages, too.

- One of the most popular and important features that will be added to many Web sites in the near future is interactive discussions and work groups. If you only have time to evaluate one new technology, that might be the one to pick. The new Netscape Communicator 4.0 package has especially strong support for group collaboration and communication.

- When you design your pages, don't assume that everyone who sees them will be using a computer. Televisions, video-telephones, game consoles, and many other devices may have access to them as well. Some of these devices have very low resolution screens (with as few as 320×200 pixels). Although it's difficult to design a Web page to look good at that resolution, you'll reach the widest possible audience if you do.

- Remember that a majority of people are still using versions 2.0 or 3.0 of Netscape Navigator and Microsoft Internet Explorer to view Web pages. If you use HTML 4.0 features such as layering and style sheets, make sure your pages still look good in browsers that don't support those features!

■ Whenever you run into something that you'd like to do on a Web page, but can't with HTML as it stands today, include a comment in the page so you can add that feature when it becomes possible in the future.

# Summary

This chapter provides a birds-eye view of the future of HTML and the new roles that HTML will play in global communications. It also outlines several applications of HTML that are likely to be much more common in the near future than they are today. Finally, it offers some advice for planning and constructing HTML pages today that will continue to serve you well into the future.

# Glossary

*by Dennis Báthory Kitsz*

# A

**ActiveX:** A technique developed by Microsoft to run applications on client Microsoft-based computers through an active Web page interface. Like plug-ins, once loaded, ActiveX remains part of the browser. *See also* **helper application**, **Java**, **plug-in**, **viewer**

**agent:** (*also called* autonomous agent, information agent, intelligent agent) An application or applet that carries the user's preferences into a virtual environment such as the Web and acts independently on those preferences. Infinitely configurable, an agent is the user's doppelgänger in cyberspace.

**American National Standards Institute (ANSI):** An organization dedicated to promoting national technology standards. ANSI is privately funded and includes both public and private members. *See also* **International Organization for Standardization**

**American Standard Code for Information Interchange (ASCII):** A code that represents a set of 256 unformatted characters—letters, numbers, symbols, and terminal actions (such as carriage returns and line feeds) in a standard format of 8 bits (although 128-character, 7-bit ASCII exists as well).

**anchor:** A portion of HTML code that identifies a specific document or a position (destination) inside a specific document. Also, the visible portion of the code, usually represented by underlined words. *See also* **hyperlink**

**ANSI:** *See* **American National Standards Institute**

**applet:** A dependent piece of computer software, usually small and compact, that requires an application with or within which to operate.

**application:** A complete piece of computer software, whether it is a compact utility consisting of a few bytes or a suite of programs that work together. An application stands alone inside its environment processor, operating system, browser, and so on.

**ASCII:** *See* **American Standard Code for Information Interchange**

**attribute:** Additional information added to element tags to specify characteristics of or render the element, such as size, color, borders, and other qualifications. Attributes are author-specified values.

**authentication:** A software technique that guarantees the identity of an individual or company; used in secure sites.

# B

**bandwidth:** The capacity to carry data. In a network, this is usually bits per second and is critical for browsing speed, especially in sites heavy in hypermedia content.

**bit:** A binary digit, the smallest atom of digital information, represented by the number 0 or 1.

**bitmap graphics:** The resolution of an image into a series of dots, represented by a map of binary digits (bits). *See also* **raster graphics**, **vector graphics**

**body:** The "visible" content of an HTML document that a browser displays.

**bookmark:** A popular term for a hyperlink name and URL that the user saves for future use in a bookmark list or hotlist.

**block element:** A tag within an HTML document that identifies the document's structural areas by grouping text content in terms of its meaning. *See also* **container, text element**

**bps:** Bits per second. *See* **Kbps**

**browser:** Client software for displaying Web pages and using hyperlinks to navigate the Web.

**byte:** A combination of eight bits that constitutes a basic digital "word" size, capable of forming 256 possible combinations of bits.

# C

**C and C++:** Advanced programming languages that dominate network applications. C is an older, structured language; C++ is its object-oriented successor.

**cable-modem:** A device that combines television and telephone technology to enable high-speed receipt of information via cable and normal-speed transmission via modem. The cable-modem is anticipated by content providers because it will make Web page (and hypermedia) downloads appear instantaneous while keeping data-thin and slower user interactions on ordinary phone lines. *See also* **modem, push**

**cache:** A temporary storage area for data. Specifically in terms of browsers, a cache is the trail of Web documents stored on the user's computer so that the user can instantaneously view a document again. Because some Web sites frequently update documents, caching can have the unwelcome side effect of holding on to "stale" pages.

**cascading style sheets (CSS):** A layout and display system for Web pages. The user can specify fonts and sizes, layouts, colors, and other viewing and printing parameters. Because CSS are optional and not part of HTML itself, they do not break HTML's platform independence for layout purposes. *See also* **frames, layers**

**cell:** A portion of a table in which information is displayed. A cell can encompass one or more of a table's rows or columns.

**CERN:** *See* **European Laboratory for Particle Physics**

**CGI:** *See* **common gateway interface**

**character encoding:** A numerical range of codes, repertoire of characters, and their mapping. *See also* **character set**

**character set:** The letters, numbers, and symbols available for display or printing. Character sets in HTML are defined to provide platform-independent consistency in all display systems for all languages.

**chunk:** A manageable piece of information. The definition is flexible but usually means the division of larger text into a single theme, concept, topic, or idea. Good "chunking" helps present nonlinear information.

**class:** The definition for a type of object in the form of a general software blueprint used in object-oriented programming. Classes may share elements with each other and may inherit characteristics of the parent blueprint. *See also* **inheritance**

**client:** A combination of computer and software capable of receiving information and instructions from a remote host computer or server.

**client-side:** Applications, activities, or events that take place on the client computer, such as image maps or applets.

**code page:** The character encoding developed for a specific language. *See also* **character encoding, character set**

**common gateway interface (CGI):** A programming interface between the client (browser) and server. CGI accepts data from the user and acts on it, sometimes returning information to the user. Common examples are forms and searches.

**compression:** The reduction of raw data by removing redundancies, making predictions, and describing events, rather than replicating them. This allows for smaller files and faster downloads but, especially in the case of audio, noticeable degradation.

**container:** An HTML element made up of an opening and closing tag. Information is contained within the tags. *See also* **block element, text element**

**content:** The information a Web page provides. Content is often highly debated and often redefined to defend a Web page creator's design. Web purists largely view content as text.

**cookie:** A line of text stored in the client browser that the server can retrieve. It may contain encoded passwords, shopping-cart contents, user identification, and so on. Cookies are controversial because commercial Web designers use them extensively to track visitors.

**copyright:** An international treaty setting the right to intellectual property. Although copyright exists the moment an idea is manifested as a work of authorship (in any medium), the nature of the Web culture has not taken copyright into account until recently.

**Cougar:** The latest W3C proposed draft for HTML specifications that distinguish between markup (content) and appearance of Web pages. Like most HTML specifications, it lags behind and attempts to codify existing practice into universally accessible definitions and incorporates significant access techniques for hypermedia. Cougar may become HTML 4.0, succeeding the present 3.2 specification.

**CSS:** *See* **cascading style sheets**

# D

**database:** An organized collection of information stored on a server.

**declaration:** A statement about a document and its structure, including its type, syntax, scope, character set, entities, naming rules, and so on.

**dialog box:** A box displayed on the screen that asks for user selections. The dialog box is a core component of a graphical user interface.

**dialup:** The method of accessing the Internet via modem and traditional telephone lines.

**DNS:** *See* **Domain Name Service**

**document type definition (DTD):** The hierarchy of elements used to define the structure of a document. The DTD is set forth in the HTML specification.

**domain name:** A name for an organization, business, or government agency expressed in word-like form. There are national domains and six major organization domain types (`.com`, `.edu`, `.org`, `.gov`, `.mil`, and `.net`). Combined with a server name, they are translated by domain name services into a numeric IP address called the "dotted quad" (such as 204.246.11.197).

**Domain Name Service (DNS):** A computer containing a cross-reference of domain names to respective numerical IP addresses.

**DTD:** *See* **document type definition**

**dynamic:** In Web parlance, particularly in terms of Web pages, dynamic refers to server responses created based on active user input (such as forms) or passive user input (such as browser identification or cookies).

**dynamic HTML:** A method that Microsoft promotes to produce pages with active or changing information.

# E

**element:** Though commonly referred to as a tag, an element is in fact a component of hierarchical structure defined by a document type definition. The element is actually described (or delimited) by the tag. This clarity is obscured, however, by elements without contents (such as line breaks), and those that may not contain other elements (such as anchors). *See also* **block element, text element**

**embedded object:** An object included as part of a document in its complete form, such as an illustration, audio file, or application. *See* **object**

**encoding (character):** *See* **character encoding**

**encryption:** A method of altering information to make it unreadable by anyone except users who possess the rules to decode it. Public-key encryption is popular because anyone can encrypt and send a message, but only the recipient can decode it.

**entity:** A character that cannot be typed on the keyboard (such as é or ©) or that has a special meaning to HTML (such as <). It is represented by its numeric form (called a character reference: &#169; for ©) or mnemonic form (&copy; for ©).

**European Laboratory for Particle Physics (CERN):** *Conseil Européan pour la Recherche Nucléaire.* This laboratory in Geneva was the birthplace of the Web concept and execution in 1989.

**event:** An incident or occurrence meaningful to a program, such as an operation's completion, a request for data, or an interruption of activity.

**event handler:** A portion of a program that responds to an event by processing its details, such as a mouse click, keyboard stroke, or "out of paper" signal.

**Extensible Markup Language (XML):** A subset of SGML that parses a document's structure and elements in terms of its document type definition.

**extension:** (1) The method of identifying the purpose of files and applications within the filename, following a dot. Common to the Web as well as UNIX and DOS operating systems, extensions can identify files such as HTML (`index.html`), MIDI (`song.mid`), images (`picture.jpg`), and so on. File extensions are not found in some operating systems, such as Macintosh.

**extension:** (2) Additions to HTML outside the existing specifications. Companies often contribute, encourage, promote, and even implement these extensions to advance features they would like to include in future releases of the HTML specification.

**extranet:** Internal web sites (intranet sites) accessible to the outside world, usually via passwords. *See also* **intranet**

**e-zine:** An online electronic publication, specifically (like a print 'zine) an amateur, artistic, or non-mainstream publication and presentation.

# F

**fat:** In reference to a client, *fat* is a general term indicating a machine that is a complete, standalone computer with an extensive operating system and powerful applications. Although such a computer can access a server, it does not require one.

**file path:** *See* **path**

**file transfer protocol (ftp):** The method for remote login to a computer to exchange files over a TCP/IP network. Ftp usually requires a username and password, but anonymous ftp can also be made available, especially with Web browsers.

**firewall:** Protective software that prevents unauthorized users or software from entering an internal network. It is used to protect theft of data and to keep out viruses but has the side effect of making Web use difficult, particularly for hypermedia.

**font:** A set of typographical characters (numbers, letters, and symbols). A complete Western (Latin) font, for example, includes upper- and lowercase letters as well as a full range of accented characters. Special software fonts such as Cherokee have helped sustain and expand their respective cultures. *See also* **kerning**, **monospaced font**, **proportional font**

**form:** An HTML component that enables Web authors to have input fields on their pages, permitting feedback from users and offering interactive options.

**format:** The presentation of a document, including fonts, voice, paging, colors, and other features. Format is also achieved by usage (such as paragraphs, lists, and titles) and logical elements. *Compare* **cascading style sheets**, **layout**, **structure**

**frames:** Valuable but confounding extensions to HTML that present information as a concurrently displayed group of pages, each with a unique URL but concatenated by a master document. Frames are a kind of simultaneous hypertext. Because they are visually organized, they are not considered platform-independent and are the subject of bitter controversy. *See also* **cascading style sheets**, **layers**

**ftp:** *See* **file transfer protocol**

# G

**GIF:** *See* **Graphics Interchange Format**

**glyph:** A character in an ideographic writing system, usually not phonetically based. Ideographic systems can use tens of thousands of unique glyphs, as opposed to the hundred or so in phonetic systems.

**gopher:** An early method of accessing information on the Internet consisting of document indexes, file transfer, database browsing, and Telnet.

**graphical user interface (GUI):** Generally, an operating environment in which icons represent files and applications on a monitor display, and a point-and-click device (such as a mouse, trackball, or pen) is used to activate them. GUIs usually employ drag-and-drop file movement and launching applications, plus buttons, toolbars, drop-down menus, and other conventions not available with line-based (keyboard) methods.

**Graphics Interchange Format (GIF):** An image compression method CompuServe developed and the first that Web browsers accommodated. Files are large and the palette is limited to 256 colors, but no information is lost in the compression.

**GUI:** *See* **graphical user interface**

# H

**handheld personal computer (HPC):** A complete computer in a small package, with a limited display. The HPC and its kin concern Web page authors because the small display and limited features call for HTML's platform independence.

**head:** Part of the HTML document containing information about the document itself, including the document title, searchability, keywords, and other contents including scripts.

**header:** The client sends the HTTP request header to the server to indicate what information it wants. Among those requests are document title, body, authorizations, contents, MIME types, and interaction with CGI.

**helper application:** A program that is not a native part of a Web browser nor a software plug-in provided for the browser. Helper applications are used to display non-text content, particularly newly developed or custom multimedia content, that goes beyond the browser's capabilities at the time of its release. *See also* **ActiveX**, **Java**, **plug-in**, **viewer**

**hex (hexadecimal) notation:** An effective method of representing binary numbers in systems with a 4-bit architectural heritage. Four binary digits (0000 through 1111) can be represented by hexadecimal numbers 0 through F; eight digits, 00 through FF; sixteen digits, 0000 through FFFF, and so on.

**hit:** A visit to a Web page or, sometimes, to each file on that page.

**host:** A server. In Web terms, a computer with a specific name on the Internet. *See also* **node**

**hotspot:** The portion of an image that is mapped to a hyperlink.

**HPC:** *See* **handheld personal computer**

**HTML:** *See* **HyperText Markup Language**

**HTTP:** *See* **HyperText Transfer Protocol**

**HyperCard:** The first practical implementation of hypertext theory in the Apple computer.

**hyperlink:** A connection between one file and another file or inside a file. It is one of the HTML anchors.

**hypermedia:** Multimedia as presented on the Web, including passive and active graphics, audio, video, virtual reality, and other media concepts under development.

**HyperTalk:** The scripting language used to create Apple HyperCard documents. *See also* **HyperCard, script**

**hypertext:** The practical and conceptual heart of the Web, hypertext is a system of relating points within and outside a text to each other nonlinearly. Hypertext, as manifested with hyperlinks, moves a user from text to text at will.

**HyperText Markup Language (HTML):** A platform-independent method of identifying a document's structure and references. In its ideal form, HTML makes no reference to the ultimate user's hardware; in practice, HTML includes presentation information as well as structural elements.

**HyperText Transfer Protocol (HTTP):** A protocol for transferring data formats between a server and client. Data formats include plain text, hypertext, images, sound, public or proprietary formats specified as a MIME type, and metainformation about the data.

# I

**icon:** A visual representation of a file or application.

**image (IMG):** Originally created to include visual images on a Web page, the IMG tag has expanded to include many types of hypermedia, including sound, video, and interactivity.

**image map (imagemap):** An image with hotspots that serve as mouse-activated hyperlinks.

**inheritance:** Characteristics of a class shared with a parent or child. *See* **class**

**integrated services digital network (ISDN):** Digital communications standards for voice, data, and video over standard phone lines at 128 Kbps. It is better established in Germany and is developing slowly in the U.S. because of anticipation of cable-modem services.

**intellectual property:** The ownership of an idea's manifestation—that is, a work put into communicable form. The communicable form can include paper, electronic media, or stone, and encompasses all forms of authorship. It has been the subject of debate and revisions to the copyright treaties because of the "Wild West" nature of the Web. *See also* **copyright**, **watermark**

**interface:** A generic term for the method used to join hardware components, software components, or users and systems. For example, a user interface is a concept and method of interaction; a printer interface consists of cabling, electronic components, and software drivers; a data interface is software to translate data formats; an equestrian interface is a saddle and reins.

**International Organization for Standardization (ISO):** Founded in 1946, this voluntary, nontreaty organization creates international standards and definitions. These standards apply to both hard and soft technologies, methods, and contents, and they are not limited to any particular group of fields or subjects. *See also* **American National Standards Institute**

**Internet:** A worldwide network of computers in communication using agreed-on protocols. A simple definition does not explain the Internet as a *concept*, but it is an opportunity for universal access to human knowledge, wherever it is distributed. *See also* **nonlinear**, **World Wide Web**

**Internet Explorer:** A Microsoft Web browser that gained popularity by being bundled with the Windows 95 and NT 4.0 operating systems.

**Internet Protocol (IP):** A system of network connections using numerical (IP) addresses. No direct connection between the sending and receiving computer is assumed; the IP address is used to establish an indirect pathway through multiple networks.

**Internet service provider (ISP):** A business that offers connection to the Internet, usually through dialup or dedicated telephone lines. ISPs can be little more than a local server, a full-featured system of various accounts including server Web space, or a commercial provider with proprietary features and chatrooms along with Internet access.

**intranet:** A network internal to an organization or corporation set up to mimic Internet features. Intranets may also connect to the Internet.

**IP:** *See* **Internet Protocol**

**IP address:** A quartet of digits separated by dots (such as 204.246.11.197) that represents a unique computer connected to the Internet. Domain names are resolved to IP addresses before information is exchanged.

**ISDN:** *See* **integrated services digital network**

**ISO:** *See* **International Organization for Standardization.** (ISO is actually not an acronym, but the prefix for the standards, derived from the Greek prefix *iso*, meaning "same.")

**ISP:** *See* **Internet service provider**

# J

**Java:** A programming language Sun Microsystems developed to permit standalone applications to run on a client computer through an active Web page interface on a "Java virtual machine." *See also* **ActiveX**, **helper application**, **plug-in**, **viewer**

**JavaScript:** A scripting language that is interpreted and runs on a client computer within an HTML document and provides active and interactive applets to Web pages.

**JavaScript style sheets:** A page formatting method that Netscape promotes and JavaScript controls. *See also* **cascading style sheets**

**Joint Photographic Experts Group Format (JPEG):** A method of compressing images; the second such method adopted to display images on the Web. The palette is large (16 million colors) and file sizes can be made small with JPEG's variable compression, but the method is *lossy*, meaning that the original image's detail is not fully restored during decompression. It is used largely for photographs, where the eye makes up for compression losses.

**JPEG** *See* **Joint Photographic Experts Group Format**

# K

**Kbps:** A thousand bits per second, often used in reference to Internet connection speeds. Early modem speeds were 300 bps (bits per second), whereas 28.8 Kbps is common today, with compression that squeezes an effective rate of 34 Kbps through the line. Other frequently encountered speeds are ISDN at 128 Kbps, T1 connections at 1.5 Mbps (million bits per second), T2 at 3 Mbps, and T3 at 45 Mbps. *See also* **bps, Mbps**

**kerning:** A typographical technique that overlaps characters for visual balance.

# L

**layers:** A Netscape-specific method of organizing multiple documents on a page, including layout features and identification of viewable content. Layers are related to frames but offer more author control. *See also* **cascading style sheets, frames**

**layout:** The visual appearance of a document. Because HTML identifies a document's structure rather than its appearance, Web authors have sought techniques to make their pages display to their tastes. Although some HTML workarounds have been developed, along with display elements within the HTML specification itself, advanced layout calls for other methods, including images and cascading style sheets. *Compare* **cascading style sheets, format, structure**

**LCD:** *See* **liquid crystal display**

**leading:** The vertical space between lines of text.

**linear:** A concept of organizing information in a known sequence. With few exceptions and until recently, this has been the method of storing, retrieving, and exchanging information throughout the history of the written word. Linear information is considered "self-contextualizing" because the references appear in a past, present, and future sequence.

**link:** *See* **hyperlink**

**Linux:** An operating system based on UNIX and created as freeware. Many small Internet servers run Linux, which independent programmers continue to maintain.

**liquid crystal display (LCD):** Low-power display hardware in which a liquid becomes semi-opaque in the presence of an electrical current.

**listserv:** An automated mailing list for exchanging messages. Documents sent to a listserv are redistributed to all its subscribers.

**LiveScript:** *See* **JavaScript**

**logical markup:** The identification of a text's characteristics, content, and structure. *Compare* **physical markup**

**Lynx:** A text-only browser found on older or slower computers, sometimes used for high-speed surfing or text-to-speech access. It has a hardcore following and is also useful for testing both the platform independence and the potential ambiguity (or complete opaqueness) of a Web page design.

# M

**map:** *See* **image map**

**markup:** The identification of a text's characteristics, content, structure, and presentation by use of language-like descriptions. *See also* **logical markup, physical markup**

**Mbps:** Million bits per second. *See* **Kbps**

**menu:** A list of choices. On Web pages, menus can be presented as hyperlinks, drop lists, check-box groups, maps, and even hypermedia controls.

**MIDI:** *See* **Musical Instrument Digital Interface**

**MIME:** *See* **Multipurpose Internet Mail Extensions**

**modem:** *Modulator-demodulator.* A device that converts digital information into a sound format that can be transmitted over acoustic phone lines.

**monospaced font:** Characters displayed or printed in equally spaced "typewriter" format.

**Moore's Law:** Originally put forward in 1965 by Intel co-founder Gordon Moore, it states that computer power doubles every 18 months. It has held true for 30 years. Software and hardware creators have exploited technological developments to the chagrin of budget-conscious users and have presented a formidable barrier to those concerned with universal access to computing power.

**Mosaic:** The first successful graphical browser, created in 1993 at the NCSA.

**Motion Picture Experts Group (MPEG):** Video and audio compression standards. There are presently three MPEG standards with several "layers" each.

**Mozilla:** From "Mosaic killer," the original prototype name for Netscape Navigator.

**MPEG:** *See* **Motion Picture Experts Group**

**multimedia:** A term expropriated from the art world (where it means a performance or art-work including several human senses), multimedia is commonly used to mean the integration of at least audio and video elements into a computer presentation. Its Net equivalent (*See* **hypermedia**) is the bane of pure HTML advocates because it does not offer platform independence.

**Multipurpose Internet Mail Extensions (MIME):** A method of encoding binary data for electronic mail transmission, including audio, graphics, video, word processing, music scores, and applications. MIME was also adopted as the standard for Web transmission.

**Musical Instrument Digital Interface (MIDI *or* Midi):** The specification of sonic parameters (such as note, volume, duration, and controllers) as a serial stream of data and the specification of the required connectivity. MIDI stepped out of the production studio onto the Web because of both the compact size of the files and its platform independence.

# N

**National Center for Supercomputing Applications (NCSA):** The University of Illinois at Urbana-Champaign center responsible for developing the original Mosaic browser.

**navigate:** To move through the Web using hyperlinks. Also, to move through Web pages using hyperlinks, droplists, toolbars, maps, hypermedia controls, and other techniques.

**NC:** *See* **Network Computer**

**NCSA:** *See* **National Center for Supercomputing Applications**

**Netscape Navigator:** Web browser created by NCSA expatriates (*See* **Mozilla**), quickly rising to popularity by a combination of aggressive giveaway marketing and the promotion of presentation-oriented Web pages, graphics, sound, and other hypermedia and a plug-in structure to accommodate new forms of media.

**Network Computer (NC):** A simplified computer (sometimes called a *thin client*) whose applications and files are stored on one or more servers, rather than locally, and without the features of a full operating system.

**news:** *See* **Usenet**

**node:** (1) The point of entrance to or exit from a Web page, considered a standalone construct.

**node:** (2) A computer connected to a network capable of generating, receiving, or forwarding data.

**nonlinear:** A concept of storing, obtaining, and exchanging information through multiple, indirect, layered, and sometimes unpredictable paths with no predefined order. Human thinking frequently follows such paths, but until modern technology made it possible, media representation of nonlinear information was virtually unknown outside its rudimentary use in printed footnotes or operatic motifs. It is now exemplified by the Web's hyperlinks.

# O

**object:** A self-contained piece of information ranging from a single byte to a complete document or application.

**object-oriented:** Programming and databases using self-contained and interchangeable software routines or data elements rather than linear (and often custom) coding. Focusing on ways of interacting with data, object orientation is based on building-block thinking.

**ODBC:** *See* **Open Database Connectivity**

**Open Database Connectivity (ODBC):** Microsoft standard for exchanging software components and data within applications.

**operating system (OS):** The software control system for a computer. It usually refers to a disk-based system, although single-board and harsh-environment computers may use ROM-based operating systems. The operating system may have several layers to create an environment (such as older Windows operating through DOS) or work directly with the computer (such as the Macintosh, Windows 95, or UNIX).

**OS:** *See* **operating system**

# P

**page:** A Web document in HTML with a single URL. Pages are usually *chunks* (*See* **chunk**), but in the case of linear information, pages can sometimes be long, text-like documents or lists of links.

**parameter:** A range of possibilities or actions in an application.

**parse:** To examine code or markup for underlying structure, grammar, and syntax; to determine whether errors are present; and to prepare the results for an action—page presentation in the case of HTML.

**password:** String of characters known only to a system or application and its user. Passwords are a simple method of keeping information confidential, but their proliferation has complicated lives for frequent computer users. Authentication methods have been proposed to replace passwords in some situations.

**path:** The trail through a computer's directory structure to a document.

**PDA:** *See* **personal digital assistant**

**Perl:** *See* **Practical Extraction and Report Language**

**personal digital assistant (PDA):** A small, handheld, computer device with a subset of the features found in larger operating systems. PDAs with Web-browsing capabilities present a challenge for page designers and HTML authors because of their small monochrome displays.

**physical markup:** The markup of a document's presentation. Physical markup is consistent with standard HTML practice in which it contributes to structure and meaning as identified in the typographical world. This remains a contentious issue, as in the case of emphasized and strong text versus italic and bold text. Some recognize the former as creating well-formed HTML with a structural meaning; others recognize the latter as creating well-formed HTML with typographical meaning.

**PICS:** *See* **Platform for Internet Content Selection**

**pixel:** From *picture element,* the pixel is the basic element on a raster display (*See* **raster graphics**), represented as a dot containing intensity and color information.

**platform:** The essential combination of hardware (microprocessor, architecture, and memory organization) and software (operating system and applications) that makes up a computer. Because hundreds of platforms exist beyond the well-known DOS, Windows, Macintosh, and UNIX systems, the HTML author strives for platform independence.

**Platform for Internet Content Selection (PICS):** Proposed standard that gives parents the technical means to block indecent material from children. It defines file formats for independent content rating, and the published results can be used by PICS-enabled software.

**platform independence:** The capability of applications or data to be used on any computer. Never actually achieved, platform independence is attempted by HTML by identifying a document's structure and liberating a document's elements from their presentation.

**plug-in:** A dependent application that extends a browser's capability to present advanced or custom content without changing the browser itself. Originally developed as helper applications, plug-ins are now provided by media content developers for the most popular browsers. *See also* **ActiveX**, **helper application**, **Java**, **viewer**

**PNG:** *See* **Portable Network Graphic**

**port:** A hardware or software entry point to a computer system, largely software ports in Internet protocol terms (HTTP uses port 80, Telnet port 23, IRC port 6667, and so on).

**Portable Network Graphic (PNG):** Compressed graphics format with a large color palette and low information loss. PNG is a public-domain technique that has been proposed as a replacement for GIF. *See also* **Graphics Interchange Format**

**Practical Extraction and Report Language (Perl):** The most popular language for programming CGI. *See* **common gateway interface**

**proportional font:** Characters presented according to their width rather than equally, as exemplified by handwriting and typesetting. Proportional fonts have become the graphics interface standard, but monospaced fonts are still used in terminals and for special circumstances.

**protocol:** A standard for network communication. Different protocols exist for unique purposes: HTTP moves Web documents, FTP transfers files, TCP manages network traffic, IP handles data packets. A group of simultaneously operating protocols is a stack. Protocols are also used for communications with peripheral devices such as printers.

**proxy gateway:** Intermediary computer and software that pass data between an isolated computer and the outside world. Proxy gateways can be configured to pass only "safe" information to the client. *See also* **firewall**

**proxy server:** A computer that stores and distributes documents it has obtained from other servers. This technique is used to lower access costs or keep frequently used documents at hand. One disadvantage is that updated Web pages might not be available to clients until the proxy server is next updated. *See also* **cache**

**pull:** Actions initiated by a client. Most browser applications request, or *pull*, information from the server.

**push:** Actions initiated by a server, especially for sending updated information to a client browser, such as news, stock quotes, and live video.

# Q

**QuickTime:** Proprietary Apple format for audio and video frequently found in CD-ROM applications and occasionally found on the Web. *See also* **MPEG**

# R

**RAM:** *Random-access memory.* Advanced clients require large amounts of high-speed RAM to handle graphics, sound, and video without requiring frequent access to a hard disk.

**raster graphics:** A method of drawing images by altering the intensity and color of an electron beam sweeping across video display terminal phosphors in a regular pattern of horizontal lines— the raster. It is an established television-style technology.

**RealAudio:** A popular audio compression system capable of streaming audio on the Internet. RealAudio offers free encoders and decoders but charges for the live-streaming servers. RealAudio automatically detects a computer's Internet connection speed and configures itself for highest audio quality.

**Request for Comments (RFC):** Published documents that include approved and proposed Internet standards, as well as agreed-upon plans and concepts. They are independently proposed by technical experts and remain RFCs even if they become standards.

**RFC:** *See* **Request for Comments**

**robot:** Automated software that performs tasks independent of users, often said to "live online." Also called a bot or an agent. *See also* **agent**

# S

**script:** A written set of instructions for performing tasks, a script is usually application-specific commands that customize an application's operations. Scripts are found in most Internet applications, with examples found in the Web's JavaScript, in dialer scripts, IRC scripts, server scripts, and so on.

**scrolling:** The movement of screen information horizontally and vertically. Scrolling is important to Web authors both as a convenience issue (vertical scrolling is expected, horizontal scrolling is considered inconvenient) or access issue (sometimes, as with WebTV, horizontal scrolling is impossible).

**search:** To use Web-based, interactive tools to locate specific information or Web sites; it is the opposite of surfing.

**Secured HyperText Transfer Protocol (SHTTP):** An HTTP protocol in which an encrypted connection is established before data is exchanged.

**security:** The preservation of privacy in data exchanges. Security usually calls for encrypting data and authenticating users and may also include passwords.

**Sequential Query Language (SQL):** Database-access and database-retrieval language used for searching large quantities of information and answering questions; pronounced "sequel." Other popular database techniques are Informix, Oracle, and Sybase.

**server:** A combination of computer, software, and network connection that acts as a central location and acts on requests for resources, such as applications, Web pages, or other data. It also processes responses to interactive pages, such as forms or searchers.

**server-side:** Applications, activities, or events that take place on the host computer or server, where information and responses are processed.

**SGML:** *See* **Standard Generalized Markup Language**

**ShockWave:** A popular browser plug-in with which to create animation and sound and, recently, other hypermedia content. Newer versions of ShockWave use streaming techniques. *See also* **streaming**

**shopping cart:** A software method to keep track of online purchases. Shopping carts are difficult to implement because the server cannot know the browser's location on the Web. Web authors resort to cookies, scripts, and other techniques to maintain shopping carts.

**SHTTP:** *See* **Secured HyperText Transfer Protocol**

**site:** *See* **Web site**

**socket:** A method for making a "virtual connection" between software processes by identifying data type, direction, and port. Originally developed for UNIX, it is now used by other systems including Windows and Macintosh.

**spider:** A searching robot that explores and indexes the contents of all local hyperlinks from a given Web page.

**SQL:** *See* **Sequential Query Language**

**Standard Generalized Markup Language (SGML):** An international standard for text information processing, distribution, search, and retrieval. SGML documents have content and structural information about content. Format is not specified in SGML.

**stream:** A continuous flow of information.

**streaming:** The use of a data stream to present time-based content (such as audio or video) as it happens, without waiting for a complete file to download. Streaming can be used with existing complete documents or "live" from digital information created on the fly.

**structure:** The organization of a document. In HTML terms, structure identifies the markup of consistent elements that identify their purpose; the definition of its content. Structuring a document frees the viewer to determine its use, particularly in a nonlinear, hypertext situation. *Compare* **format, layout**

**style sheets:** *See* **cascading style sheets**

**surf:** To browse or navigate Web sites without a specific informational goal in mind. *Compare* **search**

# T

**table:** Originally conceived as a way of marking up tabular information, the table has evolved into a document presentation element. Using borderless tables, Web designers achieve layout-like results in graphical browsers. The use of tables for design is controversial because they are used to format a display rather than to provide document structure.

**tag:** Markup instruction in an HTML document presented in angled brackets. A tag may contain a declaration, statement, and so on, as well as attributes.

**TCP:** *See* **Transport Control Protocol**

**TCP/IP:** *See* **Transmission Control Protocol/Internet Protocol**

**Telnet:** Remote login to a computer that enables a user to use a computer from a distance, including manipulating files and executing applications.

**template:** A document or file containing generic information used to build new or updated documents by "filling in the blanks" or altering variable information. Templates are particularly useful for Web sites that update information frequently, maintain an identical presentation and structure, and archive it all (such as online publications, reviews, and directories).

**terminal:** The interactive user end of a network, usually only a display, keyboard, and interface, but sometimes generally referring to any interactive end-user point on a network, including full-blown computers or, in earlier days, Teletype machines.

**text element:** A tag within an HTML document that identifies the characteristics of words or characters, rather than the structure of the content. *See also* **block element, container**

**thin:** In reference to a client, *thin* is a general term that indicates a machine without the computing capability of a complete standalone computer with an extensive operating system and powerful applications. Most of its power comes from a server.

**toolbar:** (*sometimes* **navigation bar**) A set of icons that are hyperlinks to other Web pages or hypermedia.

**Transport Control Protocol (TCP):** A means by which a connection is established between a client and a server. Data is broken into packets that are addressed to the receiving computer together with information for their reassembly.

**Transmission Control Protocol/Internet Protocol (TCP/IP):** The combination of client/server connection and data transfer (TCP) and network connection system (IP) used on the Internet. *See* **Transport Control Protocol, Internet Protocol**

**transportability:** *See* **platform independence**

# U

**UCS:** *See* **Universal Multiple-Octet Coded Character Set**

**UCS Transformation Format:** A method of switching between standard ASCII and UCS character sets within a serial stream of data.

**Unicode:** 16-bit character encoding system designed to display phonetic and ideographic languages. Although incomplete, Unicode is implemented on the latest generation of Web browsers.

**Uniform Resource Citation (URC):** A set of attributes that describe an object's characteristics, such as size, origin, authorship, copyright, data type, and so on.

**Uniform Resource Identifier (URI):** Generic set of identifications that encompasses URCs, URLs, and URNs.

**Uniform Resource Locator (URL):** The path to a specific document on the Internet that consists of the protocol (`http://`, `ftp://`, `gopher://`, `news://`, and so on), a domain name or IP address, a directory structure, and the document name.

**Uniform Resource Name (URN):** Any identifier other than a URL. This seemingly ambiguous definition leaves open the door to flexible ways of accessing Internet information in the future.

**Universal Multiple-Octet Coded Character Set (UCS):** A 32-bit character encoding system designed to accommodate phonetic and ideographic (glyph) writing systems.

**UNIX, or Unix:** The world's dominant operating system, dating from the early 1970s. UNIX is considered to provide the optimum combination of portability, flexibility, and power.

**URC:** *See* **Uniform Resource Characteristic**

**URI:** *See* **Uniform Resource Identifier**

**URL:** *See* **Uniform Resource Locator**

**URN:** *See* **Uniform Resource Name**

**Usenet:** Growing out of local electronic bulletin boards, Usenet is an informal collection of tens of thousands of thematic groups. Users post ASCII or binary messages that propagate from server to server, sometimes over a period of days. Usenet traffic ranges from authoritative to fictional, accurate to fraudulent, art to pornography.

**username:** A computer user's identification, nickname, or "handle" for a specific site, application, or connection. For security, the username is combined with a password or other authentication method.

**UTF:** *See* **UCS Transformation Format**

# V

**valid document:** Usually referring to a Web page, a valid document passes all the requirements of the particular HTML specification under which is was created, including structure, syntax, and characters.

**Validator:** An application that checks a document for validity.

**value:** A numeric or text variable that determines the range or function of a parameter. *See also* **parameter**

**VBScript:** Microsoft entry into the scripting languages for Web sites. *See also* **JavaScript**, **script**

**vector graphics:** A technique of displaying images by drawing them directly with lines and curves of changing intensity and color. *See also* **bitmap graphics**, **raster graphics**

**viewer:** A helper application originally intended for graphics, then audio. Largely superseded by the term *helper application*. *See also* **ActiveX**, **helper application**, **Java**, **plug-in**

**Viola:** An early UNIX-based browser organized on the HyperCard model.

**Virtual Reality Modeling Language (VRML):** A method of displaying, moving within, changing, and hyperlinking three-dimensional scenes. VRML deals with concepts and techniques similar to HTML but is concerned with the unique non-textual aspects of three-dimensional images, such as lighting and shadow, viewpoints, backgrounds, and the z-axis.

**virus:** A program, usually destructive or mischievous, designed to hide inside digital information, usually an application or active library, and remain outside the control of the user. Viruses usually self-replicate, hence the name, to infect other programs or systems via diskettes or networks.

**VRML:** *See* **Virtual Reality Modeling Language**

# W

**W3C:** *See* **World Wide Web Consortium**

**WAIS:** *See* **wide area information service**

**watermark:** A technique that permanently marks a digital document, usually with its creator's name and rights information. Digital watermarking is at its infant stage because of the public nature of Web documents. *See also* **copyright**, **intellectual property**

**Web:** *See* **World Wide Web**

**Web page:** *See* **page**

**Web site:** A combination of related Web pages gathered under one domain or directory, usually dealing with a single theme or personality.

**WebTV:** A television-based Web appliance, usually containing a subset of Web features, operated by remote control. WebTV concerns Web designers because of its smaller display size and lack of horizontal scrolling.

**well-formed document:** A document that not only passes HTML markup validation but also possesses a logical structure and is platform-independent.

**wide area information service (WAIS):** An early Internet method of indexing and retrieving information.

**window:** A portion of a display screen that contains an operating application or open file. Windows are often thought of as the pieces of paper on a desk (hence the term *desktop*).

**Windows:** A Microsoft operating system. Windows 3.*x* was a shell formed over DOS, whereas Windows 95 is a true operating system that also contains a Web browser and dialup software. Windows NT is a network system that is operating an increasing number of Web servers.

**World Wide Web (WWW):** The Web is a subset of the Internet that implements the concept of hyperlinks to exchange information and operates according to the HyperText Transfer Protocol. The Web is distinguished as the first widespread implementation of nonlinear information concepts.

**World Wide Web Consortium (W3C):** An industry consortium to develop common standards for the Web. Members propose standards and protocols for use of hypermedia.

**WWW:** *See* **World Wide Web**

**WYSIWYG:** What you see is what you get; simplified and largely inaccurate abbreviation for software that presents screen displays resembling a final product, such as a printed document or a Web page.

# XYZ

**XML:** *See* **Extensible Markup Language**

# HTML Quick Reference

**APPENDIX A**

This appendix is a reference to the HTML tags you can use in your documents. Unless otherwise noted, all of the tags listed here are supported by both Microsoft Explorer 3.0 and Netscape Navigator 3.0. Note that some other browsers do not support all the tags listed.

The proposed HTML style sheet specification is also not covered here. Refer to the Netscape (http://home.netscape.com/) or Microsoft (http://www.microsoft.com/) Web sites for details on this and other late-breaking changes to the HTML standard.

# HTML Tags

These tags are used to create a basic HTML page with text, headings, and lists. An (MS) beside the attribute indicates that it is only supported by Microsoft Internet Explorer.

## Comments

| | |
|---|---|
| `<!-- ... -->` | Creates a comment. Can also be used to hide JavaScript from browsers that do not support it. |
| `<COMMENT>...</COMMENT>` | The new official way of specifying comments. |

## Structure Tags

| Tag | Attribute | Function |
|---|---|---|
| `<HTML>...</HTML>` | | Encloses the entire HTML document. |
| `<HEAD>...</HEAD>` | | Encloses the head of the HTML document. |
| `<BODY>...</BODY>` | | Encloses the body (text and tags) of the HTML document. |
| | `BACKGROUND="..."` | The name or URL of the image to tile on the page background. |
| | `BGCOLOR="..."` | The color of the page background. |
| | `TEXT="..."` | The color of the page's text. |
| | `LINK="..."` | The color of unfollowed links. |
| | `ALINK="..."` | The color of activated links. |
| | `VLINK="..."` | The color of followed links. |
| | `BGPROPERTIES="..."`(MS) | Properties of background image. Currently allows only the value FIXED, which prevents the background image from scrolling. |

| Tag | Attribute | Function |
|-----|-----------|----------|
| | `TOPMARGIN="..."`(MS) | Top margin of the page, in pixels. |
| | `BOTTOMMARGIN="..."`(MS) | Bottom margin of the page, in pixels. |
| `<BASE>` | | Indicates the full URL of the current document. This optional tag is used within `<HEAD>`. |
| | `HREF="..."` | The full URL of this document. |
| `<ISINDEX>` | | Indicates that this document is a gateway script that allows searches. |
| | `PROMPT="..."` | The prompt for the search field. |
| | `ACTION="..."` | Gateway program to which the search string should be passed. |
| `<LINK>` | | Indicates a link between this document and some other document. Generally used only by HTML-generating tools. `<LINK>` represents a link from this entire document to another, as opposed to `<A>`, which can create multiple links in the document. Not commonly used. |
| | `HREF="..."` | The URL of the document to call when the link is activated. |
| | `NAME="..."` | If the document is to be considered an anchor, the name of that anchor. |
| | `REL="..."` | The relationship between the linked-to document and the current document; for example, `"TOC"` or `"Glossary"`. |
| | `REV="..."` | A reverse relationship between the current document and the linked-to document. |
| | `URN="..."` | A Uniform Resource Number (URN), a unique identifier different from the URL in `HREF`. |

*continues*

| Tag | Attribute | Function |
|-----|-----------|----------|
| | `TITLE="..."` | The title of the linked-to document. |
| | `METHODS="..."` | The method by which the document is to be retrieved; for example, FTP, Gopher, and so on. |
| `<META>` | | Indicates meta-information about this document (information about the document itself); for example, keywords for search engines, special HTTP headers to be used for retrieving this document, expiration dates, and so on. Meta-information is usually in the form of a key/value pair. Used in the document `<HEAD>`. |
| | `HTTP-EQUIV="..."` | Creates a new HTTP header field with the same name as the attribute's value; for example, `HTTP-EQUIV="Expires"`. The value of that header is specified by the `CONTENT` attribute. |
| | `NAME="..."` | If meta-data is usually in the form of key/value pairs, `NAME` indicates the key; for example, `Author` or `ID`. |
| | `CONTENT="..."` | The content of the key/value pair (or of the HTTP header indicated by `HTTP-EQUIV`). |
| `<NEXTID>` | | Indicates the "next" document to this one (as might be defined by a tool to manage HTML documents in series). `<NEXTID>` is considered obsolete. |

## Headings and Title

| Tag | Attribute | Function |
|-----|-----------|----------|
| `<H1>...</H1>` | | A first-level heading. |
| `<H2>...</H2>` | | A second-level heading. |
| `<H3>...</H3>` | | A third-level heading. |

| Tag | Attribute | Function |
|---|---|---|
| `<H4>...</H4>` | | A fourth-level heading. |
| `<H5>...</H5>` | | A fifth-level heading. |
| `<H6>...</H6>` | | A sixth-level heading. |
| `<TITLE>...</TITLE>` | | Indicates the title of the document. Used within `<HEAD>`. |

All heading tags accept the following attribute:

| | Attribute | Function |
|---|---|---|
| | `ALIGN="..."` | Possible values are CENTER, LEFT, and RIGHT. |

## Paragraphs and Regions

| Tag | Attribute | Function |
|---|---|---|
| `<P>...</P>` | | A plain paragraph. The closing tag (`</P>`) is optional. |
| | `ALIGN="..."` | Align text to CENTER, LEFT, or RIGHT. |
| `<DIV>...</DIV>` | | A region of text to be formatted. |
| | `ALIGN="..."` | Align text to CENTER, LEFT, or RIGHT. |

## Links

| Tag | Attribute | Function |
|---|---|---|
| `<A>...</A>` | | With the HREF attribute, creates a link to another document or anchor; with the NAME attribute, creates an anchor that can be linked to. |
| | `HREF="..."` | The URL of the document to be called when the link is activated. |
| | `NAME="..."` | The name of the anchor. |
| | `REL="..."` | The relationship between the linked-to document and the current document; for example, "TOC" or "Glossary". REL="..." is not commonly used. |

*continues*

| Tag | Attribute | Function |
|---|---|---|
| | REV="..." | A reverse relationship between the current document and the linked-to document (not commonly used). |
| | URN="..." | A Uniform Resource Number (URN), a unique identifier different from the URL in HREF (not commonly used). |
| | TITLE="..." | The title of the linked-to document (not commonly used). |
| | METHODS="..." | The method by which the document is to be retrieved; for example, FTP, Gopher, and so on (not commonly used). |
| | TARGET="..." | The name of a frame that the linked document should appear in. |

## Lists

| Tag | Attribute | Function |
|---|---|---|
| <OL>...</OL> | | An ordered (numbered) list. |
| | TYPE="..." | The type of numerals to label the list. Possible values are A, a, I, i, and 1. |
| | START="..." | The value with which to start this list. |
| <UL>...</UL> | | An unordered (bulleted) list. |
| | TYPE="..." | The bullet dingbat to use to mark list items. Possible values are DISC, CIRCLE (or ROUND), and SQUARE. |
| <MENU>...</MENU> | | A menu list of items. |
| <DIR>...</DIR> | | A directory listing; items are generally smaller than 20 characters. |
| <LI> | | A list item for use with <OL>, <UL>, <MENU>, or <DIR>. |

| Tag | Attribute | Function |
|---|---|---|
| | TYPE="..." | The type of bullet or number to label this item with. Possible values are DISC, CIRCLE (or ROUND) SQUARE, A, a, I, i, and 1. |
| | VALUE="..." | The numeric value this list item should have (affects this item and all below it in <OL> lists). |
| <DL>...</DL> | | A definition or glossary list. |
| | COMPACT | The COMPACT attribute specifies formatting that takes less whitespace to present. |
| <DT> | | A definition term as part of definition list. |
| <DD> | | The corresponding definition to a definition term as part of definition list. |

## Character Formatting

| Tag | Attribute | Function |
|---|---|---|
| <EM>...</EM> | | Emphasis (usually italic). |
| <STRONG>...</STRONG> | | Stronger emphasis (usually bold). |
| <CODE>...</CODE> | | Code sample (usually Courier). |
| <KBD>...</KBD> | | Text to be typed (usually Courier). |
| <VAR>...</VAR> | | A variable or placeholder for some other value. |
| <SAMP>...</SAMP> | | Sample text (not commonly used). |
| <DFN>...</DFN> | | A definition of a term. |
| <CITE>...</CITE> | | A citation. |
| <B>...</B> | | Boldface text. |
| <I>...</I> | | Italic text. |
| <TT>...</TT> | | Typewriter (monospaced) font. |

*continues*

| Tag | Attribute | Function |
|-----|-----------|----------|
| `<PRE>...</PRE>` | | Preformatted text (exact line endings and spacing will be preserved—usually rendered in a monospaced font). |
| `<BIG>...</BIG>` | | Text is slightly larger than normal. |
| `<SMALL>...</SMALL>` | | Text is slightly smaller than normal. |
| `<SUB>...</SUB>` | | Subscript. |
| `<SUP>...</SUP>` | | Superscript. |
| `<STRIKE>...</STRIKE>` | | Puts a strikethrough line in text. |

## Other Elements

| Tag | Attribute | Function |
|-----|-----------|----------|
| `<HR>` | | A horizontal rule line. |
| | `SIZE="..."` | The thickness of the rule, in pixels. |
| | `WIDTH="..."` | The width of the rule, in pixels or as a percentage of the document width. |
| | `ALIGN="..."` | How the rule line will be aligned on the page. Possible values are `LEFT`, `RIGHT`, and `CENTER`. |
| | `NOSHADE` | Causes the rule line to be drawn as a solid line instead of a transparent bevel. |
| | `COLOR="..."` (MS) | Color of the horizontal rule. |
| `<BR>` | | A line break. |
| | `CLEAR="..."` | Causes the text to stop flowing around any images. Possible values are `RIGHT`, `LEFT`, and `ALL`. |
| `<NOBR>...</NOBR>` | | Causes the enclosed text not to wrap at the edge of the page. |
| `<WBR>` | | Wraps the text at this point only if necessary. |

| Tag | Attribute | Function |
|-----|-----------|----------|
| `<BLOCKQUOTE>...` `</BLOCKQUOTE>` | | Used for long quotes or citations. |
| `<ADDRESS>...` `</ADDRESS>` | | Used for signatures or general information about a document's author. |
| `<CENTER>...` `</CENTER>` | | Centers text or images. |
| `<BLINK>...</BLINK>` | | Causes the enclosed text to blink in an irritating manner. |
| `<FONT>...</FONT>` | | Changes the size of the font for the enclosed text. |
| | `SIZE="..."` | The size of the font, from 1 to 7. Default is 3. Can also be specified as a value relative to the current size; for example, +2. |
| | `COLOR="..."` | Changes the color of the text. |
| | `FACE="..."` | Name of font to use if it can be found on the user's system. Multiple font names can be separated by commas, and the first font on the list that can be found will be used. |
| `<BASEFONT>` | | Sets the default size of the font for the current page. |
| | `SIZE="..."` | The default size of the font, from 1 to 7. Default is 3. |

## Images, Sounds, and Embedded Media

| Tag | Attribute | Function |
|-----|-----------|----------|
| `<IMG>` | | Inserts an inline image into the document. |
| | `ISMAP` | This image is a clickable image map. |
| | `SRC="..."` | The URL of the image. |

*continues*

A

HTML QUICK
REFERENCE

| Tag | Attribute | Function |
|---|---|---|
| | ALT="..." | A text string that will be displayed in browsers that cannot support images. |
| | ALIGN="..." | Determines the alignment of the given image. If LEFT or RIGHT, the image is aligned to the left or right column, and all following text flows beside that image. All other values such as TOP, MIDDLE, and BOTTOM, or the Netscape-only TEXTTOP, ABSMIDDLE, BASELINE, and ABSBOTTOM determine the vertical alignment of this image with other items in the same line. |
| | VSPACE="..." | The space between the image and the text above or below it. |
| | HSPACE="..." | The space between the image and the text to its left or right. |
| | WIDTH="..." | The width, in pixels, of the image. If WIDTH is not the actual width, the image is scaled to fit. |
| | HEIGHT="..." | The height, in pixels, of the image. If HEIGHT is not the actual height, the image is scaled to fit. |
| | BORDER="..." | Draws a border of the specified value in pixels to be drawn around the image. In the case of images that are also links, BORDER changes the size of the default link border. |
| | LOWSRC="..." | The path or URL of an image that will be loaded first, before the image specified in SRC. The value of LOWSRC is usually a smaller or lower resolution version of the actual image. |
| | USEMAP="..." | The name of an image map specification for client-side image mapping. Used with <MAP> and <AREA>. |

| Tag | Attribute | Function |
|---|---|---|
| | DYNSRC="..." (MS) | The address of a video clip or VRML world (dynamic source). |
| | CONTROLS (MS) | Used with DYNSRC to display a set of playback controls for inline video. |
| | LOOP="..." (MS) | The number of times a video clip will loop. (-1, or INFINITE, means to loop indefinitely.) |
| | START="..." (MS) | When a DYNSRC video clip should start playing. Valid options are FILEOPEN (play when page is displayed) or MOUSEOVER (play when mouse cursor passes over the video clip). |
| <BGSOUND> (MS) | | Plays a sound file as soon as the page is displayed. |
| | SRC="..." | The URL of the WAV, AU, or MIDI sound file to embed. |
| | LOOP="..." (MS) | The number of times a video clip will loop. (-1, or INFINITE, means to loop indefinitely.) |
| <SCRIPT> | | An interpreted script program. |
| | LANGUAGE="..." | Currently only JAVASCRIPT is supported by Netscape. Both JAVASCRIPT and VBSCRIPT are supported by Microsoft. |
| | SRC="..." | Specifies the URL of a file that includes the script program. |
| <OBJECT> | | Inserts an image, video, Java applet, or ActiveX control into a document. |

**NOTE**

Usage of the <OBJECT> tag is not yet finalized. Check http://www.w3.org/ for the latest attributes supported by the HTML 3.2 standard.

**A**

HTML QUICK REFERENCE

| Tag | Attribute | Function |
|---|---|---|
| `<APPLET>` | | Inserts a self-running Java applet. |
| | `CLASS="..."` | The name of the applet. |
| | `SRC="..."` | The URL of the directory where the compiled applet can be found (should end in a slash as in `http://mysite/myapplets/`). Do not include the actual applet name, which is specified with the `CLASS` attribute. |
| | `ALIGN="..."` | Indicates how the applet should be aligned with any text that follows it. Current values are `TOP`, `MIDDLE`, and `BOTTOM`. |
| | `WIDTH="..."` | The width of the applet output area, in pixels. |
| | `HEIGHT="..."` | The height of the applet output area, in pixels. |
| `<PARAM>` | | Program-specific parameters. (Always occurs within `<APPLET>` or `<OBJECT>` tags.) |
| | `NAME="..."` | The type of information being given to the applet or ActiveX control. |
| | `VALUE="..."` | The actual information to be given to the applet or ActiveX control. |
| | `REF="..."` | Indicates that this `<PARAM>` tag includes the address or location of the object. |
| `<EMBED>` (Netscape only!) | | Embeds a file to be read or displayed by a plug-in application. |

**NOTE**

In addition to the following standard attributes, you can specify applet-specific attributes to be interpreted by the plug-in that displays the embedded object.

| Tag | Attribute | Function |
|---|---|---|
| | SRC="..." | The URL of the file to embed. |
| | WIDTH="..." | The width of the embedded object in pixels. |
| | HEIGHT="..." | The height of the embedded object in pixels. |
| | ALIGN="..." | Determines the alignment of the media window. Values are the same as for the <IMG> tag. |
| | VSPACE="..." | The space between the media and the text above or below it. |
| | HSPACE="..." | The space between the media and the text to its left or right. |
| | BORDER="..." | Draws a border of the specified size in pixels to be drawn around the media. |
| <NOEMBED>...</NOEMBED> | | Alternate text or images to be shown to users who do not have a plug-in installed. |
| <MAP>...</MAP> | | A client-side image map, referenced by <IMG USEMAP="...">. Includes one or more <AREA> tags. |
| <AREA> | | Defines a clickable link within a client-side image map. |
| | SHAPE="..." | The shape of the clickable area. Currently, only RECT is supported. |
| | COORDS="..." | The left, top, right, and bottom coordinates of the clickable region within an image. |
| | HREF="..." | The URL that should be loaded when the area is clicked. |
| | NOHREF | Indicates that no action should be taken when this area of the image is clicked. |

# Forms

| Tag | Attribute | Function |
| --- | --- | --- |
| <FORM>...</FORM> | | Indicates an input form. |
| | ACTION="..." | The URL of the script to process this form input. |
| | METHOD="..." | How the form input will be sent to the gateway on the server side. Possible values are GET and POST. |
| | ENCTYPE="..." | Normally has the value application/x-www-form-urlencoded. For file uploads, use multipart/form-data. |
| | NAME="..." | A name by which JavaScript scripts can refer to the form. |
| <INPUT> | | An input element for a form. |
| | TYPE="..." | The type for this input widget. Possible values are CHECKBOX, HIDDEN, RADIO, RESET, SUBMIT, TEXT, SEND FILE, or IMAGE. |
| | NAME="..." | The name of this item, as passed to the gateway script as part of a name/value pair. |
| | VALUE="..." | For a text or hidden widget, the default value; for a checkbox or radio button, the value to be submitted with the form; for Reset or Submit buttons, the label for the button itself. |
| | SRC="..." | The source file for an image. |
| | CHECKED | For checkboxes and radio buttons, indicates that the widget is checked. |
| | SIZE="..." | The size, in characters, of a text widget. |
| | MAXLENGTH="..." | The maximum number of characters that can be entered into a text widget. |

| Tag | Attribute | Function |
|-----|-----------|----------|
| | ALIGN="..." | For images in forms, determines how the text and image will align (same as with the `<IMG>` tag). |
| `<TEXTAREA>...</TEXTAREA>` | | Indicates a multiline text entry form element. Default text can be included. |
| | NAME="..." | The name to be passed to the gateway script as part of the name/value pair. |
| | ROWS="..." | The number of rows this text area displays. |
| | COLS="..." | The number of columns (characters) this text area displays. |
| | WRAP="..." | Controls text wrapping. Possible values are OFF, VIRTUAL, and PHYSICAL. |
| `<SELECT>...</SELECT>` | | Creates a menu or scrolling list of possible items. |
| | NAME="..." | The name that is passed to the gateway script as part of the name/value pair. |
| | SIZE="..." | The number of elements to display. If SIZE is indicated, the selection becomes a scrolling list. If no SIZE is given, the selection is a pop-up menu. |
| | MULTIPLE | Allows multiple selections from the list. |
| `<OPTION>` | | Indicates a possible item within a `<SELECT>` element. |
| | SELECTED | With this attribute included, the `<OPTION>` will be selected by default in the list. |
| | VALUE="..." | The value to submit if this `<OPTION>` is selected when the form is submitted. |

# Tables

| Tag | Attribute | Function |
| --- | --- | --- |
| `<TABLE>...</TABLE>` | | Creates a table that can contain a caption (`<CAPTION>`) and any number of rows (`<TR>`). |
| | `BORDER="..."` | Indicates whether the table should be drawn with or without a border. In Netscape, `BORDER` can also have a value indicating the width of the border. |
| | `CELLSPACING="..."` | The amount of space between the cells in the table. |
| | `CELLPADDING="..."` | The amount of space between the edges of the cell and its contents. |
| | `WIDTH="..."` | The width of the table on the page, in either exact pixel values or as a percentage of page width. |
| | `ALIGN="..."` (MS) | Alignment (works like `IMG ALIGN`). Values are `LEFT` or `RIGHT`. |
| | `BGCOLOR="..."` | Background color of all cells in the table that do not contain their own `BACKGROUND` or `BGCOLOR` attribute. |
| | `BACKGROUND="..."` (MS) | Background image to tile within all cells in the table that do not contain their own `BACKGROUND` or `BGCOLOR` attribute. |
| | `BORDERCOLOR="..."` (MS) | Border color (used with `BORDER="..."`). |

| Tag | Attribute | Function |
|-----|-----------|----------|
| | BORDERCOLORLIGHT="..." (MS) | Color for light part of 3D-look borders (used with BORDER="..."). |
| | BORDERCOLORDARK="..." (MS) | Color for dark part of 3D-look borders (used with BORDER="..."). |
| | VALIGN="..." (MS) | Alignment of text within the table. Values are TOP and BOTTOM. |
| | FRAME="..." (MS) | Controls which external borders will appear around a table. Values are void (no frames), above (top border only), below (bottom border only), hsides (top and bottom), lhs (left side), rhs (right side), vsides (left and right sides), and box (all sides). |
| | RULES="..." (MS) | Controls which internal borders appear in the table. Values are none, basic (rules between THEAD, TBODY, and TFOOT only), rows (horizontal borders only), cols (vertical borders only), and all. |
| <CAPTION>...</CAPTION> | | The caption for the table. |
| | ALIGN="..." | The position of the caption. Possible values are TOP and BOTTOM. |

*continues*

| Tag | Attribute | Function |
|---|---|---|
| `<TR>...</TR>` | | Defines a table row, containing headings and data (`<TR>` and `<TH>` tags). |
| | `ALIGN="..."` | The horizontal alignment of the contents of the cells within this row. Possible values are LEFT, RIGHT, and CENTER. |
| | `VALIGN="..."` | The vertical alignment of the contents of the cells within this row. Possible values are TOP, MIDDLE, BOTTOM, and BASELINE. |
| | `BGCOLOR="..."` | Background color of all cells in the row that do not contain their own BACKGROUND or BGCOLOR attributes. |
| | `BACKGROUND="..."`(MS) | Background image to tile within all cells in the row that do not contain their own BACKGROUND or BGCOLOR attributes. |
| | `BORDERCOLOR="..."`(MS) | Border color (used with BORDER="..."). |
| | `BORDERCOLORLIGHT="..."`(MS) | Color for light part of 3D-look borders (used with BORDER="..."). |
| | `BORDERCOLORDARK="..."`(MS) | Color for dark part of 3D-look borders (used with BORDER="..."). |
| `<TH>...</TH>` | | Defines a table heading cell. |

| Tag | Attribute | Function |
|---|---|---|
| | `ALIGN="..."` | The horizontal alignment of the contents of the cell. Possible values are LEFT, RIGHT, and CENTER. |
| | `VALIGN="..."` | The vertical alignment of the contents of the cell. Possible values are TOP, MIDDLE, BOTTOM, and BASELINE. |
| | `ROWSPAN="..."` | The number of rows this cell will span. |
| | `COLSPAN="..."` | The number of columns this cell will span. |
| | `NOWRAP` | Does not automatically wrap the contents of this cell. |
| | `WIDTH="..."` | The width of this column of cells, in exact pixel values or as a percentage of the table width. |
| | `BGCOLOR="..."` | Background color of the cell. |
| | `BACKGROUND="..."` (MS) | Background image to tile within the cell. |
| | `BORDERCOLOR="..."` (MS) | Border color (used with BORDER="..."). |
| | `BORDERCOLORLIGHT="..."` (MS) | Color for light part of 3D-look borders (used with BORDER="..."). |
| | `BORDERCOLORDARK="..."` (MS) | Color for dark part of 3D-look borders (used with BORDER="..."). |
| `<TD>...</TD>` | | Defines a table data cell. |

*continues*

| Tag | Attribute | Function |
|-----|-----------|----------|
| | `ALIGN="..."` | The horizontal alignment of the contents of the cell. Possible values are LEFT, RIGHT, and CENTER. |
| | `VALIGN="..."` | The vertical alignment of the contents of the cell. Possible values are TOP, MIDDLE, BOTTOM, and BASELINE. |
| | `ROWSPAN="..."` | The number of rows this cell will span. |
| | `COLSPAN="..."` | The number of columns this cell will span. |
| | `NOWRAP` | Does not automatically wrap the contents of this cell. |
| | `WIDTH="..."` | The width of this column of cells, in exact pixel values or as a percentage of the table width. |
| | `BGCOLOR="..."` | Background color of the cell. |
| | `BACKGROUND="..."` (MS) | Background image to tile within the cell. |
| | `BORDERCOLOR="..."` (MS) | Border color (used with BORDER="..."). |
| | `BORDERCOLORLIGHT="..."` (MS) | Color for light part of 3D-look borders (used with BORDER="..."). |
| | `BORDERCOLORDARK="..."` (MS) | Color for dark part of 3D-look borders (used with BORDER="..."). |

# Frames

| Tag | Attribute | Function |
|-----|-----------|----------|
| \<FRAMESET>... \</FRAMESET> | | Divides the main window into a set of frames that can each display a separate document. |
| | ROWS="..." | Splits the window or frameset vertically into a number of rows specified by a number (such as 7), a percentage of the total window width (such as 25%), or an asterisk (*) indicating that a frame should take up all the remaining space or divide the space evenly between frames (if multiple * frames are specified). |
| | COLS="..." | Works similar to ROWS, except that the window or frameset is split horizontally into columns. |
| | BORDER="..." | Size of frame border in pixels (0 turns off borders). This tag is Netscape-specific; Microsoft IE uses FRAMEBORDER and FRAMESPACING instead. |
| | FRAMEBORDER="..." (MS) | Specifies whether to display a border for a frame. Options are YES and NO. |
| | FRAMESPACING="..." (MS) | Space between frames, in pixels. |
| \<FRAME> | | Defines a single frame within a \<FRAMESET>. |
| | SRC="..." | The URL of the document to be displayed in this frame. |

*continues*

A

| Tag | Attribute | Function |
|---|---|---|
| | NAME="..." | A name to be used for targeting this frame with the TARGET attribute in <A HREF> links. |
| | MARGINWIDTH="..." | The amount of space to leave to the left and right side of a document within a frame, in pixels. |
| | MARGINHEIGHT="..." | The amount of space to leave above and below a document within a frame, in pixels. |
| | SCROLLING="..." | Determines whether a frame has scrollbars. Possible values are YES, NO, and AUTO. |
| | NORESIZE | Prevents the user from resizing this frame (and possibly adjacent frames) with the mouse. |
| <NOFRAME>...</NOFRAME> | | Provides an alternative document body in <FRAMESET> documents for browsers that do not support frames (usually encloses <BODY>...</BODY>). |

# Character Entities

Table A.1 contains the possible numeric and character entities for the ISO-Latin-1 (ISO8859-1) character set. Where possible, the character is shown.

> **NOTE**
>
> Not all browsers can display all characters, and some browsers might even display characters different from those that appear in the table. Newer browsers seem to have a better track record for handling character entities, but be sure to test your HTML files extensively with multiple browsers if you intend to use these entities.

**Table A.1. ISO-Latin-1 character set.**

| Character | Numeric Entity | Character Entity (if any) | Description |
|---|---|---|---|
| | &#00;–&#08; | | Unused |
| | &#09; | | Horizontal tab |
| | &#10; | | Line feed |
| | &#11;–&#31; | | Unused |
| | &#32; | | Space |
| ! | &#33; | | Exclamation mark |
| " | &#34; | &quot; | Quotation mark |
| # | &#35; | | Number sign |
| $ | &#36; | | Dollar sign |
| % | &#37; | | Percent sign |
| & | &#38; | &amp; | Ampersand |
| ' | &#39; | | Apostrophe |
| ( | &#40; | | Left parenthesis |
| ) | &#41; | | Right parenthesis |
| * | &#42; | | Asterisk |
| + | &#43; | | Plus sign |
| , | &#44; | | Comma |
| - | &#45; | | Hyphen |
| . | &#46; | | Period (fullstop) |
| / | &#47; | | Solidus (slash) |
| 0–9 | &#48;–&#57; | | Digits 0–9 |
| : | &#58; | | Colon |
| ; | &#59; | | Semicolon |
| < | &#60; | &lt; | Less than |
| = | &#61; | | Equal sign |
| > | &#62; | &gt; | Greater than |
| ? | &#63; | | Question mark |
| @ | &#64; | | Commercial "at" |
| A–Z | &#65;–&#90; | | Letters A–Z |

*continues*

**Table A.1. continued**

| Character | Numeric Entity | Character Entity (if any) | Description |
|---|---|---|---|
| [ | &#91; | | Left square bracket |
| \ | &#92; | | Reverse solidus (backslash) |
| ] | &#93; | | Right square bracket |
| ^ | &#94; | | Caret |
| — | &#95; | | Horizontal bar |
| ` | &#96; | | Grave accent |
| a–z | &#97;–&#122; | | Letters a–z |
| { | &#123; | | Left curly brace |
| \| | &#124 | | Vertical bar |
| } | &#125; | | Right curly brace |
| ~ | &#126; | | Tilde |
| | &#127;–  | | Unused |
| ¡ | &#161; | &iexcl; | Inverted exclamation |
| ¢ | &#162; | &cent; | Cent sign |
| £ | &#163; | &pound; | Pound sterling |
| ¤ | &#164; | &curren; | General currency sign |
| ¥ | &#165; | &yen; | Yen sign |
| ¦ | &#166; | &brvbar; or &brkbar; | Broken vertical bar |
| § | &#167; | &sect; | Section sign |
| ¨ | &#168; | &uml; | Umlaut (dieresis) |
| © | &#169; | &copy; (Netscape only) | Copyright |
| ª | &#170; | &ordf; | Feminine ordinal |
| ‹ | &#171; | &laquo; | Left angle quote, guillemot left |
| ¬ | &#172; | &not; | Not sign |

| Character | Numeric Entity | Character Entity (if any) | Description |
|---|---|---|---|
| - | &#173; | &shy; | Soft hyphen |
| ® | &#174; | &reg; (Netscape only) | Registered trademark |
| ¯ | &#175; | &macr; | Macron accent |
| ° | &#176; | &deg; | Degree sign |
| ± | &#177; | &plusmn; | Plus or minus |
| $^2$ | &#178; | &sup2; | Superscript two |
| $^3$ | &#179; | &sup3; | Superscript three |
| ´ | &#180; | &acute; | Acute accent |
| µ | &#181; | &micro; | Micro sign |
| ¶ | &#182; | &para; | Paragraph sign |
| · | &#183; | &middot; | Middle dot |
| ¸ | &#184; | &cedil; | Cedilla |
| $^1$ | &#185; | &sup1; | Superscript one |
| º | &#186; | &ordm; | Masculine ordinal |
| › | &#187; | &raquo; | Right angle quote, guillemot right |
| $^1/_4$ | &#188; | &frac14; | Fraction one-fourth |
| $^1/_2$ | &#189; | &frac12; | Fraction one-half |
| $^3/_4$ | &#190; | &frac34; | Fraction three-fourths |
| ¿ | &#191; | &iquest | Inverted question mark |
| À | &#192; | &Agrave; | Capital A, grave accent |
| Á | &#193; | &Aacute; | Capital A, acute accent |
| Â | &#194; | &Acirc; | Capital A, circumflex accent |

*continues*

**Table A.1. continued**

| Character | Numeric Entity | Character Entity (if any) | Description |
|---|---|---|---|
| Ã | &#195; | &Atilde; | Capital A, tilde |
| Ä | &#196; | &Auml; | Capital A, dieresis or umlaut mark |
| Å | &#197; | &Aring; | Capital A, ring |
| Æ | &#198; | &AElig; | Capital AE diphthong (ligature) |
| Ç | &#199; | &Ccedil; | Capital C, cedilla |
| È | &#200; | &Egrave; | Capital E, grave accent |
| É | &#201; | &Eacute; | Capital E, acute accent |
| Ê | &#202; | &Ecirc; | Capital E, circumflex accent |
| Ë | &#203; | &Euml; | Capital E, dieresis or umlaut mark |
| Ì | &#204; | &Igrave; | Capital I, grave accent |
| Í | &#205; | &Iacute; | Capital I, acute accent |
| Î | &#206; | &Icirc; | Capital I, circumflex accent |
| Ï | &#207; | &Iuml; | Capital I, dieresis or umlaut mark |
| Ð | &#208; | &ETH; | Capital Eth, Icelandic |
| Ñ | &#209; | &Ntilde; | Capital N, tilde |
| Ò | &#210; | &Ograve; | Capital O, grave accent |

| Character | Numeric Entity | Character Entity (if any) | Description |
|-----------|----------------|---------------------------|-------------|
| Ó | &#211; | &Oacute; | Capital O, acute accent |
| Ô | &#212; | &Ocirc; | Capital O, circumflex accent |
| Õ | &#213; | &Otilde; | Capital O, tilde |
| Ö | &#214; | &Ouml; | Capital O, dieresis or umlaut mark |
| × | &#215; | &times; | Multiply sign |
| Ø | &#216; | &Oslash; | Capital O, slash |
| Ù | &#217; | &Ugrave; | Capital U, grave accent |
| Ú | &#218; | &Uacute; | Capital U, acute accent |
| Û | &#219; | &Ucirc; | Capital U, circumflex accent |
| Ü | &#220; | &Uuml; | Capital U, dieresis or umlaut mark |
| Ý | &#221; | &Yacute; | Capital Y, acute accent |
| Þ | &#222; | &THORN; | Capital THORN, Icelandic |
| ß | &#223; | &szlig; | Small sharp s, German (sz ligature) |
| à | &#224; | &agrave; | Small a, grave accent |
| á | &#225; | &aacute; | Small a, acute accent |
| â | &#226; | &acirc; | Small a, circumflex accent |

*continues*

A

HTML QUICK REFERENCE

**Table A.1. continued**

| Character | Numeric Entity | Character Entity (if any) | Description |
|---|---|---|---|
| ã | &#227; | &atilde; | Small a, tilde |
| ä | &#228; | &auml; | Small a, dieresis or umlaut mark |
| å | &#229; | &aring; | Small a, ring |
| æ | &#230; | &aelig; | Small ae diphthong (ligature) |
| ç | &#231; | &ccedil; | Small c, cedilla |
| è | &#232; | &egrave; | Small e, grave accent |
| é | &#233; | &eacute; | Small e, acute accent |
| ê | &#234; | &ecirc; | Small e, circum-flex accent |
| ë | &#235; | &euml; | Small e, dieresis or umlaut mark |
| ì | &#236; | &igrave; | Small i, grave accent |
| í | &#237; | &iacute; | Small i, acute accent |
| î | &#238; | &icirc; | Small i, circum-flex accent |
| ï | &#239; | &iuml; | Small i, dieresis or umlaut mark |
| ð | &#240; | &eth; | Small eth, Icelandic |
| ñ | &#241; | &ntilde; | Small n, tilde |
| ò | &#242; | &ograve; | Small o, grave accent |
| ó | &#243; | &oacute; | Small o, acute accent |
| ô | &#244; | &ocirc; | Small o, circumflex accent |

| Character | Numeric Entity | Character Entity (if any) | Description |
|---|---|---|---|
| õ | &#245; | &otilde; | Small o, tilde |
| ö | &#246; | &ouml; | Small o, dieresis or umlaut mark |
| ÷ | &#247; | &divide; | Division sign |
| ø | &#248; | &oslash; | Small o, slash |
| ù | &#249; | &ugrave; | Small u, grave accent |
| ú | &#250; | &uacute; | Small u, acute accent |
| û | &#251; | &ucirc; | Small u, circumflex accent |
| ü | &#252; | &uuml; | Small u, dieresis or umlaut mark |
| ý | &#253; | &yacute; | Small y, acute accent |
| þ | &#254; | &thorn; | Small thorn, Icelandic |
| ÿ | &#255; | &yuml; | Small y, dieresis or umlaut mark |

# HTML 3.2 Reference Specification

*by Dave Raggett (dsr@w3.org)*

## IN THIS APPENDIX

## Status of This Document

This document has been reviewed by W3C members and other interested parties and has been endorsed by the Director as a W3C Recommendation. It is a stable document and may be used as reference material or cited as a normative reference from another document. W3C's role in making the Recommendation is to draw attention to the specification and to promote its widespread deployment. This enhances the functionality and interoperability of the Web.

A list of current W3C Recommendations and other technical documents can be found at http://www.w3.org/pub/WWW/TR/">http://www.w3.org/pub/WWW/TR/.

# Abstract

The Hypertext Markup Language (HTML) is a simple markup language used to create hypertext documents that are portable from one platform to another. HTML documents are SGML documents with generic semantics that are appropriate for representing information from a wide range of applications. This specification defines HTML Version 3.2. HTML 3.2 aims to capture recommended practice as of early '96 and as such to be used as a replacement for HTML 2.0 (RFC 1866).

# Contents

- Introduction to HTML 3.2
- HTML as an SGML Application
- The Structure of HTML Documents
- The HEAD Element and Its Children
- The BODY Element and Its Children
- Sample SGML Open Catalog for HTML 3.2
- SGML Declaration for HTML 3.2
- HTML 3.2 Document Type Definition
- Character Entities for ISO Latin-1
- Table of Printable Latin-1 Character Codes
- Acknowledgments
- Further Reading...

# Introduction to HTML 3.2

HTML 3.2 is W3C's specification for HTML, developed in early '96 together with vendors including IBM, Microsoft, Netscape Communications Corporation, Novell, SoftQuad, Spyglass, and Sun Microsystems. HTML 3.2 adds widely deployed features such as tables, applets and text flow around images, while providing full backwards compatibility with the existing standard HTML 2.0.

W3C is continuing to work with vendors on extensions for accessibility features, multimedia objects, scripting, style sheets, layout, forms, math, and internationalization. W3C plans on incorporating this work in further versions of HTML.

## HTML as an SGML Application

HTML 3.2 is an SGML application conforming to International Standard ISO 8879—Standard Generalized Markup Language. As an SGML application, the syntax of conforming HTML 3.2 documents is defined by the combination of the SGML declaration and the document type definition (DTD). This specification defines the intended interpretation of HTML 3.2 elements and places further constraints on the permitted syntax that are otherwise inexpressible in the DTD.

The SGML rules for record boundaries are tricky. In particular, a record end immediately following a start tag should be discarded. For example:

```
<P>
Text
```

is equivalent to

```
<P>Text
```

Similarly, a record end immediately preceding an end tag should be discarded. For example:

```
Text
</P>
```

is equivalent to

```
Text</P>
```

Except within literal text (for example, the PRE element), HTML treats contiguous sequences of white space characters as being equivalent to a single space character (ASCII decimal 32). These rules allow authors considerable flexibility when editing the marked-up text directly. Note that future revisions to HTML may allow for the interpretation of the horizontal tab character (ASCII decimal 9) with respect to a tab rule defined by an associated style sheet.

SGML entities in PCDATA content or in CDATA attributes are expanded by the parser; for example, &#233; is expanded to the ISO Latin-1 character decimal 233 (a lowercase letter *e* with an acute accent). This could also have been written as a named character entity, for example, &eacute;. The & character can be included in its own right using the named character entity &amp;.

HTML allows CDATA attributes to be unquoted provided the attribute value contains only letters (*a* to *z* and *A* to *Z*), digits (0 to 9), hyphens (ASCII decimal 45), or periods (ASCII decimal 46). Attribute values can be quoted using double or single quote marks (ASCII decimal 34 and 39, respectively). Single quote marks can be included within the attribute value when the value is delimited by double quote marks, and vice versa.

Note that some user agents require attribute minimization for the following attributes: COM-PACT, ISMAP, CHECKED, NOWRAP, NOSHADE, and NOHREF. These user agents don't accept syntax such as COMPACT=COMPACT or ISMAP=ISMAP although this is legitimate according to the HTML 3.2 DTD.

The SGML declaration and the DTD for use with HTML 3.2 are given in appendices. Further guidelines for parsing HTML are given in WD-html-lex.

## The Structure of HTML Documents

HTML 3.2 documents start with a <!DOCTYPE> declaration followed by an HTML element containing a HEAD and then a BODY element:

```
<!DOCTYPE HTML PUBLIC "-//W3C//DTD HTML 3.2 Final//EN>
<HTML>
<HEAD>
<TITLE>A study of population dynamics</TITLE>
... other head elements
</HEAD>
<BODY>
... document body
</BODY>
</HTML>
```

In practice, the HTML HEAD and BODY start and end tags can be omitted from the markup as these can be inferred in all cases by parsers conforming to the HTML 3.2 DTD.

Every conforming HTML 3.2 document **must** start with the <!DOCTYPE> declaration that is needed to distinguish HTML 3.2 documents from other versions of HTML. The HTML specification is not concerned with storage entities. As a result, it is not required that the document type declaration reside in the same storage entity (that is, file). A Web site may choose to dynamically prepend HTML files with the document type declaration if it is known that all such HTML files conform to the HTML 3.2 specification.

Every HTML 3.2 document must also include the descriptive title element. A minimal HTML 3.2 document thus looks like this:

```
<!DOCTYPE HTML PUBLIC "-//W3C//DTD HTML 3.2 Final//EN>
<TITLE>A study of population dynamics</TITLE>
```

> **NOTE**
>
> The word "Final" replaces "Draft" now that the HTML 3.2 specification has been ratified by the W3C member organizations.

# The HEAD Element

This contains the document head, but you can always omit both the start and end tags for HEAD. The contents of the document head are an unordered collection of the following elements:

- The TITLE element
- The STYLE element
- The SCRIPT element
- The ISINDEX element
- The BASE element
- The META element
- The LINK element

```
<!ENTITY % head.content "TITLE & ISINDEX? & BASE?">
<!ENTITY % head.misc "SCRIPT|STYLE|META|LINK">

<!ELEMENT HEAD O O  (%head.content) +(%head.misc)>
```

The %head.misc entity is used to allow the associated elements to occur multiple times at arbitrary positions within the HEAD. The following elements can be part of the document head:

- TITLE defines the document title, and is always needed.
- ISINDEX is for simple keyword searches; see PROMPT attribute.
- BASE defines base URL for resolving relative URLs.
- SCRIPT is reserved for future use with scripting languages.
- STYLE is reserved for future use with style sheets.
- META is used to supply meta info as name/value pairs.
- LINK is used to define relationships with other documents.

TITLE, SCRIPT and STYLE are containers and require both start and end tags. The other elements are not containers so that end tags are forbidden. Note that conforming browsers won't render the contents of SCRIPT and STYLE elements.

## TITLE

```
<!ELEMENT TITLE - -  (#PCDATA)* -(%head.misc)>
```

Every HTML 3.2 document **must** have exactly one TITLE element in the document's HEAD. It provides an advisory title that can be displayed in a user agent's window caption and so on. The content model is PCDATA. As a result, character entities can be used for accented characters and to escape special characters such as & and <. Markup is not permitted in the content of a TITLE element.

Example `TITLE` element:

```
<TITLE>A study of population dynamics</TITLE>
```

## STYLE and SCRIPT

```
<!ELEMENT STYLE  - - CDATA -- placeholder for style info -->
<!ELEMENT SCRIPT - - CDATA -- placeholder for script statements -->
```

These are placeholders for the introduction of style sheets and client-side scripts in future versions of HTML. User agents should hide the contents of these elements.

These elements are defined with `CDATA` as the content type. As a result they may contain only SGML characters. All markup characters or delimiters are ignored and passed as data to the application, except for `ETAGO` (`</`) delimiters followed immediately by a name character [a-zA-Z]. This means that the element's end tag (or that of an element in which it is nested) is recognized, while an error occurs if the `ETAGO` is invalid.

## ISINDEX

```
<!ELEMENT ISINDEX - O EMPTY>
<!ATTLIST ISINDEX
        prompt CDATA #IMPLIED -- prompt message -->
```

The `ISINDEX` element indicates that the user agent should provide a single-line text input field for entering a query string. There are no restrictions on the number of characters that can be entered. The `PROMPT` attribute can be used to specify a prompt string for the input field, for example:

```
<ISINDEX PROMPT="Search Phrase">
```

The semantics for `ISINDEX` are currently well defined only when the base URL for the enclosing document is an HTTP URL. Typically, when the user presses the Enter (return) key, the query string is sent to the server identified by the base URL for this document. For example, if the query string entered is "ten green apples" and the base URL is

```
http://www.acme.com/
```

then the query generated is

```
http://www.acme.com/?ten+green+apples"
```

Note that space characters are mapped to + characters and that normal URL character escaping mechanisms apply. For further details, see the HTTP specification.

**NOTE**

Note that in practice, the query string is restricted to Latin-1 as there is no current mechanism for the URL to specify a character set for the query.

# BASE

```
<!ELEMENT BASE - O EMPTY>
<!ATTLIST BASE
        href %URL   #REQUIRED
        >
```

The BASE element gives the base URL for dereferencing relative URLs, using the rules given by the URL specification, for example,

```
<BASE href="http://www.acme.com/intro.html">
   ...
   <IMG SRC="icons/logo.gif">
```

The image is dereferenced to

```
http://www.acme.com/icons/logo.gif
```

In the absence of a BASE element, the document URL should be used. Note that this is not necessarily the same as the URL used to request the document, as the base URL may be over-ridden by an HTTP header accompanying the document.

# META

```
<!ELEMENT META - O EMPTY     -- Generic Metainformation -->
<!ATTLIST META
        http-equiv  NAME   #IMPLIED -- HTTP response header name --
        name        NAME   #IMPLIED -- metainformation name      --
        content     CDATA  #REQUIRED -- associated information    --
        >
```

The META element can be used to include name/value pairs describing properties of the document, such as author, expire date, a list of key words, and so on. The NAME attribute specifies the property name, while the CONTENT attribute specifies the property value, for example,

```
<META NAME="Author" CONTENT="Dave Raggett">
```

The HTTP-EQUIV attribute can be used in place of the NAME attribute and has a special significance when documents are retrieved via the Hypertext Transfer Protocol (HTTP). HTTP servers may use the property name specified by the HTTP-EQUIV attribute to create an RFC 822 style header in the HTTP response. This can't be used to set certain HTTP headers, though; see the HTTP specification for details.

```
<META HTTP-EQUIV="Expires" CONTENT="Tue, 20 Aug 1996 14:25:27 GMT">
```

will result in the HTTP header:

```
Expires: Tue, 20 Aug 1996 14:25:27 GMT
```

This can be used by caches to determine when to fetch a fresh copy of the associated document.

# LINK

LINK provides a media-independent method for defining relationships with other documents and resources. LINK has been part of HTML since the very early days, although few browsers as yet take advantage of it (most still ignore LINK elements).

LINK elements can be used *in principle* in the following ways:

- For document-specific navigation toolbars or menus
- To control how collections of HTML files are rendered into printed documents
- For linking associated resources such as style sheets and scripts
- To provide alternative forms of the current document

```
<!ELEMENT LINK - O EMPTY>
<!ATTLIST LINK
        href    %URL     #IMPLIED      -- URL for linked resource --
        rel     CDATA    #IMPLIED      -- forward link types --
        rev     CDATA    #IMPLIED      -- reverse link types --
        title   CDATA    #IMPLIED      -- advisory title string --
        >
```

href    Specifies a URL designating the linked resource.

rel     The forward relationship also known as the "link type." It specifies a named relationship from the enclosing document to the resource specified by the HREF attribute. HTML link relationships are as yet unstandardized, although some conventions have been established.

rev     This defines a reverse relationship. A link from document A to document B with REV=*relation* expresses the same relationship as a link from B to A with REL=*relation*. REV=made is sometimes used to identify the document author, either the author's e-mail address with a mailto URL, or a link to the author's home page.

title   An advisory title for the linked resource.

Here are some proposed relationship values:

rel=top

The link references the top of a hierarchy, for example, the first or cover page in a collection.

rel=contents

The link references a document serving as a table of contents.

rel=index

The link references a document providing an index for the current document.

`rel=glossary`

The link references a document providing a glossary of terms that are relevant to the current document.

`rel=copyright`

The link references a copyright statement for the current document.

`rel=next`

The link references the next document to visit in a guided tour. It can be used, for example, to preload the next page.

`rel=previous`

The link references the previous document in a guided tour.

`rel=help`

The link references a document offering help, for example, describing the wider context and offering further links to relevant documents. This is aimed at reorienting users who have lost their way.

`rel=search`

The link references a page for searching material related to a collection of pages

Example LINK elements:

```
<LINK REL=Contents HREF=toc.html>
<LINK REL=Previous HREF=doc31.html>
<LINK REL=Next HREF=doc33.html>
<LINK REL=Chapter REV=Contents HREF=chapter2.html>
```

# The BODY Element

This contains the document body. Both start and end tags for BODY may be omitted. The body can contain a wide range of elements:

- Headings (H1–H6)
- The ADDRESS element
- Block-level elements
- Text-level elements

The key attributes are BACKGROUND, BGCOLOR, TEXT, LINK, VLINK, and ALINK. These can be used to set a repeating background image, plus background and foreground colors for normal text and hypertext links.

```
<!ENTITY % body.content "(%heading | %text | %block | ADDRESS)*">
<!ENTITY % color "CDATA" -- a color specification: #HHHHHH @@ details? -->
```

```
<!ENTITY % body-color-attrs "
        bgcolor %color #IMPLIED
        text %color #IMPLIED
        link %color #IMPLIED
        vlink %color #IMPLIED
        alink %color #IMPLIED
        ">
<!ELEMENT BODY O O  %body.content>
<!ATTLIST BODY
        background %URL #IMPLIED  -- texture tile for document background --
        %body-color-attrs;  -- bgcolor, text, link, vlink, alink --
        >
```

Example:

```
<body bgcolor=white text=black link=red vlink=maroon alink=fuschia>
```

| | |
|---|---|
| bgcolor | Specifies the background color for the document body. See following for the syntax of color values. |
| text | Specifies the color used to stroke the document's text. This is generally used when you have changed the background color with the BGCOLOR or BACKGROUND attributes. |
| link | Specifies the color used to stroke the text for unvisited hypertext links. |
| vlink | Specifies the color used to stroke the text for visited hypertext links. |
| alink | Specifies the highlight color used to stroke the text for hypertext links at the moment the user clicks on the link. |
| background | Specifies a URL for an image that will be used to tile the document background. |

Colors are given in the sRGB color space as hexadecimal numbers (for example, COLOR="#C0FFC0"), or as one of 16 widely understood color names. These colors were originally picked as being the standard 16 colors supported with the Windows VGA palette.

*Color Names and sRGB Values*

| | |
|---|---|
| Black = "#000000" | Green = "#008000" |
| Silver = "#C0C0C0" | Lime = "#00FF00" |
| Gray = "#808080" | Olive = "#808000" |
| White = "#FFFFFF" | Yellow = "#FFFF00" |
| Maroon = "#800000" | Navy = "#000080" |
| Red = "#FF0000" | Blue = "#0000FF" |
| Purple = "#800080" | Teal = "#008080" |
| Fuchsia = "#FF00FF" | Aqua = "#00FFFF" |

# Block and Text-Level Elements

Most elements that can appear in the document body fall into one of two groups: block-level elements which cause paragraph breaks, and text-level elements which don't. Common block-level elements include H1 to H6 (headers), P (paragraphs) LI (list items), and HR (horizontal rules). Common text-level elements include EM, I, B and FONT (character emphasis), A (hypertext links), IMG and APPLET (embedded objects) and BR (line breaks). Note that block elements generally act as containers for text-level and other block-level elements (excluding headings and address elements), while text-level elements can only contain other text-level elements. The exact model depends on the element.

# Headings

```
<!--
  There are six levels of headers from H1 (the most important)
  to H6 (the least important).
-->
<!ELEMENT ( %heading )  - -  (%text;)*>
<!ATTLIST ( %heading )
        align  (left¦center¦right) #IMPLIED
        >
```

H1, H2, H3, H4, H5 and H6 are used for document headings. You always need the start and end tags. H1 elements are more important than H2 elements and so on, so that H6 elements define the least important level of headings. More important headings are generally rendered in a larger font than less important ones. Use the optional ALIGN attribute to set the text alignment within a heading, for example,

```
<H1 ALIGN=CENTER>... centered heading ...</H1>
```

The default is left alignment, but this can be overridden by an enclosing DIV or CENTER element.

# ADDRESS

```
<!ENTITY % address.content "((%text;) ¦ P)*">
<!ELEMENT ADDRESS - - %address.content>
```

The ADDRESS element requires start and end tags and specifies information such as authorship and contact details for the current document. User agents should render the content with paragraph-breaks before and after. Note that the content is restricted to paragraphs, plain text, and text-like elements as defined by the %text entity.

Example:

```
<ADDRESS>
Newsletter editor<BR>
J.R. Brown<BR>
8723 Buena Vista, Smallville, CT 01234<BR>
Tel: +1 (123) 456 7890
</ADDRESS>
```

# Block Elements

- **P** *paragraphs:* The paragraph element requires a start tag, but the end tag can always be omitted. Use the ALIGN attribute to set the text alignment within a paragraph, for example, `<P ALIGN=RIGHT>`

- **UL** *unordered lists:* These require start and end tags, and contain one or more LI elements representing individual list items.

- **OL** *ordered (numbered) lists:* These require start and end tags, and contain one or more LI elements representing individual list items.

- **DL** *definition lists:* These require start and end tags and contain DT elements that give the terms, and DD elements that give corresponding definitions.

- **PRE** *preformatted text:* Requires start and end tags. These elements are rendered with a monospaced font and preserve layout defined by whitespace and line break characters.

- **DIV** *document divisions:* Requires start and end tags. It is used with the ALIGN attribute to set the text alignment of the block elements it contains. ALIGN can be one of LEFT, CENTER, or RIGHT.

- **CENTER** *text alignment:* Requires start and end tags. It is used to center text lines enclosed by the CENTER element. See DIV for a more general solution.

- **BLOCKQUOTE** *quoted passage:* Requires start and end tags. It is used to enclose extended quotations and is typically rendered with indented margins.

- **FORM** *fill-out forms:* Requires start and end tags. This element is used to define a fill-out form for processing by HTTP servers. The attributes are ACTION, METHOD, and ENCTYPE. Form elements can't be nested.

- **ISINDEX** *primitive HTML forms:* Not a container, so the end tag is forbidden. This predates FORM and is used for simple kinds of forms which have a single text input field, implied by this element. A single ISINDEX can appear in the document head or body.

- **HR** *horizontal rules:* Not a container, so the end tag is forbidden. Attributes are ALIGN, NOSHADE, SIZE, and WIDTH.

- **TABLE** *can be nested:* Requires start and end tags. Each table starts with an optional CAPTION followed by one or more TR elements defining table rows. Each row has one or more cells defined by TH or TD elements. Attributes for TABLE elements are WIDTH, BORDER, CELLSPACING, and CELLPADDING.

# Paragraphs

```
<!ELEMENT P      - O (%text)*>
<!ATTLIST P
        align (left¦center¦right) #IMPLIED
        >
```

The P element is used to mark up paragraphs. It is a container and requires a start tag. The end tag is optional as it can always be inferred by the parser. User agents should place paragraph breaks before and after P elements. The rendering is user agent-dependent, but text is generally wrapped to fit the space available.

Example:

```
<P>This is the first paragraph.
<P>This is the second paragraph.
```

Paragraphs are usually rendered flush left with a ragged right margin. The ALIGN attribute can be used to explicitly specify the horizontal alignment:

| | |
|---|---|
| align=left | The paragraph is rendered flush left. |
| align=center | The paragraph is centered. |
| align=right | The paragraph is rendered flush right. |

For example:

```
<p align=center>This is a centered paragraph.
<p align=right>and this is a flush right paragraph.
```

The default is left alignment, but this can be overridden by an enclosing DIV or CENTER element.

## Lists

List items can contain block-level and text-level items, including nested lists, although headings and address elements are excluded. This limitation is defined via the %flow entity.

### Unordered Lists

```
<!ELEMENT UL - - (LI)+>
<!ENTITY % ULStyle "disc|square|circle">
<!ATTLIST UL -- unordered lists --
        type    (%ULStyle)  #IMPLIED   -- bullet style --
        compact (compact)   #IMPLIED   -- reduced interitem spacing --
        >
<!ELEMENT LI - O %flow -- list item -->
<!ATTLIST LI
        type    (%LIStyle)  #IMPLIED   -- list item style --
        >
```

Unordered lists take the form:

```
<UL>
    <LI>... first list item
    <LI>... second list item
    ...
    </UL>
```

The UL element is used for unordered lists. Both start and end tags are always needed. The LI element is used for individual list items. The end tag for LI elements can always be omitted. Note that LI elements can contain nested lists. The COMPACT attribute can be used as a hint to the user agent to render lists in a more compact style.

The TYPE attribute can be used to set the bullet style on UL and LI elements. The permitted values are disc, square, or circle. The default generally depends on the level of nesting for lists.

with `<li type=disc>`

with `<li type=square>`

with `<li type=circle>`

*This list was chosen to cater for the original bullet shapes used by Mosaic in 1993.*

## Ordered (Numbered) Lists

```
<!ELEMENT OL - -  (LI)+>
<!ATTLIST OL -- ordered lists --
        type        CDATA       #IMPLIED    -- numbering style --
        start       NUMBER      #IMPLIED    -- starting sequence number --
        compact     (compact)   #IMPLIED    -- reduced interitem spacing --
        >

<!ELEMENT LI - O %flow -- list item -->
<!ATTLIST LI
        type        CDATA       #IMPLIED    -- list item style --
        value       NUMBER      #IMPLIED    -- set sequence number --
        >
```

Ordered (or, *numbered*) lists take the form:

```
<OL>
    <LI>... first list item
    <LI>... second list item
    ...
    </OL>
```

The OL START attribute can be used to initialize the sequence number (by default it is initialized to 1). You can set it later on with the VALUE attribute on LI elements. Both of these attributes expect integer values. You can't indicate that numbering should be continued from a previous list, or to skip missing values without giving an explicit number.

The COMPACT attribute can be used as a hint to the user agent to render lists in a more compact style. The OL TYPE attribute allows you to set the numbering style for list items:

| Type | Numbering style |
|------|----------------|
| 1 | Arabic numbers: 1, 2, 3, ... |
| a | Lower alpha: a, b, c, ... |
| A | Upper alpha: A, B, C, ... |
| i | Lower Roman: i, ii, iii, ... |
| I | Upper Roman: I, II, III, ... |

## Definition Lists

```
<!-- definition lists - DT for term, DD for its definition -->

<!ELEMENT DL      - -  (DT¦DD)+>
<!ATTLIST DL
        compact (compact) #IMPLIED -- more compact style --
        >

<!ELEMENT DT - O  (%text)*>
<!ELEMENT DD - O  %flow;>
```

Definition lists take the form:

```
<DL>
    <DT> term name
     term definition
    ...
  </DL>
```

DT elements can only act as containers for text-level elements, while DD elements can hold block-level elements as well, excluding headings and address elements.

For example:

```
<DL>
<DT>Term 1This is the definition of the first term.
<DT>Term 2This is the definition of the second term.
</DL>
```

which could be rendered as:

Term 1    This is the definition of the first term.

Term 2    This is the definition of the second term.

The COMPACT attribute can be used with the DL element as a hint to the user agent to render lists in a more compact style.

## DIR and MENU

```
<!ELEMENT (DIR¦MENU) - - (LI)+ -(%block)>
<!ATTLIST (DIR¦MENU)
        compact (compact) #IMPLIED
        >
```

These elements have been part of HTML from the early days. They are intended for unordered lists similar to UL elements. User agents are recommended to render DIR elements as multicolumn directory lists, and MENU elements as single column menu lists. In practice, Mosaic and most other user agents have ignored this advice and instead render DIR and MENU in an identical way to UL elements.

# Preformatted Text

```
<!ELEMENT PRE - - (%text)* -(%pre.exclusion)>
<!ATTLIST PRE
        width NUMBER #implied
        >
```

The PRE element can be used to include preformatted text. User agents render this in a fixed pitch font, preserving spacing associated with white space characters such as space and newline characters. Automatic word-wrap should be disabled within PRE elements.

Note that the SGML standard requires that the parser remove a newline immediately following the start tag or immediately preceding the end tag.

PRE has the same content model as paragraphs, excluding images and elements that produce changes in font size, for example, IMG, BIG, SMALL, SUB, SUP, and FONT.

A few user agents support the WIDTH attribute. It provides a hint to the user agent of the required width in characters. The user agent can use this to select an appropriate font size or to indent the content appropriately.

Here is an example of a PRE element—a verse from Shelley ("To a Skylark"):

```
<PRE>
      Higher still and higher
        From the earth thou springest
      Like a cloud of fire;
        The blue deep thou wingest,
And singing still dost soar, and soaring ever singest.
</PRE>
```

which is rendered as:

```
      Higher still and higher
        From the earth thou springest
      Like a cloud of fire;
        The blue deep thou wingest,
And singing still dost soar, and soaring ever singest.
```

The horizontal tab character (encoded in Unicode, US ASCII, and ISO 8859-1 as decimal 9) should be interpreted as the smallest nonzero number of spaces which will leave the number of characters so far on the line as a multiple of 8. Its use is strongly discouraged since it is common practice when editing to set the tab-spacing to other values, leading to misaligned documents.

## XMP, LISTING, and PLAINTEXT

```
<![ %HTML.Deprecated [

<!ENTITY % literal "CDATA"
        -- historical, non-conforming parsing mode where
           the only markup signal is the end tag
           in full
        -->

<!ELEMENT (XMP¦LISTING) - -  %literal>
<!ELEMENT PLAINTEXT - O %literal>


]]>
```

These are obsolete tags for preformatted text that predate the introduction of PRE. User agents may support these for backwards compatibility. Authors should avoid using them in new documents!

## DIV and CENTER

```
<!ELEMENT DIV - -  %body.content>
<!ATTLIST DIV
        align    (left¦center¦right) #IMPLIED -- alignment of following text --
        >

<!-- CENTER is a shorthand for DIV with ALIGN=CENTER -->
<!ELEMENT center - -  %body.content>
```

DIV elements can be used to structure HTML documents as a hierarchy of divisions. The ALIGN attribute can be used to set the default horizontal alignment for elements within the content of the DIV element. Its value is restricted to LEFT, CENTER, or RIGHT, and is defined in the same way as for the paragraph element <P>.

Note that because DIV is a block-like element, it will terminate an open P element. Other than this, user agents are **not** expected to render paragraph breaks before and after DIV elements. CENTER is directly equivalent to DIV with ALIGN=CENTER. Both DIV and CENTER require start and end tags.

*CENTER was introduced by Netscape before they added support for the HTML 3.0 DIV element. It is retained in HTML 3.2 on account of its widespread deployment.*

## BLOCKQUOTE

```
<!ELEMENT BLOCKQUOTE - - %body.content>
```

This is used to enclose block quotations from other works. Both the start and end tags are required. It is often rendered indented, for example:

> They went in single file, running like hounds on a strong scent, and an eager light was in their eyes. Nearly due west the broad swath of the marching Orcs tramped its ugly slot; the sweet grass of Rohan had been bruised and blackened as they passed.
>
> from "The Two Towers" by J.R.R. Tolkien.

## FORM

```
<!ENTITY % HTTP-Method "GET ¦ POST"
        -- as per HTTP specification
        -->

<!ELEMENT FORM - - %body.content -(FORM)>
<!ATTLIST FORM
        action %URL #IMPLIED  -- server-side form handler --
        method (%HTTP-Method) GET -- see HTTP specification --
        enctype %Content-Type; "application/x-www-form-urlencoded"
        >
```

This is used to define an HTML form, and you can have more than one form in the same document. Both the start and end tags are required. For very simple forms, you can also use the ISINDEX element. Forms can contain a wide range of HTML markup, including several kinds of form fields such as single- and multiline text fields, radio button groups, checkboxes, and menus.

| | |
|---|---|
| action | This specifies a URL which is either used to post forms via e-mail, for example action="mailto:foo@bar.com", or used to invoke a server-side forms handler via HTTP, for example action="http://www.acme.com/cgi-bin/register.pl". |
| method | When the action attribute specifies an HTTP server, the method attribute determines which HTTP method will be used to send the form's contents to the server. It can be either GET or POST, and defaults to GET. |
| enctype | This determines the mechanism used to encode the form's contents. It defaults to application/x-www-form-urlencoded. |

Further details on handling forms are given in RFC 1867.

## HR—Horizontal Rules

Horizontal rules may be used to indicate a change in topic. In a speech-based user agent, the rule could be rendered as a pause.

```
<!ELEMENT HR    - O EMPTY>
<!ATTLIST HR
        align (left¦right¦center) #IMPLIED
        noshade (noshade) #IMPLIED
        size  %Pixels #IMPLIED
        width %Length #IMPLIED
        >
```

HR elements are not containers so the end tag is forbidden. The attributes are ALIGN, NOSHADE, SIZE, and WIDTH.

| | |
|---|---|
| align | This determines whether the rule is placed at the left, center or right of the space between the current left and right margins for align=left, align=center, or align=right, respectively. By default, the rule is centered. |
| noshade | This attribute requests the user agent to render the rule in a solid color rather than as the traditional two color "groove." |
| size | This can be used to set the height of the rule in pixels. |
| width | This can be used to set the width of the rule in pixels (for example, width=100) or as the percentage between the current left and right margins (for example, width="50%"). The default is 100%. |

# Tables

HTML 3.2 includes a widely deployed subset of the specification given in RFC 1942 and can be used to mark up tabular material or for layout purposes. Note that the latter role typically causes problems when rendering to speech or to text-only user agents.

```
<!-- horizontal placement of table relative to window -->
<!ENTITY % Where "(left¦center¦right)">

<!-- horizontal alignment attributes for cell contents -->
<!ENTITY % cell.halign
        "align (left¦center¦right) #IMPLIED"
        >

<!-- vertical alignment attributes for cell contents -->
<!ENTITY % cell.valign
        "valign (top¦middle¦bottom)  #IMPLIED"
        >

<!ELEMENT table - - (caption?, tr+)>
<!ELEMENT tr - O (th¦td)*>
<!ELEMENT (th¦td) - O %body.content>

<!ATTLIST table                         -- table element --
        align      %Where;  #IMPLIED    -- table position relative to window --
        width      %Length  #IMPLIED    -- table width relative to window --
        border     %Pixels  #IMPLIED    -- controls frame width around table --
        cellspacing %Pixels #IMPLIED    -- spacing between cells --
        cellpadding %Pixels #IMPLIED    -- spacing within cells --
        >
```

```
<!ELEMENT CAPTION - - (%text;)* -- table or figure caption -->
<!ATTLIST CAPTION
        align (top¦bottom) #IMPLIED
        >

<!ATTLIST tr                            -- table row --
        %cell.halign;                   -- horizontal alignment in cells --
        %cell.valign;                   -- vertical alignment in cells --
        >

<!ATTLIST (th¦td)                       -- header or data cell --
        nowrap (nowrap)  #IMPLIED       -- suppress word wrap --
        rowspan NUMBER   1              -- number of rows spanned by cell --
        colspan NUMBER   1              -- number of cols spanned by cell --
        %cell.halign;                   -- horizontal alignment in cells --
        %cell.valign;                   -- vertical alignment in cells --
        width   %Pixels  #IMPLIED       -- suggested width for cell --
        height  %Pixels  #IMPLIED       -- suggested height for cell --
        >
```

Tables take the general form:

```
<TABLE BORDER=3 CELLSPACING=2 CELLPADDING=2 WIDTH="80%">
<CAPTION> ... table caption ... </CAPTION>
<TR><TD> first cell <TD> second cell
<TR> ...
...
</TABLE>
```

The attributes on TABLE are all optional. By default, the table is rendered without a surrounding border. The table is generally sized automatically to fit the contents, but you can also set the table width using the WIDTH attribute. BORDER, CELLSPACING, and CELLPADDING provide further control over the table's appearance. Captions are rendered at the top or bottom of the table depending on the ALIGN attribute.

Each table row is contained in a TR element, although the end tag can always be omitted. Table cells are defined by TD elements for data and TH elements for headers. Like TR, these are containers and can be given without trailing end tags. TH and TD support several attributes: ALIGN and VALIGN for aligning cell content, ROWSPAN and COLSPAN for cells which span more than one row or column. A cell can contain a wide variety of other block- and text-level elements, including form fields and other tables.

The TABLE element always requires both start and end tags. It supports the following attributes:

align
This takes one of the case insensitive values: LEFT, CENTER, or RIGHT. It specifies the horizontal placement of the table relative to the current left and right margins. It defaults to left alignment, but this can be overridden by an enclosing DIV or CENTER element.

| | |
|---|---|
| width | In the absence of this attribute, the table width is automatically determined from the table contents. You can use the WIDTH attribute to set the table width to a fixed value in pixels (for example WIDTH=212) or as a percentage of the space between the current left and right margins (for example WIDTH="80%"). |
| border | This attribute can be used to specify the width of the outer border around the table to a given number of pixels (for example BORDER=4). The value can be set to zero to suppress the border altogether. In the absence of this attribute, the border should be suppressed. Note that some browsers also accept <TABLE BORDER> with the same semantics as BORDER=1. |
| cellspacing | In traditional desktop publishing software, adjacent table cells share a common border. This is not the case in HTML. Each cell is given its own border which is separated from the borders around neighboring cells. This separation can be set in pixels using the CELLSPACING attribute, (for example CELLSPACING=10). The same value also determines the separation between the table border and the borders of the outermost cells. |
| cellpadding | This sets the padding in pixels between the border around each cell and the cell's contents. |

The CAPTION element has one attribute, ALIGN, which can be either ALIGN=TOP or ALIGN=BOTTOM. This can be used to force the caption to be placed above the top or below the bottom of the table, respectively. Most user agents default to placing the caption above the table. CAPTION always requires both start and end tags. Captions are limited to plain text and text-level elements as defined by the %text entity. Block-level elements are not permitted.

The TR or table row element requires a start tag, but the end tag can always be left out. TR acts as a container for table cells. It has two attributes:

| | |
|---|---|
| align | Sets the default horizontal alignment of cell contents. It takes one of the case insensitive values—LEFT, CENTER, or RIGHT—and plays the same role as the ALIGN attribute on paragraph elements. |
| valign | This can be used to set the default vertical alignment of cell contents within each cell. It takes one of the case-insensitive values—TOP, MIDDLE, or BOTTOM—to position the cell contents at the top, middle, or bottom of the cell, respectively. |

There are two elements for defining table cells. TH is used for header cells and TD for data cells. This distinction allows user agents to render header and data cells in different fonts, and enables speech based browsers to do a better job. The start tags for TH and TD are always needed, but the end tags can be left out. Table cells can have the following attributes:

**B**

**HTML 3.2 REFERENCE SPECIFICATION**

| nowrap | The presence of this attribute disables automatic word wrap within the contents of this cell (for example `<TD NOWRAP>`). This is equivalent to using the ` ` entity for nonbreaking spaces within the content of the cell. |
|---|---|
| rowspan | This takes a positive integer value specifying the number of rows spanned by this cell. It defaults to one. |
| colspan | This takes a positive integer value specifying the number of columns spanned by this cell. It defaults to one. |
| align | Specifies the default horizontal alignment of cell contents, and over-rides the `ALIGN` attribute on the table row. It takes the same values: `LEFT`, `CENTER`, and `RIGHT`. If you don't specify an `ALIGN` attribute value on the cell, the default is left alignment for `<td>` and center alignment for `<th>`, although you can override this with an `ALIGN` attribute on the `TR` element. |
| valign | Specifies the default vertical alignment of cell contents, overriding the `VALIGN` attribute on the table row. It takes the same values: `TOP`, `MIDDLE`, and `BOTTOM`. If you don't specify a `VALIGN` attribute value on the cell, the default is middle although you can override this with a `VALIGN` attribute on the `TR` element. |
| width | Specifies the suggested width for a cell content in pixels excluding the cell padding. This value will normally be used except when it conflicts with the width requirements for other cells in the same column. |
| height | Specifies the suggested height for a cell content in pixels excluding the cell padding. This value will normally be used except when it conflicts with the height requirements for other cells in the same row. |

Tables are commonly rendered in bas-relief, raised up with the outer border as a bevel, and individual cells inset into this raised surface. Borders around individual cells are only drawn if the cell has explicit content. White space doesn't count for this purpose with the exception of ` `.

The algorithms used to automatically size tables should take into account the minimum and maximum width requirements for each cell. This is used to determine the minimum and maximum width requirements for each column and hence for the table itself.

Cells spanning more than one column contribute to the widths of each of the columns spanned. One approach is to evenly apportion the cell's minimum and maximum width between these columns; another is to weight the apportioning according to the contributions from cells that don't span multiple columns.

For some user agents it may be necessary or desirable to break text lines within words. In such cases a visual indication that this has occurred is advised.

The minimum and maximum width of nested tables contribute to the minimum and maximum width of the cell in which they occur. Once the width requirements are known for the top-level table, the column widths for that table can be assigned. This allows the widths of nested tables to be assigned and hence, in turn, the column widths of such tables. If practical, all columns should be assigned at least their minimum widths. It is suggested that any surplus space is then shared out proportional to the difference between the minimum and maximum width requirements of each column.

Note that pixel values for width and height refer to screen pixels, and should be multiplied by an appropriate factor when rendering to very high resolution devices such as laser printers. For instance, if a user agent has a display with 75 pixels per inch and is rendering to a laser printer with 600 dots per inch, then the pixel values given in HTML attributes should be multiplied by a factor of 8.

# Text-Level Elements

These don't cause paragraph breaks. Text-level elements that define character styles can generally be nested. They can contain other text-level elements but not block-level elements.

- Font style elements
- Phrase elements
- Form fields
- The A (anchor) element
- IMG—inline images
- APPLET *(Java Applets)*
- FONT elements
- BASEFONT elements
- BR—line breaks
- MAP—client-side image maps

## Font Style Elements

These all require start and end tags, for example:

```
This has some <B>bold text.</B>
```

Text-level elements must be properly nested; the following is in error:

```
This has some <B>bold and <I></B>italic text</I>.
```

User agents should do their best to respect nested emphasis, for example:

```
This has some <B>bold and <I>italic text</I></B>.
```

Where the available fonts are restricted or for speech output, alternative means should be used for rendering differences in emphasis.

| | |
|---|---|
| TT | Teletype or monospaced text |
| I | Italic text style |
| B | Bold text style |
| U | Underlined text style |
| STRIKE | Strike-through text style |
| BIG | Places text in a large font |
| SMALL | Places text in a small font |
| SUB | Places text in subscript style |
| SUP | Places text in superscript style |

*Note: future revisions to HTML may phase out* STRIKE *in favor of the more concise* S *tag from HTML 3.0.*

## Phrase Elements

These all require start and end tags, for example:

```
This has some <EM>emphasized text</EM>.
```

| | |
|---|---|
| EM | Basic emphasis typically rendered in an italic font |
| STRONG | Strong emphasis typically rendered in a bold font |
| DFN | Defining instance of the enclosed term |
| CODE | Used for extracts from program code |
| SAMP | Used for sample output from programs, scripts, etc. |
| KBD | Used for text to be typed by the user |
| VAR | Used for variables or arguments to commands |
| CITE | Used for citations or references to other sources |

## Form Fields

INPUT, SELECT, and TEXTAREA are only allowed within FORM elements. INPUT can be used for a variety of form fields, including single-line text fields, password fields, checkboxes, radio buttons, submit and reset buttons, hidden fields, file upload, and image buttons. SELECT elements are used for single or multiple choice menus. TEXTAREA elements are used to define multiline text fields. The content of the element is used to initialize the field.

## INPUT Text Fields, Radio Buttons, Checkboxes...

INPUT elements are not containers, so the end tag is forbidden.

```
<!ENTITY % IAlign "(top¦middle¦bottom¦left¦right)">

<!ENTITY % InputType
        "(TEXT ¦ PASSWORD ¦ CHECKBOX ¦ RADIO ¦ SUBMIT
            ¦ RESET ¦ FILE ¦ HIDDEN ¦ IMAGE)">

<!ELEMENT INPUT - O EMPTY>
<!ATTLIST INPUT
        type %InputType TEXT      -- what kind of widget is needed --
        name  CDATA #IMPLIED      -- required for all but submit and reset --
        value CDATA #IMPLIED      -- required for radio and checkboxes --
        checked (checked) #IMPLIED -- for radio buttons and check boxes --
        size CDATA  #IMPLIED      -- specific to each type of field --
        maxlength NUMBER #IMPLIED
        src    %URL  #IMPLIED     -- for fields with background images --
        align %IAlign #IMPLIED    -- vertical or horizontal alignment --
        >
```

## type

Used to set the type of input field, as follows:

### type=text (the default)

A single-line text field whose visible size can be set using the size attribute, for example size=40 for a 40 character wide field. Users should be able to type more than this limit, though, with the text scrolling through the field to keep the input cursor in view. You can enforce an upper limit on the number of characters that can be entered with the MAXLENGTH attribute. The NAME attribute is used to name the field, while the VALUE attribute can be used to initialize the text string shown in the field when the document is first loaded.

```
<input type=text size=40 name=user value="your name">
```

### type=password

This is like type=text, but echoes characters using a character like * to hide the text from prying eyes when entering passwords. You can use SIZE and MAXLENGTH attributes to control the visible and maximum length exactly as per regular text fields.

```
<input type=password size=12 name=pw>
```

### type=checkbox

Used for simple Boolean attributes, or for attributes that can take multiple values at the same time. The latter is represented by several checkbox fields with the same name

and a different value attribute. Each checked checkbox generates a separate name/
value pair in the submitted data, even if this results in duplicate names. Use the
checked attribute to initialize the checkbox to its checked state.

```
<input type=checkbox checked name=uscitizen value=yes>
```

**type=radio**

Used for attributes which can take a single value from a set of alternatives. Each radio
button field in the group should be given the same name. Radio buttons require an
explicit value attribute. Only the checked radio button in the group generates a name/
value pair in the submitted data. One radio button in each group should be initially
checked using the checked attribute.

```
<input type=radio name=age value="0-12">
<input type=radio name=age value="13-17">
<input type=radio name=age value="18-25">
<input type=radio name=age value="26-35" checked>
<input type=radio name=age value="36-">
```

**type=submit**

This defines a button that users can click to submit the form's contents to the server.
The button's label is set from the VALUE attribute. If the NAME attribute is given, then
the submit button's name/value pair will be included in the submitted data. You can
include several submit buttons in the form. See type=image for graphical submit
buttons.

```
<input type=submit value="Party on ...">
```

**type=image**

This is used for graphical submit buttons rendered by an image rather than a text
string. The URL for the image is specified with the SRC attribute. The image alignment can be specified with the ALIGN attribute. In this respect, graphical submit
buttons are treated identically to IMG elements, so you can set align to left, right, top,
middle, or bottom. The x and y values of the location clicked are passed to the server:
In the submitted data, image fields are included as two name/value pairs. The names
are derived by taking the name of the field and appending ".x" for the x value, and
".y" for the y value.

```
<p>Now choose a point on the map:
```

```
    <input type=image name=point src="map.gif">
```

*Note: image fields typically cause problems for text-only and speech-based user agents!*

**type=reset**

This defines a button that users can click to reset form fields to their initial state when
the document was first loaded. You can set the label by providing a value attribute.
Reset buttons are never sent as part of the form's contents.

```
<input type=reset value="Start over ...">
```

**type=file**

This provides a means for users to attach a file to the form's contents. It is generally rendered by text field and an associated button which when clicked invokes a file browser to select a filename. The filename can also be entered directly in the text field. Just like `type=text`, you can use the `SIZE` attribute to set the visible width of this field in average character widths. You can set an upper limit to the length of filenames using the `MAXLENGTH` attribute. Some user agents support the ability to restrict the kinds of files to those matching a comma-separated list of MIME content types given with the `ACCEPT` attribute, for example `accept="image/*"` restricts files to images. Further information can be found in RFC 1867.

```
<input type=file name=photo size=20 accept="image/*">
```

**type=hidden**

These fields should not be rendered and provide a means for servers to store state information with a form. This will be passed back to the server when the form is submitted, using the name/value pair defined by the corresponding attributes. This is a work around for the statefulness of HTTP. Another approach is to use HTTP "Cookies."

```
<input type=hidden name=customerid value="c2415-345-8563">
```

# name

Used to define the property name that will be used to identify this field's content when it is submitted to the server.

# value

Used to initialize the field, or to provide a textual label for submit and reset buttons.

# checked

The presence of this attribute is used to initialize checkboxes and radio buttons to their checked state.

# size

Used to set the visible size of text fields to a given number of average character widths, for example `size=20`.

# maxlength

Sets the maximum number of characters permitted in a text field.

# src

Specifies a URL for the image to use with a graphical submit button.

## align

Used to specify image alignment for graphical submit buttons. It is defined just like the `IMG` align attribute and takes one of the values `top`, `middle`, `bottom`, `left` or `right`, defaulting to `bottom`.

## SELECT Menus

```
<!ELEMENT SELECT - - (OPTION+)>
<!ATTLIST SELECT
        name CDATA #REQUIRED
        size NUMBER #IMPLIED
        multiple (multiple) #IMPLIED
        >

<!ELEMENT OPTION - O (#PCDATA)*>
<!ATTLIST OPTION
        selected (selected) #IMPLIED
        value  CDATA  #IMPLIED -- defaults to element content --
        >
```

`SELECT` is used to define select one from many or many from many menus. `SELECT` elements require start and end tags and contain one or more `OPTION` elements that define menu items. One from many menus are generally rendered as drop-down menus while many from many menus are generally shown as list boxes.

Example:

```
<SELECT NAME="flavor">
<OPTION VALUE=a>Vanilla
<OPTION VALUE=b>Strawberry
<OPTION VALUE=c>Rum and Raisin
<OPTION VALUE=d>Peach and Orange
</SELECT>
```

`SELECT` attributes:

| | |
|---|---|
| name | This specifies a property name that is used to identify the menu choice when the form is submitted to the server. Each selected option results in a property name/value pair being included as part of the form's contents. |
| size | This sets the number of visible choices for many menus. |
| multiple | The presence of this attribute signifies that the users can make multiple selections. By default only one selection is allowed. |

`OPTION` attributes:

| | |
|---|---|
| selected | When this attribute is present, the option is selected when the document is initially loaded. It is an error for more than one option to be so selected for one from many menus. |

value      Specifies the property value to be used when submitting the form's content. This is combined with the property name as given by the NAME attribute of the parent SELECT element.

# TEXTAREA Multiline Text Fields

```
<!-- Multi-line text input field. -->

<!ELEMENT TEXTAREA - - (#PCDATA)*>
<!ATTLIST TEXTAREA
        name CDATA #REQUIRED
        rows NUMBER #REQUIRED
        cols NUMBER #REQUIRED
        >
```

TEXTAREA elements require start and end tags. The content of the element is restricted to text and character entities. It is used to initialize the text that is shown when the document is first loaded.

Example:

```
<TEXTAREA NAME=address ROWS=4 COLS=40>
Your address here ...
</TEXTAREA>
```

It is recommended that user agents canonize line endings to CR, LF (ASCII decimal 13, 10) when submitting the field's contents. The character set for submitted data should be ISO Latin-1, unless the server has previously indicated that it can support alternative character sets.

name      This specifies a property name that is used to identify the textarea field when the form is submitted to the server.

rows      Specifies the number of visible text lines. Users should be able to enter more lines that this, so user agents should provide some means to scroll through the contents of the textarea field when the contents extend beyond the visible area.

cols      Specifies the visible width in average character widths. Users should be able to enter longer lines that this, so user agents should provide some means to scroll through the contents of the textarea field when the contents extend beyond the visible area. User agents may wrap visible text lines to keep long lines visible without the need for scrolling.

# Special Text-Level Elements

A (anchor), IMG, APPLET, FONT, BASEFONT, BR, and MAP.

## The A (anchor) Element

```
<!ELEMENT A - - (%text)* -(A)>
<!ATTLIST A
          name     CDATA    #IMPLIED    -- named link end --
          href     %URL     #IMPLIED    -- URL for linked resource --
          rel      CDATA    #IMPLIED    -- forward link types --
          rev      CDATA    #IMPLIED    -- reverse link types --
          title    CDATA    #IMPLIED    -- advisory title string --
          >
```

Anchors can't be nested and always require start and end tags. They are used to define hypertext links and also to define named locations for use as targets for hypertext links, for example:

```
The way to <a href="hands-on.html">happiness</a>.
```

They are also used to define named locations for use as targets for hypertext links, for example:

```
<h2><a name=mit>545 Tech Square - Hacker's Paradise</a></h2>
```

name
: This should be a string defining unique name for the scope of the current HTML document. NAME is used to associate a name with this part of a document for use with URLs that target a named section of a document.

href
: Specifies a URL acting as a network address for the linked resource. This could be another HTML document, a PDF file, an image, and so on.

rel
: The forward relationship also known as the "link type". It can be used to determine to how deal with the linked resource when printing out a collection of linked resources.

rev
: This defines a reverse relationship. A link from document A to document B with REV=relation expresses the same relationship as a link from B to A with REL=relation. REV=made is sometimes used to identify the document author, either the author's e-mail address with a mailto URL, or a link to the author's home page.

title
: An advisory title for the linked resource.

## IMG—Inline Images

```
<!ENTITY % IAlign "(top¦middle¦bottom¦left¦right)">

<!ELEMENT IMG    - O EMPTY --  Embedded image -->
<!ATTLIST IMG
          src      %URL      #REQUIRED   -- URL of image to embed --
          alt      CDATA     #IMPLIED    -- for display in place of image --
          align    %IAlign   #IMPLIED    -- vertical or horizontal alignment --
          height   %Pixels   #IMPLIED    -- suggested height in pixels --
          width    %Pixels   #IMPLIED    -- suggested width in pixels --
```

```
border  %Pixels  #IMPLIED   -- suggested link border width --
hspace  %Pixels  #IMPLIED   -- suggested horizontal gutter --
vspace  %Pixels  #IMPLIED   -- suggested vertical gutter --
usemap  %URL     #IMPLIED   -- use client-side image map --
ismap   (ismap)  #IMPLIED   -- use server image map --
>
```

Used to insert images. IMG is an empty element and so the end tag is forbidden. Images can be positioned vertically relative to the current textline or floated to the left or right. See BR with the CLEAR attribute for control over textflow.

`e.g. <IMG SRC="canyon.gif" ALT="Grand Canyon">`

IMG elements support the following attributes:

src
: This attribute is required for every IMG element. It specifies a URL for the image resource, for instance a GIF, JPEG or PNG image file.

alt
: This is used to provide a text description of the image and is vital for interoperability with speech-based and text only user agents.

align
: This specifies how the image is positioned relative to the current textline in which it occurs:

align=top positions the top of the image with the top of the current text line. User agents vary in how they interpret this. Some only take into account what has occurred on the text line prior to the IMG element and ignore what happens after it.

align=middle aligns the middle of the image with the baseline for the current textline.

align=bottom is the default and aligns the bottom of the image with the baseline.

align=left floats the image to the current left margin, temporarily changing this margin, so that subsequent text is flowed along the image's righthand side. The rendering depends on whether there is any left aligned text or images that appear earlier than the current image in the markup. Such text (but not images) generally forces left-aligned images to wrap to a new line, with the subsequent text continuing on the former line.

align=right floats the image to the current right margin, temporarily changing this margin, so that subsequent text is flowed along the image's lefthand side. The rendering depends on whether there is any right aligned text or images that appear earlier than the current image in the markup. Such text (but not images) generally forces right-aligned images to wrap to a new line, with the subsequent text continuing on the former line.

Note that some browsers introduce spurious spacing with multiple left- right-aligned images. As a result, authors can't depend on this being the same for browsers from different vendors. See BR for ways to control text flow.

| | |
|---|---|
| width | Specifies the intended width of the image in pixels. When given together with the height, this allows user agents to reserve screen space for the image before the image data has arrived over the network. |
| height | Specifies the intended height of the image in pixels. When given together with the width, this allows user agents to reserve screen space for the image before the image data has arrived over the network. |
| border | When the IMG element appears as part of a hypertext link, the user agent will generally indicate this by drawing a colored border (typically blue) around the image. This attribute can be used to set the width of this border in pixels. Use border=0 to suppress the border altogether. User agents are recommended to provide additional cues that the image is clickable, for example by changing the mouse pointer. |
| hspace | This can be used to provide white space to the immediate left and right of the image. The HSPACE attribute sets the width of this white space in pixels. By default HSPACE is a small, nonzero number. |
| vspace | This can be used to provide white space above and below the image The VSPACE attribute sets the height of this white space in pixels. By default VSPACE is a small, nonzero number. |
| usemap | This can be used to give a URL fragment identifier for a client-side image map defined with the MAP element. |
| ismap | When the IMG element is part of a hypertext link, and the user clicks on the image, the ISMAP attribute causes the location to be passed to the server. This mechanism causes problems for text-only and speech-based user agents. Whenever it's possible to do so, use the MAP element instead. |

Here is an example of how you use ISMAP:

```
<a href="/cgibin/navbar.map"><img src=navbar.gif ismap border=0></a>
```

The location clicked is passed to the server as follows. The user agent derives a new URL from the URL specified by the HREF attribute by appending ?, the x coordinate, and the y coordinate of the location in pixels. The link is then followed using the new URL. For instance, if the user clicked at the location x=10, y=27 then the derived URL will be "/cgibin/navbar.map?10,27". It is generally a good idea to suppress the border and use graphical idioms to indicate that the image is clickable.

Note that pixel values refer to screen pixels, and should be multiplied by an appropriate factor when rendering to very high resolution devices such as laser printers. For instance, if a user agent has a display with 75 pixels per inch and is rendering to a laser printer with 600 dots per inch, then the pixel values given in HTML attributes should be multiplied by a factor of 8.

## APPLET (Java Applets)

```
<!ELEMENT APPLET - - (PARAM | %text)*>
<!ATTLIST APPLET
        codebase %URL      #IMPLIED    -- code base --
        code     CDATA     #REQUIRED   -- class file --
        alt      CDATA     #IMPLIED    -- for display in place of applet --
        name     CDATA     #IMPLIED    -- applet name --
        width    %Pixels   #REQUIRED   -- suggested width in pixels --
        height   %Pixels   #REQUIRED   -- suggested height in pixels --
        align    %IAlign   #IMPLIED    -- vertical or horizontal alignment --
        hspace   %Pixels   #IMPLIED    -- suggested horizontal gutter --
        vspace   %Pixels   #IMPLIED    -- suggested vertical gutter --
        >

<!ELEMENT PARAM - O EMPTY>
<!ATTLIST PARAM
    name    NMTOKEN    #REQUIRED   -- The name of the parameter --
    value   CDATA      #IMPLIED    -- The value of the parameter --
    >
```

Requires start and end tags. This element is supported by all Java-enabled browsers. It allows you to embed a Java applet into HTML documents. APPLET uses associated PARAM elements to pass parameters to the applet. Following the PARAM elements, the content of APPLET elements should be used to provide an alternative to the applet for user agents that don't support Java. It is restricted to text-level markup as defined by the %text entity in the DTD. Java-compatible browsers ignore this extra HTML code. You can use it to show a snapshot of the applet running, with text explaining what the applet does. Other possibilities for this area are a link to a page that is more useful for the Java-ignorant browser, or text that taunts the user for not having a Java-compatible browser.

Here is a simple example of a Java applet:

```
<applet code="Bubbles.class" width=500 height=500>
Java applet that draws animated bubbles.
</applet>
```

Here is another one using a PARAM element:

```
<applet code="AudioItem" width=15 height=15>
<param name=snd value="Hello.au|Welcome.au">
Java applet that plays a welcoming sound.
</applet>
```

| | |
|---|---|
| codebase = *codebaseURL* | This optional attribute specifies the base URL of the applet—the directory or folder that contains the applet's code. If this attribute is not specified, then the document's URL is used. |
| code = *appletFile* | This required attribute gives the name of the file that contains the applet's compiled Applet subclass. This file is relative to the base URL of the applet. It cannot be absolute. |
| alt = *alternateText* | This optional attribute specifies any text that should be displayed if the browser understands the <APPLET> tag but can't run Java applets. |
| name = *appletInstanceName* | This optional attribute specifies a name for the applet instance, which makes it possible for applets on the same page to find (and communicate with) each other. |
| width = *pixels*<br>height = *pixels* | These required attributes give the initial width and height (in pixels) of the applet display area, not counting any windows or dialogs that the applet brings up. |
| align = *alignment* | This attribute specifies the alignment of the applet. This attribute is defined in exactly the same way as the IMG element. The permitted values are top, middle, bottom, left, and right. The default is bottom. |
| vspace = *pixels*<br>hspace = *pixels* | These optional attributes specify the number of pixels above and below the applet (VSPACE) and on each side of the applet (HSPACE). They're treated the same way as the IMG element's VSPACE and HSPACE attributes. |

The PARAM element is used to pass named parameters to applet:

```
<PARAM NAME = appletParameter VALUE = value>
```

PARAM elements are the only way to specify applet-specific parameters. Applets read user-specified values for parameters with the getParameter() method.

```
name = applet parameter name

value = parameter value
```

SGML character entities such &eacute;, &quot; and &#185; are expanded before the parameter value is passed to the applet. To include an & character, use &amp;.

*Note: PARAM elements should be placed at the start of the content for the APPLET element. This is not specified as part of the DTD due to technicalities with SGML mixed content models.*

# FONT

```
<!ELEMENT FONT - - (%text)*      -- local change to font -->
<!ATTLIST FONT
     size    CDATA    #IMPLIED    -- [+]nn e.g. size="+1", size=4 --
     color   CDATA    #IMPLIED    -- #RRGGBB in hex, e.g. red: color="#FF0000" --
     >
```

Requires start and end tags. This allows you to change the font size and/or color for the enclosed text.

The attributes are SIZE and COLOR. Font sizes are given in terms of a scalar range defined by the user agent with no direct mapping to point sizes etc. The FONT element may be phased out in future revisions to HTML.

size
This sets the font size for the contents of the font element. You can set size to an integer ranging from 1 to 7 for an absolute font size, or specify a relative font size with a signed integer value, for example size="+1" or size="-2". This is mapped to an absolute font size by adding the current base font size as set by the BASEFONT element (see following).

color
Used to set the color to stroke the text. Colors are given as RGB in hexadecimal notation or as one of 16 widely understood color names defined as per the BGCOLOR attribute on the BODY element.

Some user agents also support a FACE attribute which accepts a comma separated list of font names in order of preference. This is used to search for an installed font with the corresponding name. FACE is not part of HTML 3.2.

The following shows the effects of setting font to absolute sizes:

size=1 size=2 size=3 size=4 size=5 size=6 size=7

The following shows the effect of relative font sizes using a base font size of 3:

size=-4 size=-3 size=-2 size=-1 size=+1 size=+2 size=+3 size=+4

The same thing with a base font size of 6:

size=-4 size=-3 size=-2 size=-1 size=+1 size=+2 size=+3 size=+4

## BASEFONT

```
<!ELEMENT BASEFONT - O EMPTY      -- base font size (1 to 7) -->
<!ATTLIST BASEFONT
    size    CDATA   #IMPLIED      -- e.g. size=4, defaults to 3 --
    >
```

Used to set the base font size. BASEFONT is an empty element, so the end tag is forbidden. The SIZE attribute is an integer value ranging from 1 to 7. The base font size applies to the normal and preformatted text but not to headings, except where these are modified using the FONT element with a relative font size.

## BR

Used to force a line break. This is an empty element, so the end tag is forbidden. The CLEAR attribute can be used to move down past floating images on either margin. <BR CLEAR=LEFT> moves down past floating images on the left margin, <BR CLEAR=RIGHT> does the same for floating images on the right margin, while <BR CLEAR=ALL> does the same for such images on both left and right margins.

## MAP

The MAP element provides a mechanism for client-side image maps. These can be placed in the same document or grouped in a separate document, although this isn't yet widely supported. The MAP element requires start and end tags. It contains one or more AREA elements that specify hotzones on the associated image and bind these hotzones to URLs.

```
<!ENTITY % SHAPE "(rect¦circle¦poly)">
<!ENTITY % COORDS "CDATA" -- comma separated list of numbers -->

<!ELEMENT MAP - - (AREA)+>
<!ATTLIST MAP
    name    CDATA   #REQUIRED
    >

<!ELEMENT AREA - O EMPTY>
<!ATTLIST AREA
    shape   %SHAPE   rect
    coords  %COORDS #IMPLIED  -- defines coordinates for shape --
    href    %URL    #IMPLIED  -- this region acts as hypertext link --
    nohref (nohref) #IMPLIED  -- this region has no action --
    alt     CDATA   #REQUIRED -- needed for non-graphical user agents --
    >
```

Here is a simple example for a graphical navigational toolbar:

```
<img src="navbar.gif" border=0 usemap="#map1">

<map name="map1">
 <area href=guide.html alt="Access Guide" shape=rect coords="0,0,118,28">
 <area href=search.html alt="Search" shape=rect coords="184,0,276,28">
 <area href=shortcut.html alt="Go" shape=rect coords="118,0,184,28">
 <area href=top10.html alt="Top Ten" shape=rect coords="276,0,373,28">
</map>
```

The MAP element has one attribute, NAME, which is used to associate a name with a map. This is then used by the USEMAP attribute on the IMG element to reference the map via a URL fragment identifier. Note that the value of the NAME attribute is case sensitive.

The AREA element is an empty element, and so the end tag is forbidden. It takes the following attributes: SHAPE, COORDS, HREF, NOHREF, and ALT. The SHAPE and COORDS attributes define a region on the image. If the SHAPE attribute is omitted, SHAPE="RECT" is assumed.

```
shape=rect coords="left-x, top-y, right-x, bottom-y"
shape=circle coords="center-x, center-y, radius"
shape=poly coords="x1,y1,x2,y2,x3,y3, ..."
```

Where x and y are measured in pixels from the left/top of the associated image. If x and y values are given with a percent sign as a suffix, the values should be interpreted as percentages of the image's width and height, respectively. For example:

```
SHAPE=RECT COORDS="0, 0, 50%, 100%"
```

The HREF attribute gives a URL for the target of the hypertext link. The NOHREF attribute is used when you want to define a region that doesn't act as a hotzone. This is useful when you want to cut a hole in an underlying region acting as a hotzone.

If two or more regions overlap, the region defined first in the map definition takes precedence over subsequent regions. This means that AREA elements with NOHREF should generally be placed before ones with the HREF attribute.

The ALT attribute is used to provide text labels which can be displayed in the status line as the mouse or other pointing device is moved over hotzones, or for constructing a textual menu for nongraphical user agents. Authors are *strongly recommended* to provide meaningful ALT attributes to support interoperability with speech-based or text-only user agents.

B

HTML 3.2
REFERENCE
SPECIFICATION

# Sample SGML Open Catalog for HTML 3.2

This can be used with an SGML parser like nsgmls to verify that files conform to the HTML 3.2 DTD. It assumes that the DTD has been saved as the file HTML32.dtd and that the Latin-1 entities are in the file ISOlat1.ent.

```
-- html32.soc: catalog for parsing HTML 3.2 documents --
SGMLDECL "HTML32.dcl"
PUBLIC "-//W3C//DTD HTML 3.2 Final//EN" HTML32.dtd
PUBLIC "-//W3C//DTD HTML 3.2 Draft//EN" HTML32.dtd
PUBLIC "-//W3C//DTD HTML 3.2//EN" HTML32.dtd
PUBLIC "ISO 8879-1986//ENTITIES Added Latin 1//EN//HTML" ISOlat1.ent
```

# SGML Declaration for HTML 3.2

This uses the eight-bit ISO Latin-1 character set. The size limits on properties like literals and tag names have been considerably increased from their HTML 2.0 values, but it is recommended that user agents avoid imposing arbitrary length limits.

```
<!SGML   "ISO 8879:1986"
    --
         SGML Declaration for HyperText Markup Language version 3.2

         With support for ISO Latin-1 and increased limits
         for tag and literal lengths etc.
    --

    CHARSET
         BASESET  "ISO 646:1983//CHARSET
                  International Reference Version
                  (IRV)//ESC 2/5 4/0"
         DESCSET  0    9   UNUSED
                  9    2   9
                  11   2   UNUSED
                  13   1   13
                  14   18  UNUSED
                  32   95  32
                  127  1   UNUSED
         BASESET  "ISO Registration Number 100//CHARSET
                  ECMA-94 Right Part of
                  Latin Alphabet Nr. 1//ESC 2/13 4/1"
         DESCSET  128  32  UNUSED
                  160  96  32

    CAPACITY   SGMLREF
               TOTALCAP     200000
               GRPCAP       150000
               ENTCAP       150000

    SCOPE    DOCUMENT
    SYNTAX
         SHUNCHAR CONTROLS 0 1 2 3 4 5 6 7 8 9 10 11 12 13 14 15 16
                  17 18 19 20 21 22 23 24 25 26 27 28 29 30 31 127
         BASESET  "ISO 646:1983//CHARSET
                  International Reference Version
                  (IRV)//ESC 2/5 4/0"
         DESCSET  0 128 0

         FUNCTION
                  RE           13
                  RS           10
                  SPACE        32
                  TAB SEPCHAR   9

         NAMING   LCNMSTRT  ""
                  UCNMSTRT  ""
                  LCNMCHAR  ".-"
                  UCNMCHAR  ".-"
                  NAMECASE  GENERAL YES
                            ENTITY  NO
         DELIM    GENERAL   SGMLREF
                  SHORTREF  SGMLREF
         NAMES    SGMLREF
```

```
QUANTITY SGMLREF
         ATTSPLEN 65536
         LITLEN   65536
         NAMELEN  65536
         PILEN    65536
         TAGLVL   100
         TAGLEN   65536
         GRPGTCNT 150
         GRPCNT   64


FEATURES
   MINIMIZE
      DATATAG   NO
      OMITTAG   YES
      RANK      NO
      SHORTTAG  YES
   LINK
      SIMPLE    NO
      IMPLICIT  NO
      EXPLICIT  NO
   OTHER
      CONCUR    NO
      SUBDOC    NO
      FORMAL    YES
   APPINFO      NONE
>
```

# HTML 3.2 Document Type Definition

```
<!--
        W3C Document Type Definition for the HyperText Markup Language
        version 3.2 as ratified by a vote of W3C member companies.
        For more information on W3C look at  URL http://www.w3.org/

        Date: Tuesday January 14th 1997

        Author: Dave Raggett <dsr@w3.org>

        HTML 3.2 aims to capture recommended practice as of early '96
        and as such to be used as a replacement for HTML 2.0 (RFC 1866).
        Widely deployed rendering attributes are included where they
        have been shown to be interoperable. SCRIPT and STYLE are
        included to smooth the introduction of client-side scripts
        and style sheets. Browsers must avoid showing the contents
        of these element Otherwise support for them is not required.
        ID, CLASS and STYLE attributes are not included in this version
        of HTML.
-->

<!ENTITY % HTML.Version
        "-//W3C//DTD HTML 3.2 Final//EN"

        -- Typical usage:
```

```
                    <!DOCTYPE HTML PUBLIC "-//W3C//DTD HTML 3.2 Final//EN">
                    <html>
                    ...
                    </html>
              --
              >

<!--================== Deprecated Features Switch ==========================-->

<!ENTITY % HTML.Deprecated "INCLUDE">

<!--================== Imported Names ======================================-->

<!ENTITY % Content-Type "CDATA"
        -- meaning a MIME content type, as per RFC1521
        -->

<!ENTITY % HTTP-Method "GET | POST"
        -- as per HTTP specification
        -->

<!ENTITY % URL "CDATA"
        -- The term URL means a CDATA attribute
           whose value is a Uniform Resource Locator,
           See RFC1808 (June 95) and RFC1738 (Dec 94).
        -->

<!-- Parameter Entities -->

<!ENTITY % head.misc "SCRIPT|STYLE|META|LINK" -- repeatable head elements -->

<!ENTITY % heading "H1|H2|H3|H4|H5|H6">

<!ENTITY % list "UL | OL |  DIR | MENU">

<![ %HTML.Deprecated [
    <!ENTITY % preformatted "PRE | XMP | LISTING">
]]>

<!ENTITY % preformatted "PRE">

<!--================= Character mnemonic entities ==========================-->

<!ENTITY % ISOlat1 PUBLIC
       "ISO 8879-1986//ENTITIES Added Latin 1//EN//HTML">
%ISOlat1;

<!--================= Entities for special symbols =========================-->
<!-- &trade and &cbsp are not widely deployed and so not included here -->

<!ENTITY amp      CDATA "&#38;"   -- ampersand          -->
<!ENTITY gt       CDATA "&#62;"   -- greater than        -->
<!ENTITY lt       CDATA "&#60;"   -- less than           -->
```

```
<!--=================== Text Markup ========================================-->

<!ENTITY % font "TT ¦ I ¦ B  ¦ U ¦ STRIKE ¦ BIG ¦ SMALL ¦ SUB ¦ SUP">

<!ENTITY % phrase "EM ¦ STRONG ¦ DFN ¦ CODE ¦ SAMP ¦ KBD ¦ VAR ¦ CITE">

<!ENTITY % special "A ¦ IMG ¦ APPLET ¦ FONT ¦ BASEFONT ¦ BR ¦ SCRIPT ¦ MAP">

<!ENTITY % form "INPUT ¦ SELECT ¦ TEXTAREA">

<!ENTITY % text "#PCDATA ¦ %font ¦ %phrase ¦ %special ¦ %form">

<!ELEMENT (%font¦%phrase) - - (%text)*>

<!-- there are also 16 widely known color names although
  the resulting colors are implementation dependent:

   aqua, black, blue, fuchsia, gray, green, lime, maroon,
   navy, olive, purple, red, silver, teal, white, and yellow

These colors were originally picked as being the standard
16 colors supported with the Windows VGA palette.
-->

<!ELEMENT FONT - - (%text)*      -- local change to font -->
<!ATTLIST FONT
    size    CDATA    #IMPLIED    -- [+]nn e.g. size="+1", size=4 --
    color   CDATA    #IMPLIED    -- #RRGGBB in hex, e.g. red: color="#FF0000" --
    >

<!ELEMENT BASEFONT - O EMPTY     -- base font size (1 to 7)-->
<!ATTLIST BASEFONT
    size    CDATA    #IMPLIED    -- e.g. size=3 --
    >

<!ELEMENT BR     - O EMPTY    -- forced line break -->
<!ATTLIST BR
        clear (left¦all¦right¦none) none -- control of text flow --
        >

<!--================== HTML content models ===================================-->
<!--
    HTML has three basic content models:

        %text       character level elements and text strings
        %flow       block-like elements e.g. paragraphs and lists
        %bodytext   as %flow plus headers H1-H6 and ADDRESS
-->

<!ENTITY % block
     "P ¦ %list ¦ %preformatted ¦ DL ¦ DIV ¦ CENTER ¦
      BLOCKQUOTE ¦ FORM ¦ ISINDEX ¦ HR ¦ TABLE">

<!-- %flow is used for DD and LI -->

<!ENTITY % flow "(%text ¦ %block)*">
```

```
<!--=================== Document Body ========================================-->

<!ENTITY % body.content "(%heading ¦ %text ¦ %block ¦ ADDRESS)*">

<!ENTITY % color "CDATA" -- a color specification: #HHHHHH @@ details? -->

<!ENTITY % body-color-attrs "
        bgcolor %color #IMPLIED
        text %color #IMPLIED
        link %color #IMPLIED
        vlink %color #IMPLIED
        alink %color #IMPLIED
        ">

<!ELEMENT BODY 0 0  %body.content>
<!ATTLIST BODY
        background %URL #IMPLIED  -- texture tile for document background --
        %body-color-attrs;  -- bgcolor, text, link, vlink, alink --
        >

<!ENTITY % address.content "((%text;) ¦ P)*">

<!ELEMENT ADDRESS - - %address.content>

<!ELEMENT DIV - - %body.content>
<!ATTLIST DIV
        align    (left¦center¦right) #IMPLIED -- alignment of following text --
        >

<!-- CENTER is a shorthand for DIV with ALIGN=CENTER -->
<!ELEMENT center - - %body.content>

<!--================== The Anchor Element ===================================-->

<!ELEMENT A - - (%text)* -(A)>
<!ATTLIST A
        name     CDATA     #IMPLIED     -- named link end --
        href     %URL      #IMPLIED     -- URL for linked resource --
        rel      CDATA     #IMPLIED     -- forward link types --
        rev      CDATA     #IMPLIED     -- reverse link types --
        title    CDATA     #IMPLIED     -- advisory title string --
        >

<!--================== Client-side image maps ============================-->

<!-- These can be placed in the same document or grouped in a
     separate document although this isn't yet widely supported -->

<!ENTITY % SHAPE "(rect¦circle¦poly)">
<!ENTITY % COORDS "CDATA" -- comma separated list of numbers -->

<!ELEMENT MAP - - (AREA)*>
<!ATTLIST MAP
    name     CDATA     #IMPLIED
    >
```

```
<!ELEMENT AREA - O EMPTY>
<!ATTLIST AREA
    shape    %SHAPE  rect
    coords   %COORDS #IMPLIED  -- defines coordinates for shape --
    href     %URL    #IMPLIED  -- this region acts as hypertext link --
    nohref  (nohref) #IMPLIED  -- this region has no action --
    alt      CDATA   #REQUIRED -- needed for non-graphical user agents --
    >


<!-- ================= The LINK Element ================================== -->

<!ENTITY % Types "CDATA"
        -- See Internet Draft: draft-ietf-html-relrev-00.txt
           LINK has been part of HTML since the early days
           although few browsers as yet take advantage of it.

           Relationship values can be used in principle:

                a) for document specific toolbars/menus when used
                   with the LINK element in the document head:
                b) to link to a separate style sheet
                c) to make a link to a script
                d) by stylesheets to control how collections of
                   html nodes are rendered into printed documents
                e) to make a link to a printable version of this document
                   e.g. a postscript or pdf version
-->

<!ELEMENT LINK - O EMPTY>
<!ATTLIST LINK
        href     %URL    #IMPLIED    -- URL for linked resource --
        rel      %Types  #IMPLIED    -- forward link types --
        rev      %Types  #IMPLIED    -- reverse link types --
        title    CDATA   #IMPLIED    -- advisory title string --
        >

<!-- =================== Images ==================================== -->

<!ENTITY % Length "CDATA"    -- nn for pixels or nn% for percentage length -->
<!ENTITY % Pixels "NUMBER"   -- integer representing length in pixels -->

<!-- Suggested widths are used for negotiating image size
     with the module responsible for painting the image.
     align=left or right cause image to float to margin
     and for subsequent text to wrap around image -->

<!ENTITY % IAlign "(top|middle|bottom|left|right)">

<!ELEMENT IMG    - O EMPTY --  Embedded image -->
<!ATTLIST IMG
        src      %URL    #REQUIRED  -- URL of image to embed --
        alt      CDATA   #IMPLIED   -- for display in place of image --
        align    %IAlign #IMPLIED   -- vertical or horizontal alignment --
```

```
        height  %Pixels   #IMPLIED   -- suggested height in pixels --
        width   %Pixels   #IMPLIED   -- suggested width in pixels --
        border  %Pixels   #IMPLIED   -- suggested link border width --
        hspace  %Pixels   #IMPLIED   -- suggested horizontal gutter --
        vspace  %Pixels   #IMPLIED   -- suggested vertical gutter --
        usemap  %URL      #IMPLIED   -- use client-side image map --
        ismap   (ismap)   #IMPLIED   -- use server image map --
        >

<!-- USEMAP points to a MAP element which may be in this document
  or an external document, although the latter is not widely supported -->

<!--==================== Java APPLET tag ===================================-->
<!--
  This tag is supported by all Java enabled browsers. Applet resources
  (including their classes) are normally loaded relative to the document
  URL (or <BASE> element if it is defined). The CODEBASE attribute is used
  to change this default behavior. If the CODEBASE attribute is defined then
  it specifies a different location to find applet resources. The value
  can be an absolute URL or a relative URL. The absolute URL is used as is
  without modification and is not effected by the documents <BASE> element.
  When the codebase attribute is relative, then it is relative to the
  document URL (or <BASE> tag if defined).
-->
<!ELEMENT APPLET - - (PARAM ¦ %text)*>
<!ATTLIST APPLET
        codebase %URL     #IMPLIED    -- code base --
        code     CDATA    #REQUIRED   -- class file --
        alt      CDATA    #IMPLIED    -- for display in place of applet --
        name     CDATA    #IMPLIED    -- applet name --
        width    %Pixels  #REQUIRED   -- suggested width in pixels --
        height   %Pixels  #REQUIRED   -- suggested height in pixels --
        align    %IAlign  #IMPLIED    -- vertical or horizontal alignment --
        hspace   %Pixels  #IMPLIED    -- suggested horizontal gutter --
        vspace   %Pixels  #IMPLIED    -- suggested vertical gutter --
        >

<!ELEMENT PARAM - O EMPTY>
<!ATTLIST PARAM
        name     NMTOKEN   #REQUIRED   -- The name of the parameter --
        value    CDATA     #IMPLIED    -- The value of the parameter --
        >

<!--
Here is an example:

    <applet codebase="applets/NervousText"
        code=NervousText.class
        width=300
        height=50>
    <param name=text value="Java is Cool!">
    <img src=sorry.gif alt="This looks better with Java support">
    </applet>
-->
```

```
<!--================== Horizontal Rule =====================================-->

<!ELEMENT HR      - O EMPTY>
<!ATTLIST HR
        align (left|right|center) #IMPLIED
        noshade (noshade) #IMPLIED
        size %Pixels #IMPLIED
        width %Length #IMPLIED
        >
<!--================== Paragraphs=============================================-->

<!ELEMENT P       - O (%text)*>
<!ATTLIST P
        align   (left|center|right) #IMPLIED
        >

<!--================== Headings =============================================-->

<!--
  There are six levels of headers from H1 (the most important)
  to H6 (the least important).
-->

<!ELEMENT ( %heading )  - -  (%text;)*>
<!ATTLIST ( %heading )
        align  (left|center|right) #IMPLIED
        >

<!--================== Preformatted Text =====================================-->

<!-- excludes images and changes in font size -->

<!ENTITY % pre.exclusion "IMG|BIG|SMALL|SUB|SUP|FONT">

<!ELEMENT PRE - - (%text)* -(%pre.exclusion)>
<!ATTLIST PRE
        width NUMBER #implied -- is this widely supported? --
        >

<![ %HTML.Deprecated [

<!ENTITY % literal "CDATA"
        -- historical, non-conforming parsing mode where
           the only markup signal is the end tag
           in full
        -->

<!ELEMENT (XMP|LISTING) - - %literal>
<!ELEMENT PLAINTEXT - O %literal>

]]>

<!--================== Block-like Quotes =====================================-->

<!ELEMENT BLOCKQUOTE - - %body.content>
```

```
<!--================== Lists ==================================-->

<!--
    HTML 3.2 allows you to control the sequence number for ordered lists.
    You can set the sequence number with the START and VALUE attributes.
    The TYPE attribute may be used to specify the rendering of ordered
    and unordered lists.
-->

<!-- definition lists - DT for term, DD for its definition -->

<!ELEMENT DL     - -  (DT¦DD)+>
<!ATTLIST DL
        compact (compact) #IMPLIED -- more compact style --
        >

<!ELEMENT DT - O  (%text)*>
<!ELEMENT DD - O  %flow;>

<!-- Ordered lists OL, and unordered lists UL -->
<!ELEMENT (OL¦UL) - -  (LI)+>

<!--
        Numbering style
    1    arabic numbers      1, 2, 3, ...
    a    lower alpha         a, b, c, ...
    A    upper alpha         A, B, C, ...
    i    lower roman         i, ii, iii, ...
    I    upper roman         I, II, III, ...

    The style is applied to the sequence number which by default
    is reset to 1 for the first list item in an ordered list.

    This can't be expressed directly in SGML due to case folding.
-->

<!ENTITY % OLStyle "CDATA" -- constrained to: [1¦a¦A¦i¦I] -->

<!ATTLIST OL -- ordered lists --
        type      %OLStyle   #IMPLIED    -- numbering style --
        start     NUMBER     #IMPLIED    -- starting sequence number --
        compact  (compact)   #IMPLIED    -- reduced interitem spacing --
        >

<!-- bullet styles -->

<!ENTITY % ULStyle "disc¦square¦circle">

<!ATTLIST UL -- unordered lists --
        type     (%ULStyle)  #IMPLIED    -- bullet style --
        compact (compact)    #IMPLIED    -- reduced interitem spacing --
        >

<!ELEMENT (DIR¦MENU) - -  (LI)+ -(%block)>
<!ATTLIST DIR
        compact (compact) #IMPLIED
        >
```

```
<!ATTLIST MENU
        compact (compact) #IMPLIED
        >


<!-- <DIR>               Directory list                -->
<!-- <DIR COMPACT>       Compact list style            -->
<!-- <MENU>              Menu list                     -->
<!-- <MENU COMPACT>      Compact list style            -->

<!-- The type attribute can be used to change the bullet style
     in unordered lists and the numbering style in ordered lists -->

<!ENTITY % LIStyle "CDATA" -- constrained to: "(%ULStyle|%OLStyle)" -->

<!ELEMENT LI - O %flow -- list item -->
<!ATTLIST LI
        type    %LIStyle    #IMPLIED   -- list item style --
        value   NUMBER      #IMPLIED   -- reset sequence number --
        >


<!--================ Forms ===================================================-->

<!ELEMENT FORM - - %body.content -(FORM)>
<!ATTLIST FORM
        action %URL #IMPLIED   -- server-side form handler --
        method (%HTTP-Method) GET -- see HTTP specification --
        enctype %Content-Type; "application/x-www-form-urlencoded"
        >

<!ENTITY % InputType
        "(TEXT | PASSWORD | CHECKBOX | RADIO | SUBMIT
            | RESET | FILE | HIDDEN | IMAGE)">

<!ELEMENT INPUT - O EMPTY>
<!ATTLIST INPUT
        type %InputType TEXT      -- what kind of widget is needed --
        name CDATA    #IMPLIED    -- required for all but submit and reset --
        value CDATA   #IMPLIED    -- required for radio and checkboxes --
        checked (checked) #IMPLIED -- for radio buttons and check boxes --
        size CDATA    #IMPLIED    -- specific to each type of field --
        maxlength NUMBER #IMPLIED -- max chars allowed in text fields --
        src   %URL    #IMPLIED    -- for fields with background images --
        align %IAlign #IMPLIED    -- vertical or horizontal alignment --
        >

<!ELEMENT SELECT - - (OPTION+)>
<!ATTLIST SELECT
        name CDATA #REQUIRED
        size NUMBER #IMPLIED
        multiple (multiple) #IMPLIED
        >


<!ELEMENT OPTION - O (#PCDATA)*>
<!ATTLIST OPTION
        selected (selected) #IMPLIED
        value  CDATA  #IMPLIED -- defaults to element content --
        >
```

**B**

**HTML 3.2 REFERENCE SPECIFICATION**

```
<!-- Multi-line text input field. -->

<!ELEMENT TEXTAREA - - (#PCDATA)*>
<!ATTLIST TEXTAREA
        name CDATA #REQUIRED
        rows NUMBER #REQUIRED
        cols NUMBER #REQUIRED
        >


<!--======================= Tables =========================-->

<!-- Widely deployed subset of the full table standard, see RFC 1942
     e.g. at http://www.ics.uci.edu/pub/ietf/html/rfc1942.txt -->

<!-- horizontal placement of table relative to window -->
<!ENTITY % Where "(left|center|right)">

<!-- horizontal alignment attributes for cell contents -->
<!ENTITY % cell.halign
        "align (left|center|right) #IMPLIED"
        >

<!-- vertical alignment attributes for cell contents -->
<!ENTITY % cell.valign
        "valign (top|middle|bottom)  #IMPLIED"
        >

<!ELEMENT table - - (caption?, tr+)>
<!ELEMENT tr - O (th|td)*>
<!ELEMENT (th|td) - O %body.content>

<!ATTLIST table                        -- table element --
        align       %Where;  #IMPLIED  -- table position relative to window --
        width       %Length  #IMPLIED  -- table width relative to window --
        border      %Pixels  #IMPLIED  -- controls frame width around table --
        cellspacing %Pixels #IMPLIED   -- spacing between cells --
        cellpadding %Pixels #IMPLIED   -- spacing within cells --
        >

<!ELEMENT CAPTION - - (%text;)* -- table or figure caption -->
<!ATTLIST CAPTION
        align (top|bottom) #IMPLIED
        >

<!ATTLIST tr                       -- table row --
        %cell.halign;              -- horizontal alignment in cells --
        %cell.valign;              -- vertical alignment in cells --
        >

<!ATTLIST (th|td)                      -- header or data cell --
        nowrap (nowrap)  #IMPLIED      -- suppress word wrap --
        rowspan NUMBER   1             -- number of rows spanned by cell --
        colspan NUMBER   1             -- number of cols spanned by cell --
        %cell.halign;                  -- horizontal alignment in cell --
        %cell.valign;                  -- vertical alignment in cell --
        width   %Pixels  #IMPLIED      -- suggested width for cell --
        height  %Pixels  #IMPLIED      -- suggested height for cell --
        >
```

```
<!--================= Document Head =========================================-->

<!-- %head.misc defined earlier on as "SCRIPT¦STYLE¦META¦LINK" -->

<!ENTITY % head.content "TITLE & ISINDEX? & BASE?">

<!ELEMENT HEAD O O  (%head.content) +(%head.misc)>

<!ELEMENT TITLE - -   (#PCDATA)* -(%head.misc)
            -- The TITLE element is not considered part of the flow of text.
               It should be displayed, for example as the page header or
               window title.
            -->

<!ELEMENT ISINDEX - O EMPTY>
<!ATTLIST ISINDEX
        prompt CDATA #IMPLIED -- prompt message -->

<!--
    The BASE element gives an absolute URL for dereferencing relative
    URLs, e.g.

        <BASE href="http://foo.com/index.html">
        ...
        <IMG SRC="images/bar.gif">

    The image is deferenced to

        http://foo.com/images/bar.gif

    In the absence of a BASE element the document URL should be used.
    Note that this is not necessarily the same as the URL used to
    request the document, as the base URL may be overridden by an HTTP
    header accompanying the document.
-->

<!ELEMENT BASE - O EMPTY>
<!ATTLIST BASE
        href %URL  #REQUIRED
        >

<!ELEMENT META - O EMPTY -- Generic Metainformation -->
<!ATTLIST META
        http-equiv NAME     #IMPLIED  -- HTTP response header name  --
        name       NAME     #IMPLIED  -- metainformation name       --
        content    CDATA    #REQUIRED -- associated information      --
        >

<!-- SCRIPT/STYLE are place holders for transition to next version of HTML -->

<!ELEMENT STYLE  - - CDATA -- placeholder for style info -->
<!ELEMENT SCRIPT - - CDATA -- placeholder for script statements -->

<!-- ELEMENT STYLE  - - (#PCDATA)*  -(%head.misc) -- style info -->
<!-- ELEMENT SCRIPT - - (#PCDATA)*  -(%head.misc) -- script statements -->
```

```
<!--================ Document Structure ====================================-->

<!ENTITY % version.attr "VERSION CDATA #FIXED '%HTML.Version;'">

<![ %HTML.Deprecated [
    <!ENTITY % html.content "HEAD, BODY, PLAINTEXT?">
]]>

<!ENTITY % html.content "HEAD, BODY">

<!ELEMENT HTML O O  (%html.content)>
<!ATTLIST HTML
        %version.attr;
        >
```

# Character Entities for ISO Latin-1

```
<!-- (C) International Organization for Standardization 1986
     Permission to copy in any form is granted for use with
     conforming SGML systems and applications as defined in
     ISO 8879, provided this notice is included in all copies.
     This has been extended for use with HTML to cover the full
     set of codes in the range 160-255 decimal.
-->
<!-- Character entity set. Typical invocation:
     <!ENTITY % ISOlat1 PUBLIC
       "ISO 8879-1986//ENTITIES Added Latin 1//EN//HTML">
     %ISOlat1;
-->
    <!ENTITY nbsp   CDATA " " -- no-break space -->
    <!ENTITY iexcl  CDATA "&#161;" -- inverted exclamation mark -->
    <!ENTITY cent   CDATA "&#162;" -- cent sign -->
    <!ENTITY pound  CDATA "&#163;" -- pound sterling sign -->
    <!ENTITY curren CDATA "&#164;" -- general currency sign -->
    <!ENTITY yen    CDATA "&#165;" -- yen sign -->
    <!ENTITY brvbar CDATA "&#166;" -- broken (vertical) bar -->
    <!ENTITY sect   CDATA "&#167;" -- section sign -->
    <!ENTITY uml    CDATA "&#168;" -- umlaut (dieresis) -->
    <!ENTITY copy   CDATA "&#169;" -- copyright sign -->
    <!ENTITY ordf   CDATA "&#170;" -- ordinal indicator, feminine -->
    <!ENTITY laquo  CDATA "&#171;" -- angle quotation mark, left -->
    <!ENTITY not    CDATA "&#172;" -- not sign -->
    <!ENTITY shy    CDATA "&#173;" -- soft hyphen -->
    <!ENTITY reg    CDATA "&#174;" -- registered sign -->
    <!ENTITY macr   CDATA "&#175;" -- macron -->
    <!ENTITY deg    CDATA "&#176;" -- degree sign -->
    <!ENTITY plusmn CDATA "&#177;" -- plus-or-minus sign -->
    <!ENTITY sup2   CDATA "&#178;" -- superscript two -->
    <!ENTITY sup3   CDATA "&#179;" -- superscript three -->
    <!ENTITY acute  CDATA "&#180;" -- acute accent -->
    <!ENTITY micro  CDATA "&#181;" -- micro sign -->
    <!ENTITY para   CDATA "&#182;" -- pilcrow (paragraph sign) -->
    <!ENTITY middot CDATA "&#183;" -- middle dot -->
    <!ENTITY ccedil CDATA "&#184;" -- small c, cedilla -->
    <!ENTITY sup1   CDATA "&#185;" -- superscript one -->
    <!ENTITY ordm   CDATA "&#186;" -- ordinal indicator, masculine -->
    <!ENTITY raquo  CDATA "&#187;" -- angle quotation mark, right -->
    <!ENTITY frac14 CDATA "&#188;" -- fraction one-quarter -->
    <!ENTITY frac12 CDATA "&#189;" -- fraction one-half -->
```

```
<!ENTITY frac34 CDATA "&#190;" -- fraction three-quarters -->
<!ENTITY iquest CDATA "&#191;" -- inverted question mark -->
<!ENTITY Agrave CDATA "&#192;" -- capital A, grave accent -->
<!ENTITY Aacute CDATA "&#193;" -- capital A, acute accent -->
<!ENTITY Acirc  CDATA "&#194;" -- capital A, circumflex accent -->
<!ENTITY Atilde CDATA "&#195;" -- capital A, tilde -->
<!ENTITY Auml   CDATA "&#196;" -- capital A, dieresis or umlaut mark -->
<!ENTITY Aring  CDATA "&#197;" -- capital A, ring -->
<!ENTITY AElig  CDATA "&#198;" -- capital AE diphthong (ligature) -->
<!ENTITY Ccedil CDATA "&#199;" -- capital C, cedilla -->
<!ENTITY Egrave CDATA "&#200;" -- capital E, grave accent -->
<!ENTITY Eacute CDATA "&#201;" -- capital E, acute accent -->
<!ENTITY Ecirc  CDATA "&#202;" -- capital E, circumflex accent -->
<!ENTITY Euml   CDATA "&#203;" -- capital E, dieresis or umlaut mark -->
<!ENTITY Igrave CDATA "&#204;" -- capital I, grave accent -->
<!ENTITY Iacute CDATA "&#205;" -- capital I, acute accent -->
<!ENTITY Icirc  CDATA "&#206;" -- capital I, circumflex accent -->
<!ENTITY Iuml   CDATA "&#207;" -- capital I, dieresis or umlaut mark -->
<!ENTITY ETH    CDATA "&#208;" -- capital Eth, Icelandic -->
<!ENTITY Ntilde CDATA "&#209;" -- capital N, tilde -->
<!ENTITY Ograve CDATA "&#210;" -- capital O, grave accent -->
<!ENTITY Oacute CDATA "&#211;" -- capital O, acute accent -->
<!ENTITY Ocirc  CDATA "&#212;" -- capital O, circumflex accent -->
<!ENTITY Otilde CDATA "&#213;" -- capital O, tilde -->
<!ENTITY Ouml   CDATA "&#214;" -- capital O, dieresis or umlaut mark -->
<!ENTITY times  CDATA "&#215;" -- multiply sign -->
<!ENTITY Oslash CDATA "&#216;" -- capital O, slash -->
<!ENTITY Ugrave CDATA "&#217;" -- capital U, grave accent -->
<!ENTITY Uacute CDATA "&#218;" -- capital U, acute accent -->
<!ENTITY Ucirc  CDATA "&#219;" -- capital U, circumflex accent -->
<!ENTITY Uuml   CDATA "&#220;" -- capital U, dieresis or umlaut mark -->
<!ENTITY Yacute CDATA "&#221;" -- capital Y, acute accent -->
<!ENTITY THORN  CDATA "&#222;" -- capital THORN, Icelandic -->
<!ENTITY szlig  CDATA "&#223;" -- small sharp s, German (sz ligature) -->
<!ENTITY agrave CDATA "&#224;" -- small a, grave accent -->
<!ENTITY aacute CDATA "&#225;" -- small a, acute accent -->
<!ENTITY acirc  CDATA "&#226;" -- small a, circumflex accent -->
<!ENTITY atilde CDATA "&#227;" -- small a, tilde -->
<!ENTITY auml   CDATA "&#228;" -- small a, dieresis or umlaut mark -->
<!ENTITY aring  CDATA "&#229;" -- small a, ring -->
<!ENTITY aelig  CDATA "&#230;" -- small ae diphthong (ligature) -->
<!ENTITY ccedil CDATA "&#231;" -- small c, cedilla -->
<!ENTITY egrave CDATA "&#232;" -- small e, grave accent -->
<!ENTITY eacute CDATA "&#233;" -- small e, acute accent -->
<!ENTITY ecirc  CDATA "&#234;" -- small e, circumflex accent -->
<!ENTITY euml   CDATA "&#235;" -- small e, dieresis or umlaut mark -->
<!ENTITY igrave CDATA "&#236;" -- small i, grave accent -->
<!ENTITY iacute CDATA "&#237;" -- small i, acute accent -->
<!ENTITY icirc  CDATA "&#238;" -- small i, circumflex accent -->
<!ENTITY iuml   CDATA "&#239;" -- small i, dieresis or umlaut mark -->
<!ENTITY eth    CDATA "&#240;" -- small eth, Icelandic -->
<!ENTITY ntilde CDATA "&#241;" -- small n, tilde -->
<!ENTITY ograve CDATA "&#242;" -- small o, grave accent -->
<!ENTITY oacute CDATA "&#243;" -- small o, acute accent -->
<!ENTITY ocirc  CDATA "&#244;" -- small o, circumflex accent -->
<!ENTITY otilde CDATA "&#245;" -- small o, tilde -->
<!ENTITY ouml   CDATA "&#246;" -- small o, dieresis or umlaut mark -->
<!ENTITY divide CDATA "&#247;" -- divide sign -->
<!ENTITY oslash CDATA "&#248;" -- small o, slash -->
<!ENTITY ugrave CDATA "&#249;" -- small u, grave accent -->
```

```
<!ENTITY uacute CDATA "&#250;" -- small u, acute accent -->
<!ENTITY ucirc  CDATA "&#251;" -- small u, circumflex accent -->
<!ENTITY uuml   CDATA "&#252;" -- small u, dieresis or umlaut mark -->
<!ENTITY yacute CDATA "&#253;" -- small y, acute accent -->
<!ENTITY thorn  CDATA "&#254;" -- small thorn, Icelandic -->
<!ENTITY yuml   CDATA "&#255;" -- small y, dieresis or umlaut mark -->
```

# Table of Printable Latin-1 Character Codes

| | | | | | | | | | | | | | | | |
|---|---|---|---|---|---|---|---|---|---|---|---|---|---|---|---|
| 0 | | 32 | | 64 | @ | 96 | ` | 128 | | 160 | | 192 | À | 224 | à |
| 1 | | 33 | ! | 65 | A | 97 | a | 129 | | 161 | ¡ | 193 | Á | 225 | á |
| 2 | | 34 | " | 66 | B | 98 | b | 130 | | 162 | ¢ | 194 | Â | 226 | â |
| 3 | | 35 | # | 67 | C | 99 | c | 131 | | 163 | £ | 195 | Ã | 227 | ã |
| 4 | | 36 | $ | 68 | D | 100 | d | 132 | | 164 | ¤ | 196 | Ä | 228 | ä |
| 5 | | 37 | % | 69 | E | 101 | e | 133 | | 165 | ¥ | 197 | Å | 229 | å |
| 6 | | 38 | & | 70 | F | 102 | f | 134 | | 166 | ¦ | 198 | Æ | 230 | æ |
| 7 | | 39 | ' | 71 | G | 103 | g | 135 | | 167 | § | 199 | Ç | 231 | ç |
| 8 | | 40 | ( | 72 | H | 104 | h | 136 | | 168 | ¨ | 200 | È | 232 | è |
| 9 | | 41 | ) | 73 | I | 105 | i | 137 | | 169 | © | 201 | É | 233 | é |
| 10 | | 42 | * | 74 | J | 106 | j | 138 | | 170 | ª | 202 | Ê | 234 | ê |
| 11 | | 43 | + | 75 | K | 107 | k | 139 | | 171 | « | 203 | Ë | 235 | ë |
| 12 | | 44 | , | 76 | L | 108 | l | 140 | | 172 | ¬ | 204 | Ì | 236 | ì |
| 13 | | 45 | – | 77 | M | 109 | m | 141 | | 173 | - | 205 | Í | 237 | í |
| 14 | | 46 | . | 78 | N | 110 | n | 142 | | 174 | ® | 206 | Î | 238 | î |
| 15 | | 47 | / | 79 | O | 111 | o | 143 | | 175 | ¯ | 207 | Ï | 239 | ï |
| 16 | | 48 | 0 | 80 | P | 112 | p | 144 | | 176 | ° | 208 | Đ | 240 | ð |
| 17 | | 49 | 1 | 81 | Q | 113 | q | 145 | | 177 | ± | 209 | Ñ | 241 | ñ |
| 18 | | 50 | 2 | 82 | R | 114 | r | 146 | | 178 | ² | 210 | Ò | 242 | ò |
| 19 | | 51 | 3 | 83 | S | 115 | s | 147 | | 179 | ³ | 211 | Ó | 243 | ó |
| 20 | | 52 | 4 | 84 | T | 116 | t | 148 | | 180 | ´ | 212 | Ô | 244 | ô |
| 21 | | 53 | 5 | 85 | U | 117 | u | 149 | | 181 | µ | 213 | Õ | 245 | õ |
| 22 | | 54 | 6 | 86 | V | 118 | v | 150 | | 182 | ¶ | 214 | Ö | 246 | ö |
| 23 | | 55 | 7 | 87 | W | 119 | w | 151 | | 183 | · | 215 | × | 247 | ÷ |
| 24 | | 56 | 8 | 88 | X | 120 | x | 152 | | 184 | ¸ | 216 | Ø | 248 | ø |
| 25 | | 57 | 9 | 89 | Y | 121 | y | 153 | | 185 | ¹ | 217 | Ù | 249 | ù |
| 26 | | 58 | : | 90 | Z | 122 | z | 154 | | 186 | º | 218 | Ú | 250 | ú |
| 27 | | 59 | ; | 91 | [ | 123 | { | 155 | | 187 | » | 219 | Û | 251 | û |
| 28 | | 60 | < | 92 | \ | 124 | \| | 156 | | 188 | ¼ | 220 | Ü | 252 | ü |
| 29 | | 61 | = | 93 | ] | 125 | } | 157 | | 189 | ½ | 221 | Ý | 253 | ý |
| 30 | | 62 | > | 94 | ^ | 126 | ~ | 158 | | 190 | ¾ | 222 | Þ | 254 | þ |
| 31 | | 63 | ? | 95 | _ | 127 | | 159 | | 191 | ¿ | 223 | ß | 255 | ÿ |

# Acknowledgments

The author would like to thank the members of the W3C HTML Editorial Review Board, members of the W3C staff, and the many other people who have contributed to this specification.

# Further Reading

### The World Wide Web Consortium

Further information on W3C activities and pointers to the status of work on HTML and HTTP etc. can be found at `http://www.w3.org/`. Further information on HTML in particular can be found at `http://www.w3.org/pub/WWW/MarkUp/`.

### HTML 2.0 (RFC1866)

By Tim Berners-Lee and Dan Connolly, November 1995. Defines the Hypertext Markup Language Specification Version 2.0. Available from `ftp://ds.internic.net/rfc/rfc1866.txt`.

### Form-Based File Upload in HTML (RFC1867)

By E. Nebel and L. Masinter, November 1995. Describes extensions to HTML 2.0 (RFC1866) to support file upload from HTML forms. Available from `ftp://ds.internic.net/rfc/rfc1867.txt`.

### HTML Tables (RFC1942)

By Dave Raggett, May 1996. This defines the HTML table model. It is a superset of the table model defined by HTML 3.2. Available from `ftp://ds.internic.net/rfc/rfc1942.txt`, or as a W3C working draft at `http://www.w3.org/pub/WWW/TR/WD-tables`.

### A Lexical Analyzer for HTML and Basic SGML

By Dan Connolly, June 1996. Describes lexical considerations for parsing HTML documents. Available from `http://www.w3.org/pub/WWW/TR/WD-html-lex`.

### The Hypertext Transfer Protocol (HTTP)

Further information of HTTP can be found at `http://www.w3.org/pub/WWW/Protocols`.

### A Standard Default Color Space for the Internet—sRGB

By Michael Stokes, Mathew Anderson, Srinivasan Chandrasekar, and Ricardo Motta, November 1996. Available from `http://www.w3.org/pub/WWW/Graphics/Color/sRGB.html`. This provides a precise definition for RGB that allows sRGB images to be reproduced accurately on different platforms and media under varying ambient lighting conditions.

# CSS1 Quick Reference

*by Rick Darnell*

## IN THIS APPENDIX

This appendix provides an overview of the attributes with which you can control the appearance of your HTML documents through style sheets. The World Wide Web Consortium (W3C) set the current standard for style sheets as Cascading Style Sheets 1 (CSS1). W3C's complete recommendation for CSS is located at the W3C Web site at `http://www.w3.org/pub/WWW/TR/REC-CSS1`.

For more information on using style sheets, see Chapters 19 and 20, "Introducing Cascading Style Sheets" and "Cascading Style Sheet Usage."

# Basic Syntax

All styles within a style sheet definition follow the same basic syntax. You'll notice that there are a lot of opportunities to add other attributes or members of a group:

```
SELECTOR[.class] [,SELECTOR2[.class2]] ...
{ attribute1: value1  [;
  attribute2: value2] [;
  ... ]              [;
  attributen: valuen] }
```

The `SELECTOR` is how the style is referenced within the rest of the HTML page. It uses one of the existing HTML tags, such as `<CODE>` or `<P>`, along with an optional `class` to create additional sub-styles. A `class` is a subset of a selector, allowing the same element to have a variety of styles. For example, you could color code block quotes to identify sources or speakers.

In addition to the standard HTML tags, you can use two other values for a selector: `first-line` and `first-letter`. The `first-line` value sets the style for the first line of text in a document or several passages within a document, such as paragraph or block quote. The `first-letter` value creates drop caps and other special effects on the first letter in a document or passage.

Groups of selectors and their classes are separated by commas. A member of the group receives the same style as any other member in the group. For example, if you wanted all headings to be displayed in red, you could list H1 through H6 with the attributes to set the color to red. All other tag attributes, such as size, would remain unaffected.

Another option is contextual selectors, which tell the browser what to do with a certain tag when found nested within the parent tag.

```
OUTER_SELECTOR INNER_SELECTOR {attribute:value}
```

This means that when the `INNER_SELECTOR` is used within the `OUTER_SELECTOR`, the style is used. Otherwise, other occurrences of `INNER_SELECTOR` are handled according to browser default.

After making all of the selector and group definitions, use a curly bracket along with a series of attributes and their values. Mate each attribute with its value with a colon and separate each pair from the next pair by a semicolon. The values within a definition, such as the name of a typeface or a color value, are not case-sensitive. For example, for `font-family`, you can have `Garamond`, `garamond`, or `GARAMOND`, and it will all work out the same in the browser.

As with all good syntax, you can place style definitions in three ways within a document: with an embedded style sheet, with a linked style sheet, and with an inline style sheet.

## Embedded Style Sheet

The `<STYLE>` tags contain an embedded style sheet. As a matter of structure, the format of an HTML page with an embedded style sheet is as follows:

```
<HTML>
<HEAD>...</HEAD>
<STYLE>...</STYLE>
<BODY>...</BODY>
</HTML>
```

The `<STYLE>` tags contain the list of selectors and styles.

## Linked Style Sheet

The linked style sheet is a `.css` file that contains nothing but a set of `<STYLE>` tags and their contents. Identify the style file within an HTML document using the `<LINK>` tag in the head:

```
<HEAD>
<LINK rel=stylesheet href="filename.css" type="text/css">
</HEAD>
```

At runtime, the browser will load the style in the `.css` file and use it to format the document. If the HTML page also includes an embedded style sheet that conflicts with the linked style sheet, the embedded version also takes precedence.

## Inline Style Sheet

The last option, inline style sheets, uses style sheet syntax, although it's technically not a style sheet implementation. This option uses the style sheet nomenclature to customize single incidents of tags within the document:

```
<TAG style="attribute1:value1; ...">
```

Essentially, this is a way to customize HTML tags on a case-by-case basis. When you use all three forms of syntax, they occur in a cascading form of precedence. The highest priority is inline, followed by embedded, then linked.

# Style Attributes

Several classes of attributes are used within the definition for a selector. The following sections cover each of the attributes within a class.

# Fonts

There are no current standards for typefaces and their use on different user machines, so you'll need to choose carefully and include several options to achieve the desired effect for the user.

## The `font-family` Attribute

The `font-family` attribute lists font families in order of preference, separated by commas. Two types of variables are used: family name and generic family.

```
BODY {font-family: Garamond, Palatino, Serif}
```

A family name is the name of a specific typeface such as Helvetica, Garamond, Palatino, or Optima. Enclose font names with spaces in quotes, such as `"Gil Sans"`. The generic family is one of five choices that classifies the typeface by its style and is recommended as the last option in a `font-family` list:

- Serif: Fonts with accents at the tips of the lines (for example, Times)
- Sans-serif: Fonts without finishing accents (for example, Helvetica)
- Cursive: Scripts that more closely resemble hand-drawn calligraphy (for example, Zapf Chancery)
- Fancy: Special-use decorative fonts (for example, Comic Book Sans)
- Monospace: Fonts that maintain uniform spacing despite letter width (for example, Courier)

## The `font-style` Attribute

This attribute specifies the type of treatment a font receives and is represented by the values `normal`, `italic`, or `oblique`. The `normal` value is also referred to as Roman in some typeface references. The `oblique` value is similar to `italic` except that it is usually slanted manually by the system rather than by a separate style of the font, like italic.

```
BODY {font-style: italic}
```

## The `font-variant` Attribute

Similar to `font-style`, this attribute sets small caps. Its two values are `normal` and `small-caps`.

```
BODY {font-variant: small-caps}
```

If there is no true small caps version of the typeface, the system will attempt to scale the capital letters to a smaller size for lowercase letters. As a last resort, the text will appear in all capitals.

## The `font-weight` Attribute

A number of values for this attribute set the darkness or lightness of a typeface. The primary values are `normal` and `bold`. You can substitute these values with one of a list of values from `100` to 900. If a typeface includes a "medium" weight, it will correspond to 500. Bold is represented by 700.

```
BODY {font-weight: bold}
```

Two additional values are bolder and lighter, which increase the weight from the current parent weight by one level, such as 200 to 300 for bolder or 700 to 600 for lighter.

## The font-size Attribute

Four methods can define the size of a font in a style—absolute size, relative size, length, or percentage.

- Absolute size: This method is represented in several ways. The first is with a value that represents its size relative to other sizes within the family (xx-small, x-small, small, medium, large, x-large, xx-large). You can also use a numerical value, such as 12pt (12 points).

  ```
  BODY {font-size: 18pt}
  ```

- Relative size: This method sets the size relative to the parent style. It can be one of two values, smaller or larger, and it adjusts the size up or down the scale of sizes. If a font doesn't include a mapping to size names, a scaling of 1.5 is recommended between sizes. For example, a 10pt font would be scaled larger to 15pt or smaller to 7pt.

  ```
  P {font-size: smaller}
  ```

- Length: This method is another form of relative size that sets the size by the scale factor of the width of an em, such as 1.5em.

  ```
  P {font-size: 2em}
  ```

- Percentage: This method is also a relative specification that multiplies the size of the parent font by the percentage value to achieve the new size, such as 150%.

  ```
  H3 {font-size: 300%}
  ```

## The font Attribute

This attribute provides a shorthand for setting all of the previous attributes under one umbrella. The order of the attributes should be font-style, font-variant, font-weight, font-size, line-height, font-family. Place no commas between each of the attribute values, except for listed font families:

```
BODY {font: small-caps bold 14pt garamond, palatino, serif}
```

# Color and Background

These elements set the color values for the text (foreground) and the area behind the text (background). In addition to setting a background color, you can also define a background image. All color values are defined using the same methods as the color attribute.

## The `color` Attribute

This attribute defines the color of the text element and is specified using one of the color keywords (such as `red`). You can also define the color using a hexadecimal triplet, denoting the mix of red, green, and blue (such as `rgb(255,0,0)`).

```
BLOCKQUOTE {color: rgb(0,255,255)}
```

## The `background-color` Attribute

This attribute sets the background color for a style. You can set this attribute independently of a background color for the document to enable you to highlight text in a different manner.

```
BLOCKQUOTE {background-color: blue}
```

## The `background-image` Attribute

This attribute specifies a background image for a style element. Use it in conjunction with `background-color` to ensure a substitute effect if the image becomes unavailable. If the image is available, it will display on top of the background color.

```
BLOCKQUOTE {background-image: url(logo.gif)}
```

## The `background-repeat` Attribute

If the background image should be repeated (tiled), use this attribute to define how. Its values include `repeat`, `repeat-x`, and `repeat-y`. The `repeat` value indicates that the image should be tiled normally. The `repeat-x` value repeats the image in a single horizontal line, and the `repeat-y` value repeats the image in a vertical line.

```
BLOCKQUOTE {background-image: url(logo.gif);
            background-repeat: repeat-x}
```

## The `background-attachment` Attribute

This attribute, an extended feature of background images not seen in HTML before, sets whether the background image is attached to the foreground text (`scroll`) or anchored to the background (`fixed`). This feature is apparent only when the user scrolls across a selection of text.

```
BLOCKQUOTE {background-image: url(logo.gif);
            background-attachment: repeat-x}
```

## The `background-position` Attribute

When you use a background image through normal HTML, the starting point is always the top left of the screen. With a style sheet, you can specify a starting point anywhere within the box that contains the style content.

You can specify the image's starting position in three ways. The first way is with key word locations. For horizontal placement, your choices are `left`, `center`, or `right`. For vertical placement, your choices are `top`, `center`, or `bottom`. Alternatively, you can represent the position as a percentage of the available area, with `0% 0%` being the top left (default) and `100% 100%` being the bottom right. The last option is to specify an actual measurement in centimeters or inches.

If only one value for the placement is given, it's used as the horizontal position. If both values are given, the first is evaluated as horizontal and the second as vertical.

```
BLOCKQUOTE {background-image: url(logo.gif);
            Background-repeat: repeat-y;
            background-position: right top; }
```

## The background Attribute

This shorthand attribute, similar to `font`, enables you to define a set of values for the background in one stop. The order is `background-color`, `background-image`, `background-repeat`, `background-attachment`, and `background-position`.

```
P { background: black url(logo.gif) repeat-y fixed right top }
```

# Text

This set of style attributes covers the values that can affect the appearance of text, but not by directly changing the typeface. This includes values for spacing, underlining, blinking, and strike-through. It also supports some of the positioning attributes, including left and right justification and indents.

## The word-spacing Attribute

This attribute indicates an addition to the default amount of space between individual words and is specified in *ems*. An *em* is the space occupied by the letter "m" and is the baseline for determining widths within a font. To return the value to its default, use `0em` or `normal`.

```
BODY { word-spacing: 1em }
```

## The letter-spacing Attribute

The `letter-spacing` attribute is similar to `word-spacing`, except that `letter-spacing` adds an extra bit of spacing between individual letters. In addition to the default method the browser uses to determine spacing, additional letter spacing is also affected by text alignment.

```
BODY { letter-spacing: 0.2em }
```

## The text-decoration Attribute

This attribute is more closely related to its cousins in the `font` family. It specifies extra text flourishes, such as underline, strike-through, and blinking. The four values are `none`, `underline`, `overline`, `line-through`, and `blink`.

```
STR.blink { text-decoration: underline blink }
```

## The `vertical-align` Attribute

This attribute sets the vertical position of the text either to an absolute reference or in relation to the parent element. It supports a range of values and keywords:

- `Baseline`: Aligns the baseline of the style with the baseline of the parent element
- `Sub`: Assigns the style to a subscript relative to the parent element
- `Super`: Assigns the style to a superscript relative to the parent element
- `Text-top`: Aligns the top of the text with the top of the parent's text
- `Text-bottom`: Aligns the bottom of the text with the bottom of the parent's text
- `Middle`: Aligns the vertical halfway point of the element with the baseline of the parent plus half of the x-height of the parent (x-height is the height of the lowercase x of the font)
- `Top`: Aligns the top of the element with the tallest element on the current line
- `Bottom`: Aligns the bottom of the element with the lowest element on the current line
- `(Percentage)`: Using a positive or negative percentage value, raises or lowers the element beyond the baseline of the parent

```
SUB { vertical-align: -10% }
```

## The `text-transform` Attribute

This attribute sets the capitalization of the affected text to one of four choices: `capitalize` (first letter of every word), `uppercase` (all letters in capitals), `lowercase` (all letters in lowercase), and `none`.

```
STR.caps { text-transform: uppercase }
```

## The `text-align` Attribute

This attribute moves beyond the standard HTML `left-right-center` alignment to provide full justification (`justify` left and right). If a browser doesn't support `justify`, it will typically substitute `left`.

```
BLOCKQUOTE { text-align: justify }
```

## The `text-indent` Attribute

The `text-indent` attribute, specified in an absolute value measured in ems or inches, defines the amount of space that is added before the first line.

```
P { text-indent: 5em }
```

## The `line-height` Attribute

This attribute sets the distance between adjacent baselines using a length (in ems), multiplication factor, or percentage. Factors are indicated without any units, such as `1.5`. When you use this method, the child inherits the factor, not the resulting value.

```
DIV { line-height: 1.5; font-size: 12pt }
```

In this instance, the line height becomes 18 points and the font size remains at 12 points.

# Margins, Padding, and Borders

Each element created in a style sheet is presented in its own "box." All of the styles from the element inside the box are applied, although the box itself can have its own properties that define how it relates to adjoining elements on the page. Length is specified in inches (`in`), centimeters (`cm`), ems (`em`), points (`pt`), or pixels (`px`).

Box properties are divided into three basic categories. Margin properties set the border around the outside of the box, padding properties determine how much space to insert between the border and the content, and border properties define graphical lines around an element.

Additional properties of the box include its width, height, and physical position.

## The `margin-top`, `margin-bottom`, `margin-right`, and `margin-left` Attributes

These four attributes set the amount of space between the element and adjoining elements, whether defined by length or percentage of parent text width or handled automatically.

```
BLOCKQUOTE { margin-top: 4em;
             Margin-bottom: auto }
```

## The `margin` Attribute

The `margin` attribute provides a shorthand method for setting the four margin values.

When you specify the four values, they are applied, in order, to the top, right, bottom, and left. If you provide only one value, it applies to all sides. If you use two or three values, the missing values are copied from the opposite sides.

```
BLOCKQUOTE {margin: 4em 2em}
```

## The `padding-top`, `padding-bottom`, `padding-right`, and `padding-left` Attributes

These attributes set the distance between the boundaries of the box and the elements inside the box. It can use any of the physical measurements or a percentage of the parent's width.

```
BLOCKQUOTE {padding-top: 110%; padding-bottom: 115%}
```

## The padding Attribute

The `padding` attribute provides a shorthand method for setting the four padding values.

When you specify the four values, they are applied, in order, to the top, right, bottom, and left. If you provide only one value, it applies to all sides. If you use two or three values, the missing values are copied from the opposite sides.

```
BLOCKQUOTE {padding: 10pt 12pt}
```

## The border-top, border-bottom, border-right, and border-left Attributes

These four attributes set the style and color of each border around an element. Specify styles with one of the border style keywords: `none`, `dotted`, `dashed`, `solid`, `double`, `groove`, `ridge`, `inset`, and `outset`. For more information on these, see the information on `border-style` later in this chapter.

Specify colors using a color keyword. For more information, see the `border-color` later in this chapter.

```
BLOCKQUOTE {border-left: solid red}
```

## The border-top-width, border-bottom-width, border-right-width, and border-left-width Attributes

These attributes define a physical border around the box, similar to the border used for HTML tables. In addition to defining a specific width in ems, you can also use the keywords `thin`, `medium`, and `thick`. Using a measurement in ems results in a border whose width changes in relation to the size of the current font.

```
STR {border-right-width: 2pt;
    border-left-width: 2pt }
```

## The border-width Attribute

The `border-width` attribute provides a shorthand method for setting the width of the four borders.

When you specify the four values, they are applied, in order, to the top, right, bottom, and left. If you provide only one value, it applies to all sides. If you use two or three values, the missing values are copied from the opposite sides.

```
BLOCKQUOTE {border-width: medium 0pt 0pt thick}
```

## The border-color Attribute

This attribute sets the color of all four borders and uses one color keyword as its value. You cannot set the color of each side independently.

```
BLOCKQUOTE {border-color: yellow}
```

## The border-style Attribute

The border's appearance can take on several different settings, represented by none, dotted, dashed, solid, double, groove, ridge, inset, and outset. The last four values are represented in 3D, if the browser supports it. Alternatively, the browser also can present all of the variations as a solid line, except none.

Like border-color, the style is applied uniformly to all four sides.

```
BLOCKQUOTE {border-style: groove}
```

## The border Attribute

The border attribute provides a shorthand method for setting all of the border variables, including width, style, and color. It sets the values for all four sides at the same time, overriding any individual settings that may have been set previously for the same element.

```
BLOCKQUOTE {border: 1.5pt double black}
```

## The height Attribute

This attribute sets the overall height of the bounding box that contains either the text or image element. If the content is text, scrollbars are added as needed so that all of the material is still available to the user. If the content is an image, it's scaled to fit inside the area. You can set a physical value or use auto to let the browser allocate space as needed.

```
BLOCKQUOTE {height: 100px}
```

## The width Attribute

Similar to height, the width attribute sets the overall width of the bounding box that contains the element. If the content is text, scrollbars are added as needed so that all of the material is still available for the user. If both elements are used with an image and the value of one element is auto, the aspect ratio for the image is maintained.

```
BLOCKQUOTE {width: auto}
```

## The float Attribute

This attribute sets a value similar to the align attribute used in HTML. The three possible values are left, right, and none. The none value allows the element to fall where it may, and the other two values force the element to the left or right of the screen with text wrapping around the opposite side.

```
BLOCKQUOTE {float: right}
```

## The clear Attribute

This attribute mimics the clear attribute used with the HTML <BR> tag and uses the same keywords as float. If you use it with right or left, elements will move below any floating element on that respective side. If you set it to none, floating elements are allowed on both sides.

```
BLOCKQUOTE {clear: left right}
```

# Classification

These attributes control the general behavior of other elements more than actually specifying an appearance. In addition, classification includes the attributes for list items, identified in HTML with the <LI> tag.

## The display Attribute

This attribute identifies when and if a style element should be used. Four keywords determine its behavior:

- Inline: A new box is created within the same line as adjoining text items and is formatted according to the size and amount of content within its borders, such as an image (IMG) or text (STR).

- Block: A new box is created relative to the surrounding elements. This is common with elements such as H1 and P.

- List-item: Similar to block, only list item markers, which behave more like inline content, are added.

- None: Turns off the display of the element in any situation, including for children of the element.

```
IMG {display: inline}
BLOCKQUOTE {display: block}
```

## The white-space Attribute

The name of this attribute is a bit misleading because it relates to how spaces and line breaks are handled. The choices are normal (in which extra spaces are ignored), pre (as in preformatted HTML text), and nowrap (in which lines are broken only with <BR>).

```
BLOCKQUOTE {white-space: pre}
```

## The list-style-type Attribute

This element sets the type of markers used for a list. Your choices are disc, circle, square, decimal, lower-roman, upper-roman, lower-alpha, upper-alpha, and none. For more information on how each of these is represented onscreen, see Chapter 9, "Using Lists to Organize Information."

```
LI.outline1 {list-style-type: upper-roman}
LI.outline2 {list-style-type: upper-alpha}
LI.outline3 {list-style-type: decimal}
```

## The list-style-image Attribute

In lieu of a text marker for the list item, you can also specify the URL of an image to use. If the image is unavailable, the text marker is used as default.

```
LI.general {list-style-image: url(bullet.jpg)}
```

## The list-style-position Attribute

The two values for this attribute, inside and outside, determine the formatting of text following the list item marker. The outside value, the default value, lines up the additional lines of text beyond the first line with the first character in the first line. If you use the inside value, the second and following lines are justified with the list item marker.

```
LI {list-style-position: inside}
```

## The list-style Attribute

This attribute is a shorthand element for the list-style-type, list-style-image, and list-style-position attributes.

```
OL {list-style: lower-alpha outside}
UL {list-style: square url(bullet.jpg) inside}
```

# HTML Resources

*by David Mayhew*

## IN THIS APPENDIX

**APPENDIX D**

Because the Web is constantly changing, no book can be 100 percent up-to-date, even on the day it arrives in the bookstores. Thankfully, hundreds of resources available on the Web itself are frequently revised to keep their information current.

In this appendix, you'll find a summary of many of those resources, including their URLs and a brief description. In addition to Web pages about changes in HTML, the latest browser developments, and HTML development tools, at the end of this appendix is a guide to relevant newsgroups where hundreds of messages are posted each day.

# Information on HTML

This section gives you the details on several Web sites where you can find current HTML information.

## Netscape DevEdge OnLine

`http://developer.netscape.com/index.html`

If you use Netscape technology to develop your Internet site or intranet, you need to visit the DevEdge site frequently. DevEdge's mission is to provide "communications, tools, support, and marketing assistance to speed the planning, development, and deployment of Internet and Intranet solutions." The site is a combination of free and fee-based content. The free access is primarily through a twice-weekly news e-mail with the latest developments in Netscape technology, news of new betas, bug fixes, and so on. Premium services include early access to betas, a quarterly CD full of Netscape tools, a Netscape ONE directory link, and peer newsgroups.

## Microsoft Site Builder Network

`http://www.microsoft.com/sitebuilder/`

Here you will find a very deep resource for developing Web sites with Microsoft technology. The Site Builder Network is a multilevel program that delivers technical information, products, technologies, services, and support for the latest Internet technologies, such as new HTML extensions, ActiveX controls, and Java applets. Information is scaled to match your level of membership, but even the content available free of charge makes this site worthy of frequent visits. Of particular interest is the Workshop area, which contains hands-on information on authoring, design, programming, and server technologies.

## The World Wide Web Consortium (W3C)

`http://www.w3.org/pub/WWW/`

The W3C was founded in 1994 to develop common protocols for the evolution of the World Wide Web. The Consortium is led by Tim Berners-Lee, Director of the W3C and creator of the World Wide Web; and Jean-François Abramatic, Chairman of the W3C; and is funded by commercial members. The vendor-neutral W3C works with the global community to produce specifications and reference software that is made freely available throughout the world.

## Cougar

`http://www.w3.org/pub/WWW/MarkUp/Cougar/`

Cougar is W3C's next version of HTML.

## HTML 3.2 Reference Specification

`http://www.w3.org/pub/WWW/TR/REC-html32.html`

This site offers the final specification for HTML 3.2, written by Dave Raggett.

## HTML 2.0 Specification

`http://www.w3.org/pub/WWW/MarkUp/html-spec/html-spec_toc.html`

Tim Berners-Lee and Dan Connolly wrote the HTML 2.0 specification, located at this site.

## Cascading Style Sheets, Level 1, W3C Recommendation

`http://www.w3.org/pub/WWW/TR/REC-CSS1`

This document specifies level 1 of the Cascading Style Sheet mechanism (CSS1).

## Document Object Model (Dynamic HTML)

`http://www.w3.org/pub/WWW/MarkUp/DOM/`

This site offers an overview of materials related to the Document Object Model at W3C and around the Web. As mentioned earlier in this book, the Document Object Model (DOM) is a platform-independent and language-neutral interface that allows programs and scripts to dynamically access and update the structure, content, and style of Web pages.

## URL Descriptions

`http://www.w3.org/hypertext/WWW/Addressing/Addressing.html`

This site presents definitions of the various types of URLs as well as discussion of URIs and URNs.

## Yahoo!

`http://www.yahoo.com/Computers/World_Wide_Web`

This site exhibits links to more than 3,000 pages regarding HTML. Find links here to sites about Internet technologies such as HTML, CGI, Java, ActiveX, VBScript, VRML, and many others, as well as resources for design, programming, browser information, and server details, to name just a few.

## HTML Writers Guild

`http://hwg.org`

The HTML Writers Guild is an international organization of World Wide Web page authors and Internet publishing professionals. The more than 50,000 members enjoy a wealth of HTML resources, plus access to their newsgroups. Basic membership is free and includes access to more information than many sites give you after charging a fee. Several paid membership levels are available as well, and these offer benefits such as mentoring programs, educational classes, access to the job board, and software discounts.

## The Web Design Group

`http://www.htmlhelp.com`

This is a highly useful site for beginners and experienced developers alike. Here you will find the widely acclaimed HTML 3.2 Reference, a Cascading Style Sheets Guide, and a Character Set Overview.

## The HTML Guru

`http://members.aol.com/htmlguru/index.html`

This site offers a collection of HTML tips, tricks, and hacks covering both document authoring and Web server management, presented in a question and answer format.

# Browsers

The HTML that you create doesn't always look the way that you intended on every user's screen. The different ways that browsers interpret your HTML can be frustrating, causing your Web pages to appear flat, boring, or unreadable instead of dynamic and exciting. To counter this, you should visit the following sites frequently to keep up on the latest developments in browser technology.

## Browserwatch

`http://browserwatch.iworld.com`

This browser offers breaking news in the browser and plug-ins industry, plus browser usage statistics and a rich library of plug-ins and ActiveX components.

## Netscape

`http://home.netscape.com`

Here you will find Netscape Navigator, as well as a very rich source of information on Web-related issues.

## Microsoft Internet Explorer

`http://www.microsoft.com/ie`

Get the latest version of Microsoft's Web browser here. This site also maintains an archive of press releases and links to articles relating to Internet Explorer.

## Amaya

`http://www.w3.org/pub/WWW/Amaya/`

The follow-up to Arena, this browser was developed by Irène Vatton, Vincent Quint, and Daniel Veillard with the purpose of being a testbed for experimenting and demonstrating new specifications and extensions of Web protocols and standards.

## Arena

`http://www.yggdrasil.com/Products/Arena/`

Arena is a graphical Web browser with origins that predate proprietary packages such as Netscape Navigator, Microsoft Internet Explorer, and Mosaic. It is the source of a number of innovations that have since been copied by other Web browsers, such as HTML tables and style sheets.

## Cyberdog

`http://www.cyberdog.apple.com/`

This site presents a versatile tool that includes a Web browser, using Apple's OpenDoc technology.

## Galahad

`http://www.mcs.com/~jvwater/main.html`

Galahad is an offline Web browser.

## Lynx

`http://www.nyu.edu/pages/wsn/subir/lynx/platforms.html`

Lynx is a fully featured World Wide Web browser for users on both UNIX and VMS platforms who are connected to those systems via cursor-addressable, character-cell terminals or emulators. This text-based browser is widely used in universities, libraries, and many other situations in which there is a desire to bring the information of the World Wide Web to as wide an audience as possible.

## NCSA Mosaic

http://www.ncsa.uiuc.edu/SDG/Software/Mosaic/NCSAMosaicHome.html

This Web browser was developed at the National Center for Supercomputing Applications at the University of Illinois in Urbana-Champaign.

## Opera

http://traviata.nta.no/opera.htm

You can customize this highly configurable browser to fit the user's needs. As a bonus, you can easily configure this browser for users with a handicap, and it is also ideal for slow machines.

## SlipKnot

http://plaza.interport.net/slipknot/slipknot.html

This Web browser works without a PPP or SLIP connection.

# HTML Editors and Web Authoring Tools

Many great tools are available to make writing HTML easier and more efficient. Several *tag editors* look a lot like the text editor you might be using now, but have useful features that your text editor lacks. However, the trend recently has been toward tools that display your page in a WYSIWYG window while you work. These tools make it easy to get immediate feedback on your site's appearance and allow for manipulation of the HTML at the object level.

## HTML Tag Editors

First, take a look at the tag editors. The following headings list several of the more popular tools available.

### BBEdit

http://www.barebones.com/bbedit.html

BBEdit 4.0.4 by Bare Bones Software is available at this site.

### HomeSite

http://www.dexnet.com/homesite.html

This site is home to HomeSite 2.5, which Nick Bradbury wrote and now Allaire owns. In addition to creating HTML pages and Web sites, HomeSite also can create Cold Fusion Web applications.

## HotDog

http://www.sausage.com

The HotDog Web editor by Sausage Software is located at this site.

## HoTMetaL Pro

http://www.sq.com/products/hotmetal/hmp-org.htm

HoTMetaL by SoftQuad is located at this site.

## Webber

http://www.csdcorp.com/webber.htm

This editor from Cerebral Systems Development includes a validator program to look for invalid HTML. Also check out Webber/Active at the same URL. This product does everything Webber does, and it also includes support for ActiveX controls.

# WYSIWYG Editors

WYSIWYG editors have received more attention and more respect as powerful utilities such as FrontPage, Backstage, and PageMill have appeared. Under the following headings, you find links to a few of the most popular and most powerful products in this category.

## Netscape Composer

http://home.netscape.com/try/comprod/mirror/client_download.html

Netscape Composer is the WYSIWYG editor in the Netscape Communicator suite.

## Microsoft FrontPad

http://www.microsoft.com/ie/ie40/

FrontPad is the WYSIWYG Web page editor in Microsoft Internet Explorer 4. If you're not sure you want to take the plunge with FrontPage, FrontPad is a great way to find out for free. Although nobody at Microsoft would say that FrontPad is "FrontPage Lite," FrontPad does appear to be a scaled down version of the best-selling commercial product.

## Microsoft FrontPage 97

http://www.microsoft.com/frontpage

FrontPage 97 provides a total Web site creation solution, including site structuring, HTML editing, site maintenance, and the FrontPage Web Server.

### PageMill

http://www.adobe.com/prodindex/pagemill/overview.html

PageMill is a powerful WYSIWYG editor from Adobe, the company behind Portable Document Format (PDF) and PageMaker.

### Backstage Internet Studio

http://www.macromedia.com/software/backstage/

Backstage is Macromedia's WYSIWYG Web development tool. In addition to easily integrating multimedia components to your Web pages, Backstage offers powerful database integration features.

# Usenet Newsgroups

Usenet provides a platform for any person with Net access to express to the whole world his or her views on a topic. As you might expect, this results in a great deal of chaos. But mixed into the chaos are a lot of useful and timely ideas. The following newsgroups promise to be full of lively discussions of the latest developments in HTML, browsers, and other Web-related issues. A word of caution: Before posting your question to a newsgroup, read the group to make sure your question has not been asked and answered already. If you don't, you'll learn the unfriendly definitions of terms like *newbie* and *flame-bait*.

## The `comp.infosystems.www.authoring.html` Newsgroup

At this very useful, vibrant newsgroup, you will find information on all aspects of HTML authoring.

## The `alt.html` Newsgroup

The `alt.html` newsgroup is a much less structured, more relaxed HTML newsgroup.

## The `comp.infosystems.www.authoring.misc` Newsgroup

This newsgroup is a forum for discussion of questions not covered in the more specific authoring newsgroups.

## The `comp.infosystems.www.browsers.ms-windows` Newsgroup

This newsgroup hosts discussion of Microsoft Windows browsers.

## The `comp.infosystems.www.browsers.mac` Newsgroup

This newsgroup hosts discussion of Macintosh browsers.

## The `comp.infosystems.www.browsers.misc` Newsgroup

This newsgroup hosts discussion of all other browsers.

# What's on the CD-ROM

## IN THIS APPENDIX

APPENDIX

E

On the *HTML Unleashed* CD-ROM, you will find the sample files that were presented in this book, along with a wealth of other applications and utilities.

> **NOTE**
>
> Please refer to the readme.wri file on the CD-ROM (Windows) or the Guide to the CD-ROM (Macintosh) for the latest listing of software.

# Windows Software

## ActiveX

- Microsoft ActiveX Control Pad and HTML Layout Control

## Explorer

- Microsoft Internet Explorer 3

## Graphics, Video, and Sound Applications

- Cell Assembler
- Goldwave sound editor, player, and recorder
- MapThis image map utility
- Paint Shop Pro
- SnagIt
- ThumbsPlus
- Web graphics from The Rocket Shop

## HTML Tools

- NetObjects Fusion demo
- W3e HTML Editor
- Hot Dog 32-bit HTML editor
- HTMLed HTML editor

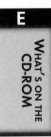

## Utilities

- Adobe Acrobat viewer
- WinZip for Windows NT/95
- WinZip Self-Extractor

# Macintosh Software

## Graphics, Video, and Sound Applications

- Graphic Converter
- GIFConverter
- Fast Player
- Sparkle
- SoundApp
- Web graphics from The Rocket Shop

## HTML Tools

- NetObjects Fusion demo
- BBEdit LITE
- HTML Web Weaver
- WebMap
- HTML.edit
- HTML Editor for the Macintosh

## Utilities

- ZipIt for Macintosh
- ScrapIt Pro
- Adobe Acrobat

# About the Software

Please read all documentation associated with a third-party product (usually contained with files named `readme.txt` or `license.txt`), and follow all guidelines.

# I
# INDEX

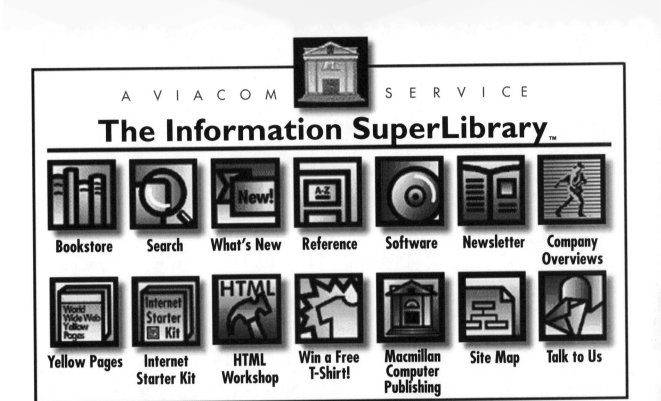

MACMILLAN COMPUTER PUBLISHING USA

A VIACOM COMPANY

## Technical ---- Support:

If you need assistance with the information in this book or with a CD/Disk
accompanying the book, please access the Knowledge Base on our Web
site at **http://www.superlibrary.com/general/support**. Our most
Frequently Asked Questions are answered there. If you do not find the
answer to your questions on our Web site, you may contact Macmillan
Technical Support **(317) 581-3833** or e-mail us at **support@mcp.com**.

# Teach Yourself Java 1.1 in 21 Days, Second Edition

—*Laura Lemay and Charles Perkins*

This updated bestseller is the definitive guide to learning Java 1.1. *Teach Yourself Java 1.1 in 21 Days, Second Edition* carefully steps you through the fundamental concepts of the Java language, as well as the basics of applet design and integration with Web presentations. You learn the basics of object-oriented programming and Java development. You learn how to create stand-alone cross-platform applications and add interactivity and animation to your Web sites with Java applets. The book's CD-ROM includes Sun's Java Development Kit 1.1, Sun's Java Development Kit 1.02 for Macintosh, and Sun's Bean Development Kit for Windows 95, Windows NT, and Solaris.

$39.99 USA/$56.95 CAN          *Internet–Programming*
1-57521-142-4                          *New–Casual*

# Teach Yourself Great Web Design in a Week

—*Anne-Rae Vasquez-Peterson and Paul Chow*

This step-by-step, full-color tutorial is loaded with graphics, tables, diagrams, and examples of what to do (and what not to do) when designing Web pages. Using this book, you will master the fundamentals of page design—from typography fan layout to use of color and graphics—and learn how to apply them to the Web. In no time, you'll be creating eye-catching Web pages that present information effectively and guide visitors through your site efficiently. The *Teach Yourself* series provides Q&A sections, week-at-a-glance previews, and real-world exercises to make learning easy and fun. The book's CD-ROM contains Internet Explorer 3.0, Microsoft ActiveX and HTML development tools, ready-to-use templates, graphics, scripts, Java applets, and ActiveX controls.

$49.99 USA/$70.95 CAN          *Internet–Web Publishing*
1-57521-253-6                          *New–Casual*

# Teach Yourself Web Publishing with HTML 3.2 in 14 Days, Professional Reference Edition

—*Laura Lemay*

This is the updated edition of Lemay's previous bestseller, *Teach Yourself Web Publishing with HTML in 14 Days, Premier Edition*. In this book, you will find all the advanced topics and updates—including adding audio, video, and animation—for Web page creation. The book includes a CD-ROM. *Teach Yourself Web Publishing with HTML 3.2 in 14 Days, Professional Reference Edition* explores the use of CGI scripts, tables, HTML 3.2, the Netscape and Internet Explorer extensions, Java applets, JavaScript, and VRML.

$59.99 USA/$84.95 CAN          *Internet–Web Publishing*
1-57521-096-7                          *New–Casual–Accomplished*

# Maximum Security: A Hacker's Guide to Protecting Your Internet Site and Network

*—Anonymous*

Now more than ever, it is imperative that users be able to protect their systems from hackers who would trash their Web sites or steal information. Written by a reformed hacker, this comprehensive resource identifies security holes in common computer and network systems, allowing system administrators to discover faults inherent within their networks and work toward a solution to those problems. *Maximum Security* explores the most commonly used hacking techniques so that users can safeguard their systems. It includes step-by-step lists and discussions of the vulnerabilities inherent in each operating system on the market. The book's CD-ROM is loaded with source code, technical documents, system logs, utilities, and other practical items for understanding and implementing Internet and computer system security on all platforms.

*$49.99 USA/$70.95 CAN*
*1-57521-268-4*          *Accomplished–Expert*

## Add to Your Sams.net Library Today
## with the Best Books for Internet Technologies

| ISBN | Quantity | Description of Item | Unit Cost | Total Cost |
|---|---|---|---|---|
| 1-57521-142-4 | | Teach Yourself Java 1.1 in 21 Days | $39.99 | |
| 1-57521-253-6 | | Teach Yourself Great Web Design in a Week | $49.99 | |
| 1-57521-096-7 | | Teach Yourself Web Publishing with HTML 3.2 in 14 Days, Professional Reference Edition | $59.99 | |
| 1-57521-268-4 | | Maximum Security: A Hacker's Guide to Protecting Your Internet Site And Network | $49.99 | |
| | | Shipping and Handling: See information below. | | |
| | | TOTAL | | |

Shipping and Handling: $4.00 for the first book, and $1.75 for each additional book. If you need to have it NOW, we can ship product to you in 24 hours for an additional charge of approximately $18.00, and you will receive your item overnight or in two days. Overseas shipping and handling adds $2.00. Prices subject to change. Call between 9:00 a.m. and 5:00 p.m. EST for availability and pricing information on latest editions.

### 201 W. 103rd Street, Indianapolis, Indiana 46290

**1-800-428-5331 — Orders     1-800-835-3202 — FAX     1-800-858-7674 — Customer Service**

Book ISBN 1-57521-299-4

# Installing
# the CD-ROM

The companion CD-ROM contains all the source code and project files developed by the authors, plus an assortment of evaluation versions of third-party products. To install, please follow these steps.

# Windows 95/NT 4 Installation Instructions

1. Insert the CD-ROM into your CD-ROM drive.
2. From the Windows 95 or NT 4 desktop, double-click the My Computer icon.
3. Double-click the icon representing your CD-ROM drive.
4. Double-click the icon titled setup.exe to run the CD-ROM installation program.

# Windows 3.x/NT 3.51 Installation Instructions

1. Insert the CD-ROM into your CD-ROM drive.
2. From File Manager or Program Manager, choose Run from the File menu.
3. Type <drive>\setup and press Enter, where <drive> corresponds to the drive letter of your CD-ROM. For example, if your CD-ROM is drive D:, type D:\SETUP and press Enter.
4. Follow the on-screen instructions.

# Macintosh Installation Instructions

1. Insert the CD-ROM into your CD-ROM drive.
2. When an icon for the CD appears on your desktop, open the disc by double-clicking its icon.
3. Double-click the icon named Guide to the CD-ROM, and follow the directions that appear.